# INTRODUCTION TO
# COMPUTER SCIENCE
## AN ALGORITHMIC APPROACH
### PASCAL EDITION

## McGraw-Hill Computer Science Series

**Ahuja:** Design and Analysis of Computer Communication Networks
**Barbacci and Siewiorek:** The Design and Analysis of Instruction Set Processors
**Ceri and Pelagatti:** Distributed Databases: Principles and Systems
**Collins:** Intermediate Pascal Programming: A Case Study Approach
**Debry:** Communicating with Display Terminals
**Donovan:** Systems Programming
**Filman and Friedman:** Coordinated Computing: Tools and Techniques for Distributed Software
**Givone:** Introduction to Switching Circuit Theory
**Goodman and Hedetniemi:** Introduction to the Design and Analysis of Algorithms
**Hayes:** Computer Architecture and Organization
**Hutchison and Just:** Programming Using the C Language
**Katzan:** Microprogramming Primer
**Keller:** A First Course in Computer Programming Using Pascal
**Kohavi:** Switching and Finite Automata Theory
**Korth and Silberschatz:** Database System Concepts
**Liu:** Elements of Discrete Mathematics
**Liu:** Introduction to Combinatorial Mathematics
**MacEwen:** Introduction to Computer Systems: Using the PDP-11 and Pascal
**Madnick and Donovan:** Operating Systems
**Manna:** Mathematical Theory of Computation
**Milenkovic:** Operating Systems: Concepts and Design
**Newman and Sproull:** Principles of Interactive Computer Graphics
**Payne:** Introduction to Simulation: Programming Techniques and Methods of Analysis
**Revesz:** Introduction to Formal Languages
**Rice:** Matrix Computations and Mathematical Software
**Salton and McGill:** Introduction to Modern Information Retrieval
**Shooman:** Software Engineering: Design, Reliability, and Management
**Su:** Database Computers: Principles, Architectures, and Techniques
**Tremblay and Bunt:** An Introduction to Computer Science: An Algorithmic Approach
**Tremblay, DeDourek, and Bunt:** An Introduction to Computer Science: An Algorithmic Approach, Pascal Edition
**Tremblay and Manohar:** Discrete Mathematical Structures with Applications to Computer Science
**Tremblay and Sorenson:** Introduction to Data Structures with Applications
**Tremblay and Sorenson:** The Theory and Practice of Compiler Writing
**Tucker:** Programming Languages
**Tucker:** Computer Science: A Second Course Using Modula-2
**Wiederhold:** Database Design
**Wiederhold:** File Organization for Database Design
**Wulf, Levin, and Harbison:** Hydra/C.mmp: An Experimental Computer System

## McGraw-Hill Series in Computer Organization and Architecture

**Bell and Newell:** Computer Structures: Readings and Examples
**Cavanagh:** Digital Computer Arithmetic: Design and Implementation
**Gear:** Computer Organization and Programming: With an Emphasis on Personal Computers
**Hamacher, Vranesic, and Zaky:** Computer Organization
**Hayes:** Computer Architecture and Organization
**Hayes:** Digital System Design and Microprocessors
**Hwang and Briggs:** Computer Architecture and Parallel Processing
**Lawrence and Mauch:** Real-Time Microcomputer System Design
**Siewiorek, Bell, and Newell:** Computer Structures: Principles & Examples
**Stone:** Introduction to Computer Organization and Data Structures
**Stone and Siewiorek:** Introduction to Computer Organization and Data Structures: PDP-11 Edition

## McGraw-Hill Series in Supercomputing and Parallel Processing

**Consulting Editor**
Kai Hwang, University of Southern California

**Hwang and Briggs:** Computer Architecture and Parallel Processing
**Quinn:** Designing Efficient Algorithms for Parallel Computers

## McGraw-Hill Series in Artificial Intelligence

**Allen:** Anatomy of LISP
**Davis and Lenat:** Knowledge-Based Systems in Artificial Intelligence
**Nilsson:** Problem-Solving Methods in Artificial Intelligence
**Rich:** Artificial Intelligence

# INTRODUCTION TO COMPUTER SCIENCE

## AN ALGORITHMIC APPROACH

### PASCAL EDITION

**JEAN-PAUL TREMBLAY**
Department of Computational Science
University of Saskatchewan
Saskatoon, Canada

**JOHN M. DeDOUREK**
School of Computer Science
University of New Brunswick
Frederickton, Canada

**RICHARD B. BUNT**
Department of Computational Science
University of Saskatchewan
Saskatoon, Canada

**McGRAW-HILL BOOK COMPANY**
New York   St. Louis   San Francisco   Auckland
Bogotá   Caracas   Colorado Springs   Hamburg   Lisbon
London   Madrid   Mexico   Milan   Montreal   New Delhi
Oklahoma City   Panama   Paris   San Juan   São Paulo
Singapore   Sydney   Tokyo   Toronto

**INTRODUCTION TO COMPUTER SCIENCE**
AN ALGORITHMIC APPROACH
PASCAL EDITION

1 2 3 4 5 6 7 8 9 0   DOC   DOC   8 9 3 2 1 0 9 8

ISBN   0-07-065174-4

This book was set in Times Roman by Publication Services.
The editors were David Shapiro and Sheila H. Gillams;
the production supervisor was Friederich W. Schulte;
the designer was Charles Carson.
R. R. Donnelley & Sons Company was printer and binder.

**Library of Congress Cataloging-in-Publication Data**

Tremblay, Jean-Paul, (date).
    An introduction to computer science: an algorithmic approach /
Jean-Paul Tremblay, John M. DeDourek, Richard B. Bunt—Pascal ed.
        p.   cm.—(McGraw-Hill computer science series)
    Includes bibliographies and indexes.
    ISBN 0-07-065174-4
    1. Electronic digital computers—Programming.   2. Algorithms.
3. Data structures (Computer science)   4. Pascal (Computer program
language)   I. DeDourek, John M.   II. Bunt, Richard B., (date).
III. Title.   IV. Series.
QA76.6.T73 1989b                                        88-3001
005—dc19                                                CIP

# ABOUT
# THE AUTHORS

**J. P. Tremblay** is Professor of Computational Science at the University of Saskatchewan in Saskatoon. He received his Ph.D. in Computer Science from Case Institute of Technology. Professor Tremblay was an Associate Professor of Computer Science at the University of New Brunswick and is co-author of the books *Discrete Mathematical Structures with Applications to Computer Science, An Introduction to Data Structures with Applications*, and *The Theory and Practice of Compiler Writing*, all part of the McGraw-Hill Computer Science Series. His research interests currently focus on data structures, compiler writing, and software engineering.

**John M. DeDourek** is Professor of Computer Science at the University of New Brunswick. He received his M.Sc. Degree in Engineering from Case Institute of Technology. His current research interests are in the area of software engineering, compilers, programming languages, and data communications.

**Richard B. Bunt** is Professor and Head of Computational Science at the University of Saskatchewan. He received his M.Sc. and Ph.D. degrees in Computer Science from the University of Toronto. His research interests are in operating systems and performance.

To Deanna Tremblay

To my father, John, and in memory of my mother, Helen DeDourek

To Gail and Andrea Bunt

# CONTENTS
# IN BRIEF

# CONTENTS

# PREFACE

The first course in a computer science curriculum is certainly one of the most important. For most students, this constitutes their initial exposure to fundamental notions such as the algorithm, as well as to the description of solutions in a manner sufficiently precise for computer interpretation. It is important that these notions be properly taught, for, as the ancient Roman poet Horace observed, "A new cask will long preserve the tincture of the liquor with which it was first impregnated."

In the mid-1960s, students in the first course became well-versed in the syntax of the instructor's favorite programming language (usually FORTRAN) and probably were given a limited view of the organization of a computer. It was assumed, however, that the students brought with them an ability to solve problems. Assistance in organizing their solutions was provided in the form of the flowchart. The emphasis was largely on the solution of numerical problems, to which the FORTRAN language was well-suited. Since the class was populated (and taught) largely by engineers, usually late in their academic programs, it seemed to fulfill their short-term requirements and there was little motivation for change.

Today the needs of such a class have changed. The emergence of computer science as an undergraduate discipline has created a need for a different orientation. The class is now generally offered in the first year of study, meaning that today's students seldom have the mathematical or problem-solving maturity of their predecessors. The increased use of computers in nonnumeric applications, such as text processing, requires the presentation of new concepts in the handling of nonnumeric data. Many curricula now require that students take courses in areas such as data structures and discrete mathematical structures early in their programs. It is important that the first course provide proper motivation for these areas by providing some knowledge of nonnumeric computation and applications.

We feel that considerations such as these dictate stringent requirements for a textbook for the first course. It must do substantially more than simply train the student in rules of syntax for a particular programming language. More emphasis must be placed on aspects of problem solving.

With this as the overriding philosophy, in 1979 we produced the first edition of *An Introduction to Computer Science: An Algorithmic Approach* (Tremblay/Bunt), which concentrated on the design of algorithms to solve problems. This book introduced a carefully considered algorithmic language with constructs appropriate to the solution of problems in both the nonnumeric and numeric domains. Considerable attention was devoted to the data structures appropriate to the applications at hand.

Since the publication of this book, computer science as a discipline has continued to evolve and mature. New concepts and shifting emphasis have led to the development of new computer science curricula. Some of these developments have had a direct bearing on the preparation of a second edition. Also, it was felt that a language-based version of the book was appropriate at this time. Pascal was selected as the language because its basic philosophy and approach align closely with that of our algorithmic language. This book is the result.

Clearly, the use of a programming language is an important part of a first course. It must not, however, obscure other important concepts. Our book is based on the premise that a student should learn to program *into* a programming language rather than *in* one. The translation of algorithmic solutions into a programming language ought to be a straightforward exercise.

In this book, students are given ample opportunity to hone their problem-solving skills, both by studying actual programs and by writing programs of their own. Each chapter contains carefully worked-out examples in which the material introduced in the chapter is applied to the solution of representative problems. The choice of applications reflects our concern with the nonnumeric aspects of computing. We have tried to choose examples and applications with care, to stimulate interest and provide the necessary motivation for learning. All programs given have been run on representative compilers to ensure their correctness. Compilers used include Borland's Turbo Pascal and Vax-11 Pascal from Digital Equipment Coroporation. As much as possible, we have attempted to adhere to ISO standard Pascal.

## SUMMARY BY CHAPTERS

Chapter 1 lays an important foundation by presenting a number of basic computing notions such as computer, computer system, hardware, and software. In addition to outlining the steps involved in using a computer to solve a problem, this chapter also examines some basic modes of computer operation.

Chapter 2 introduces the notion of the algorithm and the first constructs of the Pascal language. Some simple applications are described.

The notion of "flow of control" is introduced in Chapter 3, along with three fundamental control structures: the selection from alternative actions, the case construct, and the loop. Pascal implementations of these constructs are presented, and important variations are discussed. Solutions to several fairly elaborate applications are developed.

Chapter 4 deals with functions and procedures. Topics discussed include the correspondence of arguments and parameters and the way in which functions and procedures are invoked and values are returned. The concept of recursion is introduced. Three applications involving the use of functions and procedures are considered.

The concept of the array is the topic of Chapter 5. Processing of single-dimensional arrays, or vectors, is discussed first. Some typical applications of vectors are described. Among these are the important applications of searching and sorting, which are discussed for the first time. The notions of the time and space analysis of an algorithm are then introduced. Following this discussion, the chapter moves to a consideration of arrays of higher dimension. Applications of vectors and arrays are presented. The chapter concludes with the introduction of record structures, arrays of record structures, an introduction to sequential files, and set structures.

String processing is the topic of Chapter 6. The representation of strings in a computer and some basic operations on strings are described. A number of applications, such as text formatting and lexical analysis, are developed.

Structured design and programming style are the topics of Chapter 7. The goals of design are introduced. Module design issues involving module cohesion and coupling are discussed. Certain design heuristics and the notions of transform analysis and transactions analysis in design are described. Programming style topics discussed include considerations of program quality, defensive programming, writing readable programs, and programming as a human activity.

Chapter 8 offers an introduction to the study of linear data structures. Simple structures such as linear lists, stacks, and queues are discussed, as are basic operations on these structures. A number of important applications are described. These include the implementation of recursion, the translation of expressions, and simulation. Also discussed in this chapter are hash-table techniques.

Chapter 9 deals with nonlinear data structures. The most important nonlinear data structure is the tree. Tree topics include the binary tree, operations on binary trees, general trees, and the storage representation of trees. The application of trees to problems such as the symbolic manipulation of expressions, searching, and sorting is discussed. Graphs are then introduced briefly. The breadth-first search and depth-first search traversals of a graph are described.

Chapter 10 looks at external files. External storage devices are described, since their characteristics are important in file design and manipulation. The sequential and random file organizations are introduced.

The book concludes with appendixes pertaining to numeric calculations, recurrence relations, and the running of programs in a Pascal environment.

Extensive sets of exercises conclude each chapter and most sections. The exercises have been designed for self study as well as classroom study. For the reader's convenience, the exercises have been graded and given a level of difficulty. The ratings are as follows:

Blank  An exercise which can be answered easily

★  An average exercise which tests basic understanding of the material

★★  An exercise of moderate difficulty which can take some time

★★★  A difficult and lengthy exercise

The solutions to the exercises are included in an accompanying Instructor's Manual. The Instructor's Manual also contains a list of exercises which can be used as project assignments.

# HOW TO USE THE BOOK

This book is intended for a two-semester course with an organization similar to that advocated for courses CS1 and CS2 in the curriculum proposals of the Association for Computing Machinery. In particular, Chapters 1 through 7 align with CS1, and Chapters 8 through 10 align with CS2. The material is sufficiently modularizable, however, that it can also be used for a single-semester course. This can be accomplished in a number of ways. Certainly any course should include the material in Chapters 1 through 6. Chapters 7 and 10 are self-contained and can be included or not at the instructor's discretion. The material in Chapter 9 draws on material from Chapter 8; however, an instructor can elect to go only as far as he or she wishes. For example, an instructor wishing to introduce only linear data structures need go only as far as Chapter 8.

Material can be tailored to a specific course or set of interests in yet another way. We have made an effort in our choice of applications and exercises to cover a wide range of interests, including scientific computing, business data processing, engineering applications, societal issues, and topics of general interest. By selecting appropriate applications and problems, it is possible to realize a number of different course orientations. We have also made an effort to keep to a minimum the mathematics required to understand the material in the book. Our own course attracts some students from fields of study other than the physical sciences. We do expect, however, that most students will have had the equivalent of high school mathematics.

We advocate a laboratory environment of some sort for the parallel presentation of issues relating to the actual computing component of the course. The instructor may wish, on occasion, to deal with particularly difficult notions in class, but too much of this detracts from continuity of presentation. Students should not view the class as a class in programming. The laboratory also provides the student with the opportunity to work on programs, with assistance available readily when needed.

For convenience of presentation, we have made several assumptions as to the nature of available computing facilities. We have assumed throughout a terminal-oriented interactive environment. We recognize that this may not be the case for many students, so the dependency on such matters is minor. Should an alternative environment exist, initial guidance from the instructor should suffice to overcome any possible problems of comprehension.

# ACKNOWLEDGMENTS

We are grateful to the many people who assisted us in the preparation of this book. We owe a large debt of thanks to David Daoust, who assisted in the preparation of the manuscript, read the entire final manuscript, helped to pick out many errors, tested most of the programs, and coordinated many diverse efforts. Verna Friesen devoted a great deal of time to the reading of our notes and contributed many valuable suggestions. Grant Cheston contributed to the analysis of the algorithms throughout the book and made several suggestions based on the class testing of the manuscript. John Cooke, in addition to class testing the manuscript, suggested many improvements in style. Brad Redekopp solved many of the exercises; these solutions are in an accompanying Instructor's Manual. Deanna Tremblay proofread the manuscript. We are also grateful for the support of the Department of Computational Science at the University of Saskatchewan. We wish to acknowledge the support of the School of Computer Science of the University of New Brunswick for their assistance in the latter stages of preparation of the book. Finally, we acknowledge the many helpful comments and suggestions of instructors who used the first edition of our original book and the assistance of Lorna Bellingham (Stewart), Ken Kozar, Ram Manohar, Mike Williams, Kelly Gottlieb, Tom Austin, Doug Bulbeck, Judy Peachy (Richardson), Lyle Opseth, Dave Hrenewich, Murray Mazer, Gail Bunt, Janet Morck, Arlene Looman, and Gail Walker, who contributed in various ways to the first edition.

*Jean-Paul Tremblay*
*John M. DeDourek*
*Richard B. Bunt*

# INTRODUCTION TO
# COMPUTER SCIENCE
## AN ALGORITHMIC APPROACH
### PASCAL EDITION

# CHAPTER 1

## COMPUTERS AND SOLVING PROBLEMS

*I'm a private shamus, so I'm used to seeing peculiar sights and hearing peculiar pitches. But when a curvy girl scientist dressed in nothing but a mink wrap showed me a long, coffin-shaped box and asked me to find the million bucks worth of machinery that used to be inside, I had to smile. "Baby, that may be a computer to you," I said, "but it's just a burying-box to me."*

    *Raymond Banks,* The Computer Kill *(Toronto: Popular Library, 1961)*

It's difficult to imagine an aspect of our lives today that is not impacted by information and information processing. Found only in the largest university laboratories only a generation ago, the computer is now a common household appliance with uses ranging from recreation to household accounts to word processing. Literacy in computers is now an important part of everyone's education.

## 1-1 INTRODUCTION

Despite the fact that it is an integral part of today's society, the computer epitomizes future shock for many people. In movies, the computer is imbued with a strong personality: cold and impersonal, sinister and scheming. It is operated by a brilliant, eccentric scientist who spends night and day with the machine and, as a result, teeters on the brink of madness. With or without the aid of the scientist, the computer plots to control humanity.

    While this common scenario makes for entertaining fiction, it undermines the accomplishments of a great many computer systems and increases the distance that exists between many people and an appreciation of computers and computing. The computer was not the product of a mad scientist's warped ambition, but rather the natural culmination of humanity's growing need for fast, accurate computation—a need that has existed for thousands of years.

Since the dawn of humanity, men and women have relied on devices to assist them in performing computations. Primitive peoples counted sheep by moving sticks or stones. Clay tablets containing multiplication tables and tables of reciprocals found near Babylon are believed to have been produced about 1700 B.C. Early versions of the abacus were used in the Middle East as early as 2500 B.C. Seventeenth-century inventors such as John Napier, a Scottish nobleman, William Oughtred, an English clergyman, and Blaise Pascal, a French philosopher and mathematician, developed rather sophisticated computational aids. English physicist Charles Babbage's work in the nineteenth century laid an important foundation for today's computing industry, which, for all intents and purposes, began in the years following World War II. Rapidly increasing demands for information processing, coupled with rapidly decreasing costs for provision of computing functions, have stimulated unbelievable growth in the industry. Today the computing industry ranks with the automotive and petroleum industries as one of the cornerstones of our industrial society.

It is possible to study computers from several points of view. The technological details, while fascinating, can be overwhelming, particularly on your first exposure. The many and varied applications—scientific, industrial, and commercial—may distort an attempt to focus on the computer itself. As indicated by the title of this chapter, we are interested in the view of the computer taken by a *computer scientist*, that is, using the computer as an aid to solving problems. We will adopt a very simplified view of the computer itself, at least initially, as we focus on techniques of problem solving. As your use of the computer becomes more extensive and your problem-solving skills mature, the entire process will seem less formidable and a more detailed study of the computer itself will be possible.

As the use of computers has become more widespread, the uses to which they have been put have become more diverse. The number of people requiring numeric solutions of first-order differential equations in their day-to-day lives is small. The growth in interest in computing has been primarily in applications where numeric calculations play a very secondary role. Nonnumeric applications, such as word processing and electronic mail, while they may have significant underlying numerical problems, have paved the way for acceptance of the computer as a standard business or home commodity. The historical view of the computer as an engine for numerical calculations is far too limited in today's society. In this book we present a set of applications and problems that cover a wide spectrum of computer uses and, it is hoped, the entire spectrum of student interests as well.

The next section begins with a brief overview of computers and computer systems. Basic notions of hardware and software are introduced. We then look at some basic modes of computer operation and suggest application areas for which they are appropriate. Finally, we outline the steps involved in using a computer to solve a problem.

## 1-2 COMPUTERS AND COMPUTER SYSTEMS

A computer system is a collection of hardware and software components designed to provide an effective tool for computation. *Hardware* refers to the physical computing equipment itself; *software* refers to the programs written to provide services to the users of the system. Together, hardware and software define the *computing environment* for the user—the environment within which the user performs computations.

It is difficult to talk about a computing environment without dealing with both the hardware and the software aspects of that environment. For this reason, the term "computer system" perhaps better describes what the user interacts with than does the term "computer," which has definite hardware overtones. In the early days of computing, users interacted much more closely with the actual hardware than is common today. Many of the functions that were once performed by the users themselves are now handled by software known as the *operating system*. The operating system is essentially responsible for the processing of user requests (or user programs) by the computer system; it ensures, for example, that the appropriate hardware resources are made available as required, that software resources are supplied as needed, and that users cannot do themselves or other users irreparable harm. The operating system creates the environment in which the users can prepare their requests and have them serviced without being overly concerned with hardware details. Examples of operating systems include MS-DOS, CP/M, UNIX,[†] VMS, CMS, and MVS. For most users of computer systems, software components, such as the operating system and the programs it manages, are much more visible than the hardware components. In fact, users are often completely unaware of the hardware that is involved as their requests are processed.

Figure 1-1 depicts a typical computer system. At the core of the system is the computer hardware, about which more will be said later in this section. Typical hardware includes the central processing unit (CPU), memory, and devices (keyboards, printers, monitors, disk drives, etc.). The operating system and other software is built on this hardware to provide the user's computing environment. Typical software includes editors (to allow users to prepare programs and data), language processors (for the various programming languages supported), a file system (for storage of programs and data), communications support (to allow users to communicate with each other and the system), and application programs of every shape and form (including word processors, graphics packages, games, etc.). Users convey their requests to the system through the use of a *command language* that provides the ultimate interface between the users and the system.

---

[†] UNIX is a trademark of AT&T Bell Laboratories.

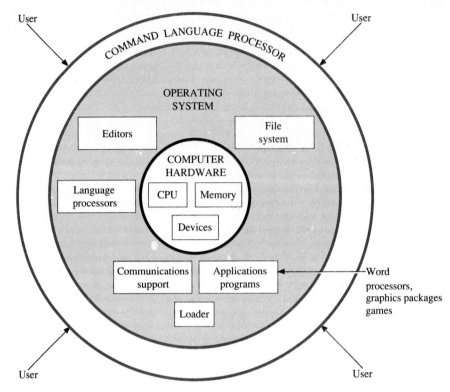

**FIGURE 1-1**
**A typical**
**computer system.**

Computer systems can be divided roughly into two main categories: *single-user systems*, such as a personal computer, and *multiuser systems*, such as a large mainframe. While the basic ideas are the same, many system-management problems become more difficult in the multiuser context. It is the function of the operating system to coordinate the sharing of the system's resources (both hardware and software) in such a way as to provide the type of service that the users require and to minimize the amount of interference that takes place among their executing programs. Central to this function is the ability of the system to allow several users to use the system simultaneously (*multiprogramming*).

Computer systems are also categorized according to the type of service they provide. As a point of fact, many systems provide several different types of services, but for the sake of simplicity, we will deal with them individually.

In a *batch processing system*, users normally submit their programs as a file, perhaps prepared using an interactive editor on the same machine or on another machine, even possibly on a personal computer. On some older systems, the program is prepared *off-line* as perhaps a deck of punched cards which are then read into the system. The job is placed in external storage by the operating system on the batch machine. The operating system chooses jobs for execution as the needed system resources become available; as jobs are completed, they release their resources and additional jobs may be selected for execution from those waiting. The output from a job is placed in external storage; it may be printed automatically or it may be held for examination by the user via the system used to prepare the program in the first place.

In an *interactive timesharing system*, users submit work to the system from individual terminals (see Fig. 1-2). These terminals normally have video displays (video display terminal—VDT, or cathode-ray tube—CRT), but some may have hard-copy capabilities. The operation is interactive in the sense that during a session at the terminal, the user is continually engaged in a dialogue with the operating system as the machine and the user cooperate in the processing of the job. Through what seems to the user to be an immediate response to his or her requests, an illusion is presented that the user has the complete and undivided attention of the computer system. In actual fact, there may be many other users simultaneously operating in a similar mode, as shown in Fig. 1-2. The operating system creates this illusion by giving to each user, in turn, a small amount of attention in the form of usable CPU time. The amount is "small" in user terms, but "large" enough in computer system terms to execute many instructions. For example, in a half a second, most computer systems could execute hundreds of thousands

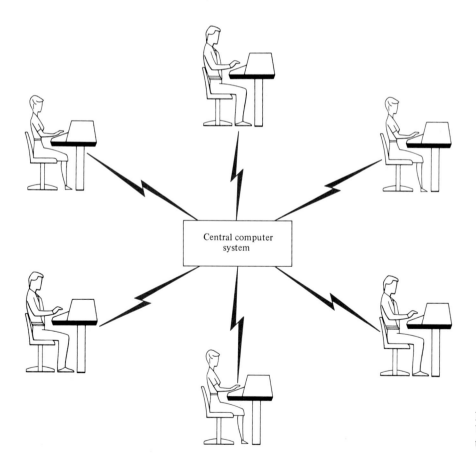

**FIGURE 1-2**
**User view of a**
**timesharing system.**

of instructions. Fast response to user requests is the dominant objective of these operating systems. Terminals connected to an interactive timesharing system can be far removed geographically from the actual computer site, transmitting data by means of communication paths such as standard telephone lines. Microwave or satellite communications may be used when very long distances are involved.

*On-line transaction systems* have a strong surface similarity to interactive timesharing systems in that user access is by means of terminals. The objectives, however, are quite different. Whereas users of timesharing systems are programmers creating and running programs, users of on-line transaction systems are not; instead, they are simply entering data to be processed by a program that runs continuously. Familiar examples of such systems are found in the areas of airline reservations and banking. In the case of a banking system, the user enters information such as account number and the nature and amount of the transaction (withdrawal, deposit, transfer). The user receives back a printed statement of the transaction showing the account updated and any cash that might have been requested. In the case of an airline system, the users are reservation clerks providing services to travelers in the form of flight information, seat reservations, and so forth. On-line transaction systems are becoming increasingly popular as a business tool to provide information and services rapidly. The design of such systems is considered as an application in a later chapter.

A *computer network* consists of a number of interconnected computer systems. These can be *local-area networks*, connecting computers (or *nodes*) in one room or one building, or *long-haul networks*, in which the computers may be quite far apart geographically. Users at any one of the nodes in the network may have work processed at any other node in the network and may thereby take advantage of some special features available at other installations. An example of a very large computer network is the ARPANET network connecting a large number of computer centers throughout the United States (see Fig. 1-3). Other popular long-haul networks include USENET, CSNET, and BITNET. It is not uncommon for a user to have access to several networks. Computer networks are expected to play an even larger role in computing in the years to come.

Although different computer systems may perform radically different functions and also may be radically different in appearance and philosophy, their basic hardware organizations are, in fact, quite similar. We turn now to a consideration of the basic hardware components of a simple, but typical, computer system.

## 1-3 COMPONENTS OF A TYPICAL COMPUTER

All computers, from the very smallest microsystem to the largest mainframe, consist of three basic components. These are memory, the central processing unit (CPU), and the input/output unit. The basic organization is depicted in Fig. 1-4. We shall now consider each of these in more detail, beginning with memory.

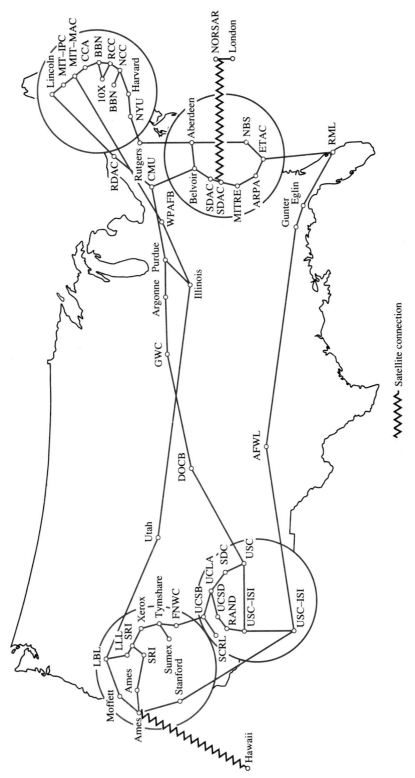

**FIGURE 1-3** ARPANET, geographic map, June 1975. (From Leonard Kleinrock, *Queueing Systems, Vol. 2: Computer Applications,* Wiley-Interscience, New York, 1976.)

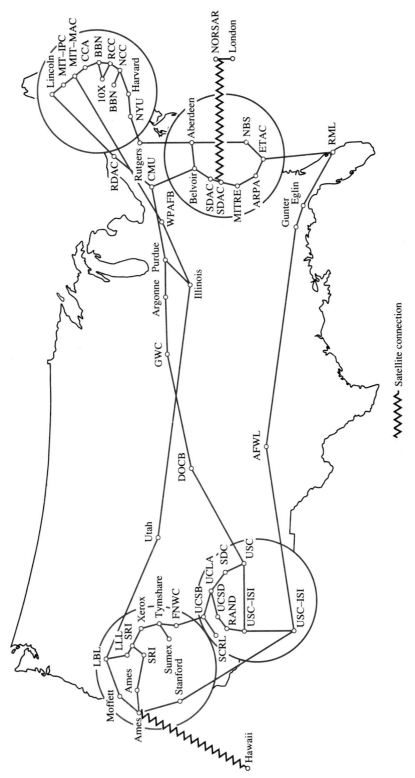Satellite connection

CPU

Control
unit

Arithmetic/logic
unit

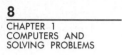

Input
device

Memory

Output
device

**FIGURE 1-4**
**The components of a**
**typical computer**
**system. (Broken lines**
**indicate control**
**signals; solid lines**
**indicate data flow.)**

## 1-3.1 MEMORY

Every computer comes with a certain amount of storage, both *internal storage*, sometimes referred to as its *memory*, and *external* (or *secondary*) *storage*, such as magnetic disk and magnetic tape devices. The two forms of storage differ in characteristics and in purpose. Programs currently in execution, along with some of the data required for execution, must reside in memory. Memory is expensive and, in most systems, a scarce resource. Information not immediately needed is normally relegated to external storage, where the capacity can be almost unlimited, although the time to retrieve the information is considerably longer. Also, the cost of external storage is low in comparison to internal storage, so information can be stored for long periods of time.

A computer's memory is divided into small, equal-sized units called *words*, each of which has a unique *address*. Each memory word is capable of holding essentially one piece of information, such as an instruction or the result of a numeric computation. The size of a word is an important design parameter of the computer and determines, for example, the largest and smallest number that can be stored. We might imagine, for example, a machine designed with a word size capable of storing up to 8 decimal digits or a machine with a word size capable of storing 16 binary digits, and so forth. The consequences of this decision are important and will be considered in more detail in App. A.

As stated, each word in memory has a unique address. Figure 1-5 illustrates how this might be represented in an arrangement similar to a set of post office boxes. The memory address serves to identify the particular word uniquely, so that the desired information can be read from it or written into it. In this way, the address serves the same function as the box number on the post office box. For purposes of illustration, the addresses in this portion of storage are shown above each word, although in practice they would not be physically present. Also, we have adopted a two-dimensional "row, column" presentation, when, in fact, memories are normally one-dimensional.

Each word in memory is directly addressable; that is to say, it can be accessed directly (by means of its address), without having first to access any words preceding it. This is in marked contrast to storage devices such as tape, for which access must be sequential. Because of this characteristic, memory is often referred to as *random-access memory*, or RAM. ROM, or *read-only memory*, is memory into which certain special information or programs are written by the manufacturer. Such memory, although it has an influence on the user, is not available for general storage and thus will not be discussed any further.

Computer memories can be built in many ways. In early machines, for example, electromagnetic relays were used. These soon gave way to vacuum-tube "flip-flops." Later, the technology of magnetized "cores" prevailed. Since the late 1960s, semiconductor memories have become increasingly popular. These technological advances have steadily improved the reliability of memories and reduced the time required to access information (thus increasing the overall speed of the computer) while at the same time vastly reducing their physical size. Despite differences in technology, the underlying principles are very similar. To illustrate how the information is actually stored, let us imagine that memory is composed of a series of two-position switches. A switch in the "on" position, by agreement, represents the binary digit 1; a switch in the "off" position represents the binary digit 0. In our illustrations we denote a switch in the "on" position by a colored rectangle; a blank rectangle denotes a switch in the "off" position.

The storage of information is based on the binary (or base 2) number system. For those of you not familiar with the binary number system, it

Word

| Address → | 0 | 1 | 2 | 3 | 4 |
|---|---|---|---|---|---|
| Contents → | | | | | |
| | 5 | 6 | 7 | 8 | 9 |
| | 10 | 11 | 12 | 13 | 14 |
| | 15 | 16 | 17 | 18 | 19 |
| | 20 | 21 | 22 | 23 | 24 |
| | 25 | 26 | 27 | 28 | 29 |
| | 30 | 31 | 32 | 33 | 34 |

FIGURE 1-5
Memory representation
of a computer.

is necessary to digress at this point for a short introduction. Readers not needing this introduction can skip ahead several paragraphs.

The binary system, like our familiar decimal (or base 10) system, is a *positional* number system. This means that the value of a digit is determined by its position in the number. In the decimal system, for example, the number 2562 has the following interpretation:

$$
\begin{aligned}
2 \times 1000 \ (10^3) &= 2000 \\
+ 5 \times \ \ 100 \ (10^2) &= \ \ 500 \\
+ 6 \times \ \ \ \ 10 \ (10^1) &= \ \ \ \ 60 \\
+ 2 \times \ \ \ \ \ \ 1 \ (10^0) &= \ \ \ \ \ \ 2 \\
&= 2562
\end{aligned}
$$

Note that the digit 2 has a different interpretation in its two occurrences in the number. The first (leftmost, or *high-order*) occurrence indicates a contribution of 2000 to the value of the number; the second occurrence (in the rightmost, or *low-order*, position) indicates a contribution of 2.

In general, the interpretation of the number *abcde* in the base *n* number system is

$$
a \times n^4 + b \times n^3 + c \times n^2 + d \times n^1 + e \times n^0
$$

The extension to higher-order digits for larger numbers proceeds in the obvious way. Thus, in a positional number system, the position of a digit in the number specifies the power by which the base of the number system (also called the *radix*) is raised to give the contribution of that digit in the final value.

In the binary number system, the radix is 2. Thus the quantity represented by (or the value of) the binary number 110101 is

$$
1 \times 2^5 + 1 \times 2^4 + 0 \times 2^3 + 1 \times 2^2 + 0 \times 2^1 + 1 \times 2^0
$$

$$
= 32 + 16 + 0 + 4 + 0 + 1
$$

$$
= 53
$$

Although straightforward methods exist for converting from decimal to binary, and vice versa, we will not go into them. To follow the examples used in this section, it will suffice to be able to perform the calculation described.

Returning to our previous discussion, Fig. 1-6 shows a portion of a memory with a "word" composed of eight consecutive switches. The settings yield the decimal values 91 for word 0, 53 for word 1, and 1 for word 2. In memory terminology, any device capable of representing a binary digit (this means that the device must have two readily identifiable states) is said to define a "bit" of information (short for *bi*nary dig*it*). Word sizes are normally quoted in bits; thus, in our example, we are dealing with a word size of 8

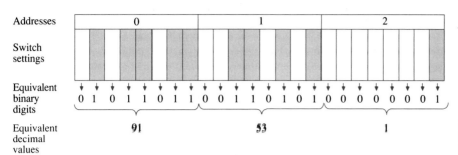

FIGURE 1-6
Information storage
in a computer.

bits. A small amount of reasoning will convince you that the largest decimal value that can be represented with $n$ bits is $2^n - 1$.

The representation of information is somewhat more complicated than we have let on. The complication arises from the fact that we wish to represent information of a variety of types. For instance, we require nonnumeric information as well as numeric information. The representation of nonnumeric (or character) information is done through a coding scheme, whereby certain patterns of bits are, by agreement, taken to stand for certain characters. Two coding schemes are most popular in the computing industry: the 8-bit EBCDIC code (Extended Binary Coded Decimal Interchange Code) and the 7-bit ASCII code (American Standard Code for Information Interchange). These are described in more detail in Chap. 6 and App. C.

With respect to numeric information, several issues remain to be considered: for example, the question of negative numbers and the distinction between integers (such as 1, 2, 3, $-1$, $-2$, $-3$) and real numbers (such as 1.8, $2\frac{3}{4}$, $-5.75$). The matter of sign is normally handled by designating one bit of the word (usually the leftmost bit) as the *sign bit*, with 0 signifying that the number is positive and 1 signifying that it is negative. If the word size is $m$ bits, this leaves $m - 1$ bits for the magnitude of the number. The representation of real numbers is considerably more complicated (involving the integer and fractional portions) and will not be dealt with here.

## 1-3.2 CENTRAL PROCESSING UNIT

The second basic component of any computer is the *central processing unit*, or CPU. The CPU contains two subcomponents: the *arithmetic/logic unit* and the *control unit*. All calculations are carried out in the arithmetic/logic unit. These may involve arithmetic operations such as addition, subtraction, multiplication, or division or logical operations such as the comparison of two values to see which is the larger. As a complex computation is performed, it is often necessary for information to be moved to and from memory during the course of the computation. The control unit is, in some sense, the heart of the computer because it controls the actions of the other components. Operating under the control of instructions from the programmer (these instructions reside in memory), the control unit causes data to be read from the input device, passes the appropriate values from storage to the arithmetic/logic unit for the required calculations, stores and retrieves data and intermediate results from main memory, and passes results to the output device for display. Broken lines in Fig. 1-4 indicate control signals that pass between the control unit and other components. Data flow is indicated by solid lines.

Instructions to the control unit must be expressed in terms of the *machine language* of the particular computer. A machine language instruction conveys the *operation* to be performed (e.g., add, subtract, load, store) and the *operands*, or memory words, that are to take part (e.g., the numbers to be added, the memory words into which a result is to be stored, etc.). The hardware circuitry of the control unit causes instructions to be read from memory one at a time and the indicated operations to be carried out on the specified operands.

Machine language programs are expressed in terms the machine understands—binary numbers and simple operations. Table 1-1, for example, gives an *instruction set* for a simple hypothetical machine. Operations are represented by 3-bit codes. A sample program written in this language is given in Table 1-2.

This machine is a "one address" machine, which means each instruction has one operand, specified by means of its address (also expressed in binary). An "accumulator" is assumed as the second operand for those instructions (load, store, add, subtract) which require two.

**TABLE 1-1** Sample Instruction Set

| Operation Code | Operation | Meaning |
|---|---|---|
| 001 | Load | Copy the value of the word addressed into the accumulator |
| 010 | Store | Copy the value of the accumulator into the word addressed |
| 011 | Add | Replace the present value of the accumulator with the sum of its present value and the value of the word addressed |
| 100 | Subtract | Replace the present value of the accumulator with the result obtained by subtracting from its present value the value of the word addressed |
| 101 | Branch | Jump to the instruction at the word addressed |
| 110 | Branch if not zero | Jump to the instruction at the word addressed only if the present contents of the accumulator are other than 0 |
| 111 | Halt | Terminate execution |

**TABLE 1-2** Sample Program

| | Instruction | |
|---|---|---|
| Address of Instruction | Operation Code | Operand |
| 0 | 001 | 01010 |
| 1 | 010 | 01100 |
| 2 | 001 | 01110 |
| 3 | 011 | 01011 |
| 4 | 010 | 01110 |
| 5 | 001 | 01100 |
| 6 | 100 | 01101 |
| 7 | 010 | 01100 |
| 8 | 110 | 00010 |
| 9 | 111 | 00000 |

To understand how the control unit processes this program requires the concept of *flow of control* through a program. Quite simply, execution proceeds sequentially through memory, from one instruction to the one physically next to it, unless a *control transfer instruction* causes control to move to a different instruction. Control transfer instructions can be unconditional (e.g., branch) or conditional (e.g., branch if not zero).

With these points in mind, you should be able to simulate the action of the control unit for this hypothetical machine and "hand execute" the simple program in Table 1-2, beginning at address 0. This program will cause the contents of several memory words (specifically, those at addresses 12 and 14) and the accumulator to change. Assume these have initial values as shown in Fig. 1-7. At program termination, they should have the values shown in Fig. 1-8.

FIGURE 1-7 Memory contents of a sample program and its associated data.

| Word | | | |
|---|---|---|---|
| Address — 0 | 1 | 2 | 3 |
| Contents (in binary) — 00101010 | 01001100 | 00101110 | 01101011 |
| 4 | 5 | 6 | 7 |
| 01001110 | 00101100 | 10001101 | 01001100 |
| 8 | 9 | 10 | 11 |
| 11000010 | 11100000 | 00000011 | 00000100 |
| 12 | 13 | 14 | 15 |
| 00000000 | 00000001 | 00000000 | 00000000 |

Accumulator:

Memory:

| 0 | 1 | 2 | 3 |
|---|---|---|---|
| 00101010 | 01001100 | 00101110 | 01101011 |
| 4 | 5 | 6 | 7 |
| 01001110 | 00101100 | 10001101 | 01001100 |
| 8 | 9 | 10 | 11 |
| 11000010 | 11100000 | 00000011 | 00000100 |
| 12 | 13 | 14 | 15 |
| 00000000 | 00000001 | 00001100 | 00000000 |

Accumulator: | 00000000 |

**FIGURE 1-8**
**Memory contents at**
**program termination.**

### 1-3.3 INPUT/OUTPUT DEVICES

Finally, any computing system that is meant to interface with the outside world must do so by means of *input* and *output devices*. Input devices provide the means by which data (and, as we shall see, instructions) is transmitted to the computer. Output devices are necessary for the display of results. There exists a wide variety of both input and output devices. Familiar input devices include terminal keyboards, magnetic tape devices, optical scanners, and punched card readers. The most common output devices are line printers, monitors, card punches, and, once again, magnetic tape devices, illustrating that some types of devices can serve as both input and output devices.

The foregoing discussion indicates how a typical computer operates. The machine language used in the example was designed solely for the purpose of illustration, yet actual machine languages have very similar properties. The role of a *program* is to provide the particular instructions under whose control the CPU is to operate to perform some required computation. Various instructions cause the movement of data from input devices or secondary storage to memory, between memory and the arithmetic/logic unit (where actual computations are performed), and from memory to the output devices (where the results of the computation are made available to the user). The task of a programmer is to produce the appropriate sequence of instructions to solve the problem at hand.

### 1-4 USING A COMPUTER

Clearly, to produce a program in raw machine language such as that used in the example of Sec. 1-3 would be a difficult and tedious task. At one time this is how things were done. Fortunately, software is now provided in most computer systems to make this task considerably easier. Programming languages are provided which allow programmers to express their ideas in a form more suited to human comprehension, and programs called *compilers* are available to translate users' programs written in this language into the machine language required for execution of the programs. Compilers for the most popular programming languages are available either from the manufacturer or from other sources, and compiler writing is an important field of computer science which is considered in more detail later in this book.

Figure 1-9 shows the steps involved in using most computer systems. The programmer begins by writing a program to solve the problem at hand. The program prepared by the programmer is referred to as the *source program* and is usually written in one of the popular programming languages, such as Pascal, Ada, LISP, PL/I, FORTRAN, Modula-2, BASIC, or COBOL. Before the steps expressed can be processed by the computer to return the required results, this source program must be translated into the machine language for the particular computer by means of a *compiler* for the programming language being used. During the translation process, the compiler checks that the rules of the language used have not been violated by the programmer in the source program. Appropriate error messages, or *diagnostics*, are issued if necessary, which may cause the programmer to revise the program and repeat this process. The result of the compilation is referred to as the *object program*—a machine-language equivalent of the programmer's original source program. Eventually, the object program is ready to be run. A piece of software known as the *loader* is called on to load the object program into memory at prescribed addresses and commence its execution.

The total time frame involved in running a program can be divided into two separate and distinct phases. *Compilation* (or *compile*) *time* relates to translation of the source program into its equivalent object program; *run time* relates to execution of the object program. Certain errors are detected at run time, often by the operating system. Run time is also the time at which the particular data that the programmer wishes to supply for the computation is made available to the program. More will be said on these types of errors later in the book.

The material in this chapter has been presented to give you a better perspective on computers and computing. We have tried to give you some idea of how a typical computer is organized and how it operates, as well as how a modern computer system is used. Clearly, we have merely scratched the surface. We could explore any of these areas in much more detail, but to do so would detract from the main purpose of this book.

The primary objective of this book is to teach you to solve problems using a computer. A computer programmer is first and foremost a solver

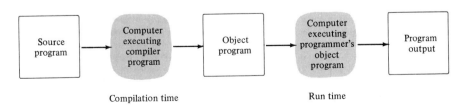

**FIGURE 1-9**
**The stages of**
**a computer run.**

of problems. To become proficient as a programmer, one must first learn to deal with problems in a rigorous, systematic fashion. Much of this book is concerned with a methodology for solving problems that is appropriate to the development of good computer programs. Central to this methodology is the notion of an *algorithm*, a notion we introduce in the next chapter.

We also shall consider the representation of these algorithms in the programming language Pascal. The basic elements of Pascal are also introduced in the next chapter.

## CHAPTER SUMMARY

The computer is a powerful problem-solving tool, one which has shaped much of our society in the past 40 years. A computing environment is a collection of hardware and software components assembled to make the problem-solving task easier for the programmer. Different types of computer systems are designed to address different sorts of needs but the underlying components are very similar.

This chapter has given a brief overview of the makeup of a typical computer and of the components that define a typical computing environment. The computer scientist is interested both in the study of the components themselves and in the effective use of computing systems in the solution of problems. In the remaining chapters, we will use the interest in problem solving as the point of departure for an introduction to the field of computer science.

## KEY TERMS

address
algorithm
arithmetic/logic unit
batch processing system
binary number system
bit
central processing unit (CPU)
command language
compile time
compiler
computer network
computer science
computer system
computing environment
control unit
diagnostics
external storage
hardware

input device
instruction set
interactive timesharing system
internal storage (memory)
loader
machine language
memory word
multiprogramming
object program
on-line transaction system
operating system
output device
program
random-access memory (RAM)
read-only memory (ROM)
run time
software
source program

# CHAPTER EXERCISES

1. Identify five circumstances in which you come into contact with computers in your normal routine. Classify the computer system involved as interactive timesharing, on-line transaction, or other.

2. Convert the following binary (base 2) numbers to their decimal (base 10) equivalent:
   - (a) 1010
   - (b) 101101
   - (c) 110110
   - (d) 1000000

3. Both the binary and decimal systems are examples of positional number systems. One very common number system is not positional. What is it?

★ 4. Derive the result that says that the largest decimal value that can be stored in an $n$-bit word is $2^n - 1$ (ignoring sign).

★ 5. If one of the bits of an $n$-bit word is used for sign, express the range of numbers that can be represented, from the largest positive number to the largest negative.

★ 6. Consider the machine language program shown in Fig. 1-7. Express in words what this program is doing.

7. List as many computer manufacturers as you can. How are you familiar with these? Do the same with programming languages.

# CHAPTER 2

# ALGORITHMS AND PROGRAMS

On your first exposure to computers, it is very easy to be overpowered by technological details. The technology is fascinating, but although it may be of interest to some of you, it is not necessary for this discussion and can obscure other important concepts. For this reason we will adopt a very simplified view of a computer, initially. As your use of computers becomes more extensive, they will seem much less formidable, and the picture will become more complete.

In this chapter we focus on the main point of this text—solving problems with the use of a computer. Some key concepts necessary to solve problems on a computer are introduced, and some simple problems are solved. The first problems may seem quite simple, but once mastered, the techniques extend easily, and will be a great aid as the complexity of the problems grows.

## 2-1 INTRODUCTION

Computers, unfortunately, do what we *tell* them to do, not necessarily what we *want* them to do. There must be no ambiguity in the instructions that we give to a computer in our programs, no possibility of alternative interpretations. The computer will always take some course of action; great care must be taken to ensure that there is only one possible course of action so that the results we get are those we intended. Although a statement such as "compute the average grade on this test" seems to specify the computation we wish to have performed, it is, in fact, much too imprecise. Too much detail is left unspecified: for example, Where are the grades? How many are there? Are the absentees to be included? and so on. Herein lies the essence of computer programming.

Most interesting problems appear to be very complex from a programming standpoint. For some problems (such as difficult mathematical problems), this complexity may be inherent in the problem itself. In many cases, however, it can be due to other factors that may be within our control: for example, incomplete or unclear specification of the problem. In the development of computer programs, as we shall see, complexity need not always be a problem if it can be properly controlled.

Computer programming can be difficult. If it were not, good programmers could not command the high salaries they receive. It is difficult largely because it itself is a complex activity, combining many mental processes. We can do a great deal, however, to make it easier. For instance, the programming task can be made much more manageable by systematically breaking it up into a number of less complex subtasks (the divide-and-conquer approach). We will use this approach of subdividing, which has seen considerable success in practice, over and over again in this book.

First, it is important that we separate the *problem-solving phase* of the task from what we will term the *implementation phase*, as shown in Fig. 2-1. In the problem-solving phase, we are concerned with the design of an ordered sequence of precise steps that describes the solution of a given problem. We call this sequence an *algorithm*. Although the term itself may be new, the concept of an algorithm should be very familiar. Directions given to a particular street constitute an algorithm for finding the street. A recipe is a very familiar form of algorithm. A blueprint serves the same purpose in a construction project. At Christmas time, many parents spend exasperating hours following algorithms for assembling their children's new toys.

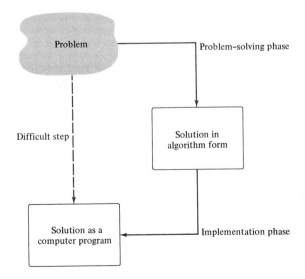

FIGURE 2-1
**Problem solving
and programming.**

In preparing volume 1 of his series *The Art of Computer Programming*, Donald Knuth attempted to track down the origins of the word "algorithm." An older form "algorism," meaning the process of doing arithmetic with Arabic numerals, was used as far back as the Middle Ages. Mathematical historians believe this word comes from the name of a famous ninth-century Arabic author of textbooks, Abu Ja'far Mohammed ibn Mûsâ al-Khowârizmî. Another word, "algebra," comes from the title of his celebrated book *Kitab al jabr w'al-muqabala* (*Rules of Restoration and Reduction*), although Knuth claims this was not a very algebraic book. Over time, the word "algorism" was somehow combined with the word "arithmetic" to become "algorithm." By the eighteenth century, the Latin phrase *algorithmus infinitesimalis* was used to denote "ways of calculation with infinitely small quantities, as invented by Leibnitz." In modern usage, the term "algorithm" has come to mean a process or method for doing something (usually with a computational flavor), but with some important features that set it apart from other processes.

We will require that our algorithms have two important properties. First, the steps in an algorithm must be simple and unambiguous and must be followed in a carefully prescribed order. Further, we will insist that algorithms be *effective*; that is, they must always solve the problem in a finite number of steps. We could ill afford to pay the computing costs if this were not the case.

In the problem-solving phase we will first formulate an algorithm with a minimum amount of detail that expresses the general manner in which the computer could produce the solution to the problem. Such an algorithm is called a *general algorithm*. We shall then add detail to this general algorithm in a step-by-step manner. The successively more detailed algorithms are called *refinements* of the general algorithm. The problem-solving phase is complete when the latest refinement is detailed enough to convince us that it is within the capabilities of a computer to execute the algorithm.

We will devote considerable space in this book to the design of algorithms. We will be presenting many problems to which computers can be (and are being) applied. Algorithms and/or Pascal programs for the solution of these problems will be carefully formulated.

We then progress to the implementation phase, which involves refining the algorithm further, that is, adding detail determined by the programming language—in this book, Pascal. The final refinement should result in an executable Pascal program. Before we can consider a method for designing algorithms, we must consider methods of expressing the algorithms. We consider these in the next section.

## 2-2 EXPRESSING ALGORITHMS

Expressing an algorithm in a clear, easy-to-follow manner aids in its development, in its subsequent transformation to a computer program, and in documentation of the program after it has been completed. This latter aspect is a particularly important stage in the programming process about which more can be said after you have had more experience developing and writing programs. In the remainder of this section we present several possible approaches to expressing algorithms.

For the purpose of illustration, consider the following problem: A student's final grade in a course is computed as the average of the four marks received on tests throughout the year. An algorithm is required to determine a student's final grade and indicate whether it is a passing or failing grade.

## 2-2.1 NARRATIVE DESCRIPTION

A straightforward method of expressing an algorithm is simply to outline its steps verbally. Recipes, for example, are normally expressed in this fashion. Since apparently very little in the way of specialized training is required for narrative description, it seems easy to do on the surface. However, this is not always the case. Natural language is wordy and imprecise and often quite unreliable as a vehicle for transferring information. It is not impossible to be precise with natural language. That it is difficult, however, ought to be clear to anyone who has ever struggled with the fine print on a contract or legal document. Comprehensibility is sacrificed for precision. The difficulty of transferring information with natural language is, in fact, the basis of a popular game that you probably played as a child. The players are seated in a circle and the game begins with one player whispering a story to his or her neighbor. That person, in turn, passes the story on to his or her neighbor, and so on around the circle. The last player then repeats the story aloud. The final version of the story usually bears shockingly little similarity to the original.

Because of the imprecision of natural language, the danger of misinterpretation or information loss looms large. Subtle nuances and shades of meaning may stimulate the reader's imagination in a novel, but in technical writing, unclear details can lead quickly to errors.

The following is an attempt to describe, in a narrative fashion, the solution to the problem posed:

*Read a set of four marks. Compute their average by summing them and dividing by 4. If this average is below 50, display the grade with a failing message; otherwise display the grade with a passing message.*

While the solution to this simple problem may be reasonably clear, you can see that solutions to larger problems rapidly become wordy and tedious. For this and the other reasons outlined, natural language is unsuitable as the sole vehicle for expressing algorithms.

## 2-2.2 THE FLOWCHART

It is often easier to convey ideas with pictures than with words. Maps provide a convenient representation of the topology of a city and are often of more value than verbal directions to people who are lost. Assembly directions for a newly acquired piece of equipment are usually much more comprehensible if diagrams are included.

An early attempt at providing a pictorial format for the description of algorithms involved the use of the *flowchart*. A flowchart shows the logic of an algorithm, emphasizing the individual steps and their interconnections, that is, the way in which control flows from one action to the next. Over the years, a relatively standard symbolism emerged (see Fig. 2-2). A computation is represented by a rectangular shape, a decision by a diamond shape, and input and output operations by shapes symbolizing the media used. The boxes are connected by directed lines indicating the order in which the operations are to be carried out. A flowchart for the problem posed is shown in Fig. 2-3.

Gradually the attitude of the computing profession toward the once popular flowchart has cooled considerably. Flowcharts do not represent certain concepts such as recursion (see Sec. 4-5 and Sec. 8-5) very well. Additionally, they are difficult to draw with enough detail to be useful. In his book of essays entitled *The Mythical Man-Month*, Frederick P. Brooks offered that "the flowchart is a most thoroughly oversold piece of documentation." A study led by Shneiderman at Indiana University raised serious questions as to the utility of detailed flowcharts. Thoughts on the flowchart vary. By some, it is considered simply as an unnecessary appendage to a program; by others, it is viewed as an instigator of bad programming habits. New generations of programmers are being schooled in new methods of program development—methods to which the flowchart in its familiar form adds little. Very often, while showing the *logic* of an algorithm, the flowchart obscures its *structure*. We feel that the structure is at least as important (and quite possibly more important). As a result, we will make very little use of flowcharts in this book. The reader who wishes more information on the subject will find it readily available.

## 2-2.3 PROGRAMMING LANGUAGES—PASCAL

Programming languages are precisely defined languages for expressing an algorithm in a form that can be processed by a compiler. When an algorithm is expressed in such a language, it can actually be run on a computer.

The programming language Pascal was designed by Professor Niklaus Wirth as a language for teaching programming as a systematic discipline. To achieve this, an attempt was made to eliminate the inconsistencies found

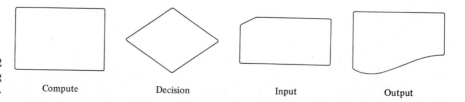

**FIGURE 2-2**
**Common flowcharting symbols.**

Compute          Decision          Input          Output

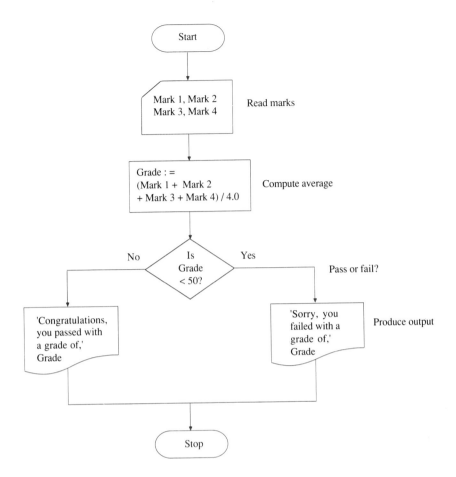

FIGURE 2-3
Simple flowchart.

in some other programming languages. Since the language was not intended as a language for implementation of large systems of programs, and in order to ensure that Pascal compilers would be small and inexpensive, some features common in other programming languages were omitted from Pascal. A preliminary version of the language was produced in 1968, and the first compiler was completed in 1970. Since then, many compilers have been built and these compilers are available for a wide range of machines. Unfortunately, many of the compilers processed slightly different versions of the language and/or gave slightly different interpretations to some of the constructs of the language. Therefore, several projects were undertaken to produce a standard definition for the language, culminating in two standards: one by the International Standards Organization (ISO) in 1982 and one approved jointly by the American National Standards Institute (ANSI) and the Institute of Electrical and Electronics Engineers (IEEE). These two definitions, hereafter referred to as the ISO and the ANSI/IEEE standards, differ in only one major area, described in Chap. 5, and a small number of minor technical issues. We shall assume the ISO definition of Pascal in this book, except where expressly noted. We will use Pascal to express the detailed algorithm which is the solution to a problem. We begin our presentation of Pascal later in this chapter.

### 2-2.4 AN ALGORITHMIC NOTATION

Loosely speaking, an algorithmic language can be viewed as an attempt to meld the expressiveness and intuitiveness of natural language with the logical precision of schemes such as the flowchart. The result enables algorithms to be described in a straightforward manner—easy to read and easy to understand. In this textbook we espouse the top-down development of programs (see Sec. 2-3). This development begins with a general statement of the algorithm. This general statement typically consists of a sequence of numbered steps, each expressed in prose. For the problem posed at the beginning of the section we might have the following general algorithm:

1. Read a set of four marks

2. Compute their average by summing them and dividing by 4

3. If the average is below 50,
   then display the grade with a failing message;
   otherwise display the grade with a passing message

4. Halt

Successive refinements of the program design add detail until a complete program in Pascal is achieved. At intermediate stages in this development, the proposed solution is exhibited in a mixture of prose and Pascal code. This mixture of the two algorithmic notations is often called *pseudocode*. Usually pseudocode uses the concept of a *program variable*. In a program such a variable represents a *named location* in the memory of the computer into which a value can be placed. This value may then be used for a later computation. Values to be placed in variables may be obtained either from an input device, e.g., a keyboard attached to the computer, or by a computation using the values of previously stored variables. In an algorithm a variable is simply a means of associating a name with a particular quantity. For example, the following might represent an intermediate stage in the development of a Pascal program for the problem posed.

1. Obtain four marks from an input device and place them into variables Mark1, Mark2, Mark3, and Mark4

2. Compute the average of the four marks by summing and dividing by 4; place the result into variable Grade

3. If Grade < 50
   then display 'Sorry. You failed with a grade of'   Grade
   else display 'Congratulations. You passed with a grade of'   Grade

4. Halt

We do not require a precise definition of pseudocode for this book because the final algorithm will be presented in Pascal. In some circumstances, however, it is useful to formalize this pseudocode into an *algorithmic language*. (See, for example, Jean-Paul Tremblay and Richard B. Bunt, *An Introduction to Computer Science: An Algorithmic Approach*, 2d ed., New York: McGraw-Hill, 1988.) Such a precise notation can be defined so that it is relatively independent of a particular programming language but similar enough to permit easy translation into a programming language. This approach is particularly valuable when it is desired to present an algorithm in sufficient detail that it is easily translated into any of several different languages.

## 2-3    A SOLUTION METHODOLOGY

As indicated in Fig. 2-1, the development of a computer program is a two-phase process. We have referred to these as the problem-solving phase, in which the objective is to produce a solution to the problem in the form of a detailed algorithm, and the implementation phase, in which the objective is to produce a complete Pascal program. The early stages of the development, however, which we classify as the problem-solving phase, constitute the harder phase, and we place emphasis on it in this book. The later stages of development, in which various details of the Pascal language are incorporated into the design, are referred to as the implementation phase. This phase is reasonably straightforward once the concepts of the Pascal language are mastered.

Problem solving is never easy. There is no simple formula, algorithm, or method which is guaranteed to find a solution to a problem. Rather, would-be problem solvers must practice their problem-solving skills and build a base of experience in order to improve their ability to find solutions to problems. Certain guiding principles have been identified which seem to help in finding solutions to problems. One of the most important, which we will emphasize throughout this book, can be summarized as "divide and conquer." Difficult problems are made easier if they are first broken down into simpler problems—problems for which a solution is more easily obtained. Once the solutions to the simpler subproblems have been developed, they are combined together in an organized way to yield a solution to the original problem.

As noted earlier, algorithms can be expressed in varying levels of detail. In fact, the statement of the problem is itself a solution, although at a very general or abstract level. The final implemented program is a solution at the most detailed level. In between are other solutions as well—at different *levels of abstraction*.

Combining this notion of levels of abstraction with the divide-and-conquer philosophy forms the basis of our solution methodology—the method of *stepwise refinement*. Each refinement adds detail as we work from general to specific.

To better illustrate the problem-solving phase, that is, the development of an algorithm to solve a particular problem, we first use a noncomputerizable problem. We will use the same method of stepwise refinement later to obtain computer algorithms that solve problems.

The problem is: weigh 1 lb of flour into a bowl. We begin by breaking this problem into separate parts and devise the following general solution to this problem:

*1.* Fetch the required items

*2.* Weigh the flour

*3.* Return the items

Here we have relied on past experience with "weighing out" types of problems to pose a feasible refinement of the problem. Recognizing the similarity of a problem to previously solved problems is another important technique in problem solving. Throughout this book we present carefully selected problems and their solutions, which we generally call "applications." Studying these solved problems and then recognizing similarities between them and problems to be solved by the reader is an important aspect of the study of computer programming.

The three steps presented as the general solution to the "weighing flour" problem must be performed in the specified order. Certainly the scale, the flour, and a vessel of some sort must be fetched before the actual weighing! Thus the order for performing the steps is obvious in this case. In more complex problem solutions, the order might not be so obvious. An important requirement in stating an algorithm is that the sequence for performing the steps be stated clearly. In our algorithm, a simple list of steps is to be performed *in the order in which they are listed*. We call this *simple sequencing*.

Let us now refine step 1 of the general algorithm. Again, experience with "weighing problems" and some consideration of this particular problem lead us to the following refinement of step 1:

*1.1.* Fetch the flour sack

*1.2.* Fetch the scales

*1.3.* Fetch the bowl

Notice that we have used a hierarchical numbering system to indicate that these three steps form a refinement of step 1 of the general algorithm.

Step 2 of the general problem is slightly more difficult. We propose, again based on previous experience with weighing, the following refinement:

*2.1.* Weigh the bowl and remember the weight

*2.2.* Put some flour into the bowl

*2.3.* While there is not exactly 1 lb of flour in the bowl:
   add or remove some flour

It happens that there are again three steps to be performed in the sequence indicated. Study the third of these steps. It indicates that some operation (*add or remove some flour*) is to be *repeated* as long as some condition *(not exactly 1 lb of flour)* holds. This is yet another type of sequencing which is important in the statement of some algorithms. Programmers use the term "loops" to denote repetitions in algorithms. The particular kind of loop that involves continuing the repetition *while* some condition holds is frequently called a *while loop*.

To illustrate that refinements can be further decomposed, we will further break step 2.3 down as follows:

*2.3.* While the weight of the bowl, as read by the scale, is not equal
to the weight of the bowl alone plus 1 lb:
*if* the weight of the bowl and flour is less than the weight of
the bowl plus 1 lb,
*then* add some flour to the bowl;
*else* remove some flour from the bowl

We have introduced another important method of controlling the sequence of an algorithm. In the form used here, a condition is given followed by two alternatives. For purposes of illustration, important words are shown in italics. *If* the condition holds true, the first alternative *(then . . .)* is performed; otherwise, the second alternative *(else . . .)* is performed. Notice that this entire alternative construct is contained within (programmers say "nested in") the while loop. Therefore, this alternative construct is repeated some number of times. Each time it is repeated, the condition is considered (programmers say "evaluated" or "computed") again. The condition may be true on some occasions and false on others as flour is added to or removed from the bowl.

We present now the entire detailed algorithm. Observe that we have refined further the third step of the general algorithm.

*1.1.* Fetch the flour sack

*1.2.* Fetch the scales

*1.3.* Fetch the bowl

*2.1.* Weigh the bowl and remember the weight

*2.2.* Put some flour into the bowl

*2.3.* While the weight of the bowl, as read by the scale, is not equal
to the weight of the bowl alone plus 1 lb:
if the weight of the bowl and flour is less than the weight of
the bowl plus 1 lb,
then add some flour to the bowl;
else remove some flour from the bowl

*3.1.* Return the scales

*3.2.* Return the flour

For simple problems this approach may seem unnecessarily tedious. However, it is important that you master the technique. As an analogy, consider the problem of long division. For simple division problems, most people arrive at the answer by inspection, without requiring the methodology of long division. Unless the scope of division problems you can hope to solve is to remain extremely limited, however, you must learn through practice the methodology of long division. The same is true of our approach. Simple algorithms (and programs) can perhaps be produced "by inspection," but more difficult problems require a much more orderly approach. The methodology that we propose extends naturally as the problems become more difficult.

We end this section with a short philosophical note on the existence of algorithms. We have been saying that a key step in the solution of any problem is the development of a suitable algorithm. We have evaded the question, "Will there always be a suitable algorithm?" Certainly this is an important issue. We do not want to waste many hours trying to construct something that cannot be constructed.

It turns out that there are many problems for which it is impossible to develop suitable algorithms, that is, algorithms that guarantee a result after the execution of a finite number of steps. We can specify an algorithm to get from point *A* to point *B* in a strange city. If the instructions are correct, we will get to point *B* eventually. Thus a suitable algorithm does exist for this problem (remember, algorithms must be effective). Suppose, however, that someone were to ask you, "How can I become a concert pianist?" A little reflection ought to convince you that there can be no suitable algorithm for this problem; the person may lack the innate talent to play the piano well, and no algorithm will ever turn that person into a concert pianist.

As you study more computer science, you will learn that there are certain classes of problems that are unsolvable or certain questions that are undecidable. The question "Does a suitable algorithm exist for this particular problem?" is a case in point. It turns out, in fact, that the very question "Is the question decidable?" is itself undecidable. Unfortunately, just about the only way of determining if a suitable algorithm exists for a given problem is to see if one can be constructed. If so, you have shown that at least one algorithm does exist—the one that you have constructed. Suppose, however, that you are unable to construct a suitable algorithm after some measure of effort. This does not mean that one does not exist; it means simply that you have not been able to construct one—not a satisfying state of affairs!

We will not say any more about this problem in this book, but it is something on which you might care to reflect. The theoretical study of algorithms is an exciting and challenging field of computer science. Rest assured that all problems and exercises in this book do have suitable algorithms, even though late some night you may think otherwise.

## EXERCISES 2-3

**1.** Develop an algorithm for changing a flat tire. Assume that a good spare tire and jack are available.

2. Develop an algorithm to get yourself out of the house in the morning. Begin from the state "asleep in bed" and include all your regular morning activities.

3. (a) Develop an algorithm for making a telephone call.
   (b) Expand part (a) to an algorithm for making a long-distance telephone call. Include the possibilities for a station-to-station call, a collect call, and a person-to-person call.

## 2-4 THE IMPLEMENTATION PHASE: AN INTRODUCTION TO THE PROGRAMMING LANGUAGE PASCAL

As an example of solving a computer-oriented problem, consider the problem of computing $9^4$, that is, nine to the fourth power, or $9 \times 9 \times 9 \times 9$, on the computer. We assume that this computation is to be specified eventually in the programming language Pascal. If a direct means for specifying that a number is to be raised to a power were provided in standard Pascal, the problem would be rather simple. (Many programming languages, and indeed some *extended* versions of Pascal, do provide such an operation.) Since standard Pascal does not, we will be forced to specify a solution to the problem in terms of operations that are available. We note that the multiplication operation is available in Pascal and will specify how to compute the fourth power in terms of a number of multiplications. The fact that a problem solution must be expressed in terms of the operations available in the programming language to be used is another principle of algorithm design.

Our first general algorithm is

1. Find $9 \times 9 \times 9 \times 9$

2. Display the result where it can be examined by the user (you!)

The second step requires some clarification. As was explained in Chap. 1, the computer computes using values stored in its memory and stores the results there. In order for the results of a computation to be available to the computer user, however, they must be transmitted to an output device. This may be a printer, which prints numbers and text on paper, or a display terminal, which shows the results on a CRT screen.

In order to store the result of the computation in step 1 and then use that result in step 2, we employ the notion of a variable. In Pascal, we specify the variable by means of a name called an *identifier*. Storing a value (say 0) into a variable (say Sum) is indicated by a statement such as

Sum := 0

which stores 0 into the variable named Sum. Using a variable Product, we can rewrite our algorithm as

1. Product := 9 * 9 * 9 * 9

2. Display the value of the variable Product

Note that we have used $*$, which in Pascal indicates multiplication instead of the usual mathematical symbol $\times$. The $\times$ is, unfortunately, not readily available on most computer equipment.

It is important to understand how we store a value into a variable and then retrieve it in a later step. Although the algorithm as developed so far could now be transformed into a Pascal program, we continue to develop the algorithm in order to illustrate further the use of variables. Consider the algorithm

*1.1.* Product : = 9

*1.2.* Product : = Product * 9

*1.3.* Product : = Product * 9

*1.4.* Product : = Product * 9

*2.* Display the value of Product

In this version, we have computed the product one step at a time. First, Product becomes the value 9. Next, Product is set to the *present value* of Product (namely, 9) times 9; thus Product becomes $9^2$, or 81. In step 1.3 Product is again set to the current value of Product (which is 81 as a result of the previous step) times 9, now giving 81 $\times$ 9, or 729 (which is $9^3$). Observe that the steps are carried out in the same order as they appear in the algorithm.

Combining this idea of computing the power one product at a time with the notion of a while loop permits us to create an algorithm which is easily modified to compute any power of some base number:

*1.* Base : = 9

*2.* Exponent : = 4

*3.* Product : = Base

*4.* Count : = 1

*5.* Repeat thru step 7 while Count < Exponent

*6.* Product : = Product * Base

*7.* Count : = Count + 1

*8.* Display the values of Base, Exponent, and Product

This algorithm is more complex than those given previously, and its execution is more difficult to understand. We therefore give a *trace table* of the algorithm, as illustrated in Table 2-1. Each line of this table shows the algorithm step number executed and the value of each variable *after execution of that step*. Also shown for step 5, which controls the loop, is the status of the test condition, whether it is "true" or "false," and the output produced by step 8.

**TABLE 2-1** Trace of Algorithm to Compute $9^4$

| Algorithm Step | Base | Exponent | Product | Count | Loop Test | Output |
|---|---|---|---|---|---|---|
| 1 | 9 | ? | ? | ? | | |
| 2 | 9 | 4 | ? | ? | | |
| 3 | 9 | 4 | 9 | ? | | |
| 4 | 9 | 4 | 9 | 1 | | |
| 5 | 9 | 4 | 9 | 1 | True | |
| 6 | 9 | 4 | 81 | 1 | | |
| 7 | 9 | 4 | 81 | 2 | | |
| 5 | 9 | 4 | 81 | 2 | True | |
| 6 | 9 | 4 | 729 | 2 | | |
| 7 | 9 | 4 | 729 | 3 | | |
| 5 | 9 | 4 | 729 | 3 | True | |
| 6 | 9 | 4 | 6561 | 3 | | |
| 7 | 9 | 4 | 6561 | 4 | | |
| 5 | 9 | 4 | 6561 | 4 | False | |
| 8 | 9 | 4 | 6561 | 4 | | 9 4 6561 |

It is important to examine this trace table closely. Notice that following step 5, either step 6 (the first step within the loop) or step 8 (the step following the loop) is executed. The choice depends on the condition evaluated *at that point*, whether it is "true" or "false." Also note that each time step 7, the last step within the loop, is completed, the algorithm returns to step 5 to reevaluate the condition.

Tracing in this way is important in finding errors in the algorithms. One of the authors is embarrassed to admit that the first attempt at this algorithm did indeed have a minor error that was discovered in producing the trace table. Try this yourself. Trace the algorithm with the operator $<$ in step 5 replaced by $\leq$. The algorithm would then produce an incorrect result. Such an error in an algorithm has come to be called a *bug*, and the process of finding such errors is known as *debugging*.

We now consider converting our algorithm into a complete Pascal program. At this point we introduce only as much of the Pascal language as is needed to construct simple programs. More complete information is provided in later chapters.

We express a Pascal program in three sections as shown in the following:

Header:          **program** . . .
Declarations:    **var**
                  .
                  .
                  .

Program body: **begin**
.
.
.

**end**.

The first section is the *header*, which gives the name of the program and indicates whether input and/or output is required. We shall call our program Power and indicate that it requires output but not input by the following program header:

**program** Power(output);

The choice of names or identifiers in Pascal programs is subject to certain rules. A small number of words are *reserved* for specific purposes. The word **program**, for example, must appear as the first word in the program and may not be used elsewhere. To emphasize the special nature of reserved words such as **program**, they are typeset in boldface throughout this book.

Nonreserved words are used as identifiers to name various elements of a program. In this example, Power is chosen as the name of the program. Since they are names of specific elements, we have chosen to show them in a sans serif typeface and capitalize the first letter of programmer-chosen identifiers. This is only our own personal convention. It is not required, however, since Pascal treats upper- and lowercase letters in identifiers as equivalent. For example, the identifiers Power and power are considered to be the same.

Certain identifiers have *predefined* meanings in Pascal. This is a different situation from that of reserved words in that a programmer may choose to use these names to define an element of the program. If such an identifier is used in a program but is not specified as naming an element of the program, then it is presumed to name some predefined object. In our example, the identifier output refers to the predefined *output stream* of the program. Text (a sequence of characters) will be transmitted to this output stream. The operating system of a computer normally arranges for the text transmitted to the output stream to be made available on the screen of a terminal or as printed pages.

There are three other symbols in this header—two parentheses and a semicolon. These might be called *punctuation* and are also part of the Pascal language. Because programming languages must be processed by a computer, the punctuation rules are much more rigid than those for a natural language such as English. Learning the specific rules for any programming language is a tedious, but unavoidable part of learning the language. In Pascal, the parentheses and semicolon must occur in exactly the positions illustrated, and no extraneous punctuation may occur.

The rules pertaining to the occurrence of blanks (sometimes called *spaces*) are much less rigorous. Three simple rules apply:

*1.* No blanks may occur within a single identifier or reserved word. We could have named our program

NineToTheFourthPower

or

Ninetothefourthpower

but not

Nine to the fourth power

*2.* One or more blanks must appear between adjacent words. Thus we write

**program** Power

and never

**program**Power

*3.* Blanks are optional everywhere else in the program.

It is important to realize that programs are read by people much more often than by computers. The *readability* of a program is a very important concern. Blanks (or "white space") are used in a program to enhance its readability. They serve to set apart the particular components of a program (identifiers, statements, etc.) so that the program's structure is more readily apparent. Imagine how (much more) difficult this book would be to read without the use of "white space" to separate paragraphs, sections, examples, figures, etc. The same is true for programs, too. We will introduce other devices later on to assist in the production of readable programs.

The second major section of a program declares various identifiers to be used in the program. At this point we introduce only declarations of variables. The variable declarations for the current program are:

**var**

| | |
|---|---|
| Base: integer; | {Number to be raised to a power} |
| Exponent: integer; | {Power to which base is to be raised} |
| Product: integer; | {Result} |
| Count: integer; | {Loop control counter} |

The variable declarations start with the reserved word **var**. Each variable is then declared by giving its identifier, followed by a colon, a type name, and a semicolon. The example contains the predefined type name **integer**, indicating that each of the variables takes on only integer values. Other predefined type names will be introduced later in this chapter.

Text enclosed in braces ("{" and "}") is called a *comment*. Comments are an important part of a program. They also serve to improve the readability and understandability of programs. Comments can appear wherever a blank can appear and are considered equivalent to a blank by the compiler. In other words, they are effectively ignored by the compiler when it processes the program. We shall use a generous number of comments in our programs, not only for pedagogical purposes, but also for understandability, and we encourage you to do likewise. The current example contains a comment for each variable declared, indicating the use of the associated variable within the program.

Pascal is very flexible in its rules for dividing a program into separate lines. A new line may begin wherever a blank may occur within a program. In fact, the computer treats the program as a continuous sequence of characters, with the characters of each line considered to be separated from the preceding line by a single blank. This prohibits splitting a word from one line to the next, because a blank is not allowed within a word.

The final section of a program, the program *body*, describes the algorithm. It starts with the reserved word **begin**. This is followed by one or more *statements*, each of which must be one of the allowable Pascal statement types. One of the most important statement types is the assignment statement, whose purpose is to assign a value to a variable. The assignment statement consists of a variable's identifier, the assignment operator ":=," and a value, as in the statement

Base : = 9

Note that the assignment operator := is a two-character symbol in which embedded blanks are not allowed.

Most programs contain several statements. To avoid confusion, these statements are separated from one another by semicolons. With two statements, for example, we interpose a single semicolon, as in

Base : = 9 ; Exponent : = 4

Frequently, statements are written on separate lines. The semicolon separators, however, are still required, since the compiler does not distinguish lines. The previous statement pair then might be written as

Base : = 9 ;
Exponent : = 4

There is a natural tendency to add an additional semicolon at the end of the last statement in the list of statements. After all, every statement in English ends with some punctuation mark! The designers of Pascal chose to use the semicolon as a statement *separator* rather than as a statement terminator. We must be careful about this, particularly because *sometimes* an extra semicolon does harm—but only sometimes.

In addition to the assignment statement, the current algorithm requires a loop. The notion of a loop was introduced earlier. In Pascal the type of loop required is specified by a construct of the following form:

**while** *condition* **do**
  **begin**
    *list of statements*
  **end**

The condition expresses a relationship that often consists of a comparison of two quantities. In Pascal, comparisons are specified by the following symbols:

| $=$ | is equal to |
| $<$ | is less than |
| $>$ | is greater than |
| $<=$ | is less than or equal to |
| $>=$ | is greater than or equal to |
| $<>$ | is not equal to |

The statements within a loop are also separated by semicolons. If there is only one statement to be repeated, then the reserved words **begin** and **end** (within the loop) may be omitted.

Our algorithm requires the loop

```
while Count < Exponent do
  begin
    Product : = Product * Base;
    Count : = Count + 1
  end
```

Note that there is no semicolon following the statement Count : = Count + 1 —there is nothing to separate it from.

The final step in this algorithm requires displaying the values of the variables Base, Exponent, and Product on a terminal screen or a printed page. The *writeln statement* is used for transmitting the values of a list of variables, in a readable (display) form, to the output stream. The desired output in the current example is specified by the statement

```
writeln (Base, Exponent, Product)
```

The parentheses surrounding the output list are required, and the variables in the list are separated by commas.

Surprisingly, writeln is not a reserved word in Pascal, but rather a predefined identifier. Our convention specifies that writeln not appear in boldface. A programmer *could* declare writeln to be the name of a variable, but that would be very unwise. The identifier writeln would then always refer to the variable, and there would now be no way to output the results! (Actually, there are some other statements that output results, but the writeln statement is too important to lose.)

The program finally ends with the reserved word **end** followed by a single period. It is easy to forget the period. Many Pascal compilers refuse to process the program correctly without it, so it is worth checking each program for its presence.

We shall normally divide the body of a program into sections, each preceded by a blank line and a comment. This considerably enhances the readability of the program. In this text, these comments frequently include step numbers for ease of reference in the accompanying program description.

We present the completed program in Fig. 2-4. Assuming you have access to a computer system, try running this program. Before you can do this, several necessary pieces of information, specific to your own computer installation, must be obtained from other sources. First, the program must be put into a form which the computer can process. Frequently, this is accomplished by using a terminal (connected to the computer) and a text editor program to enter the source program, which is subsequently stored on some magnetic recording medium (disk or tape). Next, the Pascal program must be translated by a compiler into the machine language of the machine being used. Finally, the computer must be instructed to run the resulting machine language program, including associating the output stream with an appropriate output device (terminal display or printer) so that the results may be observed. Details of all these steps are necessary before you can proceed.

```
program Power (output);
{Program to compute 9 to the fourth power}
var
    Base: integer;          {Number to be raised to a power}
    Exponent: integer;      {Power to which base is to be raised}
    Product: integer;       {Result}
    Count: integer;         {Loop control counter}
begin
    {Step 1: Initialize Base}
    Base : = 9;

    {Step 2: Initialize Power}
    Exponent : = 4;

    {Step 3: Initialize result so far}
    Product : = Base;

    {Step 4: Initialize loop counter}
    Count : = 1;

    {Step 5: Loop test}
    while Count < Exponent do
        begin

            {Step 6: Recompute result so far}
            Product : = Product * Base;

            {Step 7: Increment counter}
            Count : = Count + 1
        end;

    {Step 8: Display result}
    writeln (Base, Exponent, Product)
end.
```

**FIGURE 2-4**
**Program to**
**compute $9^4$.**

Running this example program will ensure that you become familiar with the steps involved in running a Pascal program. You also may become acquainted with the fact that it is difficult to get so many details exactly right the first time! Indeed, very few programs run correctly the first time.

One source of difficulty is the insistence of the Pascal compiler that the "punctuation rules," hereafter called *syntax rules*, of Pascal be followed *exactly*. A common mistake is misplacing the semicolons. Because it is important that you think correctly (as far as Pascal is concerned) from the beginning, let's review the rule. The statements between the **begin** and **end** of the program are *separated* by semicolons. Two statements require one semicolon; three statements, two semicolons; and so on. In counting the statements, an *entire* while–do–begin–end construct is counted as a *single statement*. Thus our Power program has six statements separated by five semicolons; here we have not counted the individual statements (or the semicolons) within the begin–end section of the while loop.

The semicolon rule is applied again within the begin–end section of the loop. In our example, two statements here require one semicolon. In order to illustrate the location of the semicolons better, we repeat the program section of Fig. 2-4 with the comments removed as Fig. 2-5.

The development of a computer program to solve a particular problem is a lot of work, perhaps more work than solving the problem by other means in some cases. Such was certainly the case for the problem of $9^4$, although in this case we wanted a simple problem to demonstrate the techniques involved. Using a computer to solve a problem is worthwhile if the problem is difficult to solve by other means, for example, analyzing Shakespeare's writings for word frequency would be enormously tedious by hand. A

```
program Power (output);
{Program to compute 9 to the fourth power}
var
    Base: integer;
    Exponent: integer;
    Product: integer;
    Count: integer;
begin
    Base := 9;
    Exponent := 4;
    Product := Base;
    Count := 1;
    while Count < Exponent do
        begin
            Product := Product *Base;
            Count := Count + 1
        end;
    writeln (Base, Exponent, Product)
end.
```

**FIGURE 2-5**
Program to compute
$9^4$ (without comments).

computer is used frequently to solve problems which require rapid calculations. Such would be the case, for example, in computing the redirection of thrust in a rocket to keep it on course. The calculation might need to be completed in a fraction of a second. Computers are fast! Finally, computer programs can be prepared to solve a class of problems rather than a single problem. For example, we can generalize our program that computes $9^4$ to one that computes $A^B$ for any integers $A$ and $B$ (subject to certain limitations to be discussed later in this chapter).

For this generalization, we introduce another type of statement, the *read statement*. Like the assignment statement, the read statement stores values in variables. In the case of the read statement, however, the values are not specified within the program. Rather, they are obtained from an input device while the program is being executed. The read statement contains a list of variables separated by commas, as in the statement

read (Base, Exponent)

This statement obtains two values from the *input stream* and stores these values, in the order obtained, in the respective variables in the list. As was the case for the writeln statement, the manner in which the input stream is associated with a particular input device is different on different systems. If we assume that the input stream is associated with a terminal, then during execution of the program a programmer must type two numbers separated by one or more blanks. The execution of a program will be temporarily suspended at the read statement until the two values have been entered before proceeding. (Some systems will require typing a carriage return before the values are transmitted to the program.)

The entire program appears in Fig. 2-6. Notice that the header line specifies both input and output streams as being used.

The previous examples have illustrated sequential control and loops in Pascal. The if–then–else construct introduced earlier allows the choice of one course of action from two alternatives. Let us see how to express this in Pascal. Suppose we wish to choose the largest of three given input numbers and output the result. One method would be to read the three numbers and do a series of comparisons. This method certainly works, but it does not generalize easily to the case of more than three numbers. It is left to the reader to consider the comparisons required to determine the largest of 10 numbers. Rather, we choose to illustrate an algorithm which, by making use of the properties of variables, finds the largest of the three given numbers. We then generalize this algorithm so that the largest of an arbitrary number of input values is found.

The approach taken is important, because it applies to the solution of several other problems throughout the book. We make use of a variable to hold the value of the largest number found so far. Then as each succeeding number is read, we will update this variable so that it still contains the largest value encountered *after considering* this new number. An algorithm for this problem follows:

```
program Power (input, output);
{Program to compute an integer to an integer power}
var
   Base: integer;          {Number to be raised to a power}
   Exponent: integer;      {Power to which base is to be raised}
   Product: integer;       {Result}
   Count: integer;         {Loop control counter}
begin
   {Step 1: Obtain input values}
   read (Base, Exponent);

   {Step 2: Initialize result so far}
   Product : = Base;

   {Step 3: Initialize loop counter}
   Count : = 1;

   {Step 4: Loop test}
   while Count < Exponent do
      begin

         {Step 5: Recompute result so far}
         Product : = Product * Base;

         {Step 6: Increment counter}
         Count : = Count + 1
      end;

   {Step 7: Display result}
   writeln (Base, Exponent, Product)
end.
```

**FIGURE 2-6**
**Program to compute**
**a given integer**
**to an integer power.**

*1.* Read the first number into the variable **Largest**

*2.* Read the second number into the variable **Current**

*3.* If **Current** > **Largest,**
   then **Largest** : = **Current**
   (otherwise **Largest** is already the largest)

*4.* Read the third number into **Current**

*5.* If **Current** > **Largest,**
   then **Largest** : = **Current**

*6.* Display the value of **Largest** as the largest of the three numbers

Observe that after step 1, **Largest** contains the value of the largest number

```
program LargestOfThree (input, output);
{Program to find the largest of three numbers}
var
    Largest: integer;      {Largest value so far}
    Current: integer;      {Current number being considered}
begin
    {Step 1: Read first number}
    read (Largest);

    {Step 2: Read second number}
    read (Current);

    {Step 3: Update largest so far}
    if Current > Largest
    then Largest : = Current;

    {Step 4: Read third number}
    read (Current);

    {Step 5: Update largest so far}
    if Current > Largest
    then Largest : = Current;

    {Step 6: Display largest value}
    writeln (Largest)
end.
```

**FIGURE 2-7**
**Program to obtain**
**the largest of**
**three numbers.**

read so far. (One value was read, so it is the largest.) Again after step 3, when two numbers have been read, Largest will still contain the largest value regardless of whether it was the first number read or the second. After step 5, Largest contains the largest of three values. Clearly, we could easily extend the algorithm to more numbers by inserting additional steps between steps 5 and 6.

The Pascal implementation of this algorithm is shown in Fig. 2-7. It is important to examine the syntax structure of the construct to select from alternative courses of action.

**if** *condition*
**then** *Statement1*
**else** *Statement2*

*Statement1* (the "true" alternative) is executed only if the condition evaluates to "true"; otherwise *Statement2* (the "false" alternative) is selected. Note that only *one* of *Statement1* or *Statement2* is executed, not both. Often the construct is used without the else part, as in

**if** *condition*
**then** *statement*

In this form the statement following the **then** is executed only if the condition is "true"; otherwise, control simply passes to the next statement. Notice that the if–then–else statement contains no semicolons. In particular, there is never a semicolon immediately preceding the **else**. In the program in Fig. 2-7 there is a semicolon following the if–then statement.

**if** Current > Largest
**then** Largest : = Current;

This semicolon is not part of the assignment statement within the alternative statement. Rather, it is present because the entire if–then statement is treated as a single statement for the purpose of placing semicolons in the program. This semicolon is present to *separate* the if–then statement from the next statement in the program, as illustrated in Fig. 2-8.

Although the program in Fig. 2-7 is easily extended to accommodate more numbers, its length grows proportionately. A program to find the largest of 1000 numbers would contain 2000 steps! A shorter program (but not a faster program) can be written using a loop, as in Fig. 2-9. This program uses an if–then statement inside the loop. We say that the if–then is *nested* within the loop. Each time the loop condition evaluates to "true," then all the statements, including the if–then statement, are reexecuted. Each time the if–then statement is executed, its condition is evaluated, and its "then" part is selected only if its condition is "true." A trace table for this program is left as an exercise.

The program in Fig. 2-9 illustrates another Pascal declaration, called a *constant definition*. The syntax of this definition is the reserved word **const** followed by one or more definitions. Each definition consists of an identifier, an equal sign, a value, and a semicolon, as in the example

**const**
  Number = 1000;

where the identifier Number is used in place of the actual number 1000 throughout the program. Such a constant declaration facility serves two purposes. First, it enhances the readability of the program, provided a suitable name is chosen for the constant's identifier. Using Number in the

**begin**
  .
  .
  .
  **if** Current > Largest ⎫ Pascal Statement
  **then** Largest : = Current; ⎬
  read (Current); ⎭ Another Pascal Statement
  .
  .
  .
**end**.

FIGURE 2-8
**The placing of semicolons in a program containing an alternative statement.**

```
program LargestOfOneThousand (input, output);
{Program to find the largest of one thousand numbers}
const
    Number = 1000;     {Number of numbers to be read}
var
    Largest: integer;       {Largest value so far}
    Current: integer;       {Current number being considered}
    Count: integer;         {Number of numbers read so far}
begin
    {Step 1: Read first number and set Count}
    read (Largest);
    Count := 1;

    {Step 2: Engage loop to read each additional number}
    while (Count < Number) do
        begin

            {Step 3: Read next number and update Count}
            read (Current);
            Count := Count + 1;

            {Step 4: Update largest so far}
            if Current > Largest
            then Largest := Current
        end; {of the while loop}

    {Step 5: Display result}
    writeln (Largest)
end.
```

**FIGURE 2-9**
**Program to obtain**
**the largest of**
**1000 numbers.**

program instead of 1000 helps the reader understand its significance. Finally, the appearance of the constant declaration at the beginning of the program allows easier modification of the program to process different amounts of data. This facility offers only a slight improvement in the current short program. In larger and more complex programs, however, considerable improvement can result. This sort of issue is discussed further in Chap. 7.

Let us now consider a problem to compute the payroll for a small company. The problem is simplified considerably as compared to a real payroll problem. The Garret Breedlove Flying School has 20 employees. Each is assigned an employee number and works for a specific rate of pay. The monthly pay is computed by multiplying the hours worked, up to a maximum of 170 hours, by the rate of pay. If employees work more than 170 hours a month, they are paid at the normal rate for the first 170 hours and at time-and-a-half for any additional hours.

A set of three numbers is prepared for each employee: namely, numbers for employee number, rate of pay, and hours worked. The input stream is supplied with a set of three numbers for the first employee, followed by three values for the second employee, etc., up to and including the three numbers for the twentieth employee. It is also required that the program print the total pay for all 20 employees for the month.

A general algorithm is as follows:

*1.* Set total pay variable to zero

*2.* Repeat thru step 6 twenty times (once for each employee)

*3.* Obtain the set of data for the current employee

*4.* Compute pay for the current employee

*5.* Display information, including total pay, for the current employee

*6.* Add current employee's pay to the total pay

*7.* Display the total pay

We wish to elaborate on (or decompose) step 4 of this algorithm. Rather than include the refinement of this step in-line in the general algorithm, we will decompose it separately as a *subalgorithm* as follows:

Subalgorithm **ComputeEmployeePay**

*1.* If the number of hours worked is less than or equal to 170,
then **PayEarned : = RateOfPay * HoursWorked;**
else **PayEarned : = RateOfPay * 170 + 1.5 * RateOfPay ***
**(HoursWorked − 170);**

*2.* Return to the main algorithm

This subalgorithm can then be invoked (or *called*) directly from step 4 of the main algorithm rather than copying these steps into the main algorithm. The importance of the subalgorithm is that the details of *how* the pay is computed for each employee do not clutter up the main algorithm. A programmer studying the main algorithm can understand the method used for computing the company's monthly payroll as long as it is understood that a subalgorithm that computes an individual's pay exists. Understanding the general algorithm requires knowing only *what* the subalgorithm does.

Also, the details of pay computations may change. With this implementation, changes would certainly be required in the subalgorithm, but the main algorithm would be unaffected. The use of subalgorithms in this way enhances considerably the *modularity* of algorithms and programs and thus is most desirable. This will be an important theme throughout the book.

The statements are expressed in terms of their *parameters*, variables local to the subalgorithm itself. At the time the subalgorithm is actually invoked, an association is established between variables in the context of the main algorithm (referred to as *arguments*) and the parameters of the subalgorithm. Details of how this is done are given in Chap. 4.

Pascal defines the concept of a *procedure*, corresponding to our algorithmic notion of a subalgorithm. A procedure corresponding to the payroll subalgorithm appears in Fig. 2-10.

Like a program, a procedure must begin with a header. The header of a procedure is somewhat more complex than that of a program. It begins with the reserved word **procedure** followed by a programmer-chosen identifier used to refer to the procedure. This is followed by a list of the *parameters* of the procedure enclosed in parentheses and, finally, a semicolon.

The parameters represent values to be transmitted to the procedure *(input parameters)* and values supplied by the procedure to the main program *(output parameters)*. We have listed each parameter in Fig. 2-10 on a separate line for reasons of clarity and readability.

An input parameter is given as an identifier, a colon, a type, and a comment, as in

EmpRate: real;     {Input, employee's rate of pay}

The example procedure introduces a new type, specified by the predefined identifier **real**. An integer variable can hold only an integral value. In the payroll example we desire the ability to specify fractional values and mixed values for the rate of pay, for example, 5.25 to represent $5.25 per hour.

An output parameter is specified in a manner similar to that used for an input parameter, except that the reserved word **var** appears immediately before *each* output parameter. It is somewhat unfortunate that Pascal uses the same reserved word for both output parameters and variable declarations because the syntax rules are considerably different.

The usual problem arises with the semicolons. Since they *separate* the parameters, the last parameter is *not* followed by a semicolon.

```
procedure ComputeEmployeePay (
    EmpRate: real;        {Input, employee's rate of pay}
    EmpHours: real;       {Input, employee's pay for the month}
    var EmpPay: real      {Output, employee's pay for the month}
                        );
{Compute monthly pay for an employee.}
begin
    {Step 1: Determine whether no overtime was worked}
    if EmpHours <= 170

    {Step 2: Compute pay if no overtime}
    then EmpPay : = EmpRate *EmpHours

    {Step 3: Compute pay if there were overtime hours}
    else EmpPay : = EmpRate *170 + 1.5 * EmpRate *(EmpHours − 170)

    {Step 4: Return to main algorithm}
end;
```

**FIGURE 2-10**
A Pascal procedure
for computing an
employee's monthly
pay.

```pascal
program Payroll (input, output);
{Monthly payroll computation}
const
    NumberOfEmployees = 20;
var
    TotalPay: real;        {Total payroll for the month}
    Number: integer;       {Current employee number}
    Rate: real;            {Current employee rate}
    Hours: real;           {Current employee hours worked}
    Pay: real;             {Current employee's pay}
    Count: integer;        {Count of employees processed so far}
{Insert procedure ComputeEmployeePay here}
begin
    {Step 1: Initialize total pay}
    TotalPay : = 0;

    {Step 2: Set up loop to process twenty employees}
    Count : = 0;
    while Count < NumberOfEmployees do
        begin

            {Step 3: Obtain the set of data for one employee}
            read (Number, Rate, Hours);

            {Step 4: Compute the pay for the current employee}
            ComputeEmployeePay (Rate, Hours, Pay);

            {Step 5: Display information about current employee}
            writeln (Number, Rate, Hours, Pay);

            {Step 6: Add this employee's pay to total and update count of
                employees processed.}
            TotalPay : = TotalPay + Pay;
            Count : = Count + 1;

        end; {of while loop}

    {Step 7: Display total pay}
    writeln (TotalPay)
end.
```

**FIGURE 2-11**
**Program for a**
**simple payroll**
**application.**

The extensive comments at the beginning of a procedure, particularly those describing the parameters, are crucial to understanding *what* the procedure does without delving into *how* it does it.

Following the procedure heading, the remainder of the procedure is similar in syntax to a program following the program header. First, there are some declarations of constants and variables which are used only by the procedure for its own purposes. These are the *local variables*. Our simple procedure requires none. Following the declarations is a list of statements, within a **begin** and **end** pair, accomplishing the purpose of the procedure. Since code will follow the procedure, the **end** is followed by a semicolon rather than the period used in a program.

The program in Fig. 2-11 implements the main program for our problem. The procedure is referenced in step 4 by a *procedure call statement*. This names the procedure and supplies a list of *argument variables* corresponding to the input and output parameters of the procedure. It is important that the arguments correspond one for one with the parameters if the procedure is to use the correct values in its computation and to set the correct variables with its results.

If the payroll program is to be run, there are two final considerations. Pascal requires that all the procedures required by a program be included between the variable declarations and the first **begin**. Finally, the program will produce its results in a peculiar notation. This is discussed later on in this chapter. We have introduced the basic ideas of algorithms and their implementation in Pascal. The remainder of this chapter considers the important notions of variables and computations using them in more detail. Chapter 3 continues with a more detailed examination of sequence of control. Chapter 4 reexamines procedures in more detail.

## EXERCISES 2-4

1. Modify the algorithm presented for computing $9^4$ so that it computes $2^8$.

2. Develop an algorithm to compute the sum of the integers from 1 to 10, that is, $1 + 2 + 3 + 4 + 5 + 6 + 7 + 8 + 9 + 10$. Use a loop to do this in a fashion similar to the loop used in the "power" algorithm.

★ 3. Develop an algorithm to compute and display successive powers of 2 from 0 to 10, that is, $2^0, 2^1, 2^2, \ldots, 2^{10}$. *Hint*: Put most of the power algorithm inside another loop.

## 2-5  DATA, DATA TYPES, AND PRIMITIVE OPERATIONS

The primary purpose of any computer is the manipulation of information or data. The data can be weekly sales figures in a department store's inventory system, names and addresses in a mailing list, final grades in a computer science class, measurements from a scientific experiment, and so on. Most computers are capable of dealing with several different types (or modes) of data. When most people think of computers, they think of numeric data. Computers are very adept at performing computations on numeric data, such as measurements from a scientific experiment, but as we will see, their capabilities extend beyond this type of data. Computers are increasingly applied to problems involving nonnumeric data, and many of these will be discussed. For example, computer processing of textual material has become quite common. The data in such instances is largely nonnumeric, involving strings of alphabetic characters.

The different types of data are represented in different ways in a computer, and in fact, the computer even has different instructions to deal with the different types. At this time it is not important to go into the details, but certain facts are important. Numeric data can be represented in two distinctly different ways: as *integer numbers* or as *real numbers*. It is important to remember that these are different representations and are handled differently by the computer.

## 2-5.1  INTEGER DATA

*Integers* correspond to whole numbers. They have no fractional or decimal component and may be either positive or negative. The following are examples of integers:

|      |     |
|------|-----|
| 13   | 7   |
| −6   | 208 |
| 7830 | 16  |
| −295 | 25  |

It should be noted that each version of Pascal will restrict integers to a certain range. The range −32768 through +32767 is common on many small computers.

## 2-5.2  REAL DATA

Many applications require numbers that go beyond the realm of integers into that of *real numbers*. In our computer representation, real numbers always contain a decimal point, or a power-of-10 exponent (described subsequently in this section), or both. Fractions must be stored in a computer as their decimal equivalent, since there is no mechanism for storing numerators and denominators. Thus the decimal portion of a real number is used to represent any fractional part. Again, the numbers can be either positive or negative. The following are examples of real numbers:

|        |          |         |
|--------|----------|---------|
| 23.8   | 3738.72  | 13.0    |
| 3.6752 | −56.321  | 0.1     |
| −8.910 | −7.7     | −0.001  |

In some scientific applications, we require a special representation to handle very large numbers, such as the mass of the sun, or very small numbers, such as the thickness of a very thin film. A computer representation of any number, however, be it integer or real, has only a certain fixed number of digits. The actual number may vary from machine to machine, but eight significant digits is typical. Thus we face a problem when we must represent a number such as 3,863,213,632 or 0.00000002857, for example. Neither of these numbers can be represented in only eight digits. Science has traditionally coped with this problem with a special notation in which a certain number of *digits of accuracy* (or precision) are expressed, followed by the magnitude of the number expressed as a power of 10. For example, we might write 3,863,213,632 to four digits of accuracy as $3.863 \times 10^9$. Although these values are clearly not the same, the second version is shorter to write and is probably sufficiently accurate for most applications. Most measuring devices have associated with them a certain limit of accuracy anyway. Try to measure the width of your thumb to five digits of accuracy on a ruler. For most applications, three or four digits of accuracy are enough. In the previous example ($3.863 \times 10^9$) we have given four. The power of 10 used (here, 9) converts the number to the correct magnitude. The conversion rule is

*1.* Decide how many digits of accuracy you wish to retain (if necessary, the last digit is rounded).

*2.* Add 1 to the power of 10 used as the multiplier for each place that you moved the decimal point to the left (the decimal point may be shown or else only implied).

Suppose that we wished to retain seven digits of accuracy. The representation is derived as follows:

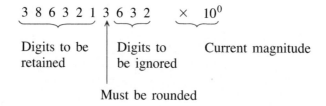

The decimal point moves three positions to the left:

$$3\ 8\ 6\ 3\ 2\ 1\ 3\ 6\ 3\ 2$$

giving us the representation

$$3\ 8\ 6\ 3\ 2\ 1\ 4 \times 10^3$$

This is the general principle for the representation of very large numbers. In actual practice, we usually carry it one step further. We always try to write the number in the same way. We will assume that in this *normalized representation* the decimal point is always placed immediately before the first significant digit. In the preceding example, this requires moving the decimal point an additional seven places to the left. Thus our final representation, to seven digits of accuracy, is

$$0 \, . \, 3 \, 8 \, 6 \, 3 \, 2 \, 1 \, 4 \quad \times \quad 10^{10}$$

Digits of accuracy          Magnitude
(precision)

We will refer to a number represented in this fashion as a *floating-point number*. This is nothing more than a special representation for real numbers. Incidentally, readers familiar with the use of logarithms will note a certain similarity in representation.

For very small numbers, we apply the same principles to get their floating-point representation. In this case, however, we shift the decimal point to the right to get the normalized representation, and as we do, we subtract 1 from the power of 10 used as the multiplier for each place moved. The rest of our conversion rule applies as stated.

For example, to represent the number 0.00000002857 (or $0.00000002857 \times 10^0$) to three digits of accuracy, we move the decimal point seven places to the right and round the 5 up to 6 to get

$$0.286 \times 10^{-7}$$

To summarize the conversion of very large or very small numbers to normalized floating-point form:

*1.* Decide how many digits of accuracy you wish to retain in the final representation. Round the last digit if necessary.

*2.* Adjust the magnitude portion of the number accordingly. For each place the decimal point is moved to the left, add 1 to the power of 10 used as multiplier; for each place moved to the right, subtract 1 from the power of 10.

These procedures may seem tiresome at this point. In fact, they are quite important. The word size of the computer places real limitations on the lengths of numbers that can be stored, as described earlier. In order to live within these limitations yet retain the ability to perform calculations with a wide range of numbers, special representations are needed. The representation described is close to the internal representation of floating-point numbers inside the computer itself. The representation has two components, called the *fraction* portion and the *exponent* portion. Each of these has an associated sign. To illustrate these terms on our earlier examples:

$$0.3863214 \times 10^{10}$$

| | |
|---|---|
| Fraction: | $+.3863214$ |
| Exponent: | $+10$ |

$$0.286 \times 10^{-7}$$

| | |
|---|---|
| Fraction: | $+.286$ |
| Exponent: | $-7$ |

The decimal point itself is not actually stored. Since it is assumed to be in the same position always (an advantage of normalized representation), we need not waste storage on it. It is inserted automatically whenever the number is read or written.

A program written in the Pascal language is meant to be entered into a computer system where it will be compiled and executed. Since most computer devices have very restricted character sets, for example, no super-scripts, Pascal uses an alternative representation for floating-point numbers. In the following, the **E** stands for "times ten to the power of."

| **Power of 10 Notation** | **Pascal Language** |
|---|---|
| $3863214 \times 10^3$ | **3863214E3** |
| $0.3863214 \times 10^{10}$ | **0.3863214E10** |
| $0.286 \times 10^{-7}$ | **0.286E−7** |

In Pascal, a real number may be written without a decimal point provided an exponent appears; thus **1.0E5** may be written **1E5**. A special restriction of Pascal is that a real number, whether or not the exponent (**E**) part is present, must have a digit both before and after the decimal point. Thus we write **0.1** instead of **.1** and **42.0E2** instead of **42.E2**.

### 2-5.3  BOOLEAN (LOGICAL) DATA

The *Boolean data type* (named after mathematician George Boole, who was one of the early developers of logic theory) is also sometimes called the *logical data type* and can take on the values "true" and "false." These values are used to perform logical operations; however, we will defer discussion of these operations until Chap. 3.

### 2-5.4  CHARACTER DATA

In addition to numbers, we are going to become extensively involved in the storage and manipulation of nonnumeric items, examples of which are the *character* and the *character string*. A character can be any of some large number of possible characters that are known to the computer: the familiar alphabetic characters (A, B, . . . , X, Y, Z, a, b, . . . , x, y, z), the digits (0, 1, 2, . . . , 8, 9), and a variety of special characters (blank, $, #, _, etc.). A character string is, as you might expect, a string of characters. A character or character string may be represented in a program as a collection of these characters beginning and ending with the special character "quote" (') so we know where the string begins and ends. We refer to the quotes as string *delimiters*. In standard Pascal, a character string that contains only one character represents a character value, whereas if it contains two or more characters, it represents a true character string. Unfortunately, standard Pascal distinguishes between a one-character value and a character string. We shall return to this problem in Chap. 6. A character string can be any length in theory, but most Pascal compilers place some limit on their length. Examples of character strings are

'Paul Tremblay'

'Rick Bunt'

'The University of Saskatchewan, Saskatoon'

'Computing science is, of course, my favorite class'

'333 + 444 gives 777'

Internally, the computer records the characters that make up the string, excluding the delimiting quotes, which are not part of the string itself.

Occasionally, we may require a quote mark itself as a character value or as part of a character string. To distinguish such a quote from one of the string delimiters, we represent it by two consecutive quotes, called an *apostrophe image*. Thus the string O'Dell is represented by

'O''Dell'

and the string representing a single quote character is

''''

Chapter 6 describes the string facilities of Pascal in more detail.

When reading this book it is sometimes difficult to distinguish actual spaces from spacing that occurs in the typesetting process. When it is important to know exactly how many blanks are present in a string, we use the character "□" to represent a single blank character. Thus we might denote a string as

'John□DeDourek'

This indicates that exactly one blank occurs between the characters n and D. When actually preparing the program for the compiler, an ordinary blank is to be used.

## 2-5.5 SYNTAX RULES

A Pascal program is composed of elements such as variables, numbers, operators, expressions, etc. We call these *constructs* of the language. The rules for writing some construct in Pascal, including the placement of punctuation, etc., are referred to as the *syntax rules*. A *syntax diagram* graphically illustrates the syntax rules of a particular Pascal construct. Figure 2-12 illustrates, for example, the syntax of an integer number, and Fig. 2-13 that of

integer number

FIGURE 2-12  Syntax diagram for integer number.

an unsigned integer number. Each diagram begins with the name of the construct being defined, in these cases "integer number" and "unsigned integer number." The diagram consists of rectangular and rounded boxes connected by arrows. A rounded box indicates an actual occurrence of the symbols contained within it. A rectangular box indicates occurrence of an instance of the construct named in the box. A particular construct is correct according to the rules of Pascal if it corresponds to a path through the syntax diagram from its entry point (the arrow that enters the diagram at the left) to its exit point (the arrow that leaves the diagram at the right). The reader is urged to trace the previous examples of integers through the syntax diagrams. We present syntax diagrams for real numbers and unsigned real numbers in Figs. 2-14 and 2-15, respectively. Finally Figs. 2-16 and 2-17 present syntax diagrams for character values and character strings, respectively. Recall that a character value consists of a single character. We shall explore the distinction between character values and character strings of length greater than 1 later.

## 2-5.6  OPERATIONS

The representation of data is only one side of the coin; computations require that we be able to manipulate these data elements as well. We are all familiar with the four basic operations on numeric data: addition, subtraction, multiplication, and division. For the nonnumeric data types, the operations are less familiar. First, let us consider the numeric operations briefly. Nonnumeric operations are dealt with in later chapters, particularly Chap. 6 on character strings.

Addition and subtraction are represented in the usual way. Multiplication, however, has a small notational problem. Because most computer devices do not have a true multiply sign ($\times$) and to avoid possible confusion with the letter $x$, the multiplication operation is denoted by " $*$ ", as in $36.8*2.59$. Division also has a notational problem. Normally, we are required to keep the entire operation confined to a single line, a constraint again dictated by limitations of traditional computer devices. This means that

unsigned integer number

FIGURE 2-13
Syntax diagram
for unsigned
integer number.

**real number**

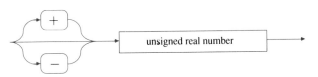

FIGURE 2-14  Syntax diagram for real number.

something like

$$\frac{8}{2}$$

cannot be written. Instead, we use the slash to denote the division operation, as in **8 / 2**.

We have been very careful to distinguish between the two types of numeric data (integer and real). We write them differently, and the computer stores them differently. As long as we continue to preserve this distinction in our mathematical operations, things remain fairly straightforward. The general rule is that the result of any operation has the same type as its two operands. For example, if we add two real numbers, we get a real result. If we multiply two integer numbers, we get an integer result. If we divide two real numbers, we get a real result. A problem may arise if we divide two integer numbers. If we followed this same rule, we would get an integer result. Thus the result of **8 / 2** would be **4**, an integer. What would happen, however, if this were **8 / 5**? We know that the answer is 1.6, but this is not an integer. There are two possibilities, in fact, for an integer result: either **1** or **2**. If the resulting answer is **1**, we say that it has been *truncated*; if it is **2**, we say it has been *rounded*.

This situation becomes even more undesirable if allowed to go unchecked. Consider the expression

$$\frac{1}{4} \times 4$$

**unsigned real number**

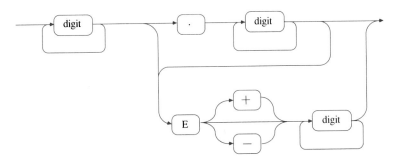

FIGURE 2-15
Syntax diagram for
unsigned real number.

character value

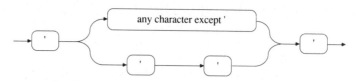

FIGURE 2-16   Syntax diagram for character value.

The obvious answer would be 1, right? Wrong! First, it would be expressed as 1/4*4. Now, since all numbers involved in the expression are integers, all results (including intermediate results) would be integers according to the previous rule. Let us suppose we carry out these operations in the normal order, from left to right, that is, dividing before multiplying. The first operation is 1/4. We know that the real answer is 0.25, but for an integer result, assuming truncation, it would be 0. We refer to this as an *intermediate* result, since we have not yet completed the calculation. The next operation is 0*4, which is clearly 0. Thus 1/4*4 would give the answer 0. Observe that this obviously undesirable situation is a direct consequence of the hazards of integer division. With real numbers, this problem would not have arisen.

Although some programming languages (for example, FORTRAN) follow the rule as described, Pascal introduces an exception to the rule in order to mitigate the effects of misuse of integer division. In Pascal, the operator "/" always returns a real result. Thus 1/4 is indeed 0.25 in Pascal. But what about (1/4)*4? If the 1/4 gives 0.25, we then have 0.25*4, which is a real times an integer. Fortunately, in Pascal (though not in some other programming languages) it is usually permissible to mix real and integer values. For the operators +, −, *, and / operating on a real and an integer value, a copy of the integer is converted to the real equivalent and the operation is performed as a real operator, yielding, of course, a real result. In our example, we have 0.25*4, which is 1.0.

There are situations, however, when a truncating integer divide is useful. Pascal uses the operator symbol **div** to indicate this operation. The result of the integer divide is alway an integer, as illustrated in these examples:

character string

FIGURE 2-17
Syntax diagram
for character string.

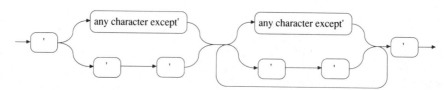

4 **div** 2 = 2
7 **div** 2 = 3
−7 **div** 2 = −3
7 **div** −2 = −3
−7 **div** −2 = 3

Notice the use of the *word symbol* **div** as an operator. Use of such word symbols is necessitated by the limited character set available on most computer devices. We often call a word symbol a *reserved word* because Pascal does not permit its use for any other purpose, such as variable identifiers. Recall that we are using boldface letters to call attention to reserved words; they are, however, typed in the normal manner when entered into a computer. The reserved words of standard Pascal are given in Table 2-2. Some compilers specify additional reserved words for defining nonstandard extensions to Pascal. It would be wise for a programmer to consult a manual or the instructor to obtain the full list for the compiler to be used.

At least one blank must precede a reserved word if it immediately follows a letter or a digit. Likewise one blank must follow a reserved word if it is immediately followed by a letter or digit. Thus we must write i **div** j and never i**div**j. Note that Pascal allows reserved words to be typed in uppercase, for example, **DIV** instead of **div**, to accommodate computer equipment that has only uppercase letters.

Related to **div** is the operator **mod**, which gives the remainder, in the "long division" sense, instead of the quotient. Thus

4 **mod** 2 = 0
7 **mod** 2 = 1
−7 **mod** 2 = 1

Note the perhaps unexpected sign of the last case. Standard Pascal defines **mod** only if the second argument (i.e., the j in i **mod** j) is positive. Further, the value of i **mod** j is $(i - k * j)$ for the integer k, making $0 \le i \text{ mod } j < j$. Use of **mod** is considered an error if the second argument is negative. Fortunately, **mod** is most useful in problems in which both arguments are positive.

**TABLE 2-2** Reserved Words in Pascal

| | | | |
|---|---|---|---|
| and | end | nil | set |
| array | file | not | then |
| begin | for | of | to |
| case | function | or | type |
| const | goto | packed | until |
| div | if | procedure | var |
| do | in | program | while |
| downto | label | record | with |
| else | mod | repeat | |

It is important to consider one restriction in the use of **div** and **mod**. Consider 8.0 **div** 2.0. The answer is not 4.0 because **div** (as well as **mod**) is defined only for integer arguments. Use of **div** with one or two real operand values results in the compiler producing an *error message* during compilation.

We now have some appreciation of the concept of data and manipulations that can be performed on numeric data. We have seen some of the basic operations that can be performed on numeric data. In later chapters we will see manipulations of nonnumeric data. Familiarity with data of all types is fundamental to success in programming.

## EXERCISES 2-5

**1.** Give the type of each of the following constants:

- *(a)* 723
- *(b)* 723.0
- *(c)* '723'
- *(d)* false
- *(e)* '7'

- *(f)* −4.032E12
- *(g)* 37E7
- *(h)* 'Question'
- *(i)* 'false'
- *(j)* '$'

**2.** Give the result and its type for each of the following expressions (assuming that the operations are performed left to right):

- *(a)* 2 * 6 + 5
- *(b)* 7 + 3 − 4.2
- *(c)* 3.0 * 4.0
- *(d)* 3 / 6.0 − 7

- *(e)* 2 / 3 − 1
- *(f)* 2 **div** 3 − 1
- *(g)* 2.0 **div** 3.0 − 1.0

**3.** Express each of the following as a real number in floating-point form with six significant figures (consult appropriate sources for the values required):

- *(a)* $\pi$
- *(b)* $e$
- *(c)* Avogadro's number

- *(d)* Mass of an electron (in kg)
- *(e)* Diameter of an atom (in cm)
- *(f)* Value of a parsec (in mi)

## 2-6   VARIABLES AND EXPRESSIONS

In the previous section some fundamental operations on numeric data were presented. We saw that it is possible to manipulate numeric data in a variety of ways and, by combining these fundamental operations, to form more elaborate expressions. In computer programs these expressions make up a major part of the specifications of a computation. In this section we explore the important concept that ties much of this together, the concept of a variable.

As was discussed earlier, a *variable* is an entity that possesses a value and is known to the program by a name (also called an *identifier*). In mathematics, the concept is very familiar. For example, if we denote the sides of a right-angled triangle by $a$, $b$, and $c$, as shown in Fig. 2-18, the pythagorean theorem gives us the following relationship between the lengths of the three sides:

$$a^2 = b^2 + c^2$$

A relationship expressed using variables in this way defines a general formula that can then be applied to specific computations. For example, if side $a$ is 5 units and side $b$ is 4 units, our formula allows us to determine the length of side $c$:

$$(5)^2 = (4)^2 + c^2$$
$$c = \sqrt{(5)^2 - (4)^2}$$
$$= \sqrt{25 - 16}$$
$$= \sqrt{9}$$
$$= 3$$

A second triangle might have the following measurements: $b$ is 5 units, $c$ is 12 units. Although this is a different triangle from the first one, the general pythagorean formula still applies and can be used to calculate the length of side $a$:

$$a^2 = (5)^2 + (12)^2$$
$$a = \sqrt{(5)^2 + (12)^2}$$
$$= \sqrt{25 + 144}$$
$$= \sqrt{169}$$
$$= 13$$

In computer programs, too, the use of variables permits the specification of a general computational formula. As in mathematical formulas, variables

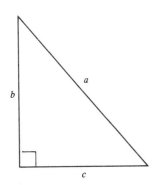

**FIGURE 2-18**
**Right-angled**
**(Pythagorean) triangle.**

in programs have names (identifiers) and take on values. In the preceding examples, we saw two different sets of values, as shown in Table 2-3. A variable can take on many different values, but at any particular time it can have only one such value, just as in Western society, where people may have many spouses as long as they have only one at a time. The names of the variables used in the pythagorean formula were simply *a*, *b*, and *c*. In computer programs we prefer more descriptive names, such as possibly Hypotenuse, Rightleg, and Leftleg in this case. This makes their purpose more apparent to the reader of the program.

Pascal's rules for naming variables are as follows: Variable identifiers may be composed of uppercase letters (A–Z), lowercase letters (a–z), and digits (0–9), but they must begin with a letter. Uppercase and lowercase letters are equivalent; thus the identifiers total and TOTAL, and even tOtAl, represent the *same variable*. Blanks may not appear within a variable identifier; we will use uppercase letters to make identifiers composed of several "words" more readable in this book. Thus we use RateOfPay rather than rateofpay. However, both would be acceptable to a Pascal compiler which adheres to the Pascal standard.

Some Pascal compilers extend the language by allowing as a legal character in variable identifiers the "break character," which appears as an underscored blank. With such a compiler we could use a convention such as rate_of_pay or RATE_OF_PAY for variable identifiers. Use of such an extension results in a Pascal program that is not so *portable*; that is, it is not so easily moved to a different compiler and/or computer. In particular, a program using "_" in variable identifiers is usable only with other compilers that permit this extension. For others, the underscores would have to be removed; this could even result in errors if, for example, the original program had two variables named numbers_pool and number_spool. These would both become the same name upon elimination of the underscore.

The following are examples of variable identifiers that violate Pascal's rules:

| | |
|---|---|
| 3file | Does not begin with a letter |
| X + Y | + is not permitted in a variable name; otherwise, how would we differentiate this from the symbol for addition? |
| Two Words | Blanks are not allowed |

**TABLE 2-3**

| Case | *a* | *b* | *c* |
|------|-----|-----|-----|
| 1 | 5 | 4 | 3 |
| 2 | 13 | 5 | 12 |

identifier

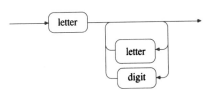

**FIGURE 2-19**  Syntax diagram for identifier.

Figure 2-19 gives the syntax diagram for identifiers. *User-defined identifiers* are used for variable names as well as for various other purposes which are described in subsequent chapters. There are two special rules regarding identifiers. First, no identifier may be identical to any of the reserved words; recall that these are listed in Table 2-2. Second, a number of identifiers are *predefined identifiers* in Pascal. Examples are "true," a Boolean value discussed in this section, and cos, a built-in function discussed in Sec. 2-6.7. Programmers may redefine these identifiers for their own purposes; however, all occurrences will then refer to the user-defined use. For example, use of cos as a variable would make all occurrences of cos in a program refer to this variable. No use could be made of the built-in function cos. In this book, references to predefined identifiers are written completely in lowercase to call attention to their use. We will avoid using any predefined identifiers for other purposes. For reference, the predefined identifiers of standard Pascal are listed in Table 2-4.

A variable stands for something, specifically, some piece of data, in an expression. In the pythagorean formula, $a$, $b$, and $c$ stood for the lengths of the sides of the right-angled triangle. In the expression

Length * Width

Length and Width might be variables standing for the sides of a rectangle.

**TABLE 2-4**  **Predefined Identifiers in Pascal**

| | | | |
|---|---|---|---|
| abs | false | pack | sin |
| arctan | get | page | sqr |
| boolean | input | pred | sqrt |
| char | integer | put | succ |
| chr | in | read | text |
| cos | maxint | readln | true |
| dispose | new | real | trunc |
| eof | odd | reset | unpack |
| eoln | ord | rewrite | write |
| exp | output | round | writeln |

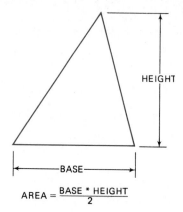

**FIGURE 2-20**
**Computing the area**
**of a triangle.**

$$\text{AREA} = \frac{\text{BASE} * \text{HEIGHT}}{2}$$

The names chosen tell us something about how we intend these variables to be used. If we give them specific values, such as **20** and **15**, the value of the expression (**300**) gives us the area of the rectangle. If we supply different values, the expression has a different result. The expression

Base * Height / 2

gives the area of a triangle if we supply the appropriate values to the variables **Base** and **Height**, as shown in Fig. 2-20. This particular expression contains a total of three data items: the variables **Base** and **Height**, and a constant, **2**. **Base** and **Height** can take on different values at different times, but the value of the constant **2** never changes.

In the previous section we introduced a number of important data types: integer, real, character, string, and Boolean. The types integer, real, character, and Boolean comprise the *predefined simple* types. They are called predefined because they are built into the definition of Pascal. For the present, we will use character strings only for output text and defer other uses until Chap. 6.

The types apply to variables as well as constants. For constants it is easy to recognize the types. Recall that an integer constant is a number with no decimal point or exponent part (for example, **2**, **41**, **6**), a real constant has a decimal point, an exponent part, or both (for example, **16.5**, **1E − 3**, **1.25E + 7**), a character constant is a single character or an apostrophe image in single quotation marks (for example, **'a'**, **'$'**, **''''**) and the Boolean constants are the names **true** and **false**, which are predefined identifiers. All the expressions in the previous section were, in fact, composed solely of constants of various types. When variables are used in expressions, they too must be of a certain type. An integer variable can take on only integer values, a real variable can take on only real values, a character variable can take on only character values, and a Boolean variable can take on only the Boolean values, namely, "true" and "false."

The types of all variables must be *declared* to the compiler by the programmer. This is necessary so that appropriate checking can be done. For the present, we will declare all variables near the beginning of a Pascal program. An example of a variable declaration is

```
var
    I: integer;
    Rate, Time: real;
    Flag: boolean;
    FirstInitial, MiddleInitial: char;
    NumberOfStudents: integer;
```

Note that a variable declaration begins with the reserved word **var**. Thereafter, each declaration is composed of a list of variables separated by commas, followed by a colon, followed by a type identifier, followed by a semicolon. The type identifiers **integer**, **real**, **boolean**, and **char** are predefined identifiers. (We will continue to refer to "character" type values and variables, but be sure to use the identifier **char** in Pascal programs!) Figure 2-21 summarizes the syntax of a variable declaration. Here assume that the "type denoter" is the name of a predefined type. Other possibilities will be introduced throughout the text. The reader is urged to trace the previous variable declaration through this diagram.

An important distinction must be made between the syntax diagrams given previously and those for variable declarations and the others to be presented in subsequent sections. The syntax diagrams for numbers (integer and real), character values, character strings, and identifiers specify construction of basic symbols of Pascal from individual characters. Notice that blanks may not appear within numbers and identifiers. The remaining syntax diagrams specify larger constructs in terms of the basic symbols: those just mentioned, reserved words, double character symbols (for example, : = ), and single-character symbols (for example, + ). Blanks may appear between these basic symbols, but they will not be explicitly shown in the syntax diagrams.

Now that we have some idea of how variables are declared and used, let us review in more detail how we give them their values. There are two ways of doing this. One way is to "read" a value into the variable by means of an input operation. We will look at the input operation later in this section along with its companion, the output operation. The other way is to "assign" the variable a value by means of the assignment operation.

**variable declaration**

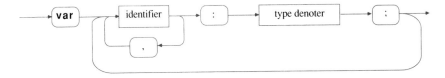

FIGURE 2-21
Syntax diagram for
variable declaration.

## 2-6.1 THE ASSIGNMENT OPERATION

The *assignment operation* specifies that a variable is to be given a new value. We simply assign that value to the variable. The assignment operation might best be denoted by a symbol such as "←," to emphasize the idea of placing a value into the variable. Since this arrow symbol is not available on most computer devices, Pascal uses the symbol := , which is typed as the two characters ":" and "=" with no blank space between them. This symbol should be read as "is assigned the value." Thus the Pascal statement

A := 3

is read as "variable A is assigned the value three." If you like, you can think of A as representing a word in the memory of the computer. After this assignment statement has been executed, this word contains the number 3 (in integer format). Notice that since a memory word can contain only one value at a time, the number 3 replaces whatever value, if any, had been previously stored in that word. We say that assignment is a *destructive* operation, since whatever value the variable possessed prior to the processing of the assignment operation has been lost; it has been replaced by the new value. Thus, if the sequence of operations

A := 16;
A := −27;
A := 1

were executed, the value of the variable A after the three operations would be 1. The values 16 and −27 have been destroyed—overwritten by subsequent assignments to the same variable. Recall that when a sequence of assignments is given, the individual operations are always executed in the order given. We will deal at greater length with the sequence in which statements are executed in later sections.

The following examples illustrate assignment statements involving variables of other types. Assume that variables Initial, Switch, and Rate are of type character, Boolean, and real, respectively.

Initial := 'J';
Switch := true;
Rate := 10.5

In the case of the variable Initial, any character constant can be assigned. In the case of Switch, however, the choice is limited to the values allowed by the definition of the variable; namely, the values "true" and "false." The real variable Rate can be assigned any real value. The following would not be allowed, assuming the same variable types, and assuming that A is not the name of another character variable and that maybe is not a Boolean variable, and would in fact produce an error diagnostic message at compile time:

| | |
|---|---|
| Initial := A; | (not a character constant, quotes are missing) |
| Initial := 'JPT'; | (not a character constant; it is a character string constant of length 3) |
| Switch := maybe; | (neither "true" nor "false") |
| Rate := '123.5' | (not a real constant; the quotes make this a character string constant) |

## 2-6.2 TYPE CONVERSIONS

Earlier we said that variables must be of a certain type and can only take on values of that type. In some of the examples in the previous subsection we were operating under the implicit assumption that **A** is an integer variable because it is being given integer values. Suppose that **B** were a real variable. **B** can then take on real values as shown in the following assignment statements:

B : = − 295.3
B : = 0.0006

Suppose that **C** were a variable of type character. We could then assign character values to **C**, as in

C : = 'T'
C : = 'B'

Note that '**B**' denotes a character value and *not* the identifier **B**. These are completely different.

As mentioned previously, the compiler will report an error during compilation if an attempt is made to assign a value of the wrong type to a variable. Pascal allows an exception to this rule: An assignment statement with a real variable on the left-hand side of the : = may have an integer value on the right-hand side. However, the value assigned to the real variable is a real value; the computer converts a copy of the integer value to the corresponding real. Thus, using **B**, assumed to be real,

B : = 11

is equivalent to

B : = 11.0

## 2-6.3 EXPRESSIONS

The form of assignment operation that we have used to this point, that of assigning a constant to a variable, is only a special case of a more general form. The right-hand side of the assignment can, in fact, be any expression, where an expression is a combination of variables, constants, and operators. The result of the evaluation of that expression is the value that is then assigned to the indicated variable. The comments on type compatibility remain in effect. The general form of the assignment operation, more commonly called the *assignment statement*, is then

*variable* : = *expression*

This is illustrated by the syntax diagram in Fig. 2-22.

**assignment statement**

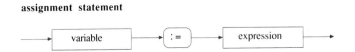

FIGURE 2-22
Syntax diagram for the assignment statement.

As an example of an expression used in an assignment statement, consider the following, in which Int is assumed to be an integer variable:

Int : = 3 + 16 + 8

We begin by evaluating the expression on the right-hand side of the assignment operator. This yields a value of **27**, which we then assign to the variable Int. The effect of this particular assignment is that the variable Int receives the calculated value **27**.

The expressions on the right-hand side in an assignment statement also may contain variables, the values of which have been previously assigned. Consider the following sequence of assignment statements, where Term1, Term2, and Result are all real variables:

Term1 : = 13.6 + 7.4;

Term2 : = 0.7 * 28.6;

Result : = Term1 / Term2

We begin by evaluating the expression **13.6 + 7.4** to get a real value **21.0**. By assignment, this becomes the value of the real variable Term1. In the second statement, the expression **0.7 * 28.6** yields the real value **20.02**, which is assigned to real variable Term2. In the third statement, we divide the value currently possessed by Term1 (21.0) by Term2 (20.02) to get **1.048951**. This is then assigned to the real variable Result.

After execution of this sequence of statements, the values of the three variables are as shown in Table 2-5. It is important to observe that the variables Term1 and Term2 have retained the values they were last assigned. The statement Result: = Term1 / Term2 does not alter the value of any variable on the right-hand side of the assignment symbol. The values of Term1 and Term2 can be used in subsequent operations.

A point worth emphasizing is that any variables used in any expression (such as the expression on the right-hand side of an assignment symbol) must have values at the time this expression is evaluated. For example, if the order of the statements in the last example were altered to read

Term1 : = 13.6 + 7.4;

Result : = Term1 / Term2;

Term2 : = 0.7 * 28.6

the program would be incorrect even though the same three statements are present. The statements are carried out in the indicated order, and at the time

| TABLE 2-5 | |
| --- | --- |
| Variable | Value |
| Term1 | 21.0 |
| Term2 | 20.02 |
| Result | 1.048951 |

the expression Term1 / Term2 is to be evaluated, the variable Term2 has not yet received its value. Thus it is not possible to compute the correct result. Some versions of Pascal detect use of a variable before assignment; other Pascal compilers simply use whatever value happens to be in the computer's memory location that has been assigned to that variable. It is the programmer's responsibility to organize the program so that all variables appearing in an expression have the correct values at the time an expression is to be evaluated. We have seen that the right-hand side of an assignment statement may be a constant, a variable, or an expression made up of variables and constants combined with operators. Notice that all these simply provide a new value to be assigned to the variable. In the remainder of this book we shall consider a constant or a variable to be merely a special case of an expression. Thus in the syntax diagram for the assignment statement in Fig. 2-22, the occurrence of "expression" is meant to include the two simpler cases. Many other Pascal constructs, to be described subsequently, require that some value be supplied. We will again use "expression" to mean that a constant, variable, or expression involving operators may be used.

## 2-6.4 MODIFYING A STORED VALUE

Suppose that we have a value stored in a variable named X (let us assume that X is an integer variable for this example). We know that if we assign a new value to that variable, it replaces the value that it had prior to the assignment. Suppose that we encounter the following sequence of statements, where A is also an integer variable.

```
X := 0;
A := 0;
X := A + 1
```

As a result of the first two statements, X and A both have the value 0. The third statement says "take the current value of the variable A (0), add 1 to it, and assign the result to the variable X." Thus, after execution of the third statement, X has a new value, 1, while A retains its value, 0.

Suppose that we had written

```
X := 0;
X := X + 1
```

How would this second statement be interpreted? It would be processed according to the same rules as all assignments are processed: "Take the current value of the variable X (which is 0), add 1 to it, and assign the result to the variable X." Thus, after execution of the second statement, X has a new value, 1. We have modified the value of the variable X by adding 1 to it. Such operations are frequently required in algorithms. It is important to realize that another variable, such as A in the previous example, is not required in order to increment the variable X.

This is a fundamental concept in computer programming. The whole point of variables is that they may hold different values at different times.

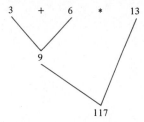

**FIGURE 2-23  Evaluation of a simple expression.**

The ability to modify these values, relative to what values the variables have, is very important indeed. Do not be perplexed by the appearance of the same variable on both sides of the assignment operator (:=). Recognize that these appearances mean different things in the processing of the statement. On the right-hand side the appearance of a variable indicates that its value is to be used; on the left-hand side it indicates that a value is to be assigned to it.

Some programming languages (for example, FORTRAN, PL/I, and BASIC) use the equal sign (=) as the symbol for assignment. Taken to mean equality, the statement X = X + 1 is nonsense mathematically. As an assignment statement, it means, simply, increase the value of X by 1. This is confusing for many beginning programmers. This is why Pascal uses the := even though it is somewhat harder to type on a keyboard; it is supposed to look somewhat like an arrow (←).

## 2-6.5  PRECEDENCE OF OPERATORS

Earlier in the book we spoke of the dangers of ambiguity. Consider the following assignment statement

SomeVar := 3 + 6 * 13

What value does SomeVar receive? There are two possible outcomes depending on the order in which the two mathematical operators (* and +) are processed. If we process them strictly left to right, that is, performing the addition before the multiplication, we get the result 117. This evaluation process can be represented diagrammatically as in Fig. 2-23.

Suppose, instead, that we performed the multiplication before the addition, as shown in Fig. 2-24. In this case, our result is 81. Which result is correct?

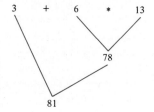

**FIGURE 2-24**
**Alternative evaluation**
**of the same**
**expression.**

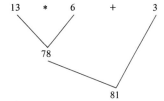

**FIGURE 2-25** Evaluating the expression written in the reverse order.

To get around such difficulties, traditional mathematics has defined some additional rules on the evaluation of expressions, specifically, on the order in which the individual operations are performed. With each operator is associated a *precedence*, or priority. While we proceed basically from left to right, operators with the highest precedence are processed first. In traditional mathematics, multiplication is given a higher precedence than addition. Thus, in the expression $3 + 6*13$, the term $6*13$ is processed first, giving **78**; then the addition operator is processed, giving the final result **81**, as shown in Fig. 2-24. Notice that with this rule, the same result is obtained if the expression is written as $13*6 + 3$ (see Fig. 2-25).

This evaluation procedure is easily applied to more complex examples. Consider the expression

$8 + 7 * 3 + 4 * 5$

We see two multiplications and two additions. The multiplications, being of higher precedence, are processed first (from left to right), yielding the intermediate results **21** and **20**. The additions are then processed to give the final result, **49**. This evaluation is shown in Fig. 2-26.

Before we give the precedences of the other mathematical operators, let us introduce one additional wrinkle, the use of parentheses. Parentheses are used to group terms as an explicit indication of the order in which the operations in an expression are to be processed. Operations in parentheses are evaluated first. For example, suppose that in the last case we had wanted the additions to be processed before the multiplications. For this we would write the expression as

$(8 + 7) * (3 + 4) * 5$

This gives the result **525**, as shown in Fig. 2-27.

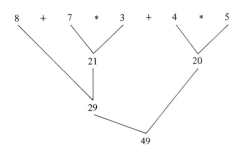

**FIGURE 2-26**
**Evaluating a more**
**complex expression**
**according to the**
**rules of operator**
**precedence.**

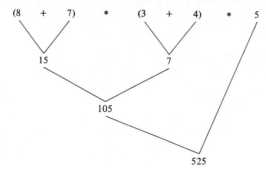

**FIGURE 2-27**
Evaluating a complex
expression containing
parentheses.

Parentheses can be nested, as in

$(3*(6+2))*8$

In this case, innermost parentheses are processed first. Thus the result of this expression is **192**, as shown in Fig. 2-28.

Now, let us look at the complete picture. The standard mathematical operators can be grouped by precedence into two classes. The higher precedence is given to the operators *, /, **div**, and **mod**. The lower precedence goes to + and −, used both for addition and subtraction and for positive and negative signs. These latter uses are called *unary plus* and *unary minus* to distinguish them from the binary (two operand) operators for addition and subtraction. Note that since unary plus has no effect on a value, it is rarely used. The operator precedences are summarized in Table 2-6.

## 2-6.6  EVALUATION OF EXPRESSIONS

Once we have precedences associated with the operators, the evaluation of an expression is straightforward. We simply scan the expression from left to right a separate time for each class of operator represented in the expression. Consider the following expression as an example:

$-3*7+2*3 \text{ div } 4-6$

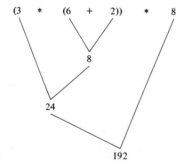

**FIGURE 2-28**
Evaluating an
expression with
nested parentheses.

**TABLE 2-6** Precedence for Standard Numerical Operators

| Class | Operators[†] | Meaning |
|-------|-----------|---------|
| 1 | *, /,**div**,**mod** | Multiplication, division (real result), integer division, integer remainder (modulus), applied left to right |
| 2 | +,− | Addition, subtraction, unary plus, and minus, applied left to right |

[†]Operators grouped together have the same precedence.

Both classes of operators are represented in this expression. This means a total of two scans is required, or two passes over the expression. On the first pass over an expression we process any of the operators *, /, **div**, and **mod** that occur. They are processed from left to right. In our example, * and **div** actually occur. The term **3 * 7** yields the intermediate result 21; the term **2 * 3 div 4** yields **6 div 4**, which then yields 1. The expression now reads

$$-21 + 1 - 6$$
$$\uparrow \quad \uparrow$$

intermediate results from first pass

On the second pass over an expression we process the addition, subtraction, and sign operators that occur. In our example there is one negative sign and one each of addition and subtraction, and we take them in turn from left to right. This gives us our final result for this expression, which is **−26**. Diagrammatically, the complete evaluation of this expression is shown in Fig. 2-29.

We mentioned earlier the use of parentheses to group terms in an expression. Since parenthesized terms are evaluated before any others, a programmer can use parentheses to overcome the effect of the standard operator precedences. For example, suppose that you were asked to represent the following fraction:

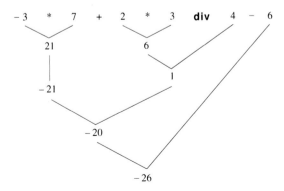

**FIGURE 2-29**
**Evaluation of another complex expression.**

$$\frac{12.0 - 2.0}{2.0 + 3.0}$$

Recall the need to write all expressions in programs on a single line. If we try to put this on one line exactly as it appears, we get

```
12.0 − 2.0 / 2.0 + 3.0
```

Because of precedence rules, however, this does not give the required value. Since the division is of higher precedence than the subtraction and addition, the calculated result would be **14.0** instead of the required **2.0**. To get the correct interpretation, we must use parentheses to indicate that the terms of the numerator and denominator are to be grouped. The correct expression is

```
(12.0 − 2.0) / (2.0 + 3.0)
```

Need a programmer ever bother to learn the rules of precedence? Through parenthesization, any order of evaluation can be imposed on an expression. Excessive use of parentheses, however, gives a strange appearance to programs and can make them hard to read. In most cases, the standard precedence rules lead to a natural interpretation. You will not find them difficult to remember as you become familiar with them.

It is worth commenting at this point that this tiresome procedure is not actually followed by the computer itself as it evaluates very simple expressions. The computer uses faster, more sophisticated methods, some of which are described in later chapters. They give the same results, however, as the "brute force" methods that we have described here.

### 2-6.7 BUILT-IN FUNCTIONS

Despite the best intentions of language designers, it is not possible to specify all operations required in programs in the form of conventional operators such as +, −, *, /, **div**, and **mod**. Quite often the conventional set is supplemented by a useful set of special operators called *built-in functions*. For example, we will use sqrt to denote the square-root operation rather than introducing another special symbol. Also, sqr designates the square of a value, that is, the value to the second power. Thus, if we know the lengths of the legs of a right-angled triangle (say, Leftleg and Rightleg), the following expression gives the length of the hypotenuse:

```
Hypotenuse : = sqrt ( sqr (Leftleg) + sqr (Rightleg))
```

Built-in functions are prewritten routines supplied by the designer of the programming language to assist the programmer in performing computations that require more than the conventional set of operators. Table 2-7 lists some of the built-in functions that are provided in standard Pascal, along with instructions for their use. Appearing in expressions, built-in functions have high precedence—higher, in fact, than all the operators.

The full syntax of expressions can now be summarized in the syntax diagrams for expression (Fig. 2-30), simple expression (Fig. 2-31), term

**TABLE 2-7** Some Typical Built-In Functions

| Function Name | Argument and Type | Meaning and Type of Result |
|---|---|---|
| abs ($\epsilon$) | $\epsilon$: a real or integer expression | Absolute value: result is $|\epsilon|$, same type as $\epsilon$ |
| sqr ($\epsilon$) | $\epsilon$: a real or integer expression | Square: result is $\epsilon^2$, same type as $\epsilon$ |
| sqrt ($\epsilon$) | $\epsilon$: a real or integer expression (must be $\geq 0$) | Square root: result is $\sqrt{\epsilon}$, type real |
| trunc ($\epsilon$) | $\epsilon$: a real expression | Truncate: result is the largest integer smaller than or equal to $\epsilon$ for positive $\epsilon$; the smallest (most negative) integer larger than or equal to $\epsilon$ for negative $\epsilon$ |
| round ($\epsilon$) | $\epsilon$: a real expression | Round: result is the largest integer smaller than or equal to ($\epsilon + 0.5$) for positive $\epsilon$; the smallest (most negative) integer larger than or equal to ($\epsilon - 0.5$) for negative $\epsilon$ |
| log ($\epsilon$) | $\epsilon$: a real or integer expression | Logarithm base $e$: result is the natural (naperian) logarithm of $\epsilon$, type real |
| exp ($\epsilon$) | $\epsilon$: a real or integer expression | Exponential: result is $e^{\epsilon}$, type real |
| sin ($\epsilon$) | $\epsilon$: a real or integer expression | Sine: result is the sine of $\epsilon$ (radians), type real |
| cos ($\epsilon$) | $\epsilon$: a real or integer expression | Cosine: result is the cosine of $\epsilon$ (radians), type real |
| arctan ($\epsilon$) | $\epsilon$: a real or integer expression | Arctangent: result is principal value in radians, type real |

**expression**

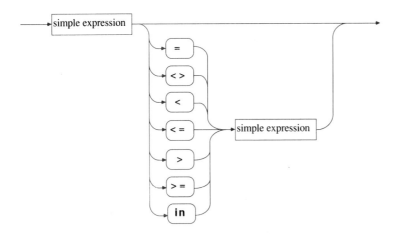

FIGURE 2-30
Syntax diagram
for expression.

simple expression

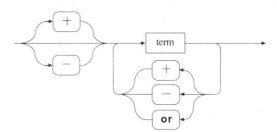

**FIGURE 2-31**
Syntax diagram for
simple expression.

(Fig. 2-32), factor (Fig. 2-33), function reference (Fig. 2-34), and unsigned constant (Fig. 2-35). Complete syntax diagrams are presented, although some features will be discussed in later chapters. So far we have introduced only *simple variables*, which are represented by identifiers; other possibilities are described in Chaps. 5 and 8. Therefore, we shall defer giving the syntax diagram for variable. The comparison operators ($=$, $<>$, $<$, $<=$, $>$, $>=$) and the logical operators (**or**, **and**, **not**) are described in Chap. 3. Set constructors and **in** are described in Chap. 5. The **nil** constant is described in Chap. 8.

## 2-6.8  INPUT AND OUTPUT

Computer calculations are of little value unless we can supply the data on which we wish the calculations to be performed and see the results of these calculations.

We define three new types of statements to handle input and output. The *read statement* allows us to read given values into indicated variables; the *write* and *writeln statements* allow us to display results. Input may come from a keyboard or from some other form of input device. Output may appear on a display screen or be printed on paper. Pascal assumes that some device has been designated as the *standard input device*, and the stream of characters obtained from this device form the *input stream*. Likewise,

term

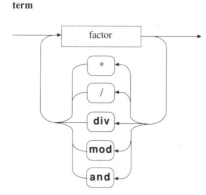

**FIGURE 2-32**
Syntax diagram
for term.

**factor**

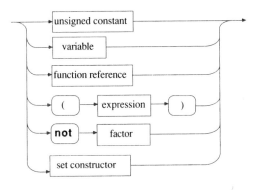

FIGURE 2-33
Syntax diagram
for factor.

some device is assumed to be designated as the *standard output device*; the characters to be displayed form the *output stream*. While we will normally assume the input device to be a keyboard and the output device to be the CRT display of a terminal, the input and output operations of Pascal are relatively independent of the actual device. We will not concern ourselves with the details of the devices.

The form of the read statement in Pascal is

read(*input variable*)

The *input variable* gives the name of the variable to which a value is to be given; it may be an integer, real, or character variable. If it is a character variable, the next unprocessed character from the input stream is assigned to the variable. Otherwise, the value is obtained by first discarding any blank characters preceding the next value and then assigning the value encountered to the variable. For an integer variable, the value must have the form of an integer number (see Fig. 2-12). For a real variable, the value must have the form of an integer number (Fig 2-12) or a real number (Fig. 2-14). If, for example, the statement is

read(A)

then the next value encountered would be given to the variable A. Following each read statement, the computer system records the "current location" in the input stream as being the character, usually a blank, following the value

**function reference**

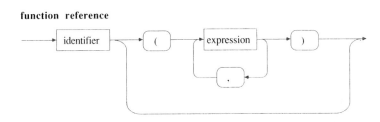

FIGURE 2-34
Syntax diagram
for function reference.

unsigned constant

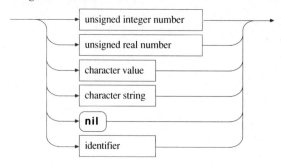

**FIGURE 2-35**
Syntax diagram for
unsigned constant.

just read. Thus the three statements

```
read(A);
read(B);
read(C)
```

read the next three values encountered and assign these values to the variables A, B, C—the first to A, the second to B, and the third to C.

As a shorthand notation, the read statement may be given a list of variables separated by commas. This is considered equivalent to three consecutive read statements. Thus

```
read (A, B, C)
```

would be equivalent to the three statements in the previous paragraph.

The input stream is assumed to be divided into lines, as for example when typed at the keyboard of a terminal. However, the read statement does not concern itself with this arrangement; only the order of the values is important. The read statement will continue processing the input stream until a value has been assigned to each variable.

Pascal treats the input as a continuous stream of input characters, each line being composed of the characters typed (not including the carriage return character) followed by an "end of line" character that is treated as a blank when processing input characters. As a consequence, a numeric value, which may not have embedded blanks, cannot be split across a line boundary. More detail on the read statement will be presented in Secs. 2-8, 3-3.2, and 5-9 and in Chap. 10.

Pascal's method of treating input data as a continuous stream is very flexible for simple programs. It frees the programmer from many considerations of how the input data should be organized into lines. There are, however, occasions when a program should be dependent on how the input is organized into lines. For such occasions, Pascal used the *readln* (read as "read line") *statement*. This will be introduced in Chap. 3 when considerations of the end of lines become important.

The output statements are like the input statement in format, but they are more general in terms of what can be specified in the *output list*. It is

possible to display any value of type: integer, real, character, Boolean, or
string. This value is specified by an expression, which may be a constant,
a variable, or any of these combined with operators. Although standard
Pascal restricts the types of values which may be displayed to integer, real,
character, Boolean, and character string, some Pascal compilers allow other
types. The general form of the write statement is

write (*output item*)

The simplest form of output item is an expression (including just a variable
or constant) of one of the permitted types. The following sequence of statements illustrates the action of a write statement. Assume that all variables
are integer.

```
Mark1 := 73;
Mark2 := 65;
Mark3 := 94;
Mark4 := 87;
Average := (Mark1 + Mark2 + Mark3 + Mark4) div 4;
write (Average)
```

The first four statements assign to the indicated variables a student's grades
on four tests. The fifth statement computes the average grade (truncating the
result to an integer). The write statement then displays this calculated result:

79

A sequence of write statements puts values on the same line. If the user or
programmer wishes to see, as well as the calculated average, the individual
grades used to compute it, we could use the sequence

```
write (Mark1);
write (Mark2);
write (Mark3);
write (Mark4);
write (Average)
```

The resulting output line would now be

73  65  94  87  79

Note that all numbers are written as integer numbers. This is so because the
variables themselves are all integer variables.

Pascal permits several consecutive write statements to be combined into
one, giving the same output. We could have written

```
write (Mark1, Mark2, Mark3, Mark4, Average)
```

Many computer systems treat an attempt to write a line longer than that
permitted on a particular output device as an error. The permitted length
varies widely among various devices. Values of 80 through 150 characters
are common. The statement

writeln

places a *new-line character* into the output stream. This causes the next output item to begin on a new line. Thus if we wish the average in the previous example to appear on a line by itself, we would use

```
write (Mark1, Mark2, Mark3, Mark4);
writeln;
write (Average);
writeln
```

Because terminating a line is a frequent occurrence, Pascal allows combining a write statement and writeln statement into one statement; the effect is to write each of the values and then output the new line character. Again, using our example, we could use

```
writeln (Mark1, Mark2, Mark3, Mark4);
writeln (Average)
```

Now, however, we have simply five numbers displayed on two lines. Looking at this output, you can see that there is nothing to tell someone reading it what the numbers signify. This could easily lead to confusion and/or misinterpretation. Suppose, instead, that we gave the following output statements:

```
writeln('Individual grades are', Mark1, Mark2, Mark3, Mark4);
writeln('Final average is', Average)
```

In this case the output would be displayed as

```
Individual grades are   73   65   94   87
Final average is   79
```

Here we have exploited the ability of a write (and writeln) statement to write character strings to provide more informative output. (Note that delimiting quotes on character strings do not appear in displayed output.) In terms of information content, the last form is definitely superior. Not only is all the information presented, but it is also clearly labeled. Those of you who receive itemized bills with particulars such as the cryptic **BX SFTY PNS** ought to appreciate the value of clear, identifiable labels. This is also important, as we will see, in the choice of variable names. Do not force your readers into word games they may not want to play.

Another feature of write and writeln statements allows more precise control of the spacing of items within an output line. Each expression specifying a value to be displayed may be followed by a colon and an output width. This width must be an integer positive-valued expression (often it is just an integer number), and it specifies the number of characters used to represent the value. If more characters are requested than are required, blanks are inserted preceding the value. (We say that the value is *right-adjusted* within the designated characters.) For example,

```
writeln (35:5, −256:6, 'ABC':6)
```

will produce the output line

When a width is not given, a default value is used. The defaults are one for a character, the actual length for a string, and the length of the value ("true" is 4 and "false" is 5) for Boolean. The default widths for integer and real are chosen by the designer of the compiler and are not necessarily the same.

If the width is specified but is too small for integer and real types, the value is displayed with the minimum required character width that will contain the entire value. Thus a width of 1 is often useful to suppress extra blanks. For example,

```
writeln ('The result is □', X:1, '□feet.')
```

would give, if X is 694,

```
The result is□694□feet.
```

and, if X is 12,

```
The result is□12□feet.
```

Boolean and character strings are truncated (eliminating rightmost characters) to the specified length.

Real values are normally printed in floating-point form. A second colon followed by a positive integer value causes conversion to fixed-point notation. The value following the second colon specifies the number of digits to follow the decimal point. For example,

```
Ratio : = 3.697;
Balance : = 24.25;
writeln (Ratio:6:2, '□$' Balance:1:2)
```

gives

```
□□3.70□$24.25
```

Another feature of standard Pascal is the *page statement*. It is intended that this statement cause all following output to be on a new page. For example,

```
writeln ('Some output');
writeln ('Some more output');
page;
writeln ('This output appears at the top of a new page')
```

Unfortunately, computer devices differ greatly in their characteristics, so the Pascal standards do not specify how the new page function is to be achieved. For example, some printer devices require a special character (sometimes called *form feed*) to cause subsequent output to begin on a new page. For these devices, the page statement simply causes that (form feed) character to be sent to the output stream. Also, the effect of **page** if the output is not directed to a printer also varies among Pascal compilers. For example, with output directed to a display terminal, **page** might cause the screen to clear, or might merely cause a blank line to be displayed, or might even be ignored completely. In fact, some well-known Pascal implementations do not include the page statement. The reader is advised to consult the documentation for the particular compiler being used.

In designing a program to satisfy the requirements of an application, some consideration must be given to the users of the program. In a batch environment, a set of input data will be prepared, and then the program will be run. The output stream will be examined later, either from a terminal or as a printed document. The usefulness of this output stream will be enhanced considerably if it is understandable without reference to another document, for example, a listing of the program. This is achieved by including more than just the results in the output. The previous paragraphs illustrated two important techniques: labeling the output and including the input values in the output stream.

Programs intended for interactive use must satisfy slightly different criteria. In the interactive environment, users of the results of a program actually run the program. They will type the input at a keyboard. The computer system will "echo" the characters typed on the display screen, where it will appear along with the output. Thus the program itself need not echo its input. However, an opportunity exists for the program to aid in correct data entry. A descriptive message, called a *prompt*, should be issued immediately before requesting each item or set of input data. For example, we might have

```
writeln ('Please enter four marks separated by blanks');
read (Mark1, Mark2, Mark3, Mark4)
```

The interaction between the output, including new lines, and the echoed input characters is system-dependent. Programmers should consult the documentation on their systems or conduct some experiments to determine satisfactory formatting of the information.

The contents and extensiveness of labels and prompts must depend on the intended users of the program. Infrequent or inexperienced users will find extensive labeling and prompting helpful. Frequent users of a program often find extensive labeling, and particularly verbose prompts, distracting and annoying. (See *Design of Man-Computer Dialogues* by Martin for a discussion of this subject.)

Finally, in designing the input portion of a program, some consideration should be given to *program robustness*. A robust program is one that produces *reasonable* results no matter what input is supplied. Robustness requires that the program check the validity of its input and take some appropriate action for unacceptable input. In a batch environment, this action might involve including appropriate messages in the output stream and terminating execution. For an interactive environment, a more appropriate action might include output of a message followed by a prompt and input of a corrected value. Checking for some types of invalid data is relatively easy. For example, negative grades should be rejected. Unfortunately, most Pascal compilers automatically terminate execution with a standard message for some types of errors. These often include illegal characters (e.g., letters or punctuation) when expecting numeric input and numbers outside the allowed range for a particular computer system. Chapter 7 considers program robustness further within the context of other design issues.

## EXERCISES 2-6

1. Give the value of the variable **Result** after execution of the following sequences of operations (assume all variables to be real):
   (a) Result := 3 * 6
   (b) X := 2;
      Y := 4;
      Result := X * Y − X
   (c) Result := 6;
      X := 3;
      Result := Result * X

2. Give the value of each of the following expressions:
   (a) 12 * 11 − 3 * 7
   (b) −4 * 3 * 2
   (c) − 2 * (3 * 2)
   (d) (24 + 2 * 6) **div** 3
   (e) 3 + 4 * (8 * (3 − (8 + 4) / 6))
   (f) 2 * 2 * 3 + 8 * 4 * 2 − 5
   (g) 8 − 32 **div** 6

★ 3. Assume that A, B, and C are real variables and that I, J, and K are integer variables. Given A = 4, B = 6, and I = 3, what is the value assigned to each of the following assignment statements?
   (a) C := A * B − I
   (b) K := I **div** 4 * 6
   (c) C := B / A + 1.5
   (d) K := trunc (B / A + 4.7)
   (e) I := round(A / (10 **div** I))
   (f) C := abs(A − B) * 3 + I

4. Write the following mathematical expressions as computer expressions:

   (a) $\frac{a}{b} + 1$

   (b) $\frac{a + b}{c - d}$

   (c) $\frac{a + \dfrac{b}{c}}{d - \dfrac{e}{f}}$

   (d) $a + \dfrac{b}{c - d}$

   (e) $(a + b)\dfrac{c}{d}$

   (f) $[(a + b)^2]^2$

   (g) $\dfrac{\dfrac{\sin a + \cos a}{\sin a}}{\cos a}$

   (h) $\dfrac{-b + \sqrt{b^2 - 4ac}}{2a}$

5. In which of the following pairs is the order of the statements important? In other words, when will changing the order of the statements change the final results? (Assume that X ≠ Y ≠ Z.)
   (a) X := Y;
      Y := Z
   (b) X := Y;
      Z := X
   (c) X := Z;
      X := Y
   (d) Z := Y;
      X := Y

## 2-7   A COMPLETE PASCAL PROGRAM

We have now presented the rules of Pascal in sufficient detail that we can again examine a complete, but very simple Pascal program. We consider the solution to the problem posed in Sec. 2-2. The complete Pascal program appears as Fig. 2-36.

The program begins with a program header line which gives the name of the program (ReportMark) and indicates that both input (for reading the term marks) and output (for displaying the results) will occur. There follows a *comment* describing the purpose of the program. A comment is composed of arbitrary text intended for the human reader of a program, but it is to be ignored by the compiler when it processes the program. Comment text is enclosed within the braces, that is, { and } . (Since some computer devices have limited character sets, most Pascal compilers accept "( *" and " *)" as equivalent to { and } , respectively.) Pascal allows a comment to appear anywhere in a program except within an identifier, number, character string, or operator. We will always begin a program with a comment stating its purpose.

Next are the declarations of the variables, with comments specifying their roles in the program. Following that is a **begin**, the statements of the program, an **end**, and a period. We shall often divide the statements of a program into logical sections and begin such sections with a comment. Although probably not required for this simple program, we have sectioned it for illustration.

**program** ReportMark (input, output);

{Given the marks achieved on four term tests (in variables Mark1, Mark2, Mark3, Mark4), this program averages them to determine the student's final course grade (Grade), along with a pass or fail indication.}
**var**
    Mark1, Mark2, Mark3, Mark4: real;   {The four term marks}
    Grade: real;                  {The final grade}
**begin**
    {Step 1: Input term marks}
    read (Mark1, Mark2, Mark3, Mark4);

    {Step 2: Compute final grade}
    Grade := (Mark1 + Mark2 + Mark3 + Mark4) / 4;

    {Step 3: Indicate status}
    **if** Grade < 50    {50 is the minimum passing grade}
    **then** writeln ('Sorry. You failed with a grade of ', Grade:8:2)
    **else** writeln ('Congratulations. You passed with a grade of', Grade:8:2)

    {Step 4: Finished}
**end**.

FIGURE 2-36
**Program to report
final mark based
on four term marks.**

Figures 2-37 and 2-38 present the complete syntax diagrams for a program and body, respectively. We note several things about the diagrams. Comments are never shown on syntax diagrams because they are allowed in so many places in Pascal. The list of identifiers between the parentheses is intended to indicate the "file variables" used to access data external to the program. For now, input and output, representing access to the standard input and output streams, will be sufficient. Files are discussed in Secs. 2-8 and 5-9, and Chap. 10. There are several kinds of declarations and definitions which might or might not be present in a program. We have so far considered only the variable declaration. Others, such as constant declaration and procedure declaration, will be described when there is a need for them.

A frequent cause for error in a Pascal program is improper placement of the semicolons. Remember, a semicolon is used to separate any two consecutive statements between **begin** and **end**. Thus we might write

**begin** I : = 2; J : = 5; writeln (I + J) **end**

Here we have three consecutive statements, thus requiring two semicolons. When the statements are shown one per line, there is a tendency to insert an extra semicolon at the end of the last statement preceding the **end**. The more correct approach is to maintain the semicolons as in the previous example. Thus we write

**begin**
  I : = 2;
  J : = 5;
  writeln (I + J)
**end**

A semicolon before the **end** would be redundant, although it would be permitted here. In this context it would indicate the presence of a fourth statement, a "null statement" specifying no operation.

We have described the rules of Pascal in sufficient detail that the reader could prepare and run a simple program. As described in Chap. 1, this typically begins with preparation of the source program, often using an interactive editor from a computer terminal. Because a wide variety of editors are in common use, we will not describe the text-preparation phase any further at this time. Following the preparation of the source program, a compiler is called on to translate the source program into machine code, and the resulting machine language program is then put into execution.

**FIGURE 2-37** Syntax diagram for a program.
program

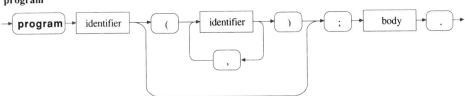

**body**

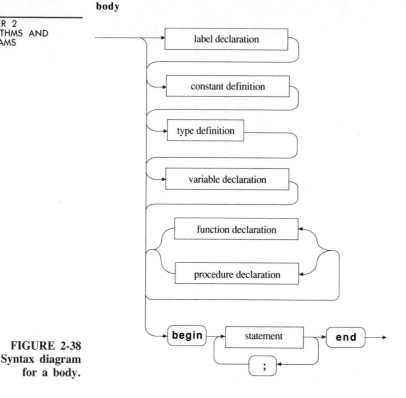

**FIGURE 2-38**
**Syntax diagram**
**for a body.**

The compilation phase often results in the production of one or more *compilation error messages* rather than the expected object program. One cause of such errors is violation of the syntax rules of Pascal. The compiler is simply a program designed using certain *compilation algorithms*. At the present state of development, these compilation algorithms require very close adherence to the syntax rules. Otherwise, the compiler will not recognize the construct as presented and will produce an error message. For example, omission of the **end** at the end of the program might produce a message

\* \* \*syntax error: end expected on line 20

The exact form of the message will depend on the particular compiler being used. Most compilers are designed to continue processing the source program after detecting an error so that subsequent syntax errors may be reported as well. A problem that arises is that the first error may cause the compiler to process subsequent text as a different Pascal construct than was intended by the programmer. This will cause the compiler to produce spurious error messages as the text is found to conflict with the syntax rules of the *assumed* construct. The compiler, of course, has no data on what the programmer *intended* to write, only what it believes the programmer has written. Thus, the programmer must examine the list of error messages carefully, together with the program text, to discover the true error.

Another source of error is type conflict. For example, the **div** operator requires integer operands. Use of **div** with a real operand might result in a message such as

∗ ∗ ∗type error: div on line 4

Again, the exact wording of the message will depend on the particular compiler being used. You must examine both the error message and the program text and determine how to modify the program to bring it into conformance with the rules of Pascal. Do not be surprised if it takes several attempts at compilation to produce an object program without compilation error messages.

After a successful compilation, you may now attempt to run the program (with input data if necessary). Rather than the expected results, however, *run-time error messages* such as

∗ ∗ ∗execution error: division by 0

may result. The errors that are deleted during execution, and the message wording, will again vary among compilers. Run-time errors can be much more insidious and thus much more difficult to detect. Basically you've done something wrong—for example, attempting to divide by a variable that presently has the value zero. Quite often, however, the actual *cause* occurs earlier in the program rather than at the point of the message. What you are seeing is the *effect* of the error.

Even a program that runs without error messages and produces results may be wrong! A program is correct only if it produces correct results for all possible valid inputs. The process of removing errors, or *bugs*, is called *debugging*. It involves eliminating compilation errors, as described previously, and detecting and eliminating run-time errors. The latter involves *testing* a program with various input data. Further information on testing programs is included in the descriptions of examples and applications throughout the text. (See, for example, Sec. 2-9.1.)

## EXERCISES 2-7

1. Throughout North America, weather offices are undergoing a conversion to the metric system. Design programs to perform the following conversions:
   (a) Read a temperature given on the Celsius scale and print its Fahrenheit equivalent (conversion formula: °F = $\frac{9}{5}$ °C + 32).
   (b) Read a rainfall amount given in inches and print its equivalent in millimeters (25.4 mm = 1 in).

★ 2. An approximation of the factorial function is given by Stirling's formula:

$$n! = \sqrt{2\pi n} \left(\frac{n}{e}\right)^n$$

Write a program that reads in a number and then uses this formula to calculate its factorial. In this problem, use variables of type real. Also use the fact that $(n/e)^n = \exp [n \times \ln (n/e)]$.

3. The following is the menu at a local hamburger emporium. Design a program that reads in the number of each item purchased and computes the total bill.

BERTHA'S BURGERS

| | | |
|---|---|---|
| Hamburger | ($1.75) | ☐ |
| Cheeseburger | ($1.95) | ☐ |
| French fries | (95¢) | ☐ |
| Soft drink | (75¢) | ☐ |
| Onion rings | ($1.05) | ☐ |
| Sundae | ($1.25) | ☐ |
| Total | | _____ |

★ 4. Write a program that reads in the time given on a 24-hour clock and converts it to the correct time on a 12-hour clock. You will read in two integers, one for the hour and one for the minutes, and print out the converted hours and minutes. You will need to use the **mod** and **div** functions, as in the following formula:

Hour12 = (Hour24 **mod** 13) + (Hour24 **div** 13)

where Hour12 is the hour on the 12-hour clock and Hour24 is the hour on the 24-hour clock. Ignore the distinction between A.M. and P.M.

5. Write a program that calculates what the world's population will be a year from now given the current population, the birth rate, and the death rate. (Assume that the birth rate and death rate are given as percentages.)

## 2-8 MORE ON INPUT AND OUTPUT

Input and output operations are a source of concern to any programmer. In this book we place more emphasis on algorithm construction than on complex input and output formats. For this reason, we often design our programs simply to read data from the input stream, perform the necessary computations, and write data to the output stream. Additional features that are dependent on the environment within which the program is to operate can be added quite easily. This would include the prompting for input in an interactive environment or the echoing of the input that is useful in a batch environment.

Many programs require only one input stream and one output stream. We shall use the standard input stream and standard output stream as described previously for all such programs. These streams are associated with some actual input and output devices on the computer system upon which the program runs. Interactive computer systems often associate these input streams with the user's terminal. This causes a problem when there is a need for printed results from the program, say, to hand in as a class assignment. Also, when a program requires a large amount of input data, it is unacceptable to require that the data be keyed in directly at the terminal every time the program is to be run, particularly during the testing phase. In these cases, it would be preferable if the input and output streams could be associated with some other device. This device might be a printer or a disk. Many independent sets of data can be stored on a disk. Each set of data is called a *file* and is referred to by its file name. Most often, it is desired to associate the output stream directly with a printer or with a file to be written on a disk and later printed. Similarly, the input stream might be associated with a file on disk that was created earlier using an editor.

Most systems provide some facilities external to the Pascal program for modifying the associations of the input and output streams. This is much preferable to incorporating the names of the input and output files directly in the program. The commands required to change the associations of input and output streams to actual devices are necessarily very system dependent. We give here some examples for widely used systems as an example of the types of facilities usually available. For example, the UNIX operating system would allow the compiled object program (usually a file called a.out) to be run with the input and output streams associated with the files infile and outfile, respectively, by the command

a.out  <infile  >outfile

This is referred to as a *redirecting* of the input or output. Similarly, a program compiled under Turbo Pascal and stored as a runnable program, say, in the file MYPROG.COM, can be run from the operating system (MS/DOS or PC/DOS) by the command

MYPROG  <INFILE.DAT  >OUTFILE.DAT

Turbo requires that a program whose output is to be redirected be compiled with the options *G* and *P*, and possibly *D*. Unfortunately, it is much less convenient to compile Turbo programs to run under the operating system. Most users prefer to run the program directly under control of the Turbo system, in which case the redirection feature is not available (see the Turbo documentation for details). Under the IBM mainframe operating system MVS, the JCL (Job Control Language) is used to adjust the associations. The user must consult the documentation for a particular compiler and computer system to determine what facilities are available.

Although it is desirable that a program be able to process input data from various sources and produce output data to various destinations without requiring that the program itself be changed, most Pascal implementations extend the language to allow an input or output stream to have its actual device association specified from within the program. Since the Pascal standard does not specify the means by which this is to be done, various Pascal compilers provide different schemes. A method commonly used involves the *reset statement* for the input stream and the *rewrite statement* for the output stream. Thus to associate the input stream with a file named infile, some Pascal compilers use

```
reset (input, 'infile');
```

Similarly, to associate the output stream with a file named outfile:

```
rewrite(output, 'outfile');
```

Other Pascal compilers use the assign statement for both input and output:

```
assign(input, 'infile');
assign(output, 'outfile');
```

Again, because the various versions of Pascal use quite different methods, the documentation on the Pascal compiler being used must be consulted for this information.

Another difficulty which arises is that some Pascal compilers require that a stream associated with a file on disk be explicity closed by statements of the form

```
close(input);
close(output);
```

before the program finishes, particularly for the output stream. The documentation for a particular Pascal compiler should warn the programmer of such nonstandard requirements.

Some Pascal compilers (e.g., the Turbo Pascal compiler) do not allow the associations of the standard input and output streams to be changed from within the program itself. Also, a program occasionally needs additional input or output streams independent of the standard streams. A Pascal program is not limited only to the predefined streams input and output. Each additional stream required is given a name chosen by the programmer. Since the stream name, called a *file variable*, is declared in a program as if it were a variable, a stream name may not be the same as a variable name. We will use the names InStream and OutStream in the following examples.

The names are included in the program header along with the standard streams if they are used by the program. For example, we would use

```
program Redirect(output, InStream, OutStream);
```

in a program that uses the input stream InStream and the output streams output and Outstream. Streams other than input and output must be declared as variables in the program. They are given the built-in type text because they are streams of textual material. (Other types of files are described in Chaps. 5 and 10.) The following is an example of such a declaration:

```
var
  InStream: text;    { input stream}
  OutStream: text;   { output stream}
```

Streams other than the built-in input and output must be prepared for input or output before they can be used. This is known as *opening* the file. The reset statement prepares a stream for reading, as in

reset(InStream)

The rewrite statement prepares a stream for writing, as in

rewrite(OutStream)

Reading and writing to these streams is similar to using the standard streams, except that each read, write, and writeln statement contains one additional parameter in its input/output list—the name of the stream. This stream name must be given first, as in the following examples:

read(InStream, Value1, Value2, Value3);
writeln(OutStream, Sum)

Figure 2-39 illustrates a simple program that reads three values from a single input stream (not input) but writes to two different output streams: the sum to a special stream and a completion message to the standard stream. These additional streams must, of course, be associated with particular devices or files when the program is run. This might be done external to the Pascal program or else by special statements recognized by a particular compiler, as described for the standard streams. In our example, we assume that this is done externally to the program.

```
program Sum3 (InStream, OutStream, output);
{Program to read three integers from an input stream and write their sum to
    an output stream.}
var
    Value1, Value2, Value3: integer;    {Values to be summed}
    Sum: integer;                       {Sum of the values}
    InStream: text;                     {Input stream for values}
    OutStream: text;                    {Output stream for sum}
begin
    {Prepare streams for processing}
    reset (InStream);
    rewrite (OutStream);

    {Read data}
    read (InStream, Value1, Value2, Value3);

    {Perform computations}
    Sum := Value1 + Value2 + Value3;

    {Write result to OutStream}
    writeln (OutStream, Sum);

    {Write completion message to standard output stream}
    writeln ('Program completed')
end.
```

**FIGURE 2-39**
**Example of use of
input and output
streams other than the
standard streams.**

## 2-9   APPLICATIONS

In this section we present three problems to which the techniques introduced to this point can be applied. We will discuss each of the applications in turn, develop a program for the solution of the problem, and give sample input and output. Some comments are made on testing the programs.

The first application involves the preparation of reports on student class performance, where a final grade is determined from a weighted combination of several factors. The second application is topical. It concerns comparing the cost of items purchased now to their cost a month ago. The result is a crude measure of the rate of inflation. The third, and final, application is the calculation of pari-mutuel payoffs at a racetrack.

### 2-9.1   REPORTING STUDENT GRADES

In a particular computer science class, the final grade is derived from a student's performance in three aspects of the year's work. There is a midterm examination which counts 30 percent toward the final grade. Laboratory work is given a mark that counts 20 percent toward the final grade. The final examination makes up the remaining 50 percent.

The problem is to compute the final grade from the supplied marks in each area. The input consists of four separate items: the student's identification number, the mark received for laboratory work, the mark received for the midterm examination, and the mark received on the final examination. Each mark is given out of a possible 100. The output should be the student's number, the three supplied marks, and the calculated final grade. So that the individual items in the output can be readily identified, we will supply appropriate headings.

The solution to this problem consists of the following steps:

*1.* Read in student's identification number and marks on the individual items

*2.* Compute and print final grade along with identification number of the student and term marks

Since this is a reasonably straightforward restatement of the original problem, we will not dwell on its verification. Based on the information at hand, we will require the following variables. The identifiers have been chosen to reflect their purpose. The types are shown in parentheses.

| | |
|---|---|
| IDNumber (integer) | Student identification number |
| LabWork (integer) | Mark on lab work |
| MidTermExam (integer) | Mark on midterm exam |
| FinalExam (integer) | Mark on final exam |
| Grade (real) | Final grade |

The variable IDNumber is clearly an integer. If we assume that the supplied marks are whole numbers, they can be integer quantities. We will, however, allow a fractional portion in the final grade.

Step 1 of our general algorithm is a straightforward read statement. Since we have introduced the needed variables, we can write this statement directly as

read(IDNumber, LabWork, MidtermExam, FinalExam)

It is worthwhile to pause at this point to ensure that the items have been given in the order that matches the actual input data.

Having verified that this is the case, we can proceed to step 2 of our original algorithm. Two basic functions are included in this step: computation of the final grade and printing of the required information with appropriate headings. Thus we could consider expressing this step as two more detailed steps:

*2.1.* Compute final grade

*2.2.* Display results

Clearly these two together perform the function of the original second step. Neither of these two steps, however, is sufficiently detailed that we can stop at this point. The calculation of the final grade involves forming an expression in which the terms are a weighted sum of the three supplied marks. Using the defined variables, we arrive at

Grade := 0.20 * LabWork + 0.30 * MidtermExam + 0.50 * FinalExam

The formulation of the appropriate output statements is straightforward. The result can be seen in the final program. Putting all of this together according to the format described in the previous section, we obtain our final program, which we will call **Report** (see Fig. 2-40).

Let us take some hypothetical input data and check the output of the program. Suppose that the following values were supplied as input:

12345  72  68  65

To this input we apply the appropriate weighting factors to determine the contribution of each of the individual items (**72**, **68**, and **65**) toward the final grade. We take 20 percent of the lab mark (**0.20 * 72** gives **14.4**), 30 percent of the mark on the midterm exam (**0.30 * 68** gives **20.4**), and 50 percent of the mark on the final exam (**0.50 * 65** gives **32.5**). We sum these to get the value assigned to **Grade** (**67.3**). Thus the following is printed:

Student I.D.:       12345
Laboratory mark:       72
Midterm examination:       68
Final examination:       65
Final grade:       67.3

```
program Report (input, output);
```
{Given individual marks in three aspects for a year's work in a course, compute the final grade with weighting of 20%, 30%, and 50% respectively. The output is a printed line giving the student's I. D. number, his or her individual marks, and final grade.}
```
  var
    IDNumber: integer;          {Student's I. D. number}
    LabWork, MidTermExam,
    FinalExam: integer;         {Three marks}
    Grade: real;                {Final grade}
  begin
    {Step 1: Input data}
    read (IDNumber, LabWork, MidTermExam, FinalExam);

    {Step 2: Compute final grade}
    Grade := 0.20 * LabWork + 0.30 * MidTermExam + 0.50 * FinalExam;

    {Step 3: Display results}
    writeln ('Student I. D.:', IDNumber);
    writeln ('Laboratory mark:', LabWork);
    writeln ('Midterm examination:', MidTermExam);
    writeln ('Final examination', FinalExam);
    writeln ('Final grade:', Grade:8:2)
  end.
```

**FIGURE 2-40**
**Program to report**
**weighted average of**
**three marks.**

Notice again that delimiting quote marks do not appear in the output of string values.

We know now that the program does produce output, but are we confident that it produces the correct output? To answer this question, we proceed to the testing of this program. Suppose that instead of a program we were testing the accuracy of the speedometer on a car. To test a speedometer, you might drive a certain number of independently measured miles at a fixed speed and compare the time you took to the time you know you should have taken. For example, if you drive 5 measured miles with the speedometer registering 60 mi/h, you know it should take exactly 5 minutes. If, in fact, it takes you more than 5 minutes, you can conclude that the speedometer reads high. You can adjust this and try again.

Likewise, it is a good practice to test a program on data that will give a known result. In this example we know that a student who receives identical marks on all three items should also receive this mark as a final grade. To verify this, let us assume that a particular student received marks of 75 on each item. For this student the lab component of his final grade is $0.20*75$, or 15.0; the midterm exam component is $0.30*75$, or 22.5; and the final exam component is $0.50*75$, or 37.5. Summing these, we get 75.0, as expected.

In testing a program, it is also important to test extreme values of the input data. Errors often result from a failure to account for the extreme values. For example, suppose that our student received a mark of 100 on all three items. This student's final grade in the course should then be 100. Does the program give this result? A little checking shows that it does. Also, suppose some unfortunate student received a mark of 0 on all items. Checking through the program shows a final grade of 0 is computed, as expected.

Testing cannot be relied on to show that a program is free of errors; at best, it shows that you have not found any errors. Either there are no errors, or they have remained hidden throughout the testing. We hope that it is the first case, but, for a program of significant complexity, we cannot be sure. Proper choice of test cases can help to increase our confidence. Errors often result from circumstances that were not anticipated. Good testers try to anticipate possible problems in their programs and force errors into revealing themselves. A sabotage mentality helps here. Errors that are revealed in the testing phase will not return to plague programmers after they have delivered their programs to the client (or instructor) with their stamp of approval. More will be said about testing in Sec. 7-5.

## 2-9.2 GAUGING INFLATION

Inflation is on everyone's mind. To get some indication of the current rate of inflation, we can compare the present price of an article with the price we paid the last time it was purchased. For the sake of uniformity, let us assume that we shop regularly once a month. The following program reads three pieces of input data: an item identification number (an integer), the price paid (in dollars and cents), and the price paid last month (again, in dollars and cents). For example,

329   2.49   2.25

shows that we paid $2.49 for item number 329 this month, whereas we paid $2.25 for the same product last month. (Note that the dollar signs are not part of the input stream but are part of the interpretation of the values found there.) Items purchased are specified by means of an integer identification number. Clearly it would be much better to read a textual description of the item rather than some mysterious number. Standard Pascal, however, does not provide a straightforward method for reading character strings. For this reason, reading character strings is deferred to Chap. 6 and a more primitive form of input will have to do for now.

For our inflation indicator we will compute two statistics. The first of these is the straight algebraic difference between the two prices. In this case the algebraic difference is $2.49 - $2.25 = $0.24. As well, we compute the percentage difference over the month. For this particular product, the percentage difference is calculated as

$$\frac{2.49 - 2.25}{2.25} \times 100\% = 10.67\%$$

Our first solution attempt has the following four steps.

*1.* Read item identification, current price, and last month's price

*2.* Compute algebraic difference in price

*3.* Compute percentage difference

*4.* Print results

From this brief description of the solution, and the problem statement, the following variables are suggested. Again, names are chosen to describe their purpose, and types are given in parentheses.

| | |
|---|---|
| Identification (integer) | Identification number of item |
| CurrentPrice (real) | Price paid this month |
| OldPrice (real) | Price paid last month |
| AlgDiff (real) | Algebraic difference |
| PCDiff (real) | Percentage difference |

The refinement of the steps in our general solution proceeds in the same way as in the previous section. Since the difficulty is roughly the same in the two cases, we will not go into details, but simply present the final program Gauge in Fig. 2-41.

For demonstration purposes, let us try three different sets of data and see what output we get. We take the following three sets of data:

```
21   4.79   4.38
22   1.57   1.54
23   0.38   0.39
```

Applying the program to the first set of input data results in the integer variable Identification getting the value 21, and the real variables CurrentPrice and OldPrice being set to 4.79 and 4.38, respectively. In step 2 OldPrice is subtracted from CurrentPrice, resulting in the value 0.41, which is assigned to the variable AlgDiff. Step 3 converts this value to a percentage of the previous month's price. The calculation is

$$\frac{0.41}{4.38} \times 100$$

which gives the value 9.36 (we will express it here to only two decimal places, although in reality, more would be computed). This is assigned to the variable PCDiff. Output is produced in step 4. For this set of data values the following output results. (Notice again that we have assumed a convenient output format. Notice also the use of the special symbols $ and %, which are supplied as string constants.)

**program** Gauge (input, output);

{This program reads in an identification of an article (Identification), the current price of the article (CurrentPrice), and its price one month ago (OldPrice). The program computes and prints the algebraic difference (AlgDiff), between the two prices and the percentage difference (PCDiff). These values may be positive or negative.}

**var**
    Identification: integer;      {Item identification}
    CurrentPrice: real;          {Price paid this month}
    OldPrice: real;              {Price paid last month}
    AlgDiff: real;               {Algebraic difference}
    PCDiff: real;                {Percentage difference}

**begin**
    {Step 1: Input}
    read (Identification, CurrentPrice, OldPrice);

    {Step 2: Compute the algebraic difference in price}
    AlgDiff := CurrentPrice − OldPrice;

    {Step 3: Compute the percentage difference}
    PCDiff := AlgDiff / OldPrice *100;

    {Step 4: Output}
    writeln ('Item purchased (identification):', Identification);
    writeln ('Price this month: $', CurrentPrice:8:2);
    writeln ('Price last month: $', OldPrice:8:2);
    writeln ('Algebraic difference: $', AlgDiff:8:2);
    writeln ('Percentage difference:', PCDiff:5:1, '%')

    {Step 5: Finished}
**end**.

**FIGURE 2-41**
**Program to**
**gauge inflation.**

| Item purchased (identification): | 21 |
|---|---|
| Price this month: $ | 4.79 |
| Price last month: $ | 4.38 |
| Algebraic difference: $ | 0.41 |
| Percentage difference: | 9.3% |

Try the program yourself on the other two sets of data values. You should get the following outputs:

| Item purchased (identification): | 22 |
|---|---|
| Price this month: $ | 1.57 |
| Price last month: $ | 1.54 |
| Algebraic difference: $ | 0.03 |
| Percentage difference: | 1.9% |

and

| Item purchased (identification): | 23 |
| Price this month: $ | 0.38 |
| Price last month: $ | 0.39 |
| Algebraic difference: $ | −0.01 |
| Percentage difference: | −2.6% |

Note in the third example the effect of the price reduction in item 23. The resulting algebraic and percentage differences are negative. In the case of the algebraic difference, this does not adapt well to our output format. How might you adjust for this?

As with any program, this one should now be thoroughly tested. From the example of the previous section, see if you can come up with an appropriate set of test cases.

### 2-9.3  PARI-MUTUEL PAYOFFS

Horse racing is one of the most popular spectator sports in North America. Wagering at most racetracks is on the pari-mutuel system, a system in which the winning bettors share the total amount wagered, less a certain percentage to the operators of the track to cover track expenses and purses for the race as well as a certain percentage to the government.

At the Ups-and-Downs racetrack, the various levels of government take a combined total of 10.6 percent of all money wagered. The track operators take an additional 12 percent. From the amount remaining in the "pool" of money wagered, payoffs are made to all those who bet on the winning horse. (We are assuming "win" bets only at this track; the calculation of payoffs for "place" and "show" bets is more complicated.) The calculation of the payoff is based on the premise that money remaining in the pool is to be divided among the winners in proportion to the amount they wagered. The payoff is normally posted for the standard $2 bet.

We require a program that takes as input the total amount wagered to win (the "win pool") for a given race, the number of the winning horse, and the amount wagered on the winning horse. The output is to be the number of the winning horse and the payoff on a $2 bet.

As our first algorithm, we come up with the following:

1. Read total amount wagered, number of winning horse, and amount bet on winning horse

2. Compute amount taken by government and track operators from total wager pool

3. Compute payoff to bettors, expressed per $2 bet

4. Print out the number of winning horse and amount of payoff

From this we generate the list of variables, appearing as the first six variable declarations in the declaration portion of Fig. 2-42.

**program** Parimutuel (input, output);

{This program reads the amount bet on a horse race (**WinPool**), the winning
horse's number (**Winner**), and the amount bet on this horse (**Bet**). The
program then calculates the amount of money that the government, the
track operators, and the bettors receive. The output consists of the number
of the winning horse and the amount to be paid out on each $2.00 winning
ticket.}

**var**

| | |
|---|---|
| WinPool: real; | {Amount of money bet on this race} |
| Winner: integer; | {Number of winning horse} |
| AmountBet: real; | {Amount bet on the winning horse} |
| GovtShare: real; | {The ponies giveth and the taxman taketh away} |
| TrackShare: real; | {Amount needed for track operation} |
| Payoff: real; | {Amount paid for each $2.00 ticket} |
| Ratio: real; | {Payoff on $1.00 bet} |

**begin**
  {Step 1: Input }
  read (WinPool, Winner, AmountBet);

  {Step 2: Calculate the government's and track's share of pool}
  GovtShare : = 0.106 * WinPool;
  TrackShare : = 0.12 * WinPool;

  {Step 3: Reduce pool accordingly}
  WinPool : = WinPool − (TrackShare + GovtShare);

  {Step 4: Calculate payoff ratio for each dollar wagered}
  Ratio : = WinPool / AmountBet;       {per $1 bet}

  {Step 5: Compute posted payoff}
  Payoff : = Ratio * 2.0;

  {Step 6: Output winning horse number and amount paid for $2.00 ticket}
  writeln ('The winning horse is number☐', Winner);
  writeln ('$2.00☐tickets☐pay☐$', Payoff:8:2)
**end.**

**FIGURE 2-42**
**Program to compute**
**pari-mutuel payoffs.**

We now proceed to refine each of these steps. Step 1 is straightforward,
so once again we can go directly to the appropriate read statement:

read (WinPool, Winner, AmountBet)

Step 2 requires a statement to generate each of the amounts taken from
the win pool: 10.6 percent goes to **GovtShare**; 12 percent goes to **TrackShare**.
This results in the following assignment statements:

GovtShare : = 0.106 * WinPool;
TrackShare : = 0.12 * WinPool

Step 3 is more involved. The money remaining in the win pool (after the deductions of step 2) must be divided among the successful bettors in proportion to the amount they bet. First, we must determine how much remains in the pool and then the correct proportion. Two steps are suggested:

*3.1.* Compute amount of win pool remaining

*3.2.* Compute payoff ratio

Referring back to our original step 3 reminds us that the payoff is to be expressed per $2 bet. Therefore, our refinement needs a third step to adjust the computed ratio (which is expressed per $1 bet) to a payoff on a $2 bet. This gives us

*3.1.* Compute amount of win pool remaining

*3.2.* Compute payoff ratio (per $1 bet)

*3.3.* Multiply payoff ratio by 2

To handle steps 3.2 and 3.3, we use the variable **Ratio**. These three steps can be expressed as the following assignment statements:

```
WinPool : = WinPool − (GovtShare + TrackShare);
Ratio : = WinPool / AmountBet;   {per $1 bet}
Payoff : = Ratio * 2.0
```

The refinement of step 4 of our general algorithm is once again straightforward. Combining all these steps, we get the program **Parimutuel** of Fig. 2-42

For demonstration purposes, we will try the program with the following sets of data values.

```
10000   1   550
24003   13   18335
```

In the first case, **WinPool**, **Winner**, and **AmountBet** get the values **10000**, **1**, and **550**, respectively, as a result of the read statement in step 1. Deductions are made in steps 2 and 3, reducing the size of the win pool from $10,000 to a final total of $7740. The return on a $1 investment is computed in step 4 to be $14.07 (**7740/550**, expressed here to two decimal figures). This represents the original $1 plus a profit of $13.07. In step 5 this is converted to a payoff on the standard $2 bet for posting purposes. The resulting output line is

```
The winning horse is number       1
$2.00 tickets pay $        28.15
```

In case 2, number 13 was a heavy favorite. As a result, much of the money bet was bet on this horse. This will mean a small payoff. The government and track take their share first. This reduces the size of the

1000 Japanese yen = 8.25 Canadian dollars

1 U.S. dollar = 1.38 Canadian dollars

Develop programs to make the following conversions:
(a) Read an amount in French francs and print the equivalent in Canadian dollars.
(b) Read an amount in Swiss francs and print the equivalent in British pounds.
(c) Read an amount in Canadian dollars and print the equivalent in both U.S. dollars and Japanese yen.
(d) Read an amount in U.S. dollars and print the equivalent in both German marks and French francs.

★ **3.** The Axel Foley Real Estate Agency pays its sales staff a salary of $400 per month plus a commission of $100 for each piece of real estate they sell plus 1 percent of the value of the sale. Each month the bookkeeper prepares a line of data for each salesperson, containing the agent's identification number, number of sales made that month, and the total value of all sales for the month. Design a Pascal program to compute and display a salesperson's salary for a given month. Test the program thoroughly on some appropriate sample data.

**4.** A system of linear equations of the form

$$ax + by = c$$

$$dx + ey = f$$

can be solved by using the following formulas:

$$x = \frac{ce - bf}{ae - bd} \quad \text{and} \quad y = \frac{af - cd}{ae - bd}$$

Design a Pascal program to read in the two sets of coefficients ($a$, $b$, and $c$, and $d$, $e$, and $f$) and print out the solution values for $x$ and $y$. Are there any cases for which this program will not work?

**5.** The cost of hail insurance in a typical farming community is 3.5 percent of the desired amount of coverage per acre multiplied by the number of acres seeded. Assuming that the crop possibilities are limited to wheat, oats, and barley, design a Pascal program that reads the desired coverage and number of acres planted for each of the three crops and computes the total cost of hail insurance for this customer.

**6.** A car traveling down a road approaches an intersection and slows down from a speed of 55 mi/h to 30 mi/h in 5 seconds. Write a Pascal program that calculates both the car's constant rate of acceleration and how long it will take for the car to stop. You will need to use the following formula to calculate acceleration:

$$a = \frac{v_f - v_i}{t}$$

where $a$ is acceleration, $t$ is time, $v_i$ is initial velocity, and $v_f$ is the final velocity.

7. The cost to the consumer of a new car is the sum of the wholesale cost of the car, the dealer's percentage markup, and the provincial or state sales tax (applied to the markup price). Assuming a dealer's markup of 12 percent on all units and a sales tax of 6 percent, design a Pascal program to read the wholesale cost of a car and print the consumer's cost.

## SELECTED REFERENCES

**Brooks**, R. P., Jr.: *The Mythical Man-Month: Essays on Software Engineering*, Addison-Wesley, Reading, Mass., 1975.

**IEEE** and ANSI/X3J9: *An American National Standard: IEEE Standard Pascal Computer Programming Language*, The Institute of Electrical and Electronics Engineers, Inc., New York, 1979.

**International** Organization for Standardization: *Specification for Computer Programming Language Pascal*, ISO 7185-1982, 1982.

**Jensen**, K., and Wirth, N.: *Pascal User Manual and Report:* 3d ed., *ISO Pascal Standard*, Springer-Verlag, New York, 1985. Third edition prepared by A. B. Mickel and J. F. Miner.

**Martin**, James: *Design of Man-Computer Dialogue*, Prentice-Hall, Englewood Cliffs, N. J., 1973.

**Shneiderman**, B., Mayer, R., McKay, D., and Heller, P.: "Experimental Investigations of the Utility of Detailed Flowcharts in Programming," *Communications of the ACM*, vol. 20, June 1977, p. 373.

**Tremblay**, J. P., and Bunt, R. B.: *An Introduction to Computer Science—An Algorithmic Approach*, 2d ed., McGraw-Hill, New York, 1988.

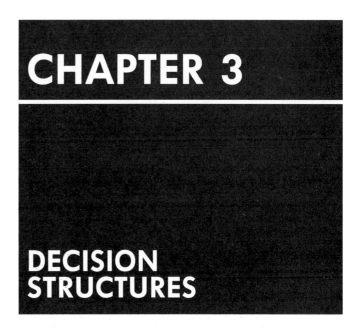

# CHAPTER 3

## DECISION STRUCTURES

In Chap. 2 we saw how to develop algorithms to solve simple problems on a computer. We then examined in greater detail algorithms that followed more or less a standard pattern: the input of some data values, a series of calculations, and the output of some results. Much of the real power of a computer, however, comes from its ability to make decisions and determine a course of action at run time based on the value of some piece of data read or on the result of some calculation.

In this chapter we examine in more detail the two powerful programming concepts that require the power of decision: the ability to select one action from a set of specified alternatives and the ability to repeat a series of actions. The Pascal syntax for these programming concepts is reviewed. Examples and applications using these new features are discussed.

## 3-1  MOTIVATION

A significant amount of manual activity is required to get any computer program running. For example, after keying in the program, through the use of a terminal, the input data also must be entered. For very simple applications, many people feel that the effort is not justified. They would rather use pen and paper or a pocket calculator. The program Report of Chap. 2, for example, is designed to compute and print the final grade for a single student. In a large class of, say, 250 students, the calculation would have to be repeated 250 times for a complete class report. As the program stands now, this would require rerunning it 250 times, each time with a new set of data. Clearly, this would be a tedious activity.

**By permission of
Johnny Hart and
Field Enterprises,
Inc.**

The concept of *flow of control* through a program refers to the order in which the individual steps of the program are executed. In this chapter we further investigate methods by which we can depart from normal linear flow through the use of *control structures*.

We will discuss several applications that are tedious or impossible to solve with only linear flow of control.

## 3-2 THE SELECTION FROM ALTERNATIVE ACTIONS

A decision is specified by a condition that can be true or false. In Pascal, we call this condition a *Boolean expression*. This type of expression is calculated in a manner analogous to a numeric expression, except that its value is true or false rather than a number. Suppose we have two numeric variables, call them $A$ and $B$, that are guaranteed to have *unequal* values, and suppose we want to print the value of the larger. If $A$ is greater than $B$, we want to print the value of $A$. On the other hand, if $B$ is greater than $A$, we want to print the value of $B$. Clearly, we have two alternative actions— print the value of A and print the value of B. The choice of which action to take rests on a decision of whether or not $A$ is greater than $B$. This structure can be illustrated by the simple flowchart shown in Fig. 3-1.

The expression $A > B$ is a Boolean expression describing a condition that we wish to test. If $A > B$ is "true," that is, if $A$ is in fact greater than $B$

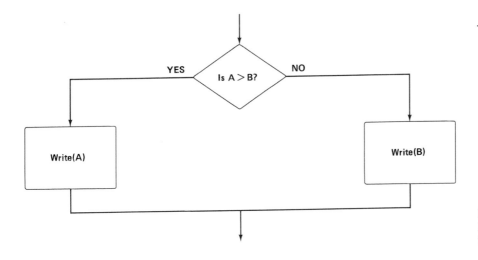

YES       Is A > B?       NO

Write(A)

Write(B)

**FIGURE 3-1**
**Flowchart of a**
**typical decision.**

with the current values of A and B (note that this is a *run-time* test), we will take the action on the left in Fig. 3-1 and print the value of A. If A > B is "false," that is, if A is not greater than B (it is less than B), we will take the action on the right and print the value of B. The result of the entire operation is that the larger of the two values is printed.

### 3-2.1 THE IF STATEMENT

Recall that the format of the if statement in Pascal is as follows:

**if** *Boolean expression*
**then** *"true" alternative*
**else** *"false" alternative*

The example in Fig. 3-1 would be written

**if** A > B
**then** writeln(A)
**else** writeln(B)

Pascal restricts each of the alternatives in the if statement to a single statement. This single statement can be a simple statement, for example, an assignment, read, or write statement, or a *structured statement*, which is composed of other statements. A very useful structured statement is the *compound statement*, which consists of any number of statements separated by semicolons and enclosed between a **begin** and **end**. For example, we might have

**if** A > B
**then begin**
        writeln (A);
        FlagA := 1;
        FlagB := 0
    **end**

```
    else begin
        writeln (B);
        FlagB : = 1;
        FlagA : = 0
    end
```

Recall the semicolon syntax rule from Chap. 2, and notice that the statements within a compound statement follow the same rule as the statements between the **begin** and **end** of a program.

The if statement is itself a statement according to the rules of Pascal; indeed it is a structured statement because it contains other statements. Notice that an if statement may therefore contain another if statement; the statements are then said to be *nested*. We will deal with this aspect in the next subsection.

A special set of operators is required to express conditions. In the preceding example, $>$ is known as a *relational operator*, because it describes a possible relation between two values. The complete set of possible relational operators is shown in Table 3-1. Notice that the two-character operators $<=$, $>=$, and $<>$ are used instead of the more traditional $\leq$, $\geq$, and $\neq$ of mathematics. This is again because of the limitations of computer devices. Simple conditions, such as $A > B$, can be joined by *logical connectives* or *logical operators*, such as **and**, **or**, and **not**, to form more complex conditions. This will be discussed in Sec. 3-4.

Relational operators can be applied to either numeric or nonnumeric data items. Their meaning in a numeric context is clear. What do they mean in connection with characters? It turns out that there is a definite sequence imposed on characters by their representation in a computer, referred to as the *collating sequence* (see Chap. 6). This will allow us, for example, to sort a list of names into alphabetical order. We will defer this material until Chap. 6. In the meantime, we will restrict our tests of characters to equality and inequality, whose interpretations are obvious.

Let us examine more carefully the flow of control through the if statement. The control structure itself is to be viewed as a complete entity that is entered at the top and exited at the bottom. The idea of a single entry point and a single exit point is an important one. Figure 3-2 shows this in diagrammatic form. The control structure is entered at the point where the condition is to be evaluated. Following evaluation of the condition, either the

**TABLE 3-1** Relational Operators

| Operator | Meaning |
|---|---|
| $>$ | Greater than |
| $<$ | Less than |
| $=$ | Equal to |
| $>=$ | Greater than or equal to |
| $<=$ | Less than or equal to |
| $<>$ | Not equal to |

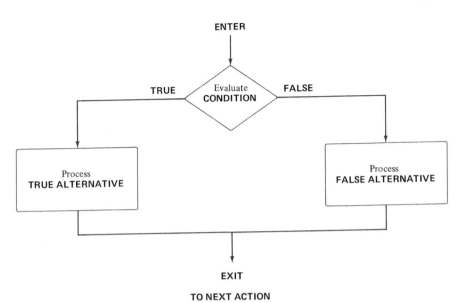

**FIGURE 3-2**
**General flowchart**
**of the selection**
**construct.**

"true" alternative or the "false" alternative is executed. After completion of the selected alternative, control passes to the next indicated action following the if statement. In some cases there may be no special action if the condition is false (that is, there is no else part). This type of structure is shown in Fig. 3-3.

Finally, we summarize the syntax of the if statement and the compound statement in the syntax charts of Figs. 3-4 and 3-5.

Consider the program in Fig. 3-6, in which an if statement is used. This is one of several ways to solve the problem of finding the largest (or

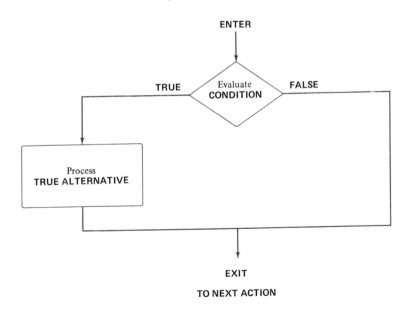

**FIGURE 3-3**
**The selection**
**construct with no**
**"false" alternative.**

**if statement**

FIGURE 3-4   Syntax diagram for the **if** statement.

smallest) of a group of numbers. This particular method is used here to illustrate a number of important points. Execution of the program begins with the reading of two values, say, −2 and 10, into Val1 and Val2, respectively. Then comes the if statement. First, the condition is evaluated. With this particular pair of data values, it turns out to be false. Thus control passes to the "false," or else, alternative. The variable Max is assigned the value of Val2 (10), and the message Second value is the largest is printed. This is the end of the execution of the if statement. We proceed to the next statement, and on through the program.

Suppose the data values were interchanged so that Val1 received the value 10 and Val2, −2. Consequently, the "true," or then, alternative would be selected. The variable Max would be assigned the value of Val1 (10) and the message First value is the largest would be printed. This is the end of this step, so we proceed directly to the statement following the entire if statement, *skipping over the statements in the else alternative.*

Note carefully the indentation scheme used in Fig 3-6. Each of the three major parts of the if structure (the if part, the then part, and the else part) begins on a new line, in the same position in fact. Additional statements in the then or else parts are lined up directly under one another. With this scheme the major components of the structure are clearly visible and the statement or statements defining each alternative are also clearly seen. We will be adopting this convention for all the programs in this book. Note also the use of a compound statement, with a **begin** and **end**, since each alternative of the if statement contains two statements.

As a second example of the use of this particular control structure, we turn to an application relating to a political nominating convention. A number of ballotings are held. A candidate is declared nominated on any given balloting only if his or her vote total exceeds the sum of the vote totals of all other candidates currently on the ballot. If no candidate can be nominated on a particular balloting, the candidate with the lowest vote total is dropped from consideration and a new balloting is conducted.

Suppose that on this particular balloting, four candidates remain in contention. We require a program to determine the outcome of the balloting.

**compound statement**

FIGURE 3-5
Syntax diagram for
the compound
statement.

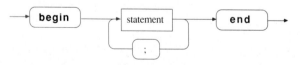

```
program Display (input, output);
{Given two integer values, this program determines the largest.}
var
    Val1: integer;    {The first value read}
    Val2: integer;    {The second value read}
    Max: integer;     {The largest value read}
begin
    {Step 1: Input data}
    read (Val1, Val2);

    {Step 2: Determine largest value}
    if Val1 > Val2
    then begin
            Max := Val1;
            writeln ('First value is the largest')
        end
    else begin
            Max := Val2;
            writeln ('Second value is the largest')
        end;

    {Step 3: Display results}
    writeln ('Value is□', Max)
end.
```

**FIGURE 3-6**
**Program to display larger integer.**

First, we will determine if the candidate with the largest vote total has a total that is higher than the sum of the other vote totals; if so, this candidate is declared nominated. If not, we must drop the candidate with the lowest vote total from the next ballot. This is a clear application of the if statement. For the sake of simplicity, the program **Nominations** in Fig. 3-7 assumes that the totals have already been sorted such that the first total read is the highest and the last is the smallest.

Let us assume that Table 3-2 gives the results of the current balloting. The data is then prepared as follows:

764    419    307    175

Table 3-3 shows the trace of the program with this data. The statements of the program have been labeled with step numbers (in comment brackets) for reference.

## 3-2.2  NESTED IFs

In some applications, one of the alternatives in an if statement may involve a further decision. For example, before you take action on a certain grade on a test, you may want to discount the possibility of a data entry error. This requires an additional check to see if the data item read is a valid item. This suggests the use of an additional if structure embedded within each (or either) of the original alternatives. Such a process is an example of *nesting*.

```
program Nominations (input, output);
{Given the vote counts for four candidates, this program determines the
    outcome according to the rules described in the text.}
var
    Count1, Count2,
    Count3, Count4: integer;    {The four vote counts}
begin
    {Step 1: Read the vote counts}
    read (Count1, Count2, Count3, Count4);

    {Step 2: Report the results}
    if Count1 > (Count2 + Count3 + Count4)
    then writeln ('First candidate is nominated')
    else writeln ('No nomination; lowest candidate is dropped from ballot')
end.
```

FIGURE 3-7
Program to determine
election outcome.

Consider the problem of determining the largest of three input values (say, A, B, and C) rather than two. These must be tested in pairs. We first test to see if A is greater than B. If so, we test to see if it is also greater than C, and so forth. The program Max3 in Fig. 3-8 solves this problem. To simplify matters, we will assume the three values to be distinct.

As a second example of the use of nesting, we present the following problem. Its solution illustrates the use of nesting to test a series of alternatives rather than just a pair.

The Genco Pura Oil Company has decided to give its deserving employees a Christmas bonus. The bonus is to be based on two criteria: the number of overtime hours worked and the number of hours the employee was absent from work. There is a set of data for each employee containing the employee's identification number, number of overtime hours worked, and number of hours absent.

The company has decided to use the following formula to calculate the bonus: subtract two-thirds of the employee's absent hours from the overtime hours, and distribute the bonus according to Table 3-4.

We require a program to read in the employee's information and calculate the amount of bonus to be paid. Clearly, we have a set of mutually exclusive alternatives; no employee can fall into more than one category.

| TABLE 3-2 | |
| --- | --- |
| Names | Vote Count |
| Friesen | 764 |
| Daoust | 419 |
| Tremblay | 307 |
| DeDourek | 175 |

| Step | Count1 | Count2 | Count3 | Count4 | Condition | Output |
|------|--------|--------|--------|--------|-----------|--------|
| 1 | 764 | 419 | 307 | 175 | | |
| 2 | 764 | 419 | 307 | 175 | False | No nomination; lowest candidate is dropped from ballot |

To determine the appropriate category, we employ nesting in a special way. Figure 3-9 contains the complete program.

Notice carefully the "cascading" test. This could also be written as a series of unnested if statements. The nested version is sometimes better, for reasons we shall now discuss.

Suppose that an employee has worked 50 hours of overtime and has been absent only 3 hours. Subtracting two-thirds of the hours absent from the overtime gives a total of 48 hours, which entitles the employee to the full bonus of $50. For this employee the first test in step 2 succeeds. Thus the then alternative is selected, and Payment is set to 50.0. Since the rest of this step is contained within the else alternative for the first test, control passes immediately to the statement following the if statement, which is a writeln statement. We have made a total of one test. If we had, instead, written

```
program Max3 (input, output);
{Given three integer numbers, this program determines the largest. The three
   numbers are assumed to be distinct (different).}
var
   A, B, C: integer;      {The three input values}
   Max: integer;          {The largest value}
begin
   {Step 1: Input data}
   read (A, B, C);

   {Step 2: Determine largest value}
   if A > B
   then if A > C
        then Max : = A     {A > B, A > C}
        else Max : = C     {C > A, A > B}
   else if B > C
        then Max : = B     {B > A, B > C}
        else Max : = C;    {C > B, B > A}

   {Step 3: Display largest}
   writeln ('Largest value is □', Max)
end.
```

**FIGURE 3-8**
**Program to find the maximum of three integers.**

| TABLE 3-4 | Bonus Schedule | |
|---|---|---|
| **Overtime − 2/3 * Absent** | | **Bonus Paid** |
| > 40 hours | | $50 |
| > 30 but ≤ 40 hours | | $40 |
| > 20 but ≤ 30 hours | | $30 |
| > 10 but ≤ 20 hours | | $20 |
| ≤ 10 hours | | $10 |

a series of unnested if statements, we would have to test each of the other categories. In the present example, each of the other tests would *also succeed*, each time causing the associated then part to be executed. The value of Payment would be successively assigned smaller values. All bonus payments would be computed as either $10 or $20! This might be fixed by reordering the tests in ascending order. The reader should verify that while this method works, it results in unnecessary assignments that waste computer time. Alternatively, compound conditions (see Sec. 3-4) could be used to make the conditions mutually exclusive. Even in this case, the number of

```
program Bonus (input, output);
{Given an employee identification number, overtime hours worked, and
    hours absent, this program determines the amount of the Christmas
    bonus.}
var
    IDNumber: integer;    {Employee identification number}
    Overtime: integer;    {Overtime hours}
    Absent: integer;      {Absent hours}
    Payment: real;        {Bonus payment in dollars}
begin
    {Step 1: Input data}
    read (IDNumber, Overtime, Absent);

    {Step 2: Compute bonus}
    if (Overtime − (2/3) * Absent) > 40.0
    then Payment : = 50.0
    else if (Overtime − (2/3) * Absent) > 30.0
        then Payment : = 40.0
        else if (Overtime − (2/3) * Absent) > 20.0
            then Payment : = 30.0
            else if (Overtime − (2/3) * Absent) > 10.0
                then Payment : = 20.0
                else Payment : = 10.0;

    {Step 3: Display bonus}
    writeln ('Bonus for employee number□', IDNumber,' □is $', Payment:8:2)
end.
```

**FIGURE 3-9**
**Calculation of**
**employee bonus.**

conditions tested will usually be greater than if nested if statements are used, and these conditions will be more complex.

Suppose that a different employee worked 30 hours of overtime but was absent for 12 hours. For this employee, the testing value [Overtime − (2/3) ∗ Absent] is 22. The first test (> 40) fails; consequently, the else alternative is chosen. This alternative begins with a second test (> 30), which also fails; consequently, its else alternative is chosen. This alternative begins with a third test (> 20), which succeeds. Since the > 30 test failed, we know now that this employee falls in the range > 20 but ≤ 30. The then alternative of this particular if statement sets Payment to 30.0. Control then passes to the writeln statement, as before.

You can see that the nesting structure employed in this program cuts down on the number of *unsuccessful* tests required to process the various cases. This is a very useful form of organization. A series of unnested if statements would require each case to be tested every time.

We could improve this program further by requiring the calculation of the testing value [Overtime − (2/3) ∗ Absent] to be performed only once. To do this, we introduce a temporary variable (let us call it TestValue) and replace the entire nested if statements of Fig. 3-9 with the program fragment of Fig. 3-10. It is also necessary to add the variable declaration

TestValue: real;     { Value tested to determine bonus}

In this version the calculated test value is stored in the variable TestValue. Rather than having it recalculated at every test point, it is simply reexamined—a much faster process. This improvement cuts down the amount of computation required and, therefore, the ultimate processing cost of the program. A good programmer is ever watchful for such improvements. At the same time, however, a programmer should be careful not to sacrifice the readability of a program for the sake of a minor gain in efficiency. A good programmer also attempts to balance efficiency and readability. We also note that many of the better compilers, often called *optimizing compilers*, would have detected the improvement described in our example and would have generated the more efficient object program automatically.

```
{Step 2.1 : Compute test value}
TestValue : = Overtime − (2/3) ∗ Absent;

{Step 2.2 : Compute bonus}
if TestValue > 40.0
then Payment : = 50.0
else if TestValue > 30.0
        then Payment : = 40.0
        else if TestValue > 20.0
                then Payment : = 30.0
                else if TestValue > 10.0
                        then Payment : = 20.0
                        else Payment : = 10.0;
```

**FIGURE 3-10**
**Alternative method**
**for employee**
**bonus calculation.**

Next we consider a seemingly trivial extension to the program Max3 that, in fact, adds considerable complexity. The problem is once again to read in three numbers, but this time to determine the minimum value as well as the maximum value. Try this problem yourself. When you are satisfied that you have a solution, examine the program MaxMin3 in Fig. 3-11.

Study Fig. 3-11 carefully. Notice that the first if statement (if A < B) has an if statement for each of its alternatives. If you are not careful, you can get quite confused with such structures. It is very important, for example, that the then and else portions are matched with the proper if test. A lack of care can lead to ambiguities whenever some of the if statements do not have "false" (else) alternatives. Consider the following example, where A, B, C, and D are integer variables.

```
if A < B
then if C < D
        then writeln ('A < B and C < D')
        else writeln ('Otherwise ?')
```

Under what condition is the second writeln statement executed? Is it when $A \geq B$, or when $A < B$ and $C \geq D$?

Notice that the following program fragment is identical to the previous one, except for the indentation of the **else**:

```
if A < B
then if C < D
        then writeln ('A < B and C < D')
else writeln ('Otherwise ?')
```

A Pascal compiler does not use indentation when analyzing a program; rather, it processes a program as a sequence of symbols. Therefore, it is unclear to the compiler whether the programmer intends that the **else** refer to the first or second **if**—an ambiguity that cannot be allowed. Such a possibility (called the *dangling else problem*) exists in several programming languages, including Pascal. To resolve the dangling else problem in Pascal, an additional syntax rule is imposed which states that in ambiguous cases, the **else** belongs to the closest previous **if** not matched by a previous **else**. Therefore, the program fragment under consideration here is interpreted as indicated by the first indentation scheme: Otherwise? is output if A < B and $C \geq D$.

To effect the other interpretation, that is, Otherwise ? is output if $A \geq B$, requires use of a compound statement as follows:

```
if A < B
then begin
        if C < D
        then writeln ('A < B and C < D')
        end
else writeln ('Otherwise ?')
```

Enclosing the inner if statement within **begin** and **end** causes the compiler

**program** MaxMin3 (input, output);
{Given three integer numbers, this program determines the largest and smallest value. The numbers are assumed to be distinct (different).}
**var**
    A, B, C: integer;    {The three input values}
    Max: integer;      {The largest value}
    Min: integer;       {The smallest value}
**begin**
    {Step 1: Input data}
    read (A, B, C);

    {Step 2: Determine largest and smallest values}
    **if** $A < B$
    **then**
        **if** $A < C$
        **then begin**
                Min : = A;        {A < B, A < C}
                **if** $B > C$
                **then** Max : = B    {A < C < B}
                **else** Max : = C    {A < B < C}
          **end**
        **else begin**
                Min : = C;        {C < A < B}
                Max : = B
          **end**
    **else**
        **if** $A > C$
        **then begin**
                Max : = A;        {A > B, A > C}
                **if** $B > C$
                **then** Min : = C    {A > B > C}
                **else** Min : = B    {A > C > B}
          **end**
        **else begin**
                Max : = C;        {C > A > B}
                Min : = B
          **end**;

    {Step 3: Display largest and smallest}
    writeln ('Largest value is ☐', Max, '☐Smallest is ☐', Min)
**end**.

**FIGURE 3-11**
**Program to find largest and smallest of three integers.**

to match the **else** with the first **if**. This is similar to using parentheses to modify the order of evaluation of operators in an expression.

### 3-2.3 SUMMARY

The if statement presented in this section is a useful and powerful programming construct. It allows a choice between two alternative courses of action. We have referred to these as the then alternative, taken when the testing condition evaluates to "true," and the else alternative, taken when the testing condition is "false." The else alternative may be omitted, in which case no special action is taken if the testing condition is "false" (see Fig. 3-3).

We also discussed the possibility of nesting, in which further tests are embedded within the alternatives. This allows us to test for a multiplicity of conditions, as illustrated in the examples, but it can quickly lead to confusion if abused. Great care must be taken to show clearly the totality of conditions in effect at any point. Appropriate comments and spacing can help considerably. Excessive nesting of if statements, however, can impede the readability of programs. This problem can often be alleviated by introducing a new control construct, called a *case statement*. This statement will be introduced in Sec. 3-5.

## EXERCISES 3-2

1. (*a*) Modify the program **Report** given in Fig. 2-40 so that a special message is printed for failing students.
   (*b*) Modify the program **Report** further so that students are given a division standing according to their final grade. Assume that the divisions are based on the following table:

| Final Grade | Division |
|-------------|----------|
| 80–100      | I        |
| 70–79       | II       |
| 60–69       | III      |
| 50–59       | IV       |
| Less than 50 | F       |

2. A utility company takes meter readings each month and charges its customers on the following basis:

| Kilowatthours | Rate |
|---------------|------|
| 0–500         | $20.00 |
| 501–1000      | $20.00 + 0.03 per kWh above 500 |
| 1001 and over | $35.00 + 0.02 per kWh above 1000 |

Write a program that reads in last month's meter reading and this month's meter reading and calculates the customer's bill.

3. Revise the program Max3 from Fig. 3-8 to account for the possibility of input values being equal.

4. Write a Pascal program to read the length of the three sides of a triangle (S1, S2, and S3) and determine what type of triangle it is, based on the following cases. Let $A$ denote the largest of S1, S2, and S3, and $B$ and $C$ the other two. Then

| | |
|---|---|
| If $A \geq B + C$ | No triangle is formed. |
| If $A^2 = B^2 + C^2$ | A right-angled triangle is formed. |
| If $A^2 > B^2 + C^2$ | An obtuse triangle is formed. |
| If $A^2 < B^2 + C^2$ | An acute triangle is formed. |

★ 5. Steve's bank's policy about loan qualifications is as follows: If the loan applicant has a checking balance of less than $1500, then the application is automatically rejected. Otherwise, the decision is based on the applicant's savings balance and number of overdrafts. If the number of overdrafts is fewer than four, then the application is approved regardless of the savings balance. However, if the number of overdrafts is four or more, then a savings balance of $1000 or more results in an approved application, whereas a savings balance of less than $1000 results in a conditionally approved application. Write a Pascal program that reads in the name, checking balance, savings balance, and number of overdrafts for a loan applicant and prints out a message indicating whether the loan was approved, conditionally approved, or rejected.

★★ 6. The following program segment was written by a confused student:

```
if x < y then if v < w
then j := x
else if x < v then if y < w then j := y
        else j := v
else begin if x < w
then j := w
end else j := x + w
```

Reconstruct this program segment so that it is more readable. Is there any way that you can make it simpler?

★ 7. Modify the program Nominations so that it does not require presorting the ballot results.

8. Write a program for a simple calculator. All that the calculator needs to do is add (+), subtract (−), multiply (∗), and divide (/). To use the calculator, you enter a number followed by an operator followed by a second number. Your program must read in the two numbers and the operator and perform the appropriate calculation. The numbers are of type real, and the operator is a character. Write out the equation with the

calculated answer. Also display any error messages for any errors that may occur. For example, the input

83.2 − 80.3

would result in the output

83.2 − 80.3 = 2.9

9. Lulu has always had difficulty deciding on her mode of transportation for getting to work in the morning. Lately, however, she has come up with a scheme to help her make this decision. If her roommate's car is available, she takes the car regardless of weather conditions. If the car is unavailable, other factors come into play. If it is raining, then she takes the bus. If it is cloudy and windy, she also takes the bus. However, if it is cloudy and not windy, or if it is sunny (regardless of wind), then she rides her bike. Write a program that reads in today's character values ('T' for true, and 'F' for false) for the variables CarAvailable, Rainy, Windy, and Cloudy and displays a message indicating how Lulu will get to work this morning.

★ 10. Write a program that calculates how much a person is charged for using a parking lot, based on the number of hours the person used the lot. The values to be read are the entry time (in hours and minutes), the departure time (in hours and minutes), the per-hour charge, and the maximum charge. The driver is charged for each full hour and is also charged for an extra hour if the car is parked for more than 10 minutes of the next hour. For example, if someone used the parking lot for 2 hours and 15 minutes, he or she would be charged for 3 hours. Assume that a 24-hour clock is used and that the lot closes at midnight. Output an appropriate message indicating the entry time, departure time, and parking fee.

## 3-3 LOOPING

Computers are particularly well-suited to applications in which an operation or series of operations is to be repeated many times. The *loop* introduced in Chap. 2 is a fundamental programming construct and can occur in a variety of forms. In this section we consider the loop in more detail.

Consider, for example, the calculation of the factorial function, an important mathematical function. For a given value $N$, the factorial of $N$ (usually written $N!$) is computed as the product $N(N − 1)(N − 2) \ldots (2)(1)$. This is nothing more than a series of repeated multiplications, where the multiplier is reduced by 1 prior to each multiplication. The program FactN in Fig. 3-12 uses a loop to compute the factorial of an input value.

The loop in this example is controlled by the while statement. Recall that this repeats the following statement (which is a compound statement) as long as the value of Multiplier remains greater than or equal to 1. This is a form of loop known as a *conditional loop*, since the process of looping is controlled by a stated condition.

```
program FactN (input, output);
{Given a nonnegative integer, this program computes the factorial.}
var
   N: integer;          {Input value}
   Product: integer;    {Product of terms computed to this point}
   Multiplier: integer; {Current term}
begin
   {Step 1: Input}
   read (N);

   {Step 2: Initialize variables}
   Product := 1;
   Multiplier := N;

   {Step 3: Engage loop}
   while Multiplier >= 1 do
      begin

         {Step 4: Compute partial product}
         Product := Product * Multiplier;

         {Step 5: Reset Multiplier}
         Multiplier := Multiplier - 1
      end;

   {Step 6: Display factorial}
   writeln ('Factorial of□', N, '□is□', Product)
end.
```

FIGURE 3-12
Calculation of
factorial of $N$ with
a conditional loop.

## 3-3.1 CONDITIONAL LOOPS

In Pascal we express a conditional loop in the following manner:

**while** *condition* **do**
   *statement*

We refer to the statement following the **do** as the *range* of the loop. This range is to be repeated as long as the stated condition remains true. The condition is evaluated prior to each pass through the loop. If it is true, the loop is executed one more time; if it is false, the loop terminates and the statement following the entire while statement (which includes the statement forming the range) is executed next. If the condition is false on the first entry into the loop, the range will be bypassed altogether. Note that since the range must be a single statement according to the syntax rules of Pascal, should several statements be required within the range of a loop, they must be made into a compound statement with a **begin** and an **end**. Figure 3-13 summarizes the syntax of the conditional loop (or while statement) using a syntax diagram.

while statement

FIGURE 3-13  Syntax diagram for the while statement.

As was the case with the if statement of the previous section, we will consider the while statement as an entity with a single entry point and a single exit point, as shown in Fig. 3-14. Entry and exit are both controlled through the condition of the while statement itself—it is both the first thing to be executed and the last. That is, the evaluation of the condition expressed in the while statement is done before any steps in the range of the loop are executed, and we exit from the loop only when the condition evaluates to false. It is the responsibility of the programmer to ensure that this does happen eventually; otherwise, the loop may run "forever," an error that is, unfortunately, all too common.

Let us trace the execution of program FactN (Fig. 3-12) with some sample data, paying particular attention to the operation of the loop. Suppose that we supplied the data value **3**. Table 3-5 shows the results of this trace. Note the introduction of a specific indication of the point at which the program terminates.

Step 1 reads the input value (**3**) and assigns it to the variable N. Step 2 initializes a pair of variables that we will be using in the loop: Product gets the value 1, and Multiplier gets the current value of N (here 3). We now come to the step controlling the loop. The first thing we do is evaluate the stated condition. Since the current value of Multiplier (**3**) is in fact greater

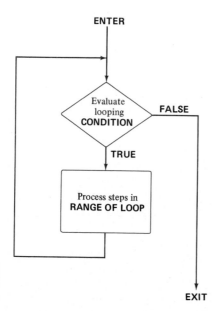

FIGURE 3-14
General flowchart of
the loop construct.

than 1, we enter into the range of the loop and proceed to step 4. In step 4 we multiply the current values of Product(1) and Multiplier(3) and assign the result (3) to Product. In step 5 we reduce the value of Multiplier by 1, so it is now 2. At this point we do not proceed ahead to step 6. Remember that we are in the range of a loop, under control of step 3 in this particular case. The only way we can get out of a loop is for the stated condition to evaluate to "false." We now return to step 3 and reevaluate this condition. The current value of the variable Multiplier is 2, which is still greater than 1, so we move once again to step 4. The current values of Product(3) and Multiplier(2) are multiplied together, and the result (6) becomes the new value of Product. Multiplier is reduced by 1 once again (to 1), and we return to reevaluate the looping condition once more. Again, the condition evaluates to "true" (Multiplier is now equal to 1), so we proceed to step 4. Once again, the current values of Product(6) and Multiplier(1) are multiplied together, and the result (6) is assigned to Product. In this case no values are actually changed. The value of Multiplier is then reduced from 1 to 0 in step 5, and we return to reevaluate the looping condition. This time the condition is "false." The current value of Multiplier (0) is neither greater than nor equal to 1. As a result, we are ready to leave the loop. We now pass automatically to the step immediately following the last step of the loop. In this case it is step 6, which produces the output

Factorial of 3 is 6

This is happily the correct result. The program then terminates.

Although this example is fairly simple, it illustrates several important points. It would be worthwhile to reread it. Of particular importance are the flow of control through the loop and the manner in which the variables

**TABLE 3-5** Trace of Program FactN

| Step | N | Product | Multiplier | Condition | Output |
|------|---|---------|-----------|-----------|--------|
| 1 | 3 | ? | ? | | |
| 2 | 3 | 1 | 3 | | |
| 3 | 3 | 1 | 3 | True | |
| 4 | 3 | 3 | 3 | | |
| 5 | 3 | 3 | 2 | | |
| 3 | 3 | 3 | 2 | True | |
| 4 | 3 | 6 | 2 | | |
| 5 | 3 | 6 | 1 | | |
| 3 | 3 | 6 | 1 | True | |
| 4 | 3 | 6 | 1 | | |
| 5 | 3 | 6 | 0 | | |
| 3 | 3 | 6 | 0 | False | |
| 6 | 3 | 6 | 0 | | Factorial of 3 is 6 |
| | | Termination | | | |

involved in the loop (**Product** and **Multiplier**) receive a succession of values. This last point can often be a source of difficulty in more complex problems. It can be helpful to tabulate the sequence of values received, as shown in Table 3-6.

To check your understanding of the foregoing discussion, run through the program **FactN** yourself. You might try **6** as the input data value. The succession of values taken on by the loop variables is shown in Table 3-7.

You might have observed by now that the value of the result in this particular program is unaffected by the last pass through the loop. Since the last pass is redundant, we could change the looping condition from **while** Multiplier $>= 1$ **do** to **while** Multiplier $> 1$ **do**. This would not alter the final result, since multiplication by 1 leaves the result unaffected. It is important, when looping, to take special care with the first pass through a loop and the last pass. Errors often result from failure to account properly for initial conditions or end conditions. They often require special attention.

In order to illustrate this point, the initial values of **Product** (1) and Multiplier(N) were carefully chosen so that the correct answer would result on certain special inputs. What happens, for example, if we input **0** as the data value? In this case, the first test of the condition Multiplier $>= 1$ evaluates to "false," since the value of Multiplier is, by assignment, 0. Thus the range of the loop is not executed at all. Control passes immediately to step 6 and the following is printed:

Factorial of 0 is 1

By definition, in mathematics, 0! is 1.

### 3-3.2 LOOP-CONTROLLED INPUT

One of the most common applications of loops is in the control of input to a computation (and, as we shall see, output from it). In all the examples presented thus far, problems have been solved for a single set of data values. By means of an appropriate loop it is possible to read additional sets of data values and repeat the computation. It is possible, for example, to process the grades for an entire class in one run or to compute the payoffs for an entire day of racing. This cuts down considerably on the amount of manual intervention required.

**TABLE 3-6** Loop Behavior of Program FactN for 3!

| Pass Through Loop | Value of **Product** | Value of **Multiplier** |
|:---:|:---:|:---:|
| 0[†] | 1 | 3 |
| 1 | 3 | 2 |
| 2 | 6 | 1 |
| 3 | 6 | 0 |

[†]The 0th pass refers to conditions in effect before the loop is entered.

**TABLE 3-7** Loop Behavior of Program FactN for 6!

**121**
3-3
LOOPING

| Pass Through Loop | Value of **Product** | Value of **Multiplier** |
|:---:|:---:|:---:|
| 0 | 1 | 6 |
| 1 | 6 | 5 |
| 2 | 30 | 4 |
| 3 | 120 | 3 |
| 4 | 360 | 2 |
| 5 | 720 | 1 |
| 6 | 720 | 0 |

To illustrate the technique, let us modify the program **Report** from Sec. 2-9.1 to compute the grades for an entire class. For convenience, we reproduce the program from Sec 2-9.1 as Fig. 3-15 here. The process of returning to read additional data is no problem now that we know about loops. The difficulty is in determining when to stop. We will discuss three ways of doing this.

One approach is to introduce one additional item of data at the front of the regular data. This item tells us how many sets of data values follow, giving us the information required to determine the number of times to loop. For example, for two students there would be two sets of data, preceded by the integer number **2**. This might appear as

```
2
26731  58  63  72
29139  77  51  60
```

We will refer to this as *counter-controlled input*. Applying this to our program **Report** gives the improved version **Report1** in Fig. 3-16.

Study this program carefully, paying particular attention to the material inserted to control the repetition. Two additional variables are used: **Students** and **Counter**. **Students** gives the number of sets of data values to be read (in this case, the number of students to be processed in total), and **Counter** is used to compute the number of sets of data values actually read. The value of **Counter** is increased by 1 each time through the loop. When **Counter** is equal to **Students**, we know that we have read all the input values and the program terminates. This is a good example of a counter-controlled input loop.

Consider processing our example data with the counter-controlled loop. The trace of this program is given in Table 3-8.

Step 1 of the program reads this first set of data and assigns the value **2** to the variable **Students**. Step 2 initializes the data counter **Counter**, to 0. In step 3 we begin the loop. The looping condition (**Counter** < **Students**) is currently true, so we enter the range of the loop. In step 4 the first actual set of data (data for student 26731) is read. Step 5 computes this student's grade, and step 6 prints the results. In step 7, we prepare to repeat the loop

**program** Report (input, output);

{Given individual marks in three aspects for a year's work in a course, this program computes the final grade with weighting of 20%, 30%, and 50%, respectively. The output is a displayed line giving the student's I.D. number, his/her individual marks, and final grade.}

**var**
  IDNumber: integer;   {Student's I.D. number}
  LabWork,
  MidTermExam,
  FinalExam: integer;   {Three marks}
  Grade: real;       {Final grade}
**begin**
  {Step 1: Input data}
  read (IDNumber, LabWork, MidTermExam, FinalExam);

  {Step 2: Compute final grade}
  Grade := 0.20 * LabWork + 0.30 * MidTermExam + 0.50 * FinalExam;

  {Step 3: Display results}
  writeln ('Student I.D.:', IDNumber);
  writeln ('Laboratory mark:', LabWork);
  writeln ('Midterm examination:', MidTermExam);
  writeln ('Final examination:', FinalExam);
  writeln ('Final grade:', Grade:8:2)
**end**.

**FIGURE 3-15**
**Program to report**
**a student's final grade.**

by updating the data counter (from 0 to 1). Control then returns to step 3 for reevaluation of the looping condition. Since Counter is still less than Students, our condition remains true, so we enter the loop a second time. In step 4 this time, we read the data set corresponding to student 29139. This student's final grade is computed in step 5 and printed in step 6. The data counter is updated in step 7, from 1 to 2, and control returns to step 3. This time, however, the value of Counter is equal to the value of Students. Since the looping condition is now false, we proceed to step 8, at which point the program terminates, having processed all the data.

The advantage of counter-controlled input is its simplicity. Should there be a large number of sets of input data, however, having to count them before running the program can be tedious and is prone to error.

A second method of controlling an input loop involves the use of an extra set of data values at the end of the regular set of data values. Something special about this set of values makes it easily identifiable, so that when it is read you know that all the normal values must already have been read. Since an element of watching is involved, we refer to the extra set that consists of these special values as a *sentinel set*. This form of input control is referred to as *sentinel-controlled input*. For our example of student

**program** Report1 (input, output);

{This is **Report** revision 1. Given individual marks in three aspects for a year's work in a course, this program computes the final grade with weighting of 20%, 30%, and 50%, respectively. The output is a displayed line giving the student's I.D. number, his/her individual marks, and final grade. The input is counter-controlled.}

**var**
```
    IDNumber: integer;      {Student's I.D. number}
    LabWork,
    MidTermExam,
    FinalExam: integer;     {Three marks}
    Grade: real;            {Final grade}
    Students: integer;      {Number of students}
    Counter: integer;       {Number of students already processed}
```
**begin**

```
    {Step 1: Read the number of students}
    read (Students);

    {Step 2: Initialize count of processed students}
    Counter: = 0;

    {Step 3: Engage counter-controlled loop}
    while Counter < Students do
       begin

          {Step 4: Read input data}
          read (IDNumber, LabWork, MidTermExam, FinalExam);

          {Step 5: Compute final grade}
          Grade : = 0.20 * LabWork + 0.30 * MidTermExam + 0.50 * FinalExam;

          {Step 6: Display results}
          writeln ('Student I. D.', IDNumber);
          writeln ('Laboratory mark', LabWork);
          writeln ('Midterm examination', MidTermExam);
          writeln ('Final examination', FinalExam);
          writeln ('Final grade', Grade:8:2);

          {Step 7: Update count of processed students}
          Counter : = Counter + 1
       end

    {Step 8: Finished}
end.
```

**FIGURE 3-16**
**Program** Report1
(**Report** revision 1) using
counter-controlled
input.

TABLE 3-8  Trace of Program Report1 (Revised for Counter-Controlled Input)

| Step | IDNumber | LabWork | MidtermExam | FinalExam | Grade | Students | Counter | Condition | Output |
|---|---|---|---|---|---|---|---|---|---|
| 1 | ? | ? | ? | ? | ? | 2 | ? | | |
| 2 | ? | ? | ? | ? | ? | 2 | 0 | | |
| 3 | ? | ? | ? | ? | ? | 2 | 0 | True | |
| 4 | 26731 | 58 | 63 | 72 | ? | 2 | 0 | | |
| 5 | 26731 | 58 | 63 | 72 | 66.5 | 2 | 0 | | |
| 6 | 26731 | 58 | 63 | 72 | 66.5 | 2 | 0 | | As specified |
| 7 | 26731 | 58 | 63 | 72 | 66.5 | 2 | 1 | | |
| 3 | 26731 | 58 | 63 | 72 | 66.5 | 2 | 1 | True | |
| 4 | 29139 | 77 | 51 | 60 | 66.5 | 2 | 1 | | |
| 5 | 29139 | 77 | 51 | 60 | 60.7 | 2 | 1 | | |
| 6 | 29139 | 77 | 51 | 60 | 60.7 | 2 | 1 | | As specified |
| 7 | 29139 | 77 | 51 | 60 | 60.7 | 2 | 2 | | |
| 3 | 29139 | 77 | 51 | 60 | 60.7 | 2 | 2 | False | |
| 8 | Termination | | | | | | | | |

marks, and presuming that no student has a real identification number of 0, we could use the following arrangement of input data:

```
26731   58   63   72
29139   77   51   60
0        0    0    0
```

Since the values of the sentinel set are not meant to be part of the calculation, but rather an indication that there are no more data values, care must be taken to ensure that they are not included in whatever calculations are taking place.

The version of program **Report** called **Report2** in Fig. 3-17 operates on sentinel-controlled input. Examine its structure carefully. There are several important ideas worthy of special note.

The program is designed so that the end of actual data is signaled by a set of data in which a value of 0 is specified for the identification number of the student. This is assumed not to be the identification number of any actual student; consequently, it serves as a good sentinel indicator. You will no doubt observe some changes in the location of the read statement over that of previous versions of the program. This is necessary for two reasons: first, to ensure that the sentinel set itself is not processed as part of the computations in the loop, and second, to allow for the possibility (albeit remote) that the sentinel set may, in fact, be the first line of data read (that is, there is no actual data). For these reasons, a read is performed immediately prior to entering the loop (step 1 in this case) to read the first set of data. If the values read constitute valid data, the loop condition will succeed and we will enter the loop to process this data. If, however, the first set of data turns out to be the sentinel set, the looping condition will fail and we will bypass the loop entirely. In the event that the loop is entered following the processing of the first set of data, the set of data for the next pass through the loop is read. This second read statement is the last step in the range of the loop (step 5). Following execution of this step, control returns to step 2 and the looping condition is reevaluated.

Notice that in this particular organization, the data read within pass $i$ of the loop (here, in step 5) is actually intended for processing in pass $i + 1$. For this reason, this is said to employ a *read-ahead scheme*. As described, a read-ahead scheme is essential whenever sentinel-controlled input is used.

To illustrate the operational differences between the two methods discussed for controlling input loops, let us take the small sample of input data illustrated previously and repeated here and examine the workings of the two versions of the program **Report**. Suppose that the following constitutes the data for a very small class:

```
26731   58   63   72
29139   77   51   60
```

This dummy set of data (no reflection on any students) occurs *after* the two actual sets of data. The important value of this set of data in this

**program** Report2 (input, output);

{This is **Report** revision 2. Given individual marks in three aspects for a year's work in a course, this program computes the final grade with weighting of 20%, 30%, and 50%, respectively. The output is a displayed line giving the student's I.D. number, his/her individual marks, and final grade. The input is sentinel-controlled. An I.D. number of 0 (with dummy values for the other three variables) signals the end of the input.}

**var**

    IDNumber: integer;   {Student's I.D. number}
    LabWork,
    MidTermExam,
    FinalExam: integer;   {Three marks}
    Grade: real;      {Final grade}

**begin**

    {Step 1: Read the first line of input data}
    read (IDNumber, LabWork, MidTermExam, FinalExam);

    {Step 2: Engage the sentinel-controlled repetition}
    **while** IDNumber <> 0 **do**
      **begin**

          {Step 3: Calculate final grade}
          Grade := 0.20 * LabWork + 0.30 * MidTermExam + 0.50 * FinalExam;

          {Step 4: Display results}
          writeln ('Student I. D.', IDNumber);
          writeln ('Laboratory mark', LabWork);
          writeln ('Midterm examination', MidTermExam);
          writeln ('Final examination', FinalExam);
          writeln ('Final grade', Grade:8:2);

          {Step 5: Read next line of input data}
          read (IDNumber, LabWork, MidTermExam, FinalExam)
      **end**

    {Step 6: Finished}
**end**.

**FIGURE 3-17**
Program **Report2**
(Report revision 2) using
sentinel-controlled
input.

example is the value of IDNumber, which must be 0. The other three values are not important but must be present nonetheless; otherwise, an input error will result when an attempt is made to read nonexistent values. The execution of this version of the program is traced in Table 3-9.

Step 1 of this program reads the first set of data (corresponding to student 26731). The loop begins in step 2. Since this is an actual set of data, the IDNumber is not 0 (in fact, it is **26731**). As a result, we are allowed to proceed into the range of the loop. The final grade for this student is calculated in step 3 and printed in step 4. In step 5 we prepare for the next pass through the loop by reading the next set of data (corresponding to student 29139). Control then returns to step 2 for reevaluation of the looping condition. Again, the value of the variable IDNumber (now **29139**) is not equal to **0**, so we are allowed to proceed. The final grade for student 29139 is computed and printed, and then, in step 5, the next set of data is read. This time it happens to be our sentinel set. Once again, control returns to step 2 for reevaluation of the looping condition. This time the value of IDNumber is **0**, so we proceed to step 6, where the program terminates.

This discussion ought to convince you that even though they are structurally different, the two methods of controlling input loops produce the same effect. When do you choose one over the other? In many cases it is hard to see an advantage, and the choice is strictly one of personal preference. Sometimes you may not know how many data values you have, and you may not be prepared to count them. In this case you may opt for a sentinel-controlled input loop. The data counter employed in counter-controlled input loops, however, often has other useful functions in a program. For example, it could be used in the calculation of the average grade in the entire class. Such a data counter also can be employed very easily in a sentinel-controlled loop. You would be wise to become comfortable with both methods of controlling input loops and let the nature of the specific application dictate the choice.

Pascal provides yet another method of controlling input loops, which we will refer to as the *end-of-file method*. A facility in Pascal provides a special end-of-data signal which is detected automatically and allows a specified action to be taken accordingly. This operates something like the sentinel method without requiring the user to include any special data.

Before we can use this facility in Pascal, we must examine the input mechanism more closely. The input may come directly from a terminal keyboard or from a text previously prepared with an interactive editor and stored in external storage. However, Pascal uses a standard scheme when processing such input. This input is considered to be a continuous stream

**TABLE 3-9**  Trace of Program Report2 (Revised for Sentinel-Controlled Input)

| Step | IDNumber | LabWork | MidtermExam | FinalExam | Grade | Condition | Output |
|------|----------|---------|-------------|-----------|-------|-----------|--------|
| 1 | 26731 | 58 | 63 | 72 | ? | | |
| 2 | 26731 | 58 | 63 | 72 | ? | True | |
| 3 | 26731 | 58 | 63 | 72 | 66.5 | | |
| 4 | 26731 | 58 | 63 | 72 | 66.5 | | As specified |
| 5 | 29139 | 77 | 51 | 60 | 66.5 | | |
| 2 | 29139 | 77 | 51 | 60 | 66.5 | True | |
| 3 | 29139 | 77 | 51 | 60 | 60.7 | | |
| 4 | 29139 | 77 | 51 | 60 | 60.7 | | As specified |
| 5 | 0 | 0 | 0 | 0 | 60.7 | | |
| 2 | 0 | 0 | 0 | 0 | 60.7 | False | |
| 6 | Termination | | | | | | |

of characters, with the characters of each line being followed by a special "new-line" character. Operation of the read statement depends on the type of the variable into which data is being read. Reading into a character variable reads the next unprocessed character into that variable. Reading into numeric variables discards blanks and new-line characters and begins processing the first nonblank character as the value to be assigned. Subsequent characters are processed until the next character cannot be a part of the value being read. For example, if the next input characters are

□□□□26731a

and the statement

read (K)

were executed, then the blanks would be discarded and the value 26731 would be placed into the variable K. The a would remain available for the next read statement. For example,

read (C)

with C, a variable of type character, would then place the character value a into the variable C.

The built-in function eof, standing for "end of file," requires no arguments and returns a Boolean value. The value will be "true" if no characters remain to be processed, and "false" otherwise.

The program in Fig. 3-18 is designed to simply read numbers and output them until the end of file is encountered. Notice the occurrence of the readln statement. This statement, when executed, causes input characters to be discarded up to and including the next new-line character. This statement is necessary to allow the program to detect end of input properly using eof.

We have also introduced the Boolean operator **not** in this program. This operator is a unary prefix operator, similar to the unary minus, except **not** is applied only to Boolean values and produces a Boolean result. Here, **not** eof is "true" when eof is "false," **not** eof is "false" when eof is "true." The **not** operator will be discussed again in Sec. 3-4 in connection with compound conditions.

Consider Fig. 3-19, the same program without the readln statement. Suppose we supply the program in Fig. 3-19 with the following data:

25
39
19

To see why this program does not work, we must consider the operation of the read statement during each execution of the loop. Remember that Pascal will consider the input to be

25 ↓ 39 ↓ 19 ↓

where we use " ↓ " to represent the new-line character.

```
program InputRight (input, output);
{Given input of integers, one per line, this program reads and displays them
  one per line. This program demonstrates the correct method of reading
  until end of file.}
var
  K: integer;
begin
  {Step 1: Engage loop}
  while not eof do
    begin

      {Step 2: Input one value}
      read (K);
      readln;

      {Step 3: Display one value}
      writeln (K)
    end
end.
```

**FIGURE 3-18**
**Correct method**
**for testing eof.**

At first execution of the **while not** eof **do**, all the characters remain to be read and so eof is "false." Therefore, the condition of the while statement, that is not eof, is "true," and the loop is entered for the first time. The read (K) will read **25** and assign this value to K. The program then writes the value for K (**25**) and returns to evaluate the condition in the while statement. The next character to be read is the new-line character ( ↓ ). Therefore, eof is "false," and the loop is entered a second time. On this pass, **39** is read and written. Note that the new-line character preceding the **39** was discarded because we are reading into a numeric variable. Again eof is "false," and the loop is entered a third time. The **19** is read and written, *leaving the final new-line character as yet unprocessed*. Now the condition is evaluated again. The eof function returns "false" because a character, the final new-line character, remains to be processed. Therefore, the loop is entered a fourth time. The read will discard the new-line character and attempt to process more characters, looking for an integer value. Encountering the end of input without being able to assign a value to the variable K causes the program to terminate with an error message. Typically, the output of this program will be

```
25
39
19
Program terminated by an attempt to read past end of file input
```

The exact wording of the error message varies among compilers.

**program** InOutWrong (input, output);
{This program is incorrect. Given input of integers, it attempts to display
   them, one per line. It fails to detect the end of file correctly. See Fig. 3-18
   for a correct solution.}
**var**
   K: integer;
**begin**
   {Step 1: Engage loop}
   **while not** eof **do**
      **begin**

         {Step 2: Input one value}
         read (K);

         {Step 3: Display one value}
         writeln (K)
      **end**
**end**.

**FIGURE 3-19**
**Incorrect method**
**for testing** eof.

Because a readln statement often immediately follows a read statement,
Pascal allows the two to be combined. The statement

readln *(variable list)*

is functionally equivalent to

read *(variable list)*;
readln

Because a readln statement discards *all characters* up to and including
the next new-line character, there is one potential difficulty with this method
for solving the **eof** problem. Suppose the input data had been organized as

25      39
19

The output would be

25
19

The **39** would have been discarded by the readln statement. Use of the readln
statement will force a certain organization of the input into lines so that all
the data is processed.
   Pascal also supplies the built-in function eoln, which takes no arguments
and returns "true" if the next character in the input stream is the new-line
character and "false" otherwise.
   Several problems arise when the read and readln statements are used
to obtain input values from the keyboard of the terminal. When a program

commences execution, it should immediately obtain the first input character from the keyboard and store it in memory. (It is stored in a *buffer*—buffers are described in Chap. 10.) This character must be available for examination by the functions eof and eoln, whose result always depends on the "next character." During subsequent execution of the program, read and readln statements consume characters and construct values for variables. Each such statement should similarly obtain one additional character and store it. Consider how this affects the normal scheme of issuing a prompt, using a write statement, for each input value required by the program. Even if the statement that displays the prompt is the first statement of the program, the input must be typed on the terminal before the prompt! The program will wait for this input, while the person at the terminal will wait for a prompt before entering data.

Some Pascal compilers implement a technique called *lazy input*. This involves deferring the operation of obtaining the next character until that character is required. Thus the program will not attempt to obtain a character until it executes an operation that examines that character. This will occur when a read or readln statement is executed or eof or eoln is called. Similarly, obtaining the extra character after each read or readln statement is deferred until the character is required. This method of handling input is considered to conform with the Pascal standard since the values of eof and eoln are determined by the *next* character to be consumed by a read or readln statement.

The following program fragment illustrates the proper way of issuing prompts for data while reading to eof. We assume that each line is to consist of two values.

```
writeln ('Enter two values'); { Issue prompt}
while not eof do
   begin
      readln (X, Y); { Read data}
         .
         . { Process data}
         .
      writeln ('Enter two values') { Issue next prompt}
   end
```

Other Pascal compilers deviate from the standard Pascal definition in the case of input from a terminal. This usually involves redefining eof and eoln to test the previously processed character rather than the next character. This requires corresponding changes in the definitions of the read and readln statements. The student should consult either documents describing the compiler or the instructor to determine what deviations are present.

Each operating system has its own scheme for generating the eof from a keyboard. A common method is to generate some control character. For example, control z is generated by typing z while pressing the "control shift" key.

These difficulties with end-of-file processing may be avoided by using sentinel-controlled input with terminals.

### 3-3.3 COUNTED LOOPS

For some applications, the conditional loop control imposed by the while statement is unnecessarily complicated. In many cases you might want a loop executed a fixed number of times, where the number is already known. For applications such as these, another form of repetition construct is in order. This construct is of the following form:

**for** *control variable* := *first value* **to** *final value* **do**
    *statement*

An example is

```
for K := 1 to 10 do
   begin
      read(X);
      writeln (X)
   end
```

In this example, the statement following the **do**, in this case a compound statement, is executed with the control variable (K) assigned the value 1, then again with the variable assigned the value 2, etc.

Each time the statement following the **do** is executed, the value of the control variable is incremented by 1 and then tested against the final value. The repeated statement is executed the final time with K assigned the value 10. Thus we have formed a loop.

The syntax diagram in Fig. 3-20 summarizes the syntax rules for the for statement. For now, the variable must be declared as an integer variable; other possibilities will be described in Sec. 3-6. The first value and final value may be any expression, including the case of a constant or a variable, of the same type as the control variable. Use of **to** indicates that after each execution of the repeated statement, the variable will be incremented. Use of **downto** indicates that the variable will be decremented instead. For example,

```
for K := 10 downto 1 do
   writeln (K)
```

**FIGURE 3-20** Syntax diagram for the for statement.

**for statement**

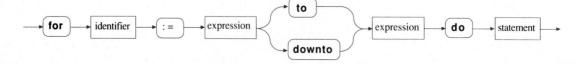

The control variable can be used as an ordinary variable in expressions within the loop, as it is in the previous example. In Pascal, however, it is considered illegal to attempt to *assign* a value to the control variable from within the repeated statement, although not all Pascal compilers report violations of this rule. Assigning to the control variable is very bad programming style, however, whether or not a particular compiler allows it.

It is possible that the statement following **do** will not be executed at all. This occurs if the final value is less than the first value in the increment (**to**) case or if the final value is greater than the first value in the decrement (**downto**) case. Two examples are

**for** K : = 10 **to** 9 **do** . . .
**for** K : = 1 **downto** 2 **do** . . .

To illustrate further the use of counted loops, we present a program that prints out the squares of the integers from 1 through 20 (see Fig. 3-21). Note carefully the structure of the loop and use of the control variable **Number**.

As another example of the use of the for statement, let us return to the factorial calculation described earlier in this section (see Fig. 3-12). An examination of its operation (see Table 3-5, for example) reveals that although it uses a while statement to control the looping, it actually executes like a counted loop, with **Multiplier** as the loop control variable. In this case, however, the programmer has taken on the burden of controlling its value directly. This program is perhaps more naturally expressed using a counted loop (see Fig. 3-22).

A for statement loop should be used whenever the number of repetitions of a loop is fixed before the loop begins. For example, the program in Fig. 3-16 making use of counter-controlled input can easily be rewritten using Pascal's for statement. This makes the intent of the program more evident to the reader. In addition, some computers generate a slightly more efficient program. The sentinel-controlled input loop in Fig. 3-17 cannot be written using the for statement, since the number of iterations is not known when the loop begins.

It should be noted that the loop limit is copied into a location that cannot be changed when the loop is begun. Thus the program segment

```
program SquaresOfIntegers (output);
{This program prints the squares of the integers from 1 to 20, that is, 1 * 1,
    2 * 2, 3 * 3, . . . , 20 * 20.}
var
    Number: integer;
begin
    {Step 1: Engage loop}
    for Number : = 1 to 20 do
        writeln (Number, '□Squared is□', sqr (Number) )
end.
```

FIGURE 3-21
Program demonstrating a for statement.

```
K := 5;
for I : = 1 to K do
    begin
       writeln (Z);
       K := 3
    end
```

will execute the writeln statement five times, as determined by the value of K when the loop begins the first time.

Standard Pascal prohibits changing the counter variable from within the loop. Thus

```
for J : = 1 to 10 do
    J : = 11;
```

is not valid. Not all compilers, however, diagnose the error.

### 3-3.4 NESTED LOOPS

Just as it was possible to have an if statement within another if statement, it is also possible to have a loop within the range of another loop. The rules

```
program FactNRevised (input, output);
{Given a nonnegative integer, this program computes the factorial. This
    revised version uses a for statement.}
var
    N: integer;          {Value read}
    Product: integer;    {Partial product}
    Multiplier: integer; {Current term}
begin
    {Step 1: Input}
    read (N);

    {Step 2: Initialize product}
    Product : = 1;

    {Step 3: Compute factorial}
    for Multiplier : = N downto 1 do
        Product : = Product * Multiplier;

    {Step 4: Output results}
    writeln ('Factorial of □', N, '□is □', Product)

    {Step 5: Finished}
end.
```

**FIGURE 3-22**
**Factorial of *N*, revised**
**to use a for statement.**

of nesting are similar in both cases. The inner construct must be completely embedded within the outer construct. There can be no partial overlapping. Figure 3-23 presents examples of proper and improper nesting.

As an example of the use of nested loops, let us modify our program FactNRevised (see Fig. 3-22) for the calculation of the factorial function to add to it an input loop. The factorial program itself uses a loop to calculate the factorial; we will be enclosing this loop with a second loop to read a series of input values. The resulting program Factorials appears in Fig. 3-24.

Examine the structure of this program carefully. You will notice that the loops are properly nested. The range of the outer loop is steps 2 through 5; the range of the inner loop is included as part of step 4. Let us examine the loop behavior as the program executes with the following two data values: 4 and 5. The loop behavior is summarized in Table 3-10.

Execution begins at step 1, which sets the outer loop in motion. Since eof is "false," the range of the loop is entered. Step 2 reads the first data value (4) and assigns it to the variable N. Notice the use of readln statement to discard the new-line character. This, of course, means that each value of input data must appear on a separate line. Step 3 initializes the variable Product to 1. Step 4 then engages the second loop. Note, however, that we are still within the range of, and under control of, the first loop and will be until step 5. Step 4 sets up a counted loop with Multiplier as the control variable. The assignment is then executed repetitively, with Multiplier receiving a succession of values 4, 3, 2, 1, as shown in Table 3-10. The value of Product grows accordingly. When the loop has been executed with the last specified value of Multiplier (1), it terminates, and control passes to step 5, where the result

Factorial of 4 is 24

is printed. Step 5 is the last step in the range of the outer loop, so control returns to step 1, the controlling statement. Since unprocessed data remains in the input stream, eof will be "false," and the range of the outer loop will be entered for a second time. Step 2 reads in the next data value (5) and assigns it to N. Next, step 3 resets the variable Product for the

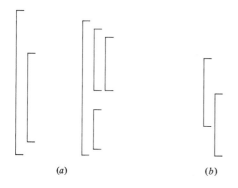

(a)                    (b)

**FIGURE 3-23**
Examples of
(*a*) proper and
(*b*) improper nesting.

```
program Factorials (input, output);
{Given a series of integers, this program computes the factorial of each.}
var
   N: integer;            {Value read}
   Product: integer;      {Accumulates the product}
   Multiplier: integer;   {Current term}
begin
   {Step 1: Engage outer loop}
   while not eof do
      begin

         {Step 2: Read in next data value}
         readln (N);

         {Step 3: Initialize Product for this particular calculation}
         Product : = 1;

         {Step 4: Loop to compute this factorial}
         for Multiplier : = N downto 1 do
            Product : = Product * Multiplier;

         {Step 5: Output results}
         writeln ('Factorial of □', N, ' □is □', Product)
      end

   {Step 6: Finished}
end.
```

**FIGURE 3-24**
**Program to compute**
**the factorial of many**
**different numbers.**

upcoming calculation. Step 4 engages the calculation loop once more. This time Multiplier gets the succession of values 5, 4, 3, 2, 1, and Product is computed accordingly. Before termination of this loop, control passes to step 5 for printing of

Factorial of 5 is 120

and back to step 1 for reevaluation of the condition. Since the last item of data has been read and the readln statement has discarded the following new-line character, eof will return "true." The outer loop terminates, and since it is the last statement of the program, the program terminates.

The concept of nested loops is an important one and can, of course, be done with either type of loop. It would be well worth your time to reread the preceding description until you are completely comfortable with what is happening. Note in particular that the two loops operate at different rates, much like a system of gears. The inner loop moves faster than the outer loop, as is shown clearly in Table 3-10. Any values required in the inner loop must be reset (as in the case of Product) before the loop is reentered. If

**TABLE 3-10** Loop Behavior in Program Factorials

**137**

3-3
LOOPING

| Pass through Outer Loop | Pass through Inner Loop | Value of N | Value of Multiplier | Value of Product |
|---|---|---|---|---|
| 1 | 1 | 4 | 4 | 4 |
|   | 2 | 4 | 3 | 12 |
|   | 3 | 4 | 2 | 24 |
|   | 4 | 4 | 1 | 24 |
| 2 | 1 | 5 | 5 | 5 |
|   | 2 | 5 | 4 | 20 |
|   | 3 | 5 | 3 | 60 |
|   | 4 | 5 | 2 | 120 |
|   | 5 | 5 | 1 | 120 |

sufficient care is not taken, you may be processing the steps in a loop with the values from the previous pass through the loop. What would happen in the program **Factorials** if step 3 were removed and inserted before step 1?

## 3-3.5 BOTTOM-TESTED CONDITIONAL LOOPS

In Sec. 3-3.1 we described conditional loops that were implemented with Pascal's while statement. Such loops have their condition tested before each execution of the range of the loop, at the "top" of the loop; hence these are called *top-tested loops*. An alternative form of loop is the *bottom-tested loop*, in which the condition is evaluated following each execution of the loop. Figure 3-25 shows the general flow of a bottom-tested conditional loop. Compare this with Fig. 3-14 showing the top-tested loop. The most

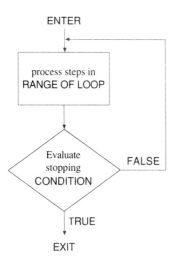

FIGURE 3-25
General flowchart of the bottom-tested conditional loop.

significant difference is that the range of the bottom-tested loop will always be executed at least once.

The Pascal repeat statement defines a bottom-tested conditional loop. It has the general form

**repeat**
  *statement₁;*
  *statement₂;*

    .

    .

    .

  *statementₙ*
**until** *condition*

Figure 3-26 summarizes the syntax with a syntax diagram. In addition to specifying a bottom-tested loop, the repeat statement differs from the while statement in two respects. First, the loop range, enclosed between the **repeat** and **until** symbols, may contain any number of statements without use of a **begin** and **end**. Second, the condition, when "true," causes termination of the loop.

The repeat statement is used less frequently than the while statement. As an example of its use, consider the following program fragment, which reads and sums integers until the sum exceeds 1000:

```
Sum := 0;
repeat
  read (K);
  Sum := Sum + K
until Sum > 1000
```

For comparison, the reader is encouraged to write a fragment performing this function using a while statement.

## 3-3.6  SUMMARY

In this section we have examined in detail the concept of a loop. We saw that there are basically two kinds of loops, distinguished by the manner in which the looping is controlled. A conditional loop is controlled by means of a condition in a while or a repeat statement. Each time the flow of control reaches the end of the range of the loop, the condition is reevaluated. Looping continues as long as the looping condition is true in the case of the while statement, or false in the case of the repeat statement.

The second type of loop we referred to as the counted loop. In a counted

**repeat statement**

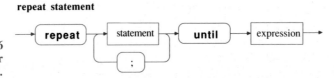

**FIGURE 3-26**
Syntax diagram for
the repeat statement.

loop (or for statement) a specially designated variable (the control variable) takes on a specified sequence of values as the looping progresses. This type of loop makes possible the repetition of a group of statements a fixed number of times.

Once again, the choice of which type of repetition construct to use should be dictated by the nature of the application. Too many programmers force one type of loop on all programs. This results in programs that are unnecessarily difficult to understand. Pascal offers a choice, and a programmer should take advantage of it.

We also considered the use of nested loops, in which the range of a loop is embedded within the range of another loop. The inner loop is executed completely (that is, all passes) on each pass through the outer loop. With both the loop and the if statement, you should avoid nesting too deeply. Programs with more than two or three levels of nesting tend to be difficult to understand and, as a result, are error-prone. One alternative to deeply nested structures is discussed in Sec. 3-4.

As a final comment on looping, we remind you that it is the responsibility of the programmer to ensure that loops will terminate. Loops that fail to do so can prove extremely costly and embarrassing to the programmer. The frequency of loops failing to terminate is probably higher with conditional loops, because the mechanism for counted loops is largely automatic. Nevertheless, it is well worth your time to double-check all loops before you run your program.

## EXERCISES 3-3

1. In each of the following program segments, indicate whether or not the loop will terminate. If it will not, why not? Assume that all variables are of type integer.

    (a) Counter : = 0;
        Total : = 0;
        **while** Counter >= 0 **do**
            Total : = Total + 2;

    (b) Counter : = 0;
        Total : = 0;
        **while** Counter <= 10 **do**
            **begin**
                Total : = Total + 2;
                Counter : = Counter + 1
            **end**

2. In each of the following segments, give the value that will be printed for the variable Result. Assume integer variables throughout.

    (a) Result : = 0;
        **for** Index : = 1 **to** 10 **do**
            Result : = Result + 1;
        writeln (Result)

(b) Result : = 0;
    **for** Index : = 1 **to** 9 **do**
        Result : = Result + 4 * Index;
    writeln (Result)

(c) Result : = 0;
    **for** Index1 : = 1 **to** 15 **do**
        **for** Index2 : = 1 **to** 8 **do**
            Result : = Result + 1;
    writeln (Result)

(d) Result : = 0;
    **for** Index : = 10 **downto** 1 **do**
        Result : = Result + 1;
    writeln (Result)

★ **3.** Write a Pascal program to compute the sum of the following series to 100 terms:

$$1 - \frac{1}{2} + \frac{1}{4} - \frac{1}{6} + \frac{1}{8} - \frac{1}{10} + \frac{1}{12} - \cdots$$

★ **4.** Saskatchewan fishing regulations impose a limit on the total weight of a day's catch. Suppose that you plan to take your portable computer terminal with you on your next fishing trip and you require a program to tell you when you have exceeded your limit. Design a program that first reads the daily limit (in pounds) and then reads input values one by one (weights of the fish recorded as they are caught) and prints a message at the point when the limit is exceeded. A weight of 0 indicates the end of input. After each fish is recorded, your program should print the total poundage caught up to that time.

★ **5.** A number is defined to be a *prime* number if it has no divisors other than 1 and the number itself. Design a Pascal program to read a number and determine whether or not the number is a prime number.

★ **6.** The Clark W. Griswald family has just returned from a motoring holiday. At each stop for gas Clark recorded his odometer reading and the amount of gas purchased (assume that he filled the tank each time). In addition, assume that gas was purchased immediately prior to leaving for the trip and immediately upon return, taking odometer readings at each point. Design a program to read first the total number of stops made by the Griswalds (including the first stop and the last) and then the data recorded for gas purchases and compute
(a) The gas mileage achieved between every pair of stops on the trip.
(b) The gas mileage achieved through the entire trip.

★★ **7.** The Who-Do-You-Trust Company plans to use a computer to prepare a report of its deposit accounts. For each customer a set of data is prepared containing information on his or her account number and balance forwarded from the previous month. This is then followed by transaction data, which contains the customer's account number and the amount of the transaction. Account withdrawals will have a negative amount of

| | |
|---|---|
| 12 | 1000.00 |
| 12 | 500.00 |
| 12 | −50.00 |
| 12 | −75.00 |
| 24 | 18075.00 |

.

.

.

Design a program to list the balance of each account after processing the transactions.

8. Modify the program obtained from Exercise 1 of Sec. 2-7 so that it prints out a table of conversions from degrees Fahrenheit to degrees Celsius. The table should print out values for every 5° increment starting at −40°F and going to 110°F.

9. Write a program to read in the final marks for a class of students and print out the number of students who got As, Bs, etc. Assume that the marks are all between 0 and 100 and that you don't know how many marks there will be in the data. Base your grade scale on the one given in Exercise 1 of Sec. 3-2.

★ 10. A proper divisor $x$ of $n$ is a positive divisor of $n$ such that $x < n$. $n$ is referred to as *perfect* if the sum of its proper divisors equals $n$. Write a program that reads in a positive integer $n$ and prints a message indicating whether or not $n$ is perfect.

★ 11. Birdy Num Num Accommodations manufactures and sells bird houses. The company makes a profit of $15.65 per house and currently sells 3500 houses per month. Operating costs of the company are fixed at $18,300 per month, and an additional $1000 is spent on advertising each month. It has been determined that doubling the amount spent on advertising will increase sales by 15 percent. You are to write a program that will find the point at which additional advertising becomes unprofitable. (At each stage, double the amount spent on advertising and multiply the previous profit by 15 percent.)

## 3-4 USE OF COMPOUND CONDITIONS

In the previous two sections we presented programming constructs that involved expression of conditions. These conditions were described in terms of simple relationships between values using the relational operators in Table 3-1. For some problems, simple relations are inadequate for describing the conditions required. The result can usually be achieved with nesting (see program Max3 in Fig. 3-8, for example), but this may make the programs unnecessarily complicated and difficult to understand.

An alternative method is the use of compound conditions. These are derived from the standard simple relations using the logical connectives **and**, **or**, and **not**. An and operation combines two simple conditions and yields a true result only if both components are true; an or operation on two simple conditions requires only one of them to be true. The not operation operates on a single simple condition and simply negates (or reverses) its value.

The meanings of these operators are best described using what is known as *truth tables*. Suppose that $c_1$ and $c_2$ represent conditions. Each may be either "true" or "false." The truth tables in Table 3-11 define **and**, **or**, and **not**. As we shall see, these definitions give natural interpretations of compound conditions.

As an example, suppose that One is a variable whose value is 1 and Two is a variable whose value is 2. Consider the following simple conditions: One $<$ 2 and Two $<$ 0. Clearly, the first relation is true and the second is false. Consider the following three compound conditions derived from these simple relationships.

*1.* (One $<$ 2) **and** (Two $<$ 0)

*2.* (One $<$ 2) **for** (Two $<$ 0)

*3.* **not** (One $<$ 2)

**TABLE 3-11**  **Truth Tables for Logical Connectives**

### (a) **and** (conjunction)

| $c_1$ | $c_2$ | $c_1$ **and** $c_2$ |
|-------|-------|---------------------|
| True  | True  | True  |
| True  | False | False |
| False | True  | False |
| False | False | False |

### (b) **or** (disjunction)

| $c_1$ | $c_2$ | $c_1$ **or** $c_2$ |
|-------|-------|--------------------|
| True  | True  | True  |
| True  | False | True  |
| False | True  | True  |
| False | False | False |

### (c) **not** (negation)

| $c_1$ | **not** $c_1$ |
|-------|---------------|
| True  | False |
| False | True  |

If we apply the truth table for the and operator to condition (1), it tells us that the value of this compound condition is "false" because the first operand is "true" but the second is "false." This makes sense intuitively. Suppose that this were used as the condition in an if statement:

**if** (One $<$ 2) **and** (Two $<$ 0)

Since One is less than 2 but Two is not less than 0, the preceding test must fail. The truth-table approach gives us the correct value, "false." Applying the appropriate truth tables to the other two examples, we get the values "true" for condition (2) and "false" for condition (3).

In the previous examples we parenthesized the individual simple conditions. While this clarifies the presentation, it is also necessary for unambiguous processing of the conditions. This is necessary because of the unusual precedences which Pascal assigns to the logical connectives in relation to the precedences of the relational operators. Table 3-12 specifies the precedences of all operators in Pascal. (The **in** operator is described in Chap. 5.) If we were to write the previous condition without parentheses, as

One $<$ 2 **and** One $<$ 0

then the operator precedence rules would force an interpretation of the form

One $<$ (2 **and** One) $<$ 0

This results in two problems: first the operands of **and** are not Boolean; second, expressions of the form $x < y < z$, where $x$, $y$, and $z$ are numeric, are not allowed in Pascal. The compiler would produce appropriate error messages.

Compound conditions can be used either in if statements or in conditional loops. The form and interpretation are the same in each case. As an example of an application using compound conditions, we will reformulate the program Max3 from Fig. 3-8. You will recall that the problem was to determine the largest of three input values A, B, and C. Our solution then involved pairwise comparisons and nested if statements. The nesting can be eliminated through the use of compound conditions. The program in Fig. 3-27 results.

You will notice that, in this case, by eliminating the nesting we produce a program that is easier to understand. The conditions in effect are clearly evident, and no comments are required. As a parenthetical remark, even though this version is shorter and easier to understand, the previous version will probably execute faster because fewer tests are required. As a general rule, we will, however, lean toward programs that are easier to read and understand. Programmer time is more valuable than computer time.

---

**TABLE 3-12**  **Operator Precedences**

| | |
|---|---|
| Highest | **not** |
| Second highest | $*$ / **div mod and** |
| Third highest | $+ -$ (binary and unary) **or** |
| Lowest | $=$  $<>$  $<$  $>$  $<=$  $>=$  **in** |

**program** Max3Version2 (input, output);
{Given three integer numbers, this program determines the largest. The numbers are assumed to be distinct. This version replaces nested if statements with compound conditions.}
**var**
  A, B, C: integer;     {The three values read}
  Max: integer;          {The largest value}
**begin**
  {Step 1: Input data values}
  read (A, B, C);

  {Step 2: Determine largest value}
  **if** (A > B) **and** (A > C)
  **then** Max : = A;
  **if** (B > A) **and** (B > C)
  **then** Max : = B;
  **if** (C > A) **and** (C > B)
  **then** Max : = C;

  {Step 3: Display largest value}
  writeln ('The largest value is □', Max);

  {Step 4: Finished}
**end**.

**FIGURE 3-27**
Program Max3Version2

As an exercise, you might try to rewrite the program MaxMin3 of Fig. 3-11 to determine the largest and smallest of three values using compound conditions.

The laws governing the interpretation of compound conditions are based on principles of formal mathematical logic, a subject into which we prefer not to venture. Just as extensive nesting can hinder understanding of a program, so too can elaborate compound conditions. In some cases we may wish to unwind a nested structure using compound conditions; in others, the complexity of the conditional expression may dictate the use of nesting instead. Even though there are formal laws governing the interpretation of complex conditional expressions (see DeMorgan's laws, for example), we prefer to restrict ourselves to expressions that are easily read and understood. A useful test of understandability is the "telephone test." Can you read the expression to someone over a telephone and have it interpreted correctly? This is a valuable test to bear in mind for any complex expression.

Up to this point, we have assumed that each compound condition is *fully* evaluated. We now introduce the concept of *partial* Boolean evaluation. For example, in the statement

**if** (X < > 0) **and** (Y / X <= 100)
**then** .

          .

          .

if the condition $X <> 0$ is "false," there is no need to evaluate the second condition $(Y / X <= 10)$, since the result of the compound condition will be "false" regardless of the truth value of the second condition. Observe that if $X = 0$, we do not want to evaluate the condition $Y / X <= 10$! Such an evaluation in this case will result in a division by 0 and will produce an error message during execution of the program. Similarly, if we have a compound condition of the form

$c_1$ **or** $c_2$

the evaluation of $c_2$ becomes unnecessary if $c_1$ has a value of "true," since the compound condition will have a value of "true" regardless of the value of $c_2$. Some Pascal compilers generate object programs that perform only *partial* Boolean evaluation. Unfortunately, standard Pascal permits the compiler designer to select whether or not partial evaluation should be done. Unless a Pascal program is to be run only with a compiler that guarantees partial evaluation, nested if statements rather than compound conditions must be used in those cases where evaluation of the second condition depends on the result of the first. The previous example would be written as

**if** $X <> 0$
**then if** $Y/X <= 10$
    **then** .
       .
       .
       .

## EXERCISES 3-4

1. Suppose that I and J are integer variables with values 6 and 12, respectively. Which of the following conditions are "true"?
   (*a*) $3 * 4 <= J$
   (*b*) $2 * I - 1 < J$
   (*c*) $(I <= 11)$ **and** $(I > 2)$
   (*d*) $(I > 20)$ **or** $(I < 6)$ **and** $(J < 25)$
   (*e*) **not** $((J < 10)$ **or** $(I > 0))$
   (*f*) **not** $(I > 6)$

2. Assume that A, B, C, and D are variables and $S_1$, $S_2$, $S_3$, and $S_4$ are statements.
   (*a*) Express the conditions necessary for the execution of $S_1$, $S_2$, $S_3$, and $S_4$ in the following statement as separate compound conditions:

    **if** $A > B$
    **then if** $B <= C$
        **then if** $C <> D$
            **then** $S_1$
            **else** $S_2$
        **else** $S_3$
    **else** $S_4$

(b) Express the following as a nested if structure using only simple conditions:

**if** ( (A < B) **and** (C <> D) ) **and** ( (B > D) **or** (B = D) ) **then** $S_1$

3. Explain why or why not the following pairs of program segments are equivalent (that is, produce the same output in all situations):

(a)
```
if X < Y                if (X < Y) and (X > 10)
  then if X > 10          then write(X)
    then write(X)        else write(Y)
  else write(Y)
```

(b)
```
if X < Y                if (X < Y) or (X > 10)
  then write(X)          then write(X)
  else if X > 10         else write(Y)
    then write(X)
    else write(Y)
```

★ 4. Students are recommended for graduate fellowships according to their overall undergraduate average. The nature of the recommendation is based on the following table:

| Average | Recommendation |
|---------|----------------|
| ≥ 90% | Highest recommendation |
| ≥ 80% but < 90% | Strong recommendation |
| ≥ 70% but < 80% | Recommended |
| < 70% | Not recommended |

A line of data is prepared for each student applicant according to the following format:

Student's identification number     Overall average

Write a Pascal program to read the data for all the applicants and prepare a list giving the identification number of each student, his or her average, and the recommendation. At the end of the list (denoted by a sentinel with student number 0), give the overall average of the applicants and a count of the number of recommendations of each type.

5. Rewrite the program of Exercise 5 in Sec. 3-2 so that compound conditions are used instead of nested if statements.

★ 6. The Wallaston Warriors hockey team has had a good season and is rewarding its players with a salary increase for the coming season. Salaries are to be adjusted as follows:

| Present Salary | Action |
|----------------|--------|
| 0–$15,000 | 20% increase |
| $15,001–$20,000 | 10% increase |
| $20,001–$28,000 | 5% increase |
| Over $28,000 | No increase |

The team roster contains 20 players. Design a program to read the number and present salary for each player and then print his number, present salary, and adjusted salary. At the end of this list, give the total payroll at present and the total payroll given the proposed adjustments.

★ 7. Students were given five examinations (A, B, C, D, E). Statistics are required to determine the number that
(a) Passed all exams.
(b) Passed A, B, and D, but not C or E.
(c) Passed A and B, C or D, but not E.
Design appropriate programs, using the end-of-file method to signal the end of input.

## 3-5   CASE STATEMENT

Earlier in this chapter it was observed that excessive nesting of if statements can impede the readability of algorithms. This section introduces a Pascal construct called a *case statement*, which can often alleviate such a problem. The case statement is an extension of the if statement that involves more than two alternative actions.

As a vehicle for the introduction of a case statement, consider a banking problem that involves an automated teller. A customer can use an automated teller according to the selection codes given in Table 3-13. The customer is allowed to make as many deposits and withdrawals as desired. The customer enters 'B' to obtain a new balance or 'C' to close the account. Each transaction is indicated by entering the appropriate selection code (a single capital letter, as shown in Table 3-13). As transactions are selected by the customer, a program is required to keep track of the customer's running balance.

Some sample customer data follows:

```
D        50.00
W        300.00
C
```

Using the approach of nested if statements, a program fragment for the processing of a customer transaction appears in Fig. 3-28.

Note that the nested if statement represents four mutually exclusive alternatives (cases), corresponding to the four selection codes: W, D, B, C.

| TABLE 3-13 | Automatic Teller Selection Codes |
|---|---|
| **Selection Code** | **Action Taken** |
| B | Obtain a new balance and end session |
| C | Close account (and end session) |
| D | Deposit into account |
| W | Withdrawal from account |

```
{Step 1: Input selection code}
read (SelectionCode);

{Step 2: Perform specified transaction}
if SelectionCode = 'W'
then begin
        read (Amount);
        Balance : = Balance − Amount;
        writeln ('Remove cash')
    end
else if SelectionCode = 'D'
        then begin
                read (Amount);
                Balance : = Balance + Amount
            end
        else if SelectionCode = 'B'
            then writeln ('Your balance is ☐', Balance)
                else if SelectionCode = 'C'
                    then begin
                            writeln ('Your closing balance is ☐', Balance, '☐Remove cash');
                            Balance : = 0
                        end
                    else writeln ('You pressed an invalid key');
readln
```

**FIGURE 3-28**
**Program segment for**
**banking problem**
**showing a deeply**
**nested if statement.**

A case statement makes a choice from among several mutually exclusive alternatives, based on the value of an expression. The program segment in Fig. 3-29 contains an example of a case statement which is intended to provide the same action as the nested if in Fig. 3-28. The observant reader will note the absence of the default case to handle error conditions. Standard Pascal does not provide a default action in a case statement. Thus, if explicit actions should be taken on every value, then every value must explicitly label a case. In this example, a case that prints an error message would be included and would be preceded by a list of every illegal character! This is inconvenient, if not impossible, in many cases. Many Pascal compilers allow, as an extension to standard Pascal, a "default" case to be specified by means of an **else** or **otherwise**. Documentation for the particular compiler will describe such an extension. We will discuss convenient ways for handling default cases in standard Pascal in Sec. 5-9.

The general format of the case statement is:

**case** *expression* **of**
    *Case value 1: statement;*
    *Case value 2: statement;*

       .

       .

    *Case value n: statement;*
**end**

```
{Step 1: Input selection code}
read (SelectionCode);

{Step 2: Perform specified transaction}
case SelectionCode of
   'W': begin
           read (Amount);
           Balance : = Balance - Amount;
           writeln ('Remove cash')
       end;
   'D': begin
           read (Amount);
           Balance : = Balance + Amount
       end;
   'B': writeln ('Your balance is □', Balance);
   'C': begin
           writeln ('Your closing balance is □', Balance, '□Remove cash');
           Balance : = 0
       end
end;
readln
```

FIGURE 3-29
Banking example using
a case statement.

The "case value" consists of one or more constants separated by commas. All the constants in the case values must be of the same type as the expression. Also, the same constant may not select more than one case of the case statement. Often, the case constants preceding a particular case consist of a contiguous set of values, for example:

1, 2, 3, 4, 5, 6:

Figure 3-30 summarizes the syntax of the case statement.

Figure 3-31 illustrates the syntax of a Pascal constant. The full syntax given includes all types of constants. However, in various contexts, certain constants are prohibited. For example, the case statement may not use constants of type "character string" to select the case. It is important to distinguish between a character type constant (whose length is exactly 1) and a character string type constant (whose length is 2 or longer). Only the character string constants are prohibited in a case statement.

FIGURE 3-30  Syntax diagram for the case statement.
**case statement**

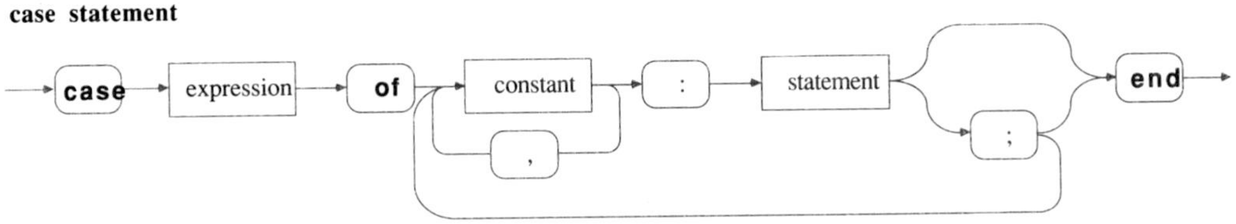

constant

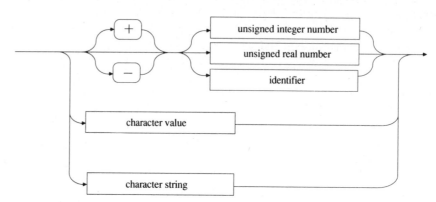

**FIGURE 3-31**
Syntax diagram for
the constant.

The execution of a case statement begins with evaluation of the expression following the case symbol. Next, the statement, which might be a compound statement, selected by that value is executed. If such a constant does not exist, an error is reported and the program is terminated. Thus, if there is no action to be performed for some of the values of the case selection expression, this must be explicitly stated by use of a null case. This case consists of the case label followed by a colon followed by a semicolon. (This indicates the presence of a *null statement*.) For example, in our example of the banking system, if a transaction code of T (for test) is to be accepted but no other action is to be performed, we could add the case

'T': ;

Following execution of the selected statement, the program continues with the statement following the **end** of the case statement. Examine the program segment in Fig. 3-29 closely and compare it with Fig. 3-28.

Most Pascal compilers implement the case statement by compiling each case into machine code and noting the address at which the code for each case begins. Then a "jump table" containing the address of each case from the minimum value to the maximum value is included in the program. Entries corresponding to values for which there is no case included are given the address of an error routine. Unfortunately, a case statement with a small number of cases for wide-ranging values will produce a very large table. For example,

```
case I of
    1: Case for value 1
    100: Case for value 100
    1000: Case for value 1000
end
```

will result in a table of 1000 entries, 997 of which specify an error routine. Much better memory utilization will be obtained by use of an if statement for such a selection. However, for selections where almost every value between the minimum and maximum corresponds to an actual case, the case statement will give better memory utilization than the if statement.

Figure 3-32 illustrates the syntax for a Pascal "statement" which therefore includes all the allowable types of statements in Pascal. Although several features are not described until later, we have chosen to give the complete syntax diagram. The optional integer and colon, called a *statement label*, should be ignored here. Also the goto statement and the with statement will be described elsewhere.

The null statement is useful when a statement is required by the syntax but no action is to be performed. Consequently, the syntax diagram in Fig. 3-33 is particularly simple.

# EXERCISES 3-5

1. Write a program that converts a date in the form DD/MM/YY into the standard form of the date (e.g.: 16/11/87 becomes November 16, 1987). Your program will read in three integers: one for the day, one for the

**FIGURE 3-32  Syntax diagram for the statement.**
statement

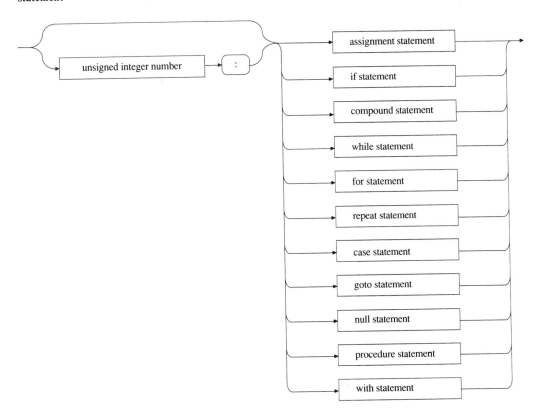

null statement

FIGURE 3-33  Syntax diagram for the null statement.

month, and one for the year. It will then print out the new form of the date.

2. Rewrite the program obtained in Exercise 8 of Sec. 3-2 so that it makes use of a case statement rather than if statements.

★ 3. The Times-R-Tough Political Party has just conducted a survey to study the population's attitude toward its newest policy. Five hundred responses have been obtained and must be analyzed. The responses to the policy have been coded as follows: **A** = strongly favorable; **B** = mildly favorable; **C** = neutral; **D** = mildly opposed; and **E** = strongly opposed. Write a program that will read in the 500 coded responses and count the number of each type of response. Also display a table that shows for each response how many of the 500 surveyed responded in that way and what percentage of the 500 responded in that way.

# 3-6 DEFINING NEW TYPES OF VALUES— ENUMERATIONS AND SUBRANGES

As we have seen, a variable in Pascal must be declared to be of a specific type. A variable's type determines which values may be assigned to the variable and which operators may operate on its value. For example, a character variable may not have the value **1.5** assigned to it nor may it be an operand of the + operator.

To this point we have used only the predefined types: integer, real, character, and Boolean. A variable's type is declared in a variable declaration (see Sec. 2-6). Each of the predefined types is named by one of the *predefined type identifiers*: integer, real, char, and Boolean. Pascal allows a programmer to introduce new types. We shall consider the enumerated and subrange types in this section. These have some use in the control structures defined in this chapter. Other programmer-defined types are considered throughout the remainder of the book.

Introduction of a programmer-defined type into a program generally involves two steps. First, the type is described and given a name in a *type definition*. Then variables of the new type are declared in variable declarations using the new type's name in the same manner as the predefined type identifiers. We first consider enumerated types.

## 3-6.1  ENUMERATED TYPES

Fanny's Fitness Emporium operates on a cashless basis, preferring to bill its customers each month. The total amount of purchases made by each customer during the month is supplied as input, along with the customer number and the type of customer. There are three types of customers, and calculation of the balance due differs for each type. Regular customers are given a 10 percent discount on the amount of purchases over $200. Senior citizens are given a 12 percent discount on the amount over $100. Students are given 8 percent discount on the total amount of purchases.

We could assign an integer code to each type of customer: 1 for regular, 2 for senior, 3 for student. Assuming that each line of input data consists of a customer number, customer type number, and total amount of purchases, the program in Fig. 3-34 will produce a report of amount due for each customer.

```
program ComputeDiscount (input, output);
{Given the customer number, customer type, and total amount of purchases,
   this program computes the amount due from each customer.}
var
   CustNumber: integer;
   CustType: integer;    {Customer type code
                    1 = regular
                    2 = senior
                    3 = student}
   AmountOfPurchases: real;
   AmountDue: real;
begin
   {Step 1: Engage loop}
   while not eof do
      begin

         {Step 2: Input data}
         readln (CustNumber, CustType, AmountOfPurchases);

         {Step 3: Compute amount due}
         case CustType of
            1:  if AmountOfPurchases > 200.00
                then AmountDue : = 200.00 + 0.90 * (AmountOfPurchases
                     − 200.00)
                else AmountDue : = AmountOfPurchases;
            2:  if AmountOfPurchases > 100.00
                then AmountDue : = 100.00 + 0.88 * (AmountOfPurchases
                     − 100.00)
                else AmountDue : = AmountOfPurchases;
            3:  AmountDue : = 0.92 * AmountOfPurchases
         end;

         {Step 4: Display amount due}
         writeln ('Customer Number ☐', CustNumber);
         writeln ('Type ☐', CustType);
         writeln ('Purchases ☐', AmountOfPurchases:8:2);
         writeln ('Due ☐☐☐☐☐☐☐', AmountDue:8:2)
      end
end.
```

FIGURE 3-34
Program to compute
amount due after
discount.

In a large program, use of integer codes requires that the programmer make frequent reference to the code lists while writing or modifying the program. In addition, use of such codes can be error-prone; it is just too easy to write the wrong code. Instead, we can introduce an *enumerated type* (also sometimes called an *enumeration* or a *scalar type*). Such a type consists of a list of identifiers. These identifiers are the *values* or *constants* of the enumerated type. For our problem, we use a type definition of the form

**type**
   KindsOfCustomer = (Regular, Senior, Student);

Variables may now be declared to be of type KindsOfCustomer. We present a revised version of program ComputeDiscount in Fig. 3-35. The revised version declares the variable CustType to be of type KindsOfCustomer. Unfortunately, this program is complicated by the restriction in standard Pascal that enumerated types may not be read from the input stream or written to the output stream. Therefore, the customer type is still read as an integer code, but use of this integer code is restricted to the input-processing step. In a larger

**program** ComputeDiscountRevised (input, output);
{Given the customer number, customer type, and total amount of purchases, this program computes the amount due from each customer. It has been revised to use an enumerated type.}
**type**
   KindsOfCustomer = (Regular, Senior, Student);
**var**
   CustNumber: integer;
   CustCode: integer;    {Used for input only
                              1 = regular
                              2 = senior
                              3 = student}
   CustType: KindsOfCustomer;
   AmountOfPurchases: real;
   AmountDue: real;
**begin**
   {Step 1: Engage loop}
   **while not** eof **do**
     **begin**

       {Step 2: Input data}
       readln (CustNumber, CustCode, AmountOfPurchases);
       **case** CustCode **of**
         1: CustType := Regular;
         2: CustType := Senior;
         3: CustType := Student
       **end**;

**FIGURE 3-35**
**Program to compute**
**amount due after**
**discount revised to**
**use enumerated types.**

program than presented here, the gain in readability is more significant, even with this restriction. Several Pascal compilers remove this restriction on input and output of enumerated types. We shall consider other methods for circumventing this restriction in Chap. 6.

We now consider the exact rules for defining and using enumerated types. The syntax diagram for a program (see Sec. 2-7) requires that the type definitions precede the variable declarations. The *type definitions* consist of the reserved word **type** followed by one or more definitions. Each definition consists of the name being given to the new type, an equal sign, and a *type denoter*. A type denoter is simply a description of the type. The type denoter of an enumerated type consists of the list of constant identifiers of the type separated by commas and enclosed in parentheses. Some examples of type definitions are as follows:

**type**
    Color = (Red, Orange, Yellow, Green, Blue, Violet, Brown, Black);
    Suit = (Spades, Hearts, Clubs, Diamonds);
    ChessPiece = (King, Queen, Bishop, Knight, Rook, Pawn);

The syntax rules for type definition, type denoter, and enumerated type

```
{Step 3: Compute amount due}
case CustType of
    Regular:   if AmountOfPurchases > 200.00
               then AmountDue : = 200.00 + 0.90 *
                   (AmountOfPurchases − 200.00)
               else AmountDue : = AmountOfPurchases;
    Senior:    if AmountOfPurchases > 100.00
               then AmountDue : = 100.00 + 0.88 *
                   (AmountOfPurchases − 100.00)
               else AmountDue : = AmountOfPurchases;
    Student:   AmountDue : = 0.92 * AmountOfPurchases
end;

{Step 4: Display amount due}
writeln ('Customer Number □', CustNumber);
case CustType of
    Regular: writeln ('Type Regular');
    Senior: writeln ('Type Senior');
    Student: writeln ('Type Student')
end;
writeln ('Purchases □', AmountOfPurchases:8:2);
writeln ('Due □□□□□□□', AmountDue:8:2);
writeln
end
end.
```

**FIGURE 3-35** *(cont.)*

type definition

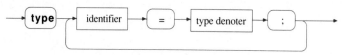

**FIGURE 3-36  Syntax diagram for type definition.**

denoters are summarized in the syntax diagrams in Figs. 3-36, 3-37, and 3-38, respectively. Type denoters for other programmer-defined types are introduced subsequently along with the types they describe.

Variables of the new types are declared just as are variables of the predefined types (see Sec. 2-6). Given the preceding type definitions, we might declare the following variables:

**var**
    Foreground, Background, Temp: Color;
    Trump: Suit;

As always, only a value of the proper type can be assigned to a variable. For an enumerated type, this must be one of the constant identifiers of that type or a value obtained from a variable of that type. All the following are valid assignments:

Foreground : = Red;
Background : = Black;
Temp : = Foreground;
Trump : = Hearts;

The following are not allowed for the reasons given, and the compiler will produce some kind of error message in each case:

type denoter

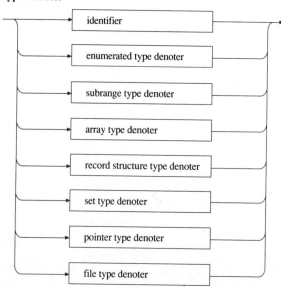

**FIGURE 3-37
Syntax diagram for
the type denoter.**

enumerated type denoter

**157**

3-6
DEFINING NEW TYPES
OF VALUES—
ENUMERATIONS AND
SUBRANGES

FIGURE 3-38  Syntax diagram for the enumerated type denoter.

| | |
|---|---|
| Foreground : = 2; | { Attempt to assign an integer value } |
| Background : = Purple; | { Not one of the enumerated values for the type } |
| Trump : = Red; | { Attempt to assign a constant of another type } |
| Color : = 'V'; | { Attempt to assign a character value } |

The only operators that apply to enumerated types are the six relational operators: $=$, $<>$, $<=$, $>=$, $<$, and $>$. The values of the enumerated type are considered ordered by their appearance in the type denoters list. Suppose a program contains the following:

**type**
   Col = (Red, White, Blue);
**var**
   C1, C2: Col;

For the enumerated type Col, Pascal defines Red $<$ White $<$ Blue since that is the order of their enumeration. Suppose that the following assignments are made:

C1 : = Red;
C2 : = Blue;

Table 3-14 presents several conditions and their values. The two values being compared must be of the same type, otherwise the compiler will produce an error message. Conditions involving enumerated types may be used anywhere a condition is permitted, for example, in the if, while, and repeat statements.

We have previously demonstrated the use of enumerated type variables in the case statements of program ComputeDiscountRevised (Fig. 3-35).

**TABLE 3-14**  Examples of Conditions Involving Enumerated Types

| Condition | Result |
|---|---|
| C1 = C2 | False |
| C1 = Red | True |
| C2 <> Red | True |
| C1 < C2 | True |
| C2 <= Blue | True |
| C2 <= White | False |

Enumerated type variables also may be used in for statements. Assuming the previous declarations of Col and C1, the following are allowed:

**for** C1 : = Red **to** Blue **do**

    .

    .

    .

or

**for** C1 : = Blue **downto** Red **do**

    .

    .

    .

There are three built-in functions which apply to variables of enumerated types. The function ord returns an integer value based on the value of the argument. In an enumerated type denoter, the first value listed corresponds to 0, the second to 1, etc. Assume the previous definitions for Col and C1 and the following assignment:

C1 : = Blue

Table 3-15 then gives some values for ord.

The built-in functions pred and succ return a value of the same enumerated type as their argument; pred returns the "predecessor" and succ returns the "successor." Assuming the same condition as in the description of ord, Table 3-16 gives some results of pred and succ. It is an error to attempt to obtain pred of the first value or succ of the last value of an enumerated type.

It is very important to consider the Pascal restriction that an identifier cannot be used for more than one purpose in a program. (Actually, this is not completely true. A more detailed discussion must be deferred until programmer-written functions and procedures are described in Chap. 4.) We have now used identifiers for variable names, for type names, and for the constants of an enumerated type. It is an error to attempt to use the same identifier for two purposes, for example, a variable and a type, or two different variables, or even as a value in two different enumerated types. For example, the following type declarations are not allowed:

| TABLE 3-15 | Sample Values Returned by ord |
|---|---|
| Expression | Value |
| ord (Red) | 0 |
| ord (White) | 1 |
| ord (Blue) | 2 |
| ord (C1) | 2 |

| TABLE 3-16 | Sample Values Returned by pred and succ |
|---|---|
| **Expression** | **Value** |
| pred (Blue) | White |
| pred (White) | Red |
| succ (Red) | White |
| pred (C1) | White |

**type**
    PrimColor = (Red, Blue, Green);
    FlagColor = (White, Red);

If it were not for this restriction, certain Pascal constructs would be ambiguous. For example, would ord (Red) be 0 or 1?

A final interesting feature of Pascal is that type Boolean is considered as if it were an enumerated type defined by

**type**
    Boolean = (false, true);

Thus we have, for example, ord (false) = 0 and false < true, etc.

## 3-6.2 SUBRANGE TYPES

The predefined types integer, character, and Boolean, along with enumerated types, are called *ordinal types*. The ord function can be used to give a unique integer for each value in these types. (Mathematically, the values of each of these types can be placed in one-to-one correspondence with some subset of the integers.) The type real is not an ordinal type.

The second programmer-defined type which we consider is the *subrange type*. A subrange type represents a contiguous subset of the values of one of the other ordinal types, which is called the subrange's *host type*. The type denoter used in a type declaration for a subrange type consists of two constants separated by the two character symbol ".." as shown in the syntax diagram in Fig. 3-39. When specifying a subrange, the two constants must be of the same type, and the first must be less than or equal to (an unusual case) the second. The following represent valid type declarations:

**type**
    ScaleLimit = −1000 .. 1000;
    ValidIdNumber = 1 .. 99999;

**subrange type denoter**

FIGURE 3-39
Syntax diagram for
the subrange type
denoter.

The types **ScaleLimit** and **ValidIdNumber** are subranges with host type integer. Other valid host types for subranges are character, Boolean, and any enumerated type. Variables of subrange types are declared in the usual way, for example:

**var**

   GaugeReading: ScaleLimit;

A variable of a subrange type may be used wherever a variable of the host type could be used. Using the preceding variable declaration, the following would be legal:

read (GaugeReading);

GaugeReading : = GaugeReading + 10;

writeln (GaugeReading)

Most Pascal compilers provide for run-time checking of values assigned to a variable of subrange type. Any attempt to assign a value outside the range will cause termination of the program with an error message. These checks are provided by including additional machine instructions in the object program. Since these will cause a program to run slower, some means is usually provided for controlling whether or not the compiler generates these checks. Various methods are used by different compilers to enable and disable the checks. The student should consult the instructor or a manual for the specific compiler for more information.

Subrange variables may be used for improved error checking in a program. For example, we might use the following declarations:

**type**

   StuNumType = 1111 .. 9999;

**var**

   StuNum: StuNumType;

Here we assume that all valid student numbers lie in the range 1111 through 9999. Any attempt to assign an illegal student number to variable **StuNum** will result in an error message (assuming that the checks have been enabled).

In using subrange variables, a common error must be avoided. Consider the program in Fig. 3-40, which is intended to read and sum 10 integers. The reader is encouraged to trace the program and discover that it attempts to assign a value of 11 to I before the loop terminates.

It is not necessary to introduce a type name (such as **StuNumType**) in a type declaration for each new type. Instead, a type denoter may be used directly in a variable declaration, as in the following examples:

**var**

   StuNum: 1111 .. 9999;

   Ran1, Ran2: 1 .. 100;

   Ran3: 1 .. 100;

However, each type denoter introduces a new type. Thus, in this example, **Ran1** and **Ran2** are of the same type, but **Ran3** is of a different type, even

```
program RangeErr (input, output);
```
{This program is incorrect. Given ten integer numbers, it attempts to compute the sum. It violates the subrange limits on I by assigning the value of 11 to I.}
```
type
   Count = 1 .. 10;
var
   Sum, D: integer;
   I: Count;
begin
   {Step 1: Initialize}
   Sum : = 0;
   I : = 1;

   {Step 2: Engage loop}
   while I <= 10 do
      begin

         {Step 3: Input data}
         read (D);

         {Step 4: Compute sum of numbers read so far}
         Sum : = Sum + D;

         {Step 5: Increment loop control variable}
         I : = I + 1
      end;

   {Step 6: Display sum}
   writeln (Sum)
end.
```

**FIGURE 3-40**
**Illustration of a common subrange error.**

though it is a subrange with the same limits as Ran1 and Ran2. In subsequent chapters we shall describe several situations, particularly in relation to subprogram parameters in Chap. 4, when variables must be of the same type. Types created by type denoters in variable declarations, which therefore have no names, are called *anonymous types*.

### 3-6.3 SUMMARY

We have introduced the concept of programmer-defined data types and described enumerated and subrange types. The types introduced to this point are known as the *simple types*. Figure 3-41 presents a taxonomy of these types. The remaining Pascal data types, namely, the structured types and the pointer types, are introduced later in the book. Use of appropriate data types can result in more straightforward solutions and thus more readable programs.

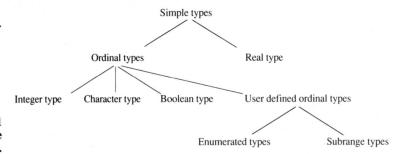

**FIGURE 3-41**
**Taxonomy of simple**
**types.**

We also have seen that there are restrictions on what values may be assigned to a variable. A value is said to be *assignment compatible* with a variable if such an assignment is legal. For the simple types, we have seen that a value is assignment compatible with a particular variable if one of the following conditions holds:

1. Both the variable and the value have the same type.
2. The value is an integer or a subrange of integer and the variable is real.
3. One of the types (of the value or the variable) is a subrange of the other or they are both subranges of the same type. In the case that the variable's type is a subrange, the value must lie within the range.

We shall introduce additional assignment compatibility rules as we introduce additional programmer-defined types.

## 3-7  CONSTANT DECLARATION

There are a number of Pascal constructs in which constants are required. The bounds in a subrange, for example, must be constants, not variables. The constant definition facility allows equating an identifier to a constant at the beginning of the program. This identifier can then be used wherever the constant is required and thus can reduce the need for "magic numbers" in a program. The use of the identifier provides an opportunity for describing the purpose of the constant at the point of its use. An additional benefit is that the value of the constant can be changed throughout the program by making only one change in the code—in the constant definition.

Constant definitions are introduced by the word **const** followed by one or more definitions. Each definition contains an identifier, an equal sign, the value, and a semicolon. For example,

```
const
   MaxScale = 1000;
   Pi = 3.14159;
```

The syntax of the constant definition is summarized in Fig. 3-42.

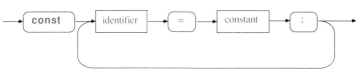

FIGURE 3-42  Syntax diagram for constant definition.

We have now seen several different types of declarations. Recall that the order of appearance of declarations in a program is constant definitions, followed by type definitions, finally followed by variable declarations.

# 3-8  APPLICATIONS

We now present a number of problems in which the techniques of this chapter are applied. Considerable attention is paid to the design of the algorithms and to the ensuing development of a Pascal program. The actual tracing of the completed programs is left as an exercise.

The first application deals with the problems faced by a college bookstore ordering textbooks for the coming term and the factors influencing its decisions. The second application is in the area of monthly mortgage payments. The third, and final, application concerns trying to reconcile checks cashed by employees of a company against those which were issued.

## 3-8.1  BOOKSTORE ORDERS

A campus bookstore would like to make an estimate of the number of books to order and its likely profit margin for the coming academic term. The number of students expected to purchase any given book is governed by a number of factors, such as the importance of the book to a course, the availability of used books, and the likelihood of groups of students sharing a single book. Since storage space is severely limited and the bookstore must pay the shipping charges on books returned to the supplier, the desire not to overstock is very strong. On the other hand, as a campus service, it must ensure that all students who want to purchase a copy of the book have the opportunity to do so.

For each book to be ordered, a line of data is prepared containing the following information:

*1.* The book identification number—a five-digit numeric code (for example, 28605)

*2.* Classification of the book, either required course text or supplementary reading

*3.* Whether or not the book is being used for the first time this term

*4.* Quantity currently in stock

5. Estimated student enrollment in the course for which the book is being ordered

6. Wholesale unit cost of the book

Bookstore studies have found that their market is dictated mainly by items 2, 3, and 5. For required texts, sales are projected at 60 percent of estimated enrollment for books that have been used in a previous term and 85 percent for new books. For books recommended as supplementary reading, the figures are 25 percent of estimated enrollment for books that have been used in a previous term and 40 percent for books that have not. These projections are used to calculate the number of books required; the quantity to order is determined by subtracting the number currently in stock. A negative result indicates the amount of excess stock that is to be returned.

The profit margin is based on the wholesale cost of the book and the bookstore's markup. From this, all bookstore expenses must be paid. There is a 25 percent markup on all books costing $10 or less and a 20 percent markup on all others.

The output required is a report of the following form:

| Identification | On Hand | To Order | Profit |
|---|---|---|---|
| 28605 | 13 | 67 | 200.00 |
| . | . | . | . |
| . | . | . | . |
| . | . | . | . |
| . | . | . | . |

Total Profit     25653.72

The algorithm to solve this problem requires a loop to read and process all the data lines and if statements to process the individual cases. We can describe this in a general or "high-level" algorithm as follows:

1. Repeat thru step 4 for each book

2. Read information for next book

3. Determine number of copies required, the size of the order, and the profit margin on this book, and print

4. Add profit margin on this book to total profit

5. Print final total

We first introduce some variables. From the general algorithm and description of the input, the variables listed in the declaration section of the program are obtained (see Fig. 3-43). We have used character variables for the **Class** and **Status** variables. The allowed one-letter codes and their interpretations are indicated in the comments in Fig. 3-43. An alternative approach would use enumerations for both these variables. We have chosen the character type because it is easier to read these values in standard Pascal.

We can proceed to the design of our final program. We will first consider processing a single book (steps 2 through 4 of the general algorithm) and incorporate the details of the input loop afterward.

The input statement is straightforward, given the preceding list of variables. It can be written directly as

readln (Ident, Class, Status, Stock, Enrollment, Cost)

Next, we must determine the number of copies required of a given book. This is a function of three integer variables: **Class**, denoting the book's classification as prescribed text or supplementary reading; **Status**, denoting whether or not this book is new this term, and **Enrollment**, denoting the estimated enrollment for the coming session. From these values the number of copies required (**NumberRequired**) is calculated as follows (notice that the result is rounded to the nearest integer through the use of the built-in function **round**):

**if** Class = 'R'
**then if** Status = 'N'
    **then** NumberRequired : = round (0.85 * Enrollment)
    **else** NumberRequired : = round (0.60 * Enrollment)
**else if** Status = 'N'
    **then** NumberRequired : = round (0.40 * Enrollment)
    **else** NumberRequired : = round (0.25 * Enrollment);

Two conditions are required before an assessment can be made. We need to know the book's classification and whether or not it is new this term. We could have used compound conditions (such as **if** Class = 'R' **and** Status = 'N'); however, a total of four tests would be required to handle the four possibilities. For this problem, the nesting approach is probably easier to understand.

Having determined the number of copies required (**NumberRequired**), it is a simple matter to determine the number to order. We use the integer variables **Stock**, denoting the number of copies currently on hand, and **Order**, denoting the number of copies that will have to be ordered to fulfill the projected requirement, in the statement

Order : = NumberRequired − Stock

Since any stock in excess of that required is to be returned to the supplier, we might issue a message to that effect if the value of **Order** turns out to be negative (note the use of the built-in function **abs**):

**if** Order < 0
**then** writeln (Ident, '□is overstocked: □', abs(Order):1, '□copies to return')

Calculation of the profit margin is based on the wholesale cost of the book (the real variable **Cost**). We use the real variable **Profit** to denote the projected profit on each copy of a particular book:

**program** Bookstore (input, output);

{Given several books' sales classifications, their status (whether they were
used last year), their stock on hand, enrollments in the courses, and the
books' costs, this program computes the quantity of books to be ordered
and the estimated profit margins.}

**var**

| | |
|---|---|
| Ident: integer; | {Book identification number} |
| Stock: integer; | {Quantity currently in stock} |
| Class: char; | {Classification of the book—required or not |
| |    'R' = Required |
| |    'O' = Optional} |
| Enrollment: integer; | {Estimated course enrollment} |
| Status: char; | {New text or used previously |
| |    'N' = New |
| |    'U' = Used} |
| Cost: real; | {Wholesale cost of the book} |
| NumberRequired: integer; | {Number of copies required} |
| Order: integer; | {Number of copies to be ordered} |
| Profit: real; | {Profit margin on the book} |
| TotalProfit: real; | {Total profit margin} |

**begin**
{Step 1: Initialize}
TotalProfit := 0.00;

{Step 2: Set up report heading}
writeln ('Identification ☐☐On☐Hand ☐☐To ☐Order ☐☐Profit ☐Margin');

{Step 3: Engage input loop}
**while not** eof **do**
   **begin**

{Step 4: read in details for each book}
readln (Ident, Class, Status, Stock, Enrollment, Cost);

FIGURE 3-43
Program BookStore.

**if** Cost $\leq$ 10.00
**then** Profit := NumberRequired * 0.25 * Cost
**else** Profit := NumberRequired * 0.20 * Cost

Within the loop, we will accumulate the total profit margin in the real
variable TotalProfit.

    For the report, we display the values of four variables for each book:
Ident (book's identification number), Stock, Order, and Profit. To read the
input values, we will use a loop controlled by an end-of-file test. After all
the data has been processed, we will display the value of TotalProfit. Putting
this all together in accordance with the general structure developed earlier
results in the program in Fig. 3-43. The input loop used in the program

```
{Step 5: Determine number of copies required}
if Class = 'R'
then {prescribed text}
    if Status = 'N'
    then NumberRequired : = round (0.85 * Enrollment)
    else NumberRequired : = round (0.60 * Enrollment)
else {supplementary reading}
    if Status = 'N'
    then NumberRequired : = round (0.40 * Enrollment)
    else NumberRequired : = round (0.25 * Enrollment);

{Step 6: Determine size of order and, if necessary, issue over-
  stocked notice}
Order : = NumberRequired − Stock;
if Order > 0
then writeln (Ident:1, '☐is overstocked: ☐', abs (Order):1,
        '☐copies to return');

{Step 7: Determine profit on this book}
if Cost <= 10.00
then Profit : = NumberRequired * 0.25 * Cost
else Profit : = NumberRequired * 0.20 * Cost;

{Step 8: Update total profit statistic}
TotalProfit : = TotalProfit + Profit;

{Step 9: Display line for this particular book and read next line}
    writeln (Ident:14, Stock:9, Order:10, Profit:13:2)
end;

{Step 10: Display total profit statistic}
writeln ('Total Profit ☐', TotalProfit:1:2)

{Step 11: Finished}
end.
```

FIGURE 3-43 (*cont.*)

is controlled by an end-of-file signal. Is this method the best suited to the application? How can the program be modified to incorporate a counter-controlled or sentinel-controlled input loop?

## 3-8.2 MORTGAGE PAYMENTS

The purchase of a home is probably the largest single investment that the average consumer will make. Many factors must be considered, not the least of which is the size of the monthly mortgage payment.

The monthly payment is based on three factors: the amount of principal owed, the interest rate for the mortgage, and the number of years for the mortgage (or the *term* of the mortgage). We want to develop a program to compute the monthly payment from the following standard formula:

$$\frac{P \times i \times (i + 1)^n}{(i + 1)^n - 1}$$

where $P$ is the amount of principal, $i$ is the monthly interest rate (in this formula interest is compounded monthly), and $n$ is the number of months in the term of the mortgage.

For our program, we will define the following variables:

Principal (real)    Amount of principal

IntRate (real)    Yearly interest rate

Term (integer)    Number of years for the mortgage

Payment (real)    Monthly payment

We will assume that these variables represent the various factors as they are normally quoted to the consumer. This means that the interest rate and term must be converted from yearly figures to monthly figures for use in the standard formula. We introduce variables J (real) and N (integer) for this purpose. This will require the statements

```
J : = IntRate / 12.0;
N : = Term * 12
```

Calculation of the monthly payment is almost a straightforward translation of the standard formula, except for the exponentiation operation. We need to compute $(J + 1)^n$. Standard Pascal does not define an exponentiation operation. We introduce the additional variables Power and P and a counted loop to compute this term:

```
P : = 1;
for Power : = 1 to N do
    P : = P * (J + 1)
```

Our formula then becomes

```
Payment : = (Principal * J * P) / (P - 1)
```

In addition to the monthly payment, we will produce a table showing a breakdown, by month, of the amount of the monthly payment going to principal and the amount going to interest. At the end of each year we will print yearly totals of amount paid to principal and interest and amount of principal outstanding. We will develop an algorithm to do this by generalizing on a particular example.

Suppose that we have a $25,000 mortgage at 10 percent per annum with a term of 25 years. If we apply the preceding computations, we get a monthly interest rate (J) of 0.10/12 and a term in months (N) of 300. Thus the value of Payment is calculated as

$$\frac{25000 \times \dfrac{0.10}{12} \times \left[\dfrac{0.10}{12} + 1\right]^{300}}{\left[\dfrac{0.10}{12} + 1\right]^{300} - 1}$$

which gives a monthly payment of \$227.17 (assume rounding to two digits). The interest for the first month of the mortgage is easy to compute. It is simply 0.10/12 of \$25,000, or \$208.33. This means that of our total monthly payment of \$227.17, \$208.33 goes to interest and the remaining \$18.84 to principal.

What happens in month 2? Our principal has been reduced by the payment in month 1, \$18.84, leaving a total of \$24,981.16. The calculation of the monthly interest/principal breakdown for this month proceeds as for the first month. Our interest payment is 0.10/12 of \$24,981.16, or \$208.18. Thus in month 2 our monthly payment of \$227.17 comprises a payment of \$208.18 to interest and \$18.99 to principal. We can continue in this fashion for the entire 25 years (or 300 months) of the mortgage.

Generalizing these calculations yields an algorithm with the following basic structure:

*1.* Read in quoted figures (amount of principal, yearly interest rate, term in years);

*2.* Compute basic monthly payment;

*3.* Repeat thru step 5 for each year of mortgage;

*4.* Repeat for each month in the year:
Compute payments to interest and principal for the month from quoted interest rate, amount of principal outstanding, and amount of monthly payment;

*5.* Compute yearly totals and amount of outstanding principal for the next year

We now proceed to supply the details. First, we will introduce some additional variables:

| | |
|---|---|
| MonthlyIntPayment (real) | Monthly payment of interest |
| MonthlyPrincPayment (real) | Monthly payment of principal |
| YearlyIntPayment (real) | Yearly payment of interest |
| YearlyPrincPayment (real) | Yearly payment of principal |

Calculation of the monthly payment has already been described. The breakdown of a monthly payment (**Payment**) is straightforward, as shown in the preceding example:

```
MonthlyIntPayment := J * Principal;
MonthlyPrincPayment := Payment — MonthlyIntPayment
```

For the year-end statistics, these components must be added to running totals YearlyIntPayment and YearlyPrincPayment.

Since the term of the mortgage is fixed, we will repeat the calculations a fixed number of times. This application is perfectly tailored to a counted loop:

**for** Year : = 1 **to** Term **do**

What happens on each pass through this loop? We begin with an outstanding principal of Principal and make 12 payments to it, computing the payment breakdown for each month as we go. For each month, then, the following calculation is made:

MonthlyIntPayment : = J * Principal;

MonthlyPrincPayment : = Payment − MonthlyIntPayment;

**program** Mortgage (input, output);
{Given the principal owing on a mortgage, the yearly interest rate, and the duration of the mortgage in years, this program computes and prints the monthly payment and a breakdown by year of the monthly payments toward interest and toward the principal.}

**var**
    Principal: real;                {Amount of principal}
    IntRate: real;                  {Yearly interest rate}
    Term: integer;               {Numbers of years for the mortgage}
    Payment: real;               {Monthly payment}
    Year: integer;
    Month: integer;
    Power, N: integer;
    MonthlyPrincPayment: real;    {Monthly payment of principal}
    MonthlyIntPayment: real;      {Monthly payment of interest}
    YearlyPrincPayment: real;     {Yearly payment of principal}
    YearlyIntPayment: real;       {Yearly payment of interest}
    J, P: real;
**begin**
    {Step 1: Input}
    read (Principal, IntRate, Term);

    {Step 2: Convert to monthly figures for use in standard formula and compute monthly payment}
    J : = IntRate / 12.0;
    N : = Term * 12;
    P : = 1;
    **for** Power : = 1 **to** N **do**
        P : = P * (J + 1);
    Payment : = (Principal * J * P) / (P − 1);
    writeln ('Monthly Payment Is $', Payment:1:2);

**FIGURE 3-44**
**Program** Mortgage.

YearlyIntPayment : = YearlyIntPayment + MonthlyIntPayment;
YearlyPrincPayment : = YearlyPrincPayment + MonthlyPrincPayment;
Principal : = Principal − MonthlyPrincPayment

In addition, the following report line is printed each month:

writeln (Year:5, Month:5, MonthlyPrincPayment:17:2, MonthlyIntPayment:25:2)

At the end of each year, a yearly summary is printed:

writeln ('Year End Summary:')
writeln ('Principal Paid:□', YearlyPrincPayment:1:2);
writeln ('Interest Paid:□', YearlyIntPayment:1:2);
writeln ('Outstanding Principal:□', Principal:1:2)

Putting all this together, we get the program in Fig. 3-44.


{Step 3: Set up table headings for the monthly reports}
writeln ('Year':6, ' Month ':6, ' Amt Paid To Principal ':24,
   ' Amt Paid To Interest ':24);

{Step 4: Engage loop to compute and print yearly payments}
**for** Year : = 1 **to** Term **do**
  **begin**

    {Step 5: Initialize yearly running totals}
    YearlyIntPayment : = 0;
    YearlyPrincPayment : = 0;

    {Step 6: Compute and print each monthly breakdown}
    **for** Month : = 1 **to** 12 **do**
      **begin**
        MonthlyIntPayment : = J * Principal;
        MonthlyPrincPayment : = Payment − MonthlyIntPayment;
        YearlyIntPayment : = YearlyIntPayment + MonthlyIntPayment;
        YearlyPrincPayment : = YearlyPrincPayment
          + MonthlyPrincPayment;
        Principal : = Principal − MonthlyPrincPayment;
        writeln (Year:5, Month:5, MonthlyPrincPayment:17:2,
          MonthlyIntPayment:25:2)
      **end**;

    {Step 7: Print yearly summary}
    writeln ('Year End Summary:');
    writeln ('Principal Paid: □', YearlyPrincPayment:1:2);
    writeln ('Interest Paid: □', YearlyIntPayment:1:2);
    writeln ('Outstanding Principal: □', Principal:1:2)
  **end**;

**end**.

FIGURE 3-44 (*cont.*)

### 3-8.3 CHECK RECONCILIATION

A line of data containing the check number and the amount of the check is prepared for every check issued to employees of Rudolph's Red Nose Winery. At the end of each month, all the cashed checks are collected from the bank and a similar line of data is prepared for each check, again containing the check number and the amount of the check. These two sets of data are merged together, by check number, to form the input to a reconciliation algorithm that is to match the checks issued against those which were cashed.

The following is typical of the input that might occur and illustrates the cases that can arise.

$$
\left.
\begin{array}{ll}
23871 & 48.50 \\
23871 & 48.50
\end{array}
\right\} \leftarrow \text{Check 23871 issued and cashed for } \$48.50
$$

$$
23872 \quad 150.00 \leftarrow \text{Check 23872 issued for } \$150.00 \text{ but not yet cashed}
$$

$$
\left.
\begin{array}{ll}
23873 & 36.20 \\
23873 & 236.20
\end{array}
\right\} \leftarrow
\begin{array}{l}
\text{Check 23873 issued and cashed for different} \\
\text{amounts}
\end{array}
$$

$$
\begin{array}{cc}
\cdot & \cdot \\
\cdot & \cdot \\
\cdot & \cdot
\end{array}
$$

The reconciliation algorithm is to list the checks issued but not yet cashed and to print the check number and two amounts of any check which is issued and then cashed at a different amount. Also, it is to print the total amount of the checks cashed and the total amount of the outstanding checks (checks issued but not yet cashed).

*Sample output:*

| Check Number | Amount | |
|---|---|---|
| 23872 | 150.00 | |
| 23873 | 36.20 | 236.20 |
| . | . | |
| . | . | |
| . | . | |

Total Cashed = $123761.42

Total Outstanding = $8731.49

This problem is typical of many problems that arise in business data processing. The techniques involved in its solution are important. The organization of read statements is somewhat different from what we have seen previously, since two lines of data are required to process each check. The first of the two lines gives us the number and amount of the check that was issued; the second line tells us what has happened to it. For example, most often the check will have been cashed normally, in which case the amount on the second line is the same as the amount on the first line (as was the case with check **23871**). On rare occasions the check may have been issued and cashed for different amounts, in which case the amounts on the two lines will be unequal (check **23873**, for example). Finally, the check may not have been cashed yet, in which case there is no second line (the case for check **23872**). How do we detect that there is no second line? We do this by comparing the check numbers of the two lines actually read. If they differ, we know that there is no second line, and, in fact, we have probably read the first line of the next pair.

Referring to the sample input, we can illustrate how this reading must work. First, we read two lines. Since they have the same check numbers (**23871**), we know that they constitute a valid pair and we proceed to process them accordingly. In this case, in fact, since the values match, the checks have been issued and cashed correctly. We then read the next two lines. In this case, however, the check numbers are different (**23872** and **23873**). This tells us immediately that since there is no second line for it, check number **23872** has not yet been cashed. We have, in fact, read the first line of the next pair. We then read one more line and find that it has a check number of **23873**, matching the other line we had just read. We can now process these two lines as a valid pair. In this instance, the check has been issued and cashed for different amounts.

As a first attempt at setting up the general structure for an algorithm to solve this problem, we might get something like the following:

*1.* Repeat thru step 4 while data lines remain to be processed

*2.* Read in two records

*3.* If the check numbers are identical,
    then if the amounts are equal,
        then the check has been correctly cashed;
        else it has been issued and cashed at different amounts

*4.* If the check numbers differ,
    then the first line read is the record of a check yet outstanding

This algorithm works correctly if the lines continue to come in as pairs. Should we encounter a case, however, where a check has yet to be cashed, we run into difficulty. In this situation, we require only one additional line; our algorithm delivers two.

To solve this particular problem, we need to introduce an additional variable that tells us which type of line is required. This will allow us to process abnormal cases as well as normal ones. For example, upon encountering an outstanding check, we will issue an appropriate message, then treat the second line as the first line of the next pair, and then set our special variable to indicate that a line of type 2 is required. This will cause us to skip over the reading of a first line. The following algorithm operates in this fashion:

*1.* LineRequired := FirstLine

*2.* Repeat thru step 4 while data lines remain to be processed;

*3.* If LineRequired = FirstLine
   then read in a "first line"
      LineRequired := SecondLine   {Now looking for a "second line"}

*4.* If data lines remain to be processed
   then Read in "second line"
      If check numbers are identical
      then if the amounts are equal
         then the check has been correctly cashed
         else it has been issued and cashed at different amounts;
         LineRequired := FirstLine   {Look for a "first line" again}
      If check numbers differ
      then identify the first line as that of an outstanding check and
         consider the second line now as a "first line"
         LineRequired := SecondLine   {Look for a "second line"}

*5.* If LineRequired ≠ FirstLine
   then identify the first line as that of an outstanding check

Returning to the sample input, since step 1 initialized LineRequired to FirstLine, the first line,

23871        48.50

is read and treated as a "first line" in step 3. More lines remain, so step 4 causes the next line,

23871        48.50

to be read as a "second line." Since the check numbers are identical and the amounts are equal, the check is noted as correctly cashed. LineRequired is then set to FirstLine to initiate a search for a new "first line." Control returns to step 2 to reevaluate the loop condition. More lines remain, so we proceed to step 3. Since LineRequired is FirstLine, the next line,

23872        150.00

is read and treated as a "first line." More lines remain, so step 4 causes the next line,

23873        36.20

to be read as a "second line." Since the check numbers of these two lines are not equal, the line with check number **23872** is recognized as that of an outstanding check, and the line with check number **23873** is now considered as a "first line." LineRequired is set to SecondLine, to indicate a search for a "second line." Control then returns to step 2. More lines remain, so control proceeds to step 3. No read occurs in step 3, since LineRequired ≠ Firstline. More lines remain, so control passes to step 4 and the next line, is read as a "second line." Since the check numbers on the two lines match but the amounts are unequal, step 4 notes this as a situation of checks being issued and cashed at different amounts. LineRequired is then set to FirstLine to indicate a search for a new pair. This approach appears to function correctly.

An additional problem with the use of two read statements is the treatment of the end of file. Since the input stream can be at end of file at either read statement, we must give some consideration to the consequences of end of file at each point. If eof is "true" when a "first line" is needed, no special action is required. If, however, it is "true" when a "second line" is being sought, we infer that the first line of a pair has been read, but there is no second line. From this we conclude that the last check has not yet been cashed and print a message to that effect. Figure 3-45 presents the complete program.

The first part of this program is straightforward. We initialize the two variables used for totals and engage the loop, indicating that a "first line" is required; we then enter the loop, unless there is no input at all! (We do not further consider the later case. The reader is encouraged to trace the program for this case.) The loop first reads a "first line" if necessary. A test for eof is not specifically required before this read because it immediately follows the loop condition. We then request a second line, but only if eof is "false." If eof is "true," indicating that the read of the "first line" in fact read the last line in the input, we bypass the read and the rest of the body of the loop. (Some Pascal compilers incorporate an *exit loop* statement. This would be an appropriate point to investigate its use if it is available to you. It could simplify this program by removing one level of testing in the loop range. ) Assuming that there is another line, then after reading it as the second line, the processing is relatively straightforward.

As you might expect, once again special action is required if there is no second line in the pair (that is, the check numbers on the two lines read are different). First, we print the required message and update the total of outstanding checks. We must then deal with the second line we did read. This is now to be treated as the first line of the next pair. Since "first line" data is to be stored in variables Check1No and Check1Amt, we must effect this by copying the values currently in Check2No and Check2Amt. The setting of the variable LineRequired to "second line" will cause us to bypass the reading of a first line in step 3 on the next pass through the loop. We will proceed instead to step 4, and we carry on processing in the normal fashion from this point. In particular, if a valid pair is encountered next, we must reset the variable LineRequired to FirstLine to allow for regular processing of subsequent lines. We will leave the complete tracing of this program as an exercise.

The program presented is not the only possible solution to the problem. The reader may wish to propose a "better" solution. However, another solution is not better if it works incorrectly for some arrangements of input data. It is important that the program never attempt to read a line of data beyond the last line. It is also important that it process the last group of data

**program** Reconcile (input, output);

{Given data on checks issued and checks cashed, this program detects discrepancies and computes the total amount cashed and outstanding. The data has been merged into one input stream. Each line contains a check number and amount. The first line of a pair was prepared at the time the check was issued. The second line, if present, was prepared after the check was cashed.}

**type**
  LineType = (FirstLine, SecondLine);
**var**
  Cashed: real;                        {Total amount of checks cashed}
  Outstanding: real;                   {Total amount of checks outstanding}
  LineRequired: LineType;              {First or second line required}
  Check1No, Check2No: integer;   {Check numbers}
  Check1Amt, Check2Amt: real;     {Check amounts}
**begin**
  {Step 1: Initialize sums and LineRequired}
  Cashed : = 0.00;
  Outstanding : = 0.00;
  LineRequired : = FirstLine;

  {Step 2: Engage loop}
  **while not** eof **do**
    **begin**

        {Step 3: Read first line only if required}
        **if** LineRequired = FirstLine
        **then begin**
              read (Check1No, Check1Amt);
              LineRequired : = SecondLine
          **end**;

        {Step 4: Check if there is more data}
        **if not** eof
        **then begin**

**FIGURE 3-45**
Program Reconcile.

correctly; in particular, if the data ends with an outstanding check, it is important that it be reported as outstanding and added to the total of outstanding checks.

Since it is very easy to overlook some of the preceding cases in the design of a program, the set of cases used to test the program should include examples of these cases. In particular, the program should be tested with data that ends with a cashed check, data that ends with an outstanding check preceded by a cashed check, and finally, data that ends with an outstanding check preceded by an outstanding check. A trace of the program in Fig. 3-45 will show that each of these tests results in a different *execution path*. An execution path is a particular sequence of execution of the statements of

```
{Step 5: Read second line}
readln (Check2No, Check2Amt);

{Step 6: Process the pair of lines}
if Check1No = Check2No
then begin
        if Check1Amt = Check2Amt
        then Cashed := Cashed + Check1Amt
        else writeln (Check1No:6, Check1Amt:8:2,
            Check2Amt:8:2);
        LineRequired := FirstLine
    end
else begin
        Outstanding := Outstanding + Check1Amt;
        writeln (Check1No:6, Check1Amt:8:2);
        Check1No := Check2No;
        Check1Amt := Check2Amt;
        LineRequired := SecondLine
    end
  end
end;

{Step 7: Process a final uncashed check}
if LineRequired = SecondLine
then begin
        Outstanding := Outstanding + Check1Amt;
        writeln (Check1No:6, Check1Amt:8:2)
    end;

{Step 8: Display final results}
writeln ('Total cashed □ = □$', Cashed:1:2);
writeln ('Total outstanding □ = □$', Outstanding:1:2)
end.
```

**FIGURE 3-45** (*cont.*)

a program and is usually dependent on the particular input data supplied. Generally, testing should check a number of different paths to improve confidence in the correctness of the program. Notice that for the program in Fig. 3-45, several *separate executions* with different data are necessary. One execution of the program will not be sufficient!

## CHAPTER SUMMARY

The material in this chapter relates to computing constructs involving a decision-making capability. Two classes of structures were introduced: one to permit selection from alternative actions (the *if–then–else* construct and the *case* construct) and one to permit repetition (the *loop*). The concept of the conditional expression is central to all of these and is explored in some depth. The *nesting* of structures within one another is discussed as well.

Within the section on loops, two forms are presented: the *conditional loop* and the *counted loop*. The application of these to the reading of sets of input data is explored. Programmer-defined types which include enumerated types and subrange types are also introduced.

## KEY TERMS

| | |
|---|---|
| anonymous type | identical types |
| assignment-compatible types | if statement |
| Boolean expression | lazy input |
| bottom-tested | logical expression |
| case statement | logical operator |
| compound condition | loop control variable |
| compound statement | nested statement |
| conditional loop | ordinal type |
| constant declaration | partial evaluation |
| control structure | relational operator |
| counter-controlled input | sentinel-controlled input |
| end-of-file method | structured statement |
| enumerated type | subrange type |
| flow of control | top-tested |
| for statement | while statement |

## CHAPTER EXERCISES

1. Write a program to display the sum of the square roots of the first 100 integers.

2. *(a)* In mathematics, the following is always true:

   $$|\sin x| \leq 1$$

   Write a program to verify this property for the built-in function sin for values of $x$ going from $-10.0$ to $+10.0$ in steps of 0.2.

   *(b)* In mathematics, the following property holds:

   $$\sqrt{x} \leq \sqrt{y} \qquad \text{whenever } x \leq y$$

   Write a program to check that this property holds for the built-in function sqrt for integral values of $x$ and $y$ in the range 0 to 100.

★ 3. Commercial fishermen are required to report monthly information on their catch to the Department of Fisheries. This data is analyzed regularly to determine the growth or reduction of the various species of fish and to indicate any possible trouble. From the catch reports and previous data, a line of data is prepared containing the following information: region fished (numerical code), species code (integer), number caught this year (integer), number caught last year (integer). For example,

16    3    20485    18760

This example indicates that in region 16, a total of 20,485 species 3 fish were caught as compared to 18,760 in the same month last year. Write a program to read the data prepared (the last line of data will contain a negative region number) and flag any unusual growth or reduction in catches. An unusual growth or reduction is defined as one in which the percentage change exceeds 30 percent, where percentage change is defined as

$$\frac{\text{(This year)} - \text{(last year)}}{\text{(Last year)}} \times 100\%$$

★ **4.** The present government of Gooba-Gooba Land instituted wage and price controls shortly after it was elected. The Prime Minister has received word from her economic advisors that future predictions, based on current trends, are that wages will continue to increase by 5 percent, the prices of essential goods and services by 10 percent, and personal taxes by 15 percent per year. Her political advisors tell her that if taxes plus the cost of essential goods and services consume more than 75 percent of their annual wage for a significant number of citizens, she will be in trouble at the next election (expected in 3 years' time), and that if this reaches 80 percent, she will be in real trouble. The Prime Minister has collected and placed in a data file the present annual wage, taxes, and cost of essential goods and services for a sample of her constituents. Write a program to determine the number and percentage of the total surveyed who will fall into the 75 percent and 80 percent categories. The number in the sample is unknown. End of input is to be determined by the end-of-file method.

★ **5.** The Saskatchewan Government Insurance agency has compiled data on all traffic accidents in the province over the past year. For each driver involved in an accident, a record has been prepared with the following three pieces of information:

> Year driver was born (integer), sex ('M' or 'F'), registration code (1 for Saskatchewan registration, 0 for everything else)

Write a program to read the records and print the following summary statistics on drivers involved in accidents:
*(a)* Percentage of drivers under 25.
*(b)* Percentage of drivers who are female.
*(c)* Percentage of drivers who are males between the ages of 18 and 25.
*(d)* Percentage of drivers with out-of-province registration.
Use the end-of-file method to signal the end of input.

★ **6.** The following table is taken from the 1985 Canadian income tax guide.

### 1985 Rates of Federal Income Tax

| Taxable Income | Federal Tax |
|---|---|
| $ 1,295 or less | 6% |
| 1,295 | $    78 + 16% on next $ 1,295 |
| 2,590 | 285 + 17% on next   2,590 |
| 5,180 | 725 + 18% on next   2,590 |
| 7,770 | 1,191 + 19% on next   5,180 |
| 12,950 | 2,176 + 20% on next   5,180 |
| 18,130 | 3,212 + 23% on next   5,180 |
| 23,310 | 4,403 + 25% on next   12,950 |
| 36,260 | 7,641 + 30% on next   25,900 |
| 62,160 | 15,411 + 34% on remainder |

Design a program to read taxable income and determine the federal income tax to be paid according to this schedule of rates.

★ **7.** The city police department has accumulated information on speeding violations over a period of time. The department has divided the city into four quadrants and wishes to have statistics on speeding violations by quadrant. For each violation, a record is prepared containing the following information:

> Vehicle registration number (integer), quadrant in which offense occurred (1–4), speed limit in miles per hour (integer), actual speed traveled in miles per hour (integer)

This set of records is terminated by a special record with vehicle registration number of 0. Write a program to produce two reports. First, give a listing of speeding fines collected, where the fine is calculated as the sum of court costs ($20) plus $1.25 for every mile per hour by which the speed limit was exceeded. Prepare a table with the following headings:

### Speeding Violations

| Vehicle Registration | Speed Recorded (mi/h) | Speed Limit (mi/h) | Fine |
|---|---|---|---|

This report is to be followed by a second report, in which an analysis of violations by quadrant is given. For each of the four quadrants give the number of violations processed and the average fine.

★ **8.** (a) Write a program to compute and tabulate the values for the function

$$f(x, y) = \frac{x^2 - y^2}{x^2 + y^2}$$

for $x = 2, 4, 6, 8$ and $y = 6, 9, 12, 15, 18, 21$.

(b) Write a program to compute the number of points with integer-valued coordinates that are contained within the ellipse

$$\frac{x^2}{16} + \frac{y^2}{25} = 1$$

*Notes:*

(**1**) Points on the ellipse are considered to be within it.

(**2**) The range of coordinate values is limited by the major and minor axes of the ellipse (that is, $-4 \le x \le 4$ and $-5 \le y \le 5$).

★ **9.** The We-Spray-Anything Company uses planes to spray crops for a variety of problems. The rates they charge farmers depend on what they are spraying for and how many acres the farmers want sprayed according to the following schedule:

Type 1: Spraying for weeds, $1 per acre

Type 2: Spraying for grasshoppers, $2 per acre

Type 3: Spraying for army worms, $3 per acre

Type 4: Spraying for all of these, $5 per acre

If the area to be sprayed is greater than 1000 acres, the farmer receives a 5 percent discount. In addition, any farmer whose bill is over $1500 receives a 10 percent refund on the amount over $1500. If both discounts apply, the acreage discount is taken first. Write a program that will read in a series of records containing the following information: farm registration number (integer), type of spraying requested (integer code 1–4), and number of acres to be sprayed (integer). For example:

645    3    950

For each record read, calculate the total cost to the farmer and display the farm number followed by the farmer's bill. Use the end-of-file method to signal the end of input.

★ **10.** (a) Write a program to compute the amount of savings you would have at the end of 10 years if you were to deposit $100 each month. Assume a constant annual interest rate of 6 percent compounded every 6 months (that is, interest in the amount of 3 percent is awarded each 6 months).

(b) We want to invest a sum of money that will grow to be $X$ dollars in $Y$ years time. If the interest rate is $R$ percent, then the amount we have to invest (the *present value* of X) is given by the formula

$$\frac{X}{(1 + 0.01 \times R)^{Y}}$$

Write a program that will display a table of the present value of $5000 at 7.5 percent interest for periods of 1 to 21 years in steps of 2 years.

★ **11.** Dandy-Dan's Computer Dating Service maintains a file of its clients. Each record in the file contains the following information:

Client number, sex ('M' or 'F'), age, height (in inches), weight (in pounds), color of eyes (1 = blue, 2 = brown, or 3 = other), color of hair (1 = brown, 2 = blonde, or 3 = other)

Write a program that will read through this file and print the client numbers of:
*(a)* All blonde-haired, blue-eyed females between 5 feet and 5 feet 2 inches weighing less than 115 pounds.
*(b)* All brown-eyed males over 6 feet tall weighing between 180 and 220 pounds.
Use the end-of-file method to signal the end of input.

★ **12.** Many professional sports teams use a computer to assist in the analysis of scouting reports on prospective players. The Warman Fuzzies hockey team has such a system. For each player scouted, a record containing the following information is prepared:

Player's number, age, height (in inches), weight (in pounds), goals scored last season, assists last season, penalty minutes last season, and league factor (real number)

The players are evaluated according to the following formula:

(goals + assists + (penalty minutes) / 4
+ (height + weight) / 5 − age) * league factor

Write a program to read in the entire file of scouting reports, listing for each player the information in his record and his evaluation figure. At the end of this list (denoted by a special record with the player number 0), give the player number and evaluation figure for the player with the highest evaluation.

# CHAPTER 4

# SUBPROGRAMS

We have emphasized throughout this book that a complex problem is best tackled by first breaking it up into a number of subproblems. Recall that problem decomposition is an important aspect of problem solving. The subprogram provides us with an important tool for the development of algorithms and programs. In this chapter we will look at two different forms of subprogram and see how they can assist us in the solution of complex problems.

## 4-1 MOTIVATION

A space launch vehicle has a great number of individual components. It is impossible to understand the interrelationships among the many components individually. Such complexity is managed by organizing these components into subassemblies, these subassemblies into modules, and so on. Thus the launch vehicle may be viewed as the first, second, and third stages. The first stage is composed of the propulsion system, the control system, etc.

An engineer working on the design of a system is concerned only with certain aspects of the subsystems comprising the system. The features of concern in the subsystems are those which affect their interconnections. A large amount of detail on the inner workings of a subsystem are of no concern when interconnecting it to others, only the details of the interface.

Subprograms provide this same ability to organize complexity in a program. A large program can be divided into a number of components, with each component implemented as a subprogram. This division must be performed in such a way that only a few details about a subprogram are needed to write the main program. The majority of details need be of concern only when designing the subprogram itself. This organization of a program into subprograms as a means of dealing with such details is one of their principal uses.

In addition to helping manage complexity, subprograms can reduce the cost of developing a program. It has been estimated that the cost of producing a standard automobile if every part had to be constructed from basic units would exceed $100,000. Automobile assembly lines take full advantage of stocks of prefabricated components to reduce the cost as well as the time required to produce a car. Similarly, in programming, we can significantly ease the production process through the use of previously written program components. Over the years, vast libraries of programs have been compiled for applications in engineering, mathematical programming, and data processing, to name just a few areas. For example, various precoded sort routines are available for data-processing applications, as are routines for such problems in mathematics as matrix inversion and the solution of differential equations. By having routines such as these available in general form, programmers of a particular problem are able instead to focus their attention on those aspects unique to their own problem.

In this chapter we discuss the concept of a subprogram. Subprograms can be loosely thought of as building blocks that can be assembled together in the process of constructing an algorithm or program. They may be precoded, as in the case of the library routines, or coded as part of the development of a suitable program for the solution of a particular problem. In either case, the use of subprograms allows programmers to focus their attention selectively, as in the divide-and-conquer philosophy, and consequently helps reduce the overall complexity of the task. We will deal with two different types of subprograms, the function and the procedure, and their use in some typical applications.

## 4-2 FUNCTIONS

Users of most programming language systems have at their disposal a supply of system-defined, or built-in, functions. Trigonometric functions such as sin (sine), cos (cosine), and atan (inverse tangent) are built into Pascal, as are other standard mathematical functions, such as abs (absolute value), sqr (square, that is, sqr(x) = x∗x), and sqrt (square root). A list of Pascal's built-in functions was given in Chap. 2. Built-in functions can be used directly in expressions, with the expected interpretation. For example, the statement

Hypotenuse := sqrt (sqr (Leftleg) + sqr (Rightleg))

computes the length of the hypotenuse of a right-angled triangle as the square root of the sums of the squares of the two legs. For a triangle with legs of 3.0 and 4.0 units, respectively, the value assigned to the variable Hypotenuse is sqrt (25.0), or 5.0. The statement

Val : = sin (Angle1) + cos (Angle2)

assigns to the variable Val the sum of the sine of Angle1 and the cosine of Angle2. If the values of Angle1 and Angle2 are $\pi/2$ (radians) and 0 (radians), respectively, the value assigned to Val is 1.0 + 1.0, or 2.0.

All these are examples of functions, in this case functions defined by the system for use by the programmer. They are used in expressions as if they were simply regular variables. Like variables, they have a single value. It is the responsibility of the programmer to supply the particular *argument* (or, in some cases, arguments) on which the function is to operate for the specific computation at hand. An argument can be any expression, and it may involve use of other (or even the same) functions. In the examples, the arguments were Leftleg, Rightleg, sqr (Leftleg) + sqr (Rightleg), Angle1, and Angle2. Arguments can be any expression, the value of which is the value on which the named function operates.

The use of subprograms (in this case, functions) affects the flow of control in a program. When a function is invoked, control passes to the instructions defining the function. Following execution of the function with the supplied arguments, control returns to the point of invocation in the calling (or main) program, with whatever values have been computed in the function. This flow of control is illustrated schematically in Fig. 4-1.

For obvious reasons, no system can hope to provide *all* possible functions. In many problems you would like to use an operation that is, unfortunately, not supplied by the system as a built-in function. It is important, too, that programmers have the ability to define their own functions. We will now see how this is done.

In mathematics, we write a function in a general form as follows:

$$f(x) = x^2 - 3x + 2$$

This particular function $f$ has been defined in terms of a *parameter* $x$. Should we wish to evaluate this function for a particular value, or *argument*, of $x$, say, $x = 3$, we substitute that value for each occurrence of the parameter $x$ in the general definition, as in the following examples:

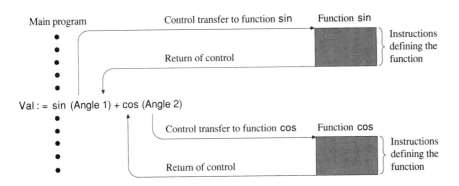

FIGURE 4-1
Effect of the use of functions on the flow of control.

$$f(3) = 3^2 - 3 \times 3 + 2 = 2$$

$$f(7) = 7^2 - 3 \times 7 + 2 = 30$$

$$f(-2) = (-2)^2 - 3 \times (-2) + 2 = 12$$

Many functions will have more than one parameter. An important part of the definition of any function is a listing of all parameters in terms of which the function is defined. For example,

$$g(x, y) = x^2 - y^2$$

$$h(x, y, z) = x^2 + 3xy + z^2$$

are functions with two and three parameters, respectively. A corresponding number of arguments is required for each evaluation. Thus,

$$g(3, 2) = 3^2 - 2^2 = 5$$

$$h(1, 2, 9) = 1^2 + 3 \times 1 \times 2 + 9^2 = 88$$

A correspondence is set up between the parameters of the definition and the arguments supplied, so that in the first case 3 is substituted for each occurrence of $x$ and 2 is substituted for each occurrence of $y$. Notice that the order is crucial; $g(3, 2)$ is *not* the same as $g(2, 3)$.

It is useful to view a function (and, as we will see later, a procedure) as an independent component of a program or algorithm, and for this reason, we will define its statements separately from those of the main part of the program. The purpose of a function is to perform some computation when we require it, under control of the main program (hence the term "*sub*program"). This computation may be required, in fact, at several places in the program. An analogy might be a song sheet, in which the chorus, although written only once, is meant to be sung after every verse. It is usually given separately from the verses and quite often, in fact, even has a different tune.

The following example is a Pascal function to compute the average of three supplied values:

```
function Average (Value1, Value2, Value3: real {Input}): real;
{The purpose of this function is to compute the average of the three values supplied by three
    input parameters.}
var
    Sum: real;
begin
    Sum := Value1 + Value2 + Value3;
    Average := Sum / 3.0
end;
```

Although this function is very simple, it serves to illustrate some key points. The syntax, the full details of which will be given shortly, is similar to that of a program. There are several important differences. The reserved word **function** replaces **program**. Following the name of the function is a list of *parameters* in parentheses—here Value1, Value2, and Value3. The type of these parameters is specified as real. We also have incorporated a comment indicating that these are "input" parameters. We will discuss other possibilities in Sec. 4-4. Following the parameters is the specification of the value type returned by the function, in this case real. The remainder of the function, called the *block* (also called the *body*), has syntax identical to the block of a program. Here Sum is declared as a variable *local* to the function. Finally, the value to be returned by the function is computed by a sequence of statements. The value to be returned is then assigned to the function name. This is a special case of the assignment statement, since the function name, rather than a variable, occurs on the left-hand side.

Any time the function is used in a program, or *called*, a correspondence is established automatically between the function parameters and the arguments of the particular function call. The nature of this correspondence is discussed more fully in Sec. 4-4; here we simply say that the values of the arguments somehow become the values of the parameters. The statements of the function are then executed. The last (possibly only) value assigned to the function name is the value returned. This value is then used as part of the expression in which the function call appears.

To illustrate, we give a program which uses the function Average in Fig. 4-2. The function itself is included, as a *function* declaration, immediately after the variable declaration. You will notice that the function is called three times in this program, once in step 2 and twice in step 4, with different arguments each time. The first call is with arguments A, B, and C. These have the values 2.0, 6.1, and 7.5, respectively. As the first function call is processed, the correspondence between the arguments and parameters is established, so that the parameters of the function, Value1, Value2, and Value3, are given the values 2.0, 6.1, and 7.5, respectively. The steps of the function itself are then executed with these values. The variable Sum in the function definition is assigned the value 15.6, and then 15.6 / 3.0, or 5.2, is returned as the value of the function in the next step. Control is returned to the calling program and the returned value (5.2) is assigned to D and displayed in step 3.

In step 4, the function is called again, twice in fact. The first of these calls is with a different ordering of the arguments. This results in Value1, Value2, and Value3 getting the values 7.5, 2.0, and 6.1, respectively. In this particular case, this results again in the value 5.2 being returned. The second call to the function in step 4 shows the versatility with which arguments can be expressed. The first argument (B) is a single variable; the second argument is a constant, 3.2; the third argument is an expression, (A + 7.0). The correspondence between arguments and parameters in this instance results in Value1, Value2, and Value3 being given the values 6.1, 3.2, and 9.0, respectively. Within the function, Sum is assigned the value 18.3, and the value 18.3 / 3.0, or 6.1, is returned as the value of the function for the second call.

```
program TestFun (output);
{This program illustrates the use of the function Average with various
    arguments.}
var
    A, B, C, D, E: real;

function Average (Value1, Value2, Value3: real {Input} ): real;
{Given three real values, this function computes their average.}
var
    Sum: real;
begin
    {Compute sum}
    Sum : = Value1 + Value2 + Value3;

    {Compute average}
    Average : = Sum/3.0
end;

begin
    {Step 1: Initialize test values}
    A : = 2.0;
    B : = 6.1;
    C : = 7.5;

    {Step 2: Function in an expression}
    D : = Average (A, B, C);

    {Step 3: Display results}
    writeln (D);

    {Step 4: Use function in a more elaborate expression}
    E : = Average (C, A, B) + Average (B, 3.2, A + 7.0);

    {Step 5: Display results}
    writeln (E)
end.
```

**FIGURE 4-2**
**Example of the**
**use of a function.**

To complete the processing of step 4 in the program TestFun, the two
function values **5.2** and **6.1** are then added together and assigned to the
variable E. Figure 4-3 summarizes the evaluation of this expression in step
4 of program TestFun. The value of E, 11.3, is then printed in step 5.

Although simple, this example illustrates several key points concerning the use of functions. Functions are defined as entities separate from
the statements of the main program, with the function parameters given in
parentheses immediately following the function name. A function returns a
single value given a particular set of arguments. The value to be returned

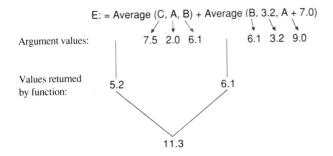

E: = Average (C, A, B) + Average (B, 3.2, A + 7.0)

Argument values:         7.5  2.0  6.1        6.1  3.2  9.0

Values returned
by function:       5.2                  6.1

                        11.3

FIGURE 4-3
Evaluation of an
expression involving
functions.

is assigned to the function name by an assignment statement within the function.

Most identifiers used in the definition of any subprogram (including the names of the parameters) are said to be *local* identifiers. This means that their names have meaning only inside the subprogram itself. For example, the names of the parameters Value1, Value2, and Value3 and the name of the variable Sum used in the definition of the function Average are local identifiers, and thus they are unknown outside the function. Only the name of the function is known outside, since it must be used in any statement invoking the function. The use of local identifiers is an important aspect of localizing the details of a subprogram. Its parameters and local variables are private and used only by the subprogram itself. Identifiers defined as constants, type names, and components of an enumerated type are similarly private (local) to the subprogram in which they are declared.

It is important to realize that the use of an identifier locally in a procedure does not preclude use of the same identifier for a *different purpose* in the calling program. In Fig. 4-4, the identifier IdA is used in the main program to store one of the values read. Within the function we have used the same identifier for the sum of the three values. Within the function, IdA represents a *completely separate* variable whose value is independent of the variable of the same name in the main program. This program, when presented with the input data

3.0   4.0   8.0

should produce the output

The average of 3.0 4.0 8.0
is 5.0

Recall that an identifier used within a subprogram refers to a parameter, constant, type, or variable declared within the subprogram, and this object is independent of any object of the same name in the main program. The identifier is said to be *local*. If an identifier is used in the subprogram but not declared there, however, then this use is considered to refer to the declaration in the calling program. Such a reference is said to be a *global* reference. Great care must be taken in using global references, either

```
program LocalIdExample (input, output);
```
{This program illustrates the use of the same identifiers in a program and in
a subprogram.}
```
var
    IdA, IdB, IdC, Aver: real;        {Real variables used in the main program}

function Average (
        Value1, Value2, Value3: real        {Input, values to be averaged}
                        ): real;
```
{Given three real values, this function computes their average.}
```
var
    IdA: real;        {Real variable used in the function}
begin
    {Compute sum}
    IdA := Value1 + Value2 + Value3;

    {Compute average}
    Average := IdA / 3.0
end;


begin
    {Step 1: Input data}
    read(IdA, IdB, IdC);

    {Step 2: Call function to compute average}
    Aver := Average(IdA, IdB, IdC);

    {Step 3: Display average}
    writeln('The average of ', IdA, IdB, IdC);
    writeln('is ', Aver)
end.
```

**FIGURE 4-4**
**Example of multiple**
**use of an identifier.**

intentionally or accidentally, say, by forgetting to include a declaration. If
we omit the declaration of IdA within the function given in Fig. 4-4, then
the sum is stored in the variable IdA in the main program. Thus executing
the program with the data

```
3.0   4.0   8.0
```

produces

```
The average of 15.0 4.0 8.0
is 5.0
```

Notice that the 3.0 has been overwritten after the calculation but before the
output statement.

A procedure or function declaration may incorporate not only local type
definitions and variable declarations, but also local function and procedure
(see the next subsection) declarations. A subprogram declared within a function

is private to it in the sense that its name (identifies) is known only within the subprogram in which it is declared and not in the main program.

As an example, consider a program to read two values, say $x$ and $y$, and compute

$$f(x, y) = x \times \left[ \sin \left( y + \frac{\pi}{2} \right) + \cos \left( y + \frac{\pi}{2} \right) \right]$$

$$+ (1 - x) \times \left[ \sin \left( y - \frac{\pi}{2} \right) + \cos \left( y - \frac{\pi}{2} \right) \right]$$

We will use the auxilary function

$$g(x) = \sin x + \cos x$$

Thus we can define $f$ in terms of $g$ as

$$f(x, y) = x \times g \left( y + \frac{\pi}{2} \right) + (1 - x) \times g \left( y - \frac{\pi}{2} \right)$$

A program containing a declaration of a function F, and nested within F the declaration of the function G, has the structure illustrated in Fig. 4-5. As in the previous examples, the declaration of function F is contained in the main program between the program's variable declarations and its executable statements (**begin** . . . **end**). Likewise, G is declared within F by placing it between F's variable declarations and its executable statements. The complete program appears in Fig. 4-6. (Although we indicated in Fig. 4-5 where the declarations for function G would be placed, G does not require any local declarations, and therefore, this section is not present within G in Fig. 4-6.)

In this example, the main program declares identifiers Pi, A, B, C, and F; these are a constant, three variables, and a function, respectively. Within the executable statements, these identifiers have the declared meanings. In turn, within the function F, the identifiers X, Y, A, T1, T2, and G are declared; these are two parameters, three variables, and a function. These particular identifiers may be used within the executable statements of function F. They are *not* available outside of F, say, in the main program. Notice that identifier A has been redeclared to represent a real variable within F; this is, as before, a different variable than A represents in the main program. The constant Pi, variables B and C, and even the function F itself are available for use within F because none of these identifiers has been redeclared.

Within function G, the identifier X is redeclared as a parameter. The identifiers Y, A, T1, T2, and G from F and Pi, B, C, and F from the main program are available in addition to the local variable X. These rules on the availability of identifiers are called *scope rules*.

It should be noted that we have sacrificed readability considerably in this example for the sake of illustrating the concept of local and global

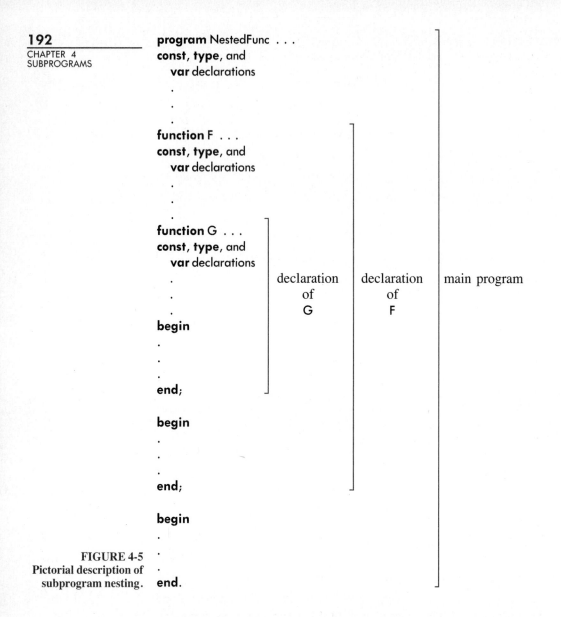

**FIGURE 4-5**
**Pictorial description of**
**subprogram nesting.**

identifiers. We again emphasize that identifiers should be chosen with some mnemonic significance. That is, they should describe the actual elements in a given application. In the context of this example, however, it makes multiple use of the same identifier unlikely.

Recall that in Chap. 2 we described reserved identifiers (**and, array,** etc.) and predefined identifiers (for example, the names of built-in functions such as abs, sqrt, and sin). The reserved words may not be used for purposes other than those defined in Pascal. Predefined identifiers, however, act as if they were declared in a "block" that contains the main program. The scope rule, as described for nested functions and procedures, determines the availability of predefined identifiers. An identifier refers to its built-in

```pascal
program NestedFunc (input, output);
{This program illustrates nested function declarations and local and global
   identifiers.}
const
   Pi = 3.14159;
var
   A, B, C: real;

function F (X, Y: real {Input} ): real;
{This function computes X * (sin (Y + π/2) + cos (Y + π/2)) +
   (1 − X) * (sin (Y − π/2) + cos (Y − π/2)).}
var
   A, T1, T2: real;

function G (X: real {Input} ): real;
{This function computes sin (X) + cos (X).}
begin     {Statements of G}
   {Perform computation}
   G := sin (X) + cos (X)
end;

begin     {Statements of F}
   {Perform computations}
   A := Y + Pi/2;
   T1 := X + G (A);
   A := Y − Pi/2;
   T2 := (1 − X) * G (A);
   F := T1 + T2
end;

begin {Statements of main program}
   {Step 1: Input data}
   read (A, B);

   {Step 2: Call function to compute result}
   C := F (A, B);

   {Step 3: Display result}
   writeln (C)
end.
```

**FIGURE 4-6**
**Example of**
**nested subprograms.**

meaning, provided that it has not been redeclared in any of the nested
blocks (program, procedure, and/or function) surrounding the identifier's
occurrence. Thus programmers may redeclare these identifiers for their own
use. Note that the predefined use thereby becomes unavailable. For example,
a program that redefines the name **cos** as a variable could not use the built-
in cosine (**cos**) function.

A function invocation or call is indicated by the presence of the function name (with appropriate arguments) in an expression. As the call is processed, a correspondence is established between the arguments of the call and the parameters specified in the function definition. In this way the values to be used in this particular execution of the function are established. Following execution of the statements in the function using these values, the *function value* is returned to the point of call.

The functions illustrated in this section all resulted in numerical values being returned to the point of call. We can refer to such functions as "numerical-valued." Since a function serves in an expression just as a regular variable, we emphasize that it is equally important that it have an associated type. We have seen that this type must be specified as part of the declaration of the function. Pascal allows functions to return only simple types (see Sec. 3-6 and Fig. 3-41) and pointer types (see Sec. 8-8). Notice that the type of a function refers to the value returned, not to the types of its parameters or arguments.

The use of subprograms allows programmers certain useful capabilities. They are able, for one thing, to extend the set of nonprimitive operations. Also, in the design of programs, programmers are able to specify *what* to do with a value (by simply indicating that a subprogram will be called) before concerning themselves with *how* that value is obtained. That decision can be deferred until the appropriate subprogram is actually designed. This ability to postpone commitments, as we will see later, can be an important factor in managing the complexity of the programming task.

## EXERCISES 4-2

1. Write a function that takes a parameter $x$ ($x \neq 0$) and returns the following value:

$$\frac{1}{x^5 \left( \dfrac{e^{1.432}}{x} - 1 \right)}$$

Recall that the built-in function **exp** can be used: **exp (1.432)** $= e^{1.432}$. Write a program to test this function by reading values for $x$ and displaying the function's result for each.

2. Write a function with two parameters, $x$ and $n$, that returns the following:

$$x + \frac{x^n}{n} - \frac{x^{n+2}}{n+2} \qquad \text{if } x \geq 0$$

$$-\frac{x^{n-1}}{n-1} + \frac{x^{n+1}}{n+1} \qquad \text{if } x < 0$$

Write a program to test this function.

3. (a) Pascal has two built-in functions for converting real values to integer. The function trunc takes a real parameter and returns the integer equivalent of the real number with everything to the right of the decimal discarded. The function round takes a real parameter and returns the integer equivalent of the real rounded off to the nearest integer number. Although convenient for programming, round is actually redundant. Write a function to perform the action of round using trunc.

(b) The function floor(x) is defined as the largest integer value not exceeding x. This is not quite the same as the trunc function. For example, floor(4.72) is 4, but floor(−16.8) is −17. Use the built-in functions listed in Chap. 2 to write a function to compute floor(x).

Test each of these functions with various arguments.

4. Write a function to take as parameters the lengths of three sides of a triangle (S1, S2, and S3) and return the area of the triangle according to the formula

$$\text{Area} = \sqrt{T(T - S1)(T - S2)(T - S3)}$$

where

$$T = \frac{S1 + S2 + S3}{2}$$

Write a program that tests your function.

★ 5. The special constant $\pi$ plays an important role in mathematics. It is not surprising that there exist many methods of achieving numeric approximations to $\pi$. Many of these involve operations on an infinite series. Three such methods are the following:

(a) $\pi = 4 \sum_{i=0}^{\infty} \frac{(-1)^i}{2i + 1} = 4\left(1 - \frac{1}{3} + \frac{1}{5} - \frac{1}{7} + \cdots\right)$

(b) $\pi = \sqrt{\sum_{i=1}^{\infty} \frac{6}{(i)^2}} = \sqrt{6 + \frac{6}{2^2} + \frac{6}{3^2} + \frac{6}{4^2} + \frac{6}{5^2} + \cdots}$

(c) $\pi = 4 \times \frac{2}{3} \times \frac{4}{3} \times \frac{4}{5} \times \frac{6}{5} \times \frac{6}{7} \times \frac{8}{7} \times \cdots$

For practical computations, infinite-series calculations must be terminated after a finite number of terms, at the expense of accuracy in the result. Write functions to calculate $\pi$ according to each of the preceding methods. Each function is to accept, as a parameter, the value N indicating the number of terms to take part in the computation. Write a program to test the three functions. This program should read a value for N and print the three values for $\pi$ and their pairwise differences.

**6.** Write a function that takes an integer number as an argument and returns the number of digits in its decimal representation. For example, the integer **1023** has four digits.

## 4-3 PROCEDURES

Although the function is a very useful programming tool, its abilities are somewhat restricted. In some situations, we may wish to specify an operation that is not conveniently stated as part of an expression. Such operations as the sorting of a list of words or the solution of a system of simultaneous linear equations have a much broader scope, and the returning of a single value for use in an expression would be somewhat artificial.

For these reasons, we introduce a second form of subprogram, which we will call a *procedure*. Although similar in most respects to the function, there are two important differences.

*1.* A procedure is invoked by means of a special statement, the *procedure statement*. (Do not confuse the procedure statement, which causes execution of the statements of a procedure, with the procedure declaration, which happens to begin with the reserved word **procedure**. To emphasize that the procedure statement invokes, or *calls*, the procedure, the procedure statement is sometimes referred to as the *procedure call statement*.) Execution of the procedure statement results in execution of the call*ing* routine being suspended and control passing to the call*ed* routine or procedure. Following execution of the steps of the procedure, control returns to the calling routine at the statement *immediately following* the procedure call statement. Execution of the calling routine then continues from this point.

*2.* There is no single returned value as in the case of a function. Any values that are to be returned by a procedure are returned through the parameter list. Any number of values can be returned.

The example in Fig. 4-7 illustrates the definition and use of a simple procedure. The procedure performs a division given two integer values and returns as results the quotient and the remainder, again integers. (We have chosen to allow the checking built into the program by the Pascal compiler to produce an error message if divide by zero is attempted. Consider how this check could be incorporated into the procedure if the compiler-supplied check were not satisfactory for the application in which the procedure is used.)

An examination of the code for the procedure **Divide** reveals that of its four parameters, two (**Dividend** and **Divisor**) cause information to be transferred from the point of call to the procedure (i.e., they are input parameters) and two (**Quotient** and **Remainder**) cause information to be transferred

```
program TestProc (output);
{This program illustrates the use of the procedure Divide.}
var
    Val1, Val2: integer;        {Test values for the procedure}
    Res1, Res2: integer;        {Results from first call}
    Res3, Res4: integer;        {Results from second call}

procedure Divide (
    Dividend, Divisor: integer;    {Input}
    var Quotient,
        Remainder: integer         {Output}
                    );
{Given two integer values, this procedure computes their quotient and
    remainder.}

begin
    {Step 1: Perform integer division}
    Quotient : = Dividend div Divisor;

    {Step 2: Determine remainder; this is slightly different from mod}
    Remainder : = Dividend — Quotient * Divisor
end; {Divide}

{Main Program}
begin
    {Step 1: Initialize test values}
    Val1 : = 5;
    Val2 : = 3;

    {Step 2: Invoke procedure for division}
    Divide (Val1, Val2, Res1, Res2);

    {Step 3: Display results}
    writeln (Res1, Res2);

    {Step 4: Invoke procedure a second time}
    Divide (Val1 * Val2 — 1, Val2 + 1, Res3, Res4);

    {Step 5: Display results}
    writeln (Res3, Res4)
end.
```

**FIGURE 4-7**
**Example of the**
**use of a procedure.**

in the opposite direction—from the procedure to the point of call (i.e., they are output parameters). We will soon see that some parameters can, in fact, be vehicles for information transfer in both directions. Pascal's mechanism for argument/parameter correspondence is sufficiently flexible to handle all possibilities. We have included comments in the *procedure heading* indicating the input and output parameters. The declaration of the output parameters also was preceded by the reserved word **var**. The need for its inclusion for output parameters will be described in the next section.

Let us examine what happens on the first call to procedure Divide (step 2 of program TestProc), noting in particular the correspondence between *arguments* and *parameters*. The first two arguments here are Val1 and Val2, which correspond positionally to Dividend and Divisor, respectively, in the procedure definition. These are *input arguments*, since the procedure requires them to arrive with values so that step 1 can be successfully executed. For this reason, they must have values at the time of the call, which they do (5 and 3, respectively). The last two arguments of the procedure statement, Res1 and Res2, will receive values from the procedure (via Quotient and Remainder). We can refer to these as *output arguments*.

As the first call is processed, the correspondence between arguments and parameters is effected as shown in Table 4-1. The steps of the procedure are executed accordingly, and following execution of the last statement in step 2 of the procedure, control returns to the point of call. The subsequent writeln statement then causes the following line to be displayed:

1    2

The procedure is called again in step 4 of the program TestProc, with a different pair of input arguments, Val1 * Val2 − 1 and Val2 + 1, and different output arguments, Res3 and Res4. Although the input arguments are somewhat more elaborate in this case, the correspondence with parameters proceeds in the same fashion. This time the correspondence established between arguments and parameters is as shown in Table 4-2. This time the following line is displayed after control returns from the procedure:

3    2

As was suggested, parameters in procedures are not always exclusively *input* or *output*. In many cases, the same parameter will act in both

**TABLE 4-1**

| Argument | | Parameter |
|---|---|---|
| Val1 | corresponds to | Dividend |
| Val2 | corresponds to | Divisor |
| Res1 | corresponds to | Quotient |
| Res2 | corresponds to | Remainder |

**TABLE 4-2**

199

4-3
PROCEDURES

| Argument | | Parameter |
|---|---|---|
| Val1 * Val2 − 1 | corresponds to | Dividend |
| Val2 + 1 | corresponds to | Divisor |
| Res3 | corresponds to | Quotient |
| Res4 | corresponds to | Remainder |

capacities. As an input parameter, it transfers information to the procedure, but, in fact, it receives a new value from the procedure that it transfers back to the point of call, thus serving also as an output parameter. Such a parameter is called an *input/output parameter*. Consider the procedure in Fig. 4-8 to interchange the values of two variables. Clearly, Val1 and Val2 serve as both input parameters and output parameters in this example. They bring the original values to the procedure but also take the new values back.

The program in Fig. 4-9 uses the procedure Exchange to sort three numbers in ascending order. Examine it carefully. Let us trace the execution of this program on some sample data, paying particular attention to the action of the procedure Exchange. Assume that we have the following three sets of input data:

| | | |
|---|---|---|
| 3 | 7 | 5 |
| 10 | 8 | 2 |
| 6 | 8 | 12   (Note that this set is already sorted.) |

```
procedure Exchange (
    var Val1: integer;    {Input/output, first value}
    var Val2: integer     {Input/output, second value}
                   );
{Given two integer arguments, this procedure interchanges their values.}
var
    Temp: integer;    {For saving one value during exchange}
begin
    {Step 1: Save the Val1 value}
    Temp : = Val1;

    {Step 2: Val1 takes on the value of Val2}
    Val1 : = Val2;

    {Step 3: Val2 takes on the previous value of Val1}
    Val2 : = Temp
end; {Exchange}
```

**FIGURE 4-8**
**Procedure to exchange**
**two values.**

```
program Sort3 (input, output);
```
{Given three integer numbers, this program sorts them into ascending (increasing) order.}

```
var
   First, Second, Third: integer; {Values to be sorted}

procedure Exchange (
      var Val1: integer;    {Input/output, first value}
      var Val2: integer     {Input/output, second value}
                     );
```
{Given two integer arguments, this procedure interchanges their values.}
```
var
   Temp: integer;      {For saving one value during exchange}
begin
   {Step 1: Save the Val1 value}
   Temp : = Val1;

   {Step 2: Val1 takes on the value of Val2}
   Val1 : = Val2;

   {Step 3: Val2 takes on the previous value of Val1}
   Val2 : = Temp
end; {Exchange}

begin
   {Step 1: Input the values}
   read (First, Second, Third);

   {Step 2: Sort by stepwise comparison}
   if First > Second
   then Exchange (First, Second);
   if Second > Third
   then Exchange (Second, Third);    {Largest value is now in Third}
   if First > Second
   then Exchange (First, Second);    {Smallest value is now in First}

   {Step 3: Display sorted values}
   writeln (First, Second, Third)
end.
```

**FIGURE 4-9**
**Example of the use of a procedure with input/output parameters.**

Table 4-3 shows the succession of values taken by the variables First, Second, and Third as these three data sets are processed. The actual exchanges are indicated by arrows. Case 2 shows the maximum possible number of exchanges; case 3, the minimum number.

Let us examine in detail the action of the procedure on the second set

**TABLE 4-3**

| Case | First | Second | Third | Output | | |
|------|-------|--------|-------|--------|---|---|
| 1 | 3 | 7 | 5 | | | |
| | 3 | 5 | 7 | | | |
| | | | | 3 | 5 | 7 |
| 2 | 10 | 8 | 2 | | | |
| | 8 | 10 | 2 | | | |
| | 8 | 2 | 10 | | | |
| | 2 | 8 | 10 | | | |
| | | | | 2 | 8 | 10 |
| 3 | 6 | 8 | 12 | | | |
| | | | | 6 | 8 | 12 |

of data, involving the greatest number of exchanges. We leave the other cases as an exercise. The initial values of First, Second, and Third are 10, 8, and 2, respectively. Since First $>$ Second, the first call to the Exchange procedure is with argument values of 10 and 8. These become associated with parameter Val1 and Val2, respectively. The procedure then interchanges these values so that immediately prior to returning, Val1 has the value 8 and Val2 the value 10. Since Val1 and Val2 correspond to arguments First and Second, respectively, upon return to the point of call, First has the value 8 and Second, the new value 10. As a result of these actions Second $>$ Third now (10 $>$ 2); thus a second call is required to interchange these values. On return from the second call, Second has the value 2 and Third, the value 10. The largest of the values is now in the variable Third. Finally, since First $>$ Second now (8 $>$ 2), a third call is required to complete the sort. On return, First has the value 2 and Second, the value 8. The action of these calls, showing the argument-parameter correspondence and the transfer of values between calling routine and procedure, is summarized in Fig. 4-10.

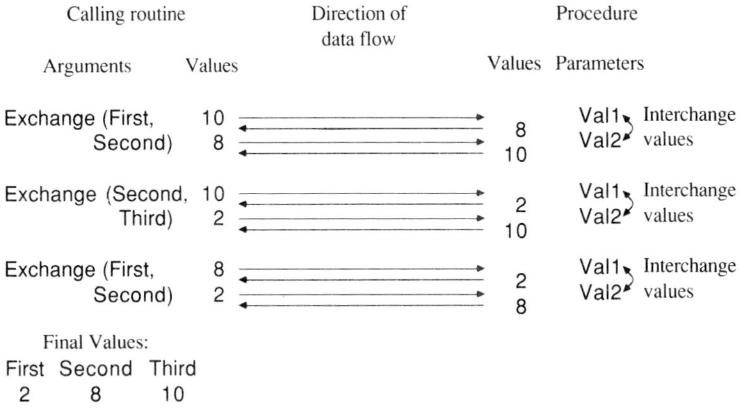

**FIGURE 4-10**
**Argument-parameter correspondence.**

# EXERCISES 4-3

1. Write a procedure to find the maximum range between values in a data collection, that is, the largest value minus the smallest value.

★ 2. Kiddies Candy Store sells all its merchandise for a price of $1 or less. Assume that all customers pay for each purchase with a $1 bill. Design a procedure that takes as a parameter the purchase price of an article and prints the number of each type of coin to be given in change so that the smallest number of coins is returned. For example, if the purchase price is 63¢, the change will be 1 quarter, 1 dime, and 2 pennies.

★ 3. A program was developed in Sec. 3-8.2 to compute and print monthly mortgage payments. Design a procedure with three input parameters:

Principal: real;     {Amount of the principal}
Term: integer;     {Number of years for the mortgage}
IntRate: real;     {Yearly interest rate}

The procedure is to compute and return to the point of call, via an output parameter, the monthly mortgage payment, calculated as in Sec. 3-8.2.

★ 4. One of the earliest applications of computers was the calculation of shell trajectories. If a shell is fired with an initial velocity $V$ (ft/s) at an angle of inclination $A$ (radians), its position in the vertical $x$, $y$ plane at time $t$ (seconds) is calculated from the following:

$$x = (V \cos A)t$$

$$y = (V \sin A)\, t - \frac{1}{2} g t^2$$

where $0 < A < \pi/2$ and $g = 32$ ft/s$^2$. Design a procedure with parameters $A$ and $V$ that will display the $x$, $y$ coordinates at intervals of 0.01 s for a particular firing, terminating the list when the shell hits the ground. Write a program to test this procedure for different values of $A$ and $V$.

★★ 5. The Gloucestershire Jockey Club's payroll has on it many part-time employees. When the payroll is processed, a check is issued for an employee only if the company owes that employee over $200 or if the employee has worked 20 or more hours since the last payroll run. Write a program to print a payroll report. Data supplied for each employee will consist of the employee's identification number (Number), the amount owed the employee from the previous payroll run (AmountOwing), the employee's hourly wage (HourlyWage), and the number of hours worked since the last payroll run (HoursWorked). Use a procedure to do the calculations for the payroll report. The parameters to this procedure will be AmountOwing, an input/output parameter (since it must be updated), HourlyWage, an input parameter, and HoursWorked, an input parameter. The report should be similar to the one below.

| Employee No. | Hours Worked | Amount Of Check | Amount Owing |
|---|---|---|---|
| 169468 | 10 | 0.00 | 145.00 |
| 239168 | 30 | 185.00 | 0.00 |

6. Life is hectic in the Computer Science Department. The professors are a harried, overworked, underpaid group of people. They have decided to develop a program to help them schedule contact hours with their students. Each professor has been asked to submit a record of how many first-year, second-year, and upper-year students the professor has this term and how many hours the professor has free for student contact each week. For example,

12 98 79 25 20

is a "workload record" that indicates that professor number 12 (in fact, Professor Bunt) has 98 first-year students, 79 second-year students, 25 upper-year students (third-year, fourth-year, and postgraduate), and 20 hours of contact time available in a week. Since there is less support available to advanced students, they generally require more contact time per student than do junior students. In fact, on average, three times as much time is required per upper-year student than per second-year student; twice as much time is required per second-year student than per first-year student.

Since it is well known that computer science professors don't program, you are asked to write a program to read a set of workload records for the 25 members of the Department of Computer Science and print out for each professor the number of minutes per student per week that the professor can spend with the first-year students, second-year students, and upper-year students. Use a procedure to do the calculations. Input parameters to this procedure will be the number of students of each level and the number of hours available, and output parameters will be the number of minutes available per student per week for each level of student.

## 4-4   ARGUMENT–PARAMETER CORRESPONDENCE

On each invocation of a procedure or function, a correspondence is established between the arguments of the particular invocation and the parameters of the procedure or function. In this section we discuss the two ways this correspondence is effected in Pascal and comment on the advantages and disadvantages of each.

The most straightforward method of associating arguments with parameters is *pass by value* (sometimes known as *call by value*). As the invocation of the procedure or function is processed, each of the arguments is evaluated. The individual values are then, in effect, assigned to their respective parameters. The parameters behave as if they were local variables, except that they are initialized to the values of the corresponding arguments. It makes no difference whether an argument is a variable, a constant, or an expression; all that matters is that it has a value. This value becomes the value of the corresponding parameter.

Figure 4-11 illustrates the pass-by-value mechanism on a procedure with three parameters. At the time the call statement is processed, each of the arguments of the call is evaluated. The value of the first argument, the variable TVal1, is 3. The value of the second argument, the constant 17, is 17. The value of the third argument, the expression TVal2 $* 2 - 1$, is 11. As execution of the procedure begins, these then become the values of the input parameters Val1, Val2, and Val3, respectively. The procedure then displays 31 as its result.

Although conceptually simple, pass by value has a major implication. Although the parameters receive the values of the arguments, they are in no other way connected to the actual arguments themselves. Changes to the parameters within the procedure do not result in corresponding changes to the arguments. In a sense, the subprogram retains no knowledge of the original arguments. Thus it is impossible to transfer values back to the point of call. In effect, such parameters are useful only as input parameters.

We have already seen cases where we require certain parameters to serve as output parameters or as input/output parameters. Consider, for example, the procedures Divide and Exchange from the previous section. With pass by value it would not be possible for the results to be returned by the

```
program PassValueExample (output);
{This program demonstrates pass-by-value parameters.}
var
   TVal1, TVal2: integer;      {Test values}
procedure PrintSumOf3 (
   Val1, Val2, Val3: integer      {Values to be summed}
                           );
{Given three integer values, this procedure displays their sum.}
begin
   {Display sum}
   writeln (Val1 + Val2 + Val3)
end;

begin
   {Step 1: Initialize variables}
   TVal1 := 3;
   TVal2 := 6;

   {Step 2: Call procedure}
   PrintSumOf3 (TVal1, 17, TVal2 * 2 - 1)
end.
```

**FIGURE 4-11**
**Example of pass-by-value parameters.**

procedure. For this reason, there is another mechanism available for associating arguments with parameters, which is referred to as *pass as variable* (also sometimes known as *call by address* or *call by reference*).

Rather than passing a value for each argument, pass as variable, in effect, passes the actual variable itself, potentially to be modified within the function or procedure. This is done by the compiler by passing the address of the argument. This address refers to the storage area where the argument variable is stored. In Pascal, the argument corresponding to a pass-as-variable parameter must be a variable.

With pass as variable, any reference to the corresponding parameter within the procedure is also a reference to the argument itself, which is, as we shall soon see, a mixed blessing. Pass as variable is illustrated in Fig. 4-12. The program outputs 11.

Although the problem that pass-by-value parameters are "input only" parameters is solved with pass as variable, a new danger is introduced. Consider the program in Fig. 4-13, which invokes a simple function SumToN, for which the processing of the parameter is done as pass as variable.

What values are printed for TVal1 and TVal2? During the processing of the function call, since pass as variable is used, the assignments to the parameter N simultaneously change the value of its corresponding argument. Thus the value of variable TVal1 is decremented by the function from 3

```
program PassVariableExample (output);
{This program demonstrates pass-as-variable parameters.}
var
    TVar: integer;          {Test variable}
procedure Increment (
    var Counter: integer     {Input-output, variable to increment}
                );
{Given an integer variable, this procedure increments its value by one.}
begin
    {Increment the value}
    Counter := Counter + 1
end;

begin
    {Step 1: Initialize}
    TVar := 10;

    {Step 2: Call procedure to increment variable}
    Increment (TVar);

    {Step 3: Display incremented variable}
    writeln (TVar)
end.
```

**FIGURE 4-12**
**Example of**
**pass-by-variable**
**parameters.**

```
program WhatsUp (output);
{This program contains an error. It attempts to display an integer and the
    sum of the integers from 1 to the specified integer.}
var
    TVar1, TVar2: integer;       {Test variables}

    function SumToN (
        var N: integer       {Input, limit value}
                        ): integer;
    {Given an integer, this function returns the sum of the integers from one to
        the given integer.}
    var
        Sum: integer;
    begin
        {Initialize}
        Sum := 0;

        {Engage loop to sum the integers}
        while N > 0 do
            begin
                Sum := Sum + N;
                N := N − 1
            end;
        SumToN := Sum
    end;

begin
    {Step 1: Initialize}
    TVar1 := 3;

    {Step 2: Call function}
    TVar2 := SumToN (TVar1);

    {Step 3: Display integer and sum}
    writeln (TVar1, TVar2)
end.
```

**FIGURE 4-13**
**Example of misuse of
pass-as-variable
parameters.**

to 0. The function returns the value 6, which is assigned to TVal2. The
program therefore prints

0    6

We refer to changes made by a function or procedure to items outside
the function or procedure itself as *side effects*. In some cases, such as the
procedures Divide and Exchange given in the previous section, the side effects
worked to our advantage. In the case of our function SumToN, however, the
side effects produced by the function are surprising and make the operation
of the program more difficult to understand. Side effects should always be

avoided except where they are clearly part of the purpose of a function or procedure. Side effects are avoided by using pass-by-value rather than pass-as-variable parameters and by avoiding use of global variables. Errors resulting from a function or procedure producing unexpected side effects are extremely difficult to locate when such a procedure is part of a very large program.

The use of pass by value prevents this type of side effect from occurring, since the function or procedure has no way of getting at the argument itself—just at its value. In Pascal, the programmer specifies for each parameter how it is to be processed—as pass as variable or pass by value. This is done by preceding the declarations of pass-as-variable parameters with the reserved word **var**. The programmer must ensure that appropriate specifications are made to eliminate possible undesirable side effects.

In this book we shall specify parameters to be *input*, *output*, or *input/output*. An input parameter supplies input to a subprogram. By convention, we will assume that an input parameter is *read-only* and shall refrain from assigning a value to it. Generally, input parameters are passed by value; exceptions will be described in Chap. 5. Output parameters provide output from a subprogram and will be considered *write-only*. Input/output parameters provide both input values to the subprogram and output values from it. Obviously, both output and input/output parameters must be *pass-as-variable* parameters.

In Pascal, we also must consider the restriction on the type of the argument in relation to the type declared for the corresponding parameter. In the case of a pass-by-value parameter, the value of the argument must be *assignment compatible* with the type of the parameter. This implies that if the argument value occurred on the right side of an assignment statement and a variable of the same type as the corresponding parameter occurred on the left, then the assignment would be allowed. For the types defined to this point, the argument and its associated parameter must be of the same type, or the argument must be an integer and its associated parameter real, or the argument and/or its associated parameter must be compatible subrange types. A subrange type is compatible with its host type, and two subranges of the same host type are compatible. If the parameter is a subrange and subrange checking is enabled (see Sec. 3-6), an error will be reported if the value of the argument is out of range for the parameter when the program is run.

A pass-as-variable parameter is more restrictive: the argument and its associated parameter must be of the *same type*. Obviously, it is important to determine when two values are of the same type. Values are provided by constants, variables, and operations on these. Integer, real, character, and Boolean constants supply values of their respective built-in types. Each operator produces a value of one of the built-in types. The only difficult cases occur when programmer-defined types occur.

We have introduced enumerated and subrange types. Each type was specified by a type denoter in a type declaration. A type denoter may be just an identifier, in which case it does not introduce a new type, but rather references some preexisting type. Otherwise, a type denoter introduces a new type, different from every other type, *even if* the two denoters "look the same." Let us study an example. Consider the following type definitions.

```
type
    QuantityType = integer;
    FruitColor = (orange, yellow);
    GradeRange = 1 .. 10;
    QualityRange = GradeRange;
    SizeRange = 1 .. 10;
```

We have introduced five type identifiers: QuantityType specifies the same (built-in) type as integer; FruitColor designates a new enumerated type; GradeRange and QualityRange designate the same subrange type; SizeRange designates a subrange type that is a different type from GradeRange and QualityRange.

These types may then be used to declare variables.

```
var
    I: integer;
    Amount: QuantityType;
    Color: FruitColor;
    Grade: GradeRange;
    Quality: QualityRange;
    Size: SizeRange;
```

Variables I and Amount are both of the built-in type integer; Color is of the enumerated type designated by FruitColor; Grade and Quality are of the same subrange type designated by GradeRange and QualityRange; Size is of the subrange type designated by SizeRange.

These types and variables are now used in a program with procedures:

```
program Test1 . . .
procedure P1 (Arg1: GradeRange);
begin
    .
    .

    .
end;
    .
    .

    .
begin
P1 (Size)
    .
    .

    .
end.
```

Program Test1 is valid because Arg1 is a pass-by-value parameter and the argument type, the type of Size, is assignment compatible with GradeRange, both being subranges of the same host type, namely integer. Consider now the following fragment:

```
program Test2  . . .
procedure P2 (var Arg1: GradeRange);
begin
      .
      .
      .
end;
      .
      .
      .
begin
P2 (Size)
      .
      .
      .
end.
```

Program Test2 is invalid because Arg1 is now a pass-as-variable parameter and the argument (Size) must be of the *same type* as Arg1. Even though both types are a subrange from 1 to 10 of type integer, because of the way they are defined (as type GradeRange and as type SizeRange, respectively), they are not of the same type. (We have used the definition of standard Pascal here. Some Pascal compilers deviate from the standard with respect to two types being the same.)

While generally flexible, there is a restriction on the ordering of the procedure and function declarations within a program. If a program contains declarations of functions F and G and only the main program contains references to the functions, then the declarations may occur in either order. If, however, the function F is also to call the function G, which is permitted, since all identifiers of the main program are available within all functions and procedures contained within the main program, as described in Sec. 4-2, then declaration of G must precede the declaration of F. The general rule states that the declaration of a function or procedure must precede all references or calls to it.

In some cases, a different ordering may be desirable to make a program more readable. Also, there may be no ordering that satisfies the general rule. Suppose, in the preceding example, that function F calls function G *and* that function G calls function F. In such a case, we say that functions F and G are *mutually recursive*. (Recursive functions are described in Sec. 4-5.) To accommodate such a situation, Pascal allows the *forward declaration* of a function or procedure. The declaration is split into two parts. The first part consists of the procedure name, parameters, and types (and result type for a function). This is followed by the *directive* forward instead of the procedure body. The body occurs later, preceded only by **procedure** (or **function**) and its name. The parameters and function result type are not repeated. Figure 4-14 presents an example of the use of a forward declaration.

We close this section with the syntax diagrams for procedure and function declarations (Figs. 4-15 and 4-16), parameters (Fig. 4-17), directive statements (Fig. 4-18), and procedure statements (Fig. 4-19). The syntax diagram for function references was given in Fig. 2-34.

```
program ForwardDec1 (input, output);
{This program illustrates use of a forward declaration  for a procedure.}
var
    N: integer;      {Input value}

procedure OutVal (V: integer {Input, value to be displayed} );
{This procedure displays a value.}
forward;

procedure Compute (X: integer {Input} );
{This procedure computes 3 * X + 5 and displays the result.}
begin
   {Compute and display}
   OutVal (3 * X + 5)
end;

procedure OutVal;
{Second part of forward declared procedure OutVal.}
var
    J: integer; {Included to illustrate where variable declarations
                    are located.}
begin
   {Display value}
   writeln ('Value☐ = ☐', V)
end;

begin
   {Step 1: Input data}
   read (N);

   {Step 2: Display value read}
   OutVal (N);

   {Step 3: Compute and display result}
   Compute (N)
end.
```

**FIGURE 4-14**
**Example of the use of**
**a forward declaration.**

**FIGURE 4-15** Syntax diagram for procedure declaration.

**procedure declaration**

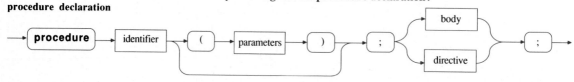

function declaration

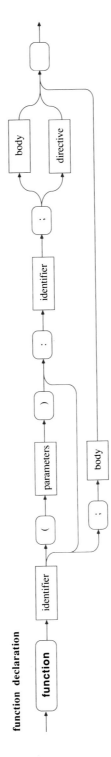

FIGURE 4-16 Syntax diagram for function declaration.

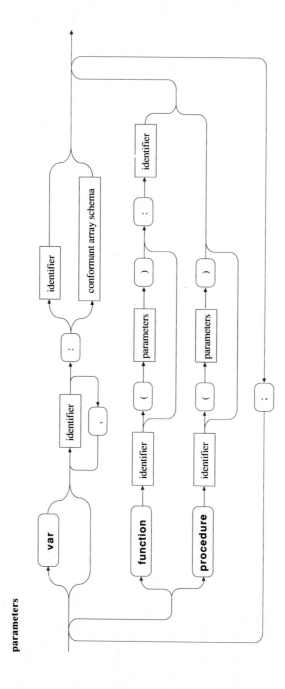

**FIGURE 4-17** Syntax diagram for parameters.

**directive**

**FIGURE 4-18**   Syntax diagram for directive statement.

**procedure statement**

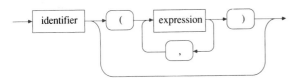

**FIGURE 4-19**   Syntax diagram for procedure statement.

# EXERCISES 4-4

1.  Consider the following:

    ```
    program A (output);
    var
        I, J: integer;
    procedure C (P, Q: integer);
    begin
        Q := I * P + Q;
        P := I;
        writeln (Q, P, J)
    end;
    procedure B (L, M: integer);
    begin
        I := 3;
        C (L, M)
    end;
    begin
        I := 10;
        J := 1;
        B (J, I)
    end.
    ```

    Give the output of program A when the arguments are passed (*a*) by value
    and (*b*) as variable (assume appropriate **var** prefixes for the procedure
    parameters).

2.  Consider the following:

    ```
    program Main (output);
    var
        X, Y, W, Z, T: integer;
    ```

```
procedure Exam (X, Y: integer);
begin
   Z := Y + 6;
   W := X * Z;
   X := X + Y;
   writeln (W, X, Y, Z)
end.
begin
   X := 2;
   Y := 1;
   W := 3;
   T := X + W;
   Exam (Y, T);
   writeln (W, X, Y)
end.
```

Give the output of program Main when the arguments are passed:

(*a*) By value.

(*b*) As variable (assume appropriate **var** prefixes for the procedure parameters).

3. Consider the following program:

```
program A (output);
var
   I, J, K: integer;
procedure C (P, Q: integer);
begin
   Q := I * P + Q;
   P := 9;
   writeln (Q, I, J)
end;
procedure B (L, M: integer);
begin
   I := 2;
   C (L, M)
end;
begin
   K := 7;
   I := 7;
   J := 1;
   B (J, K);
   writeln (I, J, K)
end.
```

Give the output of program A when the parameters are passed:

(*a*) By value.

(*b*) As variable (again assume the appropriate **var** prefix for procedure parameters).

A very useful concept in problem solving is an instance of a procedure calling another procedure. This concept is one that presents no particular problems for the programmer. In this subsection we consider a special case of this facility in which a procedure is allowed to call itself. Such a procedure is said to be *recursive*.

We will introduce the concept of recursion through several examples. Although the technique can be applied to both procedures and functions, it is somewhat simpler to illustrate with functions. Later chapters, however, contain several examples of recursion of both types of subprograms. More details of recursion will be discussed in Chap. 8.

An algorithm was developed in earlier chapters to compute the factorial of a number $n$. You will recall that the factorial of $n$, written $n!$, was defined as $n(n-1)(n-2) \ldots (1)$. The algorithm calculated each successive multiplier by subtracting 1 from the value used previously (starting with $n$), computing products until the multiplier became 1. This approach is said to be *iterative* because it iterates over successive values of the multiplier.

Consider the following alternative definition of factorial:

$$n! = \begin{cases} 1 & \text{if } n = 0 \\ n(n-1)! & \text{if } n > 0 \end{cases}$$

In this formulation, factorial is defined in terms of itself. On the surface, this may appear to be a case of circular definition, but a quick check shows that this is not so, because of the special case when $n = 0$. Let us consider a simple example, $3!$. Since $n > 0$, we apply the second line of the definition, to get

$3! = 3 * 2!$

The right-hand side, however, is not completely processed yet. Continuing, we get

| | |
|---|---|
| $3! = 3 * 2!$ | (Use line 2 of the definition) |
| $= 3 * 2 * 1!$ | (Use line 2 of the definition) |
| $= 3 * 2 * 1 * 0!$ | (Use line 2 of the definition) |
| $= 3 * 2 * 1 * 1$ | (Use line 1 of the definition) |
| $= 6$ | |

Observe that the calculation is complete when we have processed the case of $0!$ using line 1 of the definition. Thus, although the definition may appear to be circular, we can see that it is not, since it does terminate with the correct value of the factorial. This is, in fact, a recursive approach to the calculation of factorial.

Factorial is perhaps the most widely used example of a problem that is amenable to recursive formulation. Clearly, a special type of problem is needed. There are other good examples, however, for which a recursive formulation is appropriate. Before considering these, let us first consider the program specification of factorial defined recursively. The function FactRecursive follows almost immediately from the definition and is given in Fig. 4-20.

As you can see, this program is very concise. Compare it with the iterative program that requires more steps. There are evidently clear advantages for the programmer if a recursive formulation can be found for a problem. This is not to say, however, that the recursive program will execute any faster. The same computation is required, as the preceding example shows; it is simply expressed in a different way. We will defer discussion of how recursion is actually done by the computer until Chap. 8. Figure 4-21 shows the function calls required to compute FactRecursive(4) and the manner in which the results are returned as the computation proceeds. Notice that with the exception of the bottom line [FactRecursive(0)], the value of no line can be obtained until the result of the line below is received. Thus we work down a chain of calls to FactRecursive(0), which we call the *base value*, at which point no further calls are required, and then back up the chain of returns. The *depth of recursion* refers to the number of times the function or procedure is called recursively in the process of evaluating a given argument or set of arguments. For FactRecursive(4), the depth of recursion is seen to be 4.

As mentioned, factorial is only one example of a problem that can be formulated recursively; there are many other interesting examples. We now consider two of them: the computation of Fibonacci numbers and the computation of the greatest common divisor of two numbers.

The *Fibonacci series* was originally conceived by a thirteenth-century Italian merchant and mathematician Leonardo of Pisa, nicknamed Fibonacci, as a model for the breeding of rabbits. This particular series turns up again and again not only in mathematics and computer science, but also in various biological phenomena.

The series itself is very simple:

$$1, 1, 2, 3, 5, 8, 13, 21, \ldots$$

The first two terms are 1 and 1; each subsequent term is calculated as the sum of the two terms immediately preceding it. In general, $t_i = t_{i-1} + t_{i-2}$.

The problem of finding the $n$th Fibonacci number has a clear recursive formulation, which is

```
function FactRecursive (N: integer {Input} ): integer;
{Given a nonnegative integer, this function computes the factorial
  recursively.}
begin
  {Apply recursive definition}
  if N = 0
  then FactRecursive := 1
  else FactRecursive := N*FactRecursive (N − 1)
end;
```

**FIGURE 4-20**
**Recursive factorial function.**

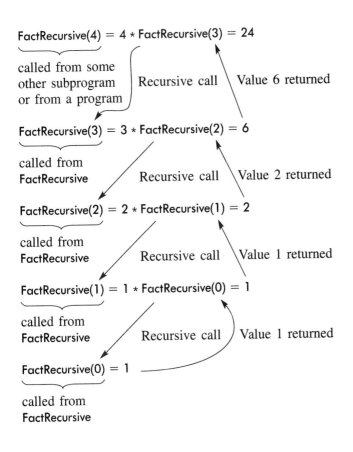

FactRecursive(4) = 4 * FactRecursive(3) = 24

called from some
other subprogram
or from a program

Recursive call    Value 6 returned

FactRecursive(3) = 3 * FactRecursive(2) = 6

called from
FactRecursive

Recursive call    Value 2 returned

FactRecursive(2) = 2 * FactRecursive(1) = 2

called from
FactRecursive

Recursive call    Value 1 returned

FactRecursive(1) = 1 * FactRecursive(0) = 1

called from
FactRecursive

Recursive call    Value 1 returned

FactRecursive(0) = 1

called from
FactRecursive

**FIGURE 4-21**
**Trace of recursive**
**factorial function.**

$$\text{Fibonacci}(N) = \begin{cases} \text{Fibonacci}(N-1) + \text{Fibonacci}(N-2) & \text{if } N > 2 \\ 1 & \text{if } N = 2 \\ 1 & \text{if } N = 1 \end{cases}$$

The recursive function Fibonacci follows directly from this definition and is presented in Fig. 4-22.

Since the function contains possibly two recursive calls, the execution trace is more complex than that for the recursive factorial. A value is obtained for the first recursive call by the same technique of following a chain of calls down to a base value and then coming back up with returned values. The process then repeats for the second recursive call. We leave this trace as an exercise.

A well-known algorithm for finding the greatest common divisor of two integers is *Euclid's algorithm*. The greatest common divisor function is defined by the following:

$$\text{GCD}(m, n) = \begin{cases} \text{GCD}(n, m) & \text{if } n > m \\ m & \text{if } n = 0 \\ \text{GCD}(n, \textbf{mod}(m, n)) & \text{if } n > 0 \end{cases}$$

where the **mod** function returns the remainder of dividing m by n. As an example, let us compute GCD(20, 6). Using the previous definition, we get

**function** Fibonacci (N: integer {Input} ): integer;
{Given a positive integer N, this function recursively computes the Nth
  Fibonacci number.}
**begin**
  {Apply recursive definition}
  **if** N = 1
  **then** Fibonacci : = 1
  **else**
    **if** N = 2
    **then** Fibonacci : = 1
    **else** Fibonacci : = Fibonacci (N − 1) + Fibonacci (N − 2)
**end**;

**FIGURE 4-22**
**Recursive Fibonacci**
**number function.**

| | | |
|---|---|---|
| GCD(20, 6) | = GCD(6, **mod**(20, 6)) | (Use line 3 of the definition) |
| | = GCD (6, 2) | (Since **mod**(20, 6) = 2) |
| GCD(6, 2) | = GCD(2, **mod**(6, 2)) | (Use line 3 of the definition) |
| | = GCD (2, 0) | (Since **mod**(6, 2) = 0) |
| GCD(2, 0) | = 2 | (Use line 2 of the definition) |

Therefore, GCD(20, 6) = 2. The recursive function GCD follows directly from
its definition and is given in Fig. 4-23.

In this section we have introduced the concept of recursion and have
given three examples of recursively defined functions. Not all programming
languages allow functions to be recursive. Although the formulation may
be somewhat awkward, it is possible to program any recursive problem by
an iterative method. Recursion does require some special sophistication to
implement, as we shall see in Chap. 8, and as a result, it is sometimes not
done. Nevertheless, it stands as an important concept of programming and
computer science in general, and one with which you should be familiar.

**function** GCD (
    M: integer;     {Input}
    N: integer     {Input}
         ): integer;
{Given two nonnegative integers, this function computes the greatest common divisor by a recursive implementation of the Euclidean algorithm.}
**begin**
  {Apply recursive definition}
  **if** N > M
  **then** GCD : = GCD (N, M)
  **else**
    **if** N = 0
    **then** GCD : = M
    **else** GCD : = GCD (N, M **mod** N)
**end**;

**FIGURE 4-23**
**Recursive function for**
**Euclidean algorithm.**

1. Trace the function **Fibonacci** (as was done in Fig. 4-21) for **N** = 4.

2. Obtain a trace (as was done in Fig. 4-21) for **GCD(20, 6)**.

## 4-6  APPLICATIONS

We conclude this chapter with three applications that illustrate the use of subprograms. The first involves the solution of quadratic equations. The second relates to the calculation of depreciation in the value of an item. The third, and final, application deals with the calculation of payroll.

### 4-6.1  SOLVING A QUADRATIC EQUATION

Finding the roots of a quadratic equation means determining those values of the free variable (say, $x$) for which the equation has the value 0. Since this calculation is used frequently in various types of numerical applications, it would be wise to write a reusable procedure. Therefore, our solution to this problem will be in the form of a procedure that can be called from a main program.

There are several ways to solve this problem, yielding either exact solutions or approximations. In this application we are seeking exact solutions.

A quadratic equation written in general form as

$$ax^2 + bx + c = 0$$

may have no roots, one root, two roots, or an infinite number of roots. The latter possibility occurs only when each of the coefficients $a$, $b$, and $c$ equals 0. Normally, if we were doing such a calculation by hand, we could arrive at a solution "by inspection." In other words, if we were given the quadratic equation

$$0x^2 + 0x + 0 = 0$$

we would immediately recognize that there is an infinite number of roots to the equation (that is, any $x$ will do). When designing an algorithm, or program, however, we cannot expect a correct answer to be given for the "obvious" cases unless we explicitly account for them in the logic of the algorithm. For this reason, it is wise to outline every situation that may occur before we embark on a formulation of the solution.

In solving a quadratic equation, we make use of the familiar formula

$$r = \frac{-b \pm \sqrt{b^2 - 4ac}}{2a}$$

where $r$ denotes a root, and $a$, $b$, and $c$ are, as before, the coefficients.

Notice that if $a = 0$, this formula cannot be used, so it is necessary to determine what occurs when $a = 0$ (that is, $bx + c = 0$). In this case, as mentioned before, if $b = 0$ and $c = 0$, then there is an infinite number of roots. If $b = 0$ and $c \neq 0$, then there are no roots. And finally, if $b \neq 0$, then there is one root $r = -(c/b)$.

For all other cases, we can use the *discriminant* $b^2 - 4ac$ to determine the number of roots. Three situations may arise:

*1.* If the discriminant $> 0$, then there are two real roots.

*2.* If the discriminant $= 0$, then there is one real root.

*3.* If the discriminant $< 0$, then there are no real roots.

In the first two cases, the formula given earlier can be used to calculate the roots.

We would like our procedure to take as input three parameters—the coefficients A, B, and C—and print out the root(s) of the equation

$$Ax^2 + Bx + C = 0$$

or a message if the number of roots is 0 or infinity.

We begin by giving a simple function (Fig. 4-24) to compute the discriminant of a quadratic. This will form part of the complete solution. We present the complete procedure Roots in Fig. 4-25.

### 4-6.2   CALCULATING DEPRECIATION

A popular method of computing depreciation is known as the *declining-balance method*. The first-year depreciation is applied to the initial cost of the item; in subsequent years, the amount of depreciation is based on the declining book value of the item. In this application, we want to design a procedure that will print the depreciation table over the lifetime of an item.

In order to produce the specified table, we will need to know the initial cost of the item and its anticipated lifetime. Then we can calculate the first-year depreciation as follows:

$$\text{Depreciation}_1 = \frac{\text{cost of item}}{\text{anticipated lifetime}}$$

```
function Discriminant (X, Y, Z: real {Input} ): real;
{Given the three coefficients of a quadratic equation, this function computes
    the discriminant.}
begin
    {Compute discriminant}
    Discriminant := sqr (Y) − 4.0 ∗ X ∗ Z
end;
```

**FIGURE 4-24**
**Discriminant function.**

```
procedure Roots (
    A, B, C: real      {Input, quadratic coeficients}
                  );
{Given the coefficients of a quadratic equation A * sqr (x) + B * x + C = 0, this
    procedure determines its roots. If no roots exist, or if an infinite number
    of roots exist, a message is displayed; otherwise the roots are displayed.}
var
    Dis: real;     {Discriminant}

{Place function Discriminant here}
begin
    {Step 1: Display heading}
    writeln ('Roots for A = □', A:1:2, '□B = □', B:1:2, '□C = □', C:1:2);

    {Step 2: Find roots when A = 0}
    if A = 0
    then
        if B = 0
        then
            if C = 0      {All three values are 0}
            then writeln ('Any X is a root')
            else {A = 0, B = 0, C <> 0}
                writeln ('There are no real roots')
        else {A = 0, B <> 0}
            writeln ('There is one real root: □', − C/B:8:2)

    {Step 3: Find roots when A <> 0}
    else begin
            Dis := Discriminant (A, B, C);
            if Dis < 0
            then writeln ('There are no real roots')
            else
                if Dis = 0
                then writeln ('There is one real root:□', − B/(2 * A):8:2 )
                else writeln ('There are two real roots:□',
                        (− B + sqrt (Dis))/(2 * A):8:2, 'and',
                        (− B − sqrt (Dis))/(2 * A):8:2)
        end
end;
```

FIGURE 4-25
Procedure to display
roots of a quadratic.

After the first year, the book value of the item will be

$$\text{Book value}_1 = \text{cost of item} - \text{depreciation}_1$$

In the second year, our calculations will be

$$\text{Depreciation}_2 = \frac{\text{book value}_1}{\text{anticipated lifetime}}$$

$$\text{Book value}_2 = \text{book value}_1 - \text{depreciation}_2$$

The method proceeds in this manner until the end of the item's lifetime is reached. For example, suppose that a small computer system, purchased for $250,000, is to be depreciated over 5 years using the declining-balance method. The amount of depreciation for each of the 5 years is given in the following table:

| Year | Depreciation | Book Value |
|------|-------------|------------|
| 0    |             | $250,000   |
| 1    | $50,000     | 200,000    |
| 2    | 40,000      | 160,000    |
| 3    | 32,000      | 128,000    |
| 4    | 25,600      | 102,400    |
| 5    | 20,480      | 81,920     |

Our procedure will accept as parameters the initial cost of the item and its anticipated lifetime and will display the depreciation table for that item. The procedure appears in Fig. 4-26.

### 4-6.3  PAYROLL PROCESSING

The Bubbly Hot Tub Company would like to computerize its weekly payroll system. Only the payroll calculations are to be programmed at this time. At a later date the company intends to automate the printing of checks.

The input to the program will contain information for each of the company's employees. This information consists of the employee's identification number, number of hours worked for the current week, hourly wage, number of dependents, and marital status. These last two items are needed in order to calculate exemptions and withholding tax. Marital status is represented using a simple one-letter code, since we are interested only in whether or not an employee is married. Character 'M' will indicate "married"; 'U' will indicate "unmarried." A payroll report including information for all the employees will be printed under the following headings:

| NUMBER | HOURLY RATE | REGULAR HOURS | OVERTIME HOURS | GROSS PAY | WITHHOLDING TAX | NET PAY |
|--------|-------------|---------------|----------------|-----------|-----------------|---------|

Overtime hours are paid at one-and-one-half times the regular pay rate. Withholding taxes are based on gross earnings minus any deductions due to exemptions.

There are three types of exemptions that must be considered when calculating deductions. First, there is a personal exemption of $40 per week which everyone can claim. Second, an exemption of $35 can be claimed for those who are married. Finally, an exemption of $50 can be claimed for each dependent.

A general algorithm for this payroll system follows:

```
procedure Depreciate (
    ItemCost: real;        {Input, initial cost}
    Lifetime: integer      {Input, lifetime in years}
                      );
```
{Given the intial cost of an item and its anticipated lifetime, this procedure displays the depreciation table over the lifetime of the item.}
```
var
    BookValue: real;       {Current book value}
    Y: integer;            {Loop control variable}
    Depreciation: real;
begin
    {Step 1: Display headings}
    writeln ('Year':4, 'Depreciation':14, 'Book Value':12);

    {Step 2: Initialize current book value}
    BookValue : = ItemCost;

    {Step 3: Engage loop}
    for Y : = 1 to Lifetime do
        begin

            {Step 4: Do computations}
            Depreciation : = BookValue / Lifetime;
            BookValue : = BookValue − Depreciation;

            {Step 5: Display results for current year}
            writeln (Y:3, '□':6, Depreciation:4:2, BookValue:13:2)
        end
end;
```

**FIGURE 4-26**
**Declining-balance**
**depreciation**
**procedure.**

1. Display payroll report headings

2. Repeat thru step 9 for each employee

3. Read details

4. Calculate gross pay

5. Calculate deductions

6. Calculate taxable income

7. Calculate withholding tax

8. Calculate net pay

9. Display paycheck details

Subprograms that contain the details of steps 4, 5, and 7 can now be formulated.

We begin by first writing a procedure (see Fig. 4-27) to compute the gross pay for an employee. The two input parameters required by this function are hours worked and rate of pay.

```
procedure CalculateGross (
    Hours: real;              {Input, hours worked}
    Rate: real;               {Input, rate of pay}
    var RegHours: real;       {Output, regular hours}
    var OtHours: real;        {Output, overtime hours}
    var Gross: real           {Output, gross pay}
                      );
```

{Given the hours worked and the hourly rate of pay, this function computes an employee's gross pay.}

```
begin
    {Step 1: Compute regular and overtime hours}
    if Hours > 40.0
    then begin
            RegHours : = 40.0;
            OtHours : = Hours − 40.0
        end
    else begin
            RegHours : = Hours;
            OtHours : = 0.0
        end;
```

FIGURE 4-27
Function to calculate
gross pay.
```
    {Step 2: Compute gross pay}
    Gross : = RegHours * Rate + 1.5 * OtHours * Rate
end;
```

We next formulate a function for calculating the deductions for an employee (see Fig. 4-28). These deductions are isolated in this particular function. In the event that exemption rates change, only this function would need to be altered; the rest of the program would remain intact.

Once the total amount of deductions is known, taxable income is calculated as follows:

Taxable income = gross pay − deductions

Now we need to compute the amount of withholding tax. Again, we will want a function to perform this task so that when tax rates change, only this function will need to be changed, not the entire program. The following table gives a breakdown of the current tax rates:

| Taxable Income | Withholding Tax |
|---|---|
| $0 to $150 | 0% |
| $151 to $200 | 10% |
| $201 to $250 | 15% |
| $251 to $300 | 18% |
| over $300 | 20% |

```
function CalculateDeductions (
    MaritalStat: char;      {Input, 'M' for married, 'U' for unmarried}
    NoDepend: integer      {Input, number of dependents}
                        ): real;
{Given the marital status and number of dependents, the function determines
    the total deductions this employee can claim, and returns this total.}
var
    MarDeduction: real;     {Marital deduction}
    DepDeduction: real;     {Dependents deduction}
begin
    {Step 1: Calculate deduction due to married exemption}
    case MaritalStat of
        'M': MarDeduction : = 35.0;
        'U': MarDeduction : = 0.0
    end;

    {Step 2: Calculate deduction due to dependents}
    DepDeduction : = NoDepend * 50.0;

    {Step 3: Calculate and return total deductions}
    CalculateDeductions : = MarDeduction + DepDeduction + 40
end;
```

**Figure 4-28**
**Function to calculate**
**payroll deductions.**

```
function CalculateTax (Taxable: real {Input, taxable income} ): real;
{Given the amount of taxable income, this function calculates withholding
    tax and returns this amount.}
begin
    {Compute tax}
    if Taxable <= 150.0
    then CalculateTax : = 0.0
    else
        if Taxable <= 200.0
        then CalculateTax : = Taxable * 0.10
        else
            if Taxable <= 250.0
            then CalculateTax : = Taxable * 0.15
            else
                if Taxable <= 300.0
                then CalculateTax : = Taxable * 0.18
                else CalculateTax : = Taxable * 0.20
end;
```

**FIGURE 4-29**
**Function to calculate**
**withholding tax.**

**program** Payroll (input, output);
{Given the identification number, hours worked in the current week, hourly
   rate, number of dependents, and marital status for each of its employees,
   this program displays a payroll report for each employee.}
**var**
   Number: integer;         {Employee identification number}
   HrsWorked: real;        {Hours worked}
   HrlyRate: real;          {Hourly rate}
   NumDependents: integer;   {Number of dependents}
   MarStatus: char;        {Marital status,
                                 M = married, U = unmarried}
   WithTax: real;           {Withholding tax}
   OtHrs: real;             {Overtime hours}
   RegHrs: real;            {Regular hours}
   GrossPay: real;          {Gross pay}
   NetPay: real;             {Net pay}
   Deductions: real;        {Total amount to be deducted from paycheck}
   TaxableIncome: real;     {Taxable income}
{Include the procedure CalculateGross and the functions CalculateDeductions,
   and CalculateTax here.}
**begin**
   {Step 1: Display headings}
   writeln ('NUMBER':6, 'HOURLY':8, 'REGULAR':9, 'OVERTIME':10, 'GROSS':8,
          'WITHHOLDING':14, 'NET':7);
   writeln ('□':6, 'RATE':7, 'HOURS':9, 'HOURS':9, 'PAY':9, 'TAX':11, 'PAY':11);

**FIGURE 4-30**
**Program to produce**
**a payroll report.**

The function, shown in Fig. 4-29, takes a single parameter—the amount of
an employee's taxable income.

    We now present the main program in Fig. 4-30. The program reads the
basic data for each employee and performs the required calculations using
this data. Note the order in which the procedure and the functions must be
declared. For output, the formatting values have been chosen to produce a
report with the information arranged in columns with some space between
columns and with two-line headings centered over the columns.

## CHAPTER SUMMARY

This chapter deals with the notion of the subprogram, specifically the *function* and the *procedure*. These are important building blocks in the construction
of large programs. Various aspects were discussed: the defining of procedures
and functions, the invoking of procedures and functions, and the passing
of data to and from the main program. The correspondence between the
parameters of a subprogram and the arguments of a particular invocation
was discussed in some detail, and two methods, *pass by value* and *pass
as variable*, were outlined. The concept of *scope* (of indentifiers) was
introduced, leading to the definition of *local* and *global* variables. Finally, the

{Step 2: Engage loop to process employees}
**while not** eof **do**
    **begin**

        {Step 3: Read data for one employee}
        read (Number, HrsWorked, HrlyRate, NumDependents);
        read (MarStatus);
        **while** MarStatus = '□' **do**      {Discard any blanks}
          read (MarStatus);
        readln;

        {Step 4: Process current employee}
        CalculateGross (HrsWorked, HrlyRate, RegHrs, OtHrs, GrossPay);
        Deductions : = CalculateDeductions (MarStatus, NumDependents);
        TaxableIncome : = GrossPay − Deductions;
        WithTax : = CalculateTax (TaxableIncome);
        NetPay : = TaxableIncome − WithTax;

        {Step 5: Display employee details}
        writeln (Number:6, HrlyRate:8:2, RegHrs:8:2, OtHrs:9:2,
            GrossPay:11:2, WithTax:11:2, NetPay:11:2)
    **end**
**end**.

**FIGURE 4-30** (*cont.*)

important concept of *recursion* was introduced for the first time. Recursion, the ability for self-invocation, is one of the fundamental concepts of computer science.

## KEY TERMS

| | |
|---|---|
| argument | pass-as-variable parameter |
| base value | pass-by-value parameter |
| function | predefined identifier |
| function call | procedure |
| function value | procedure statement |
| global reference | recursion |
| input parameter | scope rules |
| input/output parameter | side effect |
| local identifier | subprogram |
| output parameter | subprogram body |
| parameter | subprogram nesting |

## CHAPTER EXERCISES

★ **1.** Write a procedure with parameters F and Val that will determine whether the mathematical function is increasing, decreasing, or neither at the value Val. F is an integer parameter which denotes the function to be selected. The values 1 and 2 for the parameter F correspond to the built-in functions sin and cos, respectively. Val is given in radians. (*Hint:* Test the values of the functions at 0.01-radian intervals on either side of Val.) The procedure should display a message containing the tested function's name, the test value, and the result. Write a program to read in test values and call your procedure for these values.

2. A sales company pays its employees strictly on the commission from sales. Each week, data is prepared for each employee. This data consists of the employee's identification number followed by the amounts of each sale that employee made in the past week. The last amount for each employee is followed by a sentinel value of zero. The commission rate is 3.45 percent. Write a program to read and add up the sales total for each employee and compute the commission for that employee. Use a function to compute the commission for each salesperson.

3. Write a program to read a collection of positive integers and display all divisors of each, except for 1 and the number itself. If the number has no divisors, display a message saying that it is prime. Use a procedure to display all the divisors, or the prime message, for an integer.

★ 4. A toy distributor has made a bargain purchase of 10,000 small toys packaged in rectangular boxes of varying sizes. The distributor intends to put the boxes into brightly colored plastic spheres and resell them as surprise packages. The spheres come in four diameters: 4, 6, 8, and 10 inches. To place her order, the distributor needs to know how many spheres of each diameter she will need. Since the diagonal of a rectangular box with dimensions $A$, $B$, and $C$, given by

$$D = \sqrt{A^2 + B^2 + C^2}$$

is its largest measurement, the distributor must calculate the diagonal lengths of the boxes and then determine the number that are 4 in or less, 4 to 6 in, and so on. The dimensions of each box are in a data file. Write a program to read the data and determine the number of spheres of each size needed to repackage the toys. Use a function to determine the diagonal of each box. Test the program on a suitable set of data.

★ 5. The marketing office of a publishing company is faced with the task of computing the break-even point for any book they propose to publish. The break-even point is the number of copies of the book that must be sold for the sales revenue to equal production costs. Production costs consist of a fixed cost for layout, typesetting, editing, and so on, plus a per-copy cost for printing, binding, and other expenses. For each candidate for publication, a market analysis determines likely sales figures, as well as the production cost, based partly on the size of the book (number of pages) and the number of copies produced according to the formula

Production cost = fixed production cost

+ number produced × (pages × 0.0305)

An analysis of these projections is used to determine the price at which the book must be sold to break even. Data is prepared for each prospective book, containing the following information: catalog number of book (integer), sales projections, fixed production cost, and number of pages. For example, the data

6925  5000  7500  365

indicates that book number 6925, with projected sales of 5000 copies, has a fixed production cost of $7500 and is 365 pages in length. For this particular book, the cost of producing 5000 books would be

$$7500 + 5000 \times (365 \times 0.0305) = \$63,162.50$$

To break even, this book must sell for

$$\frac{\$63,162.50}{5000} = \$12.63$$

Write a program to read the data prepared for the season's prospective books and produce a line for each, giving the catalog number of the book, projected sales, and the computed break-even selling price. Use a procedure to process the individual books, passing the data read in as input arguments and returning the results as output parameters. The main program need only print headings and set up a loop to read in the data for each book, call the procedure, and display the results. Assume that the last data entry has a book catalog number of 0.

6. Write a nonrecursive function Factorial(N) that computes the factorial of the argument N (sometimes written $N!$). Recall that for an integer $N$, $N!$ is, by definition,

$$N! = N \times (N-1) \times (N-2) \times \cdots \times 1$$

Incorporate in your function the special case

$$0! = 1$$

★ 7. The number of combinations of $n$ different objects selected $r$ at a time (without regard to order) is given by

$$\binom{n}{r} = \frac{n!}{r!(n-r)!}$$

where ! denotes the *factorial* function. The number $\binom{n}{r}$ is referred to as a *binomial coefficient* and has many applications in mathematics and engineering. Write a function with parameters $n$ and $r$ that computes $\binom{n}{r}$. Use the function Factorial from Exercise 6. Write a program to read in test values, call your function, and display the test results.

★ 8. A large number of important mathematical functions have infinite series approximations. In each case, the accuracy of the approximation increases as more terms of the series are considered. Three series of this type are the following:

$$e^x = \sum_{i=0}^{\infty} \frac{x^i}{i!} = 1 + x + \frac{x^2}{2!} + \frac{x^3}{3!} + \cdots$$

$$\cos x = 1 + \sum_{i=1}^{\infty} (-1)^i \frac{x^{2i}}{(2i)!} = 1 - \frac{x^2}{2!} + \frac{x^4}{4!} - \frac{x^6}{6!} + \cdots$$

$$\sin x = \sum_{i=0}^{\infty} (-1)^i \frac{x^{2i+1}}{(2i+1)!} = x - \frac{x^3}{3!} + \frac{x^5}{5!} - \cdots$$

Write functions to compute approximations for each of these cases. Each function has a single argument $x$. Each approximation is to be obtained by adding new terms to the series until the absolute difference between two successive values is less than $10^{-3}$; that is,

$$|\text{approx}_i - \text{approx}_{i+1}| < 0.001$$

Again, use the function **Factorial** developed in Exercise 6. Test your function by writing programs that will print a table containing representative arguments, the value of your function for that argument, the value of the corresponding built-in function for the same argument, and the error. *Important:* You cannot name your functions **Exp**, **Sin**, and **Cos**; otherwise the built-in functions will be unavailable.

# CHAPTER 5

# COMPOSITE DATA STRUCTURES

Earlier we introduced the concept of a variable. Recall that a variable can have a single value such as an integer, a real number, or a character. In this chapter we extend the notion of a variable to collections of elements (e.g., values), called *arrays*, *records*, *files*, and *sets*.

The first section of the chapter deals with the general concept of a data structure. Data structures are broadly classified as primitive and nonprimitive structures. One of the most commonly used nonprimitive data structures is the array. Section 5-1 introduces the Pascal notation for one-dimensional arrays or vectors and describes referencing the elements of a vector. The counted loop control statement introduced in Sec. 3-3.3 is used throughout this section.

Section 5-2 gives the detailed rules for arrays in Pascal. The third section describes the important operations of searching and sorting with vectors. The fourth section introduces the notions of time and space analysis that can be applied to programs. Section 5-5 contains two applications of vectors.

The sixth and seventh sections extend the ideas of the previous sections to the manipulation of higher-dimensional arrays. Section 5-8 describes record structures and their use as the elements of an array. Section 5-9 contains an introduction to sequential files. Finally, Sec. 5-10 introduces the set structure.

**231**

# 5-1 ONE-DIMENSIONAL ARRAYS: VECTORS

In solving a problem with the aid of a computer, we are confronted with several interrelated subproblems. One of these subproblems is to understand the relationships among the data items that are relevant to the solution of the problem. To understand the relationships among the data items in the problem implies that we must understand the data. Data in a particular problem consists of a collection of elementary items. An item usually consists of a single element such as an integer, bit, or character or a collection of such items. A person solving a problem is concerned with structurally organizing the relevant data. Choosing items of data is a necessary and key step in defining and then solving a problem. The possible ways in which the data items or atoms are logically related define different *data structures*.

In Sec. 2-5 we introduced several primitive data structures: the integer, the real number, the character, and the Boolean value; in Sec. 3-6 we introduced enumerated types and subranges. These structures are called *primitive* or *simple* because the instruction set of a computer has low-level instructions that will manipulate these structures directly (recall Sec. 1-3). We can perform the common arithmetic operations on numbers. It also will be seen in Chap. 6 that a character string which contains a number of characters is treated as a primitive data type in some extended versions of Pascal.

Let us concern ourselves next with an example of a *nonprimitive* data structure, one that is very common. Suppose that we are given a class list for an introductory computer science course. Each entry in this list consists of a student identification number and a grade. We want to display the identification number of each student whose grade is greater than the average grade of the class.

To accomplish this task, we must scan (or read) the class list twice. On the first scan we determine the average grade obtained in the class. Once this average grade is known, a second scan of the class list is performed in which the grade of each student is compared with this average. The student's identification number is displayed if that student's grade exceeds the average. How can we perform the required task? Assuming that each number and grade is placed on one line of data, one way is to read the same data twice: once to determine the average and again to generate the required output. Not only is this approach inefficient, but in many computing systems rereading input data is not allowed. An alternative way of achieving the same goal is to store the class list in the memory of the computer and process it from there as many times as needed.

To illustrate, let us assume further that the class list contains the numbers and grades of five students. Let Number1 and Grade1 be variables that denote the number and grade, respectively, of the first student in the class list. In a similar manner, let variables Number2 and Grade2 be associated with the second student, and so forth. The required report can then be generated by the program in Fig. 5-1.

Note that this program is valid only for five students. What would the program be for a class of 100 students? Using the same approach, we would

```
program ClassStat (input, output);
{Given a class list of five students, this program produces a report which
   contains the identification numbers of each student whose grade is greater
   than the average grade of the class.}
var
   Number1, Number2, Number3,
      Number4, Number5: integer;   {Student identification numbers}
   Grade1, Grade2, Grade3,
      Grade4, Grade5: integer;      {Student grades}
   Average: real;                  {Class average}
begin
   {Step 1: Read the class list}
   read (Number1, Grade1, Number2, Grade2, Number3, Grade3,
      Number4, Grade4, Number5, Grade5);

   {Step 2: Obtain the average grade}
   Average : = (Grade1 + Grade2 + Grade3 + Grade4 + Grade5) / 5;

   {Step 3: Check the first student}
   if Grade1 > Average
   then writeln (Number1);

   {Step 4: Check the second student}
   if Grade2 > Average
   then writeln (Number2);

   {Step 5: Check the third student}
   if Grade3 > Average
   then writeln (Number3);

   {Step 6: Check the fourth student}
   if Grade4 > Average
   then writeln (Number4);

   {Step 7: Check the fifth student}
   if Grade5 > Average
   then writeln (Number5)
end.
```

**FIGURE 5-1**
**Program to report**
**on above-average**
**students.**

require 100 variables, say Number1, Number2, . . . , Number100 for student
numbers, and 100 variables for student grades, say, Grade1, Grade2, . . . ,
Grade100. The modified program to handle this case appears in Fig. 5-2.

Note that we have used the symbol " . . ." to denote missing identifiers
in the declarations and a continuation of the processing in the read statement
and in the computation in steps 1 and 2 and the symbol ":" to denote the
checking of the grades for the third through ninety-ninth student (steps 5
through 101).

**program** ClassStat1 (input, output);
{This is ClassStat revision 1. It is identical to the previous version except
   for the number of students being processed. This program handles 100
   students.}
**var**
   Number1, Number2, . . ., Number100: integer;   {Identification numbers}
   Grade1, Grade2, . . ., Grade100: integer;       {Grades}
   Average: real;                                   {Class average}
**begin**
   {Step 1: Read the class list}
   read (Number1, Grade1, Number2, Grade2, . . ., Number100, Grade100);

   {Step 2: Obtain the average grade}
   Average := (Grade1 + Grade2 + · · · + Grade100) / 100;

   {Step 3: Check the first student}
   **if** Grade1 > Average
   **then** writeln (Number1);

   {Step 4: Check the second student}
   **if** Grade2 > Average
   **then** writeln (Number2);
      .
      .
      .

   {Step 102: Check the last student}
   **if** Grade100 > Average
   **then** writeln (Number100)
**end**.

**FIGURE 5-2**
**Program to report**
**on above average**
**students revised to**
**process 100 students.**

This program for handling 100 students requires 102 steps and is clearly
absurd. If we were given a class list consisting of 200 students, a total
of 400 distinct variable names would be required for the student numbers
and grades. Furthermore, the algorithm to perform the required task would
contain some 202 steps!

A more realistic approach to solving this problem is to associate one
variable name with the entire collection of student numbers and another
variable name with the collection of student grades. Of course, we cannot
do that with the simple variables described previously, because assigning
a new value destroys the previous value. Pascal, however, provides *array
type variables* as well as simple variables. As we shall see shortly, such
variables may contain a collection of values. Let the variables Number and
Grade correspond to the collection of student identification numbers and
grades, respectively. If the class list contains five students, the variable
Number denotes an ordered set of five elements. Each element in this set
represents an integer. Using this notation, how can we refer to or select a

particular student's **Number**? We can use a *subscript* to select a particular element in the ordered set. For example, the number of the third student is denoted by **Number[3]**. Although $Number_3$ is the notational convention usually used in mathematics, Pascal uses **Number[3]** because most character alphabets on computers do not contain subscript symbols. (In fact, some computer devices do not even have the symbols [ and ]. For this reason, many Pascal compilers accept (. as equivalent to [ and .) as equivalent to ].) The variable **Number[5]** refers to the number of the fifth student in the class list, and **Grade[5]** selects that student's grade.

When we append a subscript such as 3 or 5 to the name given to an ordered set, the resulting variable is called a *subscripted variable*. The subscript associated with the collection name can itself be a variable. For example, the term **Number[K]** refers to the fifth number in the class list when K has a value of **5**. Indeed, the subscript may be any expression. For now we will use only integer-valued subscripts; other possibilities will be considered later in this section.

A *vector* is defined as an ordered collection that contains a *fixed* number of elements. An element in the vector can be, for example, an integer, a real number, or a character. Note, however, that all elements in the vector must be of the same type. A vector is also called a *one-dimensional array*.

Using this notation, we now wish to reformulate the earlier program which handled a class of five students. A general algorithm for this task has the following steps.

*1.* Read the class list

*2.* Obtain the average grade

*3.* Output the identification numbers of above-average students

We now formulate a subprogram for each of these steps. The procedure in Fig. 5-3 inputs the class data.

```
procedure ClassList (
    var Number: VectorType;    {Output, set of identification numbers}
    var Grade: VectorType;     {Output, set of grades}
    Size: integer              {Input, size of class}
                    );
{Given the class size this procedure reads and stores the class data in the
    vectors Number and Grade.}
var
    K: integer;      {Loop counter and index into vectors}
begin
    {Input data}
    for K : = 1 to Size do
        read (Number[K], Grade[K])
end;
```

FIGURE 5-3
Procedure to read
class data.

The next subprogram, which appears in Fig. 5-4, is a function that computes the average grade in the class. The procedure in Fig. 5-5 determines and displays the identification numbers of above-average students in a class.

The main program in Fig. 5-6 uses the three previous subprograms to handle a class of 5 students. A *type declaration* specifying an *array type*, VectorType, is introduced into the program. The variables Number and Grade are declared to be of this type, making these variables vectors rather than simple variables. (Type declarations are described in more detail in Sec. 5-2.) The procedure ClassList contains a loop that repeats the read statement five times. Each time that this statement is executed, two values are read from the input stream. For example, when K is 1, the number and grade on the first input line are placed in variables Number[1] and Grade[1], respectively. When K is 2, the number and grade on the second line are copied into the variables Number[2] and Grade[2], respectively. The first step of function CalculateAverage initializes the variable Sum to zero. The for loop statement accumulates the sum of the grades in the class list. Upon completion of this loop, the average grade is computed. Procedure PrintAboveAverage contains a for loop statement that checks the grade of each student against the average grade of the class.

Now, what changes are required in this program to handle a class of 100 students? The only modification required is to change the size of the constant definition. The following constant declaration handles a class of 100 students.

```
const
    ClassSize = 100;     {Size of class}


function CalculateAverage (
    Grade: VectorType;    {Input, set of grades}
    Size: integer         {Input, size of class}
                ): real;
{Given a vector of grades and the class size this function computes the
    average grade for the class.}
var
    Sum: real;            {Sum of grades}
    K: integer;           {Loop counter and index into vector}
begin
    {Step 1: Initialize running sum}
    Sum := 0;

    {Step 2: Accumulate sum of grades}
    for K := 1 to Size do
        Sum := Sum + Grade[K];

    {Step 3: Compute average grade}
    CalculateAverage := Sum / Size
end;
```

**FIGURE 5-4**
**Function to compute average grade.**

```
procedure PrintAboveAverage (
    Number: VectorType;    {Input, set of identification numbers}
    Grade: VectorType;     {Input, set of grades}
    Size: integer;         {Input, size of class}
    Average: real          {Input, average grade of class}
                        );
{Given the class data, the size of the class, and the class average, this
    procedure displays the identification numbers of above-average students.}
var
    K: integer;     {Loop counter and index into vectors}
begin
    {Display above-average students}
    for K : = 1 to Size do
        if Grade[K] > Average
        then writeln (Number[K])
end;
```

FIGURE 5-5
Procedure to display
above-average students.

Finally, can we modify the preceding program to handle various class sizes? This can be accomplished easily by having an extra piece of data that precedes all the other input. (See counter-controlled input in Sec. 3-3.2.) This piece of data is an integer which denotes the number of students in the class. The program in Fig. 5-7, in which the variable NumStudents designates the size of the class, handles this general case. This program is similar to the previous two programs. A new step has been added to obtain the size of the class first. The variable NumStudents is also used in steps 2 through 4 to denote the number of times the loops are to be performed.

An important aspect of this program concerns the possible values of NumStudents. Can this variable be arbitrarily large? If it cannot be, how large can its value be? The value for NumStudents must not be larger than the number of vector elements we have specified in the type declaration of this vector. (This is 500 in Fig. 5-7.) As will be explained in Sec. 5-2, Pascal requires that the size of an array must be specified by a constant rather than a variable. How large a vector can we specify? The size must be finite, and the precise limit on its value depends on various factors, such as how much storage the computer has at its disposal. Larger memories usually permit the use of larger vectors.

Another important aspect concerning vectors is the way in which they are organized in the memory of the computer. The elements of a vector are stored in contiguous or consecutive sequential storage locations in computer memory. For example, a 100-element integer vector could be stored from storage position (or "word") 1000 to storage position 1099 inclusive in this kind of memory representation. It is assumed that each integer would occupy one storage position. This, of course, may vary with elements of other types.

We have at this point introduced the notion of a vector and its associated subscript. We can select any element in the vector by using this subscript notation. A vector X of n elements has been defined as the sequence X[1],

```
program ClassStat2 (input, output);
```
{Given a class list of five students' identification numbers and grades, this program produces the same report as the original version of the program.}
```
const
    ClassSize = 5;      {Size of class}
type
    VectorType = array [1 .. ClassSize] of integer;
var
    Number: VectorType;    {Set of identification numbers}
    Grade: VectorType;     {Set of grades}
    Average: real;         {Class average}
```

{Include procedures ClassList, PrintAboveAverage, and function CalculateAverage here}

```
begin
    {Step 1: read the class list}
    ClassList (Number, Grade, ClassSize);

    {Step 2: Obtain the average grade}
    Average := CalculateAverage (Grade, ClassSize);

    {Step 3: Check each student in the class list}
    PrintAboveAverage (Number, Grade, ClassSize, Average)
end.
```

**FIGURE 5-6**
**Program to report on above-average students, using vectors, for five students.**

X[2], . . . , X[n]. Although the lower bound on the subscript in this instance is 1, this, in general, need not be the case. We will be discussing the general case and then proceed to describe some common operations on vectors. Such operations as assignments, input, and output will be discussed. Also, by the use of a simple example, we will introduce the important notion that a subscript referring to a particular element of a vector can have its value computed at run time.

In general, a vector X can be an ordered sequence of elements such as

X[L], X[L + 1], . . . , X[H]

where L and H are integers (L ≤ H) that denote the lower and upper bounds of the subscript, respectively. For example, the vector consisting of the elements

X[0], X[1], X[2], X[3], X[4]

contains five elements and has a lower subscript bound of 0. In this vector, X[0] denotes its first element. Another example is the vector Y, which consists of the elements

Y[− 2], Y[− 1], . . . , Y[2]

It also contains five elements and its lower subscript bound is −2. So Y[−2]

```
program ClassStat4 (input, output);
{Given a class size and the identification numbers and grades of students on
   the class list, this program produces the desired report. This program will
   handle class sizes up to 500 students.}
const
  ClassSize = 500;        {Maximum size of class}
type
  VectorType = array [1 .. ClassSize] of integer;
var
  Number: VectorType;     {Set of identification numbers}
  Grade: VectorType;      {Set of grades}
  Average: real;          {Class average}
  NumStudents: integer;   {Class size}

{Include procedures ClassList, PrintAboveAverage, and function
   CalculateAverage here}

begin
  {Step 1: Read the size of the class}
  read (NumStudents);

  {Step 2: read the class list}
  ClassList (Number, Grade, NumStudents);

  {Step 3: Obtain the average grade}
  Average : = CalculateAverage (Grade, NumStudents);

  {Step 4: Check each student in the class list}
  PrintAboveAverage (Number, Grade, NumStudents, Average)
end.
```

FIGURE 5-7
Program to report
on above-average
students, using vectors,
for 1 to 500 students.

and Y[1] denote the first and fourth elements of the vector, respectively.
Throughout the remainder of this book we will encounter examples involving
vectors with a variety of lower subscript bounds.

Actually, Pascal allows any ordinal type to specify the allowable subscript values. Therefore, a vector may have the set of integers, characters,
Boolean values, any enumerated type, or a subrange of any of these as the
set of allowable subscripts. In most Pascal compilers, however, a vector
with the set of (all) integers as allowable subscripts would represent a very
large array and so this is not allowed; subranges of integers are, of course,
always allowed, and vectors of this type are probably the most common.

As an example of other types of subscripts, suppose we have an enumerated type Day and use it to define the vector type DayVector:

```
type
  Day = (Sun, Mon, Tue, Wed, Thu, Fri, Sat);
  DayVector = array [Day] of integer;
```

Then we can use the seven elements of the enumerated type as subscripts to a vector. To illustrate this concept, suppose that we wish to store in a vector the number of hours a certain employee worked each day in a given week. This employee worked 8 hours on each of Monday, Tuesday, Wednesday, and Thursday and 4 hours on both Saturday and Sunday. We declare variables Hours and ThisDay to be of type DayVector and Day, respectively.

```
var
    Hours: DayVector;
    ThisDay: Day;
```

The following program segment would then initialize the vector Hours:

```
for ThisDay : = Mon to Thu do
    Hours[ThisDay] : = 8;
Hours[Sat] : = 4;
Hours[Sun] : = 4;
Hours[Fri] : = 0
```

In the for statement, the variable ThisDay takes on each value in the enumerated type from Mon to Thu in the order they are given in the definition. The second through fifth elements of the vector receive the value 8, while in the next two steps, the seventh and first elements of the vector receive the value 4, in that order. The sixth element of the vector (Hours[Fri]) receives the value 0. Note that the order of the enumeration is important, since it will be treated in a manner similar to the ordering of the integers when processing a subscripted vector.

Let us now restate the assignment of a value to a vector element. If we have a vector X consisting of the elements X[1], X[2], . . . , X[10], then the assignment X[5] : = 100 will assign a value of 100 to its fifth element. A subscripted variable can be used in the left part of an assignment statement in much the same way as an ordinary variable.

Processing arrays normally involves processing the individual elements of the array one at a time. You will find the counted for loop particularly useful for this purpose. For example, often in a number of applications it is required to initialize each element of a vector to the same value. For example, the vector A, consisting of the elements A[0], A[1], . . . , A[9], can be initialized to 0 by the following program fragment:

```
for K : = 0 to 9 do
    A[K] : = 0
```

Another aspect concerning vectors deals with their initialization by reading values. For example, the program fragment

```
for K : = 0 to 9 do
    read (A[K])
```

will read 10 values from the input. The first value will be placed into A[0], the second into A[1], . . . , and the tenth value into A[9].

An analogous situation arises for the output of vectors. The program

**241**

5-1
ONE-DIMENSIONAL
ARRAYS: VECTORS

fragment

```
for K := 0 to 9 do
   write (A[K])
```

will display the 10 values of the vector **A**.

As an example that involves vectors, let us formulate a program to compute the standard deviation $D$ of the elements of the vector $x$ according to the formula

$$D = \sqrt{\frac{\sum_{i=1}^{n}[x_i - \bar{x}]^2}{n - 1}}$$

```
program StandardDeviation (input, output);
```
{Given a vector of at least two input values, this program computes the standard deviation. NumValues must not be larger than 100.}
```
const
   MaxSize = 100;        {Maximum number of values}
type
   VectorType = array [1 .. MaxSize] of real;
var
   Values: VectorType;      {Input values}
   NumValues: integer;      {Number of values}
   SD: real;                {Standard deviation}
   Average: real;           {Arithmetic average}
   K: integer;              {Loop counter}
```

{Include functions CalculateAverage and CalculateSD here}

```
begin
   {Step 1: Input data}
   read (NumValues);
   for K := 1 to NumValues do
      read (Values[K]);

   {Step 2: Obtain arithmetic average}
   Average := CalculateAverage(Values, NumValues);

   {Step 3: Obtain standard deviation}
   SD := CalculateSD(Values, NumValues, Average);

   {Step 4: Display standard deviation}
   writeln ('Standard deviation is', SD)
end.
```

**FIGURE 5-8**
**Program to compute standard deviation.**

where the symbols $\sum$, $\sqrt{\phantom{x}}$, and $\bar{x}$ denote the summation operation, the square-root operation, and the average of $x$, respectively. The program in Fig. 5-8 accomplishes this task. Observe that we have used again the subprogram CalculateAverage introduced earlier. The main program also uses the function CalculateSD, which appears in Fig. 5-9.

An important concept in using vectors is the idea that a subscript can be computed. We shall illustrate this concept by considering the following problem.

The Department of Transport of British Columbia keeps records of annual rainfall at 86 different weather stations (a matter of prime interest to anglers and water-conservation authorities alike). A station number and the total depth of rain recorded at each station for this past year (in inches) have been prepared in a data file, as illustrated in Fig. 5-10. We wish to design a program that will determine the number of stations recording rainfalls in each of the groups specified in Table 5-1.

We will assume that no station receives more than 49 inches of rain in 1 year. The desired output is also illustrated in Fig. 5-10.

There are essentially two ways to attack this problem. The first method features the brute-force approach, and the second method involves the computation of a subscript. In both approaches we will let the variables StationNumber and Rainfall denote the station identification and rainfall, respectively, for the station being processed. Also common to both

```
function CalculateSD (
    Sample: VectorType;      {Input, vector of sample values}
    NumValues: integer;      {Input, number of sample values}
    Average: real            {Input, arithmetic average of sample values}
                    ): real;
{Given a vector of sample values, the number of elements, and their arith-
    metic average, this function computes the standard deviation. }
var
    Sum: real;      {Sum of values counter}
    K: integer;     {Loop counter and index into vector}
begin
    {Step 1: Initialize}
    Sum := 0;

    {Step 2: Obtain sum of squares}
    for K := 1 to NumValues do
        Sum := Sum + sqr (Sample[K] − Average);

    {Step 3: Obtain standard deviation}
    CalculateSD := sqrt (Sum / (NumValues − 1))
end;
```

**FIGURE 5-9**
**Function to compute standard deviation.**

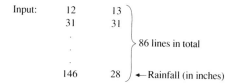

Input:

| 12 | 13 |
|----|----|
| 31 | 31 |
| . |  |
| . |  |
| 146 | 28 |

86 lines in total

←—Rainfall (in inches)

Output:

| Group | Number of Stations |
|-------|--------------------|
| 1 | 13 ← |
| 2 | 8 |
| • | • |
| • | • |
| • | • |

The number of stations recording a rainfall in the range of 0—4 inches.

FIGURE 5-10
Sample data for the annual rainfall in British Columbia.

approaches is the need for 10 counters; one counter is required to record the number of stations reporting rainfall within the same range. Let the vector Range denote this set of counters. The program in Fig. 5-11 is the result of the brute-force approach.

The program is straightforward. It first initializes the 10 range counters to 0. It then begins a loop to process the input data. In this loop, first another station's statistic is read in. Then this data is processed. Note that the station number is read but never used. When all the data has been read, eof becomes "true" and the program drops out of the loop and the report is displayed.

Let us take a close look at the sequence of if statements that update the range counters. This is accomplished by checking the Rainfall exhaustively to determine into which range it falls. This check requires 10 if statements, one for each of the intervals! Clearly, this approach is inefficient. With a little thought, we can replace these 10 if statements by the two assignments

**TABLE 5-1** Annual Rainfall Records

| Group | Range, in |
|-------|-----------|
| 1 | 0–4 |
| 2 | 5–9 |
| 3 | 10–14 |
| 4 | 15–19 |
| 5 | 20–24 |
| 6 | 25–29 |
| 7 | 30–34 |
| 8 | 35–39 |
| 9 | 40–44 |
| 10 | 45–49 |

```
program Rain (input, output);
{Given a series of input lines, each of which contains the station number and
    amount of rain reported by a station, this program produces the desired
    summary report.}
type
    RangeVector = array [1 .. 10] of integer;
var
    StationNumber: integer;      {Station identification}
    Rainfall: integer;           {For current station, inches}
    Range: RangeVector;          {Count of stations within each range}
    K: integer;                  {Loop counter}
begin
    {Step 1: Initialize the count vector}
    for K : = 1 to 10 do
        Range[K] : = 0;

    {Step 2: Process the data}
    while not eof do
        begin
            readln (StationNumber, Rainfall);
            if (0 <= Rainfall) and (Rainfall <= 4)
            then Range[1] : = Range[1] + 1;
            if (5 <= Rainfall) and (Rainfall <= 9)
            then Range[2] : = Range[2] + 1;

                 .

                 .

                 .

            if (45 <= Rainfall) and (Rainfall <= 49)
            then Range[10] : = Range[10] + 1
        end;

    {Step 3: Display the counts}
    writeln ('Group  Number of Stations');
    for K : = 1 to 10 do
        writeln (K:4, Range[K]:13)
end.
```

**FIGURE 5-11**
**Rainfall reporting**
**program, brute-force**
**method.**

```
Position : = (Rainfall div 5) + 1;
Range[Position] : = Range[Position] + 1
```

The variable Position is used to denote the particular counter that is to be updated. We also will have to add a declaration of this variable as type integer. The value of Position is determined from the Rainfall reported by the Station. Note that the **div** operator has been used to obtain the desired truncated value. The reader should verify that this computation does indeed yield the correct subscript value of the counter to be updated. There are many applications in which this technique can be used.

# 5-2 THE PASCAL ARRAY TYPE

Having considered several examples of one-dimensional arrays, in this section we summarize the detailed rules concerning their use in Pascal. First, we consider the type and variable declarations for arrays. We next consider the allowable operations on arrays. Finally, we consider the rules concerning arrays as parameters to functions and procedures.

## 5-2.1 ARRAY TYPE DEFINITIONS AND VARIABLE DECLARATIONS

In Pascal, an array type is a programmer-defined type and is similar in some ways to the previously described programmer-defined types: enumerated types and subranges (see Sec. 3-6). Thus a new array type is introduced by an array type denoter, which often occurs following an equal sign in a type definition that gives a name to the type. Several examples of type definitions involving array types are presented in the following:

```
type
    Vector = array [1 .. 100] of integer;
    Cost = array [1 .. 10] of real;
    Color = (Red, Orange, Yellow, Blue, Green, Purple);
    ColorTable = array [1 .. 4] of Color;
    ColorReference = array [Color] of integer;
    CharFreq = array [char] of integer;
```

The syntax of array type denoters is summarized in Fig. 5-12. The description of an array type involves two other types, each specified by its own type denoter contained within the array type denoter. The index type is specified by the type denoter within the square brackets. (The interpretation of a list of types separated by commas will be described in conjunction with higher-dimensional arrays in Sec. 5-6.) The index type may be any ordinal type. Recall that in Sec. 3-6 an ordinal type was defined as any of the built-in types—integer, Boolean, or character—or any programmer-defined enumeration or subrange. The index type determines two characteristics of the array. First, the number of elements in the array is equal to the number of values in the index type. Second, a subscript used in a subscripted variable referring to an array must be "assignment compatible" to its index type. (Assignment compatibility was defined in Sec. 3-6.)

**FIGURE 5-12** Syntax diagram for array type denoter.
array type denoter

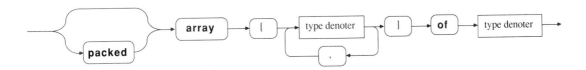

The second type denoter, appearing after the **of** in the array type denoter, is the element type. It may be of any type, and it describes the type of the elements of the array type.

An important restriction of Pascal is that an identifier used as either the index type or the element type denoter of an array type denoter must have been defined previous to its use.

The occurrence of **packed** at the beginning of a type denoter is an indication to the compiler that choices in the layout of data of this array type should be made so as to minimize the memory used, with the possible consequence of increasing the computer time used in executing the program. This Pascal feature is not used in this book except in relation to string processing. We also do not consider further the built-in procedures **pack** and **unpack**.

A variable declared to be of type

**packed array** [1 .. n] **of** char

where n is some integer constant greater than 1, is called a *string type* in standard Pascal. Several exceptions to the general rules for arrays are allowed for these string types. A string type variable may appear in a write or writeln statement, and its elements (characters) will be written to the output stream. In fact, a character string is also a string type. For example, the string 'This □string' is defined to be of type

**packed array** [1 .. 11] **of** char

String types defined by different denoters are different types, just as for other arrays. However, variables of different string types *but of the same length* are defined as compatible for assignment and comparison. Also, all six comparison operators ( =, <>, <, <=, >, >= ) are valid. In the remainder of this chapter we shall occasionally use these string types for nonnumeric data. Chapter 6 contains a more thorough treatment of character strings.

A variable of an array type might be declared either by using the name associated with an array type or by using an array type denoter itself. For example, assuming the previous type definitions, the following declare array type variables:

**var**
    Students, Marks: Vector;
    PostalRate: Cost;
    Window1, Window2: ColorTable;
    Frame1, Frame2: ColorReference;
    Chars: CharFreq;
    Inventory: **array** [1 .. 10] **of** integer;

As with other programmer-defined types, each type denoter that is not simply an identifier introduces a new array type. We shall describe some of the consequences of arrays being of different types in the next two subsections.

## 5-2.2  ARRAY OPERATIONS

The most common operation on an array type variable is that of subscripting. An array variable is subscripted by following it with a subscript expression in square brackets. This subscript expression must be of a type that is assignment compatible with the index type of the array; otherwise the compiler will report a type violation. Furthermore, if the index type of the array is a subrange, then the value of the subscript must be within the bounds of the subrange or a range error will be reported at run time if range checking is enabled.

A subscripted variable yields a "variable" of the element type of the array. Note that we refer to a "variable" rather than a value because this construct may be used in contexts where a variable is required—for example, on the left of the assignment operator or as an argument corresponding with a call as variable (**var**) parameter to a function or procedure. We have used subscripted variables throughout the previous array examples.

The value of an array-type variable may be assigned to another variable of the *same type*. This refers to assignment of the entire array, that is, all its elements. For example, given the following definitions and declarations:

**type**
   Vector = **array** [1 .. 100] **of** integer;

**var**
   V1, V2: Vector;

we could write:

V1 := V2

to copy the current value of all the elements of V2 into V1.

The only other operation permitted on array type variables is comparison for equality or inequality (= or <>, but not <, <=, >, or >=). Both operands must be of the same type.

## 5-2.3  ARRAYS AS PARAMETERS

A parameter of a function or procedure may be declared to be an array rather than a single variable. The ANSI Pascal standard requires that the corresponding argument supply a value of the *same type*. In effect, this rule requires that the argument corresponding to a parameter of an array type be a variable of the same array type. Figure 5-13 illustrates the use of arrays as parameters. Even though the parameters are of array types, the rules for argument-to-parameter correspondence described in Chap. 4 still apply.

In Fig. 5-13 we have followed our usual convention of using pass by value for input arguments and pass as variable for output (and input/output) parameters. A practical concern, however, is that the compiler will provide for a copy of the argument for all pass-by-value parameters. For simple types, such as integer and real values, the storage required by the copy is negligible. For a large array, however, this copy occupies a considerable

```
program VectorProc (input, output);
{Given two vectors, this program computes their elementwise sum.}
const
   N = 10;
type
   Vector = array [1 .. N] of integer;
var
   A, B, C: Vector;      {Sample vectors}

procedure ReadVec (var X: Vector {Output, vector to receive data} );
{This procedure reads data from the input stream into a vector. The constant
   N and the type Vector are global}
var
   K: integer;      {Loop index}
begin
   {Read vector element by element}
   for K : = 1 to N do
      read ( X[K] )
end;


procedure WriteVec (X: Vector {Input, vector to be written} );
{This procedure writes data from a vector to the standard output stream. The
   constant N and the type Vector are global.}
var
   K: integer;      {Loop index}
begin
   {Write vector element by element}
   for K : = 1 to N do
      writeln ( X[K] )
end;
```

**FIGURE 5-13**
**Example of arrays**
**as parameters.**

amount of storage. Therefore, programmers often choose pass as variable for input parameters of array types in an effort to conserve storage. This must be balanced against the care required to ensure that the function or procedure is written so as not to modify its input parameters.

An important consequence of the rules for parameters is that separate functions and parameters must be provided to process each different array type. For example, if the program in Fig. 5-13 were expanded to include the processing of vectors of real elements as well as integer elements, the ReadVec, WriteVec, and AddVec procedures could not be used for both the real and integer vectors because these vectors would be necessarily of different types.

Since the index type of an array is part of its type denoter, arrays of different index types must be of different types, just as for arrays of different element types. This is true even if the array types both have index types that are different subranges of the same host type. The following defines three different types, since three separate array denoters are involved:

```
procedure AddVec (
    X, Y: Vector;      {Input, vectors to be added}
    var Z: Vector      {Output, result}
                   );
```

{Given two vectors, this procedure computes their elementwise sum. The constant N and the type Vector are global.}

```
var
    K: integer;      {Loop index}
begin
    {Add corresponding elements}
    for K : = 1 to N do
        Z[K] : = X[K] + Y[K]
end;


begin
    {Step 1: Input data}
    ReadVec (A);
    ReadVec (B);

    {Step 2: Perform addition}
    AddVec (A, B, C);

    {Step 3: Display element-wise sum}
    WriteVec (C)
end.
```

FIGURE 5-13 (*cont.*)

```
type
    T1 = array [1 .. 10] of integer;
    T2 = array [1 .. 10] of integer;
    T3 = array [1 .. 100] of integer;
```

A program that passes arrays of these three as arguments to a procedure, say, to display the elements, must include a separate procedure for each type.

The ANSI Pascal standard provides no exception to the previous rule. The ISO Pascal standard provides the *conformant array schema* to ease this restriction. (The standard specifies, however, that this feature is an optional requirement, and therefore, a compiler may include or omit this feature and still comply with the standard.)

Figure 5-14 exemplifies this feature. The parameter to the procedure WriteVec is a conformant array schema. A parameter declared to be a conformant array schema specifies that the corresponding argument must be an array of a particular element type. The index type of the conformant array schema describing the parameters and the index type of the argument, however, need not be identical. The index type of the argument must be a subrange of the index type of the parameter or they must both be subranges of the same type. In the latter case, the upper and lower bounds of the argument's index must be within the parameter's subrange. Thus a single procedure can be written for vectors of any size, as in Fig. 5-14.

In the procedure WriteVec, the parameter X is declared to be a conformant array parameter. The identifiers M and N represent special read-only parameters to the procedure and are automatically set equal to the lower and upper bounds of the index type of the actual argument. Thus, given array variable declarations such as

**var**
  A: **array** [1 ..10] **of** integer;
  B: **array** [−100 .. +100] **of** integer;

then the calls

WriteVec (A);
WriteVec (B);

would be valid. For the first call, M and N would be assigned the values 1 and 10, respectively. For the second call, their respective values would be −100 and +100. Figure 5-15 summarizes the syntax of the conformant array schema. The appearance of **packed** requires the argument to be a **packed array**. Multiple dimensions are covered in Sec. 5-6.

As in the case of assignment, standard Pascal string types (**packed array** [1 .. n] **of** char) of the same length are compatible as parameters. That is, a procedure can be written to accept any string of a given length as a pass-by-value parameter.

Strings are described in more detail in Chap. 6. However, the **packed array** [1 .. n] **of** char form of string will be used in several of the examples later in this chapter. Recall that although the write and writeln procedures will display a value of this type, no corresponding input facility is available in standard Pascal. Figure 5-16 supplies a procedure to fulfill this need. It mimics the characteristics of the read and readln statements for integers and real values. It discards blanks preceding the value in the input stream. The string value is enclosed in single quotes, which are not part of the value.

```
procedure WriteVec (
    X: array [M .. N: integer] of integer      {Input, the vector to be written}
                         );
    {This procedure writes an integer vector of any size to the output
        stream.}
    var
    K: integer;      {Loop index}
begin
    {Write vector element by element}
    for K := M to N do
        writeln ( X[K] )
end;
```

**FIGURE 5-14**
**Example of a conformant array schema.**

conformant array schema

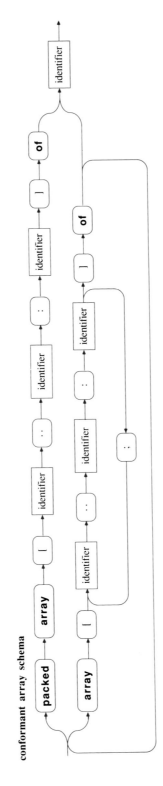

FIGURE 5-15  Syntax diagram for conformant array schema.

```
procedure ReadString(
    var S: StringType    {Output, string value read}
    );
```

{This procedure reads a string from the input stream. The string is assumed
to be enclosed in quotes and may not contain quotes. The constant
StringLength and type StringType are assumed to be global.}

```
var
    C: char;              {Input character}
    J: integer;           {Loop counter}
    K: integer;           {Loop counter}
begin
    {Step 1: Ignore characters up to opening quote}
    repeat
        read (C)
    until C = '''';

    {Step 2: Read and accumulate characters until closing quote}
    read (C);
    J := 1;
    while C <> '''' do
        begin
            S[J] := C;
            J := J + 1;
            read (C)
        end;

    {Step 3: Clear remainder of string}
    for K := J to StringLength do
        S[K] := '□'
end;
```

**FIGURE 5-16**
**Simple procedure to**
**read strings.**

No provision has been made, in this simple procedure, for an input
string to contain a single quote.

This procedure also makes use of a technique that we will use throughout the rest of the text to make subprograms more general. A program using
this procedure is expected to contain the definitions

```
const
    StringLength = n;
type
    StringType = packed array [1 .. StringLength] of char;
```

where $n$ is an integer constant specifying the string length. Thus procedure
ReadString may be used in programs using different string lengths with no
change to the procedure. In a given program, however, all string variables
read must be of the same length or else several versions of procedure
ReadString must be used.

1. Write a procedure which, given a vector of real numbers, will return the value of the largest and the second largest elements of this vector. Write a program to test this procedure.

2. Write a function which, given a vector A of real numbers and N, the number of numbers in A, will obtain the largest difference between two consecutive elements of this vector. Write a program to test this function.

3. Repeat Exercise 2 and obtain the smallest difference between two consecutive elements.

★ 4. Write functions to obtain each of the following statistics for a vector X of $n$ elements:

$$\text{Mean deviation (MD)} = \frac{1}{n} \sum_{i=1}^{n} |x_i - \bar{x}| \qquad \text{where } \bar{x} = \frac{1}{n} \sum_{i=1}^{n} x_i$$

$$\text{Root mean square (RMS)} = \sqrt{\frac{1}{n} \sum_{i=1}^{n} x_i^2}$$

$$\text{Harmonic mean (HM)} = \frac{n}{\displaystyle\sum_{i=1}^{n} \left(\frac{1}{x_i}\right)}$$

$$\text{Range (R)} = \text{Maximum}\{x_1, x_2, \ldots, x_n\} - \text{Minimum}\{x_1, x_2, \ldots, x_n\}$$

Write a program to test your functions.

★★ 5. Write a procedure that accepts an unsorted vector A of $n$ integers (input/output parameter) and outputs the vector via this parameter in the same sequence after ignoring duplicate values found in the given vector. The number of remaining elements $m$ is also required as an output parameter. For example, given the vector

| $A_1$ | $A_2$ | $A_3$ | $A_4$ | $A_5$ | $A_6$ | $A_7$ | $A_8$ | $A_9$ | $A_{10}$ |
|-------|-------|-------|-------|-------|-------|-------|-------|-------|----------|
| 15    | 31    | 23    | 15    | 75    | 23    | 41    | 15    | 31    | 85       |

of 10 integers, the compressed vector returned would be

| $A_1$ | $A_2$ | $A_3$ | $A_4$ | $A_5$ | $A_6$ |
|-------|-------|-------|-------|-------|-------|
| 15    | 31    | 23    | 75    | 41    | 85    |

with $m = 6$. Write a program to test this procedure.

★ 6. Write a procedure that takes as a parameter an integer and displays its octal (base 8) representation. The conversion is done by successive divisions. Let Number denote the integer to be converted and Base the base to which the integer is to be converted (8 in our case). For example, to compute the octal representation of 150, it is divided by 8 repeatedly and the resulting remainders are saved in order:

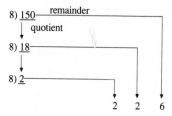

$$226_8 = 2 \times 8^2 + 2 \times 8^1 + 6 \times 8^0 = 150_{10}$$

Write a program to test your procedure.

★★ **7.** (The *"character-distance" problem*.) Examine an input stream of $n$ characters (letters of the alphabet only), and form a result stream of numeric values, one for each input character. Each position of the result stream will be occupied by a number representing a count of the characters separating the character in the corresponding input position from the nearest similar character to its left in the input stream. No distance larger than 9 will be recorded. Any character not matching anything to its left within nine positions will have a zero in the result stream. For example, the given string **AABCDBEFFEABGBWB** would yield the result **0100030013960202**. Write a program for this problem. Read the characters from the input stream and write the digits to the output stream.

★ **8.** The following formula gives the variance of the values in a vector $\bar{x}$ ($\bar{x}$ denotes the mean of the $n$ values of the vector):

$$\tau_x^2 = \frac{1}{n-1}\left[\sum_{i=1}^{n} x_i^2 - n(\bar{x})^2\right]$$

Write a procedure to accept the elements of a vector $x$ as an input parameter and compute the mean and variance of the values using this formula for variance, returning the results via output parameters. Can you see any computational advantage in computing the variance in this way, as opposed to the more familiar formula:

$$\tau_x^2 = \frac{1}{n-1}\left[\sum_{i=1}^{n} (x_i - \bar{x})^2\right]$$

Write a program to test your procedure.

★ **9.** An important problem in statistics concerns the predictability of the value of one variable from the value of another variable. Two variables that can be used in this way with a good chance of success are said to be *strongly correlated*. The strength of correlation is determined by the *correlation coefficient*. We wish to conduct an experiment to determine the strength of correlation between a student's final high school average and his or her performance in first-year university classes. Following final examinations, a set of data is prepared for each first-year student containing two real values: high school average (H) and first-year average (F). Assume that there are N students involved in this study. Write a function which, given two vectors, H[i] and F[i], i = 1, 2, . . . , N, computes the correlation coefficient $r$ according to the following formula:

$$r = \frac{N \sum H[i]F[i] - \sum H[i] \sum F[i]}{\sqrt{(N \sum H[i]^2 - (\sum H[i])^2)(N \sum F[i]^2 - (\sum F[i])^2)}}$$

Write a program that reads in the data and calls the function. If the correlation coefficient exceeds .85, a message is to be displayed saying that these variables appear to be strongly correlated.

★ 10. In any experiment there is a certain amount of error associated with any measurement. A technique known as *smoothing* can be used to reduce the effect of this error in the analysis of the results. Suppose that a series of real values has been recorded from N replications of a particular experiment. Prior to the analysis of these experimental results, the following simple smoothing operation is to be applied to the values stored in a vector V. For each value (except the first and the last, which are to remain unchanged), $V_i$ is to be replaced by

$$\frac{V_{i-1} + V_i + V_{i+1}}{3}$$

Write a program to read the initial measurements, and then display the observed values and the smoothed values.

## 5-3 SORTING AND SEARCHING WITH VECTORS

Two very important operations in computer science are those of sorting and searching. Indeed, it is estimated that computers, on average, spend up to half their time performing these operations. Although these operations are not used only with vectors, their use often occurs in conjunction with them.

Suppose that we are given an integer vector. *Sorting* such a vector is the operation of arranging its elements into sequential order according to an ordering criterion. For our example, numeric elements can be sorted into increasing or decreasing order according to the numeric value of the element. In sorting terminology, the element on which sorting (or searching) is done is often called a *key*. Assuming that the vector Vec, which contains the elements

73, 65, 52, 24, 83, 17, 35, 96, 41, 9

is to be sorted, the result of an *ascending* sort is the sequence

9, 17, 24, 35, 41, 52, 65, 73, 83, 96

while a *descending* sort would yield the sequence

96, 83, 73, 65, 52, 41, 35, 24, 17, 9

*Searching* is one of the most commonly performed operations in data processing. Basically, it involves scanning a set of items to locate a desired one. For example, in a list of names we may want to find an element with a particular name. There are many methods that can be used to search a vector. Some of these methods are more efficient than others. Invariably, the better searching methods require that the data to be searched be organized in special ways. Examples of such organizations are given in Chaps. 8, 9, and 10.

In this section we discuss some elementary sorting and searching methods involving vectors. In particular, we describe the selection sort in Sec. 5-3.1. The next subsection describes searching and applies it to a problem connected with the operation of a post office. In the last subsection, the important topic of merging and its application to sorting are discussed.

## 5-3.1 SELECTION SORT

One of the easiest ways to sort a vector is by *selection*. Suppose that we wish to sort a vector with numeric elements into ascending order. Beginning with the first element in the vector, a sequential search is performed to locate the element that has the smallest value. When this element is found, it is written out in the first position of another vector, which is to eventually have all the original elements in ascending order. In order to remember which element was selected (so as not to select it again), the smallest element in the unsorted vector is changed to some "distinguished" value. This value is assumed to be invalid as far as the given data is concerned and is thus easily recognized. Suppose we choose maxint as this value and we also assume that all data values are less than this value. (Maxint is a built-in constant identifier representing the largest integer value.) A search for the second smallest value is then carried out. This is accomplished by examining the value of each element in the given vector. If the element value is equal to the built-in constant maxint, it is not chosen because it will not be the smallest element. (Note what would happen here if the value of the smallest element had not been changed.) At the end of this searching process the second smallest value is copied into the second position of the partially sorted vector. The process of searching for the element with the next smallest value and placing it in its proper position in the partially sorted vector continues until all elements have been sorted in ascending order. The process of searching through an entire vector and selecting the element with the next smallest value is called a *pass*. If a vector consisting of *n* elements is sorted in this manner, *n* passes are required. This is so because each pass places one element in its proper location, and in the $n$th pass, the element just selected must be the largest.

A general algorithm for this sorting process is

1. Repeat step 2 a total of $n$ times

2. Examine each element in the unsorted vector and place the smallest into the next position of the partially sorted vector; once this element is found, its value is changed to maxint

(Note that elements having a special value of maxint are never selected in our search for the next smallest element.)

We will implement this algorithm as a procedure. We first introduce the parameters and some variables. The following are used (types in parentheses).

| | |
|---|---|
| InVec (array of integer) | Input parameter; vector to be sorted |
| N (integer) | Input parameter; number of elements to be sorted |
| OutVec (array of integer) | Output parameter; vector that contains the sorted elements |
| MinIndex (integer) | Position of smallest element in a particular pass |
| Pass (integer) | Current pass number |

We can now proceed to the design of our final procedure. Let us examine more closely the second step of the general algorithm. The smallest element in a particular pass can be obtained as follows:

```
MinIndex := 1;
for J := 2 to N do
    if InVec[J] < InVec[MinIndex]
    then MinIndex := J
```

Note that at the end of the loop, MinIndex contains the position of the smallest element of the current pass. The smallest element will never have a value of maxint because we have assumed that all actual values are less than maxint.

Now that we have the position of the smallest element in the unsorted vector, it can be placed in its proper output position in OutVec, the sorted vector. The selected element in InVec is then set to a value of maxint. The following program segment accomplishes the desired task:

```
OutVec[Pass] := InVec[MinIndex];
InVec[MinIndex] := maxint
```

Putting these segments together with an implementation of step 1 of the general algorithm, we obtain the Pascal procedure in Fig. 5-17.

Note that at the beginning of the search for each pass, we assume that InVec[MinIndex] = InVec[1] is the current smallest element encountered to this point. For this reason, J is always initialized to index the second

```
procedure SelectionSort (
    InVec: Vector;              {Input, vector to be sorted}
    N: integer;                 {Input, number of elements}
    var OutVec: Vector          {Output, sorted vector}
                         );
```
{Given a vector, this procedure sorts the values into ascending order in a
    second vector. It is assumed that each element of the vector is less than
    maxint.}

```
var
    MinIndex: integer;     {Position of smallest element in a particular pass}
    Pass: integer;         {Current pass number}
    J: integer;            {Loop counter}
begin
    {Step 1: Engage loop to perform N passes}
    for Pass := 1 to N do
        begin

            {Step 2: Find smallest remaining element}
            MinIndex := 1;
            for J := 2 to N do
                if InVec[J] < InVec[MinIndex]
                then MinIndex := J;

            {Step 3: Move smallest to second vector and replace by maxint}
            OutVec[Pass] := InVec[MinIndex];
            InVec[MinIndex] := maxint
        end
end;
```

**FIGURE 5-17**
**Selection sort,**
**original version.**

element. If element InVec[1] has already been selected and moved
to its proper position in the partially sorted vector OutVec, the initial test in
InVec[J] < InVec[MinIndex] still works. This is so because InVec[MinIndex]
has a value of maxint and all values in the given vector to be sorted are
assumed to be less than this special value.

We have chosen to write the selection sort as a procedure because it
might be useful in many applications. The input parameter InVec and output
parameter OutVec are declared as type Vector; a suitable definition for this
type must be supplied in the main program. For example,

```
type
    Vector = array [1 .. 100] of integer;
```

The corresponding arguments must be declared to be this type. Since InVec is
a pass-by-value parameter, the selection sort does not change the argument,
but only its own copy of the argument, to contain maxint in every element.
The output parameter is, of course, specified to be call as variable so that the
result can be returned. Recall that a detailed description of array parameters

is contained in Sec 5-2.3. We leave writing a main program to test the selection sort as an exercise.

The behavior of the selection sort on some sample data is shown in Table 5-2. Each encircled entry denotes the element with the smallest value as selected in a particular pass. The trace of each pass is given before the selected element is replaced by the special value maxint.

There are a number of obvious inefficiencies in this approach. First, we must use an additional vector in order to store the sorted vector. Second, during each pass, we must always examine all elements in the unsorted vector. Finally, the special value maxint could create a problem. This problem could arise if the valid element values are not all less than this special value. We turn now to a revised version of the previous program which eliminates all these drawbacks.

The algorithm begins as before. Beginning with the first element in the vector, a search is performed to locate the element with the smallest value. This time, however, when the smallest element is found, it is interchanged with the first element in the vector. As a result of this interchange, the element with the smallest value now sits in the first position of the vector. A search for the second smallest value is then carried out. This is accomplished by examining the values of each element from the second element onward. The element that has the second smallest value is interchanged with the element located in the second position of the vector. The process of searching for the element with the next smallest value and placing it in its proper position continues until all elements have been sorted in ascending order.

If a vector InOutVec consisting of $n$ elements is sorted in this manner, $n - 1$ passes are required. This is so because each pass places one element into its proper location and after $n - 1$ passes the last element in the vector must be the largest. Consequently, an $n$th pass is not required. Note that in the $i$th pass we concern ourselves only with the examination of the elements InOutVec[i] to InOutVec[n] inclusive, since the others have already been sorted

**TABLE 5-2** Behavior of a Selection Sort, Original Version

| | Pass Number (Pass) | | | | | | | | | |
|---|---|---|---|---|---|---|---|---|---|---|
| | 1 | 2 | 3 | 4 | 5 | 6 | 7 | 8 | 9 | 10 |
| 1 | 73 | 73 | 73 | 73 | 73 | 73 | 73 | (73) | maxint | maxint |
| 2 | 65 | 65 | 65 | 65 | 65 | 65 | (65) | maxint | maxint | maxint |
| 3 | 52 | 52 | 52 | 52 | 52 | (52) | maxint | maxint | maxint | maxint |
| 4 | 24 | 24 | (24) | maxint | maxint | maxint | maxint | maxint | maxint | maxint |
| 5 | 83 | 83 | 83 | 83 | 83 | 83 | 83 | 83 | (83) | maxint |
| 6 | 17 | (17) | maxint | maxint | maxint | maxint | maxint | maxint | maxint | maxint |
| 7 | 35 | 35 | 35 | (35) | maxint | maxint | maxint | maxint | maxint | maxint |
| 8 | 96 | 96 | 96 | 96 | 96 | 96 | 96 | 96 | 96 | (96) |
| 9 | 41 | 41 | 41 | 41 | (41) | maxint | maxint | maxint | maxint | maxint |
| 10 | (9) | maxint | maxint | maxint | maxint | maxint | maxint | maxint | maxint | maxint |

by that time. Thus each pass increases the number of sorted elements by one and decreases the number unsorted by one.

A general algorithm for this sorting process is contained in these steps:

1. Repeat thru step 3 a total of $n - 1$ times

2. Examine the remaining unsorted elements and place the smallest of these into its proper position

3. Reduce the size of the unsorted vector by one element

The procedure in Fig. 5-18 formalizes this process.

The for statement at the beginning of the procedure controls the number of passes that are required. Its range constitutes a pass. The elements to be examined in a particular pass are InOutVec[Pass] through InOutVec[N]. Note

```
procedure SelectionSort1 (
    var InOutVec: Vector;      {Input/output; on entry, an unsorted vector; upon
                                  completion, sorted into ascending order}
    N: integer                 {Input, number of elements in InOutVec}
                               );
{Given a vector of integer values, this procedure sorts them into ascending
    order.}
var
    MinIndex: integer;      {Position of smallest element in a particular pass}
    Pass: integer;          {Current pass number}
    J: integer;             {Loop counter}
    Temp: integer;          {Temporary for swapping}
begin
    {Step 1: Engage loop to perform N − 1 passes}
    for Pass := 1 to N − 1 do
        begin

            {Step 2: Find smallest value in remaining vector}
            MinIndex := Pass;
            for J := Pass + 1 to N do
                if InOutVec[J] < InOutVec[MinIndex]
                then MinIndex := J;

            {Step 3: Place smallest value into proper position}
            if MinIndex <> Pass
            then begin
                    Temp := InOutVec[MinIndex];
                    InOutVec[MinIndex] := InOutVec[Pass];
                    InOutVec[Pass] := Temp
                end
        end
end;
```

**FIGURE 5-18**
**Selection sort,**
**revision 1.**

that in the loop to search for the smallest values (**for** J := Pass + 1 **to** N), MinIndex will be changed to the value of J if the condition InOutVec[J] < InOutVec[MinIndex] is "true." Unless the element InOutVec[MinIndex] is already in its final position with respect to the ordering, the final operation in the Pass loop interchanges the contents of InOutVec[Pass] and InOutVec[MinIndex].

The behavior of this version of the selection sort is shown in Table 5-3. Each encircled entry denotes the element with the smallest value that is selected in a particular pass. The elements above the bar for a given pass are those elements that have been placed in order.

Up to this point, we have considered only the sorting of numeric elements. Sorting can be performed on nonnumeric elements. This variation of sorting will be discussed in Chap. 6.

There are many ways in which sorting can be done. We have presented the selection sort (in two variations) in this subsection. Other popular sorts include the exchange sort, the bubble sort, the shell sort, the quick sort, the heap sort, and the merge sort. These differ in the sophistication of the approach and in the cost of execution (in terms of number of operations). More efficient sorting techniques will be presented in Chaps. 8 and 9.

## 5-3.2  BASIC SEARCHING

In this section we examine two simple searching techniques. These techniques can be applied to many searching situations. An application containing an instance of searching is described.

The most straightforward method of finding a particular element in an unordered vector is the *linear search* technique. The technique simply involves scanning each element of the vector in a sequential manner (that is, one after the other in turn) until the desired element is found. The function in Fig. 5-19 performs a linear search, returning the position in the vector of

**TABLE 5-3**  Behavior of a Selection Sort, Revised Version

| | Unsorted | Pass Number (Pass) | | | | | | | | Sorted |
|---|---|---|---|---|---|---|---|---|---|---|
| $i$ | $K[i]$ | 1 | 2 | 3 | 4 | 5 | 6 | 7 | 8 | 9 |
| 1 | 73 | 9 | 9 | 9 | 9 | 9 | 9 | 9 | 9 | 9 |
| 2 | 65 | 65 | 17 | 17 | 17 | 17 | 17 | 17 | 17 | 17 |
| 3 | 52 | 52 | 52 | 24 | 24 | 24 | 24 | 24 | 24 | 24 |
| 4 | 24 | 24 | (24) | 52 | 35 | 35 | 35 | 35 | 35 | 35 |
| 5 | 83 | 83 | 83 | 83 | 83 | 41 | 41 | 41 | 41 | 41 |
| 6 | 17 | (17) | 65 | 65 | 65 | 65 | 52 | 52 | 52 | 52 |
| 7 | 35 | 35 | 35 | (35) | 52 | (52) | (65) | 65 | 65 | 65 |
| 8 | 96 | 96 | 96 | 96 | 96 | 96 | 96 | 96 | 73 | 73 |
| 9 | 41 | 41 | 41 | 41 | (41) | 83 | 83 | 83 | (83) | 83 |
| 10 | (9) | 73 | 73 | 73 | 73 | 73 | 73 | (73) | 96 | 96 |

```
function LinearSearch (
    InVec: Vector;      {Input, the vector to be searched, assumed to be an
                            array of integers}
    N: integer;         {Input the number of elements in InVec}
    Key: integer        {Input the value to be searched for}
                        ): integer;
```
{Given an unordered vector, this function searches the vector for a particular element. If the search is successful, the position of the first such element found is returned; otherwise 0 is returned.}
```
var
    NotFound: boolean;    {Loop control flag; set true if key is "not
                            found" yet}
    K: integer;           {Loop counter and index into vector}
begin
    {Step 1: Initialize}
    LinearSearch := 0;    {Return 0 if not found}
    NotFound := true;     {Initialize for loop}
    K := 1;

    {Step 2: Engage search loop}
    while NotFound and (K <= N) do
        begin

            {Step 3: Test element, quit if found}
            if InVec[K] = Key
            then begin
                    LinearSearch := K;
                    NotFound := false
                end;

            {Step 4: Increment loop control variable}
            K := K + 1
        end
end;
```

FIGURE 5-19
Linear search function.

the found element or the value 0 if the value sought is not found. Again, we leave writing a program to test this procedure as an exercise. Note that the main program must provide a suitable type definition of Vector and supply an argument of this type. The Vector type must be an array-of-integer type.

This function sequentially scans each element of the vector for Key. If this element is found, the index K is returned. In the case of an unsuccessful search, a value of 0 is returned.

One point that should be examined in this procedure is the while condition. We did not write

```
while (K <= N) and (InVec[K] <> Key) do
    K := K + 1;
if K <= N
then LinearSearch := K
```

because standard Pascal does not guarantee partial evaluation of conditions (see Sec. 3-4); therefore, this could result in a subscripting error. To see this, trace the procedure for the case where the argument corresponding to the parameter InVec is exactly full; that is, N is equal to the upper subscript limit. Consider the case that the element is not in the list. This would result in K = N + 1, and InVec[K] would represent an out-of-range subscript. (Some compilers always use partial evaluations. A program written for use only with such a compiler could use the shorter form.)

Notice that it will take, on average, $N/2$ comparisons to find a particular element in a vector containing $N$ elements. The worst case will require $N$ comparisons! This can be very time consuming when the number of elements is large and is the main drawback of this approach.

A more efficient way of performing a linear search involves introduction of a sentinel element InVec[N + 1] whose purpose is to receive the value of the element sought. The modified function appears in Fig. 5-20. Using this approach, the search will always be successful. Although the loop will still execute the same number of times, fewer operations are performed each time. The index I is never checked against N + 1, and we do not need a

```
function LinearSearch1 (
    InVec: Vector;      {Input, the vector to be searched, assumed to be
                             an array of integers}
    N: integer;         {Input, the number of elements in InVec}
    Key: integer        {Input, the value to be searched for}
                    ): integer;
{Given an unordered vector of integers, this function searches the vector for
    a particular element. If the search is successful, the position of the first
    such element is returned; otherwise the value 0 is returned. The vector
    element InVec[N + 1] must be available to be used as a sentinel element
    within this function.}
var
    I: integer;         {Loop counter}
begin
    {Step 1: Initialize}
    I := 1;

    {Step 2: Store sentinel}
    InVec[N + 1] := Key;

    {Step 3: Search vector}
    while InVec[I] <> Key do
        I := I + 1;

    {Step 4: Return appropriate value}
    if I = N + 1
    then LinearSearch1 := 0
    else LinearSearch1 := I
end;
```

FIGURE 5-20
Linear search function
(revision 1).

Boolean flag. If the index I reaches $N + 1$, then the element **Key** was not in the original vector and, consequently, the search is unsuccessful.

If the elements have previously been sorted, much more efficient searches can be conducted. (Imagine looking for someone in a telephone directory that wasn't sorted!) A relatively simple method of searching a sorted list is known as the *binary search* method. Assume that the elements in the vector are stored in ascending order. The selection sort of the previous section can be used to achieve this ordering. A search for an element with a particular value resembles the way you would search for a name in a sorted telephone directory. The approximate middle element of the vector is located and its value is examined. If this value is too high, then the value of the middle element of the first half is examined and the procedure is repeated on the first half. If the value is too low, then the value of the middle element of the second half of the vector is tried and the procedure is repeated on the second half. This process continues until the desired element is found or the search interval becomes empty.

A general algorithm for the process is as follows:

*1.* Repeat thru step 3 while the search interval is not empty

*2.* Obtain the position of the midpoint element in the current search interval

*3.* If the value of the desired element is less than the value of the midpoint element,
 then reduce the search interval to the first half of the current search interval;
 else if the value of the desired element is greater than the value of the midpoint element,
 then reduce the search interval to the second half of the current search interval
 else the search is successful

*4.* Unsuccessful search

The function in Fig. 5-21 is a formalization of this process. As an example, assume that we have the ordered vector

61, 147, 197, 217, 309, 448, 503

The behavior of the previous function for **Key** = 197 and 503 is shown in Table 5-4. The size of the vector in this example is $2^m - 1$ where $m = 3$. Since the operator **div** is used rather than /, the vector can be any size. The **div** ensures that integer division is done, truncating fractions when necessary. The behavior of the function for the sample vector

61, 147, 197, 217, 309, 448, 503, 577, 629, 701, 831

when truncating is required is shown in Table 5-5, for **Key** = 197 and 503.

Formally, an average of $\text{trunc}(\log_2 N) - 1$ comparisons are required in order to locate a specific element by means of a binary search, where $\log_2 N$

```
function BinarySearch (
    InVec: Vector;      {Input, the vector to be searched}
    N: integer;         {Input, the number of elements in InVec.}
    Key: integer        {Input, the value to be searched for}
                        ): integer;
```
{Given a vector with integer elements which are in ascending order, this
    function searches the vector for a given element. If the search is success-
    ful, the position of the found element is returned; otherwise the value 0
    is returned.}

```
var
    Low, High, Middle: integer;    {Indices of InVec}
    NotFound: boolean;             {Loop control flag}
begin
    {Step 1: Initialize}
    Low := 1;
    High := N;
    NotFound := true;

    {Step 2: Engage loop}
    while NotFound and (Low <= High) do
        begin

            {Step 3: Check middle element of current search range and adjust
                range appropriately}
            Middle := (Low + High) div 2;
            if Key < InVec[Middle]
            then High := Middle − 1
            else if Key > InVec[Middle]
                then Low := Middle + 1
                else {Key = InVec[Middle]}
                    NotFound := false
        end;

    {Step 4: Return appropriate value}
    if NotFound
    then BinarySearch := 0
    else BinarySearch := Middle
end;
```

**FIGURE 5-21**
**Binary search function.**

base denotes the logarithm to the 2 of $N$. (That is, $\log_2 N = x$, where
$2^x = N$.) The worst case will take at most $trunc(\log_2 N) + 1$ comparisons.

Intuitively it is clear that the binary search method performs as well
as or better than the linear search. Owing to the complexities of the binary
search strategy, however, additional processing steps are followed. Updating
the lower, middle, and upper indices (that is, Low, Middle, and High in the
Fig. 5-21) is an example of such overhead. Figure 5-22 shows a comparison
of the two search methods with the presence of overhead.

| TABLE 5-4 | Binary Search Behavior | | |
| --- | --- | --- | --- |
| **Iteration** | **Low** | **High** | **Middle** |
| Search for **197** | | | |
| 1 | 1 | 7 | 4 |
| 2 | 1 | 3 | 2 |
| 3 | 3 | 3 | 3 |
| Search for **503** | | | |
| 1 | 1 | 7 | 4 |
| 2 | 5 | 7 | 6 |
| 3 | 7 | 7 | 7 |

We turn now to an application of searching which involves the mailing of packages. Table 5-6 gives a recent table of costs of parcel post within the province of Saskatchewan. To be accepted, a package is subject to the following constraints:

*1.* Weight limit of 35 lb.

*2.* The rates of Table 5-6 apply to packages not exceeding 3 ft in length, width, or depth and with a combined length and girth not exceeding 6 ft; packages exceeding these dimensions are accepted, subject to a surcharge of $2.25, providing no one dimension exceeds 6 ft and the combined length and girth does not exceed 10 ft.

The girth of a package is the circumference of the package around its two smallest sides, as indicated in Fig. 5-23. Mathematically, the girth is given by the formula

| TABLE 5-5 | Binary Search Behavior | | |
| --- | --- | --- | --- |
| **Iteration** | **Low** | **High** | **Middle** |
| Search for **197** | | | |
| 1 | 1 | 11 | 6 |
| 2 | 1 | 5 | 3 |
| Search for **503** | | | |
| 1 | 1 | 11 | 6 |
| 2 | 7 | 11 | 9 |
| 3 | 7 | 8 | 7 |

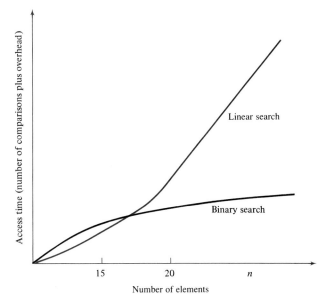

**FIGURE 5-22
Comparison of linear
search and binary
search.**

$$2 * (D1 + D2 + D3 - \text{Largest})$$

where Largest is the largest of the three package dimensions D1, D2, and D3.

We wish to design a program to process a transaction file containing one line of data for each package mailed during the week. Each line contains a transaction number, followed by the weight of the package, followed by its three dimensions (in no particular order). The end of the file is signaled by a dummy line with transaction number 0. The program must print the transaction number, weight, and postal charge for all accepted packages and the transaction number, weight, and dimensions for all rejected packages. At the end of the report, we must print the number of packages accepted and the number rejected.

This problem can be solved by storing Table 5-6 as two vectors: Weight and Cost. The postal cost of each package can then be determined by searching the Weight vector to find the required entry for a given package. The corresponding element in the Cost vector can then be selected as the basic postal cost. A general algorithm for this problem is as follows:

**TABLE 5-6** **Parcel Post Package Rate Structure**

| Packages Up To and Including: | | | | | | | | |
|---|---|---|---|---|---|---|---|---|
| Weight, lb | 2 | 3 | 4 | 5 | 6 | 7 | 8 | 9 | 10 |
| Cost, $ | 1.45 | 1.65 | 1.75 | 1.85 | 1.95 | 2.05 | 2.15 | 2.25 | 2.35 |
| Weight, lb | 11 | 12 | 13 | 14 | 15 | 20 | 25 | 30 | 35 |
| Cost, $ | 2.50 | 2.65 | 2.80 | 2.95 | 3.10 | 3.30 | 3.55 | 3.80 | 4.05 |

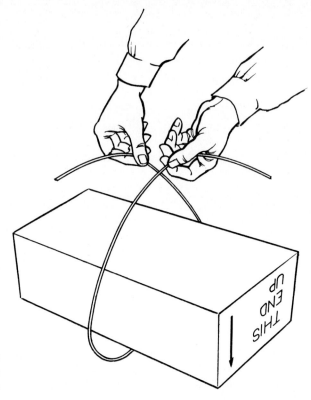

**FIGURE 5-23**
**The girth of a**
**package.**

*1.* Read a package description

*2.* Repeat thru step 4 while the last piece of data has not been encountered

*3.* If the package is too large,
   then reject the package and update rejection statistics;
   else if the package is large,
      then assess a penalty of $2.25;
      else assess no penalty
   Search the postal table for the basic postal cost
   Obtain total postal cost by adding the penalty cost to the basic
      postal cost
   Accept package and update acceptance statistics

*4.* Read another package description

*5.* Print acceptance and rejection statistics

We assume that the weight W of a package has already been rounded up to the appropriate weight category in Table 5-6. For example, an actual package weight of 2.4 lb would be recorded as 3 lb for computational purposes. It is further assumed that the dimensions of the package are given to the nearest inch.

The description of the variables required appears in the variable declaration section of Fig. 5-24. We can now proceed to the design of the final program. Let us examine more closely the third step of the general algorithm. The program segment below computes the girth of the package.

```
Largest : = Maximum (D1, D2, D3);
Girth : = 2 * (D1 + D2 + D3 − Largest)
```

where the function **Maximum** determines the largest of the three parcel dimensions **D1**, **D2**, and **D3**.

From this girth computation, we are in a position to either accept or reject the given parcel. If the parcel is acceptable, then a binary search of the postal table yields the postal cost of mailing this parcel (along with a possible penalty for an oversized parcel); otherwise, the parcel is rejected. The statements for accepting or rejecting the parcel are as follows:

```
if (W > 35) or (Largest + Girth > 120) or (Largest > 72)
then begin
        writeln ('Rejected☐package☐☐',Number:5, W:5, D1:5, D2:5, D3:5);
        NR : = NR + 1
    end
else begin
        if (Largest + Girth > 72) or (Largest > 36)
        then Penalty : = 2.25
        else Penalty : = 0.0
        Invoke routine to search table for cost, and print message
    end
```

We are now in a position to formulate a complete program. This program, which also reads the postal table, appears in Fig. 5-24.

The program begins by initializing the summary counters to 0. Then it reads in the postal table, which consists of two 18-element vectors **Weight** and **Cost**. Next it reads in the description of the first package. The while loop controls the processing of all the package data. The largest dimension and girth of a package are calculated and then the package is checked as to its acceptability. If it is acceptable, the postal cost of the package is determined. The binary search procedure is invoked to determine the subscript to the **Cost** vector. The final step in the range of the loop reads the parcel description of another package. Finally, the appropriate summaries are displayed.

## 5-3.3 MERGING AND MERGE SORTING

The process of *merging* involves taking two given sequences of, say, numbers, each of which is sorted, and combining these two sequences into a single sorted sequence. In this subsection we examine more closely the operation of merging and its application to sorting, based on successive merges.

Let us examine the merging of two sorted vectors to produce a single sorted vector. We can accomplish this process easily by successively selecting the element with the smallest value or key in either of the vectors

**program** Postal (input, output);
{Given the postal information of Table 5-6, and the parcel specifications consisting of identification number, weight, and parcel dimension, this program generates the required report described in the text. The function BinarySearch, which was presented earlier in this section, is used.}

**type**
    CostVector = **array** [1 .. 18] **of** real;
    Vector = **array** [1 .. 18] **of** integer;

**var**

| | |
|---|---|
| Weight: Vector; | {Vector which represents table of package weights} |
| Cost: CostVector; | {Vector corresponding to weight which contains tables of mailing costs} |
| Number: integer; | {Identification number of package} |
| W: integer; | {Weight of package in pounds} |
| D1, D2, D3: integer; | {Dimension (nearest inch) of package} |
| Largest: integer; | {Largest dimension of package in inches} |
| Girth: integer; | {Girth of package in inches} |
| Penalty: real; | {Penalty associated with package} |
| PostalCost: real; | {Cost of mailing package} |
| NR: integer; | {Number of rejected packages} |
| NA: integer; | {Number of accepted packages} |
| I: integer; | {Loop counter} |

{The function BinarySearch of Fig. 5-21 should be included here. A suitable implementation of the Maximum function should also be included.}

**begin**
    {Step 1: Initialize counters of accepted and rejected parcels.}
    NA := 0;
    NR := 0;

    {Step 2: Read in postal rate table.}
    **for** I := 1 **to** 18 **do**
        read (Weight[I], Cost[I]);

**FIGURE 5-24**
**An application of**
**searching.**

    {Step 3: Read first parcel description}
    read (Number, W, D1, D2, D3);

and placing this element in a new vector, thereby creating a single sorted vector of elements. For example, from the vectors

Vector 1:     13     21     39
Vector 2:      7     28

we obtain the behavior given in Table 5-7, where vector 3 is a vector that contains a trace of the desired results. This process is formalized in the

{Step 4: Engage loop to process each parcel}
**while** Number <> 0 **do**
  **begin**
    {Step 5: Find the largest dimension of the package}
    Largest := Maximum (D1, D2, D2);

    {Step 6: Compute girth of the package}
    Girth := 2 * ( D1 + D2 + D3 − Largest);

    {Step 7: Process the parcel}
    **if** (W > 35) **or** (Largest + Girth > 120) **or** (Largest > 72)
    **then begin**
        writeln ('Rejected☐package☐☐',Number:5, W:5, D1:5, D2:5,
          D3:5);
        NR := NR + 1
    **end**
    **else begin**
        **if** (Largest + Girth > 72) **or** (Largest > 36)
        **then** Penalty := 2.25
        **else** Penalty := 0.0;

        {Step 8: Search table for postal cost, and add penalty to it}
        PostalCost := Cost[BinarySearch (Weight, 18, W) ] + Penalty;
        writeln ('Accepted☐package☐☐', Number:5, W:5,
          PostalCost:7:2);
        NA := NA + 1
    **end**;

    {Step 9: Read another parcel description}
    read (Number, W, D1, D2, D3);
  **end**;

{Step 10: Display summary}
writeln ('Number accepted☐', NA:1);
writeln ('Number rejected☐', NR:1)
**end**.

FIGURE 5-24 (*cont.*)

procedure in Fig. 5-25. This merge is an example of an *inclusive merge*, in which all elements of the two vectors are included. Other forms of merge are possible; for example, duplicate elements may not be repeated. The nature of the application dictates what type of merge might be required.

Procedure SimpleMerge can be generalized to merge *k* sorted vectors into a single sorted vector. Such a merging operation is called *multiple merging* or *k-way merging*.

Multiple merging can be accomplished equivalently by performing a simple merge repeatedly. For example, if we are to merge eight vectors we

**TABLE 5-7** Sample Behavior of Merging

**Vector**

| | | | | | |
|---|---|---|---|---|---|
| 1 | 13 | 21 | 39 | | |
| | ↑ | | | | |
| 2 | 7 | 28 | | | |
| | ↑ | | | | |
| 3 | 7 | | | | |
| | ↑ | | | | |
| 1 | 13 | 21 | 39 | | |
| | ↑ | | | | |
| 2 | 7 | 28 | | | |
| | | ↑ | | | |
| 3 | 7 | 13 | | | |
| | | ↑ | | | |
| 1 | 13 | 21 | 39 | | |
| | | ↑ | | | |
| 2 | 7 | 28 | | | |
| | | ↑ | | | |
| 3 | 7 | 13 | 21 | | |
| | | | ↑ | | |
| 1 | 13 | 21 | 39 | | |
| | | | ↑ | | |
| 2 | 7 | 28 | | | |
| | | ↑ | | | |
| 3 | 7 | 13 | 21 | 28 | |
| | | | | ↑ | |
| 1 | 13 | 21 | 39 | | |
| | | | ↑ | | |
| 2 | 7 | 28 | | | |
| | | | ↑ | | |
| 3 | 7 | 13 | 21 | 28 | 39 |
| | | | | | ↑ |

can first merge them in pairs using the procedure SimpleMerge. The result of this first step yields four vectors, which are again merged in pairs to give two vectors. Finally, these two vectors are merged to give the required sorted vector. A pictorial trace of this process is given in Fig. 5-26. In this example, three separate merges are required to yield a single vector. In general, $k$ separate merges are required to merge $2^k$ separate vectors into one vector.

This same strategy can be applied to sorting. Given an unsorted vector of $n$ elements in which $n$ is an integral power of 2 (say, $2^m$), one considers this original vector to be a set of $n$ vectors, each of which contains a single element. Clearly, a vector which contains a single element is sorted. The sort requires $m$ passes where $m = \log_2 n$.

We now develop a general sorting algorithm based on this successive merging strategy and implement this algorithm as a procedure. We assume that the number of elements to be sorted in this manner is an integral power of 2 (that is, $n = 2^m$). This assumption simplifies the required algorithm. The more general procedure is more complicated (but not drastically more so) than the one that we develop. We leave this modification as an exercise.

Returning to the development of the simplified version of the desired program, we note that a merge sort requires an auxiliary storage area equal in size to that of the vector to be sorted. As mentioned previously, the sort requires $m$ passes on the data, where $m = \log_2 n$. Each pass requires a number of subpasses. This number is a function of the pass number. A subpass is essentially the same as the simple merge described previously.

In our current example, we want to sort eight elements; therefore, let us assume that three passes are required. On the first pass we have four subpasses or simple merges to perform. Each of these subpasses involves merging two single elements. In the second pass we must do two subpasses. Each of these subpasses involves merging two sets of two elements each. The final pass requires only one subpass; each of the two sets contains four elements. An informal algorithm to perform a merge sort is as follows.

*1.* Repeat thru step 3 for $m$ passes where $m = \log_2 n$

*2.* Set up control to keep track of current pass

*3.* Perform the current pass

*4.* Determine which area (the original or auxiliary) the sorted vector is in

Step 2 in this algorithm performs a very important function. This step must keep track of the number of elements to be merged in a particular subpass. Recall that this number is a function of the pass number (PassNum). Specifically, if SubSize represents the desired quantity, then its value is given by

SubSize $= 2^{\text{PassNum} - 1}$

We now give a merge sort procedure in Fig. 5-27. The first step controls the number of passes required in the sort. Because Pascal does not implement exponentiation, we use the mathematical identity

$$\log_2 n = \frac{\ln n}{\ln 2}$$

and round the (real) result to an integer. Step 2 computes the size of each subvector used in a particular pass. Again, we avoid use of exponentiation by another mathematical identity

$2^{(\text{PassNum} - 1)} = e^{(\text{PassNum} - 1) \times \ln 2}$

**procedure** SimpleMerge (

A, B: Vector;    {Input, sorted vectors to be merged}

M, N: integer;   {Input, number of elements in A and B
                      respectively}

**var** C: Vector    {Output, sorted vector containing merged values
                     from A and B}
           );

{Given two sorted vectors, this procedure merges these vectors. The type
Vector must be defined in the calling program to be an array of integers;
There must be at least M + N elements.}

**var**

  I, J, K: integer;   {Array indices}

  R: integer;      {Loop counter}

**begin**

  {Step 1: Initialize}

  I := 1;

  J := 1;

  K := 1;


  {Step 2: Compare corresponding elements and output smallest}

  **while** (I <= M) **and** (J <= N) **do**

    **if** A[I] <= B[J]

    **then begin**

        C[K] := A[I];

        I := I + 1;

        K := K + 1

    **end**


    **else begin**

        C[K] := B[J];

        J := J + 1;

        K := K + 1

    **end**;

FIGURE 5-25
Simple merge
procedure.

and note that Pascal's exp(x) gives $e^x$. Note that if PassNum is odd, then
the output area is the vector Temp; otherwise, the output area is the original
vector InOutVec. The associated vectors (InOutVec and Temp) exchange roles
in procedure MergePass. Step 4 determines which area contains the sorted
vector. If an odd number of passes was required in the sort, then the output
area contains the results. In this case, the elements in the output area Temp
are copied into InOutVec.

    Let us now turn our attention to the procedure MergePass given in Fig.
5-28. Each pass requires the execution of a number of subpasses (or simple
merges of pairs of subvectors). This quantity (NumPairs) depends on the total
number of elements (N) to be sorted and the size of a subvector (SubSize)
in a subpass:

{Step 3: Copy the remaining unprocessed elements into output area}
**if** I > M
**then** {Used all of A's elements, so copy rest of B into C}
    **for** R := J **to** N **do**
      **begin**
        C[K] := B[R];
        K := K + 1
      **end**
**else** {Used all of B's elements, so copy rest of A into C}
    **for** R := I **to** M **do**
      **begin**
        C[K] := A[R];
        K := K + 1
      **end**
**end**;

FIGURE 5-25 (*cont.*)

NumPairs := N **div** (2 * SubSize)

The procedure also must keep track of the elements that are to be merged in a particular subpass or simple merge. Notice that InVec, although it is an input parameter, is pass as variable to avoid the extra copy that pass by value would supply.

Step 1 computes the number of simple merges that must be performed during the current pass. Step 2 controls the execution of these simple merges. Step 3 keeps track of the subvector being merged during each subpass (simple merge). Step 4 invokes procedure ModifiedSimpleMerge to merge a pair of sorted subvectors. The first subvector has its first element at position LB. The position of the first element of the second subvector is given by

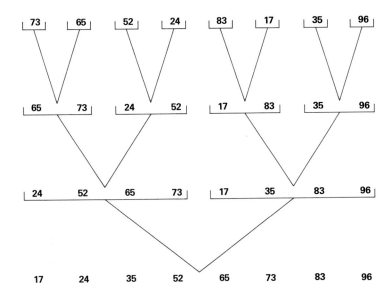

FIGURE 5-26
Two-way merge
sorting.

```
procedure MergeSort (
    var InOutVec: Vector;      {Input/output, on entry, an unsorted vector;
                                  upon completion, sorted into ascending order}
    N: integer                 {Input, the number of elements in InOutVec}
                 );
```
{Given an unsorted vector, this program performs a sort according to the method described in the text. The calling program must define the type Vector to be an array of integer, with lower bound of 1. The value of N may not be greater than the upper bound of this Vector type.}
```
var
    Temp: Vector;              {Auxiliary area to hold result of merge
                                  (on odd numbered passes) or input
                                  to merge (on even numbered passes)}
    PassNum, SubSize: integer;  {As described in the text}

    {Include procedures ModifiedSimpleMerge and MergePass here.}

begin
    {Step 1: Perform sort}
    for PassNum : = 1 to round (ln (N) / ln (2)) do
        begin

            {Step 2: Determine the size of subvector in current pass}
            SubSize : = round (exp ((PassNum − 1) * ln (2)));

            {Step 3: Perform current pass}
            if odd (PassNum)
            then MergePass (InOutVec, N, SubSize, Temp)
            else MergePass (Temp, N, SubSize, InOutVec);
        end;

    {Step 4: Ensure the result is in InOutVec}
    if odd (round (ln (N) / ln (2)))
    then InOutVec : = Temp
end;
```

**FIGURE 5-27**
**Merge sort procedure.**

the expression $LB + SubSize$. Note that since we assume that the size of the original vector is an integral power of 2, the sizes of each subvector in a given pair are always the same.

We now proceed to give the details of procedure ModifiedSimpleMerge in Fig. 5-29. This procedure is very similar to procedure SimpleMerge given earlier. The basic difference is that the two subvectors being merged are from the same vector and the lower subscript bounds of each subvector are not 1. Note that the two subvectors are always of the same size with the assumptions that we have made.

The behavior of procedure MergeSort on some sample data is shown

```
procedure MergePass (
    var InVec: Vector;         {Input, vector}
    N: integer;                {Input, number of elements in InVec}
    SubSize: integer;          {Input, number of elements in each subvector}
    var OutVec: Vector         {Output, vector}
                        );
```
{Given a vector, the number of elements it contains, and the size of the
sorted subvector, this procedure merges pairs of subvectors and places the
result in the output vector.}
```
var
    NumPairs: integer;         {Number of pairs of subvectors to be merged on
                                  this pass}
    LB: integer;               {Position of the first element of the first subvector
                                  for a simple merge}
    J: integer;                {Loop control}
begin
    {Step 1: Determine the number of pairs of subvectors to be merged}
    NumPairs := N div (2 * SubSize);

    {Step 2: Perform successive simple merges for current pass}
    for J := 1 to NumPairs do
        begin

            {Step 3: Determine lower bound position of first subvector}
            LB := 1 + (2 * J − 2) * SubSize;

            {Step 4: Perform simple merge of subvector pairs}
            ModifiedSimpleMerge (InVec, LB, SubSize, InVec, LB + SubSize,
            SubSize, OutVec, LB)
        end
end;
```

**FIGURE 5-28**
**Subpass procedure**
**for merge sort.**

in Table 5-8. The vertical strokes delineate the subtables being merged in a
particular pass. This sorting method is quite efficient. Since $\log_2 n$ passes are
required in the sort, the total number of comparisons required is proportional
to $n \times \log_2 n$. This quantity represents the worst case, as well as the average
case. An obvious disadvantage in using this method is that an output area
equal in size to the original unsorted vector is required.

In closing, we reemphasize that procedure MergeSort works only if
$n = 2^m$. This procedure can be changed to handle the general case.

# EXERCISES 5-3

1. Write a program to test the selection sort (revised) in Fig. 5-18.

2. Write a program to test the merge sort in Figs. 5-27, 5-28, and 5-29.

**procedure** ModifiedSimpleMerge (
    **var** A: Vector;               {Input, first vector}
    LBA: integer;          {Input, lower bound of first subvector in A}
    ASize: integer;        {Input, size of first subvector}
    **var** B: Vector;             {Input, second vector}
    LBB: integer;          {Input, lower bound of second subvector B}
    BSize: integer;        {Input, size of second subvector}
    **var** C: Vector;             {Output, vector}
    LBC: integer           {Input, lower bound of output subvector in C}
                           );
  {Given two sorted subvectors, this procedure merges these subvectors into a third subvector.}
  **var**
    UBA, UBB: integer;       {Upper bounds of first and second subvectors}

    APos, BPos, CPos: integer;   {Indices into subvector}
    J: integer;                {Loop Control}
  **begin**
    {Step 1: Initialize}
    UBA := LBA + ASize − 1;
    UBB := LBB + BSize − 1;
    APos := LBA;
    BPos := LBB;
    CPos := LBC;

**FIGURE 5-29**
Modified simple merge
for merge sort.

★ **3.** Given a vector X of $n$ real elements, where $n$ is odd, design a function to calculate and return the median of this vector. The median is the value such that half the numbers are greater than the value and half are less. For example, given the vector X:

| $X_1$ | $X_2$ | $X_3$ | $X_4$ | $X_5$ | $X_6$ | $X_7$ | $X_8$ | $X_9$ |
|------|------|------|------|------|------|------|------|------|
| 17.0 | −3.0 | 21.0 | 2.0 | 9.0 | −4.0 | 6.0 | 8.0 | 11.0 |

containing nine elements, the execution of your algorithm should give a value of 8.0. Write a program to test your function.

★ **4.** Procedure MergeSort given in the text works only if $n = 2^m$. Extend this procedure so that it can handle any value of $n$. A trace of this more

**TABLE 5-8** Behavior of Two-Way Merge Sorting

| Pass | $K_1$ | $K_2$ | $K_3$ | $K_4$ | $K_5$ | $K_6$ | $K_7$ | $K_8$ | $C_1$ | $C_2$ | $C_3$ | $C_4$ | $C_5$ | $C_6$ | $C_7$ | $C_8$ |
|------|------|------|------|------|------|------|------|------|------|------|------|------|------|------|------|------|
|   | 73\| | 65\| | 52\| | 24\| | 83\| | 17\| | 35\| | 96\| | — | — | — | — | — | — | — | — |
| 1 | 73 | 65 | 52 | 24 | 83 | 17 | 35 | 96 | 65 | 73\| | 24 | 52\| | 17 | 83\| | 35 | 96\| |
| 2 | 24 | 52 | 65 | 73\| | 17 | 35 | 83 | 96\| | 65 | 73 | 24 | 52 | 17 | 83 | 35 | 96 |
| 3 | 24 | 52 | 65 | 73 | 17 | 35 | 83 | 96 | 17 | 24 | 35 | 52 | 65 | 73 | 83 | 96 |
|   | 17 | 24 | 35 | 52 | 65 | 73 | 83 | 96 | 17 | 24 | 35 | 52 | 65 | 73 | 83 | 96 |

{Step 2: Compare corresponding elements and output the smallest}
**while** (APos <= UBA) **and** (BPos <= UBB) **do**
    **if** A [APos] < B[BPos]
    **then begin**
          C[CPos] : = A[APos];
          APos : = APos + 1;
          CPos : = CPos + 1
    **end**
    **else begin**
          C[CPos] : = B[BPos];
          BPos : = BPos + 1;
          CPos : = CPos + 1
    **end**;

{Step 3: Copy the remaining unprocessed elements into output area}
**if** APos > UBA
**then** {Used all of A's elements, so copy rest of B into C}
    **for** J : = BPos **to** UBB **do**
      **begin**
        C[CPos] : = B[J];
        CPos : = CPos + 1
      **end**
**else** {Used all of B's elements, so copy rest of A into C}
    **for** J : = APos **to** UBA **do**
      **begin**
        C[CPos] : = A[J];
        CPos : = CPos + 1
      **end**
**end**;

FIGURE 5-29 (*cont.*)

general two-way merge process for a vector of 10 elements is given in Fig. 5-30.

★ 5. Another familiar sorting method is the *bubble sort*. It differs from the selection sort in that instead of finding the element with the smallest value and then performing an interchange, two elements are interchanged immediately upon discovering that they are out of order. Using this approach, at most $n - 1$ passes are required. During the first pass, InOutVec[1] and InOutVec[2] are compared, and if they are out of order, they are interchanged; this process is repeated for elements InOutVec[2] and InOutVec[3], InOutVec[3] and InOutVec[4], and so on. This method will cause elements with small values to "bubble up." After the first pass, the element with the largest value will be in the $n$th position. On each successive pass, the elements with the next largest value will be placed in position $n - 1$, $n - 2$, ..., 2, respectively.

After each pass through the vector, a check can be made to determine whether or not any interchanges were made during the pass. If no

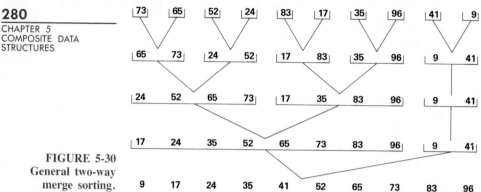

**FIGURE 5-30**
General two-way
merge sorting.

interchanges have occurred during the last pass, then the vector must be sorted and, consequently, no further passes are required. A sample behavior of this sorting process is given in Table 5-9. Write a procedure for this sorting process. Write a program to test your procedure.

★★ 6. Alter the procedure obtained in Exercise 5 to take advantage of the fact that all elements below and including the last one to be exchanged must be in the correct order; consequently, those elements do not have to be examined again.

★★ 7. Modify the procedure obtained in Exercise 6 such that alternate passes go in opposite directions. That is, during the first pass, the element with the largest value will be at the end of the vector, and during the second pass the element with the smallest value will be in the first position of the vector, and so on. A sample behavior of such a modified approach is given in Table 5-10.

★★ 8. A large firm has plants in five different cities. The firm employs a total of $n$ employees. Each employee record contains (in part) the following

**TABLE 5-9** Behavior of a Bubble Sort

| | Unsorted | | | | Pass Number | | | | | Sorted |
|---|---|---|---|---|---|---|---|---|---|---|
| i | InOutVec[i] | 1 | 2 | 3 | 4 | 5 | 6 | 7 | 8 | 9 |
| 1 | 73 | 65 | 52 | 24 | 24 | 17 | 17 | 17 | 17 | 9 |
| 2 | 65 | 52 | 24 | 52 | 17 | 24 | 24 | 24 | 9 | 17 |
| 3 | 52 | 24 | 65 | 17 | 35 | 35 | 35 | 9 | 24 | 24 |
| 4 | 24 | 73 | 17 | 35 | 52 | 41 | 9 | 35 | 35 | 35 |
| 5 | 83 | 17 | 35 | 65 | 41 | 9 | 41 | 41 | 41 | 41 |
| 6 | 17 | 35 | 73 | 41 | 9 | 52 | 52 | 52 | 52 | 52 |
| 7 | 35 | 83 | 41 | 9 | 65 | 65 | 65 | 65 | 65 | 65 |
| 8 | 96 | 41 | 9 | 73 | 73 | 73 | 73 | 73 | 73 | 73 |
| 9 | 41 | 9 | 83 | 83 | 83 | 83 | 83 | 83 | 83 | 83 |
| 10 | 9 | 96 | 96 | 96 | 96 | 96 | 96 | 96 | 96 | 96 |

**TABLE 5-10** Behavior of a Modified Bubble Sort

| i | Unsorted InOutVec[i] | Pass Number 1 | 2 | 3 | 4 | 5 | 6 | Sorted 7 |
|---|---|---|---|---|---|---|---|---|
| 1 | 73 | 65 | 9 | 9 | 9 | 9 | 9 | 9 |
| 2 | 65 | 52 | 65 | 52 | 17 | 17 | 17 | 17 |
| 3 | 52 | 24 | 52 | 24 | 52 | 24 | 24 | 24 |
| 4 | 24 | 73 | 24 | 65 | 24 | 35 | 35 | 35 |
| 5 | 83 | 17 | 73 | 73 | 65 | 52 | 52 | 41 |
| 6 | 17 | 35 | 17 | 17 | 35 | 41 | 41 | 52 |
| 7 | 35 | 83 | 35 | 35 | 41 | 65 | 65 | 65 |
| 8 | 96 | 41 | 83 | 41 | 73 | 73 | 73 | 73 |
| 9 | 41 | 9 | 41 | 83 | 83 | 83 | 83 | 83 |
| 10 | 9 | 96 | 96 | 96 | 96 | 96 | 96 | 96 |

fields:

employee identification number, city

These records are not kept in any order. Assume that the city field is coded with an integer value of 1 to 5. The information on the employees can be represented by two vectors: Number and City. Write a program which reads in, sorts, and displays all the employee records by increasing employee number within each city. That is, the format is as shown in Fig. 5-31.

★★ **9.** Management information systems are becoming more and more common. They allow an administrator to type a request for information into a computer and obtain the answer to the request. In this problem we will consider one such request: Given the number of an employee, find the department in which the employee works. These requests come in the form of the character 'D' (for department) followed by the employee's number. The last of these requests is the character 'F'.

In order to respond to such requests, the following information is available. First, there is a file of employee information. This data file contains the employee's number and the number of his or her supervisor. This information is in numerical order by employee number, and the last record in this portion of the file has a sentinel employee number of 0. The company has a large number of employees; the current number (which changes from time to time) is 134. Since the number of employees is large and the file is in numerical order by employee number, when seeking the record for a specific employee, a binary search should be used. It is known that every supervisor is also the manager of a department. Thus, in order to determine the department in which an employee works, we must determine the name of the department that the employee's supervisor manages. This information can be determined from the department portion of the data file. This file contains

First city:

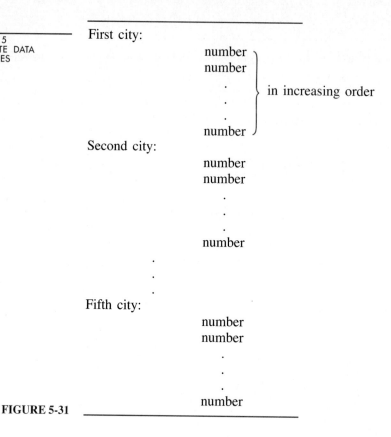

Second city:

Fifth city:

**FIGURE 5-31**

the number of each department and the number of the manager of the department. This file is ordered by department number. Note there are always less than 50 departments.

Formulate a program to respond to this type of request. For your data, assume that the department portion of the data file is preceded by a number specifying the number of records (departments) in the department file. The employee portion comes next. Last come the requests for information.

10. Andrew, Brad, and Carey like to play golf every Saturday morning at the local golf course. They have golfed together for the past few summers, always keeping track of scores and always playing to win. The winner is the one whose score is the lowest after subtracting his handicap from the number of strokes he took in the day's round (this adjusted score is called the *net* score). Andrew usually calculates these scores in his head, but Brad and Carey don't trust him anymore, so they have asked you to write a program that will do the calculations.

The method used for calculating a handicap is as follows:

handicap = max(((sum of lowest 10 scores of last 20 games) **div** 10 − 72), 0)

If this equation results in a negative value, the handicap is 0. For each of the three players, your program must read in his number (Andrew = 1, Brad = 2, and Carey = 3), his most recent 20 scores, and his gross score for the current day's round. After doing the calculations, a table should be displayed showing each player's name, gross score for the round, and net score for the round. (This table should be in decreasing order of net score so that the winner is at the top and the loser is at the bottom.) Use a function to calculate the handicap.

## 5-4 INTRODUCTION TO ALGORITHM ANALYSIS

As soon as we can design algorithms and programs, it is important to learn how to analyze them. This is an important part of being a computer scientist.

This analysis can take several forms. First, there is the question of the correctness of the algorithm that is ultimately implemented as a program. This can be determined by tracing the algorithm, reading the algorithm for logical correctness, implementing the algorithm and testing it on some data, or using mathematical techniques to prove it correct. Another question relates to the simplicity of the algorithm. Perhaps the algorithm can be expressed in a simpler way so that it is easier to implement and perform other analyses on the algorithm. The most straightforward way of solving a problem, however, is sometimes not the best one. Usually this occurs when the simplest approach involves the use of too much computer time or space. Thus it is important to be able to analyze the time and space requirements of an algorithm to see if they are within acceptable limits. For example, if an algorithm to control the trajectory of a rocket required several seconds for each trajectory adjustment, it would be unacceptable. Time and space analyses are also important for comparison of algorithms to determine the best one.

Some informal discussion of these matters has already been given. This section introduces basic concepts in analyzing the time and space requirements of an algorithm in a more rigorous fashion. The analysis will emphasize timing analysis initially and then, to a lesser extent, space analysis.

### 5-4.1 RATE OF GROWTH AND BASIC TIME ANALYSIS OF AN ALGORITHM

Unfortunately it is rarely possible to perform a simple analysis of an algorithm to determine the exact amount of time required to execute it. The first complication is that the exact amount of time will depend on the implementation of the algorithm and on the actual machine. We would usually like our analysis to be useful in as general a context as possible and be independent of the particular language or machine that might ultimately be used to implement it. As a result, we cannot expect our analysis to yield an exact value for the time required. Even if we did specify the language and machine to be used, the task of calculating the exact time required would be laborious. To do this task, we would need to know the exact instructions executed by the hardware and the time required for each instruction. Fortunately, we are normally satisfied if our analysis is capable of giving the order of magnitude for the time required.

In this subsection we examine the time required for the execution of several simple algorithms. Each of these algorithms will have a different computational cost.

Basic statements, such as assignment statements, that are executed only once (that is, do not occur in a loop) are said to execute in *constant time*. For example, the assignment statement

GrossPay : = RegularHours * PayRate + OvertimeHours * 1.5 * PayRate

will take a fixed time to execute regardless of the data elements on which it operates. Other algorithms may have time requirements that will depend directly on the amount of data that is processed. Consider, for example, the function that sums the values of a given vector, given in Figure 5-32.

An obvious approach to analyzing a program is to determine how many times each step in the program is executed. In the current example, we have the following

Step 1    1 time
Step 2    $N$ times
Step 3    1 time

Since steps 1 and 3 are performed once regardless of the value of $N$, the dominant step in the timing of the program is step 2. Consequently, as $N$ increases, we need only be concerned with this step.

```
function SumValues (
    V: Vector;      {Input, vector of real values}
    N: integer      {Input, number of elements}
                ): real;
{Given a vector of real values, this function computes the sum of the
    elements.}
var
    K: integer;     {Loop control variable}
    Sum: real;      {Sum of elements}
begin
    {Step 1: Initialize}
    Sum : = 0.0;

    {Step 2: Compute the sum}
    for K : = 1 to N do
        Sum : = Sum + V[K];

    {Step 3: Return the sum}
    SumValues : = Sum
end;
```

**FIGURE 5-32**
**Sum the values**
**of a vector.**

As remarked earlier, rather than calculating the exact execution time, we want an implementation-independent estimate of it. Another (and easier) approach to analyzing a program is to isolate a particular operation, sometimes called an *active operation*, that is central to the program and that is executed as often as or more often than any other. In the SumValues example, a good operation to isolate is the addition that occurs when another vector value is added to the partial sum; that is, the statement Sum := Sum + V[K]. The other operations in the function, the assignments, the manipulations of the index K, and the accessing of a value in the vector, occur no more often than the addition of vector values. These other operations are collectively called the *bookkeeping operations* and are generally not counted. It is important that none of the bookkeeping operations is executed significantly more often than the active operation. (Later we will see that it is not a problem if one is executed slightly more often.) After the active operation is isolated, we count the number of times that it is executed. If we follow this approach in the example, the active operation is executed a total of N times—once for each time through the loop. As long as the active operation occurs at least as often as the others, then the total execution time will increase in proportion to the number of times the active operation is executed. Thus the function SumValues has execution time proportional to N. Or, expressed another way, the time required is linearly proportional to the size of the input data.

As another example, consider the procedure for the selection sort given earlier in Sec. 5-3.1. For convenience, we reproduce revision 1 of that sort as Fig. 5-33.

Let us consider the time analysis of this procedure. We choose the comparison in the if statement contained within the inner for loop, as the active operation. Because this comparison is nested within the inner loop, it will be the most frequently executed operation. During the first pass, in which the element with the smallest value is found, $N - 1$ elements are compared. In general, for a particular pass, $N -$ Pass comparisons are required. The total number of comparisons is, therefore, the sum of the number of comparisons taken in each of the $N - 1$ passes, that is,

$$\sum_{\text{Pass}=1}^{N-1} (N - \text{Pass}) = \sum_{\text{Pass}=1}^{N-1} N - \sum_{\text{Pass}=1}^{N-1} \text{Pass}$$

$$= N \times (N - 1) - \frac{N \times (N - 1)}{2}$$

$$= \frac{N \times (N - 1)}{2}$$

$$= \frac{N^2}{2} - \frac{N}{2}$$

As N gets large, the $N^2$ term in the expression dominates. Therefore, we say that the number of comparisons is proportional to $N^2$.

```
procedure SelectionSort1 (
    var InOutVec: Vector;      {Input/output; on entry, an unsorted vector;
                                upon completion, sorted into ascending order}
    N: integer                 {Input, number of elements in InOutVec}
    );
```
{Given a vector of integer values, this procedure sorts them into ascending order.}
```
var
    MinIndex: integer;    {Position of smallest element in a particular pass}
    Pass: integer;        {Current pass number}
    J: integer;           {Loop counter}
    Temp: integer;        {Temporary for swapping}
begin
    {Step 1: Engage loop to perform N − 1 passes}
    for Pass := 1 to N − 1 do
        begin

            {Step 2: Find smallest value in remaining vector}
            MinIndex := Pass;
            for J := Pass + 1 to N do
                if InOutVec[J] < InOutVec[MinIndex]
                then MinIndex := J;

            {Step 3: Place smallest value into proper position}
            if MinIndex <> Pass
            then begin
                    Temp := InOutVec[MinIndex];
                    InOutVec[MinIndex] := InOutVec[Pass];
                    InOutVec[Pass] := Temp
                end
        end
end;
```

**FIGURE 5-33**
Selection sort,
revision 1.

To get a better appreciation for the performance of this sorting method, let us assume that we want to sort the 100,000 customers of a credit card company by customer number. If we assume that each comparison takes only $10^{-6}$ seconds, the average time to perform all the comparisons in the sort is

$$\left[\frac{100,000 \times 99,999}{2}\right] \text{ comparisons} \times 10^{-6} \text{ seconds/comparison}$$

which is slightly more than 83 minutes! Clearly, if the required sort were only one step in a complex algorithm, such a situation might become intolerable.

As a third example, let us consider a special case of the function BinarySearch given in Sec. 5-3.2. The version that we give in Fig. 5-34,

```
function BinSearch (
    InVec: Vector;      {Input, the vector to be searched}
    N: integer;         {Input, the number of elements in InVec}
    Key: integer        {Input, the value to be searched for}
                ): integer;
{Given a vector with N integer elements, where N is assumed to be an inte-
    gral power of 2, and where the elements are assumed to be in ascending
    order, this function searches the vector for a given element. If the search
    is successful, the position of the found element is returned; otherwise the
    value 0 is returned.}
var
    Low, High, Middle: integer;      {Indices of InVec}
begin
    {Step 1: Initialize}
    Low := 1;
    High := N;

    {Step 2: Engage search loop}
    while High − Low >= 1 do
        begin
            Middle := (Low + High) div 2;
            if Key <= InVec[Middle]
            then High := Middle
            else Low := Middle + 1
        end;

    {Step 3: Return correct value}
    if Key = InVec[High]
    then BinSearch := High
    else BinSearch := 0
end;
```

**FIGURE 5-34**
**Binary search function, version for timing analysis.**

while less efficient than that given earlier, is designed to make its timing analysis simple.

Consider the comparison within the loop as the active operation. This comparison (except for bookkeeping operations) is the most frequently performed operation in the function. If the size of the table is assumed to be an integral power of 2, then the size of each successive search interval is one-half its predecessor. For example, if $N = 16$, the initial search interval is 16. As the algorithm progresses, successive search interval sizes are 8, 4, 2, and 1. The number of comparisons performed in step 4 is thus $\log_2 N$. We say this algorithm executes in *logarithmic time*.

Other algorithms can be found whose timings are *polynomial*, for example, $n^2$ and $n^3$. Some algorithms have timings that are *exponential*, for example, $2^n$, $n^n$, and $n! \approx (n/2.56)^n$ (using Stirling's approximation for $n!$). Figure 5-35 plots several of these functions. As is readily apparent, some

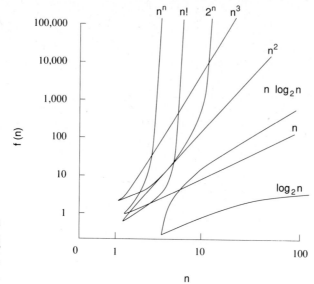

**FIGURE 5-35**
**Graph showing growth rates of several familiar functions.**

functions grow much faster than do others. To facilitate the comparison of these functions, we have used log scales for both axes in the figure. Table 5-11 contains values of several well known functions for various values of $n$. For example, assuming $n = 100$ and that a computer executes 1 million operations per second, it would take $2.96 \times 10^{144}$ years to execute 100! operations. Algorithms with polynomial time can solve reasonably sized problems if the constant in the exponent is small. For problems involving large amounts of data, it is necessary to find an algorithm whose execution time grows *linearly* (that is, proportional to $n$) or sublinearly, for instance, proportional to $\log_2 n$, or else the computation time will be unacceptably long.

## 5-4.2 ORDER NOTATION

A notation has been developed to facilitate the expression of order-of-magnitude functions. A function $f(n)$ is defined to be $O(g(n))$, that is, $f(n) = O(g(n))$, and is said to be of order $g(n)$, if there exist positive constants $n_0$ and $c$ such that

$$|f(n)| \leq c \times |g(n)| \quad \text{for all } n > n_0$$

This says that $f(n)$ is of order $g(n)$ if $f(n)$ is bounded by $g(n)$ multiplied by a constant $c$.

It is easy to verify the following:

$100n^3$ is $O(n^3)$

$6n^2 + 2n + 4$ is $O(n^2)$

**TABLE 5-11** Sample Tabulation of the Values for Several Well Known Functions that Are Used in Timing Analysis

| $n$ | $\log_2 n$ | $n$ | $n\log_2 n$ | $n^2$ | $2^n$ | $n!$ | $n^n$ |
|---|---|---|---|---|---|---|---|
| 1 | | $1.0 \times 10^{-6}$ s | | $1.0 \times 10^{-6}$ s | $2.0 \times 10^{-6}$ s | $1.0 \times 10^{-6}$ s | $1.0 \times 10^{-6}$ s |
| 2 | $1.0 \times 10^{-6}$ s | $2.0 \times 10^{-6}$ s | $2.0 \times 10^{-6}$ s | $4.0 \times 10^{-6}$ s | $4.0 \times 10^{-6}$ s | $2.0 \times 10^{-6}$ s | $4.0 \times 10^{-6}$ s |
| 10 | $3.3 \times 10^{-6}$ s | $1.0 \times 10^{-5}$ s | $3.3 \times 10^{-5}$ s | $1.0 \times 10^{-4}$ s | $1.0 \times 10^{-3}$ s | $3.63$ s | $2.78$ hr |
| 20 | $4.3 \times 10^{-6}$ s | $2.0 \times 10^{-5}$ s | $8.6 \times 10^{-5}$ s | $4.0 \times 10^{-4}$ s | $1.05$ s | Over 77,000 yr | $3.3 \times 10^{12}$ yr |
| 100 | $6.6 \times 10^{-6}$ s | $1.0 \times 10^{-4}$ s | $6.6 \times 10^{-4}$ s | $1.0 \times 10^{-2}$ s | $4.0 \times 10^{16}$ yr | $2.96 \times 10^{144}$ yr | $3.40 \times 10^{289}$ yr |

$$1 + 2 + 3 + \cdots + n = n \times (n + 1)/2 = n^2 + O(n) = O(n^2)$$

1024 is $O(1)$

$n + \log n$ is $O(n)$

$3n$ is $O(n^2)$ [and also $O(n)$]

Using the definition of a limit from calculus, the preceding definition can be shown to be equivalent to

$$\lim_{n \to \infty} \frac{|f(n)|}{|g(n)|} = c$$

for some constant $c$. In this form, L'Hôpital's rule is often useful for computing the limit. It states that if

$$\lim_{n \to \infty} f(n) = \infty \qquad \text{and} \qquad \lim_{n \to \infty} g(n) = \infty$$

then

$$\lim_{n \to \infty} \frac{f(n)}{g(n)} = \lim_{n \to \infty} \frac{f'(n)}{g'(n)}$$

where $f'$ and $g'$ are derivatives of $f$ and $g$. Thus, as an example,

$$\lim_{n \to \infty} \frac{\ln(n)}{n} = \lim_{n \to \infty} \frac{1/n}{1} = \lim_{n \to \infty} \frac{1}{n} = 0$$

so

$$\ln(n) = O(n)$$

where $\ln(n)$ is the natural logarithm of $n$. Using this notation, we have

$$T_{SV}(n) = O(n) \qquad T_{SS}(n) = O(n^2) \qquad \text{and} \qquad T_{BS}(n) = O(\log_2 n)$$

where $T_{SV}$ is the time for function SumValues, $T_{SS}$ is the time for the procedure SelectionSort, and $T_{BS}$ is the time for the function BinSearch.

## 5-4.3  MORE TIMING ANALYSIS

In this section two more algorithms will be analyzed to develop further techniques. First, consider the function to perform a linear search of a vector given in Fig. 5-19 and repeated in Fig. 5-36 for ease of reference. A reasonably active operation here is the comparison between values of InVec and Key. A problem arises, however, in counting the number of active operations executed. The answer depends on the index of the location containing Key. The best case is when Key is equal to InVec[1], since only one comparison

```
function LinearSearch (
    InVec: Vector;      {Input, the vector to be searched, assumed to be
                            an array of integers}
    N: integer;         {Input the number of elements in InVec}
    Key: integer        {Input, the value to be searched for}
                    ): integer;
```
{Given an unordered vector, this function searches the vector for a particular
  element. If the search is successful, the position of the first such element
  found is returned; otherwise 0 is returned.}
```
var
    NotFound: boolean;      {Loop control flag; set true if key is
                                "not found" yet}
    K: integer;             {Loop counter and index into vector}
begin
    {Step 1: Initialize}
    LinearSearch : = 0;     {Return 0 if not found}
    NotFound : = true;      {Initialize for loop}
    K : = 1;


    {Step 2: Engage search loop}
    while NotFound and (K <= N) do
        begin

            {Step 3: Test element, quit if found}
            if InVec[K] = Key
            then begin
                    LinearSearch : = K;
                    NotFound : = false
                end;

            {Step 4: Increment loop control variable}
            K : = K + 1
        end
end;
```

FIGURE 5-36
Linear search function.

is used. The worst case is when Key is equal to InVec[N] and N comparisons
are used. Thus we obtain

$$T_{LS}^B (N) = O(1) \qquad \text{and} \qquad T_{LS}^W (N) = O(N)$$

where $T_{LS}^B$ and $T_{LS}^W$ denote the best-case time and the worst-case time for the
linear search, respectively.

The important question is, "What time can be expected on the average?"
To answer this question, we need to know the probability distribution for
the value Key in the vector, that is, the probability of Key occurring in each
location. We will assume that Key is equally likely to be in each of the

locations. But Key might not be in the list at all. Let $q$ be the probability that Key is in the list. Then using the preceding assumption, we have

probability Key is in location J is $q/N$
probability Key is not in the vector is $1 - q$

The average time is given by

$$T_{LS}^A(N) = \sum_{s \text{ in } S} (\text{probability of situation } s) \times (\text{time for situation } s)$$

where $S$ is the set of all possible situations. Thus, for the preceding algorithm we have

$$T_{LS}^A(N) = (\text{probability of Key in location 1}) \times 1$$
$$+ (\text{probability of Key in location 2}) \times 2 + \cdots$$
$$+ (\text{probability of Key in location } N) \times N$$
$$+ (\text{probability of Key not in InVec}) \times N$$

$$= \sum_{s=1}^{N} \frac{q}{N} \times s + (1 - q) \times N$$

$$= \frac{q}{N} \sum_{s=1}^{N} s + (1 - q) \times N$$

$$= q \times \frac{(N + 1)}{2} + (1 - q) \times N \qquad \text{since} \quad \sum_{s=1}^{N} s = \frac{N(N + 1)}{2}$$

Thus, if $q = 1$ (Key *is* in the list), then

$$T_{LS}^A(N) = \frac{(N + 1)}{2}$$

and if $q = \frac{1}{2}$ (Key is as likely to be in the list as not), then

$$T_{LS}^A(N) = \frac{(N + 1)}{4} + \frac{N}{2} \approx \frac{3N}{4}$$

In either case, $T_{LS}^A(N) = O(N)$.

Unfortunately, as the preceding example indicates, average-case timing analysis is generally more difficult than best-case or worst-case timing. The difficulties begin with the need to obtain a reasonable probability distribution of the possible situations. For many problems, this is difficult to do. As a result, only the worst-case timing analysis is done for many algorithms, since it provides an upper bound on the execution time.

It is interesting to consider the alternative version of the linear search given in Fig. 5-20 and repeated in Fig. 5-37 for ease of reference. The number of comparisons between InVec and Key is the same as for the previous

```
function LinearSearch1 (
    InVec: Vector;     {Input, the vector to be searched, assumed to be
                        an array of integers}
    N: integer;        {Input, the number of elements in InVec}
    Key: integer       {Input, the value to be searched for}
                    ): integer;
```

{Given an unordered vector of integers, this function searches the vector for a particular element. If the search is successful, the position of the first such element is returned; otherwise the value 0 is returned. Vector element InVec[N + 1] must be available to be used as a sentinel element within this function.}

```
var
    I: integer;        {Loop counter}
begin
    {Step 1: Initialize}
    I := 1;

    {Step 2: Store sentinel}
    InVec[N + 1] := Key;

    {Step 3: Search vector}
    while InVec[I] <> Key do
        I := I + 1;

    {Step 4: Return appropriate value}
    if I = N + 1
    then LinearSearch1 := 0
    else LinearSearch1 := I
end
```

**FIGURE 5-37**
Linear search function
(revision 1).

program, except that one more comparison is required for the present program when Key is not in the vector. Thus using a count of executions of the active operation, we would conclude that the first program is marginally better. But for programs with the same order, the constants associated with the largest term of the timing function should be estimated. In this example, it is easy to see that there are significantly more bookkeeping operations for the first program than for the second. This results in a larger constant associated with the term for $N$ in the equation for the time of the first program. Thus the second program will be more efficient. To determine the differences in the constants would necessitate a much more detailed analysis. For such comparisons, it is sometimes better to implement and time both versions. Nevertheless, it is frequently useful to try to give an order-of-magnitude estimate for the size of the constant associated with the largest term.

## 5-4.4 SPACE ANALYSIS OF AN ALGORITHM

The analysis of the space requirements for a program or algorithm is generally easier than the timing analysis, but where necessary, the same techniques are used. Usually the space analysis is done only for the space to store the data values and hence does not include the space to store the program itself. Also, as for timing analysis, the space function is usually expressed in order notation. For example, the space requirements of the binary search function of Fig. 5-34 is $O(n)$. The space requirements of several programs will be presented in later chapters.

## EXERCISES 5-4

1. Consider a vector $X$ which contains 10 elements. Assume that the distribution of requests for each element in this vector is as shown in Table 5-12.
   (a) Compute the average number of comparisons for a sequential search of this vector.
   (b) Suggest a more efficient arrangement of the data entries. Based on this arrangement, recompute the average number of comparisons for a sequential search.

★★ 2. Suppose that we have a vector Next with data entries as follows:

| K | Next [K] |
|---|----------|
| 1 | 0 |
| 2 | 1 |
| 3 | 2 |
| . | . |
| . | . |
| . | . |

Also suppose we have a vector S of size M and a vector T of size

**TABLE 5-12**

| $i$ | $X_i$ | Distribution of Requests, % |
|-----|-------|-----------------------------|
| 1 | $X_1$ | 10 |
| 2 | $X_2$ | 5 |
| 3 | $X_3$ | 20 |
| 4 | $X_4$ | 5 |
| 5 | $X_5$ | 25 |
| 6 | $X_6$ | 10 |
| 7 | $X_7$ | 5 |
| 8 | $X_8$ | 5 |
| 9 | $X_9$ | 5 |
| 10 | $X_{10}$ | 10 |

N. Consider the program segment in Fig. 5-38. Without counting the initializations:

*(a)* In the best case, how many times is the value of J changed, and how many times is the value of K changed?

*(b)* In the worst case, how many times is the value of J changed, and how many times is the value of K changed?

Explain your answers.

3. Give the simplest and most accurate representation in order notation for the following:
   *(a)* $f(n) = 12n + 2n^3 + 3$
   *(b)* $g(n) = 6n \log_2 n + 100n$

4. *(a)* List the following functions in groups so that two functions, say, $f$ and $g$, are in the same group if and only if $f = O(g)$.

   | | |
   |---|---|
   | $n$ | $n^3$ |
   | $2^n$ | $\log n$ |
   | $n \log_3 n$ | $n^{1/2} + \log n$ |
   | $n - n^3 + 7n^5$ | $(\log n)^2$ |
   | $n^2 + \log n$ | $n!$ |
   | $n^2$ | $\ln n$ |

   *(b)* List the groups in part *(a)* from *lowest* to *highest*.

★ 5. Consider the following program segment to print out a table (all variables are of type integer):

```
for J := 1 to N do
    write (J);
writeln;
for K := 1 to M do
    begin
        read (P);
        for L := 1 to N do
            write (P * L);
        writeln
    end
```

   Give the order for the time required by the program.

★ 6. The functions in Figs. 5-39 and 5-40 take an input vector X of N real numbers and return the maximum sum found in any contiguous subvector of the input. For example, if the input vector X is

   31  −41  59  26  −53  58  97  −93  −23  84

   the functions will find the sum of X[3] to X[7] = 187 to be the largest sum, and this value will be returned by the functions. In which situations do these functions not work? Give the worst-case time complexity of

```
        J := 1;
        K := 1;
        while (J <= M) and (K <= N) do
            begin
                StopLoop := false;
                while (K > 0) and not StopLoop do
                    if S [J] <> T [K]
                    then K := Next [K]
                    else StopLoop := true;
                J := J + 1;
                K := K + 1
            end
```

FIGURE 5-38

each function using order notation. Explain how you determined the time complexity. What is the active operation?

★ 7. Given Fig. 5-41, a procedure for a bubble sort (see Exercise 5 in Sec. 5-3), what is the worst-case time complexity of this program in terms of N?

```
function MaxCon1 (X: RealVector; N: integer): real;
{Given a vector of real values, this function finds the maximum sum found
    in any contiguous subvector.}
var
    MaxSoFar, Sum: real;
    Lower, Upper, K: integer;
begin
    {Initialize}
    MaxSoFar := 0.0;

    {Engage nested loops to test each contiguous subvector}
    for Lower := 1 to N do
        for Upper := Lower to N do
            begin

                {Sum elements}
                Sum := 0.0;
                for K := Lower to Upper do
                    Sum := Sum + X[K];

                {Test sum}
                if Sum > MaxSoFar
                then MaxSoFar := Sum
            end;
    MaxCon1 := MaxSoFar
end;
```

FIGURE 5-39
Function MaxCon1.

```
function MaxCon2 (X: RealVector; N: integer): real;
{Given a vector of real values, this function finds the maximum sum found
  in any contiguous subvector.}
var
  MaxSoFar, Sum: real;
  Lower, Upper: integer;
begin
  {Initialize}
  MaxSoFar : = 0.0;

  {Engage loop to consider each element as the beginning of a subvector}
  for Lower : = 1 to N do
    begin

      {Test each possible subvector}
      Sum : = 0.0;
      for Upper : = Lower to N do
        begin
          Sum : = Sum + X[Upper];
          if Sum > MaxSoFar
          then MaxSoFar : = Sum
        end
    end;
  MaxCon2 : = MaxSoFar
end;
```

FIGURE 5-40
Function MaxCon2.

## 5-5  APPLICATIONS OF VECTORS

This section contains two applications of vectors. The first application concerns the design of routines to insert and remove elements from a table that defines the symbols used in the translation of a computer program. The second application relates to an inventory system for a blood bank.

### 5-5.1  PROCESSING SYMBOL TABLES

During the translation of many programming languages, a special table is constructed to contain relevant information about the variables encountered in processing the statements of the source programs. This table is known as a *symbol table* and contains information such as the name of a variable, its type, and its location in storage.

An entry is made into the symbol table whenever a new variable is first introduced. When the variable is subsequently used, the symbol table is interrogated for the information required by the compiler to complete the translation into executable machine language. In this subsection we investigate the use of vectors to manage a symbol table. We shall defer until later chapters string-processing considerations such as the identification and

```
procedure Bubble (
    var InOutVec: Vector;      {Input/output, integer vector to be sorted}
    N: integer                 {Input, number of elements}
            );
{Given a vector of integer elements, this procedure sorts the elements into
   ascending order.}
var
    Limit: integer;            {Index of last element for current pass}
    Cur: integer;              {Index of currently considered element}
    Swapped: boolean;          {True if an exchange was performed on the
                                  current pass}
    Temp: integer;             {Temporary used to exchange elements}
begin
    {Step 1: Initialize}
    Limit := N;
    Swapped := true;

    {Step 2: Engage loop for passes}
    while Swapped and (Limit > 1) do
        begin

            {Step 3: Initialize for pass}
            Limit := Limit - 1;
            Swapped := false;

            {Step 4: Engage loop to perform a pass}
            for Cur := 1 to Limit do

                {Step 5: Test elements and exchange if necessary}
                if InOutVec [Cur] > InOutVec [Cur + 1]
                then begin
                        Temp := InOutVec [Cur];
                        InOutVec [Cur] := InOutVec [Cur + 1];
                        InOutVec [Cur + 1] := Temp;
                        Swapped := true
                     end

        end
end;
```

**FIGURE 5-41**
Bubble sort procedure.

extraction of the variable names (or symbols) themselves from the statements of the program.

We turn first to the problem of placing a new entry into the symbol table. This occurs whenever a new variable is first introduced into a program. We will assume that a specification of the variable's type accompanies its introduction. The importance of the type as part of the symbol-table information will be seen shortly.

When a new variable is introduced, the compiler has the following responsibilities. First, it must acquire a main-storage area sufficient to hold a value of the specified type. The address of this main-storage area becomes the address of the variable that must be specified in all subsequent instructions involving the variable. Then, it must search the symbol table to ensure that no attempt has been made previously to define this same variable. Multiple definitions of a variable are not usually permitted in any programming language, and attempts to redefine a variable must be treated as a programming error. Should this attempt to define the variable prove to be legal, a new entry is made into the symbol table, consisting of the variable's name, the address of the memory area assigned to it, and an indication of its type.

Before we can design the appropriate symbol-table routines, we must concern ourselves with representational issues. For the symbol table itself, we will use vectors. In fact, we require more than one vector, since the entries have elements of different types: character string for the name of the variable, an enumeration for the variable type, and numeric for the address. We will employ "parallel" vectors. The three vectors used will represent our symbol table: a vector of type character string for the symbol name, a vector of an enumerated type for the symbol type, and a third vector of type integer for the address. This layout is shown in Fig. 5-42.

Following the specifications just given, a general algorithm for the insertion of an element into the symbol table would proceed as follows:

*1.* Search the symbol table for an element with the same name
   if found, then issue an error message and return immediately

*2.* If no match is found,
   then using the next available table position,
      insert the name, type, and address of the symbol

*3.* Return

We shall not concern ourselves in this subsection with the acquisition of main-storage space. Nor shall we be concerned with sorting the symbol table. Instead, we will assume the table to be unordered. For this reason,

| Name | Type | Address |
|------|------|---------|
| Alpha | Integer | 6030 |
| Beta | Real | 6034 |
| Gamma | Integer | 6038 |
| Letters | String | 7010 |
| • | • | • |
| • | • | • |
| • | • | • |

**FIGURE 5-42**
**Symbol-table**
**organization.**

we will be forced to rely on a linear search as described in Sec. 5-3.2. In practical compilers, the number of variable names actually processed may force the designer to a more efficient search method, such as the binary search, in which case the table would have to be sorted prior to any retrieval attempts. We will be using a modified version of the function LinearSearch, of Sec. 5-3.2, to do our insertions and retrievals.

We now give the insertion procedure. Its parameters are the name of the variable to be defined (VarName), its type (VarType), and its address (VarAddress). As mentioned, we defer until later chapters considerations of how these values are determined in practice. The program using procedure Insert must contain some definitions and declarations. Vectors SymbolVector, TypeVector, and AddressVector, as well as the variable SymbolEntries, must be contained in the main program. If instead they were declared locally in procedure Insert, their values would not be retained from one call of Insert to the next. In addition, these variables must be accessible to procedure Retrieve, as we shall see shortly. Various types of declarations associated with the symbol table also must be provided. We also assume that SymbolEntries is initialized to 0. We could require that the symbol-table vectors and SymbolEntries be passed as input-output parameters to procedure Insert. However, if we assume that a compiler has only one symbol table, then this would needlessly complicate each call. Notice that we also have chosen to return a status code (using an enumerated type) rather than print an error message directly in the procedure. The motivation for each of these decisions is further elaborated on in Chap. 7. The declarations assumed are shown in Fig. 5-43. The program also must include function LinearSearch with the Key parameter changed to be of type Symbol. Procedure Insert appears in Fig. 5-44.

Notice the use of the function LinearSearch to check for a previous definition. Rather than search all positions of the table, we need only search those in which entries have been made. This number is given by the global variable SymbolEntries.

We turn now to the problem of retrieving the information needed for

```
const
    N = 1000;        {Maximum size of symbol table}
type
    Symbol = packed array [1 .. 8] of char;   {Symbol names}
    Vector = array [1 .. N] of Symbol;        {Type used by LinearSearch}
    SymbolType = (IntegerType, RealType, StringType);
    StatusCodes = (Successful, DupDeclError, TabFullError, UnDecVarError);
var
    SymbolVector: Vector;                      {Symbol}
    TypeVector: array [1 .. N] of SymbolType;  {Table}
    AddressVector: array [1 .. N] of integer;  {Vectors}
    SymbolEntries: integer;                    {Current number of entries
                                                 in the table; must be
                                                 initialized to 0}
```

**FIGURE 5-43**
**Declarations required in a program using Insert and Retrieve.**

```
procedure Insert (
    VarName: Symbol;            {Input, variable name}
    VarType: SymbolType;        {Input, variable type}
    VarAddress: integer;        {Input, variable address}
    var Status: StatusCodes     {Output, success or error indication}
                );
```
{Given a symbol, its type, and its address, this procedure enters the new symbol into the symbol table. The three vectors comprising the symbol table (SymbolVector, TypeVector, and AddressVector) and the variable containing the number of entries currently in the symbol table (SymbolEntries) are global to this procedure.}

```
begin
    {Step 1: Return an error if the symbol is already present}
    if LinearSearch (SymbolVector, SymbolEntries, VarName) <> 0
    then Status : = DupDeclError
    else

        {Step 2: Return an error if the symbol table is full}
        if SymbolEntries = N
        then Status : = TabFullError
        else begin

            {Step 3: Enter the symbol}
            SymbolEntries : = SymbolEntries + 1;
            SymbolVector[SymbolEntries] : = VarName;
            TypeVector[SymbolEntries] : = VarType;
            AddressVector[SymbolEntries] : = VarAddress;
            Status : = Successful
        end
end;
```

**FIGURE 5-44**
**Procedure to insert into the symbol table.**

translation each time a variable name is used in a source program. Imagine that you are a compiler attempting to translate the following statement:

Alpha : = Beta * Gamma

Since this is an assignment statement, the translation must cause the following machine-level operations to be performed. First, the values of the variables Beta and Gamma must be retrieved from the appropriate memory areas (*load* operations). Since an arithmetic operation (multiplication) is indicated, a check should be made to see if the variables involved are of numeric type (integer or real). These values are then to be multiplied together and the result (in the appropriate type) is to be placed in the memory area corresponding to the variable Alpha (a *store* operation). Again, a check must be made on the type of Alpha, and if required, the result must be converted before being placed in the indicated memory area.

This sequence of actions requires three interrogations of the symbol table. The information needed consists of the addresses of the memory areas corresponding to the variables **Alpha**, **Beta**, and **Gamma** and the types of these variables. Note that we make no mention of the values of the variables. We are concerned here only with the specification in executable machine-language instructions of the steps required to perform the operations described above. The actual execution of these instructions on supplied data values will be done after the translation is complete.

For each variable name to be processed, the interrogation would be of the following form:

*1.* If the variable has not been defined,
    then return an appropriate error status

*2.* If the variable is found,
    then return to the calling program the information needed:
        specifically, the type and address

We will defer discussion of what is done by the calling routine with the information returned by this procedure.

We now give the complete retrieval procedure. Its input parameter is the name of the variable being used (**VarName**). Its output parameters are the type and address of this variable (**VarType** and **VarAddress**) as recorded in the symbol table if the search was successful. The parameter **Status** returns an indication of the success or failure of the retrieval. The procedure **Retrieve** appears in Fig. 5-45.

It should be noted here that were we to adopt a different form of table organization (that is, some form of ordered table), procedure **Retrieve** would change very little. In other words, the effects of the particular table organization have been localized. Any change to the organization would require only a call to a different procedure in step 1. The rest of the procedure is unaffected. This is a good principle of program design, about which more will be said in Chap. 7.

The operations described in this application are indicative of an important field of computer science known as *information retrieval*. In general, there is a *data base* consisting of information of interest in some application area. The users of the data base may acquire particular information by means of a retrieval operation such as that described, may add new information to the data base by means of an insertion operation similar to that given earlier, or may modify existing information by means of an update operation. Information retrieval systems are used, for example, in warehouses for parts inventories, in banks for depositors' accounts, in libraries for the whereabouts of books, or in department stores for credit card records. Properly designed, they can eliminate the need for a lot of manual clerical work, such as filing and unfiling, that is tedious, monotonous, and error-prone.

## 5-5.2 BLOOD BANK

A blood bank is a repository for blood received from donors. As in a conventional bank, blood is dispensed upon request. Clearly, many of the requirements of a blood bank are similar to those of a conventional bank.

```
procedure Retrieve (
    VarName: Symbol;            {Input, variable name}
    var VarType: SymbolType;    {Output, variable type}
    var VarAddress: integer;    {Output, variable address}
    var Status: StatusCodes     {Output, success or error indication}
                    );
{Given a symbol, this procedure searches the symbol table for the symbol
    and returns its type and address. The symbol table is organized the same
    as for procedure Insert, Fig. 5-44.}
var
    Pos: integer;       {Position of symbol in table}
begin
    {Step 1: Use procedure LinearSearch to search the table}
    Pos : = LinearSearch (SymbolVector, SymbolEntries, VarName);

    {Step 2: Check result and set output parameters}
    if Pos = 0
    then Status : = UnDecVarError
    else begin
            VarType : = TypeVector[Pos];
            VarAddress : = AddressVector[Pos];
            Status : = Successful
        end
end;
```

**FIGURE 5-45**
**Procedure to retrieve**
**information from**
**the symbol table.**

Transylvania Transfusions Limited (TTL) is implementing an automated system for managing and dispensing its many stores of blood within
hospitals. This automated inventory system must keep a running total of the
number of units of each type of blood currently in stock. A unit of blood
is 500 ml. The system must handle donations and requests, and it also must
note when levels of stock become critically low.

We have been commissioned by TTL to write a program that will implement this system. The inventory system will eventually be run on-line, but
our job is to test it with an input file that represents a typical day's transactions.

There are a number of details that must be known before we can attack
the problem. First of all, the blood types kept in stock at this blood bank
are A, B, AB, and O. Stocks of blood are considered to be critically low if
they drop below the following levels:

| | |
|---|---|
| A | 100 units |
| B | 50 units |
| AB | 30 units |
| O | 200 units |

If stock is low, action must be taken to ensure that there will be enough
blood for the next request. This action would likely consist of alerting donors

of the need and requesting their help. For now it suffices to print out a message indicating that there is a shortage of a particular type of blood.

The first line of the input file will indicate the amount of blood on hand at the beginning of the day. The line

```
250   100   80   250
```

gives us the starting inventory for a given day. The four integers denote the number of units of types A, B, AB, and O, respectively, currently on hand. When a donation is made, the input line begins with the character 'D', followed again by four integers which denote the amounts of blood of each type donated (in the order A, B, AB, and O). For example,

```
D   2   0   3   0
```

denotes a donation of 2 units of type A and 3 units of type AB. When a request is made, the input line begins with the character 'R', followed by two letters indicating the type of blood requested, followed by the number of units requested. For example,

```
RAB   5
```

informs us that 5 units of AB-type blood are needed. A 'C' in the input file marks the end of the day, at which point a report of the current inventory should be given.

We will need a four-element vector, Inventory, to keep track of the current inventory. This vector can be referenced, or subscripted, using the enumerated type

```
Blood = (A, B, AB, O)
```

We also need another vector, Low, referenced in the same way, which will contain the critical levels of types A, B, AB, and O, respectively. We present the detailed program in Fig. 5-46.

The program first initializes the vector Low. Then the totals for each blood type are read into the vector Inventory. The next portion of the program is a sentinel-controlled input loop to process deposits and requests. Notice that a readln statement is used to ensure that reading of a new transaction always begins with a new line. The transaction code must be the first character on the line. It must be followed immediately (no spaces) by the two-letter blood type for a "request." Recall from Chap. 2 that a read into a character variable always reads the next character in the input stream.

A case statement distinguishes the two transaction types. The 'C' code serves as the sentinel and causes escape from the loop. At that point, the closing inventory is displayed. Procedures are used to read and write values of enumerated type Blood. This program could be simplified if your Pascal compiler allows reading and writing of enumerated types directly.

## 5-6  HIGHER-DIMENSIONAL ARRAYS

This section first concentrates on arrays of two dimensions, or *matrices*. These arrays occur frequently in a variety of applications because of their close resemblance to tables. The second part of the discussion extends the array concept to ones having more than two dimensions. Finally we consider processing arrays of two or more dimensions in Pascal.

## 5-6.1 TWO-DIMENSIONAL ARRAYS

Each week the management of a local appliance store records the sales of the individual items in its stock. At the end of each month, these weekly summaries are sent to the head office, where they are analyzed. In a typical month, the sales might be as shown in Table 5-13.

This report is in the form of a table, with the rows denoting the weekly sales summaries and the columns denoting the sales figures for the individual appliances. We will store the sales figures, which do not include the column labeled "Week" in an array. Any individual figure in the report can be acquired simply by referring to the row and column in which it appears. For example, the number of stoves sold in the second week is given in the second row and the fourth column (not counting the "week" column) and is, in fact, 3.

The sales summary table shown in Table 5-13 is conveniently represented as an array with two subscripts: the first specifying the row and the second specifying the column. The subscripts are separated by commas. If the summary report shown is implemented as a two-dimensional array, called Report, the figure for the number of stoves sold in the second week is stored in Report[2, 4].

Each subscript of an array references a *dimension* of the array. Two-dimensional structures, such as tables, require two subscripts. Arrays of two dimensions, because they are so common, are often referred to by a special term, *matrices*.

Certain restrictions apply to higher-dimensional arrays, as they did to one-dimensional arrays. For example, as was the case with vectors, we will insist that all elements of a higher-dimensional array be of the same type.

Returning to Table 5-13, let us suppose that the head office wishes to accumulate the following statistics from the sales summary reports: first, the total number of appliances sold each week, and second, the total number of each type of appliance sold in each month. This requires totaling the values in each row of the table to get the weekly totals, as in the following:

> For each week do
>     Total the appliances sold in this week

and totaling the values in each column to get the monthly totals by appliance type, as in the following:

> For each type of appliance do
>     Total the sales for the 4 weeks

To do this, we can use nested counted loops as shown in the procedures WeeklyTotals (Fig. 5-47) and UnitTotals (Fig. 5-48).

```
program BloodBank (input, output);
```
{Given an input stream containing the data for a typical day's transactions, this program provides an inventory system for a blood bank.}
```
type
    Blood = (A, B, AB, O);
var
    Low: array [Blood] of integer;        {Critical blood levels}
    Inventory: array [Blood] of integer;  {Current blood levels}
    Code: char;                           {Transaction code
                                           D = Donation
                                           R = Request
                                           C = Close for the day}
    Amount: integer;                      {Temporary for reading donations and
                                              requests}
    BloodType: Blood;                     {Temporary}

procedure ReadBloodType (var BloodType: Blood {Output} );
```
{This procedure reads two characters from the input stream and sets the output parameter to the appropriate blood type.}
```
var
    C1, C2: char;      {Characters read}
begin
    read (C1, C2);
    case C1 of
       'A': case C2 of
               '□': BloodType : = A;
               'B': BloodType : = AB
            end;
        'B': BloodType : = B;
        'O': BloodType : = O
    end
end;

procedure WriteBloodType (BT: Blood {input} );
```
{This procedure writes two characters to the output stream corresponding to the blood type of the input parameter.}
```
begin
    case BT of
        A: write ('A□');
        AB: write ('AB');
        B: write ('B□');
        O: write ('O□')
    end
end;

begin
```
{Step 1: Initialize critical blood levels}
```
    Low [A] : = 100;
```

**FIGURE 5-46**
**Program to process blood bank inventory.**

```
Low [B] : = 50;
Low [AB] : = 30;
Low [O] : = 200;

{Step 2: Read in amounts on hand at beginning of day}
for BloodType : = A to O do
   read ( Inventory [BloodType] );
readln;

{Step 3: Read in first code}
read (Code);

{Step 4: Engage sentinel controlled input loop}
while Code <> 'C' do
  begin

    {Step 5: Process donations and requests}
    case Code of
      'D': {donation}
        for BloodType : = A to O do
          begin
            read (Amount);
            Inventory [BloodType] : = Inventory [BloodType] + Amount
          end;
      'R': {Request}
        begin
          ReadBloodType (BloodType);
          read (Amount);
          if Inventory [BloodType] − Amount > 0
          then Inventory [BloodType] : = Inventory [BloodType] − Amount
          else begin
                  write ('Not□enough□of□type□');
                  WriteBloodType (BloodType);
                  writeln ('□on□hand.')
               end;
          if Inventory [BloodType] < Low [BloodType]
          then begin
                  write ('We□are□low□on□');
                  WriteBloodType (BloodType);
                  writeln
               end
        end
    end;

    {Step 6: Read in next code}
    readln;
    read (Code)
  end;
```

**FIGURE 5-46** (*cont.*)

{Step 7: Print closing report}
writeln ('Closing inventory');
**for** BloodType : = A **to** O **do**
   **begin**
      WriteBloodType (BloodType);
      writeln (':□', Inventory [BloodType]);
   **end**
**FIGURE 5-46** (*cont.*)  **end.**

Although the loops in the procedures WeeklyTotals and UnitTotals are short, it is easy to be confused by their execution. Let us examine them carefully, paying particular attention to the order in which the individual array elements are processed.

In the procedure WeeklyTotals, the application requires that we process the array one row at a time (that is, along the rows). For the first row, then, we consider each of its columns in turn. This process continues for the second row, the third row, and finally, the fourth row. As you can see, the subscript referring to the column (the second subscript) must pass through all its values for each value of the subscript referring to the row (the first subscript). Consequently, the inner loop controls the column subscript, while the outer loop controls the row subscript. Table 5-14 shows the order in which the array elements are considered.

Turning to the second procedure, UnitTotals, here we must process the array one column at a time (that is, down the columns). For each of the columns, we look in turn at each of its rows. Thus the inner loop in this case must control the values of the row subscript, while the outer loop controls the values of the column subscript. Table 5-15 shows the order in which the array elements are considered in this instance.

Notice that we do not change the array itself, simply the *order* in which the elements are considered. The value of Report[3, 4] is always 8, regardless of the processing order. This order is determined by the manner in which values are assigned to the row and column subscripts.

The input and output of arrays can be handled in an element-by-element fashion using loops like those in the two procedures just described. For example, to write out the entire array Report by rows, we could give the following statements:

**TABLE 5-13**  **Monthly Sales Summary**

| Week | Washers | Dryers | Refrigerators | Stoves | Freezers |
|------|---------|--------|---------------|--------|----------|
| 1 | 6 | 4 | 8 | 9 | 3 |
| 2 | 7 | 7 | 10 | 3 | 5 |
| 3 | 5 | 3 | 7 | 8 | 2 |
| 4 | 8 | 10 | 15 | 12 | 5 |

```
procedure WeeklyTotals;
{Given the sales figures, stored in the global two-dimensional array Report,
  this procedure computes and displays the total sales of appliances in each
  week.}
var
  Total: integer;            {Total sales for week}
  Week, Appliance: integer;  {Loop counters}
begin
  {Step 1: Engage loop to process four weeks}
  for Week : = 1 to 4 do
    begin

      {Step 2: Compute and display total for one week}
      Total : = 0;
      for Appliance : = 1 to 5 do
        Total : = Total + Report [Week, Appliance];
        writeln ('Sales for week□', Week:1, '□were□', Total:1, '□units')
    end
end;
```

FIGURE 5-47
Procedure to
report sales for
each week.

```
for Row : = 1 to 4 do
  begin
    for Column : = 1 to 5 do
      write ( Report[Row, Column]);
    writeln
  end
```

## 5-6.2 ARRAYS OF MORE THAN TWO DIMENSIONS

It is possible to visualize three-dimensional structures, which could be represented by arrays with three subscripts. Although it is possible to have arrays with more than three subscripts, it is hard to illustrate them with realistic examples. The processes for two-dimensional arrays can easily be extended to arrays of still higher dimension. Of course, we can no longer use the terms "row" and "column," which refer to a two-dimensional table.

The Antique Car Club of Saskatoon is compiling an inventory of the antique cars in the province of Saskatchewan. For each car, a line of data is prepared with the following information: the make of car (an integer code from 0 to 30), the year of the car (from 1900 to 1950), and the car's condition (integers 1 through 4 for poor, fair, good, and excellent, respectively). To enable various analyses to be conducted, these data are stored in a three-dimensional array, as shown in Fig. 5-49.

The data structure shown in Fig. 5-49 could be represented as an array Cars with three subscripts: the first subscript gives the make of car, the second gives the year, and the third gives the condition. The value stored is the number of cars of that type found. For example, the entry shown in

**procedure** UnitTotals;

{Given the sales figures, stored in the global two-dimensional array **Report**, this procedure computes and displays the total sales of each type of appliance in a month.}

**var**
   Total: integer;              {Total sales for appliance}
   Week, Appliance: integer;   {Loop counters}
**begin**
   {Step 1: Engage loop to process all appliance types}
   **for** Appliance := 1 **to** 5 **do**
      **begin**

        {Step 2: Compute and display total for one appliance type}
        Total := 0;
        **for** Week := 1 **to** 4 **do**
           Total := Total + Report [Week, Appliance];
        writeln ('Sales for appliance□', Appliance:1, '□were□', Total:1, '□units')
      **end**
**end**;

**FIGURE 5-48**
**Procedure to report**
**total sales for**
**each appliance.**

---

**TABLE 5-14**

| Value of Row Subscript, Week | Value of Column Subscript, Appliance | Value of Array Element Considered, Report [Week, Appliance] |
|:---:|:---:|:---:|
| 1 | 1 | 6 |
|   | 2 | 4 |
|   | 3 | 8 |
|   | 4 | 9 |
|   | 5 | 3 |
| 2 | 1 | 7 |
|   | 2 | 7 |
|   | 3 | 10 |
|   | 4 | 3 |
|   | 5 | 5 |
| 3 | 1 | 5 |
|   | 2 | 3 |
|   | 3 | 7 |
|   | 4 | 8 |
|   | 5 | 2 |
| 4 | 1 | 8 |
|   | 2 | 10 |
|   | 3 | 15 |
|   | 4 | 12 |
|   | 5 | 5 |

**TABLE 5-15**

**311**
5-6
HIGHER-DIMENSIONAL
ARRAYS

| Value of Column Subscript, Appliance | Value of Row Subscript, Week | Value of Array Element Considered, Report [Week, Appliance] |
|:---:|:---:|:---:|
| 1 | 1 | 6 |
|   | 2 | 7 |
|   | 3 | 5 |
|   | 4 | 8 |
| 2 | 1 | 4 |
|   | 2 | 7 |
|   | 3 | 3 |
|   | 4 | 10 |
| 3 | 1 | 8 |
|   | 2 | 10 |
|   | 3 | 7 |
|   | 4 | 15 |
| 4 | 1 | 9 |
|   | 2 | 3 |
|   | 3 | 8 |
|   | 4 | 12 |
| 5 | 1 | 3 |
|   | 2 | 5 |
|   | 3 | 2 |
|   | 4 | 5 |

Fig. 5-49 is denoted by Cars[26, 1904, 2] and shows that six cars were found with these characteristics.

To illustrate the use of this three-dimensional array, we give the procedure in Fig. 5-50, which is given a year as an input parameter and supplies the number of cars found for that year and their average condition via output parameters. We will leave the tracing of this example as an exercise.

## 5-6.3 HIGHER-DIMENSIONAL ARRAYS IN PASCAL

Pascal treats a two-dimensional array as a vector of rows; each row is, of course, a one-dimensional array of elements. Thus the following type definitions define types T1, T2, and T3 to be two-dimensional arrays of similar shape.

**type**
    RowVector = **array** [1 .. 10] **of** integer;
    T1 = **array** [1 .. 6] **of** RowVector;
    T2 = **array** [1 .. 6] **of array** [1 .. 10] **of** integer;
    T3 = **array** [1 .. 6, 1 .. 10] **of** integer;

The array denoter associated with T3 is considered merely a shorthand for a denoter like that associated with T2.

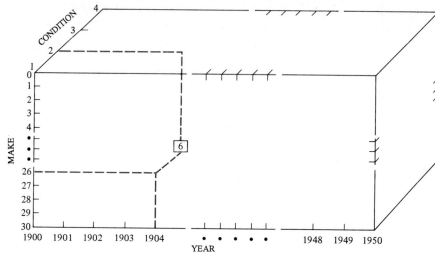

FIGURE 5-49
Pictorial
representation of a
three-dimensional
array.

Suppose the variables A, B, and C were declared as

```
var
    A: T1;
    B: T2;
    C: T3;
```

Then each of A, B, and C represents a variable of type array of array of integer, that is, a two-dimensional array. Supplying a subscript, as in A[I], B[I], or C[I], yields a variable of type array of integer, that is, a one-dimensional array. Further, because of the definitions of T1, A[I] is of type RowVector. A[I] is therefore of the same type as variables declared to be of type RowVector. Assuming X is of type RowVector, we can write assignments such as

```
A[I] := X;
A[J] := A[I];
X := A[J]
```

Since the type denoters for the rows of B and C have not been given names (they are anonymous types), it is not possible to declare variables of those types. Thus there cannot be a variable X that would allow assignments as in the previous example, since Pascal allows assignments only if the types are the *same* (see Sec. 5-2.2). The only assignments possible are of the form

```
B[I] := B[J];
C[I] := C[J]
```

Since A[I], assuming the previous declaration, represents an array-of-integer variable, then it may in turn be subscripted to select one of its elements, as in A[I][J]. The notation A[I, J] is considered an abbreviation for A[I][J]. Notice that the form used to subscript the variable, abbreviated or not, is *not* determined by whether the array denoter was abbreviated. All the

**procedure** CarReport (
    Year: integer;      {Input, year to be reported on}
    **var** Count: integer;   {Output, number of cars reported}
    **var** AvgCond: real    {Output, average condition}
              );
{Given the cars inventory, in the global three-dimensional array Cars, and a
   year this procedure computes the number of cars in inventory built in that
   year and their average condition.}
**var**
   Make, Cond: integer;     {Loop counters}
**begin**
   {Step 1: Initialize}
   Count := 0;
   AvgCond := 0;

   {Step 2: Compute sums}
   **for** Make := 0 **to** 30 **do**
      **for** Cond := 1 **to** 4 **do**
         **begin**
            Count := Count + Cars[Make, Year, Cond];
            AvgCond := AvgCond + Cond * Cars[Make, Year, Cond]
         **end**;

   {Step 3: Compute average condition}
   AvgCond := AvgCond / Count
**end**;

**FIGURE 5-50**
**Procedure to report**
**number and average**
**condition of cars**
**of a particular year.**

following forms are valid given the previous declarations:

| | | | |
|---|---|---|---|
| A[I] | B[I] | C[I] | Vectors |
| A[I, J] | B[I, J] | C[I, J] | |
| A[I][J] | B[I][J] | C[I][J] | Integers |

## EXERCISES 5-6

**1.** Given a matrix A of the form

$$\begin{bmatrix} a_{11} & a_{12} & \cdots & a_{1m} \\ a_{21} & a_{22} & \cdots & a_{2m} \\ \cdot & \cdot & & \cdot \\ \cdot & \cdot & & \cdot \\ \cdot & \cdot & & \cdot \\ a_{n1} & a_{n2} & \cdots & a_{nm} \end{bmatrix}$$

the *transpose* of A is given by

$$\begin{bmatrix} a_{11} & a_{21} & \cdots & a_{n1} \\ a_{12} & a_{22} & \cdots & a_{n2} \\ \cdot & \cdot & & \cdot \\ \cdot & \cdot & & \cdot \\ \cdot & \cdot & & \cdot \\ a_{1m} & a_{2m} & \cdots & a_{nm} \end{bmatrix}$$

That is, the transpose of a matrix is obtained by interchanging its rows and columns. Write a procedure to take as an input parameter a matrix and obtain as an output parameter its transpose. The values of $m$ and $n$ also should be input parameters. Write a program to test your procedure.

★ 2. Given the two matrices A and B, where

$$A = \begin{bmatrix} a_{11} & a_{12} & \cdots & a_{1m} \\ a_{21} & a_{22} & \cdots & a_{2m} \\ \cdot & \cdot & & \cdot \\ \cdot & \cdot & & \cdot \\ \cdot & \cdot & & \cdot \\ a_{n1} & a_{n2} & \cdots & a_{nm} \end{bmatrix} \quad \text{and} \quad B = \begin{bmatrix} b_{11} & b_{12} & \cdots & b_{1r} \\ b_{21} & b_{22} & \cdots & b_{2r} \\ \cdot & \cdot & & \cdot \\ \cdot & \cdot & & \cdot \\ \cdot & \cdot & & \cdot \\ b_{m1} & b_{m2} & \cdots & b_{mr} \end{bmatrix}$$

the *product* of A and B is given by

$$C = \begin{bmatrix} c_{11} & c_{12} & \cdots & c_{1r} \\ c_{21} & c_{22} & \cdots & c_{2r} \\ \cdot & \cdot & & \cdot \\ \cdot & \cdot & & \cdot \\ \cdot & \cdot & & \cdot \\ c_{n1} & c_{n2} & \cdots & c_{nr} \end{bmatrix}$$

where

$$c_{ij} = \sum_{k=1}^{m} a_{ik} \times b_{kj}$$

For example, given

$$A = \begin{bmatrix} 1 & 2 & 3 \\ 4 & 5 & 6 \end{bmatrix} \quad \text{and} \quad B = \begin{bmatrix} 1 & 4 \\ 2 & 5 \\ 3 & 6 \end{bmatrix}$$

the product is

$$\begin{bmatrix} 14 & 32 \\ 32 & 77 \end{bmatrix}$$

Note that it is possible to multiply matrices A and B only if the number of columns in A is equal to the number of rows in B. Write a procedure which accepts A, B, n, m, and r as input parameters and produces C via an output parameter. Write a program to test your procedure.

★★ 3. Write a program to compute and display Pascal's triangle of binomial coefficients. Such a triangle has the form

```
            1
         1   1
      1   2   1
    1   3   3   1
  1   4   6   4   1
1   5  10   10  5   1
        etc.
```

where, in general, a row is obtained by noting that each element in the row is the sum of the two elements immediately above it. Write a procedure to generate the first 10 rows of this triangle and return the results via an output parameter. The main program should display this result.

★ 4. Given a matrix Grade whose element Grade[J, K] contains the Jth student's score on the Kth problem and a weight vector Weight whose element Weight[K] denotes the weight of the Kth problem, write a program that ranks the students. The ranks are to be recorded in a vector Rank such that Rank[J] denotes the position of the Jth student in the class. The program is to read input data from N students and M problems and display the result. For example, the following arrays contain the grade, problem, and rank information for a class of five students and three problems. In this example, the average of the first student is

$$\frac{3 \times 65 + 2 \times 80 + 1 \times 85}{6} = 73.3$$

and this student is ranked fourth in a class of five students.

WEIGHT

| 3 | 2 | 1 |
|---|---|---|

GRADE

| 65 | 80 | 85 |
|-----|-----|-----|
| 80 | 60 | 90 |
| 75 | 50 | 50 |
| 100 | 50 | 75 |
| 100 | 80 | 70 |

RANK

| 4 |
|---|
| 3 |
| 5 |
| 2 |
| 1 |

★ **5.** A final examination contains 100 multiple-choice questions. Each question has five choices and only one choice can be the correct one. The examination results and student information can be represented as follows:

ANSWERS

| 1 | 2 | 3 | ... | 99 | 100 |
|---|---|---|-----|----|----|
|   |   |   | ... |    |    |

SCORE

|   | 1 | 2 | ... | 99 | 100 | NAME |
|---|---|---|-----|----|-----|------|
| 1 |   |   | ... |    |     |      |
| 2 |   |   |     |    |     |      |
| . | . | . |     | .  | .   | .    |
| . | . | . |     | .  | .   | .    |
| . | . | . |     | .  | .   | .    |
| n |   |   | ... |    |     |      |

where **Answers** contains the correct answers to the examination question, **Score** is a matrix whose row contains the answers to the 100 multiple-choice questions, and the vector **Name** contains the names of the students in the class. The answer to each question is coded as 1, 2, 3, 4, or 5. If more than one choice is marked, this possibility is recorded as a 6. Write a program that outputs the names of the students who passed. A minimum grade of 60 is required to pass.

**6.** Write a program that calculates the salary for a group of 100 salespersons. The salary of each salesperson is paid on a commission basis. Each salesperson sells 50 items. The input data consists of a number of lines of data sets each of which shows a salesperson number, item number, unit price, and units of this item which are sold. The data lines are not in any particular sequence. Use an end-of-file test to detect the end of the data. Assume a commission rate of 5 percent on all items.

★ **7.** An analysis is under way of traffic accidents in midtown Manhattan. For convenience, the streets and avenues are represented by a grid as follows:

|    | 30 | 31 | 32 | 33 | 34 | 35 | ... | 58 |
|----|----|----|----|----|----|----|-----|----|
| 1  |    |    |    |    |    |    |     |    |
| 2  |    |    |    |    |    | 9  |     |    |
| 3  |    |    |    |    |    |    |     |    |
| .  |    |    |    |    |    |    |     |    |
| .  |    |    |    |    |    |    |     |    |
| .  |    |    |    |    |    |    |     |    |
| 10 |    |    |    |    |    |    |     |    |

where the row headings denote the avenues from First Avenue to Tenth

Avenue, and the column headings denote the streets from 30th Street to
58th Street. The entries in the array denote the number of accidents occurring in that vicinity in the most recent observational period. For example,
in the case shown, nine accidents occurred near the intersection of Second Avenue and 35th Street. An unknown number of accident reports are
to be read in. Each accident is given by a pair of numbers describing its
location. For example, the pair 7, 42 denotes an accident occurring in the
vicinity of Seventh Avenue and 42nd Street. Write a program that reads
in this information and prepares an array of the form shown. Use an end-
of-file test to determine the end of the data. Incorporate a range check
to ensure that all data values lie within the range of streets and avenues
under study. Reject any invalid data with an appropriate message. Once
the data has been read and stored, produce a list of the ten most danger-
ous intersections.

★ 8. Using the three-dimensional array Cars described in this section, write
programs to compute the following statistics:
(a) The number of cars made before 1910 with condition rated good or
excellent.
(b) The most popular car, as judged by the number recorded of all the
makes.
(c) Identify the make of car that appears to be in the best average condition over all samples recorded.

9. A square matrix is said to be symmetrical if entry $(i, j)$ = entry $(j, i)$
for all $i$ and $j$ within the bounds of the matrix: that is, if A is a $4 \times 4$
matrix, then if $A(3, 4) = 17$, $A(4, 3)$ must equal 17 for A to be symmetric.
The following is an example of a symmetrical matrix:

$$\begin{bmatrix} 0 & 3 & 5 & 1 \\ 3 & 7 & 6 & 9 \\ 5 & 6 & 2 & 4 \\ 1 & 9 & 4 & 2 \end{bmatrix}$$

Write a procedure that will decide whether or not a matrix is symmetrical.
Parameters of this procedure should include N, the matrix size, and A,
the $N \times N$ matrix itself.

## 5-7 APPLICATIONS INVOLVING ARRAYS OF ONE OR MORE DIMENSIONS

In this section we present three applications involving arrays. We begin with
a problem that involves the processing of actual array elements as survey
statistics are computed for a group known as Overweights Anonymous. The
second problem deals with the preparation of league standings for a hypothetical hockey league. Finally, an application of arrays to a solution to
airline compatibility seating is described.

## 5-7.1  OVERWEIGHTS ANONYMOUS

The local branch of Overweights Anonymous is conducting a study of the effectiveness of its weight-reducing programs. Fifty members were selected at random as subjects for the study. Over the past 12 months, a record has been made of the weight of each subject at the start of the month. For each of these subjects, a line of data is prepared containing this set of 12 readings (assume that they are all rounded to the nearest pound). The branch now requires a program to analyze this information to determine the following:

*1.* The average weight change for all subjects over the entire 12-month period

*2.* The number of subjects whose total weight change exceeded the average

*3.* The average monthly weight change per subject

*4.* The number of instances during the year in which a subject lost more than the average monthly weight change during a single month

The solution of this problem requires an integer array to store the data recorded for the 50 subjects over the 12-month period. To this end, we define an integer array **Pounds** with 50 rows and 12 columns as shown in Fig. 5-51.

An algorithm to compute the required statistics has the following general form:

*1.* Repeat for each subject in the sample:
   Read 12-month history
   Add weight change for the year to running total

*2.* Compute average weight change per subject over the 12-month period

*3.* Repeat for each subject in sample:
   If total weight change exceeds average,
   then increment count
   Compute average monthly weight change
   Add to running total

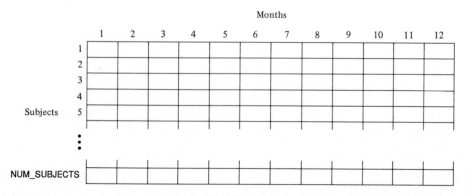

**FIGURE 5-51**
**Information layout in Overweights Anonymous.**

*4.* Compute average monthly weight change per subject

*5.* Repeat for months 2 thru 12:
Calculate number of instances where a subject experienced a weight change in the past month that exceeds the figure from step 4

This algorithm requires that we move through the elements of the array **Pounds** a total of three times (steps 1, 3, and 5). Let us consider each of the steps of this algorithm in more detail.

In step 1 we perform two important functions. We read the entire set of data values, but as we do so, we simultaneously compute the total weight change in the year. For each subject this is done by subtracting the value for month 12 from the value for month 1. In step 2 we divide this total by 50 to determine the per-subject average. In step 3 we also perform two functions as we read through the array. (In both cases, this is done to cut down on the number of times we process each array element; this can have a noticeable effect on the execution time.) First, we count the number of times that a subject's weight change for the year exceeds the per-subject average. At the same time, we compute for each subject the average monthly weight change (this requires an inner loop) and add this to a running total. In step 4 this is divided by the number of subjects to get a per-subject, per-month value. Finally, in step 5 we count the number of subjects whose weight change in any month exceeds the per-subject, per-month figure computed in step 4. Notice that the form of this step suggests column-wise processing of the array rather than the row-wise processing of the previous steps. This process is formalized in the program **OverWeights** in Fig. 5-52.

## 5-7.2 GLOBAL HOCKEY LEAGUE

Inspired by the surge of popularity of international hockey tournaments, a group of entrepreneurs has formed the Global Hockey League. A worldwide campaign for franchises has netted the following 12 teams listed alphabetically along with a team number:

*1.* The Burma Shaves

*2.* The Chile Beans

*3.* The Hammond Eggs

*4.* The Kentucky Derbies

*5.* The Labrador Retrievers

*6.* The Louisiana Purchase

*7.* The Mobile Homes

*8.* The Peking Ducks

*9.* The Scotland Yards

*10.* The Toronto Island Ferries

```
program Overweights (input, output);
{This program calculates the statistics described in the text for a sample of
    50 subjects.}
type
    WeightType = array [1 .. 50, 1 .. 12] of integer;
var
    Pounds: WeightType;      {Input data}
    PYAvg: real;             {Average weight change per subject per year}
    PMAvg: real;             {Average weight change per subject per month}
    YCount: integer;         {Number of subjects exceeding the average
                                 change per year}
    MCount: integer;         {Number of subjects exceeding the average
                                 change per month}
    Subject, Month: integer;{Loop counters}


    procedure ComputeAvg (
        Pounds: WeightType;      {Input, table of weights}
        NumSubjects: integer;    {Input, number of subjects in the table
                                     of weights}
        PYAvg: real;             {Input, per subject yearly average}
        var YCount: integer;     {Output, number of subjects exceeding
                                     the average}
        var PMAvg: real          {Output, per subject monthly weight-loss
                                     average}
                            );
    {This procedure calculates the number of subjects exceeding the average,
        and the per subject monthly weight-loss average}
    var
        Subject, Month: integer;   {Loop counters}
        Temp: real;                {Temporary sum used in computing per
                                       subject, per month change}
    begin
        {Step 1: Initialize}
        YCount := 0;
        PMAvg := 0.0;

        {Step 2: Compute per month average for each subject}
        for Subject := 1 to 50 do
            begin
                if Pounds[Subject, 1] − Pounds[Subject, 12] > PYAvg
                then YCount := YCount + 1;
                Temp := 0;
                for Month := 2 to 12 do
                    Temp := Temp + ( Pounds[Subject, Month − 1] − Pounds[Subject,
                        Month] );
                PMAvg := PMAvg + Temp / 11
            end;
```

**FIGURE 5-52**
**Program to process**
**Overweights**
**Anonymous statistics.**

{Step 3: Compute per subject monthly average}
PMAvg : = PMAvg / 50
**end**;{Compute Average}

**function** CountAboveAverage (
    Pounds: WeightType;    {Input, table of weights}
    NumSubjects: integer;    {Input, number of subjects in the table of
                              weights}
    PMAvg: real          {Input, the per subject per month
                              average weight loss}
                          ): integer;
{This function calculates the number of times that the per subject per month
  average weight was exceeded.}
**var**
    MCount: integer;        {Number of times the average weight
                              change per subject per month was exceeded}
    Subject, Month: integer;    {Loop counters}
**begin**
    {Step 1: Initialize}
    MCount : = 0;

    {Step 2: Compute total times exceeded}
    **for** Month : = 2 **to** 12 **do**
        **for** Subject : = 1 **to** 50 **do**
            **if** Pounds[Subject, Month − 1] − Pounds[Subject, Month] > PMAvg
            **then** MCount : = MCount + 1;

    {Step 3: Return result}
    CountAboveAverage : = MCount
**end**; {CountAboveAverage}

**begin**
    {Step 1: Input data and compute total yearly weight change}
    PYAvg : = 0.0;
    **for** Subject : = 1 **to** 50 **do**
        **begin**
            **for** Month : = 1 **to** 12 **do**
                read ( Pounds[Subject, Month] );
            PYAvg : = PYAvg + ( Pounds[Subject, 1] − Pounds[Subject, 12] )
        **end**;

    {Step 2: Compute yearly average per subject}
    PYAvg : = PYAvg / 50;
    writeln ('Per subject, per year weight change is □', PYAvg:1:1);

    {Step 3: Count number exceeding average and determine total average
    monthly weight change}

**FIGURE 5-52** (*cont.*)

ComputeAvg(Pounds, 50, PYAvg, YCount, PMAvg);
writeln ('Number of subjects exceeding this figure is ☐', YCount:1:1);
writeln ('Per subject, per month weight change is ☐', PMAvg:1:1);

{Step 4: Count number exceeding this average}
MCount : = CountAboveAverage(Pounds, 50, PMAvg);
writeln ('Number of times this figure was exceeded is ☐', MCount:1)

**FIGURE 5-52** (*cont.*)    **end.**

*11.* The Trafalgar Squares

*12.* The Vichy Ssoise

To enable more efficient processing of game results, which are coming from all corners of the globe, the league organizers intend to use a computer. After completion of each league game, the result is sent to league headquarters as in the following example:

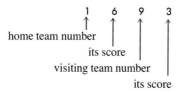

A team is awarded 2 points for each win, 1 point for each tie, and no points for a loss.

League standings are published regularly in the form given in Table 5-16. These statistics are computed from the most recently published standings, updated according to the recently arrived unprocessed game results. The teams are listed in decreasing order of points. We wish to implement a program to prepare and display the league standings.

To solve this problem, we will use two different arrays. The first will be a vector of elements of type integer and will contain the numbers of the teams as they appear in the published standings (and in the individual game reports). The second array is a two-dimensional array with integer elements. Each row of this array contains the statistics for one of the teams in the league. The columns contain the number of games played, the number of games won, the number of games lost, the number of games tied, and the total points. (Another approach would be to use five separate vectors, one for each category, and process them in parallel. We have chosen to use a two-dimensional array instead.) Although the team-number vector could be

| **TABLE 5-16** | **Standings for the Global Hockey League** | | | | |
|---|---|---|---|---|---|
| **Team** | **Games Played** | **Wins** | **Losses** | **Ties** | **Points** |
| — | — | — | — | — | — |
| — | — | — | — | — | — |

combined with the two-dimensional array, we have kept it separate because a better formulation would be to keep the names of the teams (character strings) rather than the team numbers. We leave this alternative formulation to those with a Pascal compiler containing a good string-processing extension. Figure 5-53 shows the standings after the first round of play. The order is significant. The team from Labrador (team 5) is currently in first place with a record of 6 wins, 2 losses, and 3 ties for a total of 15 points. Cold climates obviously breed a hockey tradition. The Labrador team is followed closely by the team from Toronto Island (10) with a record of 6 wins, 3 losses, and 2 ties for 14 points. At the present time, the teams from Scotland (9) and Peking (8) trail the field with identical records of 3 wins, 7 losses, and 1 tie for 7 points.

After each run of the program to compute and print the league standings, data is prepared giving the team numbers in their *current* order and their records. This serves as input to the next run, along with the results of the subsequent games.

The program must operate as follows. First, the current standings are read in and used to construct the two essential arrays (team numbers and statistics). Attention then turns to the processing of the individual game results. The data for the games is read, one at a time, and the statistics of the teams involved are updated accordingly. After all the game results have been processed, the total points for each team are recalculated. Finally, a sort into descending order of total points must be performed and the standings displayed. More formally, our algorithm has the following general structure:

**FIGURE 5-53  Global Hockey League standings after the first round of play.**

| Teams | | GamesPlayed | Wins | Losses | Ties | Points |
|---|---|---|---|---|---|---|
| 5 | ← → | 11 | 6 | 2 | 3 | 15 |
| 10 | ← → | 11 | 6 | 3 | 2 | 14 |
| 2 | ← → | 11 | 5 | 3 | 3 | 13 |
| 11 | ← → | 11 | 6 | 4 | 1 | 13 |
| 3 | ← → | 11 | 6 | 5 | 0 | 12 |
| 12 | ← → | 11 | 5 | 4 | 2 | 12 |
| 4 | ← → | 11 | 5 | 5 | 1 | 11 |
| 6 | ← → | 11 | 5 | 5 | 1 | 11 |
| 7 | ← → | 11 | 4 | 6 | 1 | 9 |
| 1 | ← → | 11 | 4 | 7 | 0 | 8 |
| 9 | ← → | 11 | 3 | 7 | 1 | 7 |
| 8 | ← → | 11 | 3 | 7 | 1 | 7 |

Array of
type integer

Array of type integer

*1.* Read and store current standings

*2.* Repeat for each new game result:
   Process the game result
   Update team statistics

*3.* Recalculate total points for all teams

*4.* Sort arrays by points

*5.* Print out new standings

Let us consider each of these steps of the algorithm in more detail. The first step, the input and storing of current standings, is actually a straightforward application of read statements. We will use an integer vector **Teams**, with 12 elements, to hold the team numbers in order of standing and a two-dimensional integer array **Stats**, with 12 rows and 5 columns, to hold the statistics. The rows of the statistics array will be numbered in correspondence with the rows of the team-number vector. The columns of the statistics array will, however, be referenced using an enumerated type. Thus **Column** is a variable of the enumerated type

(GamesPlayed, Wins, Losses, Ties, Points)

Using loops, we can now express the input statements as

```
for Row : = 1 to 12 do
   begin
      read(Teams[Row]);      {Read the team number}
      for Column : = GamesPlayed to Points do
         read (Stats[Row, Column])      {read the data for this team}
   end
```

The processing of new game results requires some further elaboration. For each set of data we must determine which rows correspond to the teams involved in the game and the appropriate adjustments to make to their statistics. From the score given, we determine the winner of the game and the loser (or possibly it was a tie). We then find the appropriate rows in the statistics table by searching the list of team numbers. For example, if the game result were

1   6   9   3

an examination of the scores tells us that Burma (team 1) has won this game and Scotland (team 9) has lost. We then search the list of numbers (Fig. 5-53) to find a match on 1 and discover that it is in row 10. We then add one more win to the statistics for this team by adding 1 to the array element Stats[10, Wins]. We also increase Stats[10, GamesPlayed] by 1 to indicate another game played. For team 9 we perform a similar process, updating Stats[11, GamesPlayed] and Stats[11, Losses] by 1. We repeat this process until all game results have been read.

```
{Flush end of line from previous input in case there are no new results}
readln;
```

```
{Process the game results}
while not eof do
  begin

      {Read the results of one game}
      readln(Team1, Score1, Team2, Score2);

      {Find positions of teams}
      for Row := 1 to 12 do
          if Teams[Row] = Team1
          then Row1 := Row
          else if Teams[Row] = Team2
                then Row2 := Row;

      {Update games played}
      Stats[Row1, GamesPlayed] := Stats[Row1, GamesPlayed] + 1;
      Stats[Row2, GamesPlayed] := Stats[Row2, GamesPlayed] + 1;
      if Score1 > Score2
      then begin
              Stats[Row1, Wins] := Stats[Row1, Wins] + 1;
              Stats[Row2, Losses] := Stats[Row2, Losses] + 1;
         end
      else
         if Score1 < Score2
         then begin
                 Stats[Row2, Wins] := Stats[Row2, Wins] + 1;
                 Stats[Row1, Losses] := Stats[Row1, Losses] + 1
            end
         else begin
                 Stats[Row1, Ties] := Stats[Row1, Ties] + 1;      {tie game}
                 Stats[Row2, Ties] := Stats[Row2, Ties] + 1
            end
  end
```

The next step is to recompute the point totals for all the teams. For this, we simply run through each row of the array **Stats**, awarding 2 points for each win and 1 point for each tie. The following loop will do this:

```
for Row := 1 to 12 do
    Stats[Row, Points] := 2 * Stats[Row, Wins] + Stats[Row, Ties];
```

After the current point totals have been computed, the teams must be sorted into descending order of points. We will use the selection sort described earlier to write a procedure that will perform this sort. We have an additional requirement, however. Because the statistics relate to particular teams, we must keep all the rows intact and preserve the correspondence between elements of the vector **Teams** and rows of the array **Stats**. This means that even though our sorting is done on the total points alone (the **Points** column of the **Stats** array), when it comes time to exchange elements, we will be moving not only all elements in that row of the Stats array, but also the corresponding element of the Teams vector. The procedure to perform this sort appears in Fig. 5-54.

The final step of our program is to print the new standings. This is no more than setting up the appropriate write statements. The analysis of this problem is now complete, and we are ready to assemble the entire program from the individual pieces that we have designed (see Fig. 5-55).

A final comment on this program concerns the control of the major

```
procedure ArraySort (
    var Teams: TeamVector;      {Input-output, teams (array of integers)}
    var Stats: StatArray;        {Input-output, statistics (array of StatRow)}
                      );
{Given the two corresponding arrays described in the text, this procedure
    sorts them into descending order based on points. Teams is assumed to be
    an array of integer; Stats to be an array of StatRow.}
var
    Pass, Row: integer;      {Loop indices}
    Top: integer;            {Index of maximum}
    TempTeams: integer;      {Temporary for exchanging Teams entries}
    TempStats: StatRow;      {Temporary for exchanging Stats rows}
begin
    {Step 1: Loop on pass index}
    for Pass : = 1 to 11 do
        begin

            {Step 2: Initialize maximum index}
            Top : = Pass;

            {Step 3: Find largest key}
            for Row : = Pass + 1 to 12 do
                if Stats[Row, Points] > Stats[Top , Points]
                then Top : = Row;

            {Step 4: Exchange rows}
            if Pass <> Top
            then begin
                    TempTeams : = Teams[Top];
                    Teams[Top] : = Teams[Pass];
                    Teams[Pass] : = TempTeams;
                    TempStats : = Stats[Top];  {Copy whole row!}
                    Stats[Top] : = Stats[Pass]; {Copy row}
                    Stats[Pass] : = TempStats  {Copy row}
                end
        end
end;
```

**FIGURE 5-54**
**Array sorting procedure for hockey standings applications.**

loop. The intention as expressed in the while statement is to perform this loop for each game result read. The use of **eof** should make this program quite easy to read and understand.

## 5-7.3 COMPATIBILITY-BASED SEAT ASSIGNMENT

How often have you been seated on an airline flight next to someone with whom you had absolutely nothing in common, leading to several painful hours of strained conversation? Inner Space Airlines is pioneering a solution to this problem by programming a slight enhancement to their flight reservation system for the purpose of seat assignment.

At the time the ticket is purchased, each Inner Space passenger is asked to state the degree of his or her feelings about a number of important factors, such as sports, movies, classical music, parties, world affairs, smoking, and artichokes. Each factor is rated according to the following codes:

1—intense like    5—mild dislike

2—moderate like    6—moderate dislike

3—mild like    7—intense dislike

4—neutral

This data is entered, along with the passenger's name and other information currently required by the reservation system. In this example, seats are to be assigned for a flight 19386 according to 3 compatibility factors. The ratings of these factors for the six passengers booked on flight 19386 are shown in Table 5-17.

The selection of a seat-mate for a given passenger requires a data-matching inquiry on the passenger file. This involves searching the rest of the passenger file for the passenger who is "most compatible." One way of doing this is to compare differences in ratings on the factors surveyed. The *least-squares* sum of the differences is a standard fitting technique for several reasons. First, it concentrates on the magnitude of the differences rather than the sign. Also, it places more importance on the large differences while tolerating small ones.

As an example, consider the first passenger with these particulars:

Rebecca Ryan    2  5  6

In computing the compatibility of potential seat-mates, the least-squares sum for each of the remaining passengers would be

For Norman Bates: $(2 - 5)^2 + (5 - 6)^2 + (6 - 3)^2 = 19$

For Marty McFly: $(2 - 2)^2 + (5 - 4)^2 + (6 - 6)^2 = 1$

For Emily Latella: $(2 - 2)^2 + (5 - 5)^2 + (6 - 7)^2 = 1$

For Jack T. Colton: $(2 - 2)^2 + (5 - 6)^2 + (6 - 7)^2 = 2$

For Joan Wilder: $(2 - 2)^2 + (5 - 4)^2 + (6 - 5)^2 = 2$

**program** Standing (input, output);

{Given the most recently published standings and the results of games played since then, this program computes and prints team standings for the Global Hockey League. The output is the revised standings sorted in decreasing order of total points.}

**type**
    ColumnTypes = (GamesPlayed, Wins, Losses, Ties, Points);
    TeamVector = **array** [1 .. 12] **of** integer;
    StatRow = **array** [ColumnTypes] **of** integer;
    StatArray = **array** [1 .. 12] **of** StatRow;

**var**
    Teams: TeamVector;          {List of team numbers in decreasing order of standings}
    Stats: StatArray;           {Team statistics corresponding to teams in TeamVector}
    Row: integer;               {Loop index}
    Column: ColumnTypes;        {Loop index}
    Team1, Team2: integer;      {Variables}
    Score1, Score2: integer;    {for processing}
    Row1, Row2: integer;        {game results}

**procedure** CalcStats (
    **var** Stats: StatArray;        {Input/Output, team statistics corresponding to teams in TeamVector}
    Row1, Row2: integer;        {Input, row-numbers in Stats}
    Score1, Score2: integer     {Input, scores}
                        );
{This procedure updates the Stats array in terms of wins, losses, and ties for the two teams involved.}
**begin**
    **if** Score1 > Score2
    **then begin**
            Stats[Row1, Wins] := Stats[Row1, Wins] + 1;
            Stats[Row2, Losses] := Stats[Row2, Losses] + 1
        **end**
    **else**
        **if** Score1 < Score2
        **then begin**
                Stats[Row2, Wins] := Stats[Row2, Wins] + 1;
                Stats[Row1, Losses] := Stats[Row1, Losses] + 1
            **end**
        **else begin**
                Stats[Row1, Ties] := Stats[Row1, Ties] + 1;
                Stats[Row2, Ties] := Stats[Row2, Ties] + 1
            **end**
**end**;

**FIGURE 5-55**
**Program to process hockey standings.**

{Include procedure ArraySort here}

**begin**
  {Step 1: Read in most recent standings}
  **for** Row : = 1 **to** 12 **do**
    **begin**
      read ( Teams[Row] );
      **for** Column : = GamesPlayed **to** Points **do**
        read ( Stats[Row, Column] )
    **end**;

  {Step 2: Flush end of line from previous input in case there are no new
    results}
  readln;

  {Step 3: Process the game results}
  **while not** eof **do**
    **begin**

      {Step 4: Read results of one game}
      readln(Team1, Score1, Team2, Score2);

      {Step 5: Search Teams vector to find row numbers of Team1 and
        Team2}
      **for** Row : = 1 **to** 12 **do**
        **if** Teams[Row] = Team1
        **then** Row1: = Row
        **else if** Teams[Row] = Team2
          **then** Row2 : = Row;

      {Step 6: Update games played}
      Stats[Row1, GamesPlayed] : = Stats[Row1, GamesPlayed] + 1;
      Stats[Row2, GamesPlayed] : = Stats[Row2, GamesPlayed] + 1;

      {Step 7: Determine game outcome}
      CalcStats(Stats, Row1, Row2, Score1, Score2);
    **end**;

  {Step 8: Compute current point totals}
  **for** Row : = 1 **to** 12 **do**
    Stats[Row, Points] : = 2 * Stats[Row, Wins] + Stats[Row, Ties];

  {Step 9: Sort the teams by decreasing order of points}
  ArraySort (Teams, Stats);

  {Step 10: Output heading}
  writeln ('Team☐☐Games☐played☐☐Wins☐☐Losses☐☐Ties☐☐Points');

**FIGURE 5-55** (*cont.*)

{Step 11: Output new standings}
**for** Row := 1 **to** 12 **do**
    writeln (Teams[Row]:3, Stats[Row, GamesPlayed]:10,
           Stats[Row, Wins]:10, Stats[Row, Losses]:7,
           Stats[Row, Ties]:7, Stats[Row, Points]:7 )

**FIGURE 5-55** (*cont.*)   **end**.

The most compatible seat-mate for Rebecca Ryan would be Marty McFly or Emily Latella, while Norman Bates is deemed the most incompatible. Either of the most compatible could be assigned.

The program does this calculation for each passenger, assigning a seat-mate, and removing both from consideration for subsequent selections. Note that the chances of finding compatible candidates can become smaller as the sample becomes smaller, making a good selection possibly more difficult for those considered later in the process.

A general algorithm for this problem follows.

*1.* Read in the flight number, number of passengers, and number of factors

*2.* Repeat for each passenger:
    Read in the passenger's profile and add to complete passenger file

*3.* Repeat thru step 8 while there remain passengers yet unmatched

*4.* Select the next candidate

*5.* Repeat for each other passenger yet unmatched:
    Compute the passenger's sum-of-squares statistic

*6.* Determine the minimum sum-of-squares statistic

*7.* Output the desired report for this matched pair of passengers

*8.* Mark the two passengers just matched as being seated

**TABLE 5-17**  **Example of Airline Seating Application Data File**

| Flight | Number of Passengers | Passenger Name | Number of Items Considered | Ratings for Items 1, 2, and 3, Respectively |
|--------|----------------------|----------------|----------------------------|---------------------------------------------|
| 19386 | 6 | | 3 | |
| | | Rebecca Ryan | | 2 5 6 |
| | | Norman Bates | | 5 6 3 |
| | | Marty McFly | | 2 4 6 |
| | | Emily Latella | | 2 5 7 |
| | | Jack T. Colton | | 2 6 7 |
| | | Joan Wilder | | 2 4 5 |

The factor ratings given by the passengers can be stored in a two-dimensional array **Rating**, each row of which represents the ratings of a particular passenger. Each element in a particular row contains the rating for a certain factor. Furthermore, we store the passenger names in a vector **Name**. We also need a Boolean vector **Seated** to keep track of which passengers have already been satisfactorily seated. A value of "true" will indicate that a passenger has been seated, while "false" will denote a passenger who has not yet been processed. Using these representations, our sample passenger data is as shown in Table 5-18. The previous comments are incorporated in the program in Fig. 5-56.

The first step of the program inputs the first line of data, which contains the flight number, the number of passengers, and the number of factors that were rated. Step 2 inputs all passenger names and ratings and sets all elements of the vector **Seated** to "false," since no one has yet been seated. Step 3 initializes the variable that keeps track of how many passengers remain to be seated (all of them) and the variable that contains the current passenger's subscript. The fourth step engages the loop, which controls the processing of all passengers. Step 5 computes the sum-of-squares statistic associated with the comparison between the current passenger and every other unprocessed passenger. The least-square statistic is found, corresponding to the passenger most compatible with the current passenger. Step 6 marks the passengers just matched as being seated, and displays a line containing their names. Step 7 prepares for reentry into the loop by decrementing the number of unprocessed passengers and finding the next unprocessed passenger. After leaving the loop, step 8 checks to see if there was an odd number of passengers, in which case someone must sit alone. (This person will be fairly incompatible with everyone to have been left to the end anyway and will undoubtedly serve everyone's needs best by sitting alone!)

## 5-8  RECORD STRUCTURES AND ARRAYS OF RECORD STRUCTURES

Thus far we have discussed elementary data structures such as the integer, real number, character, and logical value. Arrays of these elementary data

**TABLE 5-18**  Data in Form Used in Airline Seating Application

| Name | Ratings | Seated |
|------|---------|--------|
| Rebecca Ryan | 2 5 6 | False |
| Norman Bates | 5 6 3 | False |
| Marty McFly | 2 4 6 | False |
| Emily Latella | 2 5 7 | False |
| Jack T. Colton | 2 6 7 | False |
| Joan Wilder | 2 4 5 | False |

**program** SeatMate (input, output);
{Given the flight number, the number of passengers, the number of factors, and for each passenger the name and ratings, this program generates from the passenger list those pairs that are most suited to each other.}

**const**
   MaxN = 200;    {Maximum number of passengers}
   MaxM = 10;    {Maximum number of factors}

**type**
   NameType = **packed array** [1 ..20] **of** char;
   NameArray = **array** [1 .. MaxN] **of** NameType;
   RatingsType = **array** [1 .. MaxN, 1 .. MaxM] **of** integer;
   SeatedType = **array** [1 .. MaxN] **of** boolean;

**var**
| | |
|---|---|
| Flight: integer; | {Flight number} |
| N: integer; | {Number of passengers} |
| M: integer; | {Number of factors} |
| Name: NameArray; | {List of passenger names} |
| Ratings: RatingsType; | {Ratings; one row for each passenger, one column for each factor} |
| Seated: SeatedType; | {True indicates that a passenger has already been matched} |
| NumLeft: integer; | {Number of passengers remaining to be matched} |
| Current: integer; | {Subscript for passenger currently being processed} |
| CurrentMate: integer; | {Best seat mate for current passenger} |
| I, J: integer; | {Loop counters} |
| NotFound: Boolean; | {Loop flag} |

   **procedure** Compatible (
| | |
|---|---|
| Ratings: RatingsType; | {Input, ratings; one row for each passenger, one column for each factor} |
| Seated: SeatedType; | {Input, true indicates that a passenger has already been matched} |
| Current: integer; | {Input, subscript for passenger currently being processed} |
| **var** CurrentMate: integer | {Input/output, best seat mate for current passenger} |

         );
{Given the ratings table, the vector indicating already seated passengers, and the row of rating corresponding to a passenger currently being considered, this procedure determines the best, in the sense described, seat mate not yet seated.}

**var**
| | |
|---|---|
| LeastSquare: integer; | {Used to locate the least square} |
| SumOfSquares: integer; | {Sum of squares of differences for pair under consideration} |

**FIGURE 5-56**
Program for matching
airplane passengers.

```
begin
    {Step 1: Initialize}
    LeastSquare := maxint;

    {Step 2: Find most compatible seat mate}
    for I := Current + 1 to N do
        begin
            SumOfSquares := 0;
            if not Seated[I]
            then begin
                for J := 1 to M do
                    SumOfSquares := SumOfSquares +
                                        sqr (Ratings[I, J] − Ratings[Current, J]);
                if SumOfSquares < LeastSquare
                then begin
                    LeastSquare := SumOfSquares;
                    CurrentMate := I
                end
            end
        end;
end; {Compatible}


begin
    {Step 1: Input flight number, number of passengers, and number of items;
        then write heading}
    readln (Flight, N, M);
    writeln (Flight, N, M);
    writeln('Passenger list for flight', Flight);

    {Step 2: Build the table of passenger profiles}
    for I := 1 to N do
        begin
            for J := 1 to 20 do
                read (Name[I][J]); {read all 20 characters of Name[I] from the
                                        first 20 characters of the line}
            write (Name[I]);
            for J := 1 to M do begin
                read ( Ratings[I, J] ); {Read M ratings from remainder of line}
                write (Ratings[I, J]);
            end;
            readln; {Flush new line character}
            writeln;
            Seated[I] := false
        end;

    {Step 3: Initialize temporary variables}
    NumLeft := N;
    Current := 1;
```

FIGURE 5-56 (*cont.*)

{Step 4: Process all passengers: if there is an odd number, the last person must sit alone}
**while** NumLeft > 1 **do**
   **begin**

      {Step 5: Find most compatible seat-mate}
      Compatible(Ratings, Seated, Current, CurrentMate);

      {Step 6: Output and remove these 2 passengers from available list}
      Seated[Current] : = true;
      Seated[CurrentMate] : = true;
      writeln('The best matched seat-mate for□', Name[Current], '□is□',
           Name[CurrentMate] );

      {Step 7: Prepare for next pass through loop and finding the next unprocessed passenger}
      NumLeft : = NumLeft − 2;
      NotFound : = true;
      **while** NotFound **and** (Current < N) **do**
        **if** Seated[Current]
        **then** Current : = Current + 1
        **else** NotFound : = false
   **end**;

   {Step 8: Is there someone left over?}
   if NumLeft = 1
   then writeln (Name[Current], '□will be seated alone');
**end.**

**FIGURE 5-56** (*cont.*)

structures have been introduced in this chapter. An important step in problem solving is to find the proper way to structure the data involved. Different groupings of data elements specify different relationships among these data elements. For example, a student record might contain the student's name, student number, address, major, year of study, etc. In general, a record will contain data items with different types. For example, student name is of type character string, while year of study is an integer. Consequently, such a structure is *nonhomogeneous*. As we have seen, elements of arrays must all be of the same type. This limits the domain of applicability for arrays, since there are many problems for which this requirement of *homogeneity* introduces complications. In Sec. 5-7.2 (the Global Hockey League application), for example, a set of "parallel arrays" was used to circumvent this restriction (in the case that team names rather than numbers are used).

In this section we introduce a new data structure, the *record structure*, which allows us to accommodate nonhomogeneity. The introduction of records permits the natural grouping of related data elements (possibly of different types) needed for a variety of applications.

We begin by introducing the Pascal record type. As an example, the type for a complex number is specified in the following manner:

**type**
    Complex = **record**
        RealPart: real;
        ImaginaryPart: real
    **end**;

The new type, named **Complex**, which is described by the *record type denoter* following the = in the type definition, contains two *fields*. Each field is described by a name, called the *field selector*; these are **RealPart** and **ImaginaryPart** in our example. Further, each field is given a type; both fields are real in our example. (Although both fields happen to be of the same type in this simple example, this is not required for record types, as mentioned previously.)

Next, consider declaring variables of the new type, as in

**var**
    Z, X: Complex;

A variable declared with a record type takes on the structure of that type. In our example, Z has two fields. Each is selected following the variable's name by a period followed by the field selector name, as in

Z.RealPart

Z.ImaginaryPart

Each of these acts as a variable, much as each element of an array-structured variable acts as a variable. Similarly for the variable X, we have

X.RealPart

X.ImaginaryPart

Thus we may view the record variables Z and X as each representing a complex number having real and imaginary parts.

To illustrate the use of these record structures, let us formulate a procedure for simulating the addition of two complex numbers. The procedure in Fig. 5-57 performs the desired addition. The procedure statement

ComplexAdd (X, Y, Z)

invokes the procedure. X, Y, and Z must all be of the type **Complex** described previously. Values are supplied in the X and Y record structures, and the computed result is placed in the real and imaginary parts of record structure Z. Similar procedures can be written to simulate other complex arithmetic operations. Standard Pascal does not permit a function to return a record-structured value as its result. However, some compilers allow this extension to the standard language. This extension permits our complex arithmetic example to be implemented with functions instead of procedures.

The two structures just described each have two component fields which are of the same type, that is, real. In general, however, structures can be

**procedure** ComplexAdd (
   A, B: Complex;    {Input, two complex numbers to be added}
   **var** C: Complex    {Output, sum}
                        );
{Given the input parameters A and B which are record structured variables of type Complex, described in the text, this procedure adds these two complex numbers and returns the result through the output parameter C, also of type Complex.}
**begin**
   {Compute real and imaginary sums}
   C.RealPart := A.RealPart + B.RealPart;
   C.ImaginaryPart := A.ImaginaryPart + B.ImaginaryPart
**end**;

**FIGURE 5-57**
**Example of use of**
**a record structure.**

described whose components are of mixed type; indeed, a component may even be a record or array structure. As an example, the type definition in Fig. 5-58 creates a simplified structure for an employee record. We may declare a variable of this record structure by, for example

**var**
   Employee: EmployeeRecord;

The identifier Employee now refers to an entire record structure.

**type**
   EmployeeRecord =
     **record**
       Name:
         **record**
           First: **packed array** [1 ..30] **of** char;
           MiddleInit: char;
           Last: **packed array** [1 .. 30] **of** char
         **end**;
       Address:
         **record**
           Street: **packed array** [1 .. 30] **of** char;
           City: **packed array** [1 ..30] **of** char;
           Province: **packed array** [1 .. 30] **of** char
         **end**;
       Deductions:
         **record**
           NoOfDed: integer;
           DeductionName: **array** [1 ..5] **of array** [1 .. 30] **of** char;
           Amount: **array** [1 .. 5] **of** real
         **end**
     **end**;

**FIGURE 5-58**
**Example of a more**
**complex record**
**structure.**

Employee.Name refers to the part of this record dealing with the employee's name. Since this is, in turn, a record structure of three fields, we can select each of these three fields by

Employee.Name.First

Employee.Name.MiddleInit

Employee.Name.Last

The second of these is a variable of a simple type, namely, char, and is therefore called an *elementary field*. The first and third are of **packed array** [1 .. n] **of** char type (that is, standard Pascal "string" type). Individual characters could be selected by subscripts. To refer to the Jth character of the last name, we use

Employee.Name.Last[J]

which is of character type. Employee.Address and Employee.Deductions also are record structures. Two of the latter's fields are arrays. To refer to the name of the Kth deduction, we use

Employee.Deductions.DeductionName[K]

The corresponding amount is

Employee.Deductions.Amount[K]

Since the deduction name is an array of character, we can select the Jth character of the Kth name by

Employee.Deductions.DeductionName[K][J]

or equivalently

Employee.Deductions.DeductionName[K, J]

As previously defined, the EmployeeRecord type contains fields that are record structures, but these substructures are anonymous or unnamed record types. Thus it is not possible to declare variables or parameters that are of the *same* type as these substructures. If we require such parameters or variables, it will be necessary to decompose the type definition. The definition in Fig. 5-59 is equivalent to that in Fig. 5-58, except that the types are all named. Notice that the order of definition is restricted by the requirement that a type name must be defined before it is used. If a record structure contains consecutive fields of the same type, Pascal allows a shortened notation in the definition. The field selectors are separated by commas, followed by a colon and the type. We have used this notation to shorten the definition of AddressRecord.

An *array of record structures* is simply an array whose elements are record structures. These elements have identical names, levels, and subparts. For example, if a record structure MonthSalesTable were used to represent the sales performance of a salesperson for each month of the year, this type might be defined as shown in Fig. 5-60. In this definition, we have rather arbitrarily split the type definition of the array of record structures type

```
type
    String30 = packed array [1 ..30] of char;
    NameRecord =
        record
            First: String30;
            MiddleInit: char;
            Last: String30
        end;
    AddressRecord =
        record
            Street, City, Province: String30
        end;
    NameVector = array [1 .. 5] of String30;
    AmountVector = array [1 .. 5] of real;
    DedRecord =
        record
            NoOfDed: integer;
            DeductionName: NameVector;
            Amount: AmountVector
        end;
    EmployeeRecord =
        record
            Name: NameRecord;
            Address: AddressRecord;
            Deductions: DedRecord
        end;
```

**FIGURE 5-59**
Example of a complex
record with no
anonymous types.

MonthSalesTable into three definitions for readability. Additional divisions, for example, the type of the **Salesperson** field, might be required if other declarations in a program use these type definitions.

We can now declare a variable to hold sales data for the year as

```
var
    MonthSales: MonthSalesTable
```

We can refer to the sales data for the month of May by the variable MonthSales[5]. Particular parts of the May sales are referred to by the variables

```
MonthSales[5].Salesperson
```

and

```
MonthSales[5].SalesDetail
```

Likewise,

```
MonthSales[2].SalesDetail.Sales
```

refers to the sales for the month of February. Thus we have now extended

```
type
    String30 = packed array [1 .. 30] of char;
    MonthSalesRec =
        record
            Salesperson:
                record
                    Name, Region: String30
                end;
            SalesDetail:
                record
                    Quota, Sales, Commission: real
                end
        end;
    MonthSalesTable = array [1 .. 12] of MonthSalesRec;
```

**FIGURE 5-60**
**Example of an**
**array of structure**
**type.**

the concept of a Pascal variable to include both subscripts and field selectors. Such a variable may be used in any context where a variable is required, for example, on the left of an assignment statement or as an argument to a function or procedure that corresponds to a pass-as-variable parameter. The type of the variable is the type of the element (array element or record field) finally selected.

Pascal requires that the selectors (subscripts and field selectors) be given in the order that corresponds to the declaration and that all the selectors down to the level of the element being selected be specified. Some other languages relax some of the requirements. For example, PL/1 allows field selectors to be omitted as long as the reference is unique, and it also allows subscripts to be moved farther to the right from their normal position. If there were only one MonthSales variable, a PL/1 compiler would accept

SalesDetail[5].Sales

or even

SalesDetail.Sales[5]

as equivalent to

MonthSales[5].SalesDetail.Sales

Since in Pascal a field selector name always follows a variable of known type, the *scope* of a field selector is considered to be a particular record denoter rather than the program or subprogram in which it occurs. This means that a particular record structure cannot have two fields with the same name at a given level. However, the same identifier can be used for fields in different records or other uses (constant names, variables, etc.) in the program.

It is sometimes the case that some of the fields in a record are relevant only when another field has a certain value. Consider a type definition for a simplified bibliographic data base. This contains the title, author, and type (book, report, or journal article) for each reference. For books and reports, the publisher is stored, while for journal articles, the journal name, volume, and page number are stored. Pascal includes the *variant record* feature to accommodate such cases. Figure 5-61 contains the appropriate definitions.

The definition of ReferEntryRecord is divided into two parts. The part preceding the **case** defines fields applicable to all reference records. (The use of the reserved word **case** for variant records should not be confused with use of the same reserved word for the case statement.) Following **case** is the definition of a *discriminant field*, whose type must be a previously defined type identifier specifying an ordinal type. In our example, the discriminant field is Kind and is of type ReferType, an enumerated type. Pascal requires that the discriminant field be set to the appropriate value before the fields of a variant are accessed. The discriminant is followed by **of** and a list of the alternatives. Each alternative consists of one or more values of the discriminant type separated by commas, a colon, and a list of fields enclosed within parentheses. The alternatives may occur in any order. Every value of the discriminant must occur exactly once. However, the field list of an alternative may be empty.

Assuming the declaration

**var**
 References: ReferTable;

we could assign some values as follows.

```
References[1].Title : = 'An Introduction to Computer Science';
References[1].Author : = 'Tremblay, Bunt';
References[1].Kind : = Book;
References[1].Publisher : = 'McGraw-Hill';

References[2].Title : = 'The Humble Programmer';
References[2].Author : = 'Dijkstra';
References[2].Kind : = Journal;
References[2].JournalName : = 'Communications of the ACM';
References[2].Volume : = 15;
References[2].PageNumber : = 859;
```

```
type
   String50 = packed array [1 .. 50] of char;
   ReferType = (Book, Journal, Report);
   ReferEntryRecord =
      record
         Title, Author: String50;
         case Kind: ReferType of
            Book, Report: (Publisher: String50);
            Journal: (JournalName: String50; Volume, PageNumber: integer)
      end;
   ReferTable = array [1 .. 200] of ReferEntryRecord;
```

FIGURE 5-61
Example of a
variant record
structure.

The Pascal compiler allocates storage in such a way that each variant occupies the same storage. This is possible because only one variant is allowed to be active at a given time. The storage required for a record structure variable is that required for its fixed part plus that required for its longest variant.

Another form of variant record type may be defined by omitting the field selector name and colon from the discriminant. Only an ordinal type denoter appears between **case** and **of**. Such a record structure does not contain a field indicating which variant is active. However, since all the variants occupy the same memory, the programmer must use some other logic to determine which variant is active. We will not pursue this option further.

We summarize the syntax rules for a record type denoter and field list in Figs. 5-62 and 5-63. Because this is a rather complex syntax diagram, the reader is encouraged to trace the previous examples through these diagrams.

It is often necessary to refer to several fields of a record variable in consecutive statements. Pascal provides the with statement to facilitate this. The with statement specifies a record variable and an executable statement (usually a compound statement). Within the executable statement, the field names of the record may be used as variables. The assignments of the previous example may be rewritten as shown in Fig. 5-64.

Figure 5-65 presents the syntax diagram for the with statement. Note that when a list of records is given, it is as if the with statements were nested. That is, using the definitions in Fig. 5-58 and assuming that Employee is a variable of type EmployeeRecord,

**with** Employee, Deductions **do**
   NumOfDed : = NumOfDed + 1

is equivalent in effect to

**with** Employee **do**
   **with** Deductions **do**
      NumOfDed : = NumOfDed + 1

Ever wonder where TV detectives go when their shows are canceled? A group of these have banded together to form Wasteland Sleuths, the ultimate in detective agencies. The group presently includes Jim Rockford, Frank Cannon, Joe Mannix, Laura Holt, Harry Orwell, Emma Peel, Paul Drake, and Fran Belding. In the face of overwhelming demand for their services, the sleuths have decided to computerize their recordkeeping system. Files of both clients of the agency and detectives are required to maintain the information necessary for client billing and payroll. After some consideration,

**record type denoter**

**FIGURE 5-62**
**Syntax diagram for**
**record type denoter.**

**field list**

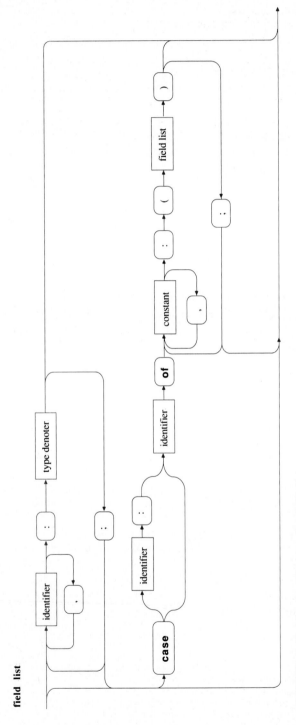

FIGURE 5-63   Syntax diagram for field list.

```
with References[1] do
    begin
        Title : = 'An Introduction to Computer Science';
        Author : = 'Tremblay, Bunt';
        Kind : = Book;
        Publisher : = 'McGraw-Hill'
    end;
with References[2] do
    begin
        Title : = 'The Humble Programmer';
        Author : = 'Dijkstra';
        Kind : = Journal;
        JournalName : = 'Communications of the ACM';
        Volume : = 15;
        PageNumber : = 859
    end
```

FIGURE 5-64
Example of the use
of the with statement.

the type definitions in Fig. 5-66 have been devised. These structures are designed to cross-reference each other. For example, the **Investigator** field of the **ClientRec** structure relates to the **Name** field of the **DetectiveRec** structure and contains the name of the detective working on the case (**Peel, Orwell, Cannon,** . . .). Note that while any given detective may be working on more than one case at a time, only one detective works on any given case.

At the end of each day, each detective submits a statement of charges, giving the number of hours he or she spent on each case on which he or she is working. For example, a set of statements for a representative day might be

| | | |
|---|---|---|
| 'Belding' | 'Cheston' | 3.5 |
| 'Belding' | 'McCalla' | 1.5 |
| 'Belding' | 'Cooke' | 2.0 |
| 'Rockford' | 'Eager' | 5.0 |
| 'Rockford' | 'Sorenson' | 1.5 |
| 'Drake' | 'Keil' | 6.5 |
| . | | |
| . | | |
| . | | |

This indicates that Fran Belding is billing 3.5 hours of this day to the Cheston case, 1.5 hours to the McCalla case, and 2.0 hours to the Cooke

**with statement**

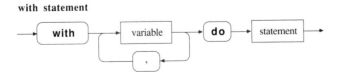

FIGURE 5-65
Syntax diagram for
with statement.

```
const
    StringLength = 30;
type
    StringType = packed array [1 .. StringLength] of char;
    ClientRec = record
        Name: record
            Last, MI, First: StringType
        end;
        Address: record
            Street, City, Province, PostalCode: StringType
        end;
        Investigator: StringType;
        BillableHours, Charge: real
    end;
    DetectiveRec = record
        Name: StringType;
        HourlyRate, HoursBilled: real
    end;
```

**FIGURE 5-66**
**Definitions for**
**detective application.**

case; Jim Rockford is billing 5.0 hours to the Eager case and 1.5 hours to the Sorenson case; Paul Drake is billing 6.5 hours to the Keil case.

Two "files" are maintained by the program, one for clients and one for detectives. These contain elements (entries) of the record types ClientRec and DetectiveRec, respectively.

Each of the "files" must be updated according to these daily statements. For example, to Belding's entry (element) is added 3.5 hours for her time spent on the Cheston case; to the Cheston entry is added 3.5 hours and a charge—3.5 hours multiplied by Belding's hourly rate (taken from her entry). A procedure is required to process the daily statements in this manner. Other procedures required include the following:

Adding a new client to the "file"

Adding a new detective to the "file"

Producing a monthly client report

Producing a monthly investigator report

Let us consider first the addition to the "files" of new clients and new detectives. While the ClientRec and DetectiveRec structures define the individual records of these "files," the "files" themselves (called Client and Detective) consist of arrays (vectors) of these record structures. A new client would be denoted by a variable of type ClientRec (say, NewClient). Similarly, NewDetective would be of type DetectiveRec.

The procedure in Fig. 5-67 reads in information for a new client and adds this information to the Client vector, a global variable. It is assumed that the Client vector is unordered and that a global variable LastClient points to the position in the vector in which the client last defined resides. The new

**procedure** AddClient;

{This procedure reads a new client name, address and investigator. If space remains in the client table, the information is added. The client table Client, and its current and maximum sizes, LastClient and MaxClients are assumed global. The user defined types are also assumed to be global.}

```
var
   NewClient: ClientRec;
begin
   with NewClient do
      begin
         with Name do
            begin
               ReadString (Last);
               ReadString (MI);
               ReadString (First)
            end;
         with Address do
            begin
               ReadString (Street);
               ReadString (City);
               ReadString (Province);
               ReadString (PostalCode)
            end;
         ReadString (Investigator);
         BillableHours : = 0.0;
         Charge : = 0.0
      end;
   if LastClient = MaxClients
   then writeln ('Client file is full')
   else begin
         LastClient : = LastClient + 1;
         Client[LastClient] : = NewClient
      end;
end;
```

FIGURE 5-67
Procedure for
adding new clients.

client will be inserted into the next position. The vector is assumed to have space for a maximum of MaxClients, a global constant. A new detective is added in a similar way. The procedure ReadString in Fig. 5-16 is used for reading the character string information.

We turn now to the procedure for processing the daily statements. Because the vectors of clients and detectives are unordered, each statement requires a linear search of each vector. Global variables LastClient and LastDetective are assumed to mark the last entry in each vector (Client and Detective). The vectors themselves are assumed to be global as well. The complete procedure appears in Fig. 5-68.

This procedure does little in the way of error checking. What else could (or should) be done? It is also noteworthy that while this procedure is simple

```
procedure DailyStatements;
```
{Given the daily statements of the detectives, this procedure updates the
  global Client and Detective vectors.}
```
var
    DetName, ClientName: StringType;    {For input of detective and client
                                              names}
    Hours: integer;                     {For input of hours on case}
    IndexD, IndexC: integer;            {Vector indices}
    NotFound: boolean;                  {Loop control flag}
begin
    {Step 1: Engage main loop}
    while not eof do
        begin

            {Step 2: Read the next statement}
            ReadString (DetName);
            ReadString (ClientName);
            readln (Hours);

            {Step 3: Find the detective in detective vector}
            IndexD := 1;
            NotFound := true;
            while NotFound do
                if DetName = Detective[IndexD].Name
                then NotFound := false
                else IndexD := IndexD + 1;

            {Step 4: Find this client in client vector}
            IndexC := 1;
            NotFound := true;
            while NotFound do
                if ClientName = Client[IndexC].Name.Last
                then NotFound := false
                else IndexC := IndexC + 1;

            {Step 5: Update vectors accordingly}
            if Client[IndexC].Investigator <> DetName
            then writeln ('Detective', DetName, 'should not be working on the ',
                              ClientName, 'case')
            else
                with Detective[IndexD], Client[IndexC] do
                    begin
                        HoursBilled := HoursBilled + Hours;
                        BillableHours := BillableHours + Hours;
                        Charge := Charge + Hours * HourlyRate
                    end
        end
end;
```

**FIGURE 5-68**
**Procedure to process**
**detectives' daily**
**statements.**

to express, it could well be very unwieldy in terms of execution time because of the frequent linear searches of both files. What could be done to improve this? What impact would this have on the segment presented to insert new clients (and the similar process for inserting new detectives)?

The next procedure is to be called each month to produce a listing of client charges. The output produced is a report in the following form

WASTELAND SLEUTHS

29 Cove Road
Malibu, California

MONTHLY CLIENT REPORT

Client      Investigator      Charges To Date

The complete procedure is presented in Fig. 5-69. A similar procedure could be produced for the monthly investigator reports.

A with statement is used to simplify the statement that writes the line of the report. This with statement must be contained *within* the range of the loop. The "address" of the record must be recomputed for each execution of the loop because it depends on the loop control variable. The program fragment

```
procedure ClientReport;
{Given the client vector (Client) and the number of entries currently in the
   vector (LastClient) as global variables, this procedure produces the monthly
   client report as described in the text.}
var
   IndexC: integer;      {Loop control variable}
begin
   {Step 1: Print headings}
   writeln ('□':26, 'WASTELAND SLEUTHS');
   writeln;     {Blank line}
   writeln ('□':28, '29 Cove Road');
   writeln ('□':25, 'Malibu, California');
   writeln;
   writeln ('□':24, 'MONTHLY CLIENT REPORT');
   writeln ('□':12, 'Client', '□':22, 'Investigator', '□':6, 'Charges To Date');
   writeln;

   {Step 2: Print one line for each client}
   for IndexC : = 1 to LastClient do
      with Client[IndexC] do
         writeln (Name.Last:30, Investigator:31, Charge:8:2)
end;
```

**FIGURE 5-69**
**Client report**
**procedure.**

with Client[IndexC] **do**

    **for** IndexC : = 1 **to** LastClient **do**

.

.

.

would be *incorrect*. This fragment specifies that the value of IndexC *before the loop* is to select a record and that all executions of the loop range should refer to this preselected record. (In the procedure ClientReport, the variable IndexC has not been assigned a value before the loop, so the subscript is in fact illegal.)

A considerable portion of the procedure is devoted to formatting the report appropriately. For example, fields of blanks are used for centering the various headings.

The complete application would require a main program that would be run once a day. This program would call the various procedures described previously. An appropriate organization might involve arranging the input stream so that each collection of input data in the input stream were preceded by an appropriate transaction code. For example, the detectives' daily statements would be preceded by 'Daily Statements', a new client's data by 'NewClient'; etc. The main program would read the transaction code and call the appropriate processing procedure.

It also will be necessary for the program to write out the Client and Detective vectors at the end of processing; these final values must be read when the program begins execution on the next day. This is best done utilizing sequential files, which are described in the next section.


## EXERCISES 5-8

1. Given the type definitions in Fig. 5-59, and the following variable declarations:

   **var**
       Deduction: DedRecord;
       Employee: EmployeeRecord;

   which of the following variable references are valid? What is the type of each valid reference?

   | | |
   |---|---|
   | (a) Deduction | (e) Employee.Name.First[1] |
   | (b) Deduction[2].Amount | (f) Deduction.DeductionName[1, 1] |
   | (c) Employee.Name | (g) Deduction.DeductionName[2] |
   | (d) Employee.Name[1] | |

★ 2. Write procedures for complex subtract, multiply, and divide similar to the add procedure given in this section. If your Pascal compiler allows functions to return record structures, implement the four operations as functions as well. Compare the usefulness of the procedure and function versions.

3. Since a complex number consists of two components of the same type (real), it may be defined as a two-element vector. Repeat Exercise 2 using the vector representation. Compare the ease of implementation of the two alternatives.

★ 4. Complete the implementation of the Wasteland Sleuths example in this section. You may read the "prior day's data" from the standard input stream and write the final data to the output stream, since we have not yet described sequential file processing.

5. A western farm currently produces several feed grains. In particular, wheat, barley, oats, canola, and flax are produced. The production level (in bushels) and the price per bushel (in dollars and cents) received during the year are recorded. Use a record structure to describe the data.

6. A university book store maintains a list of up to 20 requests for any book that is currently out of stock. The information kept for such a book consists of the book title (up to 80 characters), book price (in dollars and cents), and the requests for the book. Each request consists of a person's name (up to 40 characters) and address (100 characters). Use a record structure to describe a book with its associated information.

7. Use a record structure to represent each of the following documents:
   *(a)* Airline ticket                *(d)* Driver's license
   *(b)* Blue Cross or Medicare card   *(e)* Student identification card
   *(c)* Gasoline credit card
   Make realistic assumptions about the contents of each document.

8. A liquor store has the following kinds of alcoholic beverages on hand:

   50 brands of wine of which:
     10 brands are champagne
     5 brands are sherry
     20 brands are red
     10 brands are white
     5 brands are sparkling
   15 brands of whiskey of which:
     6 brands are rye
     6 brands are scotch
     3 brands are bourbon
   10 brands of rum
   5 brands of cognac
   7 brands of gin
   5 brands of vodka

   Write a Pascal declaration for a record structure to store this information.

9. Assume that in the Wasteland Sleuths application perks are given to the investigators in proportion to the amount of time they bill. Write a procedure to rank the investigators in terms of hours worked.

★ **10.** Write a procedure for the Wasteland Sleuths application to produce two listings of clients: one in descending order of billed hours and one in descending order of charges.

★★ **11.** The police department requires a program to assist them in determining the identities of criminals from filed descriptions supplied by their victims. The police have on file records describing known criminals. These records have the format of the following example:

| Name | Height (in inches) | Weight (in pounds) | Address |
|------|------|------|------|
| 'Bugsy Malone' | 53 | 119 | '68 Town St.' |

Design a program that first reads in the set of records giving the descriptions of known criminals and prepares a table of information on known criminals. This set of records is terminated by a special record of the form

'***'  0   0   '***'

A second set of records follows, containing descriptions of criminals participating in unsolved crimes. These records have the format of the following example:

| Description of Crime | Estimated Height of Criminal | Estimated Weight |
|------|------|------|
| '21 July: Mugging' | 68 | 155 |

This second set of records is terminated by a special record of the form

'***'  0   0

For each of the unsolved crimes, call a procedure (which you also must write) to determine possible suspects for the crime. This determination is based on the estimated height and weight of the criminals as given by the victims of the crimes. If the height is within 2 inches *and* the weight is within 10 lb of a person on the known criminals list, that person is to be listed as a possible suspect for the crime involved. The parameters of this procedure are to include the table of known criminals and the information contained in the record describing the current crime.

★★ **12.** Assume that the Saskatchewan Real Estate Board has conducted a survey of each of its licensees. Each licensee filled in a questionnaire of the form shown in Table 5-19. Write a program which analyzes these questionnaires. In particular, calculate the following for the group of respondents:

(*a*) Total number of respondents.

(*b*) Percentage brokers and percentage salespersons.

Calculate the following separately for brokers and salespersons:

(*c*) Number of respondents from each town.

| Item | Possible Values |
|---|---|
| License type (enumeration) | Broker |
| | Salesperson |
| Residence town (string) | Name of one of 800 possible towns |
| Age (integer) | Age in years |
| Sex (character) | M = male |
| | F = female |
| Education (integer) | 1 = less than high school diploma |
| | 2 = high school diploma |
| | 3 = technical institute or community college |
| | 4 = college degree |

(d) Average age.

(e) Percentage male and percentage female.

(f) Number of respondents in each educational classification.

The input data for each questionnaire consists of five questionnaire answer codes, representing license type, residence town, age, sex, and education. Use an end-of-file test to determine the end of the data.

★ 13. Universal Exports keeps a computer file of its inventory. Each record contains the following items: product number, product name, supplier name, unit price. These records are kept in a product number order. A number of queries are made concerning these inventory records. Each query takes the form: product name, product number. For each query the corresponding inventory record must be found, and the product number, product name, supplier name, and unit price are to be displayed. The query data is kept in no particular order. The data is organized as shown in Fig. 5-70. Write a program which processes the data and generates

FIGURE 5-70  Inventory program input table.

| 200 | 'Writing Pads' | 'Minto Paper Products' | 1.10 | |
|---|---|---|---|---|
| 201 | 'Memo Pads' | 'Chipman Office Products' | .50 | |
| . | . | . | . | Inventory data |
| . | . | . | . | |
| . | . | . | . | |
| 1246 | '5 Column Columner Pads' | 'Fresno Forms' | 5.00 | |

99999 ←End of inventory data

Query data

the required report. Use an end-of-file test to detect the end of the query data.

## 5-9 INTRODUCTION TO SEQUENTIAL FILES

To this point in the text we have dealt with data entities that were assumed to reside in main memory. There are at least two reasons why not all information that is processed by a computer should reside in an immediately accessible form of memory. First, some programs (and data for programs) are so large that they do not fit conveniently into main memory, which is typically a scarce resource in a computer system. Second, it is often desirable or necessary to store information from one execution of a program to the next (e.g., in a payroll system). Therefore, large volumes of data and archival data are commonly stored in external storage (usually magnetic tapes or disks) using special data-holding entities called *files*.

Recall from the previous section that a *record structure* (often called simply a *record* when discussing file processing) is a collection of information items about a particular entity. For example, a record may consist of information about a passenger on an airline flight or an article sold at a retail distribution store. A *field* (sometimes called an *item*) of a record is a unit of meaningful information about an entity. The different items of a passenger record may be the passenger's name, address, seat number, and menu restrictions. Generally, an item of a record is an integer, real, or character string data element. Items may themselves, however, be composed of aggregates of items, such as an array of items or a subcollection of nonhomogeneous items.

A *file* is a collection of records involving a set of entities with certain aspects in common and organized for some particular purpose. For example, the collection of all passenger records for the passengers on a particular flight constitutes a file.

A record item that uniquely identifies a record in a file is called a *key*. In the passenger file, individual passenger records can be uniquely identified by the passenger's name, assuming duplicate names do not occur for a particular flight. The seat-number item also can be used as a key, if desired, since seat numbers are usually uniquely assigned for a given flight.

It is a common practice to order the records in a file according to a key. Therefore, if the passenger name is selected as the key item, the record for **Adams** appears before the record for **Brown**, which appears before the record for **Camp** in a lexical ordering by surname. Some files are ordered on a particular item, termed the *sequence item*, which may not be unique for each record. For example, in a file of monthly sales for a particular company, several records containing sales information may appear for one customer. The file can be ordered by account number, with more than one occurrence of a customer sales record type for a given account number.

In a *sequential file*, records are stored (logically) one after the other on a storage device. The accessing of a record requires the scanning of all records that precede it. This form of access is called *sequential access*. Because a sequential file is conceptually simple yet flexible enough to cope with many of the problems associated with handling large volumes of data, it has been the most popular basic file structure used in the data-processing industry. In processing a sequential file, only one record is visible or accessible in main memory at any given time. When a record is read or written, it is transferred to or from an area in main memory called a *buffer*. In contrast to a sequential file, all records in an array of structures (records) are equally accessible at all times.

To facilitate the implementation of file-processing applications, we now present the facilities in Pascal for sequential files. A sequential file in standard Pascal is a sequence of elements of some type. Although Pascal permits a file element to be of any type (except that it may not itself be a file or contain a file), we shall generally only consider files of record structures. A file to be used in a program should be declared as a variable in the main program. (Files declared within procedures and functions are beyond the scope of this book.) A typical declaration would be

```
type
  FRecord =
    record
      Key, Data: integer
    end;
var
  Master = file of FRecord;
```

Standard Pascal requires that each file used (along with **input**, the standard input stream, and **output**, the standard output stream, if they are used) be listed in the program header line. Thus a program called **Example**, using the file just declared and the standard input and output files, would begin with the line

```
program Example (input, output, Master);
```

Some Pascal compilers allow the file names to be omitted.

Before a file may be used, certain system-dependent functions must be performed, e.g., allocating buffers, notifying the operating system that the file is to be used, and creating the file if it doesn't exist. Pascal defines two built-in procedures for opening a file. The reset procedure makes a file available for sequential reading, beginning at the first element (record). For example, the following statement opens the file **InputFile** for reading and loads its first record into the input buffer:

```
reset (InputFile);
```

The rewrite procedure first creates or empties the file and then makes it available for sequential writing. For example,

```
rewrite (OutputFile);
```

The first element (record) written becomes the first element of the file, the second written becomes the second, and so on.

A single record is read by the built-in read procedure. The first argument of the procedure is the file and the second is a variable into which the "next" element of the file is to be stored. Continuing our example, assuming that MRec is a variable declared to be of type FRecord, then

read (Master, MRec);

would read the next record from Master into MRec. It is important that the file's elements be of the *same type* as the variable into which the elements are read. The file must have been opened for input, using reset, prior to the execution of the read statement.

The eof function, previously described as a test for "end of file" of the standard input stream, applies to any file by supplying the file name as an argument. Thus,

eof (Master)

returns "false" if records remain to be read and "true" if all records have been processed. If eof is "true," then an attempt to read a record using the read procedure results in an error and termination of the program.

Similar to reading, writing of records is performed by the built-in write procedure. Its arguments are the file and a value to be written. The value must be of a type that is "assignment compatible" to the elements of the file; for files of record structures, this requires that the value be of the *same type* as the elements of the file. Using our example:

write (Master, MRec);

The file must be opened for output by a call to rewrite before execution of a write.

Standard Pascal has no facility for closing a file. Files are closed automatically on program termination.

A computer system will typically contain many files on its disk. Each operating system provides some sort of *directory* so that files may be accessed by name. It is convenient to allow a program to be compiled into a machine language program once and stored and then to allow the program to be run many times with different actual files as its input and output. One method for accomplishing this involves a command language external to the program. Statements in this language allow a relationship to be specified between the file variable name in the Pascal program and the directory name of the file to be used. The JCL (Job Control Language) used on many of IBM's large computers is typical.

Another scheme allows the program itself to specify the relationship just described; this is particularly common on interactive computer systems. The program can prompt for a file name on the user's terminal and read it as a character string. The program then specifies the name of the file to be used when opening the file. One common scheme uses a second parameter to the reset and rewrite built-in procedures to specify the file name. A typical example is

writeln ('Please enter master file name');

```
readln (MFileName);
reset (Master, MFileName);
```

Usually, Pascal compilers with this file-processing extension also have a character string extension. In this example, **MFileName** is assumed to be a character string variable.

Alternatively, a separate built-in procedure may associate the file name with the file prior to opening. Turbo Pascal's assign procedure is typical. We would write

```
writeln ('Please enter master file name');
readln (MFileName);
assign (Master, MFileName);
reset (Master);
```

In the remainder of this section we will ignore establishing the relationship between the Pascal file and the directory name of an actual file because the method is so system-dependent.

Let us now consider some examples of sequential file processing. As a first example, the following program fragment demonstrates the copying of a given file.

```
program Copy (OldMaster, NewMaster);
{This program copies OldMaster into NewMaster}
type
    FRecord = {Definition of record structure}
var
    OldMaster, NewMaster: file of FRecord;
    Temp: FRecord;
begin
    reset (OldMaster);
    rewrite (NewMaster);
    while not eof (OldMaster) do
        begin
            read (OldMaster, Temp);
            write (NewMaster, Temp)
        end
end.
```

As a second example, consider a simplified payroll system that produces paychecks for employees. The system also maintains a payroll master file that is kept in employee number (**EmpNum**) order. Each week a time record for each active employee is produced. These time records are sorted in employee number order and stored as a sequential file. The payroll system processes each time record against the payroll master file. When a time record matches a corresponding payroll master file record, the hourly rate of pay (and other information) is obtained from the associated master file record and a paycheck is produced. The master file record is also updated and written in a new payroll master file in such a case.

Figure 5-71 contains a program skeleton for this payroll. An important

**program** Payroll (input, output, OldPayroll, NewPayroll, TimeFile);
{Given a payroll master file and a time reports file, both sequential files, this program skeleton produces an updated payroll master file. We assume that all files are sequentially ordered on a key denoted by EmpNum.}

**type**
    MasterRecord = {Definition of master file record structure}
    TimeRecord = {Definition of time record structure}

**var**

| | |
|---|---|
| OldPayroll: **file of** MasterRecord; | {Old payroll file} |
| NewPayroll: **file of** MasterRecord; | {New payroll file} |
| TimeFile: **file of** TimeRecord; | {Time report file} |
| MRecord: MasterRecord; | {Current payroll record} |
| TRecord: TimeRecord; | {Current time record} |
| EndPayroll: boolean; | {End of OldPayroll file status flag} |
| EndTime: boolean; | {End of NewPayroll file status flag} |

**begin**
    {Step 1: Open sequential files}
    reset (OldPayroll);
    reset (TimeFile);
    rewrite (NewPayroll);

    {Step 2: Set file status flags}
    EndPayroll : = eof (OldPayroll);
    EndTime : = eof (TimeFile);

    {Step 3: Read first records from OldMaster and TimeFile, if they exist}
    **if not** EndPayroll
    **then** read (OldPayroll, MRecord);
    **if not** EndTime
    **then** read (TimeFile, TRecord);

    {Step 4: Engage loop to process while data remains in both the old payroll file and the time records file}
    **while not** EndPayroll **and not** EndTime **do**
      **begin**
        **if** TRecord.EmpNum = MRecord.EmpNum
        **then begin**

            {Step 5: Produce check for current employee and update old payroll master file record. Write out new payroll file record.}

            {Step 6: Update input file status flags}
            EndPayroll : = eof (OldPayroll);
            EndTime : = eof (TimeFile);

            {Step 7: Read next payroll master and time records, if they exist}

**FIGURE 5-71**
**Program illustrating the use of a sequential file.**

```
            if not EndPayroll
            then read (OldPayroll, MRecord);
            if not EndTime
            then read (TimeFile, TRecord)
        end
    else
```

{Step 8: Check whether current time record applies against a later
   payroll record}
```
    if MRecord.EmpNum < TRecord.EmpNum
    then begin
```

{Step 9: Copy old payroll master record into NewPayroll}
```
            write (NewPayroll, MRecord);
```

{Step 10: Update status flag of OldPayroll file}
```
            EndPayroll := eof (OldPayroll);
```

{Step 11: Read next payroll master file record, if it exists}
```
            if not EndPayroll
            then read (OldPayroll, MRecord);
        end
    else begin
```

{Step 12: No old payroll record corresponding to current
   time report}
```
            writeln (TRecord.Name, 'not in payroll file');
```

{Step 13: Update status flag for TimeFile}
```
            EndTime := eof (TimeFile);
```

{Step 14: Read next time record, if it exists}
```
            if not EndTime
            then read (TimeFile, TRecord);
        end
    end;
```

{Step 15: Copy any remaining records from OldPayroll to NewPayroll}
```
while not EndPayroll do
    begin
        write (NewPayroll, MRecord);
```

{Step 16: Update status flag and read next master record}
```
        EndPayroll := eof (OldPayroll);
        if not EndPayroll
        then read (OldPayroll, MRecord)
    end;
```

**FIGURE 5-71** (*cont.*)

{Step 17: Process any remaining time records}
**while not** EndTime **do**
   **begin**

      {Step 18: No old payroll record corresponding to current time
        report}
      writeln (TRecord.Name, 'not in payroll file');

      {Step 19: Update status flag and read next time record}
      EndTime : = eof (TimeFile);
      **if not** EndTime
      **then** read (TimeFile, TRecord)
   **end**
**FIGURE 5-71** (*cont.*)  **end**.

aspect of the program concerns end-of-file considerations. Since records that are read may not yet be processed, care must be taken to process the last records read. Observe that unless we have records yet to be processed in *both* files, we exit from the loop. Upon this exit, any remaining records in either the payroll file or time file, but not both, are processed. If a time record does not have a corresponding record in the master file, the employee's name (Name) is output.

In the interest of simplicity, we have ignored the updating of the OldPayroll file with personnel changes.

We have introduced briefly in this section the topic of sequential files. Other types of files exist. A more detailed discussion of sequential and other types of files is given in Chap. 10. This chapter also contains a description of external storage devices.

## EXERCISES 5-9

1. Modify the file copy program in this section so that it reports on the number of records copied.

2. Text files in Pascal contain "records" that are lines of text. Each of the lines may be of a different length. Many files on a computer system are best kept in this form. For example, the Pascal programs themselves are usually kept in this form. A typical computer operating system includes many utility programs for processing text files. For example, one or more editors may be supplied for creating text files. A utility may be provided for printing text files.

The sequential files discussed in this section are not usually considered text files. For example, consider a file with the record structure:

```
record
   EmployName: packed array [1..20] of char;
   EmployNumber: integer
end
```

Most Pascal compilers will store the employee number (EmployNumber) in a binary representation within the file. Processing this with a print utility will usually not result in the desired output on the printer. Likewise, a file prepared by a text editor will not be in the proper form to be read as a sequential file.

(a) Write a program that will read a standard text file as input and write a sequential file with the record structure described.

(b) Write a program that will read a sequential file with the record structure described and produce the contents in textual form suitable for display on a terminal or printer.

★ 3. Expand the program skeleton of Fig. 5-71 into a complete running program. Test the program.

★ 4. A sequential file has been prepared with numeric marks for students in a course. The record structure is of the form

**record**
    StudentId: integer;
    StudentName: **array** [1..30] **of** char;
    StudentMark: integer
**end**

Write a program that will read this file and write a new file with a letter grade appended to each record. The record structure for the output file should be

**record**
    StudentId: integer;
    StudentName: **array** [1..30] **of** char;
    StudentMark: integer;
    StudentFinalGrade: char
**end**

Letter grades are determined by the numeric mark as follows:

    A     90–100
    B     75–89
    C     55–74
    D     50–54
    F     0–49

Note that both the input file and the output file contain nontextual material, i.e., numbers stored in the binary form in which they are stored in most computers. Therefore, you may not be able to prepare the input file for the program with a text editor. Likewise, you may not be able to print the output file by the normal method for printing text files on your system. Also, write programs for creating the input file for testing your program and for displaying the output file of your program.

5. Write a program that will read the existing payroll master file and a file of new employees, and will write a new payroll master file with the new employees inserted in the appropriate positions. All of the files are kept

in order of increasing employee number. The same record structure, as described in Fig. 5-71, is used for all of these files.

## 5-10 SET STRUCTURES

In mathematics, a *set* is an unordered collection of elements. For example, if we take lower-case letters as elements, we could have the following sets:

| | |
|---|---|
| $\{a, b\}$ | Set of the two elements $a$ and $b$ |
| $\{a, c, d\}$ | Set of the three elements $a$, $c$, and $d$ |
| $\{c\}$ | Set with the single element $c$ |
| $\{\}$ | Set containing no elements; called the *empty set* and often designated by the Greek letter $\Phi$ |

Pascal implements a *set type* defined on an ordinal type called the *base type*. Recall from Chap. 3 that the ordinal types are integer, character, Boolean, enumerations, and subranges. Each of these types represent only a finite number of different values. Most Pascal compilers further restrict the *base type* of a set to an ordinal type satisfying certain constraints. Some compilers restrict base types to those ordinal types having at most some compiler-defined number of different values. Other compilers restrict base types to some specified minimum and maximum ordinal value (the value returned by the built-in function ord; see Sec. 3-6). For example, if the minimum and maximum values are 0 and 255, then the following base types are acceptable for defining sets.

| Type Denoter | Type | Minimum ord | Maximum ord |
|---|---|---|---|
| 1 .. 10 | Subrange | 1 | 10 |
| (red, white, blue) | Enumerated | 0 | 2 |
| 'A' .. 'Z' | Subrange | ord ('A') | ord ('Z') |

The following would be unacceptable as base types:

| Type Denoter | Type | Minimum ord | Maximum ord |
|---|---|---|---|
| −5 .. +5 | Subrange | −5 | +5 |
| integer | Primitive | $\leq$ −maxint | $\geq$ +maxint |
| 250 .. 260 | Subrange | 250 | 260 |

We have assumed that maxint $> 255$, as would be true for any reasonable Pascal compiler. The set types used in this book will be restricted mainly to the small nonnegative integers and small enumerations and will therefore not cause a problem with any reasonable compiler. The only problem arises with sets over the character type and its subranges. Some compilers are so restrictive that sets of characters are not acceptable. We will assume that sets of characters are allowed.

A set type is described by a *set type denoter* consisting of **set of** followed by a denoter describing the base type. Some examples of set type denoters are as follows:

**set of** 1 .. 10

**set of** (red, white, blue)

**set of** 'A' .. 'Z'

Set types may be given names, and set variables may be declared. Some examples of set type definitions and variable declarations are as follows:

**type**
    Colorset = **set of** (Black, Blue, Green, Red, White);
**var**
    RoomColors : Colorset;
    Consonants, Vowels: **set of** 'A' .. 'Z';
    Numbers: **set of** 1 .. 25;

A set value is denoted by a set constructor consisting of values and value ranges enclosed in square brackets. This is similar to the mathematical notation for sets, except that the square brackets (that is, [ and ]) are used because braces (that is, {and }) are reserved for comments. The use of the brackets to define a set can always be distinguished from their use for subscripts by the context.

The following are valid set constructors:

| | |
|---|---|
| [1, 3, 5] | Set of three integers |
| [1 .. 3, 8 .. 10] | Set of six integers, equivalent to [1, 2, 3, 8, 9, 10] |
| [ ] | Empty set |
| [I + 1 .. J − 1, 1, 3] | Assuming that I = 4 and J = 8, this defines the set [5 .. 7, 1, 3] or [5, 6, 7, 1, 3] |

Notice that the values may be expressions, which are evaluated, and that the values and ranges may appear in any order. Sets do not contain duplicates, so any duplicate elements specified in a constructor are discarded.

The syntax diagrams for set type denoter and set constructs are presented in Figs. 5-72 and 5-73.

Two set types are compatible if they have compatible base types. The base types are compatible if they are the same type, or one is a subrange of the other, or they are both subranges of the same host type. A set value

**set type denoter**

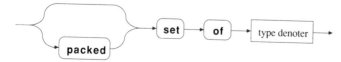

**FIGURE 5-72**
**Syntax diagram for set type denoter.**

set constructor

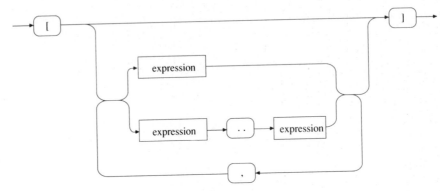

**FIGURE 5-73**
**Syntax diagram for**
**set constructor.**

may be assigned to a set variable if the types are compatible and if none of the elements present is outside the range of the base type of the variable. Thus if **S1** is of type set of 5 .. 10, then the following assignments are valid:

S1 : = [5, 7, 8];

S1 : = [ ];

S1 : = [10]

The following assignments are invalid:

S1 : = [4 .. 8];

S1 : = [1]

The operators +, −, and ∗ may be used with set operands. Their precedence is the same as for numeric operations. Their interpretation, given sets **A** and **B**, which must be of compatible types, are as follows:

| Operation | Definition | Result |
|---|---|---|
| A + B | Set union | Set containing all elements which are in A, in B, or in both |
| A − B | Set difference | Set containing all elements which are in A but not in B |
| A ∗ B | Set intersection | Set containing all elements which are in both A and B |

Four relations are defined on compatible sets:

| Relation | True Whenever: |
|---|---|
| A = B | A and B have exactly the same elements |
| A <> B | A = B is false |
| A <= B | A is a (not necessarily proper) subset of B; that is, every element in A is also in B |
| A >= B | B <= A |

A special relational operator, denoted by the reserved word **in**, may be used to test whether an element is in a set. If $e$ represents an expression and $s$ a set and $e$ is compatible with the base type of $s$, then we may write the relation $e$ **in** $s$. This relation is true only if the value represented by $e$ is in the set $s$.

The **in** operator may be used to provide a default for a case statement in standard Pascal. For the bloodbank application of Sec. 5-5.2 we could write

```
if Code in ['D', 'R']
then
    case Code of
        'D': . . . process a donation . . . ;
        'R': . . . process a request
    end
else writeln ('Illegal transaction code')
```

We now consider the applications of sets. Smith Hall, on the local university campus, has 10 classrooms numbered 1 to 10. Each classroom may be equipped with any combination of the following equipment.

Blackboard

"Green" blackboard

Slide projector

Projection screen

You are asked to write a program that produces various reports on the classrooms. One approach is to define a set variable for each type of equipment. The set elements are the room numbers in which such equipment can be placed. We use the following definitions and declarations:

```
type
    SetOfRooms = set of 1 .. 10;
var
    Blackboards, Greenboards, Projectors, Screens: SetOfRooms;
```

Rather than present a complete solution for this application, we suggest how some of the operations are performed and leave the complete program as an exercise.

We could define rooms 1 through 5 and 7 through 10 as having blackboards by

```
Blackboards := [1 .. 5, 7 .. 10]
```

If, instead, this data is to be read from the input stream, using a value of **0** as a sentinel, we could use

```
Blackboards := [];      {Initialize to empty}
read (I);
while I <> 0 do
    begin
```

Blackboards := Blackboards + [I]; {Union}

read (I)

**end**

where I is assumed to be an integer variable. Standard Pascal provides no built-in mechanism for reading or writing sets.

We use the various set operations for producing the answers to "queries," that is, for producing the information to be included in various reports. For example,

| Set Expression | Result |
| --- | --- |
| Blackboards + Greenboards | Set of rooms containing a "board" of any kind |
| Projectors * Screens | Set of rooms with projectors and screens |
| (Projectors − Screens) + (Screens − Projectors) | Rooms with projectors and no screens or screens but no projectors |

We also can use Boolean expressions (conditions) to answer "yes" or "no" types of question, as for example:

| Boolean Expression | True Whenever: |
| --- | --- |
| (Blackboards + Greenboards) = [1 .. 10] | Every room has a "board" |
| (Projectors − Screens) = [] | There are no rooms with projectors and no screens |
| 5 in Screens | Room 5 has a screen |

A set may be viewed as a Boolean vector, sometimes called a "bit string." For example, in the previous example, each of the variables may be considered to be a list string of length 10. In fact, this is exactly how many Pascal compilers implement set variables. Thus we have the examples of equivalences given in Table 5-20.

The set type, however, offers the advantage that explicit loops are not required. In fact, Pascal compilers usually make use of special bit manipulation instructions of the computer. Therefore, use of sets instead

**TABLE 5-20** Equivalence of Sets and Bit Strings

| A, B and C are **set of** [1 .. 10] | | A, B and C are **array** [1 .. 10] **of** boolean |
| --- | --- | --- |
| [T] in A | equivalent to | A[T] |
| A := [] | | **for** I := 1 **to** 10 **do** A[T] := false; |
| A := A + [T] | | A[T] := true |
| A := A − [T] | | A[T] := false |
| C := A + B | | **for** I := 1 **to** 10 **do** C[T] := A[T] **or** B[T] |

of Boolean vectors may make a program run considerably faster since the operations are performed in parallel on all (or large numbers) of bits.

## EXERCISES 5-10

1. Which of the following declarations are valid?
   
   (*a*) **var**
   
       Caps: **set of** 'A' .. 'Z';
   
   (*b*) **type**
   
       Suits = (Diamonds, Spades, Hearts, Clubs);
   
     **var**
   
       Hand: **set of** Suits;
   
   (*c*) **type**
   
       Colors = (Red, Yellow, Blue);
   
     **var**
   
       Paint: **set of** Blue
   
   (*d*) **type**
   
       Fruit = (Banana, Apple, Orange, Pineapple);
   
       FruitBowl = **set of** Fruit;
   
     **var**
   
       X: FruitBowl;
   
   (*e*) **var**
   
       Teens = **set of** 13 .. 19;

2. A, B, and C are sets assigned as follows:

   A := [2, 4, 6, 8, 10, 12, 14, 16, 18]
   B := [1, 2, 3, 5, 7, 11, 13, 17, 19]
   C := [3, 6, 9, 12, 15, 18]

   Give the result of the following set operations.
   
   (*a*)  A + B + C          (*d*) B * C + A
   
   (*b*)  A * B * C            (*e*) A * (B − C)
   
   (*c*)  (A + B) − C       (*f*) A * C

3. A and B are sets assigned as follows:

   A := [1 .. 10]
   B := [1, 3, 5, 7, 9]

   Evaluate each of the following expressions:
   
   (*a*)  B >= A            (*d*) A − B <> [2, 4, 6, 8, 10]
   
   (*b*)  5 in A             (*e*) **not** (8 in B)
   
   (*c*)  A * B <= A

4. Explain the difference between a set and an enumerated type.

5. Assume the following variable declarations:

   **var**
   UpCaseLetters: **set of** 'A' .. 'Z';
   Symbol: char;

LowCaseLetters: **set of** 'a' .. 'z';

AllCharacters: **set of** char;

Which of the following expressions are valid?

*(a)* LowCaseLetters * UpCaseLetters

*(b)* UpCaseLetters − AllCharacters

*(c)* AllCharacters − Symbol

*(d)* AllCharacters − [Symbol]

*(e)* [AllCharacters] <= [UpCaseLetters]

*(f)* Symbol − ['A']

*(g)* UpCaseLetters − ['A']

6. Write a procedure which, given an input line of characters, creates a set containing all nonalphabetic characters in the input.

7. Given the type declaration:

**type**
    SetOfRooms = **set of** 1 .. 10;

write a Pascal function with one input argument of type SetOfRooms that returns the *cardinality* of the set as an integer. Cardinality is defined as the number of elements in the set. Thus Cardinality([1, 3, 5 .. 8]) returns 6, and Cardinality([ ]) returns 0.

8. Write a procedure that accepts an input argument of type SetOfRooms, as defined in Exercise 7, and writes the room numbers to the standard output stream.

★★ 9. Implement a complete solution to the example used in this section that will produce the following reports:

*(a)* List of room numbers containing a "board" of any kind.

*(b)* List of room numbers with projectors and screens.

*(c)* List of rooms with projectors but no screens or else screens but no projectors.

## CHAPTER SUMMARY

This chapter deals with the processing of collections of data elements. A number of such collections were presented: the vector, the array, the structure, the sequential file, and the set.

Vectors and arrays are homogeneous collections; that is, all the elements must be of the same data type. Reference to individual elements is made possible by means of *subscripts*, which refer to specific positions in the collection. The use of vectors and arrays was illustrated through a variety of applications, among which were the important operations of searching, sorting, and merging.

The structure or record was the first example of a *nonhomogeneous* collection; that is, the elements need not be of the same data type. The notion was extended to include arrays of structures (and structures of arrays). A lengthy application illustrated the use of these.

Basic notions of file processing were introduced through sequential files. A *file* is a collection of information about a set of entities, organized for some paricular purpose and typically stored on some external storage medium (e.g., disk or tape). Notation was presented to deal with the processing of files and some common operations were illustrated through a simplified payroll application.

Also introduced in this chapter were the basic elements of formal algorithm analysis. Any computer scientist must consider very carefully the performance (often *expected* performance) of any algorithm he or she designs. Without some abstract way of dealing with this issue, the vagaries of different implemenations and execution environments present impossible obstacles. The concepts of time analysis were presented and illustrated through several examples. *Order notation* was introduced as a way of expressing the results of this analysis.

## KEY TERMS

active operation
algorithm analysis
array
array type
arrays of more than two dimensions
arrays of record structure
base type
binary search
bookkeeping operations
bubble sort
buffer
conformant array schema
constant time
data base
data structure
dimension
exponential time
field
field selector
file
information retrieval
key
L'Hôpital's rule
linear search
linear time
logarithmic time
matrices
merge sorting
merging
multiple merging
nonprimitive

order notation
pass
polynomial time
primitive
qualified name
read statement (for sequential file)
record structure
record type denoter
reset statement
rewrite statement (for sequential file)
searching
selection sort
sequential access
sequential file
set type
set type denoter
sorting (selection sort, bubble sort, merge sort)
sort/search key
space analysis
sublinearly
subscript
subscripted variable
symbol table
time analysis
two dimensional array
vector (one-dimensional array)
with statement
write statement (for sequential file)
worst-case analysis

## CHAPTER EXERCISES

1. Write a function Prod to compute the product of the n elements of a vector X according to the following formula (X and n are parameters of the function):

$$\prod_{i=1}^{n} x_i = x_1 \times x_2 \times \cdots \times x_n$$

2. An expression involving a variable X such as

   A[1] * X$^1$ + A[2] * X$^2$ + A[3] * X$^3$ + Constant

   can be evaluated for many values of X. For example, if

   A[1] = 3     A[2] = 1     A[3] = 0.5     and     Constant = 5.2

   then the value of the expression for X = 2 is

   (3) * (2) + 1 * (2)$^2$ + 0.5 * (2)$^3$ + 5.2 = 19.2

   Desired is a function that would calculate

   A[1] * X$^1$ + A[2] * X$^2$ + A[3] * X$^3$ + $\cdots$ + A[N] * X$^N$ + Constant

   given the value of N, a particular set of coefficients (a vector A), a Constant, and the value of X. Design a function Eval that will accept the value of N, the Constant, the coefficients (vector A), and a value for X. It will then evaluate the given expression for the value of X and return the resulting value to the point of call. Write a program to test the functions.

3. Write a procedure to accept as a parameter a vector that may contain duplicate entries. The procedure is to replace each repeated value by −1 and return to the point of call the altered vector and the number of altered entries.

★★ 4. As the shaft concrete lining was poured at a nearby potash mine, samples of the concrete were taken and tested for maximum strength. The record book of shaft depth versus concrete strength has been prepared as follows:

   The first line of input contains the starting shaft depth and the total number of test results for consecutive 1-ft increments down the shaft.

   The following input lines all contain 5 test results per line, but the last line may contain less than 5 results, depending on the total number of results taken.

   The following is an example input:

   2318   28                    [Starting depth and number of
                                    test results]

4560  3920  4350  3897  4239 [Results]

.

.

.

A running average of eight results is used as an indication of the average concrete strength and would indicate any extremely weak section in the shaft. The running average is the average of the readings at that depth and the next 7 ft below. The running average for each of the last 7 ft is the average of the remaining readings. Write a program to generate a running-average table as follows:

| DEPTH | TEST RESULT | RUNNING AVERAGE |
|-------|-------------|-----------------|
| 2318  | 4560        | 4341            |
| 2319  | 3920        | 4256            |
| .     | .           | .               |
| .     | .           | .               |
| .     | .           | .               |
| 2339  | 4820        | 4515            |
| .     | .           | .               |
| .     | .           | .               |
| .     | .           | .               |
| 2345  | 4500        | 4500            |

The "length" of the running average, in this case 8 ft, varies with each application. After you have a solution, generalize your program so that only one set of data must be changed to change the length of the average.

★ 5. A real estate company has 25 salespersons on its staff. A record is kept of each sale made by each salesperson. Each of these records contains: salesperson number, salesperson name, and amount of sale. The number of input records is unknown. The number of sales may vary from salesperson to salesperson. For example, one salesperson may have 12 sales and another 10 sales. The input records are not in sequence. Write a program that generates the total amount of sales for each salesperson. The report is to look as follows:

| SALESPERSON NO. | SALESPERSON NAME | TOTAL AMOUNT |
|-----------------|------------------|--------------|
| 1               | John Doe         | 50240.75     |
| 2               | Sue Brown        | 71326.50     |
| .               | .                | .            |
| .               | .                | .            |
| .               | .                | .            |
| 25              | Bill Smith       | 21375.00     |

The end-of-file method should be used to detect the end of the data. Special citations are to be given to the salespersons with the top two amounts. Design your program so that these two persons are specially noted.

**6.** Write a procedure that generates a yearly sales report. The report is to give a breakdown of sales for each month of the year and a yearly total. Each sales transaction is recorded in a set of data as follows: sales amount and month, where each month of the year is indicated by an integer between 1 and 12. The number of sets of input is unknown, and the input is not in any sequence. Use the end-of-file method to detect the end of the data. Write a program to test your procedure.

**7.** Write a program that inputs a class list of student names and grades and outputs a list of student names and grades in descending order of grades.

★ **8.** It has been discovered by the leaders of two international espionage organizations (called Control and Kaos) that a number of employees are on the payrolls of both groups! A secret meeting is to be held for loyal employees of Control and Kaos (that is, excluding those on both payrolls) to determine a suitable course of action to be taken against the "double agents." Write a program that will accomplish the following task. Read as input two alphabetically ordered lists of names, the first list containing the names of agents on the Control payroll and the second containing names of agents on the Kaos payroll. (Each of the two lists is followed by a sentinel name of 'ZZZZZ'.) Then scan the two lists together and print in alphabetical order the names of those agents who should be invited to the proposed meeting (that is, all those whose names appear on one list but not both).

The following is an example input:

'Armstrong', 'Black', 'Murray', 'ZZZZZ'
'Bailey', 'Murray', 'Roberts', 'Smith', ' ZZZZZ'

The output from this example would be:

Armstrong
Bailey
Black
Roberts
Smith

★ **9.** At any large school or university the task of drafting an examination timetable is both difficult and time-consuming. An aid to the development of such a timetable is an algorithm that would "check out" all students against a tentative examination timetable and determine if any examination conflicts exist (an examination conflict means the student writes more than one examination at any one time). Input to the program consists of the tentative examination timetable and student records indicating the classes taken by each student. This input is prepared as follows. The first line of data contains two numbers: the number of classes and the number of students. The next set of lines indicates the examination period for each class in the tentative schedule. The remaining data consists of sets of student names and the numbers of the classes that each student takes. Each student always takes five classes. The following example illustrates the format of the input:

```
23   180        [Number of classes and number of students]
 5  7  5  8  4  [Exam periods for classes 1 to 5]
 4  6  2  7  1  [Exam periods for classes 6 to 10]

        .
        .
        .

'Anderson' 1 4 8 3 5   [Beginning of class file]
        .
        .
        .
```

In this example, Anderson takes classes number 1, 4, 8, 3, and 5. Both classes 1 and 3 have been scheduled tentatively for examination period 5; therefore, Anderson has an examination conflict. Your program must print the names of all students who have examination timetable conflicts.

★ 10. Let **Name** and **Sex** be vectors that contain the name and sex of each member of a youth club. Male and female are denoted by 'M' and 'F', respectively. Write a program that creates two new vectors, **Males** and **Females**, such that **Males** contains the names of all males in alphabetical order and **Females** contains the names of all females in alphabetical order. Write a procedure to do the sorting of the two vectors.

11. Students at the University of Saskatchewan are classified by class and college as listed in Table 5-21. Each student is assigned a class code and a college code. Write a program that inputs the student data and

**TABLE 5-21**

| Class | Code | College | Code |
|-------|------|---------|------|
| Freshman | 1 | Agriculture | 1 |
| Sophomore | 2 | Arts and Science | 2 |
| Junior | 3 | Commerce | 3 |
| Senior | 4 | Dentistry | 4 |
| Graduate | 5 | Education | 5 |
| | | Engineering | 6 |
| | | Graduate studies | 7 |
| | | Home economics | 8 |
| | | Law | 9 |
| | | Medicine | 10 |
| | | Nursing | 11 |
| | | Pharmacy | 12 |
| | | Physical education | 13 |
| | | Veterinary medicine | 14 |

determines how many students of each class have enrolled in each college. An end-of-file test is to be used to detect the end of the data.

★ **12.** Students from 50 New Brunswick high schools take college entrance examinations. A tabulation is desired showing the scores of people from each high school that took the examination. The input has a student identification number, a high school code (from 1 to 50), and an examination score. The output is to be a tabulation showing the scores of the students from each high school. The scores from each high school should be sorted in descending order. The input is arranged by high school code. No more than 100 students per school took the examination. A sample of the output is given in Fig. 5-74.

★ **13.** The College of Arts and Science wishes to determine the age distribution of the faculty members in its various departments. In particular, they want to know for each department how many faculty members are in each of the following categories:

| | |
|---|---|
| <20 | 40–49 |
| 20–29 | 50–59 |
| 30–39 | >59 |

The following data have been prepared for the program. The first line

| HIGH SCHOOL | STUDENT NUMBER | SCORE | |
|---|---|---|---|
| 1 | — | — | |
| | — | — | Descending order |
| 2 | — | — | |
| 50 | — | — | |

**FIGURE 5-74**

gives the number of departments in the college. This is followed by the names of the departments in alphabetical order. These names are in quotes. After all the department names comes the information on the individual faculty members. This information consists of the faculty member's name (in quotes), the name of the department in which the faculty member is located, and his or her age. This information is in alphabetical order by the name of the faculty member. A set of sample data is given in Fig. 5-75.

Write a program that will use these data to output the age distribution for each department. The output should have the following format:

| DEPARTMENT | AGE CATEGORIES | | | | | |
|---|---|---|---|---|---|---|
| | $<20$ | $20-29$ | $30-39$ | $40-49$ | $50-59$ | $>59$ |
| Anatomy | 0 | 2 | 5 | 4 | 2 | 2 |
| Anthropology | 0 | 1 | 2 | 4 | 2 | 1 |
| . | | | | | | |
| . | | | | | | |
| . | | | | | | |
| Sociology | 0 | 4 | 5 | 6 | 4 | 1 |

14. A school photographer from the town of Symmetry has been asked to take a group photograph of the students in the local high school. To conform with years of tradition, the curve formed by the tops of their heads is to be as symmetrical as possible. It has been determined that an odd number of students will occupy the back row of the picture. The names of the students in the back row, ordered alphabetically, and their corresponding heights, all distinct, will be read into the parallel vectors **Student** and **Height**, respectively. To assist the photographer, you are to write a program to rearrange the students in the back row, placing their names in the vector **Pictures** in such a way that as you proceed from left to right the heights increase to the middle and then decrease to the right end. For example, given the following five students and

```
33
'Anatomy'
'Anthropology'
        .
        .
        .
'Sociology'
'Abbott'          'History'          37
'Ackerman'        'Psychology'       53
    .                 .               .
    .                 .               .
    .                 .               .
'Zook'            'Art'              42
'End'             'Data'             0
```

**FIGURE 5-75**

their corresponding heights (in centimeters)

| J | Student[J] | Height[J] |
|---|-----------|-----------|
| 1 | Bill | 179 |
| 2 | Bob | 156 |
| 3 | Jane | 169 |
| 4 | Jo | 162 |
| 5 | John | 144 |

the following is obtained:

| J | Pictures[J] |
|---|-------------|
| 1 | John |
| 2 | Jo |
| 3 | Bill |
| 4 | Jane |
| 5 | Bob |

(*Hint:* A photographer might do the operation physically by first lining the students up to form a given row along a wall in order of decreasing height and then forming the row for the group picture by first selecting the tallest student for the middle, the second tallest goes to the right of middle, the third tallest goes to the left of middle, the fourth tallest on the right, the fifth tallest on the left, and so on.)

★ 15. A magic square is a two-dimensional $m$ by $m$ array of integers in which each of the rows, columns, and diagonals adds up to the same number and all the integers from 1 to $m^2$ are used exactly once. For example, the 4 by 4 array

```
16   3   2  13
 5  10  11   8
 9   6   7  12
 4  15  14   1
```

is a magic square where each row, column, and diagonal adds up to 34. Write a function with parameters M (the dimensions of the matrix) and Matrix (the M × M matrix) that returns "true" if Matrix is an M × M magic square.

★ 16. Implement a resort selection program. This program recognizes a number of features of resorts such as golfing, surfing, skiing, etc. The program begins by reading input containing the names of well known resorts and the characteristics of each. The program then reads a set of desired features and reports on those resorts which best match the desired features. Use an enumerated type for the features, and set variables to represent the features of each resort and the desired set of features.

★ 17. Implement a resort selection program as described in Exercise 16 using Boolean arrays indexed by the features rather than set variables. Compare this solution to the solution of Exercise 16.

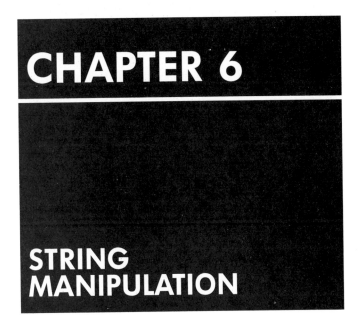

# CHAPTER 6

# STRING MANIPULATION

Computers have traditionally been associated with the solution of numeric problems such as tabulations, the calculation of the roots of an equation, and so on. In general, the primary objective of numeric computations is to obtain a numeric answer. More recently, however, a good deal of interesting work has been done using computers for essentially nonnumeric problems, such as sorting, translation of languages, text editing, pattern recognition, and symbolic manipulation of mathematical equations. Numeric answers occur infrequently in such problems. The major attributes of the computer used for these applications are its decision-making and storage capabilities rather than its ability to do arithmetic.

Although the concept of a string was brought up in Chap. 2 and again in Chap. 5, this chapter introduces the basic notions of string processing more fully and more formally. The first section deals with character information. A character is considered to be a primitive structure on most machines. The internal representation of characters in the computer's memory has important consequences in computing. Section 6-2 describes the character string facilities of standard Pascal. The assignment of a string value to a variable and the rules for comparing strings are examined. In Sec. 6-3, more powerful string-processing operations are introduced. In the following section, these facilities, as provided by two extended Pascal compilers, are described. Implementation of these operations in standard Pascal is also described. These are illustrated by means of a simple example. Several string applications are discussed in the final section.

## 6-1 CHARACTER INFORMATION

In Sec. 5-1 we introduced the notion of a primitive data structure. Recall that a primitive data structure is one that is normally operated on as a unit. For example, integer and real values are primitive data structures. Arrays, however, are nonprimitive data structures because access to the individual components (elements) is so frequent. Textual data, called character string or simply string, is sometimes viewed as primitive and sometimes as non-primitive. A string might be a person's name, a word, a line to be displayed at a terminal, or even a paragraph of text. Whenever the entire string is best handled as a single unit, viewing the string as a primitive data structure is most convenient. Many programming languages therefore include "string" as a primitive data structure in their design.

A string is more complex than integer or real data, particularly in the variability of the amount of memory required for storage. Numeric data generally is stored in fixed-size memory units. On a computer with 8-bit memory locations (bytes), for example, all integers might be stored in two bytes, thus allowing their range to be from $-32768$ to $32767$. Although small integers (in the range $-128$ to $+127$) could be stored in only one byte, the saving of one byte for those integers is not important enough in most cases to justify having to deal with multiple sizes of integers. Strings, however, may range in length from one (or sometimes zero) to many thousands of characters. Any choice of a fixed length for all strings would be too short for some applications and waste too much storage in others.

Various solutions to this dilemma have been used in the design of programming languages. The designer of Pascal chose a scheme that results in a simpler compiler but limits the convenience of strings. Pascal recognizes the character data type, representing a single character, as a primitive data type. Textual or string data is processed as an array of characters.

Although some of the issues associated with string processing are special cases of those associated with data structures generally, we devote this chapter to strings because of the importance of textual processing in computer applications. The more general issues are dealt with in Chaps. 8 and 9.

This section is therefore concerned with the character, or more generally, with a finite set of characters—an *alphabet*. An example of an alphabet is the set of English letters. Another common example is the set of decimal digits. We will give examples of certain popular alphabets which have been used in the computing industry. Furthermore, the representation (or coding) of characters within an alphabet will be described. Such representations are important to an understanding of the comparison of two strings.

Many character sets (or alphabets) have been designed for computer use over the years. The *ASCII* (American Standard Code for Information Interchange) *character set* was designed as a standard so that equipment of different manufacturers could be interconnected. This character set is used today on most small- to medium-sized computers and some larger models. In its most common form it contains 128 characters, divided into printable characters (groups 1 through 3) and control characters (group 4), as follows:

*1.* Fifty-two English *alphabet characters* in both lowercase and capital letters (a, b, . . . , z, A, B, . . . , Z)

*2.* Ten decimal *number characters* (0, 1, 2, 3, 4, 5, 6, 7, 8, 9)

*3.* Thirty-three *special characters* (space, !, '', #, $, %, &, ', (, ), *, +, ,, −, ., /, :, ;, <, =, >, ?, @, [, \, ], ^, _, ', {, |, }, ~)

*4.* Thirty-three *control characters*, such as DEL (delete or rub out), STX (start of text), ETX (end of text), ACK (acknowledge), HT (horizontal tab), VT (vertical tab), LF (line feed), CR (carriage return), NAK (negative acknowledge), SYN (synchronous idle for synchronous transmission), ETB (end of transmission block), FS (file separation), GS (group separation), and RS (record separation)

Control characters are nonprintable characters whose purpose is to perform certain specifications. The ASCII character set is often extended to 256 characters by adding special-purpose graphics characters. A revised standard is now under consideration.

The EBCDIC character-coding system is an 8-bit code developed originally for the IBM/360-370 series of mainframe computers. It consists of 256 characters divided again into printable characters and control characters. This character set has evolved over several years, and therefore, several variations exist. The most common variant includes almost all the printable characters listed previously for ASCII (groups 1 through 3) and a large number of control characters. Since there are twice as many characters in EBCDIC as there are in standard (7-bit) ASCII, a number of other characters are available in many variants of EBCDIC, including superscripts ($^0$, $^1$, $^2$, . . . , $^9$), additional special characters (¢, ≠, ≤, ≥, ±, ●), and additional control characters. Also, there are characters which are "undefined" and are therefore available for special purposes. Very few devices actually provide for the entire EBCDIC character set. Special characters such as {, }, [, and ] are often omitted.

Other character sets have been created for special-purpose applications. Many computer graphic systems, for example, use operational-type characters for the manipulation of points and lines on a cathode-ray-tube display device. For example, special characters have been used to rotate, translate, enlarge, or contract pictures on the screen. Another example of a special character set is the character set used in the APL (A Programming Language) programming system. APL, a mathematically oriented programming language designed originally by K. Iverson, is very effective for the manipulation of mathematical items such as vectors and arrays. Along with the capital letters from the English alphabet, the decimal numerals, and the special characters included in the EBCDIC and ASCII character sets, the APL character set includes some Greek letters ($\alpha$, $\Delta$, $\epsilon$, $\iota$, $\rho$, $\omega$) and a number of mathematically oriented symbols ($\subset$, $\supset$, $\cap$, $\cup$, [, ], $\leftarrow$, $\downarrow$, $\rightarrow$, $\div$, $\times$, $\because$, $\leq$, $\geq$, $\neq$, $\bigcirc$, $\square$, $\circ$), which include special operators on vectors and arrays.

Many other "special" character sets have been defined (for example, a braille character set and a kanji character set), but it is beyond the scope of this book to document all these cases.

Let us examine these character sets in terms of the functions they commonly perform. English characters, decimal number characters, and special characters can be combined to form English text. Computer applications involving natural language text are both numerous and wide-ranging. Of course, numbers are used most often in computations. Characters which are operational in nature (for example, $+, -, *, /, =$) are used in programs to represent operations in the programming language such as addition, subtraction, multiplication, and division. Control characters define operational services of a different sort, a discussion we do not wish to pursue here.

We turn now to the storage representation of character data. A character can be represented in memory as a sequence of bits (that is, a sequence of 0s and 1s), where a distinctive bit sequence is assigned to each character in the character set by the coding convention chosen.

For example, the (7-bit) ASCII representation for the letter $A$ is the bit sequence

$$
\begin{array}{ccccccc}
1 & 0 & 0 & 0 & 0 & 0 & 1 \\
2^6 & 2^5 & 2^4 & 2^3 & 2^2 & 2^1 & 2^0
\end{array}
$$

where the weight of each binary digit is given below the digit. This bit representation can be interpreted as a binary number. The decimal equivalent of the ASCII representation for $A$ is therefore

$$1 \times 2^6 + 0 \times 2^5 + 0 \times 2^4 + 0 \times 2^3 + 0 \times 2^2 + 0 \times 2^1 + 1 \times 2^0$$

$$= 1 \times 64 + 1 = 65$$

Similarly, the EBCDIC code for A is

$$
\begin{array}{cccccccc}
1 & 1 & 0 & 0 & 0 & 0 & 0 & 1 \\
2^7 & 2^6 & 2^5 & 2^4 & 2^3 & 2^2 & 2^1 & 2^0
\end{array}
$$

$$1 \times 2^7 + 1 \times 2^6 + 0 \times 2^5 + 0 \times 2^4 + 0 \times 2^3 + 0 \times 2^2 + 0 \times 2^1 + 1 \times 2^0$$

$$= 128 + 64 + 1 + 193$$

Pascal provides two built-in functions for converting between a character and an integer. The function **ord**, defined in Sec. 3-6.1 for enumerated types, also may take a character argument. In the latter case, it supplies the integer equivalent of the character code. Given an integer argument which represents a valid character, **chr** returns that character. For a Pascal compiler based on the ASCII character set:

ord ('A') = 65
chr (65) = 'A'

For a Pascal compiler based on EBCDIC, however:

ord ('A') = 193

chr (193) = 'A'

Obviously, some care must be taken when writing Pascal programs that must work correctly regardless of the character set in use!

The ordering of the characters in a character set is called its *collating sequence* and is used to determine the value of a comparison of two character values. The characters are ordered in the collating sequence by their binary equivalent values. That is, if $c_1$ and $c_2$ are two characters, then $c_1 < c_2$ if $\text{ord}(c_1) < \text{ord}(c_2)$. One unusual feature of EBCDIC is that the letters are not contiguous in the collating sequence. The letters occur in the groups a – i, j – r, s – z, A – I, J – R, and S – Z. Various special characters occur between groups. For example, the character } occurs between I and J. Therefore, the condition (C >= 'A') **and** (C <= 'Z'), where C is a character variable, is not sufficient to guarantee that C represents a capital letter. In the examples in this book, we shall assume that the capital letters (A – Z) are in proper (that is, intuitive) order, ('A'< 'B', ' B'< 'C', etc.), that the lower-case letters are similarly in proper order, and that the characters representing digits are in proper order and contiguous. This holds true for both ASCII and EBCDIC. Occasionally, the correct operation of a program will depend on constraints such as that the letters are contiguous. We shall indicate such assumptions in the text accompanying the program.

While it is worthwhile to investigate characters as primitive data structures, they are in many ways too primitive to be convenient in expressing much of the nonnumeric information that can be processed by a computer. We consider next the treatment of strings as arrays of characters in Pascal.

## 6-2   STRINGS IN STANDARD PASCAL

A character string is a string of characters. As we saw in Chap. 5, such a string can be represented as an array of characters. Recall that standard Pascal refers to a **packed array of** char whose index type is a subrange of integer with lower bound 1 and upper bound greater than 1 as a *string type*. Such a string type defines a fixed-length string:

**type**
    String20 = **packed array** [1 .. 20] **of** char;
    NameString = **packed array** [1 .. 25] **of** char;

As noted in Chap. 5, several vector operations are available: assignment by another vector of the same type and equality and inequality relations. For string types, however, Pascal allows additional operations. For assignments, Pascal allows any string type to be compatible with a different string type *of the same length*.

Different string types of the same length are also compatible for relations. In addition to the relations = and <>, the relations <, <=, >, and >= are allowed for compatible string types. The relations on strings are defined as follows. The two strings are compared character by character until a difference is found. Then the string with the "smallest" character, based on the collating sequence, is considered smaller. If there are no differences, the strings are equal. Thus, assuming either the ASCII or EBCDIC collating sequence, 'abc' < 'abd', 'xyz' > 'abc', and 'John' <= 'Rick' are all true relations. Note that we have used characters in quotation marks here. Pascal specifies that a string of $n$ characters enclosed in quotes is of type **packed array** [1 .. $n$] **of** char, provided that $n \geq 2$. Finally, Pascal allows a string type as an element in a write or writeln statement.

Consider the problem of reading a set of last names and displaying them in alphabetical order. We propose the following algorithm:

1. Repeat thru step 4 while input data remains
2. Read the name
3. Find its correct position in the vector of names read so far
4. Move following names down to make space and insert the new name into the space
5. Print the table

We give the detailed program in Fig. 6-1. We assume here that the names appear one per line and that every name consists of 30 characters; trailing blanks *must be supplied*. We have declared a string variable Name. Also, every element of the vector NameVector is a string. The program uses the >= comparison between Name and individual elements of the vector. It also performs assignments between Name and elements of the vector, as well as between different elements of the vector.

Unfortunately, Pascal is missing some important facilities for string processing. There is no provision for reading strings; hence the program in Fig. 6-1 contains a loop to read an input string character by character. Pascal compilers without the conformant array feature require that a separate procedure or function be written for every different-length string to be used. Finally, functions returning strings are not allowed. Many designers of Pascal compilers have attempted to remedy these deficiencies by defining extended Pascal features for string processing. We will next consider the concepts of strings viewed as a basic data type. Then we will consider how strings can be treated as a primitive data type and consider the most important operations on this data type.

## 6-3 STRING CONCEPTS AND TERMINOLOGY

In this section we want to concentrate on the formal notions of strings themselves as primitive data elements rather than on the characters of which they are composed. This is a form of *data abstraction*, about which we will say more in Chaps. 8 and 9. Initially, we draw an analogy between the natural number system and a string system. In so doing, the operation

```
program Names (input, output);
{Given a set of names in arbitrary order, this program arranges and displays
    the names in ascending order.}
type
   NameType = packed array [1 .. 30] of char;
var
   Name: NameType;                          {Input name}
   NameVector: array [1 .. 200] of NameType; {Complete set of names}
   N: integer;                              {Number of names in
                                              the vector}

   J, K: integer;                           {Array indices}
begin
   {Step 1: Engage loop to input and process names}
   N := 0;
   while not eof do
     begin


       {Step 2: Read a name}
       for J := 1 to 30 do
         read ( Name[J] );
       readln;


       {Step 3: Find the position in the vector for the current name}
       J := 1;
       while (J <= N) and (Name >= NameVector[J] ) do
         J := J + 1;


       {Step 4: Make room and insert new name}
       N := N + 1;
       K := N;
       while K > J do
         begin
           NameVector[K] := NameVector[K − 1];
           K := K − 1
         end;
       NameVector[J] := Name
     end;


   {Step 5: Display table}
   for J := 1 to N do
     writeln ( NameVector[J] )
end.
```

**FIGURE 6-1**
Simple example of
string processing
in standard Pascal.

of concatenation on strings will be introduced. The assignment statement is then expanded to incorporate the assignment of string values. Finally, the comparison of strings with respect to the relational operators is described.

Throughout this section and the next we are concerned with what kinds of operations can be performed on strings. We certainly expect those operations to be drastically different from the familiar arithmetic operations on numbers. Many string operations, however, are similar to some of their arithmetic counterparts. Let us examine some interesting properties for arithmetic operations over the natural numbers.

To refamiliarize ourselves with some of the properties associated with arithmetic operations, let us consider the operation of addition on the set of natural numbers. This operation can be represented in general by a functional system in two variables:

$$f(x, y) = x + y$$

where $x$ and $y$ are natural numbers. This system (the natural numbers and addition) is well known to us, and it exhibits certain interesting properties. First, the sum of any two numbers is a natural number. This property is called *closure*. Closure is a necessary property for a system (that is, a set and an operation on that set) to be classified as an algebra or algebraic system. Second, expressions such as $(x + y) + z = x + (y + z) = x + y + z$ are equivalent when $x$, $y$, and $z$ are natural numbers; the operation of addition is said to be *associative*. Third, there exists a number $i$ such that for every natural number $x$, $x + i = x$. This number is zero and is called the unit element, or *identity*, of the system. There are many other important properties, such as distributivity and commutativity, that exist when arithmetic operations such as addition and multiplication are applied to the set of natural numbers.

We have already introduced the notion of a string in Chap. 2. A string can be defined more formally in terms of an alphabet, a notion that was the topic of discussion in the previous section. A string is merely an ordered sequence of characters, each of which is a member of an alphabet. Examples of strings over the alphabet {X, Y, Z} are 'X', 'XY', 'XXYYZ', and 'ZYX'. A string can contain no characters at all. Such a string is denoted by the string '' and is called the *empty string* or *null string*. We shall use the symbol □ to denote the space (or blank) character when it is not otherwise clear that it is part of a given string. Note that the string '□' is a string that contains the space character and is not to be confused with the empty string, which contains no characters.

Let us now turn to the manipulation of character strings. Here, the operations may be less familiar than the normal numeric operations, but as we will see, they are not difficult. A very basic operation on character strings is to take two character strings and join them together to make one string. This operation is known as *concatenation*. In this section we will denote the concatenation operator initially by the symbol "○". Thus, if we have two strings, 'Mic' and 'key', the result of the operation 'Mic'○'key' is the new character string 'Mickey'. This operation is something like combining two piles of leaves on the lawn to make one bigger pile.

The empty string acts as the identity with respect to concatenation; that is, for any string x over an alphabet, $x \circ '' = '' \circ x = x$. Associativity is another property of strings with respect to concatenation; that is, for any strings x, y, and z, $(x \circ y) \circ z = x \circ (y \circ z) = x \circ y \circ z$. Finally, it is obvious that for any strings x and y, $x \circ y$ will yield a string. So the system of strings under concatenation is closed. Therefore, the system of strings under concatenation behaves in a manner similar to the set of natural numbers under addition.

The concatenation operator, like the arithmetic operators, can be applied several times in one expression. Thus the result of

'Mic' $\circ$ 'key' $\circ$ '☐Mouse'

is 'Mickey☐Mouse'. Similarly, the expression 'Edgar☐' $\circ$ 'Allan☐' $\circ$ 'Poe' gives the string 'Edgar☐Allan☐Poe'.

We now turn to the assignment of a string value to a variable. If City is a string variable, then the statement

City : = 'Saska' $\circ$ 'toon'

will assign the string value 'Saskatoon' to City. Any string variable can assume a string value whose length is a finite number. The *length* of a string is the number of characters in that string. In general, a string expression can contain string variables as well as string constants such as 'Saska' or 'toon'. For example, the sequence of assignment statements

A : = 'Computer';
B : = 'Science';
C : = A $\circ$ '☐' $\circ$ B

shows each type of element where A, B, and C are string variables and results in a value for C of 'Computer☐Science'.

We turn now to the comparison of our formal strings. In the earlier chapters the notion of testing strings for equality and inequality was introduced in an informal manner. We now wish to elaborate further on these two operators and extend the comparison of strings to the other relational operators. A test for string equality, for string variables $x = x_1, \ldots, x_n$ and $y = y_1, \ldots, y_m$, is of the form $x = y$. The condition $x = y$ is considered to be true if the following holds:

**1.** The number of characters in $x$ and $y$ are identical (that is, $n = m$).

**2.** $x_i = y_i$ for all $1 \le i \le n$.

For example, 'John' = 'John' is true while 'Bill' = 'Billy' and 'Billy' = 'Bully' are false. The inequality relation is the negation of equality. For example, 'Bill' $\ne$ 'Billy' and 'John' $\ne$ 'John☐' are both true.

It is easy to expand this comparison feature to include the other relational operators, such as $<, \le, >$ and $\ge$. The meaning of these comparisons is based on the collating sequence of a character set which was introduced in the previous section. The collating sequence for the following examples is assumed to be: A through Z, a through z. For example, 'Bill' < 'Billy', 'Ann' < 'Joan', and 'Jones' ≥ 'Bunt' are all true, while 'Tremblay' < 'Bunt', 'Computer' > 'Science', and 'Bob' ≤ 'Alan' are all false. From these examples it is obvious that the condition is tested by making a sequence of character comparisons in a left-to-right manner. Note that the presence of any character (even a space) is always considered to be greater than the omission of a character. For example,

'Science□' > 'Science'

is true.

The comparison of character strings is very important in the sorting of character data. Such a sorting operation is required in many data-processing and string-manipulation applications. The selection sort algorithm of Sec. 5-3.1 can be used directly with a vector of strings such as a list of student names.

So far, the only string operation we have introduced is that of concatenation. Clearly, if we are going to solve string-manipulation problems, we need a greater variety of string operators than this. The next section is concerned with the introduction of additional string operations and how the basic and extended string operators are introduced into Pascal.

## 6-4 EXTENDED STRING PROCESSING

In the previous section we discussed strings as a primitive data type and the operations of concatenation and relations = , ≠, ≤, <, ≥, and >, which are represented by = , <>, <=, <, >=, and >, respectively on values of this type. In this section we examine the string-processing extensions of two Pascal compilers. Both implement the operations of the previous section as well as some additional facilities. We have chosen two particular compilers to exhibit typical similarities and differences in string extensions among compilers. We then suggest the manner in which the advanced string operators can be implemented in standard Pascal. Before proceeding, we introduce a problem that we will use for comparison purposes.

### 6-4.1 A STRING-PROCESSING EXAMPLE

Consider the problem of transforming the string

'Edgar□Allan□Poe'

to the string

'Poe,□E□A'

This task can be accomplished by first scanning the name for the leftmost blank. Once we know where this blank is, the next character gives us the middle initial. By noting the position of the second blank, we can then obtain the last name. Clearly, we know the position of the first initial. Therefore, we have all the pieces required to generate the desired output.

Figure 6-2 illustrates a solution to this problem in standard Pascal. We are forced to manipulate the strings, for the most part, one character at a time using a loop. In several steps we process characters up to a '□'. This blank thus serves as a delimiter (for example, for the first name).

## 6-4.2  STRINGS IN TURBO PASCAL

The Turbo[†] Pascal compiler is available for several microcomputers. It includes a compiler that conforms in many respects to the ANSI standard, although there are both variations and significant extensions. The Turbo system also includes an interactive editor and debugging facilities (see App. E).

Turbo Pascal allows declaration of varying string types, although a maximum length must be given. Variables of this type clearly store both the current length as well as the characters contained in the string. The type denoter used is the new reserved word **string** followed by an integer constant denoting the maximum length enclosed in square brackets. For example:

```
type
    String100 = string [100];
var
    S1: String100;
    S2: string [10];
```

The maximum length must be in the range 1 through 255. Concatenation is designated by the plus sign, as in

```
'Sask' + 'atoon' + S2 + '.'
```

If S2 = ',□Sask', this gives 'Saskatoon,□Sask.'

String variables, character variables, and character strings of any length (including '' designating the empty string and strings of length one representing single characters) may participate in concatenation.

For many applications it is useful for us to be able to find the length of a given string. This operation, which Turbo denotes by the built-in function **length**, gives us this information. For example, the result of

```
length('For whom the bell tolls')
```

is **23**. At this point it is interesting to note one important fact about this function. Although the argument to this function is a string, the result is an integer. Since the result is numeric, it can be used as part of an arithmetic expression. For example, the expression

```
3 + 2 + length('Les Feux Follets')
```

has the result **21**.

---

[†] Turbo is a trademark of Borland Inc.

**program** EditName1 (input, output);

{This program reads a string which represents the name of an individual in the format described in the text. It converts it to the form of the last name followed by first and middle initials.}

**const**
  StrLength = 30;

**type**
  FixedStr = **packed array** [1 .. StrLength] **of** char;

**var**
  Name: FixedStr;          {Name as read}
  DesiredName: FixedStr;   {Name in desired format}
  Last: FixedStr;         {Last name}
  FI, MI: char;          {First and middle initials}


**procedure** ClearString (
  **var** Str: FixedStr       {Output, cleared string}
                   );
{This procedure clears a string to blanks}
**var**
  K: integer;            {Index into string}
**begin**
  **for** K := 1 **to** StrLength **do**
    Str[K] := '□'
**end**; {ClearString}


**procedure** ReadName (
  **var** Name: FixedStr    {Output, name as read}
                 );
{This procedure reads a name from the input stream}
**var**
  K: integer;            {Index for reading characters}
**begin**
  {Step 1: Clear string to blanks}
  ClearString (Name);


  {Step 2: Read and store characters to end of line}
  K := 1;
  **while** (K <= StrLength) **and not** eoln **do**
    **begin**
      read (Name[K]);
      K := K + 1
    **end**
**end**; {ReadName}

**FIGURE 6-2**
Name editing example
in standard Pascal.

```
procedure ExtractName (
    Name: FixedStr;          {Input, the name to be analyzed}
    var FI, MI: char;        {Output, the first and middle initials}
    var LastName: FixedStr   {Output, the last name}
            );
{Given the name in the input format, this procedure extracts the initials and
   last name.}
var
    NIndex: integer;         {Index into the name}
    LIndex: integer;         {Index into the last name}
begin
    {Step 1: Clear last name to blanks}
    ClearString (LastName);

    {Step 2: Initialize}
    NIndex : = 1;

    {Step 3: Obtain the first initial}
    FI : = Name[NIndex];
    NIndex : = NIndex + 1;

    {Step 4: Scan the name for the first blank}
    while Name[NIndex] <> '□' do
        NIndex : = NIndex + 1;

    {Step 5: Obtain the second initial}
    NIndex : = NIndex + 1;
    MI : = Name[NIndex];
    NIndex : = NIndex + 1;

    {Step 6: Scan the name for the second blank}
    while Name[NIndex] <> '□' do
        NIndex : = NIndex + 1;

    {Step 7: Obtain the last name}
    NIndex : = NIndex + 1;
    LIndex : = 1;
    while Name[NIndex] <> '□' do
        begin
            LastName[LIndex] : = Name[NIndex];
            LIndex : = LIndex + 1;
            NIndex : = NIndex + 1
        end
end; {ExtractName}
```

FIGURE 6-2 (*cont.*)

```
procedure ConstructName (
    Last: FixedStr;            {Input, last name}
    FI, MI: char;             {Input, first and middle initials}
    var Name: FixedStr        {Output, constructed name}
                              );
{This procedure constructs a name in the required format.}
var
    NIndex: integer;          {Index into constructed name}
    LIndex: integer;          {Index into last name}
begin
    {Step 1: Initialize}
    NIndex := 1;
    LIndex := 1;

    {Step 2: Copy last name}
    while Last[LIndex] <> '□' do
        begin
            Name[NIndex] := Last[LIndex];
            NIndex := NIndex + 1;
            LIndex := LIndex + 1
        end;

    {Step 3: Copy initials}
    Name[NIndex] := ',';
    NIndex := NIndex + 1;
    Name[NIndex] := '□';
    NIndex := NIndex + 1;
    Name[NIndex] := FI;
    NIndex := NIndex + 1;
    Name[NIndex] := '□';
    NIndex := NIndex + 1;
    Name[NIndex] := MI
end; {Construct Name}

{Main program}
begin
    {Step 1: Read input name}
    ReadName (Name);

    {Step 2: Extract initials and last name}
    ExtractName (Name, FI, MI, Last);

    {Step 3: Construct name in desired format}
    ConstructName (Last, FI, MI, DesiredName);

    {Step 4: Output the result}
    writeln (DesiredName)
end.
```

**FIGURE 6-2** (*cont.*)

Another important string operation is one which allows us to extract a specified portion of a given string. In a way, this is the reverse of the concatenation operation that combines strings to make a larger string. This new operation allows us to take smaller strings from a larger string.

The operation is known as the *substring* operation. Turbo adopts the following three-argument built-in function format:

copy ($a_1$, $a_2$, $a_3$)

where $a_1$ is the string from which we want the piece to be taken, $a_2$ is the number in the original string of the position at which the desired piece begins, and $a_3$ is the length of the desired piece. Note that $a_1$ is a string argument and $a_2$ and $a_3$ are integers. Any or all of these may be expressions themselves.

As an example, consider the following expression:

copy('Edmonton, Alberta' , 6, 3)

Note the three arguments:

$a_1$ is the string 'Edmonton, Alberta'.

$a_2$ is the number 6, indicating that we wish to extract a substring beginning at the sixth position (the character 't').

$a_3$ is the number 3, indicating that our substring will be three characters in length.

Thus the result of the indicated operation is the string 'ton'. Try one yourself. What is copy('Vancouver, B.C.' , 3, 5)?

Just as we can develop interesting and useful arithmetic expressions by combining the numeric operations (for example, $6.0 / 3 + 5 * 4$), so too can we combine string operations into one expression. Consider the following expression, for example:

copy('Edmonton' , 3, 4) + copy('Port Credit' , 7, 2) + copy('Calgary' , 2, 2)

This expression has three separate substring components or subexpressions, the result of which are concatenated to form the final result of the expression. Let us take the subexpressions one at a time.

```
              length 4
                 ↓
               ‾‾‾‾
    copy('Edmonton' , 3, 4)
                ↑
           position 3
```

The value of this subexpression is the string 'mont' .

```
              length 2
                 ↓
                ‾‾
    copy('Port Credit', 7, 2)
                ↑
           position 7
```

The value of this subexpression is the string 're' .

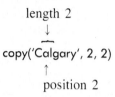

length 2
↓

copy('Calgary', 2, 2)
↑
position 2

The value of this subexpression is the string 'al' .

To get the final result of the original expression, we then concatenate these three intermediate values, 'mont' + 're' + 'al'. We can see that our final result is the string 'montreal'.

For more interesting applications, this sort of combination will be very common. Do not become flustered by the apparent complexity of the expression. Instead, concentrate on identifying and processing the various subexpressions that form the terms of the expression, as you do with numeric expressions. If you take things a step at a time, there should be no major difficulty.

To complete the definition of copy, some exceptional cases must be handled:

*1.* If $a_3 \leq 0$ (regardless of $a_2$), then the empty string is returned.

*2.* If $a_2 \leq 0$ or $a_2 > 255$ (regardless of $a_3$), then a run-time error occurs.

*3.* If $a_2 > k$ and $a_2 \leq 255$, where $k = \text{length}(a_1)$, then the empty string is returned.

*4.* If $a_2 + a_3 > k + 1$, where $k = \text{length}(a_1)$, then $a_3$ is assumed to be $k - a_2 + 1$.

Turbo actually implements the type **string** [*n*] as **array** [0 .. *n*] **of** char. Elements 1 through *n* are used to store the characters. Element 0 stores the current length converted to a character, as chr (current length). This allows selection of an individual character by an array subscript. For example, if S is of type **string** [100], then

S[K]

is equivalent to

copy (S, K, 1)

provided that the value of K $\leq$ length(S).

In many algorithms we are required to find the position of a given substring within a string. Although we are able to determine these positions by searching, using the copy function and a loop, such an approach can be somewhat tedious for the programmer. Therefore Turbo introduces a new operation to handle it, denoted by the built-in function pos. For example, the invocation of pos in

pos ('□' ,'Edgar□Allan□Poe' )

will return the position of the leftmost blank in the string 'Edgar☐Allan☐Poe' (that is, a value of 6). The function, in its general form, is

pos (P, S)

where S denotes the string which is to be examined for the leftmost occurrence of the substring given by P. The string S is quite often called the *subject string*, while P is called the *pattern string*. This process of searching for a pattern string in a subject string is commonly called *pattern matching*. If the pattern in a pos function call is not found in the subject string, then the pattern-matching process has failed. Such a failure is reported by returning a value of 0. For example, the value of pos ('☐', 'abcd') is 0. Of course, the pattern can be a string of length greater than one, as in the case of pos ('xyz', 'pqxyzzxy'), which returns a value of 3. In this case, the position of the leftmost character of 'xyz' in the subject string is returned.

It is also often useful to delete or insert a substring within a string. Turbo provides two built-in procedures for these operations. The delete procedure is called by a procedure call statement of the form

delete (St, Pos, Num)

It will delete Num characters from St, beginning at position Pos. The result is returned in St. (Thus the first parameter of delete is an *input/output parameter*.) For example, if S = 'abcdefghi', then

delete (S, 3, 4)

results in S = 'abghi'.

Similarly, the insert procedure is called by a procedure call statement of the form

insert (Obj, Target, Pos)

The string Obj is inserted into the string Target immediately before the character Pos. Again, if S = 'wxyz', then

insert ('abc', S, 2)

results in S = 'wabcxyz'. Turbo has several other useful operations which we will not consider here.

Turbo Pascal allows string expressions to appear in the write and writeln statements. In addition, a string variable may appear in a read or, more commonly, a readln statement. Unlike many other languages, and unlike the ReadString procedure in Fig. 5-14, the string is *not* enclosed in quotes in the input stream. Rather, all characters in the input stream from the next unprocessed character to, but not including, the "new-line" character are assigned to the string variable. A readln (but not a read) statement then would discard the "new-line" character. If a "new-line" character happens to be the very next unprocessed character when a read into a string variable is attempted, then the variable is set to the empty string.

We now reformulate the program EditName of the last subsection in Turbo Pascal in Fig. 6-3.

**program** EditName2 (input, output);

{Given the name of an individual in the format described in the text, this program converts it to the form of the last name followed by first and middle initials. This is the Turbo Pascal version.}

**var**
 Name: **string** [30];     {Name as read}
 DesiredName: **string** [30];  {Name in desired format}
 Last: **string** [20];     {Last name}
 FI, MI: **string** [1];      {First and middle initials}
 J: integer;          {String position}

**begin**
 {Step 1: Read input name}
 read (name);

 {Step 2: Obtain the first initial}
 FI := copy (Name, 1, 1);

 {Step 3: Obtain the position of the first blank}
 J := pos ('□', Name);

 {Step 4: Obtain the second initial}
 MI := copy (Name, J + 1, 1);

 {Step 5: Delete first name and blank}
 Name := copy (Name, J + 1, length (Name) − J);

 {Step 6: Obtain the position of the second blank}
 J := pos ('□', Name);

 {Step 7: Obtain the last name}
 Last := copy (Name, J + 1, length (Name) − J);

 {Step 8: Concatenate the strings into the desired format}
 DesiredName := Last + ',□' + FI + '□' + MI;

 {Step 9: Output the desired name}
 writeln (DesiredName)
**end**.

**FIGURE 6-3**
**Name editing example**
**in Turbo Pascal.**

# EXERCISES 6-4.2

1. Give the results of the following expression:
   *(a)* length('Alpha' + 'bet' + '□Soup')
   *(b)* copy('Harpo' + 'Chico' + 'Groucho' + 'Zeppo', 11, 7) +
       copy('Harpo' + 'Chico' + 'Groucho' + 'Zeppo', 6, 5) +

```
        copy('Harpo' + 'Chico' + 'Groucho' + 'Zeppo' , 18, 5) +
        copy('Harpo' + 'Chico' + 'Groucho' + 'Zeppo' , 1, 5)
```
(c) copy('suffix' , length('suffix' ) − 3, 4)

2. Assuming that the variable S is defined as **string** [10] and that the assignment

```
    S : = 'Chocolate'
```

has been performed, give the results of the following expressions:

(a) S[1]

(b) copy (S, 4, 4)

(c) length (S) − 3

(d) pos ('cola' , S)

(e) copy (S, pos ('cola' , S) + 4, length (S) − pos ('cola' , S) − 3)

3. Suppose that the variable Text is declared as **string** [50] and the assignment

```
    Text : = 'Why□did□the□chicken□cross□the□street?'
```

has been made. Give the result of each of the following program fragments on Text if each statement were to *immediately follow* the given assignment:

(a) insert ('not□' , Text, 21)

(b) delete (Text, 1, 1)

(c) delete (Text, 13, 7);
    insert ('goose' , Text, 13)

★ 4. Formulate a program for **pos** which uses other primitive functions (for example, **copy**). That is, construct your own version of **pos**.

★ 5. Design a function Replicate for replicating a given character string a specified number of times. For example, Replicate('Ha!□' , 3) should generate the string 'Ha!□Ha!□Ha!□'. Assume that the string parameter is of type **string** [255].

## 6-4.3 STRINGS IN VAX-11 PASCAL

The VAX-11 series of computers is manufactured by Digital Equipment Corporation. They comprise a range of computer systems from small single-user workstations through mainframes. The VAX-11 Pascal compiler processes a language that is an extension to the ISO standard Pascal. This compiler is available under the VAX/VMS[†] operating system.

Varying length strings are declared by a type denoter of the form

**varying** [*maximum length*] **of** char

For example,

**type**
    String100 = **varying** [100] **of** char;

[†] VAX and VMS are trademarks of Digital Equipment Corporation.

**var**

    S1: String100;

    S2: **varying** [10] **of** char;

The maximum length must be in the range 1 through 65535.

As in Turbo Pascal, concatenation is designated by $+$. For example,

'Saska' + 'toon'

gives 'Saskatoon'. The length function again gives the current length.

Selection of a substring is performed by the substr function, which is similar to Turbo's copy, except that if the selected substring lies outside the range of the original string, a run-time error is reported. Again, selection of a single character may be done by a subscript. The search function is called index; it is similar to Turbo's pos, except that the arguments are reversed; that is, the string to be searched is the first argument and the pattern is the second argument.

VAX-11 Pascal does not provide the delete or insert procedures. These are easily constructed using substr, however. For example, to achieve Turbo's

delete (S, P, L)

we could define the procedure

```
procedure delete (var S: varying [Len] of char; P, L: integer);
begin
    if P = 1
    then S : = substr (S, L + 1, length (S) − L)
    else
        if P + L − 1 = length (S)
        then S : = substr (S, 1, length (S) − L)
        else S : = substr (S, 1, P − 1) + substr (S,P + 1, length (S) − P − L + 1)
end;
```

Notice that some effort is required to avoid an illegal length in a call of substr when the string being deleted occurs at the beginning or end of the subject string. We have also declared the parameter S using a *conformant varying schema*, namely,

varying [Len] of char

VAX-11 Pascal uses this scheme, similar to conformant array parameters (see Sec. 5-2.3) for arrays, to allow passing a variable declared with any maximum length to the procedure. The identifier Len becomes declared as an additional implicit parameter of type integer. It takes the value of the maximum length of the argument. We leave the formulation of procedure Insert as an exercise.

We reformulate our example of the previous subsection in VAX-11 Pascal in Fig. 6-4.

```
program EditName3 (input, output);
```
{Given the name of an individual in the format described in the text, this
   program converts it to the form of the last name followed by first and
   middle initials. This is the VAX-11 Pascal version.}

```
var
   Name: varying [30] of char;        {Name as read}
   DesiredName: varying [30] of char; {Name in desired format}
   Last: varying [20] of char;        {Last name}
   FI, MI: varying [1] of char;       {First and middle initials}
   J: integer;                        {String position}
begin
   {Step 1: Read input name}
   read (name);

   {Step 2: Obtain the first initial}
   FI : = substr (Name, 1, 1);

   {Step 3: Obtain the position of the first blank}
   J : = index (Name, '□');

   {Step 4: Obtain the second initial}
   MI : = substr (Name, J + 1, 1);

   {Step 5: Delete first name and blank}
   Name : = substr (Name, J + 1, length (Name) − J);

   {Step 6: Obtain the position of the second blank}
   J : = index (Name, '□');

   {Step 7: Obtain the last name}
   Last : = substr (Name, J + 1, length (Name) − J);

   {Step 8: Concatenate the strings into the desired format}
   DesiredName : = Last + ',□' + FI + '□' + MI;

   {Step 9: Output the desired name}
   writeln (DesiredName)
end.
```

**FIGURE 6-4**
**Name editing example**
**in VAX-11 Pascal.**


## EXERCISES 6-4.3

**1.** Give the results of the following expression:
   (*a*)  length('Alpha' + 'bet' + '□Soup' )
   (*b*)  substr('Harpo' + 'Chico' + 'Groucho' + 'Zeppo', 11, 7) +

substr('Harpo' + 'Chico' + 'Groucho' + 'Zeppo' , 6, 5) +
substr('Harpo' + 'Chico' + 'Groucho' + 'Zeppo' , 18, 5) +
substr('Harpo' + 'Chico' + 'Groucho' + 'Zeppo' , 1, 5)
*(c)* substr('suffix' , length('suffix' ) $-$ 3, 4)

2. Assuming that the variable S is defined as **varying** [1..10] **of** char and that the assignment

S : = 'Chocolate'

has been performed, give the results of the following expressions:
*(a)* S[1]
*(b)* substr (S, 4, 4)
*(c)* length (S) $-$ 3
*(d)* index (S, 'cola' )
*(e)* substr (S, index (S, 'cola' ) + 4, length (S) $-$ index (S, 'cola') $-$ 3)

★ 3. Implement the procedure **delete** described in Sec. 6-4.2 in VAX-11 Pascal. Use a *conformant varying schema* so that the procedure may be passed a string of any type.

★ 4. Formulate a program for index which uses other primitive functions (for example, substr). That is, construct your own version of index.

★ 5. Implement the function Replicate from Exercise 5 of Sec. 6-4.2 in VAX-11 Pascal. Use a *conformant varying schema* to allow any string as an argument.

## 6-4.4   A STRING-PROCESSING PACKAGE
## FOR STANDARD PASCAL

For those implementations of Pascal without a string-processing extension, a set of functions and procedures can be implemented (in standard Pascal) to facilitate the programming of string-oriented applications. This subsection focuses on the design and implementation of such a set of string-manipulation routines. We also give an example of their use.

One of the first design issues is to decide how to represent strings in standard Pascal. Obviously, an array of characters is sufficient for representing the characters in a string. One of the most convenient capabilities in string manipulation, however, is the ability to put strings of different sizes into a string variable (perhaps subject to some maximum length restriction) without loss of the actual length information. One method is to associate a length (integer value) with each string value, as is done in Turbo Pascal. Alternatively, each string can have a special delimiter added to its end as a padding character. We choose to illustrate the latter approach by using the so-called null character, that is, chr(0), as the delimiter.

Several decisions must be made. First, each "string variable" will be declared as an array of characters. If a program uses arrays of various lengths, then either separate procedures must be created for each array size or the conformant array feature must be utilized (see Sec. 5-2.3 for a discussion of passing arrays as parameters). Here we choose the same size for all the string arrays. We will assume the following declarations for our subprograms:

```
const
    StrSize = 100;
type
    StrType = packed array [1 .. StrSize] of char;
```

The first procedure to be presented reads a string from the input stream. Before designing the procedure, we must decide how a string is to be delimited. Certainly, we will not use a blank because we wish to be able to read strings that contain blanks. We choose to terminate a string in the input stream by a new-line character, which will not be considered as part of the string. Many extended versions of Pascal use this method. The procedure StrRead in Fig. 6-5 will store input characters starting at the next unprocessed input character until the maximum string length is reached or a new-line character is encountered. In either case, a terminating (null) character is appended to the string. It is important to note that the new-line character should be flushed (by a readln statement) before calling procedure StrRead again; otherwise, the next call will simply return a null string.

Similarly, the procedure StrWrite in Fig. 6-6 transmits the characters of a string, up to the delimiter character, to the output stream.

The function StrLength in Fig. 6-7 returns the number of characters (up to but not including the delimiter) in a specified string. The procedure

```
procedure StrRead (
    var InString: StrType      {Output, the string read}
                    );
{Procedure to read a string from the input stream}
var
    K: integer;      {Index into InString}
begin
    {Step 1: Read characters until StrSize − 1 characters are read, or until
        the newline character is reached}
    K := 1;
    while (K < StrSize) and not eoln do
        begin
            read(InString[K]);
            K := K + 1
        end;

    {Step 2: Store the terminating null character}
    InString[K] := chr (0)
end;
```

**FIGURE 6-5**
**String read procedure.**

```
procedure StrWrite (
    OutString: StrType        {Input, the string to be written}
                      );
{Procedure to write a string to the output stream}
var
    K: integer;        {Index into OutString}
begin
    {Step 1: Output the string up to the null character}
    K := 1;
    while OutString[K] <> chr (0) do
        begin
            write (OutString[K]);
            K := K + 1
        end
end;
```

**FIGURE 6-6**
String write procedure.

StrCopy in Fig. 6-8 duplicates a specified string. Procedure StrSub in Fig. 6-9 extracts a substring from a given string. Function StrCPos in Fig. 6-10 returns the position of the leftmost occurrence of a specified character. The procedures StrNull, StrAppend, and StrCAppend perform other useful operations whose implementation is given in Figs. 6-11, 6-12, and 6-13, respectively.

Finally, the implementation of the current example using the previous string-processing routines is given in Fig. 6-14.

An extensive discussion of the implementation of a string-manipulation package in Pascal can be found in Kernigham and Plauger, *Software Tools in Pascal.*

```
function StrLength (
    InString: StrType        {Input, the string whose length is to be returned}
                      ): integer;
{Given a string, this function returns the length.}
var
    K: integer;        {Index into InString}
begin
    {Step 1: Search for null character}
    K := 1;
    while InString[K] <> chr (0) do
        K := K + 1;

    {Step 2: Return the number of characters in the string up to, but not
        including the null character}
    StrLength := K - 1
end;
```

**FIGURE 6-7**
String length function.

```
procedure StrCopy (
    var OutString: StrType;    {Output, the copy of the input string}
    InString: StrType          {Input, the string to be copied}
        );
{Given a string, this procedure makes a copy.}
var
    K: integer;      {Index into InString and OutString}
begin
    {Step 1: Copy up to null character}
    K := 1;
    while InString[K] <> chr (0) do
        begin
            OutString[K] := InString[K];
            K := K + 1
        end;

    {Step 2: Append the null character}
    OutString[K] := chr (0)
end;
```

FIGURE 6-8
String copy procedure.

## EXERCISES 6-4.4

1. Procedure StrSub in Fig. 6-9 has been carefully designed so as to do something sensible if the starting position or the end of the substring is beyond the end of the input string. What happens in these cases? Suggest other conditions that might be checked, and implement your suggestions.

2. What will happen if StrLength is given a string that does not contain the terminating null character?

### 6-4.5 SUMMARY

For string processing, standard Pascal provides only vectors of characters and a very limited set of operators directly on these. String-processing programs are certainly much easier to write if strings are considered a basic data type and a suitable set of operations on strings is supplied. Also, variables should be allowed to take on strings of differing lengths as values. Several Pascal compilers provide extensions to standard Pascal for string types. We shall assume the availability of the Turbo Pascal extensions in several of the applications in the remainder of this chapter.

## EXERCISES 6-4

1. Design a procedure that takes as an input parameter the name of a person, which is of the form

```
procedure StrSub (
    var OutString: StrType;        {Output, the substring}
    InString: StrType;             {Input, the string from which to extract the
                                        substring}

    Position: integer;             {Input, the starting position}
    Length: integer                {Input, the length of the substring}
                    );
```

{Given a string, position, and length, this procedure makes a copy of the substring beginning at the position and with the specified length.}

```
var
    OutIndex: integer;             {Index into the output string}
    InIndex: integer;              {Index into the input string}
    EndIndex: integer;             {Ending index to the input string}
    InLength: integer;             {Length of input string}
begin
    {Step 1: Initialize}
    OutIndex : = 1;
    InIndex : = Position;
    EndIndex : = Position + Length − 1;
    InLength : = StrLength (InString);
    if EndIndex > InLength
    then EndIndex : = InLength;

    {Step 2: Copy the characters}
    while InIndex <= EndIndex do
        begin
            OutString[OutIndex] : = InString[InIndex];
            InIndex : = InIndex + 1;
            OutIndex : = OutIndex + 1
        end;

    {Step 3: Append the null character}
    OutString[OutIndex] : = chr (0)
end;
```

**FIGURE 6-9**
**Substring procedure.**

'Emile☐Jean☐Paul☐Tremblay'

and places in an output parameter the following form of the name:

'Tremblay,☐E.J.P.'

Your procedure should handle an arbitrary number of names before the surname.

★ **2.** Construct a program that inputs a string and replaces all occurrences of 'Mrs.' or 'Miss' by 'Ms.' and all occurrences of 'Chairman' by 'Chairperson'.

**3.** Devise a procedure that deletes all occurrences of trailing blanks in a

```
function StrCPos (
    SearchChar: char;      {Input, character to be searched for}
    InString: StrType      {Input, string to be searched}
                ): integer;
{Given a character and a string, this function returns the position of the first
    occurrence of the character in the string and returns zero if the character
    is not found.}
var
    K: integer;      {Index into string}
begin
    {Step 1: Search string until character is found or end of string is
        reached}
    K := 1;
    while (InString[K] <> SearchChar) and (InString[K] <> chr (0)) do
        K := K + 1;

    {Step 2: Return position of character, or zero if not found}
    if InString[K] = chr(0)
    then StrCPos := 0
    else StrCPos := K
end;
```

**FIGURE 6-10**
**Function to**
**search a string**
**for a character.**

given string. For example, the string 'R.B.☐Bunt☐☐☐☐' should be transformed to the string 'R.B.☐Bunt'.

★ 4. Construct a procedure that deletes all occurrences of each character contained in one given string from another given string. The two strings are
the following input parameters:

(a) Str, the string from which deletions are to be made.

(b) List, the string providing the characters whose occurrences in Str
should be deleted.

The modified string will be contained in the output parameter NewStr. For
example, if Str = 'Thex☐eznzzxdx' and List = 'xz', the required answer is
NewStr = 'The☐end'.

★★ 5. Assuming the global definitions

```
const
    MaxStrLen = 200;
```

```
procedure StrNull (
    var OutString: StrType      {Output, string to be set to null}
                );
{Procedure to set a string to the null string}
begin
    OutString[1] := chr (0)
end;
```

**FIGURE 6-11**
**Procedure to set**
**a string to a null value.**

```
procedure StrAppend (
    var OutString: StrType;      {Input/output, string to be appended to}
    InString: StrType            {Input, string to be appended}
                    );
{Given two strings, this procedure appends the second string to the first.}
var
    OutIndex: integer;           {Index into output string}
    InIndex: integer;            {Index into input string}
begin
    {Step 1: Find the end of the output string}
    OutIndex : = StrLength (OutString) + 1;

    {Step 2: Append the second string until the null character, or until the
        maximum string size is reached}
    InIndex : = 1;
    while (OutIndex < StrSize) and (InString[InIndex] <> chr (0)) do
        begin
            OutString[OutIndex] : = InString[InIndex];
            OutIndex : = OutIndex + 1;
            InIndex : = InIndex + 1
        end;

    {Step 3: Append the null character}
    OutString[OutIndex] : = chr (0)
end;
```

**FIGURE 6-12**
Procedure to append
a string to a string.

```
procedure StrCAppend (
    var OutString: StrType;      {Input/output, string to be appended to}
    InChar: char                 {Input, character to be appended}
                    );
{Procedure to append a character to a string }
var
    OutLength: integer;          {Initial length of OutString}
begin
    {Step 1: Obtain the length of the output string}
    OutLength : = StrLength (OutString);

    {Step 2: Append character and new null character if they will fit}
    if OutLength + 1 < StrSize
    then begin
        OutString[OutLength + 1] : = InChar;
        OutString[OutLength + 2] : = chr (0)
    end
end;
```

**FIGURE 6-13**
Procedure to append
a character to a string.

```
type
    StrType = record
        StrLen: .. MaxStrLen,
        StrVal: array [1 .. MaxStrLen] of char
    end;
```

implement in standard Pascal the following functions and procedures of Turbo Pascal:

length, copy, pos, delete, insert

## 6-5 STRING APPLICATIONS

In this section we present a small representative set of three applications to illustrate string processing. The first application examines one aspect of computerized typesetting. As a second example, we discuss a simplified form-letter-generation application. The third application deals with the lexical analysis phase of compilation.

### 6-5.1 JUSTIFICATION OF TEXT

The typesetting of books, magazines, and newspapers has become very automated in recent years. Computers are used in the formatting of text through the use of a text formatter. Such a formatter has a formatting language associated with it. This language contains commands that enable the user to specify the typesetting of textual material.

Right justification is a major problem in the typesetting process. By *right justification* of text we mean that the printed form of the text is such that the right margin is aligned for all lines in the output. In text that is typeset, such as most books, right justification is achieved by first attempting to split words across lines, then by leaving a certain amount of space between words, and finally, if necessary, by expanding the spaces between letters.

Word splitting can be handled in most instances by storing the syllables of most common words along with certain simple rules which govern syllable separation. To split an "uncommon" word may require operator intervention. Once such an uncommon word is split by manual intervention, the system can store this word and its split location. This may enable the system to split the word automatically the next time it overlaps the end of a line that is to be printed.

For textual material which is printed on a typical computer printer, spacing of words must be handled in a more primitive manner. The spacing between letters is impossible to adjust at present, since these printers are fixed-print devices. That is, the amount of space between adjacent characters in such devices cannot be altered. Consequently, the spacing between words must be handled by allowing more than one blank character to be placed between words. In this subsection we discuss a solution to this problem.

**program** EditName4(input, output);

{Given the name of an individual in the format described in the text, this
program converts it to the form of the last name followed by first and
middle initials. This version uses the standard Pascal string processing
package.}

**const**
   StrSize = 30;
**type**
   StrType = **packed array** [1 .. StrSize] **of char**;
**var**

| | |
|---|---|
| Name: StrType; | {Name as read} |
| DesiredName: StrType; | {Name in desired format} |
| Last: StrType; | {Last name} |
| FI, MI: StrType; | {First and middle initials} |
| Index: integer; | {Index into name} |

{Include the string handling procedures here}

**begin**
   {Step 1: Read input name}
   StrRead (Name);

   {Step 2: Obtain the first initial}
   StrSub (FI, Name, 1, 1);

   {Step 3: Obtain the position of the first blank}
   Index := StrCPos ('□', Name);

**FIGURE 6-14**
**Name editing example**
**using string-processing**
**package.**

For this application we assume that words are not to be split between
lines and that each line is to be both left- and right-justified (except for
the last line of text). Any extra blank characters which are required in the
justification of text are to be distributed as uniformly as possible between
the words of a line. Furthermore, we assume that there are no paragraphs
and that pagination and indentation are not required. Finally, each word in
the textual material is separated from every other word by a blank or new-
line character, and each punctuation symbol is followed by a blank or new
line.

As an example, let us consider the justification of the following sample
text:

'The□business□world□is□rapidly□changing□and□our□corporation□
has□been□keeping□pace□with□the□new□requirements□forced□upon□
office□machinery.□We□are□giving□you,□Mr.□Doe,□as□a□key□figure□
in□the□Saskatoon□business□community,□an□opportunity□to□become□
familiar□with□the□latest□advancements□in□our□equipment.□'

Assuming 50 character positions per line, a right-justified equivalent of

{Step 4: Discard the first name}
StrSub (Name, Name, Index + 1, StrLength (Name) − Index);

{Step 5: Obtain the middle initial}
StrSub (MI, Name, 1, 1);

{Step 6: Obtain the position of the next blank}
Index := StrCPos ('□', Name);

{Step 7: Obtain the last name}
StrSub (Last, Name, Index + 1, StrLength (Name) − Index);

{Step 8: Construct the desired name}
StrCopy (DesiredName, Last);
StrCAppend (DesiredName, ',');
StrCAppend (DesiredName, '□');
StrAppend (DesiredName, FI);
StrCAppend (DesiredName, '□');
StrAppend (DesiredName, MI);

{Step 9: Output the desired name}
StrWrite (DesiredName);
writeln
**end**.

FIGURE 6-14 (*cont.*)

the previous text is

```
The□business□world□is□□rapidly□□changing□□and□□our
corporation□has□been□keeping□□pace□□with□□the□□new
requirements□forced□upon□office□machinery.□We□□are
giving□you,□Mr.□□Doe,□□as□□a□□key□□figure□□in□□the
Saskatoon□business□community,□□an□□opportunity□□to
become□familiar□with□the□□latest□□advancements□□in
our□equipment.
```

Note that the last line of the previous paragraph is not justified. The choice of output format for this line seems to be the most reasonable one to make.
    A general algorithmic formulation of the text-justification problem follows:

   *1.* Repeat thru step 3 while the current line is not the last

   *2.* If the current line of text is immediately right-justifiable,
        then copy this line into output area
        else determine the number of blanks to be inserted in current line
            Establish a loop to insert blanks into current line
                Distribute blanks in current line in a right-to-left manner
            Copy edited line in output area

*3.* Write current line
   Delete this line from paragraph
   If the left-most character in the remaining text is a blank,
   then delete this character

*4.* Write last line and exit

We can now formulate a list of variable names, which appears in the declaration section of Fig. 6-15.

We next develop the details of our general algorithm. The statement

**while** length (Text) $>$ RMargin **do**

controls the output of full lines of right-justified text. The last output line of text is not controlled by this statement.

The second step of the general algorithm represents the most significant portion of the desired procedure. Before developing the details of this step, however, let us examine the right justification of a line more closely.

A line of text is immediately right-justifiable if the right-most character in the line is a nonblank character and the next character is a blank. For example, assuming a line width of 25 and a text of

```
'This□book□was□authored□by□J.□E.□Doe.□He□discussed□
the□art□of□deer□hunting.□'
```

the first line of the justified text can be printed as is. In this case, the twenty-fifth character is the 'y' of 'by' and the twenty-sixth character is a blank. Consequently, no editing is required. That is, no blanks need be inserted in the current line of text. Therefore, we can write

```
This□book□was□authored□by
```

In the next line of output, however, the case is somewhat more complex. The remaining text to be printed is

```
'□J.□E.□Doe.□He□discussed□the□art□of□deer□hunting.□'
```

Since this text is to be left-justified, we eliminate the left-most blank. This operation yields the string

```
'J.□E.□Doe.□He□discussed□the□art□of□deer□hunting.□'
```

The twenty-fifth character in this string is the letter 't'. The word 'the' must be printed on the next line. Consequently, we must insert two blanks between the words in the second line. If these blanks are inserted in a right-to-left manner between the words (as evenly as possible), then the second line of output becomes

```
J.□E.□Doe.□□He□□discussed
```

The remaining text is now

```
'□the□art□of□deer□hunting.□'
```

Again, we delete the left-most blank in this string. The last output line of

```
procedure Justification (
    Text: Longstring;      {Input, input text}
    RMargin: integer      {Input, right margin, i.e., desired line length}
                       );
```
{Given a character string which contains textual material beginning with a nonblank character, and the number of characters per printed line, this procedure right-justifies the given text. The type LongString is presumed to be defined as a string type with a maximum length large enough to hold an entire paragraph. This procedure uses the Turbo Pascal string primitives.}

```
const
    MaxOutLineLen = 100;      {Maximum length of an output line}
var
    Line: string [MaxOutLineLen];   {Output line}
    Index: integer;                 {Index used to search for blanks}
```

{Include procedure InsertBlanks here}

```
begin
    {Step 1: Justify the text}
    while length (Text) > RMargin do
      begin

        {Step 2: Justify current line of text}
        if (Text [RMargin] <> '□') and (Text [RMargin + 1] = '□')
        then Line : = copy (Text, 1, RMargin) {No justification required}
        else begin
              {Blanks must be inserted in the output line}
              Index : = RMargin;
              while Text [Index] <> '□' do
                Index : = Index − 1;
              Index : = Index − 1;    {Index is now the position of the
                                       last character to be included in the
                                       output line}
              InsertBlanks (Text, RMargin, Index);
              Line : = copy (Text, 1, RMargin)
          end;

        {Step 3: Output justified line}
        writeln (Line);
        delete (Text, 1, RMargin);
        if text [1] = '□'
        then delete (Text, 1, 1) {Get rid of leading blank}
      end;

    {Step 4: Output last line}
    writeln (Text)
end;
```

**FIGURE 6-15**
**Procedure to**
**justify text.**

text is

'the□art□of□deer□hunting.□'

Since the remaining text contains 25 characters, we need not perform any right justification on this line.

From these notions we can formulate the details of editing a line of output. The statement

**if** (Text[RMargin] <> '□') **and** (Text[RMargin + 1] = '□')
**then** Line : = copy (Text, 1, RMargin) { No justification required}
**else** { Blanks must be inserted in the output line}

represents a skeleton of the required statement. To fill in the specifics of the else part of the previous statement, we must first determine the number of blanks that are to be inserted in the output line. The following program segment produces this result:

Index : = RMargin;
**while** Text[Index] <> '□' **do**
   Index : = Index − 1;
   Index : = Index − 1; { Index is not the position of the last character to be included in the output line}

The next part of the development is to distribute the required number of spaces (**Blanks**) in the output line. This may be computed by:

Blanks: = RMargin − Index

As previously mentioned, the distribution of blanks is done by scanning the line from right to left and inserting extra blanks one at a time between the words. We require a loop to control the insertion of blanks. The procedure in Fig. 6-16 carries out this operation. This procedure requires further comment. In general, we may have to scan the entire output line more than once in order to distribute all the blanks. Initially, we want to lengthen (in a right-to-left scan) every blank field (initial value of **BField**) to two blanks. If more than one entire scan is required, however, we must be careful to detect the left end of the line. Such a check is made by testing the condition Index = 0. If this condition holds, we must instigate a new scan starting from the right end of the line. Note that the position of the right-most character in the line must be calculated at this point. Before starting the second scan, we must also pad **BField** with an extra blank. So, on the second scan of the line, an occurrence of a double blank (the revised value of **BField**) is to be replaced by three blanks. This multiple scanning process continues until all blanks are distributed. A trace of the blank-distribution process is given following the detailed procedure.

The third step of the algorithm outputs the right-justified line of text and deletes a leading blank from the next line, if necessary. The following statements accomplish this task:

```
procedure InsertBlanks (
   var Text: LongString;        {Input/output, character string containing textual
                                 material}
   RMargin: integer;            {Input, right margin boundary}
   Index: integer               {Input, length of current line}
                 );

var
   BField: string [MaxOutLineLen];  {Field of blanks}
   Blanks: integer;                 {Number of blanks to be inserted}
   K: integer;                      {Loop index}
```

{Given the text to be justified, the desired output line length (right margin boundary), and the current length of the line, this procedure inserts additional blanks between words to achieve the desired length. The procedure uses the Turbo Pascal string primitives.}

```
begin
   {Step 1: Initialize}
   Blanks : = RMargin − Index;

   {Step 2: Engage loop for inserting blanks}
   BField : = '□';
   for K : = 1 to Blanks do
      begin

         {Step 3: Find next blank field separating words}
         while copy (Text, Index, length (BField) ) <> BField do
            begin
               Index : = Index − 1;
               if Index = 0
               then begin
                     Index : = RMargin − Blanks + K − 1;
                     BField : = BField + '□'
                  end
            end;

         {Step 4: Put in blank}
         insert ('□', text, Index);
         Index : = Index − 1
      end;
end;
```

FIGURE 6-16
Procedure to
insert blanks.

```
writeln (Line);
delete (Text, 1, RMargin);
if text[1] = '□'
then delete (Text, 1, 1) {Get rid of leading blank}
```

Step 4 of the general algorithm is implemented by a single statement:

```
writeln (Text)
```

The procedure for justification appears in Fig. 6-15.

Recall that the second step of the procedure performs the required editing. A test is made to determine whether or not blanks must be inserted in order to achieve right justification. If the character in position RMargin of Text is nonblank and the next character is a blank, this line can be written out directly. If the test fails, however, we must first determine the number of blanks that must be inserted in order to right-justify the line. We set Index to RMargin and then decrement it until it references a blank. (If the character in position RMargin is blank, the while condition is true initially and no decrementing is done.) We then decrement Index once more; it now represents the last character of the last word which is to appear on the output line. Once this position is found, the procedure InsertBlanks is called. There the variable Blanks is assigned the number of blanks which must be distributed between the words in the line being prepared for output. The remainder of this procedure distributes the blanks between the words.

As an example of justification, assume that Text has the value

'This□book□was□authored□by□J.□E.□Doe.□He□discussed□
the□art□of□deer□hunting.□Still□hunting□is□described□as□a...'

and RMargin is 25. Since this string contains more than 25 characters, we proceed to step 2. Because Text[25] = 'y' and Text[26] = '□', no right justification is required for the first line. Consequently, we proceed to step 3, where the first line written is

This□book□was□authored□by

The remaining text after deleting the left-most blank becomes

'J.□E.□Doe.□He□discussed□the□art□of□deer□hunting.□Still□
hunting□is□described□as□a...'

A return to step 2 indicates that Text[RMargin] = 't'. Therefore, the word 'the' cannot be printed this time. A search for the right-most blank in the second line is successful in position 24. The procedure InsertBlanks is called with RMargin = 25 and Index = 23; as a result, Blanks receives a value of 2 and BField is set to '□'. We then engage a loop to distribute these two blanks by scanning the line from position 23 from right to left. The while condition

copy (Text, Index, length (BField) ) <> BField

for Index = 23 reduces to the condition

copy (Text, 23, 1) = '□'

This condition fails because we are trying to match 'd' with '□'. We then continue to decrement Index until the match succeeds. This situation occurs when Index = 14. At that point we stop the search and exit from the loop. A blank is inserted in position 14, resulting in two blanks at this position. Now we have

'J.□E.□Doe.□He□□discussed□the□art□of□deer□hunting.□Still□
hunting□is□described□as□a...'

We now want to continue scanning the line because one more blank must be inserted. Before doing this, however, we reset Index to a position which skips over the blank field just changed. This reset operation is performed by simply decrementing Index by 1, which in our case yields a value of 13. We then resume the scan from position 13 leftward. The search for a blank is successful in position 11. We replace this blank by two blanks. The revised string now becomes

'J.□E.□Doe.□□He□□discussed□the□art□of□deer□hunting.□Still□
hunting□is□described□as□a...'

We have now inserted the required number of blanks for the second line. The procedure InsertBlanks returns control to step 2 of procedure Justification. The left-most 25 characters of Text are copied into Line and in step 3 the second line is written out as

J.□□E.□Doe.□He□□discussed

In step 3 this line and the next blank are deleted from Text. As a result, the remaining string is

'the□art□of□deer□hunting.□Still□hunting□is□described□as□a...'

A return to step 2 indicates that copy Text[RMargin] = '□'. Consequently, only one blank need be inserted into the third line in order to achieve justification. Thus the third line written is

the□art□of□deer□□hunting.

After deletion of this line and the next blank from Text, we get

'Still□hunting□□is□described□as□a...'

In step 2 copy Text[RMargin] = 'e'. The word 'described' cannot be written out on this (the fourth) line. Nine blanks must be inserted in this line; that is, Blanks = 9 and BField = '□'. A scan for the right-most blank from position 16 is successful in position 14. The substitution of two blanks here yields

'Still□hunting□□is□described□as□a...'

At this point the scan for another blank continues and a successful match occurs in position 6. The replacement of this blank by a pair of blanks gives

'Still□□hunting□□is□described□as□a...'

If we resume the scan for the next right-most blank, the search fails. This condition Index = 0 is detected in step 3 of InsertBlanks. When this situation arises, we want to repeat the scan from the right side of the line. The reset position of the scan is given by the statement

Index := RMargin − Blanks + K − 1

In our case $K = 3$, since we are presently trying to add the third blank. Therefore, Index is set to $25 - 9 + 3 - 1$, or 18. Also, note that the value of BField is '□□'. Essentially, we want to replace a field of two blanks by a string of three blanks. If we perform the entire scan, we obtain the string

'Still□□□hunting□□□is□described□as□a...'

Again, the condition Index = 0 becomes true. Since we have only distributed four blanks, we must reset the scan so that the additional blanks can be inserted. The reset position is

Index := $25 - 9 + 5 - 1$, or 20

The value of BField changes to '□□□'. We now want to replace a field of three blanks by a string of four blanks. By repeating the entire scan, we get the string

'Still□□□□hunting□□□□is□described□as□a...'

After two more scans of the line, we finally arrive at the string

'Still□□□□□hunting□□□□□□is□described□as□a...'

and the fifth output line is

Still□□□□□hunting□□□□□□is

The remaining text is then

'described□as□a...'

Assuming that this string contains less than 26 characters, we can go directly to step 4, where the last line is written out.

In this subsection we have examined only one aspect of text formatting. A number of important editing considerations, such as pagination, indentation, and underlining, have been ignored.

## 6-5.2 FORM-LETTER GENERATION

A business machine manufacturing corporation which sells equipment throughout North America controls sales from its head office but has sales people who work out of offices in each of several regions. The company sends letters annually to prospective buyers, informing them that the regional sales representative will call on them in the near future. The letters are mass-produced, but an effort is being made to personalize them by utilizing a computer.

In this subsection we wish to develop a program for generating personalized form letters. An example of the input data for a form letter is given in Fig. 6-17. Each line in the letter represents a line of data. Note that blank lines have been used to space out portions of the letter. Also present in this letter are a number of patterns or keywords such as

*DATE*

*ADDRESS*

#40 187 Main Street
#40 Winnipeg 1, Manitoba
#40 *DATE*

*X*
*ADDRESS*
*CITY*, *PROV/STATE*

Dear *Z*,

    The business world is rapidly changing and our corporation has been
keeping pace with the new requirements forced upon office machinery.
We are giving you, *Z*, as a key figures in the *CITY* business
community, an opportunity to become familiar with the latest
advancements in our equipment. A representative of our corporation in
*PROV/STATE* will be seeing you within *N* weeks. The representative will take several
machines to *CITY* that are indicative of a whole new line of office
machines we have recently developed.
    Our sales representative is looking forward to visiting *CITY*
We know that the machine we sell could become an integral part of your
office only a few days after implementation.

#40 Sincerely,


#40 Roger Smith, Manager
#40 Office Devices Corporation

**FIGURE 6-17**
**Example of input**
**to form Form Letter.**


*CITY*

*PROV/STATE*

*N*

*X*

*Z*

These patterns are to be replaced by actual and personalized information
when a particular letter is generated. For example, the patterns *DATE* and
*X* might be changed to January 1, 1987 and Ms. Mary Richards, respectively.
Also, certain lines in the form letter contain the indentation code #. The
form of this code is '#number☐' and it applies to only one line. The code
is used to indent that particular line by the specified number of spaces.

    In the interest of simplicity, we will not require the right justification
of the personalized letters, although this could be done by calling the
Justification procedure of the previous subsection. A personalized letter for
the example form letter is given in Fig. 6-18. We have assumed that each
line of the form letter after the substitution of personalized information (such
as name, city, etc.) corresponds to one line of output in the personalized
letter. Again, this assumption simplifies our problem. Finally, we assume
that several personalized letters must be produced by the program.

The data is to consist of the following:

Form letter

↑
↓

'**' An end-of-letter delimiter

First customer

{
'Date'
'Mr. (or Mrs., etc.)☐FirstName☐Surname'
'Street Address'
'City,☐ProvState'
'Number of weeks before salesperson will visit'
}

Second customer {

.
.
.

Last customer {

For example, the customer data for the personalized letter in Fig. 6-18 would be

January 1, 1987
Ms. Mary Richards
1712 N. Waverly
Minneapolis, Minnesota
four

A general algorithm for the form-letter problem is as follows:

*1.* Input the form letter

*2.* Repeat thru step 4 while input data remains to be processed

*3.* Read in data for next customer

*4.* Repeat for every line of the form letter
    Get the next line of the form letter
    Repeat for each keyword in this line
        Replace keyword with personalized data

187 Main Street
Winnipeg 1, Manitoba
January 1, 1987

Ms. Mary Richards
1712 N. Waverly
Minneapolis, Minnesota

Dear Ms. Richards,
    The business world is rapidly changing and our corporation has been
keeping pace with the new requirements forced upon office machinery.
We are giving you, Ms. Richards, as a key figure in the Minneapolis business
community, an opportunity to become familiar with the latest
advancements in our equipment. A representative of our corporation in
Minnesota will be seeing you within four weeks. The representative will take several
machines to Minneapolis that are indicative of a whole new line of office
machines we have recently developed.
    Our sales representative is looking forward to visiting Minneapolis.
We know that the machine we sell could become an integral part of your
office only a few days after implementation.

        Sincerely,

        Roger Smith, Manager
        Office Devices Corporation

**FIGURE 6-18**
**Example of a**
**generated form**
**letter.**

    If this line contains an indentation code,
    then insert the indicated number of indentation spaces
    Write out the next line of the personalized letter

Since we must produce a personalized letter for each customer, the form
letter has to be saved. To preserve the one-to-one correspondence between
each line of the form letter and the personalized letter, it is advisable to
store the form letter line by line. A vector is a convenient structure for
representing the form letter. Each string element of the vector represents
one line of the letter. In step 1, the number of lines in the form letter can
easily be determined as each line of the letter is read. On the detection of a
line which contains the string '**' in its two left-most character positions, a
transfer to step 2 is made. A list of variable names for this problem appears
in the declaration section of the program in Fig. 6-19.
    We next develop the details of our general algorithm. The specifics of
the first step for entering the form letter are as follows:

```
readln (InputLine);
NumLines : = 0;
while copy (InputLine, 1, 2) <> '**' do
begin
   NumLines : = NumLines + 1;
   Letter[NumLines] : = InputLine;
   readln (InputLine)
end;
```

**program** FormLetter (input, output);
{Given a form letter and personalized customer data according to the formats
  described in the text, this program generates a personalized letter for each
  set of customer data. This is a Turbo Pascal version.}
**const**
  MLL = 80;      {Maximum line length}
  MNL = 40;      {Maximum number of lines in a letter}
**type**
  EntryType = **string** [40];
  LineType = **string** [MLL];
**var**
  Letter: **array** [1 .. MNL] **of** LineType;
                              {Vector, each of whose elements represents
                                a line in the letter}
  NumLines: integer;          {Number of lines in the form letter}
  Date: EntryType;            {Date which is to appear on a personalized
                                letter}
  Name: EntryType;            {Name which is to appear on a personalized
                                letter}
  LastName: EntryType;        {Last name of recipient of personalized
                                letter}
  Address: EntryType;         {Street address which is to appear on a
                                personalized letter}
  Weeks: EntryType;           {Number of weeks before salesperson will
                                visit an individual}
  ProvState: EntryType;       {Prov/state which is to appear on a letter}
  City: EntryType;            {City which is to appear on a letter}
  CityProvState: EntryType;   {Input string containing both city and
                                prov/state}
  InputLine, OutLine: LineType;  {Used for processing each line of the letter}
  Blanks: LineType;           {Blanks for indentation}
  LN: integer;                {Index to process lines}
  J, K: integer;              {Miscellaneous indices}

  {Include procedures FindSubsData, Indentation, and Substitution here}


**begin**
  {Step 1: Input form letter}
  readln (InputLine);
  NumLines := 0;
  **while** copy (InputLine, 1, 2) <> '**'**do**
    **begin**
      NumLines := NumLines + 1;
      Letter [NumLines] := InputLine;
      readln (InputLine)
    **end**;

**FIGURE 6-19**
**Program to generate**
**personalized form**
**letters.**

{Step 2: Initialize blanks for indentation}
Blanks : = ''; {Null string}
**for** J : = 1 **to** MLL **do**
   insert ('□', Blanks, J);
readln (Date);

{Step 3: Engage the loop to write personalized letters}
readln (Name);
**while** Date <> '' **do**     {Null string}
  **begin**

     {Step 4: Read in data for next customer}
     readln (Address);
     readln (CityProvState);
     readln (Weeks);

     {Step 5: Split up the personalized data for one customer}
     J : = pos ('□', Name);
     K : = pos ('□', copy (Name, J + 1, length (Name) − J) );
     LastName : = copy (Name, 1, J − 1) + '□' +
              copy (Name, J + K + 1, length (Name) − J − K);
     J : = Pos (',', CityProvState);
     City : = copy (CityProvState, 1, J − 1);
     ProvState : = copy (CityProvState, J + 2, length (CityProvState) − J − 1);

     {Step 6: Generate a personalized letter for current customer}
     **for** LN : = 1 **to** NumLines **do**
      **begin**
        {Step 7: Get the next line of the form letter}
        InputLine : = Letter [LN];
        OutLine : = '';

        {Step 8: Perform all key word substitutions}
        Substitution(InputLine, OutLine, Date, Address, City, ProvState,
              Weeks, Name, LastName);

        {Step 9: Perform indentation if required}
        Indentation (OutLine, Blanks);

        {Step 10: Output next line of personalized letter}
        writeln (OutLine)
      **end**;
    readln (Date)
  **end**
**end**.

FIGURE 6-19 *(cont.)*

Note that the end of the form letter is signaled by a line which contains the string '**' in its left-most two positions.

In order to perform the indicated indentation of an output line, we need a sequence of blanks. The next step realizes this need.

```
Blanks := ''; {Null string}
for J := 1 to MLL do
    insert ('□', Blanks, J);
```

Next we must read in the date—when **Date** ='', then we have reached the end of the input.

```
readln (Date);
```

The third step controls the input:

```
while Date <> '' do {Null string}
```

Once the personalized data for a particular customer is read, we must examine the data so that the customer's last name, city, and state or province can be obtained. These items are inserted into certain lines of the personalized letter. The details of this task include

```
J := pos ('□', Name);
K := pos ('□', copy (Name, J + 1, length (Name) − J) );
LastName := copy (Name, 1, J − 1) + '□' + copy (Name, J + K + 1, length (Name) − J − K);
J := Pos (',', CityProvState);
City := copy (CityProvState, 1, J − 1);
Province := copy (CityProvState, J + 2, length (CityProvState) − J − 1);
```

The sixth step of the detailed program controls and generates a personalized letter. The control function becomes the statement

```
for LN := 1 to NumLines do
```

We generate the letter line by line. The statement

```
InputLine := Letter[LN]
```

obtains the next line of the form letter.

We must now perform all indicated substitutions of personalized information in the line which is to be output. Essentially, this involves performing a left-to-right scan on the line. This scan searches for the pattern '*KEY*', where **KEY** is any of the keywords 'DATE', 'X', 'ADDRESS', 'PROVINCE', 'CITY', 'Z', and 'N'. Each *KEY* pattern is replaced by the corresponding personalized data. More than one keyword can occur in a particular line. The procedure in Fig. 6-20 realizes this function. Figure 6-20 uses the function given in Fig. 6-21 to select which string is to be substituted for the keyword.

Finally, we must check for any indicated indentation. If the indentation code # is present in a particular line, a scan is made for the left-most blank in that line. This search isolates the string which indicates the number of indentation spaces required. This blank specification string (**Number**) is then converted to an integer (**Value**). The required number of indentation blanks is extracted from the string variable **Blanks**. The procedure in Fig. 6-22 implements this approach.

All that remains to be done is to output the edited line of the personalized letter. The previous details are contained in the program in Fig. 6-19.

## 6-5.3 LEXICAL ANALYSIS

In Sec. 1-4 we briefly described the problem of translating a higher-level language (such as the programming language used in this book) to a lower-level target language (such as machine language). In this subsection we examine certain aspects of the translation process more closely.

In an attempt to describe the translation process, let us approach the problem by first analyzing a similar task in the translation of natural languages: that is, the translation from one natural language (for example, French) into another (for example, English). It is to be stressed, however, that the analogy between programming language translation and natural language translation is valid only in an informal sense.

Consider the French-to-English translation, by a novice translator, of a string of characters that represents French text. Such a translation would probably consist of the following steps:

*1.* Recognize the French words in the given text. This step involves performing a lexical scan of the text in order to classify the words into grammatical categories (noun, adjective, verb, etc.).

*2.* Verify the grammatical structure of each sentence in the text (that is, parse each sentence).

*3.* Using a French-to-English dictionary, look up the English equivalents of the French words found in step 1. Then, according to certain rules, transform the grammatical structure obtained in step 2 into its equivalent English structure. From the latter structure, generate the translated sentences which represent the output string of English text.

Equivalently, a compiler for certain languages can be viewed as consisting of three separate tasks, as shown in Fig. 6-23. The source program is input to a *scanner* whose purpose is to separate the incoming text into words (or *tokens*) such as constants, variable names, keywords (such as **then**, **else**, and **repeat**), operators, special symbols [such as ( and )], and so on. The scanner supplies these tokens to the syntax analyzer, whose task is essentially to construct a parse of the given sentence. The output of the syntax analyzer is passed on to the code generator. Here, the parse and other things, such as symbol tables for variables and constants, are used to generate code for that sentence.

In this subsection we are concerned with the lexical analysis of source statements from a subset of Pascal. Nevertheless, many of the techniques

**procedure** Substitution (

| | |
|---|---|
| InputLine: LineType; | {Input, line of text to be processed} |
| **var** OutLine: LineType; | {Output, result of substitutions} |
| Date: EntryType; | {Input, date which is to appear on a personalized letter} |
| Address: EntryType; | {Input, street address which is to appear on a personalized letter} |
| City: EntryType; | {Input, city which is to appear on a letter} |
| ProvState: EntryType; | {Input, prov/state which is to appear on a letter} |
| Weeks: EntryType; | {Input, number of weeks before salesperson will visit an individual} |
| Name: EntryType; | {Input, name which is to appear on a personalized letter} |
| LastName: EntryType | {Input, last name of recipient of personalized letter} |

                    );
{Given a line to receive substitutions and values to be substituted, this procedure performs the substitutions.}
**var**
   IP, OP: integer;
   Key, SubsData: LineType;
**begin**
   {Step 1: Initialize]
   OutLine : = ''; {Null string}
   OP : = 1;

**FIGURE 6-20**
**Procedure to**
**substitute keywords**
**for form letters.**

presented are applicable to the lexical-analysis phase of natural language machine translation. A discussion of the syntax-analysis and code-generation passes is given in Secs. 8-5.1 and 9-4.4.

   In the discussion to follow, we consider the design of a scanner algorithm for the assignment statement of Pascal. Actually, we concern ourselves with a restricted form of this statement in which only integer arithmetic expressions are permitted. We also ignore subscripted variables, record selections, and functional references. The words or tokens for such a language are identifiers, integers, the arithmetic operators (namely, the addition, subtraction, multiplication, and division operators), and the assignment operator (:=).

   The words or tokens of this simple language are:

| | |
|---|---|
| Identifier | String of alphanumeric characters starting with a letter and whose remaining characters can be a letter or a digit |
| Integer | String of digits |
| Addition and subtraction operators | +, − |

{Step 2: Process all substitutions in line}
IP := pos ('*', InputLine);
**while** IP <> 0 **do**
   **begin**

      {Step 3: Move the part of the input line up to the substitution key
        to the output line}
      insert (copy (InputLine, 1, IP − 1), OutLine, OP);
      delete (InputLine, 1, IP);
      OP := OP + IP − 1;

      {Step 4: Find the substitution data corresponding to the key; insert
        data into output line; delete the key from the input line}
      IP := pos ('*', InputLine);
      Key := copy (InputLine, 1, IP − 1);
      delete (InputLine, 1, IP);
      SubsData := FindSubs(Key, Date, Address, City, ProvState, Weeks, Name,
                       LastName);
      insert (SubsData, OutLine, OP);
      OP := OP + Length (SubsData);

      {Step 5: Check for another key}
      IP := pos ('*', InputLine)
   **end**;

{Step 6: Copy the remaining part of the input line to the output line}
  insert (InputLine, OutLine, OP)
**end**;

FIGURE 6-20 (cont.)

| Multiplication and division operators | *, /, **div**, **mod** |
|---|---|
| Assignment operator | := |
| Left parenthesis | ( |
| Right parenthesis | ) |

In addition to these tokens, there are certain symbols which must be handled by the scanner, and yet their presence is not passed on to the syntactic analyzer. In our simple language, the blank is such a symbol (that is, A□:=□B□+□C is syntactically equivalent to A:=B+C).

Before formulating a scanning program, several observations concerning the previous classification of tokens can be made. In particular, the definition of an identifier does not make any distinction among the letters A through Z and a through z. Therefore, it is not necessary to distinguish among any of these characters; consequently, they can be treated as a single group whose generic name is "letter." Regardless of the program which we may devise,

```
function FindSubs (
    Key: LineType;              {Input, key word to be replaced}
    Date: EntryType;            {Input, date which is to appear on a personalized
                                  letter}
    Address: EntryType;         {Input, street address which is to appear on a
                                  personalized letter}
    City: EntryType;            {Input, city which is to appear on a letter}
    ProvState: EntryType;       {Input, prov/state which is to appear on a letter}
    Weeks: EntryType;           {Input, number of weeks before salesperson will
                                  visit an individual}
    Name: EntryType;            {Input, name which is to appear on a personalized
                                  letter}
    LastName: EntryType         {Input, last name of recipient of personalized
                                  letter}
    ): LineType;
{Given a key and the personalized substitution data for all the keys, this
 function returns the substitution data corresponding to the given key.}
begin
    {Test each key and return corresponding data}
    if Key = 'DATE'
    then FindSubs : = Date
    else
        if Key = 'ADDRESS'
        then FindSubs : = Address
        else
            if Key = 'CITY'
            then FindSubs : = City
            else
                if Key = 'PROV/STATE'
                then FindSubs : = ProvState
                else
                    if Key = 'N'
                    then FindSubs : = Weeks
                    else
                        if Key = 'X'
                        then FindSubs : = Name
                        else FindSubs : = LastName
end;
```

**FIGURE 6-21**
**Procedure to find**
**string corresponding**
**to keyword.**

it will not be required to perform different actions for different identifiers. A similar observation can be made about the digits 0 through 9.

In most instances it is inefficient to pass a class name, such as "integer" or "identifier," to the syntactic analyzer. Instead, we associate a unique representation number with each class, and it is this number along with the source form (for example, the integer) which is given to the syntactic

```
procedure Indentation (
    var OutLine: LineType;        {Input/output, text string to be indented}
    Blanks: LineType
                        );
var
    OP: integer;                  {Position of end of indentation value in line}
    Value: integer;               {Number of spaces for indentation}
    Number: EntryType;            {Integer which specifies the indentation spacing
                                    to be inserted in an indented line}
{Given a line of text, this procedure indents the line, if required. The
    second parameter is a string of blanks used for indentation.}
begin
    {Step 1: Test whether indentation is required}
    if OutLine[1] = '#'
    then begin


        {Step 2: Find end of indentation value (first blank)}
        OP : = pos ('□', OutLine);


        {Step 3: Convert one or two digit indentation number}
        Number : = copy (Outline, 2, OP − 2);
        Value : = 0;
        if length (Number) = 2
        then begin
                Value : = (pos (Number[1], '0123456789') − 1) * 10;
                delete (Number, 1, 1)
            end;
        Value : = Value + pos (Number, '0123456789') − 1;


        {Step 4: Delete the indentation indicator}
        delete (OutLine, 1, OP);


        {Step 5: Insert the appropriate number of blanks}
        insert (copy (Blanks, 1, Value), OutLine, 1)
    end
end;
```

FIGURE 6-22
Procedure to
perform indentation.

analyzer. For our example language, we adopt the representation numbers in Table 6-1.

For this application we will need an additional pattern matching function which we will call Span. Span matches all consecutive characters in the subject string (Subject) from the indicated cursor position (Cursor) and ending at the first character not in the pattern string (Pattern). For example, Span can be used to skip across any leading blanks in a string. With a subject string of '□□□Computers', a pattern string of '□', and a cursor position of 1,

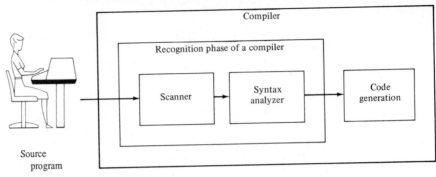

**FIGURE 6-23**
**Model of a compiler.**    Source
program

Span ('☐☐☐Computers', '☐', I, MatchStr)

where I initially has the value 1, would match and move the cursor across the left-most 3 blanks in the subject string, thus yielding the string 'Computers'. Function Span appears in Fig. 6-24.

Step 1 determines whether or not Cursor refers to a character position within the subject string. If it does not, the pattern match fails. The second step initializes the variable J to the position of the first character which is to be examined in the matching process (that is, the value of Cursor). In step 3, a search in Pattern is made for the character at position J in Subject. If this search is successful, then J is incremented by one and the search is repeated, using the next character in Subject. Encountering the end of the subject string or failing to find the specified character (of Subject) in Pattern terminates the third step. Step 4 determines whether or not any character was matched. The failure of the pattern-matching process results in an unsuccessful return from the function; otherwise, control passes to step 5, where the matched substring is copied into MatchStr and Cursor is updated appropriately. Finally, step 6 specifies a successful return from the function.

We are now prepared to give a program for scanning a source statement from the simple programming language previously described (see Fig. 6-25). The first step of the program initializes Cursor to a character position of 1.

| TABLE 6-1 | Representation Numbers of Tokens |
|---|---|
| **Token(s)** | **Representation Number** |
| Identifiers | 1 |
| Integers | 2 |
| **div** | 3 |
| **mod** | 4 |
| + | 5 |
| − | 6 |
| * | 7 |
| / | 8 |
| ( | 9 |
| ) | 10 |
| : = | 11 |

```
function Span (
    Subject: Str255;        {Input, a subject string}
    Pattern: Str255;        {Input, pattern string}
    var Cursor: integer;    {Input/output, position in Subject}
    var MatchStr: Str255    {Output, sequence matched}
         ): boolean;
```

{Given a subject string, a pattern string, and a position in the subject string, this function returns true if the character at the indicated position is contained in Pattern. In this case, successive characters are checked; again a character in the subject string matches, if it occurs in Pattern. The sequence of characters matched is returned in MatchStr and Cursor is advanced to the position of the first unmatched character in the subject string. When the first character does not match, the function returns false, Cursor is unchanged, and MatchStr is undefined. Turbo Pascal version.}

```
var
    J: integer;          {Temporary position during scanning}
    Matched: Boolean;    {True if pattern character matched the subject
                          character}
begin
    {Step 1: Does the pattern fit within the bounds of the subject string?}
    if Cursor > length (Subject)
    then Span : = false
    else begin

        {Step 2: Initialize pattern match}
        J : = Cursor;

        {Step 3: Advance J while Subject[J] is in the pattern string}
        Matched : = true;
        while (J <= length (Subject)) and Matched do
            if pos (Subject[J], Pattern ) > 0
            then J : = J + 1
            else Matched : = false;

        {Step 4: Test for unsuccessful pattern match}
        if J = Cursor
        then Span : = false
        else begin

            {Step 5: Set MatchStr and update Cursor}
            MatchStr : = copy (Subject, Cursor, J - Cursor);
            Cursor : = J;

            {Step 6: Successful return}
            Span : = true
        end
    end
end;
```

**FIGURE 6-24**
**Span function for lexical analysis program.**

**program** Scan (input, output);
{This program reads a source statement from the input stream, isolates the
statement's tokens, and finds their corresponding representation numbers
as described in the text. This is a Turbo Pascal version.}

**const**
  {Representation numbers}
  IDCode = 1;
  IntCode = 2;
  IDivCode = 3;
  ModCode = 4;
  AddCode = 5;     {Next six must be consecutive and in given order}
  SubCode = 6;
  MulCode = 7;
  DivCode = 8;
  LPCode = 9;
  RPCode = 10;
  AssCode = 11;
  {Character class definitions}
  UCLetters = 'ABCDEFGHIJKLMNOPQRSTUVWXYZ' ;
  LCLetters = 'abcdefghijklmnopqrstuvwxyz' ;
  Digits = '0123456789' ;
  Opers = '+ − */()' ;
  Ass = ':' ;

**type**
  Str255 = **string** [255];   {Type for parameter of Span}

**var**
  Source: Str255;          {Source string}
  Cursor: integer;        {Current processing position in Source}
  Letters: **string** [52];     {All letters}
  AlphaNum: **string** [62];   {All letters and digits}
  Leading: **string** [69];   {All characters which begin a token}
  Ch: char;             {Current character Source [Cursor]}
  LeadingPos: integer;   {Position of Ch in Leading}
  Token: Str255;        {Token returned by Span}
  TBool: boolean;       {Temporary}
  TString: Str255;      {Temporary}

  {Include the function Span here}

  **begin**
  {Step 1: Initialize}
  Cursor := 1;
  Letters := UCLetters + LCLetters;
  AlphaNum := Letters + Digits;
  Leading := AlphaNum + Opers + Ass;

  {Step 2: Input and output the source statement}
  readln (Source);
  writeln (Source);

**FIGURE 6-25**
**Lexical analysis**
**program.**

{Step 3: Engage the loop to scan the source statement}
**while** Cursor <= length (Source) **do**
  **begin**

     {Step 4: Obtain next token}
     **if not** Span (Source, '□', Cursor, TString) {Check for next blank
                                     character}
   **then begin**
        Ch := Source [Cursor];
        LeadingPos := pos (Ch, Leading);
        **case** LeadingPos **of**
          0: **begin**
             writeln ('Illegal character' , Ch);
             Cursor := Cursor + 1
          **end**;
         1 .. 52: **begin** {Letter}
             TBool := Span (Source, AlphaNum, Cursor, Token);
             **if** Token = 'div'
             **then** writeln (IDivCode, '□□', Token)
             **else**
               **if** Token = 'mod'
               **then** writeln (ModCode, '□□', Token)
               **else** writeln (IDCode, '□□', Token)
           **end**;
         53 .. 62: **begin** {Digits}
             TBool := Span (Source, Digits, Cursor, Token);
             writeln (IntCode, '□□' , Token)
           **end**;
         63 .. 68: **begin** { + − */()}
             writeln (AddCode + LeadingPos − 63, '□□' , Ch);
             Cursor := Cursor + 1
           **end**;
         69: **begin** {:}
             **if** Cursor = length (Source)
             **then** writeln ('Error: missing ' ' = ' ' ' )
             **else**
               **if** Source [Cursor + 1] <> ' = '
               **then** writeln ('Error missing ' ' = ' ' ' )
               **else begin**
                 writeln (AssCode, '□□:= ');
                 Cursor := Cursor + 2
              **end**
           **end**
        **end**
       **end**
   **end**
**end**.

FIGURE 6-25 (*cont.*)

Also, **Letters**, **AlphNum**, and **Leading** are set to the string of letters, of letters and digits, and of all characters which can start a token, respectively. Step 2 reads and displays the original source statement which is to be scanned. The third step controls the scanning of the source statement. Step 4 determines the next token (along with its representation number) to be output. Observe that blank characters are ignored. The first character of a potential token is copied into **Ch**. Then **Leading** is searched for the character using the pos function. Recall that **Leading** contains the set of characters which can begin a token, namely, 'A . . .Za . . .z0 . . .9 + − ∗/():'. The result of the search is used as a case statement index. Case 0 indicates an illegal character. Cases 1 through 52, the letters, indicate an identifier. The **Span** function is used to accumulate the characters of the identifier and update **Cursor**. A check is made for the reserved identifiers **div** and **mod**. Cases 53 through 62, the digits, indicate an integer number, which is again accumulated by the **Span** function. Cases 63 through 68 are the operators. Case 69, a colon (:) processes the assignment (:=). Notice the care in handling error conditions such as a missing equal sign, particularly the possibility that a colon occurs as the last character of the statement.

The output from this program for the source statement

□□A1□:=□A□+□5

is

□□A1□:=□A□+□5
1       A1
11      :=
1       A
5       +
2       5

The output from the program for the source statement

75□:=□X□Y□−□∗□Z

is

75□:=□X□Y□−□∗□Z

2       75
11      :=
1       X
1       Y
6       −
7       ∗
1       Z

In the last example, notice that the scanner is not responsible for the checking of proper syntax at the statement or sentence level. Clearly, the given statement is syntactically incorrect. The problem of parsing sentences from a programming language will be discussed in more detail in Secs. 8-5.1 and 9-4.4.

In certain compilers or translators, a token and its associated representation number are often passed to a symbol-table routine. This routine generates a number of tables, such as an identifier table, a statement-label table, a programmer-defined function table, and so on. The type of table organization that can be used depends on a number of factors, such as table size. A simple linear table such as that discussed in Sec. 5-4.1 may be used. For large symbol tables, however, more sophisticated table organization techniques must be used. Such techniques are discussed in Sec. 8-10.3.

## EXERCISES 6-5.3

1. Revise the program Scan so that it can handle the real numbers as well as integers. See Sec. 2-4 for a definition of real numbers.

2. Alter the procedure obtained in Exercise 1 such that comments can be handled. These comments should be printed by the scanner with the assignment statements, but no indication of the presence of comments should be passed to the syntactic analyzer. Therefore, the statement

   {Update A} A□: = □B□ + □C□

   should generate the following:

   | 1  | A    |
   |----|------|
   | 11 | : =  |
   | 1  | B    |
   | 5  | +    |
   | 1  | C    |

3. Modify the program Scan in the text to maintain a table that contains all tokens that are encountered in the input. Use a sequential unordered table, implemented as a vector of strings, for this purpose.

★★ 4. As an extension of Exercise 2, formulate a scanner for the Pascal language introduced so far.

## CHAPTER SUMMARY

This chapter contains an introduction to string processing. Character information and the ASCII and EBCDIC character-coding systems were discussed. Next, the concept of a string as a finite sequence of characters was presented. The assignment of string values and the rules for their comparison were introduced. A number of primitive string manipulation functions such as concatenation, length, and substring was presented. The need for these functions was motivated by examining several string-oriented applications. A string-processing system having such functions was developed in standard Pascal. Extended Pascal versions (namely, VAX-11 and Turbo Pascal) having these functions as built-in were also discussed.

## KEY TERMS

alphabet
ASCII
character set
character string
character type
closure property
collating sequence
concatenation
data abstraction
EBCDIC

empty string
justification (of text)
lexical analysis
null string
pattern matching
pattern string
pseudo-variable
string type (Pascal)
subject string
substring

## CHAPTER EXERCISES

★★ 1. (a) Construct a function for converting Roman numerals to an integer value. The input parameter is a Roman numeral, and the function is to return an integer result. Table 6-2 gives the correspondence between the two number systems.

   (b) Formulate a procedure for converting an integer value to its corresponding Roman form [that is, do the inverse of part (a)]. The input parameter is an integer and the output parameter is a string. (If your Pascal compiler allows functions to return strings as results, you may instead write a function of one argument.)

★ 2. The usual way of writing a check requires five fields to be filled in: the date, the person being paid, the amount as a number, the amount in words, and the signature of the issuer. The amount is written twice for consistency and protection. Computer-generated checks sometimes do not generate the amount in words, since it is believed by some that a machine-printed amount is more difficult to change than its handwritten counterpart. Many companies have learned, however, that such is not the

### TABLE 6-2

| Roman Symbol | Arabic Equivalent |
|--------------|-------------------|
| I | 1 |
| V | 5 |
| X | 10 |
| L | 50 |
| C | 100 |
| D | 500 |
| M | 1000 |

case; consequently, these companies do print on each check the amount in words. Formulate a procedure which, given an integer amount, will print that amount in figures as well as in words. The integer amount is given in pennies. Table 6-3 contains examples of numbers and their corresponding outputs.

★ 3. A coded message is received in groups of five letters separated by a blank. The last group of letters is followed by five 9s. The initial step in the decoding process is to replace each letter by the letter 5 positions after it (that is, A becomes F, B becomes G, C becomes H, and so forth—assume "wrap-around," that is, that A follows Z in sequence). Assume that all letters are capital letters. All nonalphabetic characters, such as numerals, punctuation, and blanks, are to remain unchanged. Write a procedure **Decode** which carries out this simple decoding process. The procedure is to have two parameters: **InString**—the character string that is in code form—and **OutString**—the decoded form of **InString**. Write a main program to test **Decode** by reading the string to be decoded and displaying the result of calling the procedure.

★★ 4. Generalize the program **FormLetter** so that the personalized letter which is produced is right-justified. State any assumptions which you made.

★ 5. Often it is important to determine the keywords in a title, that is, all those words which impart some meaning as to the nature of the document. Ordinary words such as "a," "an," "the," "to," "for," "with," "and," etc., tell little about the subject of the document. The purpose of this problem is to write a program that reads in a string containing a title and a string containing the ordinary words and then prints out the key words of the title (in their original order).

The title string contains the title of a document with blanks before the first word, between the words, and after the last word. Each ordinary word in the ordinary word string is preceded by at least one blank and followed immediately by a comma. Example input and output is

Input:     An Introduction To Computer Science And Life
           a, an, the, to, for, with, and

Output:    The key words are: Introduction, Computer, Science, Life

## TABLE 6-3

| Input (Pennies) | Amount in Figures | Amount in Words |
|---|---|---|
| 17573 | $175.73 | One hundred seventy-five and 73/100 |
| 2900 | 29.00 | Twenty-nine and 00/100 |
| 28050 | 280.50 | Two hundred eighty and 50/100 |
| 1362 | 13.62 | Thirteen and 62/100 |

Your program should make use of the procedure **Break** and the function **Span** given in the last section of this chapter. Also note that it will be necessary to convert upper-case letters to all lower-case letters before searching the test of "ordinary" words.

**6.** Write a function which returns "true" if the word it is passed as argument contains at least one pair of (adjacent) double letters; otherwise it should return "false." For example, the function should return "true" for the words 'putting' and 'Mississippi' but should return "false" for 'blast' and 'color'.

**7.** Write a procedure to find the starting position (**Start**) and length in characters (**Len**) of the longest repetition of a **Pattern** string in a **Target** string. If all the occurrences of **Pattern** in **Target** are of equal length, then **Start** should contain the starting position corresponding to the first occurrence of the **Pattern**. For example, if **Pattern** = 'xyxx' and **Target** = 'xaxyxxaxxyxxax', then **Start** will receive the value 3 and **Len** will receive the value 4. Your procedure should be able to handle variable lengths of **Pattern** and **Target**.

★★ **8.** It is becoming increasingly common to see computers employed in all phases of the text-production process. Packages are available that will assist authors in matters relating to style, whereas conventional text editors assist merely in the input of text. Write a simple authoring tool which, given a piece of text, determines

*(a)* The number of times each word in the text occurs.

*(b)* The frequency (percentage of total words) of each word.

*(c)* The readability of the text, determined by the following formula:
Readability = $\sum$ (sentence length × average word length for the sentence)/(number of sentences).

Your program should print the text, the word counts, and frequencies. The words should be printed in alphabetical order. Also print the number of sentences of the various lengths and the numerical value of the readability formula.

## REFERENCES

**Borland** International, *Turbo Pascal, Reference Manual*, version 2.0, Scotts Valley, Calif., 1983.

**Digital** Equipment Corporation, *VAX-11 Pascal Language Manual*, version 2.0, Order No. AA-H484C-TE, Maynard, Mass., Oct. 1982.

**Digital** Equipment Corporation, *VAX-11 Pascal User's Guide*, version 2.0, Order No. AA-H485C-TE, Maynard, Mass., Oct. 1982.

**Kernighan,** Brian W., and Plauger, P. J.: *Software Tools in Pascal*, Addison-Wesley, Reading, Mass., 1981.

# CHAPTER 7

# THE ENGINEERING OF COMPUTER SOFTWARE

*In programming, it is not enough to be inventive and ingenious, One also needs to be disciplined and controlled in order not to become entangled in one's own complexities.*
    Harlan D. Mills, Foreword to Programming Proverbs, *by Henry F. Ledgard, Hayden Book Company, 1975*

A computer programmer is in the business of designing solutions to problems and implementing these as computer programs. This process has both a scientific aspect and an engineering aspect and is thus often referred to as "software engineering." This chapter examines this process.

## 7-1   INTRODUCTION

Traditionally, science concerns itself with discovery of basic principles, laws, and relationships, while engineering deals with the practical application of these. Software engineering attempts to combine sound engineering principles of design, management, testing, etc. with the concepts of computer science in the production of computer software.

To a person with experience in only small programming problems, the ideas of software engineering may seem unnecessary. In programming practice, however, two facts dominate. First, practical software projects are typically anything but small. Generally, these involve many tens of thousands (or hundreds of thousands) of lines of code and teams of many programmers.

**433**

As the size of a project grows, the development cost grows more than linearly, a trend reflected by the curve shown in Fig. 7-1. This is due largely to the rapidly increasing complexity of large projects and the basic human inability to manage this complexity. Cost and time overruns are the inevitable result.

The second dominant fact is summarized in the term "software evolution." Software changes constantly, to accommodate new user requirements, to fix discovered bugs, and to fit new host systems. In many practical situations, the "maintenance time" for a piece of software vastly exceeds its development time under the presumption that it is easier to modify a piece of working software than to build something totally new. Applying Band-aids when surgery is required, however, leads to more problems than it avoids.

Much of software engineering deals with the management of complexity. In this chapter we begin by discussing in Sec. 7-2 the phases of a software project, or the "software life cycle." We turn then to the design process in Sec. 7-3 and then to implementation in Sec. 7-4. Section 7-5 looks at testing and debugging. Section 7-6 considers the effects of the human condition on the process of programming. An extensive bibliography is provided for those wishing to pursue these matters in more depth.

## 7-2   THE SOFTWARE LIFE CYCLE

A large-scale software project spans a considerable period of time. A number of distinct phases can be identified over this period of time. Together, these make up what is known as the "software life cycle."

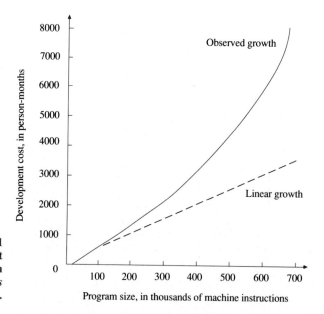

**FIGURE 7-1**
**Project development cost as a function of size** (*from Brooks 1975*).

While the actual terminology may differ, most authors identify five key phases in the software life cycle. These are

*1.* Requirements definition: The requirements of the software are established and specified.

*2.* Design: A design is developed from an analysis of the requirements.

*3.* Implementation: The design is coded in a particular programming language on a particular machine.

*4.* Testing: The implemented system is tested to see that it meets the specified requirements.

*5.* Operation and maintenance: The system is installed and used. Errors found must be repaired.

While a software project can be described in terms of these five phases, the actual development process itself is an iterative one, with both feedforward and feedback components. Each phase feeds something forward, upon which subsequent phases are based, but each phase also feeds information back to earlier phases. Implementation, for example, reveals design flaws; testing reveals implementation errors. Each phase has an input and an output—an output that must be checked carefully before being passed on.

The first phase, *requirements definition*, refers to the period during which the requirements of the system desired, that is, its functional characteristics and operational details, are specified. The input to this phase is the stated (often rather loosely stated) needs for the software. Typically, a "requirements document" is the output of this phase, a set of precisely stated properties or constraints that the final product must satisfy. This is not a design, but rather precedes the design, specifying *what* the system should do without specifying *how* it is to do it. The existence of a requirements document provides something against which a design (the next phase in the life cycle) can be validated. Sometimes a quickly developed prototype can be a useful vehicle for debugging requirements.

As with any of the phases, it is important that errors not be allowed to move into subsequent phases. An error in requirements, for example, a misstated function, leads to a faulty design and an implementation that does not do what is required. If this is allowed to proceed undetected, say, until the testing phase, the cost of repairing this error (including redesign and reimplementation) can be substantial. This is reflected in Fig. 7-2, which shows how the cost of fixing such an error grows exponentially with the phase in which it is detected. (Note the logarithmic cost scale!) Barry Boehm refers to this as the "price of procrastination" with respect to error detection. More will be said on this later. Requirements are most effectively validated by reviewing the requirements document with the client for whom the software is being developed.

The second phase, *design*, is predominantly creative. While some would argue that creativity is inherent and cannot be trained or improved, it can

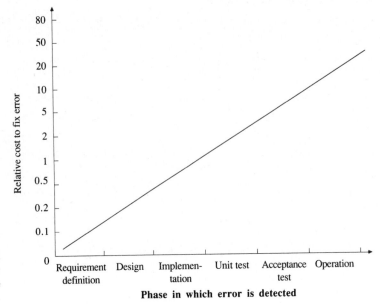

certainly be enhanced by the use of good procedures and tools. This will be discussed at length in Sec. 7-3. The input to this phase is a (debugged and validated) requirements document; the output is a design expressed in some appropriate form (for example, pseudocode). Validation of a design is important. Each requirement in the requirements document must have a corresponding design fragment to meet it. Formal verification, while possible to a limited extent, can be exceedingly difficult. More informal reviews involve the entire design team, management, and even the client.

The third phase, *implementation*, is the actual coding of the design developed in the second phase. Many aspects of this process are discussed in Sec. 7-4. The lure of this phase is strong, and many a foolhardy programmer has been drawn to it before adequately laying the groundwork in the first two phases. As a result, requirements are incompletely understood and the design is flawed. The implementation proceeds blindly, and many problems arise as a result.

The fourth phase, *testing*, is concerned with demonstrating the correctness of the implemented program. Inevitably, some testing is performed as part of the previous two phases as well. Any experienced programmer mentally tests each line as it is produced and mentally simulates the execution of any module prior to any formal testing stage. Testing is never easy. Edsger Dijkstra has written that while testing effectively shows the *presence* of errors, it can never show their *absence*. A "successful" test run means only that no errors were uncovered with the particular circumstances tested; it says nothing about other circumstances. In theory, the only way that testing can show that a program is correct is if *all* possible cases are tried (known as an *exhaustive* test), a situation technically impossible for even the simplest programs. Suppose, for example, that we have written a program to compute the average grade on an examination. An exhaustive test would require all possible combinations of marks and class sizes; it could take many years to complete the test.

Does this mean that testing is pointless? Definitely not. The programmer can do much to reduce the number of test cases to be used from the number required by an exhaustive test. With care and effort applied to the design of test cases, many superfluous cases can be eliminated and a reasonable test can possibly be made on a relatively small number of cases.

Testing a program is every bit as much an art as creating it and must be approached with the same diligence and enthusiasm. Certain principles of testing seem clear. Try to approach the testing of a program with a sabotage mentality, the type that delights in forcing an error to reveal itself. Be suspicious of everything. Test cases should be designed both from the original program specifications and from the program itself. If done only from the program, some aspect of the problem overlooked in the implementation is likely to be overlooked in the testing as well. To reduce the chances of this sort of thing happening in professional programming shops, many managers insist that persons other than the original programmer design the test cases for a program. Purchasers of programs often have their own independently developed test data ready when the program is delivered to them. Appreciate that managers view with considerable disfavor programmers whose programs fail a customer acceptance test, since this reflects badly on the entire organization and can affect its reputation in the marketplace. However it is done, a thorough test is an essential part of any programming project.

Student programmers, unfortunately, rarely become involved in the fifth stage of the programming process, *program maintenance*. Its importance in the real world, however, cannot be overemphasized, since the cost of maintaining a widely used program can match or exceed the cost of developing it. Unlike hardware maintenance, software maintenance deals not with repair of deteriorated components, but with repair of design defects, which may include the provision of added functions to meet new needs. The ability of programmers to produce *new* programs is clearly affected by the amount of time they spend maintaining *old* ones. The inevitability of maintenance must be recognized, and steps must be taken to reduce its time consumption.

The total cost of a software project is a function of the time involved and the number of people working on the project over its entire lifetime. The breakdown of the software life cycle into constituent phases provides for a finer analysis of this cost. It has been observed repeatedly that these phases contribute unequally to the total cost of a project. As has already been mentioned, for example, the maintenance phase (phase 5) may contribute as much as all the development phases (phases 1 through 4) combined. It is the job of the software engineer to keep *total* cost as low as possible. This is done by apportioning time judiciously among all the phases. Inadequate time spent in one phase (for example, testing) leads to problems in subsequent phases (here, maintenance) and increases total cost. It has been claimed that much of the maintenance effort in actual projects is due not to coding (or implementation) errors, but to changes or errors in requirements and to poor design.

In the remaining sections of this chapter we concentrate largely on issues of program design, program implementation, and program testing and debugging. We cannot, however, overlook the other components of the task as listed in this section. In practice, these are often strongly interconnected; as a result, it is difficult, and perhaps even unwise, to attempt to treat them in isolation. At times, in fact, the most important effects of a decision at some stage may well be felt most strongly in later phases of a project.

## 7-3  DESIGN ISSUES

Once the requirements of a desired system are analyzed and understood, a system can then be designed to satisfy these requirements. Next to understanding a given problem, the most important phase in developing a system is the design phase. Time spent in the design phase greatly affects the implementation, testing, and maintenance activities. It also determines how well the system resulting from the design phase will meet its requirements. The design activity is guided by several system design goals. These goals are used to evaluate a design. This section describes a set of possible design goals. Several design principles which support these design goals are described next. The remainder of the section deals with aspects of performing the activity of systems design.

### 7-3.1  BASIC SYSTEMS CONCEPTS

People often encounter complex situations (or problems) that are also either unstructured or poorly structured. To deal with complexity, we must first organize it and understand it. We must discover (or impose) some kind of order and structure. One of the most general and powerful notions of structure and order is that of a system (a word, in fact, whose Greek origin means "standing together").

We define a *system* as a set of interrelated components that can be viewed as a whole. The components of the system work together, in general, to perform several functions or to achieve several objectives. A *function* of a system is the work, activity, or task that a system performs. An *objective* of a system is the purpose or goal that the system serves in carrying out its function(s).

The solar system is an example of a well-known system, a system whose behavior is described by the laws of gravity and Kepler's laws.

A football game is another example of a system. A football game has as its major components the two teams, the playing field, the various pieces of football equipment, the officials, the actions of the players, and the score. The rules of football define the valid ways in which these components can be arranged and can interact. These rules, which are an essential part of the system, in essence define the possible relationships among the components (that is, the system structure). The function of the system is to play football. A football game may have many objectives. For example, it may entertain certain fans or provide employment to several classes of people (such as players and coaches).

In designing a computer system, it is important for each part of the system to correspond to one small, well-defined part of the problem. Furthermore, each relationship between the various parts of the problem is reflected by a corresponding relationship between the pieces of the system. This approach to design is important for several reasons, e.g., minimizing implementation and maintenance costs of a system.

One of the primary goals in the remainder of this section is to focus on the architecture of systems and programs. In the design of a system, we shall use the term "module" instead of component. Questions about the design of a system may include the following:

How should a system be organized into modules?

What is a good (or best) organization of modules?

What is a good module?

What is a bad module?

What should be the interface between modules?

The answers to such questions depend on certain design goals such as reliability, simplicity, maintainability, acceptability, and efficiency. Other factors that may influence decisions include the programming language, hardware, and software available. Design goals are described in more detail in the next subsection.

We conclude this subsection with a more precise definition of the term "module." Previously, we have used module in the general sense of a component of a program. Unfortunately, various authors have defined a module in slightly different ways. Many programming languages, e.g., FORTRAN and Pascal, directly support only one mechanism for organizing a program into components, namely, the subprogram. It is natural, when designing systems to be implemented in such languages, to equate the concept of module and subprogram. Each module becomes a subprogram, except for one module representing the main program.

Recently, it has been realized that limiting a module to be a single subprogram is too restrictive for some design methods. The more general definition allows a module to be a *collection of definitions, declarations, and operations*. A subprogram can still be a module by this definition. We now admit other possibilities, however, such as a purely *declarative module*, which makes its declarations available to other modules. Later in this chapter and in subsequent chapters we shall also consider modules which are *packages*, each containing the declarations for some data structure and subprograms representing the useful operations on that structure. Standard Pascal has no direct support for such modules. More recent languages, and some extended versions of Pascal, however, provide this support. For example, in the Ada language, a module may be a subprogram, a package, or a task. We shall assume the more general definition of a module unless stated otherwise.

## 7-3.2 GOALS OF SYSTEMS DESIGN

For systems design to be an engineering discipline, we require the definition of objectives or goals for the systems being designed. These goals lead to criteria that are used to evaluate design decisions. Goals that have proven useful in the design of systems include reliability, modifiability, understandability, utility, and efficiency. We now elaborate on each of these goals.

### Reliability

A most important goal in producing systems is that of reliability. In systems that operate with little human intervention, this goal may be critical. Reliability has recently been viewed as a problem in design. If reliability is not built into a system, it is virtually impossible to include it as an afterthought.

### Modifiability

Modifiability deals with controlled change in a given system. First, a system may have to be modified because an error that was introduced earlier in the development process must be corrected. More generally, a system is said to be *maintainable* if errors can be discovered, analyzed, and corrected in an easy manner. Second, a change in requirements for a system may require its modification. Changeability reflects the ease in modifying an existing system to accommodate such changes in requirements. That a system is modifiable implies that changes to it can be accommodated without increasing, to any significant degree, its original complexity.

### Understandability

The third goal in software design, understandability, helps in managing the complexity of systems. A system is said to be understandable if it directly reflects a natural view of the world. A characteristic of an effective system is *simplicity*. In general, a simple system can be understood more easily than can a complex one.

### Utility

*Utility* refers to the ease of use of a system. Much attention is given to utility in the early stages of software development, but its importance is sometimes forgotten in the design and implementation phases. A general lack of understanding of human factors can lead to such a situation. Implementation decisions sometimes result in poor user interfaces.

### Efficiency

The goal of efficiency is to make optimal use of scarce resources. Traditionally, efficiency has involved time and space resources. Some individuals have taken a narrow view of efficiency. In particular, efficiency is often viewed simply as increased execution speed or decreased memory requirements. In recent years, however, scarce resources have been interpreted as being not just CPU and main memory. Scarce resources also may include a variety of peripheral equipment, etc., as well as telecommunications equipment and personnel time. In some systems, time efficiency may be a very important goal; yet, in others, it may be a secondary goal.

These goals are reasonable for most systems. Such goals, however, are seldom achieved by applying just any development approach. Instead, we must use development methodologies that employ principles that support these goals. We discuss these underlying principles in the next subsection.

## 7-3.3 PRINCIPLES OF SYSTEMS DESIGN

It is well understood that one way of dealing with complexity is to chop (or decompose) a system into manageable pieces. There are many possible ways of dividing a system into modules. Some of these divisions, however, do not lead to a well-organized system. There are several design principles that support design goals. These include the principles of modularity, localization, abstraction, and information hiding.

### Modularity and Localization

Recall that an important principle that helps us deal with system complexity is modularity. Throughout this book we have attempted to use modularity to make the solution of a given problem easier. The decomposition of a solution has resulted in a set of modules (procedures and functions to this point).

In the top-down development strategy that we have used throughout the text, we have usually decomposed each successive level into different modules. Frequently, the higher-level modules have specified what actions are to be performed, while lower-level modules have defined how the actions are to be performed.

System reliability is enhanced by providing well-defined interfaces for modules. The modules that make up a system often interact with each other. The degree or strength of interconnection or *coupling* among modules is a very important notion. Loosely coupled (as opposed to tightly coupled) modules are desirable because each module can then be handled in a relatively independent manner. Another important concept that can be applied to modularity is *cohesion*. The cohesion of a module relates to how tightly bound or related the elements of the module are to each other. A well-designed module should exhibit strong cohesion. Coupling and cohesion will be described in detail in Sec. 7-3.6.

The principle of *localization* (that is, the notion of physical proximity) can help us design modules that are loosely coupled and strongly cohesive. Collecting all related elements into one module usually ensures that the module has strong cohesion. Localization then supports the independence of modules, which results in loosely coupled modules.

The principles of modularity and localization help in producing systems which are reliable, modifiable, and understandable. In a well-designed system, a given module should be understandable by itself, without requiring knowledge of the details of other modules. The localizing of design decisions to certain modules will ensure that the effects of modification will be limited to a manageable set of modules. Finally, the proper modularization of a system will result in simpler connections among modules, thus reducing the complexity of the system and enhancing its reliability.

### Abstraction and Information Hiding

The complexity of a system can be managed by using *abstraction*. Abstraction is a common principle that is applied in many situations. The main idea is to define a part of a system so that it can be understood by itself (that is, as a unit) without knowledge of its details or specifics and without knowing how this unit is used at a higher level. Most programming languages support abstraction at least through a subprogram facility (e.g., procedures and functions). This type of facility supports *procedural abstraction*. Another type of abstraction, *data abstraction*, is supported only by a few languages (such as Modula-2 and Ada).

The purpose of data abstraction is to isolate each data structure (or object) and its associated actions. For example, assume that we have some data structure (say, **Customers**) which is used in a given application to hold information about customers. Assume that the operations or actions to be performed on this data structure include those of insertion, deletion, and searching. These operations are done at the record or customer level. The isolation of **Customers** in some module, as shown in Fig. 7-3, is an example of data abstraction.

This form of module diagram is described by Grady Booch. The large rectangle represents the module itself. Along the wall of the module are several oval and rectangular shapes which represent the elements of the module accessible to other modules, its *interface*. These include objects, which are type and variable declarations, represented by ovals, and operations, which are procedures and functions, represented by the rectangles. An amorphous shape within the module represents the details of the implementation, which are hidden from its users.

In Fig. 7-3, the three rectangles represent the availability of the insert, delete, and search operations to users of the module. The correspondingly labeled rectangles within the module represent the implementation of these operations within the module. The fact that the **Customers** rectangle within the module is not named in an oval on the rectangle indicates that this object is not directly accessible to other modules. It can be manipulated only by the use of the operations provided at the module's interface. This guarantees, provided the operations are implemented correctly, that the implementation of the object remains consistent with its abstraction. (The oval object shown on the module boundary is not the object **Customers**. It might, for example, be a type declaration needed for parameter passing to the operations.)

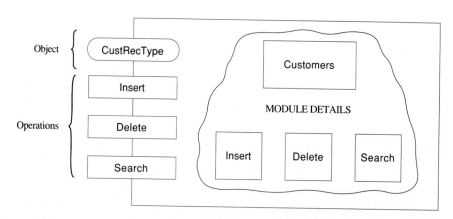

Object { CustRecType

Operations { Insert

Delete

Search

Customers

MODULE DETAILS

Insert    Delete    Search

**FIGURE 7-3**
**Example of**
**data abstraction.**

Thus we see that any reference to the object by any other module must be done by a subprogram call. This call applies one of the actions to the data object. In this example, we have also used another principle of design, namely, *information hiding*. The purpose of information hiding is to make inaccessible certain details that do not affect the other modules in the system. Thus the object and its actions constitute a closed system, the details of which are hidden from the other modules. In the current example, the data object **Customers** is *abstracted*, since it is available to other modules only through the insert, delete, and search operations that have defined results. **Customers** could be a set of parallel vectors, an array of structures, or some other data structure. To the outside world (that is, to other modules) this does not matter. The only thing that matters is the *logical view*. That is, we can insert, delete, and search on a record (or customer) basis.

Both types of abstractions (procedure abstraction and data abstraction) should be supported by a programming language to most readily achieve maintainable and reliable systems. Pascal supports procedure abstraction but has no specific support for data abstraction. However, data abstraction can be used as a design principle for modularizing a system which is to be implemented in Pascal. Each module is then implemented as a package of constant definitions, type definitions, variable declarations, procedure declarations, and function declarations. We will use this technique in the next chapter, for example, for abstracting the *stack* data structure.

Using Pascal for implementing data abstractions has several disadvantages. First, standard Pascal requires all constant definitions in a program to occur in one place, followed by all type definitions, etc. Each module implementing a data abstraction must be split into its constant, type, variable, and procedure parts, and these must be inserted in the appropriate places in the program.

The second problem is that names of constants, types, variables, procedures, and functions might conflict when several modules are included in a program. It is usually necessary to enforce some convention to prevent this.

Finally, this technique of implementing data abstraction does not enforce information hiding. Although the programmer is expected to use only the public operations of the module, the compiler cannot detect and report on violations of this policy.

Several Pascal compilers include extensions supporting data abstractions. For example, UCSD Pascal includes the concept of a *unit* to represent a module or package. Similarly, version 4.0 of Turbo Pascal provides an extension for defining modules. More recent programming languages, for example, Modula-2 and Ada, support data abstraction, as mentioned previously.

## 7-3.4 OVERVIEW OF DESIGN METHODOLOGIES

The general design principles of the previous subsection cannot be applied in a vacuum. We must arrive at a desired system structure in an organized manner. Essentially, we must formulate *criteria* for decomposing a system into a set of well-organized modules. Several design methodologies provide such decomposition criteria. These include

*1.* (Top-down) Structured design

*2.* Object-oriented design

*3.* Data-structure design

The design technique that has probably received the most attention and has been used in many projects (large and small) is referred to as *structured design*. This technique, as described by Larry Constantine, and further advanced by Edward Yourdon and Glenford Myers, is concerned with the functional decomposition of a system into a set of well-structured modules. Modularity is measured in terms of two criteria: coupling and cohesion. The main goal of structured design is to generate a system structure in which the modules are loosely coupled and highly cohesive.

It is desirable that the higher-level modules be relatively machine independent. Usually, each higher-level module specifies what action is to be taken. A lower-level module, on the other hand, specifies how the action is to be performed. Important decisions are made at the top of the hierarchy, while less important decisions are made at lower levels. The methodology is based on data flow in, out, and through a system. This flow of data (and its associated processing) is represented by *data flow diagrams*, which we shall discuss shortly. Designs are obtained from these data flow diagrams.

There are two main strategies for generating a system (or module) structure that matches the problem structure as described by data flow diagrams. In the first method, each independent data flow is regarded as a transaction that requires a special response by the system. The structure of a design contains a *transaction center*, which consists of modules that handle each type of transaction. This approach is called *transaction analysis* or *transaction-centered design*. A second approach, *transform analysis*, involves identifying important transformations (or functions) in the system. Such transformations become a *transform center* in the design structure. Structured design also provides other criteria (besides coupling and cohesion) for evaluating the quality of a design. Structured design focuses primarily on the operations or functions performed by a system, with less attention being given to the design of the data structures. More will be said on structured design in Secs. 7-3.6 and 7-3.7.

*Object-oriented design* is a relatively recent methodology which is currently being widely discussed and shows considerable promise. The scope of these discussions, however, has a range of vastly different meanings. For example, Smalltalk-80 and Ada, two extremely different programming languages, are often called object-oriented languages. Object-oriented development is based strongly on abstraction and information hiding.

The basic approach to object-oriented design is first to identify the abstract objects in a given problem. Then appropriate operations are defined for the objects. Finally, modules are developed that hide the implementation details.

Since there are many approaches to this methodology, we describe an

approach developed by R. Abbott and further advanced by Grady Booch. A **445**
summary of the steps in that approach is as follows: 7-3
DESIGN ISSUES

*1.* Define the problem specifications (essentially the requirements analysis phase of the system life cycle).

*2.* Formulate an informal strategy.

*3.* Formalize the informal strategy. This step includes the following:
   (*a*) Identifying objects and their attributes
   (*b*) Identifying operations on these objects
   (*c*) Establishing the interfaces between objects
   (*d*) Implementing the operations

We shall now describe each of these steps briefly.

The first step involves the usual step of defining the requirements for a given problem. This step is no different from that encountered in using other methodologies. For example, a data flow diagram (and its associated descriptions) could be the result of this step.

Once a basic understanding of the problem has been obtained, we proceed to give an informal strategy that parallels our view of the problem. This informal strategy is expressed in natural English descriptions which are given in terms of concepts from the problem area (or problem space). At this stage, we do not usually focus on the structure of a solution. Such a structure will evolve naturally as we proceed.

The final step in the methodology consists of formalizing the informal strategy created in the previous step. The first substep is to identify the *objects* and any associated attributes or properties. Common attributes involve constraints on an object such as a range of values. The implementation of this substep involves extracting, from the informal strategy description, nouns and any associated adjectives. The nouns and adjectives thus obtained represent objects and their associated attributes, respectively. Object-oriented programming languages contain constructs that facilitate the description of objects. Similar objects can be defined as a class. Each object is then a member of such a class. For example, in an interactive user interface we may have an object class dealing with screen windows. Particular instances of a screen window may include a workspace window, command window, message window, help window, etc.

The next substep is to identify the *operations* performed by an object or performed on an object. By extracting the verbs and adverbs from the informal strategy description, we obtain the operations and any associated attributes, respectively. The attributes of an operation specify the constraints on the operation. Examples of constraints include timing relationships, memory space, sequence of control, number of iterations, etc.

The third substep establishes the relationships among the objects. This substep involves describing the *visible* interfaces to each object. In Pascal, a subprogram (procedure or function) sees and is seen only by some (usually not all) other subprograms; objects see and are seen by other objects. Depending on the level of decomposition, certain objects may or may not be visible. In the real world, a given object interacts only with some small subset of all possible objects. Therefore, the scope and visibility of each object must be formally specified. In certain languages, such as FORTRAN or even Pascal, no provision is made for defining object interactions formally. In other languages, such as Modula-2, Smalltalk-80, and Ada, the object interfaces are specified more easily.

The fourth and final substep is the *implementation*, using a suitable programming language, of all operations associated with each object. This final substep is also accomplished more easily with a programming language with appropriate features.

The preceding methodology must be performed level by level. Thus at each successive level of decomposition, the objects and their associated operations applicable at that point of the design are identified and defined. We repeat this iterative process until we arrive at a level of decomposition which is understandable and cannot be further modularized.

The third design methodology, *data-structure design*, has become widely accepted first in Europe and recently in North America. This method has been successful in the design of business data-processing applications. Contributors to this approach to design are Jean-Dominique Warnier, Ken Orr, and Michael Jackson. The design is based on the structures of the inputs and outputs of the system. Such structures are not to be confused with the representation of data objects in memory.

We illustrate the basic notions of data-structure design by using a simple example. Suppose that we are to design a system to process and generate invoices for customers of a farm parts dealership. The input consists of a group of records for each customer. The first record in each group is a header record which contains an invoice number, the character 'H', and the customer's name and address. Each of the remaining records in the group contains the invoice number, the character 'D', the date of purchase, part name, quantity, and unit price. The output from the system is an invoice that contains an invoice number and the customer's name and address.

For each farm part purchased, a detail line containing the date of purchase, part name, quantity, unit price, and total part value is to be printed. The total part value on each detail line is obtained by multiplying quantity by unit price. The last line of the printed invoice is to contain

TOTAL SALES    TOTAL INVOICE AMOUNT

The structure of the input and output data is illustrated in Fig. 7-4. Observe that braces around a component, for example, "{group}," indicate repetition of the component.

Assuming that we process the input sequentially (that is, batch), a suitable program structure outline for the invoice system is given in Fig. 7-5. Observe that the structure of the program and the structure of the input and output data are similar. Since the input data consists of groups of records, the program also contains a loop that is executed once for each group of records. The outside loop control is based on an end-of-file test for the input file. Each group consists of a header record followed by an unknown number of

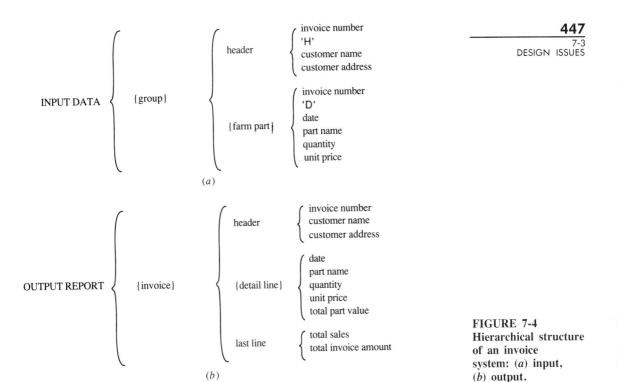

*(a)*

*(b)*

**FIGURE 7-4**
**Hierarchical structure**
**of an invoice**
**system:** (*a*) **input,**
(*b*) **output.**

detail records. Consequently, the program structure contains a sequence that processes one header record followed by a loop which handles all the detail records associated with that header record. The structure of the program in this example is also similar to the structure of the output produced.

In the current example, the structure of the system inputs and outputs was similar, and consequently, the design of a suitable program is straightforward. In more complex problems, however, the structures of the system inputs and outputs are not similar. In these situations, we have a *structure clash*. Such a clash makes the design of a suitable program more difficult. One approach in dealing with this problem is to create an intermediate form of data with a structure that does not clash with either the inputs or the outputs. The program can be divided into two parts, with the first part

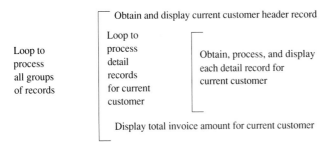

**FIGURE 7-5**
**Program structure**
**for generating invoices.**

processing the inputs to this intermediate form and the second taking the intermediate form and producing the desired outputs.

## 7-3.5 DESIGN NOTATIONS

Just as an architect uses "blueprints" to specify the design of a building (more generally, as a means of communicating the design to humans), developers of software systems need notations to show the various facets of a system throughout its life cycle. Although a computer program is the ultimate product, its use is not suitable for conveying the design of the system to a variety of people such as end users, system analysts, system designers, and programmers. To communicate effectively with such a variety of individuals requires more than one notation. A notation which is effective and understandable to a user community probably will not be suitable for the implementors of the system.

Many notations have been invented to describe a system to different groups of individuals illustrating and defining, in an organized manner, different levels of that system. In the interest of brevity, we restrict our discussion to the following complementary notations which have been used to describe a software design.

1. *Data flow diagrams*: These diagrams are used in the analysis phase (or requirements definition phase) and early design phases to portray the flow and transformation of data in, out, and within a system.

2. *Structure charts*: These charts have already been introduced informally in earlier chapters. The hierarchical diagrams show the decomposition of higher-level modules into subordinate modules. A structure chart typically contains several levels of decomposition.

3. *A problem description language*: This is usually a very high level language that contains ordinary programming language features (e.g., as in Pascal) with additional features for specifying a detailed design. Examples of such features support data abstraction and information hiding.

Data flow diagrams and structure charts are graphical notations that are ideal for illustrating the complex structure of many software systems. Occasionally, a problem description language is also graphically oriented.

### Data Flow Diagrams

During the requirements definition (analysis) phase, an analyst gathers large volumes of mostly unstructured data from several sources, such as reference manuals, interviews with potential users, sample system reports, etc. It is crucial that all this information be organized and summarized. It is required that such an organized summary serve a variety of purposes. For example, it should simplify communications between the analyst and the end users. Also, it should be in a form which is useful in supporting the remaining phases of development, particularly the design phase.

A data flow diagram can provide such an organized summary. It is a graphical notation which is meant to represent a logical model of a system.

It is meant to show *what* is being done by the system rather than *how* it is done. A data flow diagram is not concerned with hardware, software, and the data structures which eventually will be used as these are details of implementation.

Contributors to the development of data flow diagrams include Chris Gane, Trish Sarson, and Tom DeMarco. The notation that we use is similar to that developed by DeMarco.

A data flow diagram shows the transformation of inputs to outputs. In representing a system by a data flow diagram, the input and output data flows define the boundaries of the system. Four kinds of symbols are used, as shown in Fig. 7-6. A rectangle symbol represents an *external entity* (or *interface*). External entities supply inputs to the system or receive outputs from the system. The name of an external entity is written inside the rectangle box. A circle symbol (or bubble) represents a *process* which transforms data. It represents the transformation of some input data to produce some output data. A brief description of the process is written inside the bubble. This description should consist of an active verb (e.g., validate, read, search) followed by an object clause to describe the process precisely. A directed edge symbol (arrow) represents a *data flow*. The name of a data flow is written next to the edge. An open-ended square symbol denotes a *data store*. This data store is independent of physical medium, since, again, that is an implementation detail. Data flows and data stores correspond to data structures. The name of a data store is written inside the rectangle, and it should be descriptive. A data store represents information that is maintained by the system for some period of time. A data flow is a data structure in motion, while a data store is a data structure at rest. A process can be a computer program (e.g., a compiler), a manual process (e.g., a clerical operation), or anything else that performs a transformation of data. Similarly, a data store may represent a manual file, an electronic file, a table in main memory, a data base, etc.

Figure 7-7 shows a simple example of a data flow diagram for the familiar compile-execute sequence. It shows in a very high level manner a source program (along with data) being submitted by a programmer to a

External entity or
interface
(sender or recipient
of data)

Process
(transforms data)

Data flow
(data structure in motion)

Data store
(data structure at rest)

**FIGURE 7-6**
**Basic elements of a**
**data flow program.**

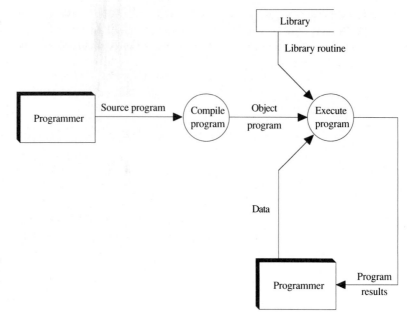

**FIGURE 7-7**
**Data flow diagram**
**for compiling and**
**executing a program.**

compiler and then the corresponding object program being executed, thereby producing results. The data store **Library** represents a set of precoded routines (such as built-in functions) which are part of the programming support system. Note that we have not included possible error reporting due to syntax, semantic, or run-time errors. Typically, such errors would be incorporated in a more detailed data flow diagram. It is sometimes desirable, for the sake of clarity and the minimizing of the crossing of data flow lines, to replicate data stores and external entities (interfaces). In the example diagram, the interface **Programmer** has been replicated.

An important way to describe and analyze the requirement specifications of a system, in conjunction with data flow diagrams, involves the use of a *data dictionary*. A data dictionary is a tool that records the definitions and composition (that is, structure) of all data flows, data stores, interfaces, and processes in a data flow diagram. Additional volume and frequency information can also be entered for the diagram components. Most current data dictionary systems are computerized, and consequently, the requirements specifications are in machine-readable form—a form that is easily modified and updated.

Data flow diagrams can be produced in a top-down fashion. A general algorithm for constructing data flow diagrams in such a way consists of the following steps:

*1.* Identify all the system's interfaces.

*2.* Identify all the inputs and outputs in the given system. (The interfaces, inputs, and outputs of a system define its boundaries. These boundaries can be represented pictorially by a *context diagram*, as shown in Fig. 7-8.)

3. Starting with each interface that produces some input, drawn on the left-hand side of the paper, draw the data flows, data stores, and processes that are required to produce the outputs received by the interfaces, drawn on the right-hand side of the paper. If this left-to-right construction strategy fails at some point in the construction process, you may want to move from the middle toward the inputs and outputs or from the outputs toward the inputs.

4. Label all data flows, data stores, and processes and include their descriptions in the data dictionary.

5. Draw a high-level free-hand diagram for the system. In the first draft, ignore error checking, exception handling, and initialization and termination (as in file processing) considerations.

6. Prepare a cleaner draft of the data flow diagram using replicated

**FIGURE 7-8   Context diagram for radiologist's billing system.**

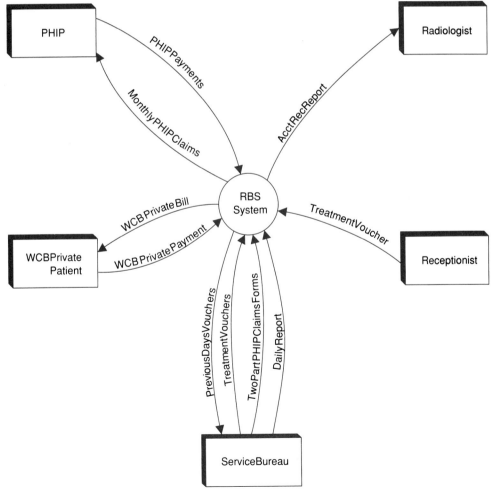

interfaces and data stores in order to minimize intersecting data flows.

7. Conduct a review of the diagram with a user and/or colleague in order to verify its correctness. Make any necessary modifications before developing more detailed diagrams.

8. For each process in the final version of the high-level data flow diagram, repeat step 9 until each process has been defined to a desired level.

9. Explode or decompose (that is, elaborate) the current process into a more detailed data flow diagram. Make any required changes to the parent diagram.

We now illustrate some of the results of applying this strategy to the development of a simple billing system for a radiologist (henceforth abbreviated **RBS**). We do not give a complete development because of its length.

A radiologist is a private doctor who provides x-ray services for patients referred to him or her by other doctors. A particular radiologist (Radiologist) and his staff of x-ray technicians treat up to 100 patients a day, although a typical daily load is 50 to 60 patients. For most patients (about 95 percent of them), the service is paid for by the Provincial Health Insurance Plan (PHIP). The remaining 5 percent of patients are about equally divided between those charged to the Workman's Compensation Board (WCBPatient) and those billed privately (PrivatePatient).

The operation of the system is as follows. When a patient arrives for a treatment, a receptionist (Receptionist) prepares a form called a treatment voucher (TreatmentVoucher) that contains information about the patient and a list of the x-ray treatments to be provided. One copy of this voucher is sent to the radiologist's accounting office. Each day the batch of vouchers for the previous day's operation (PreviousDaysVouchers) is sent to the service bureau (ServiceBureau), where PHIP claim forms (TwoPartPHIPClaimForms) are printed. The service bureau also prepares a daily treatment report (DailyReport) of the day's work, showing information for each patient and summary totals of the fees for the day, for the month to date, and for the year to date, broken down into PHIP, WCB, and private patient accounts. The vouchers (TreatmentVouchers), the two-part PHIP claim forms, and the treatment report are returned to the radiologist's accounting office for further processing and distribution. Once a month a statement of accounts receivable (AcctRecReport) is prepared manually using the summary data of new accounts from the daily reports (DailyReport) produced by the service bureau and from the payment record (PaymentRecord) contained in the receipts journal (ReceiptsJournal).

The problem to be solved is the computerization of the radiologist's accounting office. The service bureau will continue to provide its external processing services. We therefore analyze the operation of the accounting office. Applying steps 1 and 2 of the general algorithm for the production of data flow diagrams, we arrive at the context diagram in Fig. 7-8. The interfaces of the system are PHIP, Radiologist, Receptionist, ServiceBureau, and WCBPrivatePatient (the WCB and private patients combined). The input to the PHIP interface is the MonthlyPHIPClaims, and the output from PHIP is the payments made on claims (PHIPPayments). The input to the Radiologist is the monthly statement of accounts receivable. The output from the Receptionist is one copy of the treatment voucher. The service bureau has for input the vouchers sent to it for the previous day and for output the two-part PHIP claim forms, the daily treatment report, and the treatment vouchers (which it sends back after processing). The input to WCBPrivatePatient is the bills for the private and WCB patients, while the output is the payments from these patients.

You will notice that the entities PaymentRecord and ReceiptsJournal are not present in the context diagram. This is so because we do not concern ourselves with data stores and their corresponding inputs and outputs in a context diagram. These entities become visible as we apply steps 3 through 6 to produce the high-level data flow diagram in Fig. 7-9.

In this diagram, we also see the processes which are required to produce the outputs within the system. The data stores are the PHIPClaimsFile, which stores the claim forms, the PatientFile, which stores the patient records, the ReceiptsJournal, which holds payments records, and the DailyReportFile, which holds the daily treatment reports. The processes in the system are ProcessVouchers, SaveReport, MakeAcctsRecStatement, and ProcessBilling.

Each of the processes in the high-level diagram now needs to be exploded, as outlined in step 9 of the general algorithm. We choose to explode only one of these processes for the sake of illustration. Figure 7-10 is an explosion of the process ProcessBilling (from Fig. 7-9), which represents the billing activity that takes place in the radiologist's accounting office. The more detailed description of this process is as follows: A member of the accounting office staff separates the two-part claim forms (PHIPClaimForm). One copy (PHIPBills) is saved in a batch for monthly submission to PHIP, while the other copy, when attached to the matching treatment voucher, forms a patient record (PatientRecord), which is placed in a file of active patient accounts (ActivePatientFile). For accounts other than PHIP, bills (WCBBill, PrivateBill) are prepared manually and sent immediately to WCB patients (WCBPatient) or to the private patient (PrivatePatient). For these cases, the treatment voucher alone constitutes a patient record and is filed with the active patient accounts. When payments (PHIPPayments, WCBPayment, PrivatePayment) are received, the appropriate records are removed from the active account file, marked "paid," and placed in a file of paid patient accounts (PaidPatientFile). Payments are also recorded (PaymentRecord) in the receipts journal.

You will notice that we have made some changes in going from the parent diagram to this diagram. We have, in fact, exploded some of the interfaces and data flows. For instance, the data flow WCBPrivateBill has been split up into WCBBill and PrivateBill and the interface WCBPrivatePatient has been split up into WCBPatient and PrivatePatient. This diagram now gives a more in-depth view of what is being done in ProcessBilling.

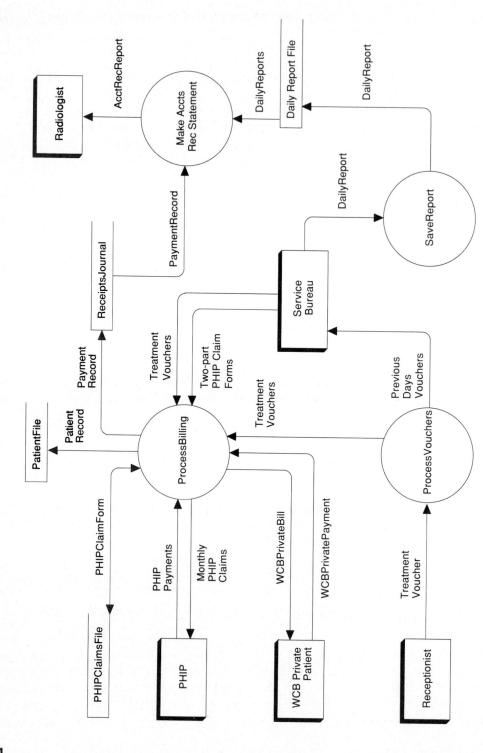

**FIGURE 7-9** Top-level data flow diagram for radiologist's billing system.

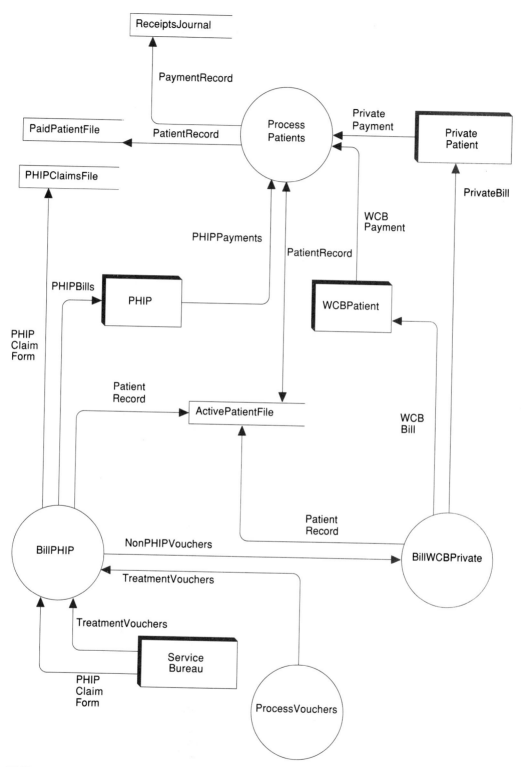

**FIGURE 7-10** Data flow diagram showing the explosion of the process Process Billing.

In a more compl63e set of specifications, we would include the composition, as well as size and volume, of all data flows and data stores. Also, we would specify the computational and logical details of each process. All this information should typically be entered into a computerized data dictionary system. Finally, observe that the error-checking and error-handling aspects of the system have also been ignored.

In closing this subsection, it should be noted that a data flow diagram does not show the following:

*1.* Decisions in the system

*2.* Loops in the system

*3.* Volume and size characteristics for data and/or processes

*4.* Calculations

*5.* How data stores are accessed, that is, on what key fields

### Structure Charts

In earlier chapters we used a form of hierarchy chart to show the partitioning of a system into modules and the hierarchy into which the modules are organized. The hierarchy chart was loosely called a structure chart. In this section we describe a structure chart more formally. In addition to showing the organization of a system into modules, a structure chart can also show the data and control interfaces among modules. Except for major decisions, a structure chart does not show the decision structure of a system.

The basic elements of a structure chart are given in Fig. 7-11. Each module in a structure chart is represented by a rectangle or box which contains a name (Fig. 7-11*a*). A module which invokes or calls another module is represented in a structure chart by a directed edge or arrow (Fig. 7-11*b*). The direction of the arrow shows which module is the superordinate module and which is the subordinate module. Where the superordinate-subordinate relationship is clear in a structure chart, we have often ignored drawing the arrowheads. A data couple is represented by a short arrow with an open

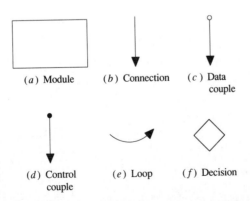

(*a*) Module     (*b*) Connection     (*c*) Data
couple

(*d*) Control     (*e*) Loop     (*f*) Decision
couple

**FIGURE 7-11**
**Basic symbols in**
**a structure chart.**

circular tail. The direction of the arrow denotes the direction of flow of the data couple (Fig. 7-11c). A *data couple* represents data which is processed. Similarly, a control couple which represents decision or logical information is represented by a short arrow with a solid circular tail (Fig. 7-11d). A *control couple* represents data which is tested (that is, not really processed) and is used for control-flow purposes. A semicircular directed edge denotes a major loop in a module (Fig. 7-11e). Finally, a diamond-shaped symbol represents a major decision within a module (Fig. 7-11f).

Examples of structure charts which exhibit the use of the basic symbols appear in Fig. 7-12. In Fig. 7-12a, module X invokes module Y, and data couple *a* travels from X to Y, data couple *c* travels from Y to X, and control couple *b* travels from Y to X. In Fig. 7-12b, module W, based on a major decision, calls either module X or Y. Module W, based on its major loop, repeatedly invokes module Z.

A structure chart does not show the internal specifications of a module, e.g., its logic and computational details and its internal data structures. Such details must be described by other means.

## Design Description Languages

A software design must be described using some form of language. Some system designers have used an existing high-level programming language such as Pascal or Ada. While this approach has the obvious advantage that the design specification is executable (assuming the availability of a compiler), it has some drawbacks. These include

*1.* Many existing high-level languages are not readily extended to include new concepts.

*2.* A system's designer may be adversely affected by the level of language constructs available in the existing high-level language being used.

*3.* Many existing high-level languages have low-level, primitive data types, structures, and operations. Some intuitively simple high-level constructs are sometimes difficult to describe in the language being used.

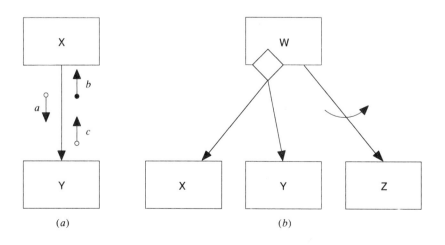

**FIGURE 7-12**
**Examples of structure charts.**
(*a*) **A simple chart.**
(*b*) **A chart containing a condition.**

**4.** If an initial design, specified in an existing programming language, has been implemented, it is difficult to reimplement a design in some other programming language.

An alternative (and better) approach to using an existing programming language for specifying a design is to use a design description language. Such languages are used specifically for documenting and specifying a design.

Design description languages usually use the control constructs available in existing high-level programming languages. Such design languages, however, permit a designer to be flexible in the description of data structures and their associated operations. English descriptions of operations are sometimes used, and additional control constructs may be created to specify certain parts of a design in attempts to improve the clarity of a design description. For example, a blend of our general algorithm approach and Pascal, augmented with a module capability, could be used as a vehicle for describing a design.

## 7-3.6  MODULE DESIGN

Although it is generally agreed that a large system should be divided or partitioned into modules if it is to be manageable, this division is no guarantee of a well-organized system. It is imperative, however, that this partitioning be carried out so as to make the modules independent of one another as much as possible. This criterion of modules independence, that is, module coupling, is examined first in this section. A second criterion for partitioning a system is that each module should carry out a single, problem-related function. This criterion of module cohesion is examined next. In addition to the criteria of coupling and cohesion, there are several other criteria or guidelines that can be used to evaluate and improve a design. A discussion of several of these guidelines concludes the section.

### Module Coupling

Recall from Sec. 7-3.3 that *coupling* refers to the degree of interdependence among modules. The degree of coupling can be used to evaluate the quality of a system design. We want to minimize coupling among modules, that is, minimize their interdependence. One extreme in coupling would be to have a system design (a hierarchy of modules) totally uncoupled. Since a system must perform some set of functions or tasks in some organized fashion, it cannot consist of a set of totally uncoupled modules. The other extreme would be to have a hierarchy of modules tightly coupled; that is, there is a high degree of dependence between each pair of modules in the design. Between these two extremes, there are many degrees of coupling.

Having a loosely coupled system facilitates:

*1.* The replacement of one module by another so that only a few modules will be affected by the change.

**2.** The tracking down of an error and the isolation of the defective module causing that error.

Having established the desirability of loosely coupled systems, we examine now the various kinds of coupling that can exist between two modules. Such a classification is given in Table 7-1. We examine the five types of coupling from the least desirable (that is, tightest coupling) to the most desirable (that is, loosest coupling). The strength of coupling between two modules is influenced by the type of connection, the type of communication between them, and the overall complexity of their interface.

**Content Coupling.** As indicated in Table 7-1, certain types of couplings are more desirable than others. The least desirable type of coupling is content coupling. Two modules exhibit *content coupling* if one module alters the other. In such a situation, the modified module is highly dependent on the modifying module. Examples of content coupling are when one module directly alters internal data within the other, when one module alters a statement within another module, or when one module transfers control (or branches) into the middle of a routine in another module. For example, Fig. 7-13 illustrates a form of content coupling where module E contains a branch to module D. This latter module, however, is supposed to be under the control of module B. Content-coupled modules are difficult to maintain. Content coupling cannot occur in programs in most programming languages, but it is possible in programs written in assembly languages.

**Common Coupling.** The degree of coupling can be reduced by placing data used by two or more modules in a global or common declarative area, such as variables declared in an outermost nested Pascal block, a FORTRAN COMMON block, or the accessible portion of an Ada package. Dependence among modules is still strong, since a change in the common data area potentially affects all modules that share the data. This type of coupling is called *common coupling*.

Drawbacks of common coupling include the following:

*1.* An error in a module sharing a common data area can affect any other module sharing that data area.

*2.* Modules that reference global data do so by actual names and not by parameters, thus requiring coordination of naming conventions among the modules involved in languages not supporting qualified naming.

*3.* Maintaining modules that share a substantial amount of common (or global) data is difficult. To maintain such modules, a programmer must

**TABLE 7-1** Classification of Module Coupling

| Type of Coupling | Degree of Coupling | Degree of Maintainability |
|---|---|---|
| Content | High (Tight) | Low |
| Common | ↑ | ↑ |
| Control | | |
| Stamp | ↓ | ↓ |
| Data | Low (Loose) | High |

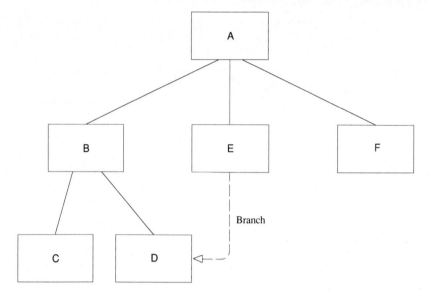

**FIGURE 7-13**
**Content coupling.**

determine what data is shared by each module and how this data is used and modified.

*4.* Changes to the global area require the determination of what modules are affected by these changes—not an easy task!

Although common coupling is preferable to content coupling, its use should be minimized.

**Control Coupling.** Two modules are said to be *control coupled* if one passes data items, called *control flags*, to the other in order to control the latter's internal logic. For example, assume that we have a module that can either perform an insertion or a retrieval in a given data structure such as an array. One of the parameters required by this module is a Boolean control flag. A value of "true" might denote an insertion and "false" might denote a retrieval. If an insertion is desired, the control flag value (that is, "true") is used by the module to control the execution of the appropriate statements which accomplish the indicated insertion. On the other hand, a control flag value of "false" ensures execution of the statements that perform a retrieval. If a subordinate module passes a control flag to a superordinate (that is, its superior), then the former controls the operation of the latter. This is usually not a desirable situation.

Control coupling between modules often indicates that the module being invoked is doing too much, that is, more than one functional task. For this reason, control-coupled modules are more difficult to maintain and to change than modules that are more loosely coupled.

**Stamp Coupling.** Two modules are said to be *stamp coupled* if a data structure is used as a communication medium. Both modules refer to the same data structure and require a knowledge of its makeup (that is, its form and contents). By a data structure here we mean a record structure consisting of several data items or, more generally, a set of nonhomogeneous elements. Stamp coupling is similar to common coupling except that the coupled modules share the data selectively. As a result, a module often gets exposed to more data than it requires to perform its assigned task. Such extraneous data can sometimes be changed inadvertently by a module with dire consequences. Also, a change in either format or structure of the data can affect all the coupled modules that refer to a common data structure—even those modules which do not use actual data items that have changed. We wish to emphasize, however, that stamp coupling is preferable to common coupling, since fewer modules need be changed when a shared data structure is altered.

**Data Coupling.** Two modules are said to be *data coupled* if they communicate through a parameter list, each parameter in the list being either a single data item or a homogeneous table (such as a vector of numbers). This is the simplest and most desirable kind of coupling between two modules. Two modules that are not even data coupled are uncoupled. The advantages of using data coupling are that we do not need to know the construction details of the other modules, data can be traced easily, and changes can be made more easily than if a tighter degree of coupling is used. In practice, a combination of data coupling and stamp coupling is probably the most desirable form of coupling between two modules.

More than one type of coupling can exist between two modules. For example, two modules could be control and common coupled. In this case, we determine their coupling as the strongest (or worst) coupling type, in this case, common coupled. They are also, however, control coupled.

The design and evaluation of a module's interface are influenced by such questions as the following:

How independently can a programmer work with respect to other programmers when implementing the particular module?

Is the module in its most usable form at a given computer installation?

Does a programmer have to be aware of certain details of other modules in the system?

## Module Cohesion

The previous subsection introduced the notion of coupling as a criterion for evaluating how well a system has been modularized. This criterion suggests that a well-modularized system is one in which the module interfaces are clear and simple. Another criterion for judging a design is to examine each module in a system and determine the strength of binding within that module. The internal strength of a module, that is, how strongly related the parts of a module are, is referred to as *cohesion*. A module whose parts are strongly related to each other and to the purpose or function of that module is said to be strongly cohesive. On the other hand, a module whose parts are not related to each other is weakly cohesive. Cohesion levels can be classified as shown in Table 7-2. We will describe each level of cohesion from the weakest (coincidental) to the strongest (informational).

**Coincidental Cohesion.** The weakest kind of cohesion occurs when the elements or parts of a module are completely unrelated to one another. Such a module is said to be *coincidentally cohesive*. For example, a module which generates the first 1000 prime numbers and produces a class list of grades in an introductory computer science class would be coincidentally cohesive. This type of situation might result from taking a long program and attempting to modularize it by segmenting it into modules of equal length, say, one page. Another possibility would be taking a group of several unrelated elements that appear in several other modules and forming a new module. Coincidentally cohesive modules have a very low maintainability.

**Logical Cohesion.** A module is said to have *logical cohesion* if its elements are related to a number of tasks of the same general kind or category. For example, consider a module designed to handle all input to a program (e.g., from terminals, disk, magnetic tape, cards, etc.) regardless of how the various items are to be used or where they are coming from. Since all parts of this module relate to the handling of input, the module is logically cohesive. Although more desirable than coincidental cohesion, the parts of a logically cohesive module are not related by either flow of data or flow of control. Since in the current example the different inputs probably serve different purposes in the program (that is, in different modules), several unrelated functions are being performed in the same module. A logically cohesive module is difficult to change and maintain. Since a logically cohesive module performs several different functions, to change one of these functions requires a search through all modules for the parts related to the functions being changed.

**Temporal Cohesion.** A module has *temporal cohesion* if its elements are involved in various activities that are related only in time. A familiar example of a temporally cohesive module is an initialization module that performs various activities at a certain time such as opening files, setting counters to zero, setting logical variables, initializing tables, etc. These activities have

---

**TABLE 7-2**  **Classification of Module Cohesion**

| Type of Cohesion | | Degree of Cohesion | Degree of Maintainability |
|---|---|---|---|
| Coincidental | | Low | Low |
| Logical | | ↑ | ↑ |
| Temporal ⎫ | Time-oriented | | |
| Procedural ⎭ | | | |
| Communicational ⎫ | Data-oriented | | |
| Sequential ⎭ | | ↓ | ↓ |
| Functional | | | |
| Informational | | High | High |

one thing in common—they are carried out at the same time. Changing and maintaining such a module are difficult, since it is tightly coupled to several other modules in the system.

**Procedural Cohesion.** In addition to being related by time, the parts of a module may have to be performed in a certain order. Such a module is said to have *procedural cohesion*. In a procedurally cohesive module, control flows from one activity to the next, and the elements in such a module are involved in different, and possibly unrelated, activities. The output produced by a procedurally cohesive module typically bears little relationship to its input data. With procedural cohesion, we have crossed the boundary from the difficult-to-maintain module with a low level of cohesion to more maintainable modules with middle levels of cohesion.

**Communicational Cohesion.** A module is *communicationally cohesive* if its elements contribute to activities that use the same input data or produce the same output data. These activities can sometimes be performed with only one tape or disk access. As an example, consider obtaining some details concerning a particular individual's income tax return. For instance, given the individual's social security number, we may wish to

Find the person's address.

Find the person's name.

Find the person's gross salary.

Find the number of dependents for that person.

These four activities are related because they all use a person's income tax record. Thus a module containing these activities is communicationally cohesive. There is a tendency in a communicationally cohesive module to share code among its activities, thereby degrading the changeability of that module. Although a communicationally cohesive module is reasonably maintainable, frequently its maintainability can be improved by splitting it into separate, more functional modules.

**Sequential Cohesion.** A module has *sequential cohesion* when its elements perform a sequence of activities such that the result or output of one activity becomes the input to the next activity in the sequence. For example, in a student record application, we might have the following sequence of four activities:

1. Read student number

2. Find student record having that student number

3. Output student information

4. Mail student information to student

Observe that the output from one step is the input to the next. This module is certainly cohesive. These four activities represent more than one functional activity. A sequentially cohesive module is easily maintained. Modules that have communicational, or sequential cohesion are data flow oriented. A sequentially cohesive module is usually loosely coupled to the other modules in a system.

**Functional Cohesion.** A module has *functional cohesion* if it performs one and only one activity. Examples of functionally cohesive modules include

> Compute the square root of a nonnegative number
>
> Compute sine of an angle
>
> Read weekly time record
>
> Verify student number
>
> Calculate final grade

Each of these modules performs a single activity. Such modules are highly cohesive. In many instances, a module performs either too many functional activities or only one part of one. Functionally cohesive modules are easily maintained and have good (that is, lowest) coupling.

**Informational Cohesion.** A module is *informationally cohesive* if it is an implementation of a nonprimitive abstract data structure and its associated operations. For example, we could have a module which implements a complex number (consisting of a real part and an imaginary part) and the four associated operations of addition, subtraction, multiplication, and division. Each operation is realized by a subprogram. Each subprogram is functionally cohesive. In an informationally cohesive module, only one functionally cohesive part of the module is executed each time the module is invoked. For example, if two complex numbers are to be added, the addition routine in the module is executed upon its invocation. Informational cohesion is the highest degree of cohesion. A module having this kind of cohesion has the best (that is, lowest) coupling and is highly maintainable. The next chapter will present several concrete examples of informationally cohesive modules.

Now that we have defined module cohesion and given some examples of it, the following question arises: How do we actually determine the level of cohesion of a given module? One good approach is to write a brief sentence that *accurately* and *completely* describes the purpose of the module. Frequently, the level of cohesion can be determined by analyzing the structure of this sentence very carefully. The following tests have been suggested by Larry Constantine:

1. If the sentence which describes a module *must be* a compound statement that contains a comma or more than one verb, then the module is probably performing more than one function. Such a module probably has sequential, communicational, or logical cohesion.

2. If the sentence contains words that are time oriented, such as "first," "next," "after," "when," "start," and "then," then the module probably has temporal, procedural, or sequential cohesion.

3. If the predicate in the sentence does not contain a single, specific object following the verb, then the module probably has logical cohesion.

4. If the sentence contains words such as "clean up" and "initialize," the module is probably temporally cohesive.

Alternatively, the decisions to determine the level of cohesion of a module are included in the following conditional statement:

If a module performs one problem-related activity,
then If this activity is one of a set of activities associated with a complex data structure,
    then we have informational cohesion
    else we have functional cohesion
else If the activities are related by data,
    then If the sequencing of activities is important,
        then we have sequential cohesion
        else we have communicational cohesion
    else If the activities are related by flow of control,
        then If sequencing is important,
            then we have procedural cohesion
            else we have temporal cohesion
        else If the activities are of the same general kind,
            then we have logical cohesion
            else we have coincidental cohesion

Modules that have functional or informational cohesion can always be described by a brief statement. A potential problem, however, is knowing how far to go in the decomposition process. Usually, a module has been sufficiently decomposed when none of its elements is useful in other parts of the system. The natural tendency (especially for beginners) is to decompose too little rather than to decompose too much.

The main goal in decomposing a system into a hierarchy of modules using the criterion of coupling is to produce a hierarchy whose modules are stamp or data coupled. Using the cohesion guideline, the elements within each module should exhibit informational or functional cohesion.

Although these two criteria are important in designing changeable and maintainable systems, other criteria or guidelines are required. For example, if we relied only on coupling as the sole criterion, we would produce a system consisting of a single module. Since there are no other modules in the system, such a system design would be very loosely coupled (that is, totally uncoupled)! The single-module system could also be highly cohesive. Therefore, we need to take into account other guidelines in the design process. The next subsection examines several additional guidelines besides coupling and cohesion.

### Additional Modularization Criteria

This section explores five additional guidelines: module size, fan-out, fan-in, scope of effect/scope of control, and factoring. The use of these guidelines may increase the modularity of a system. They are not, however, guaranteed to work. Some of these guidelines do not stand alone, and the result of their blind use can be catastrophic.

**Module Size.** Recall that in decomposing a system into a hierarchy of modules, the decomposition process should be continued until no module contains a subset of elements that can form a separate module and until each module is sufficiently small that its implementation can be understood at once. Weinberg has shown through experiments that the understandability and testability of a module decrease when its size is greater than 30 normal high-level programming statements. Usually, all the implementation of a module should be on one page or on two facing pages of an output listing. With an upper limit of 50 to 60 lines per single page, this requirement, too, sets a limit on module size.

Restricting the size of a module to between 10 and 100 high-level language statements is not a rigid rule. Some modules may contain fewer than 10 statements, while others may contain more than 100 statements. In general, we should justify separately each case of a very small or a very large module. The occurrence of a large module often indicates that the modular decomposition process has not been carried out to a sufficiently low level. Such a module may perform more than one function and suffers from logical cohesion. When a very small module is a bottom-level module in a structure chart and this module is used (that is, invoked) by several other modules, then care must be exercised in considering its elimination. If, on the other hand, the module has only one use, then it may be incorporated within its superordinate.

In the initial design phase, a designer should be fine rather than coarse in the decomposition process. If decomposition is carried out too far, resulting in too many small modules, these modules can be recombined at a later time. Modules that are useful in several places (that is, utility modules) may never be identified if the decomposition process is not sufficiently detailed (that is, is too coarse).

**Fan-out.** The *fan-out* of a module is the number of its immediate subordinates. The fan-out of module A in Fig. 7-14 is 4. As a general rule, very low or very high values of fan-out may be symptoms of poor design.

Miller has shown through extensive experimentation that people can handle or deal with only about seven objects at a time. It appears that a designer's (or problem solver's) task becomes too complex if that person has more than 7 plus or minus 2 objects or concepts to deal with at a time. Above that number, errors increase in a nonlinear manner. This phenomenon produces an error curve as shown in Fig. 7-15. This suggests that the fan-out of a module should not be more than $7 \pm 2$.

In general, we want to examine carefully any module whose fan-out is 1 or 2 or more than 10. Usually, a low fan-out for a module is less serious than a high fan-out, since the latter indicates that the module is doing too much. Such a situation often indicates a failure by the designer in defining intermediate levels. Module cohesion can be used as a guide to arriving at suitable intermediate levels.

There are many good designs that have modules with a fan-out of 1 or

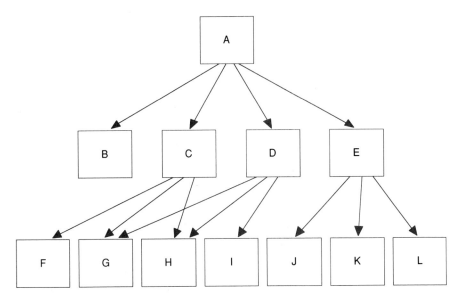

FIGURE 7-14

2. In many cases, a low fan-out for a module can be increased by splitting that module into more subordinate parts. Alternatively, a low fan-out module can be compressed or incorporated into its subordinate (providing that the module is not used by too many other modules).

**Fan-in.** The *fan-in* of a module is the number of modules that invoke (or call) it. For example, the fan-in of module **G** in Fig. 7-14 is 2. As a general rule, fan-in of modules should be as high as possible; that is, modules should be reusable. Having a module with a high fan-in means that at the implementation phase some duplicate code has been avoided.

High fan-in, however, should not be achieved at any cost. It would be unwise to maximize fan-in by combining several unrelated functions into a coincidentally cohesive "supermodule" with a high fan-in. Two guidelines can be used to restrict the use of high fan-in:

*1.* Modules should have good cohesion, for example, the ideal informational or functional cohesion. At worst, modules should have communicational or sequential cohesion.

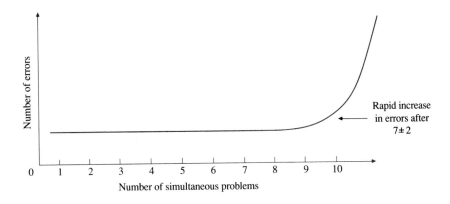

FIGURE 7-15

*2.* Each interface to a module should have the same number and types of parameters.

**Scope of Effect/Scope of Control.** Each decision in a system has some consequences in that certain processing depends on the outcome of that decision. It is important to locate the parts of a system which are affected by a given decision. A discussion of this aspect is facilitated by introducing the concepts of "scope of effect" and "scope of control." These concepts are important in determining the relative positions of modules in a given hierarchy.

The *scope of control* of a module is that module and all its subordinates. The *scope of effect* of a decision is the collection of all modules that contain code whose execution depends on that decision.

A design guideline can now be stated that associates scope of effect and scope of control. In general, the scope of effect of a decision should be within the scope of control of that decision. Following this guideline aids in attaining loosely coupled systems. In other words, we want to ensure that the modules in a design do not affect other modules over which they have no control. The following example illustrates why this consideration is important.

In Fig. 7-16, assume that the execution of a part of module C depends on the outcome of decision Y in module F. That is, the scope of effect of decision Y in module F is F and C. Either C will be control coupled to F, or the decision Y will be repeated in C. In the former approach, a control flag must be maintained and assigned a Boolean value. On the other hand, the latter approach requires duplication of some of F's code. Such duplication of code is undesirable because both copies must be altered in the event of a change to decision Y.

The scope of control of module F is F, H, and I. Therefore, in the current example, the scope of effect, that is, {F, C}, is not a subset of the scope of control, that is, {F, H, I}. This situation can be alleviated by changing the present system so that the scope of effect of decision Y is within its scope of control. We can accomplish this by moving the decision upward into C or moving the code in C affected by the decision into F (or into a module subordinate to F, that is, H or I).

Scope of effect/scope of control conflicts in a particular design can almost always be remedied easily by restructuring. The designer has the following three options:

*1.* Move the decision from a low-level module to a higher-level module.

*2.* Move a scope-of-effect module from a high-level position to a low-level position so as to place it within the scope of control.

*3.* Include (encompass) a low-level module within its superordinate module. In this case, the decision will take place high enough in the hierarchy so as to solve the scope-of-effect problem.

In summary, decision making and module structure are best related

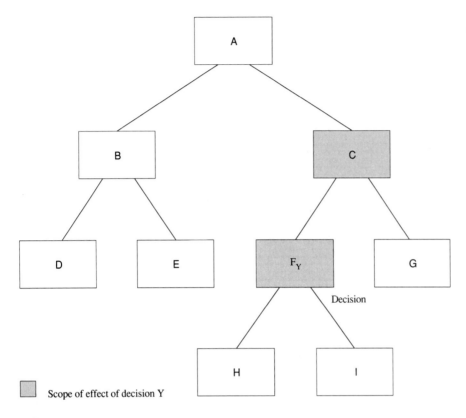

Decision

Scope of effect of decision Y

**FIGURE 7-16**
**Illustration of**
**scope of effect/scope**
**of control.**

when decisions are placed only high enough in the hierarchy so as to bring the scope of effect within the scope of control.

**Factoring.** *Factoring* is the separation of a function in one module into a new module of its own. The objectives of factoring are as follows:

*1.* To reduce module size

*2.* To make a system easier to understand, modify, and implement

*3.* To identify reusable modules

*4.* To separate work (that is, computations, data manipulations, and editing) from management (that is, control and coordination)

We now comment briefly on each of these objectives.

A module that is too large can effectively be dealt with by using factoring. Recall from the previous discussion on module size that there isn't a rigid standard for the size of a module. The question which arises in breaking modules down into subordinates is: When do you stop factoring modules? Factoring can cease when no well-defined function can be found that could be factored. Making a module out of a sequence of somewhat unrelated statements will result in procedurally or temporally cohesive modules. Factoring can also cease when a module's interface is as complex as the module itself.

Factoring can make a system easier to understand and modify. When a module contains code for doing two separate functions, such as computing a worker's gross pay and deductions, care must be exercised in changing one function without inadvertently altering the other. Using a top-down design approach will result in forming a module for each separate function. Providing that the resulting modules are loosely coupled, one module can be modified with little risk of affecting the others. Modules that are factored in this way should have informational or functional (or no worse than sequential or communicational) cohesion.

Factoring can result in minimizing duplication of code. A desirable result is to have reusable modules with high fan-in. (Recall the earlier discussion on the fan-in of a module.)

Factoring can separate work from management in a system. In well-structured organizations, a manager should control and coordinate the work of subordinates rather than do the actual work. In an analogous manner, the top-level module in a module hierarchy of a system design should, in the limiting case, contain only calls to subordinate modules (through the use of iterative and conditional statements). Most of the actual work is performed by its subordinates and, in turn, by their subordinates down to the leaf-level or atomic modules (that is, those modules which do not contain any further module calls).

Organizing a system in such a manner results in high- and medium-level modules being simple to implement, because these modules perform control and coordination functions. These modules are often very simple in content. Typically, the higher a module is in the hierarchy, the more important or significant are its decisions. The decisions that are performed by higher-level modules tend to be management decisions. Lower-level modules also can contain conditions, but they tend to deal with work-oriented rather than management matters.

The separation of work from management tends to improve the maintainability of a system. A change to a system is either a control change or a work change, but not usually both. Therefore, such changes affect one kind of module and not another. The proportion of decision making should decrease gradually from the high-level to the atomic modules.

A *completely factored system* has all its computations and data manipulations performed by atomic modules while nonatomic modules carry out only control and coordination tasks.

## 7-3.7 STRUCTURED-DESIGN TECHNIQUES

This section gives a brief description of the structured-design methodology. Its inclusion here is due to its simplicity and does not imply that structured design is more important than other design methodologies.

The approach in structured design is to convert data flow diagrams into structure charts. There are two major approaches or strategies that can be used to generate an initial design. The evaluation and refinement guidelines of the previous subsection can be used on this initial design to transform it into a better design.

The first and main design strategy, called *transform analysis* or *transform-centered design*, is applicable when most of the system's inputs are transformed in an obvious manner to the outputs. When a system processes a variety of transactions based on transaction types, the system is called a *transaction-centered system. Transaction analysis* is a strategy for designing this type of system. We proceed to describe each design strategy.

## Transform-Centered Design

Transform analysis focuses on converting a data flow diagram into a structure chart. Before describing this design strategy, we examine the various types of data flow through a module. There are four basic types of data flows (and modules), namely, input (afferent), output (efferent), transform, and coordinate. Figure 7-17 depicts the data flow (and associated module) types. The module in Fig. 7-17a processes an input flow, which it obtains from a subordinate module (shown below the module), and passes this unaltered data flow to its superordinate (shown above the module). Figure 7-17b shows an output data flow, which it obtains from its superordinate module and passes unaltered to a subordinate module. The module in Fig. 7-17c takes data from its superordinate module and transforms it into information which it then returns. Figure 7-17d shows a module which coordinates the communication of its subordinate modules. The terms "afferent" and "efferent" are often used instead of input and output, respectively. The reason for preferring these terms is to get away from the traditional tendency of associating input as something being read from some physical input medium such as a terminal and output as meaning writing or printing to some physical output medium. In general, an afferent module may not read anything and an efferent module does not necessarily write something. The terms "afferent" and "efferent" are abstractions of input and output, respectively.

A general algorithm for transform analysis consists of the following four steps:

*1.* Draw a data flow diagram for the system

*2.* Find the central transform (to be defined shortly) of the data flow diagram

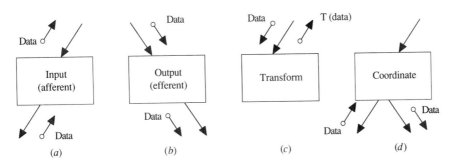

**FIGURE 7-17 Basic types of data flow (and associated modules).**

**3.** Convert the data flow diagram into an initial (high-level) structure chart

**4.** Refine this initial structure chart by using the guidelines given in Sec. 7-3.6

We proceed now to comment on each of these steps.

The first step of the general algorithm will be partly done if a structured systems analysis methodology has been followed. Following this methodology will yield a detailed set of data flow diagrams for the system. If such a methodology has not been followed, however, data flow diagrams can be drawn using the functional specifications of the system.

The data flow diagram used should not be too detailed. Staying at a level that has no more than 25 process icons is advised. More or less detail in a particular area can be incorporated or discarded as required.

A central transform of a data flow diagram is the portion of it that performs processing which is independent of the physical input and output media. Although a central transform can sometimes be identified by inspecting a data flow diagram, we recommend using the following general algorithm:

**2.1.** Identify all the major input (afferent) and output (efferent) data streams in the data flow diagram. [This includes the physical inputs and highest-level (logical) inputs and the physical outputs and highest-level (logical) outputs.]

**2.2.** Follow each input stream from the interface of the data flow diagram toward its center.

Identify each data flow that represents the input in its most logical or highest-level form, that is, in a form that has been edited or checked but not used in actual processing.

Identify the process icons between the marked data flows and their associated interfaces in the system as afferent (or input) modules. These modules are included in the afferent (input) module of the system. This part of the system is sometimes called the *input plan* because it generates the highest-level inputs from the physical inputs.

**2.3.** Trace each efferent stream from the interfaces of the data flow diagram back toward its center.

Identify each data flow that represents an output in its most logical or highest-level form, that is, at the point where the output has just been generated, but has not been formatted for report purposes.

Identify the process icons between these marked data flows and their associated interfaces in the system as efferent (or output) modules. These modules are included in the efferent module of the system. This part of the system is sometimes called the *output plan* because it produces the physical outputs from the highest-level outputs.

**2.4.** Identify the transformation processes (that is, central transform). The central part of the system is called the *transform plan*, and it generates the highest-level outputs from the highest-level inputs.

Figure 7-18 shows a simple example of partitioning a given data flow diagram by following this algorithm. In general, identifying the process icons that make up the transform plan is somewhat a value judgment on the part of the systems designer. With experience, however, most designers do not differ by more than a few process icons in their judgment of what part of the data flow diagram makes up the transform plan.

The third step of the algorithm generates an initial version of the desired structure chart. Figure 7-19*a* illustrates the form of the high-level structure chart where $M_A$, $M_T$, and $M_E$ denote the afferent (input), transform, and efferent (output) modules, respectively. $M_C$ denotes the main module, which coordinates or manages the activities of the other modules. Figure 7-19*b* shows the makeup of modules $M_A$, $M_T$, and $M_E$ in terms of the modules in the data flow diagram. Observe that, in general, the direction of data flows in a data flow diagram won't necessarily correspond to module invocation of control in the structure chart. Also, the process icons (bubbles) in a data flow diagram are redrawn as square icons in the structure chart.

**FIGURE 7-18  Partition of a data flow diagram to yield the central transform.**

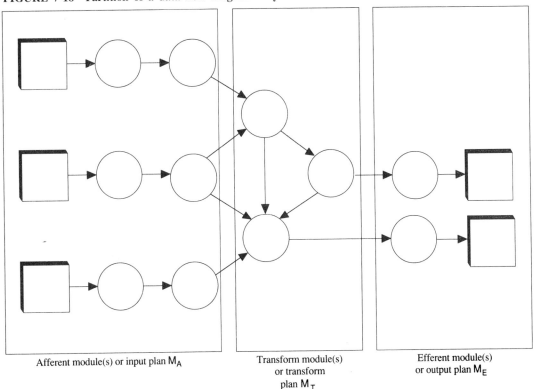

Afferent module(s) or input plan $M_A$     Transform module(s) or transform plan $M_T$     Efferent module(s) or output plan $M_E$

The fourth and final step in obtaining a structure chart is that of applying some of the guidelines discussed in the previous section. Of particular importance are the factoring and cohesion guidelines. These guidelines are to be applied to the modules in the input, central, and output plans.

As an example of the transform-analysis strategy, let us consider the data flow diagram in Fig. 7-20. A search for the central transform of this data flow diagram results in the partitioning of the diagram into an input, transform, and output plan, as shown. By introducing a new control module (System) for the entire system and connecting the central transform as well as the afferent and efferent streams to this module, we get an altered data flow diagram, as shown in Fig. 7-21. Observe that we have created a second new module (Transform) to coordinate the modules in the central transform and that the arrowheads from the data flow have been removed. Usually this type of module is required to reduce the fan-out from the module System. Fan-out has been reduced here by using factoring.

The revised data flow diagram in Fig. 7-21 can be transformed now in a structure chart, as shown in Fig. 7-22. The process icons (that is, bubbles of the data flow diagram) become the modules (represented by square boxes)

**FIGURE 7-19** (*a*) High-level structure chart. (*b*) High-level structure chart showing input, transform, and output plans.

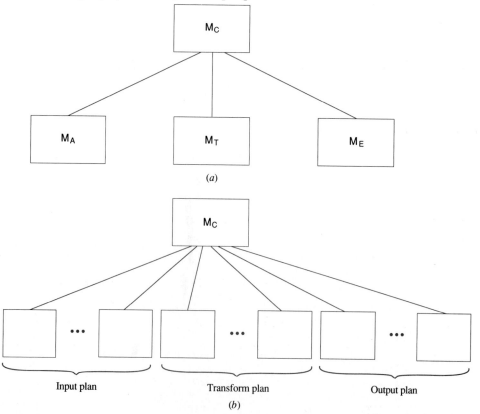

in the structure chart. Arrows for direction of call or invocation also must be added. In general, the names of the modules in the structure chart do not necessarily correspond to the names of the process icons in the data flow diagram. The name of a bubble in the data flow diagram describes its own activity, while that of the corresponding module in the structure chart should summarize the activities of its subordinate. We have also added read (such as **Read** *a*) and write modules (such as **Write** *j*) to the structure chart. Finally, we have added to the structure chart the data couples that are passed within the module hierarchy.

In a more general case, a better design can sometimes be produced from the initial structure chart by performing some or all of the following:

*1.* Factor and restructure the modules in the input and output plans.

*2.* Factor the central transform using the data flow diagram as a guideline.

*3.* Add any error-handling modules that may be required.

*4.* Check all the design guidelines against the structure chart. The structure chart should be examined (and improved) with respect to coupling, cohesion, factoring, fan-in, fan-out, and scope of effect/scope of control.

The approach used in the current example was to create a new coordinating module (**System**) in deriving a structure chart from the data flow

FIGURE 7-20  **An example data flow diagram for transform analysis.**

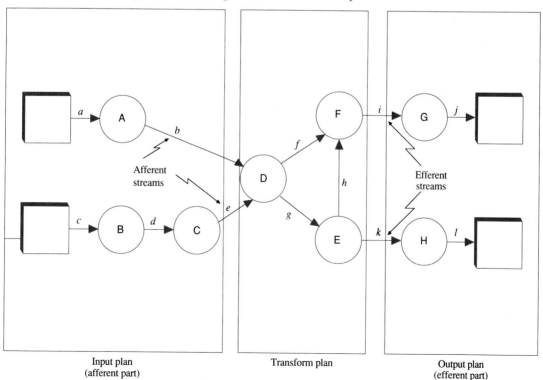

| Input plan<br>(afferent part) | Transform plan | Output plan<br>(efferent part) |

diagram. Another approach, which we will not pursue here, is to choose an existing module in the central transform to act as the chief decision maker in the system. Such a module may already exist in the system. A distinguishing feature of this module is that it does little actual processing and a substantial amount of coordination.

### Transaction-Centered Design

The transform-analysis strategy, which we have just examined, is a major strategy for converting a data flow diagram into a structure chart. The partitioning of a data flow diagram and the corresponding assignment of functions to the modules in the structure chart were based on sequence of execution. An alternative is that each module performs a different kind of function, a case that occurs frequently in a system that processes transactions. This alternative technique of design is called *transaction analysis* or *transaction-centered* design and is an important supplementary design strategy.

Transaction analysis can be used to partition a large data flow diagram into smaller, more manageable data flow diagrams—one for each different kind of transaction that a system processes. This approach allows us to use transform analysis to convert these smaller data flow diagrams to smaller, more manageable structure charts. Using the transaction-analysis strategy, we can also combine the structure charts associated with the different kinds of transactions into a larger chart which is more modifiable and maintainable.

We have used the term "transaction" informally in previous chapters. A *transaction* is a collection of data (that is, a structure) with a transaction type specified by a *transaction code*. For example, in a banking application dealing with customer checking accounts, we would have different transaction types for creating an account, closing an account, making a deposit,

**FIGURE 7-21    Modified data flow diagram in transform analysis.**

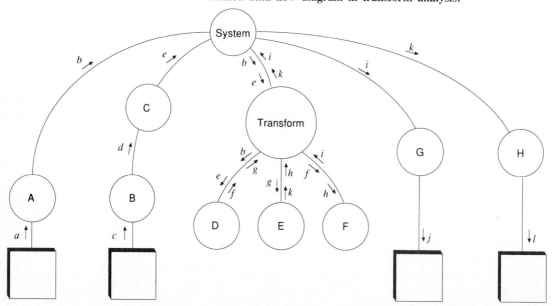

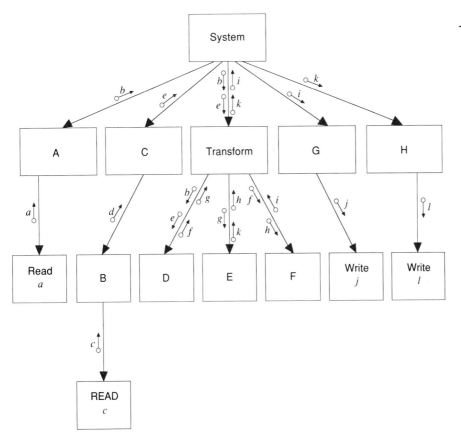

**FIGURE 7-22
First version of
structure chart
resulting from
transform analysis.**

making a withdrawal, etc. In this kind of system, each type of transaction is processed by an associated set of activities within the system.

In a typical transaction-processing system, each type of transaction has some unique processing requirements. Yet, in many instances, the processing of different types of transactions may be similar. In the past, some designers have based their designs on sharing code that is common to different types of transactions. The approach used in transaction analysis is to base a design on each transaction type and not on any common processing requirements that certain transaction types may have. A separate *transaction module* is responsible for the processing associated with each type of transaction. Another module, called the *transaction-center* module, recognizes the type of each transaction and passes control to the corresponding transaction module. This routing function is easily accomplished by using a case statement.

Figure 7-23a illustrates a transaction-driven data flow diagram that handles four different types of transactions. We assume that each transaction is to be validated in a separate way and then used to update a different master file. After each update, a log is printed of each transaction, together with the contents of each master record before and after its update. This form of diagram can be converted into a structure chart, as shown in Fig. 7-23b. Note

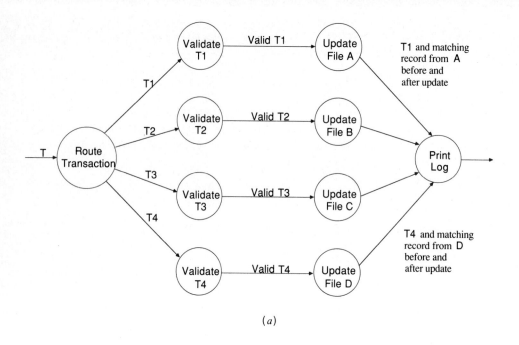

(a)

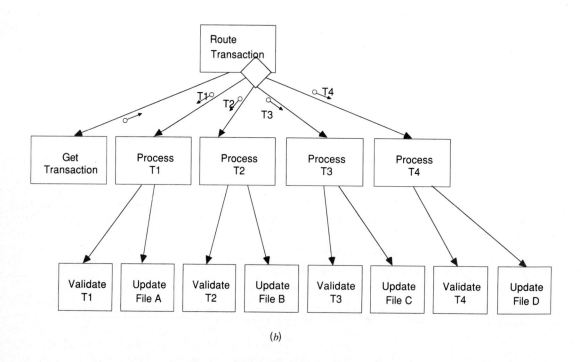

(b)

**FIGURE 7-23** (a) **Data flow diagram with four types of transactions.**
(b) **Transaction-centered structure chart.**

that because of space considerations the module that prints the log associated with each transaction update has been omitted from the structure chart.

More generally, a data flow diagram can illustrate the processing of several kinds of transactions, as shown in Fig. 7-24a. Its equivalent structure chart appears in Fig. 7-24b.

Similarities in function among transaction modules can be exploited by using factoring. Transaction-centered systems may appear to violate the guideline of fan-out. Since only one transaction is processed at one time, however, only one subordinate in the structure chart need be considered at any given time.

A general algorithm for transaction-centered design consists of the following steps:

1. Obtain a data flow diagram that shows different transactions and their associated processes.

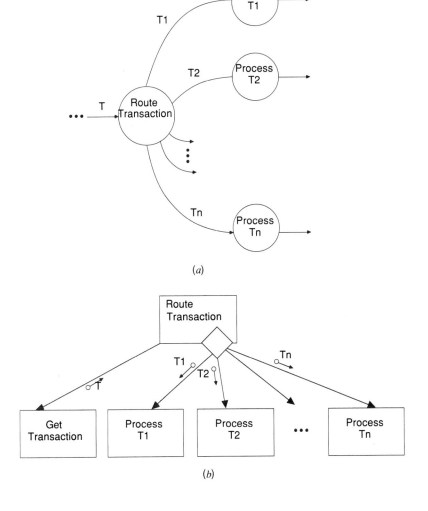

(a)

(b)

FIGURE 7-24
(a) Transaction-driven data flow diagram.
(b) Transaction-driven structure chart.

*2.* Identify any process icons where an input data flow produces several mutually exclusive data flows by transaction type.

*3.* Identify the transactions and their defining actions.

*4.* Generate a structure chart containing the transaction-center module and the transaction modules as subordinates.

*5.* Decompose transaction modules.

*6.* Refine the decomposition using the design guidelines of Sec. 7-3.6. Factoring is an important guideline here because it can exploit similarities between transaction types.

In an on-line system, it is important that transaction modules interact with users when transaction details are being entered at a terminal. In such cases, only the transaction type is entered. The determination of the transaction type then permits the appropriate routing to take place. A data flow diagram for such a system is shown in Fig. 7-25.

In closing, we summarize the primary benefits of structured design:

*1.* A data flow diagram exhibits the logical structure of a system.

*2.* The transaction-centered and transform-centered strategies translate data flow diagrams into high-level structure charts.

*3.* Design guidelines such as factoring, cohesion, and coupling (see Sec. 7-3.6) provide criteria for measuring the "goodness" of a design and comparing alternative designs for a given system.

*4.* Detailed design techniques such as stepwise refinement can be used to obtain a detailed design for each module.

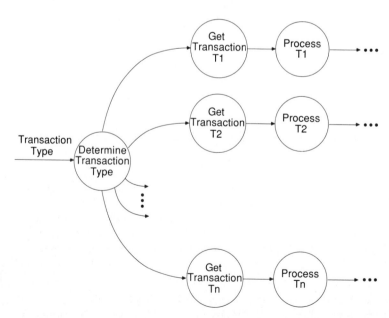

**FIGURE 7-25**
**Processing**
**transactions in an**
**on-line system.**

A significant drawback of structured design is the lack of guidance in decomposing top-level structure charts into more detailed structures. Also, because of processing-step orientation, structured design is somewhat incompatible with the design goal of information hiding.

## EXERCISES 7-3

1. The registrar of Dalmeny College, a Dr. Mark Hall, wishes to automate the annual student registration process. Operation of the system should be as follows: Department heads submit lists of classes to be offered, suggested enrollment limits for each class, and the instructors' names. From this information and a list of available rooms and their sizes (which is obtained from the Space Planning Department), a timetable is prepared. Difficulties in establishing the timetable due to conflicts in an instructor's time and/or availability of a suitable room are handled by negotiation between the registrar and the department head involved. This process is continued until a satisfactory timetable is achieved.

   A copy of the timetable and a blank registration form are mailed to each student. The student returns a completed registration form. All registration forms received by July 31 are collected and processed alphabetically, beginning at some randomly chosen letter, through to Z and then beginning again at A. A report is prepared for each student showing in which classes he or she was successfully enrolled, and any that were filled prior to processing of that student's registration form. The report, with a blank change form if some classes were full, is sent to the student. These change forms and any late registrations are processed on a first-come basis. Processing of each such form produces a report which is sent to the student. A blank change form is included if registration is still not complete.

   At the beginning of classes, a class enrollment list is produced for each instructor and a summary report on class size is produced for Dr. Hall.

   Draw a context diagram and an overall data flow diagram for the registration system.

2. Generate a structure chart for the registration system described in Exercise 1 based on a transform-centered design.

3. Hammer & Toole Contracting is a residential construction and renovation company. The partners, Mr. Mike Hammer and Mr. Joe Toole, have seen their business grow, and the paperwork to run the business is consuming a significant amount of the partners' and other employees' time. The partners have agreed that Joe Toole should work with a computer consultant to implement a computerized system for managing the company's construction jobs.

   The processing of jobs in the company is as follows: Following an inquiry from a potential customer, a construction estimator meets with the customer and discusses the requirements for the job. The estimator prepares a bid for the job and presents two copies to the customer, filing a third copy in the pending bids file. If the customer wishes to accept the bid, he or she must sign and return one of the copies within one month.

The estimator has also prepared a detailed materials list and filed it with the company's copy of the bid. When a customer accepts a bid, Mr. Mike Ozarnieski, the materials manager, retrieves the materials list and orders the necessary materials. Dave Smith, the job scheduler, schedules the crew based on Mike Ozarnieski's estimate of the delivery date of materials.

Materials are received with an invoice at the construction yard and the invoice is sent to the accounting department for payment. Also, a record of the materials' actual cost is kept with the other project documentation. One of the company's crews, headed by a foreman, is sent to do the job on the scheduled day. On completion of the job, the foreman submits a report to Dave Smith containing the actual work hours required.

Dave Smith sends a notification of job completion to accounting so that the customer may be billed. Additionally, he prepares a weekly report for the company's partners listing, for each completed job, the amount which was bid, the actual cost of materials and labor, and the net profit or loss on the job. This report is presented in two forms, one grouped by estimator's name and the other grouped by crew foreman's name.

Draw a context diagram and data flow diagram for the job-processing operation. Explode the processes into lower-level flow diagrams until a suitable level of detail is reached.

4. Prepare a structure chart based on a transform-centered approach for the job-processing operation of Exercise 3.

5. The Garden of Paradise Motel is a popular resort motel in southern California. Recently, it has experienced a growing number of customer complaints concerning poor service and mistakes, such as lack of a room for a confirmed reservation, meals billed to the wrong room, etc. Many of the problems have been attributed to a backlog of work at the front desk. It has been decided that some of the work of the front desk should be automated, thus, it is hoped, reducing the number of errors and making information available in a more timely fashion.

A description of the operations to be automated is as follows: Reservations for any days during a 6-month period commencing with the current day may be made by telephoning the front desk. A record of the number of rooms of each type (suite, two double beds, etc) booked for each day is kept. The front desk clerk will check the requested days and confirm the reservation if the rooms are available. The clerk will then make a record of the reservation and deduct the reserved rooms from the number available.

Guests checking in at the front desk will be assigned a room from a list of available and cleaned rooms. Guests checking out will receive an itemized bill; housekeeping will be notified that the room is to be cleaned. Housekeeping is also notified to clean the rooms of guests staying more than one night. The front desk is notified as soon as each room is cleaned; cleaned rooms which become vacant (guests checked out) are put on the available room list.

Several types of charges are recorded for each guest. Each morning the basic room rate is charged. Checks received from the restaurant are immediately charged to the bill. The telephone operator records long distance call charges. Finally, a computerized pay TV system is available. Guests indicate their wish to watch a movie by use of a key pad attached to the pay TV converter in their rooms. The appropriate channel is descrambled and a note of the room number and amount of charge is printed on a printer installed by the pay TV company at the front desk. That company has offered to arrange for the direct connection of a telecommunication line with its computer if the front desk is automated, permitting the charges to be billed to the guest without manual processing.

Draw a context diagram and data flow diagram for the system. Explode processes into lower-level flow diagrams until a suitable level of detail is reached.

6. Construct a structure chart, based on transaction-centered design, of the front desk system of Exercise 5. The transactions correspond to the various activities performed at the front desk, e.g., reserving a room, checking in a guest, charging the room rate, charging a meal, etc.

## 7-4    IMPLEMENTATION ISSUES

We have now considered the requirements definition and design phases of the software life cycle. We turn now to implementation. Recall that the implementation phase involves creating the source text, written in a suitable programming language, for all the modules required by the design. The design may, of course, incorporate some existing modules available from a program library as well as some new ones. You have now had some experience in implementing computer programs. The point of this section is to describe the way in which decisions made during implementation affect overall program quality and to draw to your attention some of the finer points affecting implementation. Adhering to these guidelines will produce programs of higher quality.

### 7-4.1    ASPECTS OF PROGRAM QUALITY

We want to effect good programs through our design and implementation. What do we mean by this? If you were to survey programmers for their answers to the question, "What are the characteristics of a good program?" you would probably receive a wide variety of responses, depending on the personal tastes and experiences of the individuals surveyed. A number of thoughts, however, might occur with greater frequency. In this section some common responses are analyzed.

### The Right Problem Has Been Solved

Programmers must be very careful that each module eventually implemented is the module that was, in fact, required. It is all too easy to become immersed in details and, as a result, to lose sight of original design specifications or requirements. Solving *almost* the required problem results in unsatisfied customers and/or unfortunate incidents. It is important that requirements (which may, in fact, change with time) be reviewed continually throughout implementation. The requirements themselves might be erroneous or incomplete or simply misunderstood. Be careful not to embellish the implementation with features not specifically requested (but fun to do). This introduces even further chance of error.

### The Implementation Has No Bugs

Of equal importance to solving the right problem is producing an implementation that works. It must work for all valid inputs and must produce the required response, for example, an error indication, for all invalid inputs. This seems obvious, yet it is difficult to ascertain for modules of any significant size or complexity.

Too many programmers accept bugs (or errors) as a natural consequence of the human condition and view debugging as an eternal fact of life. There is no particular reason why this should be so. Visions of evil gremlins secretly putting errors into programs spring to mind, when, in fact, the programmers themselves are usually responsible through carelessness, lack of understanding of design specifications or language features, or failure to anticipate a particular situation to which the program was applied. Programmers do not do this deliberately (nobody enjoys debugging) and, in fact, can avoid making most of these errors. Yourdon talks of a style of program development that he calls "antibugging" in which the philosophy is to avoid errors from the outset.

However it might be done, it is clearly the responsibility of the programmer to ensure that his or her program is error-free. A good deal of research in computer science has been directed toward formal, mathematical proofs of program correctness. It has been established that such proofs are possible; however, the proof procedures are lengthy and difficult—seldom practical for real applications. This being the case, the programmer must resort to other methods, such as testing, to establish the correctness of a program. More will be said about this in the next section.

### The Program Is Well-Documented

It is important that computer programs be well-documented. Documentation exists to assist in the understanding or use of a program. This can be of great value not only to those charged with maintaining or modifying a program, but also to programmers themselves. Most programmers are forced to divide their attentions among several things simultaneously, be they different programs, different parts of one program, or even different tasks of their job. Details of particular programs or particular pieces of programs are easily forgotten or confused without suitable documentation.

Documentation comes in two forms: *external documentation*, which includes such things as reference manuals, algorithm descriptions, flowcharts, project workbooks, and so on, and *internal documentation*, which is part of the source code itself (essentially, the declarations, statements, and comments). The value of internal documentation cannot be overemphasized. For any program, the source text and/or compilation listing itself constitutes the front line of program documentation. For this reason, we emphasize the importance of highly readable programs. Section 7-4.2 discusses this further.

Some external documentation will have already been produced as part of the requirements definition and design phases. Additional external documentation, however, is usually produced during the implementation. An important category of this documentation is that intended for the users of the program, who should not be required to study the source code in order to use the program. Indeed, in the case of proprietary software being sold for profit, the source code is unlikely to be available to the users. The other category of external documentation is intended for use by the implementors and maintainers and is complementary to the source text itself. More is said about the nature of external documentation in Sec. 7-4.3.

## The Program Is Efficient

The question of efficiency is a thorny one, and it has been addressed already. In the early days of computing, machines were slow and small by today's standards. Programs had to be carefully designed to make maximum use of scarce resources such as execution time and storage. Programmers would spend hours trying to chop seconds off the execution times of their programs or trying to squeeze programs into a small space in memory. A program's efficiency, most often measured by its "space-time product," was its primary figure of merit.

Today the situation has changed dramatically. Hardware costs have fallen sharply, while human costs have soared. Execution time and memory space are no longer as scarce as they once were. Whereas one should always be watchful for large savings that might result from the incorporation of a different solution technique, such as a choice to replace a linear search technique by the much more efficient binary search, it no longer makes economic sense for the normal programmer to try to squeeze every last drop of efficiency out of his or her programs. Although this might be required in a few sensitive cases, for most programs the effort simply is not justified.

Nevertheless, there are still many programmers at the altar of the space-time product, with the result of producing unnecessarily difficult program code. A program that does not work or is difficult to maintain because of such contorted code is clearly of low quality regardless of its space-time product.

As you can see, there are many facets of program quality. Clearly, it is important that a program work correctly and reliably; that is, that *all* the requirements for it have been met and unexpected errors are unlikely to occur. However, the matter does not end there. The evolution of software, as studied by Lehman and Parr, appears to be a real phenomenon. Programs require a continuing process of maintenance and modification to keep pace with changing requirements and implementation technologies. Maintainability and modifiability are essential characteristics of real programs. A program's ability to be read and understood is an important prerequisite to its maintainability and modifiability. To summarize, we want programs, and systems, that are correct, reliable, maintainable, modifiable, readable, and understandable.

## 7-4.2 PROGRAMMING STYLE

*There is no fixed set of rules according to which clear, understandable, and provable programs can be constructed. There are guidelines, of course, and good ones at that; but the individual programmer's style (or lack of it), his clarity of thought (or lack of it), his creativity (or lack of it), will all contribute significantly to the outcome.*
    Peter J. Denning, ACM Computing Surveys, *Vol. 6, December 1974*

*[We] are beginning to see a breakthrough in programming as a mental process. This breakthrough is based more on considerations of style than on detail. It involves taking style seriously, not only in how programs look when they are completed, but in the very mental processes that create them.*
    Harlan D. Mills, *Foreword to* Programming Proverbs, *by Henry F. Ledgard, Hayden Book Company, 1975*

A computer programmer is in the business of designing solutions to problems and implementing them as computer programs. It is important that beginning programmers recognize the importance of style in the practice of their craft and develop habits of programming style that will carry them in good stead in professional life. Just as a good writing style does not come simply from a thorough knowledge of the rules of English grammar, neither does a good programming style come from a thorough knowledge of the syntax of a programming language. This section is an attempt to bridge this gap.

Creative people, such as artists, composers, writers, or architects, work very hard during their early training period to master the skills of their craft. At the same time, there develops a style that is unique and identifiable to each individual. This style is not incidental to their ultimate success at their craft; for if they are to be successful, it must be preferred in the marketplace to that of their competitors.

In any field, certain styles have definite advantages. For example, certain styles of music or art have wider appeal than others. There are definite styles of writing that can communicate ideas effectively; other styles perhaps

**(By permission of King Features Syndicate, Inc.)**

are better at communicating technical detail. Certain styles of architecture are better suited than others for particular climatic conditions.

Style has important consequences in programming too, some of which we will demonstrate in this section. Quite apart from the question of professional standards, considerations of style can actually lead to improved quality of programs. For example, research has shown conclusively that stylistic practices can assist in reducing the number of errors made during the implementation of a program. At the same time, the program itself can be more easily read and understood by other programmers, who may at some time be called upon to make modifications to it. Program maintenance, that is, the "tuning" of existing programs to meet ever-changing requirements, consumes a large portion of the professional programmer's working day. Not surprisingly, there is considerable interest shown, by both programmers and their managers, in suggestions that claim to make the maintenance activity less time consuming and thus free the programmer for more original development work.

Good programming style can make an important contribution to a programmer's success. The rewards are very tangible, but a conscious effort on the part of the programmer is required. In this section we discuss a number of issues that relate to this matter of programming style. We try to provide appropriate motivation by considering in some detail the programming process itself. By examining what a programmer actually does, we can see possible problems and make suggestions as to how these might be alleviated.

In programming, as in most things, style is largely a matter of personal taste. We do not intend to impose our own style on readers simply for whimsical reasons. Instead, we will present a set of guidelines that we hope will encourage the correct attitude toward the production of programs. We will try to provide appropriate motivation by showing examples of both good and bad style.

Several short books have dealt exclusively with programming from the perspective of style, notably Kernighan and Plauger's *The Elements of Programming Style*, Ledgard's *Programming Proverbs*, and Ledgard and Tauer's *Pascal with Excellence—Programming Proverbs*. In addition to the entertaining reading they provide, these books offer suggestions on how even experienced programmers can write better programs. The material in this section is an attempt to highlight some of the ideas in books such as these.

It is understandably difficult to talk of program writing without referring to the language in which the program is being written. A command of the language being used is certainly an important factor in the production of good programs. There are, however, general issues that are largely independent of language concerns. In this section we consider both these general issues of program production and their application to Pascal.

The importance of two fundamental issues on the production of good-quality computer programs has been stressed throughout this chapter and, indeed, throughout much of the book. These are, first, the management of complexity and, second, readability. Certainly, these are not independent: If a program's complexity is kept under control, it is likely to be more readable than a program in which such care has not been taken; conversely, a readable program is more likely to be easily understood than one that is difficult to read and thus by definition is complex. Although they do approach the issue from somewhat different perspectives, they can in practice be combined effectively.

Many have recognized the fundamental importance of the management of complexity in the practice of programming. Kernighan and Plauger write:

> Controlling complexity is the essence of computer programming. We will always be limited by the sheer number of details that we can keep straight in our heads. Much of what we have tried to teach in this book is how to cope with complexity.

Dijkstra writes:

> We should recognize that ... the art of programming is the art of organizing complexity, of mastering multitude and avoiding its bastard chaos as effectively as possible.

The importance of readability has been expounded with equal force. While an important function of a program is communication with the computer, it is equally important as an aid to effective communication between human beings. Programs are read more than they are written; while debugging or modifying a program you are required to read and understand what is there before a change can be made. Readability is, as we have said, a key to understanding; programs that cannot be understood can be neither maintained nor modified and are therefore of little value. Even the author of an unreadable program, to whom it may have been clear when it was written originally, will be hard pressed to remember what is going on after a very short period of time. On the subject of readability, Kernighan and Plauger write:

> In our experience, readability is the single best criterion of program quality: if a program is easy to read, it is probably a good program; if it is hard to read, it probably isn't good.

Tremblay and Sorenson write:

> It is vital to distinguish between readability and writeability. It is important to be able to write programs easily. It is *necessary* to be able to read programs easily.

In this section we explore the question of programming style in relation to production of quality programs. Section 7-3 concerned itself with the design of a solution to a problem. Here we are concerned with the design of the program code, that is, with the *representation* of the solution in a programming language. Style issues are tied closely to the effective use of the programming language in which this implementation is being carried out (Pascal in this book). Some general principles, however, transcend language. We present four sections covering choice of identifiers, structured programming, use of type declarations, and program-presentation issues, along with a postscript. Under each of these subheadings we offer a number of suggestions, with illustrations where possible, that could lead to improving the quality of your own programs.

## Choice of Identifiers

An appropriate choice of identifiers for the names of modules, subprograms, types, variables, and other elements is crucial to producing a readable program. The programming language in use, however, may place some restrictions on the choice of identifiers.

The goal is to use *meaningful* identifiers which help the reader remember the purpose of an identifier without constantly referring to the declarations or to a variable list external to the program. Avoid cryptic abbreviations.

Unfortunately, some languages make this difficult. FORTRAN, for example (using the FORTRAN 77 definition), allows only six character identifiers. Other languages do not specify a limit on identifier length but leave it to the particular compiler. Particularly pernicious are compilers which use only a subset of the characters in the name to distinguish identifiers. Certain Pascal compilers exhibit this behavior, using only the first eight characters of the identifier. *Different* identifiers which happen to have the same first eight characters are taken to be the *same* identifier. Other compilers use the entire identifier during compilation. Some linkers, however, which combine separately compiled modules, are more restrictive. This typically places restrictions on module names and names of some types of global variables.

We suggest several general guidelines. Ledgard and Tauer offer additional considerations in their book *Pascal with Excellence—Programming Proverbs*. Longer identifiers should be used for the most significant objects in a program, as well as for those objects used in many locations, such as, for example, the name of a frequently used subprogram. Shorter identifiers should be used for strictly local objects. For example, I is useful as the index of an array in a loop; Index is not necessary. K, on the other hand, is undesirable as the name of a major data structure.

In mathematical computations, use of identifiers similar to standard mathematical notation should be encouraged. Typically, I, J, K, M, and N denote integer variables; X, Y, and Z denote real variables; and A, B, and C are coefficients or arrays. Thus the following may be used:

```
Z : = A * X * X + B * X + C
I : = (I + 1) mod N
A[I, J] : = B[I, J] + C[I, J]
```

Use capitalizaton in multiword identifiers, for example, MonthlyPay rather then MONTHLYPAY or monthlypay. If the Pascal compiler allows a *break character* in identifiers and if portability of the program to other computers is not required, the break character may be used, as in MONTHLY_PAY. Abbreviate the more common word if abbreviating multiword identifiers. Thus use BadDataMsg rather than BadDatMessage. Use a standard set of abbreviations on a project. The same program should not have InitialMsg, ErrorMes, and OverflowMesg, where Msg, Mes, and Mesg are all abbreviations for "message."

Parts of speech should be used consistently. A typical standard is as follows:

Use nouns to name data objects such as variables, constants, and types. Use Payment rather than Paid or ToPay as the value to be paid.

Use verbs to name procedures. Thus GetNextChar or ComputeNextMove are the procedures to perform these actions, rather than NextChar or NextMoveComputation.

Use forms of the verb "to be" for Boolean functions used as predicates. Thus use AreEqual, IsZero, IsReady, and IsEmpty as tests. These are used as in

**if** AreEqual(A, B)
**then** . . .

We are assuming, of course, that the = operator is not applicable to A and B, which presumably represent some programmer-defined types. Examples of data structures requiring programmer-written predicates occur in subsequent chapters.

Some authors suggest prepositions for some parameter names of procedures. Thus a procedure to get the next record from a file passed as a parameter might be defined as

**procedure** GetNextRecord (
    **var** OutRecord: MasterRec;    { Output, the next file record}
    **var** From: MasterFile    { Input/output, the file to be read and advanced}
                    );

{ The next record is obtained from the file specified by the input/output parameter From and placed into the output parameter OutRecord. The file's status is modified by advancing to the next record.}

We summarize this discussion as follows: The *identifier naming* of an object should suggest the *meaning* of the object to the reader of the program.

In addition to the choice of identifier, some programming languages give a choice as to whether certain objects are to be named. The most common case is that of constants. Suppose, for example, that we were to design a modest information-retrieval system to maintain information (or a data base) on the 37 students in a particular class in computer science. For each student, we keep the following information: name, number of lab problems completed, and lab mark to date. We choose to keep this information in an array of structures with 37 elements. The fields of the structure are a string Name, an integer LabsDone, and a real value LabMark. Routines are written to insert new lab marks, to correct marks erroneously recorded, or simply to display selected pieces of information. Each of these operations requires one or more scans through the array of structures, with a loop something like the following:

**for** K : = 1 **to** 37 **do**

We call a mysterious numeric constant that appears in a computation with little or no explanation a *magic number*. In this example, **37** is a magic number. It may appear in the array declaration or in an associated type declaration, in loop specifications as illustrated, and as an argument to subprograms which process the array. In fact, the execution of this program is heavily bound to this number.

Suppose that we wish to use this program for a different class, say, a larger class with 212 students. First, we must go through this program and change all occurrences of the number **37** which refers to the number of students to the new number **212**. We must find them all, since any we do not find will eventually (not necessarily immediately) cause an error. In addition, occurrences of related numbers, for example, **36** or **38**, may need to be changed to **211** or **213**, and so forth. (For an example of related numbers, observe that some of the sort procedures have a loop which goes to $n - 1$.) Also, we must be careful not to change any occurrences of **37** which are not dependent on the class size, for example, the maximum mark in a lab.

Recall that Pascal allows declarations of named constants, for example,

**const**
    ClassSize = 37;

Throughout the program, the identifier **ClassSize** may be used wherever a constant equal to the class size is required. Thus **37** will occur as the class size in only one place. Unfortunately, if the program requires the class size minus 1, that is, **36**, as a *constant*, say, in an array declaration, a separate constant identifier must be declared, as in

**const**
    ClassSize = 37;
    ClassSzM1 = 36;

This is so because **ClassSize** $- 1$ is considered an expression which is not an allowable constant. Many Pascal compilers relax this restriction as an extension to standard Pascal.

### Structured Programming

The last two decades have seen the emergence of an approach to programming known as *structured programming*, naively thought by some to eliminate all implementation problems. Unhappily, this is not the case. As Harlan Mills observes in an article on the growth of data processing, "There is a great deal of oversell and confusion about structured programming, primarily because an adolescent data processing community is anxious to find simple answers to complex problems."

To a large extent the "structure" of a program is determined by the constructs used to direct the flow of control. It is important to remember that while you read the program listing from top to bottom, execution of the program may proceed in a very different way. One of the main goals of structured programming is to structure the flow of control in such a way that the execution sequence is as close as possible to the reading sequence. This enforces a discipline on the programmer, in terms of control structures that can be used and, further, on the manner in which they can be used. As a first approximation, we limit ourselves to two of the control structures introduced in Chap. 3—the if–then–else construct and the while construct—and combinations of these.

According to the strict letter of the law, any program written using only these control structures is, by definition, a structured program. Unfortunately, bad programs can be written using any technique. What is more important is an adherence to the *spirit* of the law or the intent of structured programming.

Consider the program MaxMin3, which was given in Sec. 3-2 to illustrate the use of nested if statements and is repeated as Fig. 7-26.

By the strict definition of structured programming, this is, in fact, a structured program. Its readability can be improved, however, possibly at a small sacrifice in efficiency, by "unwinding" some of the nesting. The human mind has difficulty comprehending complex nested structures; it requires the retention of several different program states at the same time. Deeply nested structures are highly error-prone and normally can be avoided.

There are several ways of avoiding deeply nested structures. One method, perhaps appropriate in this particular case, is to use compound conditions in an if statement to define the specific alternatives more precisely. You must be aware, however, that the condition itself must be reasonably easy to understand or else there is little value in the change. A second method is simply to repeat code; for example, a test might be repeated. If to avoid repeating a small section of code requires a contorted structure, dues will be paid later.

The revision to the program MaxMin3 in Fig. 7-27 illustrates the application of the second of these methods.

Although the revised program is one step longer and may take longer to execute, it is probably easier to understand than the first. Do not let the fact that a program *appears* to be structured prevent you from making changes to improve it.

### Use of Type Declarations

Many modern programming languages have introduced the notion of user-defined types. This can be used to stylistic advantage because it allows a programmer to define certain composite types, e.g., record structures and arrays, and then define several objects, e.g., variables and parameters, to be of the same particular structure (type). Because there is no generally useful definition for mixing types, such as, for example, assigning a record with one integer and two character fields to, say, an array with four real elements, such operations are prohibited. Most such languages are defined so that each variable can take on values only of a single type. Such a language is said to be *strongly typed*, and violations of the type-mixing restrictions can be detected while the program is being compiled. Pascal is a strongly typed language.

It has been observed that some programming errors, such as using the wrong variable, were often flagged by compilers because they happened to cause a type mismatch. The same type of error made while using a language with less extensive type-definition facilities often required several debugging runs.

```
program MaxMin3 (input, output);
{Given three integer numbers, this program determines the largest and
    smallest value. The numbers are assumed to be distinct (different).}


var
    A, B, C: integer;           {The three input values}
    Max: integer;               {The largest value}
    Min: integer;               {The smallest value}
begin
    {Step 1: Input data}
    read (A, B, C);


    {Step 2: Determine largest and smallest values}
    if A < B
    then
        if A < C
        then begin
                Min : = A;          {A < B, A < C}
                if B > C
                then Max : = B      {A < C < B}
                else Max : = C      {A < B < C}
            end
        else begin
                Min : = C;          {C < A < B}
                Max : = B
            end
    else
        if A > C
        then begin
                Max : = A;          {A > B, A > C}
                if B > C
                then Min : = C      {A > B > C}
                else Min : = B      {A > C > B}
            end
        else begin
                Max : = C;          {C > A > B}
                Min : = B
            end;


    {Step 3: Display largest and smallest}
    writeln ('Largest value is□', Max, '□Smallest is□', Min)
end.
```

FIGURE 7-26
**Program to find
largest and smallest
of three integers.**

**program** MaxMin3Revised (input, output);
{Given three integer numbers, this program determines the largest and small-
est value. The numbers are assumed to be distinct (different).}
**var**
   A, B, C: integer;         {The three input values}
   Max: integer;             {The largest value}
   Min: integer;             {The smallest value}
**begin**
   {Step 1: Input data}
   read (A, B, C);

   {Step 2: Determine largest value}
   Max := A;
   **if** B > Max
   **then** Max := B;
   **if** C > Max
   **then** Max := C;

   {Step 3: Determine smallest value}
   Min := A;
   **if** B < Min
   **then** Min := B;
   **if** C < Min
   **then** Min := C;

   {Step 4: Display largest and smallest}
   writeln ('Largest value is□', Max, '□Smallest is□', Min)
**end**.

**FIGURE 7-27**
**Program to find**
**largest and smallest**
**of three integers**
**(revised).**

Now the trend is to define separate types for each logical class of data,
thus causing the compiler to flag each inappropriate combination of data.
Pascal allows a separate type for each programmer-defined type introduced in
a program but provides no mechanism for separate types based on a primitive
type such as integer. The programming language Ada, for example, does
allow definition of separate types even in this case.

Consider an application to process student marks. We will introduce
two Pascal vector types, one for student numbers and one for the marks, as
shown in Fig. 7-28. A procedure to average the marks of the class might be
declared using the following header.

**procedure** ClassAverage (
   Mark: MarkVector;       {Input, vector containing marks}
   N: integer;             {Input, number of students }
   **var** Aver: real        {Output, class average}
                   );

A possible programming error consists of calling the procedure with the
wrong argument, as in

```
const
    MaxNoOfStud = 100;
type
    StudNoVector = array [1 .. MaxNoOfStud] of integer;
    MarkVector = array [1 .. MaxNoOfStud] of integer;
var
    StudNos: StudNoVector;
    StudMarks: MarkVector;
    NoOfStud: integer;
    Average: real;
```

**FIGURE 7-28**
**Declarations for the**
**processing of student**
**marks.**

```
ClassAverage(StudNos, NoOfStud, Average)
```

This statement is logically incorrect, since this would average a set of student numbers. Even though the argument is an integer array of the correct size, the compiler will report a type conflict at compile time because Pascal requires identical structure types for an argument and parameter and the types StudNoVector and MarkVector are different in standard Pascal. (Some compilers use different rules, however.) This forces the programmer to reexamine this statement. Although this may seem like an unlikely error in this simple example, a program involving hundreds of modules can easily contain a few errors of this kind. As mentioned previously, the technique described here can be more rigorously applied in a language which allows new types to be derived from all types including the primitive types such as integer.

Pascal also allows subrange types to be declared. An attempt to assign a value outside the allowed range of a variable is reported as a run-time error. (Because the checking introduces additional computations and increases the execution time of the program, many compilers allow the programmer to specify whether or not these checks are to be incorporated in the program. Checking should be enabled when testing a program and even during normal operation if the speed is acceptable.) Such error reports facilitate the location of the problem.

An additional purpose for specifying value ranges is to allow the compiler to choose an appropriate internal representation for the value or to report that none is available. For example, one Pascal compiler might allow a range of $-2^{31}$ to $2^{31} - 1$ for an integer, while another might allow only a range of $-2^{15}$ to $2^{15} - 1$. A program which requires a variable Num to hold values in the range 1 to 1,000,000 might be developed and tested on the first compiler with Num declared as an integer. If the program were moved to a computer using the second compiler, the program might fail in a mysterious way (particularly if the second computer does not detect overflow in integer computations). Declaring Num as a subrange, that is,

```
var
    Num: 1 .. 1000000;
```

would allow the second compiler to report a representation problem. Alternatively, it might choose an alternate type allowing representation of the requested range. Many Pascal compilers include an additional integer type, often called *long integer*, as an extension to the standard.

The programmer should use the type-declaration facilities available in the chosen programming language to enhance the readability and reliability of programs.

### Program-Presentation Issues

The format and appearance of the program listing are not incidental to the quality of the program. More can be done here to improve the readability of a program than at almost any other point. In this subsection we consider two facets of this question: comments and paragraphing.

*Comments* constitute a major component of a program's internal documentation. They serve to help the reader understand the intent or purpose of portions of code and can also assist in explaining the logic of difficult sections. Beginning programmers are seldom given any instruction in the writing of comments, yet the writing of good comments is probably as important, and perhaps as difficult to learn, as the writing of good programs. Good comments cannot do much to improve bad code, but bad comments can seriously detract from good code.

One of the most comprehensive discussions of the use of comments is a 1976 article by Sachs. Some good material is also found in the books by Kernighan and Plauger and by Ledgard and Tauer.

Many programmers fall into one of two extreme categories: those who write few or no comments and those who overcomment. Each of these extremes detracts from the readability of the program in its own way— undercommenting by failing to provide appropriate supporting information and overcommenting by increasing the clutter. Comments should not just "parrot" the code, but should explain and support it. This requires, perhaps, that programmers approach their programs simultaneously from two points of view: that of a programmer and that of a documentor, fully appreciating the objectives of each. We have used copious comments in our programs for pedagogical reasons. By some standards, we border on overcommenting.

Much of what you can or cannot do with comments is a function of the programming language being used. Unfortunately, some languages in which comments might be most needed offer little in the way of features to support good comments. Pascal gives great freedom in the placement of comments. Care must be taken that comments are not hidden by the Pascal code. For example, a trailing comment after a statement should be separated as much as possible from the code, perhaps by moving it over to the right-hand side of the listing.

As a final point on comments, always make sure that comments and code agree. If you make a change to the code, be sure that a similar change is made to any comment relating to it. This is often overlooked.

The value of *paragraphing*, or controlled indenting of a program listing, is used, once again, in enhancing readability. In any written text, paragraphing serves two main purposes: to identify structural units of the text and to relieve the tedium of the reading process. Both apply to programs as well. The danger of unparagraphed programs is well captured in a quote from

"The Wood-Pile," by Robert Frost:

> The view was all in lines
> Straight up and down of tall slim trees
> Too much alike to mark or name a place by
> So as to say for certain I was here
> Or somewhere else;

Paragraphing can be of great assistance in revealing the logical structure of a program (or algorithm). Throughout this book, for example, we have adopted the convention that, as a rule, a new line is begun for each alternative of an if construct and that where alternatives consist of more than a single statement, subsequent statements be indented to the point of the first. This shows the alternatives clearly, as well as the conditions affecting their choice. Further, if nesting is involved, it too is clearly shown. The following example taken from Chap. 5 illustrates this scheme:

```
if Score1 > Score2
then begin
        Stats[Row1, Wins] : = Stats[Row1, Wins] + 1;
        Stats[Row2, Losses] : = Stats[Row2, Losses] + 1
      end
else
      if Score1 < Score2
      then begin
              Stats[Row2, Wins] : = Stats[Row2, Wins] + 1;
              Stats[Row1, Losses] : = Stats[Row1, Losses] + 1
            end
      else begin
              Stats[Row1, Ties] : = Stats[Row1, Ties] + 1; { tie game}
              Stats[Row2, Ties] : = Stats[Row2, Ties] + 1
            end
```

Imagine how difficult even this small section of code would be to read without the support provided by the paragraphing.

One difficulty that can arise is running out of space on a line within a very deeply nested control structure. More likely, however, this results from failure to modularize the program sufficiently. Some authors advocate that no more than four levels of nesting be allowed in a single module.

A frequent case is that a module must perform a sequence of Boolean tests. Although we have not used it in this book, a modern trend is to view this sequence of tests as a single control structure rather than nested if statements and to indent appropriately. We might indent the preceding example as follows:

```
if Score1 > Score2
then begin
        Stats[Row1, Wins] : = Stats[Row1, Wins] + 1;
        Stats[Row2, Losses] : = Stats[Row2, Losses] + 1
      end
```

```
else if Score1 < Score2
then begin
        Stats[Row2, Wins] : = Stats[Row2, Wins] + 1;
        Stats[Row1, Losses] : = Stats[Row1, Losses] + 1
    end
else begin
        Stats[Row1, Ties] : = Stats[Row1, Ties] + 1; { tie game}
        Stats[Row2, Ties] : = Stats[Row2, Ties] + 1
    end
```

Languages such as Modula-2 and Ada contain syntax specifically for writing such a control structure, namely, an elsif statement to replace **else if**, and some Pascal compilers include it as an extension to the standard. Paragraphing can also be used to delineate the range of a loop if all the statements in the range are indented under the **for, while**, or **repeat**. Statements following the loop return to the original starting position. Again, a short rephrased example from Chap. 5 illustrates this approach:

```
for Row : = 1 to 12 do
    if Teams[Row] = Team1
    then Row1: = Row
    else
            if Teams[Row] = Team2
            then Row2 : = Row;


{ Update games played}
Stats[Row1, GamesPlayed] : = Stats[Row1, GamesPlayed] + 1;
Stats[Row2, GamesPlayed] : = Stats[Row2, GamesPlayed] + 1
```

Issues of program presentation seldom *cause* errors, but they can play a large role in avoiding them. Too many programmers dismiss these matters as simply "window dressing," preferring instead to devote their energies to the more creative aspects of the job. As a key factor in the readability of the final program, its presentation serves to enhance its overall quality, in addition to giving the program a pleasing, professional appearance.

## Postscript

> *A shattered flower vase is often cheaper to replace than to repair.*
> Henry F. Ledgard, Programming Proverbs, *Hayden Book Company, 1975*

Paradoxically, it seems to be almost a law of nature that the better the module you produce, the more likely that it will at some time need to be changed. People tend to take good modules and adapt them to their own purposes rather than take the trouble to design new modules. This is not to imply that this is a bad thing—on the contrary; whenever possible, programmers should be encouraged to adapt rather than reinvent. Every change, or patch, to a module, however, increases its disorder. Before long, a module that has undergone many changes becomes a very fragile structure;

like a house of cards, if you touch it in the wrong place, it all comes tumbling down.

It is a mark of maturity for a programmer to know when it is time to replace a module. When that time comes, do not be afraid to scrap the old module and start over. This is not a defeatist attitude. As Ledgard points out, "lessons painfully learned on the old program can be applied to the new one to yield a better program in far less time with far less trouble." Rather than being subjected to the insults and abuses of disgruntled modifiers, old modules that have served well deserve a graceful retirement.

### 7-4.3 DOCUMENTATION

A computer program without documentation is like a major appliance without operating instructions. Just as the operator of the appliance needs instructions as to how to use it, so too does a user of the computer program. This forms part of what is known as *documentation*. Earlier comments (in Sec. 7-4.1) distinguished between internal documentation (in the program itself) and external documentation (separate from the program). In this section we are dealing with external documentation.

Typically, documentation serves two disparate purposes. One purpose, as mentioned, is to provide full operational instructions—for example, the form and content of any input to the program, the meaning of any output, an interpretation of error or warning messages, and a listing of limitations of the program. A separate, but equally important purpose is to provide full details of the design and implementation. This is essential for maintenance.

Because these roles are so different, separate documents are recommended. Terminology differs, but we will refer to them as the *user's manual* and the *maintenance manual*. In a large project, each of these manuals may encompass several volumes. There may be individual user's manual volumes for various classes of users and both reference and tutorial volumes. The maintenance volumes may each cover a particular subsystem, or they may have different classes of information such as data flow diagrams, data structure layouts, and output forms specifications.

Documentation should be maintained through all phases of the system life cycle, and all this documentation forms part of the documentation of the system. Certainly the requirements definition and system design are important components of the maintenance manual. Some designers advocate producing the user's manual during the design phase and reviewing it with the projected users of the system. This helps avoid proceeding with implementation of an unsatisfactory design and later attempting to patch the program to meet the users' needs.

All of us have seen examples of poor documentation. This should tip us off as to how to prepare good documentation. Organization and clarity are essential. Diagrams and charts can enhance understanding. An index can be invaluable. Once again, the availability of good tools can be a definite asset. Documentation tools include text editors, spelling checkers, formatters, charting aids, and information-retrieval packages. There is an abundance of good software on the market today to support the production of documentation.

As a piece of software evolves, so too must its documentation. Maintenance of documentation must go hand in hand with maintenance of the software. It is very frustrating when implementation and documentation disagree.

The preparation of documentation is as important to a project as preparation of the software and every bit as difficult. There is no substitute for practice and experience in becoming skilled at documentation.

## 7-5 TESTING AND DEBUGGING ISSUES

The design of a system consists of a hierarchy of modules (and associated descriptions). The next step in the development process is to convert this design into a computer program. Also, either as a separate phase or in conjunction with the programming activity, the software produced must be verified. It is widely acknowledged that approximately 50 percent of total elapsed development time and over 50 percent of total resources are expended on verifying a system. Each individual module in a system must be verified. This verification process also needs to be applied to a group of modules working as a subsystem.

In this section we first focus on strategies for programming and testing subsystems. Since the most current practical way of verifying a software system is testing, we next concentrate on test-case design techniques. The purpose of these techniques is to design a set of test cases which will expose as many errors as possible. The test-case techniques that we discuss are applied at the module level. A test case is considered to be successful if it exposes a new error. After the execution of a successful test case, the next activity deals with program debugging. Recall that this activity involves first determining the exact nature and location of an error within a program and then repairing that error. This section concludes with a more detailed discussion of debugging.

### 7-5.1 STRATEGIES FOR TESTING A SYSTEM

This subsection contains a discussion of the more common system-testing strategies. We first describe the bottom-up strategy, which is one of the traditional testing strategies. We next present the top-down testing strategy and compare it with the bottom-up approach. These pure testing strategies are then combined to form a mixed testing strategy.

#### Bottom-Up Testing Strategy
In a properly designed system, the modules are manageable "chunks" that can be programmed and tested by different individuals.

The time and cost of programming and testing a collection of modules depend on the order in which individual modules are programmed and tested. Different implementation and testing orders can greatly affect the effort required to accomplish the task. This subsection discusses one particular order of programming and testing modules. The next two subsections present different strategies leading to different orders of programming and testing.

The testing of a collection of modules that make up a system involves the following:

**1.** Program and test each individual module by itself to determine whether it meets its specifications. This activity is sometimes called a *unit test*.

**2.** Test two modules together to ensure that they function together properly. The interfaces between the two modules, such as their argument-parameter sequences and common data area, must be checked. This activity is sometimes called an *integration test*.

**3.** Test whether a subsystem (or the entire system) of modules functions properly according to its specifications. This activity is often called a *system test*.

**4.** Run the given system, under controlled conditions, in its actual or operational environment.

The *bottom-up testing strategy* involves performing these four activities in the order just given. For example, the bottom-up testing of the system of modules shown in Fig. 7-29 would result in the sequence of activities given in Fig. 7-30. Each lowest- or bottom-level module is unit tested by

**FIGURE 7-29  An example of module organization.**

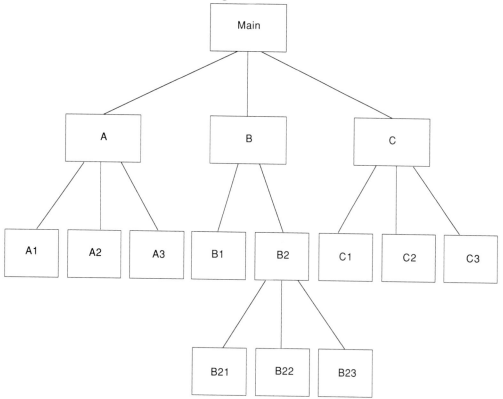

itself (Fig. 7-30a). Next, the lowest-level subsystems are tested, as shown in Fig. 7-30b. Subsystem tests are then performed for progressively higher-level subsystems until the entire system is complete. In summary, the bottom-up approach is to test the modules from the bottom to the top of the module hierarchy.

Because we wish to test lower-level modules in the absence of the actual upper-level module which uses them, we require the presence of *test drivers*.

**FIGURE 7-30**  **Basic sequence of activities in bottom-up testing.**

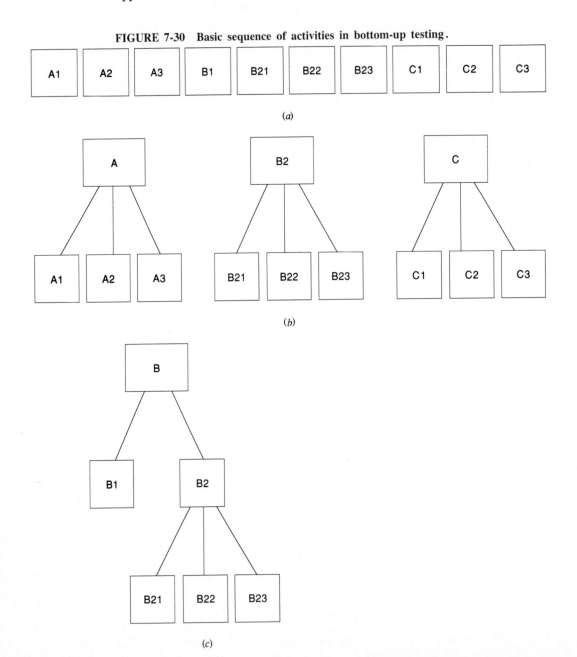

The function of a test driver is to "drive," "exercise," or invoke the module under test. A test driver is often a skeleton of a portion of the completed module which invokes the module being tested in a complete system and is usually much simpler than the actual upper-level module.

As an example of the bottom-up approach to testing, we consider the problem of processing the results of an examination. Output is to consist of the class average and the highest and lowest marks along with the names of the students making those marks. Input consists of one line for each student with his or her name followed by the exam mark, an integer from 0 to 100 inclusive. The output should also include a copy of the original input because the output is intended to be printed and filed for later reference. We will assume that no name is longer than 30 characters and that there are at most 250 students in the class.

Figure 7-31 presents a structure chart for a proposed solution to the problem. Although the problem is fairly simple, we have highly modularized the solution so as to better illustrate the principles of testing.

Our first step is to unit test procedure ReadString given in Fig. 7-32. This requires a test driver. A simple test driver would call ReadString once and report the values produced via its output parameters. Testing can be more efficiently performed, however, by designing the driver to repeatedly call procedure ReadString. The test driver in Fig. 7-33 uses this technique. Notice that Pascal requires that the constant and type declarations globally referenced by ReadString be included in the test driver.

Bottom-up testing would continue by testing procedures DisplayData, Average, HighestMark, and LowestMark and involves preparing a test driver for each. Next, testing of subsystems commences with the combination of GetOneLine and ReadString. We proceed in this manner until the entire system is tested. The complete bottom-up test of program ExamStatistics is left as an exercise.

There are two main approaches to testing a subsystem of modules. The first is a *phased approach*, which involves testing all modules in a subsystem together. For example, after unit testing modules A1, A2, and A3 in Fig. 7-29, these modules would be tested with module A as shown in Fig. 7-30b. This approach has one serious drawback. It makes the detection of interaction errors among modules more difficult than necessary. In the preceding example, throwing modules A1, A2, A3 and A into one test can result in many interaction errors.

Interaction errors can be detected more easily by using an *incremental approach*. This second approach is described using the following general algorithm:

*1.* Program and unit test each module by itself

*2.* Repeat thru step 4 until the entire system has been tested

*3.* Add a new module

*4.* Test the resulting combinations of modules

Using this approach, we are adding only one new module at a time. For

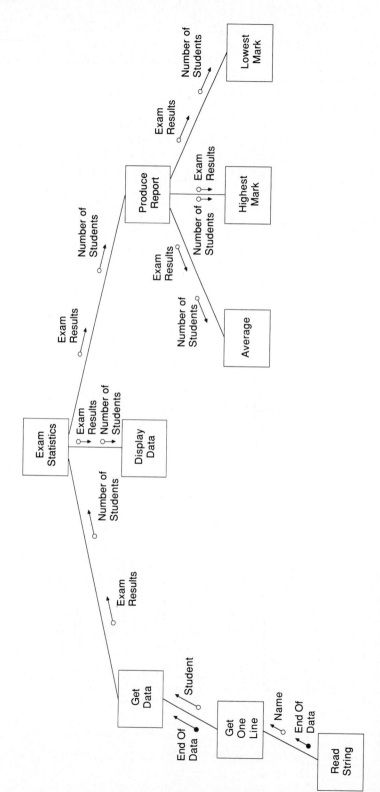

**FIGURE 7-31 Structure chart for the testing example.**

example, in the previous example, module A could be tested with module A1. When that test is complete, another module, say, A2, is added, and the new combination is tested. Finally, the third module (that is, A3) is added, and all four modules are tested together. Of course, this requires a specially modified version of module A, which does not use modules A2 or A3, or else *stub* modules, as described in the next section.

The incremental approach is clearly superior to the phased approach. In general, we start out with a combination of $n$ modules which seems to work. Note that these modules may contain undetected errors. We then add another module and test a new combination of $n + 1$ modules. If the test fails, then one or more errors have been found due to the addition of the $n + 1$st module. Quite often the error will be in (or as a result of interactions with) the most recently added module. In any case, the detection of errors has been greatly simplified.

Experience has shown that bottom-up testing of a large system is usually unsatisfactory because of the tardiness in detecting interaction and interface errors at the upper levels. Interfaces between successively larger subsystems are tested in successively later stages of the implementation and testing phase. Consequently, major interface errors are detected only late in the testing process. Frequently, such errors require the reprogramming of several modules.

Using the bottom-up strategy, the highest-level interface errors are detected and corrected (possibly) at the end of the project. Since these errors are the most difficult to fix, the entire system may not work properly even though lower-level modules have been tested. The substantial effort in fixing these errors usually results in a serious time overrun (that is, slippage past the project deadline date). It is not unusual for such overruns to cause projects to fail.

**Top-Down Testing Strategy**

The main drawback of the bottom-up testing strategy, which is testing the high-level interfaces last, can be avoided by testing the modules in a different order. The *top-down testing strategy* is to test the highest-level modules first, then proceed to test the next-highest-level modules, and continue in this fashion until the lowest-level modules in the system hierarchy are tested. Using this approach, the module organization in Fig. 7-29 would be tested in the order shown in Fig. 7-34.

Observe the interactions between levels in the module hierarchy in Fig. 7-34 in the top-down approach to testing that system. Since module Main invokes modules A, B, and C, the testing of Main requires that the latter modules be present in some form. At least the interfaces between module Main and the modules A, B, and C must be included in order to perform a test of Main. The specification of these interfaces for testing purposes is accomplished by programming a *dummy module* or *stub* for each required module.

The concept of a stub is a key aspect in the top-down testing approach. Frequently, the stub or dummy module is simply a "shell" or skeleton which

```
procedure ReadString(
    var Name: StringType;          {Output, name read}
    var EndOfData: boolean         {Output, end of data flag}
                    );
```
{This procedure reads a quoted name from the input stream. The name may not contain quotes. If the end of data is encountered before a complete string is read then true is returned for the end-of-data flag; otherwise, false is returned.}
```
var
    J: integer;
    C: char;
begin
    {Step 1: Initialize Name to blank and EndOfData to false}
    for J := 1 to StringLength do
        Name[J] := '□';
    EndOfData := false;

    {Step 2: If no more data then just set EndOfData to true}
    if eof
    then EndOfData := true
    else begin

        {Step 3: Discard leading blanks}
        read(C);
        while not eof and (C = '□') do
            read(C);
```

FIGURE 7-32
Procedure to read
a string.

does very little or no work. For example, if module C contains several input parameters and one output parameter (say, Ans), then the stub for C may contain the declarations of these parameters and an assignment statement which assigns some (constant) value to Ans. Alternatively, the stub for C might contain a statement which prints a message that indicates that module C has been invoked.

It should be emphasized, however, that the testing of module Main in Fig. 7-34a tests only the interfaces between Main and A, B, and C. The functions of modules A, B, and C are not tested at this point. In a subsequent test, the stubs for modules A, B, and C will be expanded to their final forms.

The benefits of using the incremental approach also apply to the top-down testing strategy. In fact, the incremental approach is always preferred over the phased approach regardless of which testing strategy is used.

Stubs perform a variety of actions which may include one or more of the following:

*1.* Return a particular value (e.g., assigning a constant value to Ans).

*2.* Output a message which indicates that the module has been invoked as expected.

```
{Step 4: If end of data set EndOfData to true}
if eof
then EndOfData : = true
else begin

        {Step 5: Process the string}
        if C = ''''
        then begin
                read(C);
                J : = 0;
                while not eof and (C <> '''') do
                  begin
                    J : = J + 1;
                    Name[J] : = C;
                    read(C)
                  end;
                if C <> ''''
                then begin
                        J : = J + 1;
                        Name[J] : = C
                end
            end
        end
    end
  end
end;
```

FIGURE 7-32 *(cont.)*

*3.* Return immediately to the invoking module with no processing.

*4.* Enter answers in an interactive or debugging mode.

*5.* Return a random number using a random number generator.

*6.* Calculate an approximate value(s) for the module.

*7.* Consume a specified amount of time in the module before returning to the invoking module.

Table 7-3 exhibits the stubs required in the testing of each module in Fig. 7-29. Observe that the highest-level interfaces are tested first. This approach exposes interface errors between the largest subsystems early in the testing phase. As time progresses, interface errors are detected and repaired at successively lower levels of the module hierarchy. These errors are confined to within smaller subsystems of the hierarchy. This approach tends to avoid cost and time overruns.

In order to illustrate top-down testing, we return to the exam statistics program which was used to illustrate bottom-up testing. Our first step is to test the implementation of the main program ExamStatistics (Fig. 7-35). This program cannot be run without procedures GetData, DisplayData, and ProduceReport. In fact, compilation of the main program as given will

```
program TestReadString(input, output);
{Test driver to unit test procedure ReadString.}
const
    StringLength = 30;
type
    StringType = packed array [1 .. StringLength] of char;
var
    TestString: StringType;
    EndOfData: Boolean;
{Include the procedure ReadString here}
begin
    {Read and print strings until end of data}
    repeat
        ReadString(TestString, EndOfData);
        writeln('*', TestString,'* Flag: ', EndOfData)
    until EndOfData
end.
```

**FIGURE 7-33**
**Driver to test**
**procedure ReadString.**

normally result in error messages. We therefore include the stub versions of
these procedures given in Fig. 7-36. Stubs should be as simple as possible
because the intent is to test the main program at this point. Complex stubs
might introduce errors of their own and defeat the purpose of the test. Here
we observe that the logic of the main program is devoted to calling the three
procedures in sequence and the values are merely passed on and not used in
the main program itself. Therefore, our stubs merely report that they were
activated, thus verifying the logic of the main program.

One subtlety which could cause a problem on some Pascal compilers involves use of uninitialized variables. Stub procedure GetData does
not assign values to its output parameter. We have assumed that this is
acceptable because they are never "used." However, the occurrence of variables ExamResults and NumberOfStudents as arguments corresponding to value
parameters in the last two calls is technically a use of these variables, and
some Pascal compilers may cause a run-time error message indicating the
use of uninitialized variables. It is a simple matter to add assignments to all
output parameters of each stub procedure.

Upon successful testing of the main program, top-down testing requires
testing of the next level of procedures. We will use the incremental approach
and next test procedure GetData. The header should, of course, remain
identical to that used for the stub. The body of the stub is replaced by the
actual implementation of the procedure, as shown in Fig. 7-37. We retain
the stub versions of DisplayData and ProduceReport, and we require a stub
version of procedure GetOneLine which is called by the implementation of
procedure GetData. Recall that our goal at this point is to test the logic of
GetData. A potential problem is the control coupling involving the end-of-
data flag. The stub procedure GetOneLine (Fig. 7-38) is arranged to return
student data on the first two calls and end of data on all subsequent calls.
Because Pascal lacks initialized static variables in procedures, mechanization

of this stub requires a global variable. We introduce the variable declaration

LineCounter: integer;

in the main program and the intialization

LineCounter : = 1;

temporarily for tests involving the stub GetOneLine.

**FIGURE 7-34  Basic sequence of activities in top-down testing.**

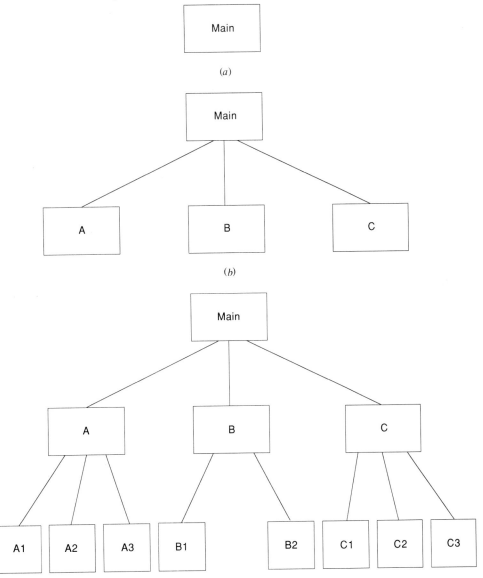

| **TABLE 7-3** Stubs Required to Test Each Module in Fig. 7-29 | |
| --- | --- |
| **Module Being Tested** | **Stubs Required** |
| MAIN | A, B, C |
| A | A1, A2, A3 |
| B | B1, B2 |
| C | C1, C2, C3 |
| B2 | B21, B22, B23 |
| All others | None |

**program** ExamStatistics(input, output);
{Given as input a set of lines each containing a student name and exam mark, this program displays the class average, and the highest and lowest mark along with the name of each student making the highest and lowest marks.}
**const**
　StringLength = 30;
　MaxNumberOfStudents = 250;
**type**
　StringType = **packed array** [1 .. StringLength] **of** char;
　StudRecType =
　　**record**
　　　Name: StringType;
　　　Mark: 0 .. 100
　　**end**;
　NumOfStudType = 1 .. MaxNumberOfStudents;
　ExamResType = **array** [NumOfStudType] **of** StudRecType;
**var**
　NumberOfStudents: NumOfStudType;
　ExamResults: ExamResType;
{Include procedure declarations here}

**begin**
　{Step 1: Get input data}
　GetData(ExamResults, NumberOfStudents);

　{Step 2: Display input data}
　DisplayData(ExamResults, NumberOfStudents);

　{Step 3: Produce the required statistical report}
　ProduceReport(ExamResults, NumberOfStudents)
**end**.

**FIGURE 7-35**
**Main program for**
**the top-down testing**
**example.**

```
procedure GetData (
    var ExamResults: ExamResType;           {Output, names and marks}
    var NumberOfStudents: NumOfStudType      {Output, actual number of students}
                  );
{This procedure reads the data for all students in the class}
{Stub version}
begin
    writeln ('GetData called')
end;


procedure DisplayData (
    ExamResults: ExamResType;              {Input, names and marks}
    NumberOfStudents: NumOfStudType        {Input, actual number of students}
                  );
{This procedure displays the data for all students in the class}
{Stub version}
begin
    writeln ('DisplayData called')
end;


procedure ProduceReport (
    ExamResults: ExamResType;              {Input, names and marks}
    NumberOfStudents: NumOfStudType        {Input, actual number of students}
                  );
{This procedure displays the average and also the highest and lowest marks
    along with the corresponding student names.}
{Stub version}
begin
    writeln('ProduceReport called')
end;
```

**FIGURE 7-36**
**Stub procedures for
testing program
ExamStatistics**.

Top-down testing next requires testing DisplayData, which does not require additional stubs. Next, ProduceReport is tested with stubs Average, HighestMark, and LowestMark. This completes the second level, and testing progresses to the third level, etc. The implementation and testing of the remainder of this example are left as an exercise.

The effort required in top-down testing is comparable to that required in the bottom-up approach. The former approach uses stubs instead of the test drivers required by the latter approach. Note that the testing of the lowest-level modules requires test drivers in the bottom-up approach but no stubs in the top-down strategy because everything is in place at that time.

## Mixed-Level Testing Strategy

The basic bottom-up testing strategy is to start testing the lowest-level modules and to proceed to higher and higher levels. Conversely, the pure top-down testing approach begins at the highest level and proceeds to successively lower levels. These basic strategies can be adhered to while, at the

```
var
  EndOfData: boolean;              {End of data flag}
  J: NumOfStudType;                {Array index}
  Student: StudRecType;            {Record of current student}
begin
  {Step 1: Initialize array index}
  J := 1;

  {Step 2: Read student data until done}
  repeat
    GetOneLine(Student, EndOfData);
    ExamResults[J] := Student;
    if J < MaxNumberOfStudents
    then J := J + 1
  until EndOfData;
  NumberOfStudents := J - 1
end;
```

FIGURE 7-37
Body of full
implementation of
procedure GetData.

same time, performing tests at higher levels in some parts of the system and at lower levels in other parts of the hierarchy.

As an example, the pure top-down sequence of tests in Fig. 7-34 can be altered so that third-level modules are tested before all modules at the second level. Figure 7-39 shows a partial testing configuration for the hierarchy in Fig. 7-29. The testing order can be Main, B, B2, C, B22.

The flexibility of the mixed-level approach is of great advantage when some modules are finished ahead of schedule or other modules are not finished on schedule. Also, certain modules (e.g., module B22 in Fig. 7-29) may be critical in the hierarchy and must be tested at an early stage. Just as high-level interface and interaction problems can cause the changing of low-level modules, problems with a critical module at a lower level can also cause the redesign of upper-level modules. The mixed-level testing approach is desirable in the latter case. Consequently, this approach facilitates the early testing of higher-level modules (and associated interfaces) and the early testing of critical lower-level modules.

## 7-5.2 SOFTWARE VERIFICATION

Regardless of how careful we are in developing software, errors do occur in the requirements specifications, design, and programming phases of development. For a system to be operationally acceptable, the effect of such errors must be reduced to an acceptable level. An important activity in attaining operational acceptability is to verify that the system operates according to the software specifications. The system-verification activity exposes errors which usually can be repaired. All too often, however, the repair of errors may require the redesign of some parts of the system. The form of verification that is used in most instances is system testing.

This section first focuses on the psychology and basic notions of testing. The reading of programs by people can be an effective error-detection

```
procedure GetOneLine (
    var Student: StudRecType;          {Output, record of one student}
    var EndOfData: boolean             {Output, end of data flag}
                    );
{This procedure reads the input data for one student, or returns an end of
    data indication.}
{Stub version}
begin
    if LineCounter = 1
    then begin
            Student.Name : = 'Name 1       ';
            Student.Mark : = 10;
            EndOfData : = false;
            LineCounter : = 2
       end
    else
        if LineCounter = 2
        then begin
                Student.Name : = 'Name 2       ';
                Student.Mark : = 20;
                EndOfData : = false;
                LineCounter : = 3
           end
        else begin
                Student.Name : = 'Invalid       ';
                Student.Mark : = 30;
                EndOfData : = true
           end
end;
```

**FIGURE 7-38**
Stub version of
procedure GetOneLine.

strategy. For this reason, we discuss the human-testing activity before the
more usual computer-based testing strategies.

### Basic Notions and Psychology of Testing

Recall that there are two broad classes of techniques that can be used to
verify the correctness of a program. One class of techniques is based on providing a formal proof for a program. The proof is usually deduced directly
from the program. Formal proofs tend to be long and complicated, even for
short programs. Furthermore, a proof can easily be wrong. Finally, proof
techniques do not take into consideration a programming language's environment, such as hardware, operating system, and users. In summary, currently, for any but the most trivial programs, formal proof techniques are not
practical, nor are they sufficient in verifying the correctness of a system.

The second class of verification technique is based on testing. *Testing*
is the activity of executing a program with the purpose of finding errors. For
each test, a program is executed for a set of input values which is called
a *test point* or *test case*. The program's observed outputs for each test case
are used to find and repair errors. Testing, as opposed to proving, does

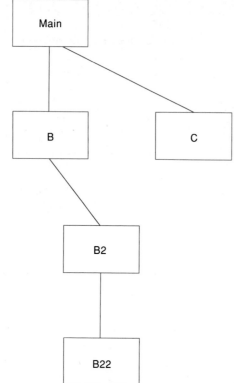

**FIGURE 7-39**
**Example configuration**
**in a mixed-level**
**testing approach.**

yield concrete information about a program's behavior in a real environment through its execution. Testing by itself, however, is usually not sufficient to verify the correctness of a program. This is so because to completely verify the correctness of a program would require (for any but the simplest programs) an astronomical number of test cases. In practice, only a small subset of possible test cases is used. A test may result in exposing an error but will not (except for trivial programs) show the absence of errors.

**Psychology of Testing.** Testing can be discussed from several viewpoints. One of its most important viewpoints, however, concerns issues of human psychology and economics. Considerations such as having the proper attitude toward testing and the feasibility of completely testing a program appear to be as important as (or maybe even more important than) purely technical issues.

Since people are usually goal-oriented, it is vitally important, from a psychological viewpoint, that a proper goal of testing be established. If the stated goal in testing is to show that a program contains no errors, then individuals will probably select test data that will not expose errors in the program. One reason for this is that such a goal is impossible or infeasible to achieve for all but the most trivial programs. Alternatively, if the stated goal is to show that a program has errors, the test data will usually have a higher probability of exposing errors. The latter approach will make the program more reliable than the former.

Earlier we defined testing as the activity of executing a program with the purpose of finding errors. This definition implies that testing is not a *constructive* process, but a *destructive* process. Since most people view things in a constructive (positive) rather than a destructive (negative) manner, this explains why many people find testing to be a difficult task. In fact, the proper testing of a program is often more difficult than its design.

It is unfortunate that in many instances testing activities are not seriously considered until software has been shown not to work properly. In designing and implementing a system, it is easy to become convinced that the solution is correct and therefore extensive testing is unwarranted. This attitude is based on viewing software development as a creative, innovative, challenging, constructive, and optimistic activity.

A proper testing attitude is, then, to view a test case as being *successful* if it exposes or detects a new error. On the other hand, a test case is *unsuccessful* if it *fails* to find a new error. Observe that the use of the words "successful" and "unsuccessful" in testing is the opposite of the common usage of these words by project managers and programmers.

The preceding definitions associated with testing make the testing attitude opposite to the design and programming attitude, since testing involves trying to destroy what a programmer has built. For this reason, it is difficult, after a programmer has created a program, to then attempt to destroy it. Consequently, many programmers cannot effectively test their own programs because they don't have the necessary mental attitude of wanting to find errors. Therefore, the verification of large systems is now performed frequently by independent testing teams.

For small systems, a reliable solution can be obtained by first designing an appropriate and suitable set of test cases. The solution can then be designed to pass these tests. More will be said about this approach in the subsections White-Box Testing and Black-Box Testing.

An important consideration concerning program testing is whether it is possible to find all errors in a given program. In general, it is impossible or impractical to locate all errors in a given program. This problem affects the way in which test cases are designed and, more generally, the economics of testing. Finally, it affects the assumptions that a test person will have to make about a given program.

**Specification-Based and Program-Based Testing Strategies.** We can classify testing methods based on how much use is made of a program's structure. In *white-box* (also called *program-based* or *logic-driven*) testing, the tester uses the internal structure of the program in the formulation of suitable test cases.

One obvious approach in attempting to exhaustively (or completely) test a program is to cause every statement in the given program to execute at least once. As we shall see later, however, this approach is grossly inadequate. Another approach is to execute, by generating a suitable set of test cases, all possible control paths through a program. By a *control path*, we mean paths containing conditional and counted-loop statements. The number of distinct logic paths in most programs tends to be extremely large. The testing of all such paths is quite often impractical. Even if we could test all possible paths, there are several reasons why the path approach to testing is not sufficient to completely test a program. An exhaustive path test is not the same as checking the specifications for the program. A program that is completely path tested could still contain many errors. The program, for example, might perform a sort instead of a search. Unless we have the program's specifications, exhaustive path testing will not detect the wrong program. Another reason is the program may contain several missing paths. Path testing would not expose the absence of necessary paths. Furthermore, an inappropriate or incorrect decision need not be exposed when a program is path tested. Finally, an incorrect calculation may not be detected when the appropriate path is tested.

A second testing strategy is *black-box* (also called *specification-based*, *data-driven*, or *input/output-driven*) testing. In using this strategy, the tester views the program as a black box whose internal structure is unknown. Test cases are generated solely from the specifications of the program and not its internal structure. Such test cases are usually extended to include invalid data so that the program can detect erroneous inputs and output appropriate error messages. A program that reacts to invalid as well as valid input data is said to be *robust*.

The exhaustive testing of a program by black-box testing requires exhaustive input testing. This requires that all possible inputs be included in a set of test cases. The verification of a program requires that a program be tested for what it is supposed to do as well as what it is *not* supposed to do. Thus a tester must include test cases that cover not only all valid inputs, but also all invalid inputs. Consequently, even for small programs, exhaustive testing requires a tester to produce essentially an infinite number of test cases.

The testing of large programs such as a Pascal or Ada compiler is even more difficult. Such compilers must detect valid as well as invalid programs. The number of such programs is clearly infinite. Programs such as operating systems, data base systems, and banking systems have "memory." The result of one test case depends on the results of previous test cases. Therefore, exhaustive sequences of test cases must be devised in order to test such programs!

From the previous discussion, we see that exhaustive input testing is not practical or possible. Therefore, we cannot guarantee that all errors in a program will be found. Also, since it is not economically feasible to exhaustively test a given program, we want to maximize the number of errors found by a finite set of test cases.

In summary, white-box and black-box testing strategies complement each other. The use of black-box tests augmented by white-box tests may in many situations be the best way of finding errors.

Since the testing of a program is incomplete (that is, we cannot guarantee that all errors have been found), a reasonable strategy is to find as many errors as possible. It is desirable to choose test cases that have a high degree of success in exposing errors. Clearly, because testing is an expensive activity, we want to find as many errors as possible with as few test cases as possible. Specific techniques for test case generation will be discussed in subsections on white-box and black-box testing.

**Testing Principles.** The following is a list of testing guidelines that are important in fostering a proper attitude to testing a program:

*1.* A program is assumed to contain errors.

*2.* Testing is performed so that errors are exposed.

*3.* Each test case should have its associated expected result.

*4.* A test case is considered to be successful if it exposes a new error; otherwise, it is unsuccessful.

*5.* Test cases should include both valid and invalid data.

*6.* Programmers should not test their own work.

*7.* The number of new errors still to be found in a program is directly proportional to the number already found.

*8.* The results of each test case must be examined carefully so that errors are not overlooked.

*9.* All the test cases should be kept for possible future use.

### Human Testing

In the early years of computing it was generally believed that the only way to test a program was to execute it on a computer. In recent years, however, the reading of programs by people has proved to be an effective way of finding errors. Human-based testing methods are applied to a program before it is tested by computers. While some of these methods are meant to involve a group consisting of several individuals, we will not focus on the makeup of such a group at this time. This section, instead, concentrates on an error checklist which is useful in inspecting programs. Although the approach to inspecting programs is simple and informal, it can contribute significantly to the productivity and reliability of a system. Errors that are found at an early stage generally are cheaper and easier to correct than those found later. At the computer-based testing stage, programmers are under greater stress than at the human-testing stage, and the result is that more mistakes are usually made in attempting to correct an error at the former stage than at the latter. Also, certain types of errors are more easily found by human testing than by computer-based testing techniques.

We present now a checklist which is useful in finding common errors in a given Pascal program. While the checklist is oriented to Pascal, many of the errors are applicable to programs in other languages. The error classes to be described in turn deal with data declaration, data reference, control flow, computation, comparison, interface, input/output, and miscellaneous syntax types of errors.

## Data-Declaration Errors

*1.* Are all constant identifiers properly defined?

*2.* Are all types properly defined? Are the definitions in the order required by Pascal? Are all types which are required for procedure and function parameters given explicit names rather than being anonymous types?

*3.* Are all variables properly declared? With the proper type?

*4.* Check for duplicate declarations of identifiers (constants, types, variables, procedure and function names, enumerated type element names, parameter names) in the same scope. If the compiler being used extracts a portion of the identifier, e.g., the first eight characters, then use the same rule in checking for duplicate identifiers.

*5.* Check for global references which refer to the wrong identifiers because another declaration for the same identifier occurs in a different scope.

*6.* Check that no predefined identifiers which are required in the program are redeclared.

*7.* Check for different identifiers with similar names. Such variables (e.g., Total and Totals) are a frequent source of errors.

## Data-Reference Errors

*1.* Verify that each variable has some value just prior to being referenced. *Undefined variables* are common programming errors.

*2.* Does every subscript in all array references have a value of the proper type? For example, a subscript may have only an integer value or an enumerated type value.

*3.* Are all subscript values in every array reference within bounds? This is another familiar source of programming errors. In particular, check each subscript for an *off-by-one* error.

## Control-Flow Errors

*1.* Check that each compound statement, each procedure and function body, and the main program have a matching **begin** and **end** pair. Also check that each **begin–end** pair corresponds to the appropriate group of statements.

*2.* Check for *dangling-else* problems. That is, check that an if-then-else construct does not have an if-then construct nested in the then part. In this case, Pascal will associate the else part with the wrong construct.

*3.* Check that every multiway-branch statement (such as a case statement) has its associated index within bounds.

*4.* Verify (informally) that each loop in a program will terminate.

*5.* Check each loop for off-by-one errors. Pay special attention to what happens the first time and last time through the loop.

6. Check the validity of a loop never executing (that is, not executing its body even once).

7. Check carefully all loops with compound conditions. For example, in the program segment

```
Found : = false;
Current : = 1;
while Current <= TableSize and not Found do
    .
    .
    .
```

what happens if **Found** is never set to "true" within the body of the loop?

8. Attempt to verify (informally) that every procedure, function, or program will terminate.

519

7-5
TESTING AND
DEBUGGING ISSUES

## Computation Errors

1. Check each division to see if it is possible to divide by zero.

2. Check each variable to ensure that its value is always within any stated bounds.

3. Check for computations that have variables whose types are not compatible. For example, the logical conjunction **or** of an integer value and a Boolean value would not be compatible.

4. Check carefully numerical computations for proper use of integer and real variables and constants and the proper use of / and **div**.

5. Check for assignment-compatible types in every assignment statement.

6. Can intermediate computations result in underflow or overflow situations?

7. Check the consequences of inaccurate computations due to roundoff and truncation errors.

8. Check the evaluation of expressions to verify that proper precedence rules are being followed.

## Comparison Errors

1. Check for comparisons of incompatible types. For example, comparing a real number to an enumerated type value is not valid.

2. Check relational operators for correctness. Relationships are often confused.

3. Check Boolean expressions for correctness. Many errors are made in using the logical operators **or**, **and**, and **not**.

4. Have relational and logical operators been mixed inadvertently? For example, the relation $A > B > C$ is usually represented by $(A > B)$ **and** $(B > C)$. Also, relations such as $0 <= J <= 50$ are usually written as $(J >= 0)$ **and** $(J <= 50)$.

5. Is the result of a comparison sensitive to the effects of roundoff and truncation?

6. Check expressions containing relational and logical operators for proper evaluation according to the rules of precedence. Remember that Pascal's precedence rules require that relations be parenthesized when joined by **and** and **or**.

7. Does a logical expression require partial evaluation? For example, in the following statement

   **if** (A <> 0) **and** (B / A = C)

   **then**

   .
   .
   .

   if A <> 0 is "false," the remainder of the expression does not need evaluation because the final result is already known to be "false." Some Pascal compilers, however, evaluate the entire expression, which, in this case, results in a division by zero.

### Interface Errors

1. Is the number of arguments in a calling statement the same as the number of parameters in the subprogram invoked?

2. Is the type of each argument corresponding to a call-by-value parameter assignment compatible to the parameters?

3. Is the type of each argument corresponding to a call-as-variable parameter of identical type to the arguments?

4. Is the order of the arguments in a calling statement the same as the order of the parameters in the subprogram invoked?

5. Is each corresponding argument-parameter pair represented in the same units? For example, an argument indicating temperature measured in Celsius degrees and its corresponding parameter assuming a temperature in Fahrenheit degrees would be an error.

6. Check all built-in function references for proper number, type, and order of arguments.

7. Are any input parameters, which were made pass-as-variable parameters for efficiency, modified?

8. Is any output parameter used before being given an initial value?

9. Does each argument corresponding to an input/output parameter have a valid value before the calling statement?

### Input/Output Errors

1. Check that each end-of-file condition is used correctly.

2. Check that an end-of-line condition is used correctly.

3. Check that all output-editing specifications are correct.

*1.* Check for proper use of semicolons.

*2.* Check that a **begin–end** is used whenever the then part or else part of an if statement or the range of a while statement has more than one statement.

### White-Box (Program-Based) Testing

Recall that it is desirable to derive test cases using specification-based (black-box) techniques and then obtain additional test cases by applying program-based techniques. Since the latter class of technique is conceptually simpler, we discuss these techniques first.

As was pointed out earlier, it is generally not feasible to path test a given program completely based on program-based methods. Based on the program structure, we want to devise test cases which will "exercise" or "cover" the various parts of a program. The simplest criterion for covering a program is to require that each statement in a program be executed at least once. As an example of this approach, consider the following procedure:

```
procedure Sample (
    X: integer;         {Input}
    Y: integer;         {Input}
    var A: integer;     {Input/output}
            );

{A simple procedure to demonstrate program-based testing.}

begin
    if (X > 10) or (Y <> 0)
    then A : = 1 + A div X;
    if (X <> 10) and (A > = 2)
    then A : = A - 1
end;
```

Using the flowchart concepts introduced in Chap. 3, this procedure can be represented graphically as shown in Fig. 7-40. In this diagram, the various possible paths that can be taken in executing this program are shown. Observe that every statement in the program can be executed by using a single test case. The test case $X = 20$, $Y = 5$, and $A = 20$ causes the statements on path *abe* to be executed.

The statement coverage criterion is very weak. For example, the logical operation in the first statement could have been **and** instead of **or**. Such an error would not be found. As another example, if the condition in the second statement should have read $A <= 2$ rather than $A >= 2$, then this error would also not be detected. Furthermore, if the value of A was supposed to be changed when path *acd* was followed, such an error would not be exposed because there are no statements at all on this path and, therefore, statement coverage testing will not generate a test case to cover this path. Clearly, the statement coverage approach is virtually useless because it fails to expose many possible errors.

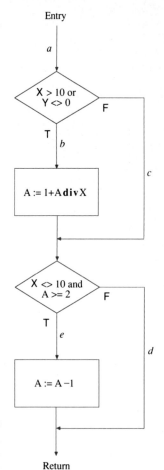

Entry

**FIGURE 7-40**
**A sample program
and its path
structure.**

A stronger criterion for testing success is *branch testing* or *decision testing*. Using this criterion, each test branch in a program is traversed at least once. Branch statements include if statements, case statements, and repeat statements.

For the sample program in Fig. 7-40, branch testing is realized by using two test cases covering paths *abe* and *acd* or *ace* and *abd*. Two test cases for the former alternative are

| | | | |
|---|---|---|---|
| X = 20 | Y = 5 | A = 20 | (path *abe*) |
| X = 10 | Y = 0 | A = 10 | (path *acd*) |

Branch-testing success usually implies that the statement covering criterion has also been satisfied. There are, however, exceptions. For example, if there are no branching decisions in a program, then no statement will be executed.

The approach that was used to branch test the current example can be used to obtain a complete set of test cases. We can obtain all the execution paths required in branch testing directly from the program. An important first step in generating test points is to calculate appropriate values at each conditional statement. The sets of such values are chosen so that all branches and all statements in the program are executed. Each set of values obtained in this way is then backtracked through the program structure to the inputs. (An example of this process occurs for A in the second if statement in Fig. 7-40.) The values of the inputs are then the test cases.

Although branch testing is superior to statement coverage, the former approach is still inadequate. For example, an error in the decision of the second if statement which would read

(X <> 10) **and** (A < = 2)

instead of

(X <> 10) **and** (A > = 2)

would go undetected if the two previous test cases were used. This occurs because the second condition (A > = 2) in the original second if statement is not tested by either test case (that is, 2 < = 2 is "true" for the first case and 10 > = 2 is also "true" for the second test case).

On the other hand, the test cases

| | | | |
|---|---|---|---|
| X = 20 | Y = 0 | A = 20 | (path *abe*) |
| X = 10 | Y = 5 | A = 0 | (path *abd*) |

test both conditions in each if statement but fail to achieve branch coverage because the *c* (that is, "false") branch of the first if statement is not followed.

In order to completely check the logic of a program, all branches and all possible outcomes of multiple conditions in each conditional construct in the program must be tested.

Another approach to testing a program called *path testing* is to ensure that every distinct path through a program is executed at least once. The distinct paths of the example in Fig. 7-40 are *abe*, *ace*, *abd*, and *acd*. The following test cases ensure path coverage for the current example:

| | | | |
|---|---|---|---|
| X = 20 | Y = 5 | A = 20 | (path *abe*) |
| X = 5 | Y = 0 | A = 10 | (path *ace*) |
| X = 10 | Y = 5 | A = 0 | (path *abd*) |
| X = 10 | Y = 0 | A = 10 | (path *acd*) |

In general, the number of distinct paths in a program may be very large.

## Black-Box (Specification-Based) Testing
The second approach to deriving test cases for a program is to ignore its structure and concentrate only on its specifications. This section focuses on specification-based testing techniques. Throughout the discussion, we assume that the program does not have memory. That is, each test case is considered to be independent of every other test case.

It has already been stated that an exhaustive black-box test of a program is usually impossible. Consequently, we want to devise a small subset of all possible test cases which will expose as many errors as possible.

The specifications for a program consist of a description of the possible inputs, the desired processing, and the possible outputs of the program. Recall that in giving these specifications we are concerned with *what* a program does, *not how* it does it. Therefore, the program can be viewed as if it were a black box (that is, we can't see inside it) which maps possible inputs into possible outputs, as shown in Fig. 7-41.

Frequently, the specifications of a program are described in a natural-language form. As an example, consider the following informal specifications for a program: "Given the three sides of a triangle $S_1$, $S_2$, and $S_3$, it is desired to compute its area by the following function:

$$\text{Area} = \sqrt{P(P - S_1)(P - S_2)(P - S_3)}$$

where $P = (S_1 + S_2 + S_3)/2$. The lengths of the sides are to be positive integers. The inputs $S_1, S_2$, and $S_3$ form a valid triangle if

$$A < B + C$$

where $A = \max(S_1, S_2, S_3)$ and $B$ and $C$ represent the other two sides. For example, input values 3, 4, and 5 represent a triangle, while input values 1, 2, and 3 do not. The valid output of the program is the area of a triangle specified by the input or some message indicating that the input values do not specify a triangle."

These specifications include the following four conditions on the input values:

**C1.** Each input contains exactly three values, that is, $S_1$, $S_2$ , and $S_3$.

**C2.** The values of $S_1$, $S_2$, and $S_3$ are greater than zero.

**C3.** The values of $S_1$, $S_2$, and $S_3$ are integers.

**C4.** $A < B + C$.

One approach to developing a minimal set of test cases for a particular program is to

*1.* Develop an appropriate set of input conditions.

*2.* Choose each test case so as to involve as many input conditions as possible.

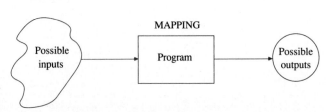

**FIGURE 7-41**
**Black-box**
**representation of**
**a program.**

Choosing an appropriate set of input conditions divides the input space (that is, *all* possible inputs) into a set of mutually disjoint sets (or *equivalence classes*) called a *partition*. The purpose of defining an equivalence class is as follows: If one test case in a particular equivalence class exposes an error, then all other test cases in that equivalence class will likely expose the same error.

The approach to obtaining a set of test cases based on equivalence partitioning of the input space is to proceed as follows:

*1.* Identify the equivalence classes based on the input conditions.

*2.* Formulate the test cases so as to cover as many equivalence classes as possible.

The equivalence classes are obtained by splitting input conditions into two or more groups. A tabular form such as that shown in Table 7-4 can be used in this process. The first column of the table contains the input conditions. The other two columns represent the valid and invalid equivalence classes based on the input conditions. A valid equivalence class represents valid inputs, while invalid equivalence classes represent invalid data.

The four input conditions of the current example are used to derive the equivalence classes. Each equivalence class is uniquely numbered, beginning with one. For example, from the input condition "number of inputs" (C1), we can obtain the equivalence class (three) consisting of all cases consisting of exactly three values. Also, invalid equivalence classes (none, one, two, $> 3$) are derived from condition C1. Similarly, from condition C2, we can obtain the valid and invalid equivalence classes $> 0$ and $\leq 0$, respectively. The other equivalence classes are obtained in a similar manner. Observe that conditions C2 and C3 are each decomposable into three conditions. For example, C2 can be restated as $S_1 > 0, S_2 > 0$, and $S_3 > 0$.

We can proceed now to the second step, which involves using the equivalence classes to formulate test cases. An approach consists of the following steps:

**TABLE 7-4** Equivalence Classes for the Area of a Triangle Example

| Input Condition | Valid Equivalence Classes | Invalid Equivalence Classes |
|---|---|---|
| C1: number of inputs | Three (1) | None (2), one (3), two (4), $> 3$ (5) |
| C2: values of $S_1, S_2, S_3$ all $> 0$ | $> 0$ (6) | $\leq 0$ (7) |
| C3: $S_1, S_2, S_3$ are all integers | Is an integer (8) | Is not an integer (9) |
| C4: $A$:$(B + C)$ | $A < B + C$ (10) | $A \geq B + C$ (11) |

1. Repeatedly formulate a new test case covering as many of the valid equivalence classes as possible until all valid equivalence classes have been covered.

2. Formulate new test cases, where possible, that cover one and only one yet uncovered invalid equivalence class until all invalid equivalences are covered.

Note that in the second step individual test cases cover each invalid equivalence class in isolation. Since invalid inputs can contain multiple errors, the detection of one error may result in other error checks not being made.

In formulating test cases, it is desirable to analyze first the boundary of each equivalence class. Rather than selecting *any* test case in an equivalence class as a representative, we can select test cases which are on the class boundary or are "close" to the boundary.

In the current example, the test case (3, 4, 5) covers valid equivalence classes 1, 6, 8, and 10 leaving classes 2, 3, 4, 5, 7, and 9. The invalid equivalence classes are covered by the following:

(2):  ( )

(3):  (3)

(4):  (3, 4)

(5):  (3, 4, 5, 6)


(7):  (0, 1, 2)

     (1, 0, 2)

     (1, 2, 0)

     (−1, 1, 2)       Note the boundary values

     (1, −1, 2)

     (1, 2, −1)


(9):  (1.5, 1, 2)

     (1, 1.5, 2)       Check for reals

     (1, 2, 1.5)

     ('A', 1, 2)

     (1, 'A', 2)       Check for strings

     (1, 2, 'A')

$$\begin{array}{c} \cdot \\ \cdot \\ \cdot \end{array} \Big\}$$ Check for other illegal types

$$\begin{array}{c} (11): (1, 2, 5) \\ (2, 3, 5) \end{array} \Big\}$$ Again, note the boundary values

Observe the test cases for the invalid equivalence classes 7 and 11. For example, in class 7, a programming error in checking, say, $S_1$ by writing $S_1 < 0$ instead of $S_1 \leq 0$ will be found. Similarly, for class 11, a programming error in writing the condition $A \leq B + C$ instead of $A < B + C$ will be found because of test case (2, 3, 5). If this test case were not used, then the error would not be exposed. The reader may want to examine how these test cases would compare with a set of test cases generated in an ad hoc manner.

In the current example, we have focused our attention on input conditions only. In general, however, output conditions must be considered. Consider a payroll example in which the input consists of an employee name, the hourly rate of pay, and the number of hours worked in a week. An output condition might be that an employee cannot receive more than some maximum weekly salary, say, $1000.00. The output space could be partitioned such that a valid weekly salary is

$$0 < PAY \leq 1000$$

and invalid classes of

$$PAY \leq 0$$

and

$$PAY > 1000$$

We then would want to devise test cases that attempt to produce weekly salaries of zero (or less) and something greater than 1000.

One weakness of equivalence-class partitioning and boundary-value analysis is that neither approach tests combinations of input values. We will not, however, explore ways of devising test cases which check for the effects of input combinations. Such methods tend to be complex.

In concluding this section, we reemphasize that specification-based testing is not sufficient. The set of test cases derived from using black-box techniques should be supplemented with additional test points obtained in using branch testing (that is, a program-based testing technique).

## 7-5.3 DEBUGGING: LOCATING AND REPAIRING ERRORS

The previous discussion dealt with testing, which is an organized approach that tries to expose the presence of errors in a given program. Frequently, this task is more difficult and tedious than that of designing the program itself. It is an unrewarding task that few programmers enjoy. Few have a natural talent for it.

Once the presence of an error has been established, its nature and location must be determined first and then the error must be fixed or repaired. Recall that this process is called *debugging* and that such an error is often called a *bug*. This subsection describes various approaches to debugging. We progress from brute-force debugging approaches to more sophisticated ones.

### Planning for Debugging

We can prepare for debugging by first assuming that the program will contain errors. Therefore, the design and programming phases should view the easy detection of errors as an important objective.

A common approach is to insert diagnostic printouts throughout a program from the start. Frequently such printouts are made conditional on special input debugging flags. It is far easier to insert these special print statements when the program is first written than at a later time. Conditional print statements often affect the structure (e.g., nesting and alignment) of a program. The placing of diagnostic printouts is easy at the initial writing of the program, since the details of its strong and weak points are fresh in the programmer's mind and it is usually a simple matter to insert a few additional statements. After the program is written, the programmer may forget some of the details, thereby making the insertion of appropriate printout statements more difficult.

Another approach to facilitate the debugging of a program is to break it up into small modules. The number (and difficulty) of bugs in a module appears to be a nonlinear function of module length. Consequently, by keeping modules small, we can locate bugs more easily. As the number of modules increases, however, we can expect an increase in bugs due to the interaction and interfacing problems among modules. The design techniques described in Sec. 7-3 should make interactions between modules more manageable.

### Debugging by Brute Force

A popular method of program debugging is the *brute-force approach*. The popularity of this rather inefficient method is perhaps due to the fact that it is the least mentally taxing of the various approaches. This method is often very time consuming and not very successful in medium-sized and larger systems.

The brute-force approach to debugging includes the following strategies:

*1.* Using storage dumps

*2.* Scattering print statements randomly throughout the program

*3.* Using automated debugging tools

The oldest debugging aid is dumping (or printing completely) the contents of memory. At any time during the execution of a program, a programmer can request the output of memory. Although a storage dump can be of assistance in finding bugs, this technique is often overused and is probably the most inefficient of the brute-force techniques. The drawbacks of the storage-dump technique include the following:

1. The difficulty of associating memory locations with program variable names because the display of memory is usually in octal (base 8) or hexadecimal (base 16) format.

2. In even the best of cases, more than 90 percent of the memory dump is useless and irrelevant. In the worst cases, the entire dump is useless.

3. A memory dump gives a snapshot or static picture of a program. To locate most errors, however, the way a program behaves over time (that is, its dynamics) must be studied.

4. The storage dump is rarely produced at the exact time when the error occurred. Therefore, the actions performed by the program (or the computer system) between the time of the error and the time of the storage dump can muddy the water.

5. There are few (if any) methodologies for analyzing a storage dump with the specific goal of finding errors.

The technique of scattering print statements throughout a program is an improvement over the storage-dump technique. It displays the contents of selected variables and facilitates the study of the program's dynamics. Some drawbacks of this technique include the following:

1. It can be a hit-or-miss approach.

2. It can be used on small programs or large programs, but the cost of using this technique can be prohibitive.

3. Its use can produce large volumes of data.

The technique of using an automated debugging aid is a third brute-force approach which is superior to the first two techniques just described. A programmer can analyze the dynamics of his or her program by using a special interactive debugging aid or taking advantage of certain language debugging constructs that are part of the programming language. Examples of such language constructs include those which produce the alteration of specified variables, the printed tracing of procedures, functions, etc., and printed traces of certain executed statements. Some system environments provide automated debugging aids that offer to a programmer a variety of commands which facilitate the following:

1. The examination and changing of variables

2. The setting and removing of breakpoints

3. A go command

4. A variety of search commands

The setting of a breakpoint (or a "stop") allows a programmer to stop the program during its execution when a specified statement or location is reached. Once a breakpoint has been reached, a programmer can, through the use of the automated aid, examine the contents of certain variables and make alterations to a program. A go command is used to resume the execution of a program after a breakpoint has been encountered. Some automated debugging aids permit the specification of conditional breakpoints and go commands. For example, a stop at a breakpoint may occur only after control has passed through it a specified number of times.

The use of an automated debugging aid can produce an excessive amount of data (much of which is useless). Also, this approach, for the most part, ignores the process of thinking. A bug can be located and repaired by first carefully analyzing the clues (or symptoms) and then piecing together the details. We now turn to strategies based on this kind of thinking.

## Debugging by Backtracking

Thus far we have discussed several brute-force approaches to debugging that require little thinking. We now examine a debugging method which requires some degree of thinking. Although this technique is of a general nature, it can be effective in locating errors, particularly in small programs.

The basic approach to backtracking is to start at the point in the program where an error has been observed (from displayed or printed results). At this point, we can deduce from the observed output the values of the program's variables (that is, the program's state). From this point, we can mentally back up the execution of the program to a previous state, that is, to a previous location (from the initial point) in the program where a new set of values for the program's variables is obtained. These new program values are inferred from the program values at the previously considered (initial) point. By repeating this basic backup process, we can often pinpoint the error easily. That is, we can isolate an error to be between the last two successive points in the program. At this point in the sequence, the state of the program (as defined by the program's variable values) is different from what was expected. Sometimes it may be necessary to collect more information by running additional test cases.

Rather than backtrack from the point at which the error was observed, we can instead track forward from the program's inputs. We wish to reemphasize that the tracking of errors (either backward or forward) often works well on small programs. If, however, the tracking of an error becomes difficult, then a more systematic and rigorous approach is required. The next subsection examines such an approach.

## Debugging by Induction

A more formal approach to locating errors is based on the principle of induction. This approach begins with a set of clues or symptoms of the error. These clues are then analyzed to produce a hypothesis of the most probable cause for the error. If the hypothesis can be verified (that is, if the hypothesized cause of the error accounts for all the clues), then the error is located; otherwise, the hypothesis must be changed.

The inductive process is summarized in the following general algorithm:

*1.* Collect the relevant data

*2.* Organize the data

*3.* Study the relationships

*4.* Attempt to devise a hypothesis
   If the attempt is not successful,
   then go to step 1

*5.* Attempt to prove the hypothesis
   If the proof attempt is not successful,
   then go to step 4

*6.* Repair the error

*7.* Verify the repair

We now elaborate on each step of this algorithm.

In the first step it is important to take into account all available data or symptoms about the problem. Test data indicating correct operation as well as data indicating incorrect operation is collected.

The second step organizes the clues or symptoms given by data so that patterns emerge. This is the inductive step, which permits us to progress from particulars to the general. Finding contradictions is an important goal in this step. A useful way of organizing (and displaying) data is shown in Table 7-5. The "What" question concerns the general symptoms of the error. The "Where" question concerns the location(s) where the symptoms were observed. The "When" question relates to the times that the symptoms occur. Finally, the "To what degree" question concerns the scope and magnitude of the symptoms. The "Is" and "Is not" columns of the table each contain the circumstances and conditions under which the error occurs or does not occur, respectively. These two columns describe potential contradictions which may lead to a hypothesis concerning the error. To obtain contradictions, it is sometimes required to use additional test points.

In steps 3 and 4, we study the relationships among the clues so that a hypothesis of most probable cause is postulated. If a hypothesis cannot be formulated, additional data is required. Additional test cases may be required at this point. At any rate, the investigation must continue.

**TABLE 7-5** A Table for Organizing Clues

| Question | Is | Is Not |
|---|---|---|
| What | | |
| Where | | |
| When | | |
| To what degree | | |

Step 5 attempts to prove the hypothesis. Failure to prove the hypothesis and attempting to repair the error may result in only a portion of the problem being corrected. The proving of the hypothesis involves verifying that it completely accounts for all clues.

Step 7 involves rerunning the case at which an error was exposed to verify that the repair has corrected the observed system. It may be advisable to run additional test cases to test the repair. Also, it is wise to rerun previously successful test cases to ensure that the repair has not created new problems (through a ripple effect). If the repair is not successful, then return to step 1.

### Debugging by Deduction

As opposed to debugging by induction, where one arrives at a hypothesis of the most probable cause for an error by examining a set of clues or symptoms for that error, debugging by deduction starts with a number of causes and by the processes of elimination and refinement arrives at the most probable cause.

The following general algorithm outlines the steps in debugging by deduction:

*1.* List all possible causes for the observed error

*2.* Use the available data to eliminate various causes

*3.* Refine the remaining hypotheses

*4.* Prove (or disprove) each remaining hypothesis

*5.* Repair the error

*6.* Verify the repair

We now elaborate on each step of this algorithm.

The first step is to compile a list of all possible causes for the error. This cause list can then be used to structure and analyze the available information.

The second step involves the analysis of the available data. Finding contradictions is an important goal in this step. Table 7-5 can again be used for this purpose. To obtain contradictions, additional test points may have to be used. In the case where more than one possible cause remains, the most likely cause is used first.

The third step involves, if necessary, using the available clues to refine the hypothesis to something more specific.

Steps 4, 5, and 6 are very similar to steps 5, 6, and 7 in the debugging by induction approach of the previous subsection.

### Debugging Example

We consider now a very simple example. Figure 7-42 presents a Pascal program to compute the average of a set of marks. The program should then display the average, the number of marks greater or equal to the average, and the number of marks below the average. A bug has been deliberately introduced into this program. Although the bug may be immediately obvious to some (probably not all) readers, we will use the formal techniques for

**program** BugExample(input, output);

{Given a set of examination marks, this program computes and displays the average mark and the number of marks greater or equal to the average, and the number of marks below the average. The marks are integers ranging from 0 through 100. Up to 100 marks are read from the input, terminated by a sentinel value of −1. A deliberate bug has been introduced into this program to illustrate debugging methods.}

**const**
    MaxNumOfMarks = 100;
    Sentinel = −1;
**type**
    MarkVector = **array**[1 .. MaxNumOfMarks] **of** integer;
**var**
    NumMarks: integer;     {Actual number of marks}
    Marks: MarkVector;     {The marks}
    Sum: integer;          {Sum of marks}
    Average: real;         {Average of marks}
    NumAbove: integer;     {Number of marks above average}
    NumBelow: integer;     {Number of marks below average}
    K: integer;            {Loop index}
**begin**
{Step 1: Read the marks}
    NumMarks := 1;
    read (Marks [NumMarks]);
    **while** Marks [NumMarks] <> Sentinel **do**
        **begin**
            NumMarks := NumMarks + 1;
            read (Marks[NumMarks])
        **end**;

{Step 2: Compute and display average}
Sum := 0;
**for** K := 1 **to** NumMarks **do**
    Sum := Sum + Marks[K];
        Average := Sum / NumMarks;
        writeln ('The average mark is', Average:6:1);

{Step 3: Count and display the number of marks above and below the average}
NumAbove := 0;
NumBelow := 0;
**for** K := 1 **to** NumMarks **do**
    **if** Marks[K] > = Average
    **then** NumAbove := NumAbove + 1
    **else** NumBelow := NumBelow + 1;
    writeln ('There were', NumAbove:1, 'marks above or the same as the average');
    writeln ('There were', NumBelow:1, 'marks below average')
**end.**

FIGURE 7-42
Erroneous program
to compute an average
set of marks.

finding the bug. A programmer must develop these techniques because not all bugs will be obvious.

The requirements for this program specified that it was to accept up to 100 integer marks, each of which was in the range 0 through 100 inclusive. The marks are to be supplied in the input stream, followed by a sentinel value of minus one. Table 7-6 presents several test cases suggested by the requirements along with the expected and actual results.

We will apply the method of debugging by induction. The pertinent data have already been presented in Table 7-6. Organizing these data exposes several symptoms of the bug. The average displayed is always less than the correct result. Further, either the number of marks above or the number of marks below average is one too great. These observations suggest a possible hypothesis: the count of marks is one too high (an off-by-one error). This would account both for the number above or below being one too large, and also for the average being too low. For example, in the first test case, an average computed as $(10 + 40 + 60 + 90)/5$ would give $200/5 = 40$. However, the actual average is 39.8. We observe that $5 * 39.8 = 199$, and conclude that the sum must have been computed incorrectly as well. The combination of the number of marks being one too high and the sum being one too low leads to our final hypothesis: the sentinel value of minus one is included in the computations as an actual mark.

Our final hypothesis can be proven either by tracing the program or by running it with some additional output statements to specifically identify the marks included in the computation of the average. Proof of the hypothesis and repair of the error are left as exercises.

## EXERCISES 7-5

1. Given the module organization in Fig. 7-43, describe the sequence of module tests for integrating the modules using a bottom-up approach and a top-down approach (with a phased approach). For each test, determine the number of drivers or stubs required.
2. Given the following procedure:

```
procedure Example(A, B, C: integer);
begin
   if (A > 10) and (B = 5)
```

**TABLE 7-6** Expected and Actual Results for Debugging Example

| Input Values | Expected Results | | | Actual Results | | |
|---|---|---|---|---|---|---|
| | Avg. | Above | Below | Avg. | Above | Below |
| 10 40 60 90 | 50.0 | 2 | 2 | 39.8 | 3 | 2 |
| 90 100 | 95.0 | 1 | 1 | 63.0 | 2 | 1 |
| 0 10 | 5.0 | 1 | 1 | 3.0 | 1 | 2 |
| 50 | 50.0 | 1 | 0 | 24.5 | 1 | 1 |

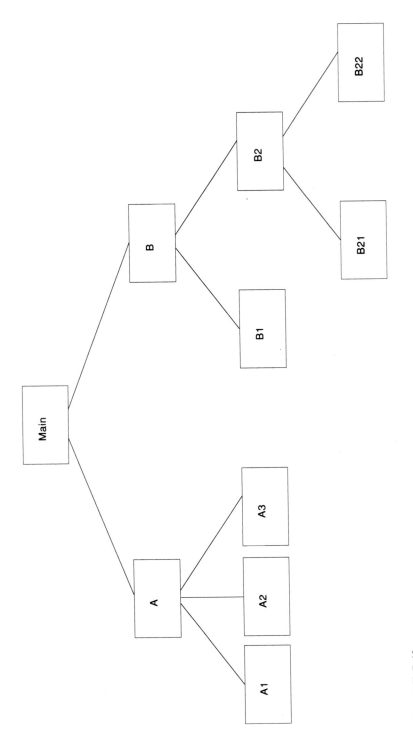

FIGURE 7-43

535

```
    then C : = 1;
    if (A = 5) or (C > 7)
      then C : = C + 2
  end;
```

devise suitable test cases to ensure

(a) Statement coverage
(b) Branch coverage
(c) Path coverage

3. Given the following program segment:

```
  .
  .
  .
Current : = 1;
NotFound : = true;
while (Current < = TableSize) and NotFound do
    if Table[Current] = SearchName
    then begin
            Found : = false;
            Current : = Current + 1
        end;
  .
  .
  .
```

devise suitable test cases to ensure the coverage of the two conditions in the while statement.

4. The real roots of a quadratic equation

$$ax^2 + bx + c = 0$$

are given by the formula

$$\frac{-b \pm \sqrt{b^2 - 4ac}}{2a}$$

where $b^2 \geq 4ac$, $a$, $b$, and $c$ are real values, and $a \neq 0$. For this problem,

(a) Develop an appropriate set of input conditions;
(b) Based on the input conditions in part (a), identify the equivalence classes;
(c) Formulate the test cases so as to cover as many equivalence classes as possible.

## 7-6  PROGRAMMING AS A HUMAN ACTIVITY

To be successful, a programmer must learn to master a wide range of different skills, from those of a creative nature such as problem analysis and solution design to purely mechanical tasks such as coding. These tasks require different abilities, yet all must be performed correctly if a correct program is to be produced. In this section we put aside technical questions and consider the effect of "the human condition" on the performance of a programmer's activities. Various aspects of the issue are considered, and suggestions are offered as to how the problem might be contained.

Programmers are not machines. They are human beings performing quite a complex task, and for this reason programmers can be expected to commit errors as a result of the basic "human condition." Human beings have real limitations in perceptual capability and performance that vary from one to another. It is important that each programmer recognize and learn to live within his or her own basic limitations.

In this section we speculate on the effects of various factors influencing a programmer writing programs on the commission of errors. We consider the causes of these errors, their ramifications, and various things that might be done to avoid or contain them. We begin by classifying the causes of error into four broad categories:

*1.* Information-processing effects

*2.* Social effects

*3.* Environmental effects

*4.* Personality effects

Material for this discussion is drawn primarily from a pair of articles by Cooke and Bunt and from books by Weinberg and by Brooks.

## 7-6.1 INFORMATION-PROCESSING EFFECTS

Errors due to information-processing effects result from inherent limitations in the reliability of human perception, memory, and cognition. Programming undeniably has a large information-processing component, the information comprising such things as the problem specifications and requirements, the rules and features of the programming language being used, and whatever parts of the program have already been written. Relevant here is the programmer's ability to input information visually, to organize the raw data (characters, spaces, etc.), and to interact effectively with the various levels of memory. Without going into details, the programmer as a human being is a very imperfect information processor: symbols are confused, language details are forgotten, the execution of routines is misunderstood, and so on. This is a frequent and important cause of error, and one to which a certain amount of attention has been devoted (see, for example, studies by Weissman and Brooks).

What can be done to reduce this source of error? The problem can be attacked on several fronts. Language designers can use the results of research in this area in the design of programming languages better suited to human information-processing limitations (see, for example, Gannon). This, however, is beyond the scope of this book and certainly beyond the control of most programmers. Individual programmers can do a great deal within the context of their own programs by maintaining an appreciation of what the potential difficulties are. For instance, an awareness of the problems of visual input suggests that the layout of a program source text and/or listing is very important. This is consistent with previous remarks on the importance of program readability. Research in eye movements suggests that effective input takes place only when the eyes fixate on some part of the display. A programmer can enhance desirable eye movements through judicious use of indentation and blank lines ("white space") to mark structural entities of the program (loops, decision alternatives, etc.). This can also assist in the perception and understanding of the structure. Perceptual speed and accuracy are heavily influenced by properties of the display. Errors increase with complexity, unfamiliarity, and clutter. This reinforces the remarks on spacing and indentation to reduce the clutter of the program listing and discourages experimentation with unfamiliar language features.

Clutter is also increased by injudicious placement of comments. Comments are certainly important in enhancing the understandability of a program, but they must be placed so as not to interfere with the perception of its important components. It is far better to have a multiline comment precede a program component than to have it interleaved within the statements of the component. Another possibility is to take advantage of space to the right of statements, if the language allows comments to be placed there.

Research on memory suggests definite upper limits on the number of "units" that can be processed effectively, where a unit can be a simple element or a related group of simple elements. For example, we might consider an operator to be a unit, or a statement, or even an entire loop or procedure. This research says something about the size of these units. If a unit, be it a procedure, a loop, or a decision alternative, is to be fully understood, its size should be limited accordingly. It might also say something about the depth of nesting before confusion sets in. As a programmer, you should try to determine your own personal limits and try not to exceed them.

An additional consequence of memory limits is that a programmer is unlikely to remember all details of a large program while working on one part of it. This suggests two things: first, that the dependencies on other parts of a program be kept to a minimum (that is, that interfaces between modules be as clean and as clear as possible), and second, that ready reference to the purpose of each module in a program be provided, either in the form of a set of comments at the head of the module or in the form of external documentation. The various design methodologies try to enforce this discipline by limiting the number and direction of intermodule references. For example, in a top-down hierarchy, modules must be unaware of other modules on the same level (that is, modules must be "blind" laterally), all references downward in the hierarchy are *control* references (that is, *do something*), and all references upward are the return of results. In addition, the top-down structure diagram serves as important external documentation.

In his paper "The Humble Programmer," Dijkstra writes of the importance of keeping programs within the "intellectual grip" of the programmer. This comment clearly relates to the information-processing capabilities of the programmer as a human being. We have suggested a number of ways in which an appreciation of these factors can reduce the chance of error. As a general rule, we encourage the practice of "defensive programming," which, like defensive driving, centers on an anticipation of errors, both your own and those of other people. The most effective programmers are those who anticipate difficulties and take steps to avoid them.

## 7-6.2 SOCIAL EFFECTS

*The practice of programming has long since passed the point where it is entirely a private activity.*
R. Conway and D. Gries, An Introduction to Programming, *Winthrop Publishers, Inc.*, 1973

Many aspects of programming involve communication between different people (directly or indirectly through shared program code). In large programming projects, programmers rarely work on a strictly individual basis. Group efforts may benefit from cooperation among the members of the group or may be hindered by excessive competition and "ego flashing." There is clearly a connection here with personality effects. Programmers in a group must be willing to accept suggestions and criticisms made for the "common good" of the project—errors must not be interpreted as public advertisements of a programmer's shortcomings.

The structure of a programming group must be designed to help overcome programmers' egos. Programmers in a group are in most cases in competition with each other for promotions, raises, and so on, yet all benefit from successful completion of the project. Brooks and Weinberg write at some length about problems of group work. Weinberg introduces the notion of "egoless" programming that has found successful application. According to this view, programs, unlike paintings or sculpture, for example, are not to be viewed as extensions of the creator's ego and thus can benefit from the suggestions and criticisms of others. The essence of the egoless approach is that each programmer in a group recognizes his or her limitations and calls on other members of the group to read his or her programs for errors and clumsiness. Systematic code perusals form a regular part of teams organized on this basis.

There appear to be definite merits to such an approach. Overall project debugging time appears to be reduced. Programs appear to be more adaptable, since more than one person must be capable of understanding what is going on. Project schedules appear to be less affected by individual programmers missing days for illness, courses, and so on. Finally, each programmer can only improve his or her programming by reading the programs of other people. This leads not only to greater job satisfaction on the part of the group members, but also to an increase in the general level of competence of the group.

## 7-6.3 ENVIRONMENTAL EFFECTS

The environment in which a programmer works has a clear effect on that programmer's effectiveness. This ranges from hardware and software support of activities relating to the development of programs to the character of office surroundings. The availability of suitable programming languages and computer systems is a definite factor, but often beyond the control of the individual programmer.

There are other valuable assists to the production of programs. For example, a good library of programs and routines can save needless "reinvention of the wheel." Computerized tools are also available to support all phases of the system life cycle. Such tools cater specifically to the needs of persons developing computer programs and, as a result, reduce the chance of error in the process.

The environment in which a person works best varies from person to person. Some people demand absolute quiet; others perform best when there is some background noise. Many programmers, by choice, are "night hawks" who relish slaving over a hot computer until the early morning hours. Some like people around at all times; others prefer privacy. It is undoubtedly the task of management to find and set the environment that maximizes the productivity of the programming personnel. Management must be prepared, however, to alter standard practices to accommodate special situations. Both Weinberg and Brooks offer amusing anecdotes concerning the discovery of suitable environments.

### 7-6.4 PERSONALITY EFFECTS

Despite their best intentions, many people may never be able to be effective programmers. In some cases this inability may be due less to information-processing limitations than to individual personality traits. Factors such as carelessness, lack of motivation, lack of organization, inability to take (or give) direction, or inability to work under stress can all lead to errors being made. Since little in the way of useful research has been conducted in this aspect of programming, it is difficult to assess its degree of impact. It is, however, something of which programmers and managers must be aware.

### 7-6.5 CONCLUDING REMARKS

We conclude our discussion of the human element in programming by observing that recognition of the problem is a large step toward its solution. Individually, each programmer must recognize and learn to live within his or her own human limitations. Management must learn to respect individual differences and recognize the effects of the human element in group activities. At the present time there has been insufficient research in the area to be able to offer concrete suggestions. The need for more activity in this important area is seen by many to be critical.

## CHAPTER SUMMARY

The programming profession is in the midst of a period of critical introspection. The need to improve the quality of programming products is real and immediate. Current thinking is that this might best be done by more formal methodologies during all phases of the software life cycle and improved appreciation of the importance of programming style.

In this chapter we have tried to give a reasonably comprehensive overview of current thoughts on the practice of software engineering. We have tried to give a working definition of program quality as well as ideas about how such quality might be achieved. A formal structure was presented for the system-development process. Suggestions were offered particularly for the design, implementation, and testing phases. Finally, some thoughts were offered on the effect of the human element.

Because of space limitations, we have only been able to scratch the surface of the field. If you wish to pursue this subject, we encourage you to refer to the list of references at the end of the chapter.

## KEY TERMS

abstraction
afferent module
black-box testing
bottom-up testing strategy
branch testing
bug
central transform
coincidental cohesion
common coupling
communicational cohesion
content coupling
context diagram
control couple
control coupling
coordinate module
data abstraction
data couple
data coupling
data description language
data dictionary
data flow
data flow diagram
data store
data-structure design
debugging
debugging by backtracking
debugging by deduction
deduction by induction
decision testing
design
efferent module

equivalence classes
external documentation
factoring
fan-in
fan-out
functional cohesion
implementation
incremental testing approach
information hiding
informational cohesion
input plan
integration test
interface
internal documentation
localization
logical cohesion
maintenance manual
mixed-level testing strategy
modifiability
modularity
module
module cohesion
module coupling
module size
object oriented design
output plan
partition
path testing
phased testing approach
procedural abstraction
procedural cohesion

process
program maintenance
programming style
reliability
requirements definition
robustness
scope of control
scope of effect
sequential cohesion
software engineering
software life cycle
stamp coupling
statement coverage testing
structure chart
structured design
structured programming
stub module

system
system test
temporal cohesion
test driver
testing
top-down testing strategy
transaction analysis
transaction-centered design
transform analysis
transform-centered design
transform module
transform plan
understandability
unit test
user's manual
utility
white-box testing

## REFERENCES

**Aktas,** A. Z.: *Structured Analysis and Design of Information Systems,* Prentice-Hall, Englewood Cliffs, N.J., 1987.

**Association for Computing Machinery:** *Computing Surveys*, special issue on programming, Peter J. Denning (ed.), vol. 6, Dec. 1974.

**Boehm,** B. W.: "Software Engineering: R and D Trends and Defense Needs," *in Research Directions in Software Technology,* ed., P. Wegner, MIT Press, Cambridge, Mass., 1979.

**Booch,** G.: *Software Engineering with Ada*, The Benjamin/Cummings Publishing Company, Menlo Park, Calif., 1983.

**Brooks,** F. P., Jr.: *The Mythical Man-Month*, Addison-Wesley, Reading, Mass., 1975.

**Brooks,** R.: "Cognitive Processes in Computer Programming," Psychology Department, Carnegie-Mellon University, 1973.

**Cooke,** J. E., and Bunt, R. B.: "Human Error in Programming as a Result of Conventional Training Methods," *Proc. IBM Scientific Symposium on Software Engineering Education*, May 1975, pp. 63–69. (*a*)

————: "Human Error in Programming: The Need to Study the Individual Programmer," *INFOR*, vol. 13, October 1975, p. 296. (*b*)

**DeMarco,** T.: *Structured Analysis and System Specification*, Yourdon Press, New York 1978.

**Dijkstra,** E. W.: "Complexity Controlled by Hierarchical Ordering of Function and Variability," in *Software Engineering*, ed. P. Naur and B. Randall, NATO Scientific Affairs Division, Brussels, 1968, p. 181.

————: "The Humble Programmer," *Communications of the ACM*, vol. 15, October 1972, p. 859.

————: "Notes on Structured Programming," in *Structured Programming*, eds. Dahl, Dijkstra, Hoare, Academic Press, New York, 1972, p. 1.

————: *A Discipline of Programming* Prentice-Hall, Englewood Cliffs, N.J., 1976.

**Dolotta,** T. A., and Mashey, J. R.: "An Introduction to the Programmer's Workbench," *Proc. Second International Conference on Software Engineering*, October 1976, p. 164.

**Fairley,** R.: *Software Engineering Concepts*, McGraw-Hill, New York, 1985.

**Gane,** C., and Sarson, T.: *Structural Systems Analysis: Tools and Techniques*, Prentice-Hall, Englewood Cliffs, N.J., 1979.

**Gannon,** J. D.: "Language Design to Enhance Programming Reliability," Technical Report CSRG-47, Computer Systems Research Group, University of Toronto, 1975.

**Gilbert,** P. : *Software Design and Development,* Science Research Associates, Palo Alto, Calif., 1983.

**Jackson,** M. A.: *Principles of Program Design,* Academic Press, New York, 1975.

**Jones,** M. P.: *The Practical Guide to Structured Systems Design,* Yourdon Press, New York, 1980.

**Kernighan,** B. W., and Plauger, P. J.: *The Elements of Programming Style,* McGraw-Hill, New York, 1974.

———, and Plauger, P. J.: *Software Tools,* Addison-Wesley, Reading, Mass., 1976.

**Ledgard,** H. F.: *Programming Proverbs,* Hayden Book Co., Rochelle Park, N.J., 1975.

———, and Tauer, J.: *Pascal with Excellence: Programming Proverbs,* Hayden Book Co., Hasbrouck Heights, N.J., 1986.

**Lehman,** M. M., and Parr, F. N.: "Program Evolution and Its Impact on Software Engineering," *Proc. Second International Conference on Software Engineering,* October 1976, p. 350.

**Miller,** G. A.: "The Magical Number Seven, Plus or Minus Two: Some Limits on our Capacity for Processing Information," *Psychological Review,* vol. 63, 1956, pp . 81–97.

**Mills,** H.: "Top Down Programming in Large Systems," in *Debugging Techniques in Large Systems,* ed. R. Rustin, Prentice-Hall, Englewood Cliffs, N.J., 1971, p. 41.

———: "Software Development," *Transactions on Software Engineering,* vol. Se-2, 1976, p. 265.

**Mosteller,** F., and Wallace, D. L.: "Inference in an Authorship Problem," *Journal of the American Statistical Association,* vol. 53, 1963, p. 275.

**Myers,** G. J.: *The Art of Software Testing,* John Wiley and Sons, New York, 1979.

**Orr,** K.: *Structured System Development,* Yourdon Press, New York, 1977.

**Pfleeger,** S. H.: *Software Engineering: The Production of Quality Software,* Macmillan, New York, 1987.

**Sachs,** J. : "Some Comments on Comments," *Systems Documentation Newsletter,* vol. 3, Dec. 1976.

**Teague,** L. C., Jr., and Pidgeon, C. W.: *Structured Analysis Methods for Computer Information Systems,* SRA, Inc., Chicago, 1985.

**Tremblay,** J.-P., and Sorenson, P. G.: *The Theory and Practice of Compiler Writing,* McGraw-Hill, New York, 1985.

**Warnier,** J. D.: *Logical Construction of Systems,* Van Nostrand/Reinhold, New York, 1981.

**Weinberg,** G. M.: *The Psychology of Computer Programming,* Van Nostrand/Reinhold, New York, 1971.

**Weinberg,** V.: *Structured Analysis,* Prentice-Hall, Englewood Cliffs, N.J., 1980.

**Weissman,** L.: "Psychological Complexity of Computer Programs: An Initial Experiment," Technical Report CSRG-26, Computer Systems Research Group, University of Toronto, 1973.

———: "A Methodology for Studying the Psychological Complexity of Computer Programs," Technical Report CSRG-37, Computer Systems Research Group, University of Toronto, 1974.

**Wirth,** N.: "Program Development by Stepwise Refinement," *Communications of the ACM,* vol. 14, April 1971, p. 221.

———: "On the Composition of Well-Structured Programs," *Computing Surveys,* vol. 6, December 1974, p. 247.

———: *Algorithms + Data Structures = Programs,* Prentice-Hall, Englewood Cliffs, N.J., 1975.

**Yourdon,** E.: *Techniques of Program Structure and Design,* Prentice-Hall, Englewood Cliffs, N.J., 1975.

———, and Constantine, L. L.: *Structured Design: Fundamentals of a Discipline of Computer Program and Software Design,* Prentice-Hall, Englewood Cliffs, N.J., 1979.

**Zurcher,** F. W., and Randell, B.: "Iterative Multi-level Modelling—A Methodology for Computer System Design," *Proc. IFIP Congress,* 1968, p. D138.

# CHAPTER 8

# LINEAR DATA STRUCTURES

The basic notions of data structures were introduced in earlier chapters. In this chapter we extend these notions to encompass the set of linear lists. All data structures introduced thus far are special subcases of a linear list. There are two ways of storing data structures in the computer's memory. The first of these storage-allocation methods, which takes advantage of the one-dimensional property of the computer's memory, is called *sequential allocation*. The second allocation method, which is based on the storage of the address or location of each element in the list, is known as *linked allocation*. Both methods of allocation are discussed in detail in this chapter. We shall see that each method of allocation has its merits.

Several subclasses of linear lists can be defined. The most important of these subclasses are called *stacks* and *queues*. These structures, along with several associated applications, are discussed at length in this chapter. In particular, certain classical applications, such as recursion and simulation, are described. Applications based on the linked storage representation of linear lists are also included in the discussion. The most important of these is the application dealing with hash-table methods.

## 8-1 LINEAR LISTS

Chapter 2 introduced several primitive data structures, such as real numbers, integers, characters, and logical values. These structures were called "primitive" because most computers have machine language instructions which manipulate them directly. Operators which operate upon, or produce, values of these types are built into Pascal and many other programming languages. Basic character string processing notions were introduced in Chap. 6. Most computers also have a variety of machine language instructions which manipulate strings. Although standard Pascal treats a string as a data structure, namely, an array of characters, many Pascal compilers, as well as those for many other programming languages, incorporate strings as a primitive data type. Chapter 1 introduced the concept of a memory address. Such an address is often called a "pointer" since it references or "points to" a storage location containing some data. A pointer can be manipulated by machine instructions and is therefore considered a "primitive" data element in many programming languages. Because of its special properties, however, the pointer is considered a separate class in Pascal.

In Chap. 5 we introduced the concept of the nonprimitive data structure and gave four examples: the array, the record structure, the file, and the set. These structures are useful in a wide variety of applications. (Several example applications appear in Chap. 5.) Furthermore, a particular scheme of implementation in terms of the primitive data structures suffices for most applications. Therefore, the designer of Pascal chose to incorporate these particular data structures into the language. Thus in Pascal we have the type classes primitive (integer, real, Boolean, character, enumerated, and subrange), structured (array, record, set, file), and pointer. Most other programming languages also incorporate nonprimitive data structures, but the ones included vary among the languages.

In this chapter and the next we continue our study of data structures with some useful structures which are not built into Pascal. The principle of data abstraction (see Chap. 7) allows us to consider first the pertinent characteristics of a data structure and the operations upon it which are useful in applications. Because these data structures are not part of the Pascal language, we go on to describe one or more possible implementations of the data structure in terms of the Pascal data types. (We shall use the array and record structure types introduced in Chap. 5 and the pointer type detailed in Sec. 8-8 most frequently.) These possible implementations differ in their storage efficiency and in the time efficiency of the operations upon them. No one method of implementation is satisfactory for all applications.

We also will describe the normal way in which Pascal's built-in data structures are implemented. We describe some alternative implementations for these structures which are useful in certain applications.

We first define the most important class of linear data structures. A *linear list* is an ordered set consisting of a variable number of elements to which additions and deletions can be made. A linear list displays the relationship of physical adjacency. Note that no deletion or addition operations can be performed on arrays. At best, we can change the value of an array element to denote an element which is to be subsequently ignored. The setting of an array element to some special value, say, zero, to denote deletion is an example of this approach. In Pascal, an array is defined as some (constant) size. Changing the size requires changing the source program and then rerunning it from the beginning. There is no provision for the size of the array to vary during execution of the program. These differences clearly distinguish a linear list from an array.

Operations performed on linear lists include those which have been introduced earlier for arrays. Arrays, however, as noted in the previous paragraph, are static in that the number of array elements is always the same. Since the size of a list can vary, insertions and deletions can be performed on a linear list. Such an insertion or deletion operation can be specified by position. As an example, we may want to delete the *i*th element of a list or insert a new element before or after the *i*th existing element. Often, it may be required to insert or delete an element whose position in a linear list depends on the values of other elements in the list (as in sorting).

Of course, we are interested in performing other important operations besides insertion and deletion. Each element in a linear list is assumed to be of some Pascal type. This might be one of the primitive types, such as integer or character. Most often it will be a programmer-defined record structure. Important operations on linear lists include the following:

*1.* Determine the size or number of elements in a list.

*2.* Search a list for a particular element which contains a field having a certain value.

*3.* Copy a list.

*4.* Sort the elements of a list into ascending or descending order, depending on the values of one or more fields within each element.

*5.* Combine two or more lists to form a new list.

*6.* Divide or split a list into several sublists.

Throughout the remainder of this chapter we will formulate algorithms for most of the operations previously described and provide implementations of the algorithms in Pascal. Such algorithms, however, depend on how a linear list is stored or organized in memory (that is, its storage structure). The next section deals with this extremely important point.

## 8-2 STORAGE STRUCTURE CONCEPTS

A *pointer* (or *link*) is an address or reference to a data structure. We illustrate the use of a pointer by considering a problem which arises in many compilers during the translation of source programs. Assume that a certain source program contains five occurrences of the string constant 'Syntax Error'. Clearly, five copies of this string could be created during the translation of this program. On most computers, less memory space is required to represent a pointer than to represent this string. From the storage efficiency point of view, it is better to create only one copy of this string and use four pointers to reference this single copy. The value of a pointer is similar to an integer. This integer value represents the location or address of a word or other unit, such as a byte, of memory in a computer (recall Sec. 1-3). If a value cannot be held in a single addressed unit (word or byte) of memory, then consecutive locations are used. The address of the first location is used as the address of the data. For example, if we assume that the string 'Syntax Error' is stored in locations 2000 through 2011, then the four pointers in question would all have as a value the address **2000**.

An important property of a pointer is its size. All possible values (or addresses) that a pointer can have are, for a particular computer system, fixed-sized integers. This uniformity permits the referencing of any data structure, regardless of its complexity, to be made in a uniform or consistent manner. In the previous example the method of referencing would be exactly the same if the four pointers referred to a logical constant, an integer constant, or a real constant, rather than a string.

There are essentially two ways to obtain the address of an element in a data structure. The first method is called the *computed-address method* and is often used in many compilers to compute the address of an element of an array. We will pursue the details of this example in the next section. The second method of obtaining an address is to store it somewhere in the computer's memory. This method of access is called a *link-* or *pointer-address method*. To access an element of a particular structure, we load a pointer value. Examples of this use occur in most object programs produced by Pascal compilers. The address of each argument of a procedure which corresponds to a var parameter is stored in memory (recall the *pass-as-variable* concept from Sec. 4-4). Also, the return address used by a procedure to return to the calling program is stored and not computed. Several data structures require a combination of computed and link addresses.

In the first part of this chapter we discuss storage structures for linear lists which are based on the computed-address method. The second part of the chapter describes storage structures based on the link-address technique.

In discussing storage structures, we are concerned with the main memory of the conventional digital computer. As mentioned in Chap. 1, main memory is organized as an ordered sequence of locations (words or bytes), each of a fixed size. Throughout this chapter and the next we will use "word" to refer to an addressable storage location. The reader is warned, however, that in much computer literature "byte" refers to an addressable storage location and "word" designates some number of bytes, usually 2 or 4.

For efficiency reasons, it is desirable to organize data in the computer's memory so that a particular element of this data can be referenced by computing its address rather than by performing a search. Many data structures (such as the array) permit the referencing of any element through its position in the structure. This referencing is accomplished through the use of an *addressing function*. Computationally, simple addressing functions are of particular interest. Several examples of these functions will be given for arrays in the next section. The storage structure for Pascal record structures and sets also will be described.

## 8-3  SEQUENTIAL STORAGE STRUCTURES FOR ARRAYS, RECORDS, AND SETS

One of the simplest data structures which makes use of the computed-address method to locate an element is a vector. As was pointed out in Chap. 1, conventional memories are organized linearly. How, then, is memory allocated to structures such as vectors and arrays? Usually, several contiguous memory locations are sequentially allocated to the vector. For an $n$-element vector, each element of which occupies one word of memory, $n$ consecutive words of memory are used. Since a vector contains a fixed number of elements, the number of memory locations required is also fixed. More generally, the sequential storage representation of a vector $A$ with a subscript lower bound of 1 can be viewed as in Fig. 8-1, where $L_0$ denotes the address of the first word allocated to the first element of $A$ and $c$ specifies the number of words occupied by each element. The position of the $i$th element of $A$ (that is, $A_i$ or $A[I]$) is given by

$$\text{loc }(A_i) = L_0 + c * (i - 1)$$

In Pascal, vectors are allocated memory at compile time since the size of each vector is declared to be a constant. (This is not exactly true, but it will suffice for the moment.) In some other programming languages, such as PL/1, the size of a vector can be specified during program execution by a computation.

It is possible to represent a higher-dimensional array by an equivalent vector by arranging the elements in some linear fashion. For example, in Pascal a two-dimensional array, A, described by the array denoter

**array** [1 .. 3, 1 .. 4] **of** SomeType

is stored sequentially by row as

A[1,1] A[1,2] A[1,3] A[1,4] A[2,1] A[2,2] A[2,3] A[2,4] A[3,1] A[3,2] A[3,3] A[3,4]

↑
$L_0$

The location of element A[$i$, $j$], assuming each element occupies 1 storage

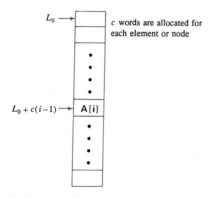

**FIGURE 8-1**
**Sequential storage representation of a vector.**

unit, is obtained from the equation

$$\text{loc } (A[i,j]) = L_0 + (i-1) * 4 + j - 1$$

As an example, the address of element A[3, 2] is given as

$$\text{loc } (A[3,2]) = L_0 + 2 * 4 + 2 - 1 = L_0 + 9$$

More generally, a two-dimensional array of $n$ rows and $m$ columns (with a subscript lower bound of 1) and an element size of $c$ which is stored row by row (that is in *row-major order*) has the location of its element A[i, j] given by the equation

$$\text{loc } (A[i,j]) = L_0 + c * ((i-1) * m + (j-1))$$

In FORTRAN, arrays are stored column by column in memory (that is, in *column-major order*) rather than row by row. The address of element A[i, j] in an array with $n$ rows and $m$ columns stored in column-major order is given by

$$\text{loc } (A[i,j]) = L_0 + c * ((j-1) * n + (i-1))$$

The representation of a two-dimensional array can be generalized further to handle arbitrary lower and upper bounds on its subscripts. Let us assume that the subscripts fall within the following ranges:

$$b_1 \le i \le u_1 \quad \text{and} \quad b_2 \le j \le u_2$$

The address of element A[i, j], assuming a row-major storage order, becomes

$$\text{loc } (A[i,j]) = L_0 + c * ((i-b_1) * (u_2 - b_2 + 1) + (j - b_2))$$

where each row in the array has $u_2 - b_2 + 1$ elements. For example, the address of A[−1, 2], when $c = 1$, $b_1 = -3$, $b_2 = 0$, and $u_2 = 2$, is

$$\text{loc } (A[-1,2]) = L_0 + 1 * ((-1 - (-3)) * (2 - 0 + 1) + (2 - 0))$$
$$= L_0 + 8$$

These notions can be extended easily to higher-dimensional arrays. As an example, consider a three-dimensional array A whose representative element is denoted by A[i, j, k] and whose subscript limits are denoted by $1 \le i \le 3$, $1 \le j \le 2$, and $1 \le k \le 4$. The row-major-order storage of this array is

$L_0$
↓

A[1,1,1] A[1,1,2] A[1,1,3] A[1,1,4] A[1,2,1] A[1,2,2] A[1,2,3] A[1,2,4]
A[2,1,1] A[2,1,2] A[2,1,3] A[2,1,4] A[2,2,1] A[2,2,2] A[2,2,3] A[2,2,4]
A[3,1,1] A[3,1,2] A[3,1,3] A[3,1,4] A[3,2,1] A[3,2,2] A[3,2,3] A[3,2,4]

A pictorial representation of this array is given in Fig. 8-2 by a cube consisting of three planes with each plane having eight points. The address of element A[i, j, k], assuming an element size of 1, is

$$\text{loc } (A[i,j,k]) = L_0 + (i-1)*8 + (j-1)*4 + k - 1$$

We can now generalize the sequential storage concept to an $n$-dimensional array with general element $A[s_1, s_2, \ldots, s_n]$ and subscript limits given by $1 \leq s_1 \leq u_1, 1 \leq s_2 \leq u_2, \ldots, 1 \leq s_n \leq u_n$, and element size $c$. The storage representation of this array in row major order has the form

| A[1, 1, . . . , 1, 1] | A[1, 1, . . . , 1, 2] | . . . | A[1, 1, . . . , 1, $u_n$] |
|---|---|---|---|
| A[1, 1, . . . , 2, 1] | A[1, 1, . . . , 2, 2] | . . . | A[1, 1, . . . , 2, $u_n$] |
| . . . . . . . . . . . | . . . . . . . . . . . | . . . | . . . . . . . . . . . |
| A[$u_1$, $u_2$, . . . , $u_{n-1}$, 1] | A[$u_1$, $u_1$, . . . , $u_{n-1}$, 2] | . . . | A[$u_1$, $u_2$, . . . , $u_{n-1}$, $u_n$] |

The address of element $A[s_1, s_2, \ldots, s_n]$ is given by

$$\text{loc } (A[s_1, \ldots, s_n]) = L_0 + cu_2 u_3 \ldots u_n(s_1 - 1) + cu_3 u_4 \ldots u_n(s_2 - 1)$$

$$+ \cdots + cu_n(s_n - 1) + c(s_{n-1} - 1)$$

It is more convenient to rewrite this equation as

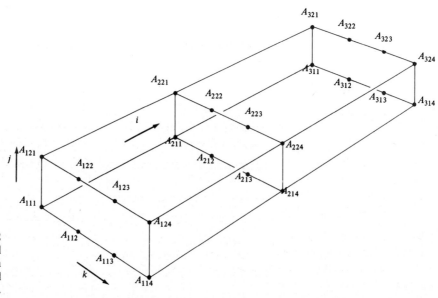

FIGURE 8-2
Pictorial
representation of a
three-dimensional
array A.

$$\text{loc } (A[s_1, s_2, \ldots, s_n]) = L_0 + c * \sum_{1 \le i \le n} p_i(s_i - 1)$$

where $p_i = \prod_{i < r \le n} u_r$ is a constant and $\sum$ and $\prod$ denote summation and

product, respectively. For arbitrary lower and upper subscript bounds $b_i \le s_i \le u_i$ for $1 \le i \le n$, the location of elements $A[s_1, s_2, \ldots, s_n]$ becomes

$$\text{loc } (A[s_1, s_2, \ldots, s_n]) = L_0 + c * \sum_{1 \le i \le n} p_i(s_i - b_i)$$

where $p_i = \prod_{i < r \le n} (u_r - b_r + 1)$

The approach just used also can be employed to store $n$-dimensional arrays in column-major order. We leave this alternative representation, however, as an exercise. It should be noted that certain compilers allocate storage in decreasing manner from the "high" end of the computer's memory. This is opposite to what we have assumed throughout our previous discussion. Clearly, both approaches are equivalent, with the exception that we subtract from the base address $L_0$ rather than add to it as we have done.

In many applications involving arrays, there are situations where only a portion of the array need be stored. An example of such a situation involves the solution of the following specialized system of equations:

$$A_{11}X_1 \qquad\qquad\qquad\qquad\qquad = b_1$$
$$A_{21}X_1 + A_{22}X_2 \qquad\qquad\qquad = b_2$$
$$A_{31}X_1 + A_{32}X_2 + A_{33}X_3 \qquad = b_3$$
$$\cdots\cdots\cdots\cdots\cdots\cdots\cdots\cdots\cdots\cdots\cdots$$
$$A_{n1}X_1 + A_{n2}X_2 + \cdots\cdots\cdots + A_{nn}X_n = b_n$$

A two-dimensional array containing $n^2$ elements can be used to represent the matrix $A$, and the system of equations can be solved using conventional techniques. If we solve these equations by those conventional methods, however, nearly half the elements in $A$ are not used. We can economize on storage by representing the "triangular" array $A$ by an equivalent vector. In so doing, we can solve a larger system of equations than is possible using the previous approach. The system under consideration has $[n(n + 1)]/2$ nonzero elements. Consequently, we can represent this array with a vector having the same number of elements.

The elements of $A$ can be stored as a Pascal vector in the following row-by-row order:

$$A_{11}A_{21}A_{22}A_{31}A_{32}A_{33} \ldots A_{nn}$$

Assuming that these elements are stored in the array AVector which has subscripts ranging from 1 to $n(n+1)/2$, then $A_{ij}$ is found at

$$\text{AVector}\left[\frac{(i-1)*i}{2}+j\right]$$

As an example, the position of element $A_{42}$ is AVector $[((4-1)*(4))/2+2]$ = AVector[8]. *Symmetric* arrays that have

$$A_{ij} = A_{ji} \qquad \text{for all } 1 \le i \le n \text{ and } 1 \le j \le m$$

also can be represented in this manner.

Record structures are normally allocated so that their fields are consecutive in memory. Because the size of each type in a Pascal program can be computed by the compiler, each field selector can be associated with a constant offset. Suppose we have defined a record type as

```
type
   ExampRecord = record
      F1, F2: integer;
      F3: real;
      F4: char
   end
```

Suppose that a particular compiler allocates 4 bytes for each integer, 8 bytes for a real, and 1 byte for a character type. Then the compiler can associate the offsets 0, 4, 8, and 16 with the field selectors F1, F2, F3 and F4, respectively. Each offset is the sum of the lengths of the preceding fields. If a variable, say, R, is declared of type ExampRecord, the compiler will allocate a total of 17 bytes of memory to this variable. Suppose that the storage for R is allocated beginning at location $L_0$. Then, for example, the address of the variable R.F2 would be $L_0 + 4$. In general, the address is computed as the *base address* of the record (address of the first byte) plus the offset associated with the field selector. We leave as an exercise the calculation of addresses for nested record structures and arrays of record structures and other similar combinations.

A complication arises on computers that require the address of certain primitive types to be located at an address which is an even multiple of some constant. For example, some computers require that an integer start at an address which is a multiple of 4. The previous example satisfies this requirement. However, if the character field had been placed first in the record, three *filler* or *pad words* would be required before the integer field to obtain the required *alignment*. The compiler automatically supplies the required filler and uses the correct field offsets. The programmer need be concerned only with alignment and filler words if an application requires very efficient use of storage.

Recall from Sec. 5-10 that sets may be represented as vectors of bits. This is, in fact, the representation usually provided by a Pascal compiler. Normally, all the bits of a word are used. Thus a computer with a word size of 8 bits would normally use 32 words to represent a set over an ordinal type of 256 distinct values. (Thirty-two words with 8 bits per word provide the necessary 256 bits.) Notice that the size of a set-type variable is determined by the number of *potential* elements, not the number of *actual* elements in the set. The bit-manipulation instructions available on most computers are used to implement the set operations. The details are beyond the scope of this book.

We have not to this point seen a general example of a linear list, although arrays may be considered linear lists of fixed size. In the next section we examine a list whose size is variable.

## EXERCISES 8-3

1. A two-dimensional array is stored column by column in memory. The row and column subscripts have the following bounds:

$$3 \le i \le 8 \quad \text{and} \quad -5 \le j \le 0$$

Obtain an equation for locating the storage position of element $A_{ij}$ assuming that the first element of the first row is stored at position $L_0$.

★ 2. Obtain the location of $A[s_1, s_2, \ldots, s_n]$ for an $n$-dimensional array with subscript bounds $b_i \le s_i \le u_i$ for $1 \le i \le n$, assuming a column-major storage order.

★ 3. Formulate a detailed program for the triangular system of equations based on the storage-representation approach given in the text.

4. In certain numerical applications a special kind of two-dimensional matrix consisting of a band of nonzero elements occurs. All other elements in the array are zero. Such an array, A, is shown in Fig. 8-3, where the elements on the leading diagonal (that is, where the row and column subscripts are equal) are nonzero. The diagonal elements immediately above and below this leading diagonal are also nonzero. If the elements in the nonzero-element band are stored as a vector B in a row-major order, then obtain an equation to determine the location of element $A_{ij}$.

5. Consider the following array:

$$\begin{bmatrix} 1 & 2 & 3 & 4 \\ 5 & 6 & 7 & 8 \\ 9 & 10 & 11 & 12 \end{bmatrix}$$

$$A = \begin{bmatrix} a_{11} & a_{12} & 0 & \cdots & \cdots & \cdots & 0 \\ a_{21} & a_{22} & a_{23} & 0 & \cdots & \cdots & 0 \\ 0 & a_{32} & a_{33} & a_{34} & \cdots & \cdots & 0 \\ \vdots & \vdots & \vdots & & & & \\ 0 & 0 & 0 & \cdots & \cdots & a_{n,n-1} & a_{nn} \end{bmatrix}$$

**FIGURE 8-3**
Band matrix.

(a) Answer each of the following assuming the array is stored in row-major order beginning at location 2000. Assume that each array element occupies 4 storage locations.

   (i) Give the value of the seventh element stored.
   (ii) Give the storage address of the value 10.
   (iii) Give the value of the element stored at location 2020.
   (iv) Give the program segment required to print the stored values in row-major order.
   (v) Give the program segment required to print the stored values in column-major order.

(b) Answer parts (i) through (v) above assuming the array is stored in column-major order.

## 8-4  STACKS

One of the most important subclasses of linear lists is the family of stack structures. In this section we first introduce the concepts associated with this subclass of linear structures. Next, several important operations, such as insertion and deletion, for a stack structure are given. In particular, we describe the implementation of these operations for a stack that is represented by a vector.

As mentioned earlier, the most general form of a linear list permits the insertion and deletion of an element at any position in the list. If we restrict occurrence of insertions and deletions to one end of a linear list, then a member of the resulting subclass of linear lists thus obtained is called a *stack*. Using stack terminology, insert and delete operations are commonly referred to as "push" and "pop" operations, respectively. The only directly accessible element of a stack is its *top* element. The least accessible element is its *bottom* element. Since insert and delete operations are performed at the same end of the stack (that is, its top end), elements can only be removed in the opposite order from that in which they were inserted onto the stack. This interesting LIFO (last-in, first-out) phenomenon will be observed in the applications to be discussed in the next section.

A familiar example of a stack, which permits the selection of only its top element, is a pile of trays in a cafeteria. This arrangement of trays is supported by a spring so that a person desiring a tray finds that only one is available at the surface of the tray counter. Such an arrangement of trays is shown in Fig. 8-4. Removal of the top tray from such a system causes the weight on the spring to lighten and the next tray on the pile to appear at the surface of the counter. Conversely, a tray that is deposited on top of the pile causes the entire pile to be pushed down and the new tray to appear above the tray counter.

Another common example of a stack is a railway system for the shunting of railway cars. In this system, which is shown in Fig. 8-5, the last railway car to be placed on the stack is the first car to leave. The repeated use of the insert and delete operations permits various arrangements of cars to be realized on the output railway line.

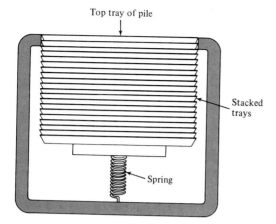

FIGURE 8-4
Cafeteria-tray holder.

The five common operations which are associated with a stack **S** are

StackInitialize (S)   Initializes stack **S**; that is, prepares **S** for use as a stack.

StackPush (S, X)   Inserts element **X** on top of stack **S** and returns the new stack. (Note that **S** is an input/output parameter to this function.)

StackPop (S, X)   Removes the top element from the stack **S** and returns the updated stack. (**S** is again an input/output parameter.) Returns the value formerly at the top of the stack as **X**.

StackEmpty (S)   Returns "true" as the function result if **S** contains no elements, or otherwise returns "false". The stack is unchanged.

StackTopVal (S)   Returns the top element of stack **S** as the function result. The stack is unchanged.

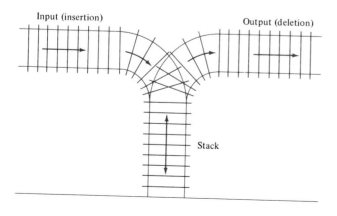

FIGURE 8-5
Railway shunting
system representation
of a stack.

The stack to be operated on is a parameter to all these operations. Each operation, as we shall see, is implemented as a Pascal subprogram. An applicaton with multiple stacks can thus be accommodated. If we were to restrict our interest solely to applications with a single stack, then that stack could be made an implicit parameter to the operations. The Pascal subprograms would reference the stack as a global variable.

Now that we know the basic operations for manipulating a stack, let us go into more detail with the railway system example. Suppose that we have four railway cars sitting on the left-hand (input) track, as shown in Fig. 8-6a. We are required to rearrange these cars so that their order is that of the right-hand (output) track in Fig. 8-6a. We will restrict our shunting system so that it typifies a stack. Therefore, once a railway car has left the left-hand (input) track for the stack, it cannot return. Likewise, once a railway car has left the stack for the right-hand (output) track, it cannot return to the stack. Clearly, at any given time, the only car that can move onto the stack is the one at the front of the input stream and the only car that can move to the output stream is the one at the top of the stack. A trace of the operations done and the state of affairs after each StackPush and StackPop required to rearrange the cars is given in Fig. 8-6b. The reader is advised to trace this carefully to understand how the stack operations work. Notice that not all permutations of the railway cars can be achieved, because of the restricted LIFO system. For example, the permutation CADB is impossible, since C must be placed on the stack before D in this case and therefore is on top of A. The only way to remove A from the stack is to take C off first. Thus C must precede A in the output. (Note: For consistency with Fig. 8-6, we have listed the sequence with the front railway car at the *right*. Thus in the sequence CADB, the car labeled B would be the first one removed from the stack and placed on the output track.) It would be helpful at this point to try various other permutations of the railway cars to see if they can be formed using the stack.

Let us turn now to the question of implementing a stack and its associated operations. A stack structure can be implemented in Pascal by using a vector whose size should be large enough to handle all insertions that could be made to the stack and a variable containing the current number of items in the stack. Such a vector representation of a stack is given in Fig. 8-7a.

The variable Top contains the number of elements currently in the stack and may be used as a subscript or as a "pointer" to the top element of the stack. For an empty stack, Top has a value of zero. Top is incremented by one prior to placing a new element on the stack. Conversely, Top is decremented by one each time an element is deleted from the stack.

An alternative and, for program-tracing purposes, a more convenient representation of a stack is shown in Fig. 8-7b. In this representation the right-most occupied element of the stack represents its top element.

For convenience in manipulating stacks in a Pascal program, we define StackType as a record structure containing the vector and the top pointer as fields (see Fig. 8-8). We include this definition, along with definitions of the constant MaxStackSize and the type StackElementType, in a program which is to use our stack operations. A stack can then be declared as a variable,

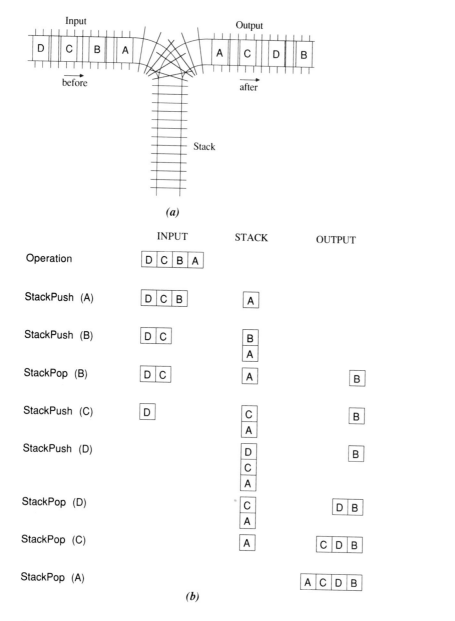

FIGURE 8-6

for example:

**var**

QuantStack: StackType;

The following implementations of the previously defined stack operations are based on this type definition. Figure 8-9 illustrates a procedure for the StackInitialize operation. This procedure is quite straightforward. Use of a subprogram provides better modularity. All the statements which are dependent on the implementation method of the stack are thus moved from the application to the suite of stack routines. After the stack S has been

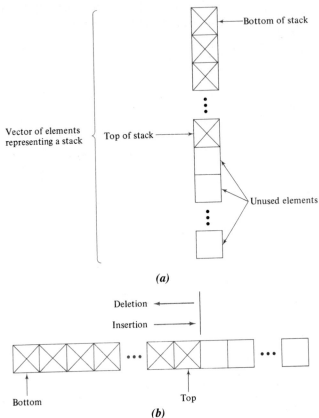

Vector of elements
representing a stack

Top of stack

Bottom of stack

Unused elements

*(a)*

Deletion

Insertion

Bottom

Top

*(b)*

**FIGURE 8-7**
*(a)* **Representation of
a stack by a vector.**
*(b)* **Alternative vector
representation of a
stack.**

initialized, the other procedures/functions dealing with stacks can be applied
to S.

Before describing the detailed implementation of the remaining stack
operations, we must consider the possibility of errors arising during these
operations. What should the StackPop operation do if the stack it is given
is already empty? We refer to this situation as a *stack underflow* error. The
program calling the stack operation can be made responsible for its own
error detection by requiring that StackPop only be called after testing for an
empty stack. That program would use

**if not** StackEmpty (S)
**then** StackPop (S, X)
**else** {handle the error appropriately}

However, consider the result if the program does not include the empty

**FIGURE 8-8**
Type definition for a
sequentially allocated
stack.

```
type
  StackType = record
    Stack: array [1 .. MaxStackSize] of StackElementType;
    Top: integer
  end;
```

**procedure** StackInitialize (**var** S: StackType {Output, initialized stack} );
{Given a sequentially allocated stack, this procedure initializes the stack to
   be empty.}
**begin**
  **with** S **do**
    {Set top pointer to indicate an empty stack}
    Top : = 0
**end**;

stack check and a call to StackPop with an empty stack occurs. The obvious
implementation for StackPop is

X : = S.Stack[S.Top];
S.Top : = S.Top − 1

An out-of-bounds subscript results because the array Stack has bounds 1 and
MaxStackSize, and Top is zero for an empty stack.

    A more subtle problem arises in our StackPush operation. Our abstract
stack model presumes no limit on the number of items which may be pushed
onto a stack. Any implementation on a real computer must have some bound
on the actual stack size. The implementation being considered here will
allow at most MaxStackSize items to be pushed. An attempt to push an item
onto a stack which already contains the maximum number of items is called
a *stack overflow error*. We could introduce a stack operation StackFull (S)
which returns "true" if the stack is full and "false" otherwise. A program
should then use StackPush in the following manner:

**if not** StackFull (S)
**then** StackPush (S, X)
**else** {handle the error appropriately}

Again, failure of the calling program to implement this test would result in
a subscript error using the obvious implementation of StackPush.

    We will incorporate underflow and overflow testing into our StackPop
and StackPush operations. This requires consideration of what should be done
when these operations detect an error. The more satisfactory solution is to
add an output parameter, say, ErrorOccurred, to each operation. It would
return a value of "true" when an error occurs and "false" otherwise. The
calling program would supply a Boolean argument corresponding to this
parameter, test the result, and handle errors in a manner appropriate to the
application.

    In order to keep parameters to a minimum in this introduction to stacks,
we choose an alternative scheme. The stack operations StackPop and
StackPush call error-handling procedures StackUnderflow and StackOverflow
when the corresponding errors are detected. We supply versions of these
procedures which display a message on the standard output stream and then
terminate the program.

    A procedure implementing the StackPush operation appears in Fig.
8-10. The first step of the procedure checks for an overflow situation. If
this situation arises, then the procedure StackOverflow is invoked.

**procedure** StackPush (
  **var** S: StackType;     {Input/output, stack structure}
  X: StackElementType     {Input, value to be pushed}
                 );
{Given a sequentially allocated stack, and a value to be pushed, this procedure makes the new top of stack be that value.}
**begin**
  **with** S **do**

     {Step 1: If stack is full call error procedure}
     **if** Top $>=$ MaxStackSize
     **then** StackOverflow

     {Step 2: Otherwise insert the new element on the stack}
     **else begin**
         Top $:=$ Top $+ 1$;
         Stack[Top] $:= $ X
    **end**
**end**;

The complementary procedure StackPop is shown in Fig. 8-11. An underflow situation is checked for in the first step of the program. Should this situation arise, procedure StackUnderflow is invoked. If this error is to be avoided, then the caller should use StackEmpty to test for an empty stack before calling StackPop, as was described earlier.

**procedure** StackPop (
  **var** S: StackType;     {Input/output, stack structure}
  **var** X: StackElementType    {Output, value popped}
                 );
{Given a sequentially allocated stack, this procedure pops the top element off the stack. The value popped is returned via the output parameter; the new stack is returned via the input/output parameter.}
**begin**
  **with** S **do**

     {Step 1: If stack is empty, call error procedure}
     **if** Top $= 0$
     **then** StackUnderflow

     {Step 2: Otherwise remove the top element of the stack}
     **else begin**
         X $:= $ Stack[Top];
         Top $:= $ Top $- 1$
    **end**
**end**;

If StackElementType were a simple type (standard Pascal allows functions to return only simple types) or if the compiler in use permits functions to return values of all types, it would be useful to make StackPop a function of one parameter, the stack. The value popped would then be returned as the function's result, allowing StackPop to be called from within an expression. Of course, StackPop changes the stack, making it one element smaller. Thus a stack pop function modifies its parameter. Recall that this is called a *side effect* (Chap. 4). Many programmers advocate avoiding side effects.

The next stack operation to be illustrated tests whether a stack is empty. We implement this as a Boolean function (see Fig. 8-12), allowing it to be used directly as the condition in, for example, a while or if statement. We have made S a pass-as-variable parameter to eliminate making a copy of the (possibly large) stack, as would happen for a pass-by-value parameter. This reduces the execution time and the space required. Notice that we have made use of a Boolean expression on the right-hand side of an assignment to the function name (of type Boolean). The parentheses in the assignment are redundant but are included for clarity.

Our final operation, StackTopVal, is implemented as a function in Fig. 8-13. Another error procedure, StackEmError is required. We again use pass as variable for the stack. In standard Pascal, the function is valid only if StackElementType is a simple type. As mentioned in the description of StackPop, some Pascal compilers do allow functions to return structured types. Alternatively, StackTopVal could be made into a procedure with an output parameter. A study of the examples in the next section will demonstrate its usefulness as a function.

Finally, we consider the implementation of the error procedures. Recall that they should display an error message and then terminate a program. A problem arises because standard Pascal provides no method for terminating a program except by allowing execution to arrive at the **end** of the main program. Fortunately, many Pascal compilers provide a built-in procedure which causes termination of the entire program. Assuming availability of such a built-in procedure, say, one called halt, Fig. 8-14 presents an implementation of StackOverflow. The procedures StackUnderflow and StackEmError are similar and are not given here.

If the error procedures are to be implemented entirely in standard Pascal, we must digress and consider another method of sequencing control available in Pascal. The goto statement forces an immediate transfer of control to some designated point in a program. In so doing, it has the power to override

**function** StackEmpty (**var** S: StackType {Input, stack to be tested} ): Boolean;
{Given a sequentially allocated stack, this function returns "true" if the stack
  is empty, "false" otherwise.}
**begin**
  {Return true if stack is empty, false otherwise}
  StackEmpty : = (S.Top = 0)
**end**;

**FIGURE 8-12**
**Function to test the**
**emptiness of a**
**sequentially allocated**
**stack.**

**function** StackTopVal (**var** S: StackType {Input, stack} ): StackElementType;
{Given a sequentially allocated stack, this function returns the value of
the top element. The stack is unchanged. It is assumed that a value of
StackElementType can be returned by a function.}
**begin**
   **with** S **do**

      {Step 1: If stack is empty, call error procedure}
      **if** Top = 0
      **then** StackEmError

      {Step 2: Otherwise return a copy of the top of stack element}
      **else** StackTopVal : = Stack[Top]
**end**;

**FIGURE 8-13**
**Function to obtain**
**the top value from a**
**sequentially allocated**
**stack.**

the actions of the other control structures described. The form of this statement is

**goto** *label*

where the *label* is an integer number between 0 and 9999 inclusive. If the
statement

**goto** 300

is executed, then the next statement to be executed will be the statement
labeled 300, rather than the statement which would be executed in the normal flow of control. This label must label exactly one statement in the program. A statement is labeled by preceding it by the label, followed by a
colon. Thus, for the previous example, the program might contain

300: writeln ('Control has transferred to statement 300');

All labels used in a program must appear in the label declaration immediately following the program header line. This declaration consists of the
reserved word **label** followed by a list of labels separated by commas. For
example,

**label** 300,310,320;

**procedure** StackOverflow;
{This procedure displays a stack overflow message and terminates execution
of the program. A built-in procedure halt, as described in the text, is
assumed to be available.}
**begin**
   writeln ('****FATAL ERROR');
   writeln ('Stack overflowed');
   writeln ('Rerun the program, increasing the constant MaxStackLength');
   halt
**end**;

**FIGURE 8-14**
**Procedure**
**StackOverflow using**
**built-in halt statement.**

In a program with subprograms (functions and procedures), statements within the body of each function and procedure, as well as the statements in the main program, may be labeled. Each program unit (that is, program, function, or procedure) must contain a label declaration listing those labels which prefix statements in that unit. This label declaration immediately follows the applicable program, function, or procedure header line. Labels follow the same scope rules as identifiers (see Chap. 4). Therefore, labels in program units are available in other program units nested within the unit containing the label. This allows, for example, a goto statement within a procedure to transfer control to a label in the main program. Such a transfer of control will terminate execution of the procedure containing the goto statement as well as the procedures, if any, which called it. A goto statement in the main program cannot access, and therefore cannot transfer control to, a label in a procedure. There are some other restrictions which disallow transferring control into a structured statement (if, while, etc) from outside it. Since we will use the goto statement in only a limited way in this book, we need not consider these restrictions further.

Our typical usage of the goto statement is illustrated in Fig. 8-15. Here the program calls a function to perform a computation. If the second argument of the function is zero, an error message is displayed and the program is terminated. The termination is achieved by placing a label (**9999**) on the last statement of the program. This statement happens to be a null statement (see Sec. 3-5 and Fig. 3-33). Placing a label at the end of a program is an important use for the null statement. Notice that the statement preceding the null statement (writeln . . .) requires a semicolon.

Unfortunately, there are a number of Pascal compilers which violate the standard definition by prohibiting goto statements which transfer control out of the program unit (program, function, or procedure) in which the goto statement occurs. This solution of the program-termination problem using a goto statement will not work with such a compiler. Fortunately, most Pascal compilers either have a program-termination built-in procedure (e.g., halt) or permit a goto statement to transfer control out of a procedure. The programmer must use whichever method is available. We illustrate a version of StackOverflow using a goto statement for termination in the example at the end of this section.

The syntax diagrams for the goto statement and label declaration are presented in Figs. 8-16 and 8-17. The syntax for statement labels was previously included in the syntax diagram for statement (Fig. 5-32). The seemingly innocuous little goto statement has been the object of an extensive controversy for many years. One camp advocates its abolition from programming; the other argues that it is a basic tool.

There is a reasonable amount of evidence to suggest that, in general, the quality of programs goes down as the number of goto statements in them goes up. Although we prefer not to be fanatical, our feeling is that if you can get along without it, you should. Since the goto statement can undermine the actions of the other control structures, the resulting logic can be very difficult to follow and the overall structure can be hard to grasp—a situation

**program** GotoExample (input, output);

{The purpose of this program is to illustrate typical use of the goto statement in this book. Given two integer values, a computation is performed and the result is displayed. If the second value is zero, the computation is aborted, an error message is displayed, and the program is terminated.}

**label**
   9999;

**var**
   In1, In2: integer;    {Input values}
   Out1: integer;     {Output value}

**function** Computlt (
   A: integer;     {Input, first argument}
   B: integer      {Input, second argument}
         ): integer;

{Given two arguments, the second of which is nonzero, this function performs a computation.}

**begin**
   {Step 1: Check second argument}
   **if** B $= 0$
   **then begin**

         {Step 2: Display message and terminate}
         writeln ('Second argument to Computlt is zero');
         writeln ('Program terminated');
         **goto** 9999
      **end**;

   {Step 3: Perform computation}
   Computlt $:= (A + 1)$ **div** B
**end**;

**begin**
   {Step 1: Input data}
   read (In1, In2);

   {Step 2: Compute}
   Out1 $:= 10 *$ Computlt (In1, In2);

   {Step 3: Display result}
   writeln ('Result is: ', Out1);

   9999:    {Labeled null statement for error termination}
**end**.

**FIGURE 8-15**
**Example of a goto statement used for program termination.**

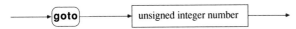

**FIGURE 8-16  Syntax diagram for the goto statement.**

that often leads to errors which are quite hard to detect. The while, repeat, for, if, and case statements described can do a great deal for you if you let them. Their execution is fairly easy to understand. Unless it complicates the solution unnecessarily, we feel that is best to avoid use of the goto statement. Certainly, any use of it must be considered very carefully! We will restrict our use of the goto statement to error termination of programs.

We now present a simple example of the use of our stack operations in Fig. 8-18. This program reads one character at a time from a line of input and pushes each character onto a stack. The end of the line is sensed by the eoln function (see Sec. 3-3.2). The characters are then popped and written out, one at a time, resulting in the line of characters appearing in reverse order.

We have used here the alternative scheme for terminating the program on an error, eliminating the need for the nonstandard built-in procedure halt, as used in Fig. 8-14. Instead, we have used a goto statement in the error procedure to transfer control to the end of the program. Thus the program of Fig. 8-18 is written completely in standard Pascal.

Applications often require more than one stack. In such applications, one stack may overflow while others are far from being full. Instead of imposing an individual maximum size for each stack, it becomes desirable to use a single vector for all stacks used in an application. In Pascal, this would require that all the stacks have the same element type or that the element type be a record structure with variants.

Figure 8-19 shows such a memory layout for the case of two stacks. The first and second stacks expand to the right and left, respectively. In such a configuration an overflow condition arises only when the combined size of the two stacks exceeds the size of the vector. Note that the bottom element of each stack is in a fixed position within the allocated memory space.

This memory-sharing configuration cannot be extended to more than two stacks while maintaining the common overflow property and the property of each stack having a fixed bottom element. The overflow property can be maintained only at the expense of the other. The amount of overhead incurred in keeping track of the bottom and top elements of several sequentially allocated stacks sharing a

label declaration

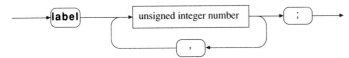

**FIGURE 8-17
Syntax diagram
for the label
declaration.**

```
program ReverseLine (input, output);
{This program uses the basic stack operations to read a line of input and
    display its characters in reverse order.}
label 9999;
const
    MaxStackSize = 200;
type
    StackElementType = char;
    StackType = record
            Stack: array [1 .. MaxStackSize] of StackElementType;
            Top: integer
        end;
var
    C: char;                {Temporary for input and output}
    LineStack: StackType;   {Characters read in}


procedure StackOverflow;
begin
    writeln ('**** FATAL ERROR');
    writeln ('Stack overflowed');
    writeln ('Rerun the program increasing the constant MaxStackLength');
    goto 9999
end;


{Procedure StackUnderflow, similar to the preceding, to be supplied.}


{Procedures StackInitialize (Fig. 8-9), StackPush (Fig. 8-10), StackPop (Fig.
    8-11), and StackEmpty (Fig. 8-12) are to be included here.}


begin
    StackInitialize (LineStack);
    while not eoln do
        begin
            read (C);
            StackPush (LineStack, C)
        end;
    readln;     {Flush end of line}
    while not StackEmpty (LineStack) do
        begin
            StackPop (LineStack, C);
            write (C)
        end;
    writeln;    {Finish output line}
9999:       {Null statement with termination label}
end.
```

**FIGURE 8-18**
**Example of the use**
**of the stack operations.**

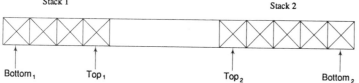

**FIGURE 8-19** Sequential allocation scheme for two stacks.

common piece of memory is very substantial. At times, entire stacks must be moved to preserve the physical adjacency relation between the elements in each stack. A more efficient storage allocation scheme for such a situation is discussed in Sec. 8-8.

Now that the basic notions of a stack have been introduced, the natural question which arises is: What is it used for? The next section examines in detail three applications that use stack structures.

## EXERCISES 8-4

★ 1. Consider the infinite set of strings

'c', 'aca', 'bcb', 'abcba', 'bacab', 'abbcbba', 'abacaba', 'aabcbaa', . . .

A typical string in this set can be specified as $wcw^R$, where $w$ contains a sequence of **a**s and **b**s and $w^R$ denotes the reverse of $w$. For example, if $w = $ 'ab', then $w^R = $ 'ba'. Given an input string $x$, formulate a program which uses a stack to determine whether or not $x$ belongs to the set of strings described by $wcw^R$.

2. Formulate a function to obtain the $i$th element from the top of a stack without deleting it. Write a program to test your function in conjunction with the other stack operations presented in this section.

3. Construct a procedure which changes the $i$th element from the top of the stack to the value contained in X. Write a program to test your procedure in conjunction with the other stack operations presented in this section.

★ 4. Figure 8-19 gave a storage representation of two stacks sharing a maximum of $m$ elements. Formulate procedures Push(J, X) and Pop(J, X) to add element X and to delete the top element from stack J, $1 \leq J \leq 2$, respectively. Note that you will need two separate variables to denote the tops of each stack. The stack vector and Top variables are global to the procedures. Write a program to test your procedures.

## 8-5   APPLICATIONS OF STACKS

This section contains three popular applications of stacks. The first deals with the conversion of symbolic infix expressions to machine code. This application of a stack structure is classical in the sense that it was one of the earliest nonnumeric applications to be attempted on computers. The second (and perhaps most important) application of stacks relates to the implementation of recursion. As was discussed in Chap. 4, recursion is a central concept of computer science and an important facility in many programming languages, including Pascal. There are many problems whose solutions are best described in a recursive manner. Instances of such problems pervade this book. The third application of stacks involves sorting. Although we do not pursue the topic here, stack structures have influenced the design of computers. In particular, several types of computers can perform stack operations (such as insertion and deletion) at the hardware or machine level.

## 8-5.1 POLISH EXPRESSIONS AND THEIR COMPILATION

We are all familiar with the standard representation of a mathematical expression, such as $a + b*c/d$, which is more formally called *infix* notation. In this form of an expression, a binary operator always lies *between* its two operands. This section examines the evaluation or compilation of infix expressions. It is found to be more efficient to evaluate an infix expression by first converting it to an alternative form and then evaluating the given expression in this latter form. Such an approach eliminates the need to scan the original infix expression repeatedly to obtain its value. Throughout this section we use examples of expressions found in higher-level programming languages. It is to be emphasized, however, that the theory developed in this section applies to any type of expression.

This section is initially concerned with introducing Polish notation. This introduction also examines a method which permits the detection of errors (that is, invalid expressions). The translation of infix expressions into Polish notation is then examined in detail. Finally, the generation of assembly language instructions for Polish expressions is discussed at some length. Certain properties of the arithmetic operators can be used in obtaining some degree of code optimization. An optimized program is one that usually contains fewer machine-level instructions than its corresponding unoptimized version.

### Polish Notation

We introduce in this subsection *Polish notation*. This notation, which is due to the Polish logician Jan Łukasiewicz, offers certain computational advantages over the more traditional infix notation. It should also be noted that certain pocket calculators require Polish expressions. The transformation of infix notation to Polish notation is informal. Formal algorithms for such conversions and their implementations are given in the next subsection. The evaluation of expressions given in Polish notation is also mentioned briefly. Finally, the notion of error detection as it pertains to Polish notation is introduced. This idea permits the identification of invalid expressions. Usually, the detection of an invalid expression is to be reported to the programmer.

First, let us consider the evaluation of unparenthesized arithmetic expressions consisting of single-letter variable names, nonnegative integers, and the four arithmetic operators $+$, $-$, $*$, and $/$. Typically, a scanner, such as that discussed in Chap. 6, has the task of isolating the symbols in the expression. The precedences of the operators $*$ and $/$ are considered to be equal and of higher value than those of $+$ and $-$ (which are also considered to have equal precedence). As an example, consider the unparenthesized expression

$$a - b/c + d*e$$

$$\underbrace{\phantom{a-b}}_{1} \underbrace{\phantom{/c}}_{2}$$

$$\underbrace{\phantom{a-b/c+}}_{3}$$

$$\underbrace{\phantom{a-b/c+d*e}}_{4}$$

To evaluate this expression in the conventional manner, as discussed in Chap. 2, it must be scanned repeatedly from left to right. The numbers associated with the subexpressions denote the steps of such an evaluation. Clearly, this process is inefficient because of the repeated scanning that must be done.

The presence of parentheses in an expression alters the order of evaluation of its subexpressions. For example, in the expression $(a + b)*(c + d)$ we first evaluate $a + b$, then $c + d$, and finally $(a + b)*(c + d)$. Parentheses can be used in writing expressions such that the order of evaluation of subexpressions is independent of the precedence of the operators. This is accomplished by parenthesizing subexpressions in such a way that there is a pair of parentheses corresponding to each operator. This pair of parentheses encloses the operator and its operands. Such an expression is said to be *fully parenthesized*. A recursive definition of fully parenthesized infix arithmetic expressions which contain single-letter names, nonnegative integers, and the four arithmetic operators follows:

*1.* Any letter (a–z) or nonnegative integer is a fully parenthesized infix expression.

*2.* If $\alpha$ and $\beta$ are fully parenthesized infix expressions, then $(\alpha + \beta)$, $(\alpha - \beta)$, $(\alpha * \beta)$, and $(\alpha / \beta)$ are fully parenthesized infix expressions.

*3.* The only fully parenthesized infix expressions are those defined by steps 1 and 2.

According to this definition, expressions such as $((a + b) * c)$ and $((a + b)*(c + d))$ are considered to be fully parenthesized, while expressions such as $x - 5$ and $(a - b/c)$ are considered to be invalid.

For a fully parenthesized expression, we can define the parenthetical level of an operator as the total number of pairs of parentheses that surround it. A pair of parentheses has the same parenthetical level as that of the operator to which it corresponds, that is, of the operator which is immediately enclosed by this pair. For example, in the fully parenthesized expression

$$(a - ((b/2)*(c + d)))$$
$$\quad 1 \quad\;\; 3 \;\; 2 \;\; 3$$

the integers below the operators specify the parenthetical level of each operator. In the evaluation of such an expression, the subexpression which contains the operator with the highest parenthetical level is evaluated first. Operators with the same parenthetical level (as in the current example) are evaluated from left to right. After the subexpressions containing operators at the highest parenthetical level have been evaluated, the remaining subexpressions which contain operators at the next highest parenthetical level are then evaluated in the same manner. Therefore, in the current example, the subexpressions are evaluated in the following order:

$$(b\,/\,2) \qquad (c+d) \qquad ((b\,/\,2)*(c+d)) \qquad (a-((b\,/\,2)*(c+d)))$$

We mention again that fully parenthesized expressions require no convention regarding operator precedence.

From the preceding discussion it is clear that a repeated scanning of the expression is still required in order to evaluate a fully parenthesized expression. This phenomenon is due to the fact that operators appear with the operands inside the expression. The notation used so far in writing expressions, that is, the operator between its operands, is called *infix notation*. This repeated scanning of an infix expression is avoided if it is converted first to an equivalent parenthesis-free, or Polish, expression in which the subexpressions have the form

| operand | operand | operator | (known as *suffix Polish* notation) |

or

| operator | operand | operand | (known as *prefix Polish* notation) |

in place of an infix form, where we have

| operand | operator | operand | (infix notation) |

It should be noted that the relative position of the two operands is the same in each form. Only the positions of the operator change.

We can directly translate a fully parenthesized infix expression to suffix or prefix notation by beginning with the conversion of the innermost parenthesized subexpression and then proceeding toward the outside of the expression. For example, to convert the fully parenthesized expression

$$(a-((b+5)\,/\,c))$$
$$\quad\;1\quad 3\quad 2$$

to suffix Polish, the innermost parenthesized subexpression at level 3 is

$$(b+5)$$

which is converted to $b5+$. This suffix subexpression becomes the first operand of the operator / at level 2. Consequently, the subexpression $b5+/c$ at level 2 is then converted to the suffix expression $b5+c/$. Finally, the expression $a\,-\,b5+c/$ is converted to the suffix expression $ab5+c/-$.

Table 8-1 gives the equivalent forms of several fully parenthesized expressions. Note that in both the prefix and suffix equivalents of such an infix expression, the variable names are all in the same relative position.

| TABLE 8-1 | Equivalent Infix, Prefix, and Suffix Forms of Expressions | |
|---|---|---|
| Infix | Prefix | Suffix |
| $((a * b) + c)$ | $+ * abc$ | $ab * c +$ |
| $((a + b) * (c + d))$ | $* + ab + cd$ | $ab + cd + *$ |
| $((a + (b * c)) - ((d/f) + e))$ | $- + a * bc + /dfe$ | $abc * + df/e + -$ |

Computer programmers, of course, rarely write expressions in fully parenthesized form. It is to be noted, however, that certain compilers convert partially parenthesized expressions to their fully parenthesized equivalent forms before ultimately performing a conversion to suffix or prefix form.

Let us now examine the conversion of a parenthesis-free arithmetic expression into suffix form. As was just mentioned, only the operators need be rearranged to generate the suffix equivalent form. In a left-to-right scan, the left-most operator having the highest precedence is the first operator encountered in the suffix string. If in an infix expression we do not specify that a left-most operator has precedence over other operators of equal precedence, then the suffix form of this expression is not unique. As an example, the expression $a * b * c$ could be converted to either $ab * c *$ or $abc * *$ if no mention was made that the left-most operator $*$ in the infix string has precedence over the remaining operator. From this observation it is clear that on scanning a suffix expression from left to right, the operators thus encountered are in the same order as the evaluation of the corresponding infix expression using the operator precedence convention. For example, the suffix equivalent of $a - b / c$ is $abc/-$. In a left-to-right scan of this suffix form we encounter the operator $/$ before the operator $-$, indicating that division is to be evaluated before subtraction. An algorithm for converting partially parenthesized infix expressions to their suffix forms will be given in the next subsection.

Let us now examine the evaluation of a suffix expression. This can be accomplished easily by scanning the expression once from left to right. For example, to evaluate the suffix expression $ab - c *$, we scan this string from left to right until we encounter $-$. The two operands $a$ and $b$, which appear to the immediate left of this operator, are its operands. The subexpression $ab -$ is then replaced by its value. Assign this value to the temporary variable $T_1$. The original suffix string now reduces to $T_1 c *$. On continuing the scanning process, we encounter the next operator, $*$. The operands of this operator are $T_1$ and $c$. The evaluation of the remaining subexpression yields a value which we denote by $T_2$.

This method of evaluation is summarized in the following general algorithm:

*1.* Repeat thru step 5 while there is an operator remaining

*2.* Find the left-most operator in the expression

*3.* Obtain the two operands which immediately precede the operator just found

*4.* Perform the indicated operation

*5.* Replace the operator and operands with the result

As a further example, the suffix expression $abc + de + * -$, which corresponds to the infix expression

$$a - (b + c) * (d + e)$$

is evaluated as shown in Table 8-2. For the values $a = 1$, $b = 2$, $c = 3$, $d = 4$, and $e = 5$ in this example, $T_1 = 5$, $T_2 = 9$, $T_3 = 45$, and $T_4 = -44$.

As mentioned earlier, certain compilers convert infix arithmetic expressions into Polish notation. In these compilers it is important to detect invalid Polish expressions. These invalid Polish expressions correspond to invalid infix arithmetic expressions. We now describe a method that detects such invalid expressions. Although the discussion applies to suffix expressions, an analogous technique also can be developed for prefix expressions.

Suffix expressions contain symbols such as variable names and constants and operators such as the arithmetic operators. Let these symbols and operators be denoted by the sets $S = \{s_1, s_2, \ldots, s_q\}$ and $O = \{o_1, o_2, \ldots, o_m\}$, respectively. The *degree* of an operator is defined as the number of operands which that operator has. For example, the multiplication operator has a degree of 2. The set of all suffix expressions is defined as follows:

*1.* Any symbol $s_i$ is a suffix expression.

*2.* If $y_1, y_2, \ldots, y_n$ are suffix expressions and $o_i$ is an operator of degree $n$, then $y_1 \, y_2 \cdots y_n o_i$ is a suffix expression.

*3.* The only valid suffix expressions are those obtained by steps 1 and 2.

For example, if the set $S$ contains the single-letter variables $(a–z)$ and the operator set $O$ consists of the standard four arithmetic operators, then the following are all valid expressions according to the previous definition:

$ab +$

$abc * +$

$ab + cd - *$

$ab * c + de/ + f -$

| TABLE 8-2 | Evaluation of the Suffix Expression $abc + de + * -$ | |
|---|---|---|
| **Suffix Form** | **Current Operator** | **Current Operands** |
| $abc + de + * -$ | $+$ | b, c |
| $aT_1 de + * -$ | $+$ | d, e |
| $aT_1 T_2 * -$ | $*$ | $T_1, T_2$ |
| $aT_3 -$ | $-$ | a, $T_3$ |
| $T_4$ | | |

Examples of invalid expressions are

| | |
|---|---|
| ab $*$ + | (Missing variable name) |
| abc + | (Missing operator) |
| abd/ + $-$ | (Missing variable name) |
| ab + cd + | (Missing operator) |

In order to detect invalid expressions, it is useful to associate a *rank* with each expression, which is defined as follows:

*1.* The rank of a symbol $s_i$ is 1.

*2.* The rank of an operator symbol $o_i$ of degree $n$ is $1 - n$.

*3.* The rank of a sequence of symbols and operators is the arithmetic sum of the ranks of the individual symbols and operators.

As an example, if the set of symbols is the English alphabet and the operator set is the four arithmetic operators, then the rank function $r$ is defined as

$$r(s_i) = 1 \quad \text{for} \quad 1 \le i \le 26$$

$$r(+) = r(-) = r(*) = r(/) = -1$$

The rank of the expression ab + cd + / is obtained by adding the ranks of each individual symbol:

$$r(\text{ab} + \text{cd} + /) = r(\text{a}) + r(\text{b}) + r(+) + r(\text{c}) + r(\text{d}) + r(+) + r(/) = 1$$

An observation to follow is very important because its use can detect invalid expressions. Before stating this observation, some basic terminology must be described. If $z = x \bigcirc y$ is a string of symbols, then $x$ is a *head* of $z$. (Recall from Chap. 6 that $\bigcirc$ designates string concatenation.) Also, $x$ is a *proper head* if $y$ is not the empty string. For example, if $z = $ 'aabcd', then the strings 'a', 'aa', 'aab', and 'aabc' are all its proper heads. The following statement is central to the detection of invalid Polish expressions:

*A suffix (prefix) expression is valid if and only if the rank of the expression is 1 and the rank of any proper head of the expression is greater than (less than) or equal to 1.*

This observation is very important in the compilation of infix expressions; it permits us to detect an invalid Polish expression and, consequently, its invalid infix counterpart. (Of course, some invalid infix expressions produce valid Polish expressions using the algorithms of the next subsection. Such errors will not be caught using this technique.) Table 8-3 contains a number of valid and invalid expressions.

**TABLE 8-3** Valid and Invalid Polish Expressions

| Infix | Suffix Polish | Validity Check Head | Validity Check Rank | Prefix Polish | Validity Check Head | Validity Check Rank | Valid or Invalid |
|---|---|---|---|---|---|---|---|
| $a - b*c$ | $abc*-$ | a | 1 | $-a*bc$ | $-$ | $-1$ | Valid |
| | | ab | 2 | | $-a$ | 0 | |
| | | abc | 3 | | $-a*$ | $-1$ | |
| | | abc$*$ | 2 | | $-a*b$ | 0 | |
| | | abc$*-$ | 1 | | $-a*bc$ | 1 | |
| $a + *b$ | $ab*+$ | a | 1 | $+*ab$ | $+$ | $-1$ | Invalid |
| | | ab | 2 | | $+*$ | $-2$ | |
| | | ab$*$ | 1 | | $+*a$ | $-1$ | |
| | | ab$*+$ | 0↓ | | $+*ab$ | 0↓ | |
| $(a+b)*(c+d)$ | $ab+cd+*$ | a | 1 | $*+ab+cd$ | $*$ | $-1$ | Valid |
| | | ab | 2 | | $*+$ | $-2$ | |
| | | ab$+$ | 1 | | $*+a$ | $-1$ | |
| | | ab$+$c | 2 | | $*+ab$ | 0 | |
| | | ab$+$cd | 3 | | $*+ab+$ | $-1$ | |
| | | ab$+$cd$+$ | 2 | | $*+ab+c$ | 0 | |
| | | ab$+$cd$+*$ | 1 | | $*+ab+cd$ | 1 | |
| $a*+bc$ | $a*bc+$ | a | 1 | | | | Invalid |
| | | a$*$ | 0↓ | | | | |
| | | a$*$b | 1 | | | | |
| | | a$*$bc | 2 | | | | |
| | | a$*$bc$+$ | 1 | | | | |

In this subsection we have introduced the notions of prefix and suffix notation. We have not, however, formulated any algorithms to convert infix expressions to their prefix and suffix forms. The next subsection is concerned with this task.

## EXERCISES

1. Using the recursive definition for fully parenthesized infix expressions given at the beginning of this section, establish the validity or invalidity of the following expressions:
   (a) $(((a*b) - c) + d)$
   (b) $(((a / b) * (c / d) + e)$
   (c) $((a + b*c) *d)$
   (d) $((((a*x) + b) *x) + c)$
   (e) $(a - b)*c$

2. Express each of the valid expressions in Exercise 1 as suffix Polish.

3. Express each of the valid expressions in Exercise 1 as prefix Polish.

4. Determine the validity or invalidity of the following suffix expressions:
   (a) $ab*c+$
   (b) $ab - cd + *$
   (c) $ab + *cd -$
   (d) $abc* + def* + *$

5. Evaluate the valid suffix expressions of Exercise 4. Assume that $a = 1$, $b = 2$, $c = 3$, $d = 4$, $e = 5$, and $f = 6$.

6. Give a general algorithm for the evaluation of prefix expressions.

7. Convert the following infix expressions to their prefix and suffix forms and in each case give a trace of the rank computation.
   (a) $a - b*c + d$
   (b) $a * (b + c - d)$
   (c) $a - b * (e + d)$

### Conversion of Infix Expressions to Polish Notation

This subsection formalizes the process of converting infix expressions into their equivalent prefix and suffix forms. The discussion is concerned primarily with the conversion of arithmetic expressions to suffix form. Initially, an algorithm is formulated for the conversion of unparenthesized expressions to suffix notation. This algorithm is then generalized to handle partially parenthesized infix expressions. Both algorithms can detect some invalid expressions. Pascal implementations of both algorithms are given. A brief discussion of the conversion of infix expressions to their prefix equivalent is then given.

Unparenthesized infix expressions are easily converted into suffix notation. Such a conversion is based on the precedence of the arithmetic operators. Also, as we shall see, a stack is required. We represent the desired output (that is, the suffix expression) by a string which will be used later in the generation of object code. Recall from the discussion of the previous subsection that the operands (variables and constants) remain in the same relative position to each other when performing the desired conversion. The operators, however, are reordered in the desired output string to reflect their relative precedence. This reordering process requires the use of a stack.

Consider the infix expressions which contain the four arithmetic operators whose precedence values are given in Table 8-4. Multiplication and division have priority over addition and subtraction. This table also contains a precedence value for single-letter variables. The reason for assigning a precedence value to variable-name symbols will be given shortly. Note that the table contains the ranks of the symbols which can occur in infix expressions. The notion of rank was discussed in the previous subsection.

Let us assume first that the stack contains a special symbol (# in Table 8-4) whose precedence value is less than that of all other symbols in the table. The purpose of this special symbol is to prevent the stack from being empty during the conversion process. We also assume that the given infix expression is padded on the right with the symbol #.

A general algorithm for the conversion process might take the following form:

*1.* Initialize stack contents to the special symbol #

*2.* Obtain the left-most symbol in the infix expression and denote it as the current input symbol

*3.* Repeat thru step 6 while the current input symbol is not #

*4.* Remove and output all stack symbols whose precedence values are greater than or equal to the precedence of the current input symbol; as each stack symbol is output, compute the rank of the output so far and indicate an error if the rank is less than 1

*5.* Push the current input symbol onto the stack

*6.* Obtain the next symbol in the infix expression and let it be the current input symbol

*7.* Remove and output all remaining symbols (except #) from the stack

*8.* If the rank ≠ 1,
then write 'Expression invalid'
otherwise write 'Expression valid'

From this general algorithm we can, in a straightforward manner, formulate the program of Fig. 8-20. The operation of this program is simple.

**TABLE 8-4**

| Symbol | Precedence Function $f$ | Rank Function $r$ |
|---|---|---|
| + , − | 1 | − 1 |
| * , / | 2 | − 1 |
| a, b, c, . . . | 3 | 1 |
| # | 0 | — |

Initially, the marker symbol # is stacked. Step 2 assigns a zero value to Rank. The third step of the program reads the left-most symbol of the infix expression and assigns this symbol to Current. Step 5 compares the precedence value of the input symbol Current to that of the top element of the stack. If the precedence value of Current is less than or equal to that of the stack top, then the latter is removed from the stack and written to the output stream. The precedence values of Current and the new element at the top of the stack are then compared. This process continues until the test fails. The rank counter is updated as each symbol is removed from the stack. If, on the other hand, the precedence value of Current is greater than that of the stack top, then the current input is stacked in step 6.

We also have introduced the error-handling function Invalid. After displaying a message, it terminates execution using a goto statement. See Sec. 8-4 for a description of other alternatives for terminating the program.

Since a variable has the highest precedence value, it is pushed onto the stack. When scanning the very next input symbol, however, such a variable on top of the stack will be deleted and written out. This is always the case because, in valid infix expressions, consecutive variable symbols cannot occur. The algorithm could be changed easily so that the precedence value of Current is tested against 3. A successful test would indicate that Current represents a variable and, therefore, could be written out without being stacked. We do not, however, pursue this approach for reasons of generality which become more important as infix expressions are permitted to be more complex.

As mentioned earlier, a current symbol whose precedence value is greater than that of the stack element will result in the stacking of the former. Such an action indicates that the operation which corresponds to the incoming operator is to be executed before all operations which correspond to the operators on the stack. The last-in, first-out (LIFO) property of a stack will indeed guarantee this behavior. Notice that when both the input and stack symbols have equal precedence, then the stack symbol is written out. This behavior ensures that in an expression which contains operators with equal precedence, the left-most operator is the one that is executed. Consequently, the current program converts $a*b*c$ to $ab*c*$ and not to $abc**$. The suffix string $ab*c*$ corresponds to the infix expression $(a*b)*c$, and $abc**$ is equivalent to the expression $a*(b*c)$. A sample trace of this program for the expression $a - b*c/d + e/f\#$ is given in Table 8-5.

We turn now to the problem of converting parenthesized infix expressions to suffix notation. Programmers do not usually write such expressions in a completely parenthesized form. Intuitively, when the current symbol is a left parenthesis, it should be pushed onto the stack. This should be done regardless of the stack contents. When a left parenthesis is on the stack, however, it should remain there until a matching right parenthesis is encountered in the input expression. At this point, the left parenthesis should be removed from the stack and the matching right parenthesis in the input should be ignored. We can force an incoming left parenthesis on the stack simply by forcing its *input precedence value* to be greater than that of any other symbol. Once on the stack, however, this same left parenthesis

```
program UnparenthesizedSuffix (input, output);
```
{Given a sequence of characters representing an infix expression whose single character symbols have precedence values and ranks as given in Table 8-4, this program converts the expression to its suffix equivalent and displays the result. The input expression is assumed to end with a #.}
```
label 9999;
const
   MaxStackSize = 25;
type
   StackElementType = char;
   StackType = record
         Stack: array [1 .. MaxStackSize] of StackElementType;
         Top: integer
      end;
var
   S: StackType;       {Operator stack}
   Rank: integer;      {Rank of suffix expression}
   Current: char;      {Current input symbol}
   TempC: char;        {Temporary}
function F (C: char {Input} ): integer;
```
{Given a symbol, this function returns the priority.}
```
begin
   {Compute priority}
   case C of
      '#'       :F:=0;
      '+','-' :F:=1;
      '*','/'   :F:=2;
      'a'..'z'  :F:=3
   end
end; {F}
function R (C: char {Input} ): integer;
```
{Given a symbol, this function returns the rank.}
```
begin
   {Compute rank}
   case C of
      '+','-','/','*' :R:=-1;
      'a'..'z'           :R:=1
   end
end; {R}
procedure Invalid;
```
{This procedure displays an error message and terminates the program.}
```
begin
   writeln;
   writeln ('Invalid expression');
   goto 9999
end; {Invalid}
```
{Include the necessary stack operations from Sec. 8-4}

**FIGURE 8-20**
Program to convert
unparenthesized infix
expressions to suffix.

```
begin
   {Step 1: Initialize stack}
   StackInitialize (S);
   StackPush (S, '#');

   {Step 2: Initialize rank count}
   Rank := 0;

   {Step 3: Read first input symbol}
   read (Current);

   {Step 4: Engage loop to translate the infix expression}
   while Current <> '#' do
      begin
         {Step 5: Remove symbols with greater or equal precedence from
            stack.}
         while F (Current) <= F (StackTopVal (S)) do
            begin
               StackPop (S, TempC);
               write (TempC);
               Rank := Rank + R (TempC);
               if Rank < 1
               then Invalid
            end;
         {Step 6: Push current symbol onto the stack and obtain next input
            symbol.}
         StackPush (S, Current);
         read (Current)
      end;
   {Step 7: Remove remaining elements from stack}
   while StackTopVal (S) <> '#' do
      begin
         StackPop (S, TempC);
         write (TempC);
         Rank := Rank + R (TempC);
         if Rank < 1
         then Invalid
      end;
   writeln;
   {Step 8: Is the suffix expression valid?}
   if Rank = 1
   then begin
           writeln;
           writeln ('Valid expression')
        end
   else Invalid;
   {Step 9: Halt}
9999:
end.
```

FIGURE 8-20 (*cont.*)

**TABLE 8-5**  Translation of Infix Expression a − b * c/d + e/f # to Suffix

| Current Input Character | Contents of Stack (Right-most Symbol Is Top of Stack) | Suffix Expression | Rank |
|---|---|---|---|
|   | # |   |   |
| a | #a |   |   |
| − | # − | a | 1 |
| b | # − b | a | 1 |
| * | # − * | ab | 2 |
| c | # − *c | ab | 2 |
| / | # − * | abc | 3 |
|   | # − / | abc * | 2 |
| d | # − / d | abc * | 2 |
| + | # − / | abc * d | 3 |
|   | # − | abc * d / | 2 |
|   | # + | abc * d / − | 1 |
| e | # + e | abc * d / − | 1 |
| / | # + / | abc * d / − e | 2 |
| f | # + / f | abc * d / − e | 2 |
| # | # + / | abc * d / − ef | 3 |
|   | # + | abc * d / − ef / | 2 |
|   | # | abc * d / − ef / + | 1 |

must have another precedence value (called its *stack precedence*), which is smaller than that of any other symbol. A stacked left parenthesis is discarded on encountering a matching right parenthesis in the infix expression. Note that this right parenthesis need never be stacked. Our previous algorithm for unparenthesized expressions can be modified easily in such a manner that the parenthesis can perform the same function as the special symbol # used earlier. Table 8-4 is easily changed to contain both an input- and a stack-precedence value for each symbol. In addition, we can get rid of the special symbol #. In so doing, the algorithm becomes more general in the sense that its complexity does not grow significantly as additional operators, such as relational, logical, and unary operators, are added to the system. Such a revised table is given in Table 8-6. Note that this table contains parentheses. Also, each symbol has both an input- and stack-precedence value, since this symbol is never stacked. The infix expressions under consideration have been expanded to contain the exponentiation operator ↑. The input precedence of each arithmetic operator (except exponentiation) is less than its corresponding stack precedence. Such a relationship preserves the desired left-to-right processing property of equal-precedence operators. The exponentiation operator, however, is right-associative. That is, the expression 2 ↑ 2 ↑ 4 is equivalent to the parenthesized expression 2 ↑ (2 ↑ 4) rather than the expression (2 ↑ 2) ↑ 4. The right-associative property is automatically enforced by having the input precedence of the exponentiation operator greater than its stack precedence.

The conversion of parenthesized infix expressions into suffix notation is very similar in operation to the previous algorithm. Initially, we place a left parenthesis on the stack and pad the given infix expression with a matching right parenthesis. A general algorithm for the revised version is formulated as follows:

1. Initialize the stack and place a left parenthesis on it
2. Initialize the output string and the rank count
3. Obtain the first input symbol
4. Repeat thru step 7 while there is still another input symbol
5. Remove and output all stack symbols whose stack precedence values are greater than the input precedence of the current input symbol; as each symbol is output, compute the rank of the output so far and indicate an error if the rank is less than 1
6. If the current symbol and top of stack symbol are matching parentheses,
   then pop the stack
   otherwise push the current symbol on the stack
7. Obtain the next input symbol
8. If the stack is not empty or rank $\neq 1$,
   then write 'Invalid expression'
   otherwise write 'Valid expression'

From this general algorithm we derive a program. The definition and declaration portion of this program is identical to that of Fig. 8-20 except for the following changes: The program name should be changed to **Suffix**. The functions F and R are replaced by new versions of F and R, and the new function G is added. Finally, the body of the program is revised in accordance with the new general algorithm. The modified program appears in Fig. 8-21.

Step 1 places a left parenthesis on the stack. The second step initializes Rank to zero. Step 3 obtains the first character in the given infix expression

**TABLE 8-6** Input- and Stack-Precedence Values for Arithmetic Expressions

| | Precedence | | |
|---|---|---|---|
| Symbol | Input Function f | Stack Function g | Rank Function r |
| $+$, $-$ | 1 | 2 | $-1$ |
| $*$, $/$ | 3 | 4 | $-1$ |
| $\uparrow$ | 6 | 5 | $-1$ |
| Single-letter variables | 7 | 8 | 1 |
| ( | 9 | 0 | — |
| ) | 0 | — | — |

**program** Suffix (input, output);
{Given a sequence of characters representing an infix expression whose single character symbols have precedence values and ranks given in Table 8-6, the program converts the expression to its suffix equivalent and displays the result. The input expression is assumed to be terminated by an extra right parenthesis followed by a blank.}

**label** 9999;

**const**
    MaxStackSize = 25;

**type**
    StackElementType = char;
    StackType = **record**
        Stack: **array** [1 .. MaxStackSize] **of** StackElementType;
        Top: integer
      **end**;

**var**
    S: StackType;      {Operator stack}
    Rank: integer;    {Rank of suffix expression}
    Current: char;    {Current input symbol}
    TempC: char;     {Temporary}

{Include neccesary stack procedures from Sec. 8-4 here as well as procedure Invalid}

**function** F (C: char {Input} ): integer;
{Given a symbol, this function returns the input priority.}
**begin**
    {Compute input priority}
    **case** C **of**
        ')'         :F:=0;
        '+','−'  :F:=1;
        '*','/'   :F:=3;
        '∧'       :F:=6;      {Note that ∧ is the usual ASCII representation
                                        for up arrow}

        'a' .. 'z'  :F:=7;
        '('        :F:=9
    **end**
**end**; {F}

**function** G (C: char {Input} ): integer;
{Given a symbol, this function returns its top of stack priority.}
**begin**
    {Compute top of stack priority}
    **case** C **of**
        '('        :G:=0;
        '+','−'  :G:=2;
        '*','/'   :G:=4;
        '∧'       :G:=5;

**FIGURE 8-21**
**Program to convert parenthesized infix expressions to suffix.**

```
        'a' .. 'z'   :G: = 8
    end
end; {G}


function R (C: char {Input} ): integer;
{Given a symbol, this function returns its rank.}
begin
    {Compute rank}
    case C of
        'a' .. 'z'   :R: = 1;
        '+', '−', '*', '/', '^' :R: = −1
    end
end; {R}


begin
    {Step 1: Initialize stack}
    StackInitialize (S);
    StackPush (S, '(');

    {Step 2: Initialize the rank count}
    Rank : = 0;

    {Step 3: Get first input symbol}
    read (Current);

    {Step 4: Engage loop to translate the infix expression}
    while Current <> '□' do
        begin
            {Step 5: Remove symbols with greater precedence on the stack.}
            if StackEmpty (S)
            then Invalid;
            while F (Current) < G (StackTopVal (S)) do
                begin
                    StackPop (S, TempC);
                    write (TempC);
                    Rank : = Rank + R (TempC);
                    if Rank < 1
                    then Invalid
                end;

            {Step 6: Are there matching parentheses?}
            if F (Current) <> G (StackTopVal (S))
            then StackPush (S, Current)
            else StackPop (S, TempC);

            {Step 7: Get the next input symbol}
            read (Current)
        end;
```

FIGURE 8-21 *(cont.)*

{Step 8: Is the expression valid?}
**if** (StackEmpty (S)) **and** (Rank = 1)
**then begin**
        writeln;
        writeln ('Valid expression')
    **end**
**else** Invalid;

{Step 9: Halt}
9999:

FIGURE 8-21 (*cont.*)    **end**.

and places it in Current. Steps 4 to 7 perform the desired translation of the given expression. The fifth step compares the current input symbol with the top element of the stack. If the precedence of the stack symbol is greater than that of the current input symbol, then we remove the former from the stack and write it out. A rank value of less than 1 implies an invalid expression and causes termination of the program. Once we remove a symbol from the stack, the entire process is repeated with the new symbol on top of the stack. When all stack symbols whose precedence values are greater than that of the current input symbol have been written out, control passes to step 6. In this step a check is made for a left parenthesis on top of the stack and a matching right parenthesis in the input. If this check fails, then the current symbol is placed on the stack; otherwise, we ignore the right parenthesis in the input and delete the corresponding left parenthesis from the stack. The final step of the program checks the validity of the expression. If the accumulated rank value of the expression is 1 and the stack is empty, then the expression is valid; otherwise, it is invalid.

A trace of the stack contents and the suffix string for the padded infix expression

$(a + b*c)*(d + e \uparrow f \uparrow a))$

is given in Table 8-7. We encourage the reader to trace the program for the padded invalid expression $((a + b / d)c + e))$. Recall from the previous subsection that an invalid infix expression which produces an invalid suffix expression will be detected. However, an invalid infix expression such as $ab + + c$ will not be detected. Modification of the program to detect all invalid infix expressions is left as an exercise.

So far we have developed algorithms for converting infix expressions to suffix notation. We turn now to the problem of converting infix expressions to prefix notation. We do not, however, formulate a Pascal program for this process. Only the general approach is discussed here.

A simple algorithm based on scanning of the infix expression from right to left can be obtained in a straightforward manner. In many cases, the entire infix expression is not available, but it is obtained one symbol at a time in a left-to-right manner. Consequently, a practical algorithm for the desired conversion should be based on a left-to-right scan of the infix string.

To facilitate such an algorithm, however, it is desirable to use two stacks instead of the one stack used in the conversion of infix to suffix. More specifically, we find it convenient to use an operator stack and an operand stack. The purpose of the latter stack is to store temporarily the intermediate operands. Recall from the previous subsection, Polish Notation, that all variables and constants retain their relative order when an infix expression is converted to prefix form. The operators, however, are reordered according to their relative precedence, and the operator stack is used in this reordering. The operand stack, on the other hand, is used for temporary storage of intermediate operands so that finally, when the associated operator is found to be applicable, it can be placed in front of the concatenated operands.

A general algorithm based on this approach follows:

**TABLE 8-7** Translation of Padded Infix Expression (a + b*c)*(d + e ↑ f ↑ a)) to Suffix

| Character Scanned | Contents of Stack (Right-most Symbol Is Top of Stack) | Suffix Expression | Rank |
|---|---|---|---|
| | ( | | |
| ( | (( | | |
| a | ((a | | |
| + | ((+ | a | 1 |
| b | ((+b | a | 1 |
| * | ((+ * | ab | 2 |
| c | ((+ *c | ab | 2 |
| ) | ((+ * | abc | 3 |
| | ((+ | abc * | 2 |
| | (( | abc * + | 1 |
| | ( | abc * + | 1 |
| * | (* | abc * + | 1 |
| ( | (*( | abc * + | 1 |
| d | (*(d | abc * + | 1 |
| + | (*(+ | abc * +d | 2 |
| e | (*(+e | abc * +d | 2 |
| ↑ | (*(+ ↑ | abc * +de | 3 |
| f | (*(+ ↑ f | abc * +de | 3 |
| ↑ | (*(+ ↑ ↑ | abc * +def | 4 |
| a | (*(+ ↑ ↑ a | abc * +def | 4 |
| ) | (*(+ ↑ ↑ | abc * +defa | 5 |
| | (*(+ ↑ | abc * +defa ↑ | 4 |
| | (*(+ | abc * +defa ↑ ↑ | 3 |
| | (*( | abc * +defa ↑ ↑ + | 2 |
| | (* | abc * +defa ↑ ↑ + | 2 |
| ) | (* | abc * +defa ↑ ↑ + | 2 |
| | ( | abc * +defa ↑ ↑ + * | 1 |
| | | abc * +defa ↑ ↑ + * | 1 |

1. Put a left parenthesis on the operator stack

2. Scan the first input symbol

3. Repeat thru step 5 while there is still some input

4. If the current input symbol is a variable or a constant,
   then push this variable or constant on the operand stack
   else Repeat while the precedence of the current input is less than
   that of the operator stack top
   Replace the two topmost operands on the operand stack by
   the operator stack top concatenated with these operands
   If the current symbol is not a right parenthesis or the symbol
   on the operator stack is not a left parenthesis,
   then push the current operator on the operator stack
   else delete the left parenthesis from the operator stack

5. Obtain the next input symbol

A trace of this general algorithm for the padded input string $(a + b) * (c + d))$ is given in Table 8-8. To avoid confusion, the operands on the operand stack have been delimited by quote symbols. When the algorithm terminates, the desired prefix expression is the top (and only) element on the operand stack. We leave the detailed algorithm to the exercises.

The notions discussed in this subsection can be extended easily to handle relational operators, logical operators, conditional statements, and many other features found in modern programming languages. A number of exercises at the end of this subsection deal with these extensions.

| **TABLE 8-8** | Translation of $(a+b)*(c+d))$ to Prefix Notation | |
|---|---|---|
| **Character Scanned** | **Operator Stack (Right-most Symbol Is Top of Stack)** | **Operand Stack (Right-most String Is Top of Stack)** |
| | ( | |
| ( | (( | |
| a | (( | 'a' |
| + | ((+ | 'a' |
| b | ((+ | 'a' 'b' |
| ) | (( | '+ab' |
| | ( | '+ab' |
| * | (* | '+ab' |
| ( | (*( | '+ab' |
| c | (*( | '+ab' 'c' |
| + | (*(+ | '+ab' 'c' |
| d | (*(+ | '+ab' 'c' 'd' |
| ) | (*( | '+ab' '+cd' |
| ) | ( | '*+ab+cd' |
| | ( | '*+ab+cd' |
| | | '*+ab+cd' |

We have been concerned until now with the conversion of infix expressions to their prefix and suffix counterparts. The motivation behind this conversion is that the latter forms can be converted into object code by a single linear scan of the prefix or suffix expression. The next subsection deals with this problem.

## EXERCISES

★ **1.** Trace (as in Table 8-5) the procedure UnparenthesizedSuffix for the following expressions:

    *(a)* $a * b - c * d / e\#$

    *(b)* $a + * b c\#$

★ **2.** Trace (as in Table 8-7) the procedure Suffix for the following input expressions:

    *(a)* $(a + b) * (c - d + e))$

    *(b)* $a * b * (c + d))$

    *(c)* $(a + b)(c + d))$

★ **3.** Consider expressions which contain relational operators. In particular, obtain the precedence functions which will handle the relational operators $<, \leq, =, \neq, >$, and $\geq$. To avoid excessive parenthesization, the relational operators should have a lower priority than the arithmetic operations.

★ **4.** As a continuation of Exercise 3, consider extending the expressions so that they contain logical operators. In particular, obtain the precedence functions that will handle the logical operators

    ~      not (use ¬ on EBCDIC machines)

    &      and

    |      or

which are given in decreasing order of priority. Assume, unlike Pascal, that these operators have lower priority than the relational and arithmetic operators.

★★ **5.** Describe how conditional statements (**if** . . . **then** . . . **else**) can be implemented in the suffix Polish framework. In particular, extend the precedence functions obtained in Exercise 4 so as to incorporate conditional statements.

★ **6.** Improve program Suffix so that invalid infix expressions such as $ab + + c$ are detected. (*Hint*: Consider what symbols can follow other symbols.)

**7.** Based on the general algorithm given in the text, formulate a program for converting infix expressions to their equivalent prefix forms.

### Conversion of Polish Expressions to Object Code

Throughout this discussion we assume that the object code desired is in the form of assembly language instructions. As a matter of convenience, we also assume that the object computer which will execute the object code produced by the translation process is a single-address, single-accumulator machine whose memory is sequentially organized into words. Such a computer was described in Chap. 1. In this subsection we assume a simple assembly language representation for the instructions introduced there. A brief description of the symbolic operations is given in Table 8-9. Note that we have added two new instructions: multiplication (MUL) and division (DIV).

An informal algorithm for the evaluation of a suffix string was given earlier. Let us consider, initially, a "brute-force" algorithm for converting suffix expressions consisting of the four basic arithmetic operators and single-letter variables to assembly language. Finally, assume that the basic arithmetic operators generate the following code:

| $a + b\,(ab+)$ | LOD | a |
| | ADD | b |
| | STO | $T_i$ |
| $a - b\,(ab-)$ | LOD | a |
| | SUB | b |
| | STO | $T_i$ |
| $a * b\,(ab*)$ | LOD | a |
| | MUL | b |
| | STO | $T_i$ |

**TABLE 8-9**  Sample Assembly Language Instruction Set

| Operations | Meaning |
|---|---|
| LOD A | Load:  Copy the value of the word addressed by A into the accumulator. |
| STO A | Store:  Copy the value of the accumulator into the word addressed by A. |
| ADD A | Add:  Replace the present value of the accumulator with the sum of its present value and the value of the word addressed by A. |
| SUB A | Subtract:  Replace the present value of the accumulator with the result obtained by subtracting from its present value the value of the word addressed by A. |
| MUL A | Multiply:  Replace the present value of the accumulator with the result obtained by multiplying its present value by the value of the word addressed by A. |
| DIV A | Divide:  Replace the present value of the accumulator with the result obtained by dividing its present value by the value of the word addressed by A. |

| a / b (ab/) | LOD | a |
| | DIV | b |
| | STO | $T_i$ |

Note that each operator generates three assembly language instructions. The third instruction in each group is of the form STO $T_i$, where $T_i$ denotes an address of a location (word) in the computer's memory that is to contain the value of the intermediate result. These addresses are to be created by the desired suffix-to-assembly language program.

A straightforward algorithm involves the use of a stack. This entails the scanning of the suffix expression in a left-to-right manner. Each variable name in the input must be placed on the stack. On encountering an operator, the topmost two operands are unstacked and used (along with the operator) to generate the desired sequence of assembly instructions. The intermediate result corresponding to the operator in question is also placed on the stack. A general algorithm based on this approach follows:

*1.* Repeat thru step 3 while there still remains an input symbol

*2.* Obtain the current input symbol

*3.* If the current input symbol is a variable,
then push this variable on the stack
else remove the two topmost operands from the stack
generate the sequence of assembly language instructions which
corresponds to the current arithmetic operator
stack the intermediate result

A program based on this general approach is given in Fig. 8-22.

Note that in this program both variable names (single letters) and temporary names (three characters long) must be pushed into the operand stack. Thus each stack element has been defined to hold a three-character string. The statements

TempS : = ' □ □ □ ' ;
TempS [1] : = Current;
StackPush (S, TempS)

are necessary to push Current on the stack because Current is a character variable, whereas StackPush requires a three-character string as its second argument. Consider how the program could be simplified using one of the string-processing extensions described in Chap. 6.

In general, variables and constants (and also operators) can be many characters long. Our stack would waste considerable storage if each stack element must be large enough to hold the maximum-length symbol. An alternative is to use a symbol table (see Secs. 5-5.1 and 8-9.3) to contain the actual symbol. A stack element would contain only the index of, or a pointer to, the symbol table entry. Indices and pointers are of a small, fixed size.

**program** AssemblyCode (input, output);
{Given a suffix expression (which contains the four basic operators and single-letter variables and is terminated by a blank), this program translates this expression to assembly language instructions as described in the text.}
**label** 9999;
**const**
　MaxStackSize = 25;
**type**
　StackElementType = **packed array** [1 .. 3] **of** char;
　StackType = **record**
　　　Stack: **array** [1 .. MaxStackSize] **of** StackElementType;
　　　Top: integer
　　**end**;
**var**
　S: StackType;　　　　　　　　　　　{Operand stack}
　TempName: StackElementType;　　　　{Name of last used temporary}
　TempS,
　Left,
　Right: StackElementType;　　　　　　{Used in pushing and popping}
　OpCode: **packed array** [1 .. 3] **of** char;　{Operation code}
　Current: char;　　　　　　　　　　{Current character being used}

{Include the necessary stack operations from Sec. 8-4}

{Include procedure IncrTemp from Fig. 8-23}

**begin**
　{Step 1: Initialize the stack and temporary name}　.
　StackInitialize (S);
　TempName : = 'T00';

　{Step 2: Obtain the first suffix symbol}
　read (Current);

　　The program in Fig. 8-22 requires a procedure which, given the previous temporary name, will generate the next one. For example, given the name T19, this procedure should return T20. A suitable procedure appears in Fig. 8-23. It has been designed so as to work no matter what character set is in use on a particular computer system. A shorter procedure could be written if some assumptions are made about the character set. (Chapter 6 describes character sets in more detail.)
　　The trace of the program for the suffix string $ab*c + def/ + *$ is given in Table 8-10. The assembly language program generated by the program is given in the right-most column of the table. Upon examination of this program, it is clear that the generated code is inefficient. First, in the output code there exist redundant pairs of instructions such as

{Step 3: Engage loop to process the suffix expression}
**while** Current <> '□' **do**
   **begin**

        {Step 4: Process the current input symbol}
        **if** Current **in** ['a' .. 'z']
        **then begin**      {Push current variable onto the stack}
            TempS := '□□□';
            TempS[1] := Current;
            StackPush (S, TempS)
      **end**
      **else begin**     {Process the current operator}
        **case** Current **of**
           '+': OpCode := 'ADD';
           '−': OpCode := 'SUB';
           '*': OpCode := 'MUL';
           '/': OpCode := 'DIV'
        **end**;
        StackPop (S, Right);
        StackPop (S, Left);
        writeln ('LOD□', Left);
        writeln (OpCode, '□', Right);
        IncrTemp (TempName);
        writeln ('STO□', TempName);
        StackPush (S, TempName)
      **end**;

    {Step 5: Obtain the next suffix symbol}
    read (Current)
  **end**;

{Step 6: Halt}
9999:
**end**.

FIGURE 8-22 (*cont.*)

```
STO T01
LOD T01
```

Second, there is no advantage taken of the commutative property of the addition and multiplication operators. An example of this occurs in the code generated for the subexpression d + e / f: namely, the sequence

```
LOD e
DIV f
STO T03
LOD d
ADD T03
STO T04
```

```
procedure IncrTemp (
    var T: StackElementType        {Input/output, temporary name}
                    );
```
{Given a temporary name of the form Tmm when mm is a two-digit integer, this procedure returns, via the input/output parameter, Tnn where nn = mm + 1.}
```
var
    I: integer;                    {Index into character string}
    Carry: Boolean;                {Set true to propagate carry into next
                                        higher "digit"}
begin
    {Initialize for the loop}
    I := 3;
    Carry := true;

    {Process digits from the right}
    while Carry do
        begin
            Carry := false;
            case T[I] of
                '0': T[I] := '1';
                '1': T[I] := '2';
                '2': T[I] := '3';
                '3': T[I] := '4';
                '4': T[I] := '5';
                '5': T[I] := '6';
                '6': T[I] := '7';
                '7': T[I] := '8';
                '8': T[I] := '9';
                '9': begin
                        T[I] := '0';
                        Carry := true
                    end
            end;
            I := I - 1
        end
end;
```

**FIGURE 8-23**
**Procedure to**
**increment temporary**
**name.**

which can be replaced by the equivalent program segment

```
LOD e
DIV f
ADD d
STO T04
```

since the right operand (ef/) is already in the accumulator and the values of d + e / f and e / f + d are identical. The last sequence of instructions takes advantage of the commutative property of addition to eliminate two instructions. Finally, there is no effort made to reduce the number of temporary locations which are required to store intermediate results. In particular, the sequence of instructions

LOD a
MUL b
STO T01
LOD T01
ADD c
STO T02

can be replaced by the equivalent sequence where all instructions are the same except for the last, which becomes STO T01. Thus, the temporary variable T02 becomes unnecessary.

The number of temporary variables required can be reduced easily by making the following simple check: Before generating the assembly

| **TABLE 8-10** | Sample Code Generated by the Program **Assembly Code** for the Suffix String **ab\*c + def / + \*** | | | |

| Character Scanned | Contents of Stack (Right-most Symbol Is Top of Stack) | Left Operand | Right Operand | Code Generated |
|---|---|---|---|---|
| a | a | | | |
| b | a, b | | | |
| * | T01 | a | b | LOD a<br>MUL b<br>STO T01 |
| c | T01, c | | | |
| + | T02 | T01 | c | LOD T01<br>ADD c<br>STO T02 |
| d | T02, d | | | |
| e | T02, d, e | | | |
| f | T02, d, e, f | | | |
| / | T02, d, T03 | e | f | LOD e<br>DIV f<br>STO T03 |
| + | T02, T04 | d | T03 | LOD d<br>ADD T03<br>STO T04 |
| * | T05 | T02 | T04 | LOD T02<br>MUL T04<br>STO T05 |

instruction for a particular operator, a check of the contents of the left (**Left**) and right (**Right**) operands associated with the operator in question can be made. For each operand which corresponds to a created variable $T_i$, the temporary variable T*mm* is decremented by 1, giving T*nn*, where $nn = mm - 1$.

The redundant pairs of store and load instructions and the unnecessary temporary storing and subsequent reloading of a right operand for commutative operators is eliminated in the following way: Instead of always storing a partial result in temporary storage, as was done in the statement

writeln (' STO☐' ,TempName)

in step 4 of program AssemblyCode, one can delay the generation of such an instruction until it is deemed absolutely necessary. The previous statement can be altered so as to place an intermediate result marker '@☐☐' on the stack instead of always generating a store instruction. If such a marker is never pushed down in the stack deeper than the next-to-top position, then an intermediate result need not be saved by the generation of a store instruction. A revised program based on the previous comments is left as an exercise.

Although in this subsection we have dealt only with the generation of code from suffix expressions, similar notions hold for generating code from prefix expressions. We leave these details to the exercises. We will next consider use of a stack to hold variables in the evaluation of recursive functions.

## EXERCISES

1. Trace (as in Table 8-10) program AssemblyCode for the following suffix expressions:
    (*a*) ab − cd + *
    (*b*) ab * c + de − −
    (*c*) abc * + de/f * −

★ 2. Based on the discussion in the text following the program AssemblyCode, write a program which will generate more efficient code when the commutativity of the operators + and * is taken into consideration.

★ 3. Modify the program obtained in Exercise 2 so that the required number of temporary positions is reduced.

★ 4. Modify the program obtained in Exercise 3 so as to incorporate the assignment operator.

★ 5. Modify the program obtained in Exercise 4 so that it will handle the unary minus operator.

★ 6. Write a program similar to program AssemblyCode for generating code for prefix expressions.

★ 7. Modify the program obtained in Exercise 6 so that advantage of the commutative operators is taken into consideration.

In Chap. 4 we gave a brief introduction to recursive subprograms. Although recursion can be applied to both functions and procedures, it was illustrated only with functions. This subsection first illustrates recursion with a recursive procedure for performing a binary search and then examines how recursion is actually done by a computer.

### An Example: Recursive Binary Search

The technique of binary search was introduced in Sec. 5.3.2 as a reasonably efficient means of searching an ordered list of items. The function BinarySearch, given there, uses an iterative method to accomplish the task.

The binary search problem also can be formulated recursively. Essentially, it amounts to dividing the list of items in half recursively and performing a binary search on the "new list." The process continues until the desired element is found or until the "list" comprises a single element. Unlike the factorial and Fibonacci problems, there exists no recursive formula from which to work. We shall proceed, instead, from a general description of the approach. Before reading further, you would be wise to review the function BinarySearch.

We assume, as before, that the list of items has been sorted into ascending order. A general formulation of the recursive solution is as follows:

1. Obtain the position of the midpoint element in the current search interval

2. If the values of the desired and midpoint elements are equal,
   then the search is successful
   else If the value of the desired element is less than the value of the midpoint element,
      then perform a binary search on the first half of current search interval (recursive call)
      else perform a binary search on the second half of current search interval (recursive call)

This algorithm will find the desired element if it is in the list, but this may not be the case. We can allow for this possibility by testing first to see if the current search interval comprises a single element that is not the desired element or if the interval has become negative. In these cases, the desired element cannot be in the list. We therefore rewrite step 1 as

1. If current search interval is a single element whose value is not equal to the value of the desired element or if the interval has become negative,
   then search is unsuccessful
   else obtain the position of the midpoint of the current search interval

Step 2 remains as before.

This formulation is clearly recursive, with two recursive calls in step 2. The function in Fig. 8-24 results from formalizing these steps.

As an example, if we wished to search the vector V, comprising elements 61, 147, 197, 217, 309, 448, and 503, for 197, we would say simply BinSearchRecursive (V, 197, 1, 7, Result). As shown in the trace in Table 8-11, the result returned would be 3.

This procedure executes somewhat differently from the previous examples of recursion. It moves down through the chain of recursive calls, dividing the search interval in half each time, until a "base condition" is reached—either the element is found or it can be determined that it is not present.

### Complexity of the Recursive Binary Search

In order to analyze the time of the binary search, we will make the comparison of Key with InVec[Middle], our active operation. We will assume that one comparison operation with a three-way branch, for $<, >$, and $=$, can be used for the branching within a call. Unfortunately, the number of comparisons depends on the location of Key. In the best case, Key will be in location $\lfloor(n + 1)/2\rfloor$, where $n$ is the number of elements in InVec, so that only one comparison is used and $T_{BS}^B(n) = O(1)$. The worst case is somewhat more complex. Let $W(\text{High} - \text{Low} + 1)$ be the function for the worst case number of comparisons in a call of BinSearchRecursive(InVec, Key, Low, High, Position). In the worst case, Key will not be equal to InVec[Middle], so that a recursive call is needed. The size of the interval in the recursive call depends on whether $\text{High} - \text{Low} + 1$ is even or odd. For $\text{High} - \text{Low} + 1$ odd, the interval sizes are

$$\text{High} - \frac{(\text{Low} + \text{High})}{2} = \frac{(\text{High} - \text{Low})}{2}$$

and

$$\frac{(\text{Low} + \text{High})}{2} - \text{Low} = \frac{(\text{High} - \text{Low})}{2}$$

For $\text{High} - \text{Low} + 1$ even, the interval sizes are

$$\text{High} - \frac{(\text{Low} + \text{High} - 1)}{2} = \frac{(\text{High} - \text{Low} + 1)}{2}$$

and

$$\frac{(\text{Low} + \text{High} - 1)}{2} - \text{Low} = \frac{(\text{High} - \text{Low} - 1)}{2}$$

Thus in the worst case we have the recurrence relation

```
procedure BinSearchRecursive (
    var InVec: Vector;        {Input, vector to be searched}
    Key: integer;            {Input, value searched for}
    Low, High: integer;      {Input, interval to be searched}
    var Position: integer    {Output, position of desired value}
                         );
```

{Given a vector of integers whose elements are in ascending order, this procedure searches an interval in the vector for a given element (Key). The interval to be searched is from Low to High. This procedure returns the position of the desired element in the vector, or 0 if the element is not present. The procedure operates recursively. It is called, initially, to search an entire vector, say A, with bounds 1 and N, for a value, say X, by the call BinSearchRecursive(A, X, 1, N, P).}

```
var
    Middle: integer;        {Midpoint of interval}
begin
    {Step 1: Check for negative interval}
    if Low > High
    then Position : = 0
    else

        {Step 2: Check for single-element interval and no match}
        if (Low = High) and (InVec[Low] <> Key)
        then Position : = 0
        else begin

            {Step 3: Obtain position of midpoint of interval}
            Middle : = (Low + High) div 2;

            {Step 4: Compare}
            if InVec[Middle] = Key
            then {Search successful}
                Position : = Middle
            else {Choose interval and search recursively}
                if InVec [Middle] < Key
                then BinSearchRecursive(InVec, Key, Middle + 1, High, Position)
                else BinSearchRecursive (InVec, Key, Low, Middle − 1, Position)
    end
end;
```

**FIGURE 8-24**
**Recursive binary search procedure.**

$$W(n) = 1 + W(\lfloor n/2 \rfloor) \text{ for } n = \text{High} - \text{Low} + 1$$

The basis condition for the relation is $W(1) = 1$. To solve the recurrence relation (see App. B), we expand the relation for a few terms, which usually gives us enough information to guess the solution:

$$W(n) = 1 + W(\lfloor n/2 \rfloor)$$
$$= 1 + 1 + W(\lfloor n/2^2 \rfloor)$$
$$= 1 + 1 + 1 + W(\lfloor n/2^3 \rfloor)$$

Thus the solution seems to be the power to which 2 must be raised to obtain a value greater than $n$, that is, $\lfloor \log_2 n \rfloor + 1$. An inductive proof can be used to verify that this is in fact true. Thus we have

$$W(n) = \lfloor \log_2 n \rfloor + 1 \text{ and } T_{BS}^W(n) = O(\log_2 n)$$

The timing analysis for the average case of the recursive binary search is difficult to perform, but the result of such an analysis is also $O(\log_2 n)$.

We now examine the space requirements of the algorithm. For the binary search algorithm, the analysis is more interesting if we assume the vector is passed by value. This means that each call of **BinSearchRecursive** has its own local storage for the vector. Thus the local storage of the routine is $O(n)$. Therefore, in the best case, when only one call is needed, the storage is $O(n)$. In the worst case and average case, $O(\log_2 n)$ calls are needed so that the storage is $O(n \log_2 n)$. On the other hand, if the vector is passed as variable (the standard approach), there is only one copy of the vector. Thus local storage is $O(1)$, so that the worst case requirement for the stack is $O(\log_2 n)$. But now $O(n)$ storage is required globally for the vector so that the total storage is

$$O(n) + O(\log_2 n) = O(n)$$

This saving of storage is one reason why arrays are normally passed as variable rather than by value, even when they are input parameters. The main reason is the time required to copy the values on procedure entry (and perhaps exit). In fact, this copy operation becomes the active operation, with time $O(n \log_2 n)$, so that the binary search is no longer useful.

**TABLE 8-11**   Trace of Recursive Binary Search

| Procedure Call | Parameters | | | | Local Variable |
| | InVec | Key | Low | High | Middle |
| --- | --- | --- | --- | --- | --- |
| 1.  BSR (V, 197, 1, 7, R) | 61 | 197 | 1 | 7 | 4 |
| | 147 | | | | |
| | 197 | | | | |
| | 309 | | | | |
| | 448 | | | | |
| | 503 | | | | |
| 2.  BSR (V, 197, 1, 3, R) | Same | Same | 1 | 3 | 2 |
| 3.  BSR (V, 197 3, 3, R) | Same | Same | 3 | 3 | 3  success |

## Implementation of Recursion

From an implementation point of view, there are special problems associated with a recursive subprogram. A recursive subprogram can be invoked either externally (that is, from outside the definition) or internally (that is, recursively). This implies that such a subprogram has to save the different return addresses, in some order, so that a return to the proper location will occur when a return to a calling statement is made. Also, the recursive subprogram must save the values of all parameters and local variables upon entry and restore these parameters and variables at completion.

It is to be emphasized here that in programming languages in which recursion is allowed, such as Pascal, these problems are handled by the associated compilers. The programmer is, therefore, relieved of these bookkeeping tasks. It is instructive, however, to examine how the compiler for a recursive language might handle these problems. Using similar techniques, a recursive environment can be simulated in a programming language which does not allow recursion.

A general algorithmic simulation model for a recursive subprogram contains the following steps:

1. [Prologue]
   Save the return address
   Save the values of the parameters and local variables

2. [Body]
   If the base criterion has been reached,
   then perform the final computation and proceed to step 3
   else perform a partial computation and proceed to step 1, i.e.,
      initiate a recursive call
      Complete the computation

3. [Epilogue]
   Restore the values of the most recently saved parameters and local variables
   Restore the most recently saved return address
   Proceed to the statement which has this address

The model consists of a prologue, a body, and an epilogue. The prologue is responsible for saving the values of the parameters and local variables. In addition, it also saves the return address. Conversely, the epilogue restores these values and the return address. Observe that the parameter values, local variable values, and return address most recently saved are the first to be restored; that is, the process operates in a last-in, first-out manner. The body of the subprogram contains an invocation to itself. In general, a recursive subprogram can contain several recursive calls to itself. Note that in the body we have distinguished between a partial computation and a final computation. The final computation gives the explicit or base definition of the process for some value(s) of the argument(s). The base criterion is a test which determines whether or not the argument value(s) is that for which an explicit definition of the process is given.

The last-in, first-out characteristics of a recursive subprogram imply that a stack is the most obvious data structure to use to implement steps 1 and 3 of the preceding general model. At each invocation of the subprogram (or level of recursion), the necessary values and return address are pushed onto the stack; upon exit from that level, the stack is popped to restore the saved values of the preceding (or calling) level.

The previous recursive mechanism is best explained by a concrete example. A program to calculate Factorial(N) recursively, which explicitly shows the recursive framework through our simulation model, is presented in Fig. 8-25.

In this example, two program units are represented. Steps 1, 2, and 8 represent the main program, and steps 3 through 7 represent the recursive factorial function. Steps 3 and 7 are the prologue and epilogue of the function, respectively. The body of the function consists of step 4, the base computation (Factorial (0) = 1), and steps 5 and 6 consist of the recursive case (Factorial (N) = N * Factorial (N − 1)). Step 5 calculates the argument (N − 1) and simulates the recursive "call." The recursive call returns to step 6, which performs the multiplication (N * Factorial (N − 1)).

Each program unit (main program, functions, and procedure) has all its variables organized in a block of storage called an *activation record*. For simplicity, in our simulation we have used the same record structure (ActRec) for the main program and the function. However, a Pascal compiler will actually generate a separate activation record structure for each program unit. The activation record contains all the local variables, the parameters, a return address, and a small amount of "bookkeeping" information for the associated program unit. Its size will be the total of the sizes of these items.

The statements of each program unit references its local variables in the activation record. A description of methods for accessing global variables is beyond the scope of this text. Certain information, however, namely, the values of arguments, the function result, and the return address, must be passed between the calling and called units. In our simulation, only one activation record is available at a time. Therefore, auxiliary variables (Result, RetAddress) are used to pass this information. A trace of the simulation is given in Fig. 8-26. Observe that the total storage required is the maximum, over all steps of the execution, of the sum of the sizes of the activation records in the stack and the current activation record. In Fig. 8-26, this maximum occurs at level 5.

The application of a stack in this subsection has been concerned with the storage of values for parameters and local variables in the evaluation of recursive functions.

In closing, we want to emphasize that the choice between iteration and recursion is not clear-cut. Although any recursive algorithm (in theory, at least) can be written iteratively, there are instances where a recursive solution is (almost) unavoidable because of the recursive nature of the problem or because of the recursive structure of the data which has to be processed. In such cases, a recursive solution is both natural and elegant. Even for cases where there is no inherent recursive structure, a recursive solution may be simpler (although sometimes more time consuming) than an iterative counterpart. On the other hand, some problems are best solved iteratively. Also, because of space and time considerations or because of the programming languages available at a particular computer installation, we may be forced to use iteration.

Finally, there are problems that can be solved just as easily by using either iteration or recursion. Whatever approach is used in solving problems, however, we want to stress the importance of thinking iteratively to formulate iterative solutions and of thinking recursively to formulate recursive solutions.

## EXERCISES 8-5.2

1. The median of a set of an odd number of scores is defined as that score which has the property that the number of scores greater than it is equal to the number of scores smaller than it. Suppose there is a set of Num scores in the array Score. Then a recursive solution to computing the median score would be to eliminate successively the highest score and the lowest score until only one score remained. That score would then be the median score. Assume Num is odd.

   Write a recursive procedure called Median which takes the parameters LowBound and HighBound that indicate that the search for the median is to take place in the part of the array Score from position LowBound to position HighBound. If there is only one value in Score between LowBound and HighBound, the procedure Median prints out that value; otherwise it finds the smallest score, exchanges it with Score[LowBound], finds the largest score, exchanges it with Score[HighBound], "shrinks" the table to exclude these two values, and repeats the procedure. Write and make use of two functions Max and Min, which each take LowBound and HighBound and return the index of the largest and smallest score, respectively, in the array Score between LowBound and HighBound.

2. The usual method used in evaluating a polynomial of the form

$$p_n(x) = a_0x^n + a_1x^{n-1} + a_2x^{n-2} + \cdots + a_{n-1}x + a_n$$

   is the technique known as *nesting*, or *Horner's rule*. This is an iterative method which is described as follows:

$$b_0 = a_0$$
$$b_{i+1} = x \cdot b_i + a_{i+1} \quad i = 0, 1, \ldots, n-1$$

   from which one can obtain $b_n = p_n(x)$.

   An alternative solution to the problem is to write

**program** FactorialExplicitRecursion (input, output);
{This program simulates a recursive computation of N!}
**label** 3, 6, 8, 9999;
**const**
   MaxStackSize = 100;
**type**
   StackElementType =
      **record**
         N, RetAdr, Factorial: integer;
      **end**;
   StackType =
      **record**
         Stack: **array** [1 .. MaxStackSize] **of** StackElementType;
         Top: integer
      **end**;
**var**
   S: StackType;                     {Activation record stack}
   ActRec: StackElementType;         {Current activation record}
   Argument: integer;                {Argument passed in when the function
                                        is called}
   ReturnAdr: integer;               {Return address passed to the function}
   Result: integer;                  {Result passed from the function}

{Include the necessary stack operations from Sec. 8-4}

**begin**
   {Step 1: Simulate the first portion of the main program. Initialize the
      stack and obtain the initial value of N.}
   StackInitialize (S);
   read (ActRec.N);

   {Step 2: Simulate a call from the main program to the factorial func-
      tion.}
   Argument : = ActRec.N;    {Pass argument}
   ReturnAdr : = 8;          {Pass return address}
   **goto** 3;                {Go to the beginning of function}

FIGURE 8-25
Simulation of a
recursive computation
of factorial using
an explicit stack.

$$p_n(x) = x \cdot p_{n-1}(x) + a_n$$

where $p_{n-1}(x) = a_0 x^{n-1} + a_1 x^{n-2} + \cdots + a_{n-2}x + a_{n-1}$

which is a recursive formulation of the problem. Formulate a recursive
function for this problem.

3. Trace the function obtained in Exercise 3 for the data $n = 3, a_0 = 1$,
   $a_1 = 3$, $a_2 = 3$, $a_3 = 1$, and $x = 3$.

{Step 3: Simulate prologue of function. Save contents of old activation record on the stack and initialize activation record with values of argument and return address.}

```
3:
StackPush (S, ActRec);
ActRec.N : = Argument;
ActRec.RetAdr : = ReturnAdr;
```

{Step 4: If base criterion of the function is satisfied, then perform the final computation.}

```
if ActRec.N = 0
then ActRec.Factorial : = 1
```

{Step 5: Otherwise make a recursive call to factorial to compute Factorial (N − 1)}

```
else begin
        Argument : = ActRec.N − 1;    {Pass argument}
        ReturnAdr : = 6;              {Pass return address}
        goto 3;                       {Go to beginning of function}
```

{Step 6: Recursive call returns here. Complete the computation for the recursive case}

```
        6:
        ActRec.Factorial : = ActRec.N * Result
    end;
```

{Step 7: Simulate epilogue of function. Pass result, restore contents of previous activation record, and go to return address.}

```
Result : = ActRec.Factorial;    {Return result}
ReturnAdr : = ActRec.RetAdr;    {Temporarily save return address}
StackPop (S, ActRec);           {Restore previous activation record}
case ReturnAdr of               {Return to caller}
    6: goto 6;
    8: goto 8
end;
```

{Step 8: Remainder of main program; display result of Factorial (N).}

```
8:
writeln ('Factorial of', ActRec.N, 'is', Result);
9999:
end.
```

FIGURE 8-25 (*cont.*)

★ 4. Consider the set of all valid, completely parenthesized, infix arithmetic expressions consisting of single-letter variable names, a digit, and the four operators +, −, *, and /. The following recursive definition specifies the set of valid expressions:

(*a*) Any single-letter variable (A–Z) or a digit is a valid infix expression.

| Level number | Description | Stack contents | Current activation record |
|---|---|---|---|
| Enter level 1 (Main program) | Step 1: read(N) <br> Step 2: call Factorial(N) | (empty) | 3 |
| Enter level 2 (Call of factorial from main) | Step 3: push ActRec and set up new current record <br> Step 5: call Factorial(N−1) | 3   Top | 3 <br> Step 8 |
| Enter level 3 (First recursive call) | Step 3: push ActRec and set up new current record <br> Step 5: call Factorial(N−1) | 3   3 (Step 8)   Top | 2 <br> Step 6 |
| Enter level 4 (Second recursive call) | Step 3: push ActRec and set up new current record <br> Step 5: call Factorial(N−1) | 3   3 (Step 8)   2 (Step 6)   Top | 1 <br> Step 6 |
| Enter level 5 (Third recursive call) | Step 3: push ActRec and set up new current record <br> Step 4: Base case Factorial = 1 | 3   3 (Step 8)   2 (Step 6)   1 (Step 6)   Top | 0 <br> Step 6 <br> 1 |
| Return to level 4 | Step 7: pop ActRec and return | 3   3 (Step 8)   2 (Step 6)   Top | 1 <br> Step 6 |

**FIGURE 8-26  A trace of the simulation of 3!.**

| Level number | Description | Stack contents | Current activation record |
|---|---|---|---|
| Complete computation at level 4 | Step 6: Factorial = n * Result | 3   3 / Step 8   2 / Step 6 (Top) | 1 / Step 6 / 1 |
| Return to level 3 | Step 7: pop ActRec and return | 3   3 / Step 8 (Top) | 2 / Step 6 |
| Complete computation at level 3 | Step 6: Factorial = N * Result | 3   3 / Step 8 (Top) | 2 / Step 6 / 2 |
| Return to level 2 | Step 7: pop ActRec and return | 3 (Top) | 3 / Step 8 |
| Complete computation at level 2 | Step 6: Factorial = N * Result | 3 (Top) | 3 / Step 8 / 6 |
| Return to level 1 (return to main program) | Step 7: pop ActRec and return | | 3 |
| Complete main program | Step 8: display result of 6 | | 3 |

FIGURE 8-26 (cont.)

*(b)* If $\alpha$ and $\beta$ are valid infix expressions, then $(\alpha + \beta)$, $(\alpha - \beta)$, $(\alpha * \beta)$, and $(\alpha\ /\ \beta)$ are valid infix expressions.

*(c)* The only valid infix expressions are those defined by steps 1 and 2. Formulate a recursive function that will input a string of symbols and output either **VALID EXPRESSION** for a valid infix expression or **INVALID EXPRESSION** for an invalid expression.

★ **5.** Write a recursive function to compute the square root of a number. Read in triples of numbers **N**, **A**, and **E**, where **N** is the number for which the square root is to be found, **A** is an approximation of the square root, and **E** is the allowable error in the result. Use as your function

$$\text{ROOT(N, A, E)} = \begin{cases} A & \text{if } |A^2 - N| < E \\ \text{ROOT}\left(N, \dfrac{A^2 + N}{2A}, E\right) & \text{otherwise} \end{cases}$$

★ **6.** The Towers of Hanoi is a game with an alleged historical basis in a ritual practiced by Brahman priests to predict the end of the world. The game begins with a series of gold rings of decreasing size stacked on a needle (the Brahman priests used 64 rings). The object is to stack all the rings onto a second needle in decreasing order of size. Before this is done, the end of the world will be upon us. A third needle is available for use as intermediate storage. The scenario is shown in Fig. 8-27. The movement of the rings is restricted by the following three rules:

*(a)* Only one ring may be moved at a time.

*(b)* A ring may be moved from any needle to any other.

*(c)* At no time may a larger ring rest on a smaller ring.

Design a recursive procedure to solve the Towers of Hanoi problem.

★ **7.** Trace the recursive operation (as in Fig. 8-26) of the procedure produced for Exercise 5 for **N** = 2.

**8.** An important theoretical function, known as *Ackermann's function*, is defined as

$$A(M,\ N) = \begin{cases} N + 1 & \text{if } M = 0 \\ A(M - 1,\ 1) & \text{if } N = 0 \\ A(M - 1,\ A(M,\ N - 1)) & \text{otherwise} \end{cases}$$

Write a recursive function for this function.

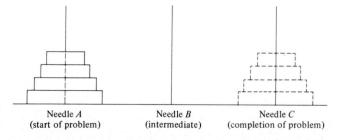

**FIGURE 8-27**
**Towers of Hanoi.**

Needle *A*
(start of problem)

Needle *B*
(intermediate)

Needle *C*
(completion of problem)

★ **9.** Evaluate the function of Exercise 8 for $M = 2$ and $N = 2$.

★★ **10.** Recursion can be used to generate all possible permutations of a set of symbols. For example, there are six permutations on the set of symbols A, B, and C; namely, ABC, ACB, BAC, BCA, CBA, and CAB. The set of permutations of $N$ symbols is generated by taking each symbol in turn and prefixing it to all the permutations which result from the remaining $N - 1$ symbols. Consequently, permutations on a set of symbols can be specified in terms of permutations on a smaller set of symbols. Formulate a recursive procedure for this problem.

★ **11.** Certain applications require a knowledge of the number of different partitions of a given positive integer $N$, that is, how many different ways $N$ can be expressed as a sum of positive integer summands. For example, $N = 5$ yields the partitions

$$1 + 1 + 1 + 1 + 1 \quad 1 + 1 + 1 + 2 \quad 1 + 2 + 2 \quad 1 + 1 + 3 \quad 1 + 4 \quad 2 + 3 \quad 5$$

If we denote by $Q_{MN}$ the number of ways in which an integer $M$ can be expressed as a sum, each summand of which is no larger than $N$, then the number of partitions of $N$ is given by $Q_{NN}$. The function $Q_{MN}$ is defined recursively as

$$Q_{MN} = \begin{cases} 1 & \text{if } M = 1 \text{ and for all } N \\ 1 & \text{if } N = 1 \text{ and for all } M \\ Q_{MM} & \text{if } M < N \\ 1 + Q_{M, M-1} & \text{if } M = N \\ Q_{M, N-1} + Q_{M-N, N} & \text{if } M > N \end{cases}$$

Formulate a recursive function for $Q_{NN}$. Implement this function in Pascal.

★ **12.** Evaluate the function $Q_{NN}$ obtained in Exercise 11 for $N = 3$ and $N = 5$.

## 8-5.3 PARTITION-EXCHANGE SORTING (QUICKSORT)

As the third application of a stack structure, we now consider a sorting technique which performs well on large tables. The approach is first to place a particular record in its final position within the sorted table. Once this is done, all records that have smaller keys precede this record while all records that have larger keys follow it (assuming a sort into ascending order). This technique partitions the original table into two subtables. The same process is then applied to each of these subtables and repeated until all records are placed in their final positions.

As an example of this approach to sorting, let us consider the placement of **73** in its final position in the following key set:

73  65  52  24  83  17  35  96  41  9

We use two index variables, J and K, with initial values of **2** and **10**, respectively. The two keys **73** and InOutVec[J] are compared, and if an exchange is required (that is, InOutVec[J] < 73), then J is incremented by 1 and the process is repeated. When InOutVec[J] ≥ 73, we proceed to compare keys InOutVec[K] and 73. If an exchange is required, then K is decremented by 1 and the process is repeated until InOutVec[K] ≤ 73. At this point, the keys InOutVec[J] and InOutVec[K] (that is, 83 and 9) are interchanged. The entire process is then repeated with K fixed and J being incremented once again. When J ≥ K, the desired key is placed in its final position by interchanging keys 73 and InOutVec[K].

The sequence of exchanges for placing 73 in its final position is given in Table 8-12, where the entries in color on each line denote the keys being compared. The original key set has been partitioned into two subtables: {41, 65, 52, 24, 9, 17, 35} and {96, 83} . The first of these contains elements less than 73, while the second contains elements greater than 73. This process can be applied to each of these subtables until the original table is sorted. Note that the partitioning process stops when we encounter a subtable of size 1. This partition-exchange technique of sorting is sometimes called *quicksort*. A general algorithm for this recursive method of sorting is:

> If the current table contains more than one element,
> then partition the current table into two subtables
> > Invoke quicksort recursively to sort left subtable
> > Invoke quicksort recursively to sort right subtable

This approach to sorting is formalized in procedure QuickSort (Fig. 8-28). Procedure Partition (Fig. 8-29) is called to partition the table into two subtables for sorting. The behavior of this procedure on the sample key set used earlier is given in Table 8-13.

Let us consider the timing analysis of this program. The analysis of procedure QuickSort is given by

$$T_{QS}(N) = P(N) + T_{QS}(\text{Split} - \text{LB}) + T_{QS}(\text{UB} - \text{Split})$$

where $P(N)$, $T_{QS}(\text{Split} - \text{LB})$, and $T_{QS}(\text{UB} - \text{Split})$ denote the times to partition

**TABLE 8-12** Sequence of Exchanges for Partition-Exchange Sorting

| | | | | | | | | | | |
|---|---|---|---|---|---|---|---|---|---|---|
| 73 | 65 | 52 | 24 | 83 | 17 | 35 | 96 | 41 | 9 | |
| 73 | 65 | 52 | 24 | 83 | 17 | 35 | 96 | 41 | 9 | |
| 73 | 65 | 52 | 24 | 83 | 17 | 35 | 96 | 41 | 9 | |
| 73 | 65 | 52 | 24 | 83 | 17 | 35 | 96 | 41 | 9 | |
| 73 | 65 | 52 | 24 | 83 | 17 | 35 | 96 | 41 | 9 | Interchange 83 and 9 |
| 73 | 65 | 52 | 24 | 9 | 17 | 35 | 96 | 41 | 83 | |
| 73 | 65 | 52 | 24 | 9 | 17 | 35 | 96 | 41 | 83 | |
| 73 | 65 | 52 | 24 | 9 | 17 | 35 | 96 | 41 | 83 | |
| 73 | 65 | 52 | 24 | 9 | 17 | 35 | 96 | 41 | 83 | Interchange 41 and 96 |
| 73 | 65 | 52 | 24 | 9 | 17 | 35 | 41 | 96 | 83 | |
| 73 | 65 | 52 | 24 | 9 | 17 | 35 | 41 | 96 | 83 | J ≥ K interchange 73 and 41 |
| 41 | 65 | 52 | 24 | 9 | 17 | 35 | 73 | 96 | 83 | |

```
procedure QuickSort (
    var InOutVec: Vector;      {Input/output, vector to be sorted}
    LB: integer;               {Input, lower bound of current subvector}
    UB: integer                {Input, upper bound of current subvector}
                );
```

{Given a vector of keys, this procedure sorts the subvector from **LB** to **UB** by the recursive QuickSort method. It is assumed that InOutVec has a dummy element InOutVec[N + 1] such that this element is larger than all the actual elements.}

```
var
    Split: integer;      {contains the position of the partitioning element}
begin
    {Step 1: Perform sort}
    if LB < UB
    then begin
            Partition(InOutVec, LB, UB, Split);
            QuickSort(InOutVec, LB, Split − 1);      {Sort left subvector}
            QuickSort(InOutVec, Split + 1, UB)       {Sort right subvector}
        end
end;
```

609
8-5
APPLICATIONS
OF STACKS

**FIGURE 8-28**
**Recursive partition exchange sort (QuickSort) procedure.**

the given table (using procedure **Partition**), sort the left subtable, and sort the right subtable, respectively. Note that the time to partition a table is $O(N)$.

The worst case occurs when, at each invocation of the procedure, the current table is partitioned into two subtables with one of them being empty (that is, **Split** = **LB** or **Split** = **UB**). Such a situation, for example, occurs when the given key set is already sorted. The sorting of the example key set $\{11, 23, 36, 42\}$ would yield the following sequence of partitions:

```
11  {23    36    42}
11   23   {36    42}
11   23    36    {42}
11   23    36     42
```

Note that in such a situation the present method of sorting is no better than the selection sort. The worst-case time analysis, assuming **Split** = **LB**, then becomes

$$T_{QS}^W(N) = P(N) + T_{QS}^W(0) + T_{QS}^W(N - 1)$$

$$= c * N + T_{QS}^W(N - 1)$$

$$= c * N + c * (N - 1) + T_{QS}^W(N - 2)$$

$$= c * N + c * (N - 1) + c * (N - 2) + T_{QS}^W(N - 3)$$

**procedure** Partition (

  **var** InOutVec: Vector;    {Input/output, vector to be sorted}

  LB: integer;    {Input, lower bound of current subvector being processed}

  UB: integer;    {Input, upper bound of current subvector being processed}

  **var** Split: integer    {Output, position of the output character}

      );

{Given a vector of keys, that includes a dummy element as described earlier, this procedure places InOutVec[LB] at its final position in the sorted table. When Done becomes true, the input subvector has been partitioned into disjoint parts.}

**var**

  Key: KeyType;    {Contains the key which is to be placed in its final position within the sorted subvector}

  ExchangeValue: KeyType;    {Temporary used when exchanging two values}

  Done: Boolean;    {Indicates the end of the process that determines final position of the element being placed}

  L: integer;    {Lower index}

  U: integer;    {Upper index}

**begin**

  {Step 1: Initialize}

  L := LB;

  U := UB + 1;

  Key := InOutVec[LB];

**FIGURE 8-29**
**Procedure to perform**
**partitioning for**
**QuickSort.**

$$= \sum_{k=1}^{N} c * k + T_{QS}^{W}(0)$$

$$= c * \frac{(N + 1)(N)}{2}$$

$$= O(N^2)$$

The worst case can sometimes be avoided by more carefully choosing the record for final placement at each stage. Rather than always choosing InOutVec[LB], as was done in the previous approach, we could choose a random position in the interval [LB, UB]. Another approach is to take the middle position in the interval, that is, $\lfloor (LB + UB) / 2 \rfloor$. Finally, the position could be chosen to be the median of the keys in the interval, although this option is costly.

    The best-case situation occurs when the table is always partitioned in half, that is, Split $= \lfloor (LB + UB) / 2 \rfloor$. The analysis becomes

{Step 2: Obtain the position of the partitioning element}
Done : = false;
**while not** Done **do**
  **begin**

    {Step 3: Scan keys from lower to higher}
    L : = L + 1;
    **while** InOutVec[L] < Key **do**
      L : = L + 1;

    {Step 4: Scan keys from right to left}
    U : = U − 1;
    **while** InOutVec[U] > Key **do**
      U : = U − 1;

    {Step 5: Perform any required intermediate interchange}
    **if** L < U
    **then begin**
        ExchangeValue : = InOutVec[L];
        InOutVec[L] : = InOutVec[U];
        InOutVec[U] : = ExchangeValue
    **end**
    **else** Done : = true
  **end**;

{Step 6: Place selected element in its final position}
ExchangeValue : = InOutVec[LB];
InOutVec[LB] : = InOutVec[U];
InOutVec[U] : = ExchangeValue;
Split : = U
**end**;

FIGURE 8-29 *(cont.)*

$$T^B_{QS}(N) = P(N) + 2T^B_{QS}(N/2) = c * N + 2T^B_{QS}(N/2)$$
$$= c * N + 2c(N/2) + 4T^B_{QS}(N/4)$$
$$= c * N + 2c(N/2) + 4c(N/4) + 8T^B_{QS}(N/8)$$
$$= 3 * c * N + 8T^B_{QS}(N/8)$$
$$\cdot$$
$$\cdot$$
$$\cdot$$
$$= (\log_2 N) * c * N + 2^{\log_2 N} * T^B_{QS}(1)$$
$$= O(N \log_2 N)$$

**TABLE 8-13** Behavior of Procedure **QuickSort** (**V** is the vector **InOutVec**)

| $V_1$ | $V_2$ | $V_3$ | $V_4$ | $V_5$ | $V_6$ | $V_7$ | $V_8$ | $V_9$ | $V_{10}$ | LB | UB |
|---|---|---|---|---|---|---|---|---|---|---|---|
| {73 | 65 | 52 | 24 | 83 | 17 | 35 | 96 | 41 | 9} | 1 | 10 |
| {41 | 65 | 52 | 24 | 9 | 17 | 35} | 73 | {96 | 83} | 1 | 7 |
| { 9 | 35 | 17 | 24} | 41 | {52 | 65} | 73 | {96 | 83} | 1 | 4 |
| 9 | {35 | 17 | 24} | 41 | {52 | 65} | 73 | {96 | 83} | 2 | 4 |
| 9 | {24 | 17} | 35 | 41 | {52 | 65} | 73 | {96 | 83} | 2 | 3 |
| 9 | 17 | 24 | 35 | 41 | {52 | 65} | 73 | {96 | 83} | 6 | 7 |
| 9 | 17 | 24 | 35 | 41 | 52 | 65 | 73 | {96 | 83} | 9 | 10 |
| 9 | 17 | 24 | 35 | 41 | 52 | 65 | 73 | 83 | 96 | | |

The average-case analysis of procedure QuickSort is difficult to perform, but the result of such an analysis is also $O(N \log_2 N)$.

Finally, consider the space analysis of procedure QuickSort. When a table is partitioned into two subtables, the left subtable is chosen to be the current subtable. Consequently, the upper and lower indices of the remaining subtable must be saved. In the worst case, the partitioning process may cause the saving of the indices for successive subtables of size 1 for later processing. In such a case, a maximum of N pairs of indices may have to be stored. This problem can be alleviated by saving the indices associated with the largest subtable and processing the smaller subtable. This approach reduces the maximum storage required to $\log_2 N$ pairs of indexes, since the smaller subtable will be no more than half the size of the subtable from which it was derived.

## EXERCISES 8-5.3

1. Describe the behavior of the procedure QuickSort (as in Table 8-13) for the sample key set:

   42  23  74  11  65  58  94  36  99  87

★★ 2. Formulate an iterative procedure for the partition-exchange method of sorting.

★ 3. Using the sample key set given in Exercise 1, trace the procedure obtained in Exercise 2.

## 8-6  QUEUES

Another important subclass of linear lists is one in which deletions are performed from the beginning (or front) of the list while insertions are performed at the end (or rear) of the list. Elements in such an organization are processed in the same order as they were received, that is on a first-in, first-out (FIFO) or a first-come, first-served (FCFS) basis. A linear list which belongs to this subclass is called a *queue*. Figure 8-30 illustrates a queue structure.

Perhaps one of the most familiar examples of a queue is a customer checkout line at a supermarket cash register. The first customer in this line is the first to be checked out and a new customer joins the end of the line.

Most computer science students have encountered another familiar example of a queue in a timesharing computer system where many users share the computer system simultaneously. Often, such a computer system has a single central processing unit and one main memory. These resources are shared by allowing one user's program to execute for a short period of time, followed by the execution of a second user's program, and so on, until there is a resumption of execution of the initial user's program. A queue is used to store the user programs which are awaiting execution. Typically, however, this waiting queue does not operate in a strict first-in, first-out manner. Rather, it operates on a complex priority scheme that is based on several factors, such as the execution time required, the number of lines of output, the compiler being used, the time of day, etc. A queue of this type is sometimes called a *priority queue*. More will be said about this type of queue in Sec. 8-7.

Most people are part of another familiar queue every day. This queue takes the form of a line of cars waiting to proceed in some direction at a street intersection. An insertion of a car in the queue involves a car joining the end of the line of existing cars waiting to proceed through the intersection, while the deletion of a car consists of the front car passing through the intersection.

The four common operations which are associated with a queue **Q** are

| | |
|---|---|
| QueueInitialize(Q) | Initializes the queue **Q** to be empty |
| QueueInsert(Q, X) | Inserts an element **X** at the rear of the queue |
| QueueDelete(Q, X) | Removes the front element from the queue and returns its value as **X** |
| QueueEmpty(Q) | Returns "true" if **Q** contains no elements; otherwise returns "false" |

As was done in the discussion of stacks, we can give a vector representation of a queue. Again, this vector is assumed to contain a sufficiently large number of elements to handle the variable-length property of a queue. Another representation, which better reflects the variable-size property of a

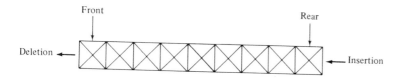

**FIGURE 8-30**
**Representation of a queue.**

queue, is given in Sec. 8-8. The vector representation of a queue requires pointers **F** and **R** to denote the present positions of its front and rear elements, respectively. Figure 8-31 illustrates the representation scheme. Using this representation, we are now in a position to formulate subprograms for the four basic queue operations.

As we did for stacks, we define a queue as a record structure containing the vector and the two pointers (subscripts) in Fig. 8-32. The integer constant MaxQueueSize and the type QueueElementType must be defined in a program using this queue definition. We then formulate the initialization procedure in Fig. 8-33. This procedure is necessary for writing modular procedures and programs in which we manipulate queues. We would like to write our basic procedures such that the programmer need not be concerned with maintenance of the variables **F** and **R**.

We first consider a procedure for queue insertion in Fig. 8-34. The first step of the procedure checks for an overflow situation. If this situation arises, then the procedure QueueOverflow is invoked. Although this procedure is application-dependent, usually its invocation generates a message which indicates that more storage is required for the queue and that the program must be rerun. We do not repeat the presentation on error-handling procedures (see Sec. 8-4). Note that in the second step a check is made for an insertion into an empty queue. In such an instance, the front pointer must be set to 1.

The corresponding deletion procedure appears in Fig. 8-35. An underflow situation is checked for in the first step of the procedure. If this situation arises, then procedure QueueUnderflow is invoked. Although this procedure is also application-dependent, attempted deletion from an empty queue may be considered a valid operation in some applications. Note that if a deletion is performed on a queue that contains a single element prior to deletion time, then the front and rear pointers are reset to zero.

Finally, we present a Boolean function (Fig. 8-36) which tests whether a queue is empty. As for the function StackEmpty, we have made the input parameter pass as variable so that the compiler does not make a copy of the queue for the procedure.

The previously described representation of a queue can be very wasteful of memory if the front pointer **F** never catches up to the rear pointer. In such a situation, a very large amount of memory would be required to accommodate the elements of the queue without encountering overflow. Therefore, this representation of a queue should be used only when the queue frequently becomes empty.

As an example of this representation of a queue, consider a vector that

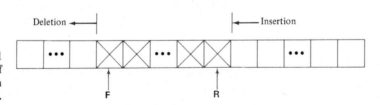

**FIGURE 8-31**
**Representation of a queue by a vector.**

```
type
    QueueType = record
        Queue: array [1 .. MaxQueueSize] of QueueElementType;
        F, R: integer
    end;
```

FIGURE 8-32    Type definition for a sequentially allocated queue.

contains five elements. Let us assume that the queue is initially empty. It is required to insert elements 'Paul', 'Rick', and 'Bob', delete 'Paul' and 'Rick', and insert 'John', 'Grant', and 'Ken'. Figure 8-37 gives a trace of the queue contents for this sequence of operations. Note that an overflow occurs on trying to insert 'Ken', even though the first two locations are not being used.

A more suitable method of representing a queue, which gets around this obvious drawback, is to arrange the elements Queue[1], Queue[2], . . . , Queue[N] in a circular fashion, with Queue[1] following Queue[N]. Figure 8-38 illustrates such a representation. The insertion and deletion procedures for a *circular queue* appear in Figs. 8-39 and 8-40, respectively. These procedures are very similar to the corresponding program for a simple queue except for wrap-around detection. The previous versions of QueueInitialize (Fig. 8-33) and QueueEmpty (Fig. 8-36) are still valid for this new representation.

Note the use of the temporary variable NewR in the insertion procedure. If R were modified directly and then queue overflow were detected, the R pointer would be left with an inappropriate value. If the application were to attempt to continue after the error, subsequent operations would produce anomalous results. This is an example of robust design of program modules.

Observe that while we have modified the way in which the queue is implemented, we have not redefined the meaning of the basic queue operations. We have only changed how the routines accomplish their task, not what they are meant to do. Thus an application using the queue operations should not require any change due to the alternative queue implementation. This is an important benefit of good program modularization.

```
procedure QueueInitialize (
    var Q: QueueType        {Output, initialized queue}
                            );
{Given a queue, this procedure initializes the queue to be empty.}
begin
    with Q do
        begin
            {Initialize front and rear pointers}
            F := 0;
            R := 0
        end
end;
```

FIGURE 8-33
Procedure to initialize
a sequentially
allocated queue.

**procedure** QueueInsert (
   **var** Q: QueueType;    {Input/output, queue}
   X: QueueElementType   {Input, value to be inserted}
         );
{Given a queue and a value, the value is inserted at the rear of the queue.}
**begin**
  **with** Q **do**

     {If overflow condition then signal error}
     **if** R >= MaxQueueSize
     **then** QueueOverflow
     **else begin**

        {Is front pointer properly set?}
        **if** F = 0
        **then** F := 1;

        {Increment rear pointer}
        R := R + 1;

        {Insert new element}
        Queue[R] := X
     **end**
**end**;

**FIGURE 8-34**
**Procedure to insert**
**at rear of a sequentially**
**allocated queue.**

An example of a circular queue capable of holding five elements is given in Fig. 8-41, where several operations are performed on an initially empty queue. Note that in this figure the queue is not shown to be circular for convenience purposes.

The preceding programs all deal with a queue that behaves in a first-in, first-out manner. A more general queue structure involves a linear list in which insertions and deletions are made to and from either end of the list. Such a structure is called a *deque* (double-ended queue) and is illustrated in Fig. 8-42. Observe that a deque is more general than either a stack or a simple queue. There are two variations of a deque: an *input-restricted deque* and an *output-restricted deque*. An input-restricted deque allows insertions only at the rear of the queue. An output-restricted deque, on the other hand, allows deletions only from the front of the queue. We leave the insert and delete algorithms for these structures as exercises.

In this section we have concentrated on the basic notions of queues. In the next section an application will be examined.

## EXERCISES 8-6

1. Construct a procedure for inserting an element into a deque. Assume a vector representation for the queue. Note that you must have a parameter that specifies at which end of the deque the insertion is to be made.

```
procedure QueueDelete (
    var Q: QueueType;          {Input/output, queue}
    var X: QueueElementType    {Output, value removed}
                );
```
{Given a sequentially allocated queue, this procedure deletes an element from the front of the queue. The value of the deleted element is returned via the output parameter.}
```
begin
    with Q do

        {If underflow, signal error}
        if F = 0
        then QueueUnderflow
        else begin

            {Return value of deleted element}
            X : = Queue[F];

            {If the last element is being deleted, reset F and R.}
            if F = R
            then begin
                F : = 0;
                R : = 0
            end

            {Otherwise increment F}
            else F : = F + 1
        end
end;
```

**FIGURE 8-35**
Procedure to delete
from the front of a
sequentially allocated
queue.

2. Repeat Exercise 1 for the deletion operation.

3. Formulate a procedure for performing an insertion into an input-restricted deque.

4. Construct a procedure for performing a deletion from an input-restricted deque. A parameter is required to denote from which end of the deque a deletion is to be made.

5. Repeat Exercises 3 and 4 for an output-restricted deque.

```
function QueueEmpty (var Q: QueueType {Input, queue} ): Boolean;
```
{Given a sequentially allocated queue, this function returns "true" if the queue is empty, and "false" otherwise.}
```
begin
    with Q do
        {Return "emptiness" of queue}
        QueueEmpty : = (R = 0)
end;
```

**FIGURE 8-36**
Function to test
whether a sequentially
allocated queue
is empty.

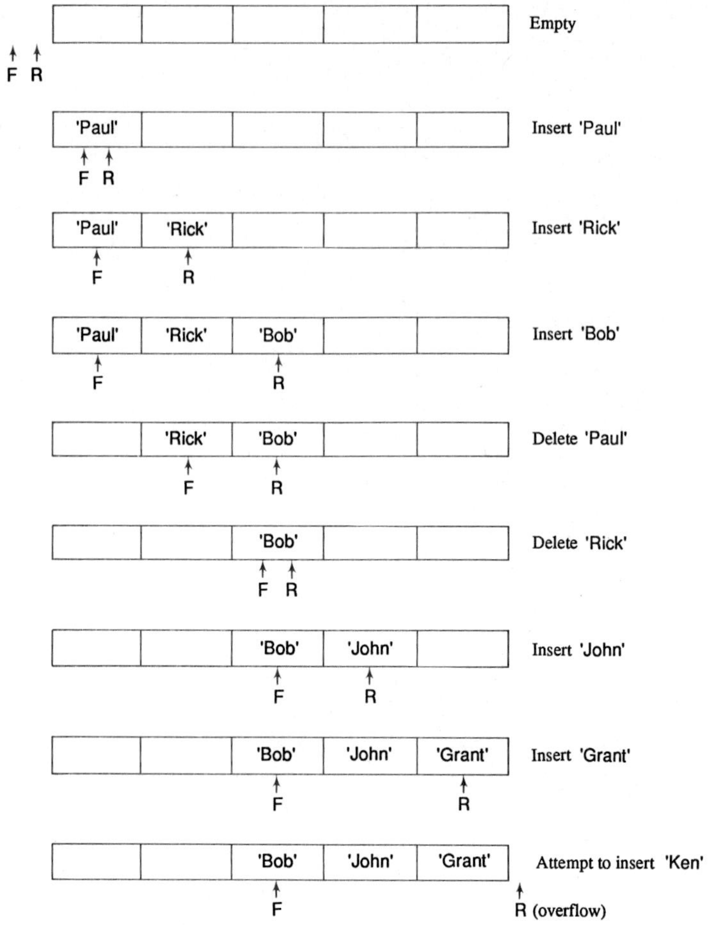

**FIGURE 8-37**
**Trace of operations**
**on a simple queue.**

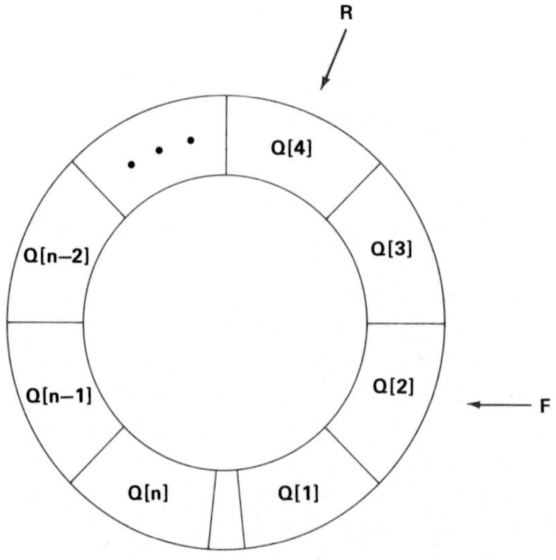

**FIGURE 8-38**
**Vector representation**
**of a circular queue.**

```
procedure QueueInsert (
    var Q: QueueType;       {Input/output, queue}
    X: QueueElementType     {Input, value to be inserted}
                        );
{Given a circular, sequentially allocated queue and a value, this procedure
    inserts the value at the rear of the queue.}
var NewR: integer;      {Temporary, for new rear pointer}
begin
    with Q do
        begin

            {Compute new rear pointer}
            if R = MaxQueueSize
            then NewR : = 1
            else NewR : = R + 1;

            {If overflow condition then signal error}
            if NewR = F
            then QueueOverflow
            else begin

                {Otherwise, insert new element}
                R : = NewR;
                Queue[R] : = X;

                {Set front pointer if queue now contains one element}
                if F = 0
                then F : = R
            end
        end
end;
```

FIGURE 8-39
Procedure to insert
at rear of a circular
sequentially allocated
queue.

6. Given the circular queue represented as in Fig. 8-38 with $F = 6$ and $R = 2$, give the values of $R$ and $F$ after *each* operation in the sequence: insert, delete, delete, insert, delete.

7. Write procedures for insertion and deletion operations on a priority queue. A priority queue operates much the same as a FIFO queue except that the position in which an element is placed depends on a key field. Elements are thus ordered by this key field. There may be many elements inserted into the queue which have the same key field. In this case, an element is placed behind the other elements with the same key field. For the insertion procedure, assume that you are given three parameters—a queue, a key field, and an information field. The queue is an input-output parameter, while the other two parameters are input parameters. The deletion procedure has an input-output parameter for the queue and output parameters for the key and information. Assume that the key is an integer.

**procedure** QueueDelete (
  **var** Q: QueueType;          {Input/output, queue}
  **var** X: QueueElementType     {Output, value removed from queue}
                    );
{Given a circular, sequentially allocated queue, this procedure deletes an
  element from the front to the queue. The value of the deleted element is
  returned via the output parameter.}
**begin**
  **with** Q **do**

      {If underflow, signal error}
      **if** R = 0
      **then** QueueUnderflow
      **else begin**

          {Otherwise, return value}
          X : = Queue[F];

          {Delete element by updating pointer}
          **if** F = R
          **then begin**      {Only element is deleted}
                  F : = 0;
                  R : = 0
              **end**
          **else**      {Increment F}
                  **if** F = MaxQueueSize
                  **then** F : = 1
                  **else** F : = F + 1
      **end**
  **end**;

FIGURE 8-40
Procedure to delete
from front of circular
sequentially allocated
queue.

## 8-7   SIMULATION

Simulation has traditionally been one of the most common applications of
computers and, therefore, one with which students of computer science
should be acquainted. Simulation involves the construction of models in the
form of computer programs—models that are used in the study of some system or phenomenon. Queues often form an integral part of computer simulation models, and that is the reason for the consideration of simulation at
this point in the book.

Any model is by nature an abstraction of reality. This abstraction serves
two purposes. First, the abstracting process itself increases our understanding
of the thing being abstracted, since it requires that we extract only the
most essential elements. Second, the model usually provides an experimental
vehicle more convenient than the real system, since it is easier for the

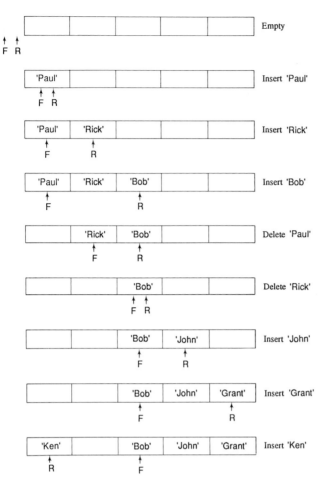

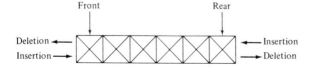

**FIGURE 8-41**
**Trace of operations**
**on a circular queue.**

experimenter to control. Both these purposes are well served by computer simulation models.

A distinguishing feature of computer simulation models is their ability to deal with the behavior of a system over a period of time. The control of time, and the way in which the system changes as time passes, is an important aspect of any simulation model. Simulation models are in fact classified according to the way this is done. A *time-driven*, or *fixed-interval*, model is one in which time is considered to pass in discrete clock ticks. At each time instant the entire system is examined and any state changes (or

**FIGURE 8-42**
**Representation**
**of a deque.**

events) that are scheduled to occur at that point in time are effected. An *event-driven*, or *next event*, model, on the other hand, maintains a schedule of events ordered by the time at which they are to occur. Time is advanced to the next scheduled event by a master scheduler. Typical driving algorithms for the two types of models are given in Fig. 8-43. A time-driven model is appropriate when events are densely scheduled in time, whereas an event-driven model is best when the schedule is sparse or when the time scale is highly variable. In that sense, the event-based approach offers greater generality. In this section we will develop an event-based simulation model.

A second essential aspect of computer simulation models is the ability to deal with stochastic elements. *Stochastic* elements (typically processes or characteristics) are those with which is associated some degree of uncertainty (or randomness). Such elements are usually described by appealing to some mathematical relationship, which is said to model the long-term characteristics of the element. For example, student grades in a course may be modeled by the normal ("bell curve") distribution, the arrival of customers to a bank is a process that may be modeled by a Poisson distribution, the flipping of a coin may be modeled by the binomial distribution, or the calling of bingo numbers may be modeled by the uniform distribution. *Deterministic* elements, on the other hand, are those with which no uncertainty is involved. The output of a deterministic process is always known precisely. The number of teller positions in a bank, the number of exams in a course, and the outcome of a toss of a "two-headed" coin would all be deterministic elements.

Stochastic elements are handled in computer simulation models through the use of a *pseudo-random number generator*. This is a specially designed subprogram (typically called something like Rand) that returns values which can be considered "random." The design of such subprograms is an inter-

```
Time : = StartTime
while Time < StopTime do
   begin
      Execute each event scheduled to occur at this time
      Time : = Time + FixedTimeIncrement
   end
```

(*a*) Time-driven model

```
while there are still scheduled events in the event queue do
   begin
      Remove the next event from queue
      Time : = time the event is scheduled to occur
      Execute this event
   end
```

**FIGURE 8-43**
**Time control in**
**simulation models.**

(*b*) Event-driven model

esting problem because the computer itself is, by design, a deterministic machine. (Imagine the ramifications to your programs were this not the case.) The values generated can be considered to be random in the sense that a long sequence of them exhibits statistical properties similar to those that a true random number sequence would display (i.e., the individual numbers appear with the same frequency). Special tricks are employed to achieve this which may involve exploiting overflow characteristics of the machine, reading values of the internal clock, etc. in some controlled way. We will not go into the details here. Instead, we will assume the existence of a function Rand which, upon repeated calls, yields a sequence of pseudo-random numbers uniformly distributed between 0.0 and 1.0 (that is, any value in that interval is equally likely). Simple transformations can be used to achieve any type of stochastic value required.

As mentioned, queues are important in simulation models. They serve several roles: as repositories for scheduled (but unexecuted) events, as holding areas for entities moving through the system, or even as service points within the system. The ability to handle queues of all types, conveniently and effectively, is important to any simulation system.

We will require both first-in, first-out (FIFO) queues and priority queues ordered on some criterion (e.g., the time at which an event is to take place). We will not concern ourselves with the actual structure or implementation of the queues, but will assume the existence of procedure QueueInsert to insert an item at the end of a FIFO queue, procedure PriQInsert to insert an item into its correct place in a priority queue, and functions QueueDelete and PriQDelete to remove the item at the head (front) of a queue of each type. The function QueueSize returns the number of elements in a queue. The function PriQEmpty returns "true" if the queue is empty and "false" otherwise.

We are now ready to consider the situation to be modeled. The mechanic at the Sunshine Cab Company, a Mr. Latka Gravas, is a bit of a problem. While he works very carefully, his work is quite slow and backlogs of vehicles needing repair pile up. The dispatcher, a Mr. Louie DePalma, becomes quite agitated when this occurs because of the ensuing loss in fares, and he has been known to say a word or two in anger to Mr. Gravas as a result.

It turns out that one of the cab drivers, a Mr. Jim Ignatowski, has had mechanic's training in the deep distant past—a fact that has only just recently come to light (even to Mr. Ignatowski). Even though his performance is quite erratic, Mr. DePalma is considering using him as a backup mechanic in times of unacceptable backlog. The potential problems with this scheme are twofold: the loss of fares during the time Mr. Ignatowski is unavailable as a driver and the high percentage of "returns" due to Mr. Ignatowski's work habits and inexperience as a mechanic. A good computer simulation will help Mr. DePalma in deciding whether or not to go ahead with this plan.

We turn first to a consideration of the elements of the system that will be incorporated into our model and the characteristics that will be associated with them. To keep things straightforward, we will be making some exceedingly simplified assumptions (for example, with respect to stochastic elements) for this presentation. We assume that the breakdown of cabs and their subsequent presentation for service are stochastic processes that can be modeled by a simple uniform distribution. The time between breakdowns is uniformly distributed in the interval 0.5 to 2.5 hours (notation: U(0.5, 2.5)). We assume that no time is taken to bring a vehicle to the garage from the point of breakdown; that is, it is available immediately for repair. Repair times and job quality vary with the two gentlemen involved. For Latka, the repair time is uniformly distributed in the interval 2 to 5 hours; 90 percent of his repairs are successful, but 10 percent return (the time of return is uniformly distributed in the interval 1 to 2 hours). For Jim, the repair time is a constant quarter hour (0.25 hours). Only 30 percent of his repairs are successful, however; 70 percent return (with the same distribution as Latka's returns). The plan is to call on Jim when the backlog of vehicles needing repair exceeds Threshold, where Threshold is a parameter of the simulation.

As a driver, Jim brings in an average of $15 per hour in fares. This, of course, is lost while he is working on repairs and must be charged to the cost of the plan. As with the vehicles, we assume that no time is taken to bring him back to the garage when needed.

The basic elements of our model are the events (that is, situations that cause the system state to change), the queues, and the stochastic processes. There are five main events:

*1.* The breakdown of a vehicle and its arrival for repair

*2.* The initiation of a repair by Latka

*3.* The initiation of a repair by Jim

*4.* The completion of a repair by Latka

*5.* The completion of a repair by Jim

Each of these alters the state of vehicles in the garage and results in the scheduling of new events in the future. Let us consider them in turn.

The "breakdown" event adds one vehicle to the pool of vehicles needing repair. A repair event may be scheduled immediately if either Latka or Jim is available (depending on the plan being simulated).

The "Latka repair" event removes one vehicle from the pool of vehicles needing repair. A repair time is determined (from the appropriate stochastic process), as is the "success factor." If the repair is unsuccessful, a new breakdown (which we will call a secondary breakdown) is scheduled (at a time that is determined from the appropriate stochastic process).

The "Jim repair" event also removes one vehicle from the pool of vehicles needing repair. The constant repair time (a deterministic process) is applied, and the "success factor" is computed. If the repair is unsuccessful, a secondary breakdown is scheduled.

The "repair completion" events return a vehicle to the usable set and free up either Latka or Jim for subsequent work.

Figure 8-44 depicts the sequencing of events in the simulation, starting from one of the "scheduled" breakdowns. The arrows indicate the scheduling of a subsequent event.

Two queues are required for this model. The first of these is the queue of scheduled events that will drive the model according to the event-driven paradigm. This is an ordered queue, in which events are queued in order of the time at which they are scheduled to take place. We will call this queue EventSchedule. The second queue is a FIFO queue for the vehicles needing repair. We will call this queue Clunkers.

There are three stochastic processes involved in this particular model, and these are summarized in Table 8-14. For the sake of simplicity, the uniform distribution has been assumed throughout. As mentioned, we are assuming the existence of a function Rand which yields a sequence of pseudo-random numbers uniformly distributed in the interval from 0 to 1 (notation: $U(0, 1)$). As shown in Table 8-14, a simple transformation converts numbers from $U(0, 1)$ to the more general $U(a, b)$. This is easily verified.

Our complete simulation model consists of a main "driver" program, subprograms representing the various events, and subprograms for "house-keeping" during the simulation. The main "driver" begins by scheduling all primary breakdowns (that is, breakdowns not a result of faulty repair) for 24 hours. The driver then turns to the queue of scheduled events. It works its way through the queue, invoking the appropriate routines, until all scheduled events have been processed. The simulation then terminates by printing various end-of-run statistics.

We begin by giving general algorithms for the important parts of the model. The main driver algorithm controls time and manages the queue of scheduled events. It takes the following form:

*1.* Schedule every "primary" breakdown at the appropriate point in time

*2.* Set Time to zero for the start of the simulation

*3.* Repeat until event queue is empty
Remove the next event from queue
Set Time to the time of its occurrence
Call the appropriate routine to effect this event

*4.* Print final statistics

**FIGURE 8-44   The sequencing of events in the Sunshine Cab Company simulation.**

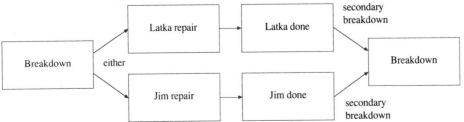

| TABLE 8-14 | Stochastic Process in the Sunshine Cab Repair Model | |
|---|---|---|
| **No.** | **Description** | **Distribution** |
| 1 | Time to next breakdown | U(0.5, 2.5) |
| 2 | Repair time for Latka | U(2, 5) |
| 3 | Re-repair return time | U(1, 2) |

*Note:* U(a, b) = a + (b − a) ∗ U (0, 1).

The "breakdown" event is effected by an algorithm with the following general form:

*1.* Increment the count of breakdowns and record the time of the breakdown

*2.* Insert the vehicle into a queue for repair

*3.* If Latka is not busy,
then schedule a Latka repair event
otherwise schedule a Jim repair event

The two algorithms for the "repair" events (Latka repair and Jim repair) are very similar, so one general algorithm will suffice:

*1.* Set a flag to indicate that this person (Latka or Jim) is busy

*2.* Remove the first vehicle for repair from queue and update statistics on its wait time (time of breakdown is stored in the queue)

*3.* Determine the time required for this repair (a stochastic variable) and schedule the appropriate "done" event accordingly

*4.* On the basis of "success factor" (a function of the repairer), determine if and when a "secondary" breakdown is to take place (both "if" and "when" are stochastic) and schedule if required

Finally, the following general algorithm serves for the two "done" events:

*1.* Clear busy flag for this person

*2.* Check the queue of vehicles needing repair
If it is not empty,
then initiate a new repair immediately

**EventType** is an enumerated type which gives the names of the events in the model:

EventType = (EvBreakdown, EvLatkaRepair, EvLatkaDone, EvJimRepair, EvJimDone)

**EventSchedule** represents the queue into which scheduled events will be inserted. The queue is a priority queue, ordered by the attribute EventTime (the time of occurrence). The queue is implemented as an array of records of type EventRecType defined by

**type**
 EventRecType =
  **record**
   EventTime: Real;
   EventName: EventType
  **end**

(EventSchedule is an array of MaxPriQSize elements of type EventRecType). Variables global to the whole program appear, with comments, in the declaration section of the program (Fig. 8-45).

 The detailed program and subprograms are well-commented and should be reasonably straightforward. Several routines, however, warrant special comment. To facilitate the scheduling of events, we assume the existence of a priority queue insert procedure PriQInsert to place an entry into the time-ordered queue of events (EventSchedule), a priority queue procedure PriQDelete to remove the next event, and an initialization procedure PriQInitialize. The design of such procedures is left to the exercises. The queue entry contains the name of the event and the time it is to occur. To accommodate the repair times of Latka and Jim, each repair "session" is effected by two events, EvLatkaRepair and EvLatkaDone (or EvJimRepair and EvJimDone), which control the start and end of the session, respectively. Breakdowns may, of course, occur during these repair sessions, but they cannot be handled until Latka or Jim is available. Status variables LatkaBusy and JimBusy are used to defer a repair until then. Note also that Jim is not scheduled for repair activities unless the size of the Clunkers queue exceeds the simulation parameter Threshold (which must, of course, be specified for each run).

 We hope that this model can assist Mr. DePalma in his difficult decision. The main program is given in Fig. 8-45. The subprograms shown are BD (Fig. 8-46), LR (Fig. 8-47), LD (Fig. 8-48), JR (Fig. 8-49), and JD (Fig. 8-50).

## EXERCISES 8-7

★ **1.** An important part of the Sunshine Cab Company simulation model is the ability to handle priority, or ordered, queues. As mentioned earlier, such queues are different from the familiar FIFO queue described in Sec. 8-6 in that elements are ordered in the queue according to the value of some criterion or key. Examples of such queues might be a queue of people ordered by height or a queue of shoppers ordered by number of items purchased. Removal of items from a priority queue takes place in the normal way, but insertion requires special treatment.

**program** Driver (input,output);

{This is the main driver of the simulation model. It has two basic functions to perform: it must initialize the simulation (variables, event queue) and it must drive the model by invoking scheduled events. When all scheduled events have been processed, final output is printed and the simulation terminates. Time is controlled by this routine and is represented in the variable Time. The procedure QueueInitialize (from Sec. 8-6) is employed to initialize the FIFO queue Clunkers, into which cars needing repair will be placed; a corresponding procedure, PriQInitialize, is assumed to initialize the priority queue EventSchedule. Insertions into this queue are accomplished by means of the procedure PriQInsert.}

**const**
    MaxQueueSize = 100;
    MaxPriQSize = 100;

**type**
    EventType = (EvBreakdown, EvLatkaRepair, EvLatkaDone, EvJimRepair,
                  EvJimDone);
    QueueElementType = real;
    EventRecType =
      **record**
        EventTime: real;
        EventName: EventType;
      **end**;
    QueueType =
      **record**
        Queue: **array** [1 .. MaxQueueSize] **of** QueueElementType;
        F, R: integer
      **end**;
    PriQType =
      **record**
        PriQ: **array** [1 .. MaxPriQSize] **of** EventRecType;
        F, R: integer
      **end**;

**var**
    Time: real;             {Time in hours (starting at 0 when simulation
                             begins)}
    Breakdowns: integer;   {Current number of breakdowns}
    Repairs: integer;      {Current number of repairs}
    TotalWaitTime: real;   {Time cabs spend waiting for repair}
    Event: EventType;     {Name of an event}
    LatkaBusy: Boolean;   {True if Latka is busy}
    Threshold: integer;    {Number of cabs awaiting repair when Jim is
                             to be activated}
    JimBusy: Boolean;    {True if Jim is busy}
    JimsTime: real;      {Time spent by Jim repairing cabs}
    Clunkers: QueueType;   {Queue containing the cabs to be repaired}
    EventSchedule: PriQType;  {Simulation event queue}

**FIGURE 8-45**
**Program Driver.**   {Add necessary procedures and functions here}

```
begin
  {Step 1: Initialize model components}
  TotalWaitTime : = 0;
  Breakdowns : = 0;
  Repairs : = 0;
  JimsTime : = 0.0;
  Time : = 0.0;
  QueueInitialize (Clunkers);
  PriQInitialize (EventSchedule);
  LatkaBusy : = false;
  JimBusy : = false;

  {Step 2: Read in the simulation parameter}
  read (Threshold);

  {Step 3: Schedule primary breakdowns}
  Time : = 0;
  while Time <= 24 do
    begin
      Time : = Time + (0.5 + 2.0*Rand); {a U(0.5,2.5) stochastic process}
      PriQInsert (EventSchedule, Time, EvBreakdown)
    end;

  {Step 4: Invoke scheduled events}
  Time : = 0.0;
  while not PriQEmpty (EventSchedule) do
    begin
      PriQDelete (EventSchedule, Time, Event);
      case Event of
        EvBreakdown: BD (Time, Breakdowns, Clunkers, LatkaBusy, JimBusy,
          Threshold, EventSchedule);
        EvLatkaRepair: LR (Time, LatkaBusy, Clunkers, TotalWaitTime,
          Repairs, EventSchedule);
        EvLatkaDone: LD (LatkaBusy, Clunkers, Time, TotalWaitTime,
          Repairs, EventSchedule);
        EvJimRepair: JR (Time, JimBusy, Clunkers, TotalWaitTime,
          Repairs, JimsTime, EventSchedule);
        EvJimDone: JD (JimBusy, Clunkers, Time, TotalWaitTime,
          Repairs, JimsTime, EventSchedule)
      end
    end;

  {Step 5: Print required statistics}
  writeln ('Sunshine Cab Company Simulation ');
  writeln ('Output for Threshold Value ', Threshold);
  writeln ('Total Breakdowns ', Breakdowns); writeln ('Total Repairs ', Repairs);
  writeln ('Average Wait Time for Repair ', TotalWaitTime/Repairs : 10 : 2);
  writeln ('Jim"s Time ', JimsTime : 10 : 2);
  writeln ('Loss in Jim"s Billing ', JimsTime*15.0 : 10 : 2)
end.
```

FIGURE 8-45  *(cont.)*

**procedure** BD (
    Time: real;                         {Input, time in hours}
    **var** Breakdowns: integer;      {Input/output, current number of break-
                                          downs}

    **var** Clunkers: QueueType;      {Input/output, queue of Cabs awaiting
                                            repair}

    LatkaBusy: Boolean;          {Input, true if Latka is busy}
    JimBusy: Boolean;            {Input, true if Jim is busy}
    Threshold: integer;           {Input, number of cabs awaiting to activate
                                          Jim}

    **var** EventSchedule: PriQType   {Input/output, simulation event queue}
        );
{Execution of this procedure causes the "breakdown" event to occur. It is called from the Driver program according to the schedule maintained in the queue EventSchedule.}

**begin**
    {Step 1 : Increment the number of breakdowns}
    Breakdowns : = Breakdowns + 1;

    {Step 2 : Insert the vehicle in the queue for repair}
    QueueInsert (Clunkers, Time);

    {Step 3 : Insert repair event into event queue}
      **if not** LatkaBusy
        **then** {start Latka if he isn't busy}
            PriQInsert (EventSchedule, Time, EvLatkaRepair)
        **else if** (QueueSize (Clunkers) >= Threshold) and **not** JimBusy
            **then** PriQInsert (EventSchedule, Time, EvJimRepair)
**end**;

FIGURE 8-46
Procedure **BD**.

Write a procedure PriQInsert to perform an insertion into a priority queue. The Key and Info fields can be assumed to be of the types dictated by the application. Assume that PriQInitialize initializes a priority queue in the same way that QueueInitialize initializes a FIFO queue.

★ 2. Implement subprograms PriQInitialize, PriQDelete, and the necessary type declarations for a sequentially allocated priority queue. Write a program to test the operation of a priority queue using these procedures and PriQInsert of Exercise 1.

★ 3. Implement the simulation of the Sunshine Cab Company using the procedures of this section and the results of Exercises 1 and 2. Obtain data for Threshold values of 2, 4, and 6. You must also write a subprogram for PriQEmpty.

4. What changes would have to be made to the subprograms for the Sunshine Cab repair simulation to change to a time-driven approach? Outline the advantages of each approach.

**procedure** LR (
    Time: real;                  {Input, event time}
    **var** LatkaBusy: Boolean;    {Input/output, true if Latka busy}
    **var** Clunkers: QueueType;    {Input/output, queue of cabs awaiting
                                    repair}
    **var** TotalWaitTime: real;    {Input/output, time cabs spend waiting for
                                    repair}
    **var** Repairs: integer;    {Input/output, current number of repairs}
    **var** EventSchedule: PriQType    {Input/output, simulation event queue}
               );
{Execution of this procedure causes the "Latka repair" event to occur. It is called from the **Driver** program according to the schedule maintained in the queue EventSchedule.}

**var**
    TimeOn: real;    {Time when cab broke down}
    WaitTime: real;    {Time cab waited from breakdown until
                    repair started}
    RepairTime: real;    {Time required to repair the cab}
    SuccessFactor: real;    {Used to determine whether a secondary
                    breakdown will occur}

**begin**
    {Step 1: Update variables}
    LatkaBusy : = true;
    QueueDelete (Clunkers, TimeOn);
    WaitTime : = Time − TimeOn;
    TotalWaitTime : = TotalWaitTime + WaitTime;
    Repairs : = Repairs + 1;

    {Step 2: Calculate repair time}
    RepairTime : = 2.0 + 3.0*Rand; {a U (2,5) stochastic process}

    {Step 3: Insert "Latka done" event into event queue}
    PriQInsert (EventSchedule, Time + RepairTime, EvLatkaDone);

    {Step 4: Calculate if and when secondary breakdown will occur and
        insert into queue}
    SuccessFactor : = Rand;
    **if** SuccessFactor >= 0.90
    **then begin**
        TimeOn : = 1.0 + 1.0*Rand; {a U (1,2) stochastic process}
        {Schedule secondary breakdown}
        PriQInsert (EventSchedule, Time + RepairTime + TimeOn, EvBreakdown)
    **end**
**end**;

**FIGURE 8-47**
**Procedure LR.**

**procedure** LD (

    **var** LatkaBusy: Boolean;    {Input/output, true if Latka busy}

    **var** Clunkers: QueueType;    {Input/output, queue of cabs awaiting repair}

    Time: real;    {Input, time in hours}

    **var** TotalWaitTime: real;    {Input/output, time cabs spend awaiting repair}

    **var** Repairs: integer;    {Input/output, current number of breakdowns}

    **var** EventSchedule:PriQType    {Input/output, simulation event queue}
    );

{Execution of this procedure causes the "Latka done" event to occur. It is called from the Driver program according to the schedule maintained in the queue EventSchedule.}

**begin**

    {Step 1: Update "Latka busy" status}

    LatkaBusy : = false;

    {Step 2: Initiate a repair if the cab queue is not empty}

    **if not** QueueEmpty (Clunkers)

    **then** LR (Time, LatkaBusy, Clunkers, TotalWaitTime, Repairs, EventSchedule)

**end**;

**FIGURE 8-48**
**Procedure LD.**

★ **5.** The company is interested in the time that cabs are off the road. Modify the program to produce a table showing the amount of time one car is in for repair, two cars, three cars, etc.

**6.** The sensitivity of a simulation model to its assumptions is an important consideration. In this model it is assumed that no time is taken to bring a broken-down cab to the garage. Suppose that this were to take a constant 10 minutes. How would this change the model? How would it change the results?

★★ **7.** A grocery store firm is considering the addition of a new service counter in one of its stores. Currently, the store has three checkouts, but customer volume has increased to the point where a new counter is warranted. To determine if the new counter should be a regular counter or an express counter (that is, eight items or less), a simulation of customer flow through the checkout area is required.

    Our initial simulation is of a checkout area consisting of one express counter and three regular checkouts. All customers with eight or fewer items are assumed to proceed to an express counter. Customers with more than eight items go to the standard checkout with the shortest waiting line.

    Customers enter the checkout area randomly, with the time of next arrival determined by adding to the present time a random number chosen

```
procedure JR (
   Time: real;                          {Input, time of event}
   var JimBusy: Boolean;                {Input/output, true if Jim busy}
   var Clunkers: QueueType;             {Input/output, cabs awaiting repair}
   var TotalWaitTime: real;             {Input/output, time cabs spend
                                           awaiting repair}
   var Repairs: integer;                {Input/output, current number of repairs}
   var JimsTime: real;                  {Input/output, time spent by Jim repairing
                                           cabs}
   var EventSchedule: PriQType          {Input/output, simulation event queue}
              );
   {Execution of this procedure causes the "Jim repair" event to occur. It is
    called from the Driver program according to the schedule maintained in
    the queue EventSchedule.}
var
   TimeOn: real;            {Time when cab broke down}
   WaitTime: real;          {Time cab waited from breakdown until
                               repair started}
   RepairTime: real;        {Time required to repair the cab}
   SuccessFactor: real;
begin
   {Step 1: Update variables}
   JimBusy : = true;
   QueueDelete (Clunkers, TimeOn);
   WaitTime : = Time − TimeOn;
   TotalWaitTime : = TotalWaitTime + WaitTime;
   Repairs : = Repairs + 1;

   {Step 2: Set repair time to constant}
   RepairTime : = 0.25;

   {Step 3: Insert "Jim done" event into event queue}
   PriQInsert (EventSchedule, Time + RepairTime, EvJimDone);

   {Step 4: Update amount of time Jim has spent doing repairs}
   JimsTime : = JimsTime + RepairTime;

   {Step 5: Calculate if and when secondary breakdown will occur and insert
      into queue}
   SuccessFactor : = Rand;
   if SuccessFactor >= 0.30
   then begin
           TimeOn : = 1.0 + 1.0*Rand;
           {Schedule secondary breakdown}
           PriQInsert (EventSchedule, Time + RepairTime + TimeOn, EvBreakdown)
       end
end;
```

**FIGURE 8-49**
Procedure **JR**.

```
procedure JD (
    var JimBusy: Boolean;              {Input/output, true if Jim busy}
    var Clunkers: QueueType;           {Input/output, cabs awaiting repair}
    Time: real;                        {Input, time of event}
    var TotalWaitTime: real;           {Input/output, time cabs spend awaiting
                                          repair}

    var Repairs: integer;              {Input/output, current number of repairs}
    var JimsTime: real;                {Input/output, time spent by Jim repairing
                                          cabs}
    var EventSchedule: PriQType        {Input/output, simulation event queue}
                );
{Execution of this procedure causes the "Jim done" event to occur. It is
 called from the Driver program according to the schedule maintained in
 the queue EventSchedule.}
begin
    {Step 1: Update "Jim busy" status}
    JimBusy : = false;


    {Step 2: Initiate a repair if cab queue is not empty}
    if not QueueEmpty (Clunkers)

    then JR (Time, JimBusy, Clunkers, TotalWaitTime, Repairs, JimsTime,
                EventSchedule)
    end;
```

**FIGURE 8-50**
**Procedure JD.**

from the range [0, 360] seconds. (0 is interpreted as a simultaneous
arrival of two customers.) The number of items bought by each customer
also can be approximated by selecting a random number in the range 1
to 40. The time taken for a customer to proceed through a checkout once
the cashier begins "ringing up" the groceries can be calculated by using
an average rate of 5 seconds per item (ringing plus wrapping time).

In setting up the simulation, we should realize that prior to bringing
a new customer into the checkout area, we must ensure that all customers
who have had their groceries processed are removed from the waiting
line. Assume that no more than 10 customers are waiting in line at any
one time for a regular checkout and no more than 15 are waiting in line
at any one time for an express checkout.

You are to design and implement a program that simulates the checkout service just described. The desired output should contain the number
of customers going through each checkout per hour, the total number
of customers handled per hour, the average time at each checkout, the
overall average waiting time in minutes, the number of items processed
at each checkout per hour, and the total number of items processed per
hour. The waiting time is the time a customer spends in the checkout
area.

Output having the following format is desirable:

| | 1 | 2 | 3 | Express | Total |
|---|---|---|---|---|---|
| Number of customers per hour | 10 | 11 | 14 | 20 | 55 |
| Average waiting time | 2.80 | 3.01 | 2.96 | 0.22 | 1.94 |
| Items processed per hour | 192 | 261 | 210 | 65 | 728 |

Simulate as well the situation in which there are four standard checkouts, using the same method of generating arrival times and number of items purchased. Your program should be designed so that the second simulation can be implemented with very few changes to the first program.

## 8-8 LINKED STORAGE ALLOCATION

Thus far in this chapter we have allocated storage for linear lists in a sequential manner. We have relied on the one-dimensional property of a computer's main memory to represent the physical adjacency relationship of the elements in a linear list. Although this method of allocating storage is adequate for many applications, there are many other applications where the sequential-allocation method is inefficient and, therefore, unacceptable. The characteristics that are often found in the latter class of applications are

*1.* Storage requirements are unpredictable. The precise amount of data storage in these applications is data-dependent; therefore, the storage requirements cannot be easily determined before the associated program is executed.
*2.* The stored data must be manipulated extensively. These applications are characterized by frequent insertion and deletion activity on the data.

In such application areas, the linked-allocation method of storage can lead to both efficient use of computer storage and computer time. Therefore, the remainder of this chapter examines the concepts of linked allocation and applies them to linear lists. In this section we introduce the basics of linked allocation.

### 8-8.1 BASIC CONCEPTS

The previous sections have dealt with how the address of an element in a linear list can be obtained through direct computation. Since the data structures were linear and this property was preserved in the corresponding storage structures by using sequential allocation, it was unnecessary for an element to specify the location of the next element in the structure.

An alternative storage-allocation approach is to use *pointers* or *links* (see Sec. 8-2) to refer to elements of a linear list. The approach is to store the address of the successor of a particular element in that element. Using this approach, the elements of the linear list need not be physically adjacent in memory. This method of allocating storage is called *linked allocation*. Let us examine how to represent a linear list by this method of allocation.

An obvious way to represent a linear list by linked allocation is to expand the element (or node structure) so as to incorporate an extra field. The field is a pointer or a link that denotes the position of the next element in the list. Such a representation is called a *singly linked linear list* or a *one-way chain*. Figure 8-51a gives a box-and-arrow representation of a linked linear list, where the pointer variable First contains the address or location of the first node in the list. Observe that each element (or node) has two parts. The first part contains the information contents of the element, and the second part contains the address of the next node in the list. Note that since the last node in the list does not have a successor, its pointer field does not contain an actual address. A special pointer value called **nil** (denoted by a diagonal line in the diagram) is assigned to the pointer field in this case. Note that **nil** is not an actual address but a special value that cannot be mistaken for a real address. The arrow emanating from the link field of a particular node terminates at its successor node. For example, Fig. 8-51b represents a four-node linear list whose elements are stored at memory locations 1000, 1500, 1400, and 1200, respectively. Note that the elements are not stored sequentially within memory. If a list contains no elements (that is, it is empty), this fact is denoted by assigning the **nil** value to First.

Let us now compare sequentially allocated and linked allocated linear lists with respect to several commonly performed operations. In particular,

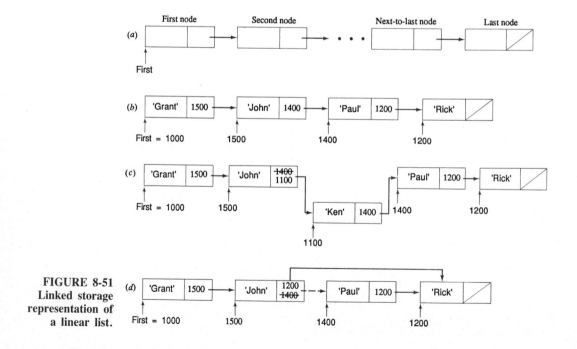

**FIGURE 8-51**
**Linked storage representation of a linear list.**

consider the operations of insertion and deletion in a sequentially allocated list. Assume that we have an $n$-element list and that it is required to insert a new element between the second and third elements. In this case, the last $n - 2$ elements of the list must be physically moved to make room for the new element. For large-sized lists which are subjected to many insertions, this insertion approach can be very costly. The same conclusion holds in the case of deletion, since all elements after the deleted element must be moved up so as to use the vacated space caused by the deletion.

An insert operation into a linked list is easy. An insertion simply involves the interchange of pointers to accommodate the new element. For example, Fig. 8-51$c$ illustrates the insertion of the new element 'Ken' between the second and third elements of a list of four elements. The new element is assumed to be stored at position 1100. The link field of the second element is changed from 1400 to 1100. Also the link field of the new node is assigned a value of 1400. Similarly, a delete operation involves changing a single pointer. Figure 8-51$d$ illustrates the deletion of the third element, 'Paul', from the original list. The link value of the second node (1400) is changed to the address of the fourth node (1200). Clearly, both insert and delete operations are more efficiently performed on linked lists than on their sequentially allocated counterparts.

These two allocation methods (linked and sequential) can be compared with respect to other operations as well. For a search operation in a linked list, we must follow the links from the first node onward until the desired node is found. This operation is certainly inferior to the computed-address method of locating an element in a sequentially allocated list. If we want to split or join two linked linear lists, then these operations involve the changing of pointer fields without having to move any nodes. Such is not the case for sequentially allocated lists.

Clearly, pointers or links consume additional memory. The cost of this additional memory becomes less important as the information contents of a node require more memory. If the memory requirements for the information contents of each node are small, it may be possible to store the information portion in one part of a memory word and store a pointer in the remaining part. At any rate, a pointer takes at least one-half word of memory on most computers. The extra cost of storing pointers is not too expensive in many applications.

In the previous discussion the actual address of a node was used in the link field for illustration purposes. In practice, however, this address may be of no concern (and indeed unknown) to the programmer. Therefore, in the remainder of our discussion of linked structures, the arrow symbol is used exclusively to denote a successor node.

In this chapter we are interested in the use of pointers only to specify the relationship of logical adjacency among elements of a linear list. This is an important point to emphasize—the notion of logical adjacency versus physical adjacency. In vector (or sequential) storage, they are the same. In linked storage, they are not. Therefore, we have more flexibility with linked storage. However, pointers can be used to specify more complex relationships, such as those found in tree and graph structures (see Chap. 9). These relationships are sometimes very difficult to specify using sequential-allocation techniques. Such complex structures are easily represented using linked allocation by placing several pointers in each node. In such instances, it is possible for a node to belong to several different structures. Chapter 9 will examine the linked representation of tree structures in detail.

From our current discussion and some of the applications to follow, it will be evident that in certain instances linked allocation is more efficient than sequential allocation. In other applications, however, the opposite is true. Yet, in other cases, both allocation methods are used.

An important consideration in both methods of allocation is the management of available storage required to perform certain operations, such as insertion and deletion. For linked allocation, a pool or list of *free* nodes called the *heap* or *availability list* must be maintained. On an insert operation, a free node is removed from the availability list and placed in the designated linear list. Conversely, a deleted node is returned to the availability list, where it can be reused for subsequent insertions. This storage-management scheme is an obvious advantage—at any particular time, the only space which is actually used is the space that is presently really required.

Storage of singly linked lists can be managed in a very straightforward manner. For more complex structures, however, this simplicity vanishes. In some of these structures a node can belong to many different structures simultaneously. Thus the deletion of a node from one structure does not imply that it can be returned to the availability list. Such complex structures are beyond the scope of this book.

The basic concepts of applying linked-storage allocation to represent linear lists have been introduced in this subsection. In the next subsection we examine the formulation of several subprograms, such as insertion, deletion, traversal, and copying, for singly linked linear lists. The following subsection describes a circularly linked representation of a linear list. Such a representation offers certain computational advantages over singly linked linear lists.

Since the traversal of a singly linked list is necessarily performed in one direction only, the deletion of an element from such a structure is inefficient. Also, several applications require the traversal of a linear list in both forward and reverse directions. For these reasons we introduce the doubly linked representation of a linear list and its associated operations in the final subsection.

## 8-8.2 SINGLY LINKED LINEAR LISTS

This subsection examines in detail the singly linked storage representation of a linear list. Several subprograms based on this representation are included. Requests and releases of nodes from and to the availability list of storage are also described.

Before proceeding to formulate programs for operations associated with linked linear lists, it is instructive to classify these operations. If the processing of data in a particular application is to be performed by a computer, we must first adequately represent the data in the computer's memory. The difficulty of this task depends to a large extent on the particular programming languages available. Pascal provides built-in management of the heap (availability list) and pointer type data. We shall describe these in this subsection.

There are three classes of operations associated with linked lists. The first class contains operations that are independent of the data values in the list nodes. Operations in this class include creation, insertion, and deletion. They are easily programmed in Pascal.

A second class of related operations concerns the conversion of raw data from a human-readable form to a corresponding machine-readable form. This class of operations also contains the inverse operation of converting a computer-stored structure into a suitable human-readable form. These are clearly data-dependent operations which depend on the interpretations associated with the structures. While some of these operations can be designed to cover a range of applications, additional operations must be programmed for each application.

The third and final class of operations relates to the data-manipulation requirements which are application-dependent. Usually these operations must be programmed. However, programmers who have at their disposal all three classes of routines will find the task of programming an application much easier.

Throughout this subsection we assume that an element or node of a list contains two fields: an information field (Info) and a pointer field (Link). NodeType represents the name of a record structure type containing these fields. The following box-and-arrow notation illustrates this node structure:

In Pascal, a pointer variable must be declared to be of a *pointer type*. A pointer type is defined by a *pointer type denoter* consisting of an up arrow ($\uparrow$) followed by the type denoter of some other type. In compilers using character sets without an up arrow, some other character is recognized for this purpose. Most often the caret ($\wedge$) is used. Some compilers also use the commercial "at" sign $@$. For the previous example, assuming an information field of integer type, we would use the definitions

**type**
    NodePointer = $\uparrow$ NodeType;
    NodeType =

```
record
    Info: integer;
    Link: NodePointer
end;
```

Now a pointer variable P, which may contain the address of a node, is declared as

```
var
    P: NodePointer;
```

Figure 8-52 presents the syntax diagram for a pointer type denoter.

Standard Pascal places two important restrictions on the addresses stored in pointer variables. First, the address, unless it is **nil**, must point to a value of the declared *domain type*, that is, the type following ↑ in the type denoter. This allows more complete type checking than is possible in languages without this restriction. Pascal allows any type as the domain type of a pointer type. In most applications, however, it will be a record type. The second restriction requires that the address assigned to a pointer variable be the address of a variable allocated from the heap (availability list) rather than the address of a local variable. Some Pascal compilers relax one or both of these restrictions as an extension to the language.

We require a notation to reference the value pointed to by a pointer variable. Pascal defines a pointer variable followed by ↑ as referencing the value pointed to by a pointer variable. Thus, given the previous variable declarations, P represents the address of a node on the heap and P ↑ represents the node itself, which is of type "record structure." Both of these can be used as variables, but they are of different types. However, it is an error to refer to P ↑ if P has the value **nil**.

We now consider referencing a field of the node (record structure). As with any record structure, we use a period followed by the field name. Thus P ↑ .Info refers to the Info field of the node pointed to by P. Similarly P ↑ .Link refers to the Link field of the node pointed to by P. These two variables (P ↑ .Info and P ↑ .Link) are of types integer and NodePointer, respectively.

We may view the ↑ as another form of variable selector similar to the field selector (.) and subscripting ([ ]). It may be appended to any variable designating a pointer type and yields a variable of the domain type. The three forms of selector may be combined provided only that the type rules are observed. Figure 8-53 summarizes the general syntax of a variable in Pascal.

A request to allocate a variable on the heap is made by calling the built-in procedure new. It is called with a single argument which must be a variable of pointer type. A sufficient amount of storage is allocated to hold a variable of the domain type of the pointer argument, and the pointer

pointer type denoter

**FIGURE 8-52**
**Syntax diagram for**
**pointer type denoter.**

variable

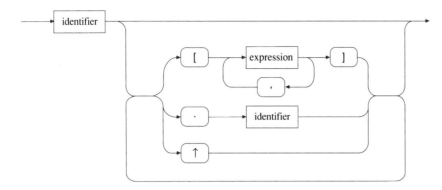

**FIGURE 8-53**
**Syntax diagram**
**for a variable.**

is assigned the address of this storage. To allocate a node for our current example, we write

new (P)

A discarded node is returned to the heap by the built-in procedure **dispose**. To dispose of the node allocated in the previous paragraph, we would write

dispose (P)

After taking this action, the node previously pointed to by **P** is assumed to be inaccessible. Any pointer reference such as **P↑** (and **Q↑** if **Q** was also pointing to the node which was returned to the heap) is considered an error until the pointer is assigned to some different node. Compilers often do not check for such errors, so the programmer should use care in designing programs that involve pointers.

Some nonstandard Pascal compilers do not provide the dispose procedure. Instead, they provide **mark** and **free** or some other facility. Readers are referred to the documentation for their particular compiler. We also will not consider a Pascal feature that allows variant record selectors as optional parameters to new and **dispose**.

We will continue our approach of providing the data structure operations in a modular fashion. Note that for singly linked linear lists the entire list is accessed through the pointer to the first node. This leads to the type definitions in Fig. 8-54, in which **ListType** is defined as a pointer to a node. The ordering of the two type definitions is crucial. The **ListType** definition must occur before the **NodeType** definition because the former is referenced

**type**
   ListType = ↑ NodeType;
   NodeType =
     **record**
       Info: InfoType;
       Link: ListType
     **end**;

**FIGURE 8-54**
**Type definitions for**
**a singly linked list.**

**procedure** LInitialize (
    **var** L: ListType    {Output, linked linear list to be initialized}
                              );
{Given a linked linear list, this procedure initializes it (to be empty) for use
  by the other list operations.}
**begin**
{Set pointer to first node to **nil**}
  L : = **nil**
**end**;

**FIGURE 8-55**
**Procedure to initialize**
**a linked linear list.**

by the latter. However, **NodeType** is also referenced by the **ListType** definition! Fortunately, Pascal accommodates such definitions by allowing the
type name following the ↑ in a type denoter to be defined later in the same
body (program or subprogram).

    Our first operation is the list initialization in Fig. 8-55. This is such a
simple operation that one is tempted to code it directly in the application
rather than using a procedure. The advantage of a procedure is that should
a decision be made later to change to a different implementation of the list
structure (see the next two subsections, for example), only the list operations
need be replaced. It would not be necessary to modify the code for the
application itself.

    Let us now consider the operation of inserting a node into a linked linear
list. Several steps are required in this operation. First, the values for the
fields of the new node are acquired through the input parameter. Second, we
must obtain a node from the heap. Finally, the values of the fields obtained
in the first step are copied into the appropriate field positions of the new
node, which is then placed in the designated linked list. The linking of a new
node to its successor node in the existing linked list is realized by setting
the pointer (**Link**) field of the former to a value that gives the address of the
latter. We present a procedure to insert an element at the front of a linked
linear list in Fig. 8-56.

    This function can be invoked repeatedly for the initial construction of
a linked linear list. Initially, the construction process begins with an empty
list. A new node is inserted by each invocation of procedure **LInsFirst**. We
can declare a list named **List** whose information field contains standard Pascal
strings of length 8 by the following sequence of definitions and declarations:

```
type
    InfoType = packed array [1 .. 8] of char;
    ListType = ↑ NodeType;
    NodeType =
        record
            Info: InfoType;
            Link: ListType
        end;
var
    List: ListType;
```

**procedure** LInsFirst (
    **var** L: ListType;   {Input/output, linked linear list}
    X: InfoType      {Input, information to be inserted}
               );
{Given a linked linear list and information to be inserted, this procedure
  creates a new node with this information and inserts it at the front of the
  list.}
**var**
  NewNode: ListType;   {Pointer to new node created}
**begin**
  {Obtain a new node}
  new (NewNode);

  {Store the information in the node}
  NewNode ↑ .Info : = X;

  {Insert the new node at the beginning of the list}
  NewNode ↑ .Link : = L;  {Set Link to point to previous first node,
                        or **nil** if list was empty.}
  L : = NewNode         {Set list head L to point to new node}
**end**;

**FIGURE 8-56**
**Procedure to insert**
**at the beginning of a**
**linked linear list.**

The following sequence of statements constructs a linked list of four nodes.

LInitialize (List);
LInsFirst (List, 'Rick☐☐☐☐');
LInsFirst (List, 'Paul☐☐☐☐');
LInsFirst (List, 'Grant☐☐☐');
LInsFirst (List, 'Bob☐☐☐☐☐')

The behavior of procedure LInsFirst is exhibited in Fig. 8-57. Note that insertions are performed in a stacklike manner.

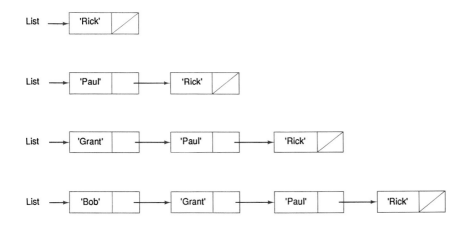

**FIGURE 8-57**
**Behavior of procedure**
**LInsFirst in the**
**construction of a**
**four-element linked**
**list.**

Rather than inserting a node at the front of an existing list, we also can insert a node at the end of a list. This operation is more difficult to formulate than procedure LInsFirst. We must deal with two situations in inserting a new node at the end of a list. The first case involves an insertion into an empty list. In such an instance, the new node merely becomes the front node of the list. In the second case, however, the existing list is not empty. To perform the desired insertion, the end node of the original list must first be found by chaining through the original list until a node with a Link field of **nil** is found. At this point, the link field of this node is assigned a value that points to the new node being inserted. The chaining operation and node insertion are accomplished by the following program segment:

```
Save : = L;
while Save ↑ .Link <>nil do
    Save : = Save ↑ .Link;    {Move to next node}
Save ↑ .Link : = NewNode
```

Observe that we exit the repeat loop when Link ↑ .Save is **nil**. We can incorporate this program segment into the procedure LInsLast in Fig. 8-58.

Note that in the case of an empty list, the address of the new node is returned via the input/output parameter, L, while in the second case the first node in the list remains the same as that before insertion, and consequently, the value of L is unchanged.

This procedure can be invoked repeatedly to construct a linked list of four nodes as follows (using the same definitions and declarations as in the previous example):

```
LInitialize (List);
LInsLast (List, 'Bob□□□□□' );
LInsLast (List, 'Grant□□□' );
LInsLast (List, 'Paul□□□□' );
LInsLast (List, 'Rick□□□□' )
```

The behavior of procedure LInsLast is portrayed in Fig. 8-59.

Observe that the performance of procedure LInsLast degenerates progressively as the number of nodes in a linear list becomes larger. In this situation the entire list must be traversed to perform the indicated insertion. We can avoid such a long search for the end element of a list by simply keeping the address of the last node that was inserted in the list. The next insertion can then be performed without traversing the entire list to find its last element. Rather, the empty link field of the previously inserted node need only be changed to the address of the new node being inserted. We can develop a revised list-processing package for this new representation. **ListType** is redefined to be a record structure containing the first and last pointers. The modified definitions appear in Fig. 8-60.

Of course, it will also be necessary to modify the implementation of **LInitialize** and **LInsFirst**. The modified procedures are left as exercises. The procedure to insert at the end of a list using this new representation is also left as an exercise.

**procedure** LInsLast (
  **var** L: ListType;    {Input/output, list}
  X: InfoType        {Input, information}
                );
{Given a pointer to the first element of a linked linear list and the information contents of a new node, this procedure creates a new node and inserts
  it at the end of the list.}
**var**
  NewNode: ListType;    {Pointer to new node created}
  Save: ListType;        {Pointer for locating end of list}
**begin**
  {Create new node}
  new (NewNode);

  {Initialize contents of new node}
  NewNode $\uparrow$ .Info : = X;
  NewNode $\uparrow$ .Link : = **nil**;

  {If the original list is empty, then "first" pointer points to new node.}
  **if** L = **nil**
  **then** L : = NewNode

  {Otherwise, find end of list}
  **else begin**
        Save : = L;
        **while** Save $\uparrow$ .Link $<>$ **nil do**
          Save : = Save $\uparrow$ .Link;

        {Make last node of list point to new node}
        Save $\uparrow$ .Link : = NewNode
    **end**
**end**;

**FIGURE 8-58**
**Procedure to insert at
end of a linked linear
list.**

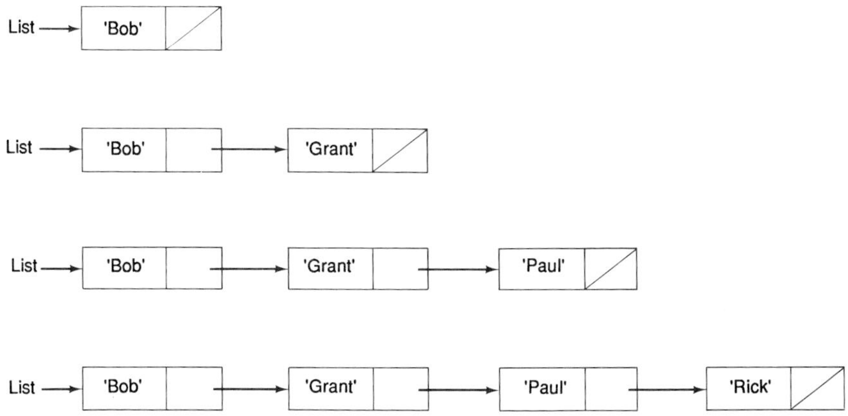

**FIGURE 8-59**
**Behavior of function
LInsLast in the
construction of a
four-element linked list.**

FIGURE 8-60
Modified type
definitions for a
linked linear list.

**type**
    ListPointerType = ↑ NodeType;
    ListType =
        **record**
            First, Last: ListPointerType
        **end;**
    NodeType =
        **record**
            Info: InfoType;
            Link: ListPointerType
        **end;**

One of the benefits of the modularization of the list-processing operations is the ease with which an application can be modified to utilize this new representation. All that is required is that the new type definitions in Fig. 8-60 be substituted for the original ones and the new operation definitions replace the originals. In the remainder of this subsection we use the original definition of a list (Fig. 8-54) and leave as an exercise the implementation for the modified structure.

Certain applications require that a linear list be maintained in order. Such an ordering is in increasing or decreasing order of data in the information field. As was the case with vectors, the maintaining of an ordered list frequently results in more efficient processing.

Let us consider first the details of an algorithm to insert into an ordered list. It is somewhat difficult to write a general procedure which is useful for all applications. In an attempt to cover a wide variety of applications, we assume that the Info field of the nodes is a record structure of one or more fields. One of these fields, named Key, is presumed to determine the ordering of the nodes. There are essentially three cases to handle for an ordered list. As before, the first case involves the insertion of an element into an empty list. Clearly, no search is required in this case. In the second case, the new element is to precede the first element in the existing list. In such a case, the new element becomes the new front element of the updated list, and the link field of the new node is assigned the address of the front node before the insertion. In the third and final case, a search is carried out to determine where the new node should be inserted. A program segment to perform this search and insertion consists of the following statements:

```
Save : = L;
NotFound : = true;
while (Save ↑ .Link <> nil) and NotFound do
    if Save ↑ .Link ↑ .Info.Key < X.Key
    then Save : = Save ↑ .Link
    else NotFound : = false;
NewNode ↑ .Link : = Save ↑ .Link;
Save ↑ .Link : = NewNode
```

where L contains the address of the front node of the list and NewNode is the address of the node being inserted. The insertion process for this third case is shown in Fig. 8-61. We assume that the node being inserted is not already in the linked list. We can now proceed to the formulation of a general algorithm:

*1.* Create the new node and set its information contents

*2.* If the linked list is empty,
   then return the address of the new node via the input/output parameter.

*3.* If the node precedes all others in the list,
   then insert the node at the front of the list and return its address

*4.* Repeat step 5 while the key of the information content of the current node in the list is less than the key of the information content of the new node

*5.* Obtain the next node in the linked list

*6.* Insert the new node in the list and return.

We present the procedure in Fig. 8-62. The procedure's steps correspond to those of the general algorithm. In step 4, Save is first initialized to point to the front element of the list. Then, in step 5, this temporary variable points to successive nodes until the value of Save ↑ .Link ↑ .Info.Key (that is, the key of the information contents of the successor to node Save) is greater than the information value of the new node or an attempt is made to "walk off" the end of the list (that is, Save ↑ .Link = **nil**). In either case, the link fields of the new node and its predecessor are set to their appropriate values.

We have examined in detail the insert operation. An equally important operation involves the deletion of a specified node from a given linked list (ordered or unordered). There are several ways of specifying which node should be deleted. For example, a node to be deleted can be specified by giving a value of some field in its information content. Another approach is to specify a pointer to the node to be deleted. We formulate a general deletion algorithm based on the latter approach:

**FIGURE 8-61   Insertion in an ordered linked list.**

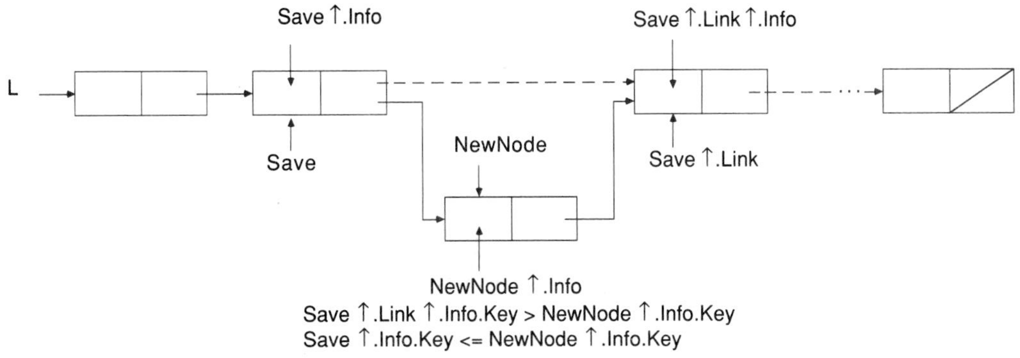

Save ↑ .Link ↑ .Info.Key > NewNode ↑ .Info.Key
Save ↑ .Info.Key <= NewNode ↑ .Info.Key

```
procedure LInsOrder (
    var L: ListType;                    {Input/output, list}
    X: InfoType                         {Input, information}
                    );
```
{Given a linked linear list, represented by a pointer to its first node, and information to be inserted, this procedure inserts a node with the information into the list. The information is assumed to be a record structure with one of its fields named Key. The list is maintained in ascending order on this field.}

```
var
    NewNode: ListType;      {Pointer to new node}
    Save: ListType;         {Search pointer}
    NotFound: Boolean;      {Loop termination flag}
begin
    {Step 1: Create a new node and store the information}
    new (NewNode);
    NewNode ↑ .Info : = X;

    {Step 2: If the list was empty, set pointer to point to new node}
    if L = nil
    then begin
            L : = NewNode;
            NewNode ↑ .Link : = nil
        end

    {Step 3: Otherwise, if new node precedes first node, then insert at front
      of list}
    else
        if L ↑ .Info.Key > X.Key
        then begin
                NewNode ↑ .Link : = L;
                L : = NewNode
            end

        {Step 4: Otherwise, initialize for search}
        else begin
                Save : = L;
                NotFound : = true;

                {Step 5: Search for the predecessor of new node}
                while (Save ↑ .Link <> nil) and NotFound do
                    if Save ↑ .Link ↑ .Info.Key < X.Key
                    then Save : = Save ↑ .Link
                    else NotFound : = false;

                {Step 6: Insert new node after node pointed to by Save}
                NewNode ↑ .Link : = Save ↑ .Link;
                Save ↑ .Link : = NewNode
            end
end;
```

**FIGURE 8-62**
**Procedure to insert a node into an ordered linked linear list.**

1. If the linked list is empty,
    then signal underflow and return

2. If the node to be deleted is at the front of the list,
    then reset the pointer to the front of the list and restore the node to the heap availability area

3. Repeat step 4 while the end of the list has not been reached and the node has not been found

4. Obtain the next node in the list

5. If the node was found,
    then delete it from the list, return the node to the heap availability area, and return
    otherwise, signal node not found and return

Since we are dealing with a specifically designated node, it does not matter if the list is ordered or not. The procedure appears in Fig. 8-63. The third parameter indicates the success or failure of the operation. Its type, RetCodeType, is assumed to be an enumerated type of the form (Success, Underflow, NotFound). This illustrates another technique for handling error conditions.

The first step of the procedure checks for an empty list condition. If this condition is "true," then we signal underflow. Step 2 determines whether or not the node to be deleted is the front node of the list. If X denotes the front node, then the second node in the list becomes its new front node. Observe that if the list contains only X, then the updated list becomes empty. The deleted node is also returned to the heap availability area in this step.

If X is not the first node of the list, then a search for its immediate predecessor (Pred) is launched. Steps 3 and 4 represent this effort. Step 5 determines whether or not the indicated node was actually found. If the search is successful, then the link field of node X is copied into the link field of Pred. The deleted node is then returned to the heap availability area. If the search fails, then this fact is reported.

Another familiar operation which is performed on a linked list is making a copy of it as follows:

1. If the list is empty, then return **nil**

2. Allocate storage for a new node and copy the information contents of the first node into it

3. Repeat thru step 5 while the end of the old list has not been reached

4. Obtain next node in the old list and record new node's predecessor node

5. Copy the node and add it to the rear of the new list

6. Set the link of the last node in the new list to null and return

Once again, the same approach applies to both ordered and unordered lists. The formulation of a detailed procedure to copy a list is left as an exercise.

```
procedure LDelete (
    var L: ListType;                {Input/output, list}
    X: ListType;                    {Input, pointer to a node in the list}
    var RetCode: RetCodeType        {Output, result of operation}
            );
{Given a linked linear list and a pointer to a node in the list, this procedure
    deletes the designated node.}
var
    Pred: ListType;                 {Pointer to predecessor of node to be deleted}
begin
    {Step 1: Check for empty list}
    if L = nil
    then RetCode : = Underflow
    else

        {Step 2: Check for deletion of first node}
        if X = L
        then begin
                L : = L ↑ .Link;
                dispose (X);
                RetCode : = Success
            end
        else begin

                {Step 3: Initialize search for predecessor of X}
                Pred : = L;

                {Step 4: Perform indicated search for X}
                while (Pred ↑ .Link <> nil) and (Pred ↑ .Link <> X) do
                    Pred : = Pred ↑ .Link;

                {Step 5: Delete indicated node, if found}
                if Pred ↑ .Link <> nil
                then begin
                        Pred ↑ .Link : = X ↑ .Link;
                        dispose (X);
                        RetCode : = Success
                    end
                else RetCode : = NotFound
            end
end;
```

**FIGURE 8-63**
Procedure to delete
selected node from a
linked linear list.

In Sec. 8-6 we discussed queues using sequential allocation. We saw that there are definite disadvantages to this method, the primary one being poor utilization of storage. A major drawback to both linear queues and circular queues was that an overflow could occur easily. The solution to this, of course, is linked or dynamic allocation. The node structure used for dynamically allocated queue elements will be the same as for singly linked lists, with a link field (Link) and an information field (Info). F and R will be pointers to the front and rear of the queue, respectively. When the queue is empty, F and R will simply be set to **nil**. Let us take a look at how changes can be made to the procedures QueueInsert and QueueDelete given in Sec. 8-6 to incorporate linked allocation. Since the queue itself cannot overflow, the first step of QueueInsert can be omitted. The allocation and initialization of a node with information field X are performed as follows:

```
new (NewNode);
NewNode ↑ .Info : = X;
NewNode ↑ .Link : = nil
```

The procedure now becomes slightly more complex because of the checks that must be done for **nil** pointers. The following steps insert the new node at the rear of the queue and adjust all the pointers as required:

```
if R = nil
then F : = NewNode
else R ↑ .Link : = NewNode;
R : = NewNode
```

Notice that when R = **nil** the queue is empty, so that **NewNode** is now the rear *and* the front node and F must be set to point to it. If R is not **nil**, then the link of the previous rear node must be set to point to the new node. In either case, R will now point to the new node.

The procedure for deleting a node from a queue also changes when linked allocation is used. The queue underflow must still be checked; in this case, underflow occurs when F = **nil**. The rest of the procedure QueueDelete translates to the following steps:

```
X : = F ↑ .Info;
OldF : = F;
F : = F ↑ .Link;
Dispose (OldF);
if F = nil
then R : = nil
```

Notice that in the first few steps, care must be taken to save the address of the node being deleted before changing the pointer F, so that it can be restored to the heap availability area. Also, a check must be done to see if the last node has been deleted, in which case R must be set to **nil**.

On reexamining some of the previous programs, such as programs LDelete and LInsOrder, we notice that the special case of an empty list must be checked for separately. We can modify the structure of a linked linear list to make this special case disappear. The next subsection explores this possibility.

## EXERCISES 8-8.2

1. Given a singly linked linear list whose typical node structure consists of an Info and a Link field, construct a procedure which counts the number of nodes in the list. (Use the type definition in Fig. 8-54 for ListType.) Test your procedure.

2. Write a procedure that changes the Info field of the $k$th node in a singly linked list to a value given by X. (Again, use Fig. 8-54.) Test your procedure.

★ 3. Construct a procedure which performs an insertion immediately before the $k$th node in a linked list. (Use Fig. 8-54 for the type definition of ListType.) Test your procedure.

★ 4. Repeat Exercise 3 for an insertion immediately after the $k$th node. (Use Fig. 8-54.) Test your procedure.

5. Given two linked lists whose front nodes are denoted by the pointers First and Second, respectively, write a procedure that will concatenate the two lists. The front-node address of the new list is to be stored in Third. (In order to avoid sharing nodes between two lists, First and Second should be input/output parameters which are set to **nil**.) Test your procedure.

6. Obtain a procedure which will deconcatenate (or split) a given linked list into two separate linked lists. The first node of the original linked list is denoted by the pointer variable First. Split denotes the address of the node which is to become the first node of the second linked list. (As in Exercise 5, the original pointer should be set to **nil**.) Test your procedure.

★ 7. Assume that you are given an ordered singly linked list whose node structure contains a Key and a Link field. The list is ordered on the Key field in increasing order. It is desired to delete a number of consecutive nodes whose Key values are greater than or equal to KMin and less than or equal to KMax. For example, an ordered seven-element linked list containing 'Andrea', 'Barb', 'Grant', 'Jennifer', 'Paul', 'Rick', and 'Susan' with KMin = 'Barb' and KMax = 'Jennifer' would result in an updated list containing 'Andrea', 'Paul', 'Rick', and 'Susan'. Assuming that the first node is denoted by the pointer variable First, write a Pascal procedure which accomplishes this task. Write a program using a key type of **packed array** [1 .. 8] **of** char to test your procedure.

★ 8. Formulate a procedure which, given a singly linked list, will return via its output parameter the list in the reverse order to which it was supplied. The original list is to remain unaltered.

★ 9. The search time for an item stored in a linear list necessarily varies with the position in the list. In many applications it is advantageous to place frequently referenced items near the start of the list. However, in many situations it cannot be determined in advance which items will be referenced most often. In cases such as these, a dynamic reorganization of the list, based on current reference activity, can reduce expected search time.

Assume that you have a singly linked linear list pointed at by the pointer variable Start. Each node consists of a search key, Key, an information field, Info, and a pointer to the next node, Next. Formulate a Boolean function Search (X, Data) that simultaneously searches and reorganizes the list in the following fashion. A node with search key X is sought. The nodes of the list are examined in turn. If the node is found, it is deleted from its current position and moved to the start of the list. Information contents of the node are then returned as parameter Data. The value of the function Search is "true," if the requested element is found and "false" if it is not.

10. Based on the list definitions in Fig. 8-60, modify the implementation of procedures LInitialize and LInsFirst.

11. Based on the list definitions in Fig. 8-60, formulate a procedure to insert an element at the end of a given list.

12. Construct a procedure that generates a copy of a given list.

## 8-8.3 CIRCULARLY LINKED LINEAR LISTS

The previous discussion dealt with linked linear lists in which the link of the last node is **nil**. A slight modification of this representation can yield an improvement in processing. The approach is to replace the **nil** pointer in the last node of a list by the pointer to its first node. Such a modified list is called a *circularly linked linear list* or, simply, a *circular list*. Figure 8-64 demonstrates the circular structure of this type of list.

Circular linked lists have several advantages over their singly linked counterparts. First, each node in a circular list is accessible from any node. That is, from a given node we can traverse the entire list. In a singly linked list we can traverse all of it only by starting at its first node. An important example of this restriction in a singly linked list is in the deletion algorithm given in the previous subsection. In that algorithm, the address of the first node of the list was required so that the predecessor of the node to be deleted could be found. This predecessor node was obtained by chaining through the

**FIGURE 8-64   Circularly linked linear list.**

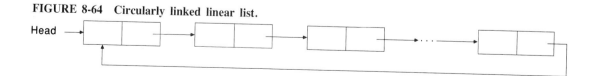

list from its first node. Clearly, the address of the first node is not needed in a circular list, since a search for the predecessor of a given node can be initiated from that node. There are certain operations, such as concatenation and splitting, which become more efficient with a circular list structure.

There is, however, a major disadvantage in using a circular list. Care must be exercised to avoid an infinite loop! Such a loop can occur if special care is not taken to detect the end of the list. One way of avoiding this loop condition is to place a special node which is permanently associated with the existence of a circular list. We call this special node the *list head* of the list. Another important advantage of using a list head is that a list can never be empty. Recall that several programs from the previous subsection require testing for an empty list condition. With a circular list representation, the need for testing this condition disappears. A representation of a circular list is given in Fig. 8-65a, where **Head** denotes the head of the list. An empty list is represented by having **Head** ↑ .**Link** = **Head**, and this possibility is shown in Fig. 8-65b. Observe that the information field in the list head node is not used. This fact is indicated by shading that field.

The following is a program segment for inserting a node at the front of a circular list:

```
new (NewNode);
NewNode ↑ .Info : = X;
NewNode ↑ .Link : = Head ↑ .Link;
Head ↑ .Link : = NewNode
```

Simplification of the previously encountered subprograms is left to the exercises.

## EXERCISES 8-8.3

1. Construct a function which counts and returns the number of nodes in a circular list with a list head. Write a program to test your function.

2. Formulate a procedure which inserts a node at the end of a circular list, that is, between the node which points to the list head and the list head. Write a program to test the procedure.

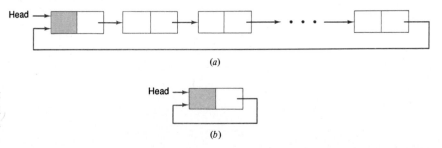

(a)

(b)

**FIGURE 8-65**
**Circularly linked**
**linear list with**
**a list head.**

3. Construct a procedure which deletes from a circular list a node whose information content is given by the variable X. Write a program to test the procedure.

★ 4. Write a procedure for the concatenation of two circular lists with list heads (see Exercise 5 in Exercises 8-8.2). (What conventions are sufficient to ensure that a node remains on only one list?) Write a program to test your procedure.

★ 5. Construct a procedure to split a circular list into two circular lists (see Exercise 6 in Exercises 8-8.2). Test your procedure.

★ 6. Write insertion and deletion procedures for a circular linked list. Test the procedures.

## 8-8.4 DOUBLY LINKED LINEAR LISTS

So far we have traversed linked linear lists in a left-to-right manner. In many applications it is required to traverse a list in both directions. This two-way motion can be realized by maintaining two link fields in each node instead of one. These links are used to denote the address of the predecessor and successor of a given node. The predecessor link is called the *left link*, and the successor link is known as the *right link*. A list whose node structure contains two link fields will be called a *doubly linked linear list* or *two-way chain*. Such a list structure is exhibited in Fig. 8-66, where Left and Right are pointer variables that denote the left-most and right-most nodes in the list, respectively. Observe that the left link of the left-most node is **nil**. The same is true of the right link of the right-most node. Finally, the left and right link fields of a node are called Lptr and Rptr, respectively.

As for singly linked linear lists, we formulate a modular package for doubly linked lists. Figure 8-67 presents the type definitions required. The ListType is defined as a record structure containing the pointers Left and Right for ease in declaring new list variables and in passing these to the procedures implementing the list operations. The definition of InfoType for the application would appear in the main program. We leave as exercises implementation of the initialize and insert/delete at front/rear operations, which are easily implemented.

Consider the problem of inserting a node into a doubly linked linear list to the right of a specified node which is pointed to by the variable M. Several cases can occur. First, the list might be empty. This is indicated by M = **nil**. In such a situation, Left and Right are both **nil**. An insertion in this

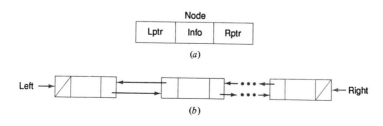

FIGURE 8-66
Doubly linked
linear list.

```
type
  ListPointerType = ↑ NodeType;
  ListType =
    record
      Left, Right: ListPointerType
    end;
  NodeType =
    record
      Lptr: ListPointerType;
      Info: InfoType;
      Rptr: ListPointerType
    end;
```

**FIGURE 8-67**
**Type definitions for**
**doubly linked linear**
**lists.**

situation involves setting **Left** and **Right** to point to the new node. Also, the left and right links of this node are set to **nil**.

A second possibility is an insertion within the list; that is, there will be a predecessor and a successor to the given node after insertion. Such a case is shown in Fig. 8-68, where **NewNode** denotes the node being inserted.

A third possibility involves the insertion to the right of the right-most node in the list, thereby requiring the pointer **Right** to be changed. The state of a list before and after insertion is given in Fig. 8-69. The procedure to insert a node to the immediate right of a specified node is left as an exercise.

The deletion of a specified node from a doubly linked list is a straightforward operation. Several cases are possible. If the list contains a single node, then the left-most and right-most pointers associated with the list must be set to **nil**. In the case of the right-most node in the list being marked

**FIGURE 8-68    Insertion within a doubly linked linear list.**

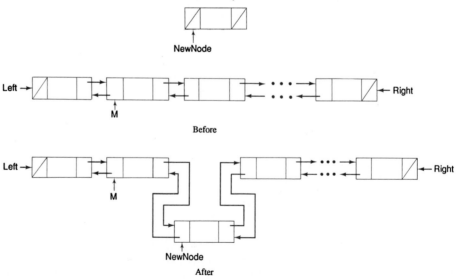

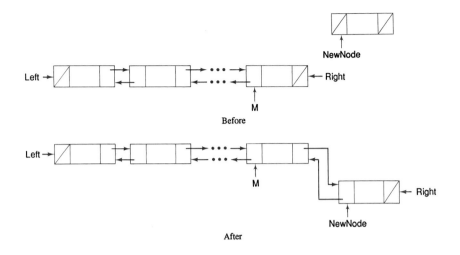

**FIGURE 8-69**
**Right-most insertion**
**in a doubly linked**
**linear list.**

for deletion, the pointer variable **Right** must be changed to point to the predecessor of the node being dropped from the list. An analogous situation is possible at the left end of the list. Finally, a deletion can occur within the list. A representation of this last case is shown in Fig. 8-70. The right link of the predecessor of **OldNode** must be set to point to the successor of **OldNode**. Also, the left link of the successor node of **OldNode** must be set to point to the predecessor node of **OldNode**. The following pair of statements accomplishes the required task:

OldNode ↑ .Lptr ↑ .Rptr : = OldNode ↑ .Rptr;
OldNode ↑ .Rptr ↑ .Lptr : = OldNode ↑ .Lptr

The deletion procedure is left as an exercise.

Observe that the deletion of a node from a doubly linked list is much more efficient, in general, than the deletion of a node from a singly linked list. In particular, in doubly linked list deletion, no search for the predecessor of the node being deleted is necessary. Given the address of the node marked for deletion, the predecessor and successor of this node are immediately known.

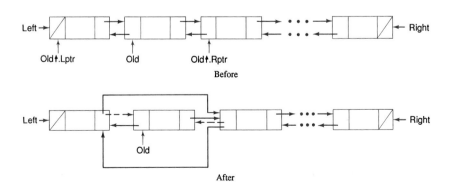

**FIGURE 8-70**
**Deletion of a**
**node from within a**
**doubly linked linear**
**list.**

A doubly linked list is well suited to represent a queue. Such a representation of a queue is shown in Fig. 8-71a, where **R** and **F** are pointer variables which denote the rear and front of the queue, respectively. The insertion of a node pointed to by **NewNode** to the rear of a nonempty queue is given in Fig. 8-71b, where **R'** denotes the rear of the queue after the insertion. A program segment for this insertion is

R ↑ .Rptr : = NewNode;
NewNode ↑ .Rptr : = **nil**;
NewNode ↑ .Lptr : = R;
R : = NewNode

In a similar way, a deletion of a node from a doubly linked queue containing at least two elements is shown in Fig. 8-71c, where **F'** denotes the front of the queue after the deletion. The following program segment accomplishes this task:

OldNode : = F;
F : = F ↑ .Rptr;
F ↑ .Lptr : = **nil**;
dispose (OldNode)

Handling the special cases is left as an exercise.

The procedures given earlier for inserting a node into and deleting a node from a doubly linked list normally have several special cases. Let us now consider the possibility of simplifying these procedures. By first introducing the notion of a list head, as was done in the previous subsection, we can eliminate once again the case of an empty list. Using this approach, an empty list will always contain the list head node. Second, if we make the list circular, this adds a certain degree of symmetry to the structure. A doubly linked circular list with a list head is shown in Fig. 8-72a, where the pointer variable **Head** denotes a pointer to the list head. In this

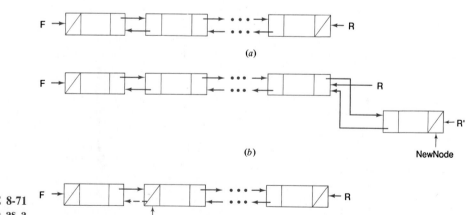

(a)

(b)

NewNode

**FIGURE 8-71**
**A queue as a**
**doubly linked list.**

F'

(c)

representation, the right pointer of the right-most information node points to the head node. Also, the left pointer of the list head points to the right-most information node. An empty list has the left and right pointers of the list head pointing to the list head. This condition is exemplified in Fig. 8-72*b*.

Based on this new doubly linked circular list representation, the insertion procedure introduced earlier becomes much simpler. The revised formulation of this procedure is presented in Fig. 8-73. This procedure consists of only one case! The reader should verify that this program works for an insertion into an empty list (that is, into a list which contains only a list head). In a similar manner, the corresponding deletion procedure can be reformulated as in Fig. 8-74.

The doubly linked method of representing list structures is used extensively. In particular, a variation of this method is used in Chap. 9 to represent tree structures. In this section we have given the basics of representing linear lists by linked-allocation techniques. The next section introduces several applications of linked structures.

## EXERCISES 8-8.4

1. Construct an insertion procedure for a deque which is represented by a doubly linked linear list with a list head node. The information associated with the new node is given by X.

2. Write a deletion procedure for deleting a node from a deque which is stored as a doubly linked list with a list head.

3. Write a program to test the procedures of Exercises 1 and 2.

4. Repeat Exercises 1, 2, and 3 for an input-restricted deque.

5. Repeat Exercises 1, 2, and 3 for an output-restricted deque.

6. Derive a function that constructs a doubly linked list with a list head from a singly linked list that is accessed through a pointer First. Note that

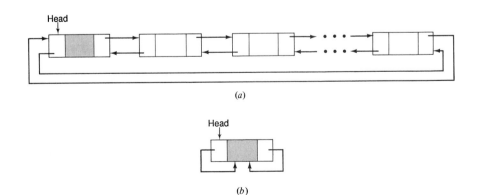

(a)

(b)

FIGURE 8-72
Doubly linked circular list with a head node.

**procedure** LInsRight (
   M: ListPointerType;   {Input, pointer to a node in the list}
   X: InfoType        {Input, information to be added}
           );
{Given a pointer to a node in a doubly linked circular list with a header
   node, this procedure inserts a new node to the "right" of the given node.}
**var**
   NewNode: ListPointerType;
**begin**
   {Step 1: Obtain a new node from the heap}
   new (NewNode);

   {Step 2: Set information contents of new node}
   NewNode ↑ .Info : = X;

   {Step 3: Insert new node to the immediate right of node M}
   NewNode ↑ .Ltpr : = M;
   NewNode ↑ .Rptr : = M ↑ .Rptr;
   M ↑ .Rptr ↑ .Lptr : = NewNode;
   M ↑ .Rptr : = NewNode
**end**;

**FIGURE 8-73**
**Insertion procedure for**
**doubly linked list**
**with header node.**

the original singly linked list need not be destroyed. Write a program
to test the procedure.

★ 7. Write a procedure which handles the updating of an ordered linear list
of computer manufacturers and their current stock market quotations.
For example, a recent list of companies and their quotations is

| | |
|---|---|
| WANG | 3.72 |
| DIGITAL | 9.83 |
| HONEYWELL | 15.21 |

**procedure** LDelete (
   OldNode: ListPointerType    {Input, pointer to node to be deleted}
           );
{Given a pointer to a node in a doubly linked circular list with a header
   node, this procedure deletes the node from the list.}
**begin**
   {Step 1: Delete the indicated node}
   OldNode ↑ .Lptr ↑ .Rptr : = OldNode ↑ .Rptr;
   OldNode ↑ .Rptr ↑ .Lptr : = OldNode ↑ .Lptr;

**FIGURE 8-74**
**Procedure to delete**
**from a doubly linked**
**linear list with header**
**node.**

   {Step 2: Return node to availability area}
   dispose (OldNode)
**end**;

| BURROUGHS | 16.13 |
|---|---|
| CONTROL DATA | 18.92 |
| IBM | 132.15 |

An input command of the form

'UPDATE' 'company name' latest quotation

should result in the updating of the list so as to preserve its order by quotation. Therefore, 'UPDATE' 'DIGITAL' 17.75 results in the new list

| WANG | 3.72 |
|---|---|
| HONEYWELL | 15.21 |
| BURROUGHS | 16.13 |
| DIGITAL | 17.75 |
| CONTROL DATA | 18.92 |
| IBM | 132.15 |

It should be assumed that the list is highly volatile in the sense that quotations are continually being changed and companies (plus quotations) are continually being added or removed from the list. Assume that a company's name is in the list. Note that a company can move *up* or *down* the list depending on the latest quotation. Therefore, choose your data structure carefully.

Note that a number of comparisons are necessary for this procedure and that to be more efficient than a straightforward deletion and reinsertion of a node, a node is to be moved only a few positions. Test your procedure.

★ 8. Give the necessary type definitions and procedures to use a linear linked list either as a stack or as a queue.

9. Based on the definitions in Fig. 8-67 and the analysis summarized in Figs. 8-68 and 8-69, formulate a procedure to insert a node to the immediate right of a specified node.

10. Write a procedure to perform a deletion of a specified node from a doubly linked list with the node structure given by the type definitions in Fig. 8-67.

## 8-9  APPLICATIONS OF LINKED LINEAR LISTS

This section discusses three applications of linked linear lists. The first application is an application of linked queues to sorting. The second application deals with the processing of rentals at a ski-rental shop. The third and final topic deals with the application of hashing functions to searching and, more generally, to the area of information organization and retrieval. The key value of a record is used in a computational way to locate that record in memory. The idea of associating a key with an address in memory is applicable to many situations which arise in computer science.

### 8-9.1 RADIX SORTING

The *radix sort* is a method of sorting which predates any digital computer. This was performed and is still performed on a mechanical card sorter. Such a sorter usually processes a standard card of 80 columns, each of which may contain a character of some alphabet. When sorting cards on this type of sorter, only one column at a time is examined. A metal pointer on the sorter is used to select any one of the 80 columns. The sorter reads cards from the bottom of the deck. For numerical data, the sorter places all cards containing a given digit into an appropriate pocket. There are 10 pockets, corresponding to the 10 decimal digits. The operator of the sorter combines in order the decks of cards from the 10 pockets. The resulting deck has the cards of pocket 0 at the bottom and those of pocket 9 on top. In general, numbers consisting of more than one digit are sorted. In such a case, an ascending-order sort can be accomplished by performing several individual digit sorts in order. That is, each column is sorted in turn, starting with the lowest-order (right-most) column first and proceeding through the other columns from right to left. This mechanical method of sorting can be implemented on a computer. If the maximum number of digits in a key is $m$, then $m$ successive passes, from the unit digit to the most significant digit, are required in order to sort the numbers.

As an example, let us consider the sorting of the following sequence of keys:

73, 65, 52, 77, 24, 83, 17, 35, 96, 62, 41, 87, 09, 11

After the first pass on the unit digit position of each number, we obtain

```
                               87
      11  62  83      35       17
      41  52  73  24  65  96  77      09
Pocket:  0   1   2   3   4   5   6   7   8   9
```

We now combine the contents of the 10 pockets in order so that the contents of the 0 pocket are on the bottom and the contents of the 9 pocket are on the top. The resulting sequence thus obtained is

41, 11, 52, 62, 73, 83, 24, 65, 35, 96, 77, 17, 87, 09

The result of performing the second pass of the sort on the higher-order digit yields the following arrangement:

```
         17                  65  77  87
      09  11  24  35  41  52  62  73  83  96
Pocket:  0   1   2   3   4   5   6   7   8   9
```

These 10 pockets are now combined in the same order as before, thus yielding the desired result.

The computerization of this mechanical process is straightforward. Two possible storage-allocation techniques for representing the data are possible. The sequential-allocation method of storage cannot be applied readily to this application, since we cannot predict the size of each pocket. Actually, a pocket could contain all the keys. Using linked allocation, however, the unpredictability of the pocket sizes causes no problems. Each pocket can be represented by a linked FIFO queue. At the end of each pass, these queues can be easily combined into the proper order. Figure 8-75a represents the state of the sort after the first pass for the sample key set just given. Note that each linked queue has an associated top pointer (denoting the rear) and bottom pointer (denoting the front). The positions of the rear elements of the 10 queues (or pockets) are kept in a vector T. Similarly, vector B contains the positions of the bottom elements of the queues. Figure 8-75b represents the state of the queues after the second pass.

More generally, keys that contain $m$ digits require $m$ successive passes, from the unit digit to the highest-order digit, in order to complete a radix sort. We now formulate an algorithm for this sorting process. We assume that a key contains the $m$ digits $b_m b_{m-1} \cdots b_1$ and that a selection mechanism is available for selecting each digit. The initial set of keys is assumed to be arranged as a singly linked list.

A general algorithm to perform a radix sort is now presented:

*1.* Repeat thru step 6 for each digit in the key

*2.* Initialize the pockets

*3.* Repeat thru step 5 until the end of the linked list

*4.* Obtain the next key and examine the currently considered digit position

*5.* Insert the record in the appropriate pocket

*6.* Combine the pockets to form a new linked list

The procedure for the sort appears in Fig. 8-76. We have chosen here to incorporate the programs for manipulating the list within the program itself. An alternative approach would make use of the modular operations of the previous section, with an additional operation to combine two lists. This approach is left as an exercise.

Step 1 of the procedure controls the number of passes required to perform the sort. The second step initializes the top and bottom pointers associated with each pocket. At the beginning of each pass the pockets are all empty. The variable Current is assigned a pointer to the first record in the table. Step 3 directs each record to the appropriate pocket (depending on the value of Digit). The fourth step combines the 10 pockets into a new linked table. This revised linked list becomes the input to the next pass. The variable First is initialized to the address of the bottom element of the first nonempty pocket.

This procedure is efficient for a table which contains keys whose lengths are short. More specifically, for a key containing $m$ digits, the radix sort requires $m * n$ key accesses.

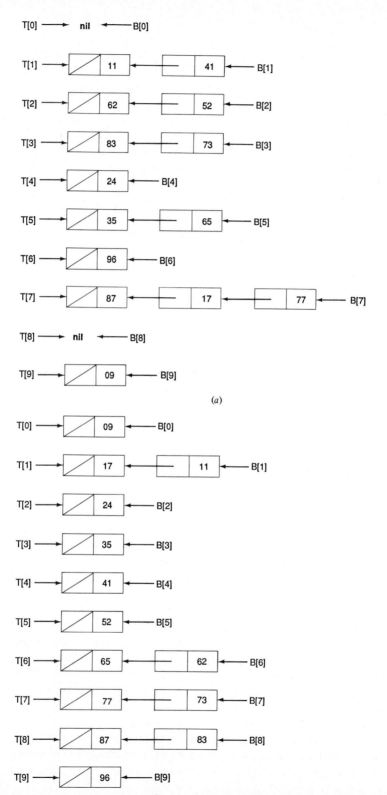

**FIGURE 8-75**
Representation of a
radix sort: (*a*) after
first pass; (*b*) after
second pass.

## 8-9.2 SKI-RENTAL SHOP

The Bonzai Boards Ski-Rental Shop has recently purchased a computer. The management is looking forward to a busy season and would like to minimize the amount of paperwork needed. The computer will be used to store information about the skis currently in the shop, those currently rented out, and those being waxed or repaired. It also will be used to maintain the record system whose description follows.

The ski shop rents out a wide range of sizes of skis on the basis of a daily rate. When a pair of skis is rented, the clerk selects a pair of the correct size from those presently in the shop. When skis are returned by the customer, they are sent to a service room where they are waxed and repaired as needed before being returned to the racks.

For clerical purposes, a record is kept for each pair of skis owned by the shop. An ID number unique to that particular pair is assigned each pair of skis and imprinted on each ski of the pair. Information on the skis is kept in three separate lists: one for skis in the shop, one for skis presently rented out, and one for skis being serviced. For each pair of skis, we will require the following information: ID number, size, rental date, and return date. The latter two pieces of information will be applicable only in the list of skis currently rented out. When a pair of skis is rented, this information is updated. When the skis are returned, the date fields are set to zero.

The list of skis in the shop is ordered according to condition. Those skis in the best condition are kept at the front of the list to ensure that wear and tear occurs evenly on all skis. The condition of a pair of skis can range from poor to excellent and is updated each time a pair of skis is returned by a customer. This will be discussed more fully later. The list of rented skis is maintained in order of date of expected return, which speeds up the search process when skis are returned. The skis in the service room being waxed or repaired are kept in a queue. Naturally, the skis will be serviced in the order that they arrive.

Rental fees must be paid *before* a customer may take the skis out of the shop. The fees are $8 a day for the first two days and $5 a day for each additional day. At the time the skis are rented, the customer pays for the number of days from the current date to the expected return date, inclusive. If the skis are returned late, the customer pays for the extra days in the usual manner. There is no penalty. However, if skis are returned *early*, no money will be refunded.

Finally, there are two special cases that can arise. First, when new skis are bought, they are added to the list of skis in the shop. Second, before releasing a pair of skis from the service room, the skis are assessed as to their condition. If they are no longer up to par, they are disposed of; otherwise, the condition code is updated and the skis are returned to the shop.

The algorithms we are about to develop will simulate this record system. An input file will be provided. This file will contain a list of the various transactions which may take place within a given time period. There are a number of operations to be performed on the list structures, depending on

```
procedure RadixSort (
    var First: ListType      {Input/output, pointer to first node of a singly
                              linked list}
    );
```
{Given a singly linked list, this procedure sorts its elements by the radix
sort algorithm. The type ListType is assumed to be globally defined as a
pointer to NodeType; the latter is a type containing a Link field and some
information content. A globally defined function, DigitSelect, is assumed
to return (as an integer value) the digit determined by the Pass number,
given a pointer to the current node. M is globally defined as the number
of digits.}
```
var
    T, B: array [0 .. 9] of ListType;   {Top and bottom pointers of pockets}
    Pass: integer;                      {The current pass number}
    Digit: integer;                     {The current digit}
    Pocket, P: integer;                 {Indices to pockets}
    Current, Next,
    Previous: ListType;                 {Pointer to list nodes}
begin
    {Step 1: Perform sort}
    for Pass : = 1 to M do
        begin

            {Step 2: Initialize the pass}
            for Pocket : = 0 to 9 do
                begin
                    T[Pocket] : = nil;
                    B[Pocket] : = nil
                end;
            Current : = First;
```

**FIGURE 8-76**
Radix sort procedure.

what type of action is denoted by the input. The variable TransactionCode
is a string variable used to read in the type of action to follow. Table
8-15 gives the possible values of TransactionCode, their meanings, the output
required, and the data items which accompany each type.

When TransactionCode equals 'RENT', it means that a customer has asked
to rent a pair of skis. The size must be known, along with the rental date
and expected date of return. From these two dates, a fee can be charged.
The algorithm calculates this fee, removes the skis from the list of skis in
the shop, and inserts them in the list of skis rented out.

A value of 'RETURN' signals a pair of skis being returned to the shop.
To find the record for these skis, the ID number must be known. Also, we
need to know the actual return date to calculate extra fees, if there are any.
The record for these skis is now deleted from the list of rented skis and
inserted in the queue of skis to be serviced.

When the string 'SERVICE' is encountered in the input, the service

{Step 3: Distribute each record in the appropriate pocket}
**while** Current <> **nil do**
    **begin**
        Digit : = DigitSelect (Current, Pass);
        Next : = Current ↑ .Link;
        **if** T[Digit] = **nil**
        **then begin**
                T[Digit] : = Current;
                B[Digit] : = Current
           **end**
        **else begin**
                T[Digit] ↑ .Link : = Current;
                T[Digit] : = Current
           **end**;
        Current ↑ .Link : = **nil**;
        Current : = Next
    **end**;

{Step 4: Combine pockets}
Pocket : = 0;
**while** B[Pocket] = **nil do**
    Pocket : = Pocket + 1;
First : = B[Pocket];
**for** P : = Pocket + 1 **to** 9 **do**
    **begin**
        Previous : = T[P − 1];
        **if** T[P] <> **nil**
        **then** Previous ↑ .Link : = B[P]
        **else** T[P] : = Previous
    **end**
  **end**
**end**;

**FIGURE 8-76** (*cont.*)

personnel just processed the pair of skis at the front of the service queue. The condition of these skis must be entered at this point, as service assesses them. If they are in poor condition, they are disposed of; otherwise, they are returned to the ski shop.

Occasionally, the ski shop will buy new skis, at which point the value read into TransactionCode is 'BUY'. These skis must be entered in the list of skis in the shop, while the values for size, ID number, and condition must be initialized.

At any time during the course of a day or week, the ski shop may wish to check the current inventory. That is, they may want a display of the skis in each of the three lists, giving the ID number and the size of each pair of skis. This can be done by entering the string 'DISPLAY' as data. No additional data is needed.

The steps involved in processing transactions for the ski shop are given in the following general algorithms, which has a very familiar form:

*1.* Initialize lists for processing

*2.* Repeat thru step 4 while there are more transactions

*3.* Read transaction type

*4.* Determine and process appropriate transaction

*5.* Save lists for next processing run

Step 4 can be further refined. This step is easily represented by a caselike statement as follows:

Select case based on transaction type

    'RENT': read and process a ski rental transaction

    'RETURN': read and process a ski return transaction

    'SERVICE': read and process a ski service transaction

    'BUY': read and process a ski purchase

    'DISPLAY': print ski inventory report

The structure chart of the proposed algorithm is given in Fig. 8-77. Note that there is a procedure associated with each possible type of transaction. (When TransactionCode = 'RENT', RentProc is called, etc.) These procedures, in turn, call other procedures or functions to insert and delete elements from the various lists. The names of these procedures are quite self-explanatory, as well (e.g., ShopDelete is a procedure for deleting an element from the linked list of skis in the shop).

**TABLE 8-15**   **Transaction Types in Ski-rental Shop**

| Value of Transaction Code | Meaning | Output to Produce | Data Items to Follow |
|---|---|---|---|
| 'RENT' | Rent skis | Message if none available Fees charged | Size, rental date expected return date |
| 'RETURN' | Return skis | Message if skis not recorded Additional fees, if any | Actual return date, ID number |
| 'SERVICE' | Skis being serviced | None | Condition |
| 'BUY' | Skis being bought | None | Size, ID number |
| 'DISPLAY' | Display lists | List names, ID numbers, and sizes | None |

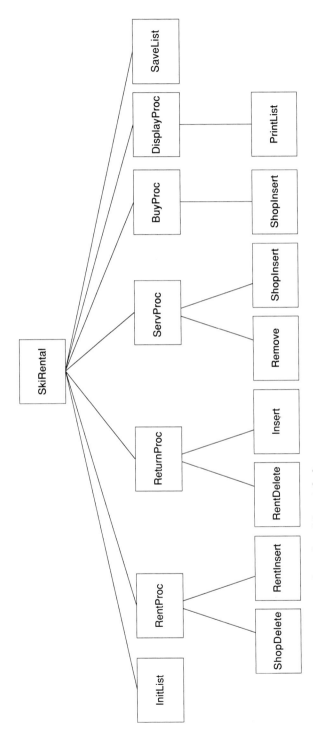

**FIGURE 8-77  Structure chart for ski-rental shop.**

The data structure naturally chosen to implement this record system is the linked list. We will, in fact, need three of them. Two will act as priority queues, while the third will be a regular FIFO queue. Priority queues are used for skis in the shop and skis rented out because they are kept in a particular order. The skis in the shop are ordered according to condition, so that the skis in the best condition will be chosen first. The skis rented out are ordered according to return date, so that the skis being returned will, it is hoped, be found very near the front of the list. The skis being serviced are kept in a FIFO queue because they are served as they are brought in—first come, first served.

The node structure for all three of these lists will be the same, to avoid the need for creating and destroying nodes as they change lists. The following node structure will be used:

| Condition | SkiSize | IDNo | Rentdate | ReturnDate | Link |
| --- | --- | --- | --- | --- | --- |

The **Condition** field will contain one of the five elements of the enumerated type

(Poor, Fair, Average, Good, Excellent)

Take note of the ordering of this type. It becomes important when inserting skis into the list of skis in the shop. The **SkiSize** field refers to the ski size (in cm) and will fall between 150 and 200. ID numbers begin at 300 and go up, so as not to confuse them with sizes. **RentDate** contains the integer between 1 and 365 denoting the day of the year the skis were rented (that is, January 1 would be 1, February 4 would be 35, etc.). The same applies to **ReturnDate**, which denotes the expected date of return. For the present application, we will disregard leap years. Also, we will assume that skiers wishing to rent skis during the Christmas holidays must return them on New Year's Eve for year-end inventory. If they wish to ski on New Year's Day, they must come back and rerent. Figure 8-78 gives an example of the three linked lists.

FIGURE 8-78   **Sample linked lists for ski-rental shop.**

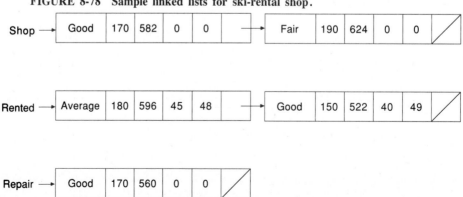

Let us now examine the various subprograms for inserting elements to and deleting elements from the various lists. Because subprograms ShopInsert and RentInsert are very similar, we present only the former in Fig. 8-79. RentInsert is obtained easily by changing Condition in step 1 in this figure to ReturnDate. Similarly, because the RentDelete and ShopDelete routines are similiar, only the former is given in Fig. 8-80. ShopDelete is obtained by changing the if conditions in steps 2 and 3 in this figure to List $\uparrow$ .SkiSize = Required Size and Current $\uparrow$ .SkiSize $<>$ RequiredSize, respectively.

The procedure Insert(List, P), given a list and a pointer to a node, inserts the node at the end of the list. It is similar to the procedure in exercise 11 of Sec. 8-8.2, except that in the present case the node has already been created and is passed to the procedure. The procedure Remove(List, P) deletes the first

```
procedure ShopInsert (
    var List: ListType;       {Input/output, the list}
    P: ListType               {Input, points to node to be inserted}
                              );
{Given a pointer to a list and a pointer to a node, this procedure inserts
    the element into the list. The list is kept ordered by decreasing value of
    Condition.}
var
    Current, Prev: ListType;    {List traversal pointer}
    NotFound: Boolean;          {Loop termination flag}
begin
    {Step 1: Find place}
    Current : = List;
    NotFound : = true;
    while (Current <> nil) and NotFound do
        if Current ↑ .Condition > P ↑ .Condition
        then begin
                Prev : = Current;
                Current : = Current ↑ .Link
            end
        else NotFound : = false;

    {Step 2: Insert in its proper place}
    if Current = List      {Front of list}
    then begin
            P ↑ .Link : = List;
            List : = P
        end
    else begin
            P ↑ .Link : = Current;
            Prev ↑ .Link : = P
        end
end;
```

**FIGURE 8-79**
Procedure **ShopInsert**.

```
function RentDelete (
    var List: ListType;        {Input/output, the list}
    ID: integer                {Input, ski ID number}
                 ): ListType;
```

{Given a pointer to a list and a specific identification number, this function searches the list for an element whose ID field equals the supplied identification number. If one is found, a pointer to it is returned and the element is deleted from the list; otherwise a value of **nil** is returned.}

```
var
    Current, Prev: ListType;        {List traversal pointers}
    NotFound: Boolean;              {Loop termination flag}
begin
    {Step 1: Empty list?}
    if List = nil
    then RentDelete : = nil
    else

        {Step 2: First node?}
        if List ↑ .IDNo = ID
        then begin
                RentDelete : = List;
                List : = List ↑ .Link
            end
        else begin

                {Step 3: Search for skis with ID number}
                Current : = List;
                NotFound : = true;
                while (Current <> nil) and NotFound do
                    if Current ↑ .IDNo <> ID
                    then begin
                            Prev : = Current;
                            Current : = Current ↑ .Link
                        end
                    else NotFound : = false;
                if Current = nil        {Not found}
                then RentDelete : = nil
                else begin
                        Prev ↑ .Link : = Current ↑ .Link;
                        RentDelete : = Current
                    end
            end
    end;
```

**FIGURE 8-80**
**Function RentDelete.**

node in the list and returns it via the output parameter P. It is similar to produce LDelete (see Sec. 8-8.2), except that it is not given a node specification (it always deletes the last node) and it returns the node to the calling routine instead of to the available space list. Construction of these routines is left as an exercise.

We are now ready to present the five primary procedures for our algorithm. Procedure RentProc is given in Fig. 8-81. Step 1 reads in the size the customer needs, as well as the current date and the expected return date. Step 2 removes a pair of skis from the Shop list, if there is one of the correct size. Note that X will receive a value of **nil** if no skis of the correct size can be found, in which case an appropriate message is displayed. Step 3 initializes the date fields for the rented pair of skis and places their record in the Rented list. Step 4 calculates the fees, charging $8 for each of the first two days and $5 a day for each additional day. We are assuming that the integer denoting the return date will always be greater than the integer denoting the rental date.

Figure 8-82 presents the ReturnProc procedure. Step 1 of this procedure reads in the actual return date and the ID number of the skis being returned. Step 2 removes the skis from the rented list, searching for the ID number. If the skis cannot be found in the list, an error message is written and control returns to the calling program. Otherwise, the difference between the actual return date and the expected return date is calculated. If this number is positive (the skis have been returned late), the customer must pay for the additional days. This payment is made in the usual manner. Notice that Days is assumed to be greater than or equal to 2. This is so because the customer will have already paid for at least one day of rental. If the skis are late, they have obviously been out for 2 or more days. Step 4 sets the date fields back to zero and inserts the record for these skis at the rear of the service queue.

Figure 8-83 presents the ServProc procedure. Step 1 of the service procedure removes a record for a pair of skis from the front of the service queue. The condition for these skis is then read in step 2. This requires a procedure to read in a condition as a string and convert it to an enumerated type. This procedure is left as an exercise. If their condition is poor, the skis are disposed of and the record is destroyed. Otherwise, the record is returned to the Shop list, with the condition field being updated.

The procedure to process new skis appears in Fig. 8-84. The first step of this procedure creates a new node for the new pair of skis. Step 2 reads in the size and ID number to be given to this pair of skis. The rental and return dates are set to zero, and the condition is set to excellent. (A new pair of skis should be in excellent condition!) The initialized record is then inserted into the Shop list in step 3.

The final procedure, which is given in Fig. 8-85, displays the current data. Notice that DisplayProc calls another procedure, PrintList. This adds to the modularity and readability of the procedure. A heading is printed, and then a procedure is called to print out the list associated with that heading. This procedure is presented in Fig. 8-86.

```
procedure RentProc (
    var Shop: ListType;        {Input/output, list of skis in the shop}
    var Rented: ListType       {Input/output, list of rented skis}
                   );
```
{Given pointers to the list of skis in the shop and to the list of rented skis,
this procedure removes a pair or skis of the proper size from the shop list
and inserts it in the rented list.}
```
var
    RequiredSize: integer;     {Required ski size}
    InRentDate: integer;       {Rental date}
    InReturnDate: integer;     {Return date}
    X: ListType;               {Pointer to node}
    Days: integer;             {Days rented}
    Fee: integer;              {Rental fee}
begin
    {Step 1: Read information}
    readln (RequiredSize, InRentDate, InReturnDate);

    {Step 2: Delete from shop list}
    X : = ShopDelete (Shop, RequiredSize);
    if X = nil
    then writeln ('No skis of size', RequiredSize, 'available')
    else begin

            {Step 3: Initialize dates and put skis in rental list}
            with X ↑ do
              begin
                RentDate : = InRentDate;
                ReturnDate : = InReturnDate
              end;
            RentInsert (Rented, X);

            {Step 4: Charge fees}
            Days : = X ↑ .ReturnDate − X ↑ .RentDate;
            Fee : = 8;
            Days : = Days − 1;
            if Days > 0     {Renting for 2 or more days}
            then begin
                    Fee : = Fee + 8;      {Second day fee}
                    Days : = Days − 1;
                    Fee : = Fee + 5*Days     {Add fee for subsequent days}
                 end;
            writeln ('The charge for', Days, 'days is $', Fee)
         end
end;
```

**FIGURE 8-81**
Procedure **RentProc.**

```
procedure ReturnProc (
    var Rented: ListType;      {Input/output, list of rented skis}
    var Repair: ListType       {Input/output, list of skis in the service room}
                        );
```
{Given a pointer to the list of skis rented out and to the list of skis in the
service room, this procedure removes a returned pair of skis from the
rented list and inserts them at the rear of the repair queue.}
```
var
    InReturnDate: integer;     {Actual return date}
    ID: integer;               {Identification number}
    X: ListType;               {Pointer to record}
    Diff: integer;             {Difference between actual days rented and days
                                   requested at rental time.}
    Days: integer;             {Actual days rented}
    Fee: integer;              {Additional fee required}
begin
    {Step 1: Read in date of return and ID number}
    readln (InReturnDate, ID);

    {Step 2: Remove from rented list}
    X : = RentDelete (Rented, ID);
    if X = nil
    then writeln ('These skis have not been recorded')
    else begin

            {Step 3: Calculate possible extra charge}
            Diff : = InReturnDate − X ↑ .ReturnDate;
            Days : = InReturnDate − X ↑ .RentDate;
            if Diff > 0      {Skis have been returned late}
            then begin
                    if Days = 2     {Will be greater than 1 if skis are late}
                    then begin
                            Fee : = 8;
                            Diff : = Diff − 1
                        end;
                    Fee : = Fee + Diff*5;
                    writeln ('The extra charge is $', Fee)
                end
            else writeln ('Fees are all paid');

            {Step 4: Set date to zero and put in repair list}
            X ↑ .ReturnDate : = 0;
            X ↑ .RentDate : = 0;
            Insert (Repair, X)
        end
end;
```

**FIGURE 8-82**
Procedure **ReturnProc.**

```
procedure ServProc (
    var Repair: ListType;    {Input/output, list of skis in the service room}
    var Shop: ListType       {Input/output, list of skis in the shop}
                    );
```
{Given pointers to the list of skis in the service room and the list of skis in the shop, this procedure removes a pair of skis from the front of the repair queue and either disposes of it, or returns it to the shop list, depending on its condition.}
```
var
    X: ListType;              {Pointer to ski record}
begin
    {Step 1: Remove skis from front of queue}
    Remove (Repair, X);

    {Step 2: Assess condition and act accordingly}
    ReadCondition (X ↑ .Condition);
    readln;
    if X ↑ .Condition = Poor
    then dispose (X)        {Get rid of skis}
    else ShopInsert (Shop, X)
end;
```

**FIGURE 8-83**
Procedure **ServProc**.

```
procedure BuyProc (
    var Shop: ListType       {Input/output, list of skis in the shop}
                    );
```
{Given a pointer to the list of skis in the shop, this program reads in data for a new pair of skis, and inserts the skis in the shop list.}
```
var
    X: ListType;       {Pointer to ski record}
begin
    {Step 1: Create a new node}
    new (X);

    {Step 2: Initialize}
    readln (X ↑ .SkiSize, X ↑ .IDNo);
    X ↑ .RentDate : = 0;
    X ↑ .ReturnDate : = 0;
    X ↑ .Condition : = Excellent;

    {Step 3: Put skis in the shop}
    ShopInsert (Shop, X)
end;
```

**FIGURE 8-84**
Procedure **BuyProc**.

```
procedure DisplayProc (
    Shop: ListType;        {Input, list of skis in the shop}
    Rented: ListType;      {Input list of rented skis}
    Repair: ListType       {Input, list of skis in the service room}
                          );
```
{Given pointers to three linked lists, this procedure prints out headings and the contents of the lists.}

```
begin
    {Step 1: Display list of skis in shop}
    writeln ('SKIS IN THE SHOP');
    PrintList (Shop);

    {Step 2: Display list of rented skis}
    writeln ('SKIS RENTED OUT');
    PrintList (Rented);

    {Step 3: Display list of skis being repaired}
    writeln ('SKIS BEING REPAIRED');
    PrintList (Repair)
end;
```

FIGURE 8-85
Procedure **DisplayProc.**

```
procedure PrintList (
    List: ListType        {Input, list to be printed}
                        );
```
{Given a pointer to a list, this procedure prints out the IDNo and SkiSize fields of each element in the list.}

```
var
    Current: ListType;      {List traversal pointer}
begin
    {Step 1: Empty list?}
    if List = nil
    then writeln ('List is empty');

    {Step 2: Print the list}
    Current := List;
    while Current <> nil do
        begin
            with Current ↑ do
                writeln (IDNo, SkiSize);
            Current := Current ↑ .Link
        end
end;
```

FIGURE 8-86
Procedure **PrintList.**

Now that these major procedures have been written, the main program, given in Fig. 8-87, is very simple. Step 2 sets up the loop which terminates when a read has failed. Step 3 reads in a transaction type code. The fourth step is made up of a nested if structure. The value of **TransactionCode** is selected from five alternatives, and control branches to the appropriate alternative. For each value of **TransactionCode**, there is an associated procedure which regulates the type of transaction specified. A default case is included so that errors in entries can be detected. (This is why a nested if structure was used instead of a case structure.)

If the processing is to be run daily, then the program should save the contents of the lists in a sequential file when the processing is completed. The next time the program is run, it can restore the lists to their status at the end of the previous run by reading this file. Steps 1 and 5 achieve this

```
program SkiRental (input, output);
{This program regulates the record system of a ski-rental shop, processing
   the day's transactions. It starts by reading the initial status of the three
   lists. It then processes transactions as described in the text. On encoun-
   tering end of file in the input stream, it saves the contents of the lists for
   the next day's processing.}
const
   StringLength = 8;
type
   ConditType = (Poor, Fair, Average, Good, Excellent);
   ListType = ↑ NodeType;
   NodeType =
      record
         Condition: ConditType;
         SkiSize: integer;
         IDNo: integer;
         RentDate: integer;
         ReturnDate: integer;
         Link: ListType
      end;
   StringType = packed array [1 .. StringLength] of char;

var
   Shop: ListType;              {List of skis in the shop}
   Rented: ListType;            {List of rented skis}
   Repair: ListType;            {List of skis in the service room}
   TransactionCode: StringType; {Transaction code}

{Include procedures ShopInsert, RentInsert, ShopDelete, RentDelete, RentProc,
   ReturnProc, ServProc, BuyProc, DisplayProc, PrintList, LInitialize, Insert,
   Remove, InitList, SaveList, ReadCondition, and ReadString here}
```

**FIGURE 8-87**
**Program to process ski rentals.**

result by calling procedures InitList and SaveList. Design of these procedures is left as an exercise.

## 8-9.3  HASH-TABLE TECHNIQUES

The best search method introduced so far (binary search) has a search time which is proportional to $\log_2 n$ for a table of $n$ entries. In this section we investigate a class of search techniques whose search times can be independent of the number of entries in a table. To achieve this goal, an entirely new approach to searching must be used. With this approach, the position of a particular entry in the table is determined by the value of the key for that entry. This association is realized through the use of a hashing function.

```
begin
    {Step 1: Initialize the lists for the beginning of the day}
    InitList (Shop, Rented, Repair);

    {Step 2: Set up the loop}
    while not eof do
        begin

            {Step 3: Read in a transaction code}
            ReadString (TransactionCode);

            {Step 4: Select proper action}
            if TransactionCode = 'RENT'
            then RentProc (Shop, Rented)
            else
                if TransactionCode = 'RETURNED'
                then ReturnProc (Rented, Repair)
                else
                    if TransactionCode = 'SERVICE'
                    then ServProc (Repair, Shop)
                    else
                        if TransactionCode = 'BUY'
                        then BuyProc (Shop)
                        else
                            if TransactionCode = 'DISPLAY'
                            then DisplayProc (Shop, Rented, Repair)
                            else writeln ('No such transaction as ', TransactionCode)
        end;

    {Step 5: Save status of lists at end of day}
    SaveList (Shop, Rented, Repair)
end.
```

**FIGURE 8-87** (*cont.*)

The notions and concepts of this new approach are first discussed. General simple hashing functions are then introduced. Unfortunately, more than one key can be mapped into the same table position. In such a case, collisions are said to occur. These collisions must be resolved using a collision-resolution technique. Two broad classes of such techniques are examined.

### Notation and Concepts

Data can be represented in many ways. In this section we are given a collection of data entities. Each entity contains, in general, several information fields. Recall from Chap. 5 that such an entity was represented by a *record structure*. The record structures are combined into a table which represents the information upon which the operations of searching, insertion, and deletion are to be performed. Each field in a record structure contains, in general, alphanumeric data. The organization of a record structure is application-dependent and has little bearing on the algorithms discussed later in the section.

A *table*, for the purposes of this presentation, is defined to be an ordered sequence of $n$ records. Each record in a table contains one or more keys. It is with respect to these keys that processing is performed. For example, the key associated with a record could be a variable name in a symbol-table application in a compiler. Equally, it could be an employee number in a payroll application. Each record, for our purpose, is assumed to contain a single key field $K_i$ and additional information which is irrelevant to the present discussion. The term "table" throughout the discussion is similar to an array of structures, which was discussed in Chap. 5. One difference between the two data structures is that a table element will have a pointer field which will denote a pointer to some other table entry.

There are many applications of tables. For example, an important part of a compiler is the construction and maintenance of a symbol table of variable names for a source program, as discussed in Sec. 5-5.1. The importance of a symbol table is best realized when we consider that every occurrence of a variable name in a program requires continual table interaction. Symbol-table access time in a Pascal-like compiler can represent a significant portion of the translation time if improper searching techniques are used. This time can be significantly reduced if a suitable table organization is chosen.

The best search method introduced so far is the binary search technique, which has a search time of $O(\log_2 n)$. The linear and binary search techniques are both based exclusively on comparing keys. Another approach, however, is to compute the location of the desired record. The nature of this computation depends on the key set (or space) and the memory-space requirements of the particular table. For example, if we have a number key whose value lies between 1 and $n$, the key value of a particular employee, used as a subscript, directly locates the employee in question. Such a convenient key-location relationship rarely exists in real-world applications. This is so because key values are chosen for many reasons, most of which are unrelated to efficient computer processing goals.

For example, in a symbol-table application involving FORTRAN, the key space involves all the valid variable names in that language. Because

FORTRAN names contain at most 6 characters, the first of which must be a
letter and the remainder of which must be letters or digits, this name space
has a size of

**681**

8-9
APPLICATIONS OF
LINKED LINEAR LISTS

$$26 + 26 \times 36 + 26 \times 36^2 + \cdots + 26 \times 36^5 \approx 1.6 \times 10^9$$

that is, 26 names of one letter, $26 \times 36$ names of two characters, and so on.
For a typical program, this name space is associated with a table space of
perhaps 100 or 200 record locations. Consequently, the problem of directly
associating a key with the storage location of its associated record in a search
is more difficult.

Formally, this *key-to-address transformation* problem is defined as a
mapping or a *hashing function H*, which maps the key space $K$ into an
address space $A$. That is, given a key value, a hashing function $H$ produces a
table address or location of the corresponding record. The function generates
this address by performing some simple arithmetical or logical operations on
the key or some part of the key.

Since, as previously indicated, the key space is usually much larger than
the address space, many keys will be matched to the same address. Such
a many-to-one mapping results in *collisions* between records. A collision-
resolution technique is required to resolve these collisions.

In the next subsection we examine some of the most popular hashing
functions. The collision-resolution problem is examined in a subsequent subsection. The most important operations performed on hash tables are those
of access and retrieval.

**Hashing Functions**

In this subsection we examine several simple hashing functions. Some of
the desirable properties of a hashing function include speed and the generation of addresses uniformly. Before describing these functions, however,
we introduce the notion of preconditioning as it relates to the key space $K$.
Each element of $K$ often contains alphanumeric characters. Some of these
characters may be arithmetically or logically difficult to manipulate. It is
sometimes convenient to convert such keys into a form that can be more
easily manipulated by a hashing function. This conversion process is often
called *preconditioning*. As an example, let us consider the preconditioning of the key RATE1. One possibility is to encode the letters as the numbers 11, 12, . . . , 36 and the set of special symbols (for example, $+$ , $-$ ,
$*$, /, . . .) as 37, 38, 39, . . . . Using this approach, RATE1 is encoded as
2811301501 (that is, the symbols R, A, T, E, and 1 are replaced by the
integers 28, 11, 30, 15, and 01, respectively).

Preconditioning is most efficiently performed by using the numerically
coded internal representation (for example, EBCDIC or ASCII) of each character in the key. For example, in ASCII, the key A1 is binary-encoded as
1000001 0110001. Interpreted as a 14-digit binary number, this has a decimal equivalent of 8369. Similarly, the EBCDIC representation of A1 is
binary-encoded as 11000001 11110001 or 49,649. In general, the preconditioned key may not fit into a word of memory. In such instances, we can

ignore certain digits of the preconditioned result. Another approach is to use a hashing function which performs a size-reduction transformation. Frequently, one hashing function generates the preconditioned result and then a second function maps this result into a table location.

We now proceed to describe four simple hashing functions. Other more complex functions exist, but they are not generally used with tables that are stored entirely in the main memory of the computer.

**The Division Method.** One of the first hashing functions, and perhaps the most widely accepted, is the *division method*, which is defined as

$$H(x) = x \bmod m + 1$$

for some integer divisor $m$. Recall that the operator **mod** denotes the modulo arithmetic system. In this system, the term $x \bmod m$ (for positive $x$ and $m$) has a value which is equal to the remainder of dividing $x$ by $m$. For example, if $x = 35$ and $m = 11$, then

$$H(35) = 35 \bmod 11 + 1 = 2 + 1 = 3$$

The division method yields a "hash value" which belongs to the set $\{1, 2, \ldots, m\}$.

In mapping keys to addresses, the division method preserves, to a certain extent, the uniformity that exists in a key set. Keys which are close to each other or clustered are mapped to unique addresses. For example, for a divisor $m = 31$, the keys **1000, 1001**, . . . , and **1010** are mapped to the addresses 9, 10, . . . , and 19. This preservation of uniformity, however, is a disadvantage if two or more clusters are mapped to the same addresses. For example, if another cluster of keys is **2300, 2301**, . . . , **2313**, then these keys are mapped to addresses 7, 8, . . . , and 20, and there are many collisions with keys from the cluster starting at **1000**. The reason for this phenomenon is that keys in the two clusters yield the same remainder when divided by $m = 31$.

In general, it is uncommon for a number of keys to yield the same remainder when $m$ is a large prime number. In practice, it has been found that odd divisors without factors less than 20 are also satisfactory. In particular, divisors which are even numbers are to be avoided because even and odd keys would be mapped to odd and even addresses, respectively (assuming an address space of $\{1, 2, \ldots, m\}$).

**The Midsquare Method.** Another hashing function which has been widely used in many applications is the *midsquare method*. In this method, a key is multiplied by itself and an address is obtained by selecting an appropriate number of bits or digits from the middle of the square. Usually, the number of bits or digits chosen depends on the table size and, consequently, can fit into one computer word of memory. The same positions in the square must be used for all products. As an example, consider a six-digit key **123456**. Squaring this key results in the value **15241383936**. If a three-digit address is required, positions 5 to 7 could be chosen, giving address 138. The midsquare method has been criticized by some, but it has given good results when applied to certain key sets.

**The Folding Method.** In the *folding method*, a key is partitioned into a number of parts, each of which has the same length as the required address, with the possible exception of the last part. The parts are then added together, ignoring the final carry, to form an address. If the keys are in binary form, the "exclusive-or" operation may be substituted for addition. As an example, assume that the key **356942781** is to be transformed into a three-digit address. In the *fold-shifting method*, 356, 942, and 781 are added to yield 079. A variation of the basic method involves the reversal of the digits in the outermost partitions. This variation is called the *fold-boundary method*. In the previous example, 653, 942, and 187 are added together, yielding 782. Folding is a hashing function which is also useful in converting multiword keys into a single word so that other hashing functions can be used.

**The Length-Dependent Method.** Another hashing technique which has been commonly used in table-handling applications is called the *length dependent method*. In this method, the length of the key is used along with some portion of the key to produce either a table address directly or, more commonly, an intermediate key which is used, for example, with the division method to produce a final table address. One function that has produced good results sums the internal binary representation of the first and last characters and the length of the key shifted left four binary places (or, equivalently, the length multiplied by 16). As an example, the key **PARTNO** becomes $215 + 214 + (6 \times 16) = 525$ assuming EBCDIC representation. If we treat 525 as an intermediate key and apply the division method with a divisor of 49, then the resulting address is 36.

Thus far we have described how to perform key-to-address transformations using hashing functions. We have, however, ignored a very important aspect relevant to this process—the problem of colliding records. In general, a hashing function is a many-to-one mapping. That is, many keys can be transformed into the same address. In practice, such a phenomenon happens because there are many more keys than there are addresses. Clearly, two records cannot occupy the same location in a table. Consequently, such collisions among keys must be resolved. We now turn our attention to this problem.

### Collision-Resolution Techniques

As mentioned earlier, a hashing function can, in general, map several keys into the same address. When this situation arises, the colliding records must be stored and accessed as determined by a *collision-resolution technique*. There are two broad classes of such techniques: open addressing and chaining. In this subsection we formulate programs from both classes. Also, we examine certain variations of these basic techniques.

The general objective of a collision-resolution technique is to attempt to place colliding records elsewhere in the table. This requires the investigation of a series of table positions until an empty one is found to accommodate a colliding record. We require a mechanism to generate the series of table positions to be examined. The main criteria for this mechanism are speed (that it determine the positions quickly), coverage (that it will try *every* table position eventually), and reproducibility (that the series produced can be produced again, namely, when it comes time to find the placed record).

With *open addressing*, if a record with key $x$ is mapped to an address location $d$ and this location is already occupied, then other locations in the table are examined until a free location is found for the new record. If a record with key $K_i$ is deleted, then $K_i$ is set to a special value called Delete, which is not equal to the value of any key. The sequence in which the locations of a table are examined can be formulated in many ways. One of the simplest techniques for resolving collisions is to use the following sequence of locations for a table of $m$ entries:

$$d, d + 1, \ldots, m - 1, m, 1, 2, \ldots, d - 1$$

An unoccupied record location is always found if at least one is available; otherwise, the search halts unsuccessfully after scanning $m$ locations. When retrieving a particular record, the same sequence of locations is examined until that record is found or until an unoccupied (or empty) record position is encountered. In this latter case, the desired record is not in the table, so the search fails. This collision-resolution technique is called *linear probing*.

We present a procedure in Fig. 8-88 which performs the table-insertion operation for a hash table using the linear probing technique just described. It is assumed that if a record location has never contained a record, then the corresponding key field has the value defined by the global constant Empty. Similarly, a location containing a deleted record has the value Delete.

In step 1 an initial position in the table is calculated. Any of the hashing functions which were discussed in the previous subsection can be used in this step. The second step sets up a loop to scan the table starting at the initial position. In step 3 the procedure checks if the record to be inserted is already in the table. If it is, an error message is displayed and the procedure is terminated. If the current position in the hash table is free, then step 4 inserts the new record at that location and terminates the procedure. Step 5 increments the position. Position 1 is considered to follow the last position. If the initial position is reached without finding a free position, then the table is full. An error message is displayed and the procedure terminates.

The lookup operation is similar to the insertion operation and is left as an exercise.

As an example of this open addressing technique, let us assume the following:

*1.* The names PAY and RATE are mapped into 1.

*2.* The name TAX is mapped into 2.

*3.* The name PENSION is mapped into 4.

*4.* The names DEDUCT, STATUS, DEPENDENTS, SEX, and SALARIED are mapped into 8.

Assume that the insertions are performed in the order PAY, RATE, TAX,
PENSION,DEDUCT, STATUS, DEPENDENTS, SEX, and SALARIED.

**685**

8-9
APPLICATIONS OF
LINKED LINEAR LISTS

Figure 8-89 represents the resulting structure with $m = 11$. Since the table is empty initially, the first key is placed in a single probe. The second key (RATE), however, must go into position 2 instead of 1, which is already occupied. TAX, which is placed in position 3, also requires two probes for its placement, since position 2 is already occupied. PENSION is placed in position 4 in one probe. DEDUCT is also placed in position 8 in one probe, but STATUS, DEPENDENTS, and SEX take two, three, and four probes, respectively. Finally, SALARIED is placed in position 5 after nine probes because positions 8, 9, 10, 11, 1, 2, 3, and 4 are all occupied. A lookup operation is completed successfully when the desired record is found or unsuccessfully if an empty record is encountered or the entire table is searched. Since all steps of the previous algorithm apply to both insertion and lookup operations, the number of probes required for lookups is the same as that for insertions.

For a uniformly distributed set of keys, the linear probing technique performs reasonably well when compared to the linear and binary search techniques, provided that the table is not too full. That is, the ratio of the number of records being entered ($n$) to the table size ($m$) must be less than approximately 0.8. This ratio is known as the *load factor*. For higher load factors, the linear probe method degenerates rapidly. This phenomenon is due to an increased number of collisions as more records are being stored in the table.

The linear probe method of collision resolution has a number of drawbacks. In particular, deletions from the table are difficult to perform. The strategy used here was to have a special table entry with a value of Delete to denote the deletion of that entry. Such an approach enables the table to be searched in a proper way. As an example, let us assume that the record with key PAY in Fig. 8-89 is marked for deletion by assigning a value of Delete to Table[1].Key. Now, if we desire to retrieve the record with a key value of RATE, the previously stated program still behaves properly. The question which arises is: Why use a special value such as Delete to denote deleted entries? If this approach were not used, duplicate entries could occur in the table. For example, in the previous case, our program would find an empty location in position 1 and assume that RATE is not in the table. It would then proceed to insert a duplicate entry for RATE. It is possible to formulate a deletion algorithm that performs deletions immediately by moving records, if necessary. Such an algorithm eliminates the necessity for having records with a value of Delete. In other words, a record position can be either occupied or empty. This approach is not taken, however, because better collision-resolution techniques (based on linked allocation) are available.

Another drawback of the linear probe method is caused by *clustering* effects, whose severity increases as the table becomes full. This phenomenon is observed by considering a trace of Fig. 8-88, which shows the state of the table after performing each insertion. This trace is given in Fig. 8-90. When the first insertion (PAY) is made, the probability of inserting this element in a particular position is 1 in 11. For the second insertion, (RATE), however, the

**procedure** OpenLpInsert (
  X: KeyType;                {Input, key of record to be
                                 inserted/retrieved}
  Info: OtherInfoType       {Input, other information}
                          );
{Given a key, and other information, this procedure performs an insertion
  into a hash table. The global hashing function Hash is used to calculate
  an initial position. Table is a global array of record structures having Key
  (of KeyType) and Data (of OtherInfoType) fields. Size is a global constant
  specifying the size of the table. Empty and Delete are global constants (of
  KeyType) specifying entries are empty or deleted.}
**var**
  J: integer;                {Loop index}
  InitPos: integer;          {Hash value}
  NotDone: Boolean;          {Loop control flag}
**begin**
  {Step 1: Calculate initial position}
  InitPos : = Hash (X);

  {Step 2: Find corresponding key}
  J : = InitPos;
  NotDone : = true;
  **while** NotDone **do**
    **begin**

      {Step 3: Check for error condition}
      **if** X = Table[J].Key
      **then begin**
            writeln ('Error in insertion—key already in table');
            NotDone : = false
      **end**
      **else begin**

**FIGURE 8-88**
**Hash table insertion.**

probability that position 2 will be selected is twice that of any other empty
position. That is, the second entry will be placed in position 2 if the second
key is hashed into either 1 or 2. Continuing in this manner, on the fourth
insertion the probability that the new entry (PENSION) is placed in position
4 is four times as likely as it being placed in any other unoccupied position.
Consequently, long sequences of occupied positions tend to become longer.
This kind of clustering phenomenon is called *primary clustering*.

The detrimental effect of primary clustering can be reduced by selecting
a different probing technique. Such a technique exists and is called *random
probing*. This method generates a random sequence of positions rather than
an ordered sequence, as was the case in the linear probing method. The random sequence generated in this fashion must contain every position between
1 and $m$ exactly once. A table is full when the first duplicate position is

```
{Step 4: Perform insertion}
if (Table[J].Key = Empty) or (Table[J].Key = Delete)
then begin
        Table[J].Key : = X;
        Table[J].Data : = Info;
        NotDone : = false
    end
end;
```

```
{Step 5: If an empty location has not been found, go to next entry}
if NotDone
then begin
        J : = J + 1;
        if J > Size
        then J : = 1;
        if J = InitPos
        then begin
                writeln('Table Overflow');
                NotDone : = false
            end
    end
end;
end;
```

FIGURE 8-88 *(cont.)*

generated. An example of a random-number generator that produces such a random sequence of position numbers is the statement

$$y \leftarrow (y + c) \bmod m$$

where $y$ is the initial position number of the random sequence and $c$ and $m$ are integers that are relatively prime to each other (that is, their greatest common divisor is 1). For example, assuming that $m = 11$ and $c = 5$, the

| | | | Number of probes |
|---|---|---|---|
| $R_1$ | PAY | | 1 |
| $R_2$ | RATE | | 2 |
| $R_3$ | TAX | | 2 |
| $R_4$ | PENSION | | 1 |
| $R_5$ | SALARIED | | 9 |
| $R_6$ | Empty | | |
| $R_7$ | Empty | | |
| $R_8$ | DEDUCT | | 1 |
| $R_9$ | STATUS | | 2 |
| $R_{10}$ | DEPENDENTS | | 3 |
| $R_{11}$ | SEX | | 4 |

**FIGURE 8-89**
**Collision resolution**
**with open addressing.**

previous statement, starting with an initial value of 2, generates the sequence 7, 1, 6, 0, 5, 10, 4, 9, 3, 8, and 2. Adding 1 to each number of this sequence transforms all numbers so that they belong to the interval [1, 11]. Procedure OpenLpInsert can easily be modified to incorporate the random probing method. This modification, however, is left as an exercise.

The deletion problem becomes more severe with random probing than is the case with linear probing. Therefore, if a table is subjected to many deletions, random probing should not be used.

Although random probing has alleviated the problem of primary clustering, we have not eliminated all types of clustering. In particular, clustering occurs when two keys are hashed into the same value. In such an instance, the same sequence of positions is generated for both keys by the random probe method. This clustering phenomenon is called *secondary clustering*.

One approach to alleviating this secondary clustering problem is to have a second hashing function, independent of the first, select the parameter $c$ in the random probing method. For example, let us assume that $H_1$ is the first hashing function, with $H_1(x_1) = H_1(x_2) = i$ for $x_1 \neq x_2$ where, $i$ is the hash value. Now, if we have a second hashing function $H_2$ such that $H_2(x_1) \neq H_2(x_2)$ when $x_1 \neq x_2$ and $H_1(x_1) = H_1(x_2)$, we can use $H_2(x_1)$ or $H_2(x_2)$ as the value of parameter $c$ in the random probe method. The two random sequences generated by this scheme are different when $H_2$ and $H_1$ are independent. The effects of secondary clustering can, therefore, be curtailed. This variation of open addressing is called *double hashing* (or *rehashing*).

As a concrete example of this method, let

$$H_1(x) = x \bmod m \qquad \text{and} \qquad H_2(x) = [x \bmod (m-2)] + 1$$

for a key $x$ and table size $m$. For a table size $m = 11$ and a key value $x = 75$,

**FIGURE 8-90** **Trace of insertions using open addressing.**

After inserting record

Contents of table after current insertion

| | | | | | | | | | | | |
|---|---|---|---|---|---|---|---|---|---|---|---|
| PAY | PAY | | | | | | | | | | |
| RATE | PAY | RATE | | | | | | | | | |
| TAX | PAY | RATE | TAX | | | | | | | | |
| PENSION | PAY | RATE | TAX | PENSION | | | | | | | |
| DEDUCT | PAY | RATE | TAX | PENSION | | | DEDUCT | | | | |
| STATUS | PAY | RATE | TAX | PENSION | | | DEDUCT | STATUS | | | |
| DEPENDENTS | PAY | RATE | TAX | PENSION | | | DEDUCT | STATUS | DEPENDENTS | | |
| SEX | PAY | RATE | TAX | PENSION | | | DEDUCT | STATUS | DEPENDENTS | SEX | |
| SALARIED | PAY | RATE | TAX | PENSION | SALARIED | | DEDUCT | STATUS | DEPENDENTS | SEX | |

$H_1(75) = 9$ and $H_2(75) = 4$. Now, the repeated application of the statement

$$y \leftarrow (y + c) \bmod 11$$

with $y = 9$ and $c = 4$ produces the sequence

$$9, 2, 6, 10, 3, 7, 0, 4, 8, 1, 5$$

Next, if we choose a key having a value of 42, then

$$H_1(42) = 9 \quad \text{[the same value as } H_1(75), \text{ but } H_2(42) = 7]$$

The repeated application of the statement

$$y \leftarrow (y + c) \bmod 11$$

with $y = 9$ and $c = 7$, yields the sequence

$$9, 5, 1, 8, 4, 0, 7, 3, 10, 6, 2$$

Note that even though $H_1(75) = H_1(42) = 9$, the two random sequences generated are different.

This double-hashing technique outperforms the linear probing method, especially as the table becomes full. For example, when a table is 95 percent full, the average number of probes for the linear probe method is 10.5, while for the double-hashing method it is 3.2—a significant improvement!

In summary, there are three main difficulties with the open addressing method of collision resolution. First, lists of colliding records for different hash values become intermixed. This phenomenon requires, on average, more probes. Second, we are unable to handle a table overflow situation in a satisfactory manner. On detecting an overflow, the entire table must be reorganized. The overflow problem cannot be ignored in many table applications where table space requirements can vary drastically. Finally, the physical deletion of records is difficult. We now turn to linked-allocation techniques to resolve these problems.

One of the most popular methods of handling overflow records is called *separate chaining*. In this method, the colliding records are chained into a special *overflow area* which is distinct from the *prime area*. This area contains that part of the table into which records are initially hashed. A separate linked list is maintained for each set of colliding records. Therefore, a pointer field is required for each record in the primary and overflow areas. Figure 8-91 shows a separate chaining representation of the sample keys used earlier in this subsection, with $m = 11$ and $n = 9$. The keys are assumed to be inserted in the order PAY, RATE, TAX, PENSION, DEDUCT, STATUS, DEPENDENTS, SEX, and SALARIED. Note that the colliding records in each linked list are not kept in alphabetical order. When a new colliding record is entered in the overflow area, it is placed at the front of those records in the appropriate linked list of the overflow area.

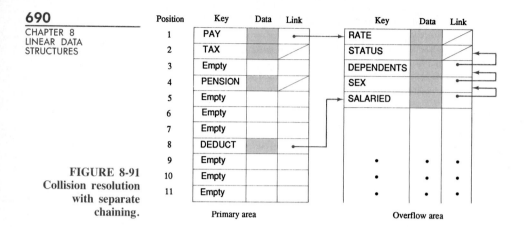

FIGURE 8-91
Collision resolution
with separate
chaining.

A useful and more efficient representation of the separate chaining technique involves the use of an intermediate table or hash table. Figure 8-92 illustrates how a hash table is used, assuming the same keys, hashing function, and collision-resolution technique as in Fig. 8-91. Note that in this representation all the records reside in the overflow area while the prime area contains only pointers. For a table having large records, this approach results in a densely packed overflow area. Furthermore, the hash table whose entries are pointers can be made large without wasting very much storage.

An algorithm for entering a key into an existing structure such as that of Fig. 8-92 is easily realized. Given a key X, which is to be entered if it is not already in the table, we first proceed to obtain its hash value. The hash-table value for this hash value can then be examined. A value of **nil** in this position indicates that the corresponding linked list is empty. Therefore, we can insert the given key into an empty list. If, however, the particular linked list in question is not empty, we can search this linked list for the

FIGURE 8-92   Separate chaining with a hash table.

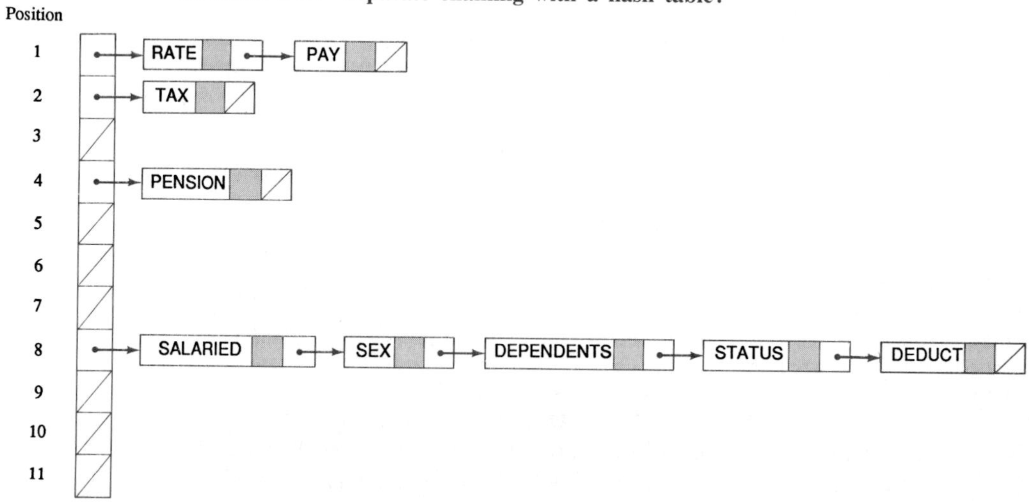

presence of the given key. If the search fails, X becomes the front entry of the updated linked list.

We first present the general algorithm for the operation:

1. Compute the hash number

2. If the pointer field referenced is empty,
    then allocate storage
        set its fields
        append the node to the front of the linked list

3. Repeat step 4 while a duplicate name is not found and the end of the linked list is not reached

4. Obtain the next name in the linked list

5. If a duplicate name was not found,
    then allocate storage
        set its fields
        append the node at the front of the linked list

6. Return

The implementation of this process is left as an exercise.

A function to search for a particular key is easily constructed and is left as an exercise. Similarly, a record can be easily deleted from its associated linked list. Also, for certain applications, such as symbol tables in compilers, it may be convenient to have all colliding records in a linked list ordered. In such applications, an alphabetical list of all variable names is desirable.

In terminating this subsection, we want to stress the importance of having a suitable hashing function. Ideally, each linked list of colliding records should have the same number of entries. The worst possible case occurs when all keys are mapped to the same hash number (that is, the same linked list), thereby causing the insertion and search operations to be no more efficient than those in a linear search method. In practice, it is a nontrivial matter to obtain a good hashing function, since the size of the linked lists of colliding records which it induces depends on the keys being used.

Another important factor pertaining to the efficiency of the separate chaining method of collision resolution is the desirability of keeping the number of records in each linked list relatively small. For example, a table of 100 entries would nicely handle 125 records in the overflow area. The average number of comparisons (assuming a uniformly distributed hashing function) for accessing a particular entry in such a situation is slightly greater than 1. From this observation it is clear that the search time in such a table organization is independent of the number of entries in the table.

Finally, since our discussion has been concerned with internal tables (that is, tables that are stored in memory at one time), the hashing function used should be simple. The response time to insert or fetch a particular entry is the sum of the times taken to evaluate the hashing function and to perform the indicated operation. It may be more efficient to allow a greater number of comparisons for performing a table operation if a significant reduction in the complexity of the hashing function results.

## EXERCISES 8-9.3

1. Using the division method of hashing with $m = 101$, obtain the hash values for the following set of keys:

   PAY

   AGE

   RATE

   NUMBER

   Assume an EBCDIC (see Sec. 6-1) representation of the keys. Recall that in EBCDIC, there are gaps in the collating sequence between I and J and between R and S. Thus A is 193, B is 194, . . . , I is 201, J is 209, . . . , R is 217, S is 226, . . . , and Z is 233.

2. Repeat exercise 1 for the ASCII representation of the keys. In this representation, A is 65, B is 66, . . . , Z is 90.

3. Assuming an open addressing method of collision resolution with linear probing, obtain the hash table (see Fig. 8-89) for the the following set of keys:

   The name **NODE** is mapped into 1.

   The name **STORAGE** is mapped into 2.

   The names **AN** and **ADD** are mapped into 3.

   The names **FUNCTION**, **B**, **BRAND**, and **PARAMETER** are mapped into 9.

   Use the division method of hashing with $m = 11$ and the ASCII collating sequence. Also, assume that the insertions are performed in the following order: **NODE**, **STORAGE**, **AN**, **ADD**, **FUNCTION**, **B**, **BRAND**, and **PARAMETER**.

★ 4. Formulate a procedure, based on the linear probe method, for deleting a record from a hash table. This procedure is not to use a special value of **Delete**. That is, each record position is to be either occupied or empty.

   One approach that can be used is first to mark the deleted record as empty. An ordered search is then made for the next empty position. If a record, say $y$, is found whose hash value is not between the position of the record just marked for deletion and that of the present empty position, then record $y$ can be moved to replace the deleted record. Then the position for record $y$ is marked as empty and the entire process is repeated, starting at the position occupied by $y$.

★ **5.** Construct a searching procedure based on double hashing.

★ **6.** Construct a function OpenLpLookup, corresponding to procedure OpenLpInsert, which locates a particular record, given its key, in a hash table consisting of an array of structures.

★ **7.** Construct a procedure Enter which inserts a record into a table with a separate hash table. The procedure has two parameters—X, the record key, and Info, additional record information.

★ **8.** Construct a function Lookup, corresponding to procedure Enter in Exercise 7, which locates a particular record, given its key, in a table with a separate hash table.

## CHAPTER SUMMARY

A new and important class of data structure is introduced in this chapter—the linear list. Unlike arrays, the size of a linear list can vary during the execution of an algorithm. Up to this point, multiple element data structures (such as vectors and arrays) have relied on and been constrained by the inherently sequential nature of computer storage. Elements *logically* adjacent (e.g., an element and its successor or predecessor) are, by and large, *physically* adjacent as well.

With linked allocation, we are no longer constrained by these physical characteristics. Individual elements can exist anywhere in memory; access is by means of links or pointers to them. For many applications this greatly simplifies the data management parts of the algorithms.

In this chapter, basic notions of linked allocation are introduced including issues of storage and representation. Implementations of two common data structures—the stack and the queue—are presented and discussed at length. Applications of each are developed and discussed. Among these are applications dealing with compilers, recursion (including its implementation), and simulation.

Various types of linked structures are described, including singly linked lists, circularly linked lists, and doubly linked lists. Basic operations on each are developed and illustrated through applications. Among these is a lengthy discussion of the important notion of hashing.

## KEY TERMS

addressing function
availability list
chaining collision resolution
circular queue
circularly linked linear list
clustering
collision

column-major order
computed-address method
controlled storage
degree of an operator
deletion
deque
deterministic element

division method of hashing
domain type
double hashing
doubly linked circular list
doubly linked linear list
dynamic allocation
event-driven (next-event) simulation
FCFS (first-come first-served)
FIFO (first-in first-out)
folding method of hashing
fully parenthesized infix expressions
goto statement
halt procedure
hash table
hashing function
heap (availability list)
infix notation
insertion
key
key-to-address transformation
label declaration
length-dependent method of hashing
linear list
linear probing
linked allocation
list
list element (node)
list head node
load factor
midsquare method of hashing
nil pointer
open addressing collision resolution
operator precedence
overflow area
partition exchange sort (quicksort)
Pascal variable notation
pointer (link)
pointer-address (link-address) method
pointer type

pointer type denoter
Polish notation
pop
preconditioning
postfix Polish notation
prefix Polish notation
primary clustering
prime area
priority queue
procedure epilogue
procedure prologue
pseudo-random number generator
push
queue
queue overflow
queue underflow
quicksort
radix sort
random probing
rank of a Polish expression
recursion
recursive binary search
row-major order
secondary clustering
separate chaining
sequential allocation
side effect
simulation
singly-linked linear list (one-way
    chain)
stack
stack overflow
stack underflow
statement label
stochastic element
suffix Polish notation
time-driven (fixed interval)
    simulation

## CHAPTER EXERCISES

★ 1. Write a recursive function which, when presented with a lower triangular
real matrix $A$ as well as its order $n > 1$, returns the value of the determinant of $A$. Recall that the determinant of a lower triangular matrix $A$

of order $n$ is the product of the element appearing in the $n$th row, $n$th column of $A$ and the determinant of the lower triangular matrix obtained by deleting the $n$th row and the $n$th column of $A$. Thus the determinant of a lower triangular matrix of order $n$ is simply the product of the elements on the main diagonal. *Note*: A matrix is lower triangular if all entries above the main diagonal are zero. The matrix $A$ given is lower triangular of order 5:

$$A = \begin{bmatrix} 1.2 & 0.0 & 0.0 & 0.0 & 0.0 \\ 2.3 & 4.6 & 0.0 & 0.0 & 0.0 \\ 1.0 & 3.3 & 9.3 & 0.0 & 0.0 \\ 5.1 & 2.4 & 8.4 & 7.6 & 0.0 \\ 2.7 & 4.9 & 8.3 & 8.6 & 2.5 \end{bmatrix}$$

★ 2. Write two queue procedures QueueInsert(Q, V, D) and QueueDelete(Q, V, D) to perform insertion and deletion, respectively, on the given queue, where Q is a stack, V is the value being inserted or deleted, and D is a status flag which is set to "true" if the operation is done and "false" otherwise. To perform these operations, you may use only the stack operations StackPop, StackPush, StackEmpty, and StackTopVal.

★★ 3. In the post office, mail is processed in a priority queue under normal conditions. As bags arrive in the receiving room, they are distributed to sorters on a first-in, first-out (FIFO) basis, subject to the priority of first class mail over second and of first and second over third.

If the bag count exceeds the capacity of the receiving room, the distribution system clogs and the receivers change strategy. Not every bag can now be seen, so they switch to handling the recent deliveries which are obscuring the earlier arrivals on a last-in, first-out (LIFO) basis. In summary, the mail room operates as a priority queue when the bag count is below some threshold and operates as a stack when the count exceeds the threshold.

Devise a data structure to represent the mail room. Define operations for receiving a bag of mail (insertion), expedition of a bag to a sorting station (deletion), finding out the number of bags in the room, and initializing the data structure. These four operations should be in the form of procedures and/or functions. Also, write a main program to read a sequence of operations and to apply the operations in order to a structure. After application of each operation, the main program should display the contents of the bag room/structure.

The data will consist of a number representing the threshold bag count followed by a sequence of codes indicating insertions, deletions, and bag counts. Following each insertion code in the data will be a description of the bag being inserted. This description will consist of a number (1, 2, or 3) indicating the class and a single letter which will serve as an identifier. Use the end-of-file method to detect the end of the input.

★★ **4.** You are required to add two sparse (containing many zeros) but large (100,000 element) vectors A and B to form a resultant vector C. However, your computer does not have enough memory to store the 100,000 elements of each vector. Since only a small portion of the vector (approximately 1 percent) is nonzero, it is possible to store the elements of each vector in a linked list as follows:

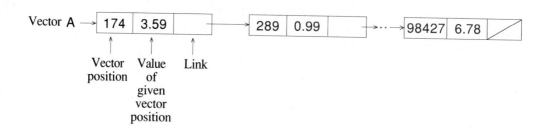

Note that the first nonzero element of vector A is $A[174] = 3.59$. Also, $A[289] = 0.99$ and the last nonzero element of A is $A[98427] = 6.78$. Each node describes one nonzero element of a vector and is defined as:

**type**
    NodePointer = ↑ NodeType;
    NodeType =
      **record**
        VectorPos: integer;
        Value: real;
        Link: NodePointer
      **end**;

Write a function Add(A, B) which will return a pointer to the new linked list resulting from the addition of the two vectors stored in the linked lists pointed to by A and B.

★ **5.** *(a)* You are to specify procedures/functions that handle the insertion and deletion operations for a priority queue with $n$ levels. The priority queue is implemented as a circular linked list in which there are $n$ pointers, one per priority level, pointing to the rear elements of each queue. In particular, the pointer Rear[i], for $1 \leq i \leq n$, points to the last element in the set of queue elements with priority level i. This arrangement is illustrated in Fig. 8-93 for $n = 3$ where element $q_{ij}$ represents the $j$th element in the set of queue elements for level i.

A *deletion* operation always involves the removal of the element in front of the nonempty queue with the highest level of priority. This Front element can always be found by examining the element pointed to by the rear element in the queue. Therefore, in Fig. 8-93, element $q_{11}$ would be deleted first followed by $q_{12}, q_{21}, q_{22}, q_{23}, q_{31}$, assuming no insertions take place.

An *insertion* of an element X into the queue at level j would involve the placement of X just after the element that is currently at the end of the list of queue elements at level j. Therefore, if X is to be inserted at level 2, it would be inserted after element $q_{23}$, as shown in Fig. 8-93.

Note that if queue j is empty, then its associated **Rear** pointer is assigned a **nil** value. Therefore, when element $q_{31}$ is deleted, **Rear[3]** is set to **nil**.

(b) Assume a priority queue of 3 levels that is initially empty and is subjected to the following sequence of operators:

Insert A at level 2.

Insert B at level 2.

Insert C at level 3.

Insert D at level 1.

Insert E at level 2.

Deletion.

Insert F at level 2.

Deletion.

Draw a schematic diagram similiar to Fig. 8-93 representing the state of the priority queue after the completion of the previous list of operations.

(c) Write a program to test your procedures/functions.

6. Given the double hashing scheme with a pair of hashing functions

$$H_1(x) = x \bmod 13 \quad \text{and} \quad H_2(x) = x \bmod 11 + 1$$

**FIGURE 8-93** **Priority queue with three levels.**

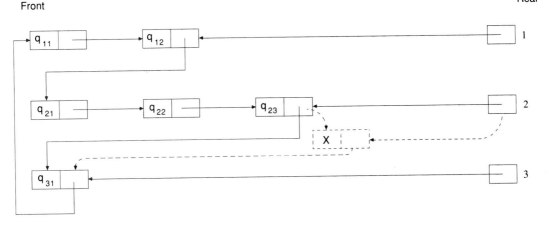

| | | |
|---|---|---|
| 0 | | |
| 1 | 27 | |
| 2 | | |
| 3 | | |
| 4 | 17 | |
| 5 | | |
| 6 | | |
| 7 | | |
| 8 | 47 | |
| 9 | 61 | |
| 10 | | |
| 11 | 37 | |
| 12 | | |

**FIGURE 8-94**

and the initial hash table given in Fig. 8-94, show the hash table before and after each of the following insertions along with the associated sequence of random probes:

82, 108, 71, 84, 51

# CHAPTER 9

# NONLINEAR DATA STRUCTURES

All data structures discussed thus far are linear. That is, the relationship that can be expressed by such data structures are essentially one-dimensional. In this chapter we introduce two classes of nonlinear data structures, namely, trees and graphs. The tree is perhaps the most important structure. A tree structure is capable of expressing more complex relationships than that of physical adjacency.

The chapter begins with a description of notation and concepts for trees. Section 9-2 discusses storage structures for binary trees, operations and manipulations that are frequently performed on binary tree structures, and implementation of these operations. Particular attention is given to linked storage structures, since, in general, they are best suited to the representation of trees that are subjected to insertions and deletions. The third section contains further discussions of general trees, including their representation by binary trees and other methods. Section 9-4 presents several applications of trees. Among these are the applications of trees to searching and sorting. Finally, Sec. 9-5 contains a brief introduction to graph structures.

## 9-1 TREE NOTATION AND CONCEPTS

In this section we first consider the definition of a general tree and its associated terminology. A number of examples of trees are given. Several equivalent forms for representing trees are introduced. For reasons of simplicity and efficiency, it is convenient to define and manipulate binary trees instead of general trees. Each general tree is easily converted to an equivalent binary tree. An informal discussion of this conversion process is presented.

Trees are very useful in describing any structures that involve hierarchical relationships. Familiar examples of such structures are family trees, the decimal classification of books in a library, the hierarchy of positions in an organization, an algebraic expression involving operations for which certain rules of precedence are prescribed, and the structure of the contents of this chapter.

There are two types of charts used in the investigation of genealogies. The first type, exhibited in Fig. 9-1a, is called a *pedigree chart*. This chart specifies a person's ancestors. In the example chart given, André's parents are Paul and Deanna. Paul's parents are Philip and Anna, who are André's grandparents on his father's side. The chart continues to the great-grandparent stage. Note that in this chart we have two-way branching. The second type of chart is called a *lineal chart*. Such a chart describes the descendants of an individual, as shown in Fig. 9-1b. In general, this chart can have many-way branching. The structure exhibited by a lineal chart is clearly different from the pedigree chart. Both are trees, however.

A partial organizational chart for a university is exemplified in Fig. 9-2. This chart exhibits the chain of command (or hierarchy) in the institution. The president is the highest level of command. The second level of command involves the academic and administrative vice presidents. The academic vice president controls a number of colleges, each of which has a

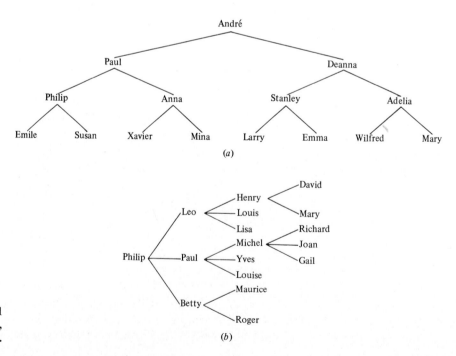

FIGURE 9-1
(a) Pedigree chart,
(b) lineal chart.

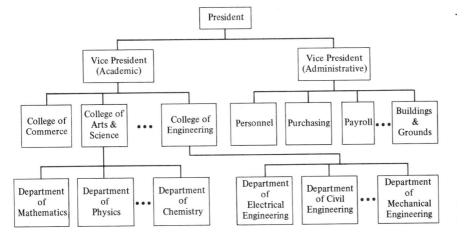

**FIGURE 9-2**
**Partial organizational chart of a university.**

dean. Each dean, in turn, controls several departments, each of which has a department head.

As a final example, consider the table of contents chart given for Chap. 9 (Fig. 9-3). This chapter contains five sections. The last four sections are each further divided into subsections.

All the tree structures introduced so far have a number of properties in common. First, in each tree there is a distinguished item or node called its *root*. For example, the root node in Fig. 9-1a is "André." A node which does not have any lines or branches emanating from it is called a *terminal node* or *leaf*; all other nodes are called *branch nodes*. Also, all trees have a finite number of nodes.

Let us now formalize the notion of a tree. Several definitions are possible. One popular definition involves defining a general graph and then restricting this graph to obtain a tree. Since we have not dealt with graphs up to this point in this book, we do not use this approach. In Sec. 9-5, however, we will see how this approach can be used to define a tree. As we shall see throughout this chapter, trees can be handled easily within a recursive framework. As a first step in that direction, a tree can be defined recursively as follows: A *tree* is a finite set of one or more nodes such that

*1.* There is a specially designated node called the *root*.

*2.* The remaining nodes are partitioned into disjoint subsets $T_1, T_2, \ldots, T_n$ $(n \geq 0)$, each of which is a tree. Each $T_i$ $(1 \leq i \leq n)$ is called a *subtree* of the root.

As an example, Fig. 9-4 represents a tree of 12 nodes. The root of the tree is $v_0$. The three subtrees of this root node are the subsets $T_1 = \{v_1, v_2, v_3, v_4, v_5, v_6\}$, $T_2 = \{v_7\}$, and $T_3 = \{v_8, v_9, v_{10}, v_{11}\}$. The subsets are themselves trees according to this definition (remember, it's recursive). The

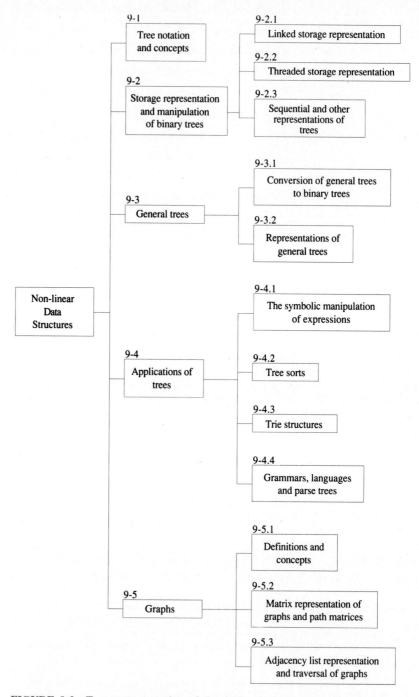

**FIGURE 9-3  Tree representation of the table of contents for Chap. 9.**

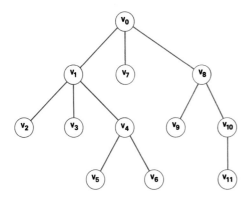

FIGURE 9-4

root of $T_1$, for example, is node $v_1$ and it has three subtrees: $T_{11} = \{v_2\}$, $T_{12} = \{v_3\}$, and $T_{13} = \{v_4, v_5, v_6\}$. The tree $T_{11}$ contains a root node (that is, $v_2$), which is a leaf. The subtree $T_{12}$ also contains a leaf node. $T_{13}$ has a root node ($v_4$) and two subtrees ($v_5$ and $v_6$). The remaining parts of the tree can be analyzed in a similar manner. Figure 9-4 is only one possible diagram for the example tree; many other diagrams are possible for the same tree. These alternative diagrams are obtained by choosing different relative positions of the nodes with respect to the root. The representation chosen here is the one that is most commonly used in the literature.

An important notion in dealing with trees is that of the level of a node. The *level* of any node is 1 plus the length of its path from the root. Consequently, the level of the root of a tree is 1, while the level of any other node is equal to 1 plus its distance from the root. Another important property of a node is its degree. The *degree* of a node is its number of subtrees. For example, the tree in Fig. 9-4 has one node of level 1, three nodes of level 2, five nodes of level 3, and three nodes of level 4. The root node has a degree of 3, and $v_{10}$ is of degree 1. The degree of a leaf is 0.

In many applications, the relative order of children of a node at any particular level is important. In a storage representation of a tree, such an order, even if it is arbitrary, is automatically implied. It is easy to impose an order on the children of a node at each level by referring to a particular node as the first child, to another node as the second child, and so on. In the diagrams the ordering may be done from left to right. A tree whose nodes at each level are so ordered is called an *ordered tree*. For example, the trees in Fig. 9-5 are equivalent as far as trees are concerned, but they represent different ordered trees. Since we are interested primarily in ordered trees in this chapter, we use the term "tree" to mean "ordered tree" unless otherwise stated.

As mentioned earlier, family trees are perhaps one of the earliest applications of trees. They have left their mark as far as terminology is concerned. In fact, much of standard tree terminology is taken from the lineal chart (such as Fig. 9-1*b*). Each root is called the parent, father, or mother of the roots of its subtrees, which in turn are denoted as siblings, brothers, or

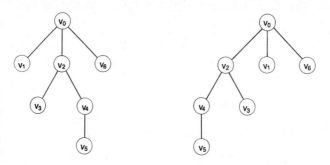

**FIGURE 9-5**
Equivalent trees
with different
ordered tree
representations.

sisters. The latter nodes are called offspring, sons or daughters, of the parent node. For example, in Fig. 9-4, $v_0$ is the parent node, which has three offspring or direct descendants. Node $v_1$, in turn, also has three offspring, $v_2$, $v_3$, and $v_4$, which are siblings. $v_0$ is the grandparent of $v_2$ and the great-grandparent of $v_5$. The node $v_1$ is an uncle or aunt of $v_9$.

If we delete the root and its associated branches which connect the nodes at level 1, we obtain a set of disjoint trees. Such a set of disjoint trees is called a *forest*. We also have seen that any node of a tree is the root of some subtree. Therefore, subtrees immediately below a certain node form a forest.

There are many other ways in which a tree can be represented graphically. These methods of representation for the tree of Fig. 9-4 are given in Fig. 9-6a through d. The first method uses a familiar technique known as *Venn diagrams* to show subtrees, the second involves the use of nested parentheses to show structure and adjacency, and the third method is the one used in the table of contents of a book. The last method, which is based on a level-number format, is similar to techniques used in programming languages such as PL/1 and COBOL for specifying hierarchical structures. Using this format, each node is assigned a number. The root of the tree has the smallest number. The number associated with a given node must be less than the numbers associated with the root nodes of its subtrees. Note that all the root nodes of the subtrees of a given node must have the same level number.

The method of representation given in Fig. 9-6b indicates how any completely parenthesized algebraic expression can be represented by a tree structure. Naturally, it is not necessary to have a completely parenthesized expression if we prescribe a set of precedence rules, as discussed in Sec. 8-5.1. As an example, consider the expression

$$v_1 - v_2 * (v_3 * v_4 + v_5 \uparrow v_6)$$

The tree corresponding to this expression is given in Fig. 9-7.

So far we have not placed any restriction on the degree of a node (that is, the number of branches which emanate from a node). If the degree of every node is less than or equal to 2, then the tree is called a *binary tree*. Furthermore, in binary trees we distinguish between the left subtree and the right subtree of each node. No such distinction between subtrees was made

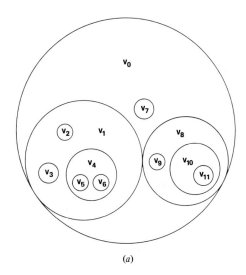

(a)

$(v_0 (v_1 (v_2) (v_3) (v_4 (v_5) (v_6))) (v_7) (v_8 (v_9) (v_{10} (v_{11}))))$

(b)

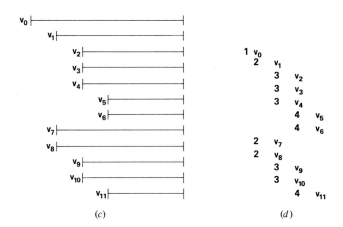

(c)                    (d)

FIGURE 9-6
Different
representations of
trees: (a) Venn
diagram; (b) nested
parentheses; (c) bar
chart; (d) level-
number notation.

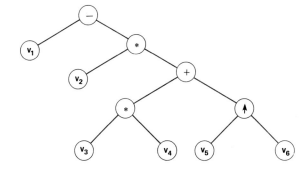

FIGURE 9-7
Tree representation
of an arithmetic
expression.

in the case of an ordered tree. The following definition incorporates these restrictions:

> *A binary tree is a finite set of m (m ≥ 0) nodes, which is either empty (m = 0) or consists of a root node which has two disjoint binary subtrees called the left subtree and the right subtree. A binary tree of zero nodes is said to be empty.*

A binary tree in which each node is of degree 0 or 2 is called a *complete binary tree*. Figure 9-8a is an example of a binary tree, Fig. 9-8b shows a complete binary tree, and Fig. 9-8c displays another binary tree. Note that although the trees of Fig. 9-8a and c are not distinct ordered trees, these two trees are certainly two distinct binary trees.

Since binary trees are easily represented and manipulated, it is convenient to convert any tree to an equivalent binary form, if possible. We shall now show that every tree can indeed be represented by an equivalent binary tree. This correspondence is a one-to-one relationship. This notation can be extended to represent a forest by a binary tree.

Figure 9-9 shows in two steps how to convert an ordered tree into its binary equivalent. In the first step, we delete all the branches originating in every node except the left-most branch. Also, we connect all siblings at the same level by branches. That is, the first sibling is connected to the second, the second is connected to the third, and so on. The second step involves choosing the left and right offspring for each node. This task is accomplished in the following manner. The left offspring is the node immediately below the given node, and the right offspring is the node to the immediate right of the given node on the same horizontal line. The resulting binary tree has an empty right subtree.

The preceding method of representing any ordered tree by a unique binary tree can be extended to an ordered forest, as shown in Figure 9-10. This correspondence is called the *natural correspondence* between ordered trees and binary trees, as well as between ordered forests and binary trees. A program to perform the indicated conversion will be given in Sec. 9-3.1.

In this section we have examined certain basic notions and concepts

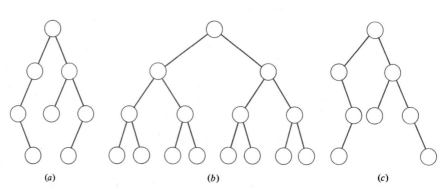

**FIGURE 9-8**
**Examples of binary trees and complete binary tree.**

(a)  (b)  (c)

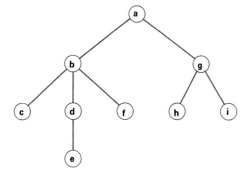

Stage 1

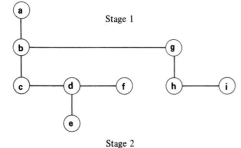

Stage 2

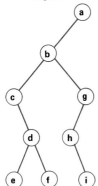

**FIGURE 9-9**
**Binary tree**
**representation of**
**a tree.**

associated with tree structures. The storage representation of binary trees will be described in the next section. A number of operations on binary trees and the implementation of these operations will be examined. Finally, several alternative representations will be briefly considered.

## EXERCISES 9-1

1. How many different trees are there with three nodes? How about ordered trees and binary trees?

2. Give an ordered tree representation of the expression

$$[(a-b)*c]/(d+f \uparrow g)$$

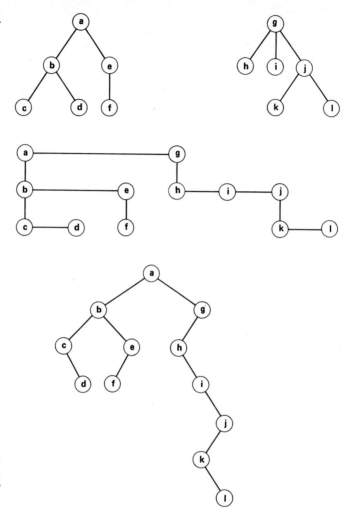

**FIGURE 9-10**
**Binary tree**
**representation of**
**a forest.**

3. Give the subtrees of the tree given in Fig. 9-11. Also, give the level and degree of each node in this tree.

4. Give the binary trees that correspond to the tree and forest in Figs. 9-11 and 9-12, respectively.

## 9-2 STORAGE REPRESENTATION AND MANIPULATION OF BINARY TREES

The previous section introduced the notions of a binary tree structure. Little mention, however, was made of how these trees are stored or of what types of operations are performed on such structures. In Chap. 8 the storage (computer) representations of certain elementary data structures such as

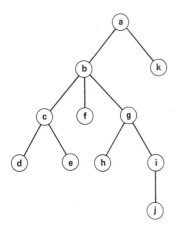

FIGURE 9-11

linear lists and arrays were presented. In this section we extend these concepts to tree structures.

Linked- and sequential-allocation techniques will be used to represent these tree structures. The advantages and disadvantages of each allocation technique also were presented in Chap. 8. In this section we will give greater emphasis to linked storage structures. These linked structures are more popular than their corresponding sequential structures because, in performing insertions and deletions, the linked structures are more easily altered. Furthermore, since the size of a tree structure is often unpredictable, linked-allocation techniques are more appropriate.

The linked storage representation of binary trees is introduced first. Based on this representation, several programs, such as those for traversing and copying tree structures, are given. The concept of "threaded" binary trees is then introduced. The storage representation of a tree based on the threading concept is efficient from the point of view of both time and space. Finally, several sequential-allocation techniques for binary trees are examined.

## 9-2.1  LINKED STORAGE REPRESENTATION

Since a binary tree consists of nodes that can have at most two offspring, an obvious linked representation of such a tree is expressed by the following Pascal type definitions:

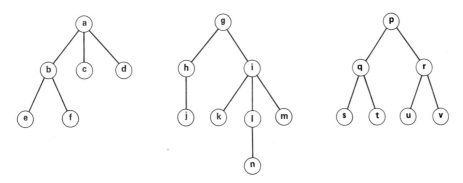

FIGURE 9-12

```
type
    BinTreeType = ↑ BinNodeType;
    BinNodeType =
        record
            Info: BinInfoType;
            Lptr, Rptr: BinTreeType
        end;
```

where **Lptr** and **Rptr** denote pointers to the left and right subtrees, respectively, of a particular root node. Empty subtrees are represented by a pointer value of **nil**. **Info** specifies the information contents of a node, which are, of course, application-specific.

Figure 9-13 contains an example of a binary tree and its linked storage representation. The pointer variable T denotes the address of the root node. The two forms are remarkably similar. This similarity illustrates that the linked storage representation of a binary tree very closely reflects the logical structuring of the data involved. This property is very useful and desirable in designing algorithms which process binary tree structures. We now introduce several of these algorithms and their implementation in Pascal.

**Traversals**

One of the most common operations performed on tree structures is that of *traversal*. This is a procedure by which each node in the tree is visited (or

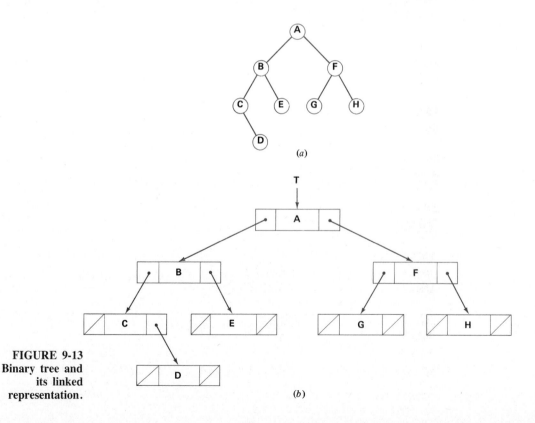

FIGURE 9-13
Binary tree and
its linked
representation.

processed) exactly once in a systematic manner. The meaning of "processed" depends on the nature of the application. For example, the tree in Fig. 9-14 represents an arithmetic expression. In this context, the processing of a node that represents an arithmetic operation would probably mean performing or executing that operation. Other applications would supply different meanings to the "processing" of a node but all involve transversals.

There are three main ways of traversing a binary tree: in inorder, in preorder, and in postorder. We now examine each traversal order. The easiest way to define each order is by using recursion.

The *inorder traversal* of a binary tree is given by the general algorithm:

*1.* If the tree is empty, then exit

*2.* Traverse the left subtree in inorder

*3.* Process the root node

*4.* Traverse the right subtree in inorder

If a particular subtree is empty (that is, a node has no left or right descendant, the traversal is performed by doing nothing. In other words, a null subtree is considered to be fully traversed when it is encountered. Otherwise, we traverse the left subtree (in inorder) and then the right. The inorder traversal of the example tree given in Fig. 9-14 results in the following processing order:

A∗B −C ↑ D + E / F

A recursive Pascal procedure for the recursive inorder traversal of a binary tree is easily formulated and is given in Fig. 9-15. A program to implement this definition is straightforward (we assume that we wish simply to print the information contents of each node). Note that the types BinNodeType and BinTreeType are global to the procedure. A trace of the inorder traversal of the sample expression is given in Table 9-1.

The *preorder traversal* of a binary tree is defined by the following general algorithm:

*1.* If the tree is empty, then exit

*2.* Process the root node

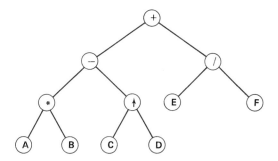

**FIGURE 9-14**
**Binary tree**
**representation of**
**an expression.**

**procedure** Rinorder (T: BinTreeType {Input, pointer to root of tree} );
{Given a binary tree represented as described, this procedure traverses the
   tree in inorder. Each node is processed by displaying its information.}
**begin**
  {Step 1: If the tree is empty, simply return}
  **if** T <> **nil**
  **then begin**

        {Step 2: Traverse the left subtree of node T}
        Rinorder (T ↑ .Lptr);

        {Step 3: Display the information contents of the root node}
        writeln (T ↑ .Info);

        {Step 4: Traverse the right subtree of node T}
        Rinorder (T ↑ .Rptr)
  **end**
**end**;

**FIGURE 9-15**
**Recursive procedure**
**for inorder traversal**
**of a binary tree.**

**TABLE 9-1**   Trace of Inorder Traversal of a Binary Tree

| Invocation Level of Inorder Procedure | Information Content of Root of Tree | Action |
|---|---|---|
| 0 (main) | '+' | |
| 1 | '−' | |
| 2 | '*' | |
| 3 | 'A' | |
| 4 | Empty subtree | Process 'A' |
| 4 | Empty subtree | Process '*' |
| 3 | 'B' | |
| 4 | Empty subtree | Process 'B' |
| 4 | Empty subtree | Process '−' |
| 2 | '↑' | |
| 3 | 'C' | |
| 4 | Empty subtree | Process 'C' |
| 4 | Empty subtree | Process '↑' |
| 3 | 'D' | |
| 4 | Empty subtree | Process 'D' |
| 4 | Empty subtree | Process '+' |
| 1 | '/' | |
| 2 | 'E' | |
| 3 | Empty subtree | Process 'E' |
| 3 | Empty subtree | Process '/' |
| 2 | 'F' | |
| 3 | Empty subtree | Process 'F' |
| 3 | Empty subtree | |

*3.* Traverse the left subtree in preorder

*4.* Traverse the right subtree in preorder

As an example, let us consider the tree given in Fig. 9-14. The preorder traversal of this tree gives the following processing order:

+ − ∗ A B ↑ C D / E F

Note that this traversal order yields the same result as the prefix Polish equivalent of the expression, as discussed in Sec. 8-5.1.

The recursive Pascal procedure given in Fig. 9-16 closely follows the general algorithm of preorder traversal.

Finally, we define the *postorder traversal* of a binary tree by the following general algorithm:

*1.* If the tree is empty, then exit

*2.* Traverse the left subtree in postorder

*3.* Traverse the right subtree in postorder

*4.* Process the root node

The postorder traversal of the sample tree gives the following processing order:

A B ∗ C D ↑ − E F / +

which is equivalent to the expression's suffix Polish form. We leave the formulation of the recursive Pascal procedure as an exercise.

```
procedure Rpreorder (T: BinTreeType {Input, pointer to root of tree} );
{Given a binary tree represented as described, this procedure traverses the
    tree in preorder. Each node is processed by displaying its information.}
begin
    {If the tree is empty, simply return}
    if T <> nil
    then begin

            {Step 1: Display the information contents of the root node}
            writeln (T ↑ .Info);

            {Step 2: Traverse the left subtree of node T}
            Rpreorder (T ↑ .Lptr);

            {Step 3: Traverse the right subtree of node T}
            Rpreorder (T ↑ .Rptr)
       end
end;
```

**FIGURE 9-16**
**Recursive procedure**
**for preorder**
**traversal of a**
**binary tree.**

We introduce at this point the notions of a predecessor and a successor which are associated frequently with tree traversals. A *successor* of a given node with respect to a particular traversal order is the next node to be processed or visited with respect to that traversal order. In the current example, the preorder successor of + is − and the inorder successor of E is /. Similarly, a *predecessor* of a given node with respect to a certain traversal order is the node that was just visited with respect to that order. In the current example, the preorder predecessor of * is − and the postorder predecessor of * is **B**. Observe that the first node of a traversal order has no predecessor and the last node of a traversal order has no successor.

If the words "left" and "right" are interchanged in the definitions for traversals, we obtain three new traversal orders, which are called *converse preorder*, *converse inorder*, and *converse postorder*, respectively. The converse traversal orders for the example tree in Fig. 9-14 are

+ / F E − ↑ D C * B A    (converse preorder)
F / E + D ↑ C − B * A    (converse inorder)
F E / D C ↑ B A * − +    (converse postorder)

We will not, however, pursue the applicability of these converse traversals in this book.

Since some programming languages do not allow recursion or implement it very inefficiently, we are sometimes forced to traverse iteratively rather than recursively, which is more natural. Iterative implementations require that we deal explicitly with much of the housekeeping detail performed automatically in the recursion. For example, it is required to descend and subsequently to ascend parts of the tree. For this reason, information that will permit movement up the tree must be temporarily saved. Downward movement in the tree is made possible through the structural links on pointers. Because movement up the tree must be made in a reverse manner from that taken in descending the tree, temporary pointer values to previously visited nodes must be stacked as the tree is traversed. A general algorithm for the iterative preorder traversal of a binary tree is now given:

*1.* If the tree is empty, then exit

*2.* Place the address of the root node of the tree on the stack

*3.* Repeat step 4 while the stack is not empty

*4.* Pop the stack and place its top element in current pointer
   Repeat while current pointer is not **nil**
      Write the data associated with current node
      If the right subtree is nonempty,
      then stack the pointer to the right subtree
      Set current pointer to address of left subtree of current node

The procedure in Fig. 9-17 iteratively traverses a binary tree in preorder printing the information contents of each node visited.

The procedure checks first for an empty tree and exits if T = **nil**. Otherwise, in step 2, it initializes the stack and stacks the address of the root node. Step 3 controls the processing of the tree. The addresses of yet untraversed subtrees are kept on the stack. In step 4 of the procedure, we process each node. The address of the right subtree, if it is not empty, is stacked and a left branch is taken. This left branching process (and the associated stacking of nonempty right subtree addresses) continues until we encounter an empty left link. At this point we unstack the address of the most recently encountered right subtree and continue processing it according to step 4. The behavior of this procedure for the binary tree in Fig. 9-13*b*

```
procedure Ipreorder (
    T: BinTreeType      {Input, pointer to root of tree}
                    );
{Given a binary tree whose root node address is given by a pointer variable
    T and whose node structure is the same as previously described, this
    procedure traverses the tree in preorder, in an iterative manner.}
var
    Current: BinTreeType;   {Denotes address of current node in the tree
                            during processing.}
    S: StackType;            {Stack of pointers to tree nodes}
{Include the stack routines StackInitialize, StackPush, StackPop, and
    StackEmpty (see Sec. 8-4).}
begin
    {Step 1: If the tree is empty, simply return}
    if T <> nil
    then begin

            {Step 2: Initialize stack}
            StackInitialize (S);
            StackPush (S, T);

            {Step 3: Process each stacked branch address}
            while not StackEmpty (S) do
                begin

                    {Step 4: Get stored address and branch left}
                    StackPop (S, Current);
                    while Current <> nil do
                        begin
                            writeln (Current ↑ .Info);
                            if Current ↑ .Rptr <> nil
                            then {Store address of nonempty right subtree}
                                StackPush(S, Current ↑ .Rptr);
                            Current := Current ↑ .Lptr {Branch left}
                        end
                end
        end
    end;
```

FIGURE 9-17
Iterative procedure
for preorder
traversal of a
binary tree.

appears in Table 9-2, where the right-most element in the stack is its top element. The notation **NB**, for example, denotes a pointer to node **B**. The processing of each node involves the output of the label associated with that node.

### Insertion

So far we have conveniently assumed that a tree somehow already exists. Let us now examine the problem of constructing a binary tree.

The approach taken in constructing a tree is often application-dependent. For example, the binary tree representation of an expression, such as that given in Fig. 9-14, depends on the left and right operands associated with each binary operator. In this particular example, an algorithm, based on the Polish notation discussion of Sec. 8-5.1, could be formulated. Rather than use the Polish-notation approach here, however, we shall assume that the desired tree is to be kept in some kind of order. The order that we choose throughout the remainder of this discussion is based on the information contents associated with each node. Suppose, for example, that a list of names is to be kept in lexical order. That is, the left subtree of the tree (or subtree) is to contain nodes whose associated names are lexically less that the name associated with the root node of the tree (or subtree). Similarly, the right subtree of the tree (or subtree) is to contain nodes whose associated names are lexically greater than the name associated with the root node of the tree (or subtree). An example of such a tree for a set of first names is given in Fig. 9-18. Note that the root node (Norma) lexically follows all names in its left subtree (Bill, John, Ken, Leo, and Maurice) and precedes all names in its right subtree (Paul and Roger). The same relationships hold for the root node of each subtree.

The tree in Fig. 9-18 can be created by the repeated use of an algorithm that can insert one node into an existing lexically ordered binary tree such that the tree is lexically ordered after insertion.

---

**TABLE 9-2** Behavior of Procedure **Ipreorder** for Fig. 9-13b

| Stack Contents | Current | "Process" Current | Output |
|---|---|---|---|
| NA | | | |
| | NA | A | A |
| NF | NB | B | AB |
| NF NE | NC | C | ABC |
| NF NE ND | nil | | |
| NF NE | ND | D | ABCD |
| NF NE | nil | | |
| NF | NE | E | ABCDE |
| NF | nil | | |
| | NF | F | ABCDEF |
| NH | NG | G | ABCDEFG |
| NH | nil | | |
| | NH | H | ABCDEFGH |

---

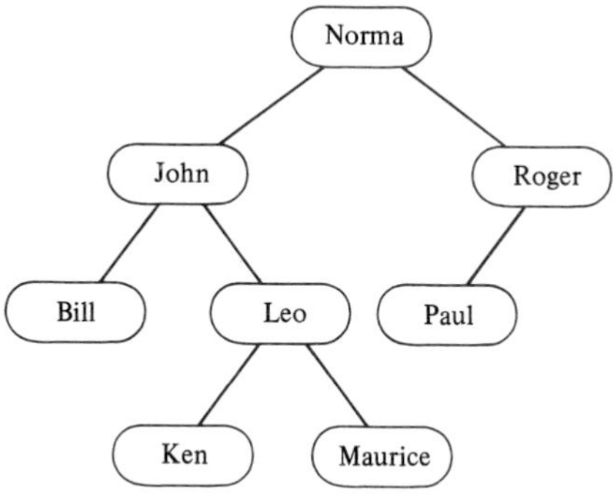

**FIGURE 9-18
Lexically ordered
binary tree of
eight names.**

A general algorithm for performing such an insertion is as follows:

*1.* If the existing tree contains no nodes,
then append the new node as the root node of the tree and exit

*2.* Set the current pointer to the root node

*3.* Repeat step 4 while the remaining tree is not empty

*4.* If the new name is lexically less than the current node's name,
then If the left subtree is not empty,
then set the current pointer to the root of the left subtree
else append the new name as a left leaf to the present tree
exit
else If the right subtree is not empty,
then set the current pointer to the root of the right subtree
else append the new name as a right leaf to the present tree
exit

It is often convenient in the manipulation of trees to have a tree with a head node as discussed in Sec. 8-8.3 for linear lists. Figure 9-19 represents a binary tree with a list head. The right link of the list head is assumed always to be **nil**. An empty binary tree takes the form of a list head whose left link is also **nil** (Fig. 9-20). Observe that we have chosen to append the tree as a left subtree to the list head node.

We now proceed to formulate a Pascal procedure that performs an insertion into a lexically ordered binary tree. We assume that the type of key associated with each node is alphabetic. We also assume that the storage representation of the ordered tree has a list head. Care must be taken to preserve order between the list head and the rest of the tree. This is accomplished easily by making the unused information field in the head node lexically greater than the information of any other node in the tree. In this way the tree will always be appended as a left subtree of the list head. The list head representation of such a lexically ordered tree is given in Fig. 9-21.

The Pascal procedure in Fig. 9-22 is a straightforward implementation of the general algorithm. Step 1 uses the function **CreateNode** to obtain and initialize a new tree node. Note that the while statement in step 2

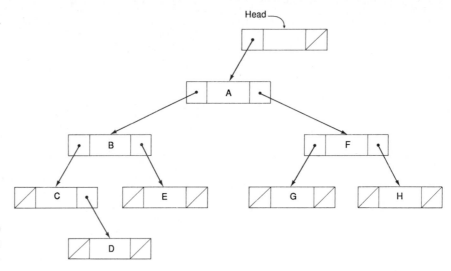

**FIGURE 9-19**
**Binary tree with**
**a list head.**

fails when the flag is set to "false." We check for empty left and right subtrees in step 3. On encountering such an empty subtree, we append the new node to the existing tree structure and set the flag to "false." Also, duplicate names are ignored (with an appropriate message being generated). The function **CreateNode** (Fig. 9-23) will be used in several of the programs and subprograms in this chapter.

The program in Fig. 9-24 invokes the procedure **IInsertNode** repeatedly in order to create a tree. The tree is then ready for processing. In this example, we merely traverse the tree in inorder. What is the result? The behavior of the insertion program in the construction of the tree given in Fig. 9-18 is exhibited in Fig. 9-25 (we have not explicitly shown the header node). assuming the following sequence of names for insertions:

Norma, Roger, John, Bill, Leo, Paul, Ken, and Maurice

This insertion procedure also can be implemented recursively. The general recursive algorithm for an insertion into a lexically ordered binary tree (with a list header, as described previously) is as follows:

*1.* If the input node's information field is lexically less than the information field of the current root node,
    then If the root node's left pointer is null,
        then insert the new node as the left subtree of the current root node and return
        else recurse on the left subtree of the current root node and return

**FIGURE 9-20   An empty binary tree with a list head.**

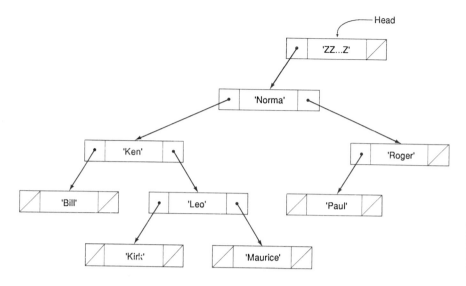

FIGURE 9-21
Lexically ordered
binary tree
with a list head.

2. If the input node's information field is lexically greater than the information field of the current root node,

then If the root node's right pointer is null,

then insert the new node as the right subtree of the current root node and return

else recurse on the right subtree of the current root node and return

3. A duplicate node has been found, so print an error message and return

Based on this general algorithm, we can now formulate the recursive Pascal procedure in Fig. 9-26.

The procedure is easy to understand. It is initially invoked with a pointer to the head node (recall that the left pointer of this node points to the root of the tree). The recursion controls the descent through the tree. Since a lexically ordered tree is such that every entry in a left subtree (or right subtree) lexically precedes (or follows) the root node, we know that whenever an empty subtree is found, this is where the new entry should go. A new node is inserted either to the left or to the right of the current root node being examined in the existing tree.

**Deletion**

Another common operation on a lexically ordered binary tree is the deletion of a designated node. Any node in the tree can be deleted, even its root. Consequently, a number of cases arise. A simple case occurs when the node marked for deletion contains an empty left and/or right subtree(s). Such a case is shown in Fig. 9-27a, where the node labeled Roger is deleted. If, however, it is required to delete a node whose left and right subtrees are nonempty, that node's inorder successor is deleted first and then used to replace the node initially marked for deletion. Note that the successor

```
procedure IInsertNode (
    Head: BinTreeType;      {Input, pointer to head node}
    X: BinInfoType          {Input, information to be added to tree}
                            );
```

{Given a pointer to the list head of a binary tree, and the information contents of a node which is to be appended to the existing tree structure, this procedure appends the indicated node as a leaf node, if it is not already there. This procedure assumes that the Info field of the header node is always greater than the value to be inserted. An iterative algorithm is used.}

```
var
    T: BinTreeType;             {Tree traversal pointer to current node}
    NewNode: BinTreeType;       {Pointer to new node}
    NotDone: Boolean;           {Loop control flag}
begin
    {Step 1: Initialize}
    T := Head;
    NewNode := CreateNode (X);

    {Step 2: Perform indicated insertion if required}
    NotDone := true;
    while NotDone do

        {Step 3: Find the location and append new node}
        if X < T ↑ .Info
        then
            if T ↑ .Lptr <> nil
            then T := T ↑ .Lptr
            else begin
                    T ↑ .Lptr := NewNode;
                    NotDone := false
                end
        else
            if X > T ↑ .Info
            then
                if T ↑ .Rptr <> nil
                then T := T ↑ .Rptr
                else begin
                        T ↑ .Rptr := NewNode;
                        NotDone := false
                    end
            else begin
                    writeln ('Duplicate node', X);
                    dispose (NewNode);
                    NotDone := false
                end
    end;
```

**FIGURE 9-22**
Iterative procedure to
insert a node into a
lexically ordered
binary tree.

```
function CreateNode (
    X: BinInfoType      {Input, information for new node}
                ):BinTreeType;
{Given information for a new binary tree node, this function creates a new
    node, initializes its information field with the given information, initializes
    its link fields to nil, and returns a pointer to the new node.}
var
    NewNode: BinTreeType;      {Pointer to new node}
begin
    {Step 1: Create a new node}
    new (NewNode);

    {Step 2: Initialize fields}
    with NewNode ↑ do
        begin
            Lptr : = nil;
            Info : = X;
            Rptr : = nil
        end;

    {Step 3: Return the new node}
    CreateNode : = NewNode
end;
```

FIGURE 9-23
Function CreateNode.

node in question always has an empty left subtree (by definition of inorder traversal). This second deletion possibility is illustrated in Fig. 9-27*b*, where John is marked for deletion. In this case, the inorder successor of John is Ken. This latter node replaces the former in the revised tree. In the deletion process, the right subtree of Ken (that is, Kirk) becomes the left subtree of Ken's parent (Leo). Also, Ken becomes the new left offspring of John's parent (that is, Norma).

We first present a general algorithm for tree deletion. In this algorithm, we again assume the existence of a header node.

*1.* Find the node marked for deletion and its parent. If the node to be deleted is the root, the head will be its parent

*2.* If the node is not found,
    then display an appropriate message and return

*3.* If the node being deleted has a left empty subtree,
    then append its right subtree to the parent node and return
    If the node being deleted has a right empty subtree,
    then append its left subtree to the parent node and return

*4.* Obtain the inorder successor of the node to be deleted and the parent of the inorder successor

```
program CreateTree (input, output);
```
{This program is an example of use of procedure IInsertNode. It creates a binary tree with list head. The input consists of a series of information items, each of which is an alphabetic string.}
```
const
    InfoLength = 8;
type
    BinInfoType = packed array [1 .. InfoLength] of char;
    BinTreeType = ↑ BinNodeType;
    BinNodeType =
        record
            Lptr: BinTreeType;
            Info: BinInfoType;
            Rptr: BinTreeType
        end;
var
    Head: BinTreeType;      {Pointer to head of tree}
    Name: BinInfoType;      {Name read}
    I: integer;             {Loop index}
```

{Include procedures IInsertNode and Rinorder here.}

```
begin
    {Step 1: Create head node for the tree}
    Head := CreateNode ('zzzzzzzz');

    {Step 2: Create desired tree}
    while not eof do
        begin
            for I := 1 to InfoLength do
                read (Name[I]);
            readln;
            IInsertNode (Head, Name)
        end;
```

**FIGURE 9-24**
**Program to create a lexically ordered binary tree.**

```
    {Step 3: Process tree in some way}
    Rinorder (Head)
end.
```

5. If the node to be deleted is the parent of its inorder successor,
   then append the left subtree of the node for deletion as the left subtree of its inorder successor (which has no left subtree)
   else append the right subtree of the successor as the left subtree of the successor's parent
   append the right subtree of the node to be deleted as the right subtree of its successor

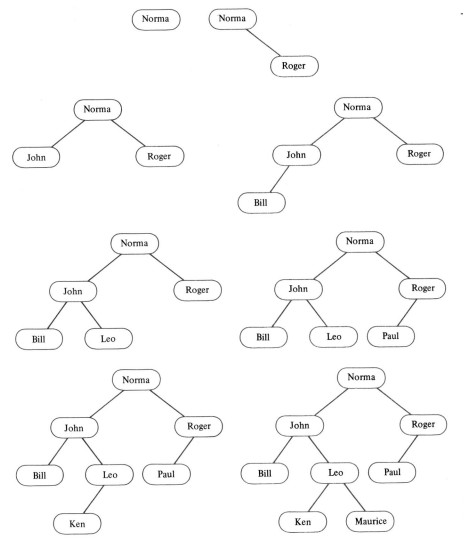

**FIGURE 9-25**
**Behavior of creating
a lexically
ordered tree.**

append the left subtree of the node to be deleted as the left
subtree of its successor
connect the parent of the node to be deleted to the inorder successor and return

The implementation of this algorithm is procedure **TreeDelete** in Fig.
9-28. This procedure calls on three other procedures to perform parts of
the deletion. Step 1 of the general algorithm is implemented as a procedure
**TreeSearch** in Fig. 9-29. Similarly, step 4 is implemented by the procedure
**FindInorderSuccessor** in Fig. 9-30. Finally, at two points in steps 3 and again
in step 5 the deleted node is disconnected from its parent and the parent

**procedure** RInsertNode (
   Root: BinTreeType;    {Input, pointer to head node}
   X: BinInfoType       {Input, information to be added to tree}
              );
{Given a pointer to the list head of a binary tree and the information contents of a node which is to be appended to the existing tree structure, this procedure appends the indicated node as a leaf node, if it is not already there. This procedure assumes the Info field of the header node is always greater than the value to be inserted. A recursive algorithm is used.}
**begin**
   {Step 1: Check left subtree}
   **if** X < Root ↑ .Info
   **then**
      **if** Root ↑ .Lptr = **nil**
      **then** Root ↑ .Lptr : = CreateNode (X)
      **else** RInsertNode (Root ↑ .Lptr, X)
   **else**

      {Step 2: Check right subtree}
      **if** X > Root ↑ .Info
      **then**
         **if** Root ↑ .Rptr = **nil**
         **then** Root ↑ .Rptr : = CreateNode (X)
         **else** RInsertNode (Root ↑ .Rptr, X)
      **else**

         {Step 3: Report duplicate node}
         writeln ('Duplicate node ', X)
**end**;

**FIGURE 9-26**
Recursive procedure to insert a node into a lexically ordered binary tree.

is connected to another node. The necessary operations are contained in ConnectToParent in Fig. 9-31.

## Copying

Another familiar operation involves making a copy of a tree. In many applications, the original tree may be destroyed during processing. In such situations, it is frequently desirable to make a duplicate copy of the original tree before processing begins. The following recursive general algorithm describes the copy operation:

*1.* If the tree is empty, then return **nil**

*2.* Create a new node and initialize information contents to that of the current node

*3.* Set the left pointer of the new node to the copy of the left subtree of the current node
Set the right pointer of the new node to the copy of the right subtree of the current node

*4.* Return address of new node

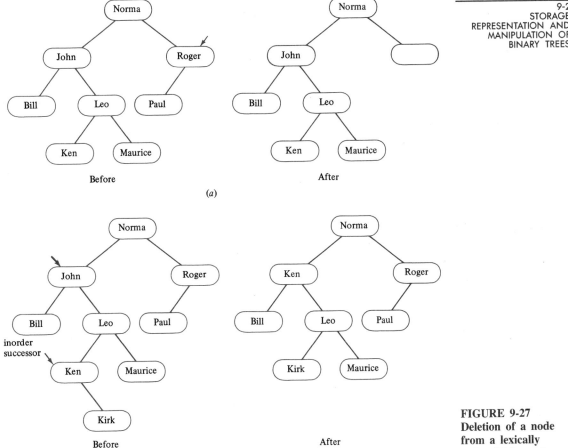

FIGURE 9-27
Deletion of a node
from a lexically
ordered binary tree.

We now give the recursive function that generates a copy of a tree in Fig. 9-32. This function is simple and requires no further comment. An iterative formulation of this operation is also possible. This version, however, is left as an exercise.

## 9-2.2 THREADED STORAGE REPRESENTATION

The wasted empty links in the storage representation of binary trees introduced in the previous subsection can be replaced by special links referred to as *threads*, which can ease subsequent manipulations.

A binary tree is *threaded* according to a particular traversal order. For example, the threads for the inorder traversal of a tree are pointers to its higher nodes. For inorder traversal, if the left link of a node **P** is normally **nil**, then this link is replaced by the address of the predecessor of **P** (inorder). Similarly, a normally **nil** right link is replaced by the address of the successor of the node in question. Because the left or right link of a node can denote either a structural link or a thread, we must somehow be able to distinguish them. A way of distinguishing a thread link from a structural link

```
procedure TreeDelete (
   Head: BinTreeType;      {Input, pointer to header node of lexically
                               ordered binary tree}
   X: BinInfoType          {Input, information content of node to be deleted
                               from tree}
                     );
```
{Given a pointer to a header node of a lexically ordered binary tree and the
information content of a node to be deleted, this procedure deletes the
node containing this information from the tree.}
```
var
   Current: BinTreeType;             {Pointer to node to be deleted}
   Parent: BinTreeType;              {Pointer to parent of node to be
                                        deleted}
   Successor, SucParent: BinTreeType;  {Pointer to the inorder successor
                                        of the node to be deleted and the
                                        successor's parent}
begin
   {Step 1: Find the node to be deleted}
   TreeSearch (Head, X, Current, Parent);

   {Step 2: Check for node not found}
   if Current = nil
   then writeln ('Node not found')
   else begin

         {Step 3: Check for an empty subtree}
         if Current ↑ .Lptr = nil
         then     {Empty left subtree}
            ConnectToParent (Current, Parent, Current ↑ .Rptr)
         else
            if Current ↑ .Rptr = nil
            then     {Empty right subtree}
               ConnectToParent (Current, Parent, Current ↑ .Lptr)
            else begin

                  {Step 4: Find inorder successor and its parent}
                  FindInorderSuccessor (Current, Successor, SucParent);

                  {Step 5: Perform deletion}
                  if Current = SucParent
                  then Successor ↑ .Lptr : = Current ↑ .Lptr
                  else begin
                        SucParent ↑ .Lptr : = Successor ↑ .Rptr;
                        Successor ↑ .Lptr : = Current ↑ .Lptr;
                        Successor ↑ .Rptr : = Current ↑ .Rptr
                     end;
                  ConnectToParent (Current, Parent, Successor)
               end;
      end;
end;
```

**FIGURE 9-28**
Procedure TreeDelete.

```
procedure TreeSearch (
    Head: BinTreeType;          {Input, pointer to header node of
                                   lexically ordered binary tree}

    X: BinInfoType;             {Input, information content of node to be
                                   found}

    var Current: BinTreeType;   {Output, pointer to desired node}
    var Parent: BinTreeType     {Output, pointer to parent of desired
                                   node}
                  );
```

{Given a pointer to the header node of a lexically ordered binary tree with the node structure previously described and the information value of a node to be found, this procedure finds the node containing that information and returns, via its output parameters, pointers to that node and its parent. Note that we have assumed the presence of a header node with an information content greater than any other tree node, and a right link of nil.}

```
var
    NotFound: Boolean;          {Loop termination flag}
begin
    {Step 1: Initialize}
    Parent : = Head;
    Current : = Head ↑ .Lptr;
    NotFound : = true;

    {Step 2: Search for node with specified information}
    while (Current <> nil) and NotFound do
        if Current ↑ .Info = X
        then NotFound : = false
        else begin
            Parent : = Current;
            if X < Current ↑ .Info
            then Current : = Current ↑ .Lptr    {Branch Left}
            else Current : = Current ↑ .Rptr    {Branch right}
        end
end;
```

FIGURE 9-29
Procedure TreeSearch.

is to have a two-valued flag for each of the left and right pointers. Using this approach, the node structure becomes that shown in Fig. 9-33, where LFlag and RFlag are the indicators associated with the left and right links, respectively. The following coding scheme is used to distinguish between a structural link and a thread:

| | |
|---|---|
| LFlag = Link | Denotes a left structural link |
| LFlag = Thread | Denotes a left thread link |
| RFlag = Link | Denotes a right structural link |
| RFlag = Thread | Denotes a right thread link |

**procedure** FindInorderSuccessor (
    Current: BinTreeType;      {Input, pointer to node to be deleted}
    **var** Successor: BinTreeType;   {Output, pointer to inorder successor of
                                    Current}

    **var** SucParent: BinTreeType   {Output, pointer to parent of Successor}
                                              );
  {Given a pointer to a node in a lexically ordered binary tree, this procedure
    returns pointers to the specified node's inorder successor and the succes-
    sor's parent.}
**begin**
    {Step 1: Initialize for search}
    SucParent : = Current;
    Successor : = Current ↑ .Rptr;

    {Step 2: Search for successor}
    **while** Successor ↑ .Lptr <> **nil do**
      **begin**
        SucParent : = Successor;
        Successor : = Successor ↑ .Lptr
      **end**
**end**;

**FIGURE 9-30**
**Procedure**
FindInorderSuccessor.

**procedure** ConnectToParent (
    **var** Current: BinTreeType;     {Input/output, pointer to node to be
                                     deleted}
    Parent: BinTreeType;         {Input, pointer to parent of Current}
    ReplaceNode: BinTreeType   {Input, pointer to node to replace Current}
                              );
  {Given a pointer to a node to be deleted, its parent, and a node to replace
    the deleted node, this procedure deletes this node and adjusts the pointers
    so that the specified node replaces the deleted node.}
**begin**
    {Step 1: Set the correct parent pointer}
    **if** Parent ↑ .Lptr = Current
    **then** Parent ↑ .Lptr : = ReplaceNode
    **else** Parent ↑ .Rptr : = ReplaceNode;

    {Step 2: Return deleted node to free space}
    **dispose** (Current)
**end**;

**FIGURE 9-31**
**Procedure**
ConnectToParent.

```
function BinCopy (
    T: BinTreeType        {Input, tree to be copied}
                ): BinTreeType;
{Given a pointer to the root node of a binary tree, this function generates a
    copy of the tree and returns the address of its root node.}
var
    NewNode: BinTreeType;      {Pointer to new node}
begin
    {Step 1: Null pointer?}
    if T = nil
    then BinCopy := nil
    else begin

            {Step 2: Create a new node}
            new (NewNode);

            {Step 3: Copy information fields}
            NewNode ↑ .Info := T ↑ .Info;

            {Step 4: Copy the left and right subtrees}
            NewNode ↑ .Lptr := BinCopy (T ↑ .Lptr);
            NewNode ↑ .Rptr := BinCopy (T ↑ .Rptr);

            {Step 5: Return pointer to new node}
            BinCopy := NewNode
        end
end;
```

**FIGURE 9-32**
**Function to copy**
**a binary tree.**

The head node (if one is present) is simply another node which serves as
the predecessor and successor of the first and last tree nodes with respect to
inorder traversal. Such an approach, in essence, imposes a circular structure
on the tree in addition to its tree structure. Figure 9-34a gives the threaded
version, for inorder traversal, of the tree in Fig. 9-19. In this diagram, a
dashed arrow denotes a thread link. Note that the tree is attached to the left
branch of the head node. Using this approach, the address of the root node
of the tree is Head ↑ .Lptr. Observe that this example tree of eight nodes
contains nine threads. Figure 9-34b denotes an empty tree, with the left link
of the head (and only) node denoting a thread.

Figure 9-35 shows the storage representation of the tree in Fig. 9-34
with the flags explicitly shown.

Given the threaded representation of a binary tree threaded with respect
to inorder traversal, it is a very simple matter to formulate a subprogram

**FIGURE 9-33  Node structure in a threaded binary tree.**

| Lptr | LFlag | Info | RFlag | Rptr |
|------|-------|------|-------|------|

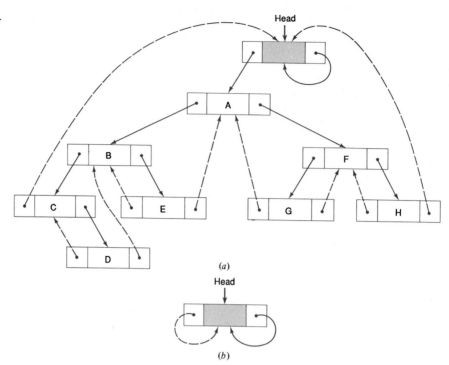

FIGURE 9-34
A threaded binary
tree for inorder
traversal.

for inorder traversal. As an intermediate step we first develop functions to obtain the inorder successor and predecessor of a designated node on such a threaded tree. Figure 9-36 presents a function to obtain the inorder successor in an inorder threaded tree. Step 1 initializes pointer P to the right link of X. If the RFlag of this node is Thread, then the inorder successor of X has been found, control passes to step 3, and the value of P is returned. If RFlag is Link, however, control passes to step 2. In this step we repeatedly branch left until a left thread is encountered. At this point we enter step 3, where the required address is returned. A function to return the inorder predecessor is presented in Fig. 9-37. This function operates in a manner similar to the function ThInorderSuc. The roles of Lptr and Rptr and LFlag and RFlag are simply interchanged.

The successor function can be used repeatedly to traverse the threaded tree in inorder. A procedure implementing this is given in Fig. 9-38. The procedure is simple. Observe that we have set up, in step 2, a repeat statement controlled by a flag. When the successor node becomes the list head, the entire tree has been traversed. At this point the flag is set to "false" and the loop terminates.

From this procedure it can be seen that the threaded tree has certain processing advantages over its unthreaded counterpart. First, the inorder traversal of a threaded tree is somewhat faster than that of its unthreaded version, since no stack is required. Second, the threaded tree representation permits the efficient determination of the predecessor and successor of a particular node. For an unthreaded tree, this task is more difficult, since a stack is

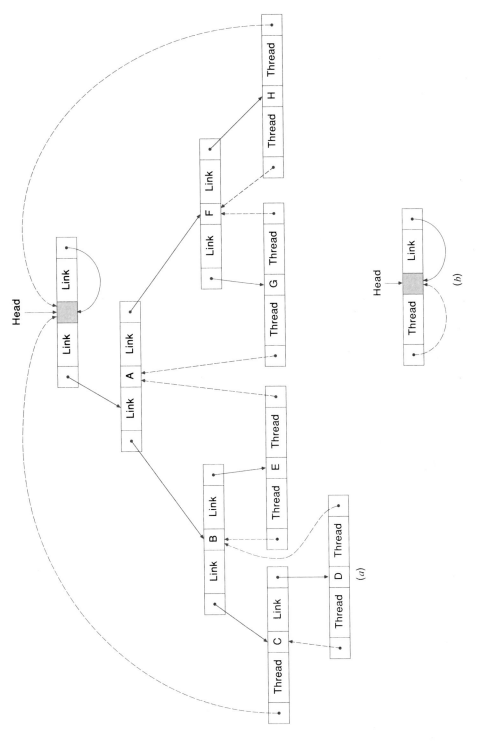

**FIGURE 9-35**

731

```
function ThInorderSuc (
    X: BinTreeType     {Input, pointer to a node in an inorder threaded
                           binary tree}
                    ): BinTreeType;
```
{Given a pointer to a node in an inorder threaded binary tree, this function
returns a pointer to the inorder successor.}
```
var
    P: BinTreeType;     {Tree traversal pointer}
begin
    {Step 1: Initialize traversal pointer and test pointer type}
    P := X ↑ .Rptr;
    if X ↑ .RFlag = Link
    then

            {Step 2: Branch left}
            while P ↑ .LFlag = Link do
                P := P ↑ .Lptr;

    {Step 3: Return address of successor}
    ThInorderSuc := P
end;
```

**FIGURE 9-36**
Function to return the
inorder successor
of a given node.

```
function ThInorderPred (
    X: BinTreeType     {Input, pointer to a node in an inorder threaded
                           binary tree}
                    ): BinTreeType;
```
{Given a pointer to a node in an inorder threaded binary tree, this function
returns a pointer to the inorder predecessor.}
```
var
    P: BinTreeType;     {Tree traversal pointer}
begin
    {Step 1: Initialize traversal pointer and test pointer type}
    P := X ↑ .Lptr;
    if X ↑ .LFlag = Link
    then

            {Step 2: Branch left}
            while P ↑ .RFlag = Link do
                P := P ↑ .Rptr;

    {Step 3: Return address of successor}
    ThInorderPred := P
end;
```

**FIGURE 9-37**
Function to return
the inorder
predecessor of a
given node.

```
procedure Tinorder (Head: BinTreeType);
{Given the address of the list head of a binary tree (Head) which has been
    threaded for inorder traversal, this procedure traverses the tree in inorder.}
var
    P: BinTreeType;      {Temporary pointer variable}
    Stop: Boolean;       {Logical flag for procedure return}
begin
    {Step 1: Initialize}
    Stop := false;
    P := Head;

    {Step 2: Traverse the threaded tree in inorder}
    repeat
        P := ThInorderSuc(P);
        if P = Head
        then Stop := true
        else writeln ('□', P ↑ .Info)
    until Stop
end;
```

FIGURE 9-38
Procedure to
traverse a threaded
binary tree in
inorder.

required to provide the upward-pointing information in the tree that threading provides.

Of course, a price must be paid for these advantages. First, threaded trees cannot share subtrees, as can unthreaded trees. Second, two additional fields are required to distinguish thread links from structural links. Finally, insertions into and deletions from a threaded tree are more time-consuming, since both thread links and structural links must be maintained.

When inserting a new node into a threaded binary tree to the left of a designated node, there are two possible cases. The easiest case involves inserting the new node as a left subtree of the designated node, if that node has an empty left subtree. The remaining (and more difficult) case inserts the new node between the given node, say, X, and the Lptr of X. The two cases are illustrated in Fig. 9-39a and b, respectively. Figure 9-40 presents a procedure to perform an insertion. The first step creates a new node and initializes its information field. Step 2 handles the case where the new node becomes the left subtree of node X. The last step handles the second insertion case where the right link of the inorder predecessor of X (before insertion) is set to a thread which points to the new node.

The notion of threading a binary tree also can be extended to preorder and postorder traversals. In these cases, however, thread pointers need not always point to higher nodes in the tree. Also, the algorithms associated with these traversals may sometimes be more complex than those obtained earlier for an inorder traversal.

## 9-2.3 SEQUENTIAL AND OTHER REPRESENTATIONS OF TREES

In this subsection we describe several representations of binary trees that are based on sequential-allocation techniques. These representations are

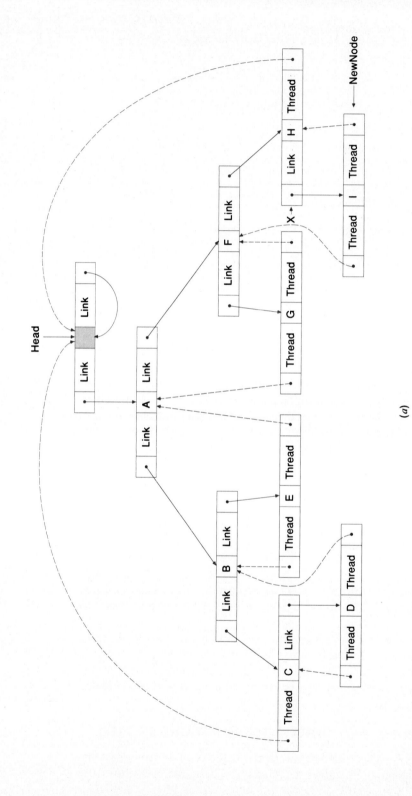

**FIGURE 9-39  Insertion into a threaded binary tree.**

(*a*)

734

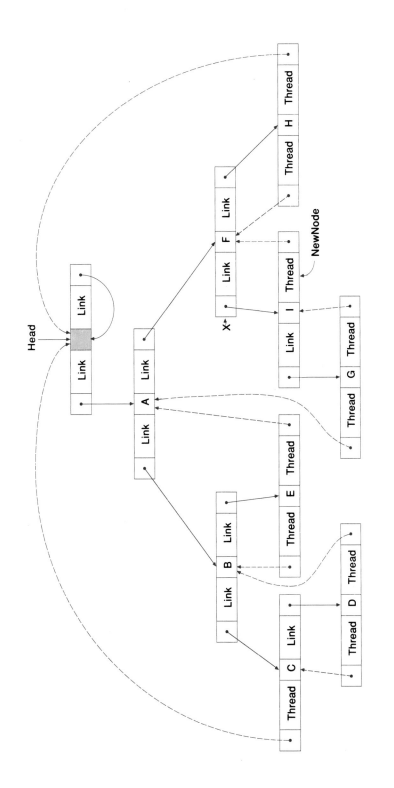

**FIGURE 9-39** (*cont.*)

(*b*)

```
procedure ThInsertLeft (
    Head: BinTreeType;      {Input, pointer to head of threaded binary tree}
    X: BinTreeType;         {Input, pointer to node designated to have the new node
                             as its left subtree}
    Data: BinInfoType       {Input, information to be contained in the new node}
                            );
```
{Given the address of the head node of an inorder threaded binary tree, the address of a designated node, and the information associated with a new node, this procedure inserts a new node to the left of the designated node.}

```
var
    NewNode: BinTreeType;   {Pointer to new node}
    Temp: BinTreeType;      {Temporary pointer variable}
begin
    {Step 1: Create new node}
    new (NewNode);
    NewNode ↑ .Info : = Data;

    {Step 2: Adjust pointer fields}
    NewNode ↑ .Lptr : = X ↑ .Lptr;
    NewNode ↑ .LFlag : = X ↑ .LFlag;
    NewNode ↑ .Rptr : = X;
    NewNode ↑ .RFlag : = Thread;
    X ↑ .Lptr : = NewNode;
    X ↑ .LFlag : = Link;

    {Step 3: Reset predecessor thread if necessary}
    if NewNode ↑ .LFlag = Link
    then begin
            Temp : = ThInorderPred(NewNode);
            Temp ↑ .Rptr : = NewNode
         end
end;
```

**FIGURE 9-40**
**Procedure to insert**
**node into an**
**inorder threaded**
**binary tree.**

efficient and convenient, provided that the tree structure does not change very much (as to insertions, deletions, etc.) during its existence. The particular representation chosen also depends on other types of application-dependent operations that are to be performed on the tree structure.

Perhaps one of the better known subclasses of binary trees is the set of full binary trees. A *full binary tree* is a binary tree in which every nonleaf node has exactly two children and all leaf nodes are at the same level. An example of such a tree structure, together with its sequential representation, is shown in Fig. 9-41. In this representation, the locations of the left and right sons of node $i$ are $2i$ and $2i + 1$, respectively. For example, in Fig. 9-41 the index of the left son of the node in position 3 (that is, E) is 6. Similarly, the index of the right son is 7. Conversely, the position of the

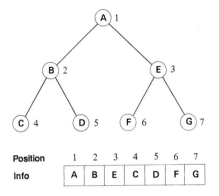

| Position | 1 | 2 | 3 | 4 | 5 | 6 | 7 |
|---|---|---|---|---|---|---|---|
| Info | A | B | E | C | D | F | G |

**FIGURE 9-41**
Sequential
representation of a
full binary tree.

parent of node $j$ is the index $j$ **div** 2. For example, the parent of nodes 4 and 5 is node 2.

In the previous example we conveniently chose a tree with $2^3 - 1$ nodes. In general, a tree with $2^n - 1$ nodes for a particular value of $n$ is easily represented by a vector of $2^n - 1$ elements. Binary trees which have more or fewer than $2^n - 1$ nodes for some $n$, however, also can be represented using the previous approach. An example of a tree that contains nine nodes is given in Fig. 9-42. Note that a substantial amount of memory is wasted in this case. Therefore, for large trees of this type, this method of representation may not be efficient in terms of storage.

Another common method for the sequential representation of binary trees uses the physical adjacency relationship of the computer's memory to replace one of the link fields in the linked representation method introduced earlier. For example, consider an alternative representation of a tree structure in which the left link (**Lptr**) from the usual doubly linked representation has been omitted. One possibility involves representing the tree sequentially,

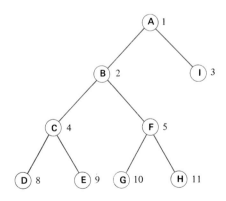

| Position | 1 | 2 | 3 | 4 | 5 | 6 | 7 | 8 | 9 | 10 | 11 | 12 | 13 | 14 | 15 |
|---|---|---|---|---|---|---|---|---|---|---|---|---|---|---|---|
| Info | A | B | I | C | F | – | – | D | E | G | H | – | – | – | – |

**FIGURE 9-42**
Sequential
representation of a
partially full
binary tree.

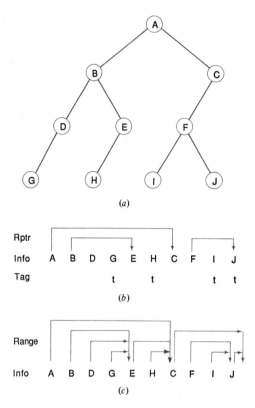

FIGURE 9-43
Preorder sequential
representations of
a binary tree.

such that its nodes appear in preorder. Using this approach, the tree in Fig. 9-43a is represented by Fig. 9-43b, where **Rptr**, **Info**, and **Tag** are the fields in an array of record structures. Notice that in Pascal the **Tree** is a vector, the nodes are **Tree[1]**, **Tree[2]**, . . ., **Tree[N]**, and **Rptr** would be an integer rather than a "pointer," referencing the appropriate element of the array. In this representation, we do not require the **Lptr** pointer, since for a nonnull link, it would point to the node to its immediate right. The Boolean vector **Tag** denotes, with a logical value of "true" (indicated by t in Fig. 9-43), a node whose left links would be **nil** in the linked allocation. This representation is wasteful of space because more than one-half of the right links are **nil**. This wasted space becomes useful by making the right link of each current node point to the node that immediately follows (with respect to preorder) the left subtree below this current node. The field **Rptr** is renamed **Range** in such a representation, as shown in Fig. 9-43c. Also, observe that we do not need a **Tag** item for a node with a null left link, since a leaf node occurs at position P when **Tree[P].Range** = P + 1.

## EXERCISES 9-2

1. Traverse the tree in Fig. 9-44 in preorder, inorder, and postorder giving a list of the nodes visited.

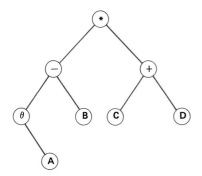

**FIGURE 9-44**

2. Give a complete trace (as in Table 9-1) of each traversal order obtained in Exercise 1.

3. Assuming an insertion sequence of Ken, Roger, Bill, Leo, Paul, Norma, Maurice, and John, construct (as in Fig. 9-25) a lexically ordered tree for this sequence of insertions.

4. Delete node **D** from the tree given in Fig. 9-45. Starting again from the original tree, delete node **G**.

★ 5. Formulate a general algorithm for finding the *k*th element in the preorder traversal of a binary tree.

6. The inorder traversal of a binary tree yields the following sequence of nodes:

   d  f  c  g  b  e  a

   Draw the tree. Is this tree unique, that is, the only binary tree with this inorder traversal?

7. Give unthreaded and threaded storage representations for the tree given in Fig. 9-46.

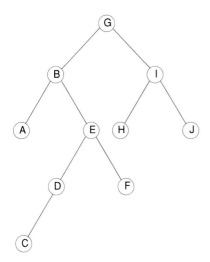

**FIGURE 9-45**

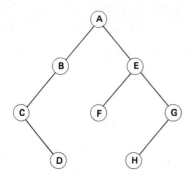

FIGURE 9-46

★ **8.** Write a recursive procedure for traversing a binary tree in postorder. Write a program to test your procedure.

 **9.** Trace the procedure Ipreorder for the tree in Fig. 9-46.

★ **10.** Write an iterative procedure for traversing a binary tree in inorder. Write a program to test your procedure.

★ **11.** Write an iterative procedure for traversing a binary tree in postorder. Write a program to test your procedure.

★ **12.** Write a function to create the "swapped" version of a binary tree. For example, Fig. 9-47 gives the swapped version of Fig. 9-46. The function should return the pointer to the root of this new tree. Write a program to test your procedure.

 **13.** Trace the procedure TreeDelete for the deletions of nodes D and then G from Fig. 9-45.

★ **14.** Given a binary tree threaded for inorder traversal, construct a procedure (similar to the procedure ThInsertLeft) for inserting a node to the immediate right of a designated node. Write a program to test your procedure.

★★ **15.** Investigate the threading of a binary tree for preorder traversal. In particular, attempt to formulate subprograms for obtaining the preorder predecessor and successor of a designated node. Write a program to test your subprograms.

★★ **16.** Repeat Exercise 15 for postorder traversal.

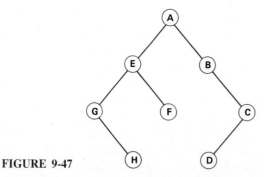

FIGURE 9-47

★ **17.** Based on the sequential representation of a full binary tree, write a procedure for its inorder traversal. Write a program to test your procedure.

★ **18.** Based on the storage representation of a binary tree given in Fig. 9-43*b*, write a procedure for its postorder traversal. Write a program to test your procedure.

★ **19.** Write a procedure for traversing, in inorder, a binary tree that is stored as in Fig. 9-43*c*. Write a program to test your procedure.

★ **20.** The *diameter* of a tree is the length of the longest path in the tree from the root to any leaf. Write a procedure that takes the value of a pointer to the root of the tree and then computes and prints the diameter of the tree and a path of that length (that is, a sequence of nodes from the root node to some leaf which is of that length). *Hint*: Try to modify the procedure obtained in Exercise 8 for your purposes.

★ **21.** Write a recursive function that has one parameter, a pointer to a binary tree in linked representation, and returns the number of leaves in the tree. Write a program to test your procedure.

★ **22.** There exists a binary tree whose nodes each contain a letter. If a postorder traversal prints

E D A C G F B H

and the number of children of the nodes are

A B C D E F G H

1 2 0 1 0 1 0 2

what does a preorder traversal print?

★★ **23.** One way to handle deletions in a lexically ordered binary tree is to have each node contain a flag that is set if the node has been deleted. If over half the nodes in the tree have been deleted, the tree is reorganized so that all nodes whose delete flags have been set are removed.

Your task is to write the following two subprograms. You should also specify which variables are global and in what manner the parameters are passed.

(*a*) A recursive function Test which, given a pointer to a binary tree with delete flags, returns "true" if more than half the delete flags have been set.

(*b*) A procedure Reorganize which, given a pointer to a binary tree with more than half the delete flags set, removes the nodes whose delete flags have been set. The procedure should be space-efficient so that the space from any removed node is reclaimed and no new space for nodes is created.

You may write other subprograms and call them from Test or Reorganize.

★ **24.** Write a procedure for LRcommon(T), where the parameter T points at a binary tree that prints out all values in the left subtree of T that also occur in the right subtree of T. You may write as many subprograms as you wish to aid in specifying the algorithm, but the procedure

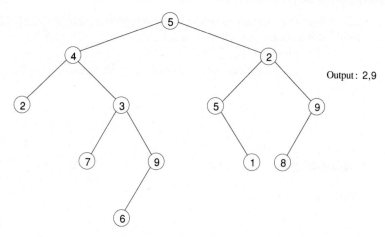

Output: 2,9

FIGURE 9-48

LRoommon(T) should be as specified. An example is given in Fig. 9-48. *Note:* You may assume that all values in each of the subtrees are distinct. Write a program to test your subprograms.

25. Recall that a full binary tree has one node at level 1, two nodes at level 2, four nodes at level 3, eight nodes at level 4, and so on. Examples of full binary trees are given in Fig. 9-49. Given the address of the head node **Head** of a linked binary tree, write a Boolean function which determines whether or not the binary tree is full.

★★ 26. (a) Write a procedure that prints the nodes at a given level (supplied as a parameter to your procedure) of a binary tree in left-to-right order. Assume that the linked list representation of the tree is already available and a pointer to the root node is a procedure parameter. *Hint:* Use recursion.

(b) Use the procedure developed in part (a) to write a procedure for doing a "level order" traversal of a binary tree. In a level-order traversal, the nodes are visited in the order of their levels; that is, the nodes at lower levels (the node at the lowest level being the root) are visited prior to the nodes at higher levels. At a given level, nodes are visited in left-to-right order. The output of your procedure should be a sequence of nodes listed in the order they are visited. For example, the procedure should produce the following output for the tree shown in Fig. 9-50:

a b c d e f g

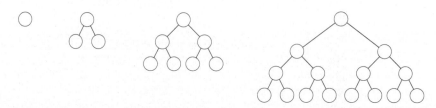

FIGURE 9-49

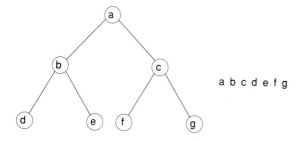

a b c d e f g

FIGURE 9-50

## 9-3   GENERAL TREES

Thus far we have been concerned with the storage representation of binary trees. Clearly, there are many applications in which the tree structures are not binary. Trees of arbitrary degree pose obvious representational problems. How many link fields do you provide? As mentioned in Sec. 9-1, more general tree structures can be converted easily to equivalent binary trees. This topic is described in detail in the next subsection.

### 9-3.1   CONVERSION OF GENERAL TREES TO BINARY TREES

Recall from Sec. 9-1 that a general tree or, more generally, a forest of trees can be converted into an equivalent binary tree. This conversion process was called the *natural correspondence* between general and binary trees. Furthermore, this correspondence is a one-to-one relationship. In this subsection we formulate a detailed program for converting general trees to binary trees. Before giving this algorithm, however, the specification of the input format is given.

Perhaps one of the most popular and convenient ways to specify a general tree (or forest) is to use a notation similar to that used in several programming languages for writing record structures. As an example, the two trees in Fig. 9-51a can be specified in the following manner:

```
1 A
    2 B
    2 C
        3 E
        3 F
    2 D
1 G
    2 H
        3 J
    2 I
```

In this notation the numbers associated with the nodes indicate the subtree relationship. For example, those nodes with an associated number of 1 denote root nodes. Those with higher numbers indicate their lower position in the tree structure. The equivalent binary tree for the forest of two trees in Fig. 9-51a is given in Fig. 9-51b.

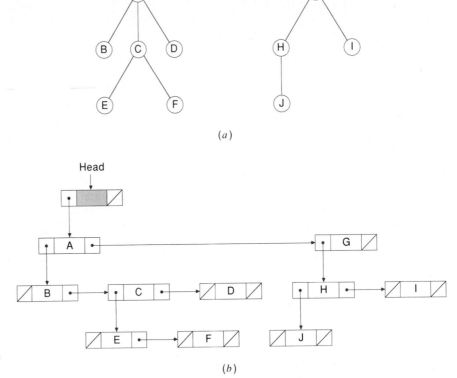

**FIGURE 9-51**
(*a*) **Forest of two**
**trees,** (*b*) **binary tree**
**representation of**
**this forest.**

In the formulation of an algorithm for converting a forest to a binary tree, we must connect a parent to its left offspring and connect from left to right all the siblings at the same level within the same tree. This latter requirement implies that a stack must be maintained. We assume that the input to the algorithm consists of a sequence of nodes for each tree in pre-order. The representation of each node takes the form of a pair of elements; the first and second elements represent the level number and name associated with that node, respectively. Each entry in the stack is made up of two items. The first item represents the level number associated with a node, and the second item denotes the address of that node.

A general algorithm for this conversion process is as follows:

1. Create a head node for the binary tree
   Push a pointer to it and a level number of 0 on the stack.

2. Repeat thru step 6 while data still remains

3. Input description of a node

4. Create a tree node and initialize its contents

5. If the level number of the current node is greater than that of the node on top of the stack,

then make the current node the left offspring of the node on top of the stack

else Remove from the stack all nodes whose level numbers are greater than that of the current node

Make the current node the right offspring of the node on top of the stack

Remove the top node (left child) from the stack

6. Push the current node description onto the stack

7. Finished

The implementation of this algorithm requires the stack operations defined in Chap. 8. The stack elements are records containing two fields— a level and a pointer to a tree node. The required type definition is

**type**
  StackElementType =
    **record**
      LevF: integer;
      PtrF: BinTreeType
    **end**

For simplicity, the information field of the tree will be a single character. The complete set of type definitions for the stack and binary tree is easily constructed.

The procedure in Fig. 9-52 implements the notion of natural correspondence. The first step of the procedure creates a list head for the required binary tree and places the level number and address of this node on the stack. Observe that a level number of zero is associated with the list head. This convenient choice will later cause the root of the first tree to be appended to the list head. Step 2 controls the input of the given forest. Step 3 inputs a pair of values that represent a node, and step 4 creates a new node and initializes its links to **nil**. The label of the new node is also copied. Step 5 compares the level of the new node with the level at the top of the stack. If the level number of the new node is greater than the level number of the topmost node on the stack, then the left link of the latter is set to point to the former. This assignment connects a parent to its left-most offspring. A transfer to step 6 then results. If, however, the level number of the new node is less than or equal to that of the stack top, then successive elements are removed from the stack until the level number of its topmost element is less than or equal to the level number of the new node. If the comparison gives a "less than" result, then an error exists in the numbering of the tree structures; otherwise, in the case of equality, the right link of the stack top node is set to **NewNode** and removed from the stack. Step 6 stacks the level number and a pointer to the new node.

Several procedures and functions are required. The function **CreateNode** allocates and initializes a new tree node and was presented in Fig. 9-23. Procedure **PushLevPtr**, which given a level and tree pointer constructs and

```
procedure TreeInput(
    var Head: BinTreeType;       {Output, pointer to head of equivalent binary
                                    tree.}
    var ErrorFlag: Boolean       {Output, flag indicating whether or not an error
                                    has occurred}
            );
```
{Given a forest of trees whose input format is in the form described in the
text, this procedure reads the input from the input stream and constructs
the equivalent binary tree representation and returns a pointer to the head
of this tree via its output parameter.}
```
var
    S: StackType;                {Levels and pointers to tree}
    Level: integer;              {Current level}
    Name: BinInfoType;           {Current node label}
    NewNode: BinTreeType;        {Pointer to new node }
    P: BinTreeType;              {Temporary tree pointer }
begin
    {Step 1: Initialize}
    Head := CreateNode ('□');
    StackInitialize(S);
    PushLevPtr (S, 0, Head);
    ErrorFlag := false;

    {Step 2: Process the input}
    while not eof and not ErrorFlag do
        begin

            {Step 3: Input a node}
            readln (Level, Name);
```

FIGURE 9-52
Procedure to convert
a general forest
to its equivalent
binary representation.

pushes a stack element, appears in Fig. 9-53. Function **TopLev**, presented
in Fig. 9-54, accesses the top stack element and returns the level value.
Function **TopPtr** is similar and is easily constructed. Procedure **DiscardTop**
pops the stack and discards the result. The stack routines are as presented
in Chap. 8, except that **StackTopVal** must be defined as a procedure with an
output parameter rather than a function. As described in Chap. 8, standard
Pascal does not permit a function to return a record value.

The behavior of this program for the forest in Fig. 9-51*a* is given in
Table 9-3, where **NA** denotes a pointer to a node with label **A**, **NB** denotes a
pointer to a node with label **B**, and so on. A stack entry written, for example,
as 1NA means that a node with level number 1, label **A**, and pointer **NA** has
been stacked. The stack top is the right-most element in the string. Note that
if a forest contains nodes with the same label, say, **B**, then each of these
nodes will be accessed by a different pointer, even though our notation refers
to each such pointer reference as **NB**. Finally, the table shows only changes
that have occurred since the previous steps.

{Step 4: Create a tree node}
NewNode : = CreateNode (Name);

{Step 5: Compare levels}
**if** Level > TopLev (S)
**then begin**
       P : = TopPtr (S);
       P ↑ .Lptr : = NewNode
  **end**
**else begin**
      **while** Level < TopLev (S) **do**
        DiscardTop (S);
      **if** Level <> TopLev (S)
      **then begin**
         writeln('Mixed level numbers');
         ErrorFlag : = true
        **end**
      **else begin**
         P : = TopPtr (S);
         P ↑ .Rptr : = NewNode;
         DiscardTop (S)
        **end**
    **end**;

{Step 6: Push a new node onto the stack}
**if not** ErrorFlag
**then** PushLevPtr (S, Level, NewNode);
  **end**
**end**;

**FIGURE 9-52** (*cont.*)

    The preorder and inorder traversals of a binary tree which corresponds to a forest have a natural correspondence with these traversals on the forest. In particular, the preorder traversal of the associated binary tree is equivalent to visiting the nodes of the forest in *tree preorder*, which is defined as follows:

*1.* Process the root of the first tree

*2.* Traverse the subtrees of the first tree in tree preorder

*3.* Traverse the remaining trees of the forest in tree preorder

The tree traversal of the forest of the two trees given in Fig. 9-51*a* gives the sequence

A B C E F D G H J I

This is exactly the same sequence obtained during the preorder traversal of the equivalent binary tree in Fig. 9-51*b*.

**procedure** PushLevPtr (

    **var** S: StackType;    {Input/output, stack for saving level number and
                                                     tree node pointers}

    Level: integer;      {Input, level number to be pushed}

    Ptr: BinTreeType    {Input, tree pointer to be pushed}
                          );

{Given a stack, level number, and pointer to a tree node, this procedure
    pushes the level and pointer on the stack.}

**var**

    Rec: StackElementType;    {Used to construct a record for the top of the
                                        stack}

**begin**

    {Construct and push new stack element}

    Rec.LevF : = Level;

    Rec.PtrF : = Ptr;

    StackPush (S, Rec)

**end**;

**FIGURE 9-53**
Procedure PushLevPtr.

Similarly, the *tree inorder* traversal of a forest is defined as follows:

*1.* Traverse the subtrees of the first tree in tree inorder

*2.* Process the root of the first tree

*3.* Traverse the remaining trees of the forest in tree inorder

The inorder traversal of the example forest in Fig. 9-51*a* yields the sequence
of labels

B E F C D A J H I G

Again, this is the same sequence as that obtained by traversing the binary
tree in Fig. 9-51*b*. No such direct correspondence exists for postorder traversal.

**function** TopLev (

    S: StackType    {Input, stack of levels and tree pointers}
                     ): integer;

{Given a stack of levels and tree pointers, this function returns the level of
    the top element of the stack. The stack is not modified.}

**var**

    Rec: StackElementType;    {Used to obtain top stack element}

**begin**

    {Obtain top element of stack and extract level number}

    StackTopVal (S, Rec);

    TopLev : = Rec.LevF

**FIGURE 9-54**
Procedure TopLev.    **end**;

**TABLE 9-3** Behavior of Program TreeInput for the Forest in Fig. 9-51a

| Current | Stack | Level | New Node | Top Level | Top Location | P↑.Lptr | P↑.Rptr |
|---------|-------|-------|----------|-----------|--------------|---------|---------|
| | 0HEAD | | | 0 | HEAD | nil | nil |
| 1, A | 0HEAD 1NA | 1 | NA | 1 | NA | NA | nil |
| 2, B | 0HEAD 1NA 2NB | 2 | NB | 2 | NB | NB | nil |
| 2, C | 0HEAD 1NA 2NC | 2 | NC | 2 | NC | nil | NC |
| 3, E | 0HEAD 1NA 2NC 3NE | 3 | NE | 3 | NE | NE | nil |
| 3, F | 0HEAD 1NA 2NC 3NF | 3 | NF | 3 | NF | nil | NF |
| 2, D | 0HEAD 1NA 2NC | 2 | ND | 2 | NC | nil | nil |
| | 0HEAD 1NA 2ND | | | 2 | ND | NE | ND |
| | | | | | | | |
| 1, G | 0HEAD 1NA | 1 | NG | 2 | ND | nil | nil |
| | 0HEAD 1NG | | | 1 | NA | NB | NG |
| | | | | | | | |
| 2, H | 0HEAD 1NG 2NH | 2 | NH | 1 | NG | NH | nil |
| 3, J | 0HEAD 1NG 2NH 3NJ | 3 | NJ | 2 | NH | NJ | nil |
| 2, I | 0HEAD 1NG 2NI | 2 | NI | 3 | NJ | nil | nil |
| | | | | 2 | NH | NJ | NI |

Now that we have discussed how to handle general trees in terms of binary trees, the topic of the next subsection is the sequential storage representation of general trees.

### 9-3.2  REPRESENTATIONS OF GENERAL TREES

A popular method of representing a general tree sequentially is based on the notion of postorder traversal. Such a representation takes the form of one vector which represents the nodes of the tree in postorder and a second vector which denotes the number of children of the nodes. An example of the postorder representation is given in Fig. 9-55. Recall that this postorder representation of a tree is useful in evaluating functions that are defined on certain nodes of the tree. Section 8-5.1 contained an example of such a case where object code was generated from the reverse Polish representation of an expression.

As a final and straightforward sequential method of representing a tree, consider a vector that contains the father of each node in the tree. As an example, the tree in Fig. 9-56 is represented as follows:

$$i \qquad\qquad 1\ 2\ 3\ 4\ 5\ 6\ 7\ 8\ 9\ 10$$

$$\text{Father}[i] \qquad 0\ 1\ 1\ 1\ 2\ 2\ 4\ 4\ 4\ 6$$

where the branches in the tree are given by

$$\{(\text{Father}[i],\ i)\} \qquad \text{for } i = 2, 3, \ldots, 10$$

Observe that the root node (1) of the tree has no father; consequently, we have used a value of zero for its father. This method of representation can be extended to represent a forest. An obvious disadvantage of this method is that it fails to reflect certain orderings of the nodes. For example, if we

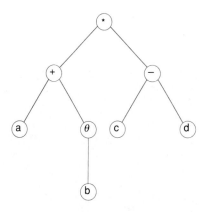

FIGURE 9-55
Postorder sequential
representation
of a tree.

| Post | a | b | $\theta$ | + | c | d | − | * |
|---|---|---|---|---|---|---|---|---|
| Degree | 0 | 0 | 1 | 2 | 0 | 0 | 2 | 2 |

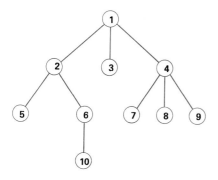

FIGURE 9-56

interchange nodes 5 and 6, the representation of this new tree is the same as that of the previous tree.

## EXERCISES 9-3

1. Using the forest in Fig. 9-10, trace (as in Table 9-3) the procedure TreeInput.

★ 2. Write a recursive procedure for converting a forest into an equivalent binary tree. Write a program to test your procedure.

★ 3. This problem concerns the operations of subtree insertion and deletion as applied to general trees. Remember that a general tree can be converted to a binary tree using the natural-correspondence algorithm discussed in this section. It is most natural to discuss insertion or deletion of a subtree in terms of its relation to the parent node. Thus we define our two operations as follows:

Delete(N, K)
Insert(N, K, T)

Delete deletes the Kth subtree of the node given by N. Insert inserts the tree with root T as the new Kth subtree of the node given by N. For example, consider the general tree shown in Fig. 9-57a. If we execute Insert(P, 2, Q), where Q identifies the tree given in Fig. 9-57b, we obtain the tree shown in Fig. 9-57c. The complementary operation for restoring our original tree is then Delete(P, 2). You are required to formulate

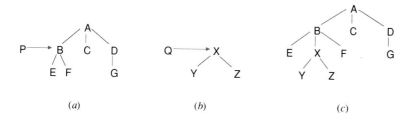

(a)        (b)        (c)        FIGURE 9-57

procedures for Insert and Delete, assuming that you are given the binary tree equivalent to the general tree (this is obtained by the natural-correspondence algorithm). State any assumptions that you make. Also examine what happens to the binary tree equivalent of the general tree when these operations are performed.

★★ **4.** *(a)* Define the complete set of type definitions needed for procedure TreeInput.

*(b)* Implement the missing procedures and functions for TreeInput.

*(c)* Design and run an appropriate set of tests for procedure TreeInput.

## 9-4 APPLICATIONS OF TREES

This section contains four applications of trees. The first application involves the symbolic manipulation of algebraic expressions—one of the earliest nonnumeric applications to which computers were applied. The second application deals with trees that are used in sorting. We describe the application of full binary trees to this process. In the third application we discuss the applicability of general trees to searching. Finally, we examine the area of syntax analysis and its relationship to parse trees.

### 9-4.1 THE SYMBOLIC MANIPULATION OF EXPRESSIONS

Several special-purpose programming languages have been designed over the years to manipulate expressions symbolically. Examples of symbolic operations performed on expressions include operations such as addition, subtraction, multiplication, and division.

The binary tree representation of expressions was introduced earlier in the chapter. Recall that a nonleaf node represents an operator and the left and right subtrees (for binary operators) are the left and right operands of that operator. The leaves of the tree are the variables and constants in the expression. Consider the representation for the expression $(a + b * \theta 2 - c/d)$, where $\theta$ is used to denote the unary minus operator. A variant record is used to distinguish between branch nodes and leaf nodes. The node structures for these types of nodes are exhibited in Fig. 9-58a and b. Note that both structures have a common field called NodeType. A branch node contains three additional fields. A leaf node, on the other hand, has one additional field. The declaration for such a tree structure follows:

**type**
   VarRec $=$
     **record**

*(a)*

| NodeType | Lptr | OpType | Rptr |
|----------|------|--------|------|

*(b)*

| NodeType | VPtr |
|----------|------|

**FIGURE 9-58**
**Variant record for**
**a symbolic expression.**

```
        Symbol: packed array [1 .. 12] of char;
        OpValue: real
    end;
Operation = (Add, Sub, Mul, Div, Neg, Expon);
NodeKind = (Op, VC);
ExpTree = ↑ TreeNode;
TablePtr = ↑ VarRec;
TreeNode =
    record
        case NodeType: NodeKind of
            Op: (Lptr: ExpTree;
                    OpType: Operation;
                    Rptr: ExpTree);
            VC: (Vptr: TablePtr)
        end;
    end;
var
  Expr: ExpTree;
```

The tree structure for $(a + b * \theta 2 - c/d)$ appears in Fig. 9-59. Note that for $\theta$, the **Neg** type of node uses **Rptr** to point to its operand.

**FIGURE 9-59   Binary tree representation of an expression.**

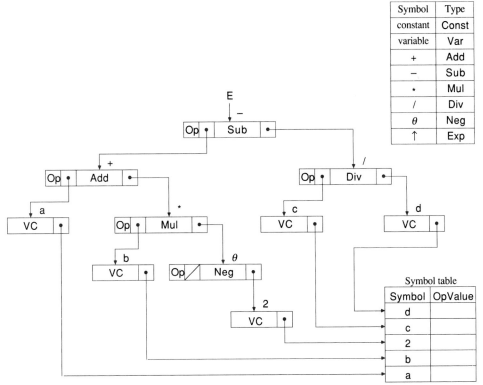

Note that the symbol table entries each contain two elements—Symbol and OpValue. Clearly, a more sophisticated representation, such as one of those given earlier in the book, could be adopted instead. The enumerated type Operation contains appropriate names for the arithmetic operators. Observe that the common field, NodeType, in the variant record structure has either a value of Op or VC, denoting a branch node or leaf node, respectively.

Let us consider first the evaluation of an expression which is represented by a binary tree. In other words, we require the (numeric) value of the expression given the values of its constituent terms. The easiest way of obtaining the desired value is by formulating a recursive solution. Such a solution is given in the recursive function in Fig. 9-60.

In this function we assume that the required type definitions appear in the main program. The function is straightforward. If the node on entering the function is a leaf (that is, NodeType is VC), then the value of the constant or variable of this node is returned. This is achieved by using the Vptr pointer of that node to reference the associated entry in the symbol table. For a nonleaf node (that is, NodeType is Op), however, the recursive evaluation of the subtree(s) of this node which represents the operand(s) of the current operator is initiated. This evaluation is accomplished by invoking the function Eval with the left and right pointers of that operator node as arguments in the case of a binary operator; otherwise, only the right pointer is used in the case of the negation operator. The process continues until a leaf node is encountered. When such a leaf node is detected, a value from its associated symbol table entry is located.

Let us now consider the symbolic addition of two arithmetic expressions. Assume that E1 and E2 are pointer variables that denote the root nodes

```
function Eval (
       E: ExpTree      {Input, root node address}
                  ): real;
{Given an expression which is represented by a binary tree with a root node
    address of E, this function returns the value of the given expression.}
begin
   case E ↑ .NodeType of
      VC: Eval : = E ↑ .Vptr ↑ .OpValue;
      Op: case E ↑ .OpType of
            Add:    Eval : = Eval (E ↑ .Lptr) + Eval (E ↑ .Rptr);
            Sub:    Eval : = Eval (E ↑ .Lptr) − Eval (E ↑ .Rptr);
            Mul:    Eval : = Eval (E ↑ .Lptr) * Eval (E ↑ .Rptr);
            Div:    Eval : = Eval (E ↑ .Lptr) / Eval (E ↑ .Rptr);
            Neg:    Eval : = − Eval (E ↑ .Rptr);
            Expon: Eval : = exp (Eval (E ↑ .Rptr) * ln (Eval (E ↑ .Lptr)))
         end
      end
end; {Eval}
```

**FIGURE 9-60**
**Eval function for**
**evaluating a symbolic**
**expression.**

of the binary trees which represent the given expressions. The desired symbolic addition is easily represented by a new binary tree by first creating a root node for the required sum and then setting the left and right pointers of this node to E1 and E2, respectively. Finally, the **OpType** field of the new root node is set to **Add**. The program statements to accomplish this construction are

```
new (P);
P ↑ .NodeType := Op;
P ↑ .OpType := Add;
P ↑ .Lptr := E1;
P ↑ .Rptr := E2
```

with **P** representing the address of the root node of the sum expression.

   In practice, we would want to make certain obvious simplifications when adding two expressions symbolically. As an example, if the two expressions being summed are constants, then we should create a new leaf node that represents this constant sum. As another example, if one of the expressions being added is zero, then no new root node is required. Similar rules can be devised for the other arithmetic operators and are left as exercises.

   As another example, let us consider the problem of deciding whether or not two expressions that are represented as binary trees are similar. Two binary trees that represent a pair of expressions are said to be *similar* if they are identical for all node types except for those which represent the commutative operators + and ∗. In the latter case we also consider two expression trees to be equivalent if the right subtree of the first tree is similar to the left subtree of the second tree and the left subtree of the first tree is similar to the right subtree of the second tree. For example, the two expression trees in Fig. 9-61 are equivalent. A program for similarity can be formulated readily by separating the operators into three categories: the binary commutative operators, the binary noncommutative operators, and the negation operator. A recursive program which uses this approach is given in Fig. 9-62.

   The first step of the program checks the types of the root nodes. If

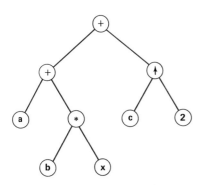
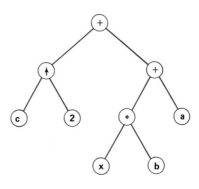

FIGURE 9-61
Two similar
expression trees.

```
function Similar (
  A: ExpTree;                    {Input, address of root node of first tree}
  B: ExpTree                     {Input, address of root node of second tree}
        ): Boolean;
{Given two expressions which are represented by binary trees with root node
  pointers A and B, respectively, this function determines whether or not
  these two binary trees are similar.}
begin
  {Step 1: Check the root nodes}
  if A ↑ .NodeType <> B ↑ .NodeType
  then Similar : = false

  {Step 2: Determine similarity}
  else
    case A ↑ .NodeType of
      {Nodes A and B are of the same type at this point}
      VC: {Compare leaf nodes}
        Similar : = (A ↑ .Vptr = B ↑ .Vptr);
      Op:
        if A ↑ .OpType <> B ↑ .OpType
        then Similar : = false
        else
          case A ↑ .OpType of
            Add, Mul:     {Check for commutativity}
              Similar : = (Similar (A ↑ .Rptr, B ↑ .Rptr) and
                Similar (A ↑ .Lptr, B ↑ .Lptr)) or
                (Similar (A ↑ .Rptr, B ↑ .Lptr) and
                Similar (A ↑ .Lptr, B ↑ .Rptr));
            Sub, Div, Expon:     {Check for identical subtrees}
              Similar : = Similar (A ↑ .Lptr, B ↑ .Lptr) and
                Similar (A ↑ .Rptr, B ↑ .Rptr);
            Neg: {Check for identical binary subtrees}
              Similar : = Similar (A ↑ .Rptr, B ↑ .Rptr)
          end     {of case on OpType}
    end     {of case on NodeType}
end; {Similar}
```

**FIGURE 9-62**
**Function for**
**determining whether**
**two expression**
**trees are similar.**

these differ, failure (that is, "false") is reported. The first case of step 2
compares leaf nodes. Identical variables (as to name and value) result in
success (that is, "true"); otherwise, failure results. This case is also applicable to constants. The second case applies to operators. If they are, then a
nested case statement is entered. Its first case applies the commutativity test
for addition and multiplication. The second case checks for identical binary
subtrees. Finally, the last case performs a test for identical unary subtrees.

There are several other classical applications involving the symbolic
manipulation of expressions. Symbolic differentiation and integration are
typical examples. The binary tree approach used in this subsection also

can handle these applications. However, we leave these investigations as exercises.

## 9-4.2 TREE SORTS

This subsection examines two sorting techniques which are based on the representation of a table by a tree. The first method, which is simple, is a binary tree sort. The second technique involves the use of a full binary tree to represent the given table. Although the second method is more complex than the first, it can also be significantly more efficient.

The basic concepts of a binary tree sort were introduced in Sec. 9-2.1, where the symbols were kept in lexical order. More specifically, the root symbol of each tree lexically followed and preceded all the symbols in its left and right subtrees, respectively. Once the binary tree for a given table has been constructed in this manner, it can then be traversed in inorder to yield the desired sorted table. For example, the key set

58, 86, 26, 44, 92, 61, 13, 39, 8, 75

yields the binary tree given in Fig. 9-63, assuming that the keys are inserted from left to right. The inorder traversal of this tree gives the desired results. The average number of comparisons for this sorting technique is $O(n\log_2 n)$ for a table of $n$ entries. In the worst case, however, the number of comparisons required is $O(n^2)$, a case that arises when the binary tree for the table is severely unbalanced. Such a case occurs if the left subtree of every node in a tree is empty. A similiar situation occurs when all right subtrees are empty.

We turn now to a completely different method of sorting, which also involves binary trees. Given $n$ keys, it takes at least $n - 1$ comparisons to obtain either the smallest or largest key value. Once the smallest or largest key is removed, however, we can obtain the next smallest or largest element in much fewer than $n - 2$ comparisons. The way of achieving this result can be explained as follows. Let us assume that a squash tournament had eight participants and was played according to the draw illustrated in Fig. 9-64. The diagram displays the outcome of the tournament, with Jane beating Lorna, Janet beating Gail, and so on, and finally Jane beating Judy in the

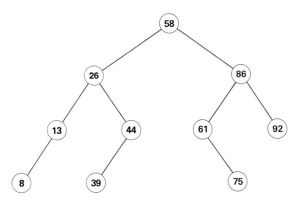

**FIGURE 9-63**
**Binary tree representation of a table of 10 keys.**

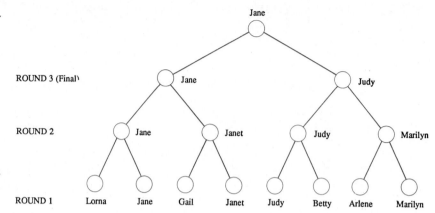

FIGURE 9-64
Outcome of a
squash tournament.

final. Jane was therefore declared to be the winner of the tournament. Suppose that it were required (for ranking purposes) to determine the second-best player as well. This player would seem to be Judy (the other finalist), but, in fact, it could be Lorna or Janet (the other players beaten by Jane). The actual second-best player can be determined by having Lorna play Janet, and the winner of this match play Judy. Using this approach, only two additional games are required to determine the second-best player. The important point to note is that a complete tournament need not be replayed with Jane absent.

We can use this tournament approach to sort a given table. First, the table is represented by a particular kind of binary tree called a *heap*. A heap is essentially a full binary tree (see Sec. 9-2.3). An example of a heap for 10 elements is given in Fig. 9-65. Note that the largest key is at the root of the tree. Similar relationships exist for the remaining keys of the table. Also note that if the number of elements in the tree is not $2^m - 1$ for some $m$, then there are fewer than $2^{l-1}$ nodes at level $l$, and these nodes occupy the left-most positions available in the tree. This phenomenon occurs depending on the value of $n$, and its presence does not make much difference in terms of the final algorithm. In general, a heap that represents a table of $n$ records satisfies the property

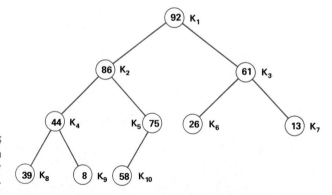

FIGURE 9-65
Heap representation
of a sample key
set of 10 numbers.

$$K_j \le K_i \qquad \text{for } 2 \le j \le n \text{ and } i = \text{trunc}(j/2)$$

where the nodes are numbered in level order. This property clearly holds for the binary tree given in Fig. 9-65.

The heap can be allocated sequentially, as was done for full binary trees in Sec. 9-2.3. Recall that in such a representation the indices of the left and right children of record $i$ (if they exist) are $2i$ and $2i + 1$, respectively. Conversely, the index of the parent of record $j$ (if it is not the root) is $\text{trunc}(j/2)$. Note that this latter operation can be shortened to ($j$ **div** 2), since what we really want is integer division. These simple relationships permit us to descend or to ascend the heap with relative ease. As a result, the sort algorithm based on a heap representation of a table tends to be relatively straightforward.

We now proceed to formulate an algorithm that constructs a heap from an unsorted sequentially allocated input table. In this construction process we start with a heap (for example, a one-record tree is a heap) and then insert a new record into the existing heap such that a new heap is formed after performing the indicated insertion. Such insertions are performed repeatedly until all records in the original table form a heap.

Let us examine the insertion process more carefully. As an example, assume that we wish to insert a new record with a key value of **92** into the existing heap given in Fig. 9-66. As indicated in the figure, the new key (**92**) is appended as a leaf to the existing tree in position 5. Clearly, the new structure is not a heap. The position of the parent of the node is (5 **div** 2), or 2. The new key is larger than the key value of its parent, so we interchange the positions of keys **92** and **58**. Since the new key is now in position 2, its new parent is in position 1. Again, the new key has a value greater than its parent (key **86**). Consequently, keys **86** and **92** interchange positions. At this point, the process terminates, with the revised tree structure in Fig. 9-66b again representing a heap.

A general algorithm is given to create the heap:

*1.* Repeat thru step 7 for each record to be placed in the heap

*2.* Obtain child to be placed at leaf level

*3.* Obtain position of parent for this child

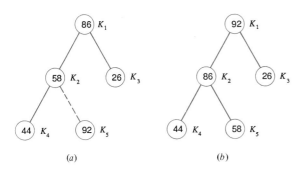

(a)                    (b)

FIGURE 9-66
Insertion of a
new record into
an existing heap.

*4.* Repeat thru step 6 while the child has a parent and the key of the child is greater than that of the parent

*5.* Move the parent down to the position of the child

*6.* Obtain the position of the new parent for the child

*7.* Copy the child record into its proper place

We now formalize the previous notions in the procedure **CreateHeap** given in Fig. 9-67.

Step 1 of the program contains an iteration statement which controls the construction, by successive insertions, of the desired heap. The second step selects the record to be inserted into the existing heap and copies the key into **NewVal**. The third step obtains the position of the parent of the new leaf node which is being inserted. Step 4 controls the placing of the new record into the existing heap. This record (initially a leaf node in the binary tree) potentially moves up the tree along the path between the new leaf and the top of the heap. This process continues (steps 5, 6, and 7) until the new record reaches a position in the tree that satisfies the definition of a heap. The copying of the new key into its proper place in the tree occurs in step 8. The behavior of the construction of the heap in Fig. 9-65 for the sample key set

58, 86, 26, 44, 92, 61, 13, 39, 8, 75

is given in Fig. 9-68. Each tree in the diagram represents the state of construction after the insertion and reconstruction process is complete.

Now that we have a heap for the given table, we can use the notion of the squash tournament to perform the sort. The record with the largest key is presently at the top of the heap, and it can be written out directly. Since we want to perform the sort in place, we can interchange the records in positions 1 and **N**. When this is done, however, we must reconstruct a new heap consisting of $N - 1$ records. This reconstruction process is realized in a manner similar to that used in procedure **CreateHeap**. In particular, the heap in Fig. 9-65 is shown in Fig. 9-69*a* after interchanging keys **92** and **58** and also after the reconstruction of a new heap. Once the key having a value of **58** is placed at the root of the tree, it must be moved down, since the present tree (Fig. 9-69*a*) is no longer a heap. This is accomplished by choosing the largest of its siblings (that is, its direct descendants), which is **86**. In this instance, **86** moves to the top of the heap. Now we examine the greatest of the left and right sons of $K_2$ (that is, **44** and **75**) and choose **75**. In order to obtain a heap, we must interchange **75** and **58**. We then get the heap in Fig. 9-69*b*. This second record can now be exchanged with the ninth record. A new heap must then be constructed for $N - 2$ records. By repeating this exchange and reconstruction process, the initial table is sorted.

We now give the general algorithm for this technique:

*1.* Create the initial heap

*2.* Repeat thru step 8 $N - 1$ times where **N** is the number of records

```
procedure CreateHeap (
    var Heap: Vector;        {Input/output, the vector to be sorted}
        N: integer           {Input, number of elements}
                        );
{Given a vector of integers, this procedure rearranges the elements to form
  a heap.}
var
    New: integer;        {Index of element being inserted into heap}
    Pos: integer;        {Index for searching for proper position}
    Par: integer;        {Index of parent of Pos}
    NewVal: integer;     {Value of element being inserted into heap}
begin
    {Step 1: Build heap}
    for New : = 2 to N do
        begin

            {Step 2: Initialize construction phase}
            Pos : = New;
            NewVal : = Heap[New];

            {Step 3: Obtain parent of new record}
            Par : = Pos div 2;

            {Step 4: Place new record in existing heap}
            while (Pos > 1) and (NewVal > Heap[Par]) do
                begin

                    {Step 5: Interchange record}
                    Heap[Pos] : = Heap[Par];

                    {Step 6: Obtain next parent}
                    Pos : = Par;
                    Par : = Pos div 2;

                    {Step 7: Check if Par subscript out of bounds}
                    if Par < 1
                    then Par : = 1
                end;

            {Step 8: Copy new record into its proper place}
            Heap[Pos] : = NewVal
        end
end; {CreateHeap}
```

**FIGURE 9-67**
**Procedure to create**
**an initial heap**
**for a key set.**

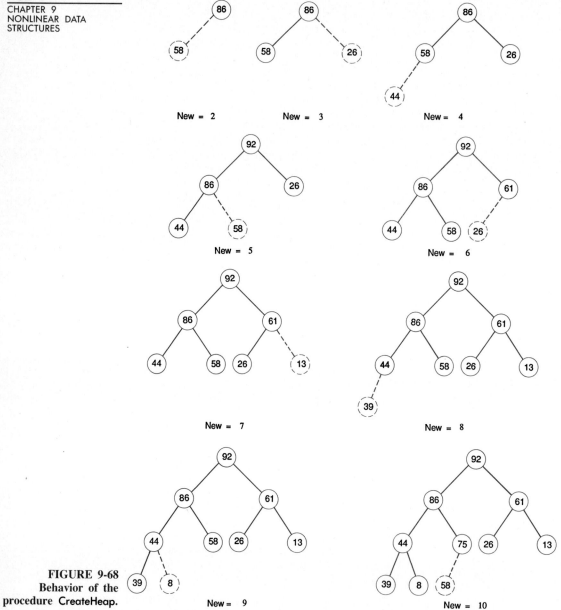

New = 2  New = 3  New = 4

New = 5

New = 6

New = 7

New = 8

FIGURE 9-68
**Behavior of the**
**procedure CreateHeap.**

New = 9

New = 10

3. Exchange the first record with the last unsorted record

4. Obtain the index of the largest son of the new record

5. Repeat thru step 8 for the unsorted elements in the heap and while the current element's key is greater than that of the first element

6. Interchange records and obtain the next left son

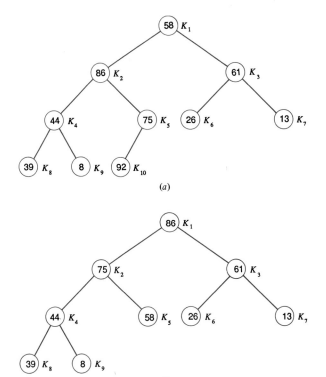

FIGURE 9-69

7. Obtain the index of the next biggest son

8. Copy the record into its proper place

The formalization of this general algorithm yields the procedure **HeapSort** in Fig. 9-70.

The behavior of procedure **HeapSort** for the heap in Fig. 9-65 is given in terms of trees in Fig. 9-71. An alternative behavior of the procedure for the same heap appears in Table 9-4.

Consider the timing analysis of the heap sort. Since we are using a full binary tree, the worst case analysis is easier than the average case. Note that the depth of a full binary tree of $n$ nodes is $\lceil \log_2 n \rceil$. Recall that to sort a given key set, we must first create a heap and then sort that heap. The worst case at each step involves performing a number of comparisons given by the depth of the tree. This observation implies that the number of comparisons is $O(n \log_2 n)$. As mentioned earlier, the average case is more complex to analyze, but it can be shown that it is also $O(n \log_2 n)$. Also, no extra working storage area, except for one record position, is required.

## 9-4.3   TRIE STRUCTURES

We have discussed the applicability of binary trees to searching. In that discussion, the branching at any level in the tree was determined by the

```
procedure HeapSort (
    var K: Vector;        {Input/output, the vector to be sorted}
    N: integer            {Input, number of elements}
                      );
```
{Given a vector of integer elements, this procedure sorts the vector in ascending order using the heap sort technique. Use is made of the procedure CreateHeap presented earlier.}
```
var
    Lim: integer;         {Limit of unsorted elements}
    Par: integer;         {Index of current parent}
    Larg: integer;        {Index of largest direct descendent of current parent}
    Key: integer;         {Current value being positioned in heap}
    Temp: integer;        {Used to swap elements}
begin
    {Step 1: Create initial heap}
    CreateHeap (K, N);

    {Step 2: Perform sort}
    for Lim := N downto 2 do
        begin

            {Step 3: Exchange record}
            Temp := K[1];
            K[1] := K[Lim];
            K[Lim] := Temp;

            {Step 4: Initialize pass}
            Par := 1;
            Key := K[1];
            Larg := 2;
```

**FIGURE 9-70
Program to perform
a heap sort.**

entire key value. In this subsection we examine briefly the feasibility of using $m$-ary trees ($m \geq 2$) for searching. Also, the branching criterion at a particular level in such a tree will be based on a portion of the key value rather than on the entire key value.

A *trie* structure is defined as a complete $m$-ary tree in which each node consists of $m$ components. Typically, these components correspond to letters and digits. Trie structures occur frequently in the area of information organization and retrieval. The method of searching in tries is analogous to the notion of digital sorting (see Sec. 8-9.1). In particular, the branching at each node of level $k$ depends on the $k$th character of a key. Table 9-5 contains an example of a trie structure for searching a set of 32 names. It consists of 12 nodes, each of which is a vector of 27 elements. Each element contains a dash, or the desired word, or a node number. A blank symbol (□) is used to denote the end of a word during the scan of a key. Node 1 is the root of the trie.

As an example, we will trace through the search for the word **PEACOCK**.

{Step 5: Obtain index of largest son of new record}
**if** Larg + 1 < Lim
**then if** K[Larg + 1] > K[Larg]
    **then** Larg : = Larg + 1;


{Step 6: Reconstruct the new heap}
**while** (Larg <= Lim − 1) **and** (K[Larg] > Key) **do**
  **begin**

      {Step 7: Interchange record}
      K[Par] : = K[Larg];

      {Step 8: Obtain next left son}
      Par : = Larg;
      Larg : = 2 * Par;

      {Step 9: Obtain index of next largest son}
      **if** Larg + 1 < Lim
      **then begin**
          **if** K[Larg + 1] > K[Larg]
          **then** Larg : = Larg + 1
        **end**
      **else if** Larg > N
          **then** Larg : = N;

      {Step 10: Copy record into its proper place}
      K[Par] : = Key
    **end**
  **end**
**end**; {HeapSort}

FIGURE 9-70 (*cont.*)

The letter **P** tells us that we should go from node 1 to node 6, since the entry which corresponds to this letter is 6. The second letter (**E**) selects the sixth component of node 6. The entry corresponding to **E** transfers us to node 12. At this node, the letter **A** is then used to find the desired word.

A general algorithm for this search technique follows:

*1.* Repeat thru step 5 for each character in the name

*2.* Obtain the index from the current character

*3.* Repeat thru step 5 until an empty location is encountered

*4.* If the calculated position contains the name,
    then return its position

*5.* If the calculated position contains a different name,
    then write 'unexpected name found' and return
    else move to this new location

*6.* Write 'name not found' and return

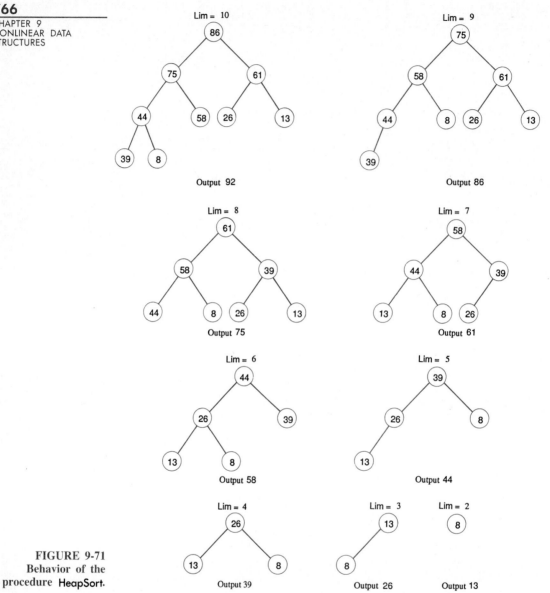

FIGURE 9-71
Behavior of the
procedure HeapSort.

The algorithm repeatedly scans the next character from the name and branches accordingly. This scanning process stops either when the given name is found or when the search fails.

The example trie given is very wasteful of memory space. Memory can be saved at the expense of running time if each class of names is represented by a linked tree. Figure 9-72 represents the trie of Table 9-5. Note that this representation is a forest of trees.

The best compromise situation in terms of space and running time occurs when only a few levels of a trie are used for the first few characters of the key and then some other structure, such as a linked list or binary tree, is used in the remainder of the search.

## 9-4.4 GRAMMARS, LANGUAGES, AND PARSE TREES

A simple model for a compiler consisting of two major phases was introduced in Sec. 6-5.3. Recall that the first phase is responsible for the syntactic recognition of a given program, while the second phase involves the generation of code for that program. The syntactic recognition phase has two subphases that deal with lexical analysis and syntax analysis. Recall that lexical analysis involves the recognition of tokens such as variable names, constants, and keywords. The syntax analyzer, however, performs higher-level recognition at the sentence level, that is, at the expression and statement levels. One approach to compiling sentences from a programming language using Polish notation was explored in Sec. 8-5.1. This subsection introduces a grammar, on the one hand, as a vehicle for precisely defining a programming language and, on the other hand, as a tool for recognizing the sentences from a given language.

Programming languages must be precisely defined. Unfortunately for some of the earlier programming languages, the existence of a particular compiler finally provided the precise definition of the language.

The proper specification of a programming language involves definition of the following:

*1.* The set of symbols (or alphabet) that can be used to construct correct programs

*2.* The set of all syntactically correct programs

*3.* The "meaning" of all syntactically correct programs

**TABLE 9-4** Behavior of the Program HeapSort

| $r$ | Initial Table $K_r$ | Initial Heap | Pass number (Lim) | | | | | | | | | Sorted |
|---|---|---|---|---|---|---|---|---|---|---|---|
| | | | 10 | 9 | 8 | 7 | 6 | 5 | 4 | 3 | 2 |
| 1 | 58 | 92 | 86 | 75 | 61 | 58 | 44 | 39 | 26 | 13 | 8 |
| 2 | 86 | 86 | 75 | 58 | 58 | 44 | 26 | 26 | 13 | 8 | 13 |
| 3 | 26 | 61 | 61 | 61 | 39 | 39 | 39 | 8 | 8 | 26 | 26 |
| 4 | 44 | 44 | 44 | 44 | 44 | 13 | 13 | 13 | 39 | 39 | 39 |
| 5 | 92 | 75 | 58 | 8 | 8 | 8 | 8 | 44 | 44 | 44 | 44 |
| 6 | 61 | 26 | 26 | 26 | 26 | 26 | 58 | 58 | 58 | 58 | 58 |
| 7 | 13 | 13 | 13 | 13 | 13 | 61 | 61 | 61 | 61 | 61 | 61 |
| 8 | 39 | 39 | 39 | 39 | 75 | 75 | 75 | 75 | 75 | 75 | 75 |
| 9 | 8 | 8 | 8 | 86 | 86 | 86 | 86 | 86 | 86 | 86 | 86 |
| 10 | 75 | 58 | 92 | 92 | 92 | 92 | 92 | 92 | 92 | 92 | 92 |

**TABLE 9-5** Trie Structure for a List

| | Node Number | | | | | |
|---|---|---|---|---|---|---|
| | 1 | 2 | 3 | 4 | 5 | 6 |
| □ | — | — | — | — | — | — |
| A | — | CANARY | EAGLE | — | — | — |
| B | — | — | — | — | — | — |
| C | 2 | — | — | — | — | — |
| D | — | — | — | — | — | — |
| E | 3 | — | — | — | — | 12 |
| F | FALCON | — | — | — | — | — |
| G | 4 | — | — | — | — | — |
| H | HAWK | — | — | — | — | PHEASANT |
| I | — | — | — | — | — | PINTAIL |
| J | — | — | — | — | — | — |
| K | KIWI | — | — | — | — | — |
| L | LOON | — | — | — | — | — |
| M | MALLARD | — | EMU | — | — | — |
| N | — | — | — | — | — | — |
| O | 5 | 9 | — | 11 | — | — |
| P | 6 | — | — | — | — | — |
| Q | — | — | — | — | — | — |
| R | 7 | 10 | — | GROUSE | ORIOLE | — |
| S | 8 | — | — | — | — | — |
| T | TEAL | — | — | — | — | — |
| U | — | — | — | GULL | — | PUFFIN |
| V | VULTURE | — | — | — | — | — |
| W | WREN | — | — | — | OWL | — |
| X | — | — | — | — | — | — |
| Y | — | — | — | — | — | — |
| Z | — | — | — | — | — | — |

In this section we shall be concerned with the first two items in the specification of programming languages.

A language $L$ can be considered a subset of the set of all strings that can be generated from a given alphabet. The language consisting of every possible string over an alphabet is not particularly interesting because it is too large. For example, if the given alphabet consists of the 26 Roman letters and the four arithmetic operators (denoted by $+$, $-$, $*$, and $/$) and we want to define a valid expression, the string (or sentence)

A + * B

is invalid syntax because of the presence of two consecutive operators, while the sentence

**TABLE 9-5** Trie Structure for a list (*cont.*)

| | Node Number | | | | | |
|---|---|---|---|---|---|---|
| | 7 | 8 | 9 | 10 | 11 | 12 |
| □ | — | — | — | — | — | — |
| A | — | SANDPIPER | — | CRANE | — | PEACOCK |
| B | — | — | — | — | — | — |
| C | — | — | — | — | — | — |
| D | — | — | — | — | — | — |
| E | REDHEAD | — | — | — | — | — |
| F | — | — | — | — | — | — |
| G | — | — | — | — | — | — |
| H | — | SHOVELLER | — | — | — | — |
| I | — | — | — | — | — | — |
| J | — | — | — | — | — | — |
| K | — | — | — | — | — | — |
| L | — | — | — | — | GOLDFINCH | PELICAN |
| M | — | — | — | — | — | — |
| N | — | — | CONDOR | — | — | — |
| O | ROBIN | — | COOT | CROW | GOOSE | — |
| P | — | SPARROW | — | — | — | — |
| Q | — | — | — | — | — | — |
| R | — | — | — | — | — | — |
| S | — | — | — | — | — | — |
| T | — | — | — | — | — | — |
| U | — | — | — | — | — | — |
| V | — | — | — | — | — | — |
| W | — | SWAN | — | — | — | — |
| X | — | — | — | — | — | — |
| Y | — | — | — | — | — | — |
| Z | — | — | — | — | — | — |

A + B

has an obvious meaning.

How can a language be represented? A language consists of a finite or an infinite set of sentences. Finite languages can be specified by exhaustively enumerating all their sentences. For infinite languages, such an enumeration is not possible. Any means of specifying a language should be finite. We are using syntax diagrams to define the syntax of Pascal in this book. Another method of specification which satisfies this requirement uses a generative device called a *grammar*.

A grammar consists of a finite nonempty set of rules or *productions* which specify the syntax of a language. Many grammars may generate the same language but impose different structures on the sentences of that

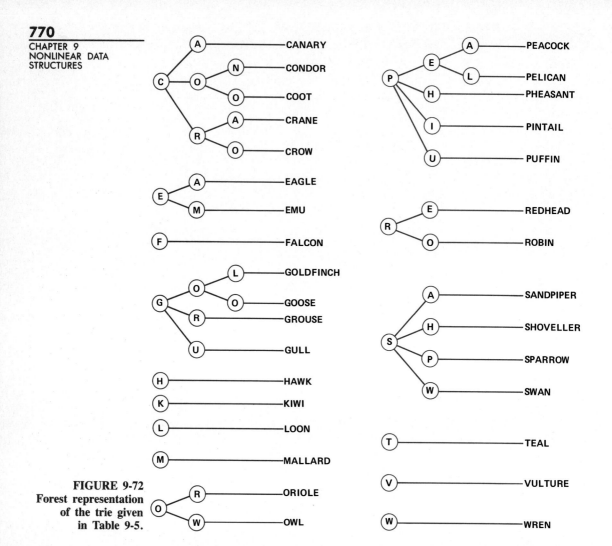

**FIGURE 9-72**
**Forest representation**
**of the trie given**
**in Table 9-5.**

language. The study of grammars constitutes an important subarea of computer science called *formal language theory*. This area emerged in the mid-1950s as a result of the efforts of Noam Chomsky, who gave a mathematical model of a grammar in connection with his study of natural languages. In 1960, the concept of a grammar became important to programmers because the syntax of ALGOL 60 was described by a grammar.

Formally, a grammar is a mathematical system for defining languages, but it is also a device for giving some useful structure to sentences in a language. The structure of a sentence will take the form of a tree. For a sentence in the English language, the structure is described in terms of subject, predicate, phrase, noun, and so on. On the other hand, for a programming language, the structure is given in terms of procedures, statements, expressions, etc. It is desirable to be able to describe all such structures and to obtain a set of all the correct or admissible sentences in a language, e.g., a set of correct sentences in English or a set of valid ALGOL programs. The grammatical structure of a language helps us determine whether a particular sentence does or does not belong to the set of correct sentences. The grammatical structure of a sentence is generally studied by analyzing the various parts of the sentence and their relationships to one another.

Consider the sentence "Lucy pets the dog." Its structure (or *parse*) is shown in Fig 9-73. This diagram of a parse displays the syntax of a sentence as a tree and is therefore called a *syntax tree* (or *parse tree*). Each node in the tree represents a phrase of the syntax. The words such as "Lucy" and "dog" are the basic symbols, or primitives, of the language.

For this example, let us consider a small subset of the English language whose syntax is described by the following rules:

*1.* <sentence> ::= <subject> <predicate>

*2.* <subject> ::= <article> <noun>

*3.* <subject> ::= <noun>

*4.* <predicate> ::= <verb> <object>

*5.* <article> ::= a

*6.* <article> ::= the

*7.* <verb> ::= holds

*8.* <verb> ::= pets

*9.* <verb> ::= sings

*10.* <noun> ::= Linus

*11.* <noun> ::= Lucy

*12.* <noun> ::= Snoopy

*13.* <noun> ::= blanket

*14.* <noun> ::= dog

*15.* <noun> ::= song

*16.* <object> ::= <article> <noun>

*17.* <object> ::= <noun>

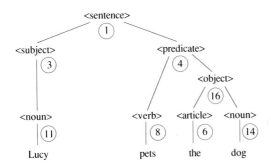

FIGURE 9-73
A parse of the sentence "Lucy pets the dog."

These rules state that a sentence in this language is composed of a <subject> followed by a <predicate>; the <subject> has two possible compositions—an <article> followed by a <noun> or simply a <noun>; a <predicate> consists of a <verb> followed by an <object>; and so on.

The structure of a language is discussed by using symbols such as <sentence>, <verb>, <article>, and <noun> which represent *syntactic classes* of elements. Each syntactic class consists of a number of alternative structures, and each structure consists of an ordered set of items which are either primitives (of the language) or syntactic classes. These alternative structures are called *productions*, or *rules of syntax*, or *replacement rules*. For example, the production

$$<\text{sentence}> ::= <\text{subject}> \quad <\text{predicate}>$$

defines a "sentence" to be composed of a <subject> followed by a <predicate>. The symbol ::= separates the syntactic class <sentence> from its definition. The syntactic class and the ::= symbol along with the interpretation of a production enable us to describe a language.

A system or language that describes another language is known as a *metalanguage*. For example, the metalanguage used to teach German at most North American universities is English, while the metalanguage used to teach English is also English. The diagram of the parse of a sentence describes its syntax but not its meaning or *semantics*. At this time, we are concerned mainly with the syntax of a language, and the device that we have just defined to give the syntactic definition of the language is called a *grammar*.

When we speak (or write) English, we use the grammatical rules of the language to help us produce correct sentences in the language. Likewise, a computer programmer is concerned with producing programs that adhere to the productions (grammatical rules) of the programming language. The compiler for a programming language, on the other hand, is faced with the problem of determining whether a given sentence (source program construct) is syntactically correct based on the given grammatical rules. If the syntax is correct, the compiler produces object code.

Consider the problem of trying to generate, or produce, the sentence "Lucy pets the dog" from the set of productions given. It is accomplished by starting first with the syntactic class symbol <sentence> and looking for a production that has <sentence> to the left of the ::= . There is only one such production, namely,

$$<\text{sentence}> ::= <\text{subject}> \quad <\text{predicate}>$$

We have replaced the class <sentence> by its only possible composition. We then take the string

$$<\text{subject}> \quad <\text{predicate}>$$

and look for a production whose left-hand side is <subject> and then replace it with the right-hand side of that production. There are two such productions, namely, productions 2 and 3. The production that we want must start with a <noun> (since "Lucy" is the first word of the given sentence). Therefore, the application of the rule

<subject> ::= <noun>

produces the string

<noun>   <predicate>

We next look for a production whose left part is <noun>, and six such productions are found. By selecting the production

<noun> ::= Lucy

and substituting the right-hand side in the string <noun> <predicate>, we obtain the string

Lucy <predicate>

This enumerative process is continued until we arrive at the correct sentence. At this point, the sentence contains only primitive or terminal elements of the language (no classes). A complete derivation or generation of the sentence "Lucy pets the dog" is as follows:

<sentence> $\Rightarrow$ <subject> <predicate>        . . . by production 1

$\Rightarrow$ <noun> <predicate>        . . . by production 3

$\Rightarrow$ Lucy <predicate>        . . . by production 11

$\Rightarrow$ Lucy <verb> <object>        . . . by production 4

$\Rightarrow$ Lucy pets <object>        . . . by production 8

$\Rightarrow$ Lucy pets <article> <noun>    . . . by production 16

$\Rightarrow$ Lucy pets the <noun>        . . . by production 6

$\Rightarrow$ Lucy pets the dog        . . . by production 14

Here the symbol $\Rightarrow$ denotes that the string on the right-hand side of the symbol can be obtained by applying one replacement rule to the previous string.

The rules for the example language can produce a large number of sentences (in fact, 972). Examples of other sentences are

"Linus holds the blanket"

"Lucy sings a song"

"The blanket sings a dog"

Note that the last of these sentences, although grammatically correct, does not make sense because of its semantics. This situation is often allowed in the specification of languages. There are many syntactically valid FORTRAN and Pascal programs that do not make sense. It turns out to be easier to define languages if certain sentences of questionable validity are allowed by the replacement rules.

The metalanguage used in the previous example is called BNF (meaning either Backus-Naur Form or Backus Normal Form). Formulated originally by John Backus (who was, in fact, the father of FORTRAN), it was first made popular when it was used to describe the syntax of ALGOL 60. It is still commonly used. Since confusion between the symbols of the metalanguage (e.g., <noun> and <verb>) and the symbols of the language itself (such as "a" and "pets") must be avoided, the three special metalinguistic symbols (<, >, ::= ) are used, which are not part of the language's alphabet. Observe that the metasymbols (or *nonterminals*) are always parenthesized with the metasymbols < and >. A *terminal symbol* is a character or a string of characters from the alphabet. For example, "a" and "the" are terminal symbols in the production for <article>. It is convenient to use a fourth metalinguistic symbol (|) to separate the right parts of productions that have a common left part. For example, the productions

$$<article> ::= a \qquad \text{and} \qquad <article> ::= the$$

can be rewritten using the metasymbol | as

$$<article> ::= a \quad | \quad the$$

We define a grammar more formally as a 4-tuple $G = (V_N, V_T, S, P)$, where $V_N$ and $V_T$ are disjoint sets of nonterminal and terminal symbols, respectively, $S$ is the distinguished symbol of $V_N$ (commonly called the *goal* or *starting* symbol), and $P$ is a finite set of productions. The set $V = V_T \cup V_N$ is called the *vocabulary* of the grammar.

For the current example, the complete specification of the grammar is

$$V_N = \{<sentence>, <subject>, <predicate>, <article>, <noun>,$$
$$<verb>, <object>\}$$

$$V_T = \{a, the, Linus, Lucy, Snoopy, blanket, dog, song, holds, pets,$$
$$sings\}$$

$$S = <sentence>$$

$$P = \text{the set of 17 productions given earlier}$$

We will refer to this grammar later as $G_1$.

There is an important thing to note concerning the generation of strings (that is, sentences) from a grammar. We have neglected (for legibility reasons) to put into the terminal symbols of the grammar the blank characters that normally appear between the words in the sentences. Throughout the current discussion, we assume, unless it is obvious from the context of the text, that a blank delimits all terminal symbols.

It should be noted that not all strings composed of terminal symbols form sentences (e.g., "Linus the a holds" is not syntactically correct). Hence it is necessary to devise a method of analyzing the various parts of a string to determine whether the string is a sentence in the language. Earlier we referred to this process as *parsing*.

How do we construct a parse? Or, equivalently, how do we derive a syntax tree? In general, there are two methods of parsing—top-down and bottom-up. Let us examine both of these methods in some detail.

In *top-down parsing*, an attempt to construct a syntax tree is initiated by starting at the root of the tree (that is, the distinguished symbol) and proceeding downward toward the leaves (that is, the symbols forming the string). The effect of such a process is to generate sentences systematically from the language until a match can be found with the string in question. Of course, if no match can be found, the string is not a sentence in the language. This generation of sentences can be mapped with the aid of a special relation $\Rightarrow$ in which $x \Rightarrow y$ is interpreted as "string $x$ produces $y$ (or $y$ reduces to $x$)" during a step of a parse. The steps in the generation of the sentence "Lucy pets the dog" given the grammatical rules for $G_1$ have already been illustrated. A circled number on the syntax tree in Fig. 9-73 represents the production number that is used in that part of the construction of the syntax tree. It is easy to see how the construction of the tree parallels the sentence-generation process just given.

In practice, the construction of a syntax tree using a top-down parsing strategy may involve a number of wrong production steps before the correct tree results. For example, the rule <subject> ::= <noun> was used in the second step of the sentence generation. We could have chosen, with the same conviction, to use the production step <subject> ::= <article> <noun>. Of course, to do so would have led to the generation of a sentence that is not the input string. This fact would have been discovered in the next production step of <article> ::= a or <article> ::= the, since neither "a" nor "the" is equivalent to "Lucy." Such errors in production selection can be recovered from relatively easily: we simply retrace our steps up the syntax tree and try an alternative production step. Such an alternative step is the application of <subject> ::= <noun>. We continue in this manner during the entire parse until the correct sentence is generated.

In the second method of parsing, *bottom-up parsing*, completion of the syntax tree is attempted by starting at the leaves and moving upward toward the root. Relating this strategy to the grammar given in the previous example, the following series of derivations results in a bottom-up parse of "Lucy pets the dog" (the notation that $x \Rightarrow y$ also means "$y$ reduces to $x$," and this is the interpretation used in bottom-up parsing):

| | | |
|---|---|---|
| <noun> pets the dog | $\Rightarrow$ Lucy pets the dog | . . . by production 11 |
| <subject> pets the dog | $\Rightarrow$ | . . . by production 3 |

| | | |
|---|---|---|
| $<$subject$>$ $<$verb$>$ the dog | $\Rightarrow$ | . . . by production 8 |
| $<$subject$>$ $<$verb$>$ $<$article$>$ dog | $\Rightarrow$ | . . . by production 6 |
| $<$subject$>$ $<$verb$>$ $<$article$>$ $<$noun$>$ | $\Rightarrow$ | . . . by production 14 |
| $<$subject$>$ $<$verb$>$ $<$object$>$ | $\Rightarrow$ | . . . by production 16 |
| $<$subject$>$ $<$predicate$>$ | $\Rightarrow$ | . . . by production 4 |
| $<$sentence$>$ | $\Rightarrow$ | . . . by production 1 |

Observe that the same syntax tree is constructed (see Fig. 9-73) and the same productions are invoked as for the top-down method; however, the production steps take place in a completely different order. In particular, because we parsed the sentence in a left-to-right manner using both methods, the productions are not applied in the reverse order. If our parsing strategy for the top-down method had worked from right to left, the productions would have been applied in the reverse order in which they were applied using the left-to-right bottom-up strategy. Similarly, a bottom-up right-to-left parse applies productions in the reverse order to that of a top-down left-to-right strategy. Because a bottom-up left-to-right parse is so commonly used in compilers for parsing statements from a programming language, it is often referred to as the *canonical parse*.

The basic parsing strategy in a canonical parse begins with the isolation of a special substring in the given input string or the resulting string that has been transformed by a number of production applications to the input string. Such a transformed string is often called a *sentential form*, and the special string that is isolated is commonly called a *handle*. In the bottom-up parse of the sentence "Lucy pets the dog," the initial string "Lucy pets the dog," the final derivation $<$sentence$>$, and all intermediate derivations are examples of sentential forms. The handle should be the left-most simple phrase (a *simple phrase* is a substring of the sentential form that matches the right-hand side of a production) corresponding to a production that can be applied given the context of the handle in the sentential form. For example, "Lucy" is the handle in the sentential form "Lucy pets the dog," and $<$verb$>$ $<$object$>$ is the handle in the sentential form $<$subject$>$ $<$verb$>$ $<$object$>$. In an example given later in this section, we illustrate how an examination of the context of a phrase affects the decision as to whether that phrase is the handle.

Once the handle has been isolated, its corresponding left-hand side (in our example, $<$noun$>$) is substituted at the position of the right-hand side to create a new sentential form (that is, the sentential form "$<$noun$>$ pets the dog" in the case of our example). This process is continued until the goal symbol ($<$sentence$>$ in the example) is reached, if possible. If the goal symbol is the only remaining symbol in the transformed string, then the original input string is a sentence from the language described by the grammar; otherwise, it is not.

The set of sentences that can be generated by the rules of the previous example is finite. Any interesting language usually consists of an infinite set of sentences. As a matter of fact, the importance of a finite device such as a grammar is that it permits the study of the structure of a language consisting of an infinite set of sentences.

The concept of recursion is very applicable to grammars. An example of a grammar that defines a simple language recursively is as follows:

$$G_2 = (V_N, V_T, S, P)$$

where $V_N = \{<\text{digit}>, <\text{no}>, <\text{number}>\}$

$V_T = \{0, 1, 2, 3, 4, 5, 6, 7, 8, 9\}$

$S = <\text{number}>$

$P = \{1 \ <\text{number}> ::= <\text{no}>$

$\qquad 2 \ <\text{no}> ::= <\text{digit}> \ | \ <\text{no}> \ <\text{digit}>$

$\qquad 3 \ <\text{digit}> ::= 0\,|\,1\,|\,2\,|\,3\,|\,4\,|\,5\,|\,6\,|\,7\,|\,8\,|\,9\}$

In the productions labeled 2, the syntactic phrase $<\text{no}>$ can be defined as $<\text{no}> \ <\text{digit}>$. This is a recursive definition. To see how it is applied, let us assume we are to generate the string '694'. We begin with the distinguished symbol $<\text{number}>$ and proceed as follows:

$<\text{number}> \Rightarrow <\text{no}>$

$\qquad\quad \Rightarrow <\text{no}> \ <\text{digit}>$

$\qquad\quad \Rightarrow <\text{no}> \ <\text{digit}> \ <\text{digit}>$

$\qquad\quad \Rightarrow <\text{digit}> \ <\text{digit}> \ <\text{digit}>$

$\qquad\quad \Rightarrow 6 \ <\text{digit}> \ <\text{digit}>$

$\qquad\quad \Rightarrow 6\,9 \ <\text{digit}>$

$\qquad\quad \Rightarrow 6\,9\,4$

The production step of $<\text{no}> ::= <\text{no}> \ <\text{digit}>$ is a very powerful one, since we are effectively creating a two-digit entity from a one-digit entity. This process of expansion allows us to express any integer we desire, regardless of its value. Of course, for a given integer, this recursive process, and hence the expansion, must ultimately cease. This occurs with the application of a nonrecursive production such as $<\text{no}> ::= <\text{digit}>$. This nonrecursive production step is called the *basis step* in the recursive process.

The power of recursive productions in a grammar should be noted and the following two statements, which can be proved as theorems (subject to some minor restriction on the grammar), illustrate this point:

*1.* Any grammar containing a recursively defined production describes an infinite language (that is, a language with an infinite number of sentences).

2. Any grammar containing no (directly or indirectly) recursively defined productions describes a finite language (that is, a language with a finite number of sentences).

Hence in this section the language described by grammar $G_2$ is infinite, while the language described by the first grammar is finite.

As another example illustrating the use of recursively defined productions, consider the problem of formulating a grammar for describing an identifier name in standard Pascal. An identifier name consists of a single alphabetical character or an alphabetical character followed by a finite number of alphabetical and numeric characters. An example grammar can be given as

$$G_3 = (V_N, V_T, S, P)$$

where $V_N = \{\text{<identifier>}, \text{<ident>}, \text{<letter>}, \text{<others>}\}$

$\qquad V_T = \{A, B, \ldots, Z, a, b, \ldots, z, 0, 1, \ldots, 9\}$

$\qquad S = \text{<identifier>}$

$\qquad P = \{1 \ \text{<identifier>} ::= \text{<ident>}$

$\qquad\qquad 2 \ \text{<ident>} ::= \text{<letter>} \mid \text{<ident>} \text{<letter>} \mid \text{<ident>} \text{<digit>}$

$\qquad\qquad 3 \ \text{<letter>} ::= A \mid B \mid C \mid \ldots \mid Z \mid a \mid b \mid c \mid \ldots \mid z$

$\qquad\qquad 4 \ \text{<digit>} ::= 0 \mid 1 \mid 2 \mid 3 \mid 4 \mid 5 \mid 6 \mid 7 \mid 8 \mid 9\}$

A syntax tree for the parse of 'Lab1' is given in Fig. 9-74.

In most programming languages, there is a practical limit to the length of an identifier name (e.g., the length of a Pascal identifier name in some implementations can be at most 31). The grammar $G_3$ allows for any length of identifier. By a slight modification in the BNF metalanguage, we can accommodate a production that is to be applied iteratively 30 times (at most).

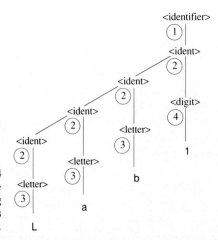

**FIGURE 9-74**
The parse of the string Lab1 using the productions of $G_3$.

The set of productions labeled 2 can be rewritten as

$$2 \quad < \text{ident} > ::= < \text{letter} > \mid < \text{letter} > [< \text{letter} > \mid < \text{others} >]^{30}$$

In general, a production of the form $x ::= y[z]^n$ is interpreted as

$$x ::= yz \mid yzz \mid yzzz \mid \ldots \mid \underbrace{yzz \ldots z}_{n \text{ times}}$$

An important question which arises in formal languages is whether a sentential form has a unique syntax tree. Consider the simple grammar $G_4$, which has the following productions:

$$< S > ::= < S > * < S >$$

$$< S > ::= a$$

where $a$ is a terminal symbol. Let us find a derivation for the sentence $a * a * a$. One such derivation is

$$<S> \Rightarrow <S> * <S> \Rightarrow <S> * <S> * <S>$$

$$\Rightarrow a * <S> * <S> \Rightarrow a * a * <S> \Rightarrow a * a * a$$

where the left-most $<S>$ in the second step has been rewritten as $<S> * <S>$. Another possibility, of course, is that the right-most $<S>$ in the same step is rewritten as $<S> * <S>$. Both possibilities are diagrammed in Fig. 9-75. It is clear that the two syntax trees are different. That is, we have two different parses for the same sentence. The existence of more than one *parse* for some sentence in a language can cause a compiler to generate a different set of instructions (object code) for different parses. Usually, this phenomenon is intolerable. If a compiler is to perform valid translations of sentences in a language, that language must be unambiguously defined. This concept leads us to the following definition: A sentence generated by a grammar is *ambiguous* if there exists more than one syntax tree for it. A grammar is ambiguous if it generates at least one ambiguous sentence.

It should be noted that we called the grammar ambiguous and not the language which it generates. There are many grammars which can generate the same language; some are ambiguous and some are not.

Let us examine another example of an ambiguous grammar. In particular, consider the grammar $G_5$ for unparenthesized arithmetic expressions consisting of the operators $+$ and $*$ with single-letter identifiers:

$$<\text{expression}> ::= i \mid <\text{expression}> + <\text{expression}>$$

$$\mid <\text{expression}> * <\text{expression}>$$

Assume that the sentence $i * i + i$ is to be parsed. Two possible derivations are as follows:

$$<expression> \Rightarrow <expression> * <expression>$$
$$\Rightarrow <expression> * <expression> + <expression>$$
$$\Rightarrow i * <expression> + <expression>$$
$$\Rightarrow i * i + <expression>$$
$$\Rightarrow i * i + i$$

$$<expression> \Rightarrow <expression> + <expression>$$
$$\Rightarrow <expression> * <expression> + <expression>$$
$$\Rightarrow i * <expression> + <expression>$$
$$\Rightarrow i * i + <expression>$$
$$\Rightarrow i * i + i$$

Their corresponding syntax trees are given in Fig. 9-76. Since there exist two distinct syntax trees for the sentence $i * i + i$, the grammar is ambiguous. Intuitively, this grammar is ambiguous because it is not known whether to evaluate $*$ before $+$ or conversely. The grammar can be rewritten in such a manner that the multiplication will have precedence over addition. This revision is accomplished using the following set of productions (grammar $G_6$):

$$<expression> ::= <term> \mid <expression> + <term>$$
$$<term> ::= <factor> \mid <term> * <factor>$$
$$<factor> ::= i$$

**FIGURE 9-75**  Two distinct syntax trees for the sentence $a * a * a$ in $G_4$.

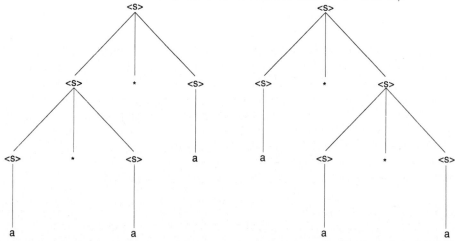

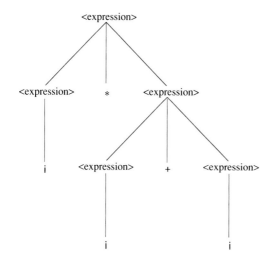

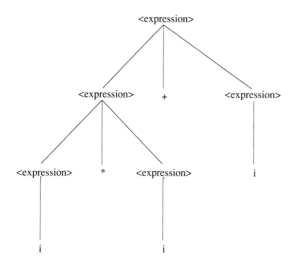

**FIGURE 9-76**
**Ambiguous syntax**
**trees for** $i * i + i$ **in** $G_5$.

Note that in this new grammar an <expression> is defined to include a <term>. A <term> can involve a multiplication but not an addition operator. Since in an <expression> all <term>'s must be resolved before <expression>'s, multiplication must have precedence over addition.

Consider the syntax diagram for the Pascal case statement, originally presented as Fig. 3-30 and repeated here as Fig. 9-77 for ease of reference. The following productions define the same portion of the Pascal language:

<case statement> ::= **case** <expression> **of** <case list> **end**

| **case** <expression> **of** <case list>; **end**

<case list> ::= <case element> | <case list>; <case element>

<case element> ::= <constant list> : <statement>

<constant list> ::= <constant> | <constant lists>, <constant>

Here, <expression>, <statement>, and <constant> are nonterminal symbols defined by other productions in the full grammar for Pascal. Notice the occurrence of two recursive productions, those for <case list> and <constant list>.

Study of these productions and the corresponding syntax diagram will demonstrate that they define exactly the same set of valid case statements. Syntax diagrams are considered by many to represent a more readable definition of language syntax rules. However, many algorithms have been developed for processing language syntax definitions in the form of grammars. For example, there are several well-known algorithms for constructing a parse tree given a grammar and a sequence of terminal symbols. (Of course, syntax diagrams can be processed as well, since they are essentially directed graphs. The processing of graphs is considered in the next section.)

The grammars we have described in this subsection are called *context-free grammars*. A context-free grammar is a grammar in which there is only one nonterminal symbol allowed on the left-hand side of a production. Parsers for context-free grammars can be very fast. In fact, several kinds of parsers exist that have a timing of $O(n)$, where $n$ is the number of tokens in a given string.

## EXERCISES 9-4

1. Based on the discussion of symbolic manipulation of expressions, construct a binary tree (and associated symbol table entries) as in Fig. 9-59 for the expression

   $a * \theta b + c / d$

2. Using the binary tree obtained in Exercise 1 and assuming values of $a = 2$, $b = 10$, $c = 8$, and $d = 4$, trace the operation of the function Eval.

3. Trace the function Similar for the pair of trees given in Fig. 9-61.

★★ 4. A classical example of symbol manipulation is finding the derivative of a formula with respect to a variable, say, $x$. This symbol-manipulation application was one of the first to be implemented on a digital

FIGURE 9-77 Syntax diagram for the case statement.

case statement

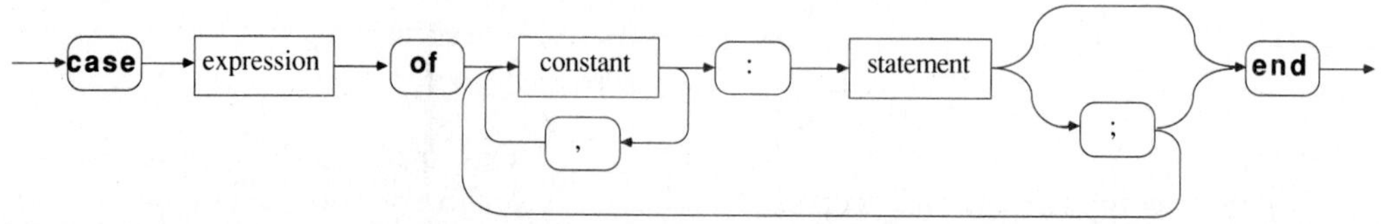

computer. Such implementations have existed since the early 1950s. This application is of great importance in many scientific application areas.

The following rules define the derivative of a formula with respect to $x$ where $u$ and $v$ denote functions of $x$:

$D(x) = 1$

$D(a) = 0$, if $a$ is a constant or a variable other than $x$

$D(\ln u) = D(u)/u$, where ln denotes the natural logarithm

$D(-u) = -D(u)$

$D(u + v) = D(u) + D(v)$

$D(u - v) = D(u) - D(v)$

$D(u*v) = D(u)*v + u*D(v)$

$D(u/v) = D(u)/v - (u*D(v))/v^2$

$D(v \uparrow u) = (v \uparrow u)*(u*D(v)/v + D(u)*\ln v)$

These rules permit evaluation of the derivative $D(y)$ for any formula $y$ composed of the preceding operations. Based on the binary tree representation of an expression given in the text, write a program which differentiates a given expression according to the differentiation rules listed above.

★★ **5.** If we apply the differentiation rules of Exercise 4 to the formula

$$y = \frac{2 \ln (x + a) + b}{x^2}$$

we obtain

$$D(y) = \frac{\left[0 \cdot \ln (x + a) + 2\left(\dfrac{1 + 0}{x + a}\right) + 0\right]}{x^2}$$
$$- \frac{\left[2 \ln (x + a) + b\right] \cdot x^2 \cdot \left(\dfrac{2 \cdot 1}{x} + 0 \cdot \ln x\right)}{(x^2)^2}$$

which is far from satisfactory. Certain redundant operations can be avoided, however, by recognizing the special cases of adding or multiplying by 0, multiplying by 1, or raising to the first power. These simplifications reduce the previous expression to

$$D(y) = \frac{2\dfrac{1}{x + a}}{x^2} - \frac{[2\ln(x + a) + b] \cdot x^2 \cdot \dfrac{2}{x}}{(x^2)^2}$$

which is somewhat more acceptable, yet not ideal. For our purposes, however, these simplifications will suffice. Modify the program obtained in Exercise 4 so that these simplifications are performed.

★★ **6.** One important task in the writing of a textbook is the construction of an index. In such an index, the major terms used in the book are presented in lexical order. Several subterms may be associated with a major term and are written in lexical order immediately following that major term. Each major term and subterm is followed by a set of ascending numbers that identify the pages where the corresponding term is discussed.

You are required to write a program to process a number of arbitrarily ordered major terms and subterms and their associated page numbers in a book and subsequently print the required index.

The input data is to consist of a sequence of input items. Each item is to represent a major term string, a subterm string, or a major term and subterm string. A subterm string always corresponds to the major term most recently encountered in the input.

As an example, some input strings are

DATA STRUCTURE@125@64@481
#VECTOR@475
DATA STRUCTURE#STACK@473@451@407

The symbols # and @ are delimiters for separating a major term from its subterm and page numbers, respectively. In this example, subterms **VECTOR** and **STACK** correspond to the major term **DATA STRUCTURE**.

To print the required index, the index must first be represented in computer memory. One possible organization is given in Fig. 9-78, where each major term corresponds to a node with four fields, which we describe as **MajorNode**. The major term name is stored in the field **Term**. The field **Mjlink** denotes a pointer to the node containing the next major term in a sequence of lexically ordered major terms. **Mjpage** specifies a pointer to a linked linear list of page numbers where the major term is discussed. **Sublist** is a pointer to a binary tree structure consisting of nodes, each of which is denoted as **SubNode**.

In each **SubNode** the field **Subtm** contains a term which is subsidiary to the major term in the **MajorNode** predecessor. **Llink** and **Rlink** point to

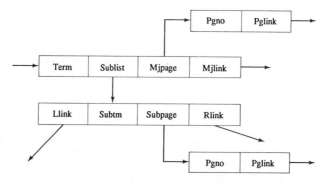

**FIGURE 9-78**
**Possible structure**
**for an index.**

the previous and successor subnodes, respectively. This linked binary tree containing subterms is lexically ordered. **SubPage** is a pointer to a linked linear list of page numbers where the subterm is discussed.

The list of page numbers contains nodes, each of which is a **PageNode**. The field **Pgno** specifies a page number for the predecessor major term or subterm. **Pglink** denotes the address of the next **PageNode**. The nodes are kept in increasing page number sequence. Using these node structures, the major term **DATA STRUCTURE** in the previous example is represented by Fig. 9-79.

7. Determine the behavior of the procedure **HeapSort** as in Table 9-4 for the following set of keys:

   43, 23, 74, 11, 65, 58, 94, 36, 99, 87

8. Construct a trie structure (as in Table 9-5) for the following set of words:

   AND, ARRAY, BEGIN, CASE, CONST, DIV, DO, DOWNTO, ELSE, END, FILE, FOR, FUNCTION, GOTO, IF, IN, LABEL, MOD, NIL, NOT, OF, OR, PACKED, PROCEDURE, PROGRAM, RECORD, REPEAT, SET, THEN, TO, TYPE, UNTIL, VAR, WHILE, and WITH

★ 9. Write a procedure for the insertion of an element into a trie structure that is organized as in Table 9-5. Write a program to test your procedure.

★ 10. Repeat Exercise 9 for the deletion of an element from a trie structure.

★ 11. Write a procedure which when given the address of a tree expression prints the equivalent infix notation of that expression such that it contains a minimum number of parentheses. Write a program to test your procedure.

★ 12. A secret message has been received from deep space on hyperchannel. Although passed through the usual decoding, the message apparently is nonsense. However, Luke Skyscraper (no relation to the famous star-hopper) has developed one ingenious method of decoding the message.

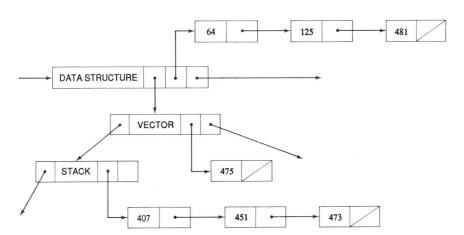

**FIGURE 9-79**
**Representation of**
**DATA STRUCTURE and**
**its subterms**
**VECTOR and**
**STACK.**

Each line of the message has the following format:

number of directions, directions, single letter

For example;

3, 'L', 'R', 'R', 'W'

L.S. has deduced the leading letters to be directions to a location in a binary tree. The last letter is to be placed at that location. For example, the preceding line would produce the following:

New node with 'W' as value

By creating the binary tree and then performing an inorder traversal, L.S. figures to read the message. You are to write a program which first builds a binary tree. Once the tree is complete (detected by the end-of-input method), you are to traverse the tree in inorder and print out the values at each node.

★ **13.** One of the earliest applications of computer science to the humanities was the verification of authorship of historic documents. Where a dispute raged between supporters of one writer and another, the issue could often be settled by analysis which compared characteristics of the document in question with known writings of each contender.

One distinctive feature of any author's writing is the frequency with which he or she uses particular words. Thus by comparing the frequency of word usage of the unknown piece with frequencies of the contending writers' known works, the authorship could be undisputably established. The counting of words is a job for a computer.

In this problem, you are to read in text and generate a list, in alphabetical order, of the words used and the number of times each appears. The input text contains no punctuation or upper-case characters, so isolating individual words is simplified. The words are to be separated and stored in a lexically ordered tree, whose nodes are of the form

| Lptr | Word | Count | Rptr |
|------|------|-------|------|

where **Word** is a string and **Count** is an integer which keeps track of the number of occurrences in the file of **Word**.

When the input is completely processed, write all the words and frequencies (that is, **Word** and **Count**) in alphabetical order by an inorder traversal of the tree. Both the insertion of words into the tree and the output by inorder traversal must be implemented as recursive subprograms.

★★ **14.** A 2-d tree is a binary tree data structure that is used to store records that have two key fields, an $x$ field and a $y$ field. Such records may hold information about a site at location $(x, y)$ (e.g., an oil well).

To insert such a record in a 2-d tree, we first compare the $x$ value of the record to the $x$ value of the record at the root of the tree. The record will be stored in the left subtree if the $x$ value is less than or equal to that of the root, otherwise the record will be stored in the right subtree. At the second level of the 2-d tree, the decision to store a record in the left or right subtree is based on the $y$ value of the record, at the third level, again by the $x$ value, and so on, alternating down the tree. An example of data and the tree produced are given in Fig. 9-80.

   (a) Write a procedure to insert a record with three fields (data, $x$, $y$) into a 2-d tree.

   (b) Write a procedure to do a range search in a 2-d tree, where a range search returns all records in a specified rectangular region. For example,

$$2 \le x \le 4, \ 5 \le y \le 10$$

   (c) Write a main program to test your procedures.

★ **15.** Construct parse trees (bottom-up or top-down as you wish) which will determine if the following input strings are sentences in the grammar

$$G = (V_N, V_T, S, P)$$

where $V_N$ = {<cliche>, <phrase>, <clause>, <subject>,

   <article>, <thing>, <connect>}

$V_T$ = {a, the, east, west, rose, is, and, or, but, best}

data $x$ $y$

(A, 50, 50)  (B, 10, 70)  (C, 80, 85)  (D, 25, 20)
(E, 40, 85)  (F, 70, 85)  (G, 10, 60)

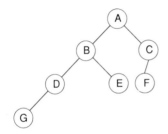

FIGURE 9-80

$$S = <\text{cliche}>$$

$$P = \{1 \quad <\text{cliche}> ::= <\text{phrase}>$$

$$2 \quad <\text{phrase}> ::= <\text{clause}> \mid <\text{phrase}> <\text{connect}>$$
$$<\text{clause}>$$

$$3 \quad <\text{clause}> ::= <\text{subject}> \text{ is } <\text{subject}> \mid$$
$$<\text{clause}> \text{ is } <\text{subject}>$$

$$4 \quad <\text{subject}> ::= <\text{thing}> \mid <\text{article}> <\text{thing}>$$

$$5 \quad <\text{article}> ::= a \mid \text{the}$$

$$6 \quad <\text{thing}> ::= \text{east} \mid \text{west} \mid \text{rose} \mid \text{best}$$

$$7 \quad <\text{connect}> ::= \text{and} \mid \text{or} \mid \text{but}\}$$

The input strings:
(a) east is east but west is best
(b) east or west is best
(c) a rose is a rose is a rose

★★ **16.** Write BNF grammars for the following languages:
  (a) $\{a^i ba^i \mid i \geq 0\}$, where $a^i$ denotes a character string of length $i$, consisting entirely of a's.
  (b) $\{w\$w^R \mid w \in \{0, 1\}^*\}$, where $w^R$ is the reverse of $w$ (that is, if $w = 001$, $w^R = 100$). $\{0, 1\}^*$ denotes the set of strings consisting entirely of zeros and ones.

★★ **17.** Write a grammar for the following language: the set of positive odd integers. Demonstrate, by means of a parse tree, that your grammar can generate the number 635.

★★ **18.** Suppose we want to implement a DDC compiler for the DDC (Decimal Digit Calculator) language which performs arithmetic operations on integer arguments. The BNF grammar description which follows was written to describe the DDC language syntactically:

$$<\text{DDC expr}> ::= <\text{DDC term}> \mid <\text{DDC expr}> <\text{op1}> <\text{DDC expr}>$$
$$<\text{DDC term}> ::= <\text{decimal arg}> \mid <\text{DDC term}> <\text{op2}> <\text{decimal arg}>$$
$$<\text{decimal arg}> ::= <\text{digit}> \mid <\text{decimal arg}> <\text{digit}>$$
$$<\text{digit}> ::= 0 \mid 1 \mid 2 \mid 3 \mid 4 \mid 5 \mid 6 \mid 7 \mid 8 \mid 9$$
$$<\text{op1}> ::= + \mid -$$
$$<\text{op2}> ::= * \mid /$$

(a) Demonstrate that the grammar is ambiguous.
(b) Correct the grammar so that it is unambiguous.
(c) According to the grammar obtained in part (b), what is the value of the expression 7 + 6 ∗ 3 / 2?
(d) If we change the BNF description of <op1> and <op2> to read

$$<\text{op1}> ::= * \mid /$$
$$<\text{op2}> ::= + \mid -$$

what is the value of the expression $7 + 6 * 3 / 2$ in the language described by this revised grammar?

★★ **19.** Study the following grammar for the if-then-else statement of a hypothetical language. Then answer the questions based on it.

$$G_{IF} = \{V_T, V_N, S, P\}$$

where $V_N$ = {\<construct\>, \<cond\>, \<oper\>, \<stmt\>, \<log\>,

      \<logc\>}

$V_T$ = {i, s, l, \<, \>, =, **and, not, or, if, then, else, begin,**

    **end, ;**}

$S$ = \<construct\>

$P$ = {1 \<construct\> ::= **if** \<cond\> **then** \<stmt\>; |

                **if** \<cond\> **then** \<stmt\> **else** \<stmt\>;

    2 \<cond\> ::= \<cond\> \<logc\> \<cond\> |

            **not** \<cond\> | i \<oper\> i | \<log\>

    3 \<oper\> ::= \< | \> | = | \<= | \>= | \<\>

    4 \<stmt\> ::= \<construct\> |

            **begin** \<construct\> **end** | s

    5 \<logc\> ::= **and** | **or**

    6 \<log\> ::= l}

(*a*) Does this grammar define a finite or infinite language?

(*b*) Do a bottom-up parse on the following valid statement (i and l are tokens, not actual variables):

if i ⇐ i and not l
then if i \< i then s else s;

(*c*) Is this grammar ambiguous? If so, give an example that illustrates the ambiguity.

## 9-5 GRAPHS

This section describes briefly another nonlinear data structure: the *graph*. The graph is more general than the tree, but similar to it in many respects. Some important differences exist.

We discuss first some basic terminology of graphs, with terms such as "graph," "vertex," "edge," "path," and "cycle." While a diagrammatic representation of a graph can be useful, such a representation is not feasible for computer processing. The second subsection presents an alternative method

of representing graphs by using matrices. This method of representation has
several advantages. It is easy to store and manipulate matrices, and hence the
graph represented by them, in a computer. Certain well-known operations of
matrix algebra can be used to obtain paths, cycles, and other characteristics
of a graph. The matrix representation of a graph, however, has several
drawbacks—especially for volatile graph structures.

The third subsection discusses the adjacency list and edge list representations for graphs. We then formulate two traversals of graphs based on
their adjacency list storage representation; these are breadth-first and depth-
first traversals.

## 9-5.1 DEFINITIONS AND CONCEPTS

Graph theory is an important branch of mathematics or theoretical computer
science that finds application in many diverse areas. In this section we give
a definition of a general graph and its associated terminology. Since there
is no standard terminology for graphs, our definitions may be somewhat
different from those used in other books.

The diagrams in Fig. 9-81 represent graphs. Very simply, a graph consists of a nonempty set $V$ of *vertices* (or *points*, or *nodes*) represented as

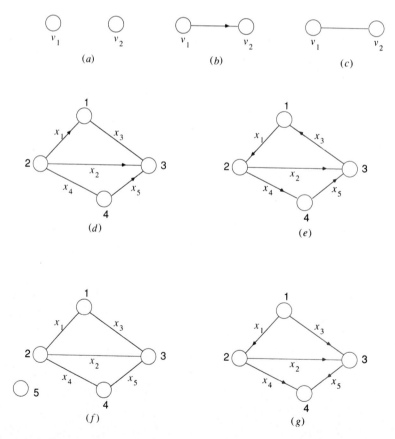

**FIGURE 9-81**
**Example of graphs.**

circles in our diagrams and sometimes labeled $v_1$, $v_2$, . . . , or 1, 2, . . . and a set $E$ of *edges* (or *arcs*) shown as lines connecting certain pairs of vertices. Either set, or both, may have labels associated with their elements. The association of edges to vertices is defined as a mapping from the set $E$ to pairs of elements in the set $V$. In Fig. 9-81$d$, for example, there are 4 vertices and 5 edges. The vertex set $V$ is {1, 2, 3, 4} and the edge set $E$ is {(2, 1), (2, 3), (1, 3), (2, 4), (4, 3)} .

As was the case with a tree, a graph is a way of representing relationships between data and thus is yet another form of data structure, somewhat more elaborate perhaps than those we have seen to date. Graphs have many applications. Suppose, for example, we represent a set of cities by vertices of a graph as in Fig. 9-82. A set of edges could represent major highways connecting these cities (Fig. 9-82$a$). For the same set of vertices, a different set of edges could represent air routes (Fig. 9-82$b$).

We shall assume throughout that both sets $V$ and $E$ of a graph are finite. It is also convenient to write a graph as $G = (V, E)$. Notice that the definition of a graph implies that to every edge of the graph $G$ we can associate a pair of nodes of the graph. If an edge $x \in E$, where the symbol $\in$ denotes set membership, is thus associated with a pair of nodes $(u, v)$, where $u, v \in V$, then we say that the edge $x$ connects or joins the nodes $u$ and $v$. Any two nodes which are connected by an edge in a graph are called *adjacent nodes*.

In a graph $G = (V, E)$, an edge which is directed from one node to another is called a *directed edge*, while an edge which has no specific direction is called an *undirected edge*. A graph in which every edge is directed is called a *directed graph*, or a *digraph*. A graph in which every edge is undirected is called an *undirected graph*. If some of the edges are directed and some are undirected in a graph, then the graph is a *mixed graph*.

In the diagrams, the directed edges are shown by means of arrows which also show the directions. The graphs given in Fig. 9-81$b$, $e$, and $g$ are directed graphs, those given in Fig. 9-81$c$ and $f$ are undirected, while the one given in Fig. 9-81$d$ is mixed. The graph given in Fig. 9-81$a$ could be considered either directed or undirected. In Fig. 9-81$f$, the nodes 1 and 2, 2 and 3, 3 and 1, 2 and 4, and 3 and 4 are adjacent.

A city map showing only the one-way streets is an example of a directed graph in which the nodes are the intersections and the edges are the streets. A

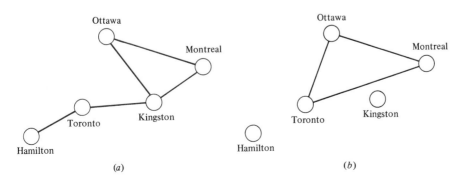

(a)          (b)

**FIGURE 9-82**
**Graphic representations of routes.**

map showing only the two-way streets is an example of an undirected graph, while a map showing all the one-way and two-way streets is an example of a mixed graph.

Let $(V, E)$ be a graph, and let $x \in E$ be a directed edge associated with the ordered pair of nodes $(u, v)$. Then the edge $x$ is said to be *initiating* or *originating* in the node $u$ and *terminating* or *ending* in the node $v$. The nodes $u$ and $v$ are also called the *initial* and *terminal* nodes of the edge $x$. An edge $x \in E$ which joins the nodes $u$ and $v$, whether it be directed or undirected, is said to be *incident* to the nodes $u$ and $v$.

An edge of a graph which joins a node to itself is called a *loop* or *sling* (not to be confused with a loop in a program). The direction of a loop is of no significance; hence it can be considered either a directed or an undirected edge.

The graphs given in Fig. 9-81 have no more than one edge between any pair of nodes. In the case of directed edges, the two possible edges between a pair of nodes which are opposite in direction are considered distinct. If there is no more than one edge between a pair of nodes (no parrallel directed edges in the case of a directed graph), then such a graph is called a *simple graph*. The graphs given in Fig. 9-81 are all simple graphs.

In some applications we might wish to associate an integer or real number (called a *weight*) with an edge. A graph in which weights are assigned to every edge is called a *weighted graph*. A graph representing a system of pipelines in which the weights assigned indicate the amount of some commodity transferred through the pipe is an example of a weighted graph. Similarly, a graph of city streets may be assigned weights according to the traffic density on each street.

In a graph, a node which is not adjacent to any other node is called an *isolated node*. A graph containing only isolated nodes is called a *null graph*. In other words, the set of edges in a null graph is empty. The graph in Fig. 9-81*a* is a null graph, while that in Fig. 9-81*f* has an isolated node. In practice, an isolated node in a graph has very little importance.

The definition of a graph contains no reference to the length or the shape and positioning of the arc joining any pair of nodes, nor does it prescribe any ordering of positions of the nodes. Therefore, for a given graph, there is no unique diagram which represents the graph. We can obtain a variety of diagrams by locating the nodes in an arbitrary number of different positions and also by showing the edges by arcs or lines of different shapes. Because of this arbitrariness, it can happen that two diagrams which look entirely different from one another may actually represent the same graph, as is the case in Fig. 9-83*a* and *b*.

In a directed graph, for any node $v$, the number of edges which have $v$ as their initial node is called the *outdegree* of the node $v$. The number of edges which have $v$ as their terminal node is called the *indegree* of $v$, and the sum of the outdegree and the indegree of a node $v$ is called its *total degree*. In the case of an undirected graph, the *total degree* or the *degree* of a node $v$ is equal to the number of edges incident with $v$. The total degree of a node that has one loop is 2 and that of an isolated node is 0. We now introduce some additional terminology associated with a simple digraph.

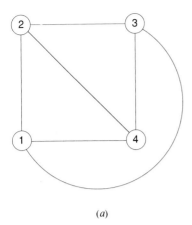

(a)

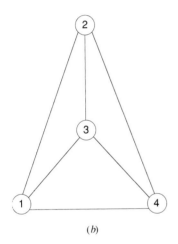

(b)

**FIGURE 9-83**

Let $G = (V, E)$ be a simple digraph. Consider a sequence of edges of $G$ such that the terminal node of any edge in the sequence is the initial node of the next edge, if any, in the sequence. An example of such a sequence is

$$((v_{i1}, v_{i2}), (v_{i2}, v_{i3}), \ldots, (v_{ik-2}, v_{ik-1}), (v_{ik-1}, v_{ik}))$$

where it is assumed that all nodes and edges appearing in the sequence are in $V$ and $E$, respectively. It is customary to write such a sequence as

$$(v_{i1}, v_{i2}, \ldots, v_{ik-1}, v_{ik})$$

Note that not all edges and nodes appearing in a sequence need be distinct. Also, for a given graph, any arbitrary set of nodes written in any order does not give a sequence as required. In fact, each node appearing in the sequence must be adjacent to the nodes appearing just before it and just after it in the sequence, except in the case of the first and last nodes.

Any sequence of edges of a digraph such that the terminal node of any edge in the sequence is the initial node of the edge, if any, appearing next in the sequence defines a *path* of the graph. A path is said to *traverse* through the nodes appearing in the sequence, *originating* in the initial node of the first edge and *ending* in the terminal node of the last edge in the sequence. The number of edges appearing in the sequence of a path is called the *length* of the path.

Consider the simple digraph given in Fig. 9-84. Some of the paths originating in node 1 and ending in node 3 are

$$P_1 = ((1, 3))$$

$$P_2 = ((1, 2), (2, 3))$$

$$P_3 = ((1, 4), (4, 3))$$

$$P_4 = ((1, 3), (3, 1), (1, 2), (2, 3))$$

A path in a digraph in which the edges are distinct is called a *simple path* (*edge simple*). A path in which all the nodes through which it traverses are distinct is called an *elementary path* (*node simple*).

Naturally, every elementary path of a digraph is also simple. The paths $P_1$, $P_2$, and $P_3$ of the digraph in Fig. 9-84 are elementary, while path $P_4$ is simple but not elementary. It can be shown that if there exists a path from a node, say, $u$, to another node $v$, then there must be an elementary path from $u$ to $v$.

A path which originates and ends in the same node is called a *cycle* (or *circuit*). A cycle is called *elementary* if it does not traverse through any node more than once.

Note that in a cycle the initial node appears twice if it is an elementary cycle. The following are some of the cycles in the graph in Fig. 9-84.

$$C_1 = ((1, 3), (3, 1))$$

$$C_2 = ((1, 2), (2, 3), (3, 1))$$

$$C_3 = ((1, 4), (4, 3), (3, 1))$$

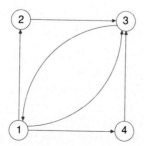

**FIGURE 9-84**

A simple digraph which does not have any cycles is called *acyclic*. A *directed tree* is an acyclic digraph which has one node, called its *root*, with indegree 0, while all other nodes have indegree 1. This definition of a tree is an alternative one to that given in Sec. 9-1. We wish to emphasize that a tree is simply a restricted graph with no cycles and having a designated vertex (the root) with no parent. Also, each of the remaining vertices has exactly one parent.

Before we can deal with graph problems, we must devise some scheme for representing the information contained in a graph in a form suitable for computer processing. The best representation for some general graph depends on the nature of the data and on the operations which are to be performed on the data. Furthermore, the choice of a suitable representation is affected by other factors, such as number of nodes, the average number of edges leaving a node, whether a graph is directed, the frequency of insertions and/or deletions to be performed, etc. In the next subsection we will examine first a strictly sequential representation of a graph by a matrix. In a later subsection we will then present a representation based on linked allocation.

## 9-5.2 MATRIX REPRESENTATION OF GRAPHS AND PATH MATRICES

Given a simple digraph $G = (V, E)$, it is necessary to assume some kind of ordering of the nodes of the graph in the sense that a particular node is called a first node, another a second node, and so on. A matrix representation of $G$ depends on the ordering of the nodes.

Let $G = (V, E)$ be a simple digraph in which $V = \{v_1, v_2, \ldots, v_n\}$ and the nodes are assumed to be ordered from $v_1$ to $v_n$. An $n \times n$ matrix $A$ whose elements $a_{ij}$ are given by

$$a_{ij} = \begin{cases} 1 & \text{if } (v_i, v_j) \in E \\ 0 & \text{otherwise} \end{cases}$$

is called the *adjacency matrix* of the graph $G$.

Any element of the adjacency matrix is either 0 or 1. Any matrix whose elements are either 0 or 1 is called a *bit matrix* or a *Boolean matrix*. Note that the $i$th row in the adjacency matrix is determined by the edges which originate in the node $v_i$. The number of elements in the $i$th row whose value is 1 is equal to the outdegree of the node $v_i$. Similarly, the number of elements whose value is 1 in a column, say, the $j$th column, is equal to the indegree of the node $v_j$. An adjacency matrix completely defines a simple digraph.

For a given digraph $G = (V, E)$, an adjacency matrix depends on the ordering of the elements of $V$. For different orderings of the elements of $V$ we get different adjacency matrices of the same graph $G$. However, any one of the adjacency matrices of $G$ can be obtained from another adjacency matrix of the same graph by interchanging some of the rows and corresponding columns of the matrix. We shall neglect the arbitrariness introduced in an adjacency matrix because of the ordering of the elements of $V$. Therefore, any adjacency matrix of the graph will satisfy a given purpose. In fact, if two digraphs are such that the adjacency matrix of one can be obtained from the adjacency matrix of the other by interchanging some of the rows and the corresponding columns, then the digraphs are equivalent.

As an example representation, consider the graphs given in Fig. 9-82, the nodes of which represent a group of five cities. In this example the order of the nodes is given as Hamilton, Toronto, Ottawa, Kingston, and Montreal. One set of edges could represent major highways connecting these cities (Fig. 9-82a): a different set of edges could represent air routes (Fig. 9-82b).

To represent this information in a form suitable for computer processing, we use an adjacency matrix. The adjacency matrix for the graph of Fig. 9-82a is given in Table 9-6.

Since we have not specified direction for the edges, this matrix is symmetrical. That is, an edge connecting Hamilton to Toronto is the same as an edge connecting Toronto to Hamilton.

Now that we have a representation of a graph appropriate for computer processing, graph problems are simply problems of array manipulation.

An important problem in graph theory is the identification of paths in a graph. Recall from the last subsection that a path was defined as a sequence of edges that begins at one node and ends at another, with no breaks in between. For example, in Fig. 9-82a, there is a path (of length 3, since three edges are involved) from Hamilton to Ottawa; in Fig. 9-82b, however, there is no path from Hamilton to Ottawa. This says that it is possible to drive from Hamilton to Ottawa, but not to fly. This sort of information is clearly important to travelers. For this section we will design a program to determine if there exists a path (of any length) between two specified nodes of a given graph.

The elements of the adjacency matrix were defined to be 0 and 1 deliberately to allow *logical* operations to take place. This is entirely appropriate to this problem; for example, if there exists a path from Hamilton to Toronto and a path from Toronto to Kingston, it follows that there exists a path from Hamilton to Kingston. We define logical bit operations $\wedge$ (and) and $\vee$ (or) in Table 9-7 by enumerating all possible calculations.

The extension of these operations to binary arrays is reasonably straightforward. Let the result of the matrix operation $A \times A$ be denoted by $A^2$, and

| TABLE 9-6 | | | | | |
|---|---|---|---|---|---|
| | HAMILTON | TORONTO | OTTAWA | KINGSTON | MONTREAL |
| HAMILTON | 0 | 1 | 0 | 0 | 0 |
| TORONTO | 1 | 0 | 0 | 1 | 0 |
| OTTAWA | 0 | 0 | 0 | 1 | 1 |
| KINGSTON | 0 | 1 | 1 | 0 | 1 |
| MONTREAL | 0 | 0 | 1 | 1 | 0 |

**TABLE 9-7**

| $\wedge$ | $\vee$ |
| --- | --- |
| $1 \wedge 0 = 0$ | $1 \vee 0 = 1$ |
| $0 \wedge 1 = 0$ | $0 \vee 1 = 1$ |
| $1 \wedge 1 = 1$ | $1 \vee 1 = 1$ |
| $0 \wedge 0 = 0$ | $0 \vee 0 = 0$ |

its $i$ $j$th entry be written as $a_{ij}^{(2)}$. Then

$$a_{ij}^{(2)} = a_{i1} \wedge a_{1j} \vee a_{i2} \wedge a_{2j} \vee \cdots \vee a_{in} \wedge a_{nj}$$

or

$$a_{ij}^{(2)} = \bigvee_{k=1}^{n} a_{ik} \wedge a_{kj}$$

By definition, if $a_{ij}^{(2)} = 1$, then there exists a path of length 2 between nodes $i$ and $j$. Similarly, $A^3 (= A^2 \times A)$ denotes the paths of length 3, $A^4$ the paths of length 4, and so on. For a graph of $n$ nodes, the longest path that can be present is of length at most $n - 1$ (assuming that we do not allow nodes to be included more than once in a path).

With this background, our search for the existence of any path between two specified nodes $i$ and $j$ of a given graph with a total of $n$ nodes whose $n \times n$ adjacency matrix is denoted by $A$ becomes the following:

1. Repeat thru step 3 for $k \leftarrow 1$ to $n$
2. Compute $A^k$
3. If $a_{ij}^{(k)} = 1$,
   then write ('**A path of length**', $k$, '**exists**') and halt
4. Write ('**No path exists**')
5. Halt

Observe that if more than one path exists between the specified nodes, this algorithm will find the shortest. Also for $k = 1$ no computation in step 2 is required since $A^k$ represents the adjacency matrix.

In the formalization of this general algorithm, we will first design a procedure to take in two binary arrays, $A$ and $B$, and return as its result $A \times B$. Clearly, such a procedure can be used to compute $A^2$ by passing as arguments $A$ and $A$; in fact for any $n$ ($n \geq 1$), it can be used to compute $A^n$ by passing as arguments $A^{n-1}$ and $A$ (assume that $A^0 = I$ and $A^1 = A$, where $I$ is the "identity" matrix, that is, 1 on the diagonal and 0 otherwise). The procedure given in Fig. 9-85 results from our earlier definition.

```
procedure BoolMul (
   A, B: Graph;          {Input, N × N arrays}
   var C: Graph;         {Output, Boolean product of A and B}
   N: integer            {Input, size of arrays}
                      );
```
{Given two Boolean arrays, this procedure computes their Boolean product.}
```
var
   I, J, K: integer;       {Loop variables}
begin
   {Step 1: Initialize result array}
   for I : = 1 to N do
      for J : = 1 to N do
         C[I, J] : = false;
   {Step 2: Compute A and B}
   for I : = 1 to N do              {Compute row elements}
      for J : = 1 to N do           {Compute column elements}
         for K : = 1 to N do        {Compute I, J element}
            C[I, J] : = C[I, J] or (A[I, K] and B[K, J])
end;
```

FIGURE 9-85
Procedure to
calculate the
Boolean product
of two arrays.

To verify that this procedure is correct, let $A$ be the adjacency matrix for the graph in Fig. 9-82a. The element corresponding to Toronto–Montreal in $A$ should be 0, since there is no path of length 1 from Toronto to Montreal. There is, however, a path of length 2 (Toronto–Kingston–Montreal). Thus the element corresponding to Toronto–Montreal in $A^2$ should be 1. Check it out. What about the same element in $A^3$?

We are now ready to formalize our complete path-finding program using the procedure BoolMul. We will assume that the data is prepared in the following manner: first, a value giving the number of nodes in the graph, followed by the elements of the adjacency matrix in row order, each element denoted by 0 or 1, followed by two numbers identifying the nodes between which a path is being sought. The program Paths given in Fig. 9-86 is to say whether or not such a path exists.

Step 1 of the program reads the input data according to the format described previously. In this step the temporary array PI is introduced. This is used to represent the "current" or most recently computed power of the adjacency matrix $A$. In step 1, it is initialized to $A$.

The search for paths is initiated in step 2. As described, there can be no path longer than $N-1$ in a graph with $N$ nodes, assuming that no nodes are visited more than once. Thus we will examine powers of the adjacency matrix from 1 (the adjacency matrix itself) to $N$, with the value of $L$ giving the path length being sought in each case.

In step 3 we test the appropriate entry of the most recently computed power of the adjacency matrix. If it is 1, then we have found a path. A message to this effect is printed and the program terminates. Otherwise, we

**program** Paths (input, output);
{Given an adjacency matrix, its size, and two specified nodes, this program
   determines whether a path exists between the specified nodes.}
**type**
   Graph = **array** [1 .. 25, 1 .. 25] **of** Boolean;
**var**
   N: integer;          {Number of nodes in the graph}
   I, J: integer;      {Nodes between which a path is sought}
   B: integer;          {Temporary for reading adjacency matrix as
                        integers 0 and 1}
   L: integer;          {Length of the path being computed}
   R, C: integer;     {Row and column index}
   A: Graph;          {Adjacency matrix of the graph}
   PI: Graph;         {Path matrix for paths of length L}
   T: Graph;          {Temporary array}
   Found: Boolean;   {Indicates if a path is found}
{Include procedure BoolMul}
**begin**
   {Step 1: Input data values and initialize temporary array}
   read (N);
   **for** R : = 1 **to** N **do**
      **for** C : = 1 **to** N **do**
         **begin**
           read (B);
           A[R, C] : = (B = 1)
         **end**;
   PI : = A;
   read (I, J);

   {Step 2: Determine all possible paths in the graph}
   Found : = false;
   L : = 1;
   **while** (**not** Found) **and** (L <= N) **do**

      {Step 3: Check for a path}
      **if** PI[I, J]
      **then** Found : = true
      **else begin**

            {Step 4: Compute next highest power of adjacency matrix}
            BoolMul (PI, A, T, N);
            PI : = T;
            L : = L + 1
      **end**;

   {Step 5: Check if path found}
   **if** Found
   **then** writeln ('A Path of Length', L: 2,' exists')
   **else** writeln ('No Path Exists')
**end**.

**FIGURE 9-86**
**Program to find**
**paths in graphs.**

proceed to step 4, in which the procedure BoolMul is called to compute the next highest power of the adjacency matrix. Upon return from the procedure, the result is assigned to Pl and the loop repeats.

If all N possibilities are tested and no path is found, control passes to step 5. A message indicating no paths is printed and the program terminates.

This approach can be generalized easily to generate the path matrix of a graph. Let $G = (V, E)$ be a simple digraph which contains $n$ nodes that are assumed to be ordered. An $n \times n$ matrix $P$ whose elements are given by

$$P_{ij} = \begin{cases} 1 & \text{if there exists a path from } v_i \text{ to } v_j \\ 0 & \text{otherwise} \end{cases}$$

is called the *path matrix* (*reachability matrix*) of the graph $G$.

Note that the path matrix shows only the presence or absence of at least one path between a pair of points and also the presence or absence of a cycle at any node. It does not show all the paths that may exist. In this sense, a path matrix does not give as complete information about a graph as does the adjacency matrix. The path matrix is, however, important in its own right.

The path matrix can be calculated directly as

$$B_n = A \vee A^2 \vee A^3 \vee \cdots \vee A^n = \bigvee_{k=1}^{n} A^k$$

We shall apply this method of calculating the path matrix to our sample problem whose graph is given in Fig. 9-82*a*.

It may be remarked here that if we are interested in knowing the reachability of one node from another, it is sufficient to calculate $B_{n-1}$, because a path of length $n$ cannot be elementary. The only difference between P calculated from $B_{n-1}$ and P calculated from $B_n$ is in the diagonal elements. For the purpose of reachability, every node is assumed to be reachable from itself. Some authors calculate the path matrix from $B_{n-1}$, while others do it from $B_n$.

The method of calculating the path matrix P of a graph by calculating first A, $A^2$, ..., $A^n$ and then $B_n$ is expensive. The computations of $A^2$, ..., $A^n$ are each $O(n^3)$. The time computation of $B_n$ is therefore $O(n^4)$. Also note that additional matrices are required as temporary storage. This method of obtaining the path matrix of a simple digraph can easily be computed by using the efficient algorithm due to Warshall. The implementation of this algorithm is given in Fig. 9-87.

To show that this program produces the required matrix, we note that step 1 produces a matrix in which P[I, J] = 1 if there is a path of length 1 from $v_l$ to $v_J$. Assume that for a fixed K, the intermediate matrix P produced by steps 3 and 4 of the program is such that the element in the Ith row and Jth column in this matrix is 1 if and only if there is a path from $v_l$ to $v_J$ through the nodes $v_1, v_2, \ldots, v_K$ or an edge from $v_l$ to $v_J$. Now with an updated value of K, we find that P[I, J] = 1 either if P[I, J] = 1 in an earlier step or if there is a path from $v_l$ to $v_J$ which traverses through $v_{K+1}$. This

```
procedure Warshall (
    A: Graph;        {Input, adjacency matrix}
    var P: Graph;    {Output, path matrix}
    N: integer       {Input, size of matrix}
            );
{Given the adjacency matrix, this procedure computes the path matrix P.
    The type Graph is an array of Boolean values.}
var
    K, I, J: integer;    {Loop variables}
begin
    {Step 1: Initialize}
    P := A;

    {Step 2: Perform a pass}
    for K := 1 to N do

        {Step 3: Process rows}
        for I := 1 to N do

            {Step 4: Process columns}
            for J := 1 to N do
                P[I, J] := P[I, J] or P[I, K] and P[K, J]
end; {Warshall}
```

**FIGURE 9-87**
**Pascal procedure**
**for Warshall's**
**algorithm.**

means that $P[I, J] = 1$ if and only if there is a path from $v_I$ to $v_J$ through the nodes $v_1, v_2, \ldots, v_{K+1}$ or an edge from $v_I$ to $v_J$.

Let us analyze procedure Warshall. Since we have a triple-nested loop, the timing analysis is clearly $O(n^3)$. The space requirement is $O(n^2)$.

Procedure Warshall can be modified further to obtain a matrix which gives the lengths of shortest paths between the nodes. For this purpose, let $A$ be the adjacency matrix of the graph. Replace all those elements of $A$ which are zero by $\infty$, which shows that there is no edge between the nodes in question. The procedure given in Fig. 9-88 produces the required matrix which shows the lengths of minimum paths.

Here, $+$ in step 4 means the ordinary adding of integers. Again, the timing of this program is $O(n^3)$. In practice we are often interested not only in the length of the minimum path between any two nodes, but also in the specific edges that make up this path. It is a simple matter to modify the previous program to obtain such a path, and therefore, it is left as an exercise.

## 9-5.3 ADJACENCY LIST REPRESENTATION AND TRAVERSAL OF GRAPHS

The use of an adjacency matrix to represent a graph as described in Sec. 9-5.2 has several drawbacks. This representation makes it difficult to store

```
procedure Minimal (
    B: Graph;          {Input, modified adjacency matrix of size N}
    var C: Graph;      {Output, minimum path matrix of size N}
    N: integer         {Input, size of graphs}
                  );
```
{Given an adjacency matrix whose zero elements are replaced by some
  large positive number, this procedure computes the minimum path matrix.
  Minimum is a function that selects the algebraic minimum of its two arguments. The type Graph is an array of integers.}
```
var K, I, J: integer;     {Loop variables}
begin
    {Step 1: Initialize}
    C := B;

    {Step 2: Perform a pass}
    for K := 1 to N do

        {Step 3: Process rows}
        for I := 1 to N do

            {Step 4: Process columns}
            for J := 1 to N do
                C[I, J] := Minimum(C[I, J], C[I, K] + C[K, J])
end; {Minimal}
```

**FIGURE 9-88**
**Procedure for**
**computing minimum-**
**path-length matrix.**

additional information about the graph. If information about a node is to be
included, it would have to be represented by an additional storage structure.
The most severe problem with using a matrix to represent a graph is its static
implementation. To use this representation requires that the number of nodes
be known beforehand so as to set up the storage array. Also, the insertion
or deletion of a node requires changing the dimensions of the array, both
difficult and inefficient with large graphs. Finally, this approach is not very
suitable for a graph that has a large number of nodes or has many nodes
which are connected to only a few edges.

A graph can be represented in many different ways, the most appropriate depending on the application at hand. In this subsection we will use
something called an *adjacency list*. An adjacency list is a listing for each
node of all edges connecting it to adjacent nodes. For a graph $G = (V, E)$,
this is formed by listing for each element $x$ of $V$ all nodes $y$ such that $(x, y)$
is an element of $E$.

If there are a number of edges between a pair of nodes and a considerable number of nodes that are connected to only a few other nodes, then
the storage representation for the adjacency list of the graph in Fig. 9-89a,
where the adjacency list is given in Fig. 9-89b, could be as shown in Fig.
9-89c. Undirected graphs also can be stored using this data structure; however, each edge will be represented twice, once in each direction. Observe that

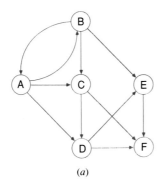

(*a*)

| A | B | C | D |
|---|---|---|---|
| B | A | C | E |
| C | D | F |   |
| D | E | F |   |
| E | F |   |   |
| F |   |   |   |

(*b*)

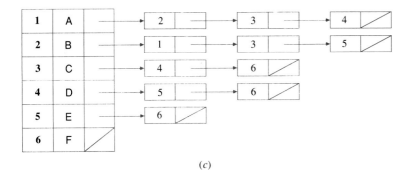

(*c*)

(A, B), (A, C), (A, D), (B, A), (B, C), (B, E), (C, D), (C, F), (D, E), (D, F), (E, F)

(*d*)

**FIGURE 9-89**
(*a*) **Sample graph;**
(*b*) **adjacency list for graph;** (*c*) **storage representation for adjacency list and;** (*d*) **edge list for graph.**

the storage representation consists of a node table directory and that associated with each entry in this directory we have an edge list. A typical node directory entry consists of a node number, the data associated with it, and a pointer field which gives the address of the list of edges for this node. Each list of edges, stored as a linked list, has an entry which contains the weight of the edge (optional) and the node number at which the particular edge terminates. For a completely dynamic representation, the node table directory could be replaced by a linked list, where the terminating node number in the edge list is changed to a pointer to the appropriate node in the linked list table directory. This representation would simplify the insertion and deletion of nodes.

Perhaps one of the conceptually simplest representations of a graph is by an *edge list*. Each pair of nodes (*u*, *v*) connected by an edge is included in the listing. If the graph being stored is a digraph, then *u* is the initiating node and *v* is the terminating node. If the graph is undirected, no ordering is imposed on the pairs. The edge list for the sample graph is given in Fig. 9-89*d*. A simple data structure to represent this listing would be a linked list. Fields could be added to this structure to store information about the edges, but adding information about the nodes would require an additional structure.

To demonstrate the effect of the choice of a graph representation on the efficiency of an algorithm, consider the following problem. Suppose we wish to determine whether a graph contains at least one edge. If the graph is stored as an adjacency matrix, the matrix must be searched until a '1' bit is found. In the worst case, there are $n^2$ elements to be examined, where $n$ is the number of nodes. If an adjacency list representation is used, each node in the node table directory must be searched to determine if a linked list is present, requiring at worst $n$ comparisons. However, if an edge list is used, all that is necessary is to check for an entry on the list: one comparison. This is not to say that this representation is best for all problems. The choice of representation, however, can have a significant impact.

We now introduce two traversal methods that will be performed on adjacency list representations of graphs.

### Breadth-First Traversal

In general, breadth-first traversal (BFT) can be used to find the shortest distance between some starting node and the remaining nodes of the graph. This shortest distance is the minimum number of edges traversed in order to travel from the start node to the specific node being examined. Starting at a node $v$, this distance is calculated by examining all incident edges to node $v$ and then moving on to an adjacent node $w$ and repeating the process. The traversal continues until all nodes in the graph have been examined.

Using the BFT strategy described above on the graph in Fig. 9-90, the traversal indicated by the dashed lines and arrows results. This traversal results in what is called a *breadth-first tree*. The tree is formed by the graph edges used to reach each node the first time during the breadth-first traversal. The traversal begins at node A, which is assigned a distance value of 0. Each

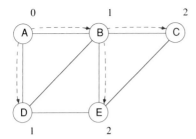

FIGURE 9-90
Breadth-first traversal
of a graph.

node adjacent to A is then visited (B first and then D) and assigned a distance value of 1. After B is visited, D is visited next. Then the nodes adjacent to B, namely, A, C, D, and E, are considered next. The nodes A and D have, of course, already been visited. Nodes C and E are visited and assigned a distance value of 2. Then the nodes adjacent to D, namely, A, B, and E, are considered. However, all these nodes have already been visited. Next, the nodes adjacent to C and then E are considered. Again, all these nodes have been previously visited. Since it has no unvisited adjacent nodes, the traversal terminates. Notice how all nodes adjacent to the current node are numbered as the traversal is conducted. This ensures that every node will be examined at least once.

The efficiency of a BFT algorithm depends on the method used to represent the graph. The adjacency list representation discussed previously is suitable for this algorithm, since finding the incident edges to the current node simply involves traversing a linked list, whereas an adjacency matrix would require searching the entire matrix many times.

We will use the data structure introduced in the previous section for implementing a BFT program. The node table directory will be represented by a vector of records with node structure as in Fig. 9-91a. Reach specifies whether a node has been reached in the traversal; its initial value is "false." NodeNo identifies the node number, Data contains the information pertaining to this node, and Dist is the variable which will contain the distance from the start node. Finally, ListPtr is a pointer to a list of adjacent edges for the node. The edges are represented by a structure of the form given in Fig. 9-91b. Destin contains the number of the terminal node for this edge, and EdgePtr points to the next edge in the list. The storage representation for the graph in Fig. 9-90 is presented in Fig. 9-92, after the BFT traversal (before

| Reach | NodeNo | Data | Dist | ListPtr |
|---|---|---|---|---|

(a)

| Destin | EdgePtr |
|---|---|

(b)

FIGURE 9-91
(a) Node table
directory structure,
(b) edge structure.

BFT traversal all **Reach** values would be "false" and **Dist** entries would be undefined).

Typical Pascal declarations for the adjacency list structure of a graph follow:

```
type
    EdgePointer = ↑ EdgeNode;
    EdgeNode =
        record
            Destin: integer;              {Terminal node number for edge}
            EdgePtr: EdgePointer          {Pointer to next edge in list}
        end;
    DirectoryNode =
        record
            Reach: Boolean;               {Tag field}
            NodeNo: integer;              {Node number}
            Data: char;                   {Node information}
            Dist: integer;                {Distance from start node}
            ListPtr: EdgePointer          {Points to node's adjacency list}
        end;
    NodeTableType = array [1 .. SizeOfTable] of DirectoryNode
```

The procedure in Fig. 9-93 to calculate BFT distances uses the three queue-handling procedures **QueueInsert**, **QueueDelete**, and **QueueEmpty** introduced in Sec. 8-6. **QueueInsert** enters a value onto the rear of a queue, in this case a node whose incident edges have not yet been examined. The procedure has two parameters, the queue name and the value to be inserted. **QueueDelete** removes a value from the front of a queue specified, placing it in **Cur**. **QueueEmpty** returns true if the queue is empty. In the program, this value is the next node which will be processed.

Using the graph representation in Fig. 9-92, the program initially places node **A** into the queue. Step 3 removes the front element from the queue (initially node **A**). Nodes **B** and **D** are placed in the queue during the list traversing loop of step 4. The program then removes **B** from the queue and begins processing its incident edges. Since the first node in the list (**A**) has already been labeled, it is ignored. This ensures that the program will not examine any node after it has been labeled. The program terminates when the queue is emptied.

**FIGURE 9-92  Storage representation of sample graph.**

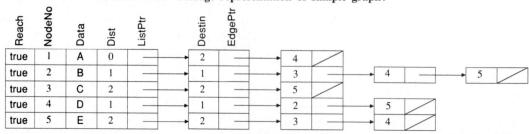

| Reach | NodeNo | Data | Dist | ListPtr | | Destin | EdgePtr | | | | | | |
|---|---|---|---|---|---|---|---|---|---|---|---|---|---|
| true | 1 | A | 0 | → | | 2 | → | 4 | | | | | |
| true | 2 | B | 1 | → | | 1 | → | 3 | → | 4 | → | 5 | |
| true | 3 | C | 2 | → | | 2 | → | 5 | | | | | |
| true | 4 | D | 1 | → | | 1 | → | 2 | → | 5 | | | |
| true | 5 | E | 2 | → | | 2 | → | 3 | → | 4 | | | |

```
procedure BFT (
    var Directory: NodeTableType;    {Input/output, node table directory}
    Start: integer                   {Input, index of initial node}
        );
```
{Given the node table directory and edge lists as described earlier, and the
initial node index, this procedure generates the shortest path for each node
from the initial node by using a breadth-first traversal. It is assumed that
the Reach field of each node has been set to false when the structure was
created. The queue operations for Sec. 8-6 are used with a queue element
type of integer.}

```
var
    Link: EdgePointer;      {Local pointer variable which is used to traverse
                                edge lists}
    Queue: QueueType;       {Queue of unprocessed nodes}
    Cur: integer;           {Index of current node}
    CurDist: integer;       {Distance of current node}
begin
    {Step 1: Initialize queue and first node's Dist number and place node in
        queue}
    QueueInitialize (Queue);
    Directory[Start].Reach := true;
    Directory[Start].Dist := 0;
    QueueInsert (Queue, Start);

    {Step 2: Repeat until all nodes have been examined.}
    while not QueueEmpty (Queue) do
        begin

            {Step 3: Remove current node to be examined from queue}
            QueueDelete (Queue, Cur);
            CurDist := Directory[Cur].Dist;

            {Step 4: Find all unlabeled nodes adjacent to current node}
            Link := Directory[Cur].ListPtr;
            while Link <> nil do
                begin

                    {Step 5: If node is not yet visited, set distance and queue it}
                    with Directory[Link ↑ .Destin] do
                        if not Reach
                        then begin
                                Dist := CurDist + 1;
                                Reach := true;
                                QueueInsert (Queue, Link ↑ .Destin)
                        end;
                    Link := Link ↑ .EdgePtr {Move down edge list}
                end
        end
end; {BFT}
```

FIGURE 9-93
Procedure for
breadth-first
traversal.

The program calculates the distance of every node from a starting node. If all that is required is the distance for one specific node, an extra condition can be inserted in the loop at step 5 comparing the current node being labeled to the specific node required. If the values are equal, the program can be stopped, saving a traversal of the remaining portion of the graph.

Let us now examine the timing analysis of procedure **BFT**. Step 1 is performed once. The then part of the if statement in step 5 is performed $n - 1$ times. This follows from the fact that the then part is executed only when the **Reach** value of a node is "false." Note that the **Reach** value is set to "true" in the then part. Hence the queue contains one node from step 1 and $n - 1$ nodes from step 4 for a total of $n$ nodes. Consequently, step 2 is repeated $n$ times. The adjacency lists contain $2 * e$ edges, where $e$ denotes the total number of edges in the graph. It then follows that the assignment statement in step 5 is performed $2 * e$ times, since all edges in the adjacency lists are examined. Consequently, the time analysis for the procedure is $O(n + e)$.

### Depth-First Traversal

A depth-first traversal (DFT) of an arbitrary graph can be used to perform a traversal of a general graph. As each new node is encountered, it is marked (in our case with "true" indicating the order in which the nodes were encountered) to show that the node has been visited. The DFT strategy is as follows. A node $s$ is picked as a start node and marked. An unmarked adjacent node to $s$ is now selected and marked, becoming the new start node, possibly leaving the original start node with unexplored edges for the moment. The traversal continues in the graph until the current path ends at a node with outdegree zero or at a node with all adjacent nodes already marked. Then the traversal returns to the last node which still has unmarked adjacent nodes and continues marking until all nodes are marked.

If we use the graph in Fig. 9-94 as an example, the DFT strategy results in the traversal indicated by the arrows, assuming each edge has been assigned a distance value of 1. This traversal results in a *depth-first tree* (denoted by the dashed lines). As in the breadth-first tree, this tree is formed by the graph edges used to reach each node the first time during the traversal. Starting at node **A**, the traversal begins numbering the nodes. Assuming **B** is the first node in **A**'s adjacency list, **B** is then visited and assigned the number

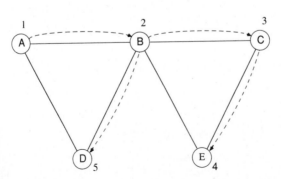

**FIGURE 9-94**
**Depth-first traversal**
**of a graph.**

2. From **B** the traversal continues to node **C**, which is assigned the number 3, and then to node **E**, which is assigned the number 4. Since all vertices adjacent to **E** have already been visited, the algorithm returns to node **C**, whose adjacent nodes also have all been marked. The algorithm then backs up further to node **B**, which still has an unlabeled adjacent node, **D**. After node **D** is labeled and assigned the number 5, the traversal is complete.

Since adjacent nodes are needed during the traversal, the most efficient representation again is an adjacency list. The same data structure as presented in algorithm **BFT** will be used, changing the **Dist** variable in the node table directory to **DFN** (for depth-first traversal number). The procedure to calculate the depth-first numbering scheme can be iterative using a stack or recursive, as shown in Fig. 9-95.

```
procedure DFT (
    var Directory: NodeTableType;     {Input/output, node table directory}
    Start: integer;                   {Input, current index into node directory
                                          table}
    var Count: integer                {Input/output, number of nodes
                                          previously visited}
              );
{Given the node table directory and edge lists, this procedure calculates the
    depth-first traversal numbers for a graph. It is assumed that the Reach field
    of each node was initialized to false when the list structure was created. A
    recursive strategy is used. A variable initialized to zero must be supplied
    as the third argument to DFT on the initial call.}
var
    Link: EdgePointer;     {Local pointer variable which is used to traverse
                              edge lists}
begin
    {Step 1: Update the depth-first traversal number; set and mark current
    node}
    Count : = Count + 1;
    Directory[Start].DFN : = Count;
    Directory[Start].Reach : = true;

    {Step 2: Set up loop to examine each neighbor of current node}
    Link : = Directory[Start].ListPtr;
    while Link <> nil do

        {Step 3: If node has not been marked, label it and make recursive call}
        begin
            if not Directory[Link ↑ .Destin].Reach
            then DFT(Directory, Link ↑ .Destin, Count);
            Link : = Link ↑ .EdgePtr {Examine next adjacent node}
        end
end; {DFT}
```

**FIGURE 9-95**
**Procedure for**
**depth-first traversal.**

The procedure checks if the **Reach** field has been set to "true" before traversing the remaining part of the graph. This will both prevent renumbering of any node and save from traversing any part of the graph twice. Once a null pointer is encountered in an edge list, the procedure returns (that is, backs up one level of recursion), repeating this until all edge lists have been traversed. Control is then returned to the calling program.

The timing analysis for this procedure is similar to that for procedure **BFT**. The worst-case analysis results in at most $n - 1$ recursive calls, since a recursive call is performed only once for each unreached node. Step 2 and the assignment statement in step 3 are performed a maximum of $2 * e$ times. Therefore, the worst-case time bound is $O(n + e)$.

## EXERCISES 9-5

1. Design a function to accept as a parameter an adjacency matrix for a graph and return to the point of call the number of edges in the graph.

★ 2. Design a function to accept as a parameter an adjacency matrix for a graph and a length $k$ and return to the point of call the number of paths of *exactly* length $k$ in the graph.

3. The regional director for a large firm has prepared a vector of cities and towns in which the firm has an office:

| | |
|---|---|
| 'EDMONTON' | 'SASKATOON' |
| 'CALGARY' | 'CHICAGO' |
| 'MINNEAPOLIS' | 'DENVER' |
| 'REGINA' | 'SPOKANE' |

Periodically, she is required to visit these sites. She has at her disposal a graph showing the air routes connecting the sites. Design a function to accept as parameters the adjacency matrix of this graph, the vector of cities and towns, the name of the city or town she is currently in, and the name of the city or town she wishes to visit. The function is to return a value of "true" if a flight exists between these two points with no more than two stops and a value of "false" otherwise.

★ 4. Formulate a procedure to
   (a) Produce a completely dynamic representation of an adjacency list as described previously in this section.
   (b) Insert a node in this structure.
   (c) Delete a node from this structure.

★ 5. Produce a procedure to transform an adjacency matrix into an adjacency list.

**6.** Consider the following undirected graph specified by means of adjacency lists:

a: f, c, d, e, j
b: f
c: a, i, g, h, k
d: f, a
e: j, a
f: h, b, a, d, i
g: c, h
h: f, c, g, l
i: c, f
j: e, a
k: c
l: h

(a) Draw a diagram of the depth-first tree that would be obtained by means of a depth-first traversal of the preceding graph starting at vertex a. As usual, the depth-first tree is formed by the graph edges used to reach each node the first time during the depth-first traversal.

(b) In general, the tree obtained in part (a) is not binary. Use the natural correspondence between general and binary trees to give the diagram for the binary tree that corresponds to the tree obtained in part (a).

**7.** Consider the breadth-first traversal of a directed graph. Recall that in a directed graph the edge from a to b and the edge from b to a are distinct edges. Give a diagram of the edges that are discovered in a breadth-first traversal starting at vertex 1 of the following directed graph (the adjacency lists are given). Denote the tree edges as solid directed lines and the nontree edges as dashed directed lines.

1: 4, 6, 9
2: 12, 10, 5
3: 8, 7
4: 6, 11
5:
6: 2, 8
7: 9, 3
8: 9
9: 1, 8
10:
11: 6, 1
12: 5

**★ 8.** You are given an undirected graph stored by means of adjacency lists, such that each vertex is labeled "left" or "right." Suppose that label (v) yields "left" or "right" for each vertex v. In the diagram of such a graph, as given in Fig. 9-96, all vertices labeled "left" are placed on the left

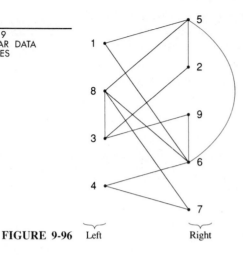

**FIGURE 9-96** Left                     Right

and all vertices labeled "right" are placed on the right. A path in such a graph is called *alternating* if the vertices on the path alternate between being left and right. For example:

| | |
|---|---|
| $1-5-8-6-4-7$ | is alternating |
| $2-3-9$ | is alternating |
| $8-6-1-5-8$ | is an alternating cycle |
| $5-6$ | is not alternating |
| $1-5-8-6-9-3$ | is not alternating |

Given two vertices $x$ and $y$, use the depth-first traversal approach to develop a procedure to determine if there is an alternating path from $x$ to $y$. If such a path exists, then the procedure should output the length of one such path.

★ **9.** Suppose we are given the adjacency list representation of a graph and wish to find the following matrix:

$$C(i, j) = \begin{cases} 1 & \text{if there is a path from } i \text{ to } j \text{ subject to the restriction} \\ & \text{that only vertices 1, 3, 7, and 9 can appear on} \\ & \text{the path between } i \text{ and } j \\ \\ 0 & \text{if no such path exists} \end{cases}$$

Assume that the vertices are 1, 2, . . . , n.
*(a)* Give an efficient procedure for the task.
*(b)* What is the order for the time required by the procedure?

★ **10.** Given a graph represented by adjacency lists, a specified vertex $v_0$ in the graph, and a set $S$ of vertices in the graph, give a program based on the breadth-first traversal to find a shortest path from $v_0$ to a vertex in $S$. The program should print out the path.

★ **11.** One way to find a cycle containing a specified vertex $v_0$ in an undirected graph is to perform a depth-first traversal from $v_0$. If, during the search, an edge is found from $p$, a vertex being searched, to $v_0$, then a cycle has been found. The cycle consists of the search path from $v_0$ to $p$ followed by the edge $(p, v_0)$. If no such edge is found, then no cycle exists. If a cycle is found, then it should be printed.

Implement a program based on a depth-first traversal to perform this task. The graph description should consist of pairs of integers, each of which represents an edge. During the reading of the pairs, an adjacency structure should be built to store the graph. The end of the edges should be indicated by the pair 0 0. Following the edges, the program should read in a set of points for which it will attempt to find cycles. *Note:* There are methods that can find all the cycles in one search. You are expected to use the preceding approach, which requires a search for each cycle determination.

## CHAPTER SUMMARY

This chapter deals primarily with the most important nonlinear data structure—the tree. We discuss the storage representation and manipulation of both binary trees and general trees. Because binary trees are easier to represent and manipulate than general trees, the former are emphasized more than the latter. Several applications of both types of trees are presented. The chapter concludes with a brief introduction to graphs. We focus on the adjacency matrix and the adjacency list representations of graphs. The presentation contains algorithms to compute path matrices, minimum path matrices, breadth-first treversals, and depth-first traversals.

## KEY TERMS

acyclic
adjacency list
adjacency matrix
adjacent nodes
ambiguous grammar
Backus-Naur Form
basis step
binary search tree
binary tree
bit matrix
Boolean matrix
bottom-up parsing
branch node
breadth-first traversal
breadth-first tree

canonical parse
circuit
complete binary tree
context-free grammar
converse inorder
converse postorder
converse preorder
cycle
degree of a node
depth-first traversal
depth-first tree
diameter of a tree
digraph
directed edge
directed graph

edge list
edges (arcs)
elementary path (node simple)
forest
formal language theory
full binary tree
general tree
goal symbol (starting symbol)
grammar
graph
graph traversal
heap
incident
indegree
initial node
initiating (originating)
inorder traversal
isolated node
level of a node
lexicographically (lexically) ordered
loop (sling)
metalanguage
minimal path matrix
mixed graph
natural correspondence
nonterminal symbol
null graph
ordered tree
outdegree
parse (parsing)
path
path matrix (reachability matrix)
points (nodes)
postorder traversal
predecessor

preorder traversal
productions (rules of syntax, replacement rules)
root
semantics
sentential form
similar binary trees
simple digraph
simple path (edge simple)
subtree
successor
syntactic classes
syntax tree (parse tree)
terminal node (leaf)
terminal symbol
terminating (ending)
threaded
threads
top-down parsing
total degree (degree)
traversal
traverse
tree
tree inorder
tree preorder
tree sort
tree structure
tree traversal
trie
undirected edge
undirected graph
vertices (nodes)
vocabulary
weight
weighted graph

# CHAPTER 10

## FILES

You will recall from Sec. 5-9 that not all information processed by a computer resides in an immediately accessible form of memory. Large volumes of data and archival data are commonly stored in external memory using files.

In this chapter we concentrate on file structures (that is, the storage representations of files referred to as file structures) and operations on files. We begin with a description of external storage devices, the media on which files normally reside. Next, some important concepts and terminology are introduced and later used in the discussion of two file organizations—sequential and direct.

## 10-1 EXTERNAL STORAGE DEVICES

The storage of information in the main or internal memory of a computer was discussed in Sec. 1-3. Any location in main memory can be accessed very quickly; a typical access time is less than 1 $\mu$s ($= 10^{-6}$ s). Main memory provides for the immediate storage requirements of the central processor for the execution of programs, including users' programs, editors, assemblers, compilers, and supervisory routines of the operating system.

The storage capacity of main memory is limited by two major factors—the cost of main memory and the technical problems in developing a large-capacity main memory. The storage requirements for programs and the data on which they operate exceed the capacity of main memory in virtually all computer systems. Therefore, it is necessary to extend the storage capabilities of a computer by using devices external to main memory.

An *external storage device* may be loosely defined as a device other than main memory on which information or data can be stored and from which the information can be retrieved for processing at some subsequent point in time. The storage and retrieval operations are referred to as *writing* and *reading*, respectively. Because of the technology employed, external storage devices have a larger capacity and are less expensive per bit of information stored than is main memory. The time required to access information, however, is much greater with these devices.

The primary uses for external storage devices include

*1.* Backup or overlay of programs during execution

*2.* Storage of programs and subprograms for future use

*3.* Storage of information in "files"

In this chapter we are concerned with the third use, although some of the techniques also may be applied to the first and second uses.

A card reader/punch can be considered as a primitive external storage device. In this section, however, we are concerned with devices that allow a more rapid transfer of data and a more convenient storage medium than punched cards. We discuss the most common external storage devices—magnetic tape, disk, and several less widely used devices. A brief description of physical characteristics as well as certain logical aspects of the first two types of devices is given.

## 10-1.1 MAGNETIC TAPE

The first compact external storage medium to be widely used was magnetic tape. A tape is made of a plastic material coated with a ferrite substance that is easily magnetized. The physical appearance of the tape is similar to that of the tape used for sound or video recording, although computer magnetic tape is typically wider. Several thousand feet of tape are wound on one reel, and information is encoded on the tape character by character. A number of channels or tracks run the length of the tape, one channel being required for each bit position in the binary-coded representation of a character.

An additional channel is usually used to detect errors in data transmission. It is possible to encode several hundred characters on one inch of magnetic tape; common encoding densities are 800 and 1600 bytes (or characters) per inch. On a 2400-foot reel of tape which stores 1600 bytes/in (a widely used standard form of tape), a maximum of 1600 bytes/in $\times$ 12 in/ft $\times$ 2400 ft $= 46,080,000$ bytes can be stored. (Assuming that 1 byte is used to store a character, such a tape can potentially store the text of 20 books the size of this one!) We will see, however, that this maximum is virtually impossible to achieve.

Reading or writing information with magnetic tape is made possible through the use of a magnetic tape drive. The tape is fed past read/write heads at a typical speed of 125 in/s (7.1 mi/h). The data transfer rate for such a tape drive when information is encoded at a density of 1600 bytes/in is, therefore, 200,000 bytes/s.

When a tape drive unit is not reading or writing information, it is in a stopped position. When a command to read or write is issued by the processor, the tape must first be accelerated to a constant speed (say, 125 in/s). Following completion of a read or write command, the tape is decelerated to a stop position. During either an acceleration or deceleration phase, a certain length of tape must be passed over. This section of tape is neither read from nor written upon. It appears between successive records (groups of data) and is called an *interrecord gap* or *IRG* (see Fig. 10-1a). An interrecord gap varies from $\frac{1}{2}$ to $\frac{3}{4}$ in, depending on the nature of the tape unit. The greater the number of interrecord gaps, the smaller the storage capacity of the tape. For example, suppose records consisting of 800 bytes each are written one at a time on a tape having a density of 1600 bytes/in. If $\frac{1}{2}$-in interrecord gaps are used, then only half the tape is actually used for storing data, since each inch of tape contains $\frac{1}{2}$ in of data record and $\frac{1}{2}$ in of interrecord gap.

To circumvent this problem, records are often grouped in *blocks*. If records are blocked, one write command can transfer a number of consecutive records to the tape without requiring interrecord gaps between them, as shown in Fig. 10-1b. Gaps appropriately called *interblock gaps (IBG)* are placed between successive blocks. The utilization of a tape's storage capacity increases as the number of records in a block (the *blocking factor*) is made larger. If the blocking factor in the previous example is 10, then

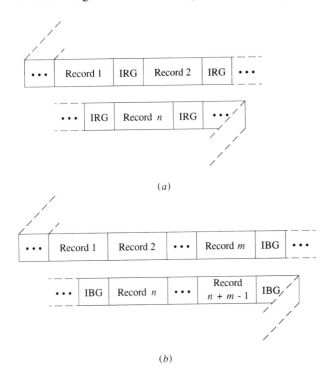

(a)

(b)

FIGURE 10-1
Record layout for
a magnetic tape.

$800 \times 10 = 8000$ bytes can be stored between gaps. Thus, the utilization increases to 10/11 from $\frac{1}{2}$.

The average time taken to read or write a record is inversely proportional to the blocking factor, since fewer gaps must be spanned and more records can be read or written per command. To utilize tape storage efficiently and to minimize read and write time, it appears that the blocking factor should be arbitrarily large. When a block of records is read or written, however, it is transferred to or from an area in main memory called a *buffer*. (More will be said about buffers in Sec. 10-4.1.) Since main memory is very often at a premium, the buffer size cannot be allowed to be arbitrarily large. Obviously, a trade-off exists between tape storage capacity and read/write time on the one hand and the amount of main memory available for buffering on the other.

A limitation of magnetic tape devices is that records must be processed in the order in which they reside on the tape. Therefore, accessing a record requires the scanning of all records that precede it. This form of access, called *sequential access*, was discussed in detail in Sec. 5-9. Operations such as rewinding a tape or backspacing a certain number of records or blocks increase the performance and flexibility of a magnetic tape device.

Magnetic tape is probably the cheapest form of external bulk storage; currently, the price of a reel of tape is around $15. In addition, a reel of tape can be easily placed on and removed from a tape drive, and hence it can be used for the off-line storage of data.

Recently, tapes enclosed in a plastic cartridge have been overtaking open-reel tapes in the data-processing industry. This is similar to cassettes replacing reel tapes in the audio market. For example, the standard IBM 3480 cartridge has a capacity of 200 megabytes (when a block size of 24000 is selected). The recording density is 1500 bytes/mm (approximately 38000 bytes/in). These tapes consume significantly less physical storage than open-reel tapes containing the same amount of recorded information and may well completely replace open-reel tapes. Cartridge tapes are also widely used for minicomputers. However, lack of industry-wide standards is hampering use of cartridge tapes for transfer of information among systems made by different manufacturers.

## 10-1.2 MAGNETIC DISKS

The magnetic disk is a direct-access storage device that has become widely used mainly because of its low cost. Disk devices provide relatively low access times and high-speed data transfer.

There are two types of disk devices, namely, fixed disks and exchangeable disks. For both types, the disk unit or pack usually consists of a number of metal platters that are stacked on top of each other on a spindle, as illustrated in Fig. 10-2. (Some small-capacity systems consist of a single platter.) The upper and lower surfaces of each platter are coated with ferromagnetic particles that provide an information storage medium. Often, the outermost surfaces of the top and bottom platters are not used for storing data, since they can be easily scratched or damaged.

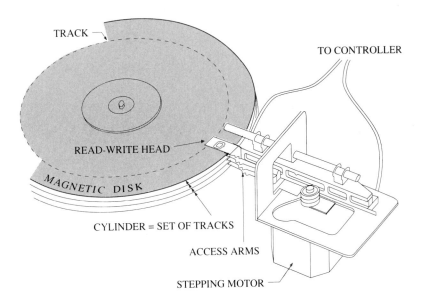

TRACK

TO CONTROLLER

READ-WRITE HEAD

MAGNETIC DISK

CYLINDER = SET OF TRACKS

ACCESS ARMS

STEPPING MOTOR

**FIGURE 10-2**
**Magnetic disk**
**access mechanisms.**

The surfaces of each platter are divided into concentric bands called *tracks* (see Fig. 10-3). Each track is further subdivided into sectors (or blocks) which are the addressable storage units. Note that although the tracks vary in size, all tracks must be capable of storing the same amount of information. To make this possible, the recording density of the inner tracks is higher than the recording density of the outer tracks. A particular sector is *directly addressable* in the sense that unlike a sequential type of device such as magnetic tape, it is not necessary to access sectors 1 to $n - 1$ in order to access sector $n$.

Information is transferred to or from a disk through read/write heads. Each read/write head floats just above or below the surface of a disk while the disk is rotating constantly at a high speed. With a fixed-disk device, the disk unit is permanently mounted on the drive. Generally, each track of each disk recording surface has its own read/write head. This allows for fast access to data.

The storage area on the disk to or from which data can be transferred without movement of the read/write heads is termed a *cylinder* or *seek area* (see Fig. 10-2). Hence a cylinder is a set of vertically aligned tracks which reside on the platters of a disk.

An exchangeable-disk device has movable read/write heads affixed to a comblike device. The heads are attached to a movable arm to form a comblike access assembly, as shown in Fig. 10-2. When data on a particular track must be accessed, the whole assembly moves to position the read/write heads over the desired track. While many heads may be in position for a read/write transaction at a given point in time, data transmission can take place only through one head at one time.

In early disk technology, the complete head assembly moved free of the disk pack, thus allowing the pack to be removed and a new pack to be

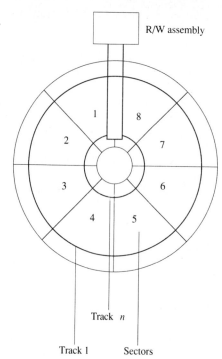

R/W assembly

Track $n$

Track 1

Sectors

**FIGURE 10-3**
**Disk surface of a**
**sector-addressable**
**disk.**

put in its place. In 1973, however, IBM revolutionized the magnetic disk industry with the introduction of what is now called *Winchester technology* in its model 3340 disk unit. With this technology, the entire set of disks and head assemblies is sealed in a "clean chamber" in which air is continuously recirculated and filtered to exclude large dust particles. Therefore, to remove a disk pack, you simply remove the entire chamber.

Disk storage can be viewed as consisting of consecutively numbered cylinders. A *seek* is a movement of the read/write head to locate the cylinder in which a particular track resides. The time for a seek is the most significant delay when accessing data on a disk. Therefore, it is always desirable to minimize the total seek time. There is also rotational delay or latency in waiting for the disk surface to rotate to a sector or block where a data transfer can commence. The *access time* $A(i)$ associated with a particular I/O operation $i$ can be expressed as the sum of the latency time $L(i)$ and the seek time $S(i)$ for $i$. That is,

$$A(i) = L(i) + S(i)$$

An additional component, called the *transmission time* $T$, is required to calculate the total time to complete a read or write operation. The transmission time, also called the *flow time*, is the time to read or write the record or series of records (as dictated by the I/O operation), given that the head is positioned over the disk location of the first record to be read or written.

The transmission time depends directly on how fast the disk rotates, as does the rotational delay. If we denote the total time to complete an operation $i$ as $\tau(i)$, then

$$\tau(i) = L(i) + S(i) + T(i)$$

Note that $\tau(i)$ varies depending on where the head is positioned and at what location the first desired record is on the track. Therefore, $\tau(i)$ will continually vary during the computer system's operation. Consequently, a more useful statistic involves the average access time, which is the sum of the average seek time and the average latency. That is,

$$\overline{A}(i) = \overline{L}(i) + \overline{S}(i)$$

Therefore, the average time to complete an I/O operation is

$$\overline{\tau}(i) = \overline{S}(i) + \overline{L}(i) + T(i) = \overline{A}(i) + T(i)$$

Characteristics of some typical magnetic disk units are summarized in Table 10-1. The IBM devices are block-oriented and hence allow variable formats for data rather than the more rigid sector approach. It also should be noted that most of the disk devices have a number of drives and hence a number of units or packs per device. The statistics given are for one unit or pack.

To illustrate the timing characteristics of a magnetic disk, assume that we have an IBM 3330 magnetic disk. Using the formula given earlier for the average time to complete an I/O operation, we obtain

$$\overline{\tau}_{\text{IBM 3330}}(\text{read 4096 bytes}) = 30 \text{ ms} + 8.3 \text{ ms} + \frac{4096 \text{ chars}}{806 \text{ chars/ms}}$$

$$= 38.3 \text{ ms} + 5.0 \text{ ms} = 43.3 \text{ ms}$$

**TABLE 10-1** Magnetic Disk Packs

| System Model | IBM | | DEC RM80 | Commodore D9090 |
|---|---|---|---|---|
| | 3330 | 3380 | | |
| Usable surfaces/unit | 19 | 15 | 7 | 6 |
| Tracks/surface | 404 | 885 | 1,122 | 153 |
| Sector size (chars) | Variable | Variable | 521 | 256 |
| Chars/track | 13,030 | 47,476 | 15,360 | 8,192 |
| Chars/unit (megabyte) | 100 | 630 | 124 | 9.5 |
| Average latency (ms) | 8.3 | 8.3 | 8.3 | 8.3 |
| Average seek time (ms) | 30 | 16 | 25 | 153 |
| Transmission rate, char/ms | 806 | 3,000 | 1,212 | 500 |

Another form of disk technology that has had a tremendous impact is the diskette commonly used with microcomputers. A diskette is a low-cost disk that is usually $3\frac{1}{2}$, $5\frac{1}{4}$, or 8 in in diameter and is coated on one or both sides with a magnetic material. There are typically between 8 and 26 sectors per track, with each sector holding from 128 to 512 bytes of data. Currently, most diskettes have a storage capacity of between 256 kilobytes and 1.5 megabytes, and transmission rates are generally in the range of 5 to 10 characters per millisecond.

Increasingly diskettes are being used primarily as an off-line form of data storage, and new and relatively inexpensive "hard disks" based on Winchester technology are becoming the standard for on-line auxiliary memory storage for most microcomputer systems.

In summary, disk storage devices are the most versatile storage devices available. They can provide large capacity and fast access time and hence satisfy the needs of most computer systems.

## 10-1.3  OTHER STORAGE DEVICES

### Magnetic Drums

A magnetic drum is a metal cylinder from 10 to 36 in in diameter which has an outside surface coated with a magnetic recording material. The cylindrical surface of the drum is divided into a number of parallel bands called *tracks*, as illustrated in Fig. 10-4. The tracks are further subdivided into either *sectors* or *blocks*, depending on the nature of the drum. The sector or block is the smallest addressable unit of a drum. A particular sector or block of a drum is directly addressable. Therefore, a drum is also a direct-access storage device.

Data is transferred to or from the drum as it rotates at a high speed past a number of read/write heads. Two schemes for arranging the read/write heads are used with magnetic drums. The most common scheme is to have *fixed* read/write heads, one for each track, as shown in Fig. 10-4. A second architecture is to have a *movable* head, in which a group of read/write heads is mounted on a rail and the heads are allowed to traverse the length of the drum. For example, a drum may have 100 tracks with a group of 5 read/write heads. Such a system permits the group of heads to be moved to any of 20 positions. Five adjacent tracks can be accessed from one position.

Magnetic drums have declined in popularity due to the success of magnetic disk devices.

### Mass Storage Devices

In the early 1960s, several computer manufacturers (NCR, IBM, ICL, and RCA) began marketing direct-access devices, called *card/strip devices*, that have storage capacities on the order of a half billion characters. A card/strip device consists of groups (decks, magazines, cells, or arrays) of magnetic cards or strips on which data is encoded. The basic principle of operation for these devices involves the selection of a card from a group and the transportation of this card to a revolving cylinder, or *capstan*. The card is

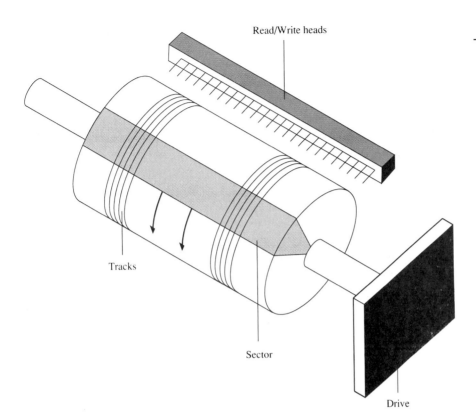

Read/Write heads

Tracks

Sector

Drive

**FIGURE 10-4**
**A magnetic drum**
**with fixed read/write**
**heads.**

wrapped around the capstan and data is then transferred to or from the card via the read/write heads.

Because they are very mechanical in operation, these devices typically have an access time that is greater than 0.5 s. Their greatest advantage is their large storage capacity; however, magnetic disk storage devices have been steadily increasing in capacity and decreasing in cost per bit, thus contributing to pushing magnetic card or strip devices into obsolescence.

### Intermediate Storage Devices

A new development in the area of external storage devices is the electronic disk. The electronic disk is named "electronic" because it provides fast access times without mechanical movement. It is an intermediate form of storage because it is being developed to fill the gap between main memory and direct-access storage. This is achieved by having a lower cost than main memory and a lower access time than is currently available with external storage devices.

The devices that currently show the greatest potential for being an acceptable electronic disk are *charge-coupled devices*. They are based on semiconductor technology, but their cost per bit should be one-third that of main memory. The average access time they provide is 60 $\mu$s.

Other candidates for electronic disks include the domain tip propagation, electron beam, and magnetic bubbles technologies.

## EXERCISES 10-1

1. Calculate the number of 80-character input records that can be stored on a magnetic tape that is 2400 ft in length, assuming
   (a) One record per block, 1600-byte/in density, and $\frac{3}{4}$-in interrecord gaps
   (b) Five records per block, 1600-byte/in density, and $\frac{3}{4}$-in interblock gaps
   (c) Twenty-five records per block, 6250-byte/in density, and $\frac{1}{2}$-in interblock gaps
   (d) One record per block, 800-byte/in density, and $\frac{1}{2}$-in interrecord gaps

★ 2. A number of standard tape densities, such as those given in Exercise 1, are used in the computer industry. Obviously, these are not effective tape density figures, since they are independent of the block size and the interblock gap size. Derive a formula for the effective tape density (expressed in effective bytes per inch) which is dependent on three factors: standard density, block size, and gap size.

3. Calculate the effective density for (a), (b), (c), and (d) of Exercise 1.

4. Suppose average tape speeds of 125 and 30 in/s are attained when reading recorded information and passing over gaps, respectively. Calculate the time required to read the tape configurations given in Exercise 1.

5. Direct-access devices are sometimes called *random-access devices*. What is the basis for this synonym type of relationship?

6. Using the data supplied in Table 10-1, compute the expected time to locate and read a particular 64-character record residing on the following disks: (a) IBM 3380, (b) DEC RM80, and (c) Commodore D9090. Suppose we are updating the record instead of reading it. In most systems, a read operation takes place immediately after a write operation. This additional read operation, which takes a time of one period of revolution, is needed to verify that the information placed in the direct-access device is correct.

## 10-2  DEFINITIONS AND CONCEPTS

Many of the definitions and terms used in the remainder of this chapter are introduced in this section. Because some of the concepts relate directly to external device characteristics, we have chosen to place this section after the discussion of external devices. Some of the terms that will be presented have been introduced previously. We reintroduce them here to provide a comprehensive and consistent overview of the hierarchy of information structures associated with file processing.

We begin with a brief review of the introduction to sequential files from Sec. 5-9. A *record* is a collection of information items about a particular entity. For example, here is the definition of a record consisting of information on an airline flight:

```
        PassengerType =
            record
                Name:
                    record
                        Initials: packed array [1 .. 2] of char;
                        Surname: packed array [1 .. 20] of char
                    end;
                Address: packed array [1 .. 60] of char;
                SeatNo: packed array [1 .. 5] of char;
                Menu: packed array [1 .. 10] of char
            end;
```

The different *items* or *fields* of this passenger record are the passenger's name, address, seat number, and menu restrictions.

Records involving a set of entities with certain aspects in common can be grouped together in *files*. A record item that uniquely identifies a record in a file is called a *key*. In the passenger file, the key could be the passenger's name, assuming duplicate names do not occur for a particular flight, or the seat number, since seat numbers are usually uniquely assigned for a given flight.

The records in many files are ordered according to a key. Other files are ordered on a *sequence item*, which may not be unique for each record. For example, in a file of monthly sales for a particular company, several records containing sales information may appear for one customer. The file can be ordered by customer account number with more than one occurrence of a customer sales record type for a given account number.

Thus far we have observed a hierarchy of information structures in which items are composed to form records and records are composed to form files. Files can be composed to form a set of files. If the set of files is used by the application programs for some particular enterprise or application area, and if these files exhibit certain associations or relationships between the records of the files, then such a collection of files is often referred to as a *database*. Figure 10-5 shows the information-structure hierarchy as it applies to file-processing applications.

Items, records, files, and databases are logical terms in the sense that they have been introduced without any indication as to how they can be realized physically on an external device. A number of file-structure concepts are associated with these logical terms. In the previous section we described how records are stored physically on several external storage devices. In particular, we pointed out that a *logical record*, as viewed by the programmer, can be grouped together with several other records to form a single physical entity called a *block* or *physical record*. The blocking of records does not affect the logical processing of those records. However, it does allow the processing to take place more efficiently because the number of read or write commands per logical record, as issued by the operating system, can be reduced significantly.

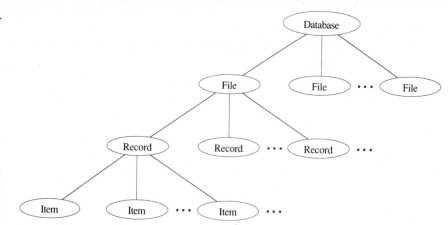

**FIGURE 10-5**
**Information structure**
**hierarchy for file**
**processing.**

The term "file" has assumed both a logical and a physical interpretation in the data-processing community. Physically, a file is considered to be a collection of physical records which must reside, often contiguously, in external memory. To provide proper access to the physical records in the file, a number of tables are kept by the storage-management routines in the operating system. These tables, along with other control information which is stored in the physical record (such as the length of the record), are transparent to the user who is working with the file at a logical level.

A physical record is composed of fields made up of bytes and words of binary-encoded information. The term "physical field" can be associated with a binary-encoded information element that corresponds to an item or field of a logical record. For simplicity and consistency, we will use the term "field" when describing the field of a physical record and the term "item" when referring to the field of a logical record. We will discover that there are some fields in a physical record, in particular fields containing system-maintained pointers, which have no counterpart items in the logical description of a record.

Having introduced most of the terminology needed for our discussion of files, let us examine some of the factors that affect the organization of a file. The prime factor that determines the organization of a file is the nature of the operations that are to be performed on the file, as dictated by the application. The operations normally performed are the same as those discussed previously in the text, namely, retrieval, addition, deletion, and update. A particular operation involving a record or set of records is called a *transaction*. For example, *delete Vernon Demerest from the passenger a list for Flight 279* is a transaction. Transactions are often processed against a file or set of files in the form of *transaction records*. These transaction records contain the keys of the records to be processed, along with the desired operation and any additional information required to complete the operation. In the sections to follow, we will see that the selection of a file organization depends not only on the operations or types of transactions, but also on the volume of transactions, the frequency with which transactions are submitted, and the response time required in the completion of a transaction or set of transactions.

The organization of a file also depends on the external storage media on which it is to reside. For example, we will discover that the file organization on a sequential device, such as a magnetic tape, differs appreciably from the file organizations that can be accommodated on a direct-access storage device, such as a magnetic disk.

## 10-3 RECORD ORGANIZATION

In the previous section we described a record as an entity composed of items or fields. In this section we concentrate on an important aspect of record organization, namely, the structure of record items.

Before discussing this aspect, the concept of the *domain* of an item must be presented. The domain of an item is simply those values which an item can assume. For example, if we are designing an application dealing with space allocation in a university, then one obvious item in a record describing the attributes of a particular room is the location of the building containing the room. The domain of values for such an item might typically represent the Administration, Agriculture, Arts, Chemistry, Commerce, Education, Engineering, Law, Medicine, Physics, and Veterinary Medicine buildings. When all the domain values for an item are known, such as in the last example, the item is said to have a *precoordinated domain*. Some record items which contain textual information are not precoordinated. For example, in a record for a bibliography system, an item may be devoted to an abstract of a book. Obviously, not all book abstracts are known prior to the establishment of a file of bibliographic information.

We now present a spectrum of methods for representing both types of items and begin with techniques for precoordinated items.

### Binary-Encoded Items

If we assume an item has a domain set of size $n$, then we can encode these item values using a binary scheme in which each element of the scheme is of length $\lceil \log_2 n \rceil$. An example of this type of encoding was given in Table 1-1 and discussed in Sec. 1-3. Basically, a binary encoding scheme is established by assigning a unique binary number to each value of the item's domain set. Table 10-2 illustrates a binary encoding represented in a bit-string notation for the example set of campus buildings.

In Pascal, we can define an enumerated type and then declare the field to be of that type. For example,

```
type
    BuildingType = (Administration, Agriculture, . . .);
    RecordType =
        record
            . . .
            Building: BuildingType;
            . . .
        end
```

**TABLE 10-2**

| Building | Encoded Value | Building | Encoded Value |
|---|---|---|---|
| Administration | 0000 | Engineering | 0110 |
| Agriculture | 0001 | Law | 0111 |
| Arts | 0010 | Medicine | 1000 |
| Chemistry | 0011 | Physics | 1001 |
| Commerce | 0100 | Veterinary Medicine | 1010 |
| Education | 0101 | | |

Unfortunately, some Pascal implementations allocate a full integer-sized field regardless of the number of values in the domain, resulting in considerable wastage of storage.

**Logically Encoded Items**

A method of logical encoding utilizes storage less efficiently than the binary encoding method just discussed but can represent more possibilities. For each possible value of a precoordinated item, a single logical value is reserved in a vector or string of logical values that constitutes the item. In the item containing the building location of a room, we can allocate a bit value for each building on campus. We let the first value represent the Administration building, the second value represent the Agriculture building, and so on, finally letting the eleventh and final value represent the Veterinary Medicine building. A record item with a value of 01000000000 in a binary notation represents the Agriculture building if the logical values of 1 and 0 are used to denote the presence and absence of item values, respectively.

A logical-valued format has the tremendous advantage of being capable of representing a multifaceted item (that is, an item that can take on more than one domain value). For example, 10001000011 indicates the Administration, Commerce, Physics, and Veterinary Medicine buildings. Of course, such a multifaceted item does not make sense in a record describing the properties of a room. However, if the item appears in the records of a file indicating the availability of certain facilities such as air conditioning, cafeteria services, libraries, etc., then a multifaceted item is needed. Note that a logically encoded item is a fixed-length item that can represent a variable number of values from the domain of an item. This is an important attribute, since variable-length records cannot be processed as efficiently as fixed-length records. Further discussion on this subject takes place at the end of this section.

In Pascal, a logically encoded item may be declared using a set type (see Chap. 5). Again using our campus building example, we would have

```
type
    RecordType =
        record
            . . .
            Building: set of BuildingType;
            . . .
        end
```

Now, if **R** is a record of **RecordType**, we could store a particular value as

R.Building : = [Administration, Agriculture];

Pascal implementations vary considerably in the storage efficiency of their set representations. Some Pascal compilers use a standard size for all sets regardless of the domain size.

### Fixed Items

When a record item has a fixed-length value and its domain is too large for an efficient bit encoding, a primitive data structure (that is, integer, real, string, etc.) format should be selected for representation of the item. For example, it is unreasonable to bit encode an item representing the net sales for the month. Instead, we can declare a record containing such an item in the programming language being used. Using our record notation, this declaration can be expressed as follows:

```
type
    MonthlyReportType =
        record
            MonthNumber: integer;
            NetSales: real;
                .
                .
                .
        end;
```

The net sales item can range in value from −999999.99 to 999999.99. It is unrealistic for the programmer to bit encode such a wide range of item values when the compiler provides an efficient encoding of an item value in binary. Since a Pascal array is of a fixed size, it also may be considered to be a fixed item. In particular, a **packed array of** char is often used for character string data.

Other examples of record items which have domains that are too large to be bit encoded are surnames and catalog numbers. Because both these items may be considered as fixed-length items, they can technically be called *precoordinated*. That is, a fixed-length item can only have a finite set of values which can be a priori enumerated. However, we reserve the term "precoordinated" for those domain sets which are completely established beforehand; in most systems dealing with surnames and catalog numbers, such a priori knowledge is not available.

Thus far we have examined record structures in which the items are of fixed length. Let us now look at some record organizations involving items that often lead to variable-length records.

### Repeating Items

Many applications arise in which the value associated with a record item may be a list of entities. For example, "the degree held" and "the programming languages used at a computer installation" are items which can assume multiple entities. In these instances, the item values may be "B.Sc., M.Sc., Ph.D." or "Ada, BASIC, COBOL, FORTRAN, Pascal," respectively.

The most popular method of handling repeating fields is to create an item that can accommodate up to some maximum number of replications. If we restrict this maximum number to three, for example, then the example items can accommodate such information as "the three most recent degrees obtained" and "the three most often used programming languages."

Standard Pascal does not have built-in facilities for handling variably repeating items.

## Tagged Items

A *tagged item* is an item that contains not only information pertinent to a particular application but also information concerning the structure of the item itself. For example, in a personnel system in which records are kept concerning the history of the employees of a company, several data items may be recorded, such as previous addresses, education, previous work experience, yearly achievement reports, etc. Instead of creating repeated items for each of these information fields, it can be more advantageous to store tags with each item. In general, a tag is used in one of two ways. One method assumes a fixed, predetermined ordering of items in the record, and tag information is used to delimit items, as shown in Fig. 10-6.

The second approach to record organization using tagged items is to include, in the tag, a description or name of the item, as shown in Fig. 10-7. When using this technique, it is not required that item values for a record occur in any predetermined order. Of course, the added flexibility of a tag that dynamically describes the record syntax results in an increase in record length.

## Textual Items

There is a final type of record item which differs from the other item forms discussed thus far. Its difference is due primarily to the size of the item. By a *textual item*, we mean an item containing a large amount of textual information such as text for a manuscript, for the abstract of a book, for a company report, or for a newspaper's classified ad. Typically, records for such items are single-item records. Because of the length of the textual record, it is not uncommon to decompose such a record and store it in several physical records or blocks. Data-compression techniques are often necessary

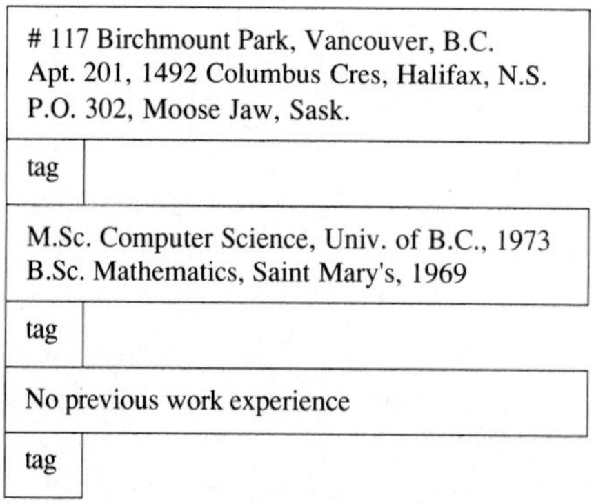

**FIGURE 10-6**
**Illustration of a preformatted personnel record with tagged items.**

```
# 117 Birchmount Park, Vancouver, B.C.
Apt. 201, 1492 Columbus Cres, Halifax, N.S.
P.O. 302, Moose Jaw, Sask.
```
tag
```
M.Sc. Computer Science, Univ. of B.C., 1973
B.Sc. Mathematics, Saint Mary's, 1969
```
tag
```
No previous work experience
```
tag

| No previous work experience | |
| --- | --- |
| 3 previous addresses | |
| # 117 Birchmount Park, Vancouver, B.C.<br>Apt. 201, 1492 Columbus Cres, Halifax, N.S.<br>P.O. 302, Moose Jaw, Sask. | |
| 2 degrees | |
| M.Sc. Computer Science, Univ. of B.C., 1973<br>B.Sc. Mathematics, Saint Mary's, 1969 | |

**FIGURE 10-7**
**Illustration of self-descriptive tagged items in a personnel record.**

to reduce the amount of storage required for textual items. One technique is to use a word-level *concordance* of positions at which that word appears in the text. In a concordance, each unique word in the text is stored along with the various positions at which that word appears in the text. For example, a concordance of the previous sentence is given in Table 10-3. Usually, the word list for the concordance is arranged in alphabetical order. To restore the text to its "natural" form, it is necessary to concatenate the common words together in an order dictated by the numbers in the position field of the concordance. The big saving in terms of compression is in multiple occurrence of common words such as "the" and "in," which are stored only once in the concordance.

There can be a significant disadvantage to storing text in a compressed format. For example, performing text editing is virtually impossible unless text is restored to an uncompressed form, and therefore, if editing operations must be performed often, compression should be avoided. In any application in which text must be manipulated frequently, compression should not be applied.

**Pointer Items**

In the remaining sections of this chapter we will discover that a very important type of record item is an item that contains information that references

**TABLE 10-3**

| Word | Position(s) | Word | Position(s) |
| --- | --- | --- | --- |
| a | 2 | stored | 11 |
| along | 12 | text | 9, 24 |
| appears | 21 | that | 19 |
| at | 17 | the | 8, 14, 23 |
| concordance | 3 | unique | 5 |
| each | 4 | various | 15 |
| in | 1, 7, 22 | which | 18 |
| is | 10 | with | 13 |
| positions | 16 | word | 6, 20 |

another record in the file. The pointer information may be in the form of a key of another record, a relative record position in a file, or an absolute physical address based on a cylinder, track, or segment (or block) address. In our discussion of direct files in Sec. 10-5, we will examine pointer items in detail and illustrate their use with some examples.

Before concluding this section, a final comment must be made concerning variable-length records. Variable-length records are used primarily in situations in which the record structure varies considerably from one record item to another in a file. They are used to save storage. Variable-length items such as repeated and tagged items are designed specifically to conserve storage. However, some additional processing time is required to encode and decode a record's format when such items are used. Usually, the development of programs to perform this encoding and decoding is left to the application programmer, since in many situations the format is application-dependent. Therefore, before adopting variable-length record formats, we should be aware of the problems that can arise.

In summary, we can say that items with a small precoordinated domain can be efficiently represented using one of the binary encoding schemes. Items with large domains can best be represented in the data-description facilities of the programming language in use. Multifaceted and replicated items generate variable-length records, unless they can be logically encoded, and textual information which is subject to very little text processing should be compressed. With our discussion of record organization completed, we can now consider how various types of items discussed in this section can be utilized to form the records that determine the organization of a file.

## EXERCISES 10-3

1. Give a practical example of a multifaceted record item for which a logical encoding would be appropriate.

2. A large multinational company manufactures its products in a number of cities. The value for an item in a record which describes a manufactured product contains one of the following city names: New York, Tokyo, Chicago, London, San Francisco, Paris, Montreal, Detroit, Dusseldorf, Mexico City, or St. Louis. Design a fixed-length binary code for the values of the item corresponding to a manufacturing location. How many more cities can be added to the list before the code length must be increased?

3. Describe how you would organize a record for a personnel file which involves the following items: (a) name, (b) address, (c) number of years with company, (d) work classification (assume a fixed number of classifications are used), (e) degrees held, and (f) previous jobs held. Create a structure description that is representative of the record.

4. Derive a word-level concordance for the first three sentences in this chapter, excluding the title.

**5.** What types of storage structures would you choose to represent the following record items?

    *(a)* The number of miles traveled by a salesperson per month

    *(b)* The days of the week

    *(c)* Aunt Matilda's favorite recipes

    *(d)* The weather conditions for the day as best described by one of the following categories: clear, cloudy, overcast, raining, snowing, hurricane, or tornado

    *(e)* The same as part *(d)*, but assume that more than one category name can be used in the daily description

    *(f)* Former places of residence

## 10-4 SEQUENTIAL FILES

Most operating systems provide a set of basic file organizations that are useful in implementing a wide range of applications. Two common types of organizations are sequential and direct, which are discussed in this section and in Sec. 10-5, respectively. The presentation of each organization begins with a description of its file structure. Next, the type of processing that can be accomplished with the file organization is examined and then illustrated by algorithms. Finally, this section contains an application that illustrates a sequential file organization.

### 10-4.1 THE STRUCTURE OF SEQUENTIAL FILES

In a sequential file, introduced in Sec. 5-9, records are stored one after the other on a storage device. Because sequential allocation is conceptually simple, yet flexible enough to cope with many of the problems associated with handling large volumes of data, a sequential file has been the most popular basic file structure used in the data-processing industry.

All types of external storage devices support a sequential file organization. Some devices, by their physical nature, can support only efficiently sequential files. For example, as described in Sec. 10-1.1, information is stored on a magnetic tape as a continuous series of records along the length of the tape. Accessing a particular record requires the accessing of all previous records in the file. Other devices which are strictly sequential in nature are paper tape readers, tape cassettes, and line printers.

Magnetic disks provide both sequential and direct access to records and hence support sequential files along with other types of file structures. A sequential file can be placed on a disk by storing the sequence of records in adjacent locations on a track. Of course, if the file is larger than the amount of space available on a track, then the records are stored on adjacent tracks. This notion of physical adjacency can be extended to cylinders and even to complete storage devices where more than one device is attached to a common control unit. Alternatively, the records of a file can be distributed in noncontiguous locations. Control information describing these locations is recorded on the disk. The operating system automatically creates this control information when a file is written. When a file is read, the operating system uses the control information to provide sequential access of the records.

The operations that can be performed on a sequential file may differ slightly, depending on the storage device used. For example, a file on magnetic tape can be either an input file or an output file, but not both at one time. A sequential file on disk can be used strictly for input, strictly for output, or for update (both input and output by the same program). Some operating systems provide file-accessing facilities which allow a file to be extended by writing records after the current last record. Also, it is sometimes possible to move backward and forward a certain number of records in the file without reading or writing. These extensions are beyond the scope of basic sequential file processing and will not be elaborated on.

Before discussing the type of processing that is normally applied to sequential files, it is important to examine how information on a file is transmitted to a user program and vice versa. In the previous sections of this chapter we defined a logical record and discussed the organization of such a record. In Sec. 10-1.1 it was suggested that it is often advantageous to group a number of logical records into a single physical record or block. Complete blocks and not individual records are transferred between main memory and the external storage.

Note, however, that the execution of a read or write statement in a Pascal program corresponds to the handling of only one logical record, as specified in the parameter list of an instruction. For example, consider the statement

```
read (Master, Employee);
```

where Employee is a suitably declared record variable. Each time this Pascal read statement is executed, the next record from the Master sequential file is moved into the variable Employee. However, each time an actual read or write operation is executed for a particular storage device, a block of logical records is transferred. The apparent difference in a program's read and write statements and the read and write operations issued for a particular device is resolved by using a *buffer* between external storage and the data area of a program. A buffer is a section of main memory which is equal in size to the maximum size of a block of logical records used by a program. The data-management routines of the operating system use buffers for the "blocking" and "deblocking" of records.

To illustrate how the blocking and deblocking of records is accomplished using a buffer, consider the use of the Master sequential file as an input file. When the first read statement is executed, a block of records is moved from external storage to a buffer. The first record in the block is then transferred to the program's data area (variable), as illustrated in Fig. 10-8. For each subsequent execution of a read statement, the next successive record in the buffer is transferred to the data area. Only after every record in the buffer has been moved to the data area, in response to read statements, does the next read statement cause another block to be transferred to the

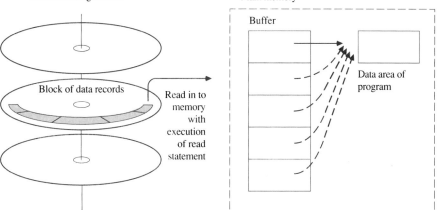

External storage device        Main memory

Buffer

Block of data records    Read in to memory with execution of read statement

Data area of program

FIGURE 10-8   Illustration of the reading in of a block of records.

buffer from external storage. The new records in the buffer are moved to the variables, as described previously, and this entire process is repeated for each block that is read.

In a similar fashion, write statements cause the transfer of program data to the buffer. When the buffer becomes full (corresponding to a block of logical records), then the block is written on the external storage device immediately after the preceding block of records.

The buffering technique just described is called *single buffering*. *Multiple buffering* makes use of a queue of buffers which is normally managed by the operating system. The need for more than one buffer arises because of the delay (which is on the order of milliseconds) necessary to read in or write out the next block of records. This delay in the execution of a program only occurs after every $n$ executions of the read or write statement, when a blocking factor of $n$ and a single buffer are used. However, if the program is executing in an environment where the desired response time is small and where processor and input/output activities need to be overlapped, then it is wise to eliminate this delay by using multiple buffers.

A circular queue of three buffers is shown in Fig. 10-9. When the first read statement is executed, the three buffers $A$, $B$, and $C$ are filled with three consecutive blocks, one block per buffer. After all the records in buffer $A$ have been processed, the execution of a subsequent read instruction results in the transfer of the first record from buffer $B$ to the program's data area. Concurrently, a read command is issued by the operating system and a block transfer from the sequential file on the external storage device to buffer $A$ is initiated. Subsequent executions of read instructions on the master file cause records to be transferred in sequence from buffer $B$ and then buffer $C$. By the time the records of buffer $C$ are being processed, buffer $A$ contains a new buffer full of records and buffer $B$ is being refilled. If the process of filling one buffer with new records is generally balanced with the process

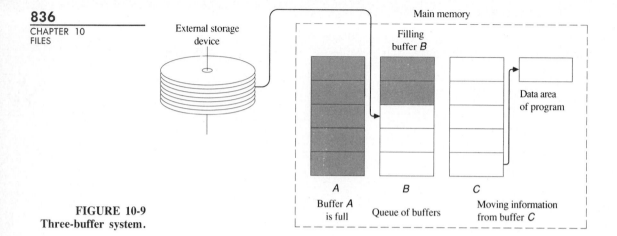

**FIGURE 10-9**
**Three-buffer system.**

of reading records from the remaining buffers, then the program should normally experience only one read or write delay, namely, when the buffers are initially being filled.

In some systems, such as an IBM mainframe system, blocks of logical records which constitute a sequential file can be either of fixed length (the case we have considered so far) or of variable length. A variable-length block contains variable-length records. Since it is not known how many records fit in a block, a maximum length is defined for the block. This maximum length is used to estimate the size of a buffer needed to hold the block, and as many records as possible are grouped into the block by the data-management facilities. Figure 10-10 shows the record format for variable-length blocked and unblocked records. Note that a BL (block length) and an RL (record length) must be stored with each block and record, respectively. These lengths are needed when unblocking the records during a read instruction.

The maximum length of a block depends on the storage device used for the file. With magnetic tape, the length depends on the maximum space available for the buffer in main memory. With disk storage, blocks are generally limited in size to the capacity of a track. Using a sector-addressable device, a block corresponds to some maximum number of sectors.

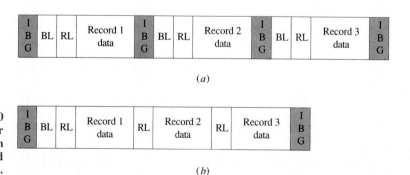

**FIGURE 10-10**
**Record format for**
**variable-length**
**(a) unblocked and**
**(b) blocked records.**

Having discussed the physical layout of a sequential file and how records are transferred to the program area from the file or vice versa, let us examine the types of processing for which sequential files are most suitable. *Serial processing* is the accessing of records one after the other according to the logical order in which they appear in the file. Obviously, it is an easy matter to process a sequential file serially. *Sequential processing* is the accessing of records one after the other in ascending order by a key index (sequence) item of the record. If, for example, a master file of employees' records is ordered by employee surname (e.g., the record for Adams is first, Baker second, . . . , and Zurcher last), then sequentially processing the file by surname is equivalent to serially processing the file. Most sequential files are ordered by a key or index item such as employee name, student identification number, or store catalog number when the file is created. The key or index item should be the item which is most often searched for when processing the file. To show the importance of key selection, assume a file of employees is ordered by employee number. Suppose we want to find the records of a number of employees given only their names. Finding the first employee's record, say, Adams, is simply a matter of serially processing the file until a record with a name item of Adams appears (ignoring the possibility of name duplications). Consider the processing of a second record, say, for Baker. Since the position of Baker's record bears no relationship to the position of Adams's record, we have no alternative but to start once again serially processing from the beginning of the master file.

On rare occasions, serial processing is all that is required on a file, irrespective of the key or item index upon which the file is ordered. For example, if we are to add a pay increase of $2 per hour to the wage item of all employees, it is irrelevant whether the file is sequenced by name or by employee number.

In sequential processing, transaction records are usually grouped together (that is, batched) and are sorted according to the same index item as records in the file. Each successive record of the file is read, compared with an incoming transaction record, and then processed in a manner that is usually dependent on whether the value of the record's index item is less than, equal to, or greater than the value of the index item of the transaction record. The payroll system introduced in Sec. 5-9 is an example of sequential processing.

Sequential and serial processing are most effective when a high percentage of the records in a file must be processed. Since every record in the file must be scanned, a relatively large number of transactions should be batched together for processing. If records are to be added to a file, it is necessary to create a new file unless the records are to be added to the end of the file. In many systems no facilities are provided to allow the direct extension of a sequential file. Records can be deleted from a sequential file by tagging them as "deleted" during a file update. However, this procedure leads to files with embedded "dummy" records, and storage is not efficiently used and processing time is increased. Usually records to be deleted are physically removed by creating a new file. While creating a new file is sometimes necessary, it should be done as infrequently as possible.

To facilitate the implementation of file-processing applications, we now review the facilities in Pascal for sequential files, which were introduced in Sec. 5-9, and describe several additional facilities. Recall that files are declared as variables in Pascal using a file type denoter whose syntax is summarized in Fig. 10-11. We have previously described the reset, rewrite, read and write statements for sequential files and the operation of the end-of-file (eof) test.

Sequential processing often requires "reading ahead" in a file. This means that one record is read from both the master and transaction files immediately after they are opened (by a reset). The index items of the master and transaction records are then compared and the result of the comparison determines the processing. Each time processing of a record is completed, the next record is read so that its index item may be examined.

Pascal provides a built-in facility for this type of processing. Whenever a file is opened for input, the first record is automatically read into a special variable called the *file buffer*. (Do not confuse the Pascal file buffer with the operating system block buffer, used for deblocking a physical block into its individual logical records.) This buffer is referenced by using the file name, followed by an up arrow ( ↑ ). Immediately after a file called Master is reset, its first record can be referenced by

Master ↑

When the current data in the file buffer has been completely processed, it is necessary to advance the file, putting the next input record into the file buffer. The built-in procedure get discards the current contents of the file buffer and stores the next input record of the file in the buffer. The observant reader will conclude that

read (Master, MRec);

is equivalent to

MRec : = Master ↑ ;
get (Master);

Recall that the eof function applied to a file returns "false" if records remain to be read and "true" if all records have been processed. If eof is "true" for a file, then the file buffer is empty. (There is no "next record!") If eof is "true," then an attempt to read a record using the read procedure or an attempt to reference data in the file buffer is an error.

file type denoter

**FIGURE 10-11**
**Syntax diagram**
**for a file type**
**denoter.**

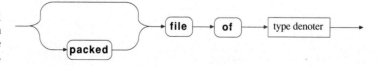

A file open for output also has a file buffer. The procedure put causes the contents of the file buffer to be written to the file. Thus

```
write (Master, MRec);
```

is equivalent to

```
Master ↑ := MRec;
put (Master);
```

where Master is assumed opened for output.

Standard Pascal has several deficiencies in its file handling. First, it has no facility for closing a file. Files are closed automatically on program termination. However, a file that has been opened for reading (reset) or writing (rewrite) can be reopened in either mode by the appropriate procedure (reset or rewrite). There is no provision for opening a file in update mode to allow each record to be read, modified, and rewritten to the same file. Often a Pascal compiler will define extensions to the language, usually in the form of additional built-in functions and procedures, to provide such facilities.

A computer system will typically contain many files on its disk. Each operating system provides some sort of *directory* so that files may be accessed by name. It is convenient to allow a program to be compiled into a machine language program once and stored and then to allow the program to be run many times with different actual files as its input and output. One method for accomplishing this involves a command language external to the program. Statements in this language allow a relationship to be specified between the file variable name in the Pascal program and the directory name of the file to be used. The JCL (Job Control Language) used on many of IBM's large computers is typical.

Another scheme allows the program itself to specify the relationship just described; this is particularly common on interactive computer systems. The program can prompt for a file name on the user's terminal and read it as a character string. The program then specifies the name of the file to be used when opening the file. One common scheme uses a second parameter to the reset and rewrite built-in procedures to specify the file name. A typical example is

```
writeln('Please enter master file name');
readln(MFileName);
reset(Master, MFileName);
```

Usually, Pascal compilers with this file-processing extension also have a character string extension. In this example, MFileName is assumed to be a character string variable.

Alternatively, a separate built-in procedure may associate the file name with the file prior to opening. The Turbo Pascal assign procedure is typical. We would write

```
writeln('Please enter master file name' );
readln(MFileName);
assign(Master, MFileName);
reset(Master);
```

In the remainder of this chapter we will ignore establishing the relationship between the Pascal file name and the directory name of an actual file because the method is so system-dependent.

Recall that we introduced the Pascal text file in Chaps. 2 and 3. There are important differences between text files and other files which should be considered in the design of file-processing programs. We briefly review the similarities and differences between these two types of files.

A text file must be declared with the built-in type identifier text, as in

**var** Messages: text;

A text file is a file whose elements are characters, that is, a **file of** char, but with certain additional properties. First, all the properties expected of a **file of** char hold for a text file. Thus the file can be opened for input or output using reset or rewrite; individual characters can be read or written using read or write; the file buffer may be accessed and is of character type; the file is advanced by get or put.

The first additional property of text files is that values of other types may be read from or written to text files. Integer, real, Boolean, and character-string values may be written. In each case, the value is converted to a string of characters (if necessary) and then written sequentially to the text file. Likewise, integer and real variables may have their values read from a text file. Characters are read sequentially until the value is obtained. The detailed rules were described in Chap. 2 in connection with the standard input and output streams, which are in fact text files.

Text files are considered to be divided into lines. Each line comprises zero or more characters followed by a "new line" character. When reading a text file, new-line characters are treated *exactly* like blank characters, except that when a new-line character is contained in the file buffer, the eoln function, with the file variable as an argument, will return "true." For example,

**if** eoln(InputFile)
**then** { End of line processing }
**else** { Not end of line processing }

Note, however, that the file buffer will still test equal to a blank. A new-line character is written by the special built-in procedure writeln, as described in Chap. 2.

The most significant difference between text files and other files is the manner in which the Pascal file relates to the physical files processed by the operating system. In some operating systems, for example Unix, (Unix is a trademark of AT&T), the operating system imposes no record structure. That is, a sequential file is a sequence of bytes. In this case, a text file and a **file of** char are almost identical except for the mandatory presence of some new-line characters in the text file. However, in operating systems which impose a record structure, it is normal to map each element of the Pascal file type into a logical record as defined by the operating system. Thus a

**file of record** . . . would store each Pascal record structure as a logical record, **file of** integer would store each integer as a logical record, and **file of** char would store each character as a separate logical record! However, the normal scheme is to store each *line* of a text file as a logical record. Therefore, a Pascal compiler implemented for an operating system with a defined record structure is responsible for translating between Pascal's notion of a text file, a sequence of characters containing new-line characters, and the operating system's record structure. An example of the use of text files is included in the billing application in the next subsection.

We now consider in detail an example of sequential file processing. A sequential file named OldMaster is read and its records are updated as specified by records in a sequential file named Transaction. The updated records are written to a sequential file named NewMaster.

Each record in the master files (OldMaster and NewMaster) contains a key field (MKey) and a data field (MData). Both fields are character strings. A transaction record similarly contains a key field (TKey) and a data field (TData), which are both character strings. Additionally, each transaction record contains a code field (TCode) whose value ranges over an enumeration with the following interpretation:

Update   The data field in the master record is replaced by the
         data field from the transaction record.

Add      A new master file record is created with the key and
         data fields from the transaction record.

Delete   The master record with the same key field as the
         transaction record is deleted.

We will assume that the value of TCode is always one of these three enumerated type values.

Recall that in a typical sequential file update application, the files are too large to be read into memory in their entirety. Therefore, we require that both the old master and transaction files be in ascending sequence of the values of the keys. We will assume that neither file contains duplicate keys. This will allow us to read one record from each of the input files, update the master record as specified by the transaction record, and write the updated master record to the new master file. Each set of records is processed in this way until the input files are exhausted.

The actual update algorithm is, as we shall see, more complex, because there may exist master records for which no transaction record is present. Such master records are to be copied to the new master file unchanged. Similarly, there may be transaction records for which no master with the same key value exists. More specifically, no master record with a key matching an "add" transaction may exist in the old master file; otherwise the transaction would represent an attempt to create a master record with the same key as an already existing master record.

A general algorithm for the sequential update is as follows:

*1.* Open the master and transaction files for input and the new master file for output

*2.* Read and process input records and write output records until all input is exhausted

Standard Pascal closes files automatically and in fact has no facility for explicitly closing files. However, some Pascal compilers, and those for many other programming languages, require that files be explicitly closed in a program. Closing the three files would form a third step in the general algorithm.

Step 1 requires no further elaboration. The essentials of the sequential update are contained in step 2, which we elaborate as follows:

*2.1*   Repeat while both the old master and transaction input files are nonempty
   Read and process old master and transaction records and write new master records

*2.2*   Repeat while the old master input file is nonempty
   Copy an old master file record to the new master file
   Obtain the next old master file record

*2.3*   Repeat while the transaction input file is nonempty
   Read and process a transaction, writing the new master record to the new master output file (Only "add" transactions are valid because the old master input file is exhausted at this point)

Observe that step 2.1 does not terminate until one (or both) of the input files is exhausted. Therefore, either (or both) of steps 2.2 and 2.3 will do no further processing.

Step 2.1 requires that we compare the keys of the "current" old master record and transaction record. Depending on whether the first is less than, equal to, or greater than the second, and depending on the transaction code of the current transaction, we may write a new master file record and "advance" one or both of the input files. Advancing an input file means making the next record be the "current" record. Obviously, the current record of each input file must always be accessible to the program in a record variable. We could arrange this by declaring a record variable for each of the input files, as was done in Sec. 5-9. The first record of an input file would be read into the associated record variable when the file is opened. An input file is "advanced" by reading the next record into the associated record variable. An additional complication arises when an advance of an input file is attempted and there are no records remaining. In this case, we shall mark the current record of this input file as "empty." This is easily accomplished by also associating a Boolean flag with each input file. This flag is set "false" on opening the file and obtaining the first record. (The flag is set "true," however, if the input file is empty when it is opened.) An advance of the input file which detects that the input file is exhausted then sets the empty buffer flag to "true."

Based on this approach, and presuming that opening the input files also initializes the current record variables and empty flags, we can elaborate step 2.1 as follows:

*2.1.1.* Repeat step 2.1.2 while there are unprocessed records in both input files

*2.1.2.* If the current master key is less than the current transaction key,
  then Write the current master record to the new master file
    Advance the old master input file
  else If the current master key equals the current transaction key,
    then Select transaction code from
       **UPDATE**: Update the master record
          Write it to the output file
          Advance both input files
       **ADD**:  Indicate an error
      **DELETE**:  Advance both input files
    else (the current master key is greater than current transaction key)
     If current transaction is an add,
     then create and write a new record
     else indicate an error

Steps 2.2 and 2.3 are straightforward and require no further elaboration.

We are now ready to implement this algorithm as a Pascal program. As indicated previously, we can make use of the built-in Pascal file buffer to simplify the program. This file buffer represents the record variable associated with each input file. The **reset** built-in procedure opens the input file and fills this buffer with the first input record. The **get** built-in procedure advances the input file, placing the next record in the file buffer. Finally, the **eof** function applied to a file returns "false" if there is a record in the buffer and "true" when the file has been advanced beyond the last record, making the buffer empty. The **eof** function therefore implements the required buffer empty flag.

If the program were to be written for a Pascal compiler not implementing the buffer variable feature, we would simply declare, for each file, a record variable to hold the current record and an empty flag. We would then incorporate the necessary statements to update these variables. Figure 5-71 uses this method for a similar application.

In Figure 10-12 we present a structure chart for the program. Figures 10-13 through 10-18 present the Pascal implementation of these modules.

Note that we have chosen to pass the files declared in the main program to the subprograms as arguments rather than accessing them by means of global references. Use of arguments better documents which subprograms

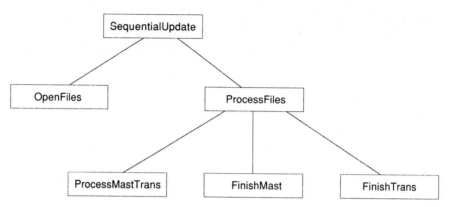

**FIGURE 10-12**
**Structure diagram**
**for sequential file**
**update.**

operate on each file, but use of global references would result in fewer arguments.

A file variable argument must be of the same type as its corresponding parameter. This requires that an identifier be defined for the file type (e.g., MasterFType and TransFType in Fig. 10-13).

The file parameters to a routine are specified as "input/output." The "input/output" specifies the parameter-passing mechanism and does not indicate whether the file is read from or written to. For example, procedure ProcessFiles in Fig. 10-15 has three file parameters which are all designated "input/output" even though the first two will be read and the third written. A file variable in Pascal represents both the contents of the file and its *state*. This state specifies whether it is closed, open for reading, or open for writing, as well as its position, that is, the next record that will be read. Almost every operation affects the state of a file. For example, a read does not affect the contents of a file but advances the position. Thus a procedure which reads from a file passed as a parameter returns the file with the position updated. A parameter whose value is to be changed is an input/output parameter! Pascal, in fact, requires that file parameters be pass-as-variable not pass-by-value, so the **var** is required in any case.

The requirement that the records in a sequential file be ordered by their keys is not essential if the file is being scanned to perform the same operation on every record.

The important points concerning the sequential processing of sequential files can be summarized as follows:

*1.* Sequential processing is most advantageous if a large number of transactions can be batched to form a single "run" on the file.

*2.* A new file should be created if any additions and/or a significant number of deletions are requested.

*3.* Quick response time should not be expected for a transaction or a batch of transactions.

*4.* The requirement that the records in a sequential file be ordered by a

```
program SequentialUpdate (output, OldMaster, Transaction, NewMaster);
{Given the files OldMaster and Transaction, this program creates a new file,
   NewMaster, by performing the operations specified by the transaction
   records.}
const
   KeySize = 10;
   DataSize = 50;
type
   TransType = (UpdateTrans, AddTrans, DeleteTrans);
   KeyType = packed array [1 .. KeySize] of char;
   DataType = packed array [1 .. DataSize] of char;
   MasterRType =
      record
         MKey: KeyType;
         MData: DataType
      end;
   TransRType =
      record
         TKey: KeyType;
         TData: DataType;
         TCode: TransType
      end;
   MasterFType = file of MasterRType;
   TransFType = file of TransRType;
var
   OldMaster: MasterFType;      {Old master file}
   Transaction: TransFType;     {Transaction file}
   NewMaster: MasterFType;      {New master file}
{Include procedures OpenFiles, ProcessFiles, ProcessMastTrans, FinishMaster,
   and FinishTrans.}

begin
   {Step 1: Open files}
   OpenFiles (OldMaster, Transaction, NewMaster);

   {Step 2: Read and process input records and write output records}
   ProcessFiles (OldMaster, Transaction, NewMaster)
end.
```

**FIGURE 10-13**
Sequential
update program.

particular key is not essential if the file is being scanned to perform the
same operation on every record (that is, serial processing).

In the following section we will see that the direct file organization is
more suitable if requirements such as quick response time and individual
transaction handling exist. If the sequential file resides on a direct-access
device, it is possible to improve the response time significantly.

```
procedure OpenFiles (
    var OldMaster: MasterFType;      {Input/output, old master file}
    var Transaction: TransFType;     {Input/output, transaction file}
    var NewMaster: MasterFType       {Input/output, new master file}
                    );
```
{This procedure opens the Master and Transaction files for input and the NewMaster file for output.}
```
begin
    {Step 1: Open the old master file for input}
    reset (OldMaster);

    {Step 2: Open the transaction file for input}
    reset (Transaction);

    {Step 3: Open the new master file for output}
    rewrite (NewMaster)
end;
```

**FIGURE 10-14**
Procedure OpenFiles.

## 10-4.3  A SMALL BILLING SYSTEM

This particular section is concerned with the analysis, design (in particular, deciding on the file structure needed in the system), and implementation of a small billing system. While this example is included primarily as an application using sequential files, it is an interesting application in its own right, since everyone, at some time, has interacted with such a system.

```
procedure ProcessFiles (
    var OldMaster: MasterFType;      {Input/output, old master file}
    var Transaction: TransFType;     {Input/output, transaction file}
    var NewMaster: MasterFType       {Input/output, new master file}
                    );
```
{Given the old master and transaction files, open for input, and the new master file, open for output, this procedure writes records to new master by performing the operations specified by the transaction records.}
```
begin
    {Step 1: Read and process records and write updated records while both
        the old master and the transaction files are nonempty}
    ProcessMastTrans (OldMaster, Transaction, NewMaster);

    {Step 2: While the old master file is nonempty, copy records to the new
        master file}
    FinishMast (OldMaster, NewMaster);

    {Step 3: While the transaction input file is nonempty process "add"
        transactions}
    FinishTrans (Transaction, NewMaster)
end;
```

**FIGURE 10-15**
Procedure ProcessFiles.

The Company of Canada, Ltd., operates a chain of small department stores. Recently, the company decided to offer a charge account service to its customers by means of credit cards. A purchase form indicating the credit card number, the items purchased, and their cost is filled out by the cashiers at the time of purchase. The form is also designed to show a customer credit in the case of returned articles. The credit card carries a six-digit customer account number, and an imprinter at the point of sale indicates the date of the transaction.

The forms are sent on an almost daily basis to the head office for processing. The head office sends out monthly statements to all credit-card–carrying customers. All payments on charge accounts are also received at the head office. The company charges interest on these accounts at the rate of 1.5 percent of that part of last month's debit balance for which payments were not received this month.

The company wishes to automate its billing system. The company is small. After some preliminary analysis, it is decided that the company, being small, could not afford the ongoing costs of its own computer, and arrangements have been made with another business to rent some magnetic disk storage and purchase some CPU time once per month.

The company would like as output from each monthly run the following information:

*1.* A listing of all credit-card–carrying customers. The listing should include for each given account number the name, address, and current balance of account, and it should be ordered by account number.

*2.* A monthly balance report, which should include the total outstanding balance owed to the company, the total of purchases made for the month, the total of payments received, the interest charged, and the new total balance owed to the company.

*3.* A daily sales report, which indicates, for each day, the total of the purchase receipts received at the head office.

*4.* Monthly statements for all customers, which should include an initial balance-forward figure, the date, name, and amount of any purchase, the date and amount of any payment on the account, the interest charged (if any), and a final current amount-owing figure. Also included is the customer's address, which is positioned on the statement so as to appear through a see-through window in the statement's envelope. The address must be no more than four lines, and a line must be fewer than 30 characters in width.

The input to the billing system includes:

*1.* Credit-card receipts, each of which includes the customer account number, date of purchase, and description and amount of items purchased.

**procedure** ProcessMastTrans (
  **var** OldMaster: MasterFType;  {Input/output, old master file}
  **var** Transaction: TransFType;  {Input/output, transaction file}
  **var** NewMaster: MasterFType  {Input/output, new master file}
  );
{Given the old master and transaction files, open for input, and the new master file, open for output, this procedure reads and processes input records and writes output records while both files are nonempty.}
**begin**
  {Step 1: Engage loop to process while both input buffers are nonempty}
  **while not** eof(OldMaster) **and not** eof(Transaction) **do**
    **if** OldMaster $\uparrow$ .MKey $<$ Transaction $\uparrow$ .TKey
    **then begin**
        NewMaster $\uparrow$ : $=$ OldMaster $\uparrow$ ;
        put(NewMaster);
        get(OldMaster)
    **end**
    **else**
      **if** OldMaster $\uparrow$ .MKey $=$ Transaction $\uparrow$ .TKey
      **then**
        **case** Transaction $\uparrow$ .TCode **of**
          UpdateTrans:
            **begin**
              NewMaster $\uparrow$ .MKey : $=$ OldMaster $\uparrow$ .MKey;
              NewMaster $\uparrow$ .MData : $=$ Transaction $\uparrow$ .TData;
              put(NewMaster);
              get(OldMaster);
              get(Transaction)
           **end**;

**FIGURE 10-16**
**Procedure**
**ProcessMastTrans.**

2. New customer credit-card applications, each of which includes the customer's name, address, and assigned account number.

3. Payment receipts, each of which includes the customer account number, the date of payment, and amount paid.

4. Customer termination information, where each termination must provide the customer account number and the date of termination.

There are some additional factors which can potentially affect the design of the system. First, all new credit cards must be issued by the head office. Second, as a service to the public, customers are allowed to indicate the termination of their accounts by writing directly to the head office or by contacting the local store and having it send in a notice of termination.

### System Design

We proceed with the system design first by deciding on the format for the inputs and outputs and then by considering the problems of how best to

```
        AddTrans:
          begin
            writeln ('Attempt to add a duplicate record for key',
              Transaction ↑ .TKey);
            get(Transaction)
          end;
        DeleteTrans:
          begin
            get(OldMaster);
            get(Transaction)
          end
    end
  else      {OldMaster ↑ .MKey > Transaction ↑ .TKey}
    case Transaction ↑ .TCode of
      AddTrans:
        begin
          NewMaster ↑ .MKey : = Transaction ↑ .TKey;
          NewMaster ↑ .MData : = Transaction ↑ .TData;
          put(NewMaster);
          get(Transaction)
        end;
      UpdateTrans, DeleteTrans:
        begin
          writeln ('Attempt to update or delete a nonexistent record',
            'with key', Transaction ↑ .TKey);
          get(Transaction)
        end
    end
  end;
```

**FIGURE 10-16** (*cont.*)

generate the desired outputs. Inputs come from two sources: the point of sale (purchase and termination slips) and the customer (applications for credit cards, payments, and termination notices).

As purchases come in from point-of-sale locations, they are keyed into the system. The following format is chosen:

Purchase record:
  Customer's account number
  Date (month, day, year)
  Amount of purchase
  Item description

The input file that is formed by the encoding of these purchases will be called Purchase. Because terminations as well as purchases arrive from the points of sale, it is decided to indicate an account termination by placing the message 'DELETE' in the description field of the Purchase record. Therefore, Purchase records also must be created for termination notices that are sent directly to the head office by the customer.

```
procedure FinishMast (
    var OldMaster: MasterFType;    {Input/output, old master file}
    var NewMaster: MasterFType     {Input/output, new master file}
                      );
```

{Given the old master file, open for input, and the new master file, open for output, this procedure copies records from the old master to the new master while the old master is nonempty. The transaction file is assumed to be exhausted.}

```
begin
    while not eof (OldMaster) do
      begin
        NewMaster ↑ : = OldMaster ↑ ;
        put (NewMaster);
        get (OldMaster)
      end
end;
```

**FIGURE 10-17**
Procedure FinishMast.

```
procedure FinishTrans (
    var Transaction: TransFType;    {Input/output, transaction file}
    var NewMaster: MasterFType      {Input/output, new master file}
                      );
```

{Given the transaction file, open for input, and the new master file, open for output, this procedure reads and processes transactions while the transaction file is nonempty. The old master file is assumed to be exhausted; therefore, only "add" transactions are valid.}

```
begin
    while not eof (Transaction) do
      case Transaction ↑ .TCode of
        AddTrans:
          begin
            NewMaster ↑ .MKey : = Transaction ↑ .TKey;
            NewMaster ↑ .MData : = Transaction ↑ .TData;
            put (NewMaster);
            get (Transaction)
          end;
        UpdateTrans, DeleteTrans:
          begin
            writeln ('Attempt to update or delete a nonexistent',
                'record with key', Transaction ↑ .TKey);
            get (Transaction)
          end
      end
end;
```

**FIGURE 10-18**
Procedure FinishTrans.

Two separate input files, **Payment** and **NewAcct**, are also created for customer payments and credit card applications, respectively.

**Payment** record:

    Customer's account number

    Date (month, day, year)

    Amount of payment

**NewAcct** record:

    Customer's account number

    Customer's name

    Customer's street or P.O. box, etc.

    Customer's city and province or state

    Customer's postal code

    Customer's initial balance (always set to zero)

An important part of any business system design is the design of output forms and reports. In this application, the greatest effort must be expended on the design of the customer's statement. A format which does satisfy the company's needs is given in Fig. 10-19. The boldface print identifies that part of the statement which is common to all statements. This common text could be preprinted on the statement by a printing shop before computer processing. This makes it necessary to print only the dates, purchases, balances, etc., for a specific customer. Such a procedure saves a tremendous amount of time and permits the generation of multicolored statements. However, for the purposes of this example, we will assume plain paper and print the headings from the program.

**FIGURE 10-19** General format of a customer's statement.

**THE COMPANY OF CANADA, LTD.**
**4141 THE STREET**
**THE CITY, PROVINCE**
**A0A 1B1**

CUSTOMER'S NAME    NUMBER
STREET OR BOX NUMBER
CITY, PROVINCE OR STATE
POS COD

| Date | TRANSACTION | DEBIT | CREDIT | BALANCE |
|------|-------------|-------|--------|---------|
| | **BALANCE FORWARD** | $DD.DD | | $BB.BB |
| MM/DD/YY | PURCHASE (ITEM) | $DD.DD | | $BB.BB |
| MM/DD/YY | PAYMENT ON ACCOUNT | | $CC.CC | $BB.BB |
| MM/DD/YY | INTEREST ON: $II.II | $DD.DD | | $BB.BB |
| MM/DD/YY | CURRENT AMOUNT OWING | | | $BB.BB |

The customer listing as required by the company should be ordered by account number, and all pertinent customer information should appear in a compact, yet readable format. To achieve this, the information pertaining to a single customer is printed on two lines with the following format:

ACCT NUM   NAME   BALANCE
STREET   or   P.O.BOX   CITY,   PROVINCE   POSTAL CODE

The monthly totals and daily payments received are printed on the same report in an easily readable format.

We now turn to the design of the program which takes the specified input and creates the desired output properly formatted. Figure 10-20 shows a data flow diagram for a possible preliminary design for the system. It is not necessarily the best design, and some improvements will be considered later in this subsection. However, it requires only the sequential file organization present in Pascal.

An obvious, yet important aspect of the system design is that each customer's current balance, along with his or her name, account number, and address, must be kept on a system file from one month's run to the next. We will call this file the **Customer** file and create it as a sequential file ordered by account number.

A conceptually simple way of handling new customers is to merge the set of new accounts with the **Customer** file and, by necessity, create a new

**FIGURE 10-20    Data flow diagram of billing system.**

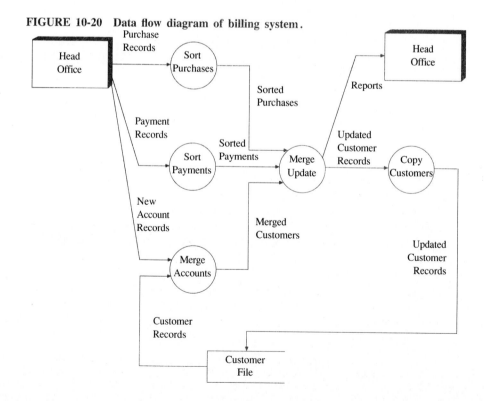

sequential file which we call MergedCustomer. In MergedCustomer, a new account will have a "current balance" field set to zero. Note that in the system we have designed, the assignment of a new account number is handled manually. While this may result in some extra bookkeeping, a sequential file ordered by account number can be created quite easily during the month for new account numbers. This ordered sequential file, called NewAcct, is the file that is merged with the Customer file to form MergedCustomer.

To generate a customer's statement, it is necessary to combine the monthly purchases and payments for a customer with his or her previous month's balance. Grouping all receipts and payments with the previous month's balance would be an inefficient, costly process if it were done using a separate run for each customer. However, by sorting the Purchase and Payment files by account number, producing files SortedPurchase and SortedPayment, and then merging the information in these two files with the information in the MergedCustomer file, we can produce all the customer statements in one run (that is, in one pass over each of the three files). The updated customer records are written to a temporary file UpdatedCustomer. The Purchase and Payment files each can be sorted by using a system sort routine or by writing your own sort procedure, as indicated in Fig. 10-20.

From the data flow diagram in Fig. 10-20, we are led to the following general algorithm for the billing system:

*1.* Sort the purchase records by customer account number

*2.* Sort the payment records by customer account number

*3.* Merge the new account records with the records in the current customer file, creating a new customer file

*4.* Perform a merge update by processing all purchases and payments

*5.* Copy the updated customer records into the permanent customer file

Steps 1 and 2 require an external sort routine. We have already encountered simple internal sort routines in Chap. 5. If the external files are large, however, these internal sort routines cannot be used directly, since all the records in an external file cannot be stored in main memory at one time. Therefore, an external sort routine must take into account that only part of a file is available in main memory during the sorting process. Usually, a system routine is available for performing an external sort on most computer systems, so we will not develop those steps further. The details for merging the new accounts (step 3) are also omitted because of the similarity between the type of processing required here and that given in program SequentialUpdate.

Step 4 of this general algorithm requires more investigation. It involves the merging of three files and is outlined in the following steps:

*4.1.* Open the files and initialize the buffers

*4.2.* Repeat thru step 4 while there are still records left in the MergedCustomer file

**4.3.** Read in a record from MergedCustomer file

**4.4.** Read in and process all Payment records with the same account number as the MergedCustomer record

**4.5.** Read in and process all Purchase records with the same account number as the MergedCustomer record

**4.6.** Calculate interest if necessary

**4.7.** Compute a new balance

**4.8.** Write a customer's statement, write a line in the customer report, and write a record to the UpdatedCustomer file

**4.9.** Write the summary report

Note that the company reports are generated during the customer file updating. A customer's account number, name, address, and balance are printed immediately after calculating a new balance during the processing of the three files. However, customer statements are printed at the same time, so care must be taken to place the company's customer list and the customer statements on separate text files for printing.

The company report containing the monthly totals is created by accumulating the totals as individual customer records are processed. The final report is output immediately after the updating of all customer records.

The daily sales report is generated by updating a vector of 31 elements, in which each element holds the accumulation of all purchases on a given day. Element $n$ holds the total of the purchase slip amounts for the $n$th day of the month.

Returning to the general algorithm, step 5 creates a new Customer file from the temporary UpdatedCustomer file. This involves nothing more than a simple record-by-record (that is, serial) copying of the records in the UpdatedCustomer file into the Customer file.

In the previous discussion, we purposely neglected the problem of handling accounts which are terminated. One possibility is physically to delete terminating accounts after the processing of these accounts has taken place. The account number is set to 000000 during the merge update before the record is written to UpdatedCustomer, and then all 000000 records are deleted when the new Customer file is created. The disadvantage with this scheme is that tardy sales slips on terminated accounts may be received the next month and the account number will already have been removed from the system. An alternative design is considered at the end of the next subsection.

The structure chart in Fig. 10-21 describes the resulting system design which is suggested by the previous algorithm refinement. The ProcessPay and ProcessPur modules represent refinements of steps 4.4 and 4.5. The module GetDate supplies today's date. Such a module is system-dependent and is not further described here. The Pascal statements which write the customer statements are mostly output-formatting statements. The required processing is heavily influenced by the layout of a customer statement. We have

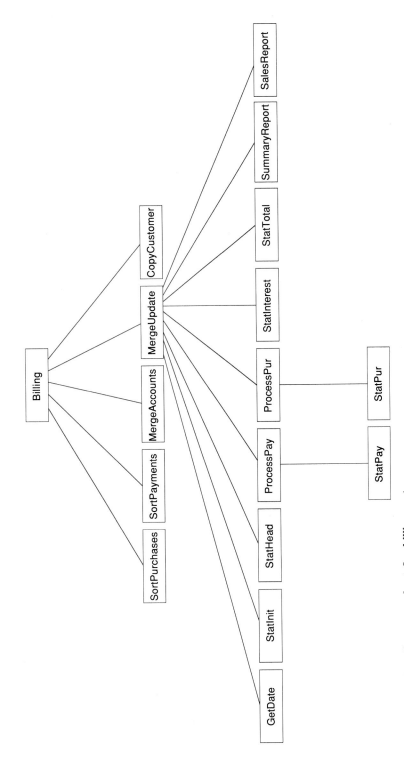

**FIGURE 10-21 Structure chart for billing system.**

segregated the production of the statements in the modules whose names begin with Stat.

### Implementation

We begin this subsection by formally defining the records and files needed for the billing application by means of the Pascal type definitions in Fig. 10-22. The records contained in the Customer, MergedCustomer, UpdatedCustomer and NewAcct files are of type CustRec. The Purchase and SortedPurchase files contain records of type PurchaseRec. The Payment and SortedPayment files contain records of type PaymentRec.

Two output text files, called Statement and Report, are also needed. Recall that text files do not contain records of a specific type, but rather, strings, integers, and reals are written to this file in a sequential manner.

```
type
    String30 = packed array [1 .. 30] of char;
    CustRec =
        record
            ID: integer;
            Name: String30;
            Address:
                record
                    Line1, Line2, PostalCode: String30
                end;
            Balance: real
        end;
    DateType =
        record
            Month, Day, Year: integer
        end;
    PurchaseRec =
        record
            ID: integer;
            PDate: DateType;
            Amount: real;
            Description: String30
        end;
    PaymentRec =
        record
            ID: integer;
            PDate: DateType;
            Amount: real
        end;
    PurFType = file of PurchaseRec;
    PayFType = file of PaymentRec;
    CustFType = file of CustRec;
    DPurType = array [1 .. 31] of real;
```

**FIGURE 10-22**
**Type definitions for the billing example.**

The format of this file is, of course, of utmost importance, since the monthly statements must follow the specifications given in the design phase. However, since the detailed characteristics of printers are very system-dependent, we will use an appropriate format for testing the program. A programmer can easily improve the formatting, given the specific characteristics of a printer and the preprinted forms to be used.

The main program Billing appears in Fig. 10-23. Step 1 consists of a series of four calls to the main modules of the billing system: SortPurchases, SortPayments, MergeAccts, and MergeUpdate. Step 2 calls the procedure to copy the updated customer file to the customer file. In a true production billing system, this operation would be conditional on successful completion of the operations performed in step 1. If any of those operations should fail, the billing system can be run again after correcting the error as long as the previous customer master file has not been destroyed. It also should be noted that most operating systems provide other methods, e.g., renaming files, for replacing the customer file by the updated customer file.

Figure 10-24 presents the MergeUpdate procedure. Step 1 obtains the date. Next, the totals for the summary and sales reports are cleared to

```
program Billing(Purchase, SortedPurchase, Payment, SortedPayment, NewAcct,
    Customer, MergedCustomer, UpdatedCustomer, Statement, Report);
{Billing program for The Company of Canada, Ltd.}
{Include the type declarations here.}
var
    Purchase: PurFType;              {File of purchases}
    SortedPurchase: PurFType;        {Sorted file of purchases}
    Payment: PayFType;               {File of payments}
    SortedPayment: PayFType;         {Sorted file of payments}
    NewAcct: CustFType;              {File of new customers}
    Customer: CustFType;             {Master file of customers}
    MergedCustomer: CustFType;       {Merged file of old and new customers}
    UpdatedCustomer: CustFType;      {Updated customer records}
    Statement: text;                 {File for statements}
    Report: text;                    {File for reports}
{Include procedures SortPurchases, SortPayments, MergeAccts, MergeUpdate,
    and CopyCustomers here.}
begin
    {Step 1: Call the procedures to do the billing}
    SortPurchases (Purchase, SortedPurchase);
    SortPayments (Payment, SortedPayment);
    MergeAccts (Customer, NewAcct, MergedCustomer);
    MergeUpdate (SortedPurchase, SortedPayment, MergedCustomer,
        UpdatedCustomer, Statement, Report);

    {Step 2: Copy the updated customer records to the customer file}
    CopyCustomer (UpdatedCustomer, Customer)
end.
```

**FIGURE 10-23**
**Billing program.**

```
procedure MergeUpdate (
    var SortedPurchase: PurFType;        {Input/output, sorted purchases}
    var SortedPayment: PayFType;         {Input/output, sorted payments}
    var MergedCustomer: CustFType;       {Input/output, customers}
    var UpdatedCustomer: CustFType;      {Input/output, updated customers}
    var Statement: text;                 {Input/output, statements}
    var Report: text                     {Input/output, reports}
    );
```

{This procedure reads records from the MergedCustomer temporary file and, for each record, processes records from the SortedPurchase and SortedPayment files which have the same ID number. A statement is produced for each customer. An entry in the customer report is produced for each customer. A monthly balance report and daily sales report are also produced.}

```
const
    IntRate = 0.015;                     {Interest rate}
var
    TotalOldBalance: real;               {Total old balances of all customers}
    TotalPayments: real;                 {Total payments of all customers}
    TotalPurchases: real;                {Total purchases of all customers}
    TotalInterest: real;                 {Total interest due from all customers}
    TotalNewBalance: real;               {Total new balances of all customers}
    DailyPurchases: DPurType;            {Total purchases for each day}
    Today: DateType;                     {Today's date}
    CurrentCustomer: CustRec;            {Current customer record}
    Day: integer;                        {Loop index}
    DeleteFlag: Boolean;                 {Flag indicating that the current customer
                                            is to be deleted}
    Interest: real;                      {Current customer interest}
    BalanceAfterPayments: real;          {Monthly balance after payments}
```

{Include procedures GetDate, StatInit, StatHead, ProcessPay, ProcessPur, StatInterest, StatTotal, StatPay, StatPur, SummaryReport, and SalesReport here.}

```
begin
    {Step 1: Initialize today's date}
    GetDate(Today);
    {Step 2: Initialize for reports}
    TotalOldBalance : = 0.0;
    TotalPayments : = 0.0;
    TotalPurchases : = 0.0;
    TotalInterest : = 0.0;
    TotalNewBalance : = 0.0;
    for Day : = 1 to 31 do
        DailyPurchases[Day] : = 0.0;
    rewrite(Report);
    {Step 3: Initialize for statements}
    StatInit(Statement);
```

FIGURE 10-24
Procedure
MergeUpdate.

```
{Step 4: Open data files}
reset(SortedPurchase);
reset(SortedPayment);
reset(MergedCustomer);
rewrite(UpdatedCustomer);
rewrite(Report);
{Step 5: Engage main loop}
while not eof(MergedCustomer) do
   begin
      {Step 6: Read the next customer record}
      read (MergedCustomer, CurrentCustomer);
      {Step 7: Perform the processing for this customer}
      StatHead(Statement, CurrentCustomer);
      TotalOldBalance : = TotalOldBalance + CurrentCustomer. Balance;
      ProcessPay(SortedPayment, Statement, CurrentCustomer, TotalPayments);
      BalanceAfterPayments : = CurrentCustomer.Balance;
      ProcessPur(SortedPurchase, Statement, CurrentCustomer, TotalPurchases,
         DailyPurchases, DeleteFlag);
      if BalanceAfterPayments > 0.0
      then begin
              Interest : = BalanceAfterPayments * IntRate;
              CurrentCustomer.Balance: = CurrentCustomer.Balance + Interest;
              TotalInterest : = TotalInterest + Interest;
              StatInterest(Statement, CurrentCustomer, Today,
                 BalanceAfterPayments, Interest)
           end;
      StatTotal(Statement, CurrentCustomer, Today, DeleteFlag);
      TotalNewBalance : = TotalNewBalance + CurrentCustomer.Balance;
      {Step 8: Write updated customer record}
      if DeleteFlag
      then CurrentCustomer.ID : = 0;
      write(UpdatedCustomer, CurrentCustomer);
      {Step 9: Write customer details to customer report}
      with CurrentCustomer do
         begin
            writeln(Report, ID:6,'':4, Name, Balance:10:2);
            with Address do
               writeln(Report, '':10, Line1, Line2, PostalCode)
         end
   end;
{Step 10: Write the summary report}
SummaryReport(Report, TotalOldBalance, TotalPayments, TotalPurchases,
   TotalInterest, TotalNewBalance);
{Step 11: Write the sales report}
SalesReport(Report, DailyPurchases)
end;
```

**FIGURE 10-24** (*cont.*)

zero. In step 3, procedure StatInit is called to initialize the preparation of customer statements. The sequential files (SortedPurchase, SortedPayment, MergeCustomer, and UpdatedCustomer) and the text file for reports are opened in step 4. The initialization having been completed, step 5 engages a loop which repeats once for each record in the MergedCustomer file. Step 7 performs the bulk of the processing. Procedures ProcessPay and ProcessPur are called to read and process all the payment and purchase transactions, respectively, for the current customer record. The summary report totals are maintained, and the interest is computed. The procedures for writing portions of the customer statement are called. Recall (see System Design) that purchase transactions containing 'DELETE' indicate that a customer account is to be deleted. ProcessPur returns a flag so that MergeUpdate can set the customer account numbers to zero in step 8 before writing the updated customer record. Step 9 completes processing of a customer record by writing the information to the customer report. After all the customer records have been processed, step 10 calls SummaryReport and step 11 calls SalesReport to write the two required reports.

Procedure ProcessPay (Fig. 10-25) reads and processes all payment transactions applying to the current customer and is quite straightforward. The file buffer associated with the SortedPayment file contains the next

```
procedure ProcessPay (
    var SortedPayment: PayFType;      {Input/output, sorted payment file}
    var Statement: text;              {Input/output, output file for statement}
    var CurrentCustomer: CustRec;     {Input/output, current customer record}
    var TotalPayments: real           {Input/output, total payments for all
                                        customers}
                  );
{This procedure processes all of the customer's current payments}
var
    PayDoneFlag: Boolean;    {True indicates that all payments of current
                              customer have been processed}
begin
    {Step 1: Initialize flag}
    PayDoneFlag : = false;

    {Step 2: Process all payments for the current customer}
    while not eof(SortedPayment) and not PayDoneFlag do
        if CurrentCustomer.ID = SortedPayment ↑ .ID
        then begin
                CurrentCustomer.Balance : = CurrentCustomer.Balance
                    − SortedPayment ↑ .Amount;
                TotalPayments : = TotalPayments + SortedPayment ↑ .Amount;
                StatPay(Statement, CurrentCustomer, SortedPayment ↑ );
                get(SortedPayment)
            end
        else PayDoneFlag : = true
end;
```

**FIGURE 10-25**
**Procedure ProcessPay.**

unprocessed payment record, if any. Reading and processing of payments continues until one is found whose account number does not match that of the current customer record or the end of file is encountered. Payment entries are written to the customer statement.

ProcessPur (Fig. 10-26) is similar to ProcessPay. The only additional feature is the setting of the deletion flag if a 'DELETE' purchase transaction is encountered for the current customer.

```
procedure ProcessPur (
    var SortedPurchase: PurFType;      {Input/output, sorted purchase file}
    var Statement: text;               {Input/output, output file for statement}
    var CurrentCustomer: CustRec;      {Input/output, current customer record}
    var TotalPurchases: real;          {Input/output, total purchases for all
                                          customers}
    var DailyPurchases: DPurType;      {Input/output, total purchases for each
                                          day}
    var DeleteFlag: Boolean            {Output, true indicates customer is to be
                                          deleted}
                    );
{This procedure processes all of the customer's current purchases}
var
    PurDoneFlag: Boolean;    {True indicates that all purchases of current
                                customer have been processed}
begin
    {Step 1: Initialize flags}
    PurDoneFlag : = false;
    DeleteFlag : = false;

    {Step 2: Process all purchases for the current customer}
    while not eof(SortedPurchase) and not PurDoneFlag do
        if CurrentCustomer.ID = SortedPurchase ↑ .ID
        then begin
            if SortedPurchase ↑ .Description =
                'Delete□□□□□□□□□□□□□□□□□□□□□□□□□□□□□□'
            then DeleteFlag : = true
            else begin
                    CurrentCustomer.Balance : = CurrentCustomer.Balance
                        + SortedPurchase ↑ .Amount;
                    TotalPurchases : = TotalPurchases + SortedPurchase ↑ .Amount;
                    DailyPurchases[SortedPurchase ↑ .PDate.Day] : =
                        DailyPurchases[SortedPurchase ↑ .PDate.Day]
                        + SortedPurchase ↑ .Amount;
                    StatPur(Statement, CurrentCustomer, SortedPurchase ↑ )
                end;
            get(SortedPurchase)
        end
        else PurDoneFlag : = true
end;
```

**FIGURE 10-26**
Procedure ProcessPur.

```
procedure StatInit (
    var Statement: text      {Input/output, file for statements}
                        );
{Initialize for producing statements.}
begin
    {Step 1: open the file}
    rewrite (Statement)
end;
```

FIGURE 10-27
Procedure StatInit.

The suite of procedures in Figs. 10-27 through 10-32 isolates the details of customer statement preparation. StatInit is called once prior to production of any statements. The version presented simply opens the text file Statement. Other operations, such as requesting the setup of special forms in the printer, could easily be added.

Each statement consists of a heading (customer name, etc.) line for each payment and each purchase, a line indicating the interest charged (if any), and finally, the totals. StatHead (Fig. 10-28) writes the heading. StatPay

```
procedure StatHead (
    var Statement: text;              {Input/output, file for statements}
        CurrentCustomer: CustRec      {Input, current customer record}
                        );
{Output statement header for current customer.}
begin
    {Step 1: Output the statement heading}
    writeln(Statement);
    writeln(Statement);
    writeln(Statement);
    writeln(Statement);
    writeln(Statement,'□':22,'The Company of Canada, Ltd.');
    writeln(Statement,'□':28,'4141 The Street');
    writeln(Statement,'□':27,'The City, Province');
    writeln(Statement,'□':32,'A0A 1B1');
    writeln(Statement);
    writeln(Statement,CurrentCustomer.Name,CurrentCustomer.ID);
    writeln(Statement,CurrentCustomer.Address.Line1);
    writeln(Statement,CurrentCustomer.Address.Line2);
    writeln(Statement,CurrentCustomer.Address.PostalCode);
    writeln(Statement);
    writeln(Statement,'Date ','□':4,
        'Transaction□□□□□□□□□□□□□□□□□□□□',
        'Debit':10,'Credit':10,'Balance':10);
    writeln(Statement);
    writeln(Statement,'□':8,'□':4,
        'Balance Forward□□□□□□□□□□□□□□□',
        CurrentCustomer.Balance:10:2,'□':10,CurrentCustomer.Balance:10:2);
end;
```

FIGURE 10-28
Procedure StatHead.

```
procedure StatPay (
   var Statement: text;              {Input/output, file for statements}
   CurrentCustomer: CustRec;         {Input, current customer record}
   Payment: PaymentRec               {Input, payment record}
                  );
{Output a payment line to the current statement.}
begin
   {Step 1: Output the payment line}
   with Payment do
      begin
         with PDate do
            write(Statement, Month:2, '/', Day:2, '/', Year:2, '□':4);
            write (Statement, 'Payment on account□□□□□□□□□□□□□□',
               '□':10, Amount:10:2)
      end;
      writeln (Statement, CurrentCustomer.Balance:10:2)
end;
```

**FIGURE 10-29**
Procedure StatPay.

(Fig. 10-29) writes a line representing a single payment and is called once for each payment transaction. Similarly, StatPur (Fig. 10-30) writes a purchase line. If interest is charged, StatInterest (Fig. 10-31) is called to write this information. Finally, the totals are written by StatTotal (Fig. 10-32).

The customer report was written line-by-line by MergeUpdate. The remaining two reports are written by SummaryReport (Fig. 10-33) and SalesReport (Fig. 10-34).

Procedure CopyCustomer, presented in Fig. 10-35, copies records from UpdatedCustomer to Customer, deleting those with an account number of zero.

To conclude this section, let us consider some design changes for the system just implemented; remember, system development is an iterative

```
procedure StatPur (
   var Statement: text;              {Input/output, file for statements}
   CurrentCustomer: CustRec;         {Input, current customer record}
   Purchase: PurchaseRec             {Input, purchase record}
                  );
{Output a purchase line to the current statement}
begin
   {Step 1: Output the purchase line}
   with Purchase do
      begin
         with PDate do
            write (Statement, Month:2, '/', Day:2, '/', Year:2, '□':4);
            write (Statement, Description, Amount:10:2, '□':10)
      end;
      writeln (Statement, CurrentCustomer.Balance:10:2)
end;
```

**FIGURE 10-30**
Procedure StatPur.

```
procedure StatInterest (
    var Statement: text;              {Input/output, file for statements}
    CurrentCustomer: CustRec;         {Input, current customer record}
    Today: DateType;                  {Input, today's date}
    BalanceAfterPayments: real;       {Input, account balance after payments}
    Interest: real                    {Input, amount of interest}
                      );
{Output an interest line to the current statement}
begin
    {Step 1: Output the interest line}
    with Today do
        write(Statement, Month:2, '/', Day:2, '/', Year:2, '□':4);
        write (Statement, 'Interest on', BalanceAfterPayments:10:2, '□':9,
        Interest:10:2, '□':10, CurrentCustomer.Balance:10:2)
end;
```

**FIGURE 10-31**
Procedure StatInterest.

process. Two major changes can be accommodated quite easily. Instead of making a separate pass over the Customer file to merge it with the NewAcct file, we can simply include this merge with the merge/update process, which involves the Payment and Purchase files. Note that the temporary file UpdatedCustomer is still used. Even if we could place the merged information from the four files immediately back into the file Customer, this would

```
procedure StatTotal (
    var Statement: text;              {Input/output, file for statements}
    CurrentCustomer: CustRec;         {Input, current customer record}
    Today: DateType;                  {Input, today's date}
    DeleteFlag: Boolean               {Input, true indicates that the current customer
                                        is to be deleted}
                      );
{Output total lines at end of statement}
begin
    {Step 1: Output the total lines}
    writeln(Statement);
    with Today do
        write(Statement, Month:2, '/', Day:2, '/', Year:2, '□':4);
        writeln(Statement, 'Current Amount Owing□□□□□□□□□□', '□':10,
        '□':10, CurrentCustomer.Balance:10:2);

    {Step 2: If the customer is being deleted, add a note}
    if DeleteFlag
    then begin
        writeln(Statement);
        writeln(Statement, 'This is your final statement');
        writeln(Statement, 'Thank you for your business')
    end
end;
```

**FIGURE 10-32**
Procedure StatTotal.

```
procedure SummaryReport (
    var Report: text;           {Input/output, file for reports}
    TotalOldBalance,
    TotalPayments,
    TotalPurchases,
    TotalInterest,
    TotalNewBalance: real     {Input, totals for report}
                      );
{Given the totals, this procedure writes the summary report.}
begin
    {Step 1: Write the totals}
    writeln(Report);
    writeln(Report);
    writeln(Report, 'Monthly Totals');
    writeln(Report);
    writeln(Report, 'Old Balance Owing□□□□□□□□', TotalOldBalance:10:2);
    writeln(Report, 'Payments Received□□□□□□□□', TotalPayments:10:2);
    writeln(Report, 'Purchases Made□□□□□□□□□□', TotalPurchases:10:2);
    writeln(Report, 'Interest Charged□□□□□□□□□', TotalInterest:10:2);
    writeln(Report, 'Current Balance Owing□□□□', TotalNewBalance:10:2)
end;
```

FIGURE 10-33
Procedure
SummaryReport.

be risky. If the computer system fails in the middle of the merge/update procedure, the Customer file would contain both updated and old records. Such a situation would make a billing system restart impossible.

A second change accommodates the problem of tardy accounts—a problem which realistically cannot be ignored. Instead of replacing a terminating account number by zero, we copy the information for the account into a

```
procedure SalesReport (
    var Report: text;               {Input/output, file for reports}
    DailyPurchases: DPurType     {Input, daily purchase totals}
                      );
{Given the total purchases for each day, this procedure writes the report of
    daily sales.}
var
    Day: integer;                   {Loop control variable}
begin
    {Step 1: Write report}
    writeln(Report);
    writeln(Report);
    writeln(Report, 'Daily Credit Sales For This Month');
    writeln(Report);
    for Day := 1 to 31 do
        if DailyPurchases[Day] <> 0.0
        then writeln(Report, Day:3, DailyPurchases[Day]:10:2)
end;
```

FIGURE 10-34
Procedure SalesReport.

```
procedure CopyCustomer (
    var UpdatedCustomer: CustFType;    {Input/output, updated customer file}
    var Cusutomer: CustFType           {Input/output, customer master file}
                        );
{Given the file of updated customer records and the master file of customer
    records, the master file is replaced by a file of updated records. Records
    with an account number of zero are discarded.}
begin
    {Step 1: Open files}
    reset(UpdatedCustomer);
    rewrite(Customer);

    {Step 2: Copy updated records into Customer file and do deletions}
    while not eof(UpdatedCustomer) do
        begin
            if UpdatedCustomer ↑ .ID <> 0
            then begin
                    Customer ↑ : = UpdatedCustomer ↑ ;
                    put(Customer)
                end;
            get(UpdatedCustomer)
        end
end;
```

**FIGURE 10-35**
**Procedure**
**CopyCustomer.**

file called **Terminated** which is retained from month to month. The terminating account record is removed from the **Customer** file. When purchases and payments are applied to an account that is not found in the **Customer** file, a search is made of the **Terminated** file. If applicable, the transactions are posted against this file and statements can be generated. Account closures can be completed based on the transactions applied to the **Terminated** file.

In this section we have presented a simplified view of a small customer billing system. Nevertheless, the system illustrates the use and importance of sequential files and provides a glimpse of the type of processing necessary in a large billing system. We turn our attention now to a discussion of another basic file organization.

## EXERCISES 10-4

1. Suppose that you are to create a sequential file which contains records describing potential new acquisitions for a library. A key which can be used to access information concerning a new book is the first author's surname. Are there any advantages or disadvantages to ordering the file by the first author's surname, assuming (*a*) search requests are not batched and (*b*) search requests are batched?

2. Suppose we are to create a sequential file which contains records describing in detail the descriptions of various course offerings at an educational institution. The class numbers can be used as a key for the file. Examples of class numbers are CMPT 250, MATH 222, and PHYS 111. Are there any advantages to ordering the files by the class number, assuming (a) search requests are not batched and (b) search requests are batched? You are to assume that almost all requests concerning classes contain legitimate keys (that is, a key for which a record exists). Can you propose a better type of ordering than by class number for the situation in which search requests are not batched?

★★★ 3. You are placed in charge of the design and implementation of a small payroll system. The system contains the following employee information:

> Employee number (integer)
>
> Employee salary (real)
>
> Social insurance number (integer)
>
> Tax exemption (real)
>
> Group insurance premium (real)
>
> Parking (real)
>
> Association dues (real)
>
> Name (up to 37 characters)

Changes to employee information are made by means of transactions which are applied to the system at the time paychecks are printed (that is, once a month). Three types of transactions are required, and these are

(a) Addition transaction, which must contain the information items for an employee, e.g.,

ADD 27823 14400 12694 01925 320 35 000 FRIESEN, V.J.

(b) Deletion transaction, which contains only an employee number, e.g.,

DEL 27823

(c) Update transaction, which contains the employee number plus an explicit indication of the items to be changed, e.g.,

UPD 27823 PARKING 48 TAXEMP 02400

On a month-end run, the system should print paychecks for each member of the staff, including an initial paycheck for an employee who is added and a final paycheck for an employee who is terminated. Payments consist of a two-part form, as illustrated in Fig. 10-36: the check itself and the statement of net earnings.

Income tax is calculated based on a graduated scale which may be approximated using the following formula ($TI$ is the taxable income; that is, $TI$ = regular pay − exemptions):

$$\text{Income tax} = \left( \frac{TI}{250} + 16 \right) \% \times TI$$

Therefore, the income tax paid by V. Friesen (after performing the update transaction above) is

$$\left( \frac{1200 - 200}{250} + 16 \right) \% \times (\$1200 - \$200) = \$200$$

Pension plan contributions are 8 percent of the income after taxes. Design in detail and then implement the payroll system just outlined. The design phase should include a detailed discussion of transaction record, employee payroll record, and output record formats. The stylized printing on the payment forms should be printed as well, even though in a production system it would be preprinted on special forms.

## 10-5   DIRECT FILES

To illustrate the type of file processing associated with a direct file, let us return momentarily to our small billing system example. We introduced the example as an application of sequential files in Sec. 10-4. In order to

**FIGURE 10-36   Sample output for payroll system.**

*J. B. REGIONAL BANK*
*3972 – 9th AVE.*
*MONTREAL, QUE.*

August 1    *19*    89

*PAY TO THE*
*ORDER OF* _____ V. J. Friesen _____  $ 889.34
EIGHT HUNDRED EIGHTY NINE...............................34 *DOLLARS*

| DATE | | |
|---|---|---|
| 08 | 01 | 89 |

*TOT. EXEMP*    $2400
*SALARY*         $14400

| | |
|---|---|
| REGULAR PAY | 1200.00 |
| INCOME TAX | 200.00 – |
| GROUP INSURANCE | 26.66 – |
| PENSION | 80.00 – |
| PARKING | 4.00 – |
| DUES | .00 |
| NET PAY | 889.34 |

| *SOCIAL INSURANCE NO.* | *EMP. NO.* |
|---|---|
| 708-312-694 | 59138 |

accommodate any form of on-line processing which concerns the status of an account, individual customer records must be accessed directly. It is also desirable to have the records ordered sequentially by account number. This is necessary to generate monthly customer bills based on receipts which are received in batches from points of sale.

It is relatively easy to hypothesize that in the near future our small company will want a billing system which does away with the process of filling out purchase slips at the point of sale and then sending these to the main office for computer processing. A simpler, but more expensive approach is to have a purchase or return posted against a customer account immediately, via on-line terminals operated by point-of-sale clerks. On-line terminals would be remote from a computer, yet tied directly to it via telephone lines. If purchases and returns can be handled at the point of sale, it would be unnecessary to batch all the customer receipts and sequentially process them against the account via the merge procedure described in Sec. 10-4. With the need for sequential processing eliminated, we can design a system that requires only the capability of direct access. In this section we consider a number of file structures which provide efficient direct access. This efficiency of access is gained because we remove the criterion that the file must be organized so that it can be accessed both sequentially and directly. The section is again divided into two parts—file structures and direct file processing.

## 10-5.1 THE STRUCTURE OF DIRECT FILES

In a *direct* (also called *random*) file, a transformation or mapping is made from the key of a record to the address of the storage location at which that record is to reside in the file. One mechanism used for generating this transformation is called a *hashing algorithm*. In Sec. 8-9.3 we examined hashing algorithms as they applied to the placement of records in a hash table. It was pointed out that a hashing algorithm consists of two components—a *hashing function*, which defines a mapping from the key space to the address space, and a *collision-resolution technique*, which resolves conflicts that arise when more than one record key is mapped to the same table location.

The hashing algorithms used for direct files are very similar to those used for tables, and therefore, it is necessary to have a complete understanding of Sec. 8-9.3 before reading this section. The main conceptual differences are due to the physical characteristics of external storage, which differ from the directly addressable storage characteristics assumed for tables in Chap. 8. In particular, the time to access a record in a table in main memory is on the order of microseconds, while the time to access a record in external memory is on the order of milliseconds. In addition, records in a file are stored in *buckets*, in which each bucket contains $b$ record locations, as opposed to just one location. The number of records in a bucket is called the *bucket capacity*. Basically, we can think of a bucket as a sector in a sector-addressable device or as a block in a block-addressable device. For a particular record to be isolated, the bucket in which the record resides must be located, the contents of the bucket brought into a buffer in memory, and then the desired record extracted from the buffer.

Let us define an *address space* $A$ of size $m$ such that $A = \{C + 1, C + 2, \ldots, C + m\}$, where $C$ is an integer constant. Each address references a bucket. Then $mb$ records can be accommodated by $A$, and the load factor for the direct file is $n/(mb)$, assuming a key set of size $n$ is mapped into the address space.

A key set of $S = \{X_1, X_2, \ldots, X_n\}$ is a subset of a set $K$ of possible keys which is called the *key space*. If the size of $K$ is equal to the number of record locations in $A$ and the keys are consecutive, then a transformation can be defined which assigns to each bucket of $A$ exactly $b$ keys from $K$. This type of one-to-one transformation is termed *direct addressing* and is an array-reference form of addressing.

In most situations, however, $S$ is a small subset of $K$, and direct addressing results in very low utilization of direct-access storage. Instead, *indirect addressing* is implemented. That is, $S$ is mapped into $A$ with the distinct possibility that enough records will be assigned to the same bucket so that a bucket *overflow* takes place. When this happens, a bucket-overflow–handling technique must be used to store any overflow records. We will discover later in this subsection that the techniques for handling bucket overflow are very similar to those for collision resolution in a table.

Having reviewed some of the concepts related to hashing algorithms, let us examine in more detail the possible organizations for a direct file. We begin by reexamining the hashing functions which can be used for address translation. A more in-depth investigation of the overflow-handling techniques is then considered.

Past hashing investigations indicated that the division method, using a prime divisor or a divisor that is relatively prime with the size of address space, yielded the best performance on average. This is not to say that, for certain key sets with certain load factors and bucket capacities, one of the other methods discussed in Sec. 8-9.3 cannot outperform the division method. For this section, we will, however, adopt the division method as the standard hashing function because it is simple to use and yields reasonable performance.

The second aspect of a hashing algorithm is the collision-resolution technique. In a direct file, the smallest addressable unit is the bucket, which may contain many records that have been mapped to the same address. Hence, in a direct file with a given bucket capacity, a certain number of collisions are expected. When there are more colliding records for a given bucket than the bucket capacity, however, then some method must be found for handling these overflow records. The term "overflow-handling technique" is used in place of collision-resolution technique, which is commonly adopted for hash-table methods.

In Sec. 8-9.3, two classes of collision-resolution techniques were given—open addressing and chaining. The same general classification can be applied to overflow-handling techniques. When we use a bucket with a capacity greater than 1, we are in fact imposing a restricted linear-probe form of open addressing. When a record is added to a bucket which is not full, the new record is added at the next open location. Of course, the next open record location is in the bucket and is already reserved for records which are mapped to that bucket address.

In the discussion to follow, we refer to the bucket referenced by the address calculation of a record as the *primary bucket* for that record. If a record is not present in the primary bucket, it is located in an *overflow bucket,* or it is not in the file.

Since the complete contents of a bucket are brought into main memory with one request, it is extremely beneficial if the desired record is located somewhere in the primary bucket. If the record is not in the primary bucket, a request must be made to bring in an overflow bucket, as determined by the overflow-handling method.

If a linear-probe open-address overflow-handling method is used, then a successive search is made of the records in the remaining buckets in the file. The search is terminated successfully when the record is located. It is terminated unsuccessfully, however, if an empty (dummy) record is encountered or if the search returns to the original bucket tested.

Neither a random-probe form of open addressing nor double hashing is a good overflow method to use for direct files. In both methods the sequences of overflow buckets which are examined do not exhibit the property of physical adjacency. That is, two buckets which are adjacent in the overflow sequence are not necessarily physically adjacent. Physical adjacency can be important, since records which are not physically adjacent have a higher probability of requiring a seek in a movable-head storage device. The extra seek time may be prohibitive.

Overflow records can be chained from the primary area to a separate overflow area. An overflow record should reside in an overflow bucket which is in the same seek area (e.g., the same cylinder) as the primary area for the overflow record. A particularly good strategy is to reserve the last few buckets of a seek area strictly for overflow records from the primary buckets in that area. However, it may be difficult to adopt such a configuration strategy, since the overflow buckets would break up the linear-addressing scheme required for direct addressing (that is, groups of prime-area buckets and overflow buckets will be interspersed throughout the file space). Therefore, an independent overflow area which is totally separate from the prime area may be required.

So far we have centered the discussion of file structures for direct files on hashing (or address-translation) techniques. There are other ways of organizing a direct file which are less popular but nevertheless may be applicable in some situations.

If the number of records in the file is relatively small and the record size is relatively large (that is, only a few records per bucket is achievable), then it may be worthwhile to consider a direct-addressing scheme. Several methods for achieving direct-address translation involve the use of cross referencing or indexing. A *cross-reference table* is simply a table of keys and addresses in which a unique external storage address is assigned to each key. Figure 10-37 illustrates a cross-reference table of surnames and external storage addresses for a sector-addressable device. Locating a record given its key is simply a matter of retrieving the external address associated with the key and then issuing an I/O command that directly retrieves the desired record. In most programming languages, however, the programmer must maintain the cross-reference table. The table can be kept as an unordered list and, therefore, can accommodate additions with ease. A linear search is then required to find an address. Alternatively, the table can be implemented as a list ordered by the key set, and a binary search can be employed to locate an address more rapidly. Record additions and deletions, however, present problems because the table must be maintained in order.

Indexing methods involving binary trees, $m$-ary trees, and trie structures also can be chosen to achieve direct addressing in direct files. With tree-structured methods (which were discussed in Secs. 9-2 and 9-4), record additions and deletions can be handled more effectively. A binary-tree indexing scheme for the cross-reference table given in Fig. 10-37 is shown, in part, in Fig. 10-38.

In the discussion throughout this subsection we have assumed that if a desired record is not located in its primary bucket, then a series of I/O commands is issued. Each command brings in an overflow bucket which is scanned in search of the required record. The search strategy just outlined is true for external memory units which are sector-addressable. Some record-addressable devices, such as the IBM 3380, however, are capable of locating, via hardware, a particular record on a given track based on the key of the record.

Let us now turn our attention to the type of processing that is associated with direct files.

## 10-5.2 PROCESSING DIRECT FILES

The processing of a direct file depends on how the key set for the records is transformed into external device addresses. In the previous subsection we

| Surname | External address (cyl., trk., sector) |
|---------|---------------------------------------|
| Ashcroft | 1,07,04 |
| Barnsley | 1,07,05 |
| Bernard | 1,08,15 |
| Duke | 1,06,09 |
| Edder | 1,07,00 |
| Groff | 1,06,10 |
| Katz | 1,06,12 |
| Murray | 1,08,13 |
| Paulsen | 1,06,00 |
| Smith | 1,06,03 |
| Thomas | 1,06,04 |
| Tollard | 1,06,11 |
| Yu | 1,07,01 |

**FIGURE 10-37**
**Cross-reference**
**table.**

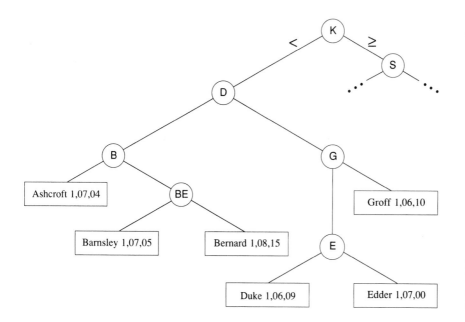

**FIGURE 10-38**
**Binary tree**
**cross-reference**
**indexing scheme.**

reviewed a number of transformation methods. It is impractical to discuss direct-file processing for each method; therefore, we have chosen to present, as a representative example, the direct processing of a file which is accessed via a hashing algorithm using chaining with separate lists for overflow handling. Programs involving the processing of this form of organization are presented in this subsection.

First, we must consider the Pascal facilities for direct access of files. Standard Pascal does not define direct-access facilities, and thus they are not available in some versions of Pascal. However, many compilers provide direct access of files as an extension to the language. Since these facilities are not part of the standard language, they differ from one compiler to the next. However, the Turbo Pascal facilities are typical of many available compilers, and we consider these next.

Direct access to Pascal files is based on the idea that a file is a sequence of elements. A built-in function **seek**, with arguments of file and element number, positions a file so that the specified element is the next one to be read or written. The first element of a file is numbered 0. This file element number is often called the *relative record number*, because it is the displacement (in records) from the beginning of the file.

Assume we are given the following definitions and declarations:

```
type
    EmployeeRecord =
        record
            Name:
                record
                    Surname: packed array [1 .. 30] of char;
                    Initials: packed array [1 .. 2] of char
```

```
        end;
    EmployeeNumber: integer;
    WagePerHr: real;
    Classification: packed array [1 .. 10] of char
  end;
var
  Master: file of EmployeeRecord;
  Employee: EmployeeRecord;
```

After opening the file for input using reset, that is,

reset(Master);

we can access record number N by

seek(Master, N);
Read(Master, Employee);

Notice that Pascal handles the mapping of the relative record number into an actual device address for accessing the file. This can be done because Pascal files are sequences of fixed-length items, so that the calculation of the device address is straightforward given the starting address of the file and the size of the items. However, direct access is not available for text files, which map variable-length lines into records within the operating system's file system.

Turbo Pascal does not implement the "file buffer" concept of standard Pascal. In several Pascal compilers that do implement the "file buffer," the seek procedure sets the next record returned by get. Because the read procedure returns the current buffer and then does a get, a seek will control the record returned by the second, not the first, read following the call to seek. The reader is warned to read carefully the manual for a particular compiler before using a nonstandard feature such as direct-access files.

We can treat Pascal direct-access files as having a bucket size of 1. The hashing function thus maps the key into a relative record number. Such a method may not give satisfactory performance if each access to a record involves an actual physical access to the disk. Often the operating system will block the records into physical blocks and read the entire block which contains the desired record. This block is then kept in memory, and should the next seek be to a record within the same block, that record can be supplied to the program without a physical input operation. Thus a judicious choice of record size, and block size if the system allows it to be controlled by the user, can result in improved performance. The block becomes a bucket holding a number of records. If the record size is 52 bytes and the block size is 260 bytes, then each block holds exactly 5 records. Records numbered 0 through 4 are in the first block, 5 through 9 in the second, and so forth. Obviously, the details vary considerably among different systems, so the reader will need to investigate the details of his or her particular system.

Output files operate similarly. A call to the seek procedure specifies the record number of the next record to be written. In some systems, the entire file is automatically filled with records marked empty by some system-dependent convention the first time it is opened. In Turbo Pascal, the user must specifically fill the file sequentially before using direct access. The user is responsible for defining the method by which a record is marked empty.

We will require the facility to open a file for *update* later in this section. This means that the file is opened for both reading and writing simultaneously. Thus a record can be read and its contents modified. A write statement then returns the updated record to the file. Standard Pascal does not define update access for files. Several versions of Pascal provide it as an extension. Typically, the file is opened by a built-in procedure, often called **update**, which is similar in operation to reset and rewrite statements, except that the file is opened for update. For our example we will use the Turbo Pascal facilities. A file opened by a reset statement must be an existing file, but once opened, it can be both read and written. *Warning*: Opening a file with rewrite creates a new file or empties an existing file, so it cannot be used to open an existing file which is to be updated. Thus we open a file called **Master** for update by

```
reset (Master);
```

When opened, the file position is set to read or write the first record. However, this position can be altered by the seek procedure just described. Both read and write operations advance the file position by one record, so it is necessary to reset the position in order to write back to the same position. Thus a particular record, say, record number **N**, can be modified by

```
seek (Master, N);
read (Master, Employee);
```

$\left. \cdot \right\}$ update information in **Employee** record

```
seek (Master, N);
write (Master, Employee);
```

We now consider how to make use of these facilities to implement an application involving direct files. Direct files are primarily processed directly. That is, a key is mapped to an address, and depending on the nature of the file transaction, a record is created, deleted, updated, or accessed at that address or possibly at some subsequent address if a collision takes place. Of course, the subsequent address is determined by the overflow-handling technique which is adopted.

We will assume that the information part of each record consists of a key and data. For simplicity, we here assume that the data part is a fixed-length character string and that the key is an integer. A fixed number of records will be grouped into a bucket. The choice of number of records which form a bucket depends on the record size and the detailed characteristics of the disk and operating system. For example, the bucket size could be chosen so that a bucket represents exactly one block on the disk and could be accessed in one physical input operation by the operating system.

When overflow handling is accommodated using chaining with separate lists, a pointer to a linked list of overflow records is included in each bucket. A representation of an overflow record in the separate list area is shown in Fig. 10-39. Each overflow location in the overflow area consists of two major parts—DRec, containing an overflow record, and Link, a pointer containing the record number of the next location in a chain. A key value of −1 represents an "empty" record. Key is the key of the record contained in DRec. Data is the data portion of the record.

A restriction imposed by Pascal is that a file must consist of a sequence of elements of the same type. Thus every record in a Pascal file is of the same record type. We will therefore use the same record format for the records in the bucket as for the overflow records described previously. The link to the overflow records will be contained in the Link field of the last record in the bucket; the Link fields of the remaining records in the bucket are unused. A value of −1 in a Link field indicates the "null" link.

In an attempt to conserve file space, one might be tempted to use Pascal's variant records to define the primary and overflow records to be of a different structure. However, most Pascal compilers will allocate file space to contain records of the size of the largest record. When a shorter variant is written to a record in the file, the extra space will be unused.

We will further presume that the file is not just a temporary file to be kept only for the duration of the execution of a single program. Rather, the file is saved and is available for access by a later execution of the same or another program. We will presume that the record size, the number of records per bucket, and the number of buckets in the primary area of the file are fixed and can be built into the programs themselves. However, the record number of the next available overflow record will vary with time and must be supplied to a program each time the program starts. Obviously, the best place to store that number is in the file itself. Therefore, we have created a special record which is placed after the primary area (buckets) of the file before the first overflow record. The Link field of this special record is maintained by the program as the record number of the next available overflow area; the remaining fields of this record are unused. Figure 10-40 contains the definitions and declarations required for an application which uses this file structure.

The procedure in Fig. 10-41 inserts a record into a direct file which is organized according to the specifications given earlier. In step 1, the key is hashed and the control flag is initialized. Step 2 obtains the overflow chain for the specified bucket; if it is not null, the bucket has previously overflowed and searching the bucket for an empty record should not be

**FIGURE 10-39**
**Representation of an overflow record.**

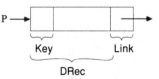

```
const
   BucketSize = 5;
   NoOfBuckets = 20;
   ControlRec = 100;      {Must be BucketSize * NoOfBuckets}
   Null = - 1;            {Null link for chains of overflow records}
   Empty = - 1;           {Key value indicating an empty record}
type
   KeyType = integer;
   DataType = packed array [1..40] of char;
   DRecType =
      record
         Key: KeyType;
         Data: DataType
      end;
   RecType =
      record
         DRec: DRecType;
         Link: integer
      end;
var
   DFile: file of RecType;
```

**FIGURE 10-40**
**Sample declarations**
**for a direct file**
**in Turbo Pascal.**

performed. Otherwise, if the overflow link is still null, there may or may not be an empty record and the bucket must be searched. In step 3, the record is placed in the bucket it is hashed to if a record location is available. Notice that it is presumed that a unique value of the key may be used to designate an empty record; here we use a key value of $-1$. If step 2 determined that an overflow chain already existed or step 3 failed to find an empty record, then step 4 determines that the information must be placed in an overflow record. Step 5 obtains the next overflow record address from the control record and updates the control record. Step 6 writes the required information, including the link to the first record on the already existing overflow chain, to the overflow record. Finally, step 7 updates the overflow pointer in the bucket to point to the new record, which is now at the front of the overflow chain.

It should be noted that a check is not made to see if the key of the record being added matches the key of a record presently in the file. This checking should be done to prevent duplicate or inconsistent data. The necessary extensions to procedure DirectInsert to effect this checking are left as an exercise.

A procedure for retrieving a record from a direct file using chaining with separate lists appears in Fig. 10-42. Step 1 hashes the key to obtain the bucket number. In step 2 the required record is assigned to DRec if it is found in the bucket. If the bucket is not full and the record is not located, then the search ends unsuccessfully. Otherwise, in step 3 each successive node of the overflow chain is examined until the record is found or the end of the linked list is encountered.

**procedure** DirectInsert(R: DRecType      {Input, record to be inserted} );
{Given a data record R containing key Key, it is required to insert R into a
   direct file with NoOfBuckets primary buckets, each containing BucketSize
   records, and with overflow records following the buckets; the overflow
   records are chained to their buckets as described in the text.}
**var**
   BucketNo: integer;      {Bucket number}
   RecNo: integer;      {Record number}
   Temp: RecType;      {Temporary for examining records}
   NotDone: Boolean;      {Control flag}
   OfPtr: integer;      {Head of overflow list}
   OfNo: integer;      {Next available overflow record}
**begin**
   {Step 1: Apply hashing function and initialize flag}
   BucketNo : = Hash(R.Key);
   NotDone : = true;

   {Step 2: Check the overflow pointer for desired bucket}
   RecNo : = BucketNo * BucketSize + BucketSize − 1;
   seek(DFile, RecNo);
   read(DFile, Temp);
   OfPtr : = Temp.Link;
   if OfPtr = Null
   **then begin**

         {Step 3: No overflow records, so search for free slot in bucket}
         RecNo : = BucketNo * BucketSize;
         **while** (RecNo < (BucketNo + 1) * BucketSize) **and** NotDone **do**
            **begin**
               seek(DFile, RecNo);
               read(DFile, Temp);
               **if** Temp.DRec.Key = Empty
               **then begin**
                     Temp.DRec : = R;
                     Temp.Link : = Null;
                     seek(DFile, RecNo);
                     write(DFile, Temp);
                     NotDone : = false
                  end;
               RecNo : = RecNo + 1
            **end**
   end;

**FIGURE 10-41**
Procedure DirectInsert
for inserting a record
in a direct file.

Because these procedures search linked lists on a disk rather than in the
main memory of the system, overflow nodes should be located in a common
seek area and, ideally, in the same area as their associated primary buckets.
This is done so that extra seeks are not required to scan a linked list of

{Step 4: If a free record was not found, put record into overflow area}
**if** NotDone
**then begin**

> {Step 5: Obtain next overflow record location from control record
>    and update the control record}
> seek(DFile, ControlRec);
> read(DFile, Temp);
> OfNo : = Temp.Link;
> Temp.Link : = OfNo + 1;
> seek(DFile, ControlRec);
> write(DFile, Temp);
>
> {Step 6: Write new record into overflow location}
> Temp.DRec : = R;
> Temp.Link : = OfPtr;
> seek(DFile, OfNo);
> write(DFile, Temp);
>
> {Step 7: Update the bucket overflow pointer}
> RecNo : = BucketNo * BucketSize + BucketSize − 1;
> seek(DFile, RecNo);
> read(DFile, Temp);
> Temp.Link : = OfNo;
> seek(DFile, RecNo);
> write(DFile, Temp)

> **end**
**end**;

**FIGURE 10-41** (*cont.*)

overflow records. However, such a file structure is very system-dependent, so we will not illustrate an actual design satisfying these criteria.

Thus far, the only type of processing we have considered for direct files is direct processing. In some instances it may be necessary to perform an identical transaction on all, or nearly all, records in the file. For example, in the small billing system, which we have often used to illustrate the material on file organization, it may be desirable to print monthly bills even though individual customer accounts can be accessed directly in an on-line mode. The generation of monthly bills can be accomplished by accessing the records in a physically sequential or serial manner.

Serial access of a direct file is not necessarily sequential access. That is, $x_1 \leq x_2$ for keys $x_1$ and $x_2$ does not imply $H(x_1) \leq H(x_2)$ for some hashing functions $H$. The fact is that we relinquished this ability of sequential access in favor of a quicker direct access.

For most direct organizations, serial access presents no problems. Access commences at the physical beginning and terminates at the physical end of the file. If the file uses a separate overflow area independent of the prime area, however, it may be difficult to access this area in a serial

```
procedure DirectRetrieve(
    Key: KeyType;              {Input, key of desired record}
    var DRec: DRecType;        {Output, record}
    var Found: Boolean         {Output, true means record was found}
                               );
{Given a key Key, it is required to retrieve the record identified by that key
    from the direct file structured as described in the text.}
var
    BucketNo: integer;         {The bucket to be searched}
    RecNo: integer;            {The record to be tested}
    Temp: RecType;             {Temporary for reading records}
    NotDone: Boolean;          {Loop control flag}
begin
    {Step 1: Apply hashing function}
    BucketNo := Hash(Key);

    {Step 2: Search the bucket indicated}
    RecNo := BucketNo * BucketSize;
    NotDone := true;
    Found := false;
    while (RecNo < BucketNo * BucketSize + BucketSize) and NotDone do
        begin
            seek(DFile, RecNo);
            read(DFile, Temp);
            if Temp.DRec.Key = Key
            then begin
                    DRec := Temp.DRec;
                    NotDone := false;
                    Found := true
                end
            else
                if Temp.DRec.Key = Empty
                then begin
                        NotDone := false;
                        Found := false
                    end
                else RecNo := RecNo + 1
        end;
```

**FIGURE 10-42**
Procedure DirectRetrieve
for retrieving a record
from a direct file.

fashion. Difficulties arise because the overflow area may be unblocked or blocked in a different manner than the prime area. A logically consistent, yet potentially time-consuming method of serial access of a separate overflow area is to read all the records in the first prime-area bucket, followed by all the overflow records for this bucket, and then return to read the next prime-area bucket, followed by its overflow records, etc., until all records in the file have been accessed.

{Step 3: If not done, that is, the key was not found and an empty
record was not found, then search the overflow chain. The start of the
chain is in the link of the last record in the bucket.}

```
RecNo : = Temp.Link;
while (RecNo <> Null) and NotDone do
  begin
    seek(DFile, RecNo);
    read(DFile, Temp);
    if Temp.DRec.Key = Key
    then begin
            DRec : = Temp.DRec;
            NotDone : = false;
            Found : = true
        end
    else RecNo : = Temp.Link
  end
end;
```

FIGURE 10-42 (*cont.*)

A final aspect of direct file processing which we should consider is file
maintenance. Many systems which support direct files simply mark deleted
records and recover the space occupied by these records only when a new
record can be added to the file at the marked location. The space occupied
by a deleted record may require needless examination in search of a record
in the prime bucket. In addition, deleted records affect performance when
probing or chaining through a file in search of an overflow record. It is
sometimes possible to remove deleted records logically, especially where
chaining is involved; however, this is rarely done. Instead, it is the programmer's responsibility to monitor the activity of the file and to reorganize it whenever performance degrades significantly. Reorganization can be
accomplished by reading the file serially and creating a new direct file that
involves only the active records of the old file.

We complete this subsection by summarizing the important properties
related to direct files:

1. Direct access to records in a direct file is rapid, especially for files with
low load factors and few overflow records.

2. Because a certain portion of the file remains unused in order to prevent an
excessive number of overflow records, the space utilization for a direct
file is poor when compared to a sequential file.

3. The performance attained using a direct file is very dependent on the
key-to-address transformation algorithm adopted. The transformation that
is used is application-dependent and is generally implemented and maintained through users' programs.

4. Records can be accessed serially but not sequentially, unless a separate
ordered list of keys is maintained.

# EXERCISES 10-5

1. In what ways does the bucket capacity affect the performance of an information system in which direct files are used?

2. In the context of direct files, list the advantages and disadvantages of chained overflow with separate lists when compared to an open-addressing technique.

★★ 3. Formulate a program for reading sequentially the records of a direct file in which chaining with separate lists is used as the overflow technique.

4. List the advantages and disadvantages of having a direct file on a record-addressable device (such as the IBM 3330) over having the file reside on a sector-addressable device.

★★ 5. Modify the procedures **DirectInsert** and **DirectRetrieve** so that each Pascal read and write statement writes an array of $m$ records (more closely simulating the concept of a bucket). How should the overflow area be handled? Investigate the performance of the two methods.

## CHAPTER SUMMARY

This chapter deals with a number of matters relating to files: devices for storing them, basic file organizations, and operations with these organizations. We look first at characteristics of common external devices—tapes, disks, and drums. Following the introduction of some fundamental terms and concepts,.we consider more carefully the structure of records in files. Finally, we turn to file organizations and deal at length with sequential files and direct files. We discuss their structure and their processing. An application involving a billing system is developed.

## KEY TERMS

access time
address space
blocking factor
blocks
bucket capacity
buckets
buffer
capstan
card/strip device
charge-coupled device
collision-resolution technique
cross-reference table
cylinder (seek area)

cylinder overflow area
data compression
database
deblocking
direct addressing
direct file (random file)
diskette
domain
eof function
eoln function
external storage device
field
file

file type denoter
fixed item
flow time
get procedure
hashing algorithm
hashing function
independent overflow area
index area
index item
indirect addressing
interblock gaps
interrecord gap
item (field)
key
key space
latency (rotational delay)
latency time
logically-encoded item
magnetic card/strip device
magnetic disk
magnetic drum
magnetic tape
magnetic tape drive
multiple buffering
overflow
overflow bucket
overflow entry
overflow handling technique
physical field
physical record
precoordinated domain
primary bucket
prime area

put procedure
random-access device
read procedure
read/write heads
reading
record
record organization
repeating item
reset procedure
rewrite procedure
sectors
seek
seek area
seek time
sequence item
sequential access
sequential device
sequential file
sequential processing
serial processing
single buffering
tagged item
text file
textual item
tracks
transaction
transaction record
transmission time
variable-length record
write procedure
writeln procedure
writing

# APPENDIX A

## NUMERIC COMPUTATIONS

One of the earliest and most important applications of computers was to the solution of numeric problems. Vast sums of money are spent each day in the solution of such problems. The study of these problems and techniques for their solution is an important field in both applied mathematics and computer science.

In this appendix we provide a brief introduction to the field. We begin by considering the important question of error in numeric calculations—what causes it, and how to deal with it. We then turn to consider techniques for the solution of a number of important problems in the field of numerical mathematics.

## A-1  ERROR

The organization of conventional computer memories imposes certain constraints on the representation of numbers. Fixed word lengths dictate not only the maximum value that these numbers can take, but also the accuracy of the representation. Because the number of decimal places that can be carried is finite, it is not possible to obtain an exact representation of many real numbers. The representation of the number $\frac{1}{3}$, for example, must be terminated after a certain number of decimal digits. In this way, an inaccuracy, or *error*, is introduced.

Any calculation involving real numbers on a computer is subject to several types of errors. Although error is always present, the case is not hopeless. Even though the error cannot be eliminated, it is possible to have it contained. There exists an extensive body of research directed toward the problem of error containment in numeric calculations, with and without the use of a computer. In this section three causes of errors are discussed. We also consider how errors are accumulated by some basic arithmetic operations. Some suggestions for minimizing the error in a calculation are presented.

## A-1.1  THE TYPES OF ERRORS

Three types of errors are common in numerical calculations. These are inherent error, truncation error, and roundoff error. Many numerical values obtained experimentally necessarily contain *inherent errors* because of the uncertainty of measurements. Generally, it is advisable to state explicitly the error limits of any experimental result. For example, a measurement of $25.4 \pm 0.05$ degrees Celsius indicates that the temperature is not less than $25.35°C$ and not more than $25.45°C$. Inherent error is also present in finite decimal approximations of such numbers as $\pi$, $e$, $\sqrt{2}$, and $\frac{1}{3}$ because they have no exact finite decimal representations. Some numbers, in fact, have a finite representation in one number system but not in another. For example, 1/10 has a finite decimal representation but not a finite binary representation, and therefore a binary computer will not give exactly 1.0 as the answer to $0.1 + 0.1 + 0.1 + 0.1 + 0.1 + 0.1 + 0.1 + 0.1 + 0.1 + 0.1$.

*Truncation errors* occur when

***1.*** An infinite mathematical process is approximated by a finite process, or

***2.*** A finite process is approximated by a smaller number of iterations

An example of type 1 is the calculation of $\sin x$ using the infinite Taylor series approximation:

$$\sin x = x - \frac{x^3}{3!} + \frac{x^5}{5!} - \frac{x^7}{7!} + \frac{x^9}{9!} - \cdots + \cdots$$

In any practical calculation, the formula must be truncated after a finite number of terms. Thus the calculated value will be inexact.

As an example of type 2, consider the summation of a large number of terms, most of which are very small. For example,

$$\sum_{n=1}^{1,000,000} \frac{1}{n!} = 1 + \frac{1}{2} + \frac{1}{6} + \frac{1}{24} + \frac{1}{120} + \frac{1}{720} + \cdots + \frac{1}{1,000,000!}$$

The terms decrease very rapidly, and such a summation would soon have to be truncated. The error that occurs when digits are dropped from a number without rounding is also called a truncation error. For example, 9.2344778 might be truncated to 9.2344, introducing an error.

*Roundoff errors* are those errors which result from rounding a number. A decimal number is rounded to $n$ decimal places by adding 5 to the

$(n + 1)$st digit to the right of the decimal point and then dropping all digits to the right of the $n$th digit. Again, since the word size of a computer is finite, roundoff errors occur frequently in computer calculations. Rounding 3.14159 to three decimal places, we get 3.142. The resulting error is $(3.14200 - 3.14159)$, which is 0.00041. When a number is rounded to $n$ places after the decimal point, the error will always be less than or equal to $5 \times 10^{-n-1}$.

Roundoff errors can also result from the shifting of values prior to a computation. Suppose, for example, that we wish to add two real numbers that differ by an order of magnitude or more, say, 999.0 and 1.12954. If we assume floating-point representation to seven decimal places, these are stored as $0.9990000 \times 10^3$ and $0.1129540 \times 10^1$. Before the calculation is actually performed, the fractional part of the smaller number will be shifted to make its exponent the same as that of the larger number. Thus $0.1129540 \times 10^1$ is changed to $0.0011295 \times 10^3$. As a result, some accuracy is lost.

## A-1.2  THE EXPRESSION AND PROPAGATION OF ERROR

An error may be expressed in absolute, relative, or percentage terms. The *absolute error* is simply the difference between the exact value of a number and the approximation. The *relative error* is the absolute error divided by the exact value. The *percentage error* is the relative error multiplied by 100 percent. Let $\bar{x}$ be an approximation of the exact value $x$. The absolute error of $\bar{x}$ is $x - \bar{x}$, the relative error of $\bar{x}$ is

$$\frac{x - \bar{x}}{x}$$

and the percentage error of $\bar{x}$ is

$$\frac{x - \bar{x}}{x} \times 100 \text{ percent}$$

Since the value $x$ is not known, it is often convenient to define the relative error to be

$$\frac{x - \bar{x}}{\bar{x}}$$

and the percentage error to be

$$\frac{x - \bar{x}}{\bar{x}} \times 100 \text{ percent}$$

When arithmetic operations are performed on two approximate numbers, the result is, of course, also an approximation; in fact, a larger error may result. In this manner, errors are said to *accumulate* or *propagate*. If the error bounds of the operands are known, however, then the error of the result can be estimated. Let $x = \bar{x} + e_x$ and $y = \bar{y} + e_y$ where $\bar{x}$ is an approximation of $x$, $\bar{y}$ is an approximation of $y$, and $e_x$ and $e_y$ are the absolute errors of $\bar{x}$ and $\bar{y}$, respectively. Consider the basic arithmetic operations: addition, subtraction, multiplication, and division.

*Addition:* For the sum of $x$ and $y$, we have

$$x + y = (\bar{x} + e_x) + (\bar{y} + e_y) = (\bar{x} + \bar{y}) + (e_x + e_y)$$

The absolute error of the sum is

$$e_{x+y} = e_x + e_y$$

and the relative error is

$$r_{x+y} = \frac{e_{x+y}}{\bar{x} + \bar{y}} = \frac{e_x + e_y}{\bar{x} + \bar{y}}$$

Notice that the relative error of the sum is intermediate between the relative errors of the two operands.

*Subtraction:* The difference between $x$ and $y$ is

$$x - y = (\bar{x} + e_x) - (\bar{y} + e_y) = (\bar{x} - \bar{y}) + (e_x - e_y)$$

Therefore,

$$e_{x-y} = e_x - e_y$$

and

$$r_{x-y} = \frac{e_{x-y}}{\bar{x} - \bar{y}} = \frac{e_x - e_y}{\bar{x} - \bar{y}}$$

Notice that when $x$ and $y$ are nearly equal, the denominator is small, and thus the relative error may become very large.

*Multiplication:* For the multiplication of $x$ and $y$,

$$xy = (\bar{x} + e_x)(\bar{y} + e_y) = \bar{x}\bar{y} + \bar{x}e_y + \bar{y}e_x + e_x e_y$$

Assuming that $e_x$ and $e_y$ are much smaller than $\bar{x}$ and $\bar{y}$, we expect the terms involving $\bar{x}$ and $\bar{y}$ to dominate. That is, we expect the term $e_x e_y$ to contribute very little to the magnitude of $e_{xy}$. Thus, the absolute error of the product is

$$e_{xy} \doteq \bar{x}e_y + \bar{y}e_x$$

where the symbol $\doteq$ is read "is approximately equal to." The relative error of the product is

$$r_{xy} = \frac{e_{xy}}{\bar{x}\bar{y}} \doteq \frac{\bar{x}e_y + \bar{y}e_x}{\bar{x}\bar{y}} = \frac{e_x}{\bar{x}} + \frac{e_y}{\bar{y}}$$

and is approximately equal to the sum of the relative errors of the operands.
*Division:* For the division of $x$ and $y$,

$$\frac{x}{y} = \frac{\bar{x} + e_x}{\bar{y} + e_y}$$

Rationalizing the denominator, we have

$$\frac{x}{y} = \frac{\bar{x}\bar{y} + \bar{y}e_x - \bar{x}e_y - e_x e_y}{\bar{y}^2 - e_y^2}$$

Again, since we expect $e_x$ and $e_y$ to be small, we can neglect the terms involving powers or products of $e_x$ and $e_y$:

$$\frac{x}{y} \doteq \frac{\bar{x}\bar{y} + \bar{y}e_x - \bar{x}e_y}{\bar{y}^2}$$

Rearranging, the quotient becomes

$$\frac{x}{y} \doteq \frac{\bar{x}}{\bar{y}} + \frac{\bar{x}}{\bar{y}}\left[\frac{e_x}{\bar{x}} - \frac{e_y}{\bar{y}}\right]$$

The absolute error of the quotient is therefore

$$e_{x/y} \doteq \frac{\bar{x}}{\bar{y}}\left[\frac{e_x}{\bar{x}} - \frac{e_y}{\bar{y}}\right]$$

The relative error of the quotient is

$$r_{x/y} = \frac{e_{x/y}}{\bar{x}/\bar{y}} \doteq \frac{e_x}{\bar{x}} - \frac{e_y}{\bar{y}}$$

and is approximately equal to the difference between the relative errors of the numerator and denominator.

Note that the sign of an error may be either positive or negative. Consequently, the previous discussion in no way implies that the errors incurred by addition and multiplication are greater than those of subtraction and division.

The various types of errors discussed combine in any numerical calculation. To illustrate, let us consider once again the Taylor series approximation for sin $x$:

$$\sin x = x - \frac{x^3}{3!} + \frac{x^5}{5!} - \frac{x^7}{7!} + \frac{x^9}{9!} - \cdots + \cdots$$

which we can also write as

$$\sin x = \sum_{n=1}^{\infty} (-1)^{n-1} \frac{x^{2n-1}}{(2n-1)!}$$

Clearly, the accuracy of this approximation increases as more terms are included or, equivalently, as the value of $n$ increases.

As the value of $n$ increases, however, the additional terms become increasingly small. Before long, roundoff error becomes significant, since it becomes increasingly difficult to represent the values accurately in the word size given. Thus the magnitude of the roundoff error grows as $n$ increases.

Clearly, the total error in this calculation is the sum of the truncation error and the roundoff error. Figure A-1 shows the behavior of these various types of errors with varying $n$. The point denoted by $\hat{n}$ represents the value of $n$ for which the total error is minimized. For values of $n$ less than $\hat{n}$, truncation error dominates; for values of $n$ greater than $\hat{n}$, roundoff error dominates.

## A-1.3  THE ITERATIVE METHOD

The total error curve in Fig. A-1 shows that it is a futile exercise to try to compute numerical results that are 100 percent accurate. Error can never be eliminated totally. This is not to say, however, that the situation is hopeless. In most cases, through the application of some carefully considered techniques, it is possible to contain the error within acceptable limits. Thus, while it may not be possible to get an "exact" result, it is usually possible to obtain a result that is close enough for the purposes required. The definition of "close enough" depends on the particular circumstances of each

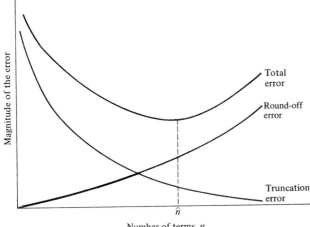

Number of terms, $n$

**FIGURE A-1**

calculation. The accuracy of the values being used (which may depend, for example, on the accuracy of measuring instruments) is certainly a factor. It is unreasonable to expect results that are more accurate than the values used to obtain them.

The study of numerical calculations centers primarily on methods that may be described as *iterative methods*. The method begins with an initial approximation to the solution of the problem. We can denote this by $S_0$. From this solution, a more accurate solution, say, $S_1$, is derived. This iterative process can continue through any number of subsequent solutions, that is, $S_2$, $S_3$, $S_4$, $\cdots$ . However, as shown in Fig. A-1, the accuracy can only improve up to a certain point, after which it gets worse. The person desiring a solution must therefore specify what he or she considers to be an acceptable error. This can be expressed in any of the forms described previously. Let us assume, for the sake of simplicity, that an absolute error has been deemed acceptable. Our iterative process is then terminated when two successive solutions agree within this error tolerance, that is, when

$$|S_i - S_{i-1}| < \epsilon$$

At this point, our technique is said to have *converged* to the result $S_i$. This criterion is satisfactory for many functions, but when the value is very small, the condition may be satisfied even when our answer, $S_i$, is 100 percent in error. A more reliable indication is the relative error criterion,

$$\left| \frac{S_i - S_{i-1}}{S_i} \right| < \epsilon$$

The study of convergence is also important in numerical computations. There may be several reasons why a particular solution technique fails to converge. For example, the specified tolerance may be set too small, or the solution technique itself may be inappropriate to the particular circumstances of the problem posed. It is often good programming practice to impose an additional stopping criterion: to terminate if convergence is not achieved after a given number of iterations.

In this section we have discussed the problem of error in numerical calculations. Although it cannot be eliminated, it can be kept under control, and acceptable answers can be obtained. Also, the iterative method of solution was introduced.

Numerical solution techniques are employed for a number of reasons. It may be, for example, that a solution cannot be obtained by other means, such as analytical techniques. For some categories of problems, analytical solution techniques simply do not exist. An example of such a problem is finding the roots of a polynomial, say, to the tenth degree. In other cases, even though analytical techniques do exist, the solution may be very difficult to derive. For example, the analytical solution of a system of 50 equations in 50 unknowns would be most tedious indeed. Numerical techniques often provide a straightforward method for computing satisfactory solutions. The use of the computer simplifies the process considerably.

In the remaining sections of this appendix we survey a number of important numerical problems and present several techniques for their solution within the framework just described. These problems have been chosen to illustrate both the type of problem that is relevant and the type of solution technique employed.

## EXERCISES A-1

1. Using the Taylor series formula for $\sin x$ given in this section, compute by hand the value of sin 1, stopping first after 3 terms, then after 5 terms and then after 10 terms. Assume six decimal digits of accuracy. Comment on the type and magnitude of the error occurring in each case. Observe that $x$ is in radians. (The correct value to six decimal places is 0.841471.)

2. Assume that you have a computer capable of storing real numbers correct to three decimal places of accuracy. Consider the execution of the following program segments where X is real and J is integer:

```
X : = 0.0
for J : = 1 to 10 do
   X : = X + 1.0 / 3.0;
write(X)
```

Hand trace this sequence of statements and comment on the value of X that is printed.

3. In conventional number systems, addition is an *associative* operation; that is, for numbers $a$, $b$, and $c$,

$$(a + b) + c = a + (b + c)$$

Unfortunately, the associative property does not always hold on a computer. Explain why this is so, and give an example where addition is not associative.

4. In addition to the associative property described in Exercise 3, addition in conventional number systems has two other important properties. First,

$$a + b = b + a$$

Also, multiplication *distributes* over addition; that is,

$$a \times (b + c) = a \times b + a \times c$$

Do these properties always hold on a computer? If not, give counterexamples.

5. Calculate the sum of the following floating-point numbers, assuming five decimal digits of accuracy. Add them first in the order given and then rearrange for maximum accuracy.

$$0.24382 \times 10^1$$
$$0.85155 \times 10^0$$
$$0.79843 \times 10^0$$
$$0.62837 \times 10^1$$
$$0.48919 \times 10^3$$

## A-2    FINDING THE ROOTS OF NONLINEAR FUNCTIONS

The *root* of a function of a single variable is defined to be that value of the variable that results in a value of zero for the function. If we graph the function in the $(x, y)$ plane, as shown in Fig. A-2, the root is the point (or points) at which the function crosses the $x$ axis.

For linear functions, the roots are easy to find algebraically. For example, the root of the function

$$f(x) = x - 3$$

is easily found by solving for the $x$ value that sets the function to 0.

$$x - 3 = 0$$
$$x = 3$$

For nonlinear functions, for example, functions with powers of $x$ greater than 1, the solution techniques are not so simple. Recall from Sec. 4-6.1 that for second-degree polynomial functions of the form

$$f(x) = ax^2 + bx + c$$

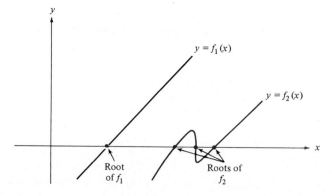

**FIGURE A-2**

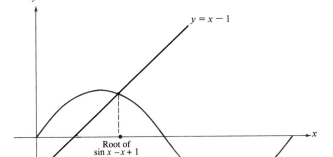

the roots are given by the quadratic formula

$$x = \frac{-b \pm \sqrt{b^2 - 4ac}}{2a}$$

Solution formulas for third- and fourth-degree polynomials are more complicated still; formulas for higher-degree polynomials do not exist. Suppose, further, that we wish to consider nonpolynomial functions of $x$, such as

$$\sin x - x + 1 = 0$$

Since there exists no general formula for the roots of this form of equation, we must resort to other solution methods. We might try rearranging the equation to

$$\sin x = x - 1$$

and graphing the two functions of the equality, as shown in Fig. A-3. The solution is then the point of intersection of the two curves. This method is clearly not acceptable for anything but rough approximations, since the accuracy is very poor. Functions involving trigonometric functions or logarithms are transcendental functions, and there are no general formulas for their roots.

We now turn to a discussion of some numerical procedures for finding the roots of functions. These are sufficiently general that they can be used for all higher-degree polynomials and also for transcendental functions.

## A-2.1 THE METHOD OF SUCCESSIVE BISECTION

Consider the function $f(x)$. We wish to find a value of $x$ for which $f(x) = 0$. We begin by choosing two $x$ values, $x_1$ and $x_2$, whose functional values have different signs; that is, one of $f(x_1)$ and $f(x_2)$ is positive and the other is negative; therefore, $f(x_1) \times f(x_2) < 0$. If we assume that $f(x)$ is continuous on $(x_1, x_2)$, there must exist a root between $x_1$ and $x_2$ that can be found by the *method of successive bisection*. Clearly, if the function never changes its sign, this method cannot be applied. Such a function never crosses the $x$ axis and thus has no real roots.

The procedure is as follows:

1. Find $r$, the midpoint of $(x_1, x_2)$, where $f(x_1)$ and $f(x_2)$ are opposite in sign.

2. If $f(r) = 0$, then the root is $r$. Also, if $|x_1 - x_2|$ is within some previously stated tolerance of 0, then the root is taken to be $x_1$ or $x_2$.

3. If $f(r)$ has the same sign as $f(x_1)$, then $r$ must be on the same side of the actual root as $x_1$; thus repeat the procedure with $x_1 = r$.

4. If $f(r)$ has the same sign as $f(x_2)$, then repeat the procedure with $x_2 = r$.

By this method, the search interval $(x_1, x_2)$ always contains the root. The length of the interval is successively halved until the functional value of the midpoint of the interval is sufficiently close to 0 or until $x_1$ and $x_2$ are very close together.

This method is illustrated in Fig. A-4. Initial values $x_1$ and $x_2$ are chosen on opposite sides of the root. A preliminary graphing of the function can be used to suggest these initial values. The point $x_3$ is derived as the midpoint of the interval $(x_1, x_2)$. As shown, $f(x_3)$ is not zero; therefore, we must continue our search. Since $f(x_3)$ has the same sign as $f(x_1)$, our new search interval becomes $(x_3, x_2)$, with $x_4$ as the midpoint. Since $f(x_4)$ has the same sign as

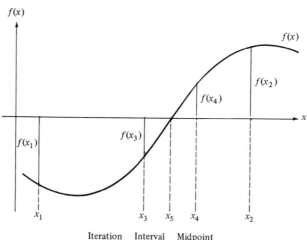

| Iteration | Interval | Midpoint | |
|-----------|----------|----------|---|
| 1 | $(x_1, x_2)$ | $x_3$ | |
| 2 | $(x_3, x_2)$ | $x_4$ | |
| 3 | $(x_3, x_4)$ | $x_5$ | (root) |

**FIGURE A-4**
**Finding the root of**
$f(x)$ **by the method**
**of successive bisection.**

$f(x_2)$, our search interval becomes $(x_3, x_4)$, with $x_5$ as the midpoint. In this case we are fortunate, since $f(x_5) = 0$, $x_5$ is the desired root.

The error associated with the root found in this manner is bounded by (that is, cannot be greater than) one-half of the length of the last interval used, or the size of the interval that would have been used had another iteration been made.

This method is almost guaranteed to converge to a root if the initial conditions are met, unless the roundoff error becomes too large. However, it converges more slowly (requires more iterations) than most other methods.

An alternative test of convergence for this particular problem is to test the function value at the computed point [that is, $f(r)$]. If it is within a specified tolerance of 0, the process is said to converge. This particular test may result in faster convergence if the interval endpoints are approximately equally spaced on either side of the root.

## A-2.2  NEWTON'S METHOD

*Newton's method* was developed by Sir Isaac Newton to assist in hand calculations of roots, but it applies well in a computing environment. In Newton's method, the curve of the function is approximated by the tangent to the curve at a certain value of $x$. The method requires only one initial guess, $x_1$. Each successive approximation of the root is the $x$-axis intersection of the tangent of the curve at the point of previous guess.

Since the derivative of the function at $x_1$ [denoted by $f'(x_1)$] is equal to the slope of the tangent line at $x_1$, we see from Fig. A-5 that

$$f'(x_1) = \frac{f(x_1)}{x_1 - x_2}$$

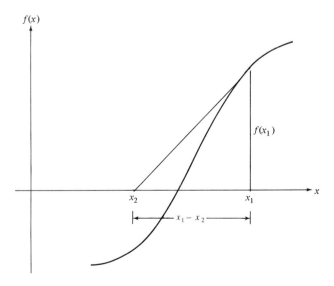

**FIGURE A-5**

which, when rearranged, yields

$$x_2 = x_1 - \frac{f(x_1)}{f'(x_1)}$$

or, more generally,

$$x_{n+1} = x_n - \frac{f(x_n)}{f'(x_n)}$$

Successive approximations are made until $f(x_n)$ is very small or until $x_n$ and $x_{n-1}$ are very close together (see Fig. A-6). In the procedure in Fig. A-7 we choose the former stopping criterion. Table A-1 shows the results of applying Newton's method to find a root of $f(x) = x^3 - x^2 - 2x + 1$ with the initial approximation $x_1 = 0.5$. The process is to terminate when the functional value of the estimated root is within $0.00001$ of zero.

Newton's method is much more efficient than the method previously discussed. However, it does have certain disadvantages: it requires the derivative of the function and it can easily go wrong (see Fig. A-8).

Newton's method requires some preliminary setup of the problem to render it amenable to solution. To illustrate, we will develop a formula for $x_{n+1}$ that could be used with Newton's method to find the square root of a nonnegative number $N$.

$$x = \sqrt{N}$$

can be written as

$$x^2 - N = 0$$

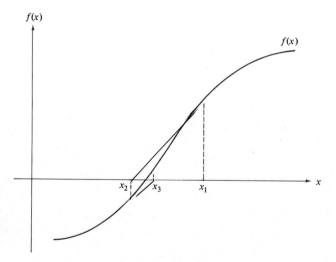

**FIGURE A-6**
**Successive**
**approximations to**
**the root of** $f(x) = 0$
**by Newton's method.**

```
procedure Newton(
    X: real;                        {Input, initial guess}
    E: real;                        {Input, desired accuracy}
    var Root: real                  {Output, the root}
        );
{Given an initial guess at the root of F, and E, the desired accuracy, this
    procedure returns the Root of the function F. The function F and its deriv-
    itive FPrime are assumed to be globally defined.}
const
    MaxIterations = 30;
var
    Iter: integer;                  {Iteration number}
    XOld: real;                     {Previous estimate}
    FAtXOld: real;                  {Value of F at XOld}
    FAtRoot: real;                  {F(Root)}
begin
    {Step 1: Initialize and compute first estimate}
    XOld : = X;
    FAtXOld : = F(XOld);
    Root : = XOld − FAtXOld / FPrime(XOld);
    FAtRoot : = F(Root);
    Iter : = 1;

    {Step 2: Engage loop to compute successive estimates}
    while (abs(FAtRoot) >= E) and (Iter < MaxIterations) do
        begin

            {Step 3: Save previous estimate}
            XOld : = Root;
            FAtXOld : = FAtRoot;

            {Step 4: Compute next estimate}
            Root : = XOld − FAtXOld / FPrime(XOld);
            FAtRoot : = F(Root);
            Iter : = Iter + 1;
        end;

    {Step 5: Display message if root was not found}
    if (abs(FAtRoot) >= E)
    then writeln('Root not found in', MaxIterations:1,
            'iterations. Root so far is', Root)
end;
```

**FIGURE A-7**
**Procedure to find a
root of F by
Newton's method.**

**TABLE A-1**  **Trace of Newton's Method**

| $n$ | $x_n$ | $f(x_n)$: $x^3 - x^2 - 2x + 1$ | $f'(x_n)$: $3x^2 - 2x - 2$ | $\dfrac{f(x_n)}{f'(x_n)}$ |
|---|---|---|---|---|
| 1 | 0.5 | −0.125 | −2.25 | 0.055556 |
| 2 | 0.444444 | 0.001373 | −2.296297 | −0.000598 |
| 3 | 0.445042 | −0.0000003 | −2.295897 | 0.0000001 |

Let

$$f(x) = x^2 - N$$

The root of $f(x) = 0$ will be the square root of $N$. For any $n$,

$$f'(x_n) = 2x_n$$

so

$$
\begin{aligned}
x_{n+1} &= x_n - \frac{x_n^2 - N}{2x_n} \\
&= \frac{x_n^2 + N}{2x_n} \\
&= \frac{1}{2}\left[ x_n + \frac{N}{x_n} \right]
\end{aligned}
$$

is the formula to be used. This is, in fact, the formula used on many electronic pocket calculators that supply a built-in square-root function. In a similar manner, formulas can be found for the cube roots, fourth roots, and so on.

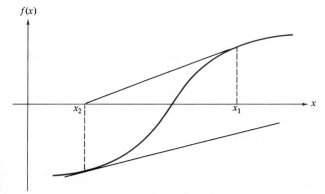

**FIGURE A-8**
**Example of how Newton's method can fail.**

# EXERCISES A-2

1. Using the method of successive bisection, compute a root of each of the following functions to an accuracy of 0.0001.
   (a) $f(x) = x^2 - 5x + 6$
   (b) $f(x) = x^3 - 4x^2 - 7x + 10$
   (c) $f(x) = xe^x - 1$

2. Using Newton's method, compute a root of each of the following functions to an accuracy of 0.0005:
   (a) $f(x) = x^2 + x - 90$
   (b) $f(x) = x^3 + 4x^2 - 17x - 60$
   (c) $f(x) = \sqrt{x} - 4 \tan(x/2)$

3. Construct an algorithm to compute the cube root of a number $N$ to an accuracy of six decimal places using Newton's method. Use $x_0 = N$ as the original estimate.

## A-3  NUMERICAL INTEGRATION

*Integration* is a standard mathematical technique for computing the area of a closed figure. Figure A-9 shows the area given by the expression

$$\int_a^b f(x)\, dx$$

where the function $f$ (which is continuous) yields the curve shown and $a$ and $b$ are two points on the $x$ axis.

There are a number of instances where numerical integration (also known as *quadrature*) must be used instead of classical analytical techniques:

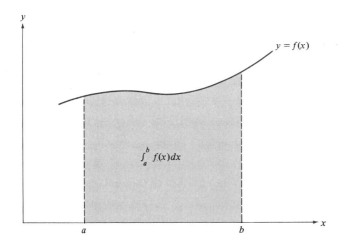

**FIGURE A-9**
$\int_a^b f(x)\, dx$ **can be thought of as the area under the curve, $f(x)$, between $a$ and $b$.**

(1) some functional values are known, but not the function itself; (2) the function would be difficult or impossible to integrate analytically; or (3) a computer is to be used to evaluate the integral.

Several numerical techniques for integration have been formulated. In this section we will present two popular methods of numerical integration.

### A-3.1 THE TRAPEZOID RULE

As an approximation to the integral, we can use the trapezoids formed by the secant line of the curve on each subinterval, that is, the line formed by joining the two endpoints of the curve on the subinterval, as shown in Fig. A-10. This approach is called the *trapezoid rule*. The area of a trapezoid (a four-sided figure with two parallel sides) is given by the average length of the parallel sides multiplied by the distance between them. Thus the area of one trapezoid, say, between $x_i$ and $x_{i+1}$, is given by the formula

$$\frac{f(x_i) + f(x_{i+1})}{2} \times (x_{i+1} - x_i) = \frac{h}{2}[f(x_i) + f(x_{i+1})]$$

and the total area, that is, the integral, is given by

$$\int_a^b f(x)\, dx \doteq \sum_{i=0}^{n-1} \frac{h}{2}[f(x_i) + f(x_{i+1})]$$

$$\doteq \frac{h}{2}[f(x_0) + f(x_1) + f(x_1) + \cdots + f(x_{n-1}) + f(x_n)]$$

$$\doteq h\left[\frac{f(x_0)}{2} + f(x_1) + f(x_2) + \cdots + f(x_{n-1}) + \frac{f(x_n)}{2}\right]$$

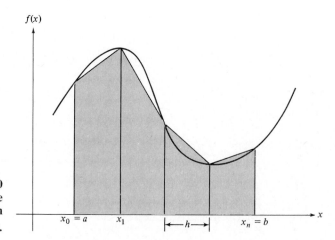

**FIGURE A-10**
**Trapezoid rule**
**approximation**
**of** $\int_a^b f(x)\, dx$.

In *Simpson's rule*, second-degree polynomials are fitted to the curve, one polynomial for each pair of subintervals, and the areas under these quadratics are calculated and added together to approximate the integral, as shown in Fig. A-11. In the trapezoid rule, the function in the interval is approximated by the secant line. For Simpson's rule, the function in the interval is approximated by a polynomial of the second degree, which coincides with the values of the function at three consecutive points.

To approximate the integral $\int_a^b f(x)\,dx$, the interval $(a,b)$ is divided into $n$ equal subintervals $(x_0, x_1), (x_1, x_2), \ldots, (x_{n-1}, x_n)$, where $n$ must be an even number. Now

$$\int_{a=x_0}^{b=x_n} f(x)\,dx = \int_{x_0}^{x_2} f(x)\,dx + \int_{x_2}^{x_4} f(x)\,dx + \cdots + \int_{x_{n-2}}^{x_n} f(x)\,dx$$

$$\doteq \frac{h}{3}[f(x_0) + 4f(x_1) + f(x_2)] + \frac{h}{3}[f(x_2) + 4f(x_3) + f(x_4)]$$

$$+ \cdots + \frac{h}{3}[f(x_{n-2}) + 4f(x_{n-1}) + f(x_n)]$$

$$\doteq \frac{h}{3}[f(x_0) + 4f(x_1) + 2f(x_2) + 4f(x_3) + \cdots + 2f(x_{n-2})$$

$$+ 4f(x_{n-1}) + f(x_n)]$$

This formula constitutes the definition of Simpson's rule. Remember that $n$ must always be an even number.

The procedure in Fig. A-12 implements Simpson's rule. Again, the iterative method is used.

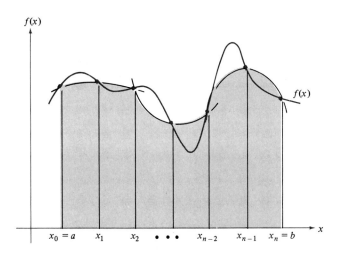

**FIGURE A-11**
Simpson's rule
approximation to
$\int_a^b f(x)\,dx$.

**procedure** Simpson (

| | |
|---|---|
| A, B: real; | {Input, endpoints of interval} |
| E: real; | {Input, prescribed accuracy} |
| **var** Simp: real | {Output, Simpson's rule approximation} |

);

{Given the endpoints of the interval of integration and the prescribed accuracy, this procedure computes the Simpson's rule approximation of $\int_a^b F(x)\, dx$, where $F$ is a global function. If the accuracy is not met after MaxIterations, a message is displayed.}

**const**
   MaxIterations = 20;

**var**

| | |
|---|---|
| N: integer; | {Number of intervals in current approximation} |
| Last: real; | {Previous approximation} |
| H: real; | {Subinterval size} |
| Sum: real; | {Simpson's rule sum} |
| NotDone: Boolean; | {Iteration control flag} |
| Iter: integer; | {Iteration number} |
| K: integer; | {Loop control} |

**begin**
   {Step 1 : Initialize}
   Simp : = 0.0;
   N : = 2;
   NotDone : = true;
   Iter : = 1;

   {Step 2 : Engage loop to compute successive approximations}
   **while** (Iter <= MaxIterations) **and** NotDone **do**
      **begin**

**FIGURE A-12**
Procedure to compute
the Simpson's rule
approximation of
an integral.

Simpson's rule is very popular for several reasons. First, the formula turns out to be exact for all polynomials of degree three and lower, because the areas in error cancel out exactly. Another reason for the wide use of the rule is its small error—only $O(h^4)$.

## EXERCISES A-3

1. Approximate the following integrals to an accuracy of 0.0001 using the rules and step sizes shown.

   (a) $\int_0^{\pi/2} \sin^2 x\, dx$, using the trapezoid rule with $h = 0.10$.

   (b) $\int_1^{\pi} \dfrac{1 - \cos x}{x}\, dx$, using Simpson's rule with $h = \pi/9$.

2. Construct an algorithm to compute the area in the first quadrant under the curve $y = x^2$ and inside the circle with unit radius. Use Simpson's rule with a step size of $h = 0.05$.

{Step 3 : Save last approximation}
Last : = Simp;

{Step 4 : Compute subinterval size}
H : = (B − A) / N;

{Step 5 : Accumulate Simpson's rule sum}
Sum : = F(A) + 4.0 * F(A + H) + F(B);
**for** K : = 0 **to** (N − 1) **div** 2 **do**
    Sum : = Sum + 2 * F(A + 2 * K * H) + 4 * F(A + (2 * K + 1) * H);

{Step 6 : Compute Simpson's rule approximation}
Simp : = H / 3.0 * Sum;

{Step 7 : Test accuracy}
**if** abs((Simp − Last) / Simp) < E
**then** NotDone : = false      {Accuracy achieved}
**else** N : = 2 * N            {Otherwise, double number of intervals}
**end**;

{Step 8 : If no convergence then display message}
**if** abs((Simp − Last) / Simp) >= E
**then** writeln('Tolerance was not met after', MaxIterations:1,
        'iterations. Current answer is', Simp)
**end**;

FIGURE A-12 (*cont.*)

3. Formulate an algorithm to compute the area of a circle with a radius of 2 units whose center has coordinates (4, 4). Use Simpson's rule with a step size of 0.01.

# APPENDIX B

## INTRODUCTION TO RECURRENCE RELATIONS

The computing time of a recursive algorithm is often expressed in terms of itself, that is, recursively. This was the case, for instance, for performing a recursive binary search (see Sec. 8-5.2) and Quicksort (see Sec. 8-5.3). We have seen that recurrence relations are useful in describing the time complexity of an algorithm. Frequently, the recurrence relations themselves are easily obtained. Having obtained a recurrence relation, we must solve it to determine its time complexity. There are several methods of solving recurrence relations. In this brief appendix, however, we concentrate on only the simplest method—substitution.

We first describe this method by means of examples. Once we have a tentative solution to a given recurrence relation, we can verify its correctness by induction. The remaining part of the appendix illustrates, through examples, this proof technique.

## B-1   SOLUTION BY SUBSTITUTION

In the substitution method of solving a recurrence relation for $T(n)$, we repeatedly use $T(n)$ to eliminate all occurrences of $T(\ )$ in the right-hand side of the relation. Once this is accomplished, the terms of the right-hand side are grouped together to obtain an expression as a function of $n$ for $T(n)$.

*Example 1:* Consider the recurrence relation for recursively traversing a binary tree in inorder and writing the information contents of each node.

$$T(n) = \begin{cases} 0 & \text{if } n = 0 \text{ (that is, the tree is empty)} \\ 1 & \text{if } n = 1 \\ 1 + T\left[\dfrac{n-1}{2}\right] + T\left[\dfrac{n-1}{2}\right] & \text{if } n > 1 \end{cases}$$

By assuming that $n = 2^k - 1$, if $n > 1$ we get

$$T(n) = 1 + 2T\left[\frac{n-1}{2}\right]$$

$$= 1 + 2T(2^{k-1} - 1)$$

If $n > 2$ then

$$T\left(\frac{n-1}{2}\right) = 1 + 2T\left[\frac{(n-1)/2 - 1}{2}\right]$$

$$= 1 + 2T\left[\frac{n-3}{2^2}\right]$$

$$= 1 + 2T(2^{k-2} - 1)$$

If $n > 3$ then

$$T\left(\frac{n-3}{2^2}\right) = 1 + 2T\left[\frac{n-7}{2^3}\right]$$

$$= 1 + 2T(2^{k-3} - 1)$$

These equalities follow immediately from the recurrence relation and the assumption that $n = 2^k - 1$. We use the equalities to obtain a nonrecursive expression for $T(n)$.

$$T(n) = 1 + 2T(2^{k-1} - 1)$$

$$= 1 + 2[1 + 2T(2^{k-2} - 1)]$$

$$= 1 + 2[1 + 2T(1 + 2T(2^{k-3} - 1))]$$

$$\vdots$$

$$= 1 + 2 + 2^2 + \cdots + 2^{k-1} + 2^k T(0)$$

Since $T(0) = 0$, we obtain

$$T(n) = \sum_{i=0}^{k-1} 2^i = 2^k - 1 = n$$

*Example 2:* Solve the following recurrence relation for $n$, a power of 3 (that is, $n = 3^k$):

$$T(n) = \begin{cases} 4 & \text{if } n = 1 \\ 3T\left[\dfrac{n}{3}\right] + 4n & \text{if } n > 1 \end{cases}$$

By assuming that $n = 3^k$ we get

$$\begin{aligned} T(3^k) &= 3T(3^{k-1}) + 4 * 3^k \\ &= 3[3T(3^{k-2}) + 4 * 3^{k-1}] + 4 * 3^k \\ &= 3^2 T(3^{k-2}) + 4 * 3^k + 4 * 3^k \\ &= 3^2[3T(3^{k-3}) + 4 * 3^{k-2}] + 4 * 3^k + 4 * 3^k \\ &= 3^3 T(3^{k-3}) + 4 * 3^k + 4 * 3^k + 4 * 3^k \end{aligned}$$

$$\vdots$$

$$= 3^i T(3^{k-i}) + i * 4 * 3^k \qquad \text{at the } i\text{th step}$$

We now set $i = k$

$$\begin{aligned} &= 3^k T(3^0) + k * 4 * 3^k \\ &= 4 * 3^k + k * 4 * 3^k \\ &= 4 * 3^k(k + 1) \\ &= 4n(\log_3 n + 1) \end{aligned}$$

*Example 3:* Solve the following recurrence relation:

$$T(3^k) = \begin{cases} 2 & \text{if } k = 0 \\ 2T(3^{k-1}) + 3^{k-1} & \text{if } k \geq 1 \end{cases}$$

Express the solution in as simple a form as possible. Again, by using substitution, we obtain

$$\begin{aligned} T(3^k) &= 2T(3^{k-1}) + 3^{k-1} \\ &= 2[2T(3^{k-2}) + 3^{k-2}] + 3^{k-1} \\ &= 2\{2[2T(3^{k-3}) + 3^{k-3}] + 3^{k-2}\} + 3^{k-1} \\ &= 2^3 T(3^{k-3}) + 2^2(3^{k-3}) + 2^1(3^{k-2}) + 2^0 3^{k-1} \end{aligned}$$

$$\vdots$$

$$= 2^k T(3^0) + \sum_{i=0}^{k-1} 2^i * 3^{k-1-i}$$

Using the base condition $T(3^0) = 2$ and rearranging terms, we get

$$T(3^k) = 2^k * 2 + \sum_{i=0}^{k-1} (\tfrac{2}{3})^i * 3^{k-1}$$

$$= 2^{k+1} + 3^{k-1} \sum_{i=0}^{k-1} (\tfrac{2}{3})^i$$

By using the equality

$$\sum_{i=0}^{m} a^i = \frac{a^{m+1} - 1}{a - 1}$$

$a = \tfrac{2}{3}$ and $m = k - 1$, we obtain

$$T(3^k) = 2^{k+1} + 3^{k-1} \left[ \frac{(\tfrac{2}{3})^k - 1}{\tfrac{2}{3} - 1} \right]$$

$$= 2^{k+1} - 3^{k-1} * 3[(\tfrac{2}{3})^k - 1]$$

$$= 2^{k+1} - 3^k[(\tfrac{2}{3})^k - 1]$$

$$= 2^{k+1} - 2^k + 3^k$$

Now that the solution of recursive relations by substitution has been illustrated, we next show how to use the principle of induction to verify a solution.

## B-2  VERIFICATION BY INDUCTION

Induction is a technique for proving a property (or predicate) $P(n)$ defined over the set of natural numbers. The approach involves the following:

*Inductive base:* Show that $P(0)$ is true.

*Inductive hypothesis:* Assume that $P(m)$ is true.

*Inductive step:* Show that $P(m+1)$ is true by using the inductive hypothesis.

We shall give here several examples to illustrate the application of the principle of mathematical induction.

*Example 1:* Show that $n < 2^n$. Let $P(n):n < 2^n$.

*Inductive base:* For $n = 0, P(0):0 < 2^0 = 1$, so that $P(0)$ is true.

*Inductive hypothesis:* For some arbitrary choice of $m$, assume that $P(m)$ holds, that is, $P(m):m < 2^m$

*Inductive step:* From the induction hypothesis, by adding 1 to both sides, we get

$$m+1 < 2^m+1 < 2^m+2^m = 2^m*2 = 2^{m+1}$$

which is exactly $P(m + 1)$. So $P(m)$ implies $P(m + 1)$. Hence, from the principle of mathematical induction, $P(n)$ is true for all natural numbers.

In the previous example we began with the base value $0$. However, this is not necessary as we can start with any natural number $n_0$. In this case, the conclusion is true for all $n > n_0$. We illustrate this variation in the next example.

*Example 2:* Show that $2^n < n!$ for $n \geq 4$. Let $P(n):2^n < n!$. Obviously, $P(1), P(2)$, and $P(3)$ are not true. We do not need them to be true.

*Inductive base:* For $n = 4$, $P(4):2^4 = 16 < 4! = 24$, so that $P(4)$ holds.

*Inductive hypothesis:* Assume that $P(m)$ holds for any $m > 4$, and so $2^m < m!$

*Inductive step:* From the inductive hypothesis, by multiplying both sides by 2 we get

$$2*2^m = 2^{m+1} < 2*(m!) < (m+1)*(m!) = (m+1)!$$

Therefore, $P(m + 1)$ holds for any $m > 3$.

The principle of induction is applied easily to prove that recurrence relations are correct. We give two examples of this approach.

*Example 3:* Use induction to prove that the solution of the recurrence relation

$$T(n) = \begin{cases} 2 & \text{if } n = 0 \\ 3 + T(n-1) & \text{if } n > 0 \end{cases} \quad \text{is} \quad T(n) = 3n + 2$$

*Inductive base:* For $n = 0$, $T(n) = 2$ and $3n + 2 = 2$.

*Inductive hypothesis:* Assume that $T(m) = 3m + 2$ for some $n, n = m$.

*Inductive step:* From the recurrence relation, we obtain $T(m + 1) = 3 + T(m)$. By using the inductive hypothesis we have $T(m + 1) = 3m + 2$. Consequently, $T(m + 1) = 3 + (3m + 2) = 3(m + 1) + 2$.

*Example 4:* Prove the solution to the recurrence relation obtained in example 2 of Sec. B-1.

*Inductive base:* For $n = 1$, that is $3^0 = 1$:

$$T(3^0) = 4 * 3^0(0 + 1)$$
$$= 4$$

*Inductive hypothesis:* Assume that $T(3^k) = 4 * 3^k(k + 1)$ for some $m = 3^k$.

*Inductive step:* From the recurrence relation we obtain

$$T(3^{k+1}) = 3 * T(3^k) + 4 * 3^{k+1}$$
$$= 3 * [4 * 3^k * (k + 1)] + 4 * 3^{k+1}$$
$$= 4 * 3^{k+1} * (k + 1) + 4 * 3^{k+1}$$
$$= 4 * 3^{k+1} * (k + 1 + 1)$$
$$= 4 * 3^{k+1}[(k + 1) + 1]$$

As mentioned earlier, the method of induction is not used to solve a recurrence relation. It is used to show that a candidate solution is correct.

# APPENDIX C

## ASCII AND EBCDIC CHARACTER CODES

The following tables contain the ASCII and EBCDIC character codes. Each character is given with its ordinal value (the value which is returned by the ord function for that character). This ordinal value is given in decimal form, which is the form most used by the Pascal programmer. It is also given in octal (that is, base 8) and hexadecimal (that is, base 16). The latter forms are commonly used in a computer device manual, as in, for example, the manual describing the operation of a particular computer printer. Where a two- or three-character abbreviation appears, this indicates that the character is defined as a control character. Its intended use is to control some feature of a computer device or communication line. For example, BEL is meant to sound an audible alarm (ring the "bell"). Some devices redefine some of the control characters for operations unique to that device. Some ASCII devices extend the ASCII character set to 256 characters by assigning characters to the ordinal values 128 through 255.

# ASCII Character Set

| Ordinal Value | | | | Ordinal Value | | | | Ordinal Value | | | | Ordinal Value | | | |
|---|---|---|---|---|---|---|---|---|---|---|---|---|---|---|---|
| Dec | Oct | Hex | Character | Dec | Oct | Hex | Character | Dec | Oct | Hex | Character | Dec | Oct | Hex | Character |
| 0 | 000 | 00 | NUL | 32 | 040 | 20 | space | 64 | 100 | 40 | @ | 96 | 140 | 60 | ` |
| 1 | 001 | 01 | SOH | 33 | 041 | 21 | ! | 65 | 101 | 41 | A | 97 | 141 | 61 | a |
| 2 | 002 | 02 | STX | 34 | 042 | 22 | " | 66 | 102 | 42 | B | 98 | 142 | 62 | b |
| 3 | 003 | 03 | ETX | 35 | 043 | 23 | # | 67 | 103 | 43 | C | 99 | 143 | 63 | c |
| 4 | 004 | 04 | EOT | 36 | 044 | 24 | $ | 68 | 104 | 44 | D | 100 | 144 | 64 | d |
| 5 | 005 | 05 | ENQ | 37 | 045 | 25 | % | 69 | 105 | 45 | E | 101 | 145 | 65 | e |
| 6 | 006 | 06 | ACK | 38 | 046 | 26 | & | 70 | 106 | 46 | F | 102 | 146 | 66 | f |
| 7 | 007 | 07 | BEL | 39 | 047 | 27 | ' | 71 | 107 | 47 | G | 103 | 147 | 67 | g |
| 8 | 010 | 08 | BS | 40 | 050 | 28 | ( | 72 | 110 | 48 | H | 104 | 150 | 68 | h |
| 9 | 011 | 09 | HT | 41 | 051 | 29 | ) | 73 | 11 | 49 | I | 105 | 151 | 69 | i |
| 10 | 012 | 0A | LF | 42 | 052 | 2A | * | 74 | 112 | 4A | J | 106 | 152 | 6A | j |
| 11 | 013 | 0B | VT | 43 | 053 | 2B | + | 75 | 113 | 4B | K | 107 | 153 | 6B | k |
| 12 | 014 | 0C | FF | 44 | 054 | 2C | , | 76 | 114 | 4C | L | 108 | 154 | 6C | l |
| 13 | 015 | 0D | CR | 45 | 055 | 2D | − | 77 | 115 | 4D | M | 109 | 155 | 6D | m |
| 14 | 016 | 0E | SO | 46 | 056 | 2E | . | 78 | 116 | 4E | N | 110 | 156 | 6E | n |
| 15 | 017 | 0F | SI | 47 | 057 | 2F | / | 79 | 117 | 4F | O | 111 | 157 | 6F | o |
| 16 | 020 | 10 | DLE | 48 | 060 | 30 | 0 | 80 | 120 | 50 | P | 112 | 160 | 70 | p |
| 17 | 021 | 11 | DC1 | 49 | 061 | 31 | 1 | 81 | 121 | 51 | Q | 113 | 161 | 71 | q |
| 18 | 022 | 12 | DC2 | 50 | 062 | 32 | 2 | 82 | 122 | 52 | R | 114 | 162 | 72 | r |
| 19 | 023 | 13 | DC3 | 51 | 063 | 33 | 3 | 83 | 123 | 53 | S | 115 | 163 | 73 | s |
| 20 | 024 | 14 | DC4 | 52 | 064 | 34 | 4 | 84 | 124 | 54 | T | 116 | 164 | 74 | t |
| 21 | 025 | 15 | NAK | 53 | 065 | 35 | 5 | 85 | 125 | 55 | U | 117 | 165 | 75 | u |
| 22 | 026 | 16 | SYN | 54 | 066 | 36 | 6 | 86 | 126 | 56 | V | 118 | 166 | 76 | v |
| 23 | 027 | 17 | ETB | 55 | 067 | 37 | 7 | 87 | 127 | 57 | W | 119 | 167 | 77 | w |
| 24 | 030 | 18 | CAN | 56 | 070 | 38 | 8 | 88 | 130 | 58 | X | 120 | 170 | 78 | x |
| 25 | 031 | 19 | EM | 57 | 071 | 39 | 9 | 89 | 131 | 59 | Y | 121 | 171 | 79 | y |
| 26 | 032 | 1A | SUB | 58 | 072 | 3A | : | 90 | 132 | 5A | Z | 122 | 172 | 7A | z |
| 27 | 033 | 1B | ESC | 59 | 073 | 3B | ; | 91 | 133 | 5B | [ | 123 | 173 | 7B | { |
| 28 | 034 | 1C | FS | 60 | 074 | 3C | < | 92 | 134 | 5C | \ | 124 | 174 | 7C | \| |
| 29 | 034 | 1D | GS | 61 | 075 | 3D | = | 93 | 135 | 4D | ] | 125 | 175 | 7D | } |
| 30 | 036 | 1E | RS | 62 | 076 | 3E | > | 94 | 136 | 5E | ^ | 126 | 176 | 7E | ~ |
| 31 | 037 | 1F | US | 63 | 077 | 3F | ? | 95 | 137 | 5F | — | 127 | 177 | 7F | DEL |

# EBCDIC Character Set

| Dec | Oct | Hex | Character | Dec | Oct | Hex | Character | Dec | Oct | Hex | Character | Dec | Oct | Hex | Character |
|---|---|---|---|---|---|---|---|---|---|---|---|---|---|---|---|
| 0 | 000 | 00 | NUL | 64 | 100 | 40 | space | 128 | 200 | 80 | | 192 | 300 | C0 | { |
| 1 | 001 | 01 | SOH | 65 | 101 | 41 | RSP | 129 | 201 | 81 | a | 193 | 301 | C1 | A |
| 2 | 002 | 02 | STX | 66 | 102 | 42 | | 130 | 202 | 82 | b | 194 | 302 | C2 | B |
| 3 | 003 | 03 | ETX | 67 | 103 | 43 | | 131 | 203 | 83 | c | 195 | 303 | C3 | C |
| 4 | 004 | 04 | SEL | 68 | 104 | 44 | | 132 | 204 | 84 | d | 196 | 304 | C4 | D |
| 5 | 005 | 05 | HT | 69 | 105 | 45 | | 133 | 205 | 85 | e | 197 | 305 | C5 | E |
| 6 | 006 | 06 | RNL | 70 | 106 | 46 | | 134 | 206 | 86 | f | 198 | 306 | C6 | F |
| 7 | 007 | 07 | DEL | 71 | 107 | 47 | | 135 | 207 | 87 | g | 199 | 307 | C7 | G |
| 8 | 010 | 08 | GE | 72 | 110 | 48 | | 136 | 210 | 88 | h | 200 | 310 | C8 | H |
| 9 | 011 | 09 | SPS | 73 | 111 | 49 | | 137 | 211 | 89 | i | 201 | 311 | C9 | I |
| 10 | 012 | 0A | RPT | 74 | 112 | 4A | ¢ | 138 | 212 | 8A | | 202 | 312 | CA | SHY |
| 11 | 013 | 0B | VT | 75 | 113 | 4B | . | 139 | 213 | 8B | | 203 | 313 | CB | |
| 12 | 014 | 0C | FF | 76 | 114 | 4C | < | 140 | 214 | 8C | | 204 | 314 | CC | |
| 13 | 015 | 0D | CR | 77 | 115 | 4D | ( | 141 | 215 | 8D | | 205 | 315 | CD | |
| 14 | 016 | 0E | SO | 78 | 116 | 4E | + | 142 | 216 | 8E | | 206 | 316 | CE | |
| 15 | 017 | 0F | SI | 79 | 117 | 4F | \| | 143 | 217 | 8F | | 207 | 317 | CF | |
| 16 | 020 | 10 | DLE | 80 | 120 | 50 | & | 144 | 220 | 90 | | 208 | 320 | D0 | } |
| 17 | 021 | 11 | DC1 | 81 | 121 | 51 | | 145 | 221 | 91 | j | 209 | 321 | D1 | J |
| 18 | 022 | 12 | DC2 | 82 | 122 | 52 | | 146 | 222 | 92 | k | 210 | 322 | D2 | K |
| 19 | 023 | 13 | DC3 | 83 | 123 | 53 | | 147 | 223 | 93 | l | 211 | 323 | D3 | L |
| 20 | 024 | 14 | RES/ENP | 84 | 124 | 54 | | 148 | 224 | 94 | m | 212 | 324 | D4 | M |
| 21 | 025 | 15 | NL | 85 | 125 | 55 | | 149 | 225 | 95 | n | 213 | 325 | D5 | N |
| 22 | 026 | 16 | BS | 86 | 126 | 56 | | 150 | 226 | 96 | o | 214 | 326 | D6 | O |
| 23 | 027 | 17 | POC | 87 | 127 | 57 | | 151 | 227 | 97 | p | 215 | 327 | D7 | P |
| 24 | 030 | 18 | CAN | 88 | 130 | 58 | | 152 | 230 | 98 | q | 216 | 330 | D8 | Q |
| 25 | 031 | 19 | EM | 89 | 131 | 59 | | 153 | 231 | 99 | r | 217 | 331 | D9 | R |
| 26 | 032 | 1A | UBS | 90 | 132 | 5A | ! | 154 | 232 | 9A | | 218 | 332 | DA | |
| 27 | 033 | 1B | CU1 | 91 | 133 | 5B | $ | 155 | 233 | 9B | | 219 | 333 | DB | |
| 28 | 034 | 1C | IFS | 92 | 134 | 5C | * | 156 | 234 | 9C | | 220 | 334 | DC | |
| 29 | 035 | 1D | IGS | 93 | 135 | 5D | ) | 157 | 235 | 9D | | 221 | 335 | DD | |
| 30 | 036 | 1E | IRS | 94 | 136 | 5E | ; | 158 | 236 | 9E | | 222 | 336 | DE | |
| 31 | 037 | 1F | ITB/IUS | 95 | 137 | 5F | ¬ | 159 | 327 | 9F | | 223 | 337 | DF | |
| 32 | 040 | 20 | DS | 96 | 140 | 60 | - | 160 | 240 | A0 | | 224 | 340 | E0 | \ |
| 33 | 041 | 21 | SOS | 97 | 141 | 61 | / | 161 | 241 | A1 | ~ | 225 | 341 | E1 | NSP |
| 34 | 042 | 22 | FS | 98 | 142 | 62 | | 162 | 242 | A2 | s | 226 | 342 | E2 | S |
| 35 | 043 | 23 | WUS | 99 | 143 | 63 | | 163 | 243 | A3 | t | 227 | 343 | E3 | T |
| 36 | 044 | 24 | BYP/INP | 100 | 144 | 64 | | 164 | 244 | A4 | u | 228 | 344 | E4 | U |
| 37 | 045 | 25 | LF | 101 | 145 | 65 | | 165 | 245 | A5 | v | 229 | 345 | E5 | V |
| 38 | 046 | 26 | ETB | 102 | 146 | 66 | | 166 | 246 | A6 | w | 230 | 346 | E6 | W |
| 39 | 047 | 27 | EXC | 103 | 147 | 67 | | 167 | 247 | A7 | x | 231 | 347 | E7 | X |
| 40 | 050 | 28 | SA | 104 | 150 | 68 | | 168 | 250 | A8 | y | 232 | 350 | E8 | Y |
| 41 | 051 | 29 | SFE | 105 | 151 | 69 | | 169 | 251 | A9 | z | 233 | 351 | E9 | Z |
| 42 | 052 | 2A | SM/SW | 106 | 152 | 6A | ¦ | 170 | 252 | AA | | 234 | 352 | EA | |
| 43 | 053 | 2B | CSP | 107 | 153 | 6B | , | 171 | 253 | AB | | 235 | 353 | EB | |
| 44 | 054 | 2C | MFA | 108 | 154 | 6C | % | 172 | 254 | AC | | 236 | 354 | EC | |
| 45 | 055 | 2D | ENQ | 109 | 155 | 6D | _ | 173 | 255 | AD | | 237 | 355 | ED | |
| 46 | 056 | 2E | ACK | 110 | 156 | 6E | > | 174 | 256 | AE | | 238 | 356 | EE | |
| 47 | 057 | 2F | BEL | 111 | 157 | 6F | ? | 175 | 257 | AF | | 239 | 357 | EF | |
| 48 | 060 | 30 | | 112 | 160 | 70 | | 176 | 260 | B0 | | 240 | 360 | F0 | 0 |
| 49 | 061 | 31 | | 113 | 161 | 71 | | 177 | 261 | B1 | | 241 | 361 | F1 | 1 |
| 50 | 062 | 32 | SYN | 114 | 162 | 72 | | 178 | 262 | B2 | | 242 | 362 | F2 | 2 |
| 51 | 063 | 33 | IR | 115 | 163 | 73 | | 179 | 263 | B3 | | 243 | 363 | F3 | 3 |
| 52 | 064 | 34 | PP | 116 | 164 | 74 | | 180 | 264 | B4 | | 244 | 364 | F4 | 4 |
| 53 | 065 | 35 | TRN | 117 | 165 | 75 | | 181 | 265 | B5 | | 245 | 365 | F5 | 5 |
| 54 | 066 | 36 | NBS | 118 | 166 | 76 | | 182 | 266 | B6 | | 246 | 366 | F6 | 6 |
| 55 | 067 | 37 | EOT | 119 | 167 | 77 | | 183 | 267 | B7 | | 247 | 367 | F7 | 7 |
| 56 | 070 | 38 | SBS | 120 | 170 | 78 | | 184 | 270 | B8 | | 248 | 370 | F8 | 8 |
| 57 | 071 | 39 | IT | 121 | 171 | 79 | ` | 185 | 271 | B9 | | 249 | 371 | F9 | 9 |
| 58 | 072 | 3A | RFF | 122 | 172 | 7A | : | 186 | 272 | BA | | 250 | 372 | FA | |
| 59 | 073 | 3B | CU3 | 123 | 173 | 7B | # | 187 | 273 | BB | | 251 | 373 | FB | |
| 60 | 074 | 3C | DC4 | 124 | 174 | 7C | @ | 188 | 274 | BC | | 252 | 374 | FC | |
| 61 | 075 | 3D | NAK | 125 | 175 | 7D | ' | 189 | 275 | BD | | 253 | 375 | FD | |
| 62 | 076 | 3E | | 126 | 176 | 7E | = | 190 | 276 | BE | | 254 | 376 | FE | |
| 63 | 077 | 3F | SUB | 127 | 177 | 7F | " | 191 | 277 | BF | | 255 | 377 | FF | EO |

*Note:* Blank characters indicate codes not assigned in the IBM standard. These often correspond to additional characters, e.g., superscripts, on various devices.

# APPENDIX D

## QUICK PASCAL REFERENCE

**Reserved Words**

| | | | | | |
|---|---|---|---|---|---|
| and | do | function | nil | program | type |
| array | downto | goto | not | record | until |
| begin | else | if | of | repeat | var |
| case | end | in | or | set | while |
| const | file | label | packed | then | with |
| div | for | mod | procedure | to | |

**Predefined Identifiers**

*Constants:*

| | | |
|---|---|---|
| false | maxint | true |

*Standard types:*

| | | | | |
|---|---|---|---|---|
| boolean | char | integer | real | text |

*Standard functions:*

| | | | | |
|---|---|---|---|---|
| abs | eof | odd | sin | trunc |
| arctan | eoln | ord | sqr | |

| chr | exp | pred | sqrt |
|-----|-----|------|------|
| cos | ln  | round | succ |

*Standard procedures:*

| dispose | pack | read | rewrite |
|---------|------|------|---------|
| get | page | readln | unpack |
| new | put | reset | write |

## Other Special Identifiers

*Standard files:*

input          output

These become automatically declared as text files in the main program if they appear in the header line of the program.

*Directive:*

forward

When the identifier forward appears in place of the body of a procedure or function, it indicates that the actual body of the routine will appear later in the program.

## Operator Precedence

Lowest      =   <>   <   <=   >   >=      **in**

$\downarrow$      +   −   **or**

      *   /   **div   mod   and**

Highest      **not**

## Syntax Diagrams

These syntax diagrams are identical with those which appear distributed throughout the text except for one addition. We originally introduced read, readln, write, and writeln as input and output statements. They are, in fact, merely calls to built-in procedures. However, these built-in procedures have some special characteristics. They may take different numbers and types of arguments, although this change does not require changes to the syntax diagrams. The write and writeln procedures can take arguments of the form

*expression : expression*

and

*expression : expression : expression*

This possibility, recognized by a modification to the syntax diagram for the procedure statement, is as follows:

procedure statement

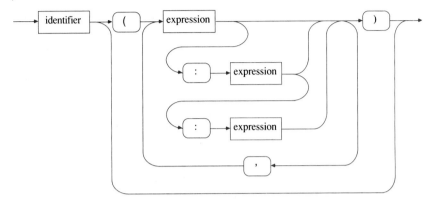

**Program Structure**

**Declarations**

**Statements**

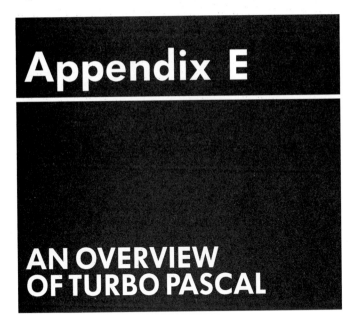

# Appendix E

# AN OVERVIEW OF TURBO PASCAL

Turbo Pascal is a very popular implementation of Pascal for personal computers. It provides many extensions to standard Pascal and introduces some deviations from the standard. In this appendix we introduce Turbo Pascal and describe the extensions most useful in conjunction with the material in this book. We also examine those deviations most likely to cause problems. No attempt is made to be comprehensive. This appendix describes Version 2.0 of Turbo Pascal. New versions of Turbo software appear frequently, however. Several of the features descibed here may not apply to new versions. The reader is referred to the Turbo Pascal Reference Manual for more information.

It is assumed that the Turbo Pascal system will be run under either the PC/DOS or MS/DOS operating system, the most popular of those under which Turbo runs. We do not present the details of the use of the operating system here because they are highly dependent on the particular computer facilities and because such information should be available from the manager of the computer facility.

This appendix is organized in a series of sections in approximately the order the material will be useful in progressing through this book. It is suggested that each section be initially read in conjunction with the chapter indicated in its heading.

## E-1   USING TURBO PASCAL (CHAP. 2)

Before Turbo is used, the operating system (PC/DOS or MS/DOS) must be activated in the manner specified by the computer facility. Next, Turbo itself must be activated; in most systems this is accomplished by typing the operating system command turbo followed by a carriage return. If this is successful, the Turbo system will display some identification information on the screen and the question

Include error messages (Y/N)?

Reply with a y without carriage return.

The operation of the Turbo system is controlled by making selections from the *main menu* whenever the Turbo prompt character > is displayed. A typical main menu is shown in Fig. E-1. Some of the information displayed depends on the computer system being used.

We illustrate the creation and execution of a simple Pascal program. First, enter the **Edit** main menu command. A main menu command is entered by typing its first character, either in upper- or lowercase. No carriage return is required. Therefore, type **e**. The editor will start, clear the screen, and request a file name to be edited. For this example, reply:

hello

Although file names must be in uppercase, Turbo allows entry in lowercase for convenience. Turbo will create an empty file **HELLO.PAS**, presuming that this file does not yet exist. The **.PAS** suffix identifies the file as a Pascal program.

The editor now awaits the entry of text and editing commands. Here we present a simple overview of the editor. More detail appears in the next section. There are two difficulties encountered in describing Turbo's editor. First, keyboards vary in the keys present, the layout of the keys, and the labeling of them. Naturally, the letters, digits, and common punctuation will be present in the expected places. But there will also be a collection of additional keys with such cryptic labels as **ESC**, **CTRL**, **F1**, ←, etc. The second problem is that the Turbo editor must be customized to work conveniently with the particular keyboard and display to be used. We assume that this has been done by the operators of the computer facility. If you must do it yourself, consult the Turbo Pascal Reference Manual.

It is necessary to understand one important feature of computer keyboards before beginning to edit. Most keys simply transmit a particular character to the editor. The shift key, however, is held down while pressing

Logged drive: A
Active directory: \

Work file:
Main file:

| Edit | Compile | Run | Save |
|------|---------|-----|------|
| Dir | Quit | compiler Options | |

**FIGURE E-1**
**Typical Turbo Pascal**
**main menu display.**

Text: 0 bytes
Free: 62903 bytes

another key and affects the character transmitted. The A transmits a, but SHIFT-A transmits A. A computer keyboard has a second shift key labeled CTRL or something similar (perhaps CNTL). CTRL-A, that is holding down the CTRL key while typing A, transmits a character different from both A and a; the character transmitted in this case is called "control A," written in this appendix as CTRL-A.

The Turbo editor displays a *cursor* on the screen. Typing an ordinary character such as a inserts the character into the text. Editor commands are specified by use of the control characters. This provides very efficient communication from the user to the editor because most editing operations require only one or two keystrokes (plus holding control). The appropriate keystrokes, however, must be memorized, since the commands are not written on the keytops.

Enter the program appearing in Fig. E-2. A line is terminated by a carriage return. The following editor commands will allow the correction of typing errors (for those who aren't perfect typists). Note that an installation may change the assignment of control keys from the Turbo standard. The facilities manager should have provided a customized list if this is the case.

CTRL-S     Move cursor left.

CTRL-D     Move cursor right.

CTRL-E     Move cursor up.

CTRL-X     Move cursor down.

Note that these keys form a diamond shape on the keyboard.

```
       E
    S     D
       X
```

If your keyboard has "arrow" keys, that is, ←, →, ↑, ↓, these may also have been defined to move the cursor. In the following commands, <DEL> stands for the key labeled DEL or, on some keyboards, RUBOUT:

<DEL>     Delete the character to the left of the cursor.

GTRL-G     Delete the character under the cursor.

Finally, we need one additional command:

CTRL-K CTRL-D     End editing and return to the Turbo prompt

The program remains in the storage of the computer when the editor is

```
program Hello(output);
begin
   writeln('Hello Dave')
end.
```

FIGURE E-2
A very simple
Turbo Pascal program.

exited. The program can be run or additional editing can be performed by reinvoking the editor.

When Turbo displays its command prompt >, it does not bother redisplaying the menu because most users will remember the common commands. Typing a carriage return, however, will redisplay the menu.

To run the program, use the run command by typing r. The program will be compiled and executed. An error detected during compilation will cause a compilation error message, after which Turbo will pause. Typing ESC (escape) will cause the editor to be automatically entered with the cursor positioned at the character where the error was *detected*. Remember that the actual error may be elsewhere. For example, if the compiler detects an extra right parenthesis at the end of an expression, it may be the result of a missing left parenthesis earlier in the expression.

The programmer may edit the program. During this time, the program is kept in the storage of the computer. If the computer is turned off or power fails, storage is cleared and the program is lost. This is avoided by typing s at intervals during an editing session. The program is saved under the name selected when the editor was invoked, discarding the previous file, if any, with that name on the disk.

Turbo is exited and control returned to the operating system by the quit command, typed as q. This discards the program in storage. If changes have been made and not saved, the user is given an opportunity to save them before the program is discarded.

For convenience, we summarize all the Turbo commands here.

**Logged Drive** L. Set the logged drive. This selects the disk on which the user's programs are stored. The user is prompted for the single-letter name of the disk device. Consult with the manager of the computer facility for a list of allowable names.

**Active Directory** A. Set the default directory or subdirectory to be used for path names not beginning with \. The user is prompted for a path name. The initial value \ indicates the main directory and will suffice for most work.

**Work File** W. Set the work file name. This is the file which will be edited when the editor is invoked. The user will be prompted for the name. If the file exists, it is loaded; otherwise, a new file is created.

**Main File** M. Set the main file name. See Sec. E-8 for more information.

**Edit** E. The editor is entered to edit the program displayed as the "work file" on the main menu. If no work file has yet been selected, the user is queried for a name. If the name given in the reply to the query is an existing file on disk, then that file is loaded; otherwise, an empty file is created.

**Compile** C. Compile the program.

**Run** R. Run the program, compiling it first, if necessary.

**Save** S. Save the program on disk.

**Dir** D. Display a list of all files on disk. The user will be prompted for a "Dir mask," that is, a *pattern*. Only those file names which match the pattern are displayed. The character ∗ matches any string of characters; ? matches any single character. For example, ∗.PAS matches all file names which are Pascal programs. Replying with just a carriage return to the pattern requests results in a list of all files on the logged disk.

**Quit** Q. Leave Turbo and return to the operating system.

**Compiler Options** O. Set certain compiler options. We will always use the default.

## E-2   THE TURBO EDITOR (CHAP. 2)

The editor was introduced in the previous section. This editor may be used for both programs and data files. Here we summarize all the editor's commands. The secret to learning efficient use of an editor is to concentrate on a few commands at a time and to become proficient in their use before attempting to learn additional commands. In the previous section we introduced a minimal set of commands. We mark with an asterisk a slightly larger set of basic commands. The user must progress to more advanced commands, however, so that he or she may efficiently work with the longer programs required by the later chapters of this book.

In the following list we give each command followed by its standard keystroke and then its alternate keystroke. The alternate keystroke is selected by the installers of the Turbo system and is chosen to be more convenient than the standard one. We have listed the most commonly chosen alternate keystroke. The manager of a computing facility should provide a list of changes to our list. Also note that if a particular control key is assigned as an alternate, then this definition takes precedence. For example, if CTRL-S is assigned as the alternate for the find (search) command, then it could no longer be used to execute the "left one character" command. A group of commands may be followed by a paragraph of supplementary information.

**Cursor Movement**

| | | |
|---|---|---|
| *Left one character | CTRL-S or CTRL-H | Left arrow |
| *Right one character | CTRL-D | Right arrow |
| *Up one line | CTRL-E | Up arrow |
| *Down one line | CTRL-X | Down arrow |
| Up one screenful | CTRL-R | PgUp |
| Down one screenful | CTRL-C | PgDn |
| Left one word | CTRL-A | CTRL-Left arrow |
| Right one word | CTRL-F | CTRL-Right arrow |
| *To beginning of line | CTRL-Q CTRL-S | Home |

| | | |
|---|---|---|
| *To end of line | CTRL-Q CTRL-D | End |
| To top of screen | CTRL-Q CTRL-E | CTRL-Home |
| To bottom of screen | CTRL-Q CTRL-X | CTRL-End |
| To top of file | CTRL-Q CTRL-R | CTRL-PgUp |
| To bottom of file | CTRL-Q CTRL-C | CTRL-PgDn |
| To previous position | CTRL-Q CTRL-P | |

### Window Movement

| | |
|---|---|
| Move window toward beginning of file | CTRL-W |
| Move window toward end of file | CTRL-Z |

The screen shows about 24 lines, a *window* into a file which may be much larger. The window moves automatically so that the cursor remains visible. These commands specifically move the window, automatically moving the cursor, if necessary, to keep it within the window.

### Deletion Commands

| | |
|---|---|
| *Delete character to left of cursor | \<DEL\> |
| *Delete character under cursor | CTRL-G |
| Delete right word | CTRL-T |
| *Delete line | CTRL-Y |
| Delete to end of line | CTRL-Q CTRL-Y |

### Insertion Commands

| | | |
|---|---|---|
| Insert mode on/off | CTRL-V | Ins |
| *Insert newline | CTRL-N | |

The editor has two modes: *insert mode* causes a noncontrol character to be *inserted* at the cursor position when typed; *overwrite mode* causes a noncontrol character to *overwrite* the character under the cursor. Inserting a new-line character breaks a line in two at the cursor.

### Block Commands

| | | |
|---|---|---|
| *Mark block begin | CTRL-K CTRL-B | F7 |
| *Mark block end | CTRL-K CTRL-K | F8 |
| Mark current word as a block | CTRL-K CTRL-T | |
| Toggle highlighting of block | CTRL-K CTRL-H | |
| *Copy block to cursor | CTRL-K CTRL-C | |
| *Move block to cursor | CTRL-K CTRL-V | |

| *Delete block | CTRL-K CTRL-Y |
| Move cursor to beginning of block | CTRL-Q CTRL-B |
| Move cursor to end of block | CTRL-Q CTRL-K |
| Write block to disk | CTRL-K CTRL-W |
| Read block from disk | CTRL-K CTRL-R |

A consecutive sequence of characters may be marked as a *block*. The block may appear highlighted on the screen, if the screen has this feature and highlighting is enabled. The block may be copied, moved, deleted, or written as a new file on disk. A file may be read from disk and inserted at the cursor; it becomes a block.

**Miscellaneous Commands**

| *End edit | CTRL-K CTRL-D |
| Tab | CTRL-I |
| *Auto indent on/off | CTRL-Q CTRL-I |
| *Restore line | CTRL-Q CTRL-L |
| *Find | CTRL-Q CTRL-F |
| Find and replace | CTRL-Q CTRL-A |
| Repeat last find | CTRL-L |
| *Abort current operation | CTRL-U |
| Control character prefix | CTRL-P |

The *tab* moves to the next *tab stop*, which is always the start of the *next word* on the *previous line*. When auto indent is *on*, <RETURN> moves to the *next line* immediately under the first nonblank character of the *current line*. The restore line restores the original contents of the current line provided that the cursor has not left the line. The *find* prompts for a search string of up to 30 characters. Terminate the search string with <RETURN>. Next, the command prompts for an option. Enter one or more of the following and <RETURN>.

| B | Backwards |
| G | Global, whole file |
| number | *n*th occurrence |
| U | Ignore upper- or lowercase distinction |
| W | Match only whole words, not parts |

The *find and replace* prompts for both a search string and a replacement string. Options are as for find, plus

| N | Replace without asking for verification |

The *repeat last find* repeats the last *find* or *find and replace* command. A control character, which is normally a command, is entered into the text being edited by preceding it with **CTRL-P**.

## E-3   MINOR DEVIATIONS FROM THE STANDARD (CHAP. 2)

Additional reserved words:

| | | |
|---|---|---|
| **absolute** | **inline** | **shr** |
| **external** | **overlay** | **string** |
| **forward** | **shl** | **xor** |

Identifiers may include an underbar, _, treated as if it were a letter. The (. and .) may be used in place of [ and ]. Likewise (* and *) may replace the { and }, that is, comment delimiters. A comment beginning with { must end with }, and one beginning with (* must end with *). Identifiers may be used in place of integers as statement labels. The label, constant, type, and variable declarations may occur repeatedly and in any order. The ∧ character is used in place of the ↑ symbol which is used in this book.

The goto statement may not jump out of a subprogram. The built-in procedure **halt** may be used to terminate a program. The **page** procedure is not available. Also, Turbo has a function **random** which returns a random value. For the exact syntax and operation of this function, see your Turbo manual.

## E-4   COMMON COMPILER DIRECTIVES (CHAP. 2)

Some features of the compiler are controlled by *compiler directives* contained in the source program itself. A compiler directive is specified by a comment beginning with a $, followed by a letter indicating the feature being controlled. Features are of two types: Boolean flags, switched *on* or *off* by following the option letter by a + or − sign and others which take an argument, such as file name, following the option letter. Examples are

{$R + }
{$U + }

The following directives will be most useful. The default setting of the option is shown when applicable.

**C—Control C and S. Default:** {$C + }. A program compiled with C+ will allow the program to be stopped while it is executing by typing **CTRL-C** as input to a read or readln statement. Also, **CTRL-S** toggles screen output on and off. Screen output runs faster with C − .

**I—I/O Error Handling Default:** {$I + }. A program compiled with I+ will terminate if an I/O error occurs during execution. An I− allows continuation. Each I/O statement, however, should be followed by exactly one call to the built-in function IOResult, which returns zero if the previous operation was successful and a nonzero error code otherwise.

**K—Stack Check Default:** {$K +} . A program compiled with K+ checks that sufficient memory is available for local variables at each procedure or function call. A K— disables the check resulting in a faster program.

**R—Index Range Check Default:** {$R —} . The R+ causes all array indices and assignments to subrange variables on the following lines to be checked during execution; R— inhibits checking and makes the program run faster. Note that the default is R—. Therefore, a program being tested should have an {$R +} near the beginning.

**V—Var-Parameter Type Check Default:** {$V +} . When a program is compiled with V+, in any following procedure or function call with a character string argument corresponding to a character string var-type parameter, the lengths must match. A V— allows length mismatches.

**U—User Interrupt Default:** {$U —} . A program compiled with U+ allows the user to interrupt the execution by typing CTRL-C at any time. This allows interrupting nonterminating loops. Therefore, programs under test should be compiled with {$U +} near the beginning. A program compiled with U— (the default) will run considerably faster.

# E-5   BASIC TEXT I/O (CHAP. 3)

Two types of file variables declared to be of the standard type text are distinguished: those associated with actual *disk files*, and those associated with *logical devices*. File variables associated with disk files closely match the text files of standard Pascal, with the following exceptions: Before the file variable is initialized for reading or writing by reset or rewrite, a disk file name must be associated with the file variable. This is done by the built-in procedure assign. Two arguments are required: first, the file variable, and second, a string containing the name of the file as listed in the disk directory. A file should also be closed after its processing is complete, by invoking the procedure Close, which takes the file variable as its only argument. Finally, the "next character" buffer, accessed, for example, by FileVar ↑ , is not available in Turbo Pascal.

Operations on file variables associated with *logical devices* deviate considerably from the standard. The logical devices provide access to the keyboard, display screen, and printer. Several different logical devices provide access to the single keyboard, but with different effects, e.g., echoing or not echoing the input to the screen. A built-in (predeclared) file variable is provided for each logical device. Alternatively, the logical device may be associated with any programmer-declared file variable of type text. This is done with the assign procedure, replacing the file name with the logical device name. The logical devices, and built-in file variable, are summarized in Table E-1.

The file variables input and output are also built in and are assigned to a logical device under control of the B compiler directive. A {$B + }, which is the default, causes input and output to be preassigned to device CON:. The directive {$B − } causes input and output to be preassigned to device TRM:. This option, if present, must precede the first declaration of any kind in the main program.

Note that the built-in file variables have been preassigned to the logical devices and readied for input and output as appropriate. Use of assign, reset, rewrite, and close on the built-in file variables, including input and output, is illegal. Thus input and output cannot be reassigned (for programs compiled in the normal way) except as provided by the B compiler directive.

There are several deviations from standard Pascal for input from logical devices. The eof and eoln functions operate differently for logical devices. In standard Pascal, and in Turbo for disk files, eof is "true" if the previous read exhausted the last input character. For a logical device, Turbo specifies that an end-of-file character CTRL-Z, ordinal value 26, follows the last data character. The eof function becomes "true" *after* this character is read and processed. In effect, eof on a disk file tests the next unprocessed character for an end of file, whereas on a logical device, the most recent previous character is tested. The eoln function similarly tests the previous character for logical devices.

| TABLE E-1 | Turbo Logical Devices | |
|---|---|---|
| **Device File** | **Variable** | **Description** |
| 'CON:' | con | The console device. When used as input, characters are read from the keyboard and echoed. An entire line, terminated by a carriage return, is read and stored in a buffer before data is transfered to the program. Typing errors may be corrected with BACKSPACE or DEL (RUBOUT). When used as output, characters are displayed on the screen. |
| 'TRM:' | trm | The terminal device. Input is from the keyboard; noncontrol characters and carriage return are echoed to the screen. Output is directed to the screen. Input is transmitted to the program on a character-by-character basis: any editing or typing correction features must be provided in the program itself. |
| 'KBD:' | kbd | The list device, which is normally a printer. Only output is allowed. |
| 'LST:' | lst | Only input, e.g., read, is allowed. Input is from the keyboard with no echoing to the screen. Processing is character-by-character, as for TRM:. |

When a read or a readln statement encounters an end of file, the program is not terminated. Instead, all the remaining variables in the read statement are processed as follows. **CTRL-Z** is assigned to each character variable. The null string is assigned to each string variable. The values of numeric variables will remain unchanged.

Input from **KBD:** and **TRM:** is processed as the characters are typed on the keyboard. A **read** terminates as soon as values are obtained for all variables. A readln statement additionally reads and discards characters through the next carriage return. The **CON:** device, however, operates in a remarkable way. Both read and readln statements wait until an entire line, including the carriage return, is typed. These characters are stored in an internal buffer. Typing errors may be corrected, before the carriage return, by use of **BACKSPACE** or **DEL**. When the carriage return is typed, it is stored as an end of file in the buffer. The readln statement will echo the carriage return to the screen, while the read statement will not. The variables of the read statement are then processed using the characters in the buffer. If the trailing end of file is encountered before all the variables are processed, then end-of-file processing occurs as described previously. Thus each line appears like an input file!

Obviously, a program using end-of-file processing must be modified to use a programmer-defined file variable to read from disk (since input is not assignable to a disk file) or must be modified to accommodate the nonstandard **eof** processing on logical devices.

## E-6 CONTROL CONSTRUCTS (CHAP. 3)

Case statements permit ranges of values as case labels. Also, a default case is provided by use of **else**. For example;

```
case K of
    2,6: writeln('Case 1');
    1,3 .. 5,7 .. 10: writeln('Case 2');
    else writeln('None of the others')
end
```

## E-7 STRINGS (CHAP. 6)

Most of the string features of Turbo Pascal are described in detail in Chap. 6. Here we summarize the built-in procedures and functions for string processing described there and some additional ones.

### Procedures

delete(St, Pos, Num)

Removes **Num** characters from **St** beginning at position **Pos**.

insert(Obj, Target, Pos)

Insert string Obj into string Target beginning at position Pos.

str(Value, St)

The integer or real Value is converted to a string of characters and stored in St.

val(St, Variable, Code)

The string St, which must be in the form of an integer or real constant, as might occur in a program, is converted to the appropriate type of value and stored in Variable. Code is set to 0 if no conversion error occurs; otherwise, it is the position in St of the first character in error.

## Functions

copy(St, Pos, Num)

Returns a string which is a copy of the substring of St beginning at Pos and Num characters long.

concat(St1, St2, . . . , StN)

Returns a string which is a concatenation of copies of the strings St1, St2, . . . , StN. This can also be written as St1 + St2 + · · · + StN.

length(St)

Returns the integer length of string St.

pos(Obj, Target)

Returns the position, an integer, of the first occurrence of Obj within Target.

## E-8   MODULAR PROGRAM CONSTRUCTION (CHAP. 7)

A large Pascal program is cumbersome to develop and maintain as a single source file. Turbo Pascal provides facilities for organizing a single program into several separate files. One file is designated the *main file* and is compiled as an ordinary program. At any point in the main file, logical inclusion of an *include file* may be indicated by a compiler directive.

Typically, a cohesive collection of constant, type, variable, procedure, and function declarations is put together in an include file. For example, a text-processing program may be organized into include files containing text justification declarations and subprograms, say, TEXTJUST.PAS, command processing declarations, say, COMMANDS.PAS, etc. Figure E-3 sketches this organization. The directive specifying inclusion of a file in the main file takes the form

{ $I filename}

A blank should separate the I from the file name, and the file name should include the extension part (part after the dot).

```
const
  LineBufSize = 200;
type
  LineBufType = string(LineBufSize);
procedure JustifyLine ( . . .);
  .
  .
  .
```

(*a*) Include file TEXTJUST.PAS

```
type
  Commands = (Break, Just, NoJust, . . .);
procedure DoCommand ( . . .);
  .
  .
  .
```

(*b*) Include file COMMMANDS.PAS

```
program Format(input, output, InFile, OutFile);
{This program formats text by interpreting embedded formatting
  commands.}
{$I TEXTJUST.PAS}   {Include line justification operations}
{$I COMMANDS.PAS}   {Include command processing operations}

  .   {Include other files required}
  .
var

  .   {Some local variables for the main program}
  .

begin
  .
  .
  .
end.
```

(*c*) Main file FORMAT.PAS

**FIGURE E-3**
**Sketch of organization**
**of a program in**
**multiple files.**

The Turbo compiler treats the program as if the contents of the include files actually replace the include directive. The program must be valid Pascal to be treated this way. To facilitate modular organization, Turbo Pascal allows multiple occurrences of constant, type, and variable declaration parts and allows these, as well as procedures and functions, to occur in any order at the beginning of the program.

From the main Turbo menu (see Sec. E-1), the M command is used to specify the name of the main file which will be compiled when the C or R commands are used. The W command specifies the file which will be loaded for editing by the **E** command. Turbo will automatically load files as appropriate. For example, the main file must be loaded at the beginning of compilation. If an error occurs while compiling an include file, the work file will be changed to specify the include file so that the error may be corrected. Turbo also automatically saves programs on disk so as to avoid loss of changes when loading a different file.

## E-9 DYNAMIC STORAGE ALLOCATION (CHAP. 8)

Turbo Pascal does not implement an available space list for the procedure **new**. Instead, storage for nodes allocated dynamically is allocated sequentially from a consecutive block of storage. Each time **new** is invoked, it returns the value of the pointer to the free space, and this pointer is incremented by the size of the new node (Fig. E-4).

The procedure **mark**, taking as an argument any type of pointer variable, records the current value of the free pointer. This same variable, when used as an argument for **release**, resets the free pointer to its recorded position. In effect, **release** returns to available space *all nodes* allocated by **new** since the corresponding **mark**. In particular, note that **release** cannot simply be substituted for Pascal's **dispose**. The latter returns *only one* node to available space.

## E-10 TYPED FILES (CHAP. 10)

Turbo refers to files other than those declared as text as *typed files*. Typically, the associated file variable is declared to be a file of some record type. Such file variables must be associated with an actual disk file, not a logical device. Turbo Pascal does not implement the file buffer, that is, *filename* ↑ . Because several of standard Pascal's built-in procedures and functions work differently with Turbo typed files, and because several additional ones are available, we present a brief summary here.

**Procedures**

assign(FilVar, Str)

The string **Str** is the disk file name to be used for file variable **FilVar**.

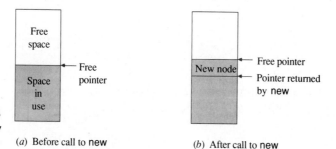

**FIGURE E-4**
**Operation of new**
**in Turbo Pascal.**

(*a*) Before call to **new**          (*b*) After call to **new**

rewrite(FilVar)

The file variable **FilVar** is prepared for I/O operations (opened). Both reading and writing are permitted (although you must write to the file before you can read from it). Any previous disk file with the assigned name (see **assign**) is discarded and a new empty file is created. The current file position is set to zero.

reset(FilVar)

The file variable **FilVar** is opened. Both reading and writing are permitted. A disk file with the assigned name must exist prior to the reset. The current file position is set to zero.

read(FileVar, Var)

The file component (record) at the current file position is placed in **Var** and the file position is advanced by one. **Var** must be of the same component type as the file. **Var** may be a list of variables, in which case one file component is read into each variable.

write(FileVar, Var)

The file component at the current file position is overwritten with the value of **Var** and the file position is advanced by one. **Var** must be of the same component type as this file. **Var** may be a list of variables, in which case one file component is written for each variable.

seek(FilVar, N)

The current file position of **FilVar** is set to be **N**, which must be an integer expression. Note that the first component is at file position zero.

close(FileVar)

Closes the file **FilVar**.

erase(FilVar)

The disk file assigned to **FilVar** is discarded. **FilVar** should be closed when **erase** is used.

rename(FilVar, Str)]

The disk file assigned to **FilVar** is renamed to the name contained in string **Str**. The new name is also assigned to **FilVar** so that any later operations on **FilVar** will use the new name.

## Functions

eof(FilVar)

Returns "true" if the current file position of **FilVar** is greater than the number of the last component ever written into the file; returns "false" otherwise.

filepos(FileVar)

Returns the integer value of the current file position of **FilVar**.

filesize(FilVar)

Returns the number of components in the disk file associated with **FilVar**. This is defined as one greater than the highest numbered component ever written to the file or zero if no components have ever been written.

# APPENDIX F

# BERKELEY PASCAL

Berkeley Pascal consists of a series of compilers for various machines running under the UNIX operating system. This appendix presents an overview of one implementation and outlines some of the differences between standard Pascal and the language accepted by these compilers. This presentation is not comprehensive, but rather concentrates on those aspects most important to the reader of this book. Further information is available in the appropriate reference manuals.

## F-1   USING BERKELEY PASCAL

One version, referred to as the interpreter version, of the Berkeley Pascal system generates machine language for a hypothetical computer rather than the actual computer in use. The resulting compiled program is then run by use of an *interpreter* program. We first explain the use of this version.

A Pascal source program is prepared using one of the text editors available on the particular UNIX system in use. The source program must be stored in a file whose name ends with the characters .p, such as, for example, example.p, which will be used in the following. This program is compiled by the command

pi example.p

producing the object program in the file named obj. The interpreter is then invoked, to run the program, by

```
px obj
```

These two steps can be combined by use of the command

```
pix example.p
```

except, in this case, no **obj** file is produced on disk.

On some systems, a second version of the compiler which produces true machine language is available. The previous example is compiled by

```
pc example.p
```

producing the object program in file **a.out** which is then executed by the command

```
a.out
```

Both compilers produce error messages on the UNIX standard output stream, which is normally the user's terminal. This output can be redirected using the UNIX operator > followed by a suitable file name. Thus, to put the error messages in file **errors**, use

```
pi example.p > errors
```

Various options are controlled from the command line by a minus sign followed immediately by a letter. For example, −l causes a full listing of the source program to be produced, as in the following examples:

```
pi −l example.p
pi −l example.p > listing
pc −l example.p
```

Another useful option for **pc** is −C, which enables various run-time checks (which are enabled by default for **pi**).

## F-2   DIFFERENCES FROM STANDARD PASCAL

The following deviations from Pascal should be noted. The first four are disabled by the use of the −s option.

*1.* Upper- and lowercase are distinguished in identifiers, making **PayRate** and **payrate** different identifiers.

*2.* Character string constants which are shorter than required by Pascal's type matching rules are padded with blanks.

*3.* Functions may return structured values.

*4.* Enumerated type values may be read and written. As input, the value is supplied as an identifier, *not* enclosed in quotes.

*5.* The following substitutions are accepted:

    #    for    '

    ~    for    not

6. Comments may be enclosed in either { and } or (* and *).

7. The contents of another file, say, defs.i, can be included logically at any point in the program with

   #include "defs.i"

   Note that the # must be the first character on the line and the name of the included file must end with .i.

8. The built-in procedure halt terminates the program.

9. The function random(x) returns a random real number uniformly distributed over the range 0.0 to 1.0. The argument is a real expression whose value is ignored.

10. The interpreter px imposes a maximum limit on the number of statements executed. A call to the built-in procedure stlimit(i), where i is an integer expression, sets the limit to i statements.

## F-3 INPUT/OUTPUT

The file variable output must be included in the program header and is automatically declared to be a text file. Except for input and output, which follow special rules described subsequently, the following apply.

1. A file variable must be declared using a file type (**file of** . . .) or the standard type text.

2. A file variable, except input and output, which are opened automatically, must be opened for input (reset) or output (rewrite) before being used.

3. A file variable opened by the standard forms of reset and rewrite statements, which have only the file variable as an argument, operate on the file whose name is associated with the file variable. A file variable not associated with a file name, that is, not listed in the program header and not previously associated with a file name (see point 4 below), will be associated with a temporary file whose name is of the form tmp.x, with x being some character. A temporary file is automatically discarded when the program exits the block in which the file variable is declared.

4. The non-standard forms

   reset(FilVar, Str)
   rewrite(FilVar, Str)

   associate the file name contained in the string Str, with trailing blanks removed, with the file variable FilVar before opening it.

   The file variable output is automatically associated with the UNIX standard output stream and can thus be rerouted by use of > on the command line which runs the program. The file variable input is automatically associated with the UNIX standard input stream and may similarly be rerouted by < followed by the input file name on the execution line. It is also possible to redirect input by method 4.

## F-4 MODULAR PROGRAMMING

The pc version of the compiler supports a form of modular programming. Constant and type definitions, variable declaration, and procedure and function declarations in a special form may be collected together in a header file whose name must end with a .h. The procedure and function declarations in this file are similar to forward declarations (Chap. 4) except that the directive forward is replaced by external. These declarations represent the externally visible portion of a module. Figure F-1, showing the contents of a file vector.h, is an example of the declarations for a module manipulating integer vectors.

The private portion of a module is stored in a file whose name must end in .p. A reasonable convention is to form the name by replacing the .h in the name of the corresponding header file by .p. This file begins with a #include of the header for the module. It may also include header files for any modules which it uses, as described in the next paragraph. The private part of the module supplies the body for each procedure and function declared in the header file. These take a form similar to the bodies of forward-declared procedures and functions, that is, procedure or function, followed by the name, a semicolon, and the local declarations and body. Figure F-2 illustrates the private file for the vector-processing module declared in Fig. F-1. Although not illustrated here, the private part could include other constant, type, variable, procedure, and function declarations which would be hidden from users of the module. The module is separately compiled using the −c option, for example,

{Integer vector package header}

```
const
    VectorSize = 10;
type
    Vector = array [1 .. VectorSize] of integer;

procedure ReadVector (var A : Vector   {Output, vector read} ); external;
procedure WriteVector (A : Vector   {Input, vector written} ); external;
function AddVector ( A, B : Vector   {Input, vectors to be added} ) : Vector;
external;
{Other procedures and functions could be added here.}
```

FIGURE F-1
Header file, vector.h,
for vector package.

which produces an object file named by replacing the .p by .o, **vector.o** in this case.

```
{Integer vector package implementation}
#include "vector.h"

procedure ReadVector;
var
   K : integer;
begin
   for K : = 1 to VectorSize do
      read (A[K])
end;

procedure WriteVector;
var
   K : integer;
begin
   for K : = 1 to VectorSize do
      writeln (A[K])
end;

function AddVector;
var
   K : integer;
   C : Vector;
begin
   for K : = 1 to VectorSize do
      C[K] : = A[K] + B[K];
   AddVector : = C
end;
```

**FIGURE F-2**
**Vector modu'e**
**implementation, file**
**vector.p**

Any module, including the main program, requiring the services of another module includes its header file. Figure F-3 illustrates a main program using the vector-processing module. The main module may also be compiled separately using the −c option, for example,

pc ⁻c vecexample.p

producing the object as **vecexample.o.** Finally, the running program **a.out** is produced by the **pc** command from all the required **.o** files. In our example, we would use

pc vecxample.o vector.o

**program** VecExample (input, output);
{This program reads two integer vectors and displays their sum using the vector module.}
#include "vector.h"
**var**
A, B : Vector;
**begin**
{Read two vectors}
ReadVector (A);
ReadVector (B);

{Compute and display sum}
WriteVector (AddVector (A, B))
**end.**

**FIGURE F-3**
**Example of the use of the vector module, file vecexample.p.**

# APPENDIX G

## VAX-11 PASCAL

VAX-11 Pascal is a compiler for use on the Digital Equipment Corp. VAX line of computers under the VAX/VMS operating system.

## G-1  USING VAX-11 PASCAL

This section presumes some familiarity with the VAX/VMS operating system. A file name is written as

*node::device:[directory]filename.type; version*

where *node* is the computer name within a network of computers, *device* is the name of the disk (or other) device, *directory* is the directory within which the file name is to be found, *filename* is a name of up to 9 characters, *type* is part of the name and is three characters, and *version* is a number from 1 to 32767 specifying which of several versions of the file to use. For example,

COMPA::DISK$USER:[SMITH]PROG1.PAS;23

Normally, suitable defaults are supplied by the operating system for node, device, and directory. The highest (most recent) version number is used for accessing an existing file, and a version number one larger than the highest existing version (if any) of the specified file is used for writing a file. Therefore, it is customary to specify only the file name, as in

PROG1.PAS

Furthermore, certain type names are customarily used to specify the types of files. Some of these are listed in Table G-1. Often the type can be omitted because it will be defaulted properly. For example, it is sufficient to specify **PROG1** to the Pascal compiler to compile **PROG1.PAS**. It is necessary to specify both the name and type when editing a file because the editor is used to preface **PAS** and **DAT** (and other) types of files.

Prepare or modify a Pascal program by using an editor, for example,

EDIT/EDT PROGEX1.PAS

When editing is complete, the program may be run by the following sequence of commands:

```
PASCAL   PROGEX1
LINK    PROGEX1
RUN    PROGEX1
```

The **PASCAL** command compiles the named source (**PROGEX1.PAS**) and produces an object file (**PROGEX1.OBJ**). This file is then linked (**LINK**) to produce an executable program (**PROGEX1.EXE**). This program is then run by the command **RUN**. Notice how the default file types have resulted in three files of different types: **PROGEX1.PAS**, **PROGEX1.OBJ**, and **PROGEX1.EXE**.

Several useful options may be appended to the compilation command immediately after **PASCAL**, such as, for example,

PASCAL/LIST PROGEX1

The options are

| /LIST | Produce a source listing on standard output. |
| /LIST = *filename* | Produce a source listing in file *filename*. |
| /CHECK = ALL | Enable all checking (subrange errors, *nil* pointers, etc.). |

**TABLE G-1**   Some Customary VAX/VMS File Types

| File Type | Usage |
| --- | --- |
| DAT | Any data file |
| EXE | Executable programs |
| LIS | Listing file from a compiler |
| MAP | Listing file from the linker |
| OBJ | Object code from a compiler |
| PAS | Pascal source file |
| PEN | Pascal environment file |

## G-2 SOME MINOR DIFFERENCES BETWEEN VAX-11 AND STANDARD PASCAL

941
G-2
SOME MINOR
DIFFERENCES BETWEEN
VAX-11 AND
STANDARD PASCAL

The following list is not complete but rather includes those differences of most importance in conjunction with the material of this book:

*1.* Identifiers may include the underbar _.

*2.* The following alternative representations are available:

| | | |
|---|---|---|
| (. and .) | for | [ and ] |
| (* and *) | for | { and } |
| ^ or @ | for | ↑ |

*3.* An exponentiation operator ** is available, with precedence below **not** but higher than the multiplying operator.

*4.* An include directive is available. The form is

%INCLUDE *'filename'*

where *filename* is any valid VAX/VMS file specification. This directive may appear wherever a comment could appear in the program and is logically replaced by the contents of the file.

*5.* **nil** is a built-in identifier rather than a reserved word.

*6.* VAX-11 Pascal relaxes the requirement that type be identical, such as between an argument and a pass-as-variable parameter. The type need only be structurally compatible. Two record types are structurally compatible if, for example, they consist of the same number of fields, and the corresponding fields are structurally compatible.

*7.* A varying-length string type is provided (see Chap. 6).

*8.* There may be multiple occurrences of the label, constant, type, and variable declarations section, and the declarations may occur in any order.

*9.* A default is available for the case statement using the reserved word **otherwise**. Note that a program using **otherwise** as a reserved word may not use it as an identifier. An example of a case statement with a default is

```
case k of
    2,6: writeln('Case 1');
    1,3 .. 5, 7 .. 10: writeln('Case 2');
    otherwise writeln('None of the others')
end
```

*10.* The build-in procedure **halt** will terminate the program.

## G-3 INPUT/OUTPUT OF FILES

The VAX/VMS operating system provides logical names, which are 1- to 63-character names. A *logical name* is associated with a filename by the ASSIGN command, in the form

ASSIGN *filename logical-name*

For example,

ASSIGN NEWMAST.DAT MASTFILE

associates the file NEWMAST.DAT with the logical name MASTFILE.

A Pascal program may specify a file variable name in the program header and declare it in the program declaration section as a file. When the file variable is opened by a reset or a rewrite statement, the file variable is associated with an actual file as follows.

*1.* If a logical name identical with the uppercase translation of the file variable exists, the associated file is used.

*2.* Otherwise, a file name is formed by appending the type .DAT to the uppercase translation of the file name.

An explicit file name may be supplied by use of the built-in function open. This should be called prior to calling reset or rewrite. Two arguments are supplied: the file variable, and a string specifying the file name. For example,

open (MASTFILE, 'NEWMAST.DAT')

associates file variable MASTFILE with the file NEWMAST.DAT. The association is canceled, and the file closed, by the built-in procedure close, as in

close (MASTFILE)

A special rule applies to input and output. If the logical name PAS$INPUT exists, the associated file is used for input; otherwise, the default system input (terminal for interactive users) is used. PAS$OUTPUT similarly specifies the file for output. Calls to the open procedure can be used for input and output only as the first executable statements of the program.

## G-4 MODULAR PROGRAMMING

VAX-11 Pascal provides a primitive module system. A module begins with a module heading in the form

module *module-name* (*field-name-list*);

followed by constant, type, variable, procedure, and function declarations, followed by

end.

Note that there are no **begin** or executable statements, as would be the case for a program. The module is compiled to give both an object file and an *environment* file by using the option

/ENVIRONMENT = *filename*

on the **PASCAL** compilation command. Access to the program or another module is provided to the declaration of the module by referencing the environment file by an *inheritance attribute*, which has the form

[INHERIT (*'filename'*)]

where *filename* specifies the environment file produced when the module was compiled. A program or module may inherit several other modules. The inheritance attribute appears ahead of the header line of the inheriting program or module. For example,

[INHERIT ('MODULE1.PEN'), INHERIT ('MODULE2.PEN')]
**program** Test12 (input, output);

.
.
.

Two limitations apply to VAX-11 Pascal modules. First, *all* the global declarations of a module, that is, those not contained within a procedure or function, are accessible to users of the module. There are no "hidden" names. Second, the names declared in a module must not be identical with any declared in the inheriting program or module. Further, if two or more modules are inherited, they may not declare identical names.

# INDEX